D1609139

THE LONDON STAGE
1890-1899:
A Calendar of Plays and Players

Volume I: 1890-1896

by

J.P. WEARING

The Scarecrow Press, Inc.

Metuchen, N.J.   1976

Library of Congress Cataloging in Publication Data

Wearing, J   P
   The London stage, 1890-1899.

   Includes index.
   1. Theater--England--London--Calendars.
I. Title.
PN2596.L6W37   792'.09421'2   76-1825
ISBN 0-8108-0910-9

For my friends

C O N T E N T S

INTRODUCTION

Modern theatre research has long been hampered by
the lack of readily accessible material which can provide a solid statistical basis for historical and
critical judgments. The purpose of this calendar,
the first of a series covering the period from 1890
to the present, is to furnish a daily listing of the
plays and players on the London stage from 1890-1899.
The basis of the calendar is a series of first-night
playbills relating to the thirty or so major London
theatres of the time. These playbills provide as much
information as can be garnered from various sources:
title of play, genre, number of acts, author, theatre,
date and length of run, performers, production staff
and references to reviews. For this calendar I have
included only performances of entire works to which
the fee-paying public were admitted. Generally, copyright and amateur performances are omitted, although,
for exceptional reasons, amateur performances are
occasionally included.
The following sample of a playbill, with a point-by-
point explanation, should make clear what readers can
expect to find in the calendar:

[*a*] 91.166 [*b*] *THE GIFTED LADY* [*c*] (SocialD,3a) [*d*]
Robert Buchanan. [*e*] AVENUE [*f*] 2/6/91-5/6/91; 9/
6/91. 5 perf.* [*g*] <u>Algernon Wormwood</u> Harry Paulton;
<u>Vitus Danse</u> W[illiam] Lestocq; <u>Vergris</u> Ivan Watson;
<u>Biler</u> R[ichard] H. Douglass; <u>Dr Plainchat</u> Sidney
Howard; <u>Charles Dangleton</u> W.H. Vernon; <u>Cabman</u>
G[eorge] Arnold. [*h*] <u>Felicia Strangeways</u> Cicely

Richards; <u>Amelia</u> Lydia Cowell; <u>Bodalia Dangleton</u>
Fanny Brough. [*i*] <u>L & MGR</u> Henry Lee; <u>Mus dir</u> Thomas
Batty; <u>Sm</u> W[illiam] Sidney; <u>Bm</u> Arthur Yates. [*j*]
REV: E 6/6/91 p7; *St* 4/6/91 p9-10; *Th* 1/7/91 p33;
Ti 4/6/91 p13. [*k*] <u>Comment</u>: Originally entitled
Heredity.

[*a*]. Playbills are arranged simply on a chronological
basis, except that when more than one play was produced
on the same day, they are arranged by theatre (on an
alphabetical basis). Thus 91.166 indicates that this
was the 166th play to be produced in 1891. This code
number is used to index every item in this playbill,
apart from characters' names and the review information. However, in the Index itself, the code numbers
have been abbreviated to save space. Thus 90.1, 90.2,
90.3 appear in the Index as <u>90</u>--1, 2, 3.
[*b*]. Full title of the play, as printed for this
particular production.
[*c*]. Genre of play and number of acts, scenes, etc.
[*d*]. Author(s). Details of adaptation and transla-
tion, where appropriate, are provided in brackets
immediately after the author.
[*e*]. Theatre. Where a play transferred to another
theatre during the course of the *same* production, this
information is also given.
[*f*]. Date, length of run and number of performances.
All dates are inclusive, and refer to the nineteenth
century unless indicated to the contrary. When a
piece has been performed prior to 1890, I give the
date of the first production on the first occasion the
play is revived during the period 1890-1899. A first
production in the 1890s (as here) is denoted by an
asterisk *. Double asterisks ** denote the revival
of a play of which the first production details have
been given earlier in the calendar. I have expressed
the length, frequency or pattern of a production in
two ways: (1) For long runs, the inclusive dates of
the complete run are given, with the frequency of
matinees and exceptions to the pattern of the production being indicated in brackets. For example:
18/1/90-1/8/90. 194 perf [w/S mat exc 18/1, 31/5;
np 4/4; add mat 7/4] indicates the run began on 18
January 1890 and terminated on 1 August 1890. There

were 194 performances. The piece was performed every weekday evening (Monday through Saturday) with regular matinees on Saturdays, with the exception of 18 January and 31 May when there were evening performances only. There was no performance on 4 April, and there was an additional matinee on 7 April. (2) For short, irregular runs the date of every performance is given. For example: 18/1/90(m); 27-29/1; 1/2/90(2). 6 perf indicates a matinee performance on 18 January, evening performances on 27, 28, 29 January, and 2 performances (matinee and evening) on 1 February for a total of six performances.

Readers should be aware of the difficulties of determing the length of runs accurately because of such factors as (1) inaccurate advertizing in newspapers and the like; (2) sudden withdrawals of productions which nevertheless remained advertized for a day or two; (3) the dearth of programmes on a day-by-day basis; (4) the existence of programmes for productions which never, in fact, came to fruition. I have tried to resolve such discrepancies as these circumstances have created, but a few cases remain intractable. Also, in some cases, the number of performances I have tabulated differs from other sources (such as *Who's Who in the Theatre*). In every case, I have based my figures on advertizements. [*g*]. Male cast. Substitutes and replacements for various roles, when known, are given after the original performer. I have endeavoured to standardize the form and spelling for each performer, but this has not always been possible. There is good evidence to suggest that many programmes were printed from information transmitted orally, and, in consequence, variations in spelling were bound to occur. This situation does not create a problem with major figures, but can provoke considerable confusion with the plethora of minor performers. It is more than likely, therefore, that I have inadvertently failed to realize when two or more names do, in fact, belong to the same performer. In using the Index to trace the career of a particular person, it will be prudent to check any other entries which resemble that person's name. For example, "John B. Smith" might well, because of the vagaries I have indicated, appear in the Index

under the following headings: Smith; Smith, J.; Smith,
J.B.; Smith, John; Smith, John B.; Smythe, etc. I
can only apologize for any confusion this state of
affairs might produce, and ask that such inconsis-
tencies be brought to my attention.

[*h*]. Female cast, with changes.

[*i*]. Production staff.

[*j*]. A short bibliography of first-night reviews. A
representative sample of daily, weekly and monthly
reviews is given.

[*k*]. Comment(s) relating to some aspect of the
production in question, such as the original title
of the piece, discrepancies in source information,
the name of a company performing the piece, and so
forth.

NB. Where information (such as production staff)
is repeated in consecutive playbills, it is listed in
full *only* in the earlier bill, to which readers are
referred. However, in the Index, such information
is indexed as though it were printed in full in each
playbill.

The second part of the calendar is the Index which
extensively cross-references every item in the playbills, with the two exceptions noted in [*a*] above.
In addition, I have also endeavoured to give birth
and death dates of performers. To save space, the
code numbers appear in modified form: 90.1, 90.2,
90.3 for a particular entry are given as 90--1, 2, 3.

The Index, of itself, should enable readers to
correlate a considerable amount of information without
reference to the main section of playbills. Simply
by turning up the title of a play, the Index will
indicate how many times that piece was produced in
a particular year. By comparing those code numbers
with the code numbers for a particular theatre and
actor, the reader could ascertain how often the play
was acted at a given theatre by a given performer.
The relevant playbill would then provide complete information. However, readers should be aware that
some plays are included in the Index as adaptations
or translations only, and not as productions. For
example, the index entry for Vanbrugh's *The Relapse*
contains a reference to the occasion when it was, in
fact, the adaptation *Miss Tomboy*. In addition, people

with more than one occupation are listed in the Index
for *all* their occupations. Hence, an actor-manager
has entries relating to both jobs: sometimes those
functions coincide, sometimes not. The reader would
need, therefore, to check the relevant playbills to
establish exactly what the Index entry indicates.

Errors and omissions are, unfortunately, in the
nature of such works as this calendar, and I would be
grateful if readers would point these out to me so
that, from time to time, a correction list can be
published--probably in *Nineteenth Century Theatre
Research*. The information in this book is based on
entries in the *Times, Era, Daily News, Daily Telegraph, Stage, Referee, Sketch, Saturday Review, Theatre,
Athenaeum*, William Archer's series of five annuals *The
Theatrical "World" of 1893* (etc.), the holdings
of the Enthoven Collection of the Victoria and Albert
Museum, London, The British Library, Birmingham Public
Library, The Folger Shakespeare Library, and the
British Theatre Museum, London. Wherever possible,
I have supplemented this information with references
from standard printed sources, and in this regard, I
owe a special debt to Allardyce Nicoll's *History of
English Drama*, Reginald Clarence's *"The Stage" Cyclo-
paedia: A Bibliography of Plays*, the *Enciclopedia
dello Spettacolo*, Walter Rigdon's *The Biographical
Encyclopedia & Who's Who of the American Theatre*,
Alfred Lowenberg's *Annals of Opera 1597-1940*, Eric
Blom's edition of *Grove's Dictionary of Music and
Musicians*, and *Who's Who in the Theatre* (edited by
John Parker, and others).

I acknowledge gratefully the assistance I have
received from the staffs of the Victoria and Albert
Museum, the British Library, the British Theatre
Museum, the Folger Shakespeare Library, the University
of Alberta Library, the University of Arizona Library,
and from Professor Joseph Donohue of the University
of Massachusetts, Amherst. The work was completed
with the aid of a Summer Research Grant from the
Department of English, the University of Arizona.

It is with pleasure that I dedicate this book to
those of my friends who have helped and supported me
while I was engaged on it: Professor and Mrs J.G.
Marino, Miss Jane Fellows, Miss Alison Wertheimer,

Miss Gillian Wilce, Miss Lesley Whitbourn, Miss Helen Buckley, and Mr P.H. Turnbull. I owe a special debt of gratitude to Mr R.B. Silverthorne, who most generously devoted part of a summer vacation to helping me check programmes and other information.

J.P.W.
University of Arizona

LIST OF ABBREVIATIONS

*	1st performance	Bsq	Burlesque
**	1st performance details given earlier in Calendar	C	Comedy
		c.	circa
		CD	Comic drama
		Ch	Choreographer
a	Act(s)	CO	Comic opera
A act mgr	Assistant acting manager	COa	Comic operetta
		Col.	Colonel
Act mgr	Acting manager	Comp	Composer, Composed
Add	Additional, Added		
		Con	Contralto
Adpt	Adapted, Adaptation	Cond	Conductor
		Cost	Costumier
Am	Assistant manager	Cpt.	Captain
		CSk	Comic Sketch
Amat	Amateur	*Cyc*	*"The Stage" Cyclopedia* (by Reginald Clarence)
Arr	Arranged		
Asm	Assistant stage manager		
Assist	Assistant	D	Drama
Ath	*The Athenaeum*	Dan	Dancer
Atr	Actor	DC	Dometic comedy
Ats	Actress	DD	Domestic drama
		DE	Domestic episode
Ba	Burletta	Dgn	Design(er)
Bar	Baritone	Dir	Director
Bm	Business manager	DomSk	Domestic sketch
Bom	Box office manager	Dram	Dramatized, dramatization

DSk	Dramatic sketch
Duol	Duologue
dy	Daily
E	*The Era*
ea	Each
Elect	Electrician
Eng	Engineer
Ent	Entertainment
Epi	Epilogue
ev	Evening
exc	Except
Ext	Extravaganza
F	Farce
FC	Farcical comedy
FCa	Farcical Comedietta
Fe	Female
fnd	Founded
FP	Farcical Play
FR	Farcical Romance
Fr	French
fr	From
Fri	Friday
Furn	Furnishings, furnisher(s)
Gen.	General
Gen dir	General director
Gen mgr	General manager
Gr	German
HistD	Historical drama
HistP	Historical play
Int	Interlude
jr	Junior
L	Lessee
Li	Licensee
Lib	Libretto, Librettist

Lieut.	Lieutenant
Lime	Limelight
LO	Light opera
Lyr	Lyrics, Lyricist
LyrP	Lyric play
M	Monday
(m), mat	Matinee
Ma	Male
Mach	Machinist
MC	Musical comedy
MCa	Musical comedietta
MCD	Musical comic drama
MD	Musical drama
MDuol	Musical duologue
Melo	Melodrama
Mez	Mezzo-soprano
MEnt	Musical entertainment
MExt	Musical extravaganza
MF	Musical farce
MFC	Musical farcical comedy
Mgr	Manager
Mjr.	Major
MMonol	Musical monologue
Monol	Monologue
MP	Musical play
MR	Musical romance
MSk	Musical sketch
Mus	Music
Mus dir	Musical director
MV	Musical vaudeville
Nicoll	Allardyce Nicoll, *History of English Drama*
Nov	Novelist
np	No performance
O	Opera

Oa	Operetta	sr	Senior
OB	Opera bouffe	*SR*	*Saturday Review*
OF	Operatic farce	*St*	*The Stage*
		supp	Supplement
P	Play		
Panto	Pantomime	T	Tragedy
Past	Pastoral	Tab	Tableau(x)
PastO	Pastoral opera	Ten	Tenor
Pd	Producer	Th	Thursday
Perf	Performance(s)	*Th*	*The Theatre*
Perfd	Performed	*Ti*	*The Times*
PoetD	Poetic drama	trans	Translated, trans-
PoetP	Poetic play		lator
Pq	Perruquier	Treas	Treasurer
Prel	Prelude	Trfd	Transferred
Prof	Professional	Tu	Tuesday
	performance	*TW93*	*Theatrical World*
Prol	Prologue		*of 1893* (William
Props	Properties		Archer)
Pp	Proprietor	*TW94*	*Theatrical World*
			of 1894
R	Romance	*TW95*	*Theatrical World*
RC	Romantic comedy		*of 1895*
RD	Romantic drama	*TW96*	*Theatrical World*
Rep	Representative		*of 1896*
REV	Reviews	*TW97*	*Theatrical World*
Revd	Revised		*of 1897*
rnd	Run not deter-		
	mined	V & A	Victoria & Albert
RO	Romantic opera		Museum, London
RP	Romantic play		(Enthoven Collect-
			ion)
S	Saturday	Vaud	Vaudeville
Sc	Scene(s),	ver	version
	scenery, scenic		
	painter	W	Wednesday
Sc dgn	Scenic design	w/	with
Sec	Secretary		
Sgt.	Sergeant		
Sing	Singer		
Sk	Sketch		
Sk	*The Sketch*		
Sop	Soprano		
Sm	Stage manager		

90.1 *TRA LA LA TOSCA; OR, THE HIGH-TONED SOPRANO AND THE VILLAIN BASE* (Bsq,2a,5sc) F.C. Burnand. ROYALTY 4/1/90; 9/1/90-22/2/90. 46 perf [w/S mat exc 4/1, 11/1].* Baron Scampia Scarpia Arthur Roberts; Spiacroni G.B. Prior; Bumblini Augustus Wheatman; Spaghetti Hampton Gordon; Maccaroni Walter Tilbury; Spermacetti William Gilbert; Raviolini James Delaney; Niuncli Robert Mason; Nianti William Lovell; Jolinosia Harry Daniels; Dogerini Arthur Dodson; Stepito Guy Fane; Tentoso Arthur Withers. Queen of Naples Amy Lyddon; Caesare Angelotti Laura Hansen; Jemmi Rino Hettie Bennett; Marchesa Tutti Tutti Morton; Contessa Lotti Totti Lily Marsden; Signorina Larki Daremo Marie Usman; Marchesa Nonpica Mesta Frances Denton; Signor Farfallone Maggie Douglas; Signorina Connie Moto Paddy St. Clare; Il Capitano Batti Batti Fannie Merton; Contessa Ann Cora Maud Royal; Admiralo Benhom Helen Stewart; Generalissimo Trombonio Gertrude Price; Anne Dante Winnie Gwynne; Ada Gio S. Collingwood; Ann Diamo Kate Price; Marchessa Fan Tutti Daisy Lennox. L Kate Santley; Mus Florian Pascal; Sc Bruce Smith; Cost L. & H. Nathan, Jacobus; Ch Paul Valentine; Mach H. Loftin; Furn Oetzmann & Co.; Lime W. Kerr; Pq William Clarkson; Songs Young, Barnett, Wal Pink; Cond George W. Byng; Asm A.E. Dodson; Bm H. Watkin. *REV: Ath 18/1/90 p94; E 11/1/90 p9; SR 11/1/90 p45-6, 18/1/90 p77; St 17/1/90 p9-10; Th 1/2/90 p111-112; Ti 10/1/90 p10.*

90.2 *THE OPERA CLOAK* ([Ca,1a]) L.D. Powles & Augustus
Harris. ROYALTY 4/1/90; 9/1-22/2/90. 40 perf. 1st
perfd Drury Lane 8/9/83. Hopley Malt J. Wilson;
Abinger Smith John Clulow; Anastatius Fitz Jones Guy
Fane; Distin Kettle G.B. Prior; Col. F.P. O'Bruin
Augustus Wheatman. Mrs Hopley Malt Hettie Bennett;
Mrs Abinger Smith Amy Liddon; Mrs O'Bruin G. Price;
Miss Lucy Malt Kate Price; Mary Maud Royal. L, Asm,
Bm as for 90.1.

90.3 *DOMESTIC ECONOMY* (F,[1a]) Mark Lemon. TOOLE'S
4/1/90-17/1/90. 12 perf. 1st perfd Adelphi 8/11/49.
John Grumley J.L. Toole; Sgt. Tom C. Wilson; Ned Nix
Charles Brunton; Joey Master Noonan. Mrs Grumley
Eliza Johnstone; Mrs Shackles Jenny Donald; Mrs Knag-
ley Mary Brough; Peggy Brown Paget; Polly Douglas. L &
MGR J.L. Toole; Bm John Donald; Sm John Billington.
REV: St 10/1/90 p10.

90.4 *A BROKEN SIXPENCE* (Ca,1a) Mrs G. Thompson & Kate
Sinclair. TOOLE'S 4/1/90; 6-10/1/90. 6 perf. 1st perfd
Ladbroke Hall 11/4/89. John Grant C. Wilson; Dick Ham-
mond C.M. Lowne. Molly Severs Effie Liston; Kitty
Severs Irene Vanbrugh; Jane Mary Brough. L & MGR,
Bm, Sm as for 90.3.

90.5 *PAUL PRY* (C,3a) John Poole. TOOLE'S 4/1/90-11/1/
90; 5-7/2/90. 10 perf [mat only 11/1]. 1st perfd Hay-
market 13/9/25. Paul Pry J.L. Toole; Col. Hardy John
Billington; Grasp George Shelton; Harry Stanley C.M.
Lowne; Frank Hardy Henry Westland; Witherton C. Wil-
son; Old Stanley Help; Simon C[harles] Brunton;
Doubledot Frank J. Arlton; Willis J. Gunn. Phoebe
Effie Liston; Marian Mary Brough; Eliza Florence Henry.
L & MGR, Bm, Sm as for 90.3. *REV: St 10/1/90 p10.*

90.6 *A SINLESS SECRET* (RD,5a) Frank Lindo. COMEDY
7/1/90 mat perf.* Pierre Leroux Oscar Adye; Col.
Von Brandstein Royston Keith; Leon Moprat Frank Lindo;
Alphonse Bohmer Ronald Power; Hans Wiesman H[enry]
Arncliffe; Roger Michel Charles Ronald; Officer E.
Gordon Taylor; Lieutenant Beresford. Rose Michel F.
Mellon; Frau Muller Dalby; Gretchen Marion Denvil;
Suzanne O'Hara; Ninette Marion Lea. L Charles H. Haw-

trey; <u>Bm</u> Gloster Armstrong; <u>Pd</u> Frank Lindo; <u>Act mgr</u>
C. St. John Denton; <u>Sm</u> T[homas] Sidney; <u>Am</u> Beresford;
<u>Cost</u> Morris Angel; <u>Pq</u> H. Hugo; <u>Mus</u> Algernon H. Lindo.
*REV: Ath 11/1/90 p58; E 11/1/90 p9; St 10/1/90 p10;
Ti 8/1/90 p8.*

90.7 *MADEMOISELLE DE LIRA* (P,1a) Mrs G. Thompson &
Kate Sinclair. COMEDY 7/1/90 mat perf.* <u>Roland Wild</u>
Royston Keith; <u>Sidney Reed</u> A. Newroy. <u>Eva Mayne</u> Mrs G.
Thompson; <u>Eva Ward</u> K[ate] Sinclair; <u>Mrs Macdonald</u> Mrs
E.H. Brooke; <u>Mary</u> A. Newroy. <u>L</u>, <u>Bm</u> as for 90.6. <u>Pd</u>
Royston Keith. *REV: 11/1/90 p9; St 10/1/90 p10.*

90.8 *THE DON* ([C,3a]) Mr & Mrs Herman C. Merivale.
TOOLE'S 11/1/90-17/1/90. 6 perf. 1st perfd Toole's
7/3/88. <u>Milliken</u> J.L. Toole; <u>Pappendick</u> John Billing-
ton; George Shelton; C.M. Lowne; C. Wilson; C[harles]
Brunton; Frank J. Arlton; J. Gunn; H[enry] Westland.
<u>Mrs Coventry Sparkle</u> Effie Liston; <u>Dora</u> Florence Hen-
ry; Eliza Johnstone; Mary Brough; Jenny Donald; Irene
Vanbrugh. <u>L & MGR</u>   Toole; <u>Bm</u> John Donald. *REV:
Observer 12/1/90 p2.*

90.9 *WAITING CONSENT* ([C,1a]) Mrs R. Fairbairn [May
Holt]. TOOLE'S 11/1/90-24/1/90. 12 perf. 1st perfd
Folly 11/6/81. <u>Hon Tom Hartley</u> Frank J. Arlton; <u>Jack
Aylmer</u> C.M. Lowne; <u>Scorcher</u> G[eorge] Shelton. <u>Grace
Hartley</u> Irene Vanbrugh. <u>L & MGR</u>, <u>Bm</u> as for 90.8. <u>Sm</u>
John Billington; <u>Mus dir</u> C.J. Hargitt.

90.10 *THE SCHOOL FOR SCANDAL* ([C,5a]) R.B. Sheridan.
VAUDEVILLE 11/1/90-8/2/90. 27 perf [w/mat 18/1, 25/1;
mat only 8/2]. 1st perfd Drury Lane 8/5/1777. <u>Moses</u>
Fred Thorne;   <u>Charles Surface</u> T.B. Thalberg; <u>Joseph
Surface</u> Cyril Maude; <u>Sir Benjamin Backbite</u> Frank Gill-
more; <u>Sir Oliver Surface</u> J.S. Blythe; <u>Rowley</u> C. Har-
bury; <u>Crabtree</u> F[red] Grove; <u>Careless</u> Oswald Yorke;
<u>Sir Peter Teazle</u> John MacLean; <u>Snake</u> J. Horton; <u>Tripp</u>
J[ohn] Wheatman; <u>Sir Harry Bumper</u> Leigh. <u>Lady Teazle</u>
Winifred Emery; <u>Maria</u> Mary Collette; <u>Mrs Candour</u>
Coralie Owen; <u>Lady Sneerwell</u> L. Bryer; <u>Lady Teazle's
Maid</u> [Lily] Hanbury. <u>L & MGR</u> Thomas Thorne; <u>Act mgr</u>
Sydney Alport; <u>Sm</u> Fred Thorne; <u>Sc</u> Walter Hann; <u>Cond</u>
A. Cooke. *REV: Ath 18/1/90 p94; E 18/1/90 p11; St*

17/1/90 p10; Ti 13/1/90 p8.

90.11 *MARJORIE* (CO) Lewis Clifton (lib) & Joseph Dilley (lib) & Walter Slaughter (mus). PRINCE OF WALES'S
18/1/80-1/8/90. 194 perf [w/S mat exc 18/1, 31/5; add
mat 7/4; np 4/4]. 1st perfd Prince of Wales's 18/7/89.
Ralf, Earl of Chestermere C. Hayden Coffin; Sir Simon
Striveling Henry Ashley; Nicolas, of Chestermere Frederick Wood; Witgills Albert James; Cpt. of the Guard
T[om] A. Shale; Martin A.T. Hendon; Gosric Harry Monkhouse.   Wilfred Agnes Huntington;   Cicely Phyllis
Broughton; Lady Alicia Mme Amadi;   Marjorie Camille
d'Arville. L & MGR Horace Sedger; Pp Edgar Bruce; Pd
Augustus Harris; Mus dir F. Stanislaus; Bm William
Greet; Act mgr Tom Pitt; Cost Alias; Cost dgn Wilhelm.
*REV: E 25/1/90 p9, 22/2/90 p10; SR 25/1/90 p109; St
24/1/90 p10; Ti 20/1/90 p8.*   Comment: V & A programme
includes *John Smith* (0a,1a), which has been deleted.

90.12 *THE BIRTHPLACE OF PODGERS* (F,1a) John Hollingshead. TOOLE'S 18/1/90-24/1/90. 7 perf [2 perf 18/1].
1st perfd Lyceum 10/3/58. Tom Cranky J.L. Toole; Erasmus Maresnest G[eorge] Shelton; Edmund Earlybird Henry
Westland; Alonzo Lexicon C.M.Lowne; 1st Photographic
Artist C. Wilson; 2nd Photographic Artist C[harles]
Brunton; Mortal Podgers Frank J. Arlton. Amelia Maresnest Florence Henry; Penelope Lexicon Mary Brough; Mrs
Cranky Eliza Johnstone.L & MGR J.L. Toole; Bm John Donald; Sm John Billington; Mus dir C.J. Hargitt. Comment:
Cast from V & A programme for 20/1/90.

90.13 *UNCLE DICK'S DARLING* (D,3a) Henry J. Byron.
TOOLE'S 18/1/90(m); 27-29/1/90; 1/2/90(2). 6 perf.
1st perfd Gaiety 13/12/69. Dick Dolland J.L. Toole;
Hon Claude Lorimer C.M. Lowne; Phipson Frank J. Arlton;
Roger C[harles] Brunton; Mr Chevenix John Billington;
Joe Lennard H[enry] Westland. Mary Belton Irene
Vanbrugh; Kate Renshaw Mary Brough; Alice Landrail
Jenny Donald; Mrs Torrington Eliza Johnstone; Servant
Douglas. L & MGR, Bm, Sm as for 90.12. Comment: as
for 90.12.

90.14 *THE BUTLER* (C,3a) Mr & Mrs Herman C. Merivale.
TOOLE'S 20/1/90-24/1/90. 5 perf. 1st perfd Theatre

Royal, Manchester 24/11/86. David Trot J.L. Toole;
Sir John Tracey John Billington; Lawrence Tracey C.
Wilson; Lord Babicombe George Shelton; Frank St. John
C.M. Lowne; A Deaf Flyman C[harles] Brunton. Lady
Tracey Eliza Johnstone; Alice Marshall Irene Vanbrugh;
Lady Anne Babicombe Florence Henry; Lavina Muddle
Effie Liston. L & M, Bm, Sm, Mus dir as for 90.12.

90.15 *ACROSS HER PATH* (P,4a) Annie Irish [fnd on Annie
Swan's novel]. TERRY'S 21/1/90 mat perf.*   Sir Adrian
Severne Oscar Adye; Jasper Leigh Henry Pagden; Mark-
ham G. Arliss; Johnson G[eorge] Belmore. Lady Severne
Josephine St. Ange; Frances Severne T. Roma; Lady
Bassett R.G. Le Thiere; Elspet Carmichael Mrs E.H.
Brooke; Barbara Dale Annie Irish. DIR W.H. Vernon;
Cost Mme Josephine; Act mgr & Treas H.T. Brickwell; L
& Mgr Edward Terry. *REV: Ath 25/1/90 p126; E 25/1/90*
p9; St 24/1/90 p10; Th 1/3/90 p153-4.

90.16 *THE TAMING OF THE SHREW* (C) William Shakespeare.
GLOBE 23/1/90-28/2/90. 14 perf [ea Th, Fri; 2 perfs
13/2, 20/2]. 1st perfd c. 1594. Petruchio F.R. Ben-
son; Baptista G[eorge] F. Black; Vincentio H. Athol
Forde; Lucentio Otho Stuart; Gremio Stephen Phillips;
Hortensio Gerald Gurney; Tranio Herbert Ross; Bion-
dello Walter Shaw; Grumio G.R. Weir; A Pedant G.M.
Howard; Tailor [Arthur] Grenville; Sugarsop H. Gordon
Tomkins; Nathaniel Charles Barwell; Nicholas C.M.
Hallard; Adam L. Rosoman; Ralph G[eorge?] Hippisley;
Gregory A.E. George; Gabriel J.B. Croft; Phillip Hugh
Meadows; Peter E[dward P.] Major; Walter Edgar Ste-
vens; Servant to Baptista Alfred Brydone. Katherina
Mrs F.R. Benson; Bianca Marion Grey; Widow Hawkins;
Curtis Alice Denvil. L & MGR F.R. Benson; Mus dir E.
Boggetti; Sm T.J. Merridew; Ch W. Ozmond; Pd Hugh Moss;
Act mgr H. Jalland. *REV: E 25/1/90 p9; SR 1/2/90 p139;*
St 31/1/90 p10; Ti 24/1/90 p9.

90.17 *THE MARRIED BACHELOR* (F,[1a]). ADELPHI 25/1/90--
10/7/90. 141 perf [np 4/4, 18/4]. 1st perfd Strand
5/3/55.

90.18 *CYRIL'S SUCCESS* (C,5a) Henry J. Byron. CRITER-
ION 25/1/90-10/2/90. 15 perf [2 perf 1/2]. 1st perfd

Globe 28/11/68. <u>Matthew Pincher</u> David James; <u>Cyril
Cuthbert</u> Leonard Boyne; <u>Mjr. Treherne</u> Arthur Elwood;
<u>Jonas Grimley</u> H. Saker; <u>Col. Rawker</u> W. Scott Buist;
<u>Mr Fitz-Pelham</u> Gerald Maxwell; <u>Pepper</u> G.B. Phillips;
<u>Viscount Glycerine</u> G[uy] Stanton; <u>Paul Bingo</u> G. Cha-
puy. <u>Mrs Cuthbert</u> Olga Brandon; <u>Mrs Singleton Bliss</u>
Compton; <u>Hon Fredk. Titeboy</u> F. Frances; <u>Miss Grannett</u>
E. Brunton; <u>Perkins</u> E[mily] Vining. <u>L & MGR</u> Charles
Wyndham; <u>Dir</u> William Duck; <u>Furn</u> Oetzmann & Co.; <u>Act
mgr</u> E. Harvey; <u>Sm</u> Edward Hastings; <u>Cond</u> B. Solomon.
*REV: Ath 1/2/90 p157-8; E 1/2/90 p16; SR 1/2/90 p139;
St 31/1/90 p10; Ti 27/1/90 p4.*

90.19 *HESTER'S MYSTERY* (Ca,1a) A.W. Pinero. TOOLE'S
25/1/90-11/2/90. 15 perf. 1st perfd Folly 5/6/80.
<u>Owen Silverdale</u> H[enry] Westland; <u>John Royle</u> C.M.
Lowne; <u>Joel</u> G[eorge] Shelton. <u>Nance Butterworth</u> Effie
Liston; <u>Hester</u> Irene Vanbrugh. <u>L & MGR</u> J.L. Toole; <u>Bm</u>
John Donald; <u>Sm</u> John Billington.

90.20 *DEARER THAN LIFE* ([C,3a]) Henry J. Byron.
TOOLE'S 25/1/90(2); 30-31/1/90. 4 perf. 1st perfd
Alexandra, Liverpool 26/11/67. <u>L & MGR</u>, <u>Bm</u> as for 90.19.

90.21 *THE SPITALFIELDS WEAVER* (Ba) Thomas Haynes Bay-
ly. TOOLE'S 25/1/90; 5-7/2/90. 4 perf. 1st perfd St.
James's 10/2/38. <u>L & MGR</u>, <u>Bm</u> as for 90.19.

90.22 *KLEPTOMANIA* (FC,3a) Mark Melford. NOVELTY 27/1/
90-1/2/90. 6 perf. 1st perfd Portland Hall, Southsea
30/4/88. <u>Gen. Blair</u> Edwin Brett; <u>Prof. Andrew Smalley</u>
Mark Melford; <u>Dr Whatley</u> Raymond Capp; <u>Mr Gathermoss</u>
Roy Byford; <u>Butler</u> James Woodbridge. <u>Lady Josephine</u>
Ruth Rutland; <u>Violet</u> Mrs Mark Melford; <u>Rosina</u> Cath-
erine Claire; <u>Mrs Gathermoss</u> Bella Cuthbert. <u>L & MGR</u>
George Turner; <u>Sm</u> Roy Byford; <u>Dir</u> Frank Rothwel; <u>Cond</u>
Hugh Sangster; <u>Furn</u> H[enry] Deares. *REV: E 1/2/90 p16.*

90.23 *THE BEST MAN WINS* (F,1a) Mark Melford. NOVELTY
27/1/90-1/2/90. 6 perf.* <u>Perks</u> Mark Melford; <u>Jopper</u>
James Woodbridge; <u>Farmer Kairns</u> Raymond Capp. <u>Car-
lotta</u> Mrs Mark Melford. <u>L & MGR</u>, <u>Sm</u>, <u>Dir</u>, <u>Cond</u>, <u>Furn</u>
as for 90.22. *REV: E 1/2/90 p16; St 31/1/90 p10.*

90.24 *ICI ON PARLE FRANCAIS; OR, FRENCH BEFORE BREAK-
FAST* (F,1a) Thomas J. Williams. TOOLE'S 27/1/90-1/2/
90; 10-11/2/90. 9 perf [2 perf on 1/2]. 1st perfd
Adelphi 9/5/59. Mr Spriggins J.L. Toole; Mjr. Rattan
H[enry] Westland; Victor Dubois C.M. Lowne. Mrs Rat-
tan Cora Poole; Mrs Spriggins Effie Liston; Angelina
Irene Vanbrugh/Florence Henry; Anna Maria Eliza John-
stone. L & MGR J.L. Toole; Bm John Donald; Sm John
Billington. Comment: Holograph note on V & A pro-
gramme gives Florence Henry for Irene Vanbrugh.

90.25 *DR. BILL* (FC,3a) Hamilton Aidé [adpt of Albert
Carré, *Le Docteur Jojo*]. AVENUE 1/2/90-20/9/90. 210
perf [w/mat 15/2, 22/2, 1/3, 5/3, 8/3, 12/3, 15/3,
22/3, 29/3, 3/5, 24/5, 13/9; np 4/4].* Dr William
Brown Fred Terry/George Alexander/J.G. Graham; George
Webster Ben Webster; Mr Horton George Capel; Baggs
Harry Grattan/C. Vernon; Mr Firmin Albert Chevalier/
Wilfred E. Shine. Louisa Brown E[lizabeth] Robins/
Lillian Hingston; Mrs Firmin Carlotta Leclercq/Mrs
Leston; Ellen Marie Linden; Jenny Firmin Laura Graves;
Miss Fauntleroy Edith Kenward; Mrs Horton Fanny Brough/
Alma Stanley. L, MGR, PD George Alexander; Sc J[oseph]
Harker; Mus dir J[ohn] Crook; Furn Oetzmann & Co.;
Bm R. d'Albertson; Asm R[obert] V. Shone; Cost Miss
Brown. *REV: Ath 8/2/90 p189-90, 22/3/90 p381; E 8/2/
90 p16, 5/4/90 p8, 9/8/90 p14; SR 8/2/90 p171; St
8/2/90 p171; Th 1/3/90 p154-5; Ti 3/2/90 p10, 17/3/90
p8.*

90.26 *FOOL'S MATE* (Ca,1a) Frederick W. Broughton.
AVENUE 1/2/90-15/3/90. 43 perf [w/mat 15/2, 22/2, 1/3,
5/3, 8/3, 12/3; mat only 15/3]. 1st perfd Toole's
12/12/89. Earl of Somerdale Fred Terry; Arthur Egerton
Nutcombe Gould. Mary Egerton Mary Kingsley; Dorothy
Gracie Murielle. L, Mgr, Pd, Cond, Asm, Bm as for
90.25. *REV: Ath 8/2/90 p190; E 8/2/90 p16; SR 8/2/90
p171; St 7/2/90 p10; Th 1/3/90 p155-6; Ti 3/2/90 p10.*

90.27 *OUR AMERICAN COUSIN* (D,4a) Tom Taylor. NOVELTY
3/2/90-8/3/90. 30 perf. 1st perfd Laura Keene's, New
York 18/10/58. Lord Dundreary George Turner; Asa
Trenchard Graham Wentworth; Sir Edward Trenchard Norman Clark; Abel Murcott D.D. Betterton; Benney Ernest

H. Patterson; Buddicombe Dermot O'Neal; Richard Coyle
Arthur Edgemore; Harry Vernon Hubert Carter. Georgina
Aida Valde; Florence Trenchard Clare Greet; Mary
Meredith E[ssex] Dane; Mrs Montchessington Adeline
Lester; Skillett Bertha Bingham. L & MGR George
Turner. *E 8/2/90 p16; St 7/2/90 p10.*

90.28 *THE SECRET.* NOVELTY 3/2/90-8/3/90. 30 perf.
Comment: Sources [*E, St*] differ on length of run.

90.29 *A NOBLE BROTHER* (CD,4a) W.J. Summers. OPERA
COMIQUE 3/2/90-15/2/90. 12 perf. 1st perfd Shakes-
peare, Liverpool 28/10/89. Col. Richard Leigh George
Lester Herbert; Harry Travers E[dward?] Rochelle;
Jack Ellsworth Charles Weir; Detective Howard Henry
W. Vaughan; Jerry W.J. Summers. Nana Leigh Ellen
Boucher; Rosie Rapid Clara Rose; Mrs Leigh Pattie
Bell. L F.J. Harris; Mgr H. Gittus Lonsdale; Mus Fred
Wright; Cond W.F. Glover; Gen mgr Charles Terry;
Treas E. Clifford. *REV: Ath 8/2/90 p190; E 8/2/90
p16; St 7/2/90 p10; Ti 4/2/90 p7.*

90.30 *CHAWLES; OR, A FOOL AND HIS MONEY* ([C,3a])
[Henry J. Byron]. TOOLE'S 3-4/2/90. 2 perf. 1st perfd
Globe 17/1/78. Comment: Mentioned only in *Ti*. Orig-
inal title: *A Fool and His Money.*

90.31 *OFF THE LINE* ([F,1a]) [Clement Scott]. TOOLE'S
3-4/2/90; 8/2/90(2). 4 perf. 1st perfd Gaièty 1/4/
71. Comment: Mentioned only in *Ti*.

90.32 *MERRY WIVES OF WINDSOR* (C,[5a]) William Shakes-
peare. HAYMARKET 5/2/90; 26/2/90. 2 mat perf. 1st
perfd 1596. Sir John Falstaff H.B. Tree; Mr Ford
[James] Fernandez; Master Slender [C.H.E.] Brook-
field; Dr Caius [Henry] Kemble; Host of "The Garter"
C[harles] Collette; Sir Hugh Evans E.M. Robson;
Pistol Charles Allan; Justice Shallow Perceval-Clarke;
Mr Page Gurney; Bardolph Hargreaves; Nym Robb Harwood;
Fenton Fuller Mellish; Simple [Alfred] Wigley; John
Rugby Leith. Mistress Ford Lingard; Mistress Page
Rose Leclercq; Anne Page Mrs H.B. Tree; Robin Alyward;
Mistress Quickly Lindley. L & MGR H.B. Tree; Mus Sir
Arthur Sullivan; Bom W.H. Leverton; Sm A.B. Tapping;

Mus dir Carl Armbruster; Bm & Sec F[rederick] Harrison.

90.33 *CLARISSA* (D,4a) Robert Buchanan [fnd on Samuel
Richardson's novel]. VAUDEVILLE 6/2/90-18/4/90. 68
perf [w/S mat exc 12/4; mat only 6/2; add mat 7/4;
np 3-4/4].* Philip Belford Thomas Thorne; Lovelace
T.B. Thalberg; Mr Solmes Cyril Maude; Cpt. Harlowe
Oswald Yorke; Stokes J.S. Blythe; Mr Harlowe C. Har-
bury; Sir Harry Tourville F[red] Grove; Aubrey Frank
Gillmore; Cpt. Macshane Fred Thorne; Watchman [John]
Wheatman; Richards C[ecil] Ramsey; Coffee-Stall Keep-
er Bray; Drawer [A] Austin. Clarissa Harlowe Winifred
Emery; Jenny Mary Collette; Mrs Osborne Coralie Owen;
Bab Lawrence L. Bryer; Lady May Lawrence Florence
Wemyss; Hetty Belford Ella Bannister; Sally Lily Han-
bury. L & MGR Thomas Thorne; Act mgr Sydney Alport;
Sm Fred Thorne; Sc Walter Hann, [William] Perkins,
[W.T.] Hemsley; Cost dgn Karl; Cost Nathan; Mus
Crooke, Robert H. Lyon. *REV: Ath 15/2/90 p221; E 8/2/
90 p10; Th 1/3/90 p157-8; SR 15/2/90 p198; St 14/2/90
p10.*

90.34 *NEW LAMPS FOR OLD* (FC,3a) Jerome K. Jerome.
TERRY'S 8/2/90-19/7/90. 160 perf [w/S Mat exc 8/2,
15/2, 22/2; add mat 21/5; np 4/4].* Buster W.S. Penley; Edwin Honeydew Bernard Gould; Jorkins W[illiam]
Lestocq; Postlethwaite Frederick Kerr. Elvira Honeydew Cissy Grahame; Jemima Houston; Octavia Gertrude
Kingston. L Edward Terry; Mgr Cissy Grahame; Mus dir
J. Bayliss; Dir W.H. Vernon; Sc Jetley; Act mgr H.T.
Brickwell; Asm George Belmore. *REV: Ath 15/2/90
p221-2; E 15/2/90 p16; St 14/2/90 p10; Th 1/3/90
p156-7; Ti 10/2/90 p7.*

90.35 *THE PARTING OF THE WAYS* (RusticC,1a) Frederick
Bowyer & W. Edwardes-Sprange. TERRY'S 8/2/90-28/3/90.
42 perf.* Rev Arthur Ellis Oscar Adye; Harold Cony-
beare Yorke Stephens. Margaret Grey M.A. Giffard;
Edith Hastings Helen Leyton; Nance Rose Dearing. L,
Mgr, Act mgr, Mus dir, Asm as for 90.34. *REV: E 15/2/
90 p16; St 14/2/90 p10; Th 1/3/90 p157.*

90.36 *THE SERIOUS FAMILY* ([C,3a]) Morris Barnett
[adpt fr *Le Mari à la Campagne*]. TOOLE'S 8/2/90(2). 2
perf. 1st perfd Haymarket 30/]0/49. L & MGR J.L.
Toole; Bm John Donald. Comment: For probable cast
see 91.182.

90.37 *ARTFUL CARDS* (FC,3a) F.C. Burnand. TOOLE'S 10/
2/90-11/2/90. 2 perf. 1st perfd Gaiety 24/2/77. Robert
Spicer Romford J.L. Toole; Fred Flutter C.M. Lowne;
Prince Ivanous Fordorsoff C. Wilson; M. Le Baron von
Teufelgarten G[eorge] Shelton; Foxcraftleigh C[harles]
Brunton; Sir Haircut Shortleigh John Billington; In-
spector of Police Johnson; Footman Speirs; Gamblers
Granville, Tyler, Shepherd, Howard. Countess Aster-
iski Effie Liston; Countess Maybloom Jenny Donald;
Dora Stewart Irene Vanbrugh; Dobson Mary Brough; Mrs
Spicer Romford Eliza Johnstone; Gamblers Orford, Dia-
mond, Wadmere, Paget. L & MGR J.L. Toole; Bm John
Donald; Sm John Billington. *REV: Ti 12/2/90 p10.*

90.38 *OUR BOYS.* (C,3a) Henry J. Byron. CRITERION 11/2/
90-21/3/90. 39 perf [w/S mat]. 1st perfd Vaudeville
16/1/75. Perkyn Middlewick David James; Charles
Middlewick Leonard Boyne; Sir Geoffrey Champneys
Arthur Elwood; Talbot Champneys E.W. Gardiner; Kemps-
ter L. Chapuy; Poddles Hood. Mary Melrose Olga Bran-
don; Clarissa Champneys E. Brunton; Violet Melrose
F. Frances; Belinda E[mily] Vining. L & MGR Charles
Wyndham; Sm Edward Hastings; Cond B. Solomon; Dir
William Duck; Furn Oetzmann & Co.; Act mgr E. Harvey.
REV: Ath 15/2/90 p222; E 15/2/90 p16; St 14/2/90 p10.

90.39 *SWEETHEART, GOOD BYE* (Ca,1a) Mrs R. Fairbairn.
CRITERION 11/2/90-21/3/90. 34 perf. 1st perfd Theatre
Royal, Scarborough 10/10/81. Reginald Rothsey W. Scott
Buist; Frank Penrhyn G[uy] Stanton; Farmer Wort H.
Saker; Joe L. Chapuy. Mrs Wort E. Brunton; Effie Ella-
line Terriss; Martha E[mily] Vining. L & MGR, Sm, Dir,
Act mgr as for 90.38.

90.40 *LOCKED IN* (Oa) Walter Frith & Alfred J. Caldicott (mus). COMEDY 14/2/90 mat perf. 1st perfd Savoy
28/5/89. Christopher Rutland Barrington. Sophie Jessie
Bond; Schoolmistress Jane Sullivan. SM Julian Cross.

REV: St 21/2/90 p10.

90.41 *THE HOME FEUD* (DD,3a) Walter Frith. COMEDY 14/
2/90 mat perf.* Mr Joliffe Stewart Dawson; Cpt. Hargreaves Nutcombe Gould; Hon George Beilby William
Herbert; Hon John Beilby W. Scott Buist; Horace Tennant Wilfred Draycott; Cawley Shackleton. Louise
Brunton Gertrude Kingston; Helen Joliffe May Whitty;
Alice Joliffe Eva Moore; Jane Winter. *REV: Ath 22/2/
90 p253; St 21/2/90 p9-10; Ti 15/2/90 p12.*

90.42 *ISALDA* (P,1a) Fred Horner. TOOLE'S 14/2/90-22/
3/90. 41 perf [w/W, S mat exc 15/2. 19/2].* Don
Antonio Bassett Roe; Comte Henri Matthew Brodie; Pedro
R[eginald] Stockton. Isalda Vane Featherston. MGR
Fred Horner; Pd Richard [S.] Boleyn; Sc Lill Hart;
Furn Procter & Co., Fur Store, Williams & Bach; Pq
C.H. Fox; Act mgr & Treas J. E[dward] Hollingshead;
A act mgr W.H. Archer; Mus dir C.J. Hargitt; Sm
Alfred Rousby. *REV: Ath 22/2/90 p253; E 22/2/90 p16;
St 21/2/90 p10; Ti 15/2/90 p12.*

90.43 *MY BROTHER'S SISTER* (P,3a) Leonard Grover.
GAIETY 15/2/90; 22/2/90. 2 mat perf. 1st perfd
Prince's, Manchester 3/9/88 as *Nadine*. Achille Henri
de la Bernadet John MacLean; Richard Livingston
Wallace Erskine; Waldcoffer Grosserby Herbert Spar-
ling; Mr Parker C.W. Allison; Officer Schultz George
Bernage. Nadine/Jimmy Tyson/Mabel Parker/Dashing
Naval Cadet Minnie Palmer; Mrs Livingston Helen Pal-
grave; Geraldine Previous Gladys Homfrey; Mary Ann
Cecilia Beaucliffe. L & MGR George Edwardes; Furn
Oetzmann & Co.; Sm W.J. Robertson; Cond Warwick Will-
iams; Rep Douglas Cox; Act mgr C.J. Abud; Bom A.P.
Oxley. *REV: Ath 22/2/90 p253; E 22/2/90 p11; St
21/2/90 p10; Ti 17/2/90 p18.*

90.44 *LES CLOCHES DE CORNVILLE* (CO) H.B. Farnie & R.
Planquette. OPERA COMIQUE 17/2/90-19/4/90. 60 perf
[w/S mat exc 22/3, 29/3, 19/4; add mat 7/4; np 4/4].
1st perfd Folly 23/2/78. Gaspard Shiel Barry; Henri,
Marquis de Corneville H. Gittus Lonsdale; The Bailie
Tom Paulton; Gobo Charles Ashford; Grenicheux
L[lewelyn] Cadwaladr. Christopher Florence Lonsdale;

Serpolette Irene Verona; Germaine Helen Capet; Manette
P. Marshall; Jeame Buckland; Lisette Zaranski; Suzame
Dare; Marie Vitu; Gertrude Lynn. L F.J. Harris; Mgr
H. Gittus Lonsdale; Sc [T.E.] Ryan, [Edward] Banks;
Cost Alias, Mme Fitzjames; Pq William Clarkson; Act
mgr & Treas William Hogarth; Cond W.F. Glover. *REV:*
E 22/2/90 p16; St 21/2/90 p10; Ti 18/2/90 p10, 17/3/
90 p8.

90.45 *QUICKSANDS* (C,4a) Charlotte E. Morland [adpt of
Mrs Lovett Cameron's novel *The Devout Lover*]. COMEDY
18/2/90 mat perf.* Matthew Dane Walter Russell; John
Halliday Edwin Gilbert; Geoffrey Dane Laurence Caut-
ley; Albert Trichet Gilbert Yorke; Miles Faulkner
Edgar Smart; Horace Lessiter Charles Kent; M. de Bre-
four/Leon de Brefour Ivan Watson; Footman Grafton
Granville. Angel Halliday Charlotte E. Morland; Dulcie
Halliday Florence Bright; Martine Mrs B.M. de Solla;
Maid Grant; Rose de Brefour Robins. *REV: Ath 22/2/90*
p254; E 22/2/90 p10; St 21/2/90 p10.

90.46 *TABITHA'S COURTSHIP* (Ca) Eva & Florence Bright.
COMEDY 18/2/90 mat perf.* Prof Joseph Juggins Cecil
[H.] Thornbury; Harry Juggins R. Saunders; Charlie
Mordaunt Edgar Smart; William Master J. Daniell. Tab-
itha Mrs B.M. de Solla; Kate Preston Florence Bright.
REV: St 21/2/90 p10.

90.47 *ALL ABROAD* (Oa,1a) Arthur Law (lib) & Alfred J.
Caldicott (mus). PRINCE OF WALES'S 21/2/90-1/8/90.
138 perf [np 4/4].* Mr Bunting Frederick Wood;
Charles Templer Saxe; Winkles Albert James. Mrs Bunt-
ing Amy Abbott; Jeannette Florence Darley. L & MGR
Horace Sedger. *REV: E 1/3/90 p16; St 28/2/90 p13.*

90.48 *A PAIR OF SPECTACLES* (C,3a) Sydney Grundy [adpt
of Eugene Labiche & Delacour, *Les Petits Oiseaux*].
GARRICK 22/2/90-28/2/91. 323 perf [w/mat 19/4, 26/4,
17/5, 24/5, 31/5, 7/6, 21/6, 28/6, 12/7, 23/8, 13/9,
27/9, 1/11, 15/11/90, 21/2/91; mat only 9/8, 3/12,
10/12/90, 14/1/91, 21/1, 28/1, 4/2, 14/2; np 31/3-4/4,
24-25/12/90, 8/1/91].* Benjamin Goldfinch John Hare;
Uncle Gregory Charles Groves; Joyce R[owley] Cathcart; Dick Sydney Brough; Lorimer Charles Dodsworth;

Bartholomew F. Hamilton Knight; <u>Percy</u> Rudge Harding;
<u>Shoemaker</u> John Byron. <u>Lucy Lorimer</u> Blanche Horlock/
[Annie] Webster; <u>Charlotte</u> F. Hunter; <u>Mrs Goldfinch</u>
Kate Rorke. <u>L & MGR</u> John Hare; <u>Act mgr</u> C.G. Compton;
<u>Cond</u> Schoening; <u>Asm</u> R[owley] Cathcart; <u>Sc</u> William
Harford. *REV: E 1/3/90 p16, 21/6/90 p8, 4/10/90 p9;
Ath 1/3/90 p286; SR 1/3/90 p260-1; St 28/2/90 p12;
Th 1/4/90 p208-9.*

90.49 *DREAM FACES* (Dramatic Fancy,1a) Wynn Miller.
GARRICK 22/2/90-28/2/91. 325 perf [w/mat 19/4, 26/4,
17/5, 24/5, 31/5, 7/6, 21/6, 28/6, 12/7, 23/8, 13/9,
27/9, 1/11, 15/11/90, 21/2/91; mat only 9/8, 3/12,
10/12/90, 14/1/91, 21/1, 28/1, 4/2, 14/2; np 31/3-
4/4, 24-5/12/90, 8/1/91, 11/2]. 1st perfd Sanger's,
Ramsgate 18/10/88. <u>Robert</u> Johnston Forbes-Robertson;
<u>Philip</u> Sydney Brough; <u>Servant</u> Stanley Pringle. <u>Lucy</u>
Blanche Horlock; <u>Margaret</u> Carlotta Addison. <u>L & MGR</u>,
<u>Act mgr</u>, <u>Cond</u>, <u>Asm</u>, <u>Sc</u> as for 90.48. *REV: Ath 1/3/90
p286; St 28/2/90 p12; Th 1/4/90 p209-10.*

90.50 *AS YOU LIKE IT* (C,5a) William Shakespeare. ST.
JAMES'S 24/2/90-30/4/90. 58 perf [w/mat 12/4, 19/4;
mat only 26/4; np 4/4]. 1st perfd c. 1598-1600.
<u>Jaques</u> Henry Arncliffe/Arthur Bourchier; <u>Orlando</u>
Laurence Cautley; <u>Dennis</u> G[ilbert] Yorke; <u>Adam</u> Fred
A. Everill; <u>Touchstone</u> Charles Sugden; <u>Duke</u> Charles
Fulton; <u>1st Lord</u> Norman Forbes; <u>Silvius</u> Matthew Bro-
die; <u>Duke Frederick</u> George Canninge; <u>Le Beau</u> Ernest
Lawford; <u>Amiens</u> Ager Grover; <u>Charles</u> E. Teale Ling-
ham; <u>Oliver</u> Walter Gay; <u>Corin</u> Roydon Erlynne; <u>William</u>
Erskine Lewis. <u>Celia</u> Amy McNeil; <u>Audrey</u> Marion Lea;
<u>Phoebe</u> Beatrice Lamb; <u>Hymen</u> Violet Armbruster; <u>Rosa-
lind</u> Mrs Langtry. <u>L & MGR</u> Mrs Langtry; <u>Sc</u> Bruce Smith,
W[illiam] Perkins; <u>Ch</u> John d'Auban; <u>Mus & Cond</u> Will-
iam Corri, jr; <u>Cost</u> Nathan, Mrs Lintott; <u>Pq</u> William
Clarkson; <u>Bm</u> Gilbert Tate; <u>Dir</u> Lewis Wingfield; <u>Sm</u>
Lewis Sealy; <u>Treas</u> F.C. Griffith. *REV: Ath 1/3/90
p286; E 1/3/90 p16; SR 1/3/90 p258; St 28/2/90 p12;
Th 1/4/90 p210-11; Ti 25/2/90 p10.*

90.51 *ADRIENNE LECOUVREUR* (P,5a) Eugene Scribe &
Ernest Legouvé. GLOBE 25/2/90 mat perf. 1st perfd
Théâtre de la République, Paris, 14/4/49. <u>Maurice</u>

de Saxe Fred Terry; Prince de Bouillon Gerald Maxwell;
Abbe de Chazeuil Sydney Herberte Basing; Michonner
Julian Cross; Poission H. Athol Forde; Quinault Walter
Shaw; Call Boy Master River. Princess de Bouillon
Vane; Duchesse d'Aumont Cowen; Marquise de Sancerre
J. Earle; Countess de Beauveau Violet Armbruster; Ad-
rienne Lecouvreur [Ellen Lancaster] Wallis [Mrs Lan-
caster]; Mlle Jouvent Adrienne Dairolles; Mlle Dange-
ville Ada Laurence; Maid May Conrade. L & MGR F.R.
Benson; Cost Mrs May; Pq William Clarkson; Furn Oezt-
mann & Co.; Sm Julian Cross; Hon Sec Cpt. Jephson; Bm
Harrington Baily. *REV: E 1/3/90 p11; St 28/2/90 p12-3.*

90.52 *ON A DOOR STEP* (DSk) Clement Scott. GLOBE 25/2/
90 mat perf. [1st perf ?]. Vera Beringer; Minnie
Terry. L & MGR F.R. Benson. *REV: St 28/2/90 p13.*

90.53 *MEADOW SWEET* (C,1a) "Terra Cotta" [Miss C.M.
Prevost]. VAUDEVILLE 5/3/90-26/7/90. 122 perf [np
3-4/4].* Benjamin Barnes J.S. Blythe; John Cyril
Maude; Fred Topliff Frank Gillmore; Jokel Fred Thorne.
Julia Topliff [Lily] Hanbury; Margery Meadows Ella
Banister. L Thomas Thorne; Act mgr Sydney Alport; Sm
Fred Thorne. *REV: Ath 8/3/90 p318; E 8/3/90 p11; St
7/3/90 p12; Th 1/4/90 p211-2.*

90.54 *HAMLET* (T,5a) William Shakespeare. GLOBE 6/3/90-
18/4/90. 13 perf [ea Th, Fri; add mat 13/3; np 3-4/4].
1st perfd Globe 1602. Claudius Charles Cartwright;
Hamlet F.R. Benson; Polonius [George] F. Black; Laer-
tes Herbert Ross; Horatio Otho Stuart; Rosencrantz
Arthur Grenville; Guildenstern G.M. Howard; Osric
Gerald Gurney; Francisco C.M. Hallard; Reynaldo L.
Rosoman; Priest Walter Shaw; 2nd Gravedigger H. Athol
Forde; 1st Gravedigger G.R. Weir; 1st Actor Alfred
Brydone; 2nd Actor Edward P. Major; 5th Actor Charles
Barwell; 4th Actor Hugh Meadows; Bernardo E. Sherard;
Messenger G. Harrod; Marcellus E. Perry; Ghost Ste-
phen Phillips. Gertrude Ada Ferrar; 3rd Actor Edith
Selwyn; Ophelia Mrs F.R. Benson. L & MGR F.R. Benson;
Sc [W.T.] Hemsley; Props H. Skelly; Mus dir E. Bog-
getti; Sm T.J. Merridew; Pd Hugh Moss; Act mgr H.
Jalland. *REV: Ath 8/3/90 p349; E 8/3/90 p11; SR 15/
3/90 p315-6; St 14/3/90 p12; Th 1/4/90 p 212-3; Ti*

7/3/90 p10.

90.55 *THE FAVOURITE OF THE KING* (HistP,4a) F.S. Boas.
COMEDY 11/3/90-15/3/90. 5 mat perf.* <u>Francis</u> Thomas
Lewen; <u>George Villiers</u> Royce Carleton; <u>Dr Lambe</u> Bas-
set Roe; <u>John Felton</u> J.R. Crauford; <u>Sir Roger Aston</u>
Allen Beaumont; <u>Philip Barton</u> Lawrence d'Orsay. <u>Helen</u>
<u>Aston</u> Dorothy Dene; <u>Lady Katherine Manners</u> Annie Rose;
<u>Cecilia</u> Mrs C.L. Carson; <u>Lady Villiers</u> Louise Moodie.
[<u>Singer</u> in Act IV Templer Saxe]. <u>L</u> Charles H. Hawtrey;
<u>Songs</u> C.A. Lee; <u>Ch</u> Katti Lanner; <u>Chorus dir</u> John Fitz-
Gerald; <u>Cost</u> J.A. Harrison, Mme M. & H. Gothon; <u>Pq</u>
William Clarkson; <u>Furn</u> W.S. Lyon; <u>Mus dir</u> J[ames] M.
Glover. *REV: Ath 15/3/90 p350; E 15/3/90 p8; St 14/3/*
90 p12; Th 1/4/90 p213-4.

90.56 *THE HUNCHBACK* ([P,5a]) James Sheridan Knowles.
ADELPHI 13/3/90 mat perf. 1st perfd Covent Garden
5/4/32. <u>Master Walter</u> Julian Cross; <u>Sir Thomas Clif-</u>
<u>ford</u> Luigi Lablache; <u>Lord Tinsel</u> A. Rodney; <u>Earl Roch-</u>
<u>dale</u> R. de Fonblanque; <u>Modus</u> Ben Greet; <u>Falhorn</u> Bel-
lew; <u>Stephen</u> McManns. <u>Julia</u> Emmerson; <u>Helen</u> Mrs Patrick Campbell. <u>L</u> A. & S. Gatti; <u>Sm</u> Robert Soutar; <u>Mus</u>
<u>dir</u> Henry Sprake; <u>Act mgr</u> Charles A. Jecks.

90.57 *DELICATE GROUND* (CD,1a) Charles Dance. ADELPHI
13/3/90 mat perf. 1st perfd Lyceum 27/11/49. <u>Citizen</u>
<u>Sangfroid</u> Arthur Dacre; <u>Alphonse de Grandier</u> Heinrich
Varna. <u>Pauline</u> Amy Roselle. <u>L</u>, <u>Sm</u>, <u>Mus dir</u>, <u>Act mgr</u>
as for 90.56.

90.58 *MISS CINDERELLA* (Ca,1a) W.R. Walkes. AVENUE
15/3/90-21/5/90; 16/6/90-20/9/90. 144 perf [w/mat
22/3, 29/3, 3/5; np 4/4].* <u>Mr Wriothesley</u> Nutcombe
Gould; <u>Lord Raemore</u> Ben Webster. <u>Mrs Wriothesley</u> Mrs
Leston; <u>Hester</u> Lillie Young; <u>Margery</u> Laura Graves. <u>MGR</u>
& PD George Alexander; <u>Act mgr</u> R. d'Albertson; <u>Cond</u>
John Crook; <u>Sm</u> R[obert] V. Shone. *REV: Ath 22/3/90*
p381-2; E 22/3/90 p9; SR 22/3/90 p349-50; St 21/3/90
p12; Ti 17/3/90 p8.

90.59 *CORISANDE* (P,4a) Charles H. Hoyt. COMEDY 17/3/90
mat perf. Leonard Boyne; Cyril Maude; Alfred Bishop;
Waller. Olga Brandon; Beatrice Lamb; Agnes Thomas.

Comment: Mentioned only in *Ath 8/3/90 p318*.

90.60 *MY AUNT'S ADVICE* (C,1a). DRURY LANE 17/3/90 mat
perf. [1st perf ?]. Cpt. Howard Leslie E.S. Willard;
Charles Arundel Herbert Waring. Lucy Arundel Mrs E.S.
Willard; Servant [Violet] Armbruster. L & MGR Augus-
tus Harris; Treas Arthur Yates; Private sec Fred G.
Latham; Sec Miss A. Josephs; Mus dir Walter Slaughter;
Cost Mrs May, L. & H. Nathan, J.A. Harrison; Pq C.H.
Fox, William Clarkson. *REV: E 22/3/90 p9; St 21/3/90
p12.*

90.61 *WAITING* (Dramatic Eccentricity,1a). DRURY LANE
17/3/90; 2/6/90. 2 mat perf. 1st perfd Theatre Royal,
Edinburgh 29/4/87. Harry Harry Monkhouse. Phyllis
Phyllis Broughton. L & MGR, Treas, Private sec, Sec,
Mus dir, Cost, Pq as for 90.60. *REV: E 7/6/90 p14;
St 21/3/90 p12, 6/6/90 p12.*

90.62 *MISS TOMBOY* (C,3a) Robert Buchanan [based on
Vanbrugh's *The Relapse*]. VAUDEVILLE 20/3/90-3/5/90.
12 mat perf [20/3, 28/3, 2/4, 8-9/4, 12/4, 16/4, 19/4,
23/4, 26/4, 30/4, 3/5]. 6/5/90-26/7/90. 86 perf [w/W,
S mat exc 4/6, 28/6, 2/7, 5/7, 9/7, 12/7, 16/7, 19/7,
23/7, 26/7; add mat 26/5].* Lord Foppington Thomas
Thorne; Lory Cyril Maude; Tom Fashion Frank Gillmore;
Sir George Matcham J.S. Blythe; Hyde [C.] Harbury;
Sir Tunbelly Clumsy Fred Thorne; Squire Ditch [A.]
Austin; Lavarole O[swald] Yorke; Jabez J[ohn] Wheat-
man; Jacob C[ecil] Ramsey; Rev Mr Quiverwit T. Grove;
Mendlegs J. Crichton; Glitter S. Freeman; Coates S.
Lawrence; Tierce T. Walters. Fanny Hoyden Winifred
Emery; Mrs Sentry Sylvia Hodson; Nancy Ditch Lily
Hanbury; Dolly Primrose Mary Collette. L Thomas Thorne;
Act mgr Sydney Alport; Sm Fred Thorne. *REV: Ath 29/3/
90 p414; E 22/3/90 p8; SR 22/3/90 p350; St 28/3/90
p12; Th 1/5/90 p256-8; Ti 21/3/90 p11.*

90.63 *DAVID GARRICK* (C,3a) T.W. Robertson. CRITERION
22/3/90-3/5/90; 31/5/90(m). 43 perf [w/S mat exc 22/3;
np 4/4]. 1st perfd Prince of Wales's, Birmingham 4/64.
David Garrick Charles Wyndham; Squire Chivey George
Giddens; Smith William Blakeley; Brown Sydney Valentine; Jones S[tanley] Hewson; Thomas F[rank] Atherley;

George F. Emery; <u>Simon Ingot</u> William Farren. <u>Mrs</u>
<u>Smith</u> Ffolliott Paget/Emily Vining; <u>Araminta Brown</u>
Emily Miller/M.A. Victor; <u>Ada Ingot</u> Mary Moore. <u>L &</u>
<u>MGR</u> Charles Wyndham; <u>Cond</u> B. Solomon; <u>Sc</u> Bruce Smith;
<u>Decorations</u> Maple & Co.; <u>Act mgr</u> E. Harvey; <u>Sm</u> Edward
Hastings. *REV: Ath 29/3/90 p414; St 28/3/90 p11.*

90.64 *A PRETTY PIECE OF BUSINESS* (Ca,1a) Thomas Morton. CRITERION 22/3/90-3/5/90. 36 perf [np 4/4]. 1st
perfd 12/11/53. <u>Cpt. Felix Merryweather</u> Frank Atherley; <u>Dr Launcelot Shee</u> George Giddens. <u>Mrs Grantley</u>
Fanny Moore; <u>Miss Charlotte Shee</u> E[leanore] Leyshon;
<u>Dobson</u> Emily Vining. <u>L & MGR</u>, <u>Act mgr</u>, <u>Sm</u>, <u>Sc</u>, <u>Decora-</u>
<u>tions</u> as for 90.63.

90.65 *NUMBER TWO* (FC,3a) Harry Croft Hiller. VAUDE-
VILLE 24/3/90-25/3/90. 2 mat perf.* <u>Larry O'Larrigan</u>
Fred Shepherd; <u>Peter Jump</u> Charles Medwin; <u>Fred Darcy</u>
Norman V. Norman; <u>Harry Brompton</u> Richard Brennand;
<u>Jack Cramp</u> Adolphus Ellis; <u>Suetonius Lippy</u> Edgar
Smart; <u>Hinton Biffkins</u> Fowler Thatcher; <u>Mr Ralston</u>
George Hughes. <u>Lady Magrath</u> Mary Stuart; <u>Emily Jemima</u>
<u>Jump</u> Mrs Henry Leigh; <u>Emily Jump</u> Gertrude Lovell;
<u>Mabel Brompton</u> Rose Dearing; <u>Daisy Dove</u> Vinnie Ben-
nett. *REV: Ath 29/3/90 p414; E 29/3/90 p8; St 28/3/90*
p12.

90.66 *ANDROMEDA* (T,1a) Rose Seaton. VAUDEVILLE 24/3/
90-25/3/90. 2 mat perf.* <u>Cleon</u> Leonard Outram. <u>Nes-</u>
<u>trina</u> Josephine St. Ange; <u>Ismene</u> Mrs Wyatt; <u>Andro-</u>
<u>meda</u> Rose Seaton. *REV: As for 90.65.*

90.67 *JESS* (D,4a) Eweretta Lawrence & J.J. Bisgood
[fr H. Rider Haggard's novel]. ADELPHI 25/3/90 mat
perf.* <u>Silas Croft</u> J.D. Beveridge; <u>John Niel</u> T.B.
Thalberg; <u>Frank Muller</u> Charles Dalton; <u>Hans Coetzee</u>
Julian Cross; <u>Carolus</u> J[ohn] Clulow; <u>Jan</u> Gilbert Yorke;
<u>Jantze</u> H. Athol Forde; <u>Moute</u> [Sydney] Jerram; <u>Hendrik</u>
Calvert. <u>Mrs Neville</u> [Josephine] St. Ange; <u>Bessie</u>
<u>Croft</u> Helen Forsyth; <u>Jess</u> Eweretta Lawrence. <u>L</u> A. & S.
Gatti; <u>Dir</u> J.D. Beveridge; <u>Mus dir</u> Henry Sprake; <u>Act</u>
<u>mgr</u> Charles A. Jecks. *REV: Ath 29/3/90 p414; E 29/3/*
90 p8; SR 29/3/90 p378-9; St 28/3/90 p12; Ti 26/3/90
p8.

90.68 *PEDIGREE* (C,3a) C. Clement Bowring & F.H. Court.
TOOLE'S 28/3/90 mat perf.[1st prof]. Sydney Calthorpe
Yorke Stephens; Hon Guy Spavin Compton Coutts; Cpt.
John Pollard Liugi Lablache; Robert E.M. Robson; Lord
Martingale Lawrence d'Orsay; Sir Jabez Blair Edward
Righton. Kitty Clifton Vane Featherston; Mrs Fitz-
patrick Robertha Erskine; Jane Helen Leyton; Diana
Eva Moore; Nora Sylvia Grey. DIR W.H. Vernon; Mus
C.J. Hargitt; Bm [J.] Edward Hollingshead; Bom Monte;
Mgr Fred Horner. *REV: Ath 5/4/90 p446; E 29/3/90 p7;
St 4/4/90 p10.*

90.69 *HENRY IV, PART I* (HistP,5a) William Shakespeare.
LYCEUM 29/3/90 mat perf. 1st perfd 1598. King Henry IV
Arthur Ayers; Henry Ben Webster; Prince John Arthur
Fry; Westmoreland John Pullman; Sir Walter Blunt Hugh
Chisholm; Thomas Percy F.R[awson] Buckley; Henry Percy
William Bell; Hotspur Frank Halden; Edmund Mortimer
F.H. Roberts; Archibald F. Harvey; Owen Glendower S.
A. Boulton; Sir Richard Vernon H. Stockley; Sir John
Falstaff Augustus Littleton; Poins F. Sherbrooke;
Gadshill C.H. Owen; Peto C.J. Kent; Bardolph J.O.
Grout; Francis J.B. Edwards; Travellers W. Belford,
F. Robinson; Carriers W.S. Campbell, J. Corbould;
Sheriff Arthur Pullman; Chamberlain B. Williams. Lady
Percy Webster; Lady Mortimer Eleanor Rees; Mrs Quick-
ly Mrs William Bell. L & MGR Henry Irving; Dir H.D.
Shepard; Props A.G. Hamilton; Cost H. & L. Nathan; Pq
C.H. Fox. *REV: Ath 5/4/90 p445; E 5/4/90 p9; SR 5/4/
90 p413; St 4/4/90 p9; Ti 31/3/90 p8.* Comment: Perfd
by the Irving Amateur Dramatic Club.

90.70 *FOR HER CHILD'S SAKE* (DE,1a) Sir Charles Young.
TERRY'S 29/3/90-25/6/90. 75 perf [np 4/4]. [1st prof].
Stephen Ormonde Oscar Adye; Mr Marsham A. Ellis; Aub-
rey Verschoyle J[ames] Nelson. Edith Ormonde M.A.
Giffard; Geraldine Helen Leyton. L Edward Terry; Mgr
Cissy Graham; Act mgr H.T. Brickwell; Sec C. [St.
John] Denton; Mus dir J. Bayliss; Asm George Belmore.
*REV: Ath 5/4/90 p446; E 5/4/90 p14; St 4/4/90 p9; Ti
31/3/90 p8.*

90.71 *A VILLAGE PRIEST* (P,5a) Sydney Grundy [fr William Busnach & Cauvin, *La Secret de la Terreuse*]. HAY-

MARKET 3/4/90-12/7/90; 6/10/90-6/11/90. 131 perf [w/S
mat exc 5/4, 12/7, 18/10, 1/11; add mat 23/4, 30/4,
21/5; np 4/4, 3/11].*Abbé Dubois H.B. Tree; Jean Tor-
quenie James Fernandez; Armand d'Arcay Fred Terry;
Cpt. of Gendarmes [Charles] Allan. Mme d'Arcay Mrs
Gaston Murray; Countesse de Tremeillan Rose Leclercq;
Marguerite Mrs H.B. Tree/Julia Neilson; Jeanne Tor-
quenie [Rose] Norreys; Madeline Mrs E.H. Brooke. L &
MGR H.B. Tree; Bom W.H. Leverton; Cond Carl Armbruster;
Sc Walter Hann, Walter Johnstone; Sm A.B. Tapping; Bm
& Sec F[rederick] Harrison. *REV: Ath 12/4/90 p477-8;
E 5/4/90 p8; SR 12/4/90 p436-7; St 11/4/90 p12, 10/
10/90 p14-5; Th 1/5/90 p258-9; Ti 4/4/90 p8.*

90.72 *ROMEO AND JULIET* (O,Prol,4a) Charles Gounod.
DRURY LANE 5/4/90, 9/4, 14/4/90. 3 perf. 1st perfd
Théâtre-Lyrique, Paris, 27/4/67. Romeo Barton Mc-
Guckin; Mercutio F[rank] H. Celli; Tybalt John Child;
Friar Lawrence Abramoff; Duke of Verona E. Albert;
Benvolio Ellis; Capulet Max Eugene; Paris Wilfred Es-
mond. Stephano Kate Drew; Juliet Zelie de Lussan;
Gertrude Annie Cook. L & MGR Augustus Harris; Cond
Eugene I. Goossens; Mgr dir Augustus Harris, Henry
Bruce. *REV: Ath 12/4/90 p477; E 12/4/90 p7; SR 19/4/
90 p474; St 11/4/90 p11; Ti 7/4/90 p6.* Comment: Carl
Rosa Opera Company.

90.73 *THE SENTRY* (MV,1a) Felix Remo & T. Malcolm Wat-
son. LYRIC 5/4/90-17/5/90. 37 perf.* Col. Pettigrew
Frank [M.] Wood; Sgt.-mjr. F.L. Scates; Tim O'Brien
John Le Hay. Peggy Maud Holland; Polly Burchett Ellis
Jeffreys; Mrs Pettigrew Adelaide Newton. L & MGR
Henry J. Leslie; Mus Ivan Caryll; Song W. Yardley.
REV: E 12/4/90 p14; St 11/4/90 p12; Ti 7/4/90 p11.

90.74 *DICK VENABLES* (D,4a) Arthur Law. SHAFTESBURY
5/4/90-17/5/90. 40 perf [w/mat 7/4, 16/4, 23/4].*
Dick Venables E.S. Willard; Archdeacon Jellicoe Alfred Bishop; Cpt. Lankester Arthur Elwood; Dr Pagan-
stecher E.W. Garden; Peters H[enry] Cane; Charles
Kirby Henry V. Esmond; Clifford Royston Keith; Mori-
arty E.W. Thomas; Atkinson Hugh Harting. Lady Harriet
Jellicoe Mrs [George] Canninge; Helen Jellicoe Annie
Rose; Wilson Annie Hill; Mrs Lisle Olga Brandon;

Horner Groeme; <u>Lister</u> Beckett. L & MGR E.S. Willard,
John Lart; <u>Dir</u> E.S. Willard; <u>Act mgr</u> W.H. Griffiths;
<u>Bom</u> [F.] Forbes; <u>Sc</u> Walter Hann, Bruce Smith; <u>Treas</u>
Gilbert Tate; <u>Mus dir</u> Edward Jones; <u>Asm</u> [C.H.] Rimbault; <u>Pp</u> John Lancaster. *REV: Ath 12/4/90 p478; E*
12/4/90 p14; SR 12/4/90 p438; St 11/4/90 p12; Th 1/5/
90 p260-1; Ti 7/4/90 p11.

90.75 *DOMESTIC ECONOMY* (COa) F.C. Burnand & Edward
Soloman (mus). COMEDY 7/4/90-3/5/90. 24 perf.* <u>John</u>
<u>Grumley</u> Ells Dagnall; <u>Tom Smith</u> William Lugg; <u>Joey</u>
Master S. Solomon. <u>Mrs Shackles</u> Alice Yorke; <u>Miss Knag-</u>
<u>ley</u> Mary Glover; <u>Mrs Grumley</u> Alma Stanley. *REV: E 12/*
4/90 p14; St 11/4/90 p12; Ti 8/4/90 p5.

90.76 *CARMEN* (O,4a) Georges Bizet. DRURY LANE 7/4/90,
12/4(m), 16/4, 19/4(m), 24/4, 3/5, 7/5, 10/5/90. 8
perf. 1st perfd Opéra-Comique, Paris, 3/3/75. <u>José</u>
Barton McGuckin; <u>Escamillo</u> Leslie Crotty; <u>Dancairo</u>
Aynsley Cook; <u>Remendado</u> Wilfred Esmond; <u>Zuniga</u> E.
Albert; <u>Morales</u> P. Somers; <u>Lilas Pastia</u> C. Stewart.
<u>Michaela</u> Amanda Fabris; <u>Mercedes</u> Lucille Saunders;
<u>Fransquita</u> Kate Drew; <u>Carmen</u> Zelie de Lussan. L & MGR
Augustus Harris; <u>Mgr dir</u> Augustus Harris, Henry Bruce;
<u>Cond</u> Eugene I. Goossens. *REV: Ath 12/4/90 p477; E 12/*
4/90 p7; SR 19/4/90 p474; St 11/4/90 p11; Ti 8/4/90
p5. <u>Comment</u>: Carl Rosa Opera Company.

90.77 *THE BOHEMIAN GIRL* (O,3a) Michael Balfe. DRURY
LANE 7/4/90(m), 11/4, 21/4, 23/4(m), 2/5, 7/5(m),
21/5/90(m). 7 perf. 1st perfd Drury Lane 27/11/43.
<u>Thaddeus</u> John Child; <u>Count Arnheim</u> Frank H. Celli;
<u>Florestine</u> Wilfred Esmond; <u>Devilshoof</u> Aynsley Cook.
<u>Queen of the Gypsies</u> Mlle Tremelli; <u>Buda</u> Annie Cook;
<u>Arline</u> Fanny Moody. L & MGR Augustus Harris; <u>Cond</u>
Claude Jaquinot. *REV: As for 90.76.* <u>Comment</u>: Carl
Rosa Opera Company.

90.78 *NIXIE* (P,3a) Mrs Frances Hodgson Burnett &
Stephen Townsend. TERRY'S 7/4/90-2/5/90. 20 mat perf
[np ea S].* Trfd GLOBE 5/5/90-17/5/90. 14 perf [w/S
mat]. <u>Basil Belasys</u> Lewis Waller; <u>Bill Hutchens</u>
Julian Cross; <u>Dr Armstead</u> Walter Russell; <u>Bryan Law-</u>
<u>rence</u> William Herbert; <u>Blackett</u> Frederick Knight.

<u>Kitty</u> Helen Forsyth; <u>Mrs Belasys</u> Ruth Rutland; <u>Miss</u>
<u>Pinch</u> Caroline Ewell; <u>Miss Macgregor</u> Charlotte E. Mor-
land; <u>Nixie</u> Lucy Webling; <u>Mary</u> Grace Astle. <u>L</u> Edward
Terry; <u>Mgr</u> Cissy Grahame; <u>Pd</u> Hugh Moss; <u>Bm</u> R. Redford.
REV: Ath 12/4/90 p478; E 12/4/90 p8; St 11/4/90 p13;
Th 1/5/90 p261-2; Ti 14/4/90 p10.

90.79 *FAUST* (O,5a) Charles Gounod. DRURY LANE 8/4/90,
18/4, 26/4(m), 30/4, 6/5/90. 5 perf. 1st perfd Théâtre-Lyrique, Paris, 19/3/59. <u>Faust</u> Runcio; <u>Valentine</u>
Leslie Crotty; <u>Mephistopheles</u> Abramoff; <u>Wagner</u> Charles
Campbell. <u>Siebel</u> Lucille Saunders; <u>Martha</u> Annie Cook;
<u>Marguerita</u> Georgina Burns. <u>L & MGR</u> Augustus Harris;
<u>Cond</u> Eugene I. Goossens. *REV: Ath 12/4/90 p477; E 12/*
4/90 p7; St 11/4/90 p11-2; Ti 11/4/90 p7. <u>Comment</u>:
Carl Rosa Opera Company.

90.80 *APRIL SHOWERS* (C,3a) G. Somers Bellamy & F. Ro-
mer. COMEDY 9/4/90(m), 12/4(m), 16/4(m), 18/4(m),
23/4(m), 26/4(m); 5-23/5/90. 23 perf. 1st perfd
Terry's 24/1/89. <u>Lord Lacy</u> Nutcombe Gould; <u>Frank Lacy</u>
H. Reeves-Smith; <u>Mr Clincher</u> Ells Dagnall; <u>Charlie</u>
<u>Clincher</u> Walter Everard. <u>Mrs Lawrence</u> E. Brunton; <u>Miss</u>
<u>Lawrence</u> Maude Millett; <u>Miss Lacy</u> Annie Hughes. <u>L</u>
Charles H. Hawtrey; <u>Dir</u> William Duck; <u>Bm</u> Gloster Armstrong. *REV: Ath 12/4/90 p478; E 12/4/90 p8; St 11/4/*
90 p12-3; Ti 10/4/90 p8.

90.81 *RELEASED* (D,1a) Charles H. Dickinson. COMEDY
9/4/90(m), 12/4(m), 16/4(m), 18/4(m), 23/4(m), 26/4
(m); 5-23/5/90. 23 perf.* <u>Cpt. Paul Vallete</u> Luigi
Lablache; <u>Victor Leroux</u> Bassett Roe; <u>Corporal Georges</u>
Julian Cross. <u>Mme Lasalle</u> Ada Neilson; <u>Marie Lasalle</u>
Emmerson; <u>Nanette</u> Hetty Dene. <u>L</u>, <u>Dir</u>, <u>Bm</u> as for 90.80.
REV: Ath, E, St as for 90.80.

90.82 *MIGNON* (O,3a) Ambroise Thomas. DRURY LANE 10/4/
90; 10/5/90(m). 2 perf. 1st perfd Opéra-Comique, Paris
17/11/66. <u>Wilhelm</u> John Child; <u>Lothario</u> Frank H. Celli;
<u>Laertes</u> Wilfred Esmond; <u>Giarno</u> Charles Campbell. <u>Fi-</u>
<u>lina</u> Amanda Fabris; <u>Frederick</u> Lucille Saunders; <u>Mignon</u>
Fanny Moody. <u>L & MGR</u> Augustus Harris; <u>Cond</u> Eugene I.
Goossens. *REV: Ath 19/4/90 p508; E 12/4/90 p7; SR*
19/4/90 p474; St 18/4/90 p12; Ti 11/4/90 p7. <u>Comment</u>:

Carl Rosa Opera Company.

90.83 *THE PRINCE AND THE PAUPER* (P,4a) Mrs Oscar Be-
ringer [adpt fr Mark Twain]. GAIETY 12/4/90(m),
19/4(m), 26/4(m), 3/5(m), 10/5(m), 17/5(m). 6 mat
perf.* Henry VIII W.H. Vernon; Miles Hendon J.H. Bar-
nes; John Canty J.G. Taylor; Earl of Hertford Edmund
Gurney; Lord St. John Ernest Hendrie; Father Andrews
John Beauchamp; Bat A. Wood; Dot-go-one [H.C.] Barry;
Sgt. Francis; Sentry Hill; Gaoler [C.] Walker; 1st.
Courtier Kelly; Herald Sirrell; Prince [in Acts I &
IV] Master Alfred Field-Fisher. Edward, Prince of
Wales/Tom Canty Vera Beringer; Mrs Canty Annie Irish;
Lady Jane Grey Ethel Matthews. L & MGR George Edward-
es; Dir W.H. Vernon; Sm Frank Parker; Mus W. Meyer
Lutz; Cost Harrison; Bom A.P. Oxley. *REV: Ath 19/4/*
90 p509; E 19/4/90 p8; SR 19/4/90 p470-1; St 18/4/90
p12-3; Ti 14/4/90 p10.

90.84 *LURLINE* (RO,3a) Vincent Wallace. DRURY LANE
12/4/90; 15/4/90. 2 perf. 1st perfd Covent Garden 23/
2/60. Count Rudolph Durward Lely; The Baron Aynsley
Cook; Wilhelm Frank M. Wood; The Gnome Max Eugene;
Rhineberg Leslie Crotty. Ghiva Grace Digby; Liba
Jeanie Mills; Lurline Georgina Burns. L & MGR Augustus
Harris; Mgr dir Augustus Harris, Henry Bruce; Cond
Eugene I. Goossens; Cost dgn Wilhelm; Cost Mrs East,
Drew; Ch Katti Lanner; Dir Augustus Harris. *REV: Ath*
19/4/90 p508; E 19/4/90 p7; SR 19/4/90 p474; St 18/4/
90 p12; Ti 14/4/90 p10. Comment: Carl Rosa Opera
Company.

90.85 *THE BELLS* (D,3a) Leopold Lewis [adpt of Erckmann-
Chatrian *Le Juif Polonais*]. LYCEUM 12/4/90, 19/4, 26/4,
3/5, 10/5, 12-17/5, 24/5, 26/5, 20/12, 27/12/90, 24/1/
91, 31/1, 21/2/91. 17 perf. 1st perfd Lyceum 25/11/71.
Mathias Henry Irving; Walter [Henry] Howe; Hans [Sam]
Johnson; Christian [William] Haviland; Dr Zimmer [G.]
Black/John Martin Harvey; Notary Gurney; President of
the Court Frank Tyars; Clerk Lacy; Mesmerist [John]
Archer. Catherine Pauncefort; Sozel Kate Phillips;
Annette Coleridge. L & MGR Henry Irving; Sm H.J. Love-
day; Mus dir [J.] Meredith Ball; Act mgr Bram Stoker.

90.86 *THE KING AND THE MILLER; OR, CRAMOND BRIG* (D,1a)
William H. Murray. LYCEUM 12/4/90, 19/4, 26/4, 3/5,
10/5, 12-17/5, 24/5, 26/5, 20/12, 27/12/90, 24/1/91,
31/1, 7/2, 14/2, 21/2, 27-28/2, 7/3, 9/3, 14/3, 16/3,
21/3, 28/3, 30/3, 11/4, 18/4/91. 30 perf. 1st perfd
Theatre Royal, Edinburgh 27/2/26 [as *Cramond Brig*].
James V of Scotland Frank Tyars; James Birkie John
Martin Harvey; Jock Howieson [Sam] Johnson; Cpt. of
King's Guard Lacy; King's Page Master Harwood. Tib-
bie Howieson Pauncefort; Marion Foster. L & MGR, Sm,
Mus dir, Act mgr as for 90.85. REV: E 14/2/91 p9.

90.87 *SHE STOOPS TO CONQUER* (C,5a) Oliver Goldsmith.
VAUDEVILLE 15/4/90(m); 19/4/90-5/5/90. 15 perf. 1st
perfd Covent Garden 15/3/1773. Hardcastle [Henry]
Kemble; Sir Charles Marlow [C.] Harbury; Young Marlow
T.B. Thalberg; Hastings Frank Gillmore; Diggory Fred
Thorne; Jeremy J[ohn] Wheatman; Stingo J.S. Blythe;
Jack Slang F[red] Grove; Mat Muggins Rogers; Tom Twist
C]ecil] Ramsey; Tony Lumpkin Thomas Thorne. Miss
Hardcastle Winifred Emery; Miss Neville Ella Banister;
Maid Lily Hanbury; Mrs Hardcastle Mrs John Billington.
L Thomas Thorne; Act mgr Sydney Alport; Sm Fred Thorne;
Mach S. Trewen. REV: Ath 19/4/90 p510; E 19/4/90 p9;
St 18/4/90 p12; Ti 16/4/90 p8.

90.88 *TWO ROSES* (C,3a) James Albery. CRITERION 16/4/
90(m), 30/4(m), 21/5/90(m). 3 mat perf. 1st perfd
Vaudeville 4/6/70. Jack Wyatt Charles Wyndham; Digby
Grant William Farren; Caleb Deecie George Giddens;
Our Mr Jenkins Edward Righton; Mr Furnival William
Blakeley. Our Mrs Jenkins Mrs E[dmund] Phelps; Mrs
Cups E[mily] Vining; Ida F. Frances; Lotty Mary Moore.

90.89 *JUANNA* (T,3a) W.G. Wills. OPERA COMIQUE 16/4/90
mat perf. 1st perfd Court 7/5/81. Don Carlos de Nar-
cisso Norman V. Norman; Friar John Leonard Outram;
Friar Philip Sam Johnson; Pedro Ivan Watson; The Prior
W.L. Branscombe; The Provost George Hughes; 1st Monk
W.H. Cavendish; 2nd Monk Arthur Lovell; 3rd Monk
Charles Terric. Juanna Esteban Frances Ivor; Dame
Garcia Mrs John Billington; Clara Perez Adrienne Dai-
rolles; Katrina Sybil Baird. L F.J. Harris; Mgr H.
Gittus Lonsdale; Dir Leonard Outram; Cost Victor Bar-

the; Pq William Clarkson; Bm C. St. John Denton; Sm
George Hughes. *REV: Ath 19/4/90 p509; E 19/4/90 p9;
St 18/4/90 p13.*

90.90 *THE LINENDRAPER* (FC,3a) J.R. Brown & J.F. Thorn-
thwaite. COMEDY 17/4/90 mat perf.* Benjamin Bazin
Edward Righton; Squire de Broke Guise; Cpt. Harold de
Broke W. Scott Buist; Reginald Maitland Walter McEwen;
Lush Frank [M.] Wood; George H[enry W.] Brame. Sarah
Cicely Richards; Elinor March Vane Featherston; Mary
Bazin [Mina?] Le Bert; Mrs Maitland Susie Vaughan.
*REV: Ath 26/4/90 p541; E 19/4/90 p9; St 25/4/90 p12;
Ti 18/4/90 p5.*

90.91 *THE STAR OF THE NORTH (L'Etoile du Nord)* Giacomo Meyerbeer. DRURY LANE 17/4/90, 19/4(m), 25/4/90.
3 perf. 1st perfd Opéra-Comique, Paris, 16/2/54.
Peter the Great Frank H. Celli; Danilowitz John Child;
George Skavrouski Wilfred Esmond; Gritzenko Aynsley
Cook; Tchesemeleff Belton; Yesmailoff Charles Camp-
bell; Ismailoff [P.] Somers. Prascovia Kate Drew; Nat-
alie Marion Drew; Ekimono Violet Kranski; Catherine
Georgina Burns. L & MGR Augustus Harris; Cond Eugene
I. Goossens. *REV: Ath 26/4/90 p539; E 19/4/90 p7; St
25/4/90 p11; Ti 19/4/90 p12.* Comment: Carl Rosa Opera
Company.

90.92 *CERISE & CO.* (FC,3a) Mrs H. Musgrave. PRINCE OF
WALES'S 17/4/90 mat perf.* Penguine Vanderbone F.H.
Kerr; Mr Styleman Eric Lewis; Lord Adolphus Perfect
H.H. Morell; Mr Flutter Gilbert Trent; Barlow John Le
Hay; Servant [Philip] Sefton. Lady Kilkenny Myra Kem-
ble; Mrs Obadiah Vanderbone Emily Thorne; Virginia
Sutch Lottie Venne; Miss Blunt Josephine St. Ange;
Miss Prettyman Sylvia Grey; Miss Sweet Ettie Williams.
L Horace Sedger; Pp Edgar Bruce; Cost John Barker &
Co.; Cost dgn Mrs T.P. Hill; Furn Oetzmann & Co.; Pq
William Clarkson; Cond F. Stanislaus; Bm Tom Pitt.
REV: Ath 26/4/90 p541; E 19/4/90 p8; Ti 18/4/90 p5.

90.93 *THE GREEN BUSHES* (D,3a) J.B. Buckstone. ADELPHI
19/4/90-12/7/90. 73 perf. 1st perfd Adelphi 27/1/45.
Connor O'Kennedy Frank [Kemble] Cooper; George W.L.
Abingdon; Wild Murtogh J.D. Beveridge; Muster Grin-

nidge John L. Shine; <u>Jack Gong</u> Lionel Rignold; <u>Cpt.</u>
<u>Dartois</u> Arthur Styan; <u>Paddy Kelly</u> Howard Russell;
<u>Dennis</u> Marshall Moore; <u>Larry</u> James East; <u>Ned Keogh</u> W.
Northcote; <u>Darty Donovan</u> J[ohn] Northcote; <u>Edwards</u>
E[rnest] Bantock; <u>Liitle Bear</u> Victor; <u>Rattlesnake</u>
Collins. <u>Miami/Mme St. Aubert</u> Mary Rorke; <u>Geraldine</u>
Ada Ferrar; <u>Nelly O'Neil</u> Kate James; <u>Meg</u> Mrs Brunton;
<u>Tigertail</u> Clara Jecks; <u>Louise</u> Constance Beaufoy; <u>Eve-</u>
<u>leen</u> Jenny Humm. <u>L</u> A. & S. Gatti; <u>Sc</u> Bruce Smith; <u>Pd</u>
William Sidney; <u>Cost</u> J.A. Harrison; <u>Mus dir</u> Henry
Sprake; <u>Act mgr</u> Charles A. Jecks. *REV: Ath 26/4/90*
p541; E 26/4/90 p16; St 25/4/90 p12; Ti 21/4/90 p6.

90.94 *A MERE BLIND* (Oa) Jacques Offenbach [English
ver by J.G. Taylor]. GAIETY 21/4/90 mat perf. <u>Patachon</u>
<u>White</u> J.G. Taylor; <u>Theodore Black</u> J. Furneaux Cook.
<u>L & MGR</u> George Edwardes; <u>Sm</u> Frank Parker. *REV: E 26/*
4/90 p11; St 25/4/90 p12-3.

90.95 *LONDON ASSURANCE* (C,5a) Dion Boucicault. AVENUE
22/4/90 mat perf. 1st perfd Covent Garden 4/3/41. <u>Sir</u>
<u>Harcourt Courtley</u> F.H. Macklin; <u>Cool</u> Charles H.E.
Brookfield; <u>Max Harkaway</u> Charles Groves; <u>Dazzle</u> Sydney Valentine; <u>Simpson</u> Sydney Brough; <u>Mr Spanker</u>
Charles Dodsworth; <u>Solomon Isaacs</u> W[illiam] Lestocq;
<u>Charles Courtley</u> Yorke Stephens; <u>Mark Meddle</u> Arthur
Williams; <u>Martin</u> Montague. <u>Grace Harkaway</u> Kate Rorke;
<u>Pert</u> Lottie Venne; <u>Lady Gay Spanker</u> Mrs F.H. Macklin.
<u>PD</u> Edward Hastings; <u>Bm</u> C. Irvine Bacon. *REV: E 26/4/*
90 p11; St 25/4/90 p13.

90.96 *THORGRIM* (RO,4a) Frederick H. Cowen (mus) & Joseph Bennett (lib). DRURY LANE 22/4/90, 28/4, 1/5,
5/5, 9/5/90. 5 perf.* <u>Thorgrim</u> Barton McGuckin;
<u>Harold (King of Norway)</u> Frank H. Celli; <u>Eric (a Jarl)</u>
Max Eugene; <u>Thorir (a Jarl)</u> [P.] Somers; <u>Herald</u> E.
Albert; <u>Helgi</u> Leslie Crotty. <u>Amora (wife of Eric)</u> Tremelli; <u>Nanna</u> Kate Drew; <u>Olof (daughter of Thorir)</u>
Zelie du Lussan. <u>L & MGR</u> Augustus Harris; <u>Cond</u> Frederick H. Cowen; <u>Sc</u> [Robert] Caney. *REV: Ath 26/4/90*
p539-40, 3/5/90 p579; E 26/4/90 p8; SR 3/5/90 p534-5;
St 25/4/90 p11-2; Ti 23/4/90 p10. <u>Comment</u>: Carl Rosa
Opera Company.

90.97 *THE VIOLIN MAKERS* (PoetP,1a) Alfred Berlyn [adpt
of François Coppée, *Le Luthier de Cremone*]. SHAFTES-
BURY 22/4/90-17/5/90. 23 perf.* <u>Filippo</u> E.S. Willard;
<u>Ferrari</u> Alfred Bishop; <u>Sandro</u> [Arthur] Elwood. <u>Gian-
nina</u> Olga Brandon. <u>L & MGR</u> E.S. Willard, John Lart;
<u>Act mgr</u> W.H. Griffiths; <u>Pp</u> John Lancaster; <u>Bom</u> [F.]
Forbes; <u>Mus dir</u> Edward Jones; <u>Treas</u> Gilbert Tate. *REV:
Ath 26/4/90 p541; E 26/4/90 p16; St 25/4/90 p12; Ti
23/4/90 p10.*

90.98 *THE CABINET MINISTER* (F,4a) A.W. Pinero. COURT
23/4/90-8/8/90;11/10/90-14/2/91. 199 perf [w/mat 21/
1/91; mat only 12/7/90, 19/7, 26/7, 2/8, 20/12/90,
10/1/91, 17/1, 24/1, 28/1, 31/1, 14/2; np 22-25/12/
90].* <u>Sir Julian Twombley</u> Arthur Cecil; <u>Joseph Leban-
on</u> Weedon Grossmith; <u>Valentine White</u> Herbert Waring/
Frank Rodney; <u>MacPhail</u> Brandon Thomas; <u>Brooke Twombley</u>
E. Allan Aynesworth; <u>Earl of Drumdurris</u> Richard Saunders; <u>Mr Mitford</u> Frank Farren; <u>Munkittrick</u> John Clulow; <u>Probyn</u> Ernest Paton. <u>Dowager Countess of Drum-
durris</u> Roma Guillon Le Thiere/Carlotta Leclercq; <u>Mrs
Gaylustre</u> Rosina Filippi; <u>Imogen</u> Florence Tanner;
<u>Countess of Drumdurris</u> Eva Moore; <u>Angele</u> Marianne
Caldwell; <u>Lady Euphemia Vibart</u> Isabel Ellissen; <u>Miss
Munkittrick</u> Florence Harrington; <u>Lady MacPhail</u> Mrs
Edmund Phelps; <u>Lady Twombley</u> Mrs John Wood. <u>L & MGR</u>
Mrs John Wood, Arthur Chudleigh; <u>Sc</u> T.W. Hall; <u>Mus</u>
Andrew Levey; <u>Cost</u> Russell & Allen, Scott Adie, Na-
than. *REV: Ath 26/4/90 p541, 18/10/90 p521; E 26/4/
90 p16, 11/10/90, p11; SR 26/4/90 p501-2; St 2/5/90
p12; Ti 24/4/90 p5.*

90.99 *DELICATE GROUND* (CD,1a) Charles Dance. CRITER-
ION 23/4/90(m); 14/5/90(m); 5/7/90-2/8/90. 27 perf.**
<u>Citizen Sangfroid</u> Charles Wyndham; <u>Alphonse de Grand-
ier</u> George Giddens. <u>Pauline</u> Mary Moore. <u>L</u> Charles
Wyndham; <u>Act mgr</u> E. Harvey; <u>Sm</u> Edward Hastings; <u>Cond</u>
B. Solomon. *REV: Ath 26/4/90 p542; E 26/4/90 p9; St
25/4/90 p13; Ti 24/5/90 p5.*

90.100 *TRYING IT ON* (F,1a) William Brough. CRITERION
23/4/90(m); 14/5/90(m). 2 mat perf. 1st perfd Lyceum
3/5/53. <u>Walsingham Potts</u> Charles Wyndham; <u>Mr Jobstock</u>
W[indham] Guise; <u>Mr Tittlebat</u> S[tanley] Hewson. <u>Mrs</u>

Jobstock Ffolliott Paget; Fanny E[leanore] Leyshon;
Lucy E. Penrose. L, Act mgr, Sm, Cond as for 90.99.
REV: As for 90.99.

90.101 *WHY WOMEN WEEP* (Ca,1a) Frederick W. Broughton.
CRITERION 23/4/90 mat perf. 1st perfd Criterion 24/
1/88. Arthur Chandos F. Emery; Frank Dudley C. Crof-
ton; Fritz George Giddens. Madge E[leanore] Leyshon;
Dora F. Frances. L, Act mgr, Sm, Cond as for 90.99.
REV: St 25/4/90 p13.

90.102 *MARITANA* (RO,3a) Vincent Wallace. DRURY LANE
23/4/90, 30/4(m), 8/5/90. 3 perf. 1st perfd Drury Lane
15/11/45. Don Cesar de Bazan John Child; Don José
Leslie Crotty; Charles II Max Eugene; Marquis de Monte-
fiore C. Stewart. Marchioness de Montefiore Annie
Cook; Maritana Georgina Burns; Lazarillo Grace Digby.
L & MGR Augustus Harris; Mgr dir Augustus Harris,
Henry Bruce; Cond Claude Jaquinot; Dir Augustus Harris.
REV: E 26/4/90 p15; Ti 28/4/90 p8.

90.103 *OTHELLO* (T,5a) William Shakespeare. GLOBE 24/
4/90-25/4/90. 2 perf. 1st perfd 1/11/1604. Duke of
Venice Stephen Phillips; Brabantio Alfred Brydone;
Gratiano A.E. George; Lodovico Gerald Gurney; Othello
F.R. Benson; Cassio Herbert Ross; Iago Charles Cart-
wright; Montano H. Athol Forde; Roderigo Arthur Gren-
ville; Messenger from the Galleys G.M. Howard; Julio
C.M. Hallard; Officer G[eorge?] Hippisley; Herald L.
Rosoman; Clown H. Gordon Tomkins. Desdemona Mrs F.R.
Benson; Emilia Rose Mellor; Bianca Mabel Henry. L F.R.
Benson; Act mgr H. Jalland; Sc [W.T.] Hemsley; Props
[H.] Skelly; Mus dir E. Boggetti; Sm T.J. Merridew.
*REV: Ath 3/5/90 p580; E 26/4/90 p11; St 2/5/90 p12;
Ti 25/4/90 p12.*

90.104 *CHANGES* (C,3a) John Aylmer. TOOLE'S 25/4/90 mat
perf.* Sir Timothy Evergreen Adolphus Ellis; John
Hewitt Reginald Stockton; Mr Flimsleigh Ernest H.
Patterson; Mjr. Jungle John Aylmer; Bob Migley Walter
Arnauld. Mrs Cranbury Croker Josephine St. Ange; Lady
Una Scatterton Alice Yorke; Ethel Evergreen Mary Col-
lette. MGR Fred Horner; Bm J. E[dward] Hollingshead;
Pd Alfred Rousby. *REV: Ath 3/5/90 p580; E 26/4/90 p15;*

St 2/5/90 p12.

90.105 *LOHENGRIN* (O,[3a]) Richard Wagner. DRURY LANE 26/4/90, 29/4, 3/5/90(m). 3 perf. 1st perfd Court, Weimar 28/8/50. Lohengrin Barton McGuckin/Runcio; Henry the Fowler Henry Pope; Herald D. Ffrangcon Davies/Charles Campbell; Telramund Max Eugene. Ortrud Tremelli; Elsa Amanda Fabris; Duke Gottfried Martha Mayall; Pages Laubach, Annie Cook, Skard, Neuwirth. MGR Augustus Harris; Cond Eugene I. Goossens. *REV: Ath 3/5/90 p579; E 3/5/90 p9; St 2/5/90 p12; Ti 28/4/ 90 p8.* Comment: Carl Rosa Opera Company.

90.106 *LOUIS XI* (5a) Dion Boucicault [adpt fr Casimir Delavigne's play]. LYCEUM 3/5/90(m); 19-23/5/90. 6 perf. 1st perfd Princess's 13/1/55. Louis XI Henry Irving; Nemours William Terriss; Cottier F.H. Macklin; Philip de Commines [Henry] Howe; Tristan L'Ermite [Frank] Tyars; Francois de Paule [William] Haviland; Dauphin John Martin Harvey; Marcel [Sam] Johnson; Oliver de Dain [John] Archer; Cardinal W.J. Lorriss; de Dreux [G.] Black; Montjoie Lacy; de Lude [H.W.] Cushing; de Dunis [R.P.] Tabb; Richard [T.] Reynolds; Didier [W.] Marion; Officer [H.] Graham; Attendant Clifford; Toison d'Or Lindsay. Martha Kate Phillips; Jeanne Foster; Marie [Amy] Coleridge. L & MGR Henry Irving; Mus dir J. Meredith Ball; Sm H.J. Loveday; Act mgr Bram Stoker; Bom Joseph Hurst.

90.107 *ESTHER SANDRAZ* (P,3a) Sydney Grundy [adpt of Adolphe Belot, *La Femme de Glace*]. ST. JAMES'S 3/5/ 90-7/6/90. 32 perf [w/mat 17/5; mat only 24/5, 31/5]. 1st perfd Prince of Wales's 11/6/89. Henri Vandelle Charles Sugden; Olivier Deschamps Arthur Bourchier; Fourcanade Fred A. Everill; Boisgommeux Herman de Lange; Justin Erskine Lewis; Joseph [Arthur] Munro; Jules Lambarte. Esther Sandrez Mrs Langtry/Amy McNeil; Mme Fourcanade Mrs Charles Calvert; Henriette Marion Lea; Clarisse Carrie Benton; Berthe Lena Meyers; Blanche Ettie Williams/Violet Armbruster. L Mrs Langtry; Mus dir W[illiam] Corri, jr; Sm Lewis Sealy; Asm F[rank] Weathersby; Treas F.C. Griffith; Bm Gilbert Tate. *REV: Ath 10/5/90 p617; E 10/5/90 p14; SR 10/5/ 90 p571-2; St 9/5/90 p11; Th 1/6/90 p310-1.*

90.108 *THE TIGER* (MF,1a) F.C. Burnand & Edward Solo-
mon (mus). ST. JAMES'S 3/5/90-23/5/90. 18 perf.*
Philip Fuller Charles Colnaghi; Mjr. Stirling W.F.
Stirling; Jacob Nutt J.G. Taylor. L, Mus dir, Sm, Asm,
Treas, Bm as for 90.107. *REV: E 10/5/90 p14; St 9/5/
90 p11; Th 1/6/90 p311.*

90.109 *THE BEGGAR* (C,1a) Frederick W. Broughton. COM-
EDY 5/5/90-23/5/90. 17 perf. 1st perfd Strand 8/7/89.
Martin Harringay William Lugg; Luke Raspin Ells Dagnall; Rev Arthur Selwyn W. Scott Buist. Hetty Harringay Ellaline Terriss; Kate Neville E. Brunton. L
Charles H. Hawtrey; Dir William Duck; Bm Gloster Armstrong; Cond James M. Glover; Sm Edward Hastings.

90.110 *A MISER* (D,1a) Julian Cross. GLOBE 5/5/90-17/
5/90. 12 perf. 1st perfd Theatre Royal, Brighton, 16/
11/87. Gabriel Brandon Julian Cross; Harold F[red-
erick] Knight; Philip H[arold] Eden; Dr Wilding Walter
Russell; Dr Butler T. Enfield. Amy Ruby West; Abegail
[Caroline] Ewell. L F.R. Benson; Mgr R. Redford. *REV:
E 10/5/90 p14.*

90.111 *THEODORA* (P,6a,7tab) Robert Buchanan [adpt fr
Victorien Sardou's play]. PRINCESS'S 5/5/90-27/5/90;
9/6/90-21/6/90. 34 perf [w/mat 14/5, 18/6]. 1st perfd
Theatre Royal, Brighton 18/11/89. Justinian W.H. Ver-
non; Marcellus Charles Cartwright; Belisarius Cecil
Morton York; Euphrates George Bernage; Caribert
George W. Cockburn; Timocles Alfred B. Cross; Agathon
Howard Sturge; Faber Henry de Solla; Styrax Charles
Lander; Executioner Charles Forsey; Mundus Henry Lud-
low; Priscus W.H. Gunn; Lycostrates Walter Lawrence;
Orythes Charles Anson; Amron George Lake Grange; Cal-
chas Thomas Blacklock; 1st Lord William Price; 2nd
Lord C. Downey; 3rd Lord Thomas Harris; 4th Lord
Arthur Prior; Chief of the Ostiaries George Aubrey;
Andreas Leonard Boyne. Michael Mabel Champion; An-
tonia Clarice Trevor; Tamyris Dolores Drummond;
Calhirhoe Marie Stuart; Macedonia Alice de Wynton;
Iphis A. Lloyd; Alexis Dora de Wynton; Columba Bar-
bara Meade; Zena Lucy O'Connor; Theodora Grace Haw-
thorne. L Grace Hawthorne; Mgr W.W. Kelly; Dir W.H.
Vernon; Sc Bruce Smith, Richard C. Durant, H[arry]

Potts; <u>Cost</u> Duquesnel; <u>Mus</u> Jules Massenet, E. Boggetti;
<u>Bom</u> A[rthur] Frye; <u>Mach</u> J.W. Cawdray; <u>Furn</u> J.S. Lyons;
<u>Mus dir</u> E. Boggetti; <u>Act mgr</u> E.H. Robotham; <u>Asm</u> T.C.
Dwyer. *REV: Ath 10/5/90 p617-8; E 10/5/90 p14; SR 10/*
5/90 p572; St 9/5/90 p11-2; Ti 6/5/90 p9.

90.112 *STAGE STRUCK* (F,1a) William Dimond. LYRIC 6/5/
90 mat perf. 1st perfd English Opera House 12/11/35.
<u>Tom Tape</u> Arthur Williams; <u>Sir Matthew Scraggs</u> Frank
[M.] Wood; <u>Count Storiaux</u> Charles [S.] Fawcett. <u>Sally</u>
<u>Scraggs</u> Lottie Harcourt; <u>Lady Scraggs</u> Mrs Henry Leigh;
<u>Poplin</u> Annie Goward. *REV: E 10/5/90 p7; St 9/5/90 p12.*

90.113 *THE GAVOTTE* (Ca) Minnie Bell. LYRIC 6/5/90 mat
perf. 1st perfd Steinway Hall 1/4/90. Sylvia Grey;
Mrs William Greet. *REV: As for 90.112.*

90.114 *COMEDY AND TRAGEDY* (P,1a) W.S. Gilbert. HAY-
MARKET 7/5/90, 14/5(m); 31/5-12/7; 6/10-6/11; 17/11,
24/11/90. 68 perf [np 15/10]. 1st perfd Lyceum 26/1/
84. <u>D'Aulnay</u> Fred Terry; <u>Dr Choquart</u> Charles Allan;
<u>Duc d'Orleans</u> Lewis Waller?/Nutcombe Gould; <u>Abbe Du-</u>
<u>bois</u> Leith; <u>De Grancy</u> Warden; <u>De la Ferte</u> Robb Har-
wood; <u>De Courcelles</u> [Rankin?] Duval; <u>Viscomte de</u>
<u>Mauzun</u> Paton; <u>De Broglio</u> Ashby; <u>Joseph</u> [J.] Montagu.
<u>Pauline</u> Aylward; <u>Clarice</u> Julia Neilson. <u>L & MGR</u> H.B.
Tree; <u>Cost</u> L. & H. Nathan; <u>Cond</u> Carl Armbruster; <u>Sm</u>
A.B. Tapping; <u>Bm & Sec</u> Frederick Harrison. *REV: Ath*
11/10/90 p492; E 10/5/90 p8; SR 10/5/90 p572.

90.115 *THE BALLAD-MONGER* (RP,1a) Walter Besant &
Walter Herries Pollock [adpt of Theodore de Banville,
Gringoire]. HAYMARKET 7/5/90 mat perf. 1st perfd Hay-
market 15/9/87. <u>Gringoire</u> H.B. Tree; <u>Louis XI</u> [C.H.
E.] Brookfield. <u>Loyse</u> Mrs H.B. Tree. *REV: SR 10/5/90*
p572; St 9/5/90 p12.

90.116 *RACHEL* (DSk) Clotide Graves. HAYMARKET 7/5/90
mat perf.* <u>Rachel</u> Laura Villiers; <u>Rose</u> Aylward. *REV:*
E 10/5/90 p8; St 9/5/90 p12.

90.117 *A MODERN MARRIAGE* (P,4a) Neville Doone. COMEDY
8/5/90 mat perf.* <u>Henry Edwards</u> Lewis Waller; <u>Cpt.</u>
<u>Gossett</u> Sydney Herberte Basing; <u>Walter Trevor</u> Royce

Carleton; <u>Wilson</u> H[arold] Eden; <u>Sir Richard Arling-</u>
<u>ford</u> John Beauchamp; <u>John Middleton</u> Julian Cross;
<u>Mjr. Sportington</u> C[harles] Kent. <u>Lilian Arlingford</u>
Alma Murray; <u>Lady Blessington</u> Robertha Erskine; <u>Eva</u>
<u>Arlingford</u> Ellaline Terriss. *REV: Ath 17/5/90 p650;*
E 10/5/90 p9; St 16/5/90 p12; Th 1/6/90 p314-5.

90.118 *SHE STOOPS TO CONQUER* (C,3a) Oliver Goldsmith.
CRITERION 10/5/90-4/7/90. 49 perf [w/mat 17/5].**
<u>Young Marlow</u> Charles Wyndham; <u>Hardcastle</u> William
Blakeley; <u>Sir Charles Marlow</u> F[rank] Atherley; <u>Has-</u>
<u>tings</u> W[ilfred] Draycott; <u>Tony Lumpkin</u> George Giddens;
<u>Diggory</u> Sydney Valentine; <u>Roger</u> S[tanley] Hewson;
<u>Ralph</u> C[harles] Steyne; <u>Gregory</u> L. Chapuy; <u>Stingo</u> J.
Francis; <u>Tom Tickle</u> C. Edmonds; <u>Tom Twist</u> F. Emery;
<u>Jack Slang</u> W[indham] Guise; <u>Mat Muggins</u> H. Esmond.
<u>Mrs Hardcastle</u> M.A. Victor; <u>Miss Neville</u> Eleanore
Leyshon; <u>Miss Hardcastle</u> Mary Moore; <u>Maid</u> E. Penrose;
<u>Barmaid</u> R. McNeill. L Charles Wyndham; <u>Sc</u> Bruce
Smith; <u>Cost</u> Nathan, [Victor] Barthe; <u>Act mgr</u> E. Harvey; <u>Sm</u> Edward HAstings; <u>Cond</u> B. Solomon. *REV: Ath*
17/5/90 p650; E 17/5/90 p14; St 16/5/90 p12; Th 1/6/
90 p311-2; Ti 12/5/90 p10.

90.119 *LIVING TOO FAST* (Ca,1a) A.C. Troughton. CRIT-
ERION 10/5/90-4/7/90. 48 perf. 1st perfd Princess's
9/10/54. <u>Charles Prudent</u> Frank Atherley; <u>Cpt. Hon</u>
<u>Craven Plausible</u> Wilfred Draycott; <u>Mr Cotton</u> Windham
Guise; <u>William</u> Stanley Hewson. <u>Julia</u> F. Frances; <u>Mary</u>
R. McNeill. <u>L</u>, <u>Act mgr</u>, <u>Sm</u> as for 90.118.

90.120 *PAUL KAUVAR* (D,4a) James Steele MacKaye. DRURY
LANE 12/5/90-7/6/90. 24 perf. 1st perfd Standard, New
York 24/12/87 [as *Anarchy; or, Paul Kauvar*]. <u>Paul</u>
<u>Kauvar</u> William Terriss; <u>Honore Albert Maxime</u> Henry
Neville; <u>Gen. Delaroche</u> Arthur Stirling; <u>Marquise de</u>
<u>Vaux</u> Charles Hudson; <u>Carrac</u> Ernest Hendrie; <u>Col. La</u>
<u>Hogue</u> Wallace Moir; <u>Dodolphe Potin</u> Victor Stevens;
<u>1st Orderly</u> Herbert Lewin; <u>2nd Orderly</u> J.L. Stoner;
<u>Gen. Kleterre</u> Acton Bond. <u>Nanette</u> Edith Bruce; <u>Scar-</u>
<u>lotte</u> Mrs H. Clifton; <u>Diane de Beaumont</u> [Jessie]
Millward. <u>MGR</u> Augustus Harris; <u>Mus</u> Claude Jaquinot;
<u>Sc</u> [Robert] Caney; <u>Bom</u> John Kemp. *REV: Ath 17/5/90*
p650; E 17/5/90 p14; SR 17/5/90 p600-1; St 16/5/90

p12; Th 1/6/90 p315-6; Ti 13/5/90 p9.

90.121 *THE MARRIED RAKE* (F,1a) Charles Selby. DRURY
LANE 12/5/90-7/6/90. 24 perf. 1st perfd Queen's 9/2/
35. Mr Flighty Victor Stevens. Hettie Bennett; French;
Sybil Grey; [May Lever] Palfrey. MGR, Bom as for 90.
120. *REV: St 16/5/90 p12; Th 1/6/90 p316.*

90.122 *THE FERRY GIRL* (Oa,2a) Dowager Marchioness of
Downshire. SAVOY 13/5/90 mat perf.* Carlo Cpt. Ri-
cardo; Rinaldo Louis Mantell; Dancer C.P. Colnaghi;
Conte Montebello David Bispham; Pietro C.R. Rose;
Francesco P. Burbank. Dancer Lady Augusta Fane; Coun-
tess Montebello Mervyn Keating; Martha Mrs Godfrey
Pearse; Marietta [Cissie] Saumarez; Giovanna [Nellie]
Lawrence. MUS Lady Arthur Hill; Cond Francois Cellier;
Act mgr G.F. Bashford. *REV: E 17/5/90 p8; Ti 14/5/90
p7.* Comment: *Ti* indicates add mat on 14/5/90.

90.123 *AS LARGE AS LIFE* (F,3a) Arthur Shirley. TERRY'S
13/5/90 mat perf.* Ulysses Tinkler G.H. Kersley;
Mulready Splurge James Nelson; Joshua Bimble Sam
Johnson; Bertie Fitz Bunnyon Horace Mills; Raccio
Henry Bedford; Graccio Ivan Watson; Higgs George Bern-
age; Esau H. Landeck. Mrs Morency Adrienne Dairolles;
Mrs Splurge Irene Rickards; Elsie Lena Greville; Mrs
Fitz Bunnyon Madge Stavart; Marian Blanche Wolsley.
L Edward Terry; Mgr Cissy Grahame; Sm H.E. Russell;
Mus dir J. Bayliss; Act mgr & Sec C. St. John Denton;
Sc G[eorge] A. Toplis; Cost Harrison; Pq William
Clarkson; Bom F.H. Innes. *REV: E 17/5/90 p8; St 16/5/
90 p12.*

90.124 *IN LOVE* (Ca,1a). TERRY'S 13/5/90 mat perf.*
Valentine Falcon Edward Lennox; Cpt. Findlay Fred
Tyrrell; Dr Barton Henry Belding. Amabel Irene Rickards; Bessie Lena Greville. L, Mgr, Sm, Mus dir, Act
mgr & Sec, Bom as for 90.123. *REV: As for 90.123.*

90.125 *A HOUSEHOLD FAIRY* (DomSk) Francis Talfourd.
CRITERION 14/5/90 mat perf. 1st perfd St. James's
24/12/59. Comment: Advertized only in *Ti*.

90.126 *THE BARRISTER* (FC,3a) George Manville Fenn &

J.H. Darnley. ROYALTY 17/5/90-6/6/90. 18 perf. 1st
perfd Grand, Leeds 19/3/87. Arthur Maxwell Fred Mer-
vin; Cpt. Arthur Walker Lawrance d'Orsay; Mjr. Dray-
ton Robert Medlicott; Tom Price Fred Emney; Waiter
H.O. Cleary; Mr Jenkins H[enry] W. Brame; Sgt. Crisp
Fred Burton; Jack Roderick Walter McEwen. Miss Foster
Susie Vaughan; Mrs Maxwell Alice Yorke; Ellen Fayre
Mary Kingsley; Kittie Drayton Delia Carlyle; Jane
Clara Ellison. L Kate Santley; Mgr Violet Melnotte;
Pd Fred Mervin; Bm H. Jalland; Act mgr & Treas Henry
Brandon; Cond Louis Strelitskie; Sm Fred Mervin; Furn
J.S. Lyon. *REV: Ath 24/5/90 p684; E 24/5/90 p14; St
23/5/90 p13; Ti 19/5/90 p12.*

90.127 *THE BAILIFF* (Ca,1a) Frederick W. Broughton.
ROYALTY 17/5/90-6/6/90. 18 perf. 1st perfd Theatre
Royal, Bath 5/4/90. Benjamin Grattan Robert Medlicott;
Frank H[enry] Arncliffe; Daniel Grattan Walter McEwen.
Minnie Mary Kinsley. L, Mgr, Bm, Act mgr & Treas,
Cond, Sm as for 90.126. *REV: E, St, Ti as for 90.126.*

90.128 *FAUST* (O[5a]) Charles Gounod. COVENT GARDEN
19/5/90, 26/5, 30/5, 17/6, 28/6, 23/7/90. 6 perf.**
Faust Jean de Reske/Sebastian Montariol/Luigi Ravelli;
Valentino Francesco d'Andrade/Franceschetti; Wagner
Antonio de Vaschetti; Mephistopheles Orme Darvall/
Edouarde de Reske. Siebel Sofia Scalchi; Marta Mathilde Bauermeister; Marguerite de Nouvina/Lillian Nordica. L & MGR Augustus Harris; Cond Enrico Bevignani.
*REV: Ath 24/5/90 p 682; E 24/5/90 p7, 31/5/90 p7; SR
24/5/90 p639; St 23/5/90 p12; Ti 20/5/90 p11, 28/5/90
p10.*

90.129 *THE WRONG DOOR* (FC,3a) Ina Leon Cassilis. COM-
EDY 20/5/90 mat perf.* John Sherman E[rnest] H. Pat-
terson; Dexter Gilbert Yorke; Albert Verner Charles
Lander; Rev Abinadab Vesey Cecil H. Thornbury; Josiah
Pringle Ernest Hendrie. Marie Leroy Agnes Thomas;
Martha Leroy Fanny Robertson; Mrs Scatterby Lena
Young; Cissy Grantley Nellie Lingard; Lizzie Lisa
Leonards. L Charles H. Hawtrey; Dir William Duck; Sm
J.A.E. Malone; Bm Gloster Armstrong. *REV: Ath 24/5/90
p683-4; E 24/5/90 p9; St 23/5/90 p13.*

90.130 *CARMEN* (O[4a]) Georges Bizet. COVENT GARDEN
20/5/90, 4/6, 16/6, 25/6, 28/7/90. 5 perf.** Don
José Fernando Valero/Jean de Reske/Luigi Ravelli;
Escamillo Francesco d'Andrade/Jean Lassalle; Dancairo
Bieletto; Remendado Rinaldini; Morales Miranda;
Zuniga Antonio de Vaschetti. Carmen Zelie de Lussan;
Michaela Virginia Colombati/Regina Pinkert/Margaret
MacIntyre; Frasquita Mathilde Bauermeister; Mercedes
Longhi. L & MGR Augustus Harris; Cond Alberto Ran-
degger. *REV: Ath 24/5/90 p682, 2/8/90 p170; E 24/5/90
p7; St 23/5/90 p12.*

90.131 *MY MOTHER* (F,3a) Amy Steinberg [Mrs John Doug-
lass].TOOLE'S 20/5/90 mat perf.* Adonis Featherfield
Yorke Stephens; Tom Meredith James Nelson; Sir Dallas
Dallas B.P. Seare; Josiah Sparkle A[dolphus] Ellis;
Waiter E[dward] Cranston; Job Turner Henry Bedford;
Dennis McCarthy Harry Monkhouse. Amy Darlington Vane
Featherston; Florence Jean Vanderbilt; Mary Jane Eva
Eden; Mrs Compass Elsie Chester; Felicite Blobbs Amy
Steinberg. PD John Douglass; Mgr Fred Horner; Bm C.
St. John Denton. *REV: E 24/5/90 p8; St 23/5/90 p13;
Th 1/7/90 p29-30.*

90.132 *TIME'S REVENGES* (P,1a) W. Edwardes-Sprange.
TOOLE'S 20/5/90 mat perf.* Prince Alexis Neirska
Oscar Adye; Paul Petrovitch Adolphus Ellis; Gen. Dom-
aloff W.H. Brame; Michael Boralak Sutton Vane; Nathan
B.P. Seare; Gerald Leigh James Nelson. Sophie d'Est-
erie Helen Leyton; Countess Berstal Elsie Chester;
Vera Vassaliski Marie Illington. MGR, Bm as for 90.
131. Pd Sutton Vane. *REV: As for 90.131.*

90.133 *THE BRIDE OF LOVE* (PoetP,4a) Robert Buchanan.
ADELPHI 21/5/90(m);* trfd LYRIC 9/6/90-11/7/90. 31
perf [w/mat 18/6, 25/6]. Methonos Alfred Brydone;
Atalantos Leonard Outram; Lycas Bassett Roe; Zephyros
Lionel Rignold; Eros T.B. Thalberg; Nassrad E. Lennox;
King of Circassia C.M. Hallard; King of Thule Henry
Bayntun; Glaucus H[enry] Arncliffe. Princess Psyche
Harriett Jay; Aphrodite Ada Cavendish; Euphrosyne
Letty Lind; Eridon Clara Jecks; Hyla Frances Ivor;
Crensa Ada Ferrar; Erotion Marie Fraser; Cupidon
Jenny Humm; Phosphoros A. Somerset; 2 Young Zephyrs

Stead, Beatrice Ferrar. <u>MGR</u> A. & S. Gatti/Henry J.
Leslie; <u>Choral Odes</u> Dr A.C. MacKenzie; <u>Mus</u> Walter
Slaughter;<u>Cost dgn</u> Karl; <u>Cost</u> Nathan; <u>Sc</u> F.G. Fenton;
<u>Act mgr</u> Charles A. Jecks; <u>Pq</u> William Clarkson; <u>Sm</u> E.
B. Norman. *REV: Ath 24/5/90 p683; E 24/5/90 p9, 14/6/*
90 p14; St 23/5/90 p12-3, 13/6/90 p12; Th 1/7/90 p26-
9; Ti 22/5/90 p8.

90.134 *THE GRANDSIRE* (P,3a) Archer Woodhouse [adpt of
Jean Richepin, *Le Flibustier*]. AVENUE 21/5/90 mat perf.
1st perfd Terry's 15/5/89. <u>Francois Legoez</u> George Alexander; <u>Jacquemin</u> Nutcombe Gould; <u>Pierre</u> Ben Webster.
<u>Janik</u> Marie Linden; <u>Marie Anne</u> Carlotta Leclercq.*REV:*
E 24/5/90 p10; St 23/5/90 p13.

90.135 *THE WILL AND THE WAY* (Duol) Justin Huntly
McCarthy. AVENUE 21/5/90-31/5/90. 10 perf [mat only
21/5].* <u>Stanley Grant</u> Ben Webster. <u>Sibyl Wisdom</u>
Elizabeth Robins. <u>MGR & PD</u> George Alexander; <u>Cond</u>
John Crook; <u>Sm</u> Robert V. Shone; <u>Bm</u> R. d'Albertson.
REV: E 24/5/90 p11; St 23/5/90 p13.

90.136 *JUDAH* (P,3a) H.A. Jones. SHAFTESBURY 21/5/90-
26/9/90. 122 perf [w/mat 11/6, 18/6, 21/6, 25/6,
28/6, 9/7, 23/7, 26/7, 30/7, 6/8, 13/8, 21/8, 17/9,
24/9; np 6/9, 8-9/9].* <u>Earl of Asgarby</u> Charles J.
Fulton; <u>Prof Jopp</u> Sant Matthews; <u>Mr Prall</u> H[arry]
Cane; <u>Juxon Prall</u> Frederick Kerr; <u>Mr Dethic</u> Royce
Carleton;<u>Mr Papworthy</u> E.W. Thomas; <u>Roper</u> H[ugh] Hart-
ing; <u>Judah Llewellyn</u> E.S. Willard. <u>Lady Eve</u> Bessie
Hatton; <u>Sophie Jopp</u> Gertrude Warden; <u>Mrs Prall</u> Ade-
laide Bowering; <u>Vashti Dethic</u> Olga Brandon/Eleanor
Calhoun. <u>L & MGR</u> E.S. Willard, John Lart; <u>Pp</u> John
Lancaster; <u>Sc</u> Walter Hann; <u>Act mgr</u> W.H. Griffiths;
<u>Bom</u> Forbes;<u>Dir</u> E.S. Willard; <u>Furn</u> Lyon; <u>Treas</u> Gilbert
Tate; <u>Mus dir</u> Edward Jones; <u>Asm</u> [C.H.] Rimbault. *REV:*
Ath 24/5/90 p683; E 24/5/90 p14, 2/8/90 p9; SR 24/5/
90 p640; St 23/5/90 p12, 30/5/90 p11-2; Th 1/7/90 p
24-6; Ti 22/8/90 p6.

90.137 *I PESCATORI DI PERLE (LES PECHEURS DE PERLES)*
(O[3a]) Georges Bizet. COVENT GARDEN 22/5/90. 1 perf.
1st perfd Théâtre-Lyrique, Paris 30/9/63. <u>Zurga</u>
Eugene Dufriche; <u>Nurabad</u> Miranda; <u>Nadir</u> Fernando Val-

ero. <u>Lelia</u> Ella Russell. <u>L & MGR</u> Augustus Harris;
<u>Cond</u> Luigi Mancinelli. *REV: Ath 31/5/90 p712-3; E 24/
5/90 p7; St 30/5/90 p11.*

90.138 *A RIVERSIDE STORY* (P,2a) Mrs S.B. Bancroft.
HAYMARKET 22/5/90 mat perf.*   <u>Harold Brandon</u> Sydney
Brough; <u>Tom Harrington</u> Leonard Boyne; <u>Joe Evans</u> George
Giddens. <u>Lady Carlton</u> Rose Leclercq; <u>Mrs Harrington</u>
Mrs E.H. Brooke; <u>Susie Leyton</u> Kate Rorke; <u>Alice</u> Annie
Hughes; <u>Sarah Grebe</u> Maria Daly; <u>Polly</u> Kate Phillips;
<u>Kitty</u> Mary Collette; <u>Hetty</u> Georgina Kuhe; <u>Jenny</u> Fog-
erty; <u>Tilly</u> Clive; <u>Mother Sibby</u> Robertha Erskine. <u>L &
MGR</u> H.B. Tree; <u>Bom</u> W.H. Leverton; <u>Sc</u> Walter John-
stone; <u>Sm</u> S.B. Bancroft; <u>Act mgr</u> G.F. Bashford; <u>Pq</u>
William Clarkson, C.H. Fox; <u>Mach</u> Oliver Wales; <u>Cond</u>
Carl Armbruster. *REV: Ath 31/5/90 p714; E 24/5/90 p8;
SR 24/5/90 p641; St 30/5/90 p12; Th 1/7/90 p30-1; Ti
23/5/90 p5.*

90.139 *SUGAR AND CREAM* (Ca) James P. Hurst. HAYMARKET
22/5/90 mat perf. 1st perfd Theatre Royal, Windsor
13/1/83. <u>Mr Wentworth</u> Arthur Bourchier; <u>Frank</u> Sir
Augustus Webster. <u>Spruce</u> Violet Armbruster; <u>Mrs Mir-
field</u> Lady Augusta Fane. <u>L & MGR</u>, <u>Bom</u>, <u>Act mgr</u> as for
90.138; <u>Sm</u> William Cathcart. *REV: E, St, Ti as for
90.138.*

90.140 *THE UP TRAIN* (Ca) C.P. Colnaghi. HAYMARKET 22/
5/90 mat perf.*   <u>Guard</u> Eustace Ponsonby; <u>Gentleman</u> C.
P. Colnaghi. <u>Lady</u> Lottie Venne. <u>L & MGR</u>, <u>Bom</u>, <u>Act
mgr</u> as for 90.138. *REV: E 24/5/90 p9; St 30/5/90 p12.*

90.141 *GRETNA GREEN* (CO,3a) T. Murray Ford & John(lib)
Storer (mus). OPERA COMIQUE 22/5/90; 24/5/90-7/6/90.
17 perf [w/mat 24/5, 31/5, 7/6; mat only 26/5]. 1st
perfd Comedy 4/12/89. <u>John Bramble</u> L[lewelyn] Cad-
waladr; <u>Justice Nettle</u> H. Gittus Lonsdale; <u>Robin Bates</u>
William Hogarth; <u>Barnes</u> Eric Thorne; <u>Peter Pong</u>
Charles Collette; <u>John Paisley</u> C. Jameson. <u>Ruth Ferns</u>
Leonora Braham; <u>Widow Ferns</u> Marion Erle; <u>Cicely
Barnes</u> Florence Lonsdale; <u>Phyllis Ferns</u> Villa Knox. <u>L</u>
F.J. Harris; <u>Mgr</u> H. Gittus Lonsdale; <u>Act mgr & Treas</u>
Charles Terry; <u>Dir</u> Hugh Moss; <u>Cond</u> W.F. Glover; <u>Sc</u>
[Edward] Banks; <u>Cost</u> Mme May; <u>Pq</u> William Clarkson.

REV: E 24/5/90 p14; St 30/5/90 p12; Ti 23/5/90 p5.

90.142 *MESMERISM* (F,1a) Carrol Clyde. OPERA COMIQUE
22/5/90-7/6/90. 14 perf [np 26/5].* <u>Sidney Shy</u> Eric
Thorne; <u>Jack Sharp</u> Maitland Marler. <u>Mrs Grey</u> Florence
Lonsdale. <u>L</u>, <u>Bm</u> as for 90.141. *REV: E, St as for 90.
141.*

90.143 *LOHENGRIN* (O[3a]) Richard Wagner. COVENT GARDEN
23/5/90, 5/6, 10/6, 9/7, 18/7/90. 5 perf.** <u>Lohengrin</u>
Jean de Reske/Antonio d'Andrade; <u>Enrico l'Uccellatore</u>
Edouard de Reske; <u>Telramonde</u> Francesco d'Andrade;
<u>L'Araldo del Re</u> Abramoff; <u>Ortrudo</u> Emma Fursch-Madi;
<u>Elsa di Brabante</u> Magaret MacIntyre/Nellie Melba. <u>L &
MGR</u> Augustus Harris; <u>Cond</u> Luigi Mancinelli. *REV: Ath
31/5/90 p713; E 14/6/90 p13; Ti 9/6/90 p6, 12/6/90
p11.*

90.144 *QUEEN'S COUNSEL* (F,3a) James Mortimer [adpt fr
Victorien Sardou *Les Pommes du Voisin*]. COMEDY 24/5/
90-3/6/90. 9 perf.* <u>Joseph Twitterton</u> E.M. Robson;
<u>Robert Keene</u> Edmund Maurice; <u>Mr Blizzard</u> Julian Cross;
<u>Tapp</u> William Lugg; <u>Waiter</u> Ells Dagnall; <u>Constable</u> F.
G. Richards. <u>Katarina</u> Marie Lewes; <u>Mrs Rumbleby</u> E.
Brunton; <u>Miss Tuffon</u> Maria Daly; <u>Angela</u> Maria Fraser;
<u>Polly</u> Lydia Cowell. <u>L</u> Charles H. Hawtrey; <u>Dir</u> William
Duck; <u>Bm</u> Gloster Armstrong. *REV: Ath 31/5/90 p714; E
31/5/90 p14; St 30/5/90 p12; Ti 26/5/90 p5.* <u>Comment</u>:
Cast from V & A programme for 31/5/90.

90.145 *THE CLOCKMAKER'S HAT* (Ca) T.W. Robertson. COM-
EDY 24/5/90-3/6/90. 9 perf. 1st perfd Adelphi 8/3/55
[as *Betty Martin*]. <u>Col. Capstick</u> William Lugg;
<u>Christopher Capstick</u> Ells Dagnall; <u>Mr Duplex</u> R[obert]
Soutar; <u>Fubbs</u> F.G. Richards. <u>Mrs Capstick</u> M. Merton;
<u>Sally Smart</u> Lydia Cowell. <u>L</u>, <u>Dir</u>, <u>Bm</u> as for 90.144.
REV: E, St as for 90.144.

90.146 *IL TROVATORE* (O[4a]) Giuseppe Verdi. COVENT
GARDEN 24/5/90, 1/7/90. 2 perf. 1st perfd Teatro
Apollo, Rome, 19/1/53. <u>Il Conte di Luna</u> Francesco
d'Andrade; <u>Ferrando</u> Orme Darvall; <u>Manrico</u> Rawner;
Bieletto; Palermini. <u>Leonora</u> Eva Tetrazinni; <u>Agucena</u>
Sofia Scalchi; Mathilde Bauermeister. <u>Premiere Dan-</u>

seuse Palladino. L & MGR Augustus Harris; Cond Enrico
Bevignani. *REV: Ath 31/5/90 p713; E 31/5/90 p7; St
30/5/90 p11.*

90.147 *THE FAST COACH* (F) Robert Soutar & J.G. Taylor.
ST. JAMES'S 26/5/90-7/6/90. 11 perf [np 31/5]. 1st
perfd 29/9/73. Jerry Bolt/Prof Walker J.G. Taylor;
Felix Phastley Norman Forbes; Mr Whiffleblinks W.F.
Stirling. Miss Laura Lena Myers; Mary Miffs Carrie
Benton. L Mrs Langtry; Mus dir W[illiam] Corri, jr;
Sm Lewis Sealy; Treas F.C. Briffith; Asm F[rank]
Weathersby; Bm Gilbert Tate.

90.148 *ADOPTION* (Matrimonial Mixture,1a) "Richard
Henry" [Richard Butler & H. Chance Newton]. TOOLE'S
26/5/90-26/6/90. 36 perf [w/W, S mat exc 4/6].*
Barnabas Blockle Compton Coutts; Theodosius Reginald
Stockton; Glumber Alfred Balfour. Barbara Blockle
Cicely Richards; Constantia Marie Illington; Whisker
Mary Jocelyn. MGR Fred Horner; Act mgr & Treas J.
E[dward] Hollingshead; A act mgr W.H. Archer; Mus dir
C.J. Hargitt; Asm S. Jefford. *REV: Ath 31/5/90 p714;
E 31/5/90 p15; St 30/5/90 p12; Th 1/7/90 p31-2; Ti
27/5/90 p10.*

90.149 *LES HUGUENOTS* (O[5a]) Giacomo Meyerbeer. COVENT
GARDEN 27/5/90, 9/6, 24/6, 7/7, 16/7, 25/7/90. 6 perf.
1st perfd Opéra, Paris 29/2/36. Conte di San Bris
Eugene Dufriche/Jean Lassalle; Conte di Nevera
Francesco d'Andrade; Marcello Edouarde de Reske;
Raoul di Nangis Guillaume Ybos/Luigi Ravelli. Valentina Eva Tetrazzini/Lillian Nordica/Ella Russell;
Margherita di Valois Ella Russell/Regina Pinkert; Urbano Sofia Scalchi; Dama d'Onore Mathilde Bauermeister. L & MGR Augustus Harris; Cond Enrico Bevignani. *REV: Ath 31/5/90 p713, 2/8/90 p170; E 31/5/90
p7; St 30/5/90 p11; Ti 28/5/90 p10, 12/6/90 p11, 28/
7/90 p8.*

90.150 *OLIVIA* (P,4a) W.G. Wills. LYCEUM 27/5/90-31/5/
90. 5 perf. 1st perfd Court, 30/3/78. Dr Primrose
Henry Irving; Squire Thornhill William Terriss; Mr
Burchell F.H. Macklin; Moses Gordon Craig; Farmer
Flamborough H[enry] Howe; Leigh F[rank] Tyars. Olivia

Ellen Terry; <u>Sophia</u> Annie Irish; <u>Polly Flamborough</u>
N. de Silva; <u>Phoebe</u> Foster; <u>Gipsy</u> Agnes Barnett; <u>Mrs</u>
<u>Primrose</u> Mrs Pauncefort; <u>Dick/Bill</u> Holland, Pearle.
<u>L & MGR</u> Henry Irving; <u>Mus dir</u> J. Meredith Ball; <u>Sm</u>
H.J. Loveday; <u>Act mgr</u> Bram Stoker; <u>Bom</u> Joseph Hurst.
REV: St 6/6/90 p12; Ti 2/6/90 p7.

90.151 *THE NEW WING* (FC,3a) H. Arthur Kennedy. STRAND
27/5/90 mat perf.* <u>George Slab</u> Charles Collette; <u>Sir</u>
<u>Edward Strangeways</u> Frank Gillmore; <u>Gen. Singleside</u> H.
Athol Forde; <u>Jobbings</u> Eardley Turner; <u>Bobbie Bulton</u>
Herbert Ross. <u>Hester Singleside</u> Gertrude Lovell;
<u>Precilla Singelside</u> Mrs Henry Leigh; <u>Flossie Trivett</u>
Adah Barton. *REV: Ath 31/5/90 p714; E 31/5/90 p8; St
30/5/90 p12-3; Th 1/7/90 p32-3.*

90.152 *A THROW OF THE DICE* (Sk) H. Arthur Kennedy.
STRAND 27/5/90 mat perf.* <u>Lucius Aemilius</u> Leonard
Outram; <u>Caradoc</u> Oswald Yorke. <u>Mona</u> Gertrude Lovell.
REV: Ath 31/5/90 p714; E 31/5/90 p8; St 30/5/90 p13.

90.153 *WANTED A WIFE* (FC,3a) J.H. Darnley. TERRY'S
28/5/90 mat perf. 1st perfd Theatre Royal, Edinburgh
4/11/89. <u>Edward Carlton</u> Arthur Williams; <u>Silvester</u>
<u>Down</u> Sutton Vane; <u>Walter Boyne</u> Yorke Stephens; <u>Cpt.</u>
<u>Bagshot</u> Leslie Corcoran; <u>Gilman Gaunt</u> Walter McEwen;
<u>Frederick Mason</u> James Nelson; <u>Young Harry Carlton</u>
Harry Eversfield; <u>Dixon</u> Adolphus Ellis; <u>Dawes</u> W.
Brame; <u>William</u> F[rederick] Glover; <u>Norman</u> G[eorge]
Belmore. <u>Mrs Boyne</u> Helen Leyton; <u>Mrs Carlton</u> M.A.
Giffard; <u>Mary</u> Rose Dearing; <u>Mrs Mason</u> Ethel Norton;
<u>Young Mrs Carlton</u> Alice Bruce. *REV: Ath 31/5/90 p714;
E 31/5/90 p9; St 30/5/90 p12; Th 1/7/90 p33-4; Ti
29/5/90 p6.*

90.154 *THE DEAR DEPARTED* (Oa) Martyn van Lennep (mus)
& Walter Parke (lib) [fnd on *Le Clou aux Maris*]. COM-
EDY 29/5/90 mat perf.* <u>Philip Dormer</u> Templer Saxe;
<u>Didymus Doolittle</u> F.W. Stanley; <u>Mjr. Maroon</u> Charles
Rowan. <u>Catherine Dormer</u> Annie Schuberth; <u>Cassandra</u>
<u>Doolittle</u> Florence Marryatt. <u>DIR</u> Eugene O. Stafford.
REV: E 31/5/90 p9; St 6/6/90 p12-3; Ti 30/5/90 p7.

90.155 *HEAD OR HEART* (Oa) Arthur Chapman (lib) & Mar-

tyn van Lennep. COMEDY 29/5/90 mat perf.* <u>Legras</u>
Frank Lindo; <u>Francois</u> B.P. Seare; <u>Victor de Merimac</u>
Templer Saxe. <u>Adele Legras</u> Annie Schuberth; <u>Julie</u>
Olga Lovell. <u>DIR</u> Eugene O. Stafford. *REV: E 31/5/90*
p9; St 6/6/90 p12; Ti 30/5/90 p7.

90.156 *MURDER DETECTED* (SensationalSk). COMEDY 29/5/
90 mat perf. <u>DIR</u> Eugene O. Stafford. <u>Comment</u>: Mentioned only in *Ti.*

90.157 *LA SONNAMBULA* (O[2a]) Vincenzo Bellini. COVENT
GARDEN 29/5/90. 1 perf. 1st perfd Teatro Carcano,
Milan 6/3/31. <u>Il Conte</u> Edouard de Reske; <u>Aleasio</u>
Rinaldini; <u>Un Notaro</u> Bieletto; <u>Elvino</u> Luigi Ravelli.
<u>La Sonnambula</u> Etelka Gerster; <u>Lisa</u> Mathilde Bauer-
meister; <u>Teresa</u> Clarice Sinico. <u>L & MGR</u> Augustus
Harris; <u>Cond</u> Alberto Randegger. *REV: Ath 7/6/90 p744;*
E 31/5/90 p7; St 6/6/90 p12; Ti 2/6/90 p10.

90.158 *MARRIED LIFE* (C,3a) J.B. Buckstone. VAUDEVILLE
29/5/90 mat perf. 1st perfd Haymarket 20/8/34.   <u>Mr</u>
<u>Dove</u> Thomas Thorne; <u>Mr Younghusband</u> H. Reeves-Smith;
<u>Mr Dismal</u> Arthur Williams; <u>Lionel Lynx</u> Henry Neville;
<u>Mr Coddle</u> William Blakeley. <u>Mrs Younghusband</u> Lucy
[Isabella] Buckstone; <u>Mrs Lionel Lynx</u> Dorothy Dene;
<u>Mrs Dove</u> Kate Phillips; <u>Maid</u> Ellen Terry; <u>Mrs Coddle</u>
Emily Thorne; <u>Mrs Dismal</u> Eleanor Bufton. *REV: E 31/5/*
90 p7; St 6/6/90 p13.

90.159 *TRYING IT ON* (F,1a) William Brough. VAUDEVILLE
29/5/90 mat perf.** <u>Walsingham Potts</u> Charles Wyndham;
<u>Mr Jobstock</u> W[indham] Guise; <u>Mr Tittlebat</u> S[tanley]
Hewson. <u>Mrs Jobstock</u> F. Frances; <u>Fanny</u> Eleanore Leyshon; <u>Lucy</u> E. Penrose. *REV: As for 90.158.*

90.160 *IN A DAY* (PoetD,3a) Augusta Webster. TERRY'S
30/5/90 mat perf.* <u>Myron</u> Matthew Brodie; <u>Olymnios</u>
Stephen Phillips; <u>Euphranor</u> Roydon Erlynne; <u>Rufus</u> T.
J. Merridew; <u>Tertius</u> C.M. Hallard; <u>Bion</u> David Cours;
<u>Lysis</u> Master Sidney Speller. <u>Klydone</u> Davies Webster;
<u>Ione</u> Lilian Revell; <u>Rhoda</u> Etta Claire; <u>Myrrlia</u> F.M.
Wilson; <u>Earine</u> Edith Vincent. <u>L</u> Edward Terry; <u>Mgr</u>
Cissy Grahame; <u>Sec</u> C. St. John Denton; <u>Sm</u> T.J. Merri-
dew; <u>Songs</u> Mary Carmichael; <u>Sc dgn</u> E.J. Poynter, Wal-

ter Crane; <u>Sc</u> T.W. Hall; <u>Bm</u> Harrington Baily; <u>Act mgr</u>
<u>Mus dir</u> J. Bayliss; <u>Asm</u> George Belmore. *REV: E 31/5/*
90 p9; St 6/6/90 p13.

90.161 *LA TRAVIATA* (O[3a]) Giuseppe Verdi. COVENT GAR-
DEN 31/5/90, 3/7/90. 2 perf. 1st perfd Teatro La Fe-
nice, Venice 6/3/53. <u>Germont</u> Palermini; <u>Gaston</u> Iginio
Corsi; <u>Il Marchesse</u> Bieletto; <u>Il Barone</u> Antonio de
Vaschetti; <u>Il Dottore</u> Miranda; <u>Alfredo</u> Sebastian Mon-
tariol; <u>Giuseppe</u> Cernusco. <u>Violetta</u> Ella Russell;
<u>Flora</u> Longhi; <u>Annina</u> Mathilde Bauermeister. <u>L & MGR</u>
Augustus Harris; <u>Cond</u> Alberto Randegger. *REV: Ath*
7/6/90 p744; E 7/6/90p7; St 6/6/90 p12; Ti 2/6/90 p10.

90.162 *DON GIOVANNI* (O[2a]) W.A. Mozart. COVENT GARDEN
2/6/90, 11/6, 20/6, 9/7/90. 4 perf. 1st perfd Prague
29/10/1787. <u>Don Ottavio</u> Luigi Ravelli; <u>Leporello</u> Jacques Isnardon; <u>Massetto</u> Miranda; <u>Il Commendatore</u>
Plunkett Greene; <u>Don Giovanni</u> Francesco d'Andrade/Jean
Lassalle. <u>Zerlina</u> Zelie de Lussan; <u>Donna Anna</u> Marie
Tavary; <u>Donna Elvira</u> Lillian Nordica. <u>L & MGR</u>, <u>Cond</u>
as for 90.161. *REV: Ath 7/6/90 p744; E 7/6/90 p7; St*
6/6/90 p12; Ti 4/6/90 p8.

90.163 *THE ARTFUL DODGE* (F,1a) E.L. Blanchard. DRURY
LANE 2/6/90 mat perf. 1st perfd Olympic 21/2/42. <u>De-</u>
<u>mosthenes Dodge</u> Arthur Williams; <u>Hon Frederick Flam-</u>
<u>well Fitz Fudge</u> Charles Hudson; <u>Gregory Grudge</u> John
Carter; <u>Timothy Trundle</u> Herbert Shelley; <u>Budge</u> H.
Shelley; <u>Nudge</u> H. Legerton. <u>Emily Wilton</u> Olive Stet-
tith; <u>Susan Smudge</u> Clara Jecks. <u>MGR</u> Augustus Harris.
REV: E 7/6/90 p14; St 6/6/90 p12.

90.164 *A LOST THREAD* (Sk) Mrs Hugh Bell. DRURY LANE
2/6/90 mat perf. 1st perfd Prince's Hall 20/5/90.
Arthur Dacre. Amy Roselle. <u>MGR</u> Augustus Harris. *REV:*
Ath 7/6/90 p746; E 7/6/90 p14; St 6/6/90 p12.

90.165 *TRYING IT ON* (F,1a) William Brough. DRURY LANE
2/6/90 mat perf.** <u>Walsingham Potts</u> Charles Wyndham.
<u>MGR</u> Augustus Harris. *REV: As for 90.164.*

90.166 *LA LUTTE POUR LA VIE* (5a,6tab) Alphonse Daudet.
HER MAJESTY'S 2/6/90-7/6/90. 7 perf [w/mat 7/6]. 1st

perfd Gymnase-Dramatique, Paris 30/10/89. Paul Astier
Marais; Chemineau Noblet; Vaillant Paul Devaux; Conte
Adriani Paul Plan; Marchand Adrien; Antonin Caussade
Burguet; Lortigue Hirch; Heurtebize Lagrange; Le
Notaire Ricquier; Duc de Bretigny Seiglet; 1ere Cha-
sseur Torin; 2eme Chasseur Alphonse; Commissionaire
Boudier; Valet Sorianne. Maria Antonia Pasca; La Mare-
chale de Seleny Desclauzas; Lydie Vaillant Darlaud;
Esther de Seleny Demarsy; Mme de Foder Auge; Mme de
Rocanère Varly. MGR M.L. Mayer. *REV: Ath 7/6/90 p745;
E 7/6/90 p9; SR 7/6/90 p698-9; St 6/6/90 p12; Ti 3/6/
90 p5.* Comment: Gymnase Company.

90.167 *ROMEO ET JULIETTE* (O[5a]) Charles Gounod. COV-
ENT GARDEN 3/6/90, 12/6, 19/6, 30/6, 26/7/90. 5 perf.**
Frere Laurent Edouard de Reske; Capulet Cobalet; Ty-
balt Sebastian Montariol; Mercutio Eugene Dufriche/
Plunkett Greene; Romeo Jean de Reske; Duc de Verone
Plunkett Greene; Gregorio Miranda; Benvoglio Rinal-
dini. Juliette Nellie Melba; Stephano Regina Pinkert;
Gertrude Mathilde Bauermeister. L & MGR Augustus
Harris; Cond Luigi Mancinelli. *REV: Ath 7/6/90 p744;
E 7/6/90 p7; Ti 4/6/90 p8.*

90.168 *SOWING AND REAPING* (C,2a) C. Vernon. CRITERION
5/6/90(m), 3/7(m), 5/7; 7/7/90-2/8/90. 27 perf.*
Harry Grahame Charles Wyndham; Joseph Shenston George
Giddens; Sampson Paley William Blakeley; Dick Hobbs
Sydney Valentine; Robert C. Edmonds; John F. Emery.
Mrs Charity Smith M.A. Victor; Mrs Sampson Paley
E[leanore] Leyshon; Julia Mary Moore; Mrs Watkins
Emily Vining. L & MGR Charles Wyndham; Act mgr E. Har-
vey; Sm Edward Hastings; Cond B. Solomon. *REV: Ath
12/7/90 p75; E 12/7/90 p14; St 11/7/90 p10; Th 1/8/90
p87-8; Ti 7/7/90 p10.*

90.169 *LOCKED IN* (Oa) Walter Frith (lib) & Alfred J.
Caldicott (mus). CRITERION 5/6/90 mat perf.**
[Christopher] Rutland Barrington. [Schoolmistress]
Jennie Hervey; [Sophie Burchell] Jessie Bond. Comment:
Mentioned only in *Ti*.

90.170 *WAITING* (Duol). CRITERION 5/6/90 mat perf.**
[Harry] Harry Monkhouse. [Phyllis] Phyllis Broughton.

REV: Ath 7/6/90 p746; E 7/6/90 p8.

90.171 *A SWARRY DANSONG* (OF) Rutland Barrington (lib)
& Edward Solomon (mus). CRITERION 5/6/90 mat perf.*
Rutland Barrington. Jessie Bond. *REV: As for 90.170.*

90.172 *A BURIED TALENT* (CD,1a,3tab) Louis N. Parker.
VAUDEVILLE 5/6/90 mat perf. 1st perfd Digby Hotel,
Sherborne 3/12/86. Maris Ben Greet; Pietro Bassett Roe;
Felix Roland Atwood; Count von Friedeberg Murray Haw-
thorne. Stella Maris Mrs Patrick Campbell. *REV: Ath
14/6/90 p779; E 7/6/90 p9; St 13/6/90 p12.*

90.173 *IN OLDEN DAYS* (Cavalier Incident, 1a) Mrs
Agatha Hodgson & Archibald Hodgson. VAUDEVILLE 5/6/90
mat perf. 1st perfd Philharmonic Hall, Southampton
8/2/90. Cpt. Desborough Archibald Hodgson; Jocelyn
Durant C. Forbes Drummond. Damaris Nethercliffe Violet
Raye. *REV: As for 90.172.*

90.174 *PICKING UP THE PIECES* (Duol) Julian Sturgis.
VAUDEVILLE 5/6/90 mat perf. 1st perfd Court 14/11/82.
Lord Dawlish Ben Greet. Mrs Melton Mrs Onslow. *REV:
As for 90.172.*

90.175 *LUCIA DI LAMMERMOOR* (O[3a]) Gaetano Donizetti.
COVENT GARDEN 6/6/90, 21/6, 10/7/90. 3 perf. 1st perfd
San Carlo, Naples, 26/9/35. Ashton Palermini/Fran-
cesco d'Andrade; Raimonde Abramoff; Edgardo Luigi
Ravelli; Normanno Bieletto; Arturo Iginio Corsi. Lucia
Nellie Melba; Alice Mathilde Bauermeister. L & MGR
Augustus Harris; Cond Enrico Bevignani. *REV: 14/6/90
p777; St 13/6/90 p12; Ti 9/6/90 p6.*

90.176 *NERVES* (FC,3a) J.W. Comyns Carr [adpt fr Ernest
Blum & Raoul Toché, *Les Femmes Nerveuses*]. COMEDY
7/6/90-13/11/9-. 136 perf.* Buxom Brittle H[enry]
Kemble; Hippolyte Caramel Edward Righton; Cpt. Armi-
tage Charles H. Hawtrey; James G. Kennedy; Commiss-
ionaire William Wyes; Customer P.S. Champion. Violet
Armitage Maude Millett; Mrs Buxom Brittle Sophie Lar-
kin; Emma Lydia Cowell; Iphigenie Ethel Matthews; Mme
Zephyr Elaine Lottie Venne; Clarisse Eleanor May;
Juliette Jennie Coppinger; Anna Carrie Hunt; Lady

Helen Lambert. L & MGR Charles H. Hawtrey; Bm E.F.
Bradley; Sc Walter Johnstone; Asm Charles Milton; Mus
dir James M. Glover. *REV: Ath 14/6/90 p779; E 14/6/90*
p14; SR 14/6/90 p731; St 13/6/90 p12; Th 1/7/90 p34;
Ti 9/6/90 p5.

90.177 *A BAD PENNY* (D,1a) W[illiam] Lestocq. COMEDY
7/6/90-17/10/90. 113 perf. 1st perfd Vaudeville 13/7/
82. Charles Hyde William Wyes; Harry Godwin P.S.
Champion; Richard Hyde William H. Day; Hopkins A.W.
Aysom. May Hyde Ethel Matthews. L & MGR, Bm, Asm, Mus
dir as for 90.176. *REV: E 14/6/90 p14.*

90.178 *DIE MEISTERSINGER* (O[3a]) Richard Wagner. COV-
ENT GARDEN 7/6/90, 14/6, 2/7, 22/7/90. 4 perf. 1st
perfd Munich 21/6/68. Walther Jean de Reske; David
Sebastian Montariol; Viet Pognor Abramoff; Sizus Beck-
messer Jacques Isnardon; Fritz Winogradoff; Hermann
Plunkett Greene; Hans Sachs Jean Lassalle; Kunz Vogel-
sang Iginio Corsi; Balthazar Zorn Rinaldini; Konrad
Delasco; Hans Schawrs Miranda; Ulrich Bieletto;
Augustin Uberti; Hans Foltz Cernusco. Magdalena Ma-
thilde Bauermeister; Eva Marie Tavary. L & MGR
Augustus Harris; Cond Luigi Mancinelli. *REV: Ath 14/*
6/90 p777; E 14/6/90 p13; Ti 9/6/90 p6.

90.179 *PARIS FIN DE SIECLE* (P,5a) Ernest Blum & Raoul
Toché. HER MAJESTY'S 9/6/90-14/6/90. 7 perf [w/mat
14/6]. 1st perfd Gymnase, Paris 22/2/90. Alfred,
Vicomte de Mirandol Noblet; Duc de Linarès Paul Plan;
La Faloise [Armand] Numes; Marquis de Boissy-Godet
Lagrange; Roger de Kerjoel Burguet; La Fauchette
Hirch; Rivolet Nicolini; Valet Seiglet;1er Garcon de
Café Debray; Jules Franck; M des Epiglottes Renoux;
Domestique Ricquier; Adrien Torin; 2eme Garcon de
Café Alphonse. Claire de Chancenay Sisos; Marquise de
Boissy-Godet Desclauzas; Berthe Depoix; Mme des Epi-
glottes Demarsy; Judith Fripier Darlaud; Mme de Val
Chevrette Varly; Mme de la Verpilliere Augé; Mme de
la Roche qui Pleure Lecuyer; Albertine Arbel; Une
Caissiere Miramont; Mme Fripier Renard; Juliette
Sorianne; Femme de Chambre Davenay. MGR M.L. Mayer.
REV: Ath 14/6/90 p779; E 14/6/90 p8; SR 14/6/90 p735;
St 13/6/90 p11; Ti 11/6/90 p10.

90.180 *BY THE SEA* (D,1a) "Alec Nelson" [E.B. Aveling; fr Theuriet's *Jean Marie*]. LYRIC 9/6/90-11/7/90. 29 perf. 1st perfd Ladbroke Hall 15/12/85. Jamie Leonard Outram; Robin Gray Alfred Brydone. Jeanie Francis Ivor. L & MGR Henry J. Leslie; Sm E.B. Norman. *REV: St 13/6/90 p12.*

90.181 *JOAN; OR, THE BRIGANDS OF BLUEGORIA* (CO,2a) Robert Martin (lib) & Ernest Ford (mus). OPERA COMIQUE 9/6/90-14/6/90. 7 perf [w/mat 13/6].* Bilboss David Bispham; Kyrle F. Kinsey Peile; Alphonse George Power; Uriah Elijah Skinner Charles H. Lamb; Coppero Robert Martin; Lumbero Cosmo Gordon Lennox; Herald F. Althaus; Brigands Ernest Enthoven, Paul Monckton, Ernest Little, Cpt. Sinclair, W. Wilson, Evan Fryers, Cecil Haig, Rennell Coleridge, Luther Munday, F. Althaus, Algernon Nugent, Bell, Villegos, I. Malcolm, P. Edmunds, Brand. Bonda Nicholson; Natalie Mrs Godfrey Pearse/Margaret Chetwynd; Annette Aimee Lowther; Joan Douilly; Peasants Douglas, Mrs F. Kinsey Peile, Mrs Nixon, Margot Tennant, Humm Webster, Chetwynd, O'Brien, Langley, Cohen, Douglas Willan, Maxwell, Ross. Dancers Charles Colnaghi. Lady Augusta Fane, Savile Clark. L F.J. Harris; Sm C.W.A. Trollope; Cond Ernest Ford; Dir F. Kinsey Peile; Act mgr Arthur Donald; Ch John d'Auban; Cost dgn Percy Anderson; Cost C.H. Fox. *REV: E 14/6/90 p7.*

90.182 *OLD FRIENDS* (P,1a) Lady Violet Greville. OPERA COMIQUE 9/6/90-14/6/90. 7 perf [w/mat 13/6].* Jack Fitzroy Matthew Brodie; Cpt. Mowbray G[ilbert] Farquhar. Alice Annie Irish; Dolly Helen Forsyth. L, Sm, Act mgr as for 90.181.

90.183 *CASTING THE BOOMERANG* (EccentricC,4a) Augustin Daly [adpt of Franz von Schonthan, *Schwabenstreich*]. LYCEUM 10/6/90-23/6/90; 11/8/90-16/8/90. 21 perf [w/ S mat]. 1st perfd Daly's, New York 24/2/83. Courtney Corliss John Drew; Launcelot Bargiss James Lewis; Paul Hollyhock George Clark; Palmiro Tamborini Frederick Bond; Prof Gasleigh Charles Leclercq; Postman Charles Wheatleigh; Jobbins Edward P. Wilks. Floss Ada Rehan; Hypatia Bargiss Mrs G.H. Gilbert; Dora Hollyhock Adelaide Prince; Jessie Kitty Cheatham. L

Henry Irving; <u>Bom</u> Joseph Hurst; <u>Bm</u> Edward Brown; <u>Act</u>
<u>mgr</u> Richard Dorney; <u>Sm</u> John Moore; <u>Sc</u> T.E. Ryan; <u>Furn</u>
Maple & Co., Lyon; <u>Pq</u> C.H. Fox; <u>Dir</u> Augustin Daly.
*REV: Ath 14/6/90 p779; E 14/6/90 p14, 23/3/90 p9; St
13/6/90 p12, 22/8/90 p12; Th 1/7/90 p35; Ti 11/6/90
p10, 14/8/90 p6, 18/8/90 p6.* Comment: Daly's company.

90.184 *A PEOPLE'S HERO* (D,4a) W. Howell-Poole [fnd on
Ouida's *Tricotrin*].VAUDEVILLE 12/6/90 mat perf. 1st
perfd Grand,Glasgow 21/2/89. <u>Duke de Vigne</u> B.P. Searle;
<u>Earl Charteris</u> E. Hoggan-Armadale; <u>Viscount Lascelles</u>
Arthur Raynor; <u>Lioncoeur</u> W.Howell-Poole; <u>Glaucus Rio</u>
Wallace Moir; <u>Guido Rienzi</u> William Felton; <u>Pierre</u>
<u>Daudet</u> Charles Hargrave; <u>Garton</u> A.E. Maskell; <u>Alphon-</u>
<u>se</u> James Adams. <u>Héloise</u> Alice Raynor; <u>Duchess de</u>
<u>Vigne</u> Gertrude Lesage; <u>Lola</u> Laura Hansen; <u>Florette</u>
Etta Claire; <u>Mere Verite</u> Emily Turtle. *REV: Ath 21/6/
90 p810; E 14/6/90 p8; St 20/6/90 p12.*

90.185 *LA FAVORITA* (O[4a]) Gaetano Donizetti. COVENT
GARDEN 13/6/90, 11/7/90. 2 perf. 1st perd Opéra, Paris
2/12/40. <u>Alphonse</u> Cobalet; <u>Balthazar</u> Abramoff; <u>Gas-</u>
<u>par</u> Iginio Corsi; <u>Fernand</u> Sebastian Montariol. <u>Leo-</u>
<u>nore</u> Hélène Richard; <u>Ines</u> Mathilde Bauermeister; <u>1ere</u>
<u>Danseuse</u> Palladino. <u>L & MGR</u> Augustus Harris; <u>Cond</u>
Enrico Bevignani; <u>Ch</u> Katti Lanner. *REV: Ath 21/6/90
p809; E 21/6/90 p13; St 20/6/90 p12.*

90.186 *ROMEO AND JULIET* (T) William Shakespeare. GLOBE
17/6/90-9/8/90. 48 perf [w/mat 4/8]. 1st perfd 1597.
<u>Romeo</u> Otis Skinner; <u>Friar Laurence</u> John Nesbitt; <u>Cap-</u>
<u>ulet</u> George F. Black; <u>Apothecary</u> J.F. Graham; <u>Tybalt</u>
Edwin Wilde; <u>Benvolio</u> John Humphries; <u>Escalus</u> J.H.
Manley; <u>Paris</u> S.C. Henry; <u>Montague</u> Fred Wells; <u>Peter</u>
G.B. Phillips; <u>Balthasar</u> Moreton Baker; <u>Friar John</u>
Edward Boddy; <u>Mercutio</u> Mark Quinton; <u>Sampson</u> T. Mow-
bray; <u>Gregory</u> B. Simes; <u>Abram</u> David Cowis. <u>Juliet</u>
Adelaide Moore; <u>Lady Capulet</u> May Protheroe; <u>Nurse</u>
Mrs Charles Calvert; <u>Lady Montague</u> Nelly Duncan. <u>L</u> W.
B. Moore; <u>Pd</u> Hugh Moss; <u>Ch</u> W. Ozmond; <u>Cost</u> May & Co.;
<u>Pq</u> William Clarkson; <u>Sm</u> J.F. Graham; <u>Mus dir</u> E. Bog-
getti. *REV: Ath 21/6/90 p810; E 21/6/90 p14; St 20/6/
90 p12; Ti 18/6/90 p9.*

90.187 *LE NOZZE DI FIGARO* (O[4a]) W.A. Mozart. COV-
ENT GARDEN 18/6/90. 1 perf. 1st perfd Burgtheater,
Vienna 1/5/1786. Il Conte Eugene Dufriche; Bartolo
Jacques Isnardon; Basilio Rinaldini; Don Curzio
Bieletto; Antonio Miranda; Figaro Francesco d'An-
drade. La Contessa Marie Tavary; Susanna Ella Russell;
Cherubino Sofia Scalchi; Marcellina Mathilde Bauer-
meister. L & MGR Augustus Harris; Cond Alberto Ran-
degger. *REV: Ath 21/6/90 p809; E 21/6/90 p13; Ti 19/*
6/90 p7.

90.188 *LE PROPHETE* (O[5a]) Giacomo Meyerbeer. COVENT
GARDEN 23/6/90, 27/6, 5/7, 15/7, 19/7/90. 5 perf.
1st perfd Opéra, Paris 16/4/49. Jean de Leyde Jean
de Reske; Oberthal Cobalet; Jonas Sebastian Montari-
iol; Mathisen Miranda; Zacharie Edouard de Reske;
Sergent Rinaldini. Fides Hélène Richard; Berthe de
Nuovina; 1ere Danseuse Palladino. L & MGR Augustus
Harris; Cond Luigi Mancinelli; Ch Katti Lanner. *REV:*
Ath 28/6/90 p840; E 28/6/90 p13; Ti 24/6/90 p10.

90.189 *JEANNE D'ARC* (Drame Légende,3parts,6tab) Jules
Barbier. HER MAJESTY'S 23/6/90-5/7/90. 12 perf [w/mat
28/6; mat only 5/7; np 4/7]. 1st perfd Gaité, Paris
8/11/73. Barwick Garnier; Jacques d'Arc Lacroix;
Lahire Rebel; Thibaut Rosny; Laurent Guesdon Besson;
Siward Herbert; Un Vieillard Perrier; Nicholas Loy-
seleur Piron; Roi Charles VIII Deneubourg; De Thouars
Albert Darmont; Dunois Darlès; Xountrailles Carter-
eau; Pierrolo Prevost; Gordon Duberry; Maitre Jean
Mallet; Manchon Jegu; Jean d'Estivet Legrand. Jeanne
d'Arc Sarah Bernhardt; Iseult Jane Méa; Isabelle
Romée Marie Grandet; Mengette Seylor; Loys Andran.
MGR M.L. Mayer; Mus Charles Gounod. *REV: Ath 28/6/90*
p841; E 28/6/90 p8; St 27/6/90 p9-10; Ti 24/6/90 p10.

90.190 *ART AND LOVE* (C,1a) A.W. Dubourg. AVENUE 24/6/
90 mat perf. 1st perfd Opera Comique 17/2/77. Mr Jackson Arthur Stirling; Harry Sidney Herberte Basing;
Servant H.A. Saintsbury. Lucy [Ellen Lancaster]
Wallis.Lĭ G[eorge] Paget; Mgr George Alexander; Act
mgr A. Darville. *REV: E 28/6/90 p14; St 27/6/90 p10;*
Th 1/8/90 p78-9.

90.191 *PUNCHINELLO* (P,1a) Dr G.H.R. Dabbs. AVENUE 24/
6/90 mat perf.* Oliver Retherdon W.H. Vernon; Roly
Reverie Ben Webster; Lord Reverie Bassett Roe. Nina
E[lizabeth] Robins. MGR, Act mgr as for 90.190; Pq
C.H. Fox. *REV: AS for 90.190.*

90.192 *STAGE STRUCK* (F,1a) William Dimond. AVENUE 24/
6/90 mat perf.** Tom Tape Lionel Rignold. Sally
Scraggs Clara Jecks. MGR, Act mgr as for 90.190. *REV:
E, Ti as for 90.190.*

90.193 *NANCY AND CO* (EccentricC,4a) Augustin Daly
[based on Gr by Julius Rosen]. LYCEUM 24/6/90-7/7/90.
14 perf [w/S mat]. 1st perfd Daly's, New York 24/2/
86. Ebenezer James Lewis; Kiefe O'Kiefe John Drew;
Stockslow Frederick Bond; Tippy Brasher Burr MacKintosh; Renseller Eugene Ormond; Julius William Sampson.
Nancy Ada Rehan; Mrs Dangery Mrs G.H. Gilbert; Daisy
Isabel Irving; Oriana Edith Crane; Betsy Kitty Cheatham. L Henry Irving; Act mgr Richard Dorney; Bm Edward Brown; Dir Augustin Daly; Bom Joseph Hurst; Sm
John Moore; Sc T.E. Ryan; Furn Maple & Co., Lyon; Pq
C.H. Fox. *REV: Ath 28/6/90 p841; E 28/6/90 p14; St
27/6/90 p10; Th 1/8/90 p79-80; Ti 26/6/90 p13.* Comment: Daly's Company.

90.194 *RIGOLETTO* (O[3a]) Giuseppe Verdi. COVENT GAR-
DEN 26/6/90, 4/7, 14/7/90. 3 perf. 1st perfd Teatro
la Fenice, Venice 11/3/51. Rigoletto Jean Lassalle;
Sparafucile Abramoff; Il Duca Fernando Valero. Gilda
Nellie Melba; Maddalena Sofia Scalchi; Giovanna
Mathilde Bauermeister. MGR Augustus Harris; Cond
Luigi Mancinelli. *REV: Ath 5/7/90 p41; E 28/6/90 p13;
St 4/7/90 p9; Ti 28/6/90 p15.*

90.195 *YOUR WIFE* (FC,3a) Justin Huntly McCarthy
[adpt of Maurice Desvallières, *Prête-moi Ta Femme*].
ST. JAMES'S 26/6/90-12/7/90. 15 perf.* Jack Daryl
Arthur Bourchier; Appleton Crabbe [Fred A.] Everill;
Arminius Pappenberg Herman de Lange; Tom Verity
Ernest Lawford. Amy Edith Chester; Lucy Annie Irish;
Josephine Adrienne Dairolles. L Mrs Langtry; Mgr
Arthur Bourchier; Sc Phil W. Goatcher; Furn Oetzmann
& Co.; Act mgr H. Jalland; Mus dir William Corri, jr;

Sm Lewis Sealy; Asm Frank Weathersby; Bm Gilbert Tate;
Bom George Reid. *REV: Ath 5/7/90 p42; E 28/6/90 p14;
St 4/7/90 p9-10; Th 1/8/90 p80-1; Ti 28/6/90 p15.*

90.196 *OLD FRIENDS* (P,1a) Lady Violet Greville. ST.
JAMES'S 26/6/90-12/7/90. 15 perf.** Dick Fitzroy
Laurence Cautley; Cpt. Mowbray Gilbert Farquhar. Alice
Annie Irish; Dolly Marie Illington. L, Mgr, Act mgr,
Mus dir, Sm, Asm, Bm, Bom as for 90.195. *REV: Ath
5/7/90 p42; E 28/6/90 p14; Th 1/8/90 p81.*

90.197 *NEARLY SEVERED* (Ca,1a) James P. Hurst. TERRY'S
26/6/90-5/11/90. 111 perf [np 21-23/7]. 1st perfd
Comedy, Manchester 31/8/85. Fred Middleton James
Nelson; Sam Eckersley William Lestocq. Hannah Eckers-
ley M.A. Giffard; Carrie Sprent Helen Leyton. MGR
Cissy Grahame; Sm Ernest Cathcart; Sec C. St. John
Denton; Act mgr Arthur Yates.

90.198 *CYRENE* (Dramatic Fancy,3a) Alfred C. Calmour.
AVENUE 27/6/90 mat perf.* Fantea Henry Neville; Bran-
cho Edmund Gurney; Gustrell F. Hamilton Knight; Drega
P.J. Kirwan; Zembra John Carter; Moretus Arthur Stir-
ling. Ciprissa Lillian Hingston; Nina Clara Jecks;
Cyrene Marion Terry. MUS Frederick H. Cowen, John
Crook; Ch Sylvia Grey. *REV: Ath 5/7/90 p42; E 28/6/
90 p7; St 4/7/90 p10; Th 1/8/90 p81-2; Ti 30/6/90 p12.*

90.199 *PAPA'S HONEYMOON* (C,3a) Sylvain Mayer & W.B.
Tarpey. CRITERION 28/6/90 mat perf.* Arthur Hale
George Giddens; Benjamin Bush William Blakeley; Mar-
tin Sydney Valentine; Walter Emden S[tanley] Hewson;
Joseph Sniffle J.T. Graham. Amelia Clutterbuck M.A.
Victor; Ida Angela Cudmore; Annette Helen Forsyth;
Agnes Ellaline Terriss; Lucy Mabel Hardinge; Caroline
E[mily] Vining. L Charles Wyndham; Act mgr E. Harvey;
Sm Edward Hastings; Cond B. Solomon. *REV: Ath 5/7/90
p42; E 5/7/90 p8; St 4/7/90 p10; Th 1/8/90 p82-3.*

90.200 *VERA* (Russian Story,4a) M. Ellis Smith. GLOBE
1/7/90-5/7/90. 5 mat perf.* Baron Alexis Edmund Gurney; Leon d'Arblay Cecil Morton Yorke; Feodor Shap-
iroff Alfred B. Cross; Gen. Vladimir Roydon Erlynne;
Count Olgaff J.A. Bentham; Messenger from the Palace

F. Lake; <u>Aloski</u> E. Dillon Shallard; <u>Cpt. Burlmitz</u> Algernon Newark; <u>Petrovitch</u> F. Shelley; <u>Orloff</u> L. Sheldon. <u>Isadora</u> Violet Thornycroft; <u>Mme Petrolsky</u> Therese Mayer; <u>Narska</u> Edith Dixey; <u>Vera de Saviloff</u> Anna de Naucaze. <u>L</u> W.B. Moore; <u>Pd</u> Anna de Naucaze; <u>Bm</u> Ernest H. Fishbourne; <u>Sm</u> Herman de Lange; <u>Asm</u> Fitzroy Morgan. *REV: E 5/7/90 p9; St 4/7/90 p10; Th 1/8/90 p83.*

90.201 *FAZIO* (T,5a) Henry Hart Milman. STRAND 1/7/90 mat perf. 1st perfd Surrey 22/12/16. <u>Fazio</u> Lewis Waller; <u>Bartoldo</u> John Carter; <u>Piero</u> Charles Milton; <u>Gonsalvo</u> Thomas Blacklock; <u>Philario</u> A. Courtenay; <u>Aurio</u> Harold Eden; <u>Falsetto</u> Orlando Barnett; <u>Theodore</u> K. Gran; <u>Antonio</u> Frederic Jacques; <u>Duke of Florence</u> Julian Cross. <u>Bianca</u> Claire Ivanova; <u>Aldabella</u> Mrs Bennett; <u>Clara</u> Henrietta Cross. DIR Julian Cross; <u>Mgr</u> Harrington Baily. *REV: Ath 5/7/90 p42; E 5/7/90 p8; St 4/7/90 p10; Th 1/8/90 p83-4.*

90.202 *THE VIOLIN MAKERS* (PoetP,1a) Alfred Berlyn [adpt fr François Coppée, *Le Luthier De Cremone*]. CRITERION 3/7/90 mat perf.** <u>Filippo</u> E.S. Willard; <u>Ferrari</u> Harry Cane; <u>Sandro</u> Charles J. Fulton; <u>Giannina</u> Olga Brandon.

90.203 *A HOUSEHOLD FAIRY* (DSk) Francis Talfourd. CRITERION 3/7/90 mat perf.** <u>Julian de Clifford</u> George Giddens. <u>Katherine</u> E. Penrose.

90.204 *ILLUSION* (P,3a) Pierre Leclercq. STRAND 3/7/90 mat perf.* <u>Mr Lullworth</u> W.H. Vernon; <u>Hon Fred Slawson</u> Fuller Mellish; <u>Earl of Bramber</u> Lawrence d'Orsay; <u>Count de Buci</u> Ivan Watson; <u>Joseph Revellin</u> Henry Arncliffe; <u>Eyres Higginson</u> G. Foss; <u>Mr Arterberry</u> Fred Grove; <u>Bob</u> Cecil Ramsey; <u>John Revellin</u> Lewis Waller; <u>Page</u> Master Brooke. <u>Blanche Faneuse</u> Rose Leclercq; <u>Matilda</u> Florence Bright; <u>Una Revellin</u> Marion Lea. DIR Fred Mervin; <u>Mgr</u> Harrington Baily; <u>Mus</u> William Wallace; <u>L</u> Willie Edouin; <u>Pp</u> J.S. Clarke. *REV: Ath 12/7/90 p75-6; E 5/7/90 p9; St 11/7/90 p11; Th 1/8/90 p84-5; Ti 7/7/90 p10.*

90.205 *THE SOLICITOR* (F,3a) J.H. Darnley. TOOLE'S 3/7/90-7/11/90; 29/11/90-12/12/90. 146 perf [w/mat 30/7, 9/8, 16/8, 23/8, 30/8, 6/9, 13/9, 17/9, 20/9, 24/9, 27/9, 1/10, 4/10, 8/10, 11/10, 15/10, 18/10, 22/10, 25/10, 29/10, 1/11, 3/12, 6/12, 10/12]. 1st perfd

Court, Liverpool 5/5/90. <u>Gilbert Brandon</u> John Tresa-
har/[Fred?] Mervin; <u>Cpt. Midhurst</u> Graham Wentworth;
<u>Private Manners</u> Lawrence d'Orsay; <u>Lieut. Arlington</u> A.
B. Francis; <u>Peter Flagan</u> Henry Bedford; <u>Hobson</u> Henry
W. Brame; <u>Baxter</u> Fred Burton; <u>Col. Sterndale</u> F. Kaye.
<u>Mrs Brandon</u> Susie Vaughan; <u>Mrs Midhurst</u> Blanche Wols-
ley; <u>Mary Kingston</u> Clara Ellison; <u>Bella</u> Delia Carlyle; <u>Mrs Sterndale</u> Ruth Rutland; Leslie Bell; Violet
Thornycroft. <u>L</u> J.L. Toole; <u>Mgr</u> Violet Melnotte; <u>Act
mgr & Treas</u> Henry Brandon; <u>Sec</u> Charles Campbell; <u>Cond</u>
Edward Crosse. *REV: Ath 12/7/90 p75, 6/12/90 p785; E
5/7/90 p14; Th 1/8/90 p85-6; Ti 7/7/90 p10.*

90.206 *THE BAILIFF* (Ca,1a) Frederick W. Broughton.
TOOLE'S 3/7/90-7/11/90. 110 perf.** <u>Benjamin Grattan</u>
Henry Bedford; <u>Frank</u> A.B. Francis; <u>Daniel Grattan</u>
Henry W. Brame; <u>Minnie</u> Irene Richards. <u>L</u>, <u>Mgr</u>, <u>Act
mgr & Treas</u>, <u>Sec</u> as for 90.205.

90.207 *ADRIENNE LECOUVREUR*(D,5a) Eugene Scribe & Ernest Legouvé. HER MAJESTY'S 4/7/90, 7/7/90. 2 perf.**
<u>Michonnet</u> Lacroix; <u>Maurice de Saxe</u> Rebel; <u>Le Prince
de Bouillon</u> Munié; <u>L'Abbé de Chazeuil</u> Thefer; <u>Quin-
ault</u> Piron; <u>Poisson</u> Deneubourg; <u>L'Avertisseur</u> Mortimer; <u>Valet</u> Cartereau. <u>Adrienne Lecouvreur</u> Sarah Bernhardt; <u>Princesse de Bouillon</u> Marie Grandet; <u>Athenais</u>
Jane Méa; <u>La Marquise</u> Merle; <u>La Baronne</u> Fortin; <u>Mlle
Jouvenot</u> Latour; <u>Mlle Dangerville</u> Seylor; <u>Femme de
Chambre</u> Simonson. <u>MGR</u> M.L. Mayer. *REV: E 12/7/90 p8.*

90.208 *MISS HOYDEN'S HUSBAND* (C,1a) Augustin Daly [fr
Sheridan's *Trip to Scarborough*]. SHAFTESBURY 4/7/90
mat perf. 1st perfd Daly's, New York 26/3/90. <u>Lord
Foppington</u> Charles Leclercq; <u>Young Fashion</u> George
Clarke; <u>Sir Tunbelly Clumsy</u> Charles Wheatleigh; <u>Col.
Townley</u> Eugene Ormond; <u>Lory</u> Frederick Bond; <u>Nicode-
mus</u> Hobart Bosworth; <u>Servant</u> Ralph Nisbett; <u>Servant</u>
William Sampson. <u>Miss Hoyden</u> Ada Rehan; <u>Miss Hoyden's
Nurse</u> May Sylvie; <u>Mistress Coupler</u> Adelaide Prince.
<u>MGR</u> E.S. Willard, John Lart; <u>Pp</u> John Lancaster; <u>Sm</u>
Robert V. Shone, Edward P. Wilks, C.H. Rimbault, Lew-
is Sealy; <u>Mus dir</u> John Crook, Edward Jones; <u>Act mgr</u>
W.H. Griffiths, Silvanus Dauncey. *REV: E 5/7/90 p13;
SR 12/7/90 p46; St 11/7/90 p10-1.* <u>Comment</u>: Daly's Co.

90.209 *KIT MARLOWE* (P,1a) W.L. Courtney. SHAFTESBURY
4/7/90 mat perf.* <u>Kit Marlowe</u> Arthur Bourchier; <u>Ned</u>
<u>Alleyne</u> Erskine Lewis; <u>Henry Chettle</u> Cyril Maude; <u>Fran-</u>
<u>cis Archer</u> Charles J. Fulton; <u>Thomas Nash</u> R.G. Legge.
<u>Nan</u> Annie Irish. <u>MGR</u>, <u>Pp</u>, <u>Sm</u>, <u>Mus dir</u>, <u>Act mgr</u> as for
90.208. *REV: E, SR, St as for 90.208; Ath 12/7/90 p75.*

90.210 *VANITY OF VANITIES* (Duol) Justin Huntly McCarthy. SHAFTESBURY 4/7/90 mat perf.* <u>Morris Hastings</u>
Herbert Waring; <u>Princess Nicholas</u> May Whitty. <u>MGR</u>, <u>Pp</u>,
<u>Sm</u>, <u>Mus dir</u>, <u>Act mgr</u> as for 90.208. *REV: E, St as for*
90.208.

90.211 *LA DAME AUX CAMELIAS* (D,5a) Alexandre Dumas,
fils. HER MAJESTY'S 5/7/90, 8/7/90. 2 perf. 1st perfd
Vaudeville, Paris 2/2/52. <u>Armand Duval</u> Dumeny; <u>Gas-</u>
<u>ton Rieux</u> Angelo; <u>Georges Duval</u> Piron; <u>de Varville</u>
Rebel; <u>St. Gaudens</u> Munié; <u>Gustave</u> Thefer; <u>Comte de</u>
<u>Giray</u> Deneubourg; <u>Docteur</u> Lacroix; <u>Commissionnaire</u>
Mortimer; <u>Domestique</u> Cartereau. <u>Marguerite Gauthier</u>
Sarah Bernhardt; <u>Prudence</u> Marie Grandet; <u>Olympe</u> Jane
Méa; <u>Nichette</u> Seylor; <u>Nanine</u> Simonson; <u>Arthur</u> Fortin;
<u>Anais</u> Merle. <u>MGR</u> M.L. Mayer. *REV: E 12/7/90 p8.*

90.212 *THE WALL OF CHINA* (F) Arthur Matthison. CRIT-
ERION 5/7/90-2/8/90. 25 perf. 1st perfd Criterion
15/4/76. <u>Peter Pottle</u> Frank Atherley. <u>Rose Petal</u>
F. Frances; <u>Landlady</u> Emily Vining. <u>L</u> Charles Wyndham;
<u>Act mgr</u> E. Harvey; <u>Sm</u> Edward Hastings; <u>Cond</u> B. Solo-
mon. *REV: E 12/7/90 p14; St 11/7/90 p10.*

90.213 *THE TAMING OF THE SHREW* (C,5a) William Shakespeare. LYCEUM 8/7/90-14/7/90. 6 perf.** <u>Petrucio</u> John
Drew; <u>Grumio</u> James Lewis; <u>Baptista</u> Charles Fisher;
<u>Lord</u> George Clarke; <u>Christopher Sly</u> Charles Wheat-
leigh; <u>Gremio</u> Charles Leclercq; <u>Tranio</u> Frederick Bond;
<u>Vincentio</u> John Moore; <u>Lucentio</u> Eugene Ormond; <u>Horten-</u>
<u>sio</u> Sidney Herbert; <u>Pedant/Page</u> William Sampson;
<u>Huntsmen</u> Ralph Nisbett, Hobart Bosworth, McCauley;
<u>Players</u> Frederick Bond, John Moore; <u>Biondello</u> Edward
P. Wilks; <u>Tailor</u> Hobart Bosworth. <u>Katherine</u> Ada Rehan;
<u>Curtis</u> Mrs G.H. Gilbert; <u>Bianca</u> Edith Crane; <u>Widow</u>
Adelaide Prince; <u>Hostess</u> May Sylvie; Kitty Cheatham.
<u>L</u> Henry Irving; <u>Act mgr</u> Richard Dorney; <u>Sm</u> John Moore;
<u>Bom</u> Joseph Hurst; <u>Sc</u> T.R. Hann, James Roberts, Henry

Hoyt; <u>Furn</u> Hampton & Sons, Lyon; <u>Pq</u> C.H. Fox; <u>Dir</u> Augustin Daly. *REV: Ath 12/7/90 p75; E 12/7/90 p14; St 11/7/90 p10; Ti 10/7/90 p4.* <u>Comment</u>: Daly's Company.

90.214 *LA TOSCA* (D,5a,6tab) Victorien Sardou. HER MAJESTY'S 9/7/90-12/7/90. 5 perf [w/mat 12/7]. 1st perfd Porte-Saint-Martin, Paris 1887. <u>Baron Scarpia</u> Garnier; <u>Mario Cavaradossi</u> Dumeny; <u>Eusebe</u> Lacroix; <u>Spoletta</u> Rebel; <u>Marquis Attavanti</u> Munié; <u>De Trevilhac</u> Thefer; <u>Schiaronne</u> Piron; <u>Caesare Angelotti</u> Angelo; <u>Trivulce</u> Deneubourg; <u>Ceccho</u> Cartereau; <u>Paisello</u> Durand; <u>Sgt.</u> Mortimer; <u>Colometti</u> Remy. <u>Floria Tosca</u> Sarah Bernhardt; <u>Reine Marie Caroline</u> Jane Méa; <u>Gennarino</u> Seylor; <u>Princesse Orlonia</u> Merle; <u>Scafarelli</u> Fortin; <u>Luciana</u> Simonson. <u>MGR</u> M.L. Mayer. *REV: E 12/7/90 p8.*

90.215 *FROU FROU* (C,5a) Henri Meilhac & Ludovic Halévy. ST. JAMES'S 10/7/90 mat perf. 1st perfd Gymnase, Paris 30/10/69. <u>Brigard</u> Arthur Bourchier; <u>Comte de Valreas</u> Fred Terry; <u>Baron de Cambri</u> Gilbert Farquhar; <u>Pitou</u> Forbes Dawson; <u>Vincent</u> Charles Milton; <u>Henry Sartorys</u> Henry Neville; <u>Georgie</u> Master Eric Field-Fisher. <u>Baronne de Cambri</u> Fanny Brough; <u>Louise</u> Gertrude Kingston; <u>Pauline</u> Edith Chester; <u>Governess</u> Florence Cole; <u>Gilberte</u> Mrs Charles Kettlewell. <u>DIR</u> Henry Neville; <u>Sm</u> Manson; <u>Act mgr</u> W.H. Griffiths, Gilbert Tate. *REV: Ath 12/7/90 p76; E 12/7/90 p9.*

90.216 *THE LITTLE SENTINEL* (Ca,1a) Thomas J. Williams. ADELPHI 11/7/90-12/7/90; 12/8/90-20/6/91. 266 perf [np 25/12/90, 27/3/91, 4-6/5/91]. 1st perfd St. James's 4/5/63. <u>Wheedleton Coaxer</u> J[ohn] Northcote; <u>Cpt. Clarence Courtington</u> James East; <u>Sim</u> W. Northcote. <u>Letty Hawthorne</u> Essex Dane; <u>May</u> Clara Jecks. <u>L</u> A. & S. Gatti; <u>Sm</u> William Sidney; <u>Mus dir</u> Henry Sprake; <u>Act mgr</u> Charles A. Jecks. <u>Comment</u>: Cast from V & A programme for 2/8/90.

90.217 *ESMERALDA* (O[4a]) A. Goring Thomas. COVENT GARDEN 12/7/90, 17/7, 24/7/90. 3 perf. 1st perfd Drury Lane 26/3/83. <u>Claude Frollo</u> Jean Lassalle; <u>Quasimodo</u> Eugene Dufriche; <u>Gringoire</u> Sebastian Montariol; <u>Clopin</u> Winogradoff; <u>Phoebus</u> Jean de Reske; <u>De Chevreuse</u> Antonio de Vaschetti. <u>Esmeralda</u> Nellie Melba; <u>Fleur-de-Lys</u> Regina Pinkert; <u>1ere Danseuse</u> Palladino. <u>L & MGR</u> Augustus Harris; <u>Cond</u> Alberto Randegger; <u>Ch</u> Katti Lanner. *REV: 19/7/90 p106; E 19/7/90 p13; Ti 14/7/90 p12.*

90.218 *SWEET NANCY* (C,3a) Robert Buchanan [fnd on Rhoda Broughton's "Nancy"]. LYRIC 12/7/90-2/8/90; 6/10/90-17/11/90. 55 perf.* <u>Sir Roger Tempest</u> Henry Neville/Yorke Stephens; <u>Frank Musgrave</u> [Alfred] Bucklaw/C.H. Garthorne; <u>Mr Grey</u> Ernest Hendrie; <u>Algernon Grey</u> Henry V. Esmond; <u>Robert Grey</u> C.M. Hallard; <u>James Grey</u> Master Walter Highland; <u>Pendleton</u> [Frank] Smithson; <u>Footman</u> A.R. Bennett. <u>Barbara Grey</u> Harriett Jay; <u>Nancy Grey</u> Annie Hughes; <u>Mrs Grey</u> Ethel Hope; <u>Teresa Grey</u> B[eatrice] Ferrar; <u>Mrs Huntley</u> Frances Ivor/ Jennie McNulty. <u>L</u> Henry J. Leslie; <u>Mus dir</u> Walter Slaughter; <u>Sm</u> E.B. Norman; <u>Act mgr</u> Charles Bernard. *REV: Ath 19/7/90 p107-8; E 19/7/90 p14, 11/10/90 p9; St 18/7/90 p10, 10/10/90 p15; Th 1/8/90 p88-9; Ti 14/ 7/90 p4.*

90.219 *AN OLD MAID'S WOOING* (Ca,1a) Arnold Goldsworthy & E.B. Norman. LYRIC 12/7/90-1/8/90. 18 perf. 1st perfd St. George's Hall 28/1/88. <u>Rev James Braithwaite</u> E.B. Norman; <u>Henry Higgins</u> Ernest Hendrie; <u>George Gammon</u> Henry Bayntun. <u>Hester Grayson</u> Ethel Hope; <u>Naomi Wild</u> B[eatrice] Ferrar. <u>L</u>, <u>Sm</u>, <u>Mus dir</u>, <u>Act mgr</u> as for 90.218. *REV: 19/7/90 p14; St 18/7/90 p10; Ti 14/7/90 p4.*

90.220 *THE BEST PEOPLE* (C,4a) Mrs Fairfax. GLOBE 14/ 7/90 mat perf.* <u>Hon Cpt. Lester</u> H. Percival; <u>Mr Skinner</u> Tom Squire; <u>Lord Pierrepoint</u> H[enry] Pagden; <u>Spicer Mummery</u> Compton Coutts; <u>George Mawler</u> W. Scott Buist; <u>Pat</u> John Le Hay; <u>Mr Ball</u> H. Clarey. <u>Lady Pierrepoint</u> Mrs Fairfax; <u>Lady Diana Fane</u> Sophie Larkin; <u>Signora Parrini</u> Adrienne Dairolles; <u>Edith Lester</u> Essex Dane; <u>Lucy Latimer</u> Rhoda Larkin; <u>Lady Blemish</u> Pettie Cleaver. <u>L</u> W.B. Moore; <u>Sm</u> Malcolm Bell; <u>Bm</u> Gilbert Tate; <u>Mus dir</u> E. Boggetti. *REV: Ath 19/7/90 p108; E 19/7/90 p8; St 18/7/90 p10.*

90.221 *AS YOU LIKE IT* (C,5a) William Shakespeare. LYCEUM 15/7/90-4/8/90. 21 perf [w/mat 19/7, 23/7,

26/6].** <u>Orlando</u> John Drew; <u>Touchstone</u> James Lewis;
<u>Denis</u> R[alph] Nisbett; <u>Jacques</u> George Clarke; <u>Adam</u>
Charles Fisher; <u>Frederick</u> Frederick Bond; <u>Duke</u> Charles
Wheatleigh; <u>Corin</u> Charles Leclercq; <u>Oliver</u> Eugene Or-
mond; <u>Le Beau</u> Sidney Herbert; <u>Charles</u> H[obart] Bos-
worth; <u>Amiens</u> McCauley; <u>Lord</u> Hobart; <u>Jacques</u> W[illiam]
Sampson; <u>Silvius</u> Frederick Bond; <u>William</u> Edward P.
Wilks. <u>Rosalind</u> Ada Rehan; <u>Audrey</u> Isabel Irving;
<u>Phoebe</u> Edith Crane; <u>Hymen</u> Kitty Cheatham; <u>Page</u> Flo-
rence Conron; <u>Page</u> Louise Smith; <u>Celia</u> Adelaide
Prince. <u>L</u> Henry Irving; <u>Cond</u> Henry Widmer; <u>Dir</u> Augustin Daly; <u>Act mgr</u> Richard Dorney; <u>Sm</u> John Moore; <u>Sc</u>
Bruce Smith, James Roberts, Henry Hoyt; <u>Pq</u> C.H. Fox;
<u>Bom</u> Joseph Hurst. *REV: Ath 19/7/90 p108; E 19/7/90
p14; SR 19/7/90 p73-4, 26/7/90 p105-6, 30/8/90 p253;
St 18/7/90 p9-10; Th 1/8/90 p90; Ti 16/7/90 p5.* <u>Com-
ment</u>: Daly's Company.

90.222 *COSI FAN TUTTE* (O,2a) W.A. Mozart. SAVOY 16/7/
90 mat perf. 1st perfd Burgtheater, Vienna 26/1/1790.
<u>Ferrando</u> Edward G. Branscombe; <u>Gratiano</u> John Sand-
brook; <u>Don Alfonso</u> Charles J. Magrath. <u>Isidora</u> Ella
Walker; <u>Dorabella</u> Ethel Webster; <u>Maid</u> Maggie Davies.
<u>Cond</u> C. Villiers Stanford. *REV: E 19/7/90 p7; Ti 17/
7/90 p9.*

90.223 *OFF DUTY* (DC,1a) T. Edgar Pemberton. LYCEUM
17/7/90 mat perf. 1st perfd Toole's 9/9/84. <u>Ben Bloss</u>
Lionel Brough; <u>Negus</u> Percy Everard; <u>Sam Medley</u> Alfred
Matthews; <u>Scrope</u> Percy Brough. <u>Mrs Tinkler</u> Kate Hod-
son; <u>Millie</u> Mary Brough. <u>L & MGR</u> Henry Irving; <u>Bom</u>
Joseph Hurst; <u>Sm</u> George Clarke; <u>Mus dir</u> Henry Widmer;
<u>Cond</u> J. Meredith Ball; <u>Pq</u> William Clarkson, C.H. Fox.
REV: E 19/7/90 p9.

90.224 *HAMLET* (O[5a]) Ambroise Thomas. COVENT GARDEN
21/7/90. 1 perf. 1st perfd Opéra, Paris 9/3/68. <u>Ham-
let</u> Jean Lassalle; <u>Claudius</u> Jacques Isnardon; <u>Laerte</u>
Sebastian Montariol; <u>L'Ombre du Roi</u> Orme Darvall;
<u>Marcellus</u> Iginio Corsi; <u>Horatio</u> Miranda. <u>La Reine
Gertrude</u> Hélène Richard; <u>Ophelie</u> Nellie Melba; <u>1ere
Danseuse</u> Palladino. <u>L & MGR</u> Augustus Harris; <u>Cond</u>
Enrico Bevignani; <u>Ch</u> Katti Lanner. *REV: Ath 26/7/90
p138; E 26/7/90 p13; Ti 23/7/90 p4.*

90.225 *A GOLD MINE* (C,3a) Brander Matthews & George
H. Jessop. GAIETY 21/7/90-8/8/90. 17 perf. 1st perfd
Fifth Avenue, New York 4/3/89. Silas K. Wolcott Nat
C. Goodwin; Sir Everard Foxwood William Farren; George Foxwood Harry Eversfield; Wilson Eric Thorne;
Julius Krebs Frank [M.] Wood; Gerald Riordan, M.P.
Charles Glenney. Hon Mrs Meredith Kate Forsyth; Miss
Una Foxwood Jennie McNulty; Mrs Vandervas Carlotta
Leclercq. L & MGR George Edwardes; Furn Oetzmann &
Co.; Mus dir W.W. Lutz,jr; Sm Frank Parker; Act mgr
C.J. Abud; Bom A.P. Oxley. *REV: Ath 26/7/90 p139-40;
E 26/7/90 p14; SR 26/7/90 p107-8; St 25/7/90 p10;
Th 1/9/90 p129-30; Ti 22/7/90 p8.*

90.226 *THE WOMAN'S WONT* (F). LYCEUM 23/7/90(m); 5/8/
90-9/8/90. 6 perf. Father-in-Law James Lewis; Husband
George Clarke; Servant Frederick Bond. Wife Isabel
Irving; Woman Kitty Cheatham; Mother-in-Law Mrs G.H.
Gilbert. L & MGR Henry Irving; Bom Joseph Hurst; Act
mgr Richard Dorney; Sm John Moore; Sc Bruce Smith,
James Roberts, Henry Hoyt; Pq C.H. Fox. *REV: E 26/7/
90 p9; SR 26/7/90 p108; St 25/7/90 p10; Th 1/9/90
p137.* Comment: Daly's Company.

90.227 *THE JUDGE* (FP,3a) Arthur Law. TERRY'S 24/7/90-
13/9/90;* trfd to OPERA COMIQUE 15/9/90-3/1/91. 166
perf [w/S mat exc 26/7; add mat 22/10, 10/11, 3/12,
10/12, 26/12, 31/12/90; np 22-25/12/90]. Sir John
Pye W.S. Penley; Herbert Stryver William Herbert/
Charles Cooper; Algernon Pringle Frank H. Fenton;
Mowle Mark Kinghorne; Mr Shuttleworth W[illiam] Lestocq; Jacob Ricketts G[eorge] Belmore/A.J. Leigh.
Daphne Pye Cissy Grahame; Mrs Shuttleworth Emily
Thorne; Mrs Ricketts Elsie Chester; Chloe Pye Helen
Leyton. SC Jetley; Cost Marie Watkins; Treas H. Gunn;
Sec C. St. John Denton; Mus dir J. Bayliss; Sm W[ill-
iam] Lestocq/Ernest Cathcart; L Edward Terry; Mgr
Cissy Grahame; Act mgr H.T. Brickwell/Arthur Yates.
*REV: Ath 2/8/90 p172; E 26/7/90 p14, 20/9/90 p9; SR
2/8/90 p137-8; St 1//8/90 p9-10, 24/10/90 p12; Th
1/9/90 p130-1; Ti 26/7/90 p16, 16/9/90 p4.*

90.228 *LITTLE NOBODY* (C,3a) Mary Righton. VAUDEVILLE
24/7/90 mat perf.* Cpt. Trayton Kenward Louis Freeman;

Sir Dennis Hargraves J.R. Crauford; Col. Forbes Walter
Russell; Dolly Bruce A. Rowney; Dennison Orlando Barnett; Smith G.B. Phillips; Lord Tryon Dyer Williams;
Hon Will Saunders Clifford Leigh. Mrs Forbes Isa Johnson; Georgie Grahame Sylvia Southgate; Fay "Little
Nobody" Mary Righton. L Thomas Thorne; Bm Louis Weigh-
ton. *REV: E 26/7/90 p8; St 1/8/90 p10; Th 1/9/90 p131-
2.*

90.229 *DEAR FRIENDS* (Ca,1a) Mary Righton. VAUDEVILLE
24/7/90 mat perf. 1st perfd Ladbroke Hall 16/3/88.
Violet Woodfield Annie Howard; Daisy Greenacre Sylvia
Southgate. L, Bm as for 90.228. *REV: As for 90.228.*

90.230 *THE VIOLIN MAKERS* (PoetP,1a) Alfred Berlyn
[adpt of François Coppée, *Le Luthier de Cremone*].
SHAFTESBURY 25/7/90 mat perf.** Filippo E.S. Willard;
Ferrari H[arry] Cane; Sandro [Charles J.] Fulton.
Giannina Annie Hill. *REV: E 26/7/90 p7; Th 1/9/90 p
132-3.*

90.231 *IN HONOUR BOUND* (C,1a) Sydney Grundy. SHAFTES-
BURY 25/7/90 mat perf. 1st perfd Prince of Wales's
25/9/80. Sir George Carlyon Edgar Bruce; Philip Graham Ernest Lawford. Rose Dalrymple Edith Chester;
Lady Carlyon Dorothy Dene. *REV: As for 90.230.*

90.232 *HOW IT HAPPENED.* SHAFTESBURY 25/7/90 mat perf.
Kate Vaughan. Comment: Mentioned only in *Ti.*

90.233 *SWEET WILL* (C,1a) H.A. Jones. SHAFTESBURY 25/
7/90 mat perf. 1st perfd New Club, Covent Garden 5/3/
87. Will Darbyshire Lewis Waller. Betty Emma Rivers;
Mary Darbyshire Annie Hill; Judith Loveless Rose Norreys; Mrs Darbyshire Fanny Coleman. *REV: Ath 2/8/90
p172; E 26/7/90 p7; SR 2/8/90 p138; Th 1/9/90 p132-3;
Ti 28/7/90 p8.*

90.234 *GUY FAWKES, ESQ.* (Bsq,3a) "A.C. Torr" [Fred
Leslie] & Herbert F. Clark. GAIETY 26/7/90 mat perf.
1st perfd Theatre Royal, Nottingham 7/4/90. Guy Faw-
kes Arthur Roberts; James I W.H. Rawlins; Badcorn
Sam Wilkinson; Francis Tresham Walter Sealby; Grovel
G.B. Prior; Extras W. Clark, A. Jackson, R. Holding,

W. Palmer, Oscar Grey, T. Laroney. Robert Catesby
Fanny Marriott; Viviana Radcliffe Amelia Gruhn; Ruth
Ipgreve Amy Lyddon; Lord Mounteagle Alice Ford;
Steenie Ethel Blenheim; Angelica Minnie Thurgate;
Bates Agnes Taylor; Sgt. Louie Fay; Policeman Louise
Norman; Extras Lily Marsden, Mildred Talbot, Amy Gor-
don, Louise Norman, Eva Milton, Marie Carr, Fanny
Herve, Octavia Rivers, Millie Garthorne, Lillie Mer-
ville, Lucy Wade, Florence Dene, Ella Johnson, Clara
Davies, Mercy Merrick. L & MGR George Edwardes; Mus
George W. Byng; Lyr Doss Childerdoss; Cost dgn Stew-
art Browne; Cost Alias; Pq William Clarkson; Ch Paul
Martinette; Props H. Skelly; Pyrotechnics James Pain
& Sons; Sm W.H. Rawlins; Mus dir George W. Byng; Act
mgr Neil Carlton. *REV: Ath 2/8/90 p172; E 2/8/90 p14;
St 1/8/90 p10; Ti 28/7/90 p8.*

90.235 *THAT GIRL* (C,3a) Henry Hamilton & Mrs Oscar
Beringer [adpt of story by Clementina Black]. HAY-
MARKET 30/7/90 mat perf.* Cpt. Wentworth C.W. Somer-
set; Philip Challoner H. Reeves-Smith; Alexander Mc-
Nab Earle Douglas; Frank Hillyard Rudge Harding;
Harold Leigh Granville Kingsland; Lumley Brereton E.
W. Gardiner. Iris Wentworth Rose Norreys; Aphrodite
Dodge Vera Beringer; Mrs Cyrus P. Dodge Helen Leigh;
Caroline Murthwaite Houston; Fraulein Schwabe Mrs E.
H. Brooke. MGR H.B. Tree; Bm Henry Ball; Sm Ernest
Hendrie. *REV: Ath 9/8/90 p204; E 2/8/90 p9, 27/2/92
p8, 5/3/92 p12, 12/3/92 p10; St 1/8/90 p9; Th 1/9/90
p133-4; Ti 31/7/90 p7.*

90.236 *THE ENGLISH ROSE* (D,4a) George R. Sims & Rob-
ert Buchanan. ADELPHI 2/8/90-2/5/91. 238 perf [w/mat
3/1/91, 10/1, 28/2; np 25/12/90, 27/3/91].* Harry
O'Mailley Leonard Boyne; Knight of Ballyveeney J.D.
Beveridge; Sgt. O'Reilley John L. Shine; Father
Michael O'Mailley T.B. Thalberg; Cpt. Macdonell W.L.
Abingdon; Nicodemus Dickenson Lionel Rignold; Randall
O'Mara Charles Dalton; Sir Philip Kingston Bassett
Roe; Cassidy J[ohn] Northcote; Larry MacNulty James
East; Shaun W. Northcote; O'Brien E[rnest] Bantock;
Farmer Flannigan H[arwood] Cooper; O'Shea J. Howe.
Ethel Kingston Olga Brandon; Patsie Blake Kate James;
Louisa Ann Ferguson Clara Jecks; Judy Essex Dane;

Biddy Madge Mildren; Bridget O'Mara Mary Rorke; Norah
Janette Reeve; Mary Nellie Carter. MGR A. & S. Gatti;
Sc Bruce Smith, Phil W. Goatcher, W[illiam] Perkins;
Cost J. Harrison; Sm & Pd William Sidney; Mus dir
Henry Sprake; Act mgr Charles A. Jecks. *REV: Ath 9/8/*
90 p203-4; E 9/8/90 p14; SR 9/8/90 p167; St 8/8/90
p9-10; Th 1/9/90 p134-5; Ti 4/8/90 p10, 28/11/90 p7.

90.237 *THIS WOMAN AND THAT* (P,3a) Pierre Leclercq.
GLOBE 2/8/90 mat perf.* Sir George Ingleside Mark
Quinton; Percy Gauntlett Otis Skinner; Charles Tetter-
ton J.H. Manley; Funge J.F. Graham; Blight E[dward]
Boddy. Eve Fleurier Adelaide Moore; Lady Ingleside
Emilie Calhaem; Paskins M. Baker. L W.B. Moore; Dir
Hugh Moss. *REV: Ath 9/8/90 p204; E 9/8/90 p8; St 8/8/*
90 p10; Th 1/9/90 p135-6; Ti 4/8/90 p10.

90.238 *THE CORSICAN BROTHERS* (SensationalD,4a) Dion
Boucicault [adpt of Dumas, *Les Frères Corses*]. NOV-
ELTY 4/8/90. Rnd. 1st perfd Princess's 24/2/52.
Fabien/Louis Charles Sennett; Chateau Renard George
Byrne; Alfred Meynard Henry Crane; Le Baron Giordano
Martelli Norman Clarke; Le Baron Montgeron Druce;
Gartano Orlando R. Robertson; Marco Colomia Russell;
Griffo S. Charles; Antonio Sanolo T. Brownlow; Blaze
Charles Steyne; Tomaso H. Moss; Surgeon W. Blake.
Emile de l'Esparre Jessie Robertson; Mme Dei Franchi
Mrs J.F. Brian; Gran d'Or Ada Pitt; Pomponnetti Kate
Long; Marie Marie Brian. L S.T. Tolhurst; Act mgr
Thomas Crawford; Mgr & dir Joseph A. Cave; Mus & cond
Henri G. French; Mechanical effects Walter Lee; Elect
J. Wells; Sc W.H. Drury.

90.239 *THE GREAT UNKNOWN* (EccentricC,3a) Augustin
Daly [fr Gr of Franz von Schonthan & Gustave Kadel-
burg]. LYCEUM 5/8/90-9/8/90. 6 perf [w/mat 9/8]. 1st
perfd Daly's, New York 22/10/89. Cousin Ned John
Drew; Jeremiah Jarraway James Lewis; O'Donnell Don
Frederick Bond; Tom Prowde Eugene Ormond; Patrick
William Sampson. Etna Ada Rehan; Aunt Penelope Mrs G.
H. Gilbert; Pansy Isabel Irving; Shirley Munkittrick
Edith Crane; Mrs Arabella Jarraway May Sylvie; Miss
Twitters Florence Conron; Mlle Agathe Adelaide Prince.
L & MGR Henry Irving; Bom Joseph Hurst; Cond Henry

Widmer; <u>Act mgr</u> Richard Dorney; <u>Sm</u> John Moore; <u>Sc</u> T. E. Ryan; <u>Furn</u> Hampton, Lyons; <u>Pq</u> C.H. Fox. *REV: Ath 9/8/90 p204; E 9/8/90 p14; SR 9/8/90 p167; St 8/8/90 p10; Th 1/9/90 p136-7; Ti 6/8/90 p8.* <u>Comment</u>: Daly's Company.

90.240 *WELCOME LITTLE STRANGER* (C,3a) James Albery. CRITERION 6/8/90-11/9/90. 31 perf.* <u>Cranberry Buck</u> William Blakeley; <u>Darrtell Roe</u> Edmund Maurice; <u>James Paragon</u> George Giddens. <u>Mrs Amelia Buck</u> M.A. Victor; <u>Mrs Cecilia Roe</u> Helen Forsyth; <u>Fanny</u> Emily Vining; <u>Ann</u> F. Frances; <u>Mrs Llorencourt</u> Vane Featherston. <u>L</u> Charles Wyndham; <u>Act mgr</u> E. Harvey; <u>Sm</u> Edward Hastings; <u>Cond</u> B. Solomon. *REV: Ath 9/8/90 p204; E 9/8/90 p14; SR 9/8/90 p167; St 15/8/90 p12; Th 1/9/90 p137-8; Ti 8/8/90 p6.*

90.241 *JILTED* (CD,2a) Alfred Maltby. CRITERION 6/8/90-11/10/90. 58 perf. 1st perfd Prince of Wales's, Liverpool 18/6/77. <u>Samuel Potts, jr</u> George Giddens; <u>Samuel Potts, sr</u> Sydney Valentine; <u>Hon Henry St. Cloud</u> Frank Atherley; <u>Mr Equity Transfer</u> F. Emery. <u>Mrs Daulton</u> E[mily] Miller; <u>Marguerite</u> F. Frances; <u>Topham</u> E[mily] Vining; <u>Carrie Dalrypple</u> E[llaline] Terriss. <u>L</u>, <u>Act mgr</u>, <u>Sm</u>, <u>Cond</u> as for 90.240. *REV: E 9/8/90 p14; St 19/9/90 p11-2; Th 1/9/90 p138.*

90.242 *THE BOOKMAKER* (C,3a) J.W. Pigott. GAIETY 9/8/90-26/8/90. 15 perf. 1st perfd Terry's 19/3/89. <u>Sir Joseph Trent</u> Nat C. Goodwin; <u>Earl of Harborough</u> William Farren, jr; <u>Gerald, Lord Maidment</u> H. Reeves-Smith; <u>Hon Jack Carew</u> Charles Glenney; <u>Mr Mortmain</u> Eric Thorne; <u>Bubbles</u> Frank [M.] Wood; <u>James</u> C. Walker; <u>Marquis of Budleigh</u> George Dalziel. <u>Polly</u> Jennie McNulty; <u>Lady Jessie Harborough</u> Christine Mayne; <u>Sybil Hardwicke</u> Adelaide Gunn; <u>Lady Harborough</u> Carlotta Leclercq. <u>L & MGR</u> George Edwardes; <u>Dir</u> J.W. Pigott; <u>Mus dir</u> W.W. Lutz, jr; <u>Sm</u> Frank Parker; <u>Act mgr</u> C.J. Abud. *REV: Ath 16/8/90 p235-6; E 16/8/90 p9; St 15/8/90 p12; Th 1/9/90 p139; Ti 11/8/90 p8.*

90.243 *CAPTAIN THERESE* (CO,3a) Alexandre Bisson (lib) & F.C. Burnand (lib) & Robert Planquette (mus). PRINCE OF WALES'S 25/8/90-5/12/90. 103 perf [w/S mat].*

Vicomte Tancrede de la Touche C. Hayden Coffin; <u>Philip</u>
<u>de Bellegarde</u> Joseph Tapley; <u>Col</u>. Sombrero Henry Ash-
ley; <u>Marquis de Vardeuil</u> Harry Parker; <u>Cpt</u>. Boulignac
T[om] A. Shale; <u>Lieut</u>. Campastro A.T. Hendon; <u>Duvet</u>
Harry Monkhouse; <u>Coupecourt</u> J[ohn] Ettinson; <u>Mjr. de</u>
<u>la Gonfrière</u> George Marler; <u>Sgt</u>. Vadeboncoeur T.
Arthur; <u>Sgt. La Tulipe</u> A. Thomas; <u>Extras</u> Betjemann,
[W.] Burt, [Alfred] Wigley, Feltham, Burch, Aldridge,
Gregory, Pearse, Ewing, Scales, Hogan, Bottrill,
[Philip] Sefton, Miller, Edwards. <u>Mlle Thérèse</u> Attalie
Claire; <u>Mme la Chanoinesse</u> Amadi; <u>Marceline</u> Phyllis
Broughton; <u>Claudine</u> Florence Darley; <u>Extras</u> L. Cope,
Neil, Tate, M. Spencer, Jones, F. Cope, Sinclair,
Shepherd, [Ivy] Hertzog, Laurie, [Amy] Abbott, Daw-
son, L. Spencer, Levine, Bentley, Clifton, Harris,
Edwards, Bright, Fitzherbert, Bell, Rees, Stanley,
Franklyn, Johnson, Heilbrow, Hall, Marsden, Gordon,
Conway, Wilton, Wallace, Storey, K. Howe, Elton,
Robinson, J. Langton, Habet, Hertie, M. Langton, Up-
perton. <u>MGR</u> Horace Sedger; <u>Mus dir</u> John Crook; <u>Pp</u>
Edgar Bruce; <u>Pd</u> Charles Harris; <u>Ch</u> W[illie] Warde;
<u>Sc</u> [William] Telbin, [William] Perkins, [Edward]
Banks; <u>Cost</u> Auguste, Nathan, Alias; <u>Pq</u> William Clark-
son; <u>Bm</u> William Greet; <u>Act mgr</u> Tom Pitt; <u>Mgr dir</u>
Augustus Harris, Henry Bruce. *REV: Ath 30/8/90 p299;*
E 30/8/90 p13; St 29/8/90 p12; Th 1/10/90 p183-4; Ti
26/8/90 p8. <u>Comment</u>: Carl Rosa Light Opera Company.

90.244 *ALL ABROAD* ([Oa,1a]) Arthur Law (lib) & Alfred
J. Caldicott (mus). PRINCE OF WALES'S 26/8/90. 1
perf.** <u>Mr Bunting</u> J[ohn] Ettinson; <u>Charles</u> Philip
Sefton; <u>Winkles</u> W. Burt. <u>Mrs Bunting</u> Amy Abbott;
<u>Jeanette</u> Florence Darley. <u>L</u>, <u>Pp</u>, <u>Bm</u>, <u>Act mgr</u> as for
90.243.

90.245 *THE VIOLIN MAKERS* (PoetP,1a) Alfred Berlyn
[adpt of François Coppée, *Le Luthier de Cremone*].
SHAFTESBURY 27/8/90, 3/9/90. 2 mat perf.** [<u>Filippo</u>]
E.S. Willard; [<u>Ferrari</u> Harry] Cane; [<u>Sandro</u> Charles
J.] Fulton. [<u>Giannina</u>] Mrs E.S. Willard.

90.246 *THE DEACON* (CSk,2a) H.A. Jones. SHAFTESBURY
27/8/90, 3/9/90. 2 mat perf.* <u>Abraham Boothroyd</u> E.S.
Willard; <u>Tom Dempster</u> C[harles J.] Fulton; <u>Tibbetts</u>

Hugh Harting. <u>Rosa Jervoise</u> Annie Hill; <u>Mrs Boling-</u>
<u>broke</u> Mrs F.H. Macklin. *REV: Ath 30/8/90 p300; E 30/*
8/90 p9; St 29/8/90 p12; Th 1/10/90 p185-6; Ti 28/8/
90 p3.

90.247 *LIGHT O' DAY* (CD,4a) Brien McCullough. NOVELTY
30/8/90-26/9/90; 28/3/91. c. 36 perf. 1st perfd
Gaiety, Burnley 18/6/88. <u>Adam Ainsworth, jr</u> Percy
Gwynne; <u>Adam Ainsworth, sr</u> Rex Russell; <u>Dr Harness</u>
Horace Newland; <u>Dr John Manley</u> Hugh Cannon; <u>Bartholo-</u>
<u>mew Brown</u> Brien McCullough; <u>Old Joe Denton</u> Charles
Lerigo; <u>Jonathan O'Grady</u> H. Buckstone Clair; <u>Gilbert</u>
<u>Muddle</u> H. Jackson; <u>Col. Harrington Hastings</u> [W. Aub-
rey] Chandler; <u>Meek</u> Dudley Smith; <u>Dixon</u> Stinton;
<u>Lunacy Commissioners</u> Wybert, Giles; <u>Guardians of the</u>
<u>Poor</u> Everhard, Ross, [Clement] Flint. <u>Mabel Masters</u>
Daisy Gwynne; <u>Lillian Hastings</u> Marie Brian; <u>Mrs Den-</u>
<u>ton</u> Mrs W. Aubrey; <u>Tiddy Dunn</u> Nelly Nelson. MGR Mrs
J.F. Brian; <u>L</u> S.T. Tolhurst; <u>Act mgr</u> Walter Blount;
<u>Treas & Sec</u> W.R. Pope; <u>Cond</u> Henry T. Parkes; <u>Mechan-</u>
<u>ical effects</u> Walter Lee; <u>Dir</u> Brien McCullough. *REV:*
E 6/9/90 p9; St 5/9/90 p12.

90.248 *THE SPITALFIELDS WEAVER* (F) Thomas Haynes Bay-
ly. 30/8/90. [run probably as for 90.247].** Alfred
Tate; H. Buckstone Clair; John Darrell; Charles
Lerigo. Frances Harrold. <u>MGR</u>, <u>L</u>, <u>Act mgr</u>, <u>Treas &</u>
<u>Sec</u>, <u>Cond</u>, <u>Mechanical effects</u>, <u>Dir</u> as for 90.247.

90.249 *THE MERCHANT OF VENICE* (C,5a) William Shakes-
peare. ROYALTY 30/8/90. 1 perf. 1st perfd 1596. <u>Shy-</u>
<u>lock</u> Charles Cameron; <u>Duke of Venice</u> George Wray;
<u>Prince of Morocco</u> Percy Wright; <u>Antonio</u> Ernest N.
Abbott; <u>Bassanio</u> Norman Clark; <u>Gratiano</u> Roydon Er-
lynne; <u>Salanio</u> Richard Norton; <u>Salarino</u> J. Lewis
Lloyd; <u>Lorenzo</u> Frank Herbert; <u>Tubal</u> W. Lane; <u>Launce-</u>
<u>lot Gobbo</u> Fred Winn; <u>Old Gobbo</u> E. Graham; <u>Leonardo</u>
F. Davies; <u>Gaoler</u> E. Bersford. <u>Portia</u> Olive Stettith;
<u>Balthazar</u> Marie King; <u>Stephano</u> Amy Dewsnap; <u>Nerissa</u>
Mrs Gordon-Ascher; <u>Jessica</u> Violet Langley. *REV: Ath*
6/9/90 p332; E 6/9/90 p9; St 5/9/90 p12.

90.250 *A KISS IN THE DARK* ([F,1a]) J.B. Buckstone.
ROYALTY 30/8/90. 1 perf. 1st perfd Haymarket 13/6/40.

Pettibone Fred Winn. *REV: 5/9/90 p12.*

90.251 *A MILLION OF MONEY* (Military, Sporting & Spec-
tacular Drama,5a) Henry Pettitt & Augustus Harris.
DRURY LANE 6/9/90-13/12/90;* trfd to COVENT GARDEN
15/12/90-17/1/91. 117 perf [w/mat 20/9, 25/10, 26/12/
90; np 25/12/90]. Harry Dunstable Charles Warner;
Frank Hastings Mark Quinton; Tom Cricklewood Harry
Nicholls; Geoffrey St. Clair Charles Glenney; Rev
Gabriel Maythorne Allen Beaumont; Mjr. Belgrave Her-
bert Standing; Dick Bounder Fred Shepherd; John Paw-
ter Fred Dobell; Lord Weatherdown Guy Stanton; Daniel
Whetstone Alfred P. Phillips; Francois Ronald Power;
Reginald Beaumont F. Stoner; Sir Herbert Beechwood
Frank Harrison. Mary Maythorne Jessie Millward;
Hetty Nestledown Fanny Brough; Stella St. Clair Alice
Lingard; Nancy Lee Lizzie Claremont; Elsie Drummond
Helena Dacre; Lady Sandson Lilian Audrie; Mrs Marlow
[Geraldine] Olliffe; Mme Ribob May Palfrey; Ada
Brooks Lily Martin. MGR & DIR Augustus Harris; Sc
R[obert] Caney, W[illiam] Perkins; Cost Mrs Atkins,
Auguste, Mme Oliver Holmes, Stagg & Mantle, [Morris]
Angel, Miss Palmer; Pq William Clarkson; Mach M. Far-
rell; Props R. Hicks; Mus Oscar Barrett; Mus dir P.
Bucalossi; Sm Arthur P. Collins; Treas Fred G. La-
tham. *REV: Ath 13/9/90 p363; E 13/9/90 p9; St 12/9/
90 p12; Th 1/10/90 p186-90; Ti 8/9/90 p6.*

90.252 *THE MIDDLEMAN* (P,4a) H.A. Jones. SHAFTESBURY
6/9/90-9/9/90. 3 perf. 1st perfd Shaftesbury 27/8/89.
Cyrus Blenkarn E.S. Willard; Sir Seaton Umfraville
Sant Matthews; Joseph Chandler C. Harbury; Jesse
Pegg E.W. Gardiner; Cpt. Julian Chandler C[harles J.]
Fulton; Batty Todd H[arry] Cane; Epiphany Danks E.W.
Thomas; Postman S[ydney] Jerram; Servant Hugh Harting;
Daneper [C.H.] Rimbault; Vachell Cleveland. Nancy
Bessie Hatton; Maud Chandler Annie Hill; Felicia
Umfraville Graeme; Mrs Chandler Adelaide Bowering;
Lady Umfraville Josephine St. Ange; Mary Mrs E.S.
Willard. PP John Lancaster; L & Mgr E.S. Willard;
Bom [F.] Forbes; Act mgr W.H. Griffiths; Treas Gil-
bert Tate; Mus dir Edward Jones; Asm [C.H.] Rimbault.
REV: E 4/10/90 p9; St 12/9/90 p12.

90.253 *TRUTH* (C,3a) Bronson Howard. CRITERION 11/9/90-
11/10/90. 27 perf. 1st perfd Hooley's, Chicago 27/5/
78. John Penryn George Giddens; Sir Patridge Compton
William Blakeley; Alfred Sterry T.G. Warren; Frederick
Fry A[ubrey] Boucicault. Dorothy Sterry Helen Forsyth;
Mrs McNamara Emily S. Fitzroy; Mrs Tuttle Maria Daly;
Lady Compton F. Frances; Prudence Ellaline Terriss;
Patience M[abel] Hardinge; Jumps E[mily] Vining. L
Charles Wyndham; Act mgr E. Harvey; Sm Edward Hast-
ings; Cond B. Solomon. *REV: Ath 20/9/90 p395; E 13/9/
90 p8; St 19/9/90 p11; Th 1/10/90 p190-1.*

90.254 *RAVENSWOOD* (P.4a) Herman C. Merivale [fr Sir
Walter Scott, *The Bride of Lammermoor*]. LYCEUM 20/9/
90-3/1/91; 9/1/91, 16/1, 23/1, 30/1, 31/1(m), 6/2,
13/2, 20/2/91. 99 perf [w/mat 6/12/90; mat only 20/
12/90, 27/12/90, 3/1/91; np 25/12/90].* Edgar Henry
Irving; Hayston of Bucklaw [William] Terriss; Caleb
Balderstone William MackIntosh; Craigengelt [Thomas
E.] Wenman; Sir William Ashton Alfred Bishop; Marquis
of Athole F.H. Macklin; Bide-the-Bent H[enry] Howe;
Henry Ashton Gordon Craig; Moncrieff F[rank] Tyars;
Thornton of Lyddall [William] Haviland; Priest Lacy;
Lockhard Davis. Lady Ashton [Roma Guillon] Le Thiere;
Ailsie Gourlay Marriott; Annie Winnie Mrs Pauncefort;
Lucy Ashton Ellen Terry. L & MGR Henry Irving; Mus
Dr A.C. MacKenzie; Sc Hawes Craven, Joseph Harker;
Cost dgn Seymour Lucas, Mrs J.W. Comyns Carr; Cost
Auguste, May, Mrs Reid; Cond J. Meredith Ball; Chorus
master [R.P.] Tabb; Pq C.H. Fox; Mach Fillery; Furn
Perry & Co., Arnott; Bom Joseph Hurst; Sm H.J. Love-
day; Act mgr Bram Stoker. *REV: Ath 27/9/90 p425; E
27/9/90 p11; SR 27/9/90 p367, 1/11/90 p501; St 26/9/
90 p12; Th 1/10/90 p191-4; Ti 22/9/90 p6.*

90.255 *THE BLACK ROVER* (MelodramaticO,3a) Luscombe
Searelle. GLOBE 23/9/90-7/11/90. 40 perf.* The Black
Rover William Ludwig; Pedro Guzman Charles Collette;
Patronio William Hogarth; Jacob John Le Hay; Moro
Royden Erlynne; Felix Maurice Mancini; Chickanaque
Shiel Barry; Negro Slaves & Pirates Adams, Aldridge,
G. Almonte, J. Almonte, Benwell Boissonade, A. Bolton,
Burry, Buthin, C. Canning, G. Canning, Dear, Fishe,
Ford, Gray, Henrihart, Hunt, Judd, Laguerre, Laming,

Lowe, Morris, Newman, Owen, C. Romaine, Weston, Winn-
ing, Workman; <u>Planters & Soldiers</u> Cairns, [David]
Cowis, d'Alberti, Davies, Ellis, Fraser, Hawthorn,
Hilsden, Pitts, F. Pritchard, H. Pritchard, Skinner,
H. Vernon, Vining, Wadey, Ward, Wood. <u>Sabina</u> Effie
Chapuy; <u>Annetta</u> Florence Lloyd; <u>Isidora</u> Blanche Fen-
ton; <u>School Girls</u> Benson, Dudleigh, Goodricke, R.
Maitland, [Lucy] Montrose, [M.] Wentworth; <u>Cocoa Girls</u>
Cleaver, A. Maitland, Meredith, Waltham, Stuart;
<u>Cotton Girls</u> Chase, Julian, Reynolds, Swannell, Viz-
ard, Wynter; <u>Fruit Girls</u> Adams, Courtenay, Denton,
Dipnell, [E.] Faulkner, O'Connor, Wallis; <u>Negresses</u>
Adare, [Marie] Deloitte. <u>L</u> F.R. Benson; <u>Pd</u> Hugh Moss;
<u>Sc</u> W.T. Hemsley; <u>Cost</u> Harrison; <u>Cost dgn</u> Glindoni;
<u>Mus dir</u> Luscombe Searelle; <u>Asm</u> Herbert Stanley; <u>Dir</u>
George Paget; <u>Bm</u> A. Talbot; <u>Ch</u> Osmond; <u>Pq</u> Fox. *REV:*
Ath 27/9/90 p425; E 27/9/90 p9; St 26/9/90 p12, 10/
10/90 p15; Th 1/11/90 p231-2; Ti 13/10/90 p4.

90.256 *THE STRUGGLE FOR LIFE* (D,4a) Robert Buchanan &
Fred Horner [adpt of Alphonse Daudet, *La Lutte pour*
la Vie]. AVENUE 25/9/90-25/10/90. 27 perf.* <u>Paul</u>
<u>Astier</u> George Alexander; <u>Chemineau</u> Albert Chevalier;
<u>Count Andriani</u> Ben Webster; <u>Vaillant</u> Nutcombe Gould;
<u>Antonin Caussade</u> Frederick Kerr; <u>Vedrine</u> [Alfred]
Bucklaw; <u>Heurtebrise</u> George Capel; <u>Duc de Bretigny</u>
Batson; <u>Noblet</u> Alfred Holles; <u>Stenne</u> E.H. Kelly;
<u>Paskowitch</u> A[rthur?] Royston. <u>Esther de Sélény</u> Alma
Stanley; <u>La Maréchale de Sélény</u> Kate Phillips; <u>Lydie</u>
Laura Graves; <u>Mme Paul Astier</u> Genvieve Ward; <u>Count-</u>
<u>ess Fodore</u> Lillian Hingston; <u>Mme de Quincampoix</u>
Charlotte Granville; <u>La Marquise de Rocanère</u> Stuart;
<u>Marie</u> Melitta. <u>MGR</u> George Alexander; <u>Li</u> George Paget;
<u>Sc</u> Joseph Harker; <u>Furn</u> Hampton & Sons, Oetzmann & Co.,
Frank Giles & Co.; <u>Mus</u> John Crook; <u>Cost</u> Maison Felix,
Deamarsy, Savage, Perkins, Morris Angel & Son; <u>Pq</u>
C.H. Fox; <u>Mus dir</u> F. Sydney Ward; <u>Sm</u> Robert V. Shone;
<u>Bm</u> Alwyn Lewis. *REV: Ath 4/10/90 p457-8; E 27/9/90*
p9; SR 27/9/90 p372-3; St 3/10/90 p12; Th 1/11/90 p
232-4; Ti 26/9/90 p7.

90.257 *MAN PROPOSES* (Ca,1a) Sydney Grundy. AVENUE 25/
9/90-25/10/90; 1/11/90-29/1/91. 102 perf [np 24-25/
12/91]. 1st perfd Duke's 18/3/78. <u>Cpt. Huntington</u>

Ben Webster. Dinah Lillian Hingston; Bell Huntington
Marie Linden. MGR, Sm, Bm as for 90.256.

90.258 *SELF; OR, MEN OF THE WORLD* Brien McCullough.
NOVELTY 29/9/90-?17/10/90. c. 18 perf. 1st perfd
Theatre Royal, Bolton 6/83 [as *Self; or, Man's In-
humanity*]. Farmer Bainbridge Charles Lerigo; Gilbert
Morton C. Walter Chamberlain; Harry Davenport H. Buck-
stone Clair; Simon Medwin Hugh Cannon; Walter Mason
E[dwin] Fergusson; George Sculthorpe Alfred Clives;
"Yours truly, Walker Wallop" Brien McCullough; Tim-
othy Willing Charles Daley; Philip Redfern [W. Aub-
rey] Chandler; Teddy Sharp R. Greenwood; Jarvis John
E. Rodgers; Percy Cute Arthur Witherton; Magistrate
Swinbank; Cabman S. Read. Lucy Bainbridge Marie Brian;
Mrs Bainbridge Mrs Allwon; Marion Medwin Nellie Nel-
son; Mrs Copp Mrs W. Aubrey. L S.T. Tolhurst; Act mgr
Walter Blount; Treas & Sec W.R. Pope; Cond Henry T.
Parkes; Dir Brien McCullough; Mechanical effects Wal-
ter Leigh.

90.259 *A KISS IN THE DARK* (F,1a) J.B. Buckstone. NOV-
ELTY 29/9/90-?17/10/90. c. 18 perf.** Stafford;
Alfred Clives. Marie Brian; Nellie Nelson. L, Act
mgr, Treas & Sec, Cond, Mechanical effects, Dir as for
90.258.

90.260 *SWEET LAVENDER* (DD,3a) A.W. Pinero. TERRY'S
29/9/90-21/11/90. 53 perf [w/S mat exc 15/11]. 1st
perfd Terry's 21/3/88. Geoffrey Wedderburn W.H.
Vernon; Clement Hale H. Reeves-Smith; Dr Delaney
Julian Cross; Dick Phenyl Edward Terry; Horace Bream
Henry Dana; Mr Maur Fred W. Irish; Mr Bulger Prince
Miller. Mrs Gilfillian Dolores Drummond; Minnie Marie
Linden; Ruth Rolt Mrs F.H. Macklin; Lavender Eleanore
Leyshon. MGR Edward Terry; Bm H.T. Brickwell; Sm
George Belmore; Mus dir J. Bayliss. *REV: E 4/10/90
p11; St 3/10/90 p12; Th 1/11/90 p234-5.*

90.261 *CARMEN UP TO DATA* (Bsq,2a) George R. Sims &
Henry Pettitt. GAIETY 4/10/90-4/7/91. 240 perf [w/mat
25/10, 8/11, 22/11, 27/12/90, 10/1/91, 17/1, 7/2,
21/2; np 24-25/12/90, 27/3/91]. 1st perfd Shakespeare,
Liverpool 4/10/90. José E.J. Lonnen; Lillius Pasta

George T. Minshull; Dancairo E.H. Haslem; Remendado
Horace Mills; Cpt. Zuniga Arthur Williams. Carmen
Florence St. John; Escamillo Jenny Dawson; Michaila
Maria Jones; Alphonze Katie Barry; Frasquita Florence
Levy/Sylvia Grey; Juanita Maude Wilmot; Inez Eva
Greville; Zorah Alice Gilbert/Eva Wilson; Intimidado
Maude Hobson/Day Ford; Morales Blanche Massey; Lar-
ranaga Grace Wixon/Madge Mildren; Partagas Hetty
Hammer; Mercedes Letty Lind; Hidalgos Flo Henderson,
E. Robina, Minnie Ross, Madge Mildren/Lilly Harold.
L & MGR George Edwardes; Mus Meyer Lutz; Cost Miss
Fisher, Harrison; Cost dgn Percy Anderson; Sc Walter
Hann, T.E. Ryan; Ch John d'Auban; Pq Charles H. Fox;
Cond W. Meyer Lutz; Sm Frank Parker; Act mgr C.J.
Abud; Dir Thomas W. Charles. *REV: E 11/10/90 p9, 7/2/*
91 p9; SR 11/10/90 p424; St 10/10/90 p15, 9/4/91 p12;
Th 1/11/90 p237-9; Ti 6/10/90 p12, 4/2/91 p3. Comment:
The following parts were added during the run: Manuela
Florence Levy; Manuelita Jessie Hassan; Donna Fan-
dango M. Simmons].

90.262 *PEPPER'S DIARY* (Ca,1a) Arthur Morris. ROYALTY
6/10/90-17/11/90. 37 perf.* Hon Robert St. John
Ernest Hendrie; Mjr. Bunderput Henry V. Esmond; Pepper
[Frank] Smithson. Mrs Dorothy Pringle Jenny McNulty;
Letty Mary Jocelyn. L Kate Santley; Mgr Harriett Jay;
Furn Oetzmann & Co.; Cond Walter Slaughter; Sm E.B.
Norman; Act mgr Charles Bernard. *REV: E 11/10/90 p9;*
St 10/10/90 p15. Comment: Cast from V & A programme
for 14/10/90.

90.263 *THE CRUSADER AND THE RAVEN* (Medieval 0a,1a) W.
Allison (lib) & Percy Reeve (mus). GLOBE 7/10/90-
7/11/90. 28 perf.* Sir Rupert Maelvoisie William Ho-
garth; Blondel Fitz Osborne John Le Hay. Dame Alice
Effie Chapuy. *REV: Ath 18/10/90 p520; E 11/10/90 p9;*
St 10/10/90 p15; Ti 13/10/90 p4.

90.264 *THE SIXTH COMMANDMENT* (RD,5a) Robert Buchanan.
SHAFTESBURY 8/10/90-14/11/90. 33 perf.* Fedor Ivan-
ovitch Lewis Waller; Arthur Merrion William Herbert;
Prince Zosimoff Herbert Waring; Arcadius Snaminski
[C.D.] Marius; Gen. Skobeloff Ivan Watson; Alexis
Alexandrovitch Reginald Stockton; Gen. Wolenski W.

Russell; <u>Moustoff</u> M. Byrnes; <u>Kriloff Kriloffski</u> George
Seldon; <u>Petrovitch</u> G[uy] Fane; <u>Father Abramoff</u> Herman
de Lange; <u>Landlord</u> Sydney Herberte Basing; <u>Sgt. of
Cossacks</u> C[harles] Lander; <u>Sgt. of Police</u> F.H. Morton;
<u>Ivan</u> H[enry] Bayntun. <u>Liza</u> Elizabeth Robins; <u>Sophia</u>
Marion Lea; <u>Anna</u> Ellen Lancaster Wallis; <u>Princess
Orenburg</u> Mrs Richardson; <u>Pulcheria Ivanovna</u> Cowen;
<u>Catherine Petroska</u> Maude Brennan; <u>Katel</u> Christine
Bernard; <u>Marfa</u> Josephine St. Ange. <u>PP & MGR</u> John Lan-
caster; <u>Sc</u> Walter Hann; <u>Sm</u> [C.D.] Marius; <u>Bom</u> [F.]
Forbes; <u>Act mgr</u> W.H. Griffiths; <u>Cost</u> L. & H. Nathan,
Debenham & Freebody, Marshall & Snelgrove; <u>Furn</u> Lyon;
<u>Pq</u> William Clarkson; <u>Lime</u> [W.] Kerr; <u>Mus & Mus dir</u>
Arthur E. Godfrey. *REV: Ath 11/10/90 p492; E 11/10/90
p9; SR 11/10/90 p423-4; St 10/10/90 p14, 17/10/90 p12,
1/1/91 p12; Th 1/11/90 p235-6; Ti 9/10/90 p9, 20/10/
90 p4.*

90.265 *LA CIGALE* (CO,3a) F.C. Burnand (lib) & Ivan
Caryll (mus) [fr Fr by Henri Chivot, Alfred Duru &
Edmond Audran]. LYRIC 9/10/90-12/12/91. 417 perf
[w/S mat exc 11/10/90, 21/3/91, 16/5, 6/6, 27/6, 27/7,
1/8, 8/8, 15/8, 22/8, 29/8, 5/9, 12/9, 19/9, 26/9,3/10,
10/10; add mat 5/11/90, 12/11, 19/11, 26/11, 26/12/90,
30/3/91; np 25/12/90, 18/3/91, 27/3/91].* <u>Mathew
Vanderkoopen</u> Lionel Brough/Harry Monkhouse; <u>William</u>
E.W. Garden/Gilbert Porteous; <u>Vincent Knapps</u> Michael
Dwyer/John Peachey; <u>Duke of Fayensberg</u> Eric Lewis;
<u>Curfew Watch</u> John Peachey/T. Crook; <u>Mendicant</u> George
Mudie; <u>Chevalier Franz de Bernheim</u> Chevalier Scovel/
C. Hayden Coffin; <u>Cavalier</u> Francis Barnard/C. Crook;
<u>Chorus (male)</u> Atkins, Arthur, Barnes, C. Crook, T.
Crook, Crofton, Josey, Leaver, Mantell, Mullen, Mum-
ford, Narabloni, Pink, Guadri, Ryley, Selby, Seymour,
Stockwell, Upperton, Wells, White, Wood. <u>Marton</u>
Geraldine Ulmar/Marie Halton; <u>Charlotte</u> Effie Clements; <u>Duchess of Fayensburg</u> Annie Rose [Mrs Horace
Neville]; <u>Aunt Catherine</u> Adelaide Newton; <u>La Frivo-
lini</u> Mimi St. Cyr; <u>Juliette Grisenbach</u> Ethel Carling-
ton/Mabel Love; <u>Alizia</u> Gwynne; <u>Zitanella</u> Lillie Co-
myns/Edith Charteris; <u>Tamburina</u> M. Branard; <u>Cecilia
de Monti</u> Jannette Desborough/M. Greet; <u>Francoise</u> Mabel
Love; <u>Rosina</u> Florence Melville; <u>Manetta</u> Ellis Jeff-
reys/Florence Melville; <u>Leila</u> Charlotte Hope; <u>Camille</u>

Duburri May Sinclair/Ellis Jeffreys; <u>Gervaise Trufle-</u>
<u>boom</u> Julie Couteur; <u>Annetta</u> Florence Lewis; <u>Liza</u> May
Scarlett; <u>Chorus</u> Albert, Austin, Bayley, Braham,
Campbell, Cartwright, Clark, Chapman, Chase, Chesson,
Cranford, Edmonds, Fenton, Ferrar, Fitzgerald, Goss,
Glenn, Hamilton, Hicks, Herrick, Hilton, Howe, Josey,
King, Maxwell, Monmouth, Northcott, Raymond, Reguies,
Rowe, Talbot, Teesdale, Thorne, Union, Wingfield. <u>L &</u>
<u>MGR</u> Horace Sedger; <u>Mus dir</u> Ivan Caryll; <u>Mach</u> S. Tre-
wen; <u>Cost</u> Alias, Auguste & Cie; Miss Fisher, Mme
Champion, Mme Manning, Mme Atkins, Wilhelm, A.C. Con-
rade, Howell Russell, Percy Anderson; <u>Pq</u> William
Clarkson; <u>Ch</u> John d'Auban; <u>Props</u> Labhart; <u>Bm</u> William
Greet. *REV: Ath 18/10/90 p520; E 11/10/90 p11, 17/1/*
91 p11, 4/4/91 p11, 17/10/91 p15; SR 8/11/90 p531,
28/2/91 p263; St 17/10/90 p11-2, 9/4/91 p12, 28/5/91
p12, 6/8/91 p10; Th 1/11/90 p240-1; Ti 10/10/91 p7.

90.266 *STILL WATERS RUN DEEP* (C,3a) Tom Taylor [fnd on
de Bernard, *Le Gendre*]. CRITERION 13/10/90-22/11/90.
42 perf [w/S mat]. 1st perfd Olympic 14/5/55. <u>John</u>
<u>Mildmay</u> Charles Wyndham; <u>Cpt. Hawksley</u> A[rthur] El-
wood; <u>Mr Potter</u> William Blakeley; <u>Dunbilk</u> S[ydney]
Valentine; <u>Gimlet</u> F. Emery; <u>Langford</u> F[rank] Atherley;
<u>Markham</u> S[tanley] Hewson; <u>Jessop</u> G.B. Phillips. <u>Mrs</u>
<u>Mildmay</u> Mary Moore; <u>Mrs Sternhold</u> Mrs Bernard Beere.
<u>L</u> Charles Wyndham; <u>Act mgr</u> E. Harvey; <u>Cond</u> B. Solo-
mon. *REV: Ath 18/10/90 p521; E 18/10/90 p9; St 17/10/*
90 p12; Ti 14/10/90 p5.

90.267 *DEAREST MAMMA* (Ca[1a]) Walter Gordon. CRITER-
ION 13/10/90-11/3/91. 123 perf [np 24-26/11/90, 24-
25/12/90, 9/3/91(?)]. 1st perfd Olympic 14/5/60.
<u>Harry Clinton</u> F[rank] Atherley; <u>Nettle Croker</u> Edmund
Maurice; <u>Browser</u> William Blakeley; <u>Jones</u> F. Emery.
<u>Mrs Breezely Fussell</u> M.A. Victor; <u>Edith Clinton</u> Ella-
line Terriss; <u>Mrs Honeywood</u> F. Frances/Mary Moore(?).
<u>L</u>, <u>Act mgr</u>, <u>Cond</u> as for 90.266. *REV: 18/10/90 p9;*
SR 28/2/91 p262.

90.268 *HIS LAST CHANCE* (Oa) Herbert Harraden (lib) &
Ethel Harraden (mus). GAIETY 13/10/90-4/7/91. 225
perf [np 24-25/12/90, 27/3/91].* <u>Charles Chester</u>
George T. Minshull. <u>Alice Montrose</u> Loie Fuller. <u>L &</u>

MGR George Edwardes; Act mgr C.J. Abud; Sm Frank Parker; Mus dir W. Meyer Lutz. *REV: Ti 14/10/90 p5.*

90.269 *THAT DREADFUL DOCTOR* ([Ca,1a]) Sir Charles L.
Young. HAYMARKET 15/10/90. 1 perf. MGR H.B. Tree.
Comment: Advertized in *Ti* for this date.

90.270 *MADCAP* (Ca,1a) "Alec Nelson" [Dr E.B. Aveling].
COMEDY 17/10/90-28/1/91. 82 perf [np 13-14/11/90,
15-17/12/90, 24-25/12/90].* John Read G. Kennedy/
Leonard Outram; Jack Barton P.S. Champion. Ada Eleanor May; Mrs Barton Helene Lambert; Daphne Rhoda Larkin. MGR Charles H. Hawtrey; Bm E.F. Bradley; Asm
Charles Milton; Mus dir James M. Glover. *REV: Ath
25/10/90 p557; E 25/10/90 p9; St 24/10/90 p12; Ti 20/
10/90 p4.*

90.271 *AIDA* (O[4a]) Giuseppe Verdi. COVENT GARDEN 18/
10/90, 22/10/90. 2 perf. 1st perfd Cairo 24/12/71.
Ramfis Meroles; Amonasro Antonio Galassi; Radamès
Ferruccio Giannini; Il Re Camillo Fiegna; Messaggiero
Rinaldini. Aida Sofia Ravogli; Amneris Giulia Ravogli;
Sacerdotessa Inverni; Dancers Louise Loveday, Jessie
Smiles. MGR Lago; Cond Enrico Bevignani. *REV: Ath 25/
10/90 p556; E 25/10/90 p15; St 24/10/90 p12; Ti 20/
10/90 p10.*

90.272 *BROUGHT TO LIGHT* (CD) Edward Darbey. NOVELTY
18/10/90. Rnd. 1st perfd Theatre Royal, Rotherham 12/
8/89. Brien McCullough. Comment: Play advertized in
V & A programme for 29/9/90.

90.273 *THE GYPSIES* (Oa,1a) Basil Hood (lib) & Wilfred
Bendall (mus). PRINCE OF WALES'S 18/10/90-6/12/90;
26/12/90-6/1/91; 9/2/91-7/8/91. 207 perf [w/mat 20/6/
91; np 27/3/91].* Black Dan Leon Roche/A.T. Hendon;
Albert Tom [A.] Shale; Percival Philip Sefton. Miss
Christine Lightfoot Amy Abbott; Zitella Florence Darley. MGR Horace Sedger. *REV: 1/11/90 p9; St 31/10/90
p12; Ti 27/10/90 p8.* Comment: Advertized in *Ti* for this
date; other sources indicate 1st perf was 25/10/90.

90.274 *LES HUGUENOTS* (O[5a]) Giacomo Meyerbeer. COVENT
GARDEN 20/10/90, 28/10, 12/11/90. 3 perf.** Raoul di

Nangis Julius Perotti; Conte di San Bris Antonio Ga-
lassi; Conte di Nevers Mariano Padilla; Marcello
Meroles; Soldier G. Testa; Tavennes Iginio Corsi; De
Retz Rinaldini; Maurevert Orlandini; De Cosse Moro.
Valentina Maria Peri/Emma Albani; Margherita di Valois
Emma Stromfeld; Urbano Giulia Ravogli; Dama d'Onore
Florenza. MGR Lago; Cond Luigi Arditi. *REV: Ath 25/*
10/90 p556, 15/11/90 p670; E 24/10/90 p15; SR 25/10/
90 p478-9; St 24/10/90 p12; Ti 21/10/90 p9, 31/10/90
p4, 18/11/90 p8.

90.275 *THE SENTRY* (MF,1a) Felix Remo & T. Malcolm Wat-
son. LYRIC 20/10/90-3/3/91. 115 perf [np 25/12/90].**
Col. Pettigrew George Mudie; Tim O'Brien E.W. Garden;
Sgt.-mjr. Jones. Peggy Annie Schuberth; Polly Burch-
ett Ellis Jeffreys; Mrs Pettigrew Adelaide Newton.
L & MGR Horace Sedger; Mus Ivan Caryll; Bm William
Greet.

90.276 *FAUST E MARGHERITA* (O[5a]) Charles Gounod. COV-
ENT GARDEN 21/10/90, 27/10, 7/11, 15/11, 26/11/90. 5
perf.** Mephistopheles Franco Novara; Valentino Mariano Padilla; Faust Suane; Wagner Moro. Margherita
Fanny Moody/Margaret MacIntyre; Siebel Costanzi; Marta
Florenza. MGR Lago; Cond Enrico Bevignani; Bom E.
Hall; Sec J.D. McLaren. *REV: 25/10/90 p557; 1/11/90*
p593; E 25/10/90 p15; SR 25/10/90 p478-9, 1/11/90
p504-5; Ti 23/10/90 p8, 31/10/90 p4.

90.277 *BARBARA* (Ca,1a) Jerome K. Jerome. OPERA COMI-
QUE 22/10/90 mat perf. 1st perfd Globe 19/6/86. Cecil
H. Reeves-Smith; Funnicum [William] Lestocq. Annie
Hughes; Cissy Grahame. *REV: St 24/10/90 p12.*

90.278 *IL TROVATORE* (O[4a]) Giuseppe Verdi. COVENT
GARDEN 23/10/90, 1/11, 19/11/90. 3 perf.** Manrico
Ferruccio Giannini; Ferrando Camillo Fiegna; Conte di
Luna Antonio Galassi; Ruiz Rinaldini. Leonora Sofia
Ravogli; Azucena Giulia Ravogli; Inez Florenza. MGR
Lago; Cond Enrico Bevignani. *REV: Ath 1/11/90 p593;*
Ti 25/10/90 p7.

90.279 *LUCIA DI LAMMERMOOR* (O[3a]) Gaetano Donizetti.
COVENT GARDEN 24/10/90, 4/11/90. 2 perf.** Edgardo

Suane/Dimitresco; Ashton Mariano Padilla; Raimondo
Camillo Fiegna; Normanno Rinaldini; Arturo Iginio
Corsi. Lucia Emma Stromfeld; Alice Florenza. MGR
Lago; Cond Luigi Arditi. *REV: Ath 1/11/90 p593; SR
1/11/90 p504-5; Ti 25/10/90 p7.*

90.280 *ROBERTO IL DIAVOLO* (O[5a]) Giacomo Meyerbeer.
COVENT GARDEN 25/10/90, 31/10, 21/11/90. 3 perf. 1st
perfd Opéra, Paris 21/11/31. Roberto Julius Perotti;
Rambaldo Pedro Guetary; Bertramo Charles Manners;
Alberto Orlandini; Prior Boccolini; Cavaliers Iginio
Corsi, Rinaldini, Moro, G. Testa. Alice Fanny Moody;
Isabella Emma Stromfeld; Lady of Honour Vita; Elena
Louise Loveday. MGR Lago; Cond Luigi Arditi. *REV: Ath
1/11/90 p593; E 1/11/90 p15; SR 1/11/90 p504-5; Ti
27/10/90 p8.*

90.281 *HAND IN HAND* (CD,4a) Edward Darbey. NOVELTY
25/10/90-c. 23/11/90. c. 24 perf. 1st perfd Theatre
Royal, Rotherham 5/8/89. Edgar Hartington Edwin Fer-
gusson; Herbert Hartington H. Buckstone Clair; Ben
Drummond Charles Lerigo; Ted Ward Charles Daley;
Billy Barton Brien McCullough; P.C. Foot Alfred Tate;
P.C. X92 Percy Astor. Jack Marie Brian; Polly Nellie
Nelson; Elsie Marchand Julia Listelle; Grace Edmond-
son Ada Douglas. L S.T. Tolhurst; Act mgr Walter
Blount; Mechanical effects G. Sewell; Treas & Sec
W.R. Pope; Dir Brien McCullough; Cond Henry T. Parkes.
REV: E 1/11/90 p9; St 31/10/90 p12.

90.282 *THE JEALOUS WIFE* (F[5a]) George Colman the
Elder. NOVELTY 25/10/90. Rnd. 1st perfd Drury Lane
12/2/1761. Alfred Tate; Charles Daley; H. Buckstone
Clair. Constance Selos; Georgie Harris. L, Act mgr,
Mechanical effects, Treas & Sec, Dir, Cond as for 90.
281.

90.283 *DIVORCONS* (C,3a) Victorien Sardou & Emile de
Najac. ST. JAMES'S 27/10/90-1/11/90. 7 perf [w/mat
1/11]. 1st perfd Palais-royal, Paris 6/12/80. Des
Prunelles Jaeger; Clavignac Lenormant; Adhermar de
Gratignan Hurtaux; Bafourdin Ricquier; Bastien La-
grange; Jamarot Daumerie; Joseph Millaud. Cyprienne
Chaumont; Mlle de Lusignan Gaudin; Mme de Valfontaine

Davryl; <u>Mme de Brionne</u> Cheller; <u>Josepha</u> Brunet. <u>L</u>
Mrs Langtry; <u>Mgr</u> M.L. Mayer; <u>Mus dir</u> W.C. Lamartine.
*REV: Ath 1/11/90 p596; E 1/11/90 p10; SR 8/11/90 p
531; St 31/10/90 p12; Ti 28/10/90 p6.*

90.284 *MONSIEUR MOULON; OR, THE SHADOW OF DEATH* (P,4a)
Charles Hannan. SHAFTESBURY 28/10/90 mat perf. 1st
prof thus. <u>Jacques Moulon</u> Luigi Lablache; <u>Gustave
Rochefort</u> Sydney Herberte Basing; <u>Henri Raymond</u> C.M.
Hallard; <u>Victor Raymond</u> Frank H. Fenton; <u>Vicomte
Maurice Ongré</u> M[ervyn] Herapath; <u>Pierre Carot</u> Charles
Sugden; <u>Grandfather Lupin</u> A. Wood; <u>Jean</u> E.M. Robson;
<u>Servant</u> V. Everard; <u>Doctor</u> Mervyn. <u>Marquise de Cham-
bery</u> Vane; <u>Jeannette</u> Adrienne Dairolles; <u>Justine
Raymond</u> Georgina Kuhe; <u>Adèle Lecour</u> Mary Barton;
<u>Cherie</u> Amy Bowman, Lucy Webling; <u>Marie Lupin</u> Alma
Murray. <u>PP & MGR</u> John Lancaster; <u>Dir</u> Charles Hannan,
Arthur Deakin; <u>Sm</u> E.B. Norman; <u>Mus</u> Walter Slaughter;
<u>Cost</u> L. & H. Nathan, Auguste & Cie; <u>Pq</u> William Clark-
son; <u>Act mgr</u> W.H. Griffiths. *REV: Ath 1/11/90 p595;
E 1/11/90 p10; St 31/10/90 p12.*

90.285 *LA GIOCONDA* (O[4a]) Amilcare Ponchielli. COV-
ENT GARDEN 29/10/90, 3/11/90. 2 perf. 1st perfd
Teatro alla Scala, Milan, 8/4/76. <u>Barnaba</u> Antonio
Galassi; <u>Enzo</u> Suane/Dimitresco; <u>Alvise</u> Camillo Fieg-
na; <u>Zuane</u> Moro; <u>Isepo</u> Rinaldini; <u>Pilot</u> Boccolini.
<u>La Gioconda</u> Maria Peri; <u>Laura</u> Giulia Ravogli; <u>La
Cieca</u> Grace Damian; <u>Dancers</u> Louise Loveday, Jessie
Smiles. <u>MGR</u> Lago; <u>Cond</u> Enrico Bevignani. *REV: Ath
1/11/90 p593-4; E 1/11/90 p15; SR 1/11/90 p504-5;
Ti 31/10/90 p4.*

90.286 *MOTHS* (RD,4a) Henry Hamilton [adpt of Ouida,
Moths]. LYRIC 29/10/90 mat perf. 1st perfd Globe
25/3/82. <u>Prince Zouroff</u> R[ichard] S. Boleyn; <u>Duke
of Mull & Cantyre</u> Sidney Brough; <u>Lord Jura</u> F.H. Mack-
lin; <u>Raphael de Correze</u> Lewis Waller; <u>Ivan</u> Sydney
Herberte Basing. <u>Princess Nadine Nelaguine</u> Henrietta
Lindley; <u>Duchesse de Sonnaz</u> Adrienne Dairolles; <u>Lady
Dolly Vanderdecken</u> Carlotta Addison; <u>Vere Herbert</u>
Beatrice Lamb; <u>Fuschia Leach</u> Fanny Brough. <u>L & MGR</u>
Horace Sedger; <u>Pq</u> William Clarkson; <u>Furn</u> Oetzmann; <u>Sm</u>
R[ichard] S. Boleyn; <u>Bm</u> William Greet. *REV: Ath 1/11/*

90 p596.

90.287 *LA TRAVIATA* (O[3a]) Giuseppe Verdi. COVENT GAR-
DEN 30/10/90. 1 perf.** <u>Alfredo Germont</u> Ferruccio
Giannini; <u>Giorgio Germont</u> Mariano Padilla; <u>Marchese</u>
Moro; <u>Baron Duphol</u> Fiegna; <u>Gastone</u> Iginio Corsi;
<u>Dottore Grenvil</u> Meroles. <u>Violetta</u> Emma Albani; <u>Flora</u>
<u>Bervoix</u> Inverni; <u>Annina</u> Florenza. <u>MGR</u> Lago; <u>Cond</u>
Enrico Bevignani. *REV: E 1/11/90 p15; Ti 30/10/90 p4.*

90.288 *SUNLIGHT AND SHADOW* (P,3a) R.C. Carton. AVENUE
1/11/90-29/1/91;* trfd to ST. JAMES'S 31/1/91-21/2/
91. 111 perf [w/S mat exc 8/11/90, 31/1/91; add mat
26/12/90, 21/1/90, 4/2/90; np 24-25/12/90]. <u>George</u>
<u>Addis</u> George Alexander; <u>Dr Latimer</u> Nutcombe Gould;
<u>Mr Bamfield</u> Ben Webster; <u>Scollick</u> Alfred Holles; <u>Mark</u>
<u>Denzil</u> Yorke Stephens. <u>Maud</u> Maude Millett; <u>Janet Fel-</u>
<u>ton</u> Ada Neilson; <u>Helen</u> Marion Terry. <u>LI</u> George Paget;
<u>Mgr</u> George Alexander; <u>Mus dir</u> F. Sydney Ward; <u>Sm</u>
Robert V. Shone; <u>Bm</u> Alwyn Lewis; <u>Sc</u> Joseph Harker;
<u>Furn</u> Oetzmann & Co.; <u>Pq</u> C.H. Fox. *REV: Ath 8/11/90*
p633-4; E 8/11/90 p9; SR 8/11/90 p527-8; St 7/11/90
p11-2; Th 1/12/90 p277-9; Ti 3/11/90 p12, 2/2/91 p7.

90.289 *BEAU AUSTIN* (C,4a) Robert Louis Stevenson &
William Ernest Henley. HAYMARKET 3/11/90, 27/11,
24/11, 1/12, 10/12(m), 17/12(m); 30/12/90-10/1/91.
17 perf [np 5/1/91].* <u>George Frederick Austin</u> H.B.
Tree; <u>Menteith</u> Charles H.E. Brookfield; <u>John Fenwick</u>
Fred Terry; <u>Anthony Musgrave</u> Edmund Maurice; <u>Royal</u>
<u>Duke</u> Robb Hardwood. <u>Evelina</u> Rose Leclercq; <u>Barbara</u>
<u>Ridley</u> Aylward; <u>Dorothy Musgrave</u> Mrs H.B. Tree. <u>L &</u>
<u>MGR</u> H.B. Tree; <u>Sc</u> Walter Johnstone; <u>Cost</u> L. & H.
Nathan; <u>Cond</u> Carl Armbruster; <u>Sm</u> Edward Hastings; <u>Bm</u>
<u>& Sec</u> F[rederick] Harrison. *REV: Ath 8/11/90 p634;*
E 3/11/90 p10, 3/1/91 p11; SR 8/11/90 p532; St 7/11/
90 p12; Th 1/12/90 p279-81; Ti 4/11/90 p9.

90.290 *LES REVOLTEES* (C,1a) Edmond Gondinet. ST.
JAMES'S 3/11/90-8/11/90. 7 perf [w/mat 8/11/90]. 1st
perfd Gymnase, Paris 30/11/65. <u>M. de Brion</u> Lenormant; <u>M. Dargis</u> Rouvenat. <u>Mme de Brion</u> Chaumont; <u>Mme</u>
<u>Dargis</u> Stuard. <u>L</u> Mrs Langtry; <u>Mgr</u> M.L. Mayer; <u>Mus dir</u>
W.C. Lamartine. *REV: E 8/11/90 p8; SR 8/11/90 p531;*

St 7/11/90 p12.

90.291 *L'AUTOGRAPHIE* (C,1a) Henri Meilhac. ST.JAMES'S
3/11/90-8/11/90. 7 perf [w/mat 8/11]. 1st perfd Gymnase, Paris 27/11/58. Chastenay Lenormant; Comte
Riscara Rouvenat; Flavio Lagrange, *fils*. Julie Chaumont; La Comtesse Fromant. L, Mgr, Mus dir as for 90.
290. *REV: As for 90.290.*

90.292 *LOLOTTE* (C,1a) Henri Meilhac & Ludovic Halévy.
ST. JAMES'S 3/11/90-8/11/90. 7 perf [w/mat 8/11]. 1st
perfd Vaudeville, Paris 4/10/79. Croisilles Hurtaux;
Le Baron Pouf Rouvenat; Domestique Debarsa. Lolotte
Chaumont; Julie Brunet; La Baronne Pouf Stuard. L,
Mgr, Mus dir as for 90.290. *REV: E 8/11/90 p8.*

90.293 *NORMA* (O[2a]) Vincenzo Bellini. COVENT GARDEN
5/11/90. 1st perfd Teatro alla Scala, Milan 26/12/31.
Polione Ferruccio Giannani; Oroveso Meroles; Flavio
Iginio Corsi. Norma Maria Peri; Adalgisa Costanzi;
Clotilde Florenza. MGR Lago; Cond Luigi Arditi. *REV:*
SR 15/11/90 p561.

90.294 *MY FRIEND JARLET* (P,1a) Arnold Goldsworthy &
E.B. Norman. TERRY'S 5/11/90-14/3/91. 125 perf [w/S
mat exc 8/11, 15/11, 22/11; add mat 26/12, 29/12/90,
1/1/91, 8/1/91; np 22-25/12/90, 2-4/3/91]. 1st perfd
Old Stagers, Canterbury 2/8/87. Emile Jarlet Julian
Cross; Paul Latour Henry Dana; Prussian Officer
Arthur Wellesley. Marie Leroux Elinore Leyshon. L &
MGR Edward Terry; Bm H.T. Brickwell; Sm George Belmore; Mus dir J. Bayliss. *REV: Ath 8/11/90 p634; E*
8/11/90 p9; St 7/11/90 p12; Th 1/12/90 p281; Ti 6/
11/90 p7.

90.295 *ORFEO [Orfeo, ed Euridice]* C.W. Gluck. COVENT
GARDEN 6/11/90, 11/11, 17/11, 22/11, 27/11, 29/11/
90(m). 6 perf. 1st perfd Burgtheater, Vienna 5/10/1762.
Euridice Sofia Ravogli; L'Amore [Eros] Otta Brony;
Orfeo Giulia Ravogli; Dancers Louise Loveday, Jessie
Smiles. MGR Lago; Cond Enrico Bevignani. *REV: Ath*
15/11/90 p670; E 8/11/90 p15; SR 15/11/90 p561; Ti
7/11/90 p3.

90.296 *SMOKE* (Ca,1a) Benjamin Webster the younger.
OPERA COMIQUE 6/11/90-3/1/91. 47 perf [np 22-25/12/90].
1st perfd Adelphi 26/12/70. Reuben Armstrong R[ichard]
S. Boleyn; James Brown Compton Coutts; Richard Burton
W[illiam] Lestocq. Ellen Armstrong Cissy Grahame;
Abigail Armstrong M.A. Giffard. MGR Cissy Grahame;
Sm Ernest Cathcart; Act mgr Arthur Yates. *REV: Ath*
15/11/90 p672; E 8/11/90 p9; St 14/11/90 p12; Th 1/
12/90 p281-2; Ti 7/11/90 p3.

90.297 *LOHENGRIN* (O[3a]) Richard Wagner. COVENT GAR-
DEN 8/11/90, 14/11, 24/11/90. 3 perf.** Lohengrin
Julius Perotti; Federico di Telramondo Antonio Ga-
lassi; Enrico l'Uccellatore Franco Novara; l'Araldo
del Re Camillo Fiegna. Elsa di Brabante Emma Albani/
Ella Russell; Ortrud Giulia Ravogli. MGR Lago; Cond
Luigi Arditi; Sec J.D. McLaren. *REV: Ath 15/11/90*
p670; SR 22/11/90 p586-7; Ti 12/11/90 p7, 18/11/90 p8.

90.298 *TWO RECRUITS* (FC,3a) Frank Wyatt. TOOLE'S
8/11/90-26/11/90. 18 perf [w/mat 19/11, 26/11]. 1st
prof. Mr Eldred Albert Chevalier; Frank Selwyn
H[arry] Eversfield; Col. Gunning W[illiam] Cheesman;
Jack Selwyn W[indham] Guise; Thomas Gurgles Henry W.
Brame; Joe Gurgles F. Kaye. Mrs Eldred Ruth Rutland;
Violet Fane Violet Thornycroft; Sally Flapper Julia
Seaman; Martha Mrs Henry Leigh; Tricksey Delia Car-
lyle. MGR Violet Melnotte; Pd Frank Wyatt; Cost Morris
Angel & Son; Pq C.H. Fox; Cond Edward Crosse; Act mgr
& Treas Henry Brandon; Sec Charles Campbell. *REV: Ath*
15/11/90 p671-2; E 15/11/90 p9; St 14/11/90 p12; Th
1/12/90 p282-3; Ti 10/11/90 p8.

90.299 *RIGOLETTO* (O[3a]) Giuseppi Verdi. COVENT GARDEN
10/11/90, 13/11/90. 2 perf.** Rigoletto Antonio
Galassi/Victor Maurel; Duke Dimitresco; Sparafucile
Meroles; Marullo Rinaldini; Monterone Orlandini; Borsa
Iginio Corsi; Conte de Ceprano Moro. Gilda Emma Stromfeld; Maddalena Louise Lablache; Giovanna Florenza;
Contessa di Ceprano Vita. MGR Lago; Cond Enrico Bevignani; Sec J.D. McLaren. *REV: Ath 22/11/90 p706; SR*
15/11/90 p561, 22/11/90 p586-7; Ti 12/11/90 p7.

90.300 *CALLED BACK* (P,Prol,3a) Hugh Conway & J.W.

Comyns Carr. HAYMARKET 10/11/90-29/12/90. 42 perf [w/
S mat; np 17/11, 24/11, 1/12, 8/12, 15/12, 22/12, 24-
25/12]. 1st perfd Prince of Wales's 20/5/84. Paolo
Macari H.B. Tree; Dr Ceneri [James] Fernandez; Gil-
bert Vaughan Fred Terry; Arthur Kenyon Frederick
Kerr; Anthony March [E.] Webster Lawson; Petroff
Charles Hudson; Bolski Mark Paton; Chief of Russian
Police [A.B.] Tapping; Mjr. Markeloff [Charles] Allan;
Cpt. Varlamoff Robb Harwood; Sgt. of Cossacks Leith;
Warder Kedril [J.] Montagu; Nicholas Martin; Wood-
ford Warden; Wolynski [Alfred] Wigley. Pauline Julia
Neilson; Mary Vaughan Blanche Horlock; Mrs Wilkins
Mrs E.H. Brooke; Susan Aylward. L & MGR H.B. Tree;
Bom W.H. Leverton; Sc Walter Hann, Walter Johnstone;
Cond Carl Armbruster; Sm Edward Hastings; Bm & Sec
F[rederick] Harrison. *REV: Ath 15/11/90 p672; E 15/*
11/90 p9; St 14/11/90 p11-2; Th 1/12/90 p283-4; Ti
11/11/90 p7.

90.301 *L'AMI DES FEMMES* (C,5a) Alexandre Dumas. ST.
JAMES'S 10/11/90-15/11/90. 7 perf [w/mat 15/11]. 1st
perfd Gymnase, Paris 5/3/64. De Ryons Valbel; De
Montegre Lenormant; De Simerose Rouvenat; Des Tar-
gettes Ricquier; Leverdet Daumerie; De Chantrin
Lagrange, *fils*; Joseph Debarsa. Jane de Simerose
Stuart; Mme Leverdet Gaudin; Mlle Hackendorf Cheller;
Balbine Leverdet Davryl; Justine Brunet. L Mrs Lang-
try; Mgr M.L. Mayer; Mus dir W.C. Lamartine. *REV:*
E 15/11/90 p11; St 14/11/90 p12; Ti 12/11/90 p8.

90.302 *MAY AND DECEMBER* (FC,3a) Sydney Grundy [based
on S. Grundy & Joseph MacKay's version of *La Petite*
Marquise]. COMEDY 15/11/90-13/12/90. 29 perf. 1st
prof perfd Criterion 25/4/87. Cpt. L'Estrange Charles
H. Hawtrey; Sir Archibald Ffolliott Charles H.E.
Brookfield; Babbington Jones J.F. Graham; Simpson
W[illiam] Wyes; Telegraph Messenger A.W. Aysom. Lady
Ffolliott [Rose] Norreys; Jane Lydia Cowell; Dolly
Ethel Matthews; Judy Belsize Lottie Venne. MGR Charles
H. Hawtrey; Pd F[rederick] Glover; Bm E.F. Bradley;
Asm Charles Milton; Mus dir James M. Glover. *REV:*
Ath 22/11/90 p708; E 22/11/90 p9; SR 22/11/90 p587-8;
St 21/11/90 p12-3; Th 1/12/90 p282-3; Ti 18/11/90 p4.

90.303 *THE PHARISEE* (P,3a) T. Malcolm Watson & Mrs
Ellen Lancaster Wallis. SHAFTESBURY 17/11/90-13/2/91.
85 perf [w/mat 29/11, 10/12, 26/12, 31/12/90, 7/1/91,
14/1, 21/1, 28/1/91; np 24-25/12/90].* Lord Helmore
Lewis Waller; Geoffrey Landon Herbert Waring; Cpt.
James Darrell [C.D.] Marius/W.H. Vernon; Mr Pettifer
John Beauchamp/Edmund Gurney; Graham Maxwell Henry V.
Esmond; Brooke Sydney Herberte Basing. Kate Landon
Mrs Ellen Lancaster Wallis; Miss Maxwell Sophie
Larkin; Maud Marion Lea; Katie Minnie Terry; Martin
Winifred Dennis. PP & MGR John Lancaster; Sc Walter
Hann; Furn Lyon, Labhart; Dir [C.D.] Marius; Bom
[F.] Forbes; Act mgr W.H. Griffiths; Asm Sydney Her-
berte Basing. *REV: Ath 22/11/90 p708; E 22/11/90 p9;
SR 22/11/90 p587; St 21/11/90 p12; Th 1/12/90 p285-6;
Ti 18/11/90 p6.*

90.304 *TANNHAUSER* (O[3a]) Richard Wagner. COVENT GAR-
DEN 18/11/90, 20/11, 29/11/90. 3 perf. 1st perfd
Dresden 19/10/45. Tannhauser Julius Perotti; Herman I
Meroles; Walther Pedro Guetary; Biterolf Orlandini;
Heinrich Rinaldini; Reinmar Camillo Fiegna; Wolfram
Victor Maurel. Elizabeth Emma Albani; Venus Sofia
Ravogli; Young Shepherd Cecile Brani. MGR Lago; Cond
Enrico Bevignani. *REV: Ath 22/11/90 p706; Ti 21/11/
90 p14.*

90.305 *ANTONY AND CLEOPATRA* (T,5a) William Shakespeare. PRINCESS'S 18/11/90-21/2/91. 96 perf [w/mat
6/12, 13/12, 20/12, 26/12, 31/12/90, 10/1/91, 14/1,
21/1, 24/1, 28/1, 4/2, 7/2, 14/2, 18/2/91; np 25/12/
90]. 1st perfd 1608. Antony [Charles F.] Coghlan;
Sextus Pompeius Kenneth Black; Enobarbus Arthur Stir-
ling; Octavius Caesar F[rank] Kemble Cooper; 2nd
Soldier A. Watson; 1st Soldier W. Clifton; Clown
F[red A.] Everill; Soothsayer Arthur Munro; Proculeius
Henry Loraine; Mardian Harry Fenwicke; Eros Charles
Burleigh; Seleucus Henry J. Carvill; Messenger Oscar
Adye; Ventidius H[ubert] Druce; Scarus A.T. Hilton;
Alexas [Frank] MacVickar; Mecaenas W.S.Parkes; Menas
H. Yardley; Thyreus [Walter] Gay; Varrius Stanley
Pringle; Lepidus P.C. Beverley. Cleopatra Mrs Lang-
try; Octavia Frances Ivor; Charmian Amy McNeil; Iras
F. Harwood; Day Emma d'Auban; Night Madge Greet.

MGR Mrs Langtry; Mus Edward Jakobowski; Sc Bruce
Smith, [Edward] Banks, Joseph Harker, Perkins; Ch
John d'Auban; Cost Bianchini, Landolf & Cie, Alias,
Mrs Lintott; Armour Gurperle & Cie, Kennedy; Props
Burdett; Pq William Clarkson; Dir Lewis Wingfield;
Bom Hamilton; Mach J.W. Cawdray; Lime Jones, [W.]
Kerr; Mus dir W[illiam] Corri, jr; Asm W. Lintott; Bm
Gilbert Tate. *REV: Ath 22/11/90 p707-8; E 22/11/90*
p11; SR 22/11/90 p584-5; St 21/11/90 p12; Th 1/12/90
p287-8.

90.306 *A PAIR OF LUNATICS* (Ca,1a) W.R. Walkes. SHAFT-
ESBURY 19/11/90 mat perf. 1st perfd Drury Lane 11/4/
89. He George Alexander. She Maude Millett. MGR John
Lancaster; Mus dir Arthur E. Godfrey; Act mgr W.H.
Griffiths; Sm [C.D.] Marius.

90.307 *HIS LAST CHANCE* (Oa) Herbert & Ethel Harraden.
SHAFTESBURY 19/11/90 mat perf.** Mr Chester G.T.
Minshull. Miss Montrose Loie Fuller. PP & MGR, Sm,
Mus dir, Act mgr as for 90.306.

90.308 *IN CHANCERY* (F,3a) A.W. Pinero. TERRY'S 22/11/
90-28/2/91. 99 perf [w/S mat exc 22/11; add mat 26/
12, 30/12/90, 1/1/91, 8/1/91; np 22-25/12/90]. 1st
perfd Lyceum, Edinburgh 19/9/84. Montague Joliffe
Edward Terry; John Henry Dana; Mr Hinxman Prince
Miller; Cpt. Dionysius McCafferty Julian Cross; Dr
Titus Fred W. Irish; Mr Buzzard Robert Soutar; Mr
Gawge George Belmore. Mrs Smith Elinore Leyshon;
Patricia McCafferty Kate Mills; Kittles Rose Dearing;
Walker Violet Armbruster; Mrs Marmaduke Jackson Alice
Yorke; Amelia Ann Buzzard Jessie Danvers. L & MGR
Edward Terry; Bm H.T. Brickwell; Sm George Belmore;
Mus dir J. Bayliss. *REV: Ath 29/11/90 p748; E 29/11/*
90 p9; St 28/11/90 p12; Th 1/1/91 p37-40; Ti 24/11/90
p8.

90.309 *NEVER DESPAIR* (CD,Prol,4a) George Comer. NOVEL-
TY 23/11/90-c. 5/12/90. c. 12 perf. 1st perfd Gaiety,
Halifax 5/5/87. Horatio Spriggins Brien McCullough;
Harry Brierly Edwin Fergusson; Dan Brierly Charles
Lerigo; Joe Dyson Alfred Tate; Desmond Adair H. Buck-
stone Clair; Phipps King Bolton. Lottie Smith Nellie

Nelson; <u>Ned Adair</u> Julia Listelle; <u>Mary Adair</u> Mrs Edward Hallows; Marian Brian. *REV: St 28/11/90 p12.*

90.310 *QUEER LODGERS* (F,1a) Alfred A. Wilmot. NOVELTY
23/11/90 [probably ran until c. 24/12/90]. 1st perf
Park Town Hall, Battersea 1/3/90. <u>George Delbarre</u>
[H. Buckstone] Clair; <u>Frank Wilson</u> [Owen] Wynne; <u>Sgt.
Nailem</u> [Alfred] Tate. <u>Mrs Slummers</u> Georgie Harris;
<u>Mrs Delbarre</u> C[onstance] Selos. *REV: St 28/11/90 p12.*

90.311 *MY LADY HELP* (Ca,1a) Arthur Macklin. SHAFTES-
BURY 24/11/90-14/2/91. 69 perf [np 24-25/12/90]. *
<u>Benjamin Pennygrass</u> John Beauchamp/Edmund Gurney;
<u>Jack Desborough</u> Henry V. Esmond. <u>Lady Eva Desborough</u>
Florence West. <u>PP & MGR</u> John Lancaster; <u>Sm</u> W.H. Vernon; <u>Asm</u> Sydney Herberte Basing; <u>Bom</u> [F.] Forbes; <u>Act
mgr</u> W.H. Griffiths. *REV: Ath 29/11/90 p748; E 29/11/
90 p9; St 28/11/90 p12; Th 1/1/91 p40; Ti 28/11/90 p7.*

90.312 *L'ETOILE DU NORD* (O,3a) Giacomo Meyerbeer.
COVENT GARDEN 25/11/90, 28/11/90. 2 perf.** <u>Danilo-
witz</u> Pedro Guetary; <u>Peter</u> Victor Maurel; Iginio Corsi;
Giuseppe Ciampi; Camillo Fiegna; Orlandini; Lesta;
Rinaldini. <u>Catherine</u> Emma Stromfeld; <u>Prascovia</u> Norini;
Cecile Brani; Florenza. <u>MGR</u> Lago; <u>Cond</u> Luigi Arditi.
*REV: Ath 29/11/90 p746-7; E 29/11/90 p15; Ti 27/11/90
p6.*

90.313 *LONDON ASSURANCE* (C,5a) Dion Boucicault. CRI-
TERION 27/11/90-25/2/91. 90 perf [w/S mat; add mat
28/1/91, 4/2/91; np 24-25/12/90].** <u>Dazzle</u> Charles
Wyndham; <u>Sir Harcourt Courtly</u> William Farren; <u>Dolly
Spanker</u> George Giddens; <u>Charles Courtly</u> Arthur Bourchier; <u>Mark Meddle</u> William Blakeley; <u>Cool</u> Cyril
Maude; <u>Max Harkaway</u> H.H. Vincent; <u>Martin</u> Frank Atherley; <u>James</u> S[tanley] Hewson; <u>Solomon Isaacs</u> F. Emery.
<u>Grace Harkaway</u> Mary Moore; <u>Pert</u> E[mily] Vining; <u>Lady
Gay Spanker</u> Mrs Bernard Beere/Emily [S.] Fitzroy.
<u>MGR</u> Charles Wyndham. *REV: Ath 6/12/90 p785; E 29/11/
90 p9; St 5/12/90 p12; Th 1/1/91 p41-3; Ti 28/11/90
p7.*

90.314 *THE BALLADMONGER* (RP,1a) Walter Besant & Walter
Herries Pollock [adpt of Theodore de Banville, *Grin-*

goire]. 1/12/90; 30/12/90-10/1/91. 11 perf [np 5/1/
91].** Gringoire H.B. Tree; Louis XI [James] Fernandez; Olivier Charles Allan; Simon Leith. Loyse Mrs
H.B. Tree; Nicole Hethcote. L & MGR H.B. Tree; Cond
Carl Armbruster; Sm Edward Hastings; Bm & Sec Frederick Harrison. Comment: Cast from Birmingham Public
Library programme for c. 30/12/90.

90.315 *THE PENALTY* (D,3a) Julian Cross. TERRY'S 2/12/
90 mat perf.* Cirio Antonelli Julian Cross; John
Bentry Henry Bedford; Sir Lionel Drillinghurst Robert
Soutar; Guy Drillinghurst Graham Wentworth; George
Loombe Henry Dana; Jack Barnard A. Wood; Sam George
Belmore. Alice Bentry Marie Linden; Lawretta Bentry
Kate Bealby; Iris Loombe Elinore Leyshon; Lizzie
Willis Rose Dearing; Cora Montez Ruth Rutland. *REV:
Ath 6/12/90 p785-6; E 6/12/90 p10; St 5/12/90 p12.*

90.316 *THE PEOPLE'S IDOL* (D,4a) Wilson Barrett & Vic-
tor Widnell. OLYMPIC 4/12/90--2/1/91. 28 perf [w/S
mat; np 24-25/12/90].* Lawrence St. Aubrey Wilson
Barrett; Arthur St. Aubrey H. Cooper Cliffe; Mjr.
Duncan T.W. Percyval; Mr Dolroyd Edward Irwin; Dr
Wheeler W. Lionel Belmore; Jim Stevens Austin Melford;
Mr Hackett Ambrose Manning; Buster W.A. Elliott/Geo-
rge Barrett; Sam Purkiss Stafford Smith; Tom Spate
P[aul] Belmore; Jack Burdock A.E. Field; George Far-
gate Franklin McLeay; Sneedon Horace Hodges; James
Cecil Duncan; Gabriel Stevens George Barrett. Grace
Duncan Winifred Emery; Myra Keith Lillie Belmore;
Lydia Maud [C.] Jeffries; Mrs St. Aubrey Alice Cooke;
Blanche Louie Bassett Wilmot; Rose Lowdham Lily Han-
bury; Mrs Melway Alice Belmore; Jane Batts Bessie
Carlyon; Sarah Kibworth Harrietta Polini; Jane Alice
Gambier. L & MGR Wilson Barrett; Bom A[rthur] Frye;
Pp Charles Wilmot; Pd Wilson Barrett; Sc Walter Hann,
Bruce Smith, Stafford Hall; Pq William Clarkson; Cost
Elita & Cie; Mus & Cond Michael Connelly; Bm G.M.
Polini; Act mgr F. Vagg Walter; Sm Charles Cathcart.
*REV: Ath 13/12/90 p823, 20/12/90 p864; E 6/12/90 p11;
St 12/12/90 p12; Th 1/1/91 p43-5; Ti 5/12/90 p7, 6/
12/90 p4.*

90.317 *A CLERICAL ERROR* (Ca,1a) H.A. Jones. OLYMPIC

5/12/90-2/1/91. 23 perf [np 24-25/12/90]. 1st perfd
Court 13/10/79. Rev Richard Capel W.A. Elliott;
Richard Capel T.W. Percyval; Perry Austin Melford.
Minnie Heritage Lily Hanbury. L & MGR, Pp, Bom, Bm,
Act mgr, Sm, Mus dir as for 90.316.

90.318 *THE MOCK DOCTOR* (CO,3a) Charles Gounod. GLOBE
6/12/90-12/12/90. 6 perf. 1st perfd Théâtre-Lyrique,
Paris 15/1/58. Leander King Morgan; Geronte Sebastian
King; Valere Joseph Wilson; Lucas Kelson Trueman; M.
Robert W. Barker; Hellebore Edward Thirlby; Sganarelle
Richard Temple; Chorus Lee Williams, C. Jameson, R.
Massow, J. Bowen, Hy Passy, W. Fletcher, James Lewis,
Victor Thornleigh, J. Moore, W. Barker, W. Percy,
Arthur Wiseman, D. Preston, J. Roby. Lucinda Effie
Chapuy; Martine Susetta Fenn; Jacqueline Annie Dwelley;
Chorus [Marie] Deloitte, May Clark, Lillian Thirlby,
M. Nilen, E. Clinton, M. Gow, J. Holles, R. Adair,
E. Faulkner, Nellie Richardson, M. Wentworth, F.
Hewett, F. Bromley, K. Elsie, M. Wilson, Lucy Mont-
rose, Ada McAckland; Dancers Hamilton, Matthews,
Barnett, Richards, Day, Lawford, Powelle, French,
Evans, Rockwell, Fairland, Martin. L F.R. Benson; Dir
Richard Temple; Cost May; Cost dgn Tony Johannot; Mus
dir Victor Champion; Pq William Clarkson; Ch Paul
Valentine; Sm Edward Thirlby; Bm E. Lockwood.

90.319 *CUPS AND SAUCERS* (Oa) George Grossmith. GLOBE
6/12/90-12/12/90. 6 perf. 1st perfd Opera Comique
5/8/78. Gen. Deelah Joseph Wilson. Mrs Nankeen Worcester Marie Deloitte. L, Dir, Mus dir, Sm, Bm as for 90.
318.

90.320 *THE SHAUGHRAUN* (D,4a) Dion Boucicault. NOVELTY
6/12/90-2/1/91. c. 25 perf. 1st perfd Wallack's, New
York 14/11/74. Cpt. Molineux Edwin Fergusson; Robert
Ffolliott Gilbert Vernon; Father Dolan Watty Brunton;
Corry Kinchela H. Buckstone Clair; Harvey Duff Al-
fred Tate; Sgt. Jones [Owen] Wynne; Reilly G. Wallace;
Sullivan A. Willmore; Mangan Clement Flint; Doyle
Walter Moore; Conn Brien McCullough. Claire Ffolliott
Marie Brian; Arte O'Neil Florence Worth; Mrs O'Kelly
Mrs W[atty] Brunton; Bridget Madigan Georgie Harris;
Nancy Malone Gibson; Moya Nellie Nelson. L S.T. Tol-

hurst. *REV: E 13/12/90 p9, 3/1/91 p9.*

90.321 *THE REDLAMP* (D,4a) W. Outram Tristram. HAYMAR-
KET 8/12/90, 22/12/90, 5/1/91. 3 perf. 1st perfd
Comedy 20/4/87. <u>Demetrius</u> H.B. Tree; <u>Ivan Zazzulic</u>
James Fernandez; <u>Gen. Morakoff</u> Kemble; <u>Alexis Valerian</u>
Fred Terry; <u>Allan Villiers</u> Fred Kerr; Charles Hudson;
Robb Harwood; J. Hastings Batson; Leith. <u>Princess
Claudia</u> Mrs H.B. Tree; <u>Felise</u> Floyd; Julia Neilson;
Mrs E.H. Brooke; Aylward; Rosina Filippi. <u>MGR</u> H.B.
Tree. *REV: Ath 13/12/90 p823-4.*

90.322 *CAPTAIN SWIFT* (P,4a) C. Haddon Chambers. HAY-
MARKET 15/12/90, 29/12/90. 2 perf. 1st perfd Haymarket
20/6/88. <u>Wilding</u> H.B. Tree; <u>Marshall</u> James Fernandez;
<u>Seabrook</u> H[enry] Kemble; <u>Gardiner</u> Fred Terry; <u>Michael
Ryan</u> Charles Allan; <u>Harry Seabrook</u> E. Webster Lawson;
[<u>Bates</u> J.] Montagu. <u>Mrs Seabrook</u> Lady Monckton; <u>Lady
Staunton</u> Rose Leclercq; <u>Stella Darbisher</u> Mrs H.B.
Tree; <u>Mabel Seabrook</u> Aylward; [Blanche] Horlock. <u>MGR</u>
H.B. Tree. *REV: Ath 20/12/90 p864; E 20/12/90 p10.*

90.323 *THE LADY OF LYONS* (D,5a) Edward Bulwer Lytton.
OLYMPIC 17/12/90, 24/12, 31/12/90, 7/1/91. 4 mat perf.
1st perfd Covent Garden 15/2/38. <u>Claude Melnotte</u>
Wilson Barrett; <u>Col. Damas</u> George Barrett; <u>Beauscant</u>
H. Cooper Cliffe; <u>Glavis</u> T.W. Percyval; <u>M. Deschap-
pelles</u> Franklyn McLeay; <u>Gaspard</u> Murray Carson; <u>Land-
lord</u> Horace Hodges; <u>Cpt. Gervais</u> E[dward] Irwin;
<u>Mjr. Desmoulins</u> W. [Lionel] Belmore; <u>Lieut. Dupont</u>
A.E. Field. <u>Pauline</u> Winifred Emery; <u>Mme Deschappelles</u>
Mrs Henry Leigh; <u>Widow Melnotte</u> Alice Cooke. <u>L & MGR</u>
Wilson Barrett; <u>Pp</u> Charles Wilmot; <u>Bom</u> A[rthur] Frye;
<u>Mus</u> Edward Jones; <u>Cost</u> D. Bernstein; <u>Bm</u> G.M. Polini;
<u>Act mgr</u> F. Vagg Walter; <u>Sm</u> Charles Cathcart; <u>Mus dir</u>
Michael Connelly. *REV: Ath 20/12/90 p864; E 20/12/90
p11; St 19/12/90 p10; Ti 20/12/90 p14.*

90.324 *JANE* (F,3a) Harry Nicholls & W[illiam] Lestocq.
COMEDY 18/12/90-4/7/91. 191 perf [w/S mat exc 20/12/
90, 10/1/91, 18/4, 25/4, 30/5, 6/6, 13/6, 20/6, 27/6;
add mat 28/1/91, 4/2, 18/2, 4/3, 18/3; np 24-25/12/90,
27/3/91].* <u>William</u> Charles H.E. Brookfield; <u>Mr Ker-
shaw</u> H[enry] Kemble; <u>Pixton</u> E.M. Robson; <u>Charles</u>

Shakleton Charles H. Hawtrey; Claude Master R[ichard]
Saker. Lucy Norton Ethel Matthews; Mrs Chadwick
[Caroline] Ewell; Mrs Pixton Ada Murray; Jane Lottie
Venne. MGR Charles H. Hawtrey; Bm E.F. Bradley; Asm
Charles Milton; Mus dir James M. Glover. *REV: 27/12/*
90 p899; E 20/12/90 p9; SR 27/12/90 p734; St 26/12/90
p10; Th 1/2/90 p89-91; Ti 19/12/90 p8, 2/2/91 p7

90.325 *A HAPPY PAIR* (Ca,1a) S. Theyre Smith. CRITERION
19/12/90 mat perf. 1st perfd St. James's 2/3/68.
[Mr Honeyton] Arthur Bourchier. [Mrs Honeyton] Mary
Moore. *REV: St 26/12/90 p10.*

90.326 *THE ROSE AND THE RING* (Panto) Henry Saville
Clarke [fr W.M. Thackeray]. PRINCE OF WALES'S 19/12/
90-24/12/90; 5 mat perf; 26/12/90-6/1/91; 20 perf [2
perf dy]; 7/1/91-31/1/91; 22 mat perf. Total perf 47.*
Valoroso Harry Monkhouse; Bulbo John Le Hay; Glum-
boso/Padella W[illiam] Cheesman; Tommaso/Count Spin-
achi Tom A. Shale; Count Hedzoff A.T. Hendon; Jenkins
Gruffanuff S. Solomon; Count Hogginarmo G[eorge]
Marler; Jester R. Bernard. Prince Gigho Violet Cameron;
Betsinda/Rosalba Attalie Claire; Angelica Maud Holland;
Countess Gruffanuff Amadi; Fairy Blackstick Isa Bow-
man; Queen of Paflagonia Ada Doree; Polly/Gen. Punch-
ikoff Empsie Bowman. MUS Walter Slaughter; Pd Augus-
tus Harris, Charles Harris; Ch John d'Auban; Mus dir
John Crook; Sc William Telbin; Mach S. Trewen; Cost
Alias, Auguste, Miss Fisher, Champion, Manning, At-
kins; Cost dgn Wilhelm, Howell Russell; Pq William
Clarkson; Props Labhart; Bm William Greet; Act mgr
C.P. Levilly. *REV: E 27/12/90 p9; SR 27/12/90 p738;*
St 26/12/90 p10; Th 1/2/91 p91-2; Ti 22/12/90 p13.

90.327 *BEAUTY AND THE BEAST* (Panto,17sc) William
Yardley & Augustus Harris. 26/12/90-4/4/91. 149 perf
[2 perf dy exc 26/12/90, 10/2/91, 17/2, 20/2, 24/2,
26-27/2, 3/3, 5-6/3, 10/3, 12-13/3, 17/3, 19-20/3,
24/3, 26/3, 31/3, 2-3/4; np 27/3/91].* Mary Anne
Harry Nicholls; Sarah Jane Herbert Campbell; Lom-
barde Streete Dan Leno; Beast John d'Auban; Montmorency Charles Wallace; Private Block Fred Walton;
Old Bogie George Temple; McSkipper Tom Pleon; Envy/
Hatred/Malice/Slander/Lying Leopold Troupe; Maxwel-

ton J. Griffiths; Sheepshead F. Griffiths; Lieut. Gen.
Shrimp Master Coleman; Postman Terriss; "Harlequinade"
Whimsical Walker, Harry Leopold, Fred Leopold, Joseph
Leopold. King Courage Vesta Tilley; Fairy Rosebud
Florence Paltzer; King of Diamonds Sybil Grey;
Vivandiere Retta Walton; Fairy Chamberlain Emma d'Au-
ban; Beauty Belle Bilton; King's Chamberlain Ethel
Salisbury; Field Marshall Baton Nicholls; Mjr. Gen.
Plume Violet Ellicot; Lieut. Col. Filbert Benton; Mjr.
Key C. Mabel Coates; Cpt. Jinks Violet Granville;
Lieut. Wright Daisy Baldry; Ensign Flagg Moore; Field
Marshalless Baton Cissy St. George; "Harlequinade"
Georgina Cook. L & MGR & DIR Augustus Harris; Mus P.
Bucalossi; Ch John d'Auban; Sm Arthur P. Collins; Sec
& Treas Fred G. Latham; Sc [Robert] Caney, [T.E.]
Ryan, Kautsky, [William] Perkins; Cost Edel & Russell,
Auguste, Alias, Harrison, M. Landolf, Miss Palmer, Mrs
Atkins, Kennedy, Phillips; Pq William Clarkson; Mach
M. Farrell; Props R. Hicks; Chorus master Stedman.
REV: Ath 3/1/91 p29; E 3/1/91 p8.

90.328 *ALADDIN UP TO DATA* (Bsq) Brien McCullough &
Frank Green. NOVELTY 26/12/90 [ran until at least 7/
2/91]. Abanazar H. Buckstone Clair; Vizier [Owen]
Wynne; Emperor Ski-Cri Charles Lerigo; Ching Chow
Watty Brunton; Widow Crankey Brien McCullough/J.G.
Wilton. Beppo Nellie Nelson/Georgie Harris; Slave of
the Lamp Annie Shelby/Clifford; Aladdin Marie Brian;
Princess Ada Douglas; Geni of the Ring Georgie Harris/
Annie Selby. L S.T. Tolhurst; Act mgr [H.J.] Borley;
Treas & Sec W.R. Pope; Cond Henry T. Parkes; Mach G.
Sewell. *REV: E 3/1/91 p9; St 1/1/91 p12-3.*

*   *   *   *   *

PLAYBILLS

1 8 9 1

91.1 *A SOCIAL PEST* (DD,4a) Frederick Vanneck. NOVELTY
3/1/91-c.16/1/91. c.8 perf.* <u>Paul Veriker</u> Edwin
Fergusson; <u>Cpt. Gilbert Redman</u> Gilbert Vernon; <u>Sir</u>
<u>William Clifford</u> H. Buckstone Clair; <u>George Bartlett</u>
Brien McCullough; <u>Phillips</u> Watty Brunton; <u>Scarred</u>
<u>Face Jim</u> [Owen] Wynne; <u>Weasel</u> Charles Lerigo;
<u>Inspector</u> Hugh Cannon; <u>Policeman</u> Walter Moore. <u>Mabel</u>
<u>Clifford</u> Evelyn Nelson; <u>Julianna Clifford</u> Marie
Brian; <u>Lucy Barlett</u> Julia Listelle; <u>Carrotty Eliza</u>
Mrs [Watty] Brunton. *REV: E 10/1/91 p9; St 8/1/91
p12.*

91.2 *THE SILVER KING* (D,5a) H.A. Jones & Henry Herman.
OLYMPIC 3/1/91-7/2/91. 31 perf. 1st perfd Princess's
16/11/82. <u>Wilfred Denver</u> Wilson Barrett; <u>Jaikes</u>
George Barrett; <u>Frank Selwyn</u> Edward Irwin; <u>Geoffrey</u>
<u>Ware</u> T.W. Percyval; <u>Samuel Baxter</u> Stafford Smith;
<u>Cpt. Herbert Skinner</u> H. Cooper Cliffe; <u>Henry Corkett</u>
Ambrose Manning; <u>Elijah Coombe</u> Austin Melford; <u>Cripps</u>
W.A. Elliott; <u>Parkyn</u> Hutton; <u>Binks</u> P[aul] Belmore;
<u>Bronson</u> W. [Lionel] Belmore; <u>Bilcher</u> Santon; <u>Teddy</u>
Gale; <u>Tubbs</u> A.E. Field; <u>Gaffer Pottle</u> [Horace] Hod-
ges; <u>Passenger</u> Abe; <u>Newsboy</u> H. Norton; <u>Cabman</u>
F[ranklin] McLeay; <u>Leaker</u> Curfew; <u>Servant</u> [Cecil]
Duncan; <u>Inspector</u> Lynd. <u>Nelly Denver</u> Winifred Emery;
<u>Cissie</u> Edie King; <u>Ned</u> Mary Smith; <u>Olive Skinner</u> Maud
[C.] Jeffries; <u>Tabitha Durden</u> Alice Cooke; <u>Susy</u>
Lillie Belmore; <u>Lady Passenger</u> Alice Gambier; <u>Mrs</u>
<u>Gammage</u> Mrs Strickland. L & MGR Wilson Barrett; <u>Bm</u>

G.M. Polini; Act mgr F. Vagg Walter; Sm Charles Cathcart; Mus dir Michael Connelly; Bom A[rthur] Frye.
REV: Ath 10/1/91 p60; E 10/1/91 p9; Ti 5/1/91 p7.

91.3 *THE COLOUR-SERGEANT* (P,1a) Brandon Thomas. OLYM-
PIC 3/1/91-7/2/91. 31 perf. 1st perfd Princess's
26/2/85. William Honour W.A. Elliott; Harry Honour
Edward Irwin; Bob Atkins Austin Melford; Charley
Tucker H[orace] Hodges; Boy Master Norton. Nellie
Lily Hanbury. L & MGR, Bm, Act mgr, Sm, Mus dir, Bom
as for 91.2. *REV: E 10/1/91 p9.*

91.4 *MUCH ADO ABOUT NOTHING* (C,5a) William Shakespeare.
LYCEUM 5/1/91-3/3/91; 9/3, 17/3, 31/3, 4/4, 6-7/4,
11/4(m), 13-14/4, 20/4, 2/5(m); 25/7/91. 53 perf [mat
only 24/1, 7/2, 14/2; np 9/1, 16/1, 23/1, 30-31/1,
6/2, 13/2, 20/2, 27/2]. 1st perfd 1600. Don Pedro
[F.H.] Macklin; Don John [William] Haviland; Claudio
William Terriss; Benedick Henry Irving; Leonato
[Thomas E.] Wenman; Antonio H[enry] Howe; Borachio
[Frank] Tyars; Conrade John Martin Harvey; Friar
Francis Alfred Bishop; Dogberry [William] MackIntosh;
Verges Davis; Seacoal [John] Archer; Oatcake [W.J.]
Lorriss; Sexton [T.] Reynolds; Messenger Gordon Craig;
Balthazar J. Robertson; Boy Master Harwood. Hero Annie
Irish; Beatrice Ellen Terry; Margaret Kate Phillips;
Ursula [Amy] Coleridge. L & MGR Henry Irving; Sc
Hawes Craven, W. Cuthbert, William Telbin; Mus & Mus
dir J. Meredith Ball; Cost Auguste, L. & H. Nathan,
Mrs Reid, Mrs Nettleship; Mach Fillery; Furn Arnott;
Sm H.J. Loveday; Act mgr Bram Stoker. *REV: Ath 10/1/
90 p60; E 10/1/91 p9; SR 10/1/91 p44-5, 1/8/91 p135;
St 8/1/91 p12; Th 1/2/91 p94-5; Ti 6/1/91 p7, 27/7/
91 p8.*

91.5 *PRIVATE ENQUIRY* (FC,3a) F.C. Burnand [fr Albert
Valabrègue, *La Sécurité des Familles*]. STRAND 7/1/91-
13/2/91. 38 perf [w/S mat]. 1st perfd Opera House,
Leicester 25/11/90. Richard Wrackham Alfred Maltby;
John Buckleigh John Beauchamp; Louis Herbert Sparling;
Harry Hooker Willie Edouin; Toby Trimlett Master H.
Buss; Blunt William Lugg; Alexander Robert Nainby;
2nd Waiter A. Perkins. Mrs Buckleigh May Whitty; Mrs
Wrackham Marie Linden; Mrs Finch Ruth Rutland; Fanny

Finch Georgie Esmond; Bennett Venie Bennett. PP J.S.
Clarke; L Willie Edouin; Bom H[enry] L. Boss; Sm J.A.
E. Malone; Cond Ernest Bucalossi; Bm George Bryer.
REV: Ath 10/1/91 p60; E 10/1/91 p9; St 15/1/91 p13;
Th 1/2/91 p93-4; Ti 2/2/91 p7.

91.6 *DAGGERS DRAWN* (Ca,1a) Pryce Seaton. STRAND 7/1/
91-18/4/91. 89 perf [w/mat 4/4, 11/4, 18/4; np 26-27/
3].* Sir George Grantley William Lugg; Cpt. J. Grantley Sydney Barraclough. Mrs Gerald Deering Ruth Rutland; Alice Deering Georgie Esmond; Ford Lillian Milward. PP, L, Bom, Sm, Cond, Bm as for 91.5. *REV: St*
15/1/91 p13; Th 1/2/91 p95-6.

91.7 *WOODBARROW FARM* (C,3a) Jerome K. Jerome. VAUDE-
VILLE 13/1/91-14/3/91. 62 perf [w/S mat exc 14/2,
21/2; add mat 18/2, 25/2]. 1st perfd Comedy 18/6/88.
Piffin Thomas Thorne; Allen Rollitt Bernard Gould;
Luke Cranbourne Cecil M. York; Hon Tom Gussett Frank
Gillmore; Mr Purtwee J.S. Blythe; Mike Stratton [F.]
Hamilton Knight; Baron von Schorr F[red] Grove; Icha-
bod C[ecil] Ramsey; Peters J[ohn] Wheatman; Col. Jack
Dexter Fred Thorne; Richard Hanningford [F.] Hamilton
Knight. Clara Dexter, Vane; Mrs Rollitt Emily Thorne;
Rachael Williamson; Deborah Deacon Ella Bannister.
L & MGR Thomas Thorne; Act mgr Sydney Alport; Sm
Fred Thorne; Cond Charles Dubois. *REV: Ath 17/1/91*
p97; E 17/1/91 p9; St 15/1/91 p12; Th 1/2/91 p96-8;
Ti 14/1/91 p5.

91.8 *THE NOTE OF HAND* (P,1a) Herbert Keith. VAUDEVILLE
13/1/91-4/4/91. 63 perf [np 16-17/3, 23-28/3].* Rev
J. Merton F[red] Grove; Solomon Fred Thorne. Mabel
Annie Hill; Mrs Peckover C[oralie] Owen. L & MGR,
Act mgr, Sm, Cond as for 91.7. *REV: St 15/1/91 p12-3;*
Th 1/2/91 p98. Comment: *We Two* by R. Annandale was
announced for performance on 24/2/91, but was appa-
rently cancelled at the last moment.

91.9 *THE DANCING GIRL* (P,4a) H.A. Jones. HAYMARKET
15/1/91-27/6/91; 5/10/91-15/1/92. 266 perf [w/S mat
exc 17/1, 7/3/91, 9/1/92; add mat 25/2, 30/3, 8/4,
15/4, 22/4; np 23/2, 27/3, 24-25/12].* Duke of Guise-
bury H.B. Tree; Hon Reginald Slingsby Fred Kerr;

Augustus Cheevers [J.H.] Batson; David Ives [James]
Fernandez; John Christison Fred Terry; Mr Crake Allan;
Mr Goldspink Robb Harwood; Cpt. Leddra Charles Hudson;
Charles Leith; Herr Poniatowski Warden. Lady Bawtry
Rose Leclercq; Lady Brislington Adelaide Gunn; Sybil
Crake Rose Norreys; Drusilla Ives Julia Neilson/
Beatrice Lamb; Faith Ives Blanche Horlock; Mrs
Christison [Margaret] Ayrtoun; Mrs Leddra Mrs E.H.
Brooke; Sister Beatrice Hethcote. L & MGR H.B. Tree;
Sc Walter Hann, Walter Johnstone; Cost L. & H. Nathan,
Lewis & Allenby; Furn Emile Godfrey; Pq William Clark-
son; Bom W.H. Leverton; Sm Edward Hastings; Mus dir
Carl Armbruster; Bm F[rederick] Harrison. *REV: Ath*
24/1/91 p131; E 17/1/91 p10, 10/10/91 p9; SR 24/1/91
p99-100, 14/3/91 p326, 10/10/91 p414-5; St 22/1/91
p12-3, 8/10/91 p12; Th 1/2/91 p98-100; Ti 16/1/91 p3.

91.10 *THE REAL LITTLE LORD FAUNTLEROY* (P,3a) Mrs
Frances Hodgson Burnett. TERRY'S 15/1/91 mat perf.
1st perfd Terry's 14/5/88. Lord Dorincourt Alfred
Bishop; Havisham Henry Pagden; Higgins H.L. Brans-
combe; Thomas G[eorge] Hughes. Mrs Errol Elizabeth
Robins; Minnie Elsie Chester; Lord Fauntleroy Vera
Beringer. MGR Edward Terry. *REV: E 17/1/91 p10.*

91.11 *THE HOLLYTREE INN* (P,1a) Mrs Oscar Beringer
[adpt fr Charles Dickens]. TERRY'S 15/1/91 mat perf.*
Jabez Cobbs Ernest Hendrie; Cpt Walmers H. Reeves-
Smith; Tom Fred Baxter. Mrs Cobbs Mrs E.H. Brooke;
Norah Minnie Terry; Betty Mary Collette; Harry Vera
Beringer. MGR Edward Terry. *REV: E 17/1/91 p10.*

91.12 *JOAN OF ARC* (Bsq,2a) John L. Shine & Adrian Ross.
OPERA COMIQUE 17/1/91-18/7/91. 173 perf [w/S mat exc
17/1, 21/2, 30/5, 6/6, 13/6, 20/6, 27/6, 4/7, 11/7,
18/7; np 27/3].* Charles VII John L. Shine; Jacques
Darc Charles Danby; Arthur de Richemont Arthur Rob-
erts; Fill-up the Good E[rnest] Bantock; Bishop of
Bovril/Schoolmaster Willie Warde; Mayor of Orleans
G. Moore. New York Herald E[thel] Blenheim; Joan of
Arc Emma Chambers; Marie Grace Pedley; Talbot Alma
Stanley; Isabelle Darc Louise Gourlay; Yolande of Bar
Linda Verner; Blanche Darc Katie Seymour; Catherine
of Rochelle Phyllis Broughton. L & MGR George Ed-

wardes; <u>Mus</u> F. Osmond Carr; <u>Sc</u> H[enry] Emden, Bruce
Smith; <u>Dir</u> Richard Barker; <u>Cost dgn</u> Percy Anderson;
<u>Cost</u> Miss Fisher, Alias; <u>Ch</u> Willie Warde; <u>Props</u> Lab-
hart; <u>Pq</u> C.H. Fox; <u>Furn</u> Atkinson & Co.; <u>Mus dir</u> F.
Stanislaus; <u>Sm</u> John Ettinson; <u>Act mgr</u> M. Russell
Rosse; <u>Bom</u> A[rthur] Donald. *REV: Ath 24/1/91 p131-2;*
E 24/1/91 p9; St 22/1/91 p13; Th 1/2/91 p100-1; Ti
19/1/91 p7, 11/6/91 p12.

91.13 *A PAIR OF LUNATICS* (Ca,1a) W.R. Walkes. LYRIC
20/1/91 mat perf.** <u>He</u> George Alexander. <u>She</u> Maude
Millett. <u>PP</u> Henry J. Leslie; <u>L & Mgr</u> Horace Sedger.
REV: E 24/1/91 p8.

91.14 *ALL THE COMFORTS OF HOME* (FC,3a) William Gil-
lette & H.C. Duckworth [adpt of *Ein Toller Einfall*].
GLOBE 24/1/91-13/2/91. 18 perf. Museum, Boston 3/3/90.
<u>Egbert Pettibone</u> Frederick Glover; <u>Alfred Hastings</u>
Norman Forbes; <u>Tom</u> Willie Phillips; <u>Christopher Dab-</u>
<u>ney</u> Ian Robertson; <u>Judson Langhorn</u> Lawrance d'Orsay;
<u>Theodore Bender</u> Harry Paulton; <u>Augustus McDonald</u>
Herman de Lange; <u>Victor Smythe</u> Gerald Gurney. <u>Rosa-</u>
<u>belle Pettibone</u> Stella Maris; <u>Emily Pettibone</u> Sybil
Carlisle; <u>Fifi Oritanski</u> Lily Linfield; <u>Josephine</u>
<u>Bender</u> Fanny Coleman; <u>Evangeline Bender</u> Mary Ansell;
<u>Kate</u> Adrienne Dairolles; <u>Gretchen</u> Eva Murray. <u>L & MGR</u>
Norman Forbes; <u>Sc</u> W[illiam] Telbin; <u>Cond</u> C.J. Har-
gitt; <u>Act mgr</u> [W.] Conyers d'Arcy; <u>Sm</u> Frederick
Glover. *REV: Ath 31/1/91 p161-2; E 31/1/91 p11; SR*
31/1/91 p131-2; St 29/1/91 p12; Th 1/3/91 p138-40; Ti
26/1/91 p4.

91.15 *GRINGOIRE* W.G. Wills [adpt of Fr by François
Coppée]. GLOBE 24/1/91-13/2/91; 18/2/91-14/3/91. 40
perf. 1st perfd Prince of Wales's 22/6/85. <u>Louis XI</u>
Ian Robertson; <u>Pierre Gringoire</u> Norman Forbes; <u>Simon</u>
<u>Fourniez</u> George Bernage; <u>Olivier</u> Herman de Lange.
<u>Louise</u> Mary Ansell; <u>Suzan</u> Adrienne Dairolles. <u>L & MGR</u>,
<u>Cond</u>, <u>Act mgr</u>, <u>Sm</u> as for 91.14. <u>Sc</u> W[illiam] Harford;
<u>Cost</u> Edwin Abbey. *REV: Ath, E, St, Ti as for 91.15;*
Th 1/3/91 p140-1.

91.16 *THE REFUGEES* (F,1a) J.M. Campbell. OPERA COMIQUE
27/1/91-9/3/91. 36 perf. 1st perfd Adelphi 19/7/88.

Lord Charles Linklater Harry Grattan; Peter Poddleson
Ernest Bantock; Pomponsseau Hill. Mme Nanichette Linda
Verner; Marie Toulouse Ethel Blenheim. L & MGR George
Edwardes; Mus dir F. Stanislaus; Sm John Ettinson;
Act mgr M. Russell; Bom A[rthur] Donald.

91.17 *A DOLL'S HOUSE* (P,3a) Henrik Ibsen [trans Will-
iam Archer]. TERRY'S 27/1/91 mat perf. 1st perfd
Novelty 7/6/89. Torvald Helmer C. Forbes Drummond: Dr
Rank William Herbert; Nils Krogstad Charles J. Ful-
ton; Porter Kelly. Mrs Linden Elizabeth Robins; Anna
Rose Evelyn; Ellen Mary Jocelyn; Einar Mabel Hoare;
Emmie E. Harding; Nora Marie Fraser. PP & MGR Edward
Terry; Mus dir J. Bayliss; Sm Fitzroy Morgan; Bm C.
St. John Denton, H.T. Brickwell. *REV: Ath 31/1/91
p162; E 31/1/91 p11; St 29/1/91 p12; Ti 29/1/91 p14.*

91.18 *OUR REGIMENT* (FC,3a) Henry Hamilton [adpt of
Gustav von Moser & Franz von Schonthan *Krieg im
Frieden*]. TOOLE'S 27/1/91-11/4/91. 87 perf [w/W, S
mat exc 28/1; add mats 30/3, 6/4; np 27/3]. 1st perfd
Vaudeville 13/2/83. Mr Dobbinson Willie Drew; Mr
Ellaby Earle Douglas; Cpt. Fetherston Alfred J. Byde;
Guy Warrener W.S. Penley; Rev. John Talbot H. Reeves-
Smith; Batters Sydenham Dixon. Mrs Dobbinson Fanny
Robertson; Olive Florence McKenzie; Enid Thurston
Fanny Brough; Maud Ellaby Violet Thornycroft. L J.L.
Toole; Mgr Florence McKenzie; Gen mgr Alfred J. Byde;
Act mgr Fred Fernandez; Sec A.H. Cree; Sm Willie Drew;
Asm G. Claremont; Mus dir F. Sydney Ward. *REV: E 31/
1/91 p11; St 29/1/91 p12-3; Th 1/3/91 p141-2; Ti 29/
1/91 p14.*

91.19 *A HUSBAND IN CLOVER* (F,1a) H.C. Merivale. TOOLE'S
27/1/91-14/2/91. 17 perf. 1st perfd Lyceum 26/12/73.
Horace Sydenham Dixon. Lydia Eugenie Vernie. L, Mgr,
Gen mgr, Act mgr, Sec, Sm, Asm, Mus dir as for 90.18.

91.20 *THE STRANGER* (P,3a) [Benjamin Thompson; adpt of
August Kotzebue]. OLYMPIC 28/1/91, 10/2/91. 2 mat perf.
1st perfd Drury Lane 24/3/1798. Stranger Wilson
Barrett; Count Wintersen T.W. Percyval; Baron Stein-
fort W.A. Elliott; Solomon Austin Melford; Peter
George Barrett; Tobias Stafford Smith; Francis H.

Cooper Cliffe; George P[aul] Belmore. Countess Winter-
sen Lily Hanbury; Mrs Haller Winifred Emery; Charlotte
Lillie Belmore; Annette Maud C. Jeffries; Claudine
Alice Gambier; Susan Lily Twyman. L & MGR Wilson
Barrett; Bm G.M. Polini; Act mgr F. Vagg Walter; Sm
Charles Cathcart; Mus dir Michael Connelly; Bom
A[rthur] Frye. *REV: Ath 31/1/91 p162; E 31/1/91 p11;
St 29/1/91 p13; Th 1/3/91 p142; Ti 29/1/91 p8.*

91.21 *FOR CHARITY'S SAKE* (DC,1a) Charles S. Fawcett.
COMEDY 29/1/91-17/8/91. 170 perf [np 27/3, 6/7].*
Nicholas Nubbles William Wyes; Zeberdy Benjamin Cat-
terpole W.F. Hawtrey; Edward Esher Wilfred Draycott;
Inspector Jones Charles Milton; Young Nick Master C.
G. Holmes. Charity Lydia Cowell. MGR Charles H. Haw-
trey; Bm & Act mgr E.F. Bradley; Asm Charles Milton;
Mus dir James M. Glover. *REV: E 31/1/91 p11; St 5/2/
91 p13; Th 1/3/91 p143; Ti 2/2/91 p7.*

91.22 *IVANHOE* (RO,3a) Julian Sturgis (lib) & Arthur
Sullivan (mus). ROYAL ENGLISH OPERA HOUSE 31/1/91-
31/7/91. 160 perf [w/mat 28/3, 2/5, 9/5, 16/5, 23/5,
30/5, 6/6; mat only 27/6, 4/7; np 6/2, 17/2, 27/3].*
Richard Coeur de Lion Norman Salmond/Franklin Clive;
Prince John Richard Green/Wallace Brownlow; Brian de
Bois-Gilbert Eugene Oudin/Francois Noije; Maurice de
Bracey Charles Kenningham; Lucas de Beaumont Adams
Owen; Cedric the Saxon D. Ffrangcon Davies/W.H. Bur-
gon; Wilfred, Knight of Ivanhoe Ben Davies/Joseph
O'Mara; Friar Tuck Avon Saxon; Isaac Charles Copland;
Locksley W.H. Stephens; The Squire F[rederick] Bovill;
Wamba [David] Cowis. Lady Rowena Esther Palliser/
Lucile Hill; Ulrica Marie Groebl; Rebecca Margaret
MacIntyre/Thuddicum/Lucile Hill. PP & MGR Richard
d'Oyly Carte; Mus dir Francois Cellier; Cond Francois
Cellier, Ernest Ford; Sm Hugh Moss; Sc Hawes Craven,
T.E. Ryan, Joseph Harker, William Telbin; Mach W.P.
Dando; Cost dgn Percy Anderson; Cost Miss Fisher,
Cooling & Lawrence, Harrison, Alias, Gutperle, Nathan;
Pq William Clarkson; Props [H.] Skelly; Bm R. Redford;
Am Charles Corry. *REV: Ath 7/2/91 p193-4, 14/2/91
p226, 21/2/91 p258; E 7/2/91 p11, 25/4/91 p15; SR
7/2/91 p161; St 5/2/91 p12; Th 1/3/91 p158-61; Ti 6/
2/91 p13, 26/5/91 p10.*

91.23 *EAST LYNNE; OR, A MOTHER'S LOVE* (4a). NOVELTY
31/1/91-6/2/91. 6 perf. Archibald Carlyle E[dwin]
Fergusson; Francis Levison Gilbert Vernon; Bullseye
F. Wilton; Lord Mountsevern H. Buckstone Clair;
Justice Hare Watty Brunton; Richard Hare [Owen] Wynne;
Lawyer Dill King Bolton; Willie Carlyle Master Bertie
Jones. Lady Isabel Carlyle/Mme Vine [Julia] Listelle;
Joyce Marie Brian; Susanne [Annie] Selby; Wilson
[Georgie] Harris; Cornelia Carlyle [Mrs Watty] Brun-
ton; Barbara Hare Ada Douglas. L S.T. Tolhurst; Act
mgr [H.J.] Borley; Treas & Sec W.R. Pope; Cond Henry
T. Parkes; Mach G. Sewell.

91.24 *THE GAY LOTHARIO* (C,1a) Alfred C. Calmour. ST.
JAMES'S 31/1/91-21/2/91; 16/3/91-15/5/91. 71 perf
[np 27/3].* Also played DRURY LANE 23/4/91 mat perf.
Sir Harry Lovell George Alexander; Sparks Ben Webster.
Letty Laura Graves; Amanda Goldacre Maude Millett.
L & MGR George Alexander; Bom W. Benedict; Sm Robert
V. Shone; Mus dir Walter Slaughter; Bm Alwyn Lewis.
*REV: Ath 7/2/91 p195; E 7/2/91 p9, 25/4/91 p8; St
5/2/91 p12-3; Th 1/3/91 p143-3.*

91.25 *MAID MARIAN* (CO,3a) Harry B. Smith (lib) & Reg-
inald de Koven (mus). PRINCE OF WALES'S 5/2/91-14/4/
91. 65 perf [w/S mat exc 21/2, 21/3, 4/4, 11/4; add
mat 30/3; np 27/3]. 1st prof. Robert, Earl of Hunt-
ingdon C. Hayden Coffin; Friar Tuck Harry Parker;
Will Scarlet Egbert Roberts; Little John Leonard
Russell; Sir Guy John Le Hay; Sir Tristram Testy Harry
Monkhouse; Mach Tom A. Shale; Maid o'-the-Mill Collini.
Allan-a-Dale Violet Cameron; Annabel Attalie Claire;
Dame Durden Amadi; Bend-the-Bow Florence Darley; Maid
Marian Marian Manola. PP Edgar Bruce; L & Mgr Horace
Sedger; Dir Charles Harris; Mus dir John Crook; Sc
W[illiam] Telbin, H[enry] Emden, W[illiam] Perkins;
Mach S. Trewen; Cost Auguste, Alias, Harrison; Cost
dgn Percy Anderson; Pq William Clarkson; Ch [John]
d'Auban; Props Labhart; Bm William Greet; Act mgr C.P.
Levilly. *REV: E 7/2/91 p11; St 12/2/91 p13; Th 1/3/91
p144-5.*

91.26 *MONTECRISTO* (RD,5a) [adpt fr Alexandre Dumas].
AVENUE 7/2/91-28/2/91. 19 perf. 1st perfd Adelphi

17/10/68. Edmund Dantes Charles Warner; Fernand J.G.
Graham; Albert E.H. Vanderfelt; Danglars Luigi Labla-
che; Caderouse J.G. Taylor; M de Villefort J.R. Crau-
ford; Father Dantes Charles J. Fulton; Abbe Faria
George Warde; M Morel J.A. Howell; Brigadier Thomas
W. Ford; Noirtier Henry Lee; Governor of Chateau d'If
George Osborne; Commissary Harold Foster; 1st Agent
O'Shea; 2nd Agent Alfred P. Phillips; 1st Jailor
George Arnold; 2nd Jailor N. Johnson; Germain Arthur
Godfrey; Servant B. Raikes; Penelon Rodney Miller;
Sentinel L. Lanty. Carconte Elsie Chester; Mlle Dan-
glars Helena Dacre; Mercedes Jessie Milward. L & MGR
Henry Lee; Sc Joseph Harker, Richard Halley, T.E.
Ryan; Sm William Sidney; Cond Barter Johns; Bom W.T.
Pierce; Bm Arthur Yates; Cost May; Pq C.H. Fox. *REV:*
Ath 14/2/91 p227; E 14/2/91 p9; St 12/2/91 p13; Th
1/3/91 p145-7; Ti 9/2/91 p8.

91.27 *THE LYONS MAIL* (Melo,3a) Charles Reade [adpt of
Emile Moreau, Giraudin & A.C. Delacour, *Le Courrier*
de Lyon]. LYCEUM 7/2/91, 14/2, 27-28/2, 7/3, 9/3,
14/3, 16/3, 21/3, 4/4(m), 11/4, 25/4/91. 12 perf. 1st
perfd Princess's 26/5/54 [as *The Courier of Lyons*].
Lesurques/Dubosc Henry Irving; Courriol William Ter-
riss; Choppard S[am] Johnson; Fouinard [John] Archer;
Jerome Lesurques [Thomas E.] Wenman; Dorval [Frank]
Tyars; Didier [William] Haviland; Joliquet John Martin
Harvey; Guerneau Gordon Craig; Lambert Lacy; Post-
master Davis; Durochat Lorriss; Coco [T.] Reynolds;
Commissary [H.W.] Cushing; Postillion [J.H.] Allen;
Waiter [W.] Marion. Julie Lesurques [Amy] Coleridge;
Marie Foster; Jeanette Frances Ivor; Niece to Post-
master Brown. L & MGR Henry Irving; Sm H.J. Loveday;
Mus dir J. Meredith Ball; Act mgr Bram Stoker. *REV:*
Ath 14/2/91 p227; E 14/2/91 p9; St 12/2/91 p12; Th
1/3/91 p148-9; Ti 16/2/91 p4.

91.28 *THE WILD PRIMROSE* (CD,4a). NOVELTY 7/2/91-14/2/
91. 6 perf.* Senor Wiggano Charles Warren; Walter
Gale Edwin Fergusson; Ross Purcell H. Buckstone Clair;
Benjamin Barnet J.G. Wilton; Robert Burton Gilbert
Vernon. Helen Purcell Madge Denzil; Maggie Burton
Julia Listelle; Arethusa Blivens Eleanor Lloyd; Rosa
Marguerite Fish. *REV: E 14/2/91 p9; St 12/2/91 p13-4.*

91.29 *THE SPECTRE BRIDEGROOM* ([F,2a]) [W.T. Moncrieff].
NOVELTY 7/2/91-14/2/91. 6 perf. 1st perfd Drury Lane
2/7/21. [Owen] Wynne; [Gilbert] Vernon; [J.G.] Wilton. *REV: St 21/2/91 p14.*

91.30 *THE LIGHTS O' LONDON* (Melo,5a) George R. Sims.
OLYMPIC 9/2/91-11/4/91. 52 perf [w/mat 14/2, 21/2,
4/3; np 23-27/3]. 1st perfd Princess's 10/9/81. Harold
Armytage Wilson Barrett; Clifford Armytage H. Cooper
Cliffe; Seth Preene Austin Melford; Squire Armytage
W.A. Elliott; Marks Stafford Smith; Philosopher Jack
Ambrose Manning; Jarvis George Barrett; Skeffington
Wensleydale; Cutts Franklin McLeay; Waters A.E. Field;
Constables W. [Lionel] Belmore, Warren; Man P[aul]
Belmore; Brown C[ecil] Duncan; Smith T.W. Percyval;
Trotters E[dward] Irwin; Percy-de-Vere Horace Hodges;
Porter Lloyd; Joey Master Wright; Jim King. Bess
Winifred Emery; Hetty Preene Lily Hanbury; Annie Maud
C. Jeffries; Sal Harrietta Polini; Shakespeare Jarvis
Louie [Bassett] Wilmot; Mrs Jarvis Mrs Henry Leigh;
Janet Alice Gambier. L & MGR Wilson Barrett; Bom
A[rthur] Frye; Act mgr F. Vagg Walter; Sm Charles
Cathcart; Mus dir Michael Connelly; Bm G.M. Polini.
REV: Ath 14/2/91 p227-8; E 14/2/91 p9; St 12/2/91 p12-
3; Th 1/3/91 p150-1; Ti 10/2/91 p9.

91.31 *TOMMY* (Ca) Mrs E.S. Willard ["Rachel Penn"].
OLYMPIC 9/2/91-8/5/91. 71 perf [np 23-27/3, 20/4].*
Peter Horace Hodges; Nicodemus Simpkins Ambrose Mann-
ing; Solomon Paul Belmore. Sister Rachel Alice Cooke;
Martha Alice Gambier; Sarah Slocum Lily Twyman; Tommy
Lillie Belmore. L & MGR, Bm, Act mgr, Sm, Mus dir, Bom
as for 91.30. *REV: E 14/2/91 p9; St 12/2/91 p13; Th*
1/3/91 p147-8.

91.32 *TURNED UP* (FC,3a) Mark Melford. STRAND 14/2/91-
18/4/91. 64 perf [w/S mat exc 14/2; add mat 18/3,
30/3; np 26-27/3]. 1st perfd Grand, Glasgow [as *Too*
Much Married]. Gen. Baltic John Beauchamp; Cpt. Medway
Alfred Maltby; George Medway Charles S. Fawcett; Nod
Steddam Sydney Barraclough; Tom Lobb Robert Nainby;
Carraway Bones Willie Edouin; Ephraim Master Hackney.
Mary Medway Ruth Rutland; Sabina Medway May Whitty;
Ada Baltic Georgie Esmond; Mrs Pannall Emily Dowton;

Cleopatra Annie Goward. PP J.S. Clarke; L Willie Ed-
ouin; Bom Henry L. Boss; Sm J.A.E. Malone; Cond
Ernest Bucalossi; Bm George Bryer. *REV: E 21/2/91 p9;
St 19/2/91 p12-3; Th 1/3/91 p149-50; Ti 18/2/91 p4.*

91.33 *LEAH.* NOVELTY 16/2/91-14/3/91. 24 perf. Comment:
Mentioned in *St.*

91.34 *SUMMER CLOUDS* (Ca,1a) Neville Doone. TOOLE'S
16/2/91-11/4/91. 47 perf [np 27/3].* Rev Philip Marston Sydney Herberte Basing; Harry Temple Philip Cunningham; Sir Richard Rigby Charles F. Caravoglia. Mary
Marston Eugenie Vernie. *REV: Ath 21/1/91 p260; E 21/
2/91 p9; St 19/2/91 p13; Ti 18/2/91 p4.*

91.35 *THE PARVENU* (C,3a) G.W. Godfrey. GLOBE 18/2/91-
14/3/91. 23 perf [w/mat 28/2]. 1st perfd Court 8/4/82.
Mr Ledger Harry Paulton; Charles Tracey Charles Sugden; Claude Glynne William Herbert; Sir Fulke Pettigrew Ian Robertson; A Waterman Frank Vancrossen; Servant Richard Cave. Lady Pettigrew Fanny Coleman; Mary
Ledger Laura Linden; Gwendolen Pettigrew Lucy Isabella
Buckstone. L & MGR Norman Forbes; Sc Walter Johnstone;
Cond C.J. Hargitt; Act mgr Arthur Twiss; Sm Frederick
Glover. *REV: Ath 21/2/91 p259; E 21/2/91 p9; St 19/2/
91 p12; Th 1/3/91 p151-2; Ti 19/2/91 p5.*

91.36 *A YORKSHIRE LASS; OR, THE ROLL OF THE DRUM* (D,
4a) J. Wilton Jones. OLYMPIC 18/2/91, 25/2/91. 2 mat
perf.* Gen. Sir Gilbert Selwyn Charles J. Fulton;
Jack Selwyn Arthur Bourchier; Cpt. Stewart Digby
R[ichard] S. Boleyn; Stephen Milsom F.H. Macklin; Dick
Blosser George Barrett; Maurice Thorne Herbert Sparl-
ing; Gabriel Oxtoby A.G. Leigh; Inspector Exley W.
L[ionel] Belmore; Sgt. Kackles Paul Belmore. Faith
Mary Eastlake; Elise de Mornay Gertrude Warden; Kate
Grantley Gwendolyn Floyd; Patty Kate Phillips; John
Selwyn, jr Christine Bernard. L & MGR Wilson Barrett;
Bm G.M. Polini; Act mgr F. Vagg Walter; Sm Charles
Cathcart; Mus dir Michael Connelly; Bom A[rthur] Frye.
*REV: Ath 21/2/91 p259; E 21/2/91 p10; St 19/2/91 p12;
Th 1/3/91 p152-3; Ti 19/2/91 p5.*

91.37 *THE SCHOOL FOR SCANDAL* ([C,5a]) Richard Brinsley

Sheridan. ADELPHI 19/2/91 mat perf.** Sir Peter Tea-
zle Hermann Vezin; Sir Oliver Surface Fred Thorne;
Sir Benjamin Backbite H.A. Saintsbury; Joseph Surface
Edmund Gurney; Charles Surface H.B. Conway; Crabtree
[Mark] Kinghorne; Rowley Maitland Dicker; Careless
Sydney Herberte Basing; Moses G.B. Phillips; Snake
Cyril Hayward; Trip Philip Cunningham. Lady Teazle
Mrs Patrick Campbell; Mrs Candour Eleanor Bufton;
Lady Sneerwell Violet Thornycroft; Maria Agnes Verity.
L A. & S. Gatti; Sm Robert Soutar; Mus dir Henry
Sprake; Act mgr Charles A. Jecks.

91.38 *THE ROUNDHEAD* (RD,3a) Bernard F. Bussy & W.T.
Blackmore. TERRY'S 20/2/91 mat perf. 1st perfd Crystal
Palace 12/6/83. Col. Leighton Edwin Gilbert; Cpt.
Glynne Edward O'Neill; Reuben Lightfoot Welton Dale;
Sgt. Ireton R. Cole-Aspinall; 1st Trooper Graham;
Archibald Warrington H.A. Saintsbury; Troopers Tiere,
Gibbs, Holmes. Constance Edith Jordan; Alice Lillian
Millward. *REV: Ath 28/2/91 p289; E 21/2/91 p11; St
26/2/91 p12.*

91.39 *RICHARD'S PLAY* (Ca,1a) Mary C. Rowsell & Joseph
J. Dilley. TERRY'S 20/2/91 mat perf. 1st prof. Richard
Maitland Edwin Gilbert; Admiral Sandilands Cecil
Thornybury; Postboy Graham. Sylvia Deloraine Madelaine
Rowsell; Prudence Maitland Mrs Conyers d'Arcy. *REV:
As for 91.38.*

91.40 *ROSMERSHOLM* (D,4a) Henrik Ibsen. VAUDEVILLE
23/2/91, 5/3/91. 2 mat perf. 1st English perf. Rosmer
F.R. Benson; Kroll H. Athol Forde; Brendal Charles
Hudson; Mortensgard John Wheatman. Helseth May
Protheroe; Rebecca West Florence Farr [Mrs E. Emery].
L & MGR Thomas Thorne; Act mgr A.L. Baldry; Sm [Dr
John] Todhunter; Cond Ernest Lake; Cost Claude; Pq
William Clarkson. *REV: Ath 28/2/91 p289; E 28/2/91
p10; St 26/2/91 p11-2; Th 1/4/91 p196; Ti 24/2/91 p10.*

91.41 *SOWING AND REAPING* (C,2a) C. Vernon. CRITERION
25/2/91-21/3/91. 26 perf [w/W, S mat exc 25/2, 4/3;
np 9/3, 16/3].** Harry Grahame Charles Wyndham;
Joseph Shenston George Giddens; Sampson Paley William
Blakeley; Dick Hobbs S[ydney] Valentine; Robert C.

Edmonds; John F. Emery. Mrs Charity Smith M.A. Victor;
Mrs Sampson Paley Beatrice Lamb; Mrs Watkins E[mily]
Vining; Julia Mary Moore. MGR Charles Wyndham; Furn
Oetzmann; Mus dir Theodore Ward; Act mgr E. Harvey.
REV: E 28/2/91 p9; SR 28/2/91 p262; Ti 26/2/91 p7.

91.42 *TRYING IT ON* (F,1a) William Brough. CRITERION
25/2/91-21/3/91. 26 perf [w/W, S mat exc 25/2, 4/3;
np 9/3, 16/3].** Walsingham Potts Charles Wyndham;
Jobstock Sydney Valentine; Tittlbat S[tanley] Hewson.
Mrs Jobstock F. Frances; Fanny E[llaline] Terriss;
Lucy M[abel] Hardinge. MGR, Furn, Mus dir, Act mgr as
for 91.41. *REV: As for 91.41.*

91.43 *THE MOCK DOCTOR* (CO,3a) Charles Gounod. AVENUE
26/2/91. 1 perf.** Sganarelle E. Allen Taussig;
Leander C.M.J. Edwards; Geronte Bert Mayne; Lucas John
Fletcher; Valere Ernest Delsart. Martine Violet Rob-
inson; Jacqueline Hannah Jones; Lucinda Virginie
Cheron. COND Alberto Randegger; Pd G.H. Betjemann.
REV: Ath 7/3/91 p320. Comment: Royal Academy of Music.

91.44 *THE IDLER* (P,4a) C. Haddon Chambers. ST. JAMES'S
26/2/91-17/7/91; 30/9/91-4/11/91. 173 perf [w/S mat
exc 28/2, 28/3, 4/7, 11/7, 3/10, 10/10; add mat 8/4,
15/4; np 27/3]. 1st perfd Lyceum, New York 11/11/90.
Mark Cross George Alexander; Sir John Harding Herbert
Waring; Simeon Strong John Mason; Gen. Merryweather
Nutcombe Gould; Bennett Alfred Holles. Lady Harding
Marion Terry; Mrs Cross Lady Monckton; Mrs Glynn-
Stanmore Gertrude Kingston; Kate Merryweather Maude
Millett. L & MGR George Alexander; Sm Robert V. Shone;
Bm Alwyn Lewis; Sc Walter Hann, Walter Johnstone,
Joseph Harker; Furn Frank Giles; Mus & Mus dir Walter
Slaughter; Cost Girodin, Savage & Perkins; Bom W.
Benedict. *REV: Ath 7/3/91 p321; E 28/2/91 p11; SR
7/3/91 p291-2, 3/10/91 p389-90; St 5/3/91 p12, 8/10/
91 p12; Th 1/4/91 p197-9; Ti 27/2/91 p3, 28/2/91 p15.*

91.45 *LADY BARTER* (C,3a) Charles F. Coghlan. PRIN-
CESS'S 28/2/91-20/3/91. 19 perf [w/mat 18/3].* Col.
Pearce Charles F. Coghlan; Gen. Peters Arthur Stirling;
Archdeacon Short Fred Everill; Lord Brent Lewis
Waller; Wright Hubert Druce; Servant Kingscote. Lady

Barter Mrs Langtry; Hon Mary Brent Helen Forsyth;
Justine Ethel Hope. PP Mrs Harriet Gooch; L & Mgr Mrs
Langtry; Bm & treas Henry Ball; Sc Harry Potts; Furn
Oetzmann; Pq William Clarkson; Mach W.J. Cawdray;
Props Louis Labhart; Gas & Lime Jones & [W.] Kerr; Sm
E.B. Norman; Mus dir William Corri, jr; Asm W. Lin-
tott. *REV: Ath 7/3/91 p321; E 7/3/91 p9; SR 7/3/91
p295; St 5/3/91 p12; Th 1/4/91 p199-200.*

91.46 *RACHEL'S MESSENGER* (P,1a) T. Malcolm Watson.
PRINCESS'S 28/2/91-20/3/91. 18 perf.* Bruce Holden
Oscar Adye; Richard Gleddin E.B. Norman; Stephen
Hedley S.H. Lechmere. Rachel Vicary Amy McNeil; Ruth
Gleddin Ethel Hope; May Gleddin Hetty Dene. PP, L &
mgr, Bm, Sm, Mus dir, Asm as for 91.45. *REV: E, St
as for 91.45; Th 1/4/91 p200-1.*

91.47 *CHANGES AND CHANCES* (DC,2a). AVENUE 2/3/91-7/3/
91. 6 perf.* Fred Harrison James Nelson; Harry Ver-
non Acton Bond; Mr Harbinger A. Ellis; Mr Dodson
Sydney Herberte Basing. Mrs Harbinger Julia Seaman;
Rachel Beatrice Adair; Servant Montagu; Deborah
Schubert. MGR Henry Lee; Bm Arthur Yates; Bm for
Burlesque Co. C. St. John Denton; Mus dir Barter
Johns; Sm W[illiam] Sidney. *REV: E 7/3/91 p9; St 5/3/
91 p12; Ti 4/3/91 p13.*

91.48 *MADEMOISELLE CLEOPATRA* (Bsq,1a) Walter Sapte,
jr (lib) & James M. Glover (mus). AVENUE 2/3/91-7/3/
91. 6 perf.* Scarus Willie Drew; Octavius Caesar
W.F. Hawtrey; Marc Antony J.J. Dallas; Enobarbus
Frank Lindo; Spoofsayer Bernard Traille; Pantalon
Vernon Cooper; Extras Cubitt, Moore, Leighton, Cullen,
Villiers. Alexas Stella Scott; Cleopatra Floy Vita;
Lepidus Laura Hansen; Charmian Edith Kenward; Iras
Edith Charteris; Octavia Julia Seaman; Eros Eva Eden;
Thyreus Nellie Palmer; Extras Wood, Thorn, Montagu,
Mordaunt, Marsh, Pasbach, Campbell, Murray, Hamilton,
Blanchard, P. Blanchard, Spence, Holland, Ormonde,
Hardwick, Hochheimer, Seymour, Delderfield, Stewart,
Swonnell. MGR, Bm, Mus dir, Sm as for 91.47; Dir
Fitzroy Morgan. *REV: E 7/3/91 p9; SR 7/3/91 p296; St
5/3/91 p12-3; Ti 4/3/91 p13.*

91.49 *ZEPHYR* (C,4a) Mrs Bernard Wishaw. AVENUE 3/3/91
mat perf.* OPERA COMIQUE 5/5/91 mat perf. Lord Kyr-
connell Arthur Forrest; Sir Anthony Montague R.F.
Eden; Tom Edge Horace Mills; Page Master George Arnold;
Mr Winn A[rthur] Godfrey. Zephyrina Winn Loie Fuller;
Lady Eleanor Montague Mrs Gordon-Ascher; George
Montague Sylvia Grey; Lady Hester O'Connor Annie All-
iston; Lady Marth O'Connor Isabel Grey; Lily Everitt
Georgie Esmond; Mabel Montague Beatrice Patrice. *REV:*
Ath 7/3/91 p322; E 7/3/91 p8; SR 7/3/91 p296; St
5/3/91 p13.

91.50 *TWO OR ONE?* (FCa,1a) Mrs Bernard Wishaw. AVENUE
3/3/91 mat perf.* OPERA COMIQUE 5/5/91 mat perf.
Douglas McDougal [George T.] Minshull; Tiger Master
George Arnold. Fanny Campbell Loie Fuller. *REV: E, St*
as for 91.49. Comment: This play was later retitled
Will He Come Home Again?

91.51 *OUR ANGELS* (D,3a,4tab) Dr G.H.R. Dabbs & Edward
Righton. VAUDEVILLE 3/3/91, 16/3/91. 2 mat perf.*
Blinker W.H. Vernon; Morton Farquharson Lewis Waller;
Rupert Cardwell Ben Webster; Tarbard Ernest Hendrie;
Sir Beevor Vandyke Lawrance d'Orsay; Inspector
[William] Wyes; Jock Edward Righton; Percy Fortescue
H[arry] Eversfield; Dr McRobin Sydney Herberte Bas-
ing; Hotel Manager [A.W.] Aysom; Hamish Sydney; Sandy
W. Riley. Lily Beatrice Lamb; Maud Fanny Brough. L &
MGR Thomas Thorne; Act mgr Sydney Alport; Dir Edward
Righton; Mus C.J. Hargitt; Pq & Cost C.H. Fox. *REV:*
E 7/3/91 p10; SR 7/3/91 p296; St 5/3/91 p13; Ti 5/3/
91 p13. Comment: Cast from V & A programme for 16/3/
91.

91.52 *CHARLES I* (P,4a) W.G. Wills. LYCEUM 4/3/91-7/3/
91; 11-14/3; 18-21/3; 1-3/4; 8-10/4; 15-18/4; 21/4,
1/5, 8-9/5, 1/7(m), 4/7/91(m).   28 perf [mat
only 7/3, 14/3, 18/4, 9/5]. 1st perfd Lyceum 28/9/72.
Charles I Henry Irving; Lord Huntley [Henry] Howe;
Lord Moray William Terriss; Oliver Cromwell [Thomas
E.] Wenman; Ireton [Frank] Tyars; 1st Cavalier Lacy;
2nd Cavalier [W.] Belford; Attendant R.P. Tabb;
Queen's Page John Martin Harvey. Princess Elizabeth
Minnie Terry; Prince James [Grace] Webb; Lady Elea-

nor Annie Irish; Queen Henrietta Maria Ellen Terry;
King's Page [Mrs S.] Holland. L & MGR Henry Irving;
Sc Hawes Craven, Joseph Harker; Cost dgn Seymour
Lucas; Cost Auguste, Mrs Nettleship, Mrs Reid; Armour
Kennedy & Co.; Mach Fillery; Furn Arnott; Sm H.J.
Loveday; Mus dir J. Meredith Ball; Act mgr Bram
Stoker. *REV: E 7/3/91 p11; SR 7/3/91 p296; St 12/3/91
p10; Th 1/4/91 p201; Ti 6/3/91 p12.*

91.53 *LOVE AND LAW* (Oa,1a) Frank Latimer (lib) & Ivan
Caryll (mus). LYRIC 4/3/91-12/12/91. 242 perf [np
18/3, 27/3].* Lord Belgravia Michael Dwyer; Robert
Sheepskin George Mudie. Lady Belgravia Annie Schuberth; Justina Taper Adelaide Newton. L & MGR Horace
Sedger; Bm William Greet. *REV: E 7/3/91 p9; SR 7/3/91
p296; St 12/3/91 p10; Ti 5/3/91 p5.*

91.54 *CULPRITS* (F,3a) Arthur Law. TERRY'S 5/3/91-14/
3/91. 11 perf [w/mat 7/3, 14/3]. 1st perfd Prince of
Wales's, Liverpool 29/8/90. Mjr. Rackshaw Edward
Terry; Sir Joseph Pendlecoop Fred Kaye; Hon & Rev
Oriel Fanlight Walter Everard; Edward Pendlecoop
Henry V. Esmond; Count Octave de Loreauzane Herman de
Lange; Burton Robert Soutar; Phillip Ashton A[lfred]
Kendrick; Gardener R.E. Sythe. Lady Pendlecoop Sophie
Larkin; Mary Seymour Elinore Leyshon; Countess de
Loreauzane Alice Yorke; Gwendoline Fanlight Eva
Moore; Mrs Rackshaw Susie Vaughan. PP & MGR Edward
Terry; Bm H.T. Brickwell; Sm George Belmore; Mus dir
J. Bayliss. *REV: Ath 14/3/91 p354; E 7/3/91 p9; St
12/3/91 p10; Th 1/4/91 p204-5; Ti 7/3/91 p5.*

91.55 *LADY BOUNTIFUL* (P,4a) A.W. Pinero. GARRICK 7/3/
91-22/5/91. 65 perf [w/mat 11/4, 16/5; mat only 9/5;
np 17/3, 26-27/3].* Roderick Heron John Hare; Dennis
Heron Johnston Forbes-Robertson; John Veale Charles
Groves; Sir Richard Philliter C.W. Somerset; Ped-
grift R[owley] Cathcart; Sir Lucian Brent Gilbert
Hare; Wimple John Byron; Floyce R. Power; Villager
Henry Rivers. Camilla Brent Kate Rorke; Miss Brent
Carlotta Addison; Margaret Veale Marie Linden; Mrs
Veale Dolores Drummond; Beatrix Brent Beatrice Ferrar;
Amelia [Annie] Webster; Mrs Hodnutt Caroline Elton;
Villager E[mily] Turtle. MGR John Hare; Bom E. Cand-

ler; Act mgr C.G. Compton; Sc William Harford; Mus
dir Schoening; Asm Rowley Cathcart. *REV: Ath 14/3/91
p354; E 14/3/91 p9; SR 14/3/91 p321-2; St 12/3/91
p9-10; Th 1/4/91 p202-4.*

91.56 *BEN-MY-CHREE* (D,5a) Hall Caine & Wilson Barrett.
OLYMPIC 7/3/91, 12/3, 14/3/91. 3 mat perf. 1st perfd
Princess's 17/5/88. Dan Mylrea Wilson Barrett; Ewan
Mylrea H. Cooper Cliffe; Thorkell Mylrea W.A. Elliott;
Gilchrist Mylrea Austin Melford; Davy Fayle George
Barrett; Billy Quilleash Stafford Smith; Ned Teare
E[dward] Irwin; Jim Callow Owen Cooper; Michael Lov-
ney Paul Belmore; Jabez Gawn W. [Lionel] Belmore;
Harcourt T.W. Percyval; Jim Curphey Franklin McLeay;
Hommy Beg Horace Hodges; Coroner A.E. Field. Kitty
Lillie Belmore; Liza Teare Harrietta Polini; Kathleen
M[aud] C. Jeffries; Bridget A[lice] Gambier. L & MGR
Wilson Barrett; Bm G.M. Polini; Act mgr F. Vagg Wal-
ter; Sm Charles Cathcart; Mus dir Michael Connelly;
Bom A[rthur] Frye; Mus Michael Connelly; Cost V[ic-
tor] Barthe, Miss [W] Bernstein; Sc Walter Hann; Pq
William Clarkson; Dir Wilson Barrett. *REV: E 14/3/91
p9; SR 14/3/91 p326; St 12/3/91 p10.*

91.57 *LOVE AND ART; OR, THE ARTIST'S GHOST* (Ca,1a) Alf-
red A. Wilmot. NOVELTY 9/3/91-23/3/91. 12 perf. 1st
perfd Lyric,Hammersmith 28/3/89. Sir Pompos Penygrin
J.G. Wilton; Lester Durnstead H.Buckstone Clair. Mrs
Lestrange M[adge] Denzil; Ethel Ferndale Georgie
Harris; Smartly Dorothy Vernon. ACT MGR H.J. Borley;
Sec & Treas W.R. Pope. *REV: E 21/3/91 p9.*

91.58 *CRIME AND CHRISTENING* (F) "Richard Henry" [Rich-
ard Butler & H. Chance Newton]. OPERA COMIQUE 10/3/91-
15/7/91. 112 perf [np 27/3].* Prowle E[rnest] Bantock; Gribble J[ohn] Ettinson; Algernon S. Hill. Mrs
Townley Linda Verner; Mrs Prowle Ethel Blenheim;
Lucinda Katie Seymour. L & MGR George Edwardes; Mus
dir F. Stanislaus; Sm G[eorge] Capel; Act mgr G.F.
Bashford; Bom A[rthur] Donald. *REV: E 14/3/91 p9.*

91.59 *NINE POINTS OF THE LAW* (C,1a) Tom Taylor. CRI-
TERION 12/3/91-21/3/91; 18/5/91-13/6/91. 32 perf
[np 16/3]. 1st perfd Olympic 11/4/59. Rodomont

Rollingstone George Giddens; <u>Joseph Ironside</u> William
Blakeley; <u>Mr Cunningame</u> Cyril Maude; <u>John Britton</u>
F[rank] Atherley; <u>John</u> Terric. <u>Mrs Smylie</u> F. Frances;
<u>Katie Mapelson</u> M[abel] Hardinge; <u>Sarah Jane</u> Ellaline
Terriss. <u>L & MGR</u> Charles Wyndham; <u>Mus dir</u> Theodore
Ward; <u>Act mgr</u> E. Harvey; <u>Furn</u> Oetzmann. *REV: St 21/
5/91 p10.*

91.60 *GHOSTS* (FamilyD,3a) Henrik Ibsen [trans William
Archer]. ROYALTY 13/3/91. 1 perf.* <u>Oswald Alving</u>
Frank Lindo; <u>Pastor Manders</u> Leonard Outram; <u>Jacob
Engstrand</u> Sydney Howard. <u>Mrs Alving</u> Mrs Theodore
Wright; <u>Regina</u> Edith Kenward. <u>L</u> Kate Santley; <u>Mgr &
Founder</u> J.T. Grein; <u>Mus dir</u> Jan Mulder; <u>Bm</u> Frank
Lindo; <u>Act mgr</u> Charles Hoppe; <u>Pq & Cost</u> C.H. Fox;
<u>Furn</u> J.S. Lyon. *REV: Ath 21/3/91 p387-8; E 21/3/91
p10; SR 21/3/91 p350-1; St 19/3/91 p10; Th 1/4/91 p
205-6; Ti 14/3/91 p7.* <u>Comment</u>: Independent Theatre
Society.

91.61 *THE VOLCANO* (F,3a) R.R. Lumley. COURT 14/3/91-
2/5/91. 43 perf [w/mat 18/4; mat only 2/5; np 27/3].*
<u>Duke of Donoway</u> Arthur Cecil; <u>Viscount Ratcliffe</u>
Weedon Grossmith; <u>Gilbert Stukeley</u> E. Allan Aynes-
worth; <u>Cpt. Roland Gurney</u> Brandon Thomas; <u>Daniel
Pultebeck</u> Fred Cape; <u>Ponter</u> John Clulow; <u>Veeley</u>
Master Wilson; <u>Gridd</u> Master Sidney Westgate. <u>Duchess
of Donoway</u> Carlotta Leclercq; <u>Lady Barbara</u> Marianne
Caldwell; <u>Lady Mabel</u> Perdita Hudspeth; <u>Mrs Delancey
Valentine</u> Mrs John Wood. <u>MGR</u> Mrs John Wood & Arthur
Chudleigh; <u>Mus dir</u> Andrew Levey; <u>Sc</u> T.W. Hall, Walter
Hann. *REV: Ath 21/3/91 p388; E 21/3/91 p9; SR 28/3/
91 p351; St 19/3/91 p9-10, 9/4/91 p12; Th 1/4/91 p
206-7; Ti 16/3/91 p3.*

91.62 *SPRING LEAVES* (Ca,1a) J.T. Grein & C.W. Jarvis.
COURT 14/3/91-20/3/91. 6 perf.* <u>Leonard Fairweather</u>
Charles Rock. <u>Florence</u> Perdita Hudspeth; <u>Harriett
Courtley</u> Isabel Ellissen; <u>Martha</u> Mrs Edmund Phelps.
<u>MGR</u>, <u>Sc</u>, <u>Mus dir</u> as for 91.61. *REV: E 21/3/91 p9;
St 19/3/91 p10; Ti 16/3/91 p3.*

91.63 *THE COLLEEN BAWN; OR, THE BRIDES OF GARRYOWEN*
(D,3a) Dion Boucicault [fnd on Gerald Griffen *The*

Collegians]. NOVELTY 16/3/91-28/3/91. 12 perfs. 1st
perfd Laura Keene's, New York 28/3/60. E[dwin] Fergusson; H. Buckstone Clair; G[ilbert] Vernon; O[wen]
Wynne; G[eorge] Clanville; J.G. Wilton. Marie Brian;
M[adge] Denzil; M[arion] Lacy; D[orothy] Vernon;
G[eorgie] Harris; Eleanor Lloyd. Comment: Mentioned
in *St* & *The Referee*.

91.64 *THE BALLAD-MONGER* (RP,1a) Walter Besant & Wal-
ter Herries Pollock [adpt of Theodore de Banville,
Gringoire]. HAYMARKET 18/3/91 mat perf.** Gringoire
H.B. Tree; Louis XI James Fernandez; Olivier Charles
Allan; Simon Leith. Loyse Mrs H.B. Tree; Nicole
Kildare. MGR H.B. Tree.

91.65 *A SWARRY DANSONG* (MusicalDuo1) Rutland Barrington (lib) & Edward Solomon (mus). HAYMARKET 18/3/91
mat perf.** Robert Plushley Rutland Barrington.
Harriet Mantell Jessie Bond. MGR H.B. Tree.

91.66 *DIAMOND DEANE* (P,4a) Henry J.W. Dam. VAUDEVILLE
18/3/91-21/3/91; 30/3/91-4/4/91. 11 perf [w/mat
30/3].* Rev Donald Grant Thomas Thorne; Henry Denni-
son H.B. Conway; Robert Dennison W. Scott Buist;
Lord Sheldon Lawrance d'Orsay; John Murray J.S.
Blythe; Lyons C[ecil] Ramsey; Johnson Fred Thorne.
Mary Dennison Dorothy Dorr; Mrs Maclane Mrs [George]
Canninge; Miss Young Jessie Millward. L & MGR ¬Thomas
Thorne; Act mgr Sydney Alport; Sm Fred Thorne; Pq
William Clarkson; Sc Maple, W.T. Hemsley. *REV: Ath
21/3/91 p388; E 21/3/91 p9; St 19/3/91 p10, 26/3/91
p10; Th 1/4/91 p207-8; Ti 20/3/91 p3.*

91.67 *FATHER BUONAPARTE* (P,3a) Charles Hudson. OLYM-
PIC 19/3/91, 21/3/91. 2 mat perf.* Abbé Buonaparte
Wilson Barrett; Stephano S. Miller Kent; Dr Fénélon
Austin Melford; Gen. Morivart Edward Irwin; Colnaghi
Franklin McLeay; Soldier Aubrey. Countess d'Osa
Frances Ivor; Luzette Alice Cooke; Mattea Lillie
Belmore; Adèle Winifred Emery. L & MGR Wilson Barrett;
Act mgr F. Vagg Walter; Sm Charles Cathcart; Mus &
Mus dir Michael Connelly; Bom A[rthur] Frye; Bm G.M.
Polini; Cost Miss W. Bernstein; Pq William Clarkson.
REV: E 21/3/91 p10; St 26/3/91 p10; Ti 20/3/91 p3.

91.68 *MISS TOMBOY* (C,3a) Robert Buchanan [adpt fr
Vanbrugh, *The Relapse*].   VAUDEVILLE 20/3/91 mat perf.**
Lord Foppington Thomas Thorne; Tom Fashion Frank
Gillmore; Sir George Matcham J.S. Blythe; Sir Tunbelly
Clumsy Fred Thorne; Squire Ditch [A.] Austin; Lava-
role O[swald] Yorke; Lory Cyril Maude; Jabez [John]
Wheatman; Jacob [Cecil] Ramsey; Rev Quiverwit T.
Grove; Mendlegs J. Crichton; Glitter S. Freeman; Hyde
[C.] Harbury; Coates S. Lawrence; Tierce T. Walters.
Fanny Hoyden Winifred Emery; Mrs Sentry Sylvia Hod-
son; Nancy Ditch [Lily] Hanbury; Dolly Primrose
[Mary] Collette. L & MGR Thomas Thorne; Act mgr Syd-
ney Alport; Sm Fred Thorne.

91.69 *A MUTUAL MISTAKE* (F,1a) W.H. Denny. COURT 21/3/
91-31/7/91; 21/10/91-31/10/91; 5/11/91-1/12/91. 143
perf [np 27/3, 2-5/5].*   John Charles Rock; Owen Smith
John Clulow. Letitia McGilligan Susie Vaughan. MGR
Mrs John Wood, Arthur Chudleigh; Mus dir Andrew
Levey; Sc T.W. Hall, Walter Hann. *REV: E 28/3/91 p9;
St 9/4/91 p12.*

91.70 *OUR DOCTORS* (FC,3a) Sir Randal Roberts & Joseph
MacKay. TERRY'S 24/3/91 mat perf.*   Jack Worthington
Henry V. Esmond; Joshua Morley Fred Kaye; Charles
Merton Oscar Adye; Dr Corbyn Conyers Edmund Gurney;
Dr Barber Robert Soutar; Jiggers A.E. Chapman. Vir-
ginia Morley Florence Haydon; Lucy Morley Sybil Grey;
Susan Cicely Richards. PP & MGR Edward Terry; Bm
H.T. Brickwell; Sm George Belmore; Mus dir J. Bayliss.
REV: St 26/3/91 p10.

91.71 *THE BOOKMAKER* (C,3a) J.W. Pigott. GLOBE 25/3/91-
9/5/91. 51 perf [w/S mat exc 28/3; np 27/3, 4/5].**
Sir Joseph Trent Harry Paulton; Earl of Harborough
W[illiam] Farren, jr; Gerald Lord Maidment Acton Bond;
Jack Carew Charles K. Cooper; Mr Mortmain Albert E.
Drinkwater; Bubbles Charles Goold; James F[rank] Van-
crossen; Marquis of Budleigh J.W. Pigott. Lady Jessie
Violet Raye; Sybil Hardwicke Mary Ansell; Polly Les-
lie Bell. L & MGR Norman Forbes; Cond C.J. Hargitt;
Act mgr Arthur Twiss; Sm J.W. Pigott. *REV: E 28/3/91
p9; St 2/4/91 p12; Ti 26/3/91 p7.*

91.72 *A MONTH AFTER DATE* (CD,1a) Sylvanus Dauncey.
GLOBE 25/3/91-9/5/91. 38 perf [np 27/3, 4/5]. 1st
perfd Jewish Institute, Highbury 18/10/85 [as *A
Divided Duty*]. Benjamin Cumber Albert E. Drinkwater;
Frank Clive Frank Vancrossen; Whimple Charles Goold.
Rosy Mary Ansell. L & MGR, Cond, Act mgr, Sm as for
91.71. *REV: E 28/3/91 p9; St 2/4/91 p12; Ti 26/3/91
p7.*

91.73 *GRAU-A-AILLE* (DSk). NOVELTY 25/3/91. 1 perf.*
Pat O'Connor R.C. Lyons; J.G. Wilton. Mona Kate Gurney; [Madge] Denzil. *REV: E 28/3/91 p9.*

91.74 *THE HENRIETTA* (C,4a) Bronson Howard. AVENUE
28/3/91-23/5/91. 57 perf [w/S mat exc 16/5, 23/5; add
mat 30/3, 17/4]. 1st prof. Nicholas Vanalstyne W.H.
Vernon; Dr Parke Wainwright Yorke Stephens; Nicholas
Vanalstyne, jr Lewis Waller; Bertie Vanalstyne John
L. Shine; Lord Arthur Trelawney Earle Douglas; Rev
Dr Murray Hilton Donald Robertson; Watson Flint
Henry Lee; Musgrave Charles J. Fulton. Mrs Cornelia
Opdyke Fanny Brough; Rose Vanalstyne Florence West;
Agnes Lockwood Marion Lea; Lady Arthur Trelawney Mary
Jocelyn. L & MGR Henry Lee; Sc Joseph Harker, R[ich-
ard] Halley; Sm W[illiam] Sidney; Act mgr Arthur
Yates; Mus dir Barter Johns. *REV: Ath 4/4/91 p451; E
4/4/91 p9; SR 4/4/91 p415; St 2/4/91 p11-2; Th 1/5/
91 p250-3; Ti 30/3/91 p11.*

91.75 *THE BELLS* (D,3a) Leopold Lewis [adpt of Erckmann-Chatrian, *Le Juif Polonais*]. LYCEUM 28/3/91,
30/3, 18/4, 20/6, 18/7(m), 24/7/91. 6 perf.** Mathias
Henry Irving; Walter [Henry] Howe; Hans [Sam] Johnson; Christian [William] Haviland; Dr Zimmer John
Martin Harvey; Notary Gurney; President of the Court
F[rank] Tyars; Clerk of the Court Lacy; Mesmerist
[John] Archer. Catherine Mrs Pauncefort; Sozel Kate
Phillips; Annette [Amy] Coleridge. L & MGR Henry Irving; Sm H.J. Loveday; Mus dir J. Meredith Ball; Act
mgr Bram Stoker.

91.76 *THE ROCKET* (CD,3a) A.W. Pinero. TERRY'S 30/3/91-
13/5/91. 45 perf [w/S mat]. 1st perfd Prince of
Wales's, Liverpool 30/7/83. Chevalier Walkinshaw

Edward Terry; <u>Lord Leadenshall</u> Henry V. Esmond; <u>Jos-lyn Hammersmith</u> Philip Cunningham; <u>John Mable</u> Ian Robertson; <u>Clement</u> Robert Soutar; <u>Chatwood</u> George Belmore; <u>Bingle</u> A. Ringworth. <u>Florence</u> Eleanore Ley-shon; <u>Rosaline Fabrequette</u> Adrienne Dairolles; <u>Georgette</u> Rose Dearing; <u>Lady Hammersmith</u> Sophie Lar-kin. <u>PP & MGR</u> Edward Terry; <u>Bm</u> H.T. Brickwell; <u>Sm</u> George Belmore; <u>Mus dir</u> J. Bayliss; <u>Furn</u> Lyons; <u>Pq</u> C.H. Fox; <u>Sc</u> [W.T.] Hemsley. *REV: E 4/4/91 p9; St 2/ 4/91 p12; Ti 31/3/91 p3.*

91.77 *L'ENFANT PRODIGUE* (MP without words,3a) Michel Carré, *fils* & André Wormser (mus). PRINCE OF WALES'S 31/3/91-14/4/91 [13 mat perf]; 15/4/91-29/10/91 [w/ M, W, S mat exc 13/7, 20/7, 27/7, 29/7, 3/8, 10/8, 17/8, 24/8, 31/8, 2/9, 5/9, 7/9, 12/9, 14/9, 19/9, 21/9, 26/9, 28/9, 3/10, 5/10, 10/10, 12/10, 17/10, 19/10, 24/10, 26/10: 210 perf]. 223 perf. 1st perfd Cercle funambulesque, Paris 14/6/90. <u>Pierrot, sr</u> [V.] Courtès; <u>Le Baron</u> Louis Gouget; <u>Servant</u> Jean Arceuil. <u>Pierrot, jr</u> Jane May; <u>Mme Pierrot</u> Schmidt; <u>Phrynette</u> Francesca Zanfretta. <u>PP</u> Edgar Bruce; <u>L & Mgr</u> Horace Sedger; <u>Pianist</u> Emil Artaud; <u>Regisseur</u> de Gasperi; <u>Mus dir</u> John Crook; <u>Cost</u> Julian & Cie, Lan-dolf; <u>Pq</u> William Clarkson; <u>Furn</u> Oetzmann; <u>Bm</u> William Greet; <u>Act mgr</u> C.P. Levilly, J.S. Fleming. *REV: Ath 4/4/91 p451-2, 11/4/91 p481; E 4/4/91 p11; SR 25/4/91 p505; St 2/4/91 p12; Th 1/5/91 p264-6; Ti 1/4/91 p4.* <u>Comment</u>: Cast from V & A programme for 4/4/91.

91.78 *THE SCHOOL FOR SCANDAL* (C,5a) R.B. Sheridan. CRITERION 1/4/91-16/5/91. 46 perf [w/S mat exc 9/5].** <u>Charles Surface</u> Charles Wyndham; <u>Sir Peter Teazle</u> William Farren; <u>Joseph Surface</u> Arthur Bourchier; <u>Care-less</u> George Giddens; <u>Crabtree</u> William Blakeley; <u>Sir Oliver Surface</u> H.H. Vincent; <u>Sir Benjamin Backbite</u> Cyril Maude; <u>Moses</u> Sydney Valentine; <u>Sir Harry Bumper</u> Frank Atherley; <u>Snake</u> S[tanley] Hewson; <u>Rowley</u> F. Emery; <u>Sir Toby</u> [Arthur] Playfair; <u>Trip</u> Meadows; <u>Ser-vant</u> Shelley. <u>Maria</u> Mary Moore; <u>Mrs Candour</u> M.A. Vic-tor; <u>Lady Sneerwell</u> E[mily] S. Fitzroy; <u>Maid</u> Ellaline Terriss; <u>Lady Teazle</u> Mrs Bernard Beere. <u>MGR</u> Charles Wyndham; <u>Sc</u> Bruce Smith, Walter Johnstone, Amable & Gardy; <u>Ch</u> Louis d'Egville; <u>Cost</u> Pitts & Richards, Mrs

Nettleship, Nathan; Pq C.H. Fox; Mus dir Theodore
Ward; Act mgr E. Harvey. *REV: Ath 4/4/91 p452; E 4/4/
91 p9; SR 11/4/91 p442; St 9/4/91 p12; Th 1/5/91 p253;
Ti 2/4/91 p4.*

91.79 *MR BARNES OF NEW YORK* Hal Collier-Edwards. NOV-
ELTY 4/4/91-c.11/4/91. c.6 perf. 1st perfd Marylebone
23/6/88. Mr Barnes Edwin Fergusson; Danella Gilbert
Vernon; De Belloc H. Buckstone Clair; Anstruther
George Clanville; Tommaso J.G. Wilton. Marina [Jessie]
Robertson; Enid Madge Denzil; Lady Charteris Marian
Lacy; Maude Marie Brian. *REV: St 9/4/91 p12-3.*

91.80 *WHITTINGTON; OR, THE GIRL THAT WAS UP TO DICK.*
NOVELTY 4/4/91-c.11/4/91. c.6 perf. Idle Jack J.G.
Wilton; Cook George Clanville; Bogie Man Owen Wynne;
Cat Master [Buck] Williams; Cpt. Flyback H. Mottley;
Alderman Fitzwarren H. Buckstone Clair. Dick Marie
Brian; Alice Dorothy Vernon. *REV: St 9/4/91 p12-3.*

91.81 *ORFEO* (O[4a]) C.W. Gluck. COVENT GARDEN 6/4/91,
14/4, 28/4, 14/5, 28/5, 9/7/91. 6 perf.** Orfeo
Giulia Ravogli; L'Amore [Eros] Mathilde Bauermeister;
Euridice Sofia Ravogli. MGR Augustus Harris; Cond
Luigi Mancinelli/Enrico Bevignani. *REV: Ath 11/4/91
p481; E 11/4/91 p15; SR 11/4/91 p438; St 9/4/91 p11-2;
Ti 7/4/91 p10, 17/4/91 p12.*

91.82 *BREAKING THE SPELL* (COa,1a) Jacques Offenbach.
GAIETY 6/4/91 mat perf. Old Matthew [E.H.] Haslem;
Peter Bloom Fred Wood. Jenny Wood Alice Aynsley Cook.
L & MGR George Edwardes; Hon sec C.J. Abud; Sm
[Frank] Parker; Cond F. Stanislaus, W. Meyer Lutz.
REV: E 11/4/91 p12.

91.83 *GOOD FOR NOTHING* (CD,1a) J.B. Buckstone GAIETY
6/4/91 mat perf. 1st perfd Haymarket 4/2/51. Tom
Dibbles Arthur Williams; Harry Collier J.D. Beveridge;
Charley [John] Tresahar; Young Mr Simpson [Fred]
Emney; Servant [C.] Walker. Nan Nellie Farren. L & MGR,
Hon sec, Sm, Cond as for 91.82. *REV: E 11/4/91 p12.*

91.84 *FAUST* (O[5a]) Charles Gounod. COVENT GARDEN
7/4/91, 13/4, 25/4, 16/5, 30/5, 3/6, 11/6, 17/6, 30/6,

10/7, 16/7, 22/7/91. 12 perf.** Faust Julius Perotti/
Jean de Reske/Ernest van Dyck/Luigi Ravelli; Valentino Ceste/Devoyod/Victor Maurel/Jean Lassalle; Wagner Antonio de Vaschetti/Miranda; Mephistopheles
Victor Maurel/Edouard de Reske/Pol Plancon. Siebel
Olimpia Guercia/Agnes Janson/Passama; Marguerite
Emma Eames; Marta Mathilde Bauermeister; 1ere Danseuse Palladino. MGR Augustus Harris; Cond Luigi Man-
cinelli/Enrico Bevignani.*REV: Ath 11/4/91 p481,18/4/91
p513, 6/6/91 p741; E 11/4/91 p15, 6/6/91 p13; SR
11/4/91 p438, 13/6/91 p715; St 9/4/91 p12, 16/4/91
p12; Ti 13/4/91 p12, 17/4/91 p12, 1/6/91 p4.*

91.85 *MY LADY HELP* (Ca,1a) Arthur Macklin. AVENUE
8/4/91-13/5/91. 31 perf.** Jack Desborough Arthur
Godfrey; Benjamin Pennyglass F. Hamilton Knight. Lady
Eva Desborough Mary Jocelyn. L & MGR Henry Lee; Act
mgr Arthur Yates; Sm W[illiam] Sidney; Mus dir Thomas
Batty. *REV: E 11/4/91 p9; St 9/4/91 p12.* Comment:
Ath indicates these cast differences: Jack Desborough
Lewis Waller; Eva Florence West.

91.86 *LINDA GREY* (P,5a) Sir Charles L. Young. PRIN-
CESS'S 8/4/91-17/4/91. 9 perf. 1st perfd Theatre
Royal, Margate 9/6/85. Victor Broughton Bernard
Gould; Lord Parkhurst Herbert Standing; Zed Jay Fred
[A.] Everill; Cpt. Beaufort Edmund Maurice; Sir
Dennis Broughton E.B. Norman; Ashby S.H. Lechmere;
Wilson Hubert Druce; Dean Kingscote. Linda Grey Mrs
Langtry; Lady Broughton May Whitty; Priscilla Royal
Laura Linden; Jane Ethel Hope. L & MGR Mrs Langtry:
Pp Mrs Harriet Gooch; Bom Winkley; Mus W[illiam]
Corri, jr; Sc Harry Potts; Furn Oetzmann; Sm E.B.
Norman; Bm Henry Ball; Pq William Clarkson; Mach W.J.
Cawdrey; Props Louis Labhart; Gas & Lime Jones &
[W.] Kerr. *REV: Ath 11/4/91 p482; E 11/4/91 p9; SR
11/4/91 p443-4; St 9/4/91 p12; Th 1/5/91 p254-5.*

91.87 *CARMEN* (O[4a]) Georges Bizet. COVENT GARDEN
9/4/91, 16/4, 4/5, 18/5, 13/6, 19/6, 4/7/91. 7 perf.**
Escamillo F[rank] H. Celli/Eugene Dufriche/Devoyod/
Jean Lassalle; Dancairo Giuseppe Ciampi; Remendado
Rinaldini; Morales Miranda; Zuniga Antonio de Vas-
chetti; Don Jose Albert Lubert/Jean de Reske. Carmen

Carmen Giulia Ravogli/Zelie de Lussan; Frasquitta
Mathilde Bauermeister; Mercedes Agnes Janson; Michaela Sofia Ravogli/Katerina Rolla/Nellie Melba; 1ere
Danseuse Palladino. MGR Augustus Harris; Cond Alberto
Randegger. *REV: Ath 18/4/91 p512, 9/5/91 p614; E 11/
4/91 p15, 9/5/91 p15, 11/7/91 p13; SR 11/4/91 p438,
9/5/91 p561-2, 27/6/91 p772-3; St 16/4/91 p12, 23/4/
91 p12, 9/7/91 p9; Ti 13/4/91 p12, 17/4/91 p12, 18/5/
91 p3, 6/7/91 p8.*

91.88 *THE BABY; OR, A WARNING TO MESMERISTS* (Sk,1a)
Lady Violet Greville [based on a story in Max Adler,
Elbow Room]. TERRY'S 9/4/91-13/5/91. 35 perf [w/S
mat exc 11/4; add mat 7/5]. 1st perfd Theatre Royal,
Brighton 31/10/90. Jack Turtledove Henry V. Esmond;
Zachary Inkhorn Robert Soutar; Doddles George Belmore.
Selina Turtledove Rose Dearing. MGR Edward Terry; Bom
A. Evans. *REV: E 11/4/91 p9; St 16/4/91 p13; Ti 11/4/
91 p15.* Comment: Cast from V & A programme for 7/5/
91.

91.89 *MONEY* (C,5a) Edward Bulwer Lytton. VAUDEVILLE
9/4/91-2/5/91 [w/mat 11/4, 16/4, 18/4, 25/4, 2/5];
5-6/5(m), 11/5(m), 13/5(m), 19/5(m), 21/5(m), 25/5,
29/5/91(m). 34 perf.1st perfd Haymarket 8/12/40.
Alfred Evelyn H.B. Conway; Sir John Vesey Fred Thorne;
Stout Edward Righton; Sir Frederick Blount Lawrence
d'Orsay; Cpt. Dudley Smooth Arthur Elwood; Lord
Glossmore Oswald Yorke; Sharp Fred Grove; Old Member
J[ohn] Wheatman; John C[ecil] Ramsey; Graves Thomas
Thorne; Green H. Palmer; Flat M. Wilson; Servant A.
Austin. Clara Douglas Dorothy Dorr; Georgina Ella
Banister; Lady Franklin Kate Phillips. L & MGR
Thomas Thorne; Act mgr Sydney Alport; Sm Fred Thorne.
*REV: Ath 18/4/91 p513; E 11/4/91 p9; SR 18/4/91 p473;
St 16/4/91 p12;. Ti 11/4/91 p15.*

91.90 *LOHENGRIN* (O[3a]) Richard Wagner. COVENT GARDEN
11/4/91, 17/4, 23/4, 29/4, 11/5, 25/5, 6/6, 22/6,
27/7/91. 9 perf.** Federico di Telramondo Victor
Maurel/Eugene Dufriche; Enrico l'Uccellatore Edouard
de Reske; L'Araldo del Re Abramoff; Lohengrin Jean de
Reske/Julius Perotti/Eugene Dufriche/Alec Marsh.
Elsa di Brabante Emma Eames/Marie Tavary/Nellie Melba;

Ortruda Giulia Ravogli. <u>MGR</u> Augustus Harris; <u>Cond</u>
Luigi Mancinelli. *REV: Ath 18/4/91 p512-3; E 18/4/91
p15; St 16/4/91 p12; Ti 13/4/91 p12.*

91.91 *IT'S NEVER TOO LATE TO MEND* (D,4a) Charles
Reade. DRURY LANE 11/4/91-23/5/91. 37 perf. 1st perfd
Theatre Royal, Leeds 1864. <u>Tom Robinson</u> Charles
Warner; <u>Peter Crawley</u> Harry Nicholls; <u>George Fielding</u>
Edmund Gurney; <u>Mr Merton</u> Edwin Shepherd; <u>William
Fielding</u> Frank MacVicar; <u>Isaac Levi</u> Henry Loraine;
<u>Fry</u> W.S. Parkes; <u>Mr Hawes</u> Julian Cross; <u>Rev Mr Eden</u>
Mark Quinton; <u>Jacky</u> Harry Fischer; <u>Mr Meadows</u> Albert
Marsh; <u>Evans</u> Robert Shaw; <u>Black Will</u> F. Johnson;
<u>Hudson</u> G. Williams; <u>Hitchen</u> Arthur Gregory; <u>Abner</u>
Alfred P. Phillips; <u>Black Jack</u> F. Campbell; <u>Carter</u>
Anderson; <u>Groom</u> Archer; <u>Nigger Boy</u> Master Freddie
French. <u>Josephs</u> Kate MacCabe; <u>Mary</u> Constance Wallace;
<u>Susan Merton</u> Jessie Millward. <u>L & MGR</u> Augustus Harris;
<u>Sec & Treas</u> F[red] G. Latham; <u>Sm</u> Arthur P. Collins;
<u>Dir</u> Augustus Harris; <u>Cond</u> P. Bucalossi; <u>Sc</u> William
Perkins, R[ichard] C. Durant. *REV: Ath 18/4/91 p513;
E 18/4/91 p9; SR 18/4/91 p473; St 16/4/91 p12; Ti
13/4/91 p10.*

91.92 *HAMLET* (T) William Shakespeare [arr Wilson Bar-
rett]. OLYMPIC 13/4/91-18/4/91; 4-5/5; 8/5/91. 10
perf.** <u>Hamlet</u> Wilson Barrett; <u>Claudius</u> Austin Melford; <u>Laertes</u> H. Cooper Cliffe; <u>Ghost</u> W.A. Elliott;
<u>Polonius</u> Stafford Smith; <u>Horatio</u> S. Miller Kent; <u>1st
Gravedigger</u> George Barrett; <u>Rosencrantz</u> A.E. Field;
<u>Guildenstern</u> Franklin McLeay; <u>Marcellus</u> A. Manning;
<u>Bernardo</u> W. [Lionel] Belmore; <u>Francisco</u> Paul Belmore;
<u>1st Actor</u> Edward Irwin; <u>2nd Actor</u> Charles Fredericks;
<u>Osric</u> T.W. Percyval; <u>Priest</u> Lynd; <u>2nd Gravedigger</u>
Horace Hodges. <u>Gertrude</u> Louise Moodie; <u>Player Queen</u>
Lily Hanbury; <u>Ophelia</u> Winifred Emery. <u>MGR</u> Wilson
Barrett; <u>Bom</u> A[rthur] Frye; <u>Mus</u> Edward Jones; <u>Cost</u>
V[ictor] Barthe, D. Bernstein; <u>Sc</u> Stafford Hall,
Walter Hann; <u>Bm</u> G.M. Polini; <u>Act mgr</u> Fred W. Crellin;
<u>Sm</u> Charles Cathcart; <u>Mus dir</u> Michael Connelly. *REV:
Ath 18/4/91 p513; E 18/4/91 p9; St 16/4/91 p12.*

91.93 *ROMEO ET JULIETTE* (O[5a]) Charles Gounod. COVENT
GARDEN 15/4/91, 21/4, 1/5, 9/5, 2/6, 12/6, 15/6,

21/7/91. 8 perf.** <u>Romeo</u> Jean de Reske; <u>Frère Laur-</u>
<u>ent</u> Edouard de Reske/Pol Plancon; <u>Mercutio</u> Ceste;
<u>Capulet</u> Eugene Dufriche; <u>Tybalt</u> Sebastian Montariol/
Iginio Corsi; <u>Duke</u> Armand Castelmary/Conti; <u>Gregorio</u>
Miranda; <u>Benvoglio</u> Rinaldini. <u>Nurse</u> Mathilde Bauermeister; <u>Juliette</u> Emma Eames/Nellie Melba; <u>Stephano</u>
Regina Pinkert/Agnes Janson. <u>MGR</u> Augustus Harris;
<u>Cond</u> Luigi Mancinelli. *REV: Ath 18/4/91 p513, 6/6/91*
p741; E 18/4/91 p15; St 23/4/91 p12; Ti 17/4/91 p12,
3/6/91 p5.

91.94 *OUR DAUGHTERS* (C,3a) T.G. Warren & Willie Edouin.
STRAND 15/4/91(m); 22/4/91-9/5/91. 20 perf [w/S mat].
1st perfd Theatre Royal, Portsmouth 30/6/90 [as
Daughters]. <u>Richard Mayhew</u> John Beauchamp; <u>Barnaby</u>
<u>Trotter</u> Willie Edouin; <u>Harold Winyard</u> H. Reeves-Smith/
Charles S. Fawcett; <u>Bob Bounder</u> Percy F. Marshall;
<u>Fred Danby</u> Sydney Barraclough; <u>Montague Jarvis</u> Herbert
Sparling; <u>Postman</u> Hackney/Robert Nainby. <u>Nellie May-</u>
<u>hew</u> May Whitty; <u>Mimi Mayhew</u> Alice Atherton; <u>Mrs Dolly</u>
<u>Danby</u> Lilian Millward; <u>Mrs Courteney</u> Ruth Rutland;
<u>Marie</u> Ina Goldsmith. <u>L & MGR</u> Willie Edouin; <u>Pp</u> J.S.
Clarke; <u>Sm</u> J.A.E. Malone; <u>Bm</u> George Bryer; <u>Cond</u>
Ernest Bucalossi; <u>Bom</u> H[enry] L. Boss. *REV: Ath 18/*
4/91 p513-4; E 18/4/91 p10; SR 18/4/91 p473; St 16/4/
91 p12-3; Th 1/5/91 p255-6; Ti 16/4/91 p7, 24/4/91 p5.

91.95 *THE LADY GUIDE;OR,BREAKING THE BANK*(C,3a).TERRY'S
15/4/91 mat perf.* <u>Hon Peter F. Chomleigh</u> William
Cheesman; <u>Hercules Lebeau</u> H. Austin; <u>Allan Armitage</u>
Alfred B. Cross; <u>M. le Commissaire</u> H[enry] Bayntun.
<u>Mrs Rushforth</u> Elsie Chester; <u>Queenie</u> Cissie Wade;
<u>Miss Whilem Chetwood</u> Florence Wade. <u>PD</u> Florence Wade.
REV: Ath 18/4/91 p514; E 18/4/91 p11; St 16/4/91 p13.

91.96 *RICHARD SAVAGE* (P,4a) J.M. Barrie & H.B. Marri-
ott Watson. CRITERION 16/4/91 mat perf.* <u>Richard</u>
<u>Savage</u> Bernard Gould; <u>Sir Richard Steele</u> Cyril Maude;
<u>Col. Jocelyn</u> Leonard Outram; <u>Jacob Tonson</u> Compton
Coutts; <u>Aynston</u> E. Webster Lawson; <u>Sir George Sandys</u>
F. Brandon; <u>Will</u> William Lugg. <u>Prue</u> Phyllis Broughton;
<u>Betty Steele</u> Helen Forsyth; <u>Lady Yuill</u> Marie Fraser;
<u>Lady Macclesfield</u> Louise Moodie. <u>MGR</u> Charles Wyndham;
<u>Cost</u> Nathan; <u>Pq</u> C.H. Fox; <u>Sm</u> George R. Foss; <u>Act mgr</u>

E. Harvey; <u>Mus dir</u> Theodore Ward. *REV: Ath 25/4/91 p545-6; E 18/2/91 p11; SR 18/4/91 p470; St 23/4/91 p13; Th 1/5/91 p256-7; Ti 17/4/91 p12.*

91.97 *TANNHAUSER* (O[3a]) Richard Wagner. COVENT GARDEN 18/4/91, 24/4, 6/5, 12/5/91. 4 perf.** <u>Tannhauser</u> Julius Perotti; <u>Walter</u> Pedro Guetary; <u>Biterolf</u> Camillo Fiegna; <u>Langravio</u> Abramoff; <u>Wolframo</u> Victor Maurel; <u>Heinrich</u> Rinaldini; <u>Reinmar</u> Miranda. <u>Elizabeth</u> Emma Albani; <u>Venus</u> Sofia Ravogli; <u>Pastore</u> Mathilde Bauermeister. <u>MGR</u> Augustus Harris; <u>Cond</u> Enrico Bevignani. *REV: Ath 25/4/91 p544; E 25/4/91 p15; SR 25/4/91 p502-3; St 23/4/91 p12; Ti 22/4/91 p7.*

91.98 *LA TRAVIATA* (O[3a]) Giuseppe Verdi. COVENT GARDEN 20/4/91, 30/4, 1/7, 24/7/91. 4 perf.** <u>Germont</u> Victor Maurel; <u>Alfredo</u> Sebastian Montariol/Albert Lubert; <u>Gaston</u> Iginio Corsi; <u>Il Marchese</u> Bieletto; <u>Il Barone</u> Antonio de Vaschetti; <u>Il Dottore</u> Miranda; <u>Guiseppe</u> Cernusco. <u>Violetta</u> Emma Albani/Emma Teleky; <u>Flora</u> Florenza; <u>Annina</u> Mathilde Bauermeister; <u>lere Danseuse</u> Palladino. <u>MGR</u> Augustus Harris; <u>Cond</u> Alberto Randegger. *REV: Ath 25/4/91 p544-5; E 25/4/91 p15; SR 2/5/91 p529; St 23/4/91 p12, 30/7/91 p9; Ti 22/4/ 91 p7, 27/7/91 p14.*

91.99 *CHATTERTON.* GAIETY 20/4/91 mat perf. [<u>Chatterton</u>] Wilson Barrett; [<u>Nat Boaden</u>] George Barrett. [<u>Lady Mary</u>] Lily Hanbury; [<u>Cecilia</u>] Lillie Belmore; [<u>Mrs Angel</u>] Mrs Belmore. *REV: 25/4/91 p546.*

91.100 *A QUIET RUBBER* (C,1a) Charles F. Coghlan [adpt of *Une Partie de Piquet*]. GAIETY 20/4/91 mat perf. 1st perfd Court 2/1/76. [<u>Lord Kilclare</u>] John Hare; [<u>Charles</u>] Gilbert Hare; [<u>Mr Sullivan</u>] Charles Groves. [<u>Mary</u>] Webster. *REV: Ath 25/4/91 p546.*

91.101 *HEDDA GABLER* (P,4a) Henrik Ibsen [trans Edmund Gosse & William Archer]. VAUDEVILLE 20/4/91 mat perf.* <u>Judge Brack</u> Charles Sugden; <u>George Tesman</u> W. Scott Buist; <u>Ejlbert Lovborg</u> Arthur Elwood. <u>Mrs Elvsted</u> Marion Lea; <u>Juliana Tesman</u> Henrietta Cowen; <u>Bertha</u> Patty Chapman; <u>Hedda Tesman</u> Elizabeth Robins. <u>L & MGR</u> Thomas Thorne; <u>Act mgr</u> Sydney Alport; <u>Sm</u> George R.

Foss; Cond Charles Dubois. *REV: Ath 25/4/91 p546; E
25/4/91 p11; SR 25/4/91 p498, 9/5/91 p562; St 23/4/
91 p12; Th 1/5/91 p257-9; Ti 21/4/91 p10.*

91.102 *THE ACROBAT* (D,4a) Wilson Barrett [adpt of
Adolphe d'Ennery & Marc Fournier, *La Paillasse*].
OLYMPIC 21/4/91-2/5/91; 6-7/5/91. 14 perf [w/mat
25/4].* Belphegor Wilson Barrett; Duke de Montbazon
Austin Melford; Lavarennes H. Cooper Cliffe; Count de
Blangy W.A. Elliott; Grela Stafford Smith; Viscount
d'Arpignol Ambrose Manning; Viscount Hercule Horace
Hodges; Flip Flap George Barrett; Marquis de Cour-
gemont T.W. Percyval; Gen. Pouffiere Edward Irwin;
Jason Paul Belmore; Servant W. [Lionel] Belmore;
Servant Lloyd. Mlle de Vermandois Mrs Henry Leigh;
Flora Lillie Belmore; Catherine Lily Hanbury; Anas-
tasia Harrietta Polini; Fanny Louie [Bassett] Wilmot;
Madeline Winifred Emery; Henri Edie King; Jeanette
Pollie Smith; Therese Alice Gambier. MGR Wilson Bar-
rett; Bom A[rthur] Frye; Sc Walter Hann, Stafford
Hall; Cost Elita & Cie, Miss D. Bernstein; Mus & Mus
dir Michael Connelly; Ch Henri Dewinne; Bm G.M. Pol-
ini; Act mgr Fred W. Crellin; Sm Charles Cathcart.
*REV: Ath 25/4/91 p546; E 25/4/91 p9; SR 25/4/91 p503;
St 23/4/91 p12; Th 1/5/91 p259-60; Ti 22/4/91 p7.*

91.103 *A NIGHT IN TOWN* (FC,3a) H.A. Sherburn. STRAND
21/4/91 mat perf.* Mr Babbicombe Arthur Williams;
Fred Cecil Ramsey; Mr Dovedale Albert E. Drinkwater;
Frank Darlington Reginald Stockton; Mr Culpepper
William Lockhart; Jorkins Frederic Jacques; Policeman
H. Shelley. Mrs Babbicombe Madeline l'Estrange; Mrs
Dovedale Muriel Wylford; Mabel Alice Maitland; Bea-
trice Kate Bealby; Mme Cuthbert Marie Lewes; Polly
Parker Julia Warden; Mrs Pegwell May Protheroe; Mlle
Anastasie Mrs Gordon-Ascher; Simmons Phyllis Ayrian.
*REV: Ath 25/4/91 p546; E 25/4/91 p11; St 23/4/91 p
12-3; SR 25/4/91 p503.*

91.104 *LOVE'S YOUNG DREAM* (CD,1a) Eva Bright. STRAND
21/4/91 mat perf.* Sir Geoffrey Vansittart Acton
Bond; George Frederic Jacques. Edith de Brissey Amy
McNeil; Iris de Brissey Florence Bright; Anne Mrs
E.H. Brooke. *REV: Ath, E, St as for 91.103.*

91.105 *RIGOLETTO* (O[3a]) Giuseppe Verdi. COVENT GARDEN
22/4/91, 5/6, 18/6, 2/7, 13/7/91. 5 perf.** Rigoletto
Victor Maurel; Sparafucile Abramoff; Il Duca Sebastian
Montariol/Luigi Ravelli; Marullo Cernusco; Monterone
Antonio de Vaschetti; Borsa Rinaldini; Conte di
Ceprano Bieletto. Gilda Emma Albani/Nellie Melba;
Maddalena Olimpia Guercia/Giulia Ravogli; Giovanna
Mathilde Bauermeister. MGR Augustus Harris; Cond
Enrico Bevignani. *REV: Ath 25/4/91 p545, 13/6/91 p*
774; E 25/4/91 p15, 13/6/91 p13; SR 13/6/91 p715; St
23/4/91 p12, 30/4/91 p12; Ti 8/6/91 p13.

91.106 *OLIVIA* (P,4a) W.G. Wills. LYCEUM 22/4/91-7/5/
91; 24/6(m), 27/6(m), 8/7(m), 23/7/91. 16 perf [mat
only 25/4; np 1-2/5].** Dr Primrose Henry Irving;
Moses Gordon Craig; Thornhill William Terriss; Burchell [F.H.] Macklin; Farmer Flamborough [Henry] Howe;
Leigh [Frank] Tyars. Gipsy Agnes Barnett; Mrs Primrose Mrs Pauncefort; Olivia Ellen Terry; Polly Flamborough N. de Silva; Phoebe Foster; Dick Minnie
Terry; Bill Grace Webb; Sophia Annie Irish. L & MGR
Henry Irving; Sm H.J. Loveday; Mus dir J. Meredith Ball; Act mgr Bram Stoker. *REV: Ath 25/4/91*
p546; E 25/4/91 p9; SR 25/4/91 p503; St 30/4/91 p12.

91.107 *BACK IN FIVE MINUTES* (F,1a) Henry T. Johnson.
STRAND 22/4/91-9/5/91. 16 perf. 1st perfd Parkhurst
16/2/91. Roscoe Robinson Sydney Barraclough; Bedford Roe William Lugg; Peterkin Prosser Robert Nainby. Mary Maybud Georgie Esmond; Theresa Tompkins
Lilian Millward. PP J.S. Clarke; L Willie Edouin; Bom
H[enry] L. Boss; Sm J.A.E. Malone; Cond Ernest Bucalossi; Bm George Bryer. *REV: E 25/4/91 p9.*

91.108 *CUT OFF WITH A SHILLING* (Ca,1a) S. Theyre
Smith. DRURY LANE 23/4/91 mat perf. 1st perfd Prince
of Wales's 10/4/71. Sam Gaythorne Sydney Brough; Col.
Berners Charles Collette. Kitty Gaythorne Fanny Brough.
REV: 25/4/91 p8.

91.109 *HIS LAST CHANCE* (Oa,1a) Herbert & Ethel Harra-
den. DRURY LANE 23/4/91 mat perf.** Charles Chester
George T. Minshull. Alice Montrose Loie Fuller. *REV:*
E 25/4/91 p8.

91.110 *THE UPPER CRUST* (C,3a) Henry J. Byron. TOOLE'S
23/4/91-13/5/91. 20 perf [w/mat 25/4, 2/5]. 1st perfd
Folly 31/3/80. Barnaby Doublechick J.L. Toole; Lord
Hesketh John Billington; Sir Robert Bootleton Henry
Westland; Walter Wrentmore C.M. Lowne; Tibthorpe
Frank J. Arlton. Lady Bootleton Eliza Johnstone;
Norah Doublechick Irene Vanbrugh; Kate Vennimore
Effie Liston. MGR J.L. Toole; Sm John Billington; Bm
George Lee; Cost Harrisons; Furn Lyons; Mus dir Will-
iam Robins. *REV: E 25/4/91 p9; SR 2/5/91 p531; Ti
24/4/91 p5.*

91.111 *HESTER'S MYSTERY* (CD,1a) A.W. Pinero. TOOLE'S
23/4/91-13/5/91. 20 perf [w/mat 25/4, 2/5].**   Owen
Silverdale Henry Westland; John Royle C.M. Lowne;
Joel G[eorge] Shelton. Nance Butterworth Eliza Johnstone; Hester Irene Vanbrugh. MGR, Sm, Bm, Mus dir
as for 91.110; Bom G.C. Oliver. *REV: E, SR as for 91.
110.*

91.112 *A PAIR OF SPECTACLES* (C,3a) Sydney Grundy [adpt
of Eugene Labiche & Delacour, *Les Petites Oiseaux*].
GARRICK 25/4/91(m); 23/5/91-26/6/91. 31 perf [mat
only 30/5, 6/6, 13/6, 20/6, 24/6].**   Benjamin Gold-
finch John Hare; Gregory Goldfinch Charles Groves;
Joyce John Byron/R[owley] Cathcart; Dick Sydney
Brough; Percy Rudge Harding; Lorimer G[ilbert] Trent/
[Charles] Dodsworth; Bartholomew John Byron/Tarleton;
Shoemaker W[illiam] Cathcart. Lucy Lorimer Annie
Webster; Mrs Goldfinch Kate Rorke; Charlotte F. Hunter
MGR John Hare; Asm R[owley] Cathcart; Mus dir Schoen-
ing; Sc William Harford; Act mgr C.G. Compton. *REV:
Ath 30/5/91 p710; St 28/5/91 p12; Ti 25/5/91 p6.*

91.113 *A QUIET RUBBER* (Ca,1a) Charles F. Coghlan [adpt
of *Une Partie de Piquet*]. GARRICK 25/4/91(m); 23/5/
91-5/6/91. 13 perf [mat only 30/6].**   Lord Kilcare
John Hare; Charles Gilbert Hare; Mr Sullivan Charles
Groves. Mary Annie Webster. MGR, Mus dir, Asm, Sc,
Act mgr as for 91.112. *REV: As for 91.112.*

91.114 *LE PROPHETE* (O[5a]) Giacomo Meyerbeer. COVENT
GARDEN 27/4/91, 5/5, 13/5/91. 3 perf.**   Jean de Leyde Jean de Reske; Oberthal Eugene Dufriche; Jonas

Sebastian Montariol; <u>Mathisen</u> Miranda; <u>Sergent</u> Rinaldini; <u>Zacharie</u> Edouard de Reske. <u>Berthe</u> Katerina
Rolla; <u>Fides</u> Hélène Richard; <u>lere Danseuse</u> Palladino.
<u>MGR</u> Augustus Harris; <u>Cond</u> Luigi Mancinelli. *REV: Ath*
2/5/91 p580; E 2/5/91 p15; SR 2/5/91 p529; Ti 4/5/91
p13.

91.115 *HUSBAND AND WIFE* (FC,3a) F.C. Phillips & Percy
Fendall. CRITERION 30/4/91 mat perf.* <u>Adolphus Green-</u>
<u>thorne</u> George Giddens; <u>Montrevor Smith</u> William Blake-
ley; <u>Alfred Stepit</u> James Nelson; <u>Inspector Thickhead</u>
Sydney Valentine; <u>Waiter</u> Shelley; <u>Phillip Softdown</u>
Stanley Hewson; <u>Mr Delamere</u> F. Emery. <u>Mrs Springfield</u>
Laura Linden; <u>Mrs Greenthorne</u> Carlotta Addison; <u>Mrs</u>
<u>Montrevor Smith</u> M.A. Victor; <u>Mrs Phillip Softdown</u>
Ellaline Terriss; <u>Mrs Delamere</u> Annie Hill; <u>Mary</u> Edith
Kenward. <u>MGR</u> Charles Wyndham; <u>Act mgr</u> E. Harvey; <u>Mus</u>
<u>dir</u> Theodore Ward. *REV: E 2/5/91 p9; SR 2/5/91 p532;*
St 7/5/91 p12; Th 1/6/91 p301; Ti 1/5/91 p10.

91.116 *ALL ABOUT A BONNET* (MCa,1a) Herbert Harraden
(lib) & Ethel Harraden (mus). TERRY'S 30/4/91 mat
perf.* <u>Herbert</u> Herbert Harraden. <u>Ethel</u> Ethel Harraden.
<u>MGR</u> Edward Terry; <u>Bm</u> Gilbert Tate; <u>Mus dir</u> Barter
Johns; <u>Sm</u> George Belmore; <u>Act mgr</u> H.T. Brickwell.
REV: E 2/5/91 p11; St 7/5/91 p12; Ti 2/5/91 p9.

91.117 *AUNT AGATHA'S DOCTOR* (MCa,1a) Herbert Harraden
(lib) & Ethel Harraden (mus). TERRY'S 30/4/91 mat
perf.* <u>Dr Miller</u> Herbert Harraden. <u>Agatha Goodman</u>
Ethel Harraden; <u>Rosie</u> [Lizzie] St. Quinten. <u>MGR</u>, <u>Bm</u>,
<u>Mus dir</u>, <u>Sm</u>, <u>Act mgr</u> as for 91.116. *REV: As for 90.116.*

91.118 *CHARLIE* (MCa,1a) Herbert Harraden. TERRY'S 30/
4/91 mat perf.* <u>Kitty</u> [Lizzie] St. Quinten; <u>Lizzie</u>
Loie Fuller. <u>MGR</u>, <u>Bm</u>, <u>Mus dir</u>, <u>Sm</u>, <u>Act mgr</u> as for
91.116. *REV: E, St as for 90.116.*

91.119 *THAT WOMAN IN PINK* (MCa,1a) Herbert Harraden
(lib) & Ethel Harraden (mus). TERRY'S 30/4/91 mat perf.*
<u>Jack</u> George T. Minshull. <u>Florrie</u> Loie Fuller. <u>MGR</u>,
<u>Bm</u>, <u>Mus dir</u>, <u>Sm</u>, <u>Act mgr</u> as for 91.116. *REV: E, St*
as for 91.116.

91.120 *MEFISTOFELE* (O,Prol,4a,Epi) Arrigo Boito. COVENT GARDEN 2/5/91, 8/5/91. 2 perf. 1st perfd Teatro alla Scala, Milan 5/3/68. Mefistofele Edouard de Reske; Nereus Rinaldini; Faust Julius Perotti/Sebastian Montariol; Wagner Rinaldini. Margherita/Elena Emma Albani; Maria/Pantalio Olimpia Guercia. MGR Augustus Harris; Cond Luigi Mancinelli. *REV: Ath 9/5/91 p614; E 9/5/91 p15; SR 9/5/91 p561; St 7/5/91 p12; Ti 4/5/91 p13.*

91.121 *POOR JO* (D,4a) [H. Davenport; adpt of Charles Dickens, *Bleak House*]. NOVELTY 2/5/91-15/5/91. 11 perf. 1st perfd Theatre Royal, Southampton 25/2/78. Sir Leicester Dedlock W. Garrett; Mr Tulkinghorn G[ilbert] Vernon; Bucket Edwin Fergusson; Rev Mr Chadband H. Buckstone Clair; Mr Snagsby J.G. Wilton; Mr Guppy Owen Wynne; Coroner Edgerton; Beadle G. Sewell; Policeman Johnson; Footman James. Jo Marie Brian; Lady Dedlock Madge Denzil; Esther Summerson Dorothy Vernon; Mrs Snagsby Mrs Chandler; Hortense Eleanor Lloyd. *REV: E 9/5/91 p9; St 7/5/91 p13.*

91.122 *THE ANONYMOUS LETTER* (C,3a) Mark Ambient & Frank Latimer. LYRIC 5/5/91, 13/5, 21/5/91. 3 mat perf.* Ernest Sinclair Lewis Waller; Charles Credit Eric Lewis; Sir Daniel Dollary George Mudie; Thomas Cecil Frere; Baron Goldschein W.H. Vernon. Lady Dollary Vane; Mrs Sinclair Annie Rose; Paterson Alexes Leighton; Helen Grant Florence West. MGR Horace Sedger; Dir W.H. Vernon. *REV: Ath 9/5/91 p616; E 9/5/91 p11; SR 9/5/91 p562; St 7/5/91 p12; Th 1/6/91 p301-2.*

91.123 *BETRAYED BY A KISS* (C,1a) H.A. Saintsbury ["Jay Nibb"]. OPERA COMIQUE 5/5/91 mat perf.* Achille de Tremont Leonard Outram; Maurice de Vernois H.A. Saintsbury; Jean Licard J.G. Taylor. Comtesse de Cardillac Marie de Valge; Gabrielle St. Aubert Loie Fuller; Adele de Vernois Maud Digby; Cerise Degeon Mrs Campbell Bradley. *REV: E 9/5/91 p7; St 7/5/91 p12.*

91.124 *THE LATE LAMENTED* (F,3a) Fred Horner [adpt of Alexandre Bisson, *Feu Toupinal*]. COURT 6/5/91-31/7/91; trfd to STRAND 1/8/91-7/1/92. 230 perf [w/mat

23/5/91; w/S mat at Strand exc 31/10/91, 26/12/91,
2/1/92].* <u>Stuart Crosse</u> Arthur Cecil/Willie Edouin;
<u>Mjr. Joseph Marshall</u> Herbert Standing; <u>Richard Webb</u>
E. Allan Aynesworth/Harry Eversfield; <u>Parker</u> Fred
Cape; <u>Mr Fawcett</u> Gilbert Farquhar/George P. Hawtrey;
<u>Jansen Smith</u> Charles Rock/Sydney Barraclough; <u>Porter</u>
John Clulow/Akermann May. <u>Mrs Richard Webb</u> Rosina
Filippi/Eva Moore/Beatrice Lamb; <u>Kate Morgan</u> Mrs
Edmund Phelps; <u>Mary</u> Florence Harrington/Venie
Bennett; <u>Mrs Stuart Crosse</u> Mrs John Wood/Fanny Brough/
Cicely Richards. <u>MGR</u> Mrs John Wood & Arthur Chudleigh/
Willie Edouin; <u>Mus dir</u> Andrew Levey/Ernest Bucalossi;
<u>Sm[Strand]</u> J.A.E. Malone; <u>Bm[Strand]</u> J.T. Mackay
Robertson. *REV: Ath 16/5/91 p647; E 9/5/91 p9, 8/8/
91 p7; SR 9/5/91 p559-60; St 7/5/91 p12, 14/5/91 p12;
Th 1/6/91 p302-3, 1/9/91 p137-8; Ti 7/5/91 p7.*

91.125 *THE STREETS OF LONDON* (D,Prol,4a) Dion Bou-
cicault. ADELPHI 7/5/91-20/6/91. 39 perf. 1st perfd
Wallack's, New York 8/12/57 [as *The Poor of New York*].
<u>Badger</u> Leonard Boyne; <u>Crawley</u> Frederick Glover;
<u>Puffy</u> Lionel Rignold; <u>Paul</u> T.B. Thalberg; <u>Cpt.Fair-</u>
<u>weather</u> Charles Dalton; <u>Mark Livingstone</u> Frank Gill-
more; <u>James</u> J[ohn] Northcote; <u>Count</u> James East; <u>Craft</u>
W. Northcote; <u>Edwards</u> H[arwood] Cooper. <u>Dan</u> Clara
Jecks; <u>Alida</u> Ada Ferrar; <u>Mrs Puffy</u> Mrs Henry Leigh;
<u>Lucy</u> Olga Brandon. <u>PP & MGR</u> A. & S. Gatti; <u>Mus dir</u>
Henry Sprake; <u>Act mgr</u> Charles A. Jecks. *REV: E 9/5/
91 p9; SR 16/5/91 p591; St 14/5/91 p13; Th 1/6/91
p304-5; Ti 8/5/91 p10.*

91.126 *DON GIOVANNI* (O[2a]) W.A. Mozart. COVENT GAR-
DEN 7/5/91, 15/5, 21/5, 1/6, 23/6/91. 5 perf.** <u>Don</u>
<u>Giovanni</u> Victor Maurel; <u>Leporello</u> Jacques Isnardon/
Edouard de Reske; <u>Masette</u> Giuseppe Ciampi; <u>Il Com-</u>
<u>mendatore</u> Abramoff; <u>Don Ottavio</u> Sebastian Montariol/
Luigi Ravelli. <u>Donna Anna</u> Marie Tavary; <u>Donna Elvira</u>
Katerina Rolla; <u>Zerlina</u> Zelie de Lussan. <u>MGR</u> Augustus
Harris; <u>Cond</u> Enrico Bevignani/Alberto Randegger.
*REV: Ath 16/5/91 p646; E 9/5/91 p15; SR 9/5/91 p562;
St 14/5/91 p12; Ti 18/5/91 p3.*

91.127 *DAVID GARRICK* (C,3a) T.W. Robertson. GARRICK
7/5/91 mat perf.** <u>David Garrick</u> Charles Wyndham;

Simon Ingot William Farren; <u>Squire Chivy</u> George Giddens; [<u>Smith</u>] William Blakeley; [<u>Brown</u>] Sydney Valentine; [<u>Jones</u>] S[tanley] Hewson; [<u>Thomas</u>] Frank Atherley; [<u>George</u>] F. Emery. [<u>Mrs Smith</u>] M.A. Victor; [<u>Araminta Brown</u>] E[mily] Miller; <u>Ada Ingot</u> Mary Moore. *REV: Daily Telegraph 8/5/91 p3.*

91.128 *THE DIRECTOR* (F,3a) Harry Greenbank. TERRY'S 7/5/91 mat perf.* <u>Sydenham Sudds</u> Edward Terry; <u>Augustus</u> Henry V. Esmond; <u>Joseph Jonquil</u> E.M. Robson; <u>Charlie Chiffins</u> Robert Ganthony; <u>Tom Ashford</u> Philip Cunningham; <u>John Gibbons</u> A[lfred] Kendrick. <u>Caroline Sudds</u> Mrs Charles Calvert; <u>Dolly</u> Alice Maitland; <u>Gertie Gimcrack</u> Rose Dearing; <u>Millie Mackintosh</u> Mrs Gordon-Ascher; <u>Maudie Mackintosh</u> Mary Marden; <u>Jane</u> Jessie Danvers; <u>Rebecca Sudds</u> Sophie Larkin. PP & MGR Edward Terry; <u>Act mgr</u> H.T. Brickwell; <u>Sm</u> George Belmore; <u>Mus dir</u> J. Bayliss. *REV: Ath 16/5/91 p648; E 9/5/91 p10; St 14/5/91 p12; Th 1/6/91 p304.*

91.129 *LEAH.* VAUDEVILLE 7/5/91 mat perf. <u>Rudolf</u> Alfred B. Cross; <u>Nathan</u> Bassett Roe; <u>Father Herman</u> Oswald Yorke; <u>Lorenz</u> F[red] Grove; <u>Ludwig</u> Fred Thorne; <u>Jacob</u> C[ecil] Ramsey; <u>Abraham</u> J[ohn] Wheatman. <u>Leah</u> Bessie Byrne; <u>Sarah</u> Cahill; <u>Madalena</u> Annie Hill; C[oralie] Owen; Lilian Everard; Binder. *REV: St 14/ 5/91 p12.*

91.130 *CONFUSION* (FC,3a) Joseph Derrick. VAUDEVILLE 8/5/91, 13/5, 15/5, 18/5, 20/5, 28/5/91 [6 mat perf]; 1/6/91-13/6/91 [14 perf; w/mat 6/6, 13/6, 20/6]. Total: 21 perf. 1st perfd Vaudeville 17/5/83. <u>Christopher Blizzard</u> Thomas Thorne; <u>Mortimer Mumpleford</u> H.B. Conway; <u>Rupert Sunbury</u> Oswald Yorke; <u>Dr Jones</u> F[red] Grove; <u>Muzzle</u> J[ohn] Wheatman; <u>James</u> Fred Thorne. <u>Rose</u> Ella Banister; <u>Violet</u> Annie Hill; <u>Maria</u> Kate Lee; <u>Lucreta</u> Sophie Larkin. L & MGR Thomas Thorne; <u>Act mgr</u> Sydney Alport; <u>Sm</u> Fred Thorne; <u>Mus dir</u> [Charles] Dubois. *REV: E 9/5/91 p9; St 14/5/91 p12; Th 1/6/91 p305.* <u>Comment</u>: Cast from V & A programme for 1/6/91.

91.131 *CHATTERTON.* OLYMPIC 9/5/91. 1 perf.** <u>Chatterton</u> Wilson Barrett; <u>Nat Boaden</u> George Barrett.

Lady Mary Lily Hanbury; Cecilia Lillie Belmore; Mrs
Angel Alice Cooke. *REV: E 16/5/91 p7; St 14/5/91 p13.*

91.132 *THE MISER* (Fantasy,1a) Dr S. Weir Mitchell.
OLYMPIC 9/5/91. 1 perf.* Miser Wilson Barrett; Death
Austin Melford; Satan H. Cooper Cliffe, Woman Lillie
Belmore. *REV: As for 91.131.*

91.133 *THE COLOUR-SERGEANT* (P,1a) Brandon Thomas.
OLYMPIC 9/5/91. 1 perf.** William Honor W.A. Elli-
ott; Harry Edward Irwin. *REV: As for 91.131.* Comment:
Possibly as revival of 91.3 (q.v.).

91.134 *THE LADY FROM THE SEA* (D,5a) Henrik Ibsen
[trans Eleanor Marx Aveling]. TERRY'S 11/5/91-15/5/
91. 5 mat perf.* Dr Wangel Oscar Adye; Arnholm
Leonard Outram; Lyngstrand Herbert Sparling; Balle
sted Ernest H. Patterson; Stranger Charles Dalton.
Ellida Wangel Rose Mellor; Bolette Violet Armbruster;
Hilde Edith Kenward. PP & MGR Edward Terry; Act mgr
H.T. Brickwell; Sm George Belmore; Mus dir J. Bay-
liss; Dir "Alec Nelson" [E.B. Aveling]; Bm C. St.
John Denton. *REV: Ath 16/5/91 p647-8; E 16/5/91 p11;
SR 16/5/91 p591; St 14/5/91 p12-3; Th 1/6/91 p306-7;
Ti 12/5/91 p12.*

91.135 *DELICATE GROUND* (CD,1a) Charles Dance. CRI-
TERION 12/5/91 mat perf.** Citizen Sangfroid Charles
Wyndham; Alphonse de Grandier George Giddens. Pauline
Mary Moore. *REV: St 14/5/91 p13.*

91.136 *ON LEASE* (Oa) Cotsford Dick. CRITERION 12/5/91
mat perf.* Sir Charles La Rose C.P. Colnaghi; Col.
Fitz Bluster Walkes; Registrar Cotsford Dick. Lady
La Rose Mrs Godfrey Pearse. *REV: St 14/5/91 p13.*

91.137 *THE CORSICAN BROTHERS* (D,3a) Dion Boucicault
[fr Dumas, *Les Frères Corses*]. LYCEUM 12/5/91-17/7/
91. 57 perf [w/mat 16/5, 23/5, 30/5, 6/6; mat only
20/6, 11/7; np 24/6, 27/6, 1/7, 4/7, 8/7].** Louis
de Franchi/Fabien de Franchi Henry Irving; M de Chateau William Terriss; Orlando [Thomas E.] Wenman;
Colonna S[am] Johnson; Giordano Martelli [Frank]
Tyars; Boisses [T.] Reynolds; Tomaso [R.P.] Tabb;

Baron de Montgiron [F.H.] Macklin; Alfred Meynard
[William] Haviland; Antonio Sanola John Martin Harvey;
Griffo [John] Archer; Verner Lacy; Beauchamp Gordon
Craig; Surgeon Gurney. Emilie de l'Esparre Annie
Irish; Coralie Kate Phillips; Marie N. de Silva; Rose
Clive; Mme de Franchi Mrs Pauncefort; Estelle Amy
Coleridge; Celestine Foster; Eugenie [E.?] Oldcastle.
L & MGR Henry Irving; Sc Hawes Craven, Joseph Harker;
Ch Espinosa; Bom Joseph Hurst; Cost Auguste, Mrs
Nettleship, Mrs Reid; Mach Fillery; Furn Arnott; Sm
H.J. Loveday; Mus dir J. Meredith Ball; Act mgr Bram
Stoker. *REV: Ath 16/5/91 p648; E 16/5/91 p9; SR*
16/5/91 p591-2, 23/5/91 p624; St 14/5/91 p12; Th 1/
6/91 p307-9; Ti 13/5/91 p5.

91.138 *NANCE OLDFIELD* (C,1a) Charles Reade. LYCEUM
12/5/91-1/6/91; 20/6/91-18/7/91; 24/7/91. 42 perf
[w/mat 16/5, 23/5, 30/5; mat only 20/6, 11/7, 18/7;
np 24/6, 27/6, 1/7, 4/7, 8/7]. 1st perfd Olympic
24/2/83. Nathan Oldfield [Thomas E.] Wenman; Alexander
Oldworthy Gordon Craig. Mrs Oldfield Ellen Terry;
Susan Oldfield Kate Phillips. L & MGR, Bom, Sm, Mus
dir, Act mgr as for 91.137. *REV: Ath, E, St, Ti as*
for 91.137; SR 16/5/91 p592; Th 1/6/91 p309.

91.139 *PAUL PRY* (C,3a) John Poole. TOOLE'S 14/5/91-
29/5/91. 15 perf [w/mat 23/5].** Paul Pry J.L. Toole;
Col. Hardy John Billington; Whitherton H[enry] J.
Carvill; Old Stanley Frank J. Arlton; Harry Stanley
C.M. Lowne; Frank Hardy Henry Westland; Willis Will-
iams; Grasp George Shelton; Simon Charles Brunton.
Mrs Subtle Effie Liston; Eliza Irene Vanbrugh; Phoebe
Eliza Johnstone; Marian Polly Brough. L & MGR J.L.
Toole; Bom G.C. Oliver; Sm John Billington; Bm
George Lee; Mus dir William Robins. *REV: E 16/5/91*
p9; SR 23/5/91 p624-5.

91.140 *A BROKEN SIXPENCE* (Ca,1a) Mrs G. Thompson &
Kate Sinclair. TOOLE'S 14/5/91-27/5/91. 13 perf [w/
mat 23/5].** John Grant H[enry] J. Carvill; Dick
Hammond C.M. Lowne. Molly Severs Effie Liston; Kitty
Severs Irene Vanbrugh; Jane Mary Brough. L & MGR,
Bom, Sm, Bm, Mus dir as for 91.139.

91.141 *THE BIRTHPLACE OF PODGERS* (F,1a) John Hollingshead. TOOLE'S 14/5/91-29/5/91; 24/6/91. 16 perf
[w/mat 23/5].** <u>Tom Cranky</u> J.L. Toole; <u>Old Maresnest</u>
George Shelton; <u>Edmund Earlybird</u> Henry Westland;
<u>Allonzo Lexicon</u> C.M. Lowne; <u>1st Photographer</u> H[enry]
J. Carvill; <u>2nd Photographer</u> Frank J. Arlton; <u>Old
Podgers</u> Williams. <u>Mrs Cranky</u> Eliza Johnstone; <u>Pene-
lope Lexicon</u> Polly Brough; <u>Amelia</u> Irene Vanbrugh.
<u>L & MGR</u>, <u>Bom</u>, <u>Sm</u>, <u>Bm</u>, <u>Mus dir</u> as for 91.139. *REV: E
16/5/91 p9.*

91.142 *UNCLE TOM'S CABIN* (D,4a). [Fnd on Mrs Harriet
Beecher Stowe's novel]. NOVELTY 16/5/91-29/5/91. 21
perf. <u>Phineas Fletcher</u> J.G. Wilton; <u>Shelby/Wilson</u>
George Clanville; <u>Augustus St. Clair</u> W. Garrett;
<u>George Harris</u> Edwin Fergusson; <u>Dan Haley</u> H. Buckstone
Clair; <u>Simon Legree</u> Gilbert Vernon; <u>Marks</u> Owen Wynne;
<u>Uncle Tom</u> R.B. Lewis; <u>Tom Locker</u> Clinton Baddeley.
<u>Little Harry</u> Swan; <u>Aunt Ophelia</u> Mrs J.F. Brian; <u>Mrs
Shelby</u> Rose Crawford; <u>Marie St. Clair</u> Jackson; <u>Em-
meline</u> Alice Belmont; <u>Carry</u> Nolan; <u>Eliza Harris/Cassy</u>
Eleanor Lloyd; <u>Aunt Chloe</u> Eally Brown; <u>Topsy</u> Marie
Brian; <u>Little Eva</u> Lena Lewis. *REV: E 23/5/91 p7.*

91.143 *THE SILVER KING* (D,5a) H.A. Jones & Henry Herman. OLYMPIC 16/5/91-23/5/91. 8 perf [w/mat 13/5].**
[<u>Wilfred Denver</u>] Wilson Barrett; [<u>Elijah Coombe</u>] Austin
Melford; [<u>Cpt. Herbert Skinner</u>] H. Cooper Cliffe;
[<u>Cripps</u>] W.A. Elliott; [<u>Henry Corkett</u>] Ambrose Manning; [<u>Samuel Baxter</u>] Stafford Smith; [<u>Gaffer Pottle</u>]
Horace Hodges; [<u>Jaikes</u>] George Barrett. [<u>Olive Skin-
ner</u>] Maud C. Jeffries; [<u>Tabitha Durden</u>] Alice Cooke;
Louie Bassett Wilmot; Lily Hanbury. <u>MGR</u> Wilson Barrett.
REV: Ath 23/5/91 p678. <u>Comment</u>: Probably a revival of
91.2 (q.v.).

91.144 *HANDFAST* (CD,3a) Henry Hamilton & Mark Quinton.
SHAFTESBURY 16/5/91-1/7/91. 42 perf [w/mat 23/5,
30/5]. 1st perfd Prince of Wales's 13/12/87. <u>Earl of
Cirencester</u> Lewis Waller; <u>Comte de Preville</u> William
Herbert; <u>Lambert d'Arcy</u> W.L. Abingdon; <u>Mr Barnard</u>
John Beauchamp; <u>Marmaduke Marsh</u> H. Reeves-Smith;
<u>Vicomte de Jarnac</u> Herman de Lange; <u>Dr Stubley</u> John
Gibson; <u>Austin Woodville</u> Cyril Maude. <u>Mme de Ligniac</u>

Winifred Emery; <u>Mrs Trefusis</u> Carlotta Leclercq; <u>Irene Kingston</u> Annie Hughes; <u>Servant</u> [Mary] Bessle. MGR Cuthbert Rathbone; <u>Gen mgr</u> Sydney Herberte Basing; <u>Act mgr</u> W.H. Griffiths; <u>Sc</u> Walter Hann, Harry Potts, Jetley; <u>Sc dgn</u> Edward Banks; <u>Mus</u> Walter Slaughter; <u>Mus dir</u> Arthur E. Godfrey; <u>Asm</u> Walter Barnard; <u>Bom</u> [F.] Forbes; <u>PP</u> John Lancaster. *REV: Ath 23/5/91 p678; E 23/5/91 p7; SR 30/5/91 p654; St 21/5/91 p10; Th 1/6/91 p310-1; Ti 18/5/91 p8.*

91.145 *WILD OATS* (C,3a) John O'Keeffe. CRITERION 18/5/91-13/6/91. 26 perf [w/mat 23/5, 30/5]. 1st perfd Covent Garden 16/4/1791. <u>Rover</u> Charles Wyndham; <u>John Dory</u> David James; <u>Sir George Thunder</u> Edward Righton; <u>Harry Thunder</u> W.E. Gregory; <u>Ephraim Smooth</u> William Blakeley; <u>Sim</u> George Giddens; <u>Banks</u> F[rank] Atherley; <u>Farmer Gammon</u> Sydney Valentine; <u>Lamp</u> S[tanley] Hewson; <u>Twitch</u> F. Emery; <u>Landlord</u> J. Francis; <u>Trap</u> W. Dale; <u>Ruffians</u> Jones, Terric. <u>Ameila</u> Mrs J.C. Smith; <u>Jane</u> Ellaline Terriss; <u>Lady Amaranth</u> Mary Moore; <u>Milkmaid</u> M[aria?] Saker; <u>Rachel</u> M. Howard. MGR Charles Wyndham; <u>Sc</u> Bruce Smith; <u>Mus dir</u> Theodore Ward; <u>Act mgr</u> E. Harvey. *REV: Ath 23/5/91 p678; E 23/5/91 p7; SR 23/5/91 p624; St 21/5/91 p10.*

91.146 *MANON* (O[5a]) Jules Massenet. COVENT GARDEN 19/5/91, 22/5, 26/5, 8/6/91. 4 perf. 1st perfd Opéra Comique, Paris 19/1/84. <u>Lescaut</u> Eugene Dufriche; <u>Le Comte des Grieux</u> Jacques Isnardon; <u>Guillot</u> Juteau; <u>De Bretigny</u> Ceste; <u>Le Chevalier des Grieux</u> Ernest van Dyck. <u>Manon Lescaut</u> Sybil Sanderson; <u>Poussette</u> Regina Pinkert; <u>Javotte</u> Olimpia Guercia; <u>Rosette</u> Agnes Janson. MGR Augustus Harris; <u>Cond</u> Luigi Mancinelli. *REV: Ath 23/5/91 p677; E 23/5/91 p13; SR 23/5/91 p 623, 6/6/91 p684; St 21/5/91 p9-10; Ti 20/5/91 p7, 25/5/91 p13.*

91.147 *LES HUGUENOTS* (O[5a]) Giacomo Meyerbeer. COVEN[T] GARDEN 20/5/91, 27/5, 4/6, 9/6, 20/6, 29/6, 11/7, 20/ 7/91. 8 perf.** <u>Conte di San Bris</u> Jean Lassalle; <u>Conte di Nevers</u> Victor Maurel; <u>Marcello</u> Edouard de Reske; <u>Raoul di Nangis</u> Jean de Reske/Luigi Ravelli; <u>Huguenot Soldier</u> Iginio Corsi; <u>Maurevert</u> Antonio de Vaschetti; <u>Tavannes</u> Bieletto; <u>De Cosse</u> Rinaldini; <u>De</u>

Retz Miranda. Valentina Emma Albani; Margherita di
Valois Eugenia Mravina; Urbano Giulia Ravoli; Dama
d'Onore Mathilde Bauermeister; lere Danseuse Palladino. MGR Augustus Harris; Cond Enrico Bevignani.
*REV: Ath 23/5/91 p677-8; E 23/5/91 p13; SR 23/5/91
p623, 30/5/91 p654; St 28/5/91 p12; Ti 25/5/91 p13.*

91.148 *CASTE* (C,3a) T.W. Robertson. TERRY'S 21/5/91
mat perf. 1st perfd Prince of Wales's 6/4/67. Eccles
Edward Righton; George d'Alroy Philip Cunningham;
Sam Gerridge Harding Cox; Cpt. Hawtrey J.W. Pigott.
Marquise de St. Maur Fanny Coleman; Esther Eccles
Violet Raye; Polly Olga Garland. *REV: E 23/5/91 p9;
St 28/5/91 p12-3.*

91.149 *SWEEPSTAKES* (MC) Ernest Lake. TERRY'S 21/5/91
mat perf.* Bertie Grant Richie Ling; Courtnay Holmes
Kingston. Chrissie Melton Mrs Harding Cox. *REV: As for
91.148.*

91.150 *DIE MEISTERSINGER* (O[3a]) Richard Wagner. COV-
ENT GARDEN 23/5/91, 29/5/91. 2 perf.** Walther de
Stolzing Jean de Reske; Hans Sachs Jean Lassalle;
David Sebastian Montariol; Veit Pogner Abramoff;
Sixus Beckmesser Jacques Isnardon; Fritz Kothner Eu-
gene Dufriche; Kunz Vogelsang Iginio Corsi; Hermann
Ortel Antonio de Vaschetti; Balthazar Zorn Rinaldini;
Hans Schwars Miranda; Konrad Nachtigal Camillo Fiegna;
Ulrich Eisslinger Bieletto; Hans Foltz Cernusco;
Augustin Moser Uberti. Magdalena Mathilde Bauermeister;
Eva Emma Albani. MGR Augustus Harris; Cond Luigi Man-
cinelli. *REV: Ath 30/5/91 p708-9; E 30/5/91 p13; SR
30/5/91 p650-1; St 28/5/91 p12; Ti 25/5/91 p13.*

91.151 *MIGNON* (O,3a) Ambroise Thomas. ROYALTY 23/5/91.
1 perf.** Wilhelm William Green; Laertes D. Pughe
Evans; Lothario Smallwood Metcalfe; Giarno Frank
Fisher; Zaffari C[harles] Edwards; Antonio E. Hart.
Filina Magaret Eden; Frederick Marie Garcia; Mignon
Florence Eason. L Kate Santley; Dir Gustave Garcia;
Cond Henry J. Wood; Ch B. Soutten; Assistant J. Mill-
ard; Assistant Master in Acting E[dgar] B. Skeet; Cost
May; Pq William Clarkson; Furn Oetzmann. *REV: E 30/5/
91 p7; St 28/5/91 p12; Ti 25/5/91 p6.*

91.152 *THE NETTLE* (Ca,1a) Ernest Warren. ROYALTY 23/5/
91. 1 perf. 1st perfd Court 13/10/86. Guy Charlton
Edgar B. Skeet. Dulcie Meredith Emily Arnold. L Kate
Santley.

91.153 *STAGE STRUCK* (F,1a) William Dimond. GAIETY 25/
5/91 mat perf.** Sir Matthew Scraggs F[red] Emney;
Count Glorieux George T. Minshull; Tom Tape Arthur
Williams. Lady Scraggs Maria Jones; Poplin Linda
Verner; Sally Scraggs Clara Jecks. L & MGR George Ed-
wardes; Cond W. Meyer Lutz, Norfolk Megone; Sm Frank
Parker; Pq C.H. Fox; Cost J. Harrison. *REV: E 30/5/91
p8; St 28/5/91 p13.*

91.154 *ROBERT MACAIRE* (Bsq,1a) Henry J. Byron. GAIETY
25/5/91 mat perf. 1st perfd Globe 16/4/70. Germieul
Henry Nelson; Dumont Mark Kinghorne; Robert McCaire
E.J. Lonnen; Jacques Strop Lonnen Meadows; Charles
Walter Gray; Pierre C[harles] Goold; Sgt. Loupy C.M.
Lowne; Louis McNamara. Marie Harriett Clifton; Cle-
mentine Florence Harwood; Dancers Wilmot, Adelaide
Astor, L. & A. Davies, Alice Lethbridge. L & MGR,
Cond, Sm, Pq, Cost as for 91.153; Ch John d'Auban.
REV: As for 91.153.

91.155 *HUBBY* (FC,2tab) H.A. Sherburn. SHAFTESBURY 25/
5/91-1/7/91. 33 perf. 1st perfd Lyric Hall, Ealing,
22/4/84. Mjr. O'Braggerty Fred Mervin; Mr Hopscotch
Walter Everard; Bobbins Fawdon Vokes. Mrs O'Braggerty
Victoria Vokes; Mrs Hopscotch Lillian Hingston; Mrs
Cattermole Annie Fawdon. MGR Cuthbert Rathbone; Gen
mgr Sydney Herberte Basing; Act mgr W.H. Griffiths;
Bom F. Forbes; PP John Lancaster. *REV: E 30/5/91 p7;
St 28/5/91 p12; Th 1/7/91 p28; Ti 26/5/91 p10.*

91.156 *FORMOSA* (D,3a) Dion Boucicault. DRURY LANE 26/
5/91-20/6/91. 23 perf. 1st perfd Drury Lane 5/8/69.
Tom Burroughs Charles Glenney; Compton Kerr Mark
Quinton; Mjr. Jorum Austin Melford; Dr Doremous Walter
Russell; Sam Boker Julian Cross; Spooner Cecil Crof-
ton; Byfield Ronald Power; Bob Saunders Harry Nich-
olls; Bancroft H. Martin; Sadler F. Bolton; Cutts R.
Kemble; Hervey H. Lillford; Merivale Drelincourt;
Lord Talbot Faulkner; Burbage J. [L.] Stoner; Dudley

Clifford Leigh; <u>Policeman</u> [Frank] MacVicars; <u>Murray</u>
Frank Damser; <u>Cobb</u> Thomas Terriss; <u>Welch</u> James Dar-
ington. <u>Jenny Boker</u> Jessie Millward; <u>Mrs Boker</u> Mrs
John Billington; <u>Nelly Saunders</u> Mary Ansell; <u>Lord</u>
<u>Eden</u> Katie James; <u>Mrs Lestelle</u> Conroy; <u>Mrs Dudley</u>
Alice Kingsley; <u>Sybil Fletcher</u> Bartlett; <u>Maud Lester</u>
Alice Selby; <u>Mabel Grace</u> L[ily] Brooking; <u>Countess</u>
Winter; <u>Constance Beresford</u> [Constance] Wallace; <u>Edith</u>
<u>Burroughs</u> [Mina?] Le Bert. <u>L & MGR</u> Augustus Harris;
<u>Dir</u> Augustus Harris; <u>Sc</u> [Robert] Caney, [Richard C.]
Durant, William Perkins; <u>Cond</u> P. Bucalossi; <u>Sec &</u>
<u>Treas</u> F[red] G. Latham; <u>Sm</u> Arthur P. Collins. *REV:*
Ath 30/5/91 p710; E 30/5/91 p7; SR 30/5/91 p654; St
28/5/91 p12; Th 1/7/91 p27-8; Ti 28/5/91 p14.

91.157 *MISS TOMBOY* (C,3a) Robert Buchanan [fnd on John
Vanbrugh, *The Relapse*]. VAUDEVILLE 26/5/91(m); 15/6/
91-19/6/91. 6 perf.** <u>Lord Foppington</u> Thomas Thorne;
<u>Tom Fashion</u> H.B. Conway; <u>Sir George Matcham</u> J[ohn]
Wheatman; <u>Sir Tunbelly Clumsy</u> Fred Thorne; <u>Squire</u>
<u>Ditch</u> [A.] Austin; <u>Lavarole</u> Oswald Yorke; <u>Lory</u> Law-
rance d'Orsay; <u>Jabez</u> [Cecil] Ramsey; <u>Jacob</u> Terric;
<u>Rev Mr Quiverwit</u> F[red] Grove; <u>Mendlegs</u> J. Crichton;
<u>Glitter</u> [S.] Freeman; <u>Hyde</u> Lewis; <u>Coates</u> S. Lawrence;
<u>Tierce</u> T. Walters. <u>Fanny Hoyden</u> Ella Bannister; <u>Mrs</u>
<u>Sentry</u> C[oralie] Owen; <u>Nancy Ditch</u> Hilda Hanbury;
<u>Dolly Primrose</u> Annie Hill. *REV: E 30/5/91 p8; SR 30/*
5/91 p654; St 28/5/91 p13, 18/6/91 p10; Ti 28/5/91
p14.

91.158 *A WINNING DEFEAT* (D,4a) Duncan Campbell & Mar-
cus Quare. NOVELTY 30/5/91-5/6/91. 6 perf.* <u>Geoffrey</u>
<u>Rolliston</u> H. Buckstone Clair; <u>Frank Rolliston</u> Edwin
Fergusson; <u>Talbot Rolliston</u> Gilbert Vernon; <u>Dr Shine</u>
W. Garrett; <u>Stephen Clewson</u> T. Norton; <u>Sam Baxter</u>
George Clanville; <u>Jim Warble</u> J.G. Wilton; <u>Joe Grimble</u>
Owen Wynne; <u>Ned Jones</u> George Edgerton; <u>1st Lad</u> [G.]
Sewell; <u>Landlord</u> Laurence. <u>Alice Beaumont</u> Marie Brian;
<u>Miss Rolliston</u> Eleanor Lloyd; <u>Laura</u> Evelyn Nelson;
<u>Mrs Grimble</u> Mrs J.F. Brian. *REV: E 6/6/91 p7; St 4/6/*
91 p10.

91.159 *CHAWLES; OR, A FOOL AND HIS MONEY* (C,3a) Henry
J. Byron. TOOLE'S 30/5/91-5/6/91. 7 perf [w/mat 30/5].**

Brabazon Vandaleur H[enry] Westland; Mr Pentland
G[eorge] Shelton; Chawles J.L. Toole; Percival Ransome
C.M. Lowne; Mulligan Frank J. Arlton. Kate Vandaleur
Irene Vanbrugh; Mary Draper Eliza Johnstone; Mrs Rum-
sey Effie Liston; Jane Mary Brough. L & MGR J.L.
Toole; Sm John Billington; Bm George Lee. *REV: E 6/6/*
91 p8.

91.160 *IBSEN'S GHOST; OR, TOOLE UP TO DATE* (Bsq,1a)
J.M. Barrie. TOOLE'S 30/5/91-27/6/91. 27 perf [w/mat
30/5, 13/6, 20/6; np 6/6].* George Tesman (an Idiot)
George Shelton; Peter Terence (Thea's Grand Papa)
J.L. Toole. Thea Tesman (George's wife for the Pres-
ent) Irene Vanbrugh; Delia Terence (Peter's Doll)
Eliza Johnstone. L & MGR, Sm, Bm as for 91.159; Pq
C.H. Fox. *REV: E 6/6/91 p8; SR 6/6/91 p682-3; St*
4/6/91 p10; Th 1/7/91 p28-30; Ti 1/6/91 p4.

91.161 *A REGULAR FIX* (F,1a) John Maddison Morton. LY-
CEUM 1/6/91-20/6/91. 19 perf [w/mat 6/6]. 1st perfd
Olympic 11/10/60. Hugh de Drass William Terriss;
Surplus Alfred Bishop; Charles Surplus John Martin
Harvey; Abel Quick Gordon Craig; Smiler [John] Archer;
Porter [T.] Reynolds. Emily A[my] Coleridge; Mrs
Deborah Carter Roma Guillon Le Thiere; Matilda Jane
Kate Phillips. L & MGR Henry Irving; Bom Joseph Hurst;
Sm H.J. Loveday; Mus dir J. Meredith Ball; Act mgr
Bram Stoker.

91.162 *THE LOVE CHASE* (C,3a) James Sheridan Knowles.
SHAFTESBURY 1/6/91-5/6/91. 5 mat perf. 1st perfd
Haymarket 9/10/37. Master Wildrake E.H. Vanderfelt;
Sir William Fondlove George Warde; Master Trueworth
William Calvert; Master Waller Henry Arncliffe; Master
Neville A[rthur] Grenville; Stephen Sam T. Pearce;
Master Humphrey Philip Vincent; Lash Fenton Boyd.
Constance Fortesque; Lydia Helen Ferrers; Amelia S. de
Groot; Widow Green Kate Hodson. MGR Cuthbert Rathbone;
Gen mgr Sydney Herberte Basing; Bom F. Forbes; Act
mgr W.H. Griffiths; Pp John Lancaster. *REV: Ath 6/6/*
91 p742; E 6/6/91 p9; SR 6/6/91 p683; St 4/6/91 p10;
Th 1/7/91 p32; Ti 2/6/91 p10.

91.163 *A NIGHT'S FROLIC* (FC,3a) Gus Thomas & Helen

Barry [adpt fr Gustav von Moser]. STRAND 1/6/91-20/
6/91. 21 perf [w/S mat].* Commodore Stanton Willie
Edouin; Oakley Sedley Percy F. Marshall; Cpt. Alfred
Chandon Charles S. Fawcett; Claude d'Elmont Sydney
Barraclough; Phil Sawyer William Lugg. Mrs Sophie
Sedley Florence West; Nellie Stanton Georgie Esmond;
Sarah Venie Bennett; Lady Betty Vane Alice Atherton.
PP J.S. Clarke; L Willie Edouin; Bom H[enry] L. Boss;
Sm J.A.E. Malone; Cond Ernest Bucalossi; Bm George
Bryer. *REV: E 6/6/91 p7; SR 6/6/91 p683; St 4/6/91
p10; Th 1/7/91 p30-2; Ti 2/6/91 p10.*

91.164 *DAGGER'S DRAWN* (Ca,1a) Pryce Seaton. STRAND
1/6/91-20/6/91. 18 perf.** Sir George Grantley Will-
iam Lugg; Cpt. Jack Grantley Sydney Barraclough; Tom
Trip Robert Nainby. Mrs Gerald Deering Ruth Rutland;
Alice Deering Georgie Esmond; Ford Lillian Milward.
PP, L, Bom, Sm, Cond, Bm as for 91.163.

91.165 *PERFECTION* (C,1a). VAUDEVILLE 1/6/91-19/6/91.
17 perf. Sir Lawrence Paragon Oswald Yorke; Charles
Paragon Lawrence d'Orsay; Sam Fred Thorne. Kate
O'Brien Dorothy Dorr; Susan Annie Hill. L & MGR Thomas
Thorne; Act mgr Sydney Alport; Sm Fred Thorne; Mus
dir Charles Dubois. *REV: SR 6/6/91 p683; St 4/6/91
p10.*

91.166 *THE GIFTED LADY* (SocialD,3a) Robert Buchanan.
AVENUE 2/6/91-5/6/91; 9/6/91. 5 perf.* Algernon Worm-
wood Harry Paulton; Vitus Danse W[illiam] Lestocq;
Vergris Ivan Watson; Biler R[ichard] H. Douglass; Dr
Plainchat Sidney Howard; Charles Dangleton W.H. Ver-
non; Cabman G[eorge] Arnold. Felicia Strangeways
Cicely Richards; Amelia Lydia Cowell; Bodalia Dangle-
ton Fanny Brough. L & MGR Henry Lee; Mus dir Thomas
Batty; Sm W[illiam] Sidney; Bm Arthur Yates. *REV:
E 6/6/91 p7; St 4/6/91 p9-10; Th 1/7/91 p33; Ti 4/6/
91 p13.* Comment: Originally entitled *Heredity.*

91.167 *THE VIPER ON THE HEARTH* (D,1a) J.M. Campbell.
AVENUE 2/6/91-5/6/91; 9/6/91. 5 perf. 1st perfd
Criterion 15/5/88. John Baxendale John L. Shine; John
Lydyard W[illiam] Lestocq; George Heriot Ivan Watson.
Hesketh Price Cicely Richards; Ethel Lydyard Eleanor

May. L & MGR, Mus dir, Sm, Bm as for 91.166; Pq C.H.
Fox. *REV: E 6/6/91 p7; St 4/6/91 p10.*

91.168 *A DOLL'S HOUSE* (P,3a) Henrik Ibsen [trans
William Archer]. CRITERION 2/6/91 mat perf.** Dr
Rank W.L. Abingdon; Nils Krogstad Charles J. Fulton;
Ivar Eric Field-Fisher; Thorval Helmer Frank Rodney;
Porter Brooke. Mrs Linden Lucia Harwood; Anna Mrs E.
H. Brooke; Emmie Caryl Field-Fisher; Nora Rose
Norreys; Servant Brooke. L & MGR Charles Wyndham; Bm
Arthur Blackmore; Ch John d'Auban; Dir Emilie Leices-
ter; Mus dir Theodore Ward. *REV: E 6/6/91 p10; SR
6/6/91 p683; St 4/6/91 p10; Th 1/7/91 p33-4; Ti 4/6/
91 p13.*

91.169 *IN WANT OF AN ENGAGEMENT* (MSk) Nellie Ganthony.
VAUDEVILLE 3/6/91 mat perf.* Nellie Ganthony. *REV:
St 4/6/91 p10.*

91.170 *ROSENCRANTZ AND GUILDENSTERN* (Bsq,3tab) W.S.
Gilbert. VAUDEVILLE 3/6/91 mat perf.* Hamlet Frank
Lindo; Guildenstern C. Lambourne; Rosencrantz Sidney
Herberte Basing; Claudius Alexander Watson; 1st Play-
er C. Stewart. Gertrude Mrs Theodore Wright; Ophelia
Mary Bessle. MGR Thomas Thorne; Dir W.S. Gilbert.
*REV: Ath 6/6/91 p742; E 6/6/91 p9; SR 6/6/91 p683;
St 4/6/91 p10; Th 1/7/91 p34-5; Ti 4/6/91 p12.*
Comment: Gilbert letter on the play in *Daily Tele-
graph 18/5/91 p3.*

91.171 *SHATTERED UN* BsqSk) Albert Chevalier. VAUDE-
VILLE 3/6/91 mat perf.* Shattered 'Un Frank Lindo;
Bold'un Charles F. Barrett. Mary Edith Kenward. MGR
Thomas Thorne; Sm George Barrett. *REV: E, SR, St,
Th, Ti as for 91.170.*

91.172 *GOOD OLD QUEEN BESS* (Bsq,1a) Walpole Lewin.
VAUDEVILLE 3/6/9] mat perf.* Queen Bess Charles H.
Kenny; Lord Burleigh J.W. Handley; Julius the Jester
Frank Smithson. Don Spainindo Oniano Emily Spiller;
Lady Maude Minnie Thurgate; Earl of Leicester Julia
Egley; Earl of Essex Winnie Elliot; Lady Jane Amy
Farrell; Sir Walter Raleigh Lydia Lisle. MGR Thomas
Thorne; Mus William Robins; Cost Harrison; Pq William

Clarkson. *REV: E, SR, St, Th as for 91.170.*

91.173 *A TRIP TO GRETNA* (Ca,2a) W. Barrington d'Al-
meida. VAUDEVILLE 3/6/91 mat perf.* John Smith J.T.
MacMillan; Richard Travers Charles Bedells; Tom Spud
Robson Paige; Col. Beauchamps P.C. Beverley; Charles
Beauchamps Roydon Erlynne; Sgt. Arthur St. George.
Kate Beauchamps Mrs Bennett; Belinda Dare Cissy Far-
rell. MGR Thomas Thorne. *REV: E, SR, St, Th as for*
91.170.

91.174 *SERGE PANINE* (P,5a) J.H. Thorp [fr Georges
Ohnet, *Serge Panine*]. AVENUE 4/6/91 mat perf.*
Prince Serge Panine Lewis Waller; Pierre de la Rue
[E.] Webster Lawson; Henry Desvarrennes Compton
Coutts; Herzog F. Hamilton Knight; Marechal H[enry]
Dana; Jules [Willie] Drew; Cayrol W.H. Vernon. Mme
Desvarrennes Genevieve Ward; Michelene Webster;
Cecile Baines; Jeanne Estelle Burney. MGR Henry Lee;
Act mgr Arthur Yates; Dir W.H. Vernon. *REV: E 6/6/91*
p9; SR 13/6/91 p711; St 11/6/91 p10; Th 1/7/91 p35-6;
Ti 5/6/91 p8.

91.175 *THE LADIES' BATTLE* (C,3a) Charles Reade [fr
Eugene Scribe & Ernest Legouvé, *La Bataille des Dames*].
OPERA COMIQUE 5/6/91 mat perf. 1st perfd Olympic 7/5/
51. Gustave de Grignon A[dolphus] Vane-Tempest;
Henri de Flavigneul H. Lechmere Stuart; Brigadier
E.M. Wood; Servant Hill; Baron de Montrichard [Char-
les] Sugden. Countess d'Autreval Henrietta Lindley;
Leonie de la Villegoutier [Jennie] McNulty. L George
Edwardes; Cost L. & H. Nathan; Pq Willian Clarkson,
C.H. Fox; Cond F. Stanislaus; Sm G[eorge] Capel; Mgr
G.F. Bashford. *REV: St 11/6/91 p10.*

91.176 *THE HIGHWAYMAN* (Ca) Justin Huntly McCarthy.
OPERA COMIQUE 5/6/91 mat perf.* Sir Harry Bellairs
C.P. Colnaghi. Lady Betty Bassett Letty Lind. L, Cost,
Pq, Cond, Sm, Mgr as for 91.175. *REV: SR 13/6/91 p711;*
St 11/6/91 p10.

91.177 *EAST LYNNE.* NOVELTY 6/6/91-26/6/91. 18 perf.
Comment: Mentioned in *The Referee.*

91.178 *HIGH LIFE BELOW STAIRS* ([F,2a]) Rev James Townley. NOVELTY 6/6/91-26/6/91. 18 perf. 1st perfd Drury
Lane 31/10/1759. Comment: As for 91.177.

91.179 *THE LANCASHIRE SAILOR* (CD,1a) Brandon Thomas.
TERRY'S 6/6/91-31/7/91;* trfd to SHAFTESBURY 3/8/91-
17/10/91; trfd to TOOLE'S 19/10/91-28/11/91. 152 perf
[w/mat 11/7, 21/11, 28/11; np 4/7]. Ralph Ormerod
W.L. Branscombe; Alfred Brandon Thomas;Erasmus Eller-
by Compton Coutts. Alice Ormerod Edith Chester/Rose
Norreys; Martha Remnant Dolores Drummond. PP Edward
Terry; Mgr George Edwardes; Mus dir & Mus Edward Jones;
Sm J. Ettinson; Bm C.J. Abud. *REV: Ath 13/6/91 p775-6;
E 13/6/91 p7, 8/8/91 p7, 24/10/91 p9; SR 13/6/91 p714;
St 11/6/91 p9-10, 22/10/91 p12; Th 1/7/91 p36-7; Ti
8/6/91 p11.*

91.180 *A COMMISSION* (C,1a) Weedon Grossmith. TERRY'S
6/6/91-31/7/91;* trfd to SHAFTESBURY 3/8/91-17/10/91;
trfd to TOOLE'S 19/10/91-28/11/91. 152 perf [w/mat
11/7, 21/11, 28/11; np 4/7]. Marshall Forbes Dawson;
Shaw Weedon Grossmith; Gloucester Brandon Thomas. Mrs
Hemmersley Lily Hanbury/Beatrice Lamb; Parker Day
Ford. PP, Mgr, Mus dir & Mus, Sm, Bm as for 91.179.
REV: As for 91.179.

91.181 *A PANTOMIME REHEARSAL* (Bsq,1a) Cecil Clay.
TERRY'S 6/6/91-31/7/91;* trfd to SHAFTESBURY 3/8/91-
17/10/91; trfd to TOOLE'S 19/10/91-28/11/91. 152 perf
[w/mat 11/7, 21/11, 28/11; np 4/7]. Jack Deedes W.G.
Elliott; Sir Charles Grandison A. Danemore; Lord
Arthur Pomeroy Weedon Grossmith; Cpt. Tom Robinson
Brandon Thomas; Tomkins Johnson. Lady Muriel Beauclerc
Helena Dacre; Miss Lily Laura Linden; Miss Violet
Edith Chester; Miss May Ruby Tyrrell; Miss Rose
Tyrrell; Lady Sloane-Willery Day Ford. PP, Mgr, Mus
dir & Mus, Sm, Bm as for 91.179. *REV: Ath, E, SR, St,
Ti as for 91.179; Th 1/7/91 p37-8.*

91.182 *THE SERIOUS FAMILY* (C,3a) Morris Barnett [adpt
fr *Le Mari à la Campagne*]. TOOLE'S 6/6/91-27/6/91.
20 perf [w/mat 13/6, 20/6, 24/6].** Aminadab Sleek
J.L. Toole; Cpt. Murphy Maguire John Billington;
Charles Torrens C.M. Lowne; Danvers Frank J. Arlton;

Frank Vincent H[enry] J. Carvill. <u>Lady Sowerby Cream-</u>
<u>ly</u> Eliza Johnstone; <u>Mrs Charles Torrens</u> Irene Van-
brugh; <u>Mrs Ormsby Delmaine</u> Effie Liston; <u>Emma Torrens</u>
Mary Brough; <u>Graham</u> Ethel Bland. <u>L</u> & <u>MGR</u> J.L. Toole;
<u>Sm</u> John Billington; <u>Bm</u> George Lee. *REV: E 20/6/91 p8.*

91.183 *DREAM FACES* (Dramatic Fancy,1a) Wynn Miller.
GARRICK 8/6/91-26/6/91. 15 perf [mat only 24/6; np
13/6, 20/6].** <u>Robert</u> Johnston Forbes-Robertson;
<u>Philip</u> Sydney Brough; <u>Servant</u> John Byron. <u>Margaret</u>
Carlotta Addison; <u>Lucy</u> [Annie] Webster. <u>L</u> & <u>MGR</u> John
Hare; <u>Bom</u> E. Candler; <u>Act mgr</u> C.G. Compton; <u>Mus dir</u>
Schoening; <u>Asm</u> R[owley] Cathcart; <u>Sc</u> William Harford.

91.184 *LEAVE IT TO ME* (F,1a) Arthur Williams. STRAND
8/6/91 mat perf. 1st perfd Surrey 26/12/70. <u>Joe</u>
<u>Sprouts</u> Arthur Williams; George T. Minshull; Philip
Cunningham; Fred Emery. Kate James; Violet Raye.
REV: St 11/6/91 p10.

91.185 *THE SILVER LINE* (WordlessSk) C.D. Marius.STRAND
8/6/91(m); CRITERION 2/7/91(m). 2 mat perf. C.D. Marius. *REV: St 11/6/91, 9/7/91 p10.* <u>Comment</u>: Nicoll,
probably incorrectly, gives 1st perf as Gaiety 25/5/
91.

91.186 *MIREILLE* (O[5a]) Charles Gounod. COVENT GARDEN
10/6/91, 16/6, 25/6/91. 3 perf. 1st perfd Théâtre-
Lyrique, Paris 19/3/64. <u>Vincent</u> Albert Lubert; <u>Mai-</u>
<u>tre Ramon</u> Jacques Isnardon; <u>Ourrias</u> Victor Maurel.
<u>Mireille</u> Emma Eames; <u>Taven</u> Passama; <u>Le Berger</u> Regina
Pinkert; <u>Clemence</u> Mathilde Bauermeister. <u>MGR</u> Augustus
Harris; <u>Cond</u> Enrico Bevignani. *REV: Ath 13/6/91 p774-*
5; E 13/6/91 p13; St 18/6/91 p9; Ti 13/6/91 p16.

91.187 *THE MISCHIEF MAKER* (FC,3a) Edith Henderson.
GLOBE 12/6/91 mat perf.* <u>Percival Loggerhead</u> W. Scott
Buist; <u>Dr Middleton</u> Frederic Jacques; <u>Keith Denby</u>
Reginald Stockton; <u>Oliver Tapperton</u> A[lbert] E.
Drinkwater; <u>John</u> Frank Damer; <u>Bates</u> George Highland.
<u>Mrs Loggerhead</u> Mary Ansell; <u>Lucy Wentworth</u> Phyllis
Ayrian; <u>Anastasia Page</u> Sallie Booth; <u>Alice</u> Madge
Herrick; <u>Mary</u> Eva Murray. <u>L</u> Norman Forbes; <u>Dir</u> Albert
E. Drinkwater; <u>Mus dir</u> C.J. Hargitt. *REV: E 13/6/91*

p10; SR 20/6/91 p745.

91.188 *ICI ON (NE) PARLE (PAS) FRANCAIS* (WordlessF)
William Robins (mus). TOOLE'S 13/6/91-27/6/91. 15
perf [w/mat 13/6, 20/6].* Mr Spriggins J.L. Toole;
Mjr. Regulas Rattan H[enry] Westland; Victor Dubois
C.M. Lowne. Mrs Mjr. Regulas Rattan Mary Brough;
Angelina Irene Vanbrugh; Mrs Spriggins Effie Liston;
Anna Maria Eliza Johnstone. L & MGR J.L. Toole; Sm
John Billington; Bm George Lee. *REV: E 20/6/91 p8; SR
20/6/91 p745; Ti 15/6/91 p6.*

91.189 *DAVID GARRICK* (C,3a) T.W. Robertson. CRITERION
15/6/91-21/7/91. 36 perf [w/mat 20/6, 27/6, 4/7,
21/7].**   David Garrick Charles Wyndham; Simon Ingot
W[illiam] Farren; Squire Chivey George Giddens; Smith
William Blakeley; Brown Sydney Valentine; Jones
S[tanley] Hewson; William Frank Atherley; George F.
Emery. Mrs Smith M.A. Victor; Araminta Brown Emily
Miller; Ada Ingot Mary Moore. MGR Charles Wyndham;
Act mgr E. Harvey; Mus dir Theodore Ward. *REV: SR
20/6/91 p744.*

91.190 *HEADS OR TAILS?* (Ca,1a) J. Palgrave Simpson.
CRITERION 15/6/91-21/7/91. 33 perf [w/mat 20/6]. 1st
perfd Olympic 29/6/54. Wrangleworth Sydney Valentine;
Harold Dyecaster Stuart; Christopher Quaile S[tanley]
Hewson. Rosamond Ellaline Terriss; Bridget F. Frances.
MGR, Act mgr, Mus dir as for 91.189.

91.191 *MARIAGE BLANC* (D,3a) Jules Lemaitre. ROYALTY
15/6/91, 17/6/91. 2 perf. 1st perfd Comédie-française,
Paris 20/3/91. Jacques de Tievre F. Febvre; Docteur
Doliveux Laroche. Simone Reichenberg; Mme Aubert
Fayolle; Marthe Du Minil. L Kate Santley; Mgr M.L.
Mayer; Act mgr Gaston Mayer. *REV: Ath 20/6/91 p807-8;
SR 20/6/91 p741; St 18/6/91 p9-10; Ti 16/6/91 p10.*

91.192 *THE POISON FLOWER* (DSk,3a) Dr John Todhunter
[adpt of Nathaniel Hawthorne, *Rappacini's Daughter*].
VAUDEVILLE 15/6/91-19/6/91. 5 mat perf.* Giacomo
Rappacini Brandon Thomas; Giovanni Guasconti Bernard
Gould; Celio Ruffini Malcom Bell. Beatrice Rappacini
Florence Farr; Lisabetta Retus; Spirit Voice Beaton.

L & MGR Thomas Thorne; Act mgr S. Sherrington Chinn;
Mus dir Ernest Lake; Sm, Dir, & Sc A.L. Baldry; Pq
William Clarkson; Cost [Victor] Barthe, William
Clarkson; Mus B. Luard Selby. *REV: E 20/6/91 p11; SR
20/6/91 p745; St 18/6/91 p10.*

91.193 *A SICILIAN IDYLL* (Past,2sc) Dr John Todhunter.
VAUDEVILLE 15/6/91-19/6/91. 5 mat perf. 1st perfd
Club Theatre, Bedford Park 5/5/90. Alcander T.B.
Thalberg; Daphnis Cecil Crofton; Alexis Malcolm Bell;
"Prologue" Bernard Gould; Chorus Augustus Bingham,
W. Ensall, Richie Ling, Pinder, W.H. Roe. Amaryllis
Florence Farr; Thestylis Lily Linfield; Praxinoe
Constance Leveson; Chorus Retus, Alice Suter, Mabel
Lenway, Beaton, E[thel] Daymond, M. Daymond, Violet
Jones, Giddens, Brennard. L & MGR, Act mgr, Mus dir,
Sm, Dir, & Sc, Pq, Cost, Mus as for 91.192. *REV: E,
SR as for 91.192.*

91.194 *ESTHER SANDRAZ* (P,3a) Sydney Grundy [adpt of
Adolphe Belot's novel, *La Femme de Glace*]. CRITERION
16/6/91 mat perf.** Henri Vandelle Bassett Roe;
Olivier Deschamps H. Reeves-Smith; Fourcanade Willie
Drew; Boisgommeaux Herman de Lange; Justin Gordon
Harvey; Jules Newark; Joseph G. Doughty. Henriette
Eleanore Leyshon; Mme Fourcanade M.A. Victor; Clarisse
H[elen] Vicary; Berthe Darley; Blanche M. Leyshon;
Esther Sandraz Violet Thornycroft. L & MGR Charles
Wyndham; Sm Herman de Lange; Bm Willie Drew; Act mgr
E. Harvey; Mus dir Theodore Ward; Pq C.H. Fox. *REV:
E 20/6/91 p8; SR 20/6/91 p744-5; St 18/6/91 p10.*

91.195 *PEPA* (C,3a) Henri Meilhac & Louis Ganderay.
ROYALTY 16/6/91. 1 perf. 1st perfd Théâtre-français,
Paris 31/10/88. Raymond de Chambreuil F. Febvre;
Jacques de Guerche Boucher; Ramiro Vasquez Leloir;
Jean Roger; Benito [J.] Deroy. Pépa Vasquez Reichen-
berg; Mosquita Bertiny; Yvonne Chambreuil Du Minil.
MGR M.L. Mayer. *REV: St 18/6/91 p10.*

91.196 *A GOLDEN SORROW* (D,3a) Albert E. Drinkwater.
GLOBE 17/6/91 mat perf. 1st perfd Victoria Hall,
Ealing 2/2/91. Mr Bellamy C.W. Somerset; Mr Leigh W.
Scott Buist; Philip Denzil Albert E. Drinkwater; Sig-

nor Barozzi Sydney Valentine; Caesarini Ronald Bayne;
Mr Sunderland C[harles] Dodsworth; Harris Frank
Damer. Mary Bellamy Lilian Revell; Francesca Alice
Yorke; Angelina Annie Goward. L Norman Forbes; Bm
Harrington Baily. *REV: Ath 20/6/91 p808; E 20/6/91 p9;
SR 27/6/91 p774; St 18/6/91 p10.*

91.197 *SHYLOCK AND CO* (F,3a) George Canninge & Albert
Chevalier [adpt of Baitaille & Feguere, *L'Article 7*].
CRITERION 18/6/91 mat perf. 1st perfd Park, Camden
Town 5/12/90 [as *I.O.U.*]. Elijah Quarm William Blake-
ley; Dr Gossage Sydney Valentine; Prince Zannibulu
H[arry] Eversfield; Hector Rolleston Henry V. Esmond;
Sgt. Bonser A. Leigh; Burton F. Emery, Mrs Gossage
Marie Illington; Minnie Ellaline Terriss; Mrs Quarm
F. Frances; Lucy Mabel Hardinge. *REV: Ath 27/6/91
p840; E 20/6/91 p13; SR 27/6/91 p774; St 25/6/91 p10.*

91.198 *LES PETITES OISEAUX* (C,3a) Eugene Labiche &
Alfred-Charlemagne Delacour. ROYALTY 18/6/91. 1 perf.
1st perfd Vaudeville, Paris 1/4/62. Blandinet E.-A.-
H. Coquelin [*cadet*]; Francois Leloir; Roger; Villain;
Gravolet. Du Minil; Bertiny. MGR M.L. Mayer. *REV: St
25/6/91 p10.*

91.199 *LE BONHOMME JADIS* (C,1a) Henri Murger. ROYALTY
18/6/91. 1 perf. 1st perfd Français, Paris 21/4/52.
Boucher; Leloir. Reichenberg.

91.200 *AS YOU LIKE IT* (C) William Shakespeare. SHAFT-
ESBURY 18/6/91 mat perf.** Duke Leonard Outram; Fred-
erick Bassett Roe; Amiens Henry Cooper; Jaques Herbert
Pearson; Le Beau Gerald Gurney; Charles Cecil Morton
York; Oliver Stratton Rodney; Jaques Nutcombe Gould;
Orlando Frank Worthing; Adam Albert E. Drinkwater;
Touchstone Ben Greet; Corin Murray Hawthorne; Silvius
Roland Atwood; William W[illiam] Lockhart. Rosalind
Mrs Patrick Campbell; Ceclia Violet Raye; Phebe
Florence Tanner; Audrey Alexes Leighton. *REV: E 20/6/
91 p7; St 25/6/91 p10.*

91.201 *LE MONDE OU L'ON S'ENNUIE* (C,3a) Edouard
Pailleron. ROYALTY 19/6/91, 20/6/91(m). 2 perf. 1st
perfd Français, Paris 25/4/81. Paul Raymond Boucher;

Saint Reault Joliet; Francois Roger; Le General Villain; Bellac Gravollet; Roger de Ceran Leitner; Toulonnier Gavoret; Desmillets [J.] Deroy; Virot Rhode.
Jeanne Raymond Reichenberg; La Duchesse de Reville
Fayolle; Lucy Watson Du Minil; Suzanne de Villiers
Bertiny; Mme de Ceran Malck; Mme Arriego Degredes; Mme
de Loudan Amel. L Kate Santley; Mgr M.L. Mayer; Act
mgr Gaston Mayer.

91.202 *CHAMILLAC* (C,5a) Octave Feuillet. ROYALTY 20/
6/91, 23/6, 29/6/91. 3 perf. Théâtre-français, Paris
9/4/86. Chamillac C.-B. Coquelin [*ainé*]; Le General
F. Febvre; La Bartherie Joliet; Hugonnet Jean Coquelin; Robert Gavoret; Chanteloup Roger; Gaillard Villain; Maurice Leitner; Carville [J.] Deroy. Jeanne
Du Minil; Clotide Fayolle; Lopeic Bertiny; La Comtesse
Malck; La Baronne Amel; Mlle Godemer Degredes. L, Mgr,
Act mgr as for 91.201. *REV: E 27/6/91 p6; St 25/6/91
p10.*

91.203 *DICK WILDER* (C,4a) Mrs H. Musgrave. VAUDEVILLE
20/6/91 mat perf.* Sir Harry Heathcote Fred Thorne;
Lord St. Maur Lawrence d'Orsay; Eustace Davenport/Dick
Wilder H.B. Conway; Jacob Fred Grove. Molly Heathcote
Dorothy Dorr; Barbara Morris Adrienne Dairolles; Mar-
garet Clark C[oralie] Owen. L & MGR Thomas Thorne;
Act mgr Sydney Alport; Sm Fred Thorne; Cost Nathan;
Pq William Clarkson; Sc W.T. Hemsley; Mus dir Charles
Dubois. *REV: E 27/6/91 p10; St 25/6/91 p10; Ti 22/6/
91 p12.*

91.204 *MARGOT* (C,3a) Henri Meilhac. ROYALTY 22/6/91,
26/6/91. 2 perf. 1st perfd Comédie-français, Paris
18/1/90. Boisvillette F. Febvre; Jean Roger; Leridan
Villain; Francois Leitner; Georges Gravollet; Pilard
Gavoret. Margot Reichenberg; Carline Du Minil; Mme
Monin Fayolle; Valentine Bertiny; Adele Degredes;
Mme d'Arcy Febvre-Brindeau. L Kate Santley; Mgr M.L.
Mayer; Act mgr Gaston Mayer. *REV: E 27/6/91 p6; St
25/6/91 p10; Ti 27/6/91 p6.*

91.205 *DRINK* (D,7a) Charles Reade [adpt of William
Busnach & Gastineau's ver of Emile Zola, *L'Assommoir*].
DRURY LANE 23/6/91-4/8/91. 37 perf. 1st perfd Prin-

cess's 2/6/79. <u>Coupeau</u> Charles Warner; <u>Lantier</u> Charles
Glenney; <u>Gouget</u> Edmund Gurney; <u>Poisson</u> Julian Cross;
<u>Mes Bottes</u> William Morgan; <u>Bec Sali</u> Alfred P. Phillips;
<u>Jacques</u> Herbert Terriss; <u>Adolphe</u> Ronald Power; <u>Bibi</u>
[W.] Staunton; <u>Pierre Colombe</u> Reginald Cox. <u>Gervais</u>
Jessie Millward; <u>Virginie</u> Ada Neilson; <u>Mme Rouge</u> Mrs
John Billington; <u>Juliet</u> Alice Kingsley; <u>Phoebe Sage</u>
Kate James; <u>Little Nana</u> Little Daisy Stratton; <u>Louise</u>
Alice Selby; <u>Delphine</u> Lily Brooking. L & MGR Augustus
Harris; <u>Cond</u> P. Bucalossi; <u>Dir</u> Augustus Harris; <u>Sm</u>
Arthur P. Collins; <u>Asm</u> N[apier] Barry; <u>Sec & Treas</u>
F[red] G. Latham. *REV: E 27/6/91 p7; SR 27/6/91 p*
774; St 25/6/91 p9-10; Th 1/8/91 p79; Ti 25/6/91 p13.

91.206 *WATCHING AND WAITING* (C,3a) Agatha & Archibald
Hodgson. TERRY'S 23/6/91 mat perf. 1st prof. <u>Hugh</u>
<u>Helstone</u> Julian Cross; <u>Julian Dalziel</u> Philip Cunning-
ham; <u>Gilbert Marsden</u> Gerald Gurney; <u>Rev Angelus And-</u>
<u>erson</u> Sydney Jerram; <u>Montague Helstone</u> Cecil Crofton.
<u>Evelyn Helstone</u> Annie Hill; <u>Mrs Loxdale</u> Gertrude War-
den; <u>Mrs Anderson</u> Emily Miller; <u>Norah Marsden</u> Lily
Linfield; <u>Jane</u> Kathleen Hill. MGR Fred W. Crellin.
REV: E 27/6/91 p10; St 25/6/91 p10.

91.207 *LUCIA DI LAMMERMOOR* (O[3a]) Gaetano Donizetti.
COVENT GARDEN 24/6/91, 6/7/91. 2 perf.** <u>Ashton</u>
Devoyod; <u>Raimondo</u> Abramoff; <u>Normano</u> Bieletto; <u>Arturo</u>
Iginio Corsi; <u>Edgardo</u> Luigi Ravelli. <u>Lucia</u> Nellie
Melba; <u>Alice</u> Mathilde Bauermeister. MGR Augustus
Harris; <u>Cond</u> Enrico Bevignani. *REV: E 27/6/91 p13;*
St 2/7/91 p10.

91.208 *MADEMOISELLE DE LA SEIGLIERE* (C,4a) Jules Sandeau. ROYALTY 24/6/91, 2/7/91. 2 perf. 1st perfd
Comédie-française,Paris, 4/11/51. C.-B. Coquelin
[*ainé*]; Leitner; Jean Coquelin; Gravollet; Roger. Du
Minil; Fayolle. MGR M.L. Mayer.

91.209 *WAITING CONSENT* ([C,1a]) [Mrs R. Fairburn; May
Holt]. TOOLE'S 24/6/91. 1 perf.** MGR J.L. Toole.
<u>Comment</u>: Advertized in *Ti* for this date.

91.210 *L'AMI FRITZ* (C,3a) "Erckmann-Chatrian" [Emile
Erckmann & Louis-Gratien-Charles-Alexandre Chatrian].

ROYALTY 25/6/91, 27/6/91(2). 3 perf. 1st perfd Comédie-
française, Paris 4/12/76. David Sichel C.-B. Coquelin
[*aîné*]; Fritz Kobus F. Febvre; Christel Villain; Frederic Joliet; Hanezo Jean Coquelin; Joseph Gravollet.
Suzel Reichenberg; Catherine Febvre-Brindeau; Catherine Bassett. *REV: E 27/6/91 p6; Ti 29/6/91 p7.*

91.211 *CLEOPATRA* (FC,3a) Arthur Shirley [adpt of *Les
Amours de Cléopatre*]. SHAFTESBURY 25/6/91 mat perf.*
Simon Rawkins Harry Paulton; Edwin Vane Fred Mervin;
Bob Lupton W. Scott Buist; Jelks Algernon Newark;
Landlord of the "Compass" E. Stirling; Policeman Ste-
phen Caffrey; Montague Mowler Herman de Lange. Milly
Rawkins Lilian Hingston; Cleopatra Collins Maud Mil-
ton. SM Fred Mervin. *REV: E 27/6/91 p8; SR 4/7/91
p20; St 2/7/91 p10; Th 1/8/91 p80.*

91.212 *JASPER'S REVENGE* (CD,1a) Wynn Miller. SHAFTES-
BURY 25/6/91 mat perf.* Jasper Langley Lionel Brough;
Earl of Denesbrook John Beauchamp; Ernest Bagot Chum-
ley Sydney Brough. Mary Langley Webster. *REV: E, SR,
St as for 91.211; Th 1/8/91 p80-1.*

91.213 *MARTHA* [*MARTHA ODER DER MARKT VON RICHMOND*]
(O[4a]) Friedich von Flotow. COVENT GARDEN 26/6/91,
7/7/91. 2 perf. 1st perfd Karntnertor-Theater, Vienna
25/11/47. Lionello Luigi Ravelli; Plumketto Edouard
de Reske; Sir Tristano Giuseppe Ciampi. Nancy Giulia
Ravogli; Marta Eugenia Mravina; 1ere Danseuse Palladino. MGR Augustus Harris; Cond Enrico Bevignani.
REV: E 4/7/91 p13.

91.214 *THE OCTOROON* (P,5a) Dion Boucicault. NOVELTY
27/6/91-9/7/91. c.11 perf. 1st perfd Winter Garden,
New York 6/12/59. Comment: Mentioned in *St.*

91.215 *KATTI* (DomesticF,3a) Charles S. Fawcett [fr
Henri Meilhac, *Gotte*]. STRAND 27/6/91-25/7/91; 28-29/
7/91. 31 perf [w/S mat exc 27/6]. 1st perfd Princess's
Glasgow 30/9/87. Kinnikin Fluffy Willie Edouin;
Richard Fluffy Ells Dagnall; Bob Harry Eversfield; Dr
Easyman Sydney Barraclough; Joliffe T[homas] Sidney.
Katti Alice Atherton; Mrs Finnikin Fluffy Marie Ill-
ington; Mrs Richard Fluffy Ruth Rutland; Alice Somers

Georgie Esmond; <u>Miss Perkins</u> Venie Bennett. <u>PP</u> J.S.
Clarke; <u>L</u> Willie Edouin; <u>Bom</u> H[enry] L. Boss; <u>Bm</u>
J.T. Mackay Robertson; <u>Sm</u> J.A.E Malone; <u>Cond</u> Ernest
Bucalossi. *REV: E 4/7/91 p7; SR 4/7/91 p20; St 2/7/*
91 p10; Ti 29/6/91 p7.

91.216 *BACK IN FIVE MINUTES* (F,1a) Henry T. Johnson.
STRAND 27/6/91-7/1/92. 162 perf [np 27/7, 30-31/7,
24-25/12/91]. <u>Roscoe Robinson</u> Sydney Barraclough;
<u>Bedford Roe</u> T[homas] Sydney/George P. Hawtrey; <u>Peter-</u>
<u>kin Prosser</u> Ells Dagnall/Robert Nainby; <u>Mary Maybud</u>
Georgie Esmond/Ina Goldsmith; <u>Theresa Tompkins</u> Venie
Bennett. <u>PP</u>, <u>L</u>, <u>Bom</u>, <u>Bm</u>, <u>Sm</u>, <u>Cond</u> as for 91.215.

91.217 *LES FOURBERIES DE SCAPIN* (C) Molière. ROYALTY
30/6/91. 1 perf. <u>Comment</u>: Advertized in *Ti* for this
date.

91.218 *LA JOIE FAIT PEUR* (C,1a) Delphine de Girardin.
ROYALTY 30/6/91. 1 perf. 1st perfd Théâtre-français,
Paris 25/2/54. <u>Comment</u>: As for 91.217.

91.219 *THE NAUTCH GIRL; OR, THE RAJAH OF CHUTNEYPORE*
George Dance (lib) & Edward Solomon (mus). SAVOY
30/6/91-16/1/92. 200 perf [w/S mat; np 24-25/12/90].*
<u>Punka</u> Rutland Barrington; <u>Indru</u> Courtice Pounds;
<u>Pyjama</u> Frank Thornton; <u>Baboo Currie</u> Frank Wyatt; <u>Bumbo</u>
W.H. Denny. <u>Suttee</u> Cissie Saumarez; <u>Chinna Loofa</u>
Jessie Bond; <u>Cheetah</u> Nellie Lawrence; <u>Hollee Beebee</u>
Lenore Snyder; <u>Banyan</u> Louise Rowe; <u>Kalee</u> Annie Cole;
<u>Tiffin</u> Cora Tinnie. <u>MGR</u> Richard d'Oyly Carte; <u>Lyr</u>
George Dance, Frank Desprez; <u>Sc</u> T.E. Ryan, Joseph
Harker; <u>Dir</u> Charles Harris; <u>Mus dir</u> Francois Cellier;
<u>Assistant</u> Ernest Ford; <u>Ch</u> John d'Auban; <u>Cost dgn</u>
Percy Anderson; <u>Cost</u> Miss Fisher, Auguste, Alias; <u>Pq</u>
William Clarkson; <u>Props</u> [H.] Skelly; <u>Mach</u> Sheldon;
<u>Elect</u> Lyons; <u>Act mgr</u> J.W. Beckwith; <u>Sm</u> W.H. Seymour.
REV: E 4/7/91 p9; SR 4/7/91 p14-5; St 2/7/91 p9-10;
Th 1/8/91 p98-101.

91.220 *THE RULE OF THREE* (Melo,4a) Pierre Leclercq.
SHAFTESBURY 30/6/91 mat perf.* <u>Valentine Mayhood</u>
Fuller Mellish; <u>David Banks</u> Julian Cross; <u>Tom Chant-</u>
<u>ler</u> Walter Everard; <u>Dr Banvil</u> John Carter; <u>Stephen</u>

Banks Henry Nelson; Arnold Seago Fred Mervin. Gertrude
Banks Mary Jocelyn; Annie Phyllis Ayrian; Bernice
Seago Alma Murray. *REV: Ath 4/7/91 p44; E 4/7/91 p8;
SR 4/7/91 p20; St 2/7/91 p10; Th 1/8/91 p81-2.*

91.221 *MRS ANNESLEY* (CD,3a) J.F. Cooke. CRITERION
1/7/91 mat perf.* Mr Brandreth Bassett Roe; Father
Andre William Herbert; Mr Annesley John Beauchamp;
Dr Ellis Charles Allan; Rackstraw Compton Coutts;
Frank Seagrave Frederick Harrison; Waiter [Rankin?]
Duval; William Warden. Estelle Brandreth May Whitty;
Mrs Annesley Beatrice Lamb. *REV: Ath 4/7/91 p44; E
4/7/91 p9; SR 4/7/91 p20; St 2/7/91 p10-1; Th 1/8/91
p82-3.*

91.222 *MOONFLOWERS* (A Cobweb,WordlessP) Ivan Caryll
(mus). GAIETY 1/7/91 mat perf.* A Student Herbert
Pearson; A Young Man E. Webster Lawson. Girl Norreys.
L & MGR George Edwardes; Cond W. Meyer Lutz; Pq C.H.
Fox; Cost Mrs May; Sm Frank Parker; Act mgr C.J. Abud.
*REV: E 4/7/91 p9; SR 4/7/91 p20; St 2/7/91 p10; Ti
2/7/91 p12.*

91.223 *A PANTOMIME REHEARSAL* (Bsq,1a) Cecil Clay.
GAIETY 1/7/91 mat perf.** Jack Deedes [W.G.] Elliott;
Sir Charles Grandison C.P. Little; Lord Arthur Pomeroy
Weedon Grossmith; Cpt. Tom Robinson Brandon Thomas;
Tomkins [F.] Vaughan. Lady Muriel Beauclerc Helena
Dacre; Miss Lily Laura Linden; Miss Violet Edith Ches-
ter; Miss May Ruby Tyrrell; Miss Rose Tyrrell; Lady
Sloane-Willery Day Ford; "Duet" Edith Chester, Lizzie
Ruggles. L & MGR, Cond, Pq, Cost, Sm, Act mgr as for
91.222. *REV: E, St as for 91.222.*

91.224 *LA MASCOTTE* (CO,3a) Edmond Audran (mus) & H.B.
Farnie (lib) & Robert Reece (lib). GAIETY 1/7/91 mat
perf. 1st perfd Theatre Royal, Brighton 19/9/81.
Laurent XVII Arthur Roberts; Pippo Frank H. Celli;
Prince Fritellini Lytton Grey; Rocco Arthur Williams;
Guiseppe C. Walker. Tito Hetty Harmer; Fiammetta
Phyllis Broughton; Bettina Florence St. John; Angelo
Maude Hobson; Luigi Blanche Massey; Paola Sedgwick;
Francesca Capel; Bianca Maud Wilmot. L & MGR, Cond,
Pq, Cost, Sm, Act mgr as for 91.222; Dir Charles

Harris. REV: E, St as for 91.222.

91.225 *LE DEPUTE DE BOMBIGNAC* (C,3a) Alexandre Bisson.
ROYALTY 1/7/91. 1 perf. 1st perfd Théâtre-français,
Paris 28/5/84. C.-B. Coquelin [aîné]; Jean Coquelin.
Fayolle; Du Minil; Bertiny. MGR M.L. Mayer. Comment:
Advertized in Ti for this date.

91.226 *A PAIR OF LUNATICS* (Ca,1a) W.R. Walkes. CRITER-
ION 2/7/91 mat perf.** He George Alexander. She
Maude Millett. REV: St 9/7/91 p10.

91.227 *IN SEARCH OF AN ENGAGEMENT* (MSk) Nellie Ganthony. CRITERION 2/7/91 mat perf.** Nellie Ganthony.
REV: St 9/7/91 p10. Comment: Apparently an alternative
title to *In Want of an Engagement*.

91.228 *MR AND MRS WHITE* (F). NOVELTY 2/7/91. 1 perf.
1st perfd Strand 15/5/54. Peter White Fred Bird;
Mjr. Pepper [Henry] Belding; Frank [Edwin] Fergusson.
Widow White Mrs J.F. Brian; Mrs White Marie Brian;
Kitty Ida Douglas. MGR Mrs J.F. Brian; Dir Gilbert
Vernon, Charles A. Welch. REV: E 4/7/91 p7; St 9/7/91
p10.

91.229 *HER FIRST APPEARANCE* (MCa). NOVELTY 2/7/91. 1
perf. Arthur Lloyd; A.J. Damer; Delarme Lloyd. Annie
King-Lloyd; Lizzie Nelson. MGR, Dir as for 91.228.
REV: As for 91.228.

91.230 *FOR CLAUDIA'S SAKE* (CD,3a) Mabel Freund-Lloyd.
VAUDEVILLE 2/7/91 mat perf.* Sir Lionel Urquhart
H.A. Saintsbury; Lord Vivian Acton Bond; Cpt. Chart-
eris Alfred B. Cross; Stonewall Leo Leather; Gardener
Foster Courtenay. Sylvia Talbot Edith Jordan; Claudia
Talbot Ida Logan; Lady Charteris Laura Laughton; Mrs
Simmons Mabel Freund-Lloyd; Hannah Marlowe. L & MGR
Thomas Thorne; Bm Oswald Brand; Sm George Hughes; Mus
dir W.W. Meadows. REV: E 4/7/91 p9; St 9/7/91 p10.

91.231 *SACRIFICED* (D,1a) Mabel Freund-Lloyd. VAUDEVILLE
2/7/91 mat perf.* Sir Gilbert Trevor George Hughes;
Hugh Berington H.A. Saintsbury; Tom Locksley Leo
Leather. Elsie Berington Rhoda Larkin; Helen Percival

Helen Bayard; <u>Sarah Ann</u> Kate Brand. <u>L & MGR</u>, <u>Bm</u>, <u>Sm</u>, <u>Mus dir</u> as for 91.230. *REV: As for 91.230.*

91.232 *FIDELIO* (O[2a]) Ludwig van Beethoven. COVENT GARDEN 3/7/91. 1 perf. 1st perfd Theater auf der Wieden, Vienna 20/11/05. <u>Rocco</u> Pol Plançon; <u>Pizzaro</u> Devoyod; <u>Giachino</u> Rinaldini; <u>Il Munstro</u> Alec Marsh; <u>Florestano</u> Luigi Ravelli. <u>Leonora</u> Marie Tavary; <u>Marcellina</u> Mathilde Bauermeister. <u>MGR</u> Augustus Harris; <u>Cond</u> Alberto Randegger. *REV: E 11/7/91 p13; St 9/7/91 p9; Ti 6/7/91 p8.*

91.233 *LE GENDRE DE MONSIEUR POIRIER* (C,4a) Emile Augier & Jules Sandeau. ROYALTY 3/7/91. 1 perf. 1st perfd Gymnase, Paris 8/4/54. <u>Poirier</u> C.-B. Coquelin [*aîné*]; <u>Le Marquis</u> Valbel; <u>Verdelet</u> Jean Coquelin; <u>Francois</u> Roger; <u>Vatel</u> [J.] Deroy; <u>Hector</u> Gavoret. <u>Antoinette</u> Du Minil. <u>MGR</u> M.L. Mayer. *REV: E 11/7/91 p9.*

91.234 *LES SURPRISES DU DIVORCE* (C,3a) Alexandre Bisson & Antony Mars. ROYALTY 4/7/91(2). 2 perf. 1st perfd Vaudeville, Paris 2/3/88. <u>Henri Duval</u> C.-B. Coquelin [*aîné*]; <u>Champeaux</u> Jean Coquelin; <u>Corbulon</u> Leitner; <u>Bourganeuf</u> [J.] Deroy. <u>Diane</u> Du Minil; <u>Mme Bonivard</u> Patry; <u>Gabrielle</u> Depoix; <u>Victoria</u> Brunet. *REV: E 11/7/91 p9.*

91.235 *THE MISCHIEFMAKER* (FC,3a) Edith Henderson. VAUDEVILLE 4/7/91-5/9/91; trfd to TOOLE'S 7/9/91-25/9/91. 89 perf [w/S mat exc 4/7, 19/9; add mat 3/8, 5/8, 12/8, 19/8, 26/8, 2/9, 9/9].** <u>Oliver Tapperton</u> Harry Paulton; <u>Percival Loggerhead</u> Charles S. Fawcett; <u>Keith Denby</u> Philip Cunningham; <u>Dr Middleton</u> John Carter; <u>Bates</u> J[ohn] Wheatman; <u>John</u> H[enry] Nelson; <u>Alfred</u> Master C.T. Smith. <u>Lucy Wentworth</u> Phyllis Ayrian; <u>Alice</u> Alice Bruce; <u>Mary</u> B[lanche?] Eversleigh; <u>Miss Pryce</u> Florence Haydon; <u>Amy Loggerhead</u> Edith Bruce. <u>L</u> Thomas Thorne; <u>MGR</u> Harrington Baily; <u>Dir</u> Julian Cross; <u>Mus dir</u> Charles Dubois. *REV: E 11/7/91 p7; St 9/7/91 p10; Ti 6/7/91 p8.*

91.236 *GABRIEL'S TRUST* (DD,1a) Alfred C. Calmour. VAUDEVILLE 4/7/91-14/7/91. 9 perf.* <u>Gabriel Stroud</u>

Alfred C. Calmour; George Field Philip Cunningham;
Thomas Rhodes H[enry] Nelson; Constable J[ohn] Wheatman. Mary Mason Alice Bruce; Janet Florence Haydon.
L, Mgr, Mus dir as for 91.235. *REV: E, St, Ti as for*
91.235; Th 1/8/91 p83-4.

91.237 *HUSBAND AND WIFE* (FC,3a) F.C. Philips & Percy
Fendall. COMEDY 7/7/91-17/10/91. 89 perf.** Sir
George Muddle Charles H.E. Brookfield; Montrevor
Smith W.F. Hawtrey; Alfred Stepit James Nelson; Phil-
lip Softdown Gerald Gurney; Delamere S.H. Lechmere;
Inspector Thickhead William Wyes; Adolphus Green-
thorne George Giddens; Waiter S. Handel; Clerk E[rn-
est] Cosham; Usher C[harles] Milton; P.C. Blunt G.A.
Vaughan. Mrs Greenthorne Vane Featherstone; Mrs
Montrevor Smith Ada Murray; Mrs Delamere Ethel Matt-
hews; Mary Edith Kenward; Mrs Phillip Softdown Ethel
Norton; Mrs Springfield Lottie Venne. MGR Charles H.
Hawtrey; Bm & Act mgr E.F. Bradley; Asm Charles Milton; Mus dir James M. Glover. *REV: Ath 11/7/91 p76;*
E 11/7/91 p7; SR 11/7/91 p48-9, 25/7/91 p108; St
9/7/91 p10; Th 1/8/91 p84-5; Ti 13/7/91 p3.

91.238 *THE SCAPEGOAT* (P,4a) J. Wilton Jones [adpt of
the novel by Gertrude Warden]. GLOBE 7/7/91. 1 perf.*
Aubrey de Vaux Lewis Waller; Bruce Laidlaw William
Herbert; Mr Smith Sidney Herberte Basing; Dr Marsden
John Beauchamp; Burton Algernon Newark. Lola Florence
West; Mabyn Laidlaw Annie Hughes; Lady Ermyntrude
Laidlaw Carlotta Leclercq; Marquise de Vaux Mrs
Theodore Wright; Ella Granville Gertrude Warden; Miss
Fox-Willoughby Adela Houston; Jennings Florence. SM
Herman de Lange; Mus dir Arthur E. Godfrey. *REV: E*
11/7/91 p8; St 9/7/91 p10; Th 1/8/91 p84-6; Ti 8/7/
91 p10.

91.239 *HUMANITY* (D). NOVELTY 11/7/91-23/7/91. c. 11
perf. Joshua Langley George Clanville; Jacob Cuthbert
Edwin Fergusson; Jacob Silvani/Hassan Cleopatra John
Lawson; Nugget Ned/Tootler Clinton Baddeley; 59 Laurence; Binks/Brassy Loudtone J.G. Wilton; Owen Meredith Gilbert Vernon; Ernest Redfern W. Garrett; Reuben Crane Horton Tree; Blowit Edgerton; Tootler G.
Sewell; Ben Barton H. Buckstone Clair; Bob Charles

Fitzgerald; <u>Knowall</u> W. Westwood. <u>Angel</u> <u>Aggie</u> Georgie
Harris; <u>Grace Barton</u> Marie Brian; <u>Mrs Rowstock</u> Mrs
J.F. Brian; <u>Mrs Naggle</u> Eleanor Lloyd; <u>Lucy Moore</u>
Ida Douglass; <u>Mary</u> Mayo. *REV: E 18/7/91 p7; St 16/7/
91 p10.*

91.240 *HIGH LIFE BELOW STAIRS* (F,2a) Rev James Town-
ley. NOVELTY 11/7/91-23/7/91. c.11 perf.** <u>Duke</u> H.
Buckstone Clair; <u>Sir Harry</u> J.G. Wilton; [<u>Lovel</u>]
Edwin Fergusson; W. Garrett. <u>Kitty</u> Marie Brian. *REV:
As for 91.239.*

91.241 *A MIGHTY ERROR* (RD,2a) Leonard Outram [suggest-
ed by Robert Browning, "In a Balcony"]. AVENUE 14/7/
91. 1 perf.* <u>Amadis</u> Leonard Outram; <u>Miguel</u> Frank
Worthing; <u>Xante</u> Sydney Herberte Basing. <u>Joan</u> Frances
Ivor; <u>Inez</u> Mary Ansell. *REV: Ath 18/7/91 p107; E 18/
7/91 p7; SR 25/7/91 p111-2; St 16/7/91 p10; Th 1/8/91
p86-7; Ti 15/7/91 p5.*

91.242 *A SUMMER'S DREAM* (DD,1a) Rose Meller. AVENUE
14/7/91. 1 perf.* <u>Garth</u> Henry Dana; <u>Farmer Fielding</u>
F. Rawson Buckley. <u>Joan</u> Mrs Bennett; <u>Dahlia</u> Isabel
Maude. *REV: E, SR, St, Ti as for 91.241; Ath 25/7/91
p140; Th 1/8/91 p88.*

91.243 *AIDA* (O[4a]) Giuseppe Verdi. COVENT GARDEN
14/7/91, 17/7/91. 2 perf.** <u>Amonasro</u> Devoyod/Tschern-
off; <u>Il Re</u> Miranda; <u>Ramfis</u> Abramoff; <u>Messaggiero</u>
Rinaldini; <u>Radames</u> Luigi Ravelli. <u>Aida</u> Lillian Nordica; <u>Amneris</u> Olimpia Guercia. MGR Augustus Harris;
<u>Cond</u> Enrico Bevignani. *REV: E 18/7/91 p13; St 16/7/
91 p10; Ti 16/7/91 p10.*

91.244 *OTELLO* (O[4a]) Giuseppe Verdi. COVENT GARDEN
15/7/91, 18/7, 23/7, 25/7/91. 4 perf. 1st perfd
Teatro alla Scala, Milan 5/2/87. <u>Otello</u> Jean de Reske;
<u>Iago</u> Victor Maurel/Eugene Dufriche; <u>Cassio</u> Sebastian
Montariol/Pedro Guetary; <u>Ludovico</u> Abramoff; <u>Roderigo</u>
Iginio Corsi; <u>Montano</u> Miranda. <u>Emilia</u> Passama; <u>Des-</u>
<u>demona</u> Emma Albani/Emma Eames. MGR Augustus Harris;
<u>Cond</u> Luigi Mancinelli.*REV: E 18/7/91 p13; SR 18/7/91
p77-8; St 16/7/91 p10, 23/7/91 p9-10; Ti 16/7/91 p10,
27/7/91 p14.*

91.245 *THE SEQUEL* (P,1a) Louis N. Parker. VAUDEVILLE 15/7/91-5/9/91;* trfd to TOOLE'S 7/9/91-25/9/91. 74 perf [w/mat 8/8, 12/8, 15/8, 19/8, 22/8, 26/8, 29/8, 2/9, 5/9, 9/9, 12/9]. Lord Henry Somerville Philip Cunningham; Mr Foljambe Charles S. Fawcett; Peters H[enry] Nelson. Clarissa Alma Murray; Mary Alice Bruce. L Thomas Thorne; Mgr Harrington Baily; Mus dir Charles Dubois. *REV: Ath 25/7/91 p140; E 18/7/91 p7; SR 25/7/91 p11; St 16/7/91 p10; Th 1/8/91 p88; Ti 18/7/91 p7.*

91.246 *MOLIERE* (CD,1a) Walter Frith. ST. JAMES'S 17/7/91; 30/9/91-10/10/91. 11 perf.* Molière George Alexander; Marquis Ben Webster; Baron Alfred Holles; Dr Dacquin Herbert Waring; L'Epine V[ernon] Sansbury; 1st Chairman Howard Russell; 2nd Chairman George Gamble. Catherine Laura Graves; Armande Molière Marion Terry. *REV: Ath 25/7/91 p138-9; E 25/7/91 p7; SR 25/7/91 p111; St 23/7/91 p10, 8/10/91 p12; Th 1/8/91 p89; Ti 18/7/91 p7*

91.247 *RAVENSWOOD* (P,4a) Herman C. Merivale. LYCEUM 20/7/91, 21/7/91. 2 perf.** Edgar Henry Irving; Hayston William Terriss; Caleb Balderstone William Mackintosh; Craigengelt [Thomas E.] Wenman; Sir William Ashton Alfred Bishop; Marquis of Athole [F.H.] Macklin; Bide-the-Bent [Henry] Howe; Henry Ashton Gordon Craig; Moncrieff [Frank] Tyars; Thornton [William] Haviland; Priest Lacy; Lockhard Davis. Lucy Ashton Ellen Terry; Ailsie Gourlay Marriott; Lady Ashton Roma Guilllon Le Thiere; Annie Winnie Mrs Pauncefort. L & MGR Henry Irving; Mus Dr A.C. Mackenzie; Sm H.J. Loveday; Mus dir J. Meredith Ball; Act mgr Bram Stoker; Bom Joseph Hurst. Comment: Possibly an add perf on 22/7/91.

91.248 *THAT DREADFUL DOCTOR* (Ca,1a) Sir Charles L. Young. OPERA COMIQUE 20/7/91 mat perf.** Dr Mars Arthur Bourchier; Edmund Beauchamp S.H. Lechmere. Mrs Beauchamp Lena Ashwell. SEC Walter Pallant, C.J. Abud; Act mgr G.F. Bashford; Sm George Capel, J[ohn] Ettinson, J.A.E. Malone; Mus dir F. Stanislaus, Edward Jones, James M. Glover, George W. Byng; Pq C.H. Fox, William Clarkson; Lime W. Kerr. *REV: E 25/7/91 p6;*

St 23/7/91 p10.

91.249 *A PANTOMIME REHEARSAL* (Bsq,1a) Cecil Clay.
OPERA COMIQUE 20/7/91 mat perf.** Jack Deedes [W.G.]
Elliott; Sir Charles Grandison C.P. Little; Lord
Arthur Pomeroy Weedon Grossmith; Cpt. Tom Robinson
Brandon Thomas; Tomkins [F.] Vaughan. Lady Muriel
Beauclerc Helena Dacre; Miss Lily Laura Linden; Miss
Violet Edith Chester; Miss May Ruby Tyrrell; Miss
Rose Tyrrell; Lady Sloane-Willery Day Ford; "Fairies
Duet" Edith Chester, Lizzie Ruggles. SEC, Act mgr, Sm,
Mus dir, Pq, Lime as for 91.248. *REV: St 23/7/91 p10.*

91.250 *GUY FAWKES, ESQ* (Bsq,3a) "A.C. Torr" [Fred Les-
lie] & Herbert F. Clarke. OPERA COMIQUE 20/7/91 mat
perf.** Guy Fawkes Arthur Roberts; James I J.J. Dallas; Badcorn Sam Wilkinson; Grovel G.P. Prior; Tresham H[arry] Grattan. Viviana Radcliffe Amelia Gruhn;
Ruth Ipgreve Linda Verner; Robert Catesby Fanny Marriott; Steinie E[va] Milton; Lord Mounteagle Phoebe
Carlo. SEC, Act mgr, Sm, Mus dir, Pq, Lime as for 91.
248. *REV: As for 91.248.*

91.251 *MISS DECIMA* (OperaticC,3a) F.C. Burnand [fr
Edmond Audran & Maxime Boucheron]. CRITERION 23/7/91-
25/11/91;* trfd to PRINCE OF WALES'S 26/11/91-16/1/
92. 178 perf [w/S mat; np 25/12/91]. Rev Dr Jeremie
Jackson David James; Peter Paul Rolleston Charles
Conyers/C. Hayden Coffin; Chevalier Patrick Julius
O'Flanagan Chauncey Olcott; Bertie Brown Templer Saxe/
Leonard Russell; Marmaduke Jessop Welton Dale; Donald
McQuord R. Sesnon; Jules H. Gordon. La Senora de Var-
ganaz M.A. Victor; Senora Inez Josephine Findlay/
Annie Schuberth;Jeannie F. Frances/Edith Fielding;
Flora Lucy [Isabella] Buckstone; Decima [Juliette]
Nesville/Decima Moore; Rosa A. McRae; Mlle Coralie
B[ertha] Vere. L & MGR Charles Wyndham; Lyr Percy
Reeve; Dir [C.D.] Marius; Mus dir F. Stanislaus; Sc
T.E. Ryan; Cost dgn Alfred Maltby; Cost Alias, Pitts
& Richards; Act mgr E. Harvey; Sm S.H.S Austin. *REV:
E 25/7/91 p7; SR 1/8/91 p134; St 30/7/91 p10; Th 1/9/
91 p130-3; Ti 24/7/91 p9.*

91.252 *RIGHT AGAINST MIGHT* (CD,3a) M. White. NOVELTY

27/7/91-1/8/91. 6 perf.* Sir Roger Marsden W. Aubrey
Chandler; Lieut. Geoffrey Marsden William Glenney;
Lieut. Richard Armstrong Charles Terric; Cpt. Reginald
Brentwood J.P. Dryden; Count d'Esmay Herbert Boyle;
Mr Johnston Robert Barton; Tim Maloney Fred Winn; Joe
Percy Sydney; Jones Edwin Evans; Thomas Thomas Martin;
Rev Mr Brown Barithwaite; Martin Slopper Ben Shore;
Jack Robertson E. Lyob. Violet Armstrong Winifred
Elliott; Madge Marston Jessie Chandler; Nora O'Connor
Mabel Hardy; Mrs O'Connor Josephine McMahon. *REV:
E 1/8/91 p7; St 6/8/91 p10.*

91.253 *FATE AND FORTUNE; OR, THE JUNIOR PARTNER* (Melo,
4a) James J. Blood. PRINCESS'S 27/7/91-7/8/91. 12
perf [w/mat 3/8].* Mr Glendon Henry Pagden; Ralph
Glendon Bassett Roe; Walter Halmshaw W.R. Sutherland/
Henry Dana; Kopain W.L. Abingdon; Bob Tranter George
Barrett/Frank M. Wood; Tom Woolett W[illiam] Chees-
man; Blister T.F. Doyle; Marklow Stephen Caffrey;
Swagg Henry Bedford; Springe Huntley Wright; Swadler
John M. East; Docker C. Medwyn; Mr Lambsdown W.F.
Antcliffe. Grace Hasluck May Whitty; Mrs Tranter
Sallie Turner; Matilda Jane Tranter Cicely Richards;
Madge Gracie Muriel; Mrs Prowse May Protheroe; Miss
Flick B. Wildmere. PP Mrs Harriet Gooch; Mgr Sidney
Herberte Basing; Pd T.F. Doyle, James J. Blood; Act
mgr William Craston; Sm T.F. Doyle; Mus dir Arthur
E. Godfrey; Mach J.W. Cawdray; Bom [F.] Forbes; Furn
Oetzmann; Cost Morris Angel & Son; Lime Oxy-Hydrogen
Light Co. *REV: Ath 1/8/91 p171; E 1/8/91 p7; SR 1/8/
91 p134-5; St 30/7/91 p10; Th 1/9/91 p133-4; Ti 28/
7/91 p8.*

91.254 *THE PLEBIAN* (CD,4a) Miss Costello. VAUDEVILLE
28/7/91 mat perf.* Thomas Armstrong Julian Cross;
Dick Everard Reginald Stockton; Robert Lefroy Orlando
Barnett; Servant Henry Nelson; Lord Helham T. Hill;
Col. Lefroy John Carter. Norah Lefroy Mrs Bennett;
Pauline Lefroy Kate Bealby; Cecily Deane Phyllis
Ayrian; Miss d'Arcy Florence Haydon; Lottie Lefroy
Henrietta Cross. L Thomas Thorne; Mgr Harrington Bai-
ly; Bom W. Allcroft; Dir Julian Cross. *REV: E 1/8/91
p8; St 30/7/91 p10; Th 1/9/91 p134-5.*

91.255 *THE TRUMPET CALL* (D,4a) George R. Sims & Robert Buchanan. ADELPHI 1/8/91-9/4/92; 16/4/92-21/4/92. 220 perf [np 25/12/91, 20/1/92].* <u>Cuthbert Cuthbertson</u> Leonard Boyne; <u>Sgt.-Mjr. Milligan</u> J.D. Beveridge; <u>Prof Ginnifer</u> Lionel Rignold; <u>Richard Featherston</u> Charles Dalton; <u>Tom Dutton</u> Richard H. Douglass; <u>Col. Englehardt</u> Howard Russell; <u>Sir William Barton</u> Arthur Leigh; <u>Flash Bob</u> Royston Keith; <u>James Redruth</u> James East; <u>Tompkins</u> Willie Drew; <u>Deputy of Doss House</u> J[ohn] Northcote; <u>Cpt. Sparks</u> W. Northcote; <u>Spriggins</u> H[arwood] Cooper; <u>Mummy</u> E.F. Saxon; <u>Corporal Plummer</u> F.O. Anderson; <u>Bill</u> H[arwood] Cooper, jr. <u>Bertha</u> Mrs Patrick Campbell; <u>Mrs Wicklow</u> Mrs H. Leigh; <u>Lavinia Ginnifer</u> Clara Jecks; <u>Constance</u> Elizabeth Robins/Evelyn Millard; <u>Lill</u> [Helen] Vizitelly; <u>Lucy</u> E. Heffer; <u>Mary</u> Alice Bronse; <u>Little Cuthbert</u> Daisy Stratton. <u>PP & MGR</u> A. & S. Gatti; <u>Sc</u> Bruce Smith, Walter Hann; <u>Mus dir</u> Henry Sprake; <u>Act mgr</u> Charles A. Jecks; <u>Mach</u> H. Loftin. *REV: Ath 8/8/91 p203; E 8/8/91 p9, 26/3/92 p10; St 6/8/91 p9-10; Th 1/9/91 p136-7; Ti 3/8/91 p6, 27/11/91 p7.*

91.256 *THEODORA* (P,6a,8tab) Robert Buchanan [adpt of Sardou]. OLYMPIC 1/8/91-8/9/91. 33 perf [w/mat 3/8; np 31/8].** <u>Andreas</u> Fuller Mellish; <u>Justinian</u> Murray Carson; <u>Belisarius</u> Frederick Victor; <u>Marcellus</u> George W. Cockburn; <u>Euphratus</u> T.W. Percyval; <u>Caribert</u> Theodore Alker; <u>Timocles</u> G.H. Binney; <u>Agathon</u> Henry Ludlow; <u>Faber</u> C.A. Gillig; <u>Styrax</u> Henry de Solla; <u>Executioner</u> W. Baker; <u>Mundus</u> W. Joseph King; <u>Priscus</u> Leslie Corcoran; <u>Orythes</u> Charles Anson; <u>Lywstrates</u> Richard Warton; <u>Amrou</u> W.J. Monckton; <u>Calchas</u> John Franklin; <u>1st Lord</u> William Price; <u>2nd Lord</u> C. Downey; <u>3rd Lord</u> Thomas Hunter; <u>4th Lord</u> Arthur Prior; <u>Chief of the Ostiaries</u> H. Benham. <u>Theodora</u> Grace Hawthorne; <u>Michael</u> Willis Cartland; <u>Alexis</u> Amy Verity; <u>Antonina</u> Bertie Willis; <u>Tamyris</u> Louisa Wyatt; <u>Callirhoe</u> Lilian Seccombe; <u>Macedonia</u> Forbes Dawson; <u>Iphis</u> Louis [Bassett] Wilmot; <u>Columba</u> Barbara Meade; <u>Zena</u> Lucy O'Connor. <u>PP</u> Charles Wilmot; <u>Mgr</u> W.W. Kelly; <u>Bom</u> Arthur Frye; <u>Bm</u> H. Lawrence Harris; <u>Dir</u> W.H. Vernon; <u>Cond</u> William Robins; <u>Lyr</u> Murray Carson; <u>Mus</u> George W. Cockburn; <u>AssistantBm</u> George Stone; <u>Asm</u> T.C. Dwyer; <u>Mach</u> R. Warton. *REV: E 8/8/91 p7; St 6/8/91 p10.*

91.257 *MULDOON'S PICNIC; OR, IRISH LIFE IN AMERICA*
(F) Harry Pleon. NOVELTY 3/8/91-c.15/8/91. c.12 perf.
1st perfd Marylebone 8/11/86. Comment: Mentioned in
St.

91.258 *THE FIFTEENTH OF OCTOBER* (Military Farcical Oa,
1a) E. Leterrier & Albert Vanloo. PRINCE OF WALES'S
8/8/91-29/10/91. 71 perf. 1st perfd Alhambra 22/3/75.
Durandal Leonard Russell; Larry Owen Harry Parker;
Capier G[eorge] Marler.Miss Camille Cissy Cranford.
PP Edgar Bruce; L & Mgr Horace Sedger; Lyr G. Capel;
Mus G[eorges] Jacobi; Bm William Greet; Act mgr C.P.
Levilly, J.S. Fleming. REV: E 15/8/91 p7; St 13/8/
91 p9-10; Th 1/9/91 p143-4; Ti 10/8/91 p8.

91.259 *TWO IN THE BUSH* (F,1a) Murray Carson ["Thornton Clark"]. OLYMPIC 15/8/91-8/9/91; 11/9/91-26/9/91.
34 perf.* Cyrus Carr Leslie Corcoran; Mjr. Frere
Murray Carson; Harry Draycott T.W. Percyval. Nettie
Carr Louie [Bassett] Wilmot. REV: Ath 22/8/91 p268;
E 22/8/91 p7; SR 5/9/91 p276; St 20/8/91 p9. Comment:
Newspaper advertisements simply describe the accomp-
anying piece to *Theodora* as "farce"; I have taken this
to be *Two in the Bush*.

91.260 *HOUPLA* (Ca,1a) T.G. Warren. COMEDY 18/8/91-5/9/
91; 7/9/91-7/12/91. 93 perf [np 19-21/10].* Chev-
alier Maurice Maroni William Wyes; Owen Fleetwood
Gerald Gurney; Great Little Sammy Ernest Cosham; Mr
Fleetwood's Tiger Master C.G. Holmes; Bill E. Copping;
Jack J.R. Hale/T. Wynne; Tom H. Hudson. Rosabel Jenny
Dawson; Lena Helen Lambert. MGR Charles Wyndham; Bm
E.F. Bradley; Asm Charles Milton; Mus dir James M.
Glover. REV: Ath 22/8/91 p268; St 20/8/91 p9. Comment:
Renamed *Rosabel* on 7/9/91.

91.261 *OTHELLO* (T,5a) William Shakespeare. AVENUE 25/
8/91. 1 perf.** Duke of Venice George Wallack; Iago
George Hughes; Othello Lion Margrave; Cassio H.A.
Saintsbury; Roderigo Frank Hibbert; Brabantio W.R.
Staveley; Montano Barnett Adams; Gratiano Charles
Terric; Lodovico William Lockhart; Antonio E. Leeds.
Emilia Alice Yorke; Desdemona Frances Ivor. DIR & GEN
Leonard Outram; Furn Oetzmann; Pq C.H. Fox; Cost Mrs

May, Victor Barthe; Act mgr Gilbert Tate; Mus dir J.
Kornfeld. *REV: Ath 29/8/91 p300; E 29/8/91 p8; St 27/
8/91 p9-10; Th 1/10/91 p177; Ti 26/8/91 p5.*

91.262 *THE FIAT OF THE GODS* (Roman Idyl,1a) Leonard
Outram. AVENUE 25/8/91. 1 perf.* Flavian Acton Bond;
Galba Austin Melford. Faustina Frances Ivor; Nesdamia
Sybil Baird. DIR & GEN MGR, Act mgr, Mus dir as for
91.261. *REV: Ath, E, St, Ti as for 91.261; Th 1/10/91
p175-7.*

91.263 *NED'S CHUM* (CD,3a) David Christie Murray. GLOBE
27/8/91. 1 perf. 1st perfd Opera House, Auckland, New
Zealand 4/4/90 [as *Chums*]. John Furlong David Christie
Murray; Mr Brocklehurst A. Wood; Ned Fellowes H.
Reeves-Smith; Dr Wentworth George Alison; Stuart Will-
ougby David James, jr; Bob Clancey Ells Dagnall; Bill
J. Hatfield; Trooper Frank Damer; Harold Master Leo
Byrne. Lucy Draycott Violet Raye; Araminta Rose Dear-
ing; Mrs Brocklehurst Emily Miller. MGR Fred Stanmaur;
Mus C.J. Hargitt. *REV: Ath 5/9/91 p329-30; E 29/8/91
p9; SR 5/9/91 p275-6; St 3/9/91 p10; Th 1/10/91 p177-
8; Ti 28/8/91 p4.*

91.264 *ARRAH-NA-POGUE: OR, THE WICKLOW WEDDING* (D,3a)
Dion Boucicault. PRINCESS'S 29/8/91-7/11/91. 78 perf
[w/W, S mat exc 29/8, 5/9, 4/11, 7/11]. 1st perfd
Theatre Royal, Dublin 5/11/64. Beamish McCoul Arthur
Dacre; Col. Bagenal O'Grady Henry Neville; The Sec-
retary John Carter; Shaun-the-Post Wilfred E. Shine;
Michael Feeny Charles Ashford; Sgt. Henry Bedford;
Mjr. Coffin Bassett Roe; Oiny Farrell T[homas] Kings-
ton; Winterbottom T[homas] Verner; Sentry [Percy]
Ames; Regan C[harles] Steuart; Patsey W. [F.] Ant-
cliffe; Lanagan L[ouis] Warner; Corporal George Aubrey.
Fanny Power Amy Roselle/Julia Warden; Katty Mrs John
Carter; Arrah Meelish Ellaline Terriss. PP Mrs Harri-
et Gooch; L & Mgr Sydney Herberte Basing; Sc A.E.
Shelton, W. Finch Leicester; Mach J.W. Cawdery; Mus
dir Michael Connelly; Asm T[homas] Verner; Bom [F.]
Forbes; Mus W.C. Levey; Dir Isaac Cohen; Lime Oxy-
Hydrogen Light Co.; Furn Oetzmann; Cost Morris Angel
& Son; Pq William Clarkson. *REV: E 5/9/91 p9; SR 5/9/
91 p276; St 3/9/91 p9; Th 1/10/91 p180-2; Ti 31/8/91*

p2.

91.265 *A SAILOR'S KNOT* (D,4a) Henry Pettitt. DRURY
LANE 5/9/91-5/12/91. 74 perf [w/mat 7/11].*   Jack
Westward Charles Warner; Harry Westwood Charles Glen-
ney; Andre Delaunay Edmund Gurney; Peter Pennycad
Julian Cross; Ben Charker Fred Dobell; Joe Strawbones
Harry Nicholls; Col. Scarlett Frank MacVicars/Dawson;
Sgt. O'Grady Alfred P. Phillips; George Seafield
Thomas Terriss; Mjr. Vivian Ronald Power; Tom Luard
W. Staunton; Cpt. Vernon William Lugg. Marie Delaunay
Jessie Millward; Margery Briarwood Fanny Brough; Jose-
phine Ethel Bland. L & MGR Augustus Harris; Dir Augus-
tus Harris; Sm Arthur P. Collins; Asm Napier Barry;
Mus dir John Crook; Sec & Treas F[red] G. Latham. *REV:
Ath 12/9/91 p363-4; E 12/9/91 p11; SR 19/9/91 p334;
St 10/9/91 p12; Th 1/10/91 p178-80; Ti 7/9/91 p5.*

91.266 *MY SWEET HEART* (MC,2a) William Gill. VAUDEVILLE
7/9/91-10/10/91. 35 perf [w/S mat]. 1st perfd Prin-
cess's, Glasgow 4/6/83. Tony Faust C.J. Murton; Joe
Shotwell William Farren, jr; Dudley Harcourt Herbert
Sparling; Dr Oliver W.J. Robertson; Farmer Hatzell
George Bernage; George Washington Snow Harry Halley.
Tina Minnie Palmer; Miss Fleeter Marie Lewes; Mrs
Hatzell Jane Grey; Daisy Hatzell Daisy Hatzell [sic];
Peek-a-boo Little Jo. L & MGR Thomas Thorne; Act mgr
Douglas Cox; Bom W. Allcroft; Furn Oetzmann; Sm W.J.
Robertson; Mus dir Warwick Williams. *REV: E 12/9/91
p9; SR 12/9/91 p300; St 10/9/91 p12; Ti 8/9/91 p4.*

91.267 *WELL MATCHED* (Ca,1a) Philip Havard. VAUDEVILLE
7/9/91-10/10/91. 30 perf. 1st perfd Public Hall, Ealing
26/3/87. Earl of Bamford William Farren, jr; Blinker
Harry Halley. Mrs Nye Count Smyth Josephine St. Ange.
L & MGR, Act mgr, Bom, Sm, Mus dir, Furn as for 91.266.
REV: E 12/9/91 p9.

91.268 *A NIGHT OFF; OR, A PAGE FROM BALZAC* (C,4a)
Augustin Daly [adpt fr Franz von Schoenthan *Der Raub
der Sabinerinnen*]. LYCEUM 9/9/91-19/9/91. 11 perf
[w/mat 12/9; mat only 19/9]. 1st perfd Daly's, New York
4/3/85. Justinian Babbit James Lewis; Jack Mulberry
John Drew; Harry Damask Herbert Gresham; Lord Mulberry

Charles Wheatleigh; <u>Marcus Brutus Snap</u> Charles Le-
clercq; <u>Prowl</u> [William] Sampson. <u>Nisbe</u> Ada Rehan; <u>Mrs</u>
<u>Zantippe</u> Mrs G.H. Gilbert; <u>Angelica Damask</u> Adelaide
Prince; <u>Susan</u> Isabel Irving; <u>Maria</u> Lulu Smith. L & MGR
Henry Irving; <u>Dir</u> Augustin Daly; <u>Sm</u> George Clarke;
<u>Mus dir</u> Henry Widmer; <u>Bm</u> Richard Dorney; <u>Bom</u> Joseph
Hurst. *REV: E 12/9/91 p9; SR 12/9/91 p300; St 17/9/91
p9; Ti 10/9/91 p4.* <u>Comment</u>: Daly's Company.

91.269 *A ROYAL DIVORCE* (RD,5a) W.G. Wills. OLYMPIC
10/9/91-c.6/1/92. c.136 perf. 1st perfd Avenue, Sunderland 1/5/91. <u>Napoleon I</u> Murray Carson; <u>Talleyrand</u>
T.W. Percyval; <u>Marquis de Beaumont</u> George W. Cockburn;
<u>Gen. Augereau</u> Eardley Turner; <u>Dr Corvisart</u> Powell;
<u>Grimaud</u> James A. Welch; <u>Marshal Murat</u> Frederick Turn-
er; <u>Marshall Ney</u> J[ohn] M. East; <u>Brigadier Antoine</u>
T.C. Dwyer; <u>Bridgadier Pierre</u> Henry Ludlow; <u>Brigadier</u>
<u>Jacques</u> Henry de Solla; <u>Servants</u> J[ames] Caversham,
Campbell; <u>Officer</u> Theodore Alker. <u>Marie Louise</u> Leslie
Bell; <u>Stephanie de Beauharnais</u> Bertie Willis; <u>Blanche</u>
<u>de Hervas</u> Louie [Bassett] Wilmot; <u>Angelique de Var-</u>
<u>ennes</u> Lilian Seccombe; <u>Gouvernante of King of Rome</u>
Louisa Wyatt; <u>Mme dé Campan</u> Madge Herrick; <u>Jeanne La</u>
<u>Terreur</u> Henrietta Watson; <u>Little King of Rome</u> Ethel
Patrick. <u>L</u> Murray Carson; <u>Mgr</u> W.W. Kelly; <u>Dir</u> Henry
Herman; <u>Cost</u> Morris Angel; <u>Mus</u> William Robins; <u>Sc</u>
Richard C. Durant, W.H. Dixon; <u>Mus dir</u> William Robins;
<u>AssistBm</u> George Stone; <u>Asm</u> T.C. Dwyer; <u>Mach</u> R. Warton;
<u>Bom</u> Arthur Frye; <u>Bm</u> H. Lawrence Harris. *REV: Ath 19/
9/91 p396; E 12/9/91 p9; SR 19/9/91 p334-5; St 17/9/
91 p10, 26/11/91 p12; Th 1/10/91 p182-3; Ti 11/9/91
p4.* <u>Comment</u>: The play was advertized only sporadically
in newspapers.

91.270 *YVETTE* (MP,without words,4a) Michel Carré &
Henri Remond. AVENUE 12/9/91-19/9/91. 7 perf.* <u>Mathias</u>
Chautard; <u>Gontran</u> Fordyce; <u>Baron Karp</u> Dubois; <u>William</u>
Sidney Harcourt; <u>John</u> W[indham] Guise; <u>Restaurant</u>
<u>Porter</u> Wray. <u>Pierrot</u> Milly Dathenes; <u>Yvette</u> Julie Avo-
cat; <u>Eva</u> Laborie; <u>Claire</u> Dupressoir; <u>Mme Chalumet</u>
Marsden; <u>Suzanne</u> Garcia. <u>MGR & PD</u> Gaston Mayer; <u>Mus</u>
Andre Gedalge; <u>Act mgr</u> W.H. Griffiths. *REV: E 19/9/91
p9; SR 19/9/91 p335; St 17/9/91 p9-10; Th 1/10/91
p193-4; Ti 14/9/91 p7.*

91.271 *THE TWO BLIND* (Oa,la) Jacques Offenbach. AVE-
NUE 12/9/91-19/9/91. 7 perf. 1st perfd Bouffe-Paris-
iens, Paris, 5/7/55 [as *Les Deux Aveugles*]. Buffles
W[indham] Guise; Morgan Sidney Harcourt. MGR, Act
mgr as for 91.270; Cond Perpignan. *REV: St 17/9/91
p10.*

91.272 *SCHOOL* (C,4a) T.W. Robertson. GARRICK 19/9/91-
19/12/91. 90 perf [w/S mat exc 19/9, 10/10, 19/12].
1st perfd Prince of Wales's 16/1/69. Lord Beaufoy
H.B. Irving; Dr Sutcliffe H.H. Vincent; Beau Farin-
tosh W[illiam] Mackintosh; Jack Poyntz C.W. Garthorne;
Mr Krux Gilbert Hare; Vaughan Hilton. Mrs Sutcliffe
Fanny Robertson; Bella Kate Rorke; Naomi Tighe Annie
Hughes; Tilly Constance Robertson; Milly Beatrice
Ferrar; Mary Kathleen Dene; Laura Gertrude Baines;
Lucy Lena Dene; Clara Winifred Fraser; Kitty Kathleen
Hill; Hetty Kate Grattan; Sybil Jessie Ferrar; Fanny
Grattan; Ethel Lyndall. L & MGR John Hare; Sc Will-
iam Harford; Bom E. Candler; Act mgr C.G. Compton;
Asm R[owley] Cathcart; Mus dir A. Arnstein. *REV:
Ath 26/9/91 p425; E 26/9/91 p10; SR 26/9/91 p363; St
24/9/91 p10; Th 1/10/91 p186-8.*

91.273 *THE LAST WORD* (C,4a) Augustin Daly [fr Franz
von Schoenthan, *Das Letzte Wort*]. LYCEUM 19/9/91-
2/11/91; 13/11/91(2). 46 perf [w/S mat exc 19/9].
1st perfd Daly's, New York 28/10/90. Harry Rutherell
John Drew; Alexander Airey James Lewis; The Secretary
George Clark; Prof Rutherell Charles Wheatleigh;
Moses Mossop Charles Leclercq; Boris Bouraneel Sidney
Herbert; Baron Stuyve Sidney Bowkett; Jordan William
Sampson. Baroness Vera Ada Rehan; Faith Rutherell
Isabel Irving; Winnifred Kitty Cheatham; Paul Lulu
Smith; Mlle Lida May Sylvie. L & MGR Henry Irving;
Sm George Clarke; Mus dir Henry Widmer; Bm Richard
Dorney. *REV: Ath 26/9/91 p425-6; E 26/9/91 p9; SR
26/9/91 p362-3; St 24/9/91 p9-10; Th 1/10/91 p185-6;
Ti 14/11/91 p9.* Comment: Daly's Company.

91.274 *CAPTAIN BILLY* (Oa,la) Harry Greenbank (lib) &
Francois Cellier (mus). SAVOY 23/9/91-16/1/92. 98
perf [np 24-25/12/91].* Cpt. Billy H[elier] Lemaistre;
Christopher Jolly C.R. Rose; Samuel Chunk Rudolph

Lewis. <u>Polly</u> Decima Moore; <u>Widow Jackson</u> Rosina Brand-
ram. <u>PP & MGR</u> Richard d'Oyly Carte; <u>Mus dir</u> Francois
Cellier, Ernest Ford; <u>Sm</u> W.H. Seymour; <u>Act mgr</u> J.W.
Beckwith. *REV: E 26/9/91 p11; St 1/10/91 p12.*

91.275 *LISCHEN AND FRITZCHEN* (Oa,1a) Jacques Offenbach.
CRITERION 26/9/91-25/11/91. 52 perf. 1st perfd Ems
21/7/63. <u>Fritzchen</u> W.R. Shirley. <u>Lischen</u> B[ertha]
Vere. <u>MGR</u> Charles Wyndham; <u>Sm</u> S.H.S. Austin; <u>Act mgr</u>
E. Harvey.

91.276 *THE AMERICAN* (P,4a) Henry James. OPERA COMIQUE
26/9/91-4/12/91. 69 perf [w/S mat exc 26/9]. 1st perfd
Winter Gardens, Southport 3/1/91. <u>Christopher Newman</u>
Edward Compton; <u>Comte Valentin de Bellegarde</u> Clarence
Blakiston; <u>M Nioche</u> Young Stewart; <u>Marquis de Belle-
garde</u> Sydney Paxton; <u>Lord Deepmere</u> C.M. Hallard; <u>M de
Marignac</u> Harrison Hunter; <u>Doctor</u> Fred W. Permain;
<u>Servant</u> W.G. Gunninghame. <u>Marquise de Bellegarde</u> Kate
Bateman [Mrs Crowe]; <u>Mrs Bread</u> Louise Moodie; <u>Noemie
Nioche</u> Adrienne Dairolles; <u>Sister of Charity</u> C. Lindsay; <u>Claire</u> Elizabeth Robins. <u>L & MGR</u> Edward Compton;
<u>Sc</u> Joseph Harker; <u>Furn</u> Frank Giles & Co.; <u>Cost</u> Deben-
ham & Freebody, Mme Patrick, Miss Nimmo; <u>Bom</u> Miss
Niven; <u>Mus dir</u> W.A. Lutz; <u>Sm</u> Lewis Ball; <u>Bm</u> J.H. Savile. *REV: Ath 3/10/91 p461; E 3/10/91 p9; SR 3/10/91
p389; St 1/10/91 p12; Th 1/11/91 p226-9; Ti 28/9/91
p8.*

91.277 *A DEAD LETTER* (DD,1a) W.A. Brabner. OPERA COM-
IQUE 26/9/91-13/11/91. 42 perf. 1st perfd Gaiety,
Dublin 17/4/91. <u>Ben Somers</u> Lewis Ball; <u>Mr Chadwick</u>
Sydney Paxton; <u>Fred Armstrong</u> Harrison Hunter. <u>Polly</u>
Evelyn McNay. <u>L & MGR</u>, <u>Bom</u>, <u>Mus dir</u>, <u>Sm</u>, <u>Bm</u> as for
91.276. *REV: As for 91.276.*

91.278 *JOAN OF ARC* (Bsq,2a) John L. Shine & Adrian
Ross. GAIETY 30/9/91-19/12/91; trfd to SHAFTESBURY
21/12/91-16/1/92. 96 perf [w/mat 17/10, 31/10, 14/11;
np 25/12/91].** <u>Arthur de Richemont</u> Arthur Roberts;
<u>Charles VII</u> [C.D.] Marius/Ernest Bantock; <u>Jacques Darc</u>
F[red] Emney; <u>Fill-up the Good</u> E[rnest] Bantock/A.
Rolph; <u>Bishop of Bovril</u> Willie Warde; <u>Schoolmaster</u>
E.D. Wardes; <u>Mayor of Orleans</u> A. Rolph. <u>Talbot</u> Alma

Stanley/Agnes Hewitt; New York Herald Agnes Hewitt;
Marie Florence Dysart; Yolande Linda Verner; Cath-
erine Alice Lethbridge; Duchess d'Alencon Day Ford;
Aline Violet Monckton; Isabelle Darc Louise Gourlay/
Maria Jones; Blanche Darc Katie Seymour; French
Officer Lily Harold; Joan of Arc Marion Hood/Grace
Pedley; Pages Phoebe Carlo, E. Williams, Louie
Pounds, E. Goss, J. Davis, W. Westlake, A. Bilton.
L & MGR George Edwardes; Mus F. Osmond Carr; Sc Henry
Emden, Bruce Smith; Ch Willie Warde; Cost Miss Fisher,
Alias; Pq C.H. Fox; Bom A.P. Oxley; Dir [C.D.] Marius;
Mus dir W. Meyer Lutz; Asm J[ohn] Ettinson; Act mgr
C.J. Abud. *REV: E 3/10/91 p9, 26/12/91 p9; SR 10/10/*
91 p415, 7/11/91 p526; St 1/10/91 p12; Ti 1/10/91 p4.

91.279 *CARMEN* (O[4a]) Georges Bizet. DRURY LANE 3/10/
91 mat perf.** Escamillo George Fox; Zuniga Whyte;
Dancairo Gilbert King; Remendado Wilfred Esmond; Don
Jose Durward Lely; Morales H. Harrison. Carmen Daria
Farini; Frasquita Kate Merton; Mercedes Agnes Janson;
Michaela Mathilde Bauermeister. MGR Augustus Harris;
Cond John Crook. *REV: 3/10/91 p15; St 1/10/91 p12.*
Comment: A V & A programme indicates there was also
a perf on 26/9/91, but I have been unable to verify
this.

91.280 *THE FIRST MATE* (DD,2a) "Richard Henry" [Richard
Butler & H. Chance Newton]. GAIETY 5/10/91-19/12/91.
66 perf. 1st perfd Gaiety 31/12/88. Farmer Braddock
W.E. Richardson; John Braddock A. Rolph; Mr Brogden
Frank Lacy; Slive E.D. Wardes; Fred Finch Fred Emney.
Mrs Braddock Linda Verner; Letty Lansdell Katie Sey-
mour; Deborah Agnes Hewitt. L & MGR George Edwardes;
Asm J[ohn] Ettinson; Act mgr C.J. Abud.

91.281 *THE WINGS OF THE STORM* (Melo,Prol,3a) R.J.
Barlow & William North. GLOBE 5/10/91. 1 perf.*
Cpt. Barton Price William Glenney; Charles Price
Charles F. Barrett; Mizral Norman Clark; Rev Jedediah
Gradder T.J. Guthrie; Mark Skinner Robson Paige; Puddy
Gorman J.G. Wilton; Silas Silkstone R[obert] Barton;
Pierre Dubosquet Edwin Evans; Tom Davies; Telegraph
Lad Gunners. Mabel Collingwood Cissy Farrell; Cora
Price Winifred Elliott; Jeanne Dubosquet Josephine

MacMahon; <u>Kitty Waffles</u> Lydia Lisle; <u>Alice</u> Lilian
Lewis. <u>DIR</u> F.J. Leslie. *REV: E 10/10/91 p10; SR 10/10/
91 p415; St 8/10/91 p12.*

91.282 *THE SCRIBE; OR, LOVE AND LETTERS* (Oa,1a) Philip
Hayman. GLOBE 5/10/91. 1 perf.* <u>Vacani</u> Philip Hayman;
<u>Beppo</u> E. Dillon Shallard; <u>Tonino</u> Llewelyn Cadwaladr.
<u>Rita</u> Amy Farrell. <u>DIR</u> F.J. Leslie. *REV: As for 91.281.*

91.283 *SLIGHTLY SUSPICIOUS* (F) Josiah Byron. GLOBE
5/10/91. 1 perf.* <u>William Green</u> Norman Clarke; <u>Joe</u>
<u>Jones</u> Robson Paige; <u>P.C. 2 1/4</u> John Robinson Harry
Maynard. <u>Martha Green</u> Winifred Elliott; <u>Mrs Tabitha</u>
<u>Williamson</u> Mrs Robinson; <u>Agnes de Vere</u> Josephine Mac-
Mahon; <u>Mary Muggins</u> Lydia Lisle. <u>DIR</u> F.J. Leslie.
REV: E, St as for 91.281.

91.284 *THERESE RAQUIN* (D,4a) Emile Zola [trans A. Tei-
xeira de Mattos, rev George Moore]. ROYALTY 9/10/91;
14/10/91-28/10/91. 16 perf [w/mat 17/10, 24/10, 28/
10].* <u>Laurent</u> W.L. Abingdon; <u>Grivet</u> Herman de
Lange; <u>Camille</u> Sydney Herberte Basing; <u>Michaud</u> John
Gibson. <u>Mme Raquin</u> Mrs Theodore Wright; <u>Therese Ra-</u>
<u>quin</u> Laura Johnson; <u>Suzanne</u> Clarice Shirley. <u>L</u> Kate
Santley; <u>Mgr & Treas</u> J.T. Grein; <u>Act mgr</u> Charles
Hoppe; <u>Mus dir</u> Jan Mulder; <u>Mgr</u> Sydney Herberte Basing;
<u>Dir</u> Herman de Lange. *REV: Ath 17/10/91 p525; E 17/10/
91 p10; SR 17/10/91 p444-5; St 15/10/91 p12; Th 1/11/
91 p231-3; Ti 10/6/91 p262.* <u>Comment</u>: Independent
Theatre Society.

91.285 *THE BOHEMIAN GIRL* (O[3a]) Michael Balfe. DRURY
LANE 10/10/91(m), 17/10/91(m). 2 mat perf.** <u>Count</u>
<u>Arnheim</u> George Fox; <u>Devilshoof</u> Gilbert King; <u>Flores-</u>
<u>tein</u> Wilfred Esmond; <u>Thaddeus</u> Durward Lely. Queen of
the Gypsies Agnes Janson; <u>Arline</u> Daria Farini/Reba
Henderson. <u>MGR</u> Augustus Harris; <u>Cond</u> John Crook. *REV:
E 17/10/91 p15; St 15/10/91 p12.*

91.286 *THE PARSON* (FC,3a) S.J. Adair Fitzgerald. GLOBE
10/10/91. 1 perf.* <u>Benjamin Scuggles</u> J.G. Wilton;
<u>Josiah Hedgehog</u> Charles F. Barrett; <u>Mjr. Miggle</u> [Rob-
ert] Barton; <u>Rev Septimus Simpleton</u> William Glenney;
<u>Cutely Sharpe</u> Norman Clark; <u>Postman</u> Davies. Mrs Matil-

da Hagglethorpe Mabel Pate; Mrs Jane Hedgehog Lydia
Lisle; Miss Bootleby Winifred Elliott; Mrs Smith Mrs
Robinson; Maria Cissy Farrell. DIR F.J. Leslie. *REV:*
E 17/10/91 p11; St 15/10/91 p12-3.

91.287 *FOILED* (DSk) J.R. Alberton. GLOBE 10/10/91.
1 perf.* Mr Richlee P. Barton; Jack Verance C[harles]
F. Barrett; Mr Downie Norman Clark. Pollie Lillian
Lewis; Mabel Weston Winifred Elliott. DIR F.J. Leslie.
REV: As for 91.286.

91.288 *THE PRINCE AND THE PAUPER* (CD,4a) Joseph Hatton
[fr Mark Twain]. VAUDEVILLE 12/10/91-31/10/91. 18
perf.* Miles Hendon Forbes Dawson; John Canty Mark
Kinghorne; Antony Gorse Bassett Roe; Lord Seymour
Charles [J.] Fulton; Hugh Gallard Cecil Crofton; Cpt.
of Palace Guard A.T. Hendon; Earl of Hertford H. Howe;
Archbishop Cranmer G. Wilsonia; Landlord W. Birch;
Ruffler H[enry] Nelson. Nan Canty Laura Linden; Princess Elizabeth Marie Linden; Mrs Canty Mrs [F.H.]
Macklin; Prince of Wales/Tom Canty Bessie Hatton. L
Thomas Thorne; Mgr Horace Sedger; Mus Alfred J. Caldicott; Cost Harrison, Mrs Nettleship; Furn Oetzmann;
Bom W. Allcroft; Bm William Greet; Act mgr C.P. Levilly. *REV: Ath 17/10/91 p525; E 17/10/91 p11; SR 17/
10/91 p445; St 15/10/91 p12; Th 1/11/91 p233-4; Ti
13/10/91 p4.* Comment: Sources differ on production
date and length of run.

91.289 *HIS LAST CHANCE* (MCa) Ethel & Herbert Harraden.
ROYALTY 14/10/91-3/11/91. 18 perf.** Charles Chester
Sydney Herberte Basing. Alice Montrose [Lizzie] St.
Quinten. PP Kate Santley; L & Mgr Sydney Herberte
Basing; Bom Carpenter; Mus dir Arthur E. Godfrey; Sec
& Treas F. Forbes; Sm Herman de Lange; Asm W[illiam]
Bonney; Act mgr Frederic Baugh.

91.290 *CRISPINO E LA COMARE* (CO) Luigi & Federico
Ricci. SHAFTESBURY 19/10/91, 21/10, 23/10, 26/10,
28/10, 30/10, 31/10(m), 6/11, 7/11(2), 11/11, 14/11(m),
18/11, 21/11(m), 26/11/91. 15 perf. 1st perfd San
Benedetto, Venice 28/2/50. Crispino Giuseppe Ciampi;
Fabrizio Buti; Mirabolana Caracciolo; Contino del
Fiore Grossi; Don Asdrubale Moro; Bortolo Polacco.

Annetta Laura Zagury; La Comare Biancoli. MGR Lago;
Pp John Lancaster. REV: E 24/10/91 p15; St 22/10/91
p12; Ti 20/10/91 p4.

91.291 *CAVALLERIA RUSTICANA* (O[1a]) Pietro Mascagni.
SHAFTESBURY 19/10/91, 21/10, 23/10, 26/10, 28/10,
30/10, 31/10(m), 2/11, 4/11, 6/11, 7/11(2), 9/11,
11/11; 13/11-12/12/91 [w/S mat]. 45 perf. 1st perfd
Teatro Costanzi, Rome 17/5/90. Turiddu Francesco
Vignas; Alfio Brombara. Santuzza Adelaide Mariani;
Lola Marie Brema; Mamma Lucia Grace Damian. MGR
Lago; Pp John Lancaster; Cond Luigi Arditi. REV: E
10/10/91 p15, 24/10/91 p15; SR 24/10/91 p473, 9/12/
93 p651; St 22/10/91 p12; Th 1/11/91 p242-3; Ti 20/
10/91 p4.

91.292 *ROMEO ET JULIETTE* (O[5a]) Charles Gounod. COV-
ENT GARDEN 20/10/91, 2/11, 12/11/91. 3 perf.** Frere
Laurent Abramoff; Capulet Tyssière; Tybalt Pedro
Guetary; Mercutio Eugene Dufriche; Duc de Verone
Armand Castelmary; Gregorio Miranda; Romeo Emile
Cossira. Juliette Manette Simmonet; Stephano Agnes
Janson; Gertrude Laurent. MGR Augustus Harris; Cond
Leon Jehin. REV: E 24/10/91 p15; St 22/10/91 p12.

91.293 *LA CENERENTOLA* (O,4a) Gioacchino Rossini.
SHAFTESBURY 20/10/91. 1 perf. 1st perfd Valle, Rome
25/1/17. Don Magnifico Giuseppe Ciampi; Dandini Buti;
Alidoro Moro; Don Ramiro Chinelli. Cenerentola
Guerrina Fabbri; Tisbe Cecile Brani; Clorinda Biancoli. PP John Lancaster; Mgr Lago; Cond Bimboni; Act
mgr J.D. McLaren. REV: E 24/10/91 p15; Ti 23/10/91 p3.

91.294 *PALMISTRY* (Ca,1a) R.R. Lumley. VAUDEVILLE 20/
10/91-31/10/91. 11 perf. 1st perfd Prince of Wales's
13/4/88. L Thomas Thorne; Mgr Horace Sedger.

91.295 *PAMELA'S PRODIGY* (C,3a) Clyde Fitch. COURT 21/
10/91-31/10/91. 11 perf.* Algernon Serious George
Giddens; Samuel Bogle Donald Robertson; Sir Timothy
Iggins Charles Rock; Jennings Seymour Hicks; James
John Clulow; Edward Hamilton Percy Brough; Adolphus
Todd Edward Righton. Lady Iggins Mrs Edmund Phelps;
Lucinda Mitts Emily Miller; Clarissa Podkins Mary

Jocelyn; <u>Marie</u> Marianne Caldwell; <u>Lady of Title</u> Jessie
Lee; <u>Mrs Pamela Podkins</u> Mrs John Wood; <u>Seraphina</u>
Daisy Stratton. <u>MGR</u> Mrs John Wood, Arthur Chudleigh;
<u>Sc</u> William Callcott; <u>Cost dgn</u> Percy Anderson; <u>Cost</u>
Cooling & Lawrence, Miss Fisher; <u>Mus dir</u> Andrew Levey.
REV: E 24/10/91 p9; SR 24/10/91 p474; St 29/10/91 p13;
Th 1/11/91 p236; Ti 22/10/91 p6.

91.296 *THE LIAR* (C,2a) Samuel Foote. OPERA COMIQUE
21/10/91, 28/10, 4/11, 11/11, 18/11, 25/11, 2/12
[7 mat perf]; 5/12/91-11/12/91 [6 perf]. Total 13
perf. 1st perfd Covent Garden 12/1/1762. <u>Jack Wilding</u>
Edward Compton; <u>Mr Wilding</u> Lewis Ball; <u>Sir James</u>
<u>Elliott</u> Clarence Blakiston; <u>Papillion</u> Sydney Paxton;
<u>John</u> Fred W. Permain; <u>William</u> W.G. Gunninghame. <u>Miss</u>
<u>Grantham</u> Evelyn McNay; <u>Miss Godfrey</u> Elinor Aickin.
<u>L & MGR</u> Edward Compton; <u>Mus dir</u> W.A. Lutz; <u>Sm</u> Lewis
Ball; <u>Bm</u> J.H. Savile. *REV: E 24/10/91 p11; St 22/10/*
91 p12; Th 1/11/91 p235-6; Ti 22/10/91 p6.

91.297 *THE QUEEN'S ROOM* (PoetP,1a) F. Frankfort Moore.
OPERA COMIQUE 21/10/91, 28/10, 4/11, 11/11, 18/11,
25/11, 2/12 [7 mat perf]; 5/12/91-7/1/92 [27 perf;
np 24-25/12/91]. Total 34 perf.* <u>Father Allen</u> Edward
Compton; <u>Chastelard</u> Clarence Blakiston; <u>Henry, Lord</u>
<u>Darnley</u> Harrison Hunter; <u>Cpt.</u> W.G. Gunninghame. <u>Mary</u>
<u>Stuart</u> Ellen Lancaster Wallis; <u>Mary Beaton</u> Evelyn Mc-
Nay. <u>L & MGR</u>, <u>Mus dir</u>, <u>Sm</u>, <u>Bm</u> as for 91.296. *REV:*
E, St, Ti as for 91.296; SR 24/10/91 p474-5; Th 1/11/
91 p235.

91.298 *GODPAPA* (FC,3a) F.C. Philips & Charles H.E.
Brookfield. COMEDY 22/10/91-14/1/92. 72 perf [w/mat
2/1/92; np 24-25/12/91].* <u>Reginald</u> Charles H. Haw-
trey; <u>Sir George Tanworth</u> James Nelson; <u>Pygmalion</u>
William Wyes; <u>Mr Craven</u> W.F. Hawtrey; <u>Mr Bunbury</u>
Charles H.E. Brookfield; <u>Servant</u> Ernest Cosham. <u>Mrs</u>
<u>St. Germain</u> Annie Irish; <u>Mrs Craven</u> Vane Featherston/
[Helen] Lambert; <u>Mary Browne</u> Lottie Venne/Florence
Fordyce; <u>Violet Bunbury</u> Violet Armbruster; <u>Trixie</u>
Helen Lambert; <u>German Lady</u> Eva Williams; <u>Daughter of</u>
<u>Country Squire</u> Stella Maris; <u>Flossie/Maude</u> Mrs Ashford
Griffith. <u>MGR</u> Charles H. Hawtrey; <u>Act mgr & Bm</u> E.F.
Bradley; <u>Asm</u> Charles Milton; <u>Mus dir</u> James M. Glover.

REV: Ath 31/10/91 p593; E 24/10/91 p9; SR 31/10/91 p501; St 29/10/91 p12-3; Th 1/11/91 p236-7; Ti 23/10/91 p3.

91.299 *CARMEN* (O[4a]) Georges Bizet. COVENT GARDEN 22/10/91, 27/10, 17/11, 21/11/91, 4 perf.** <u>Escamillo</u> Lorrain; <u>Dancairo</u> Jouanne; <u>Remendado</u> Iginio Corsi; <u>Morales</u> Miranda; <u>Zuniga</u> Mazani; <u>Don Jose</u> Pierre Emile Engel. <u>Carmen</u> Blanche Deschamps-Jehin; <u>Frasquita</u> Florence Paltzer; <u>Mercedes</u> Mallet; <u>Michaela</u> Manette Simmonet. <u>MGR</u> Augustus Harris; <u>Cond</u> Leon Jehin. *REV: E 24/10/91 p15; St 29/10/91 p12; Ti 26/10/91 p4.*

91.300 *ERNANI* (O[4a]) Giuseppe Verdi. SHAFTESBURY 22/10/91, 2/11, 4/11, 14/11, 21/11, 27/11/91. 6 perf. 1st perfd Teatro La Fenice, Venice 9/3/44. <u>Carlo V</u> R. Blanchard; <u>Silva</u> Giulio Rossi; <u>Jago</u> Moro; <u>Scudiero</u> <u>Don Ricardo</u> Polacco; <u>Ernani</u> Bertini. <u>Elvira</u> Giulia Valda; <u>Anna</u> Biancoli. <u>PP</u> John Lancaster; <u>Mgr</u> Lago; <u>Cond</u> Bimboni; <u>Act mgr</u> J.D. McLaren. *REV: E 24/10/91 p15; Ti 23/10/91 p3.*

91.301 *PHILEMON ET BAUCIS* (O[3a]) Charles Gounod. COVENT GARDEN 24/10/91, 30/10, 31/10, 4/11, 10/11, 13/11, 14/11, 18/11/91. 8 perf. 1st perfd Théâtre-Lyrique, Paris 18/2/60. <u>Philemon</u> Pierre Emil Engel; <u>Jupiter</u> Max Bouvet; <u>Vulcan</u> Lorrain. <u>Baucis</u> Manette Simmonet. <u>MGR</u> Augustus Harris; <u>Cond</u> Leon Jehin. *REV: E 31/10/91 p15; St 29/10/91 p12; Th 1/12/91 p287-8; Ti 26/10/91 p4.*

91.302 *FAUST* (O) Charles Gounod. COVENT GARDEN 24/10/91, 3/11/91. 2 perf.** <u>Faust</u> Demaureux/Emile Cossira; <u>Mephistopheles</u> Lorrain; <u>Valentine</u> Eugene Dufriche; <u>Wagner</u> Miranda. <u>Siebel</u> Agnes Janson/de Spagni; <u>Marguerite</u> Marta Petrina/Martini; <u>Marta</u> Laurent. <u>MGR</u>, <u>Cond</u> as for 91.301. *REV: E 31/10/91 p15, 7/11/91 p15; St 29/10/91 p12, 5/11/91 p12; Ti 26/10/91 p4, 30/10/91 p6, 9/11/91 p8.*

91.303 *IL BARBIERE DI SIVIGLIA* (O[2a]) Gioacchino Rossini. SHAFTESBURY 24/10/91, 29/10, 6-7/11, 11/11, 16/11, 18/11, 25-27/11, 28/11/91(m). 11 perf. 1st perfd Teatro Argentina, Rome 20/2/16. <u>Figaro</u> Buti;

Almaviva Chinelli; Giuseppe Ciampi; Giulio Rossi;
Moro. Rosina Giuseppina Gargano; Berta Biancoli.
PP John Lancaster; Mgr Lago; Cond Luigi Arditi. *REV:*
Ti 28/10/91 p7.

91.304 *THE TIMES* (C,4a) A.W. Pinero. TERRY'S 24/10/91-
26/3/92. 157 perf [w/S mat exc 24/10, 31/10; add mat
28/12, 31/12/91, 4/1/92, 6/1, 13/1, 27/1/92; np 24-
25/12/91].* Percy Egerton-Bompas Edward Terry; Trim-
ble [W.G.] Elliott; Howard Henry V. Esmond; Denham
W.T. Lovell; Jelf Albert Sims; McShane Fred Thorne.
Miss Cazalet Helena Dacre; Beryl Annie Hill; Mrs
Hooley Alexes Leighton; Countess of Ripstow M. Talbot;
Lucy Tuck Hetty Dene; Honoria Laura Barradell; Mrs
Egerton-Bompas Fanny Brough. PP & MGR Edward Terry;
Bm H.T. Brickwell; Sc T.W. Hall; Furn M.W. Edgley;
Cost Russell & Allen; Pq C.H. Fox; Mus dir Tom Smythe;
Sm George Belmore. *REV: Ath 31/10/91 p593; E 31/10/91*
p9; SR 31/10/91 p500-1, 13/2/92 p183; St 29/10/91
p12; Th 1/11/91 p238; Ti 26/10/91 p7.

91.305 *LES HUGUENOTS* (O[5a]) Giacomo Meyerbeer. COVENT
GARDEN 26/10/91, 9/11/91. 2 perf.** Comte de St. Bris
Lorrain; Comte de Nevers Max Bouvet/Tyssière; Marcel
Armand Castelmary; Raoul de Nangis Emile Cossira;
Huguenot Soldier Iginio Corsi. Valentine Martini/
Marta Petrina; Marguerite Bresolles; Urbaine de Spag-
ni. MGR Augustus Harris; Cond Leon Jehin. *REV: E 14/*
11/91 p15; St 12/11/91 p12; Ti 14/11/91 p13.

91.306 *IL VASCELLO FANTASMA [DER FLIEGENDE HOLLANDER]*
(O[3a]) Richard Wagner. SHAFTESBURY 27/10/91, 31/10,
5/11, 10/11, 17/11, 24/11/91. 6 perf. 1st perfd
Dresden 2/1/43. Erik Dorini; Dalando Franco Novara;
Pilota Philip Newbury; Vander Decken R. Blanchard.
Senta Magaret MacIntyre; Mary Grace Damian. PP John
Lancaster; Mgr Lago; Cond Luigi Arditi. *REV: E 31/10/*
91 p11; SR 31/10/91 p501-2; Ti 20/10/91 p7.

91.307 *LE RÊVE* (O[4a]) Alfred Bruneau. COVENT GARDEN
29/10/91, 6/11/91. 2 perf. 1st perfd Opéra-Comique,
Paris 18/6/91. Jean d'Hautecoeur Max Bouvet; Hubert
Lorrain; Felicien Pierre Emile Engel. Angelique Manette Simmonet; Hubertine Blanche Deschamps-Jehin.

MGR Augustus Harris; Cond Leon Jehin. *REV: E 31/10/91
p15, 21/11/91 p15; St 5/11/91 p12; Ti 30/10/91 p6,
9/11/91 p8.*

91.308 *EAST LYNNE* (4a) John C. Chute [adpt of Mrs
Henry Wood's novel]. ROYALTY 29/10/91-7/11/91. 10
perf [w/mat 31/10]. 1st perf?. Cpt. Levison W.L.
Abingdon; Archibald Carlyle Fuller Mellish; Lawyer
Dill Herman de Lange; Bullock Thomas Verner; Lord
Mountsevern John Carter; Richard Hare Frank H. West-
erton; Justice Hare John Gibson; Willie Carlyle Mas-
ter Eric Field-Fisher. Lady Isabel Frances Ivor;
Barbara Hare Nina Williams; Cornelia Carlyle Brunton;
Wilson Dolland; Joyce Miller; Susan [Mrs John] Carter.
PP Kate Santley; L & Mgr Sydney Herberte Basing; Bom
Carpenter; Mus dir Arthur E. Godfrey; Sec & Treas F.
Forbes; Sm Herman de Lange; Asm W[illiam] Bonney; Act
mgr Frederic Baugh. *REV: E 7/11/91 p9; St 5/11/91 p13.*

91.309 *THE PLANTER* (FC,3a) William Yardley [adpt of
Maurice Ordonneau, *La Plantation Thomassin*]. PRINCE
OF WALES'S 31/10/91-21/11/91. 21 perf [w/mat 7/11,
14/11].* Reginald Robinson T.G. Warren; Donald Mac
Haddock Fred Kaye; Theodore Thompson William H. Day;
Don Lopez Charles Groves; Angus MacHaddock Gerald
Kennedy; Cpt. Clay Charles Gilbert; Patrick Pheelan
Harry Parker; Whitewashington Tom Edwardes. Mrs Reg-
inald Robinson Helen Forsyth; Maggie Mac Haddock
Natalie Brande; Mrs Tunnard Amadi. PP Edgar Bruce;
L & Mgr Horace Sedger; Pd [C.D.] Marius; Furn Oetzmann;
Bm William Greet; Act mgr C.P. Levilly; Sm Harry Par-
ker; Mach S. Trewen. *REV: Ath 7/11/91 p626; E 7/11/91
p9; SR 7/11/91 p526; St 5/11/91 p13; Th 1/12/91 p273-
4; Ti 2/11/91 p14.*

91.310 *THE GYPSIES* (Oa,1a) Basil Hood (lib) & Wilfred
Bendall (mus). PRINCE OF WALES'S 31/10/91-21/11/90.
19 perf.** Black Dan A.T. Hendon; Albert T.A. Shale;
Percival H[owell] Russell. Christine Lightfoot Cissy
Cranford; Zirella Ellis Jeffreys. PP, L & Mgr, Bm,
Act mgr, Sm, Mach as for 91.309. *REV: E 7/11/91 p9.*

91.311 *THE CRUSADERS* (D,3a) H.A. Jones. AVENUE 2/11/91-
29/1/92. 91 perf [w/S mat exc 7/11; add mat 2/12,

16/12, 28/12, 30/12/91, 6/1/92, 13/1/92; np 24-25/12/
91; 20/1/92].* Lord Burnham Arthur Cecil; Hon Dick
Rusper Yorke Stephens; Philos Ingerfield Lewis Waller;
Mr Palsam Weedon Grossmith; Mr Burge-Jawle Henry Kem-
ble; Mr Figg Sant Matthews; Rev Algernon Portal E.
Allan Aynesworth; Worrell G.L. Leith. Cynthia Green-
slade Winifred Emery/Maude Millett; Mrs Campion-Blake
Lady Monckton; Queen of the Marshall Niels Lillie
Belmore; Lady Gloire de Dijon Ettie Williams; Victor-
ine Thérèse Mayer; Una Dell Olga Brandon. L H.A. Jones;
Bom Melton; Bm George D. Day; Furn William Morris &
Co.; Cond Wurm; Sm C[harles] M. Appleby; Sc Walter
Hann. *REV: Ath 7/11/91 p626; E 7/11/91 p11; SR 7/11/
91 p525-6; St 5/11/91 p13; Th 2/11/91 p274-6; Ti 3/
11/91 p7, 17/11/91 p6.*

91.312 *AS YOU LIKE IT* (C,5a) William Shakespeare.
LYCEUM 3/11/91-12/11/91. 10 perf [w/mat 7/11].**
Orlando John Drew; Touchstone James Lewis; Jacques
George Clarke; Duke Charles Wheatleigh; Corin Charles
Leclercq; Frederick John Craig; Amiens Laporte; A
Lord/Charles Hobart Bosworth; Oliver Sidney Bowkett;
Le Beau Sidney Herbert; Jacques Ralph Nisbet; Adam
Tyrone Power; Dennis Ralph Nisbet; Silvius Collin
Kemper; William William Sampson. Rosalind Ada Rehan;
Celia Adelaide Prince; Audrey Isabel Irving; Hymen
Kitty Cheatham; Phoebe Florence Conron. L & MGR Henry
Irving; Bom Joseph Hurst; Mus & Mus dir Henry Widmer;
Sm George Clarke; Bm Richard Dorney. *REV: Ath 7/11/
91 p626; E 7/11/91 p9; SR 7/11/91 p526; Ti 4/11/91
p7.* Comment: Daly's Company.

91.313 *THE BASOCHE* (O,3a) Augustus Harris, Eugene
Oudin (lib) [adpt of Albert Carré] & André Messager
(mus). ROYAL ENGLISH OPERA HOUSE 3-5/11/91, 10-11/11,
14/11(2), 16/11(2), 17/11, 19-20/11, 21/11(2), 23-
27/11/91; 5/12/91-16/1/92 [w/S mat exc 5/12/91]. 60
perf [np 25/12/91].* Louis XII W.H. Burgon; Duc de
Longueville David Bispham/Wallace Brownlow; Clement
Marot John McCaulay/Ben Davies/Joseph O'Mara; Jeban
L'Eveille Charles Kenningham; Roland Charles Cop-
land; Master Guillot John Le Hay; Chancellor of the
Basoche Frederick Bovill; Equerry of the King Wilson
Sheffield; Grand Provost [Walter?] Uridge; Jacquet

David Cowis; Page Carrington; Watchman Godwin Hunt.
Marie d'Angleterre Esther Palliser/Esme Lee; Colette
Lucille Hill/Carrie Donald; Jeanette Esme Lee/
Stephanie Seymour; Clarice Kate Vito/Annie Temple.
MGR Richard d'Oyly Carte; Mus dir Francois Cellier;
Dir Hugh Moss; Sc William Perkins, W.T. Hemsley, Will-
iam Telbin; Asm [Herbert] Stanley; Ch Osmond; Cost dgn
Bianchini; Cost Alias, Mme Leon; Pq William Clarkson;
Props [H.] Skelly; Mach Peter White; Bm R. Redford;
Am A.D. Corry. *REV: E 7/11/91 p11, 12/12/91 p15; SR
7/11/91 p524-5; St 5/11/91 p12-3; Th 1/12/91 p285-7;
Ti 4/11/91 p6, 7/12/91 p12.*

91.314 *ORFEO* (O[3a]) C.W. Gluck. SHAFTESBURY 3/11/91,
9/11, 13/11, 20/11/91; 28/11/91-12/12/91 [w/mat 5/12,
12/12]. 19 perf.** Orfeo Guerrina Fabbri; Eurydice
Rita Elandi; L'Amore Cecile Brani. PP John Lancaster;
Mgr Lago; Cond Bimboni; Act mgr J.D. McLaren. *REV:
E 7/11/91 p15; Ti 5/11/91 p11, 5/12/91 p10.*

91.315 *THE CAN'T SING GIRL* (Travestie) Arthur Garland.
ROYALTY 4/11/91-7/11/91. 4 perf.* Algernon Newark;
Fuller Mellish. Amanda Aubrey; Lilly Linfield. MGR
Sydney Herberte Basing; Mus Arthur E. Godfrey. Comment: Advertized in *Ti* thus. Nicoll indicates the
play was licensed for the Princess's 2/11/91, but
does not list this production.

91.316 *AUNT JACK* (F,3a) Ralph R. Lumley. COURT 5/11/
91-1/12/91. 23 perf. 1st perfd Court 13/7/89. S. Berk-
eley Brue George Giddens; Caleb Cornish H. Reeves-
Smith; Col. Tavenor Seymour Hicks; Lord St. John
Brompton Gerald Maxwell; Swoffer W.T. Riley; Justice
Mundle Charles Rock; Associate W.H. Quinton; Usher
F. Fair; Joseph Percy Brough; Foreman of Jury John
Clulow; Mr Juffin Edward Righton. Mrs Ephraim B. Van-
streek Susie Vaughan; Mildred Ethel Matthews; Joan
Bryson Mrs John Wood. MGR Mrs John Wood, Arthur Chud-
leigh. *REV: E 7/11/91 p9; St 12/11/91 p12; Th 1/12/
91 p277; Ti 6/11/91 p9.*

91.317 *A PAIR OF THEM* (Oa,1a) Peyton Wray (lib) & W.
Meyer Lutz (mus). GAIETY 5/11/91 mat perf. 1st perfd
Gaiety 1/3/79. E. Cotte. Maude Venna. L & MGR George

Edwardes; <u>Mus dir</u> W. Meyer Lutz, John Crook, Walter
Slaughter, John Fitzgerald, Gallico, J. Hamilton
Clarke, Edward Jones; <u>Dir</u> C.D. Marius; <u>Cost & Pq</u>
Mrs May, William Clarkson, C.H. Fox; <u>Bom</u> A.P. Oxley;
<u>Act mgr</u> C.J. Abud. *REV: St 12/11/91 p13.*

91.318 *THE BALLAD-MONGER* (RP,1a) Walter Besant & Wal-
ter Pollock [adpt of Theodore de Banville, *Gringoire*].
GAIETY 5/11/91 mat perf.** <u>Louis XI</u> [James] Fernan-
dez; <u>Gringoire</u> H. Beerbohm Tree; <u>Olivier</u> Charles
Allan; <u>Simon</u> Robb Harwood. <u>Loyse</u> Julia Neilson; <u>Nicole</u>
Hethcote. <u>L & MGR</u>, <u>Mus dir</u>, <u>Dir</u>, <u>Cost & Pq</u>, <u>Bom</u>, <u>Act</u>
<u>mgr</u> as for 91.317. *REV: St 12/11/91 p13.*

91.319 *WAITING* (Sk). GAIETY 5/11/91 mat perf.** <u>Harry</u>
Harry Monkhouse. <u>Phyllis</u> Phyllis Broughton. <u>L & MGR</u>,
<u>Mus dir</u>, <u>Dir</u>, <u>Cost & Pq</u>, <u>Bom</u>, <u>Act mgr</u> as for 91.317.
REV: St 12/11/91 p13.

91.320 *IVANHOE* (O,3a) Arthur Sullivan (mus) & Julian
Sturgis (lib). ROYAL ENGLISH OPERA HOUSE 6/11/91,
7/11, 9/11, 12-13/11, 18/11/91. 6 perf.** <u>King Rich-</u>
<u>ard</u> Norman Salmond; <u>Prince John</u> Wallace Brownlow; <u>Sir</u>
<u>Brian de Bris Guilbert</u> Eugene Oudin; <u>Maurice de Bracy</u>
Charles Kenningham; <u>The Grand Master</u> Adams Owen; <u>Ced-</u>
<u>ric</u> D. Ffrangcon Davies; <u>Ivanhoe</u> Barton McGuckin;
<u>Friar Tuck</u> Avon Saxon; <u>Isaac the Jew</u> Charles Copland.
<u>The Lady Rowena</u> Medora Henson; <u>Ulrica</u> Marie Groeble;
<u>Rebecca</u> I. Thuddicum. <u>MGR</u> Richard d'Oyly Carte; <u>Cond</u>
Ernest Ford. *REV: E 14/11/91 p15; Ti 9/11/91 p8.*

91.321 *LOHENGRIN* (O[3a]) Richard Wagner. COVENT GAR-
DEN 7/11/91, 11/11, 16/11/91. 3 perf.** <u>Federico</u>
<u>di Telramondo</u> Eugene Dufriche; <u>Enrico l'Uccellatore</u>
Lorrain; <u>L'Araldo del Re</u> Abramoff/D. Ffrangcon Davies; <u>Lohengrin</u> E. Charles Hedmont/Edward Scovel.
<u>Elsa di Brabante</u> Martini; <u>Ortruda</u> de Spagni; <u>MGR</u> Au-
gustus Harris; <u>Cond</u> Leon Jehin. *REV: E 14/11/91 p15,*
21/11/91 p15; St 12/11/91 p12, 19/11/91 p12; Ti 9/11/
91 p8, 20/11/91 p3.

91.322 *LORD ANERLEY* (P,4a) Mark Quinton & Henry Hamilton. ST. JAMES'S 7/11/91-23/12/91. 45 perf [w/S mat
exc 7/11, 19/12].* <u>Rupert Lee</u> George Alexander; <u>Earl</u>

of Edgehill Nutcombe Gould; Norman, Lord Anerley
Arthur Bourchier; George Beaufort Ben Webster; Travers
E.W. Gardiner; Evans Alfred Holles; Hervey Lester
Herbert Waring. Mme de Sivori Gertrude Kingston; Hon
Esme de Burgh Laura Graves; Evelyn Carew Marion Terry.
MGR George Alexander; Sc H.P. Hall; Mus & Mus dir
Walter Slaughter; Furn Frank Giles; Cost Girodin,
Savage & Purdue, Morris Angel; Pq C.H. Fox; Sm Robert
V. Shone; Bm Alwyn Lewis.*REV:Ath 14/11/91 p657;E 14/11/*
91 p9; St 12/11/91 p12; Th 1/12/91 p277-9; Ti 9/11/91
p8.

91.323 *AFTER DARK: A TALE OF LONDON LIFE* (D,5a) Dion
Boucicault. PRINCESS'S 9/11/91-19/12/91. 45 perf [w/
W, S mat exc 11/11, 16/12, 19/12]. 1st perfd Princess's
12/8/68. Old Tom Henry Neville; Chandos Bellingham
W.L. Abingdon; Dicey Morris Wilfred E. Shine; Gordon
Chumley Sidney Herberte Basing; Area Jack Henry
Bedford; Sir George Medhurst Fuller Mellish; Pointer
Charles Steuart; Crumpets Thomas Verner; 1st Player
Thomas Kingston; 2nd Player H.E. Yeo; 1st Marker
Percy Ames; 2nd Marker William Clifford; Servant
Knox-Ord; Jem Louis Warner; "Music hall scene" Alec
Hurley, George Robey, George Aubrey, McOllive, Mc-
Kane. Rose Egerton Ellaline Terriss; Eliza Beatrice
Selwyn; Street Urchin Bella Orchard; Waitress Gladys
Courtenay; "Music hall scene" Harriet Vernon, Bessie
Bonehill, Susie Harvey. PP Mrs Harriet Gooch; L &
MGR Sidney Herberte Basing; Sc H. Norman, C. Grimani
& sons, G. Harcourt; Mach J.W. Cawdrey; Gas effects
D. Jones; Sm Isaac Cohen; Mus dir Michael Connelly;
Asm Thomas Verner; Act mgr F. Forbes; Sec Cecil Bre-
ton; Lime [W.] Kerr; Furn Oetzmann; Cost Morris Angel,
E.J. Smith; Pq William Clarkson. *REV: E 14/11/91 p9;*
SR 14/11/91 p559; St 12/11/91 p12; Th 1/12/91 p279-80.

91.324 *GLORIANA* (C,3a) James Mortimer [adpt of Henri
Chivot & Alfred Duru, *Le Truc d'Arthur*]. GLOBE 10/11/
91-2/2/92. 97 perf [w/S mat exc 14/11/91, 13/2/92; np
24-25/12/91, 20/1/92; add mat 31/12/91, 6/1/92, 27/1/
92].* Count Vladimir Evitoff W.H. Vernon; Spinks
W[illiam] Lestocq; Timothy Chadwick Harry Paulton/
George Barrett; Leopold Fitz Jocelyn Forbes Dawson;
Richards James A. Welch; Baron Kronikoff C. Howell;

Mjr. Stonidoff J.W. Valsoff. Mrs Gloriana Lovering
Florence West; Jessie Chadwick Georgie Esmond; Kitty
Lydia Cowell. MGR Murray Carson; Sm W[illiam] Lestocq;
Asm R.E. Watson; Mus dir John Storer; Dir W.H. Vernon;
Act mgr W.H. Griffiths; Treas James A. Welch. *REV:
Ath 14/11/91 p657; E 14/11/91 p9; SR 14/11/91 p559;
St 12/11/91 p12; Th 1/12/91 p280-2; Ti 12/11/91 p4.*

91.325 *COUSIN JACK* (FC,3a) Hermann Vezin [adpt fr Roderick Benedix]. OPERA COMIQUE 12/11/91 mat perf. 1st
perfd Assembly Room, Worthing 30/9/91. Cousin Jack
Hermann Vezin; Dunn George R. Foss; Frank Dunn Gerald
Gurney; Charles Sharpe Alfred Courtenay; John Sullivan. Bob Dunn Lucie; May Scott Beatrice Lamb; Daisy
Dunn Elsie Chester. L & MGR Edward Compton; Sm George
R. Foss; Act mgr C. St. John Denton. *REV: Ath 21/11/
91 p694; E 14/11/91 p11; St 19/11/91 p12.*

91.326 *THE PERUVIAN* (CD,1a) Anna de Naucaze. OPERA
COMIQUE 12/11/91 mat perf.* Maurice de Travey Brandon
Hurst. Princess Tcherinchoff Mrs Kemmis; Sylvia de
Torello Anna de Naucaze. L & MGR, Sm, Act mgr as for
91.325. *REV: E, St as for 91.325.*

91.326B *IL MATRIMONIO SEGRETO* (O[2a]) Domenico Cima-
rosa. SHAFTESBURY 12/11/91, 19/11/91. 2 perf. 1st
perfd Burgtheater, Vienna 7/2/1792. Paolino Chinelli;
Count Robinson Buti; Geronimo Giuseppe Ciampi. Fidal-
ma Guerrina Fabbri; Elisetta Guilia Valda; Carolina
Giuseppina Gargano. PP John Lancaster; Mgr Lago; Cond
Bimboni; Act mgr J.D. McLaren. *REV: E 14/11/91 p15;
SR 21/11/91 p585; Ti 14/11/91 p13.*

91.327 *TWO IN THE BUSH* (F,1a) Murray Carson. GLOBE
14/11/91-16/12/91. 29 perf [w/mat 21/11].** Cyrus
Carr Henry de Solla; Mjr Frere James A. Welch; Harry
Draycott T.W. Percyval. Nettie Carr Georgie Esmond.
MGR Murray Carson; Act mgr & Bom W.H. Griffiths; Treas
James A. Welch; Mus dir John Storer.

91.328 *HOOK AND EYE* (Ca) Eille Norwood. OPERA COMIQUE
14/11/91-11/12/91; 9/1/92-14/1/92. 29 perf. 1st perfd
Grand, Leeds 22/3/87. Joshua Gedling Young [M.]
Stewart; Ned Fairleigh Clarence Blakiston; Harry Sel-

bourne Harrison Hunter. <u>Sylvia Selbourne</u> Evelyn McNay.
<u>L & MGR</u> Edward Compton; <u>Mus dir</u> W.A. Lutz; <u>Sm</u> Lewis
Ball; <u>Bm</u> J.H. Savile. *REV: E 21/11/91 p9; St 19/11/91
p12, 14/1/92 p15.*

91.329 *TOMMY* (C,1a) "Rachel Penn" [Mrs E.S. Willard].
AVENUE 16/11/91-29/1/92. 62 perf [np 24-25/12/91,
20/1/92].** <u>Peter</u> Philip Cunningham; <u>Mr Simpkins</u>
Charles Dodsworth; <u>Solomon</u> G.L. Leith. <u>Sister Rachel</u>
Terese Mayer; <u>Martha</u> Mary Callon; <u>Sarah</u> Lily Twyman.
<u>MGR</u> H.A. Jones; <u>Bm</u> George D. Day.

91.330 *FAUVETTE* (CO,3a) Alfred Rae (lib) & Andre
Messager (mus) [adpt of *La Fauvette du Temple*]. ROYAL-
TY 16/11/91-21/11/91. 6 perf. 1st perfd Lyceum, Edin-
burgh 18/5/91. <u>St Angenor</u> W.H. Rawlins; <u>Ahmed</u> West-
lake Perry; <u>Pierre</u> Harry Child; <u>Cransac</u> George Mudie;
<u>Joseph</u> Horace Lingard; <u>Trecourt</u> Fuller Allen; <u>Malek</u>
Bernard Morgan; <u>Ali</u> H. Burgoyne. <u>Fauvette</u> Florence
Burns; <u>Zelie</u> Belle Harcourt; <u>Eugenie</u> Ivy Ambrose;
<u>Tarata</u> Maud Durand; <u>Rosetta</u> Lancaster [?Ellen Lancas-
ter Wallis]. <u>MGR</u> Sidney Herberte Basing; <u>Cond</u> Arthur
E. Godfrey. *REV: 21/11/91 p12; St 19/11/91 p12; Ti
17/11/91 p6.*

91.331 *BESS* (D,3a) Mrs Oscar Beringer. NOVELTY 17/11/
91. 1 perf[?].*

91.332 *LEAH* (5a). PRINCESS'S 19/11/91 mat perf. <u>Lorenz</u>
John Beauchamp; <u>Rudolf</u> Acton Bond; <u>Father Herman</u>
George R. Foss; <u>Ludwig</u> Henry Bedford; <u>Jacob</u> T[homas]
Kingston; <u>Nathan</u> Bassett Roe; <u>Abraham</u> Henry de Solla.
<u>Madalena</u> Annie Rose [Mrs Horace Neville]; <u>Mother Gros-
chen</u> Mrs B.M. de Solla; <u>Rosel</u> Marjorie Field-Fisher;
<u>Leah (child)</u> Little Caryl Field-Fisher; <u>Leah</u> du Barry;
<u>Sarah</u> Agnes B. Cahill. <u>PP</u> Mrs Harriet Gooch; <u>L</u> Sidney
Herberte Basing; <u>Pq</u> William Clarkson; <u>Mus dir</u> Michael
Connelly; <u>Gen mgr</u> V.R. de Magistris. *REV: St 26/11/91
p12.*

91.333 *THE ROUNDHEAD* (RD,3a) Bernard F. Bussy & W.T.
Blackmore. TERRY'S 20/11/91 mat perf.** <u>Col. Leighton</u>
Edwin Gilbert; <u>Cpt. Glynne</u> Edward O'Neill; <u>Reuben
Lightfoot</u> Welton Dale; <u>Sgt. Ireton</u> R. Cole-Aspinall;

1st Trooper Graham; Troopers Gibbs, Holmes, Tiere;
Archibald Warrington H.A. Saintsbury. Alice Lilian
Millward; Constance Edith Jordan. PP & MGR Edward
Terry; Cost Samuel May, Mrs Davies; Pq William Clark-
son; Sc [W.T.] Hemsley; Furn J.S. Lyons; Mus Edwin
Brett; Sm H.A. Saintsbury; Asm J. Bowden Haswell; Act
mgr W. Conyers d'Arcy; Bm H.T. Brickwell; Cond J.
Bayliss.

91.334 *RICHARD'S PLAY* (Ca,1a) Mary C. Rowsell & Joseph
J. Dilley. TERRY'S 20/11/91 mat perf.** Richard Maitland Edwin Gilbert; Admiral Sandilands Cecil Thornybury; Postboy Graham. Sylvia Deloraine Madelaine Rowsell; Prudence Maitland Mrs Conyers d'Arcy. PP & MGR,
Sm, Asm, Act mgr, Cond, Bm as for 91.333.

91.335 [Deleted]

91.336 *L'ELISIR D'AMORE* (O[2a]) Gaetano Donizetti.
SHAFTESBURY 23/11/91. 1 perf. 1st perfd Teatro della
Canobbiana, Milan 12/5/32. Chinelli; Buti; Caracciolo.
Giuseppina Gargano; Cecile Brani. PP John Lancaster;
Mgr Lago; Cond Bimboni.

91.337 *THE PRANCING GIRL* (Travestie of Modern Drama)
Campbell Rae-Brown & B. Brigata (mus). PRINCE OF
WALES'S 26/11/91-19/12/91. 21 perf.* Duke of Goose-
berry Arthur Playfair; Hon Slaugsby Tom A. Shale;
David B-Hives F. Emery; John Whiskison Harry Parker;
Goldspink A.T. Hendon. Lady Boko Adelaide Newton;
Midget Crake Cissy Cranford; Priscilla B-Hives Ellis
Jeffreys. L & MGR Horace Sedger; Pp Edgar Bruce; Cost
Morris Angel; Furn Oetzmann; Bm William Greet; Act
mgr C.P. Levilly; Mus dir A[lfred] J. Caldicott; Sm
Harry Parker. *REV: SR 5/12/91 p638; St 3/12/91 p12;
Ti 27/11/91 p7.*

91.338 *HER OATH* (D,4a) Mrs Henry Wylde. PRINCESS'S
26/11/91 mat perf.* Frank Danvers Henry Neville; Gen.
Danvers Henry Bedford; Col. Westbridge J[ohn] Gibson;
Rajah of Dustnugger W.L. Abingdon; Ali Jan Ivan Wat-
son; Rajah of Saidpore Charles Steuart; Prince Mirza
Kingston; Brahmin Priest L.J. Munro; Count Theodor
Austin Melford; Max Herman de Lange; Sentinel Percy

Ames. Nubian Page [E.] Roydall; Renee Beatrice Lamb;
Josephine Clara Jecks; Marquise de Pontarlier [Cla-
rice?] Sinico; An Ayah Frances Ivor. L & MGR Sidney
Herberte Basing; Dir Henry Heville. *REV: SR 28/11/91
p613; St 3/12/91 p12; Ti 27/11/91 p7.*

91.339 *BRIGHTON* (C,4a) Bronson Howard. CRITERION 1/12/
91-4/2/92; 21/3/92-9/4/92. 77 perf [w/mat 19/12/91,
2/1/92, 26/3, 2/4, 9/4/92; np 25/12/91, 15/1/92, 20/
1/92]. 1st perfd Fifth Avenue, New York 21/12/70.
Bob Sackett Charles Wyndham; Mr Vanderpump William
Blakeley; W. Carter Sydney Valentine; Sir Lewis Park
Walter Everard; Columbus Drake Cecil Crofton; Fred
Carter S[tanley] Hewson; Mjr. Whist W.R. Shirley;
Frank Littlefield Akerman May/R. Sesnon; Jack Benedict Frank Atherley; Waiter C. Edmonds. Kate Livingston Charlotte Granville/L. Gordon; Virginia Vanderpump Mary Ansell/Mabel Hardinge; Mrs Olivia Alston
F. Frances; Mrs Vanderpump Caroline Ewell/Mrs Edmund
Phelps; Mrs W. Carter Emilie Grattan; Jenny Ogden
Sybil Carlisle/Stella Maris; Laura Tracy Nellie Gregory; Effie Remmington Mary Moore. MGR Charles Wyndham; Mus dir Theodore Ward; Sm S.H.S. Austin; Act mgr
E. Harvey. *REV: E 5/12/91 p9; SR 5/12/91 p638, 26/3/
92 p361; St 3/12/91 p12; Th 1/1/91 p50-2; Ti 2/12/91
p6.* Comment: *Th* describes this play as "a localized
version by Frank Marshall of Bronson Howard's *Sara-
toga.*"

91.340 *HEADS OR TAILS* (Ca) J. Palgrave Simpson. CRI-
TERION 1/12/91-4/2/92; 12/2/92-26/2/92; 3/3/92-23/4/
92. 111 perf[np 25/12/91, 15/1/92, 20/1, 15/4/92].**
Wrangleworth Sydney Valentine; Harold Dyecaster Frank
Atherley; Christopher Quaile S[tanley] Hewson. Rosamond Sybil Carlisle/Mabel Hardinge; Bridget F. Fran-
ces/E[mily] Vining. MGR, Mus dir, Sm, Act mgr as for
91.339. *REV: E 5/12/91 p9.*

91.341 *MRS M.P.* (F,3a) Hermann Vezin [adpt of Julius
Rosen, *Kanonenfrutter*]. OPERA COMIQUE 1/12/91 mat
perf. 1st perfd Assembly Rooms, Worthing 28/9/91.
Sir John Loveday Graham Wentworth; Frank Cope Hermann
Vezin; Buzzard George R. Foss; Samuel Orlando Bar-
nett; Thomas Sidney Burt. Mrs Masterman Elsie Chester;

Constance Violet Thornycroft; Emma Alice Maitland;
Mary Agatha Kelly. L & MGR Edward Compton; Sm George
R. Foss; Bm J.J. Killingsworth; Mus dir W.A. Lutz;
Sm Lewis Ball; Bm J.H. Savile. *REV: E 5/12/91 p10;*
St 3/12/91 p12; Th 1/1/92 p52-3.

91.342 *A BREACH OF PROMISE* (Ca,1a) Mabel Freund-Lloyd.
OPERA COMIQUE 1/12/91 mat perf.* Jack Greythorpe
Orlando Barnett; Cpt. Heriot Graham Wentworth. Lin-
olia Greythorpe Mary Mordaunt; Winifred Stanley Alice
Maitland; Mrs Grimley Eleanor Bufton. L & MGR, Sm, Bm,
Mus dir, Act mgr as for 91.341. *REV: As for 91.341.*

91.343 *A PANTOMIME REHEARSAL* (Bsq,1a) Cecil Clay.
COURT 2/12/91-2/4/92; 27/4/92-15/10/92. 290 perf [w/
S mat exc 5/12/91, 11/6/92, 25/6, 9/7, 16/7, 23/7,
30/7, 6/8, 13/8, 20/8, 27/8, 3/9, 1/10/92; add mat
27/1/92, 3/2, 10/2, 17/2, 24/2(?), 9/3, 16/3, 23/3,
30/3/92; mat only 27/8/92, 3/9/92; np 24-25/12/91,
20/1/92].** The Gifted Author [Jack Deedes] C.P.
Little; Lord Arthur Pomeroy Weedon Grossmith; Cpt. Tom
Robinson Brandon Thomas; Sir Charles Grandison Wilfred
Draycott; Tomkins [F.] Vaughan. Lily Eaton-Belgrave
Rose Norreys/Ellaline Terriss; Violet Eaton-Belgrave
Edith Chester/Decima Moore/Briant; Mary Russell-
Portman May Palfrey; Rose Russell-Portman Maude Mc-
Naught/Christine Noel/[Stella] Berridge; Lady Muriel
Beauclerc Carlotta Addison/Gertrude Kingston. PP Mrs
John Wood, Arthur Chudleigh; Dir Brandon Thomas; Bm
Leonard Lillies; Cost Russell & Allen; Mus dir Edward
Jones. *REV: SR 16/1/92 p70-1; St 10/12/91 p13; Ti*
28/4/92 p10.

91.344 *A COMMISSION* (C,1a) Weedon Grossmith. COURT
2/12/91-2/4/92. 129 perf [w/S mat exc 5/12/91; add
mat 27/1/92, 3/2, 10/2, 17/2, 24/2(?), 9/3, 16/3,
23/3, 30/3/92; np 24-25/12/91, 20/1/92].** Mr Marshall Wilfred Draycott; Shaw Weedon Grossmith; Gloucester Brandon Thomas. Mrs Hemmersley Edith Chester;
Parker May Palfrey. PP, Dir, Mus dir, Bm as for 91.
343. *REV: St 10/12/91 p13.*

91.345 *GOOD FOR NOTHING* (CD,1a) J.B. Buckstone. COURT
2/12/91-26/1/92. 52 perf [w/S mat exc 5/12/91; np

24-25/12/91, 20/1/92].** Tom Dibbles Brandon Thomas;
Harry Collier [W.L.] Branscombe; Charley Wilfred
Draycott; Young Mr Simpson Compton Coutts; Servant
[W.H.] Quinton. Nan Rose Norreys. PP, Dir, Bm, Mus
dir as for 91.343. *REV: SR 19/12/91 p695; St 10/12/91 p13.*

91.346 *A MISUNDERSTANDING* (WordlessP). LYRIC 2/12/91
mat perf. [C.D.] Marius. Mlle Marie. *REV: St 3/12/91 p12.*

91.347 *THE RECKONING* (P,4a) Silvanus Dauncey. GLOBE
3/12/91 mat perf.* Cpt. Philip Conway Lewis Waller;
Mr Leach Murray Carson; Rigby Nicks Wilfred E. Shine;
Frank Gibbon T.W. Percyval; Sir William Deacon Ed-
ward Lennox; Dr McPherson James A. Welch; Rev Samuel
Oliver Frederick Victor; Slisher J[ohn] Willes; Duck-
ett James Caversham. Dora Deacon Gracie Warner; Janet
Lillie Belmore; Mrs Chilcot Lena Ashwell; Constance
Oliver Florence West. L & MGR Murray Carson; Sm
W[illiam] Lestocq; Pq William Clarkson; Furn Oetzmann;
Act mgr W.H. Griffiths; Treas James A. Welch; Asm R.
E. Warton. *REV: Ath 12/12/91 p809; E 5/12/91 p10; St
10/12/91 p12-3; Th 1/1/92 p53-4; Ti 4/12/91 p11.*

91.348 *MY SWEETHEART* (MC,3a) William Gill. NOVELTY
4/12/91. Rnd [probably played earlier than this].**
Tony Johnstone Gould; Dr Oliver W. Garrett; Joe Shot-
well H. Buckstone Clair; G. Brooke; G.M. Slater.
Tina Marie Brian; Mrs Chandler; Eleanor Lloyd. *REV:
St 10/12/91 p13.*

91.349 *THE GAMBLER* (D,3a) James Wimsett Boulding. ROY-
ALTY 5/12/91. 1 perf.* Cpt. John Dudley Leonard Out-
ram; Gen. Dudley John Carter; Albert Montrose Richard
Saunders; William Fraser Cecil H. Thornbury; Bob
Blackley Hamilton Hine; Dick Wildman Hugh Fleming;
Joe Darnley Howard Thompson. Little Jack Little Maudie
Marshall; Maud Stainton [Anna] de Naucaze; Kathleen
Octavia Kenmore; Jane [Amy?] Elstob; Mary Agnes Im-
lay; Victoria Mrs Bennett. BM J.J. Killingsworth.*REV:
E 12/12/91 p11; St 10/12/91 p12.*

91.350 *THE END OF A DAY* (Ca,1a) Herbert Burnett. ROY-

ALTY 5/12/91. 1 perf.* <u>Rev Frank Thornton</u> H.A. Saintsbury; <u>Sir Geoffrey Carlyon</u> Kenneth Rivington; <u>Archie, Lord Fielding</u> Thomas Terriss; <u>James</u> Russell Vaun. <u>Evelyn</u> Violet Thornycroft. <u>BM</u> as for 91.349. *REV: As for 91.349.*

91.351 *A BREEZY MORNING* (Ca,1a) Eden Phillpotts. COMEDY 8/12/91-14/1/92; 23/1/92-17/2/92. 53 perf [np 24-25/12/91]. 1st perfd Grand, Leeds 27/4/91. <u>Mr Goldie</u> Sam Sothern. <u>Mrs Goldie</u> Florence Fordyce. <u>MGR</u> Charles H. Hawtrey; <u>Act mgr & Bm</u> E.F. Bradley; <u>Asm</u> Charles Milton; <u>Mus dir</u> James M. Glover. *REV: E 12/12/91 p9; SR 12/12/91 p667; St 10/12/91 p12.*

91.352 *MARGARET BYNG* (P,4a) F.C. Phillips & Percy Fendall. CRITERION 8/12/91 mat perf.* <u>Bazano</u> Charles H.E. Brookfield; <u>Col. Heathcote</u> John Beauchamp; <u>Cpt. Frederick Dornton</u> Ben Webster; <u>J. Dornton</u> H[enry] Dana; <u>Francois</u> Charles Milton; <u>Braddick</u> William Wyes; <u>Sharker</u> Ernest Cosham; <u>Gutteridge</u> A.W. Ayson; <u>Mr Byng</u> William Herbert. <u>Margaret Byng</u> Estelle Burney; <u>Mary</u> Helen Lambert; <u>Francine</u> Maud Durand; <u>Mrs Dornton</u> Lizzie Webster. <u>L & MGR</u> Charles Wyndham; <u>Dir</u> Charles Milton; <u>Cost</u> Nathan; <u>Pq</u> C.H. Fox; <u>Mus dir</u> Theodore Ward. *REV: E 12/12/91 p10; SR 12/12/91 p667; St 10/12/91 p12; Ti 9/12/91 p10.*

91.353 *THE ROAD TO RUIN* (C,4a) Thomas Holcroft. OPERA COMIQUE 9/12/91(m); 12/12/91-7/1/92. 27 perf [w/mat 16/12/91, 19/12, 26/12, 28/12/91, 2/1/92; np 24-25/12/91]. 1st perfd Covent Garden 18/2/1792. <u>Charles Goldfinch</u> Edward Compton; <u>Mr Dornton</u> Lewis Ball; <u>Harry Dornton</u> Clarence Blakiston; <u>Sulky</u> Sydney Paxton; <u>Smith</u> Fred W. Permain; <u>Jack Milford</u> Harrison Hunter; <u>Silky</u> Young Stewart; <u>Williams</u> W.G. Gunninghame; <u>Jacob</u> Sharp; <u>Sheriff's Officer</u> William Riach; <u>John</u> Flexmore. <u>Jenny</u> C. Lindsay; <u>Widow Warren</u> Elinor Aickin; <u>Sophia Freelove</u> Evelyn McNay. <u>L & MGR</u> Edward Compton; <u>Mus dir</u> W.A. Lutz; <u>Sm</u> Lewis Ball; <u>Bm</u> J.H. Savile. *REV: E 12/12/91 p9; SR 19/12/91 p695; St 10/12/91 p13; Ti 14/12/91 p14.*

91.354 *THE BARBER OF BAGDAD* (O) Rev Marmaduke E. Browne (lib) & Peter Cornelius (mus). SAVOY 9/12/91

mat perf.* Caliph John Sandbrook; Baba Mustapha
William White; Noureddeen William Green; Aboul Hassan
Ali Eben Bekar Charles J. Magrath. Morgiana Una H.
Bruckshaw; Bostana Pattie Hughes. Cond C. Villiers
Stanford; Sm C.H.E. Brookfield. *REV: E 12/12/91 p7;
SR 12/12/91 p668; Ti 10/12/91 p10.* Comment: Royal
College of Music.

91.355 *ON AN ISLAND* (Sk) J. Wilton Jones. AVENUE 10/
12/91 mat perf. 1st perfd Theatre Royal, Bradford
8/3/79. Charles Cooper. Lillie Belmore. *REV: 17/12/91
p12.*

91.356 *THE YOUNG PRETENDER* (FC,3a) Barton White. OPERA
COMIQUE 10/12/91 mat perf. 1st perfd Sanger's, Rams-
gate 3/7/90. Matthew Honeybun John Tresahar; Hugh
Jones James Nelson; Davies Alexander Loftus; Benja-
min Honeybun Gilbert Trent; Prof Bluejohn Fossil
Frederick Kaye. Aunt Harriett Sophie Larkin; Min Nina
Williams; Dolly Fossil Isabel Ellissen; Maud Honeybun
Nora Williamson. L & MGR Edward Compton; Sm John Tre-
sahar; Act mgr & Dir C. St. John Denton; Mus dir W.A.
Lutz; Bm J.H. Savile. *REV: E 12/12/91 p11; St 17/12/
91 p12.*

91.357 *COCK ROBIN & JENNY WREN* (Ent,1a) M.C. Gilling-
ton (lib) & Florian Pascal (mus). ROYALTY 12/12/91-
2/1/92;* trfd to VAUDEVILLE 4/1/92-11/1/92. 24 mat
perf [np 25/12/91, 9/1/92]. Cock Robin Master E. Pow-
er; Cuckoo Master William Kelly; Sparrow Master Will-
ie Sewell; Fly Master Horatio Gregg; Rook Master
Walter Wray. Jenny Wren Daisy Gilpin; Owl Marie All-
wood; Bull Julia Johnson; Beetle Elaine Lawson;
Chronista Gracie Murielle. PP Kate Santley; Dir John
Donald, C. Burleigh-Tesseman; Singing Mistress Mrs
Fitzgerald; Dancing Master W. Osmond; Cond J[ohn]
Fitzgerald; Cost Harrison; Pq C.H. Fox; Furn Oetzmann;
Bm John Donald.*REV: E 19/12/91 p9; SR 19/12/91 p695;
St 17/12/91 p12; Ti 14/12/91 p14.* Comment: London
Juvenile Opera Company.

91.358 *OLD KING COLE AND GOOD QUEEN COLE* (Ent,1a)
William Younge (lib) & Florian Pascal (mus). ROYALTY
12/12/91-2/1/92;* trfd to VAUDEVILLE 4/1/92-11/1/92.

24 mat perf [np 25/12/91, 9/1/92]. Old King Cole Master F.W. Allwood; Lord Chamberlain Master Horatio Gregg; Fiddlers Master Walter Wray, Master E. Lord, Master E. King; Pipers Master E. Power, Master William Kelly, Master G. Croxon; Drummers Master M. Allwood, Master E. Brewer, Master D. Moran; Smokers Master Willie Sewell, Master N. Baker, Master C. Hammond. Good Queen Cole Gracie Murielle; Mistress of the Robes Victoria Allwood; Nurses Daisy Gilpin, Elaine Lawson, D. Kaines; Housemaids J. Bromley, S. Breslauer, B. Harding; Cooks Julia Johnson, L. Safferine, M. Wilds; Laundresses Violet Hart, L.Gee, Daisy Hart; Pages M. Stephens, M. Jamieson, G. Reed, L. Breslauer, A. Thompson; Maids of Honour F. Farmer, A. Tupholine, E. Braham, N. Dillon, D. Nolan, C. Pratt, E. Coles, A. Jowers. PP, Dir, Singing Mistress, Dancing Master, Cond, Cost, Pq, Furn, Bm as for 91.357. *REV: As for 91.357.* Comment: As for 91.357.

91.359 *AN OLD FASHIONED HARLEQUINADE.* ROYALTY 12/12/ 91-2/1/92; trfd to VAUDEVILLE 4/1/92-11/1/92. 24 mat perf [np 25/12/91, 9/1/92]. Policeman Master E. King; Pantaloon Master Horatio Gregg; Sailor's Hornpipe F.W. Allwood; Clown Master Harry Paulo. Columbine Marie Allwood; Harlequine Victoria Allwood; Skipping Rope Dance Julia Johnson. "Incidental songs & dances" Fred Allwood, Harry Paulo, Marie Allwood, Victoria Allwood. PP, Dir, Singing Mistress, Danicng Master, Cond, Cost, Pq, Furn, Bm as for 91.357. *REV: SR, St, Ti as for 91.357.* Comment: As for 91.357.

91.360 *THE BOHEMIAN GIRL* (O,3a) Michael Balfe. SHAFT-ESBURY 16/12/91 mat perf.** Thaddeus Wilfrid Acfield; Florestein Patrick O'Connor; Count Arnheim Albert Thorn; Devilshoof Charles Hinchliff; Cpt. of the Guard Edward Epstein. Arline Frederica Smith/Eugenia Morgan; Queen of the Gipsies Jessie Browning; Buda Jenny H. Smith. Cond Neill O'Donovan. *REV: E 19/12/ 91 p7.* Comment: Guildhall School of Music.

91.361 *THROUGH THE FIRE* (Ca,1a) W[illiam] Lestocq & Yorke Stephens. GLOBE 17/12/91-16/2/92. c.50 perf [np 24-25/12/91, 20/1/92]. 1st perfd Strand 25/2/88. Jack Wonlock Frederick Victor; George Todd T.W.

Percyval; <u>Old Wenlock</u> J[ohn] Willes; <u>William</u> A.H.
Brooke. <u>Mrs Wenlock</u> Kate Robertson; <u>Daisy Lane</u> Georgie
Esmond; <u>Dolly</u> Lena Ashwell. <u>MGR</u> Murray Carson; <u>Sm</u>
W[illiam] Lestocq; <u>Asm</u> R.E. Warton; <u>Mus dir</u> John Stor-
er. <u>Comment</u>: Possibly also perfd 17/2-22/2.

91.362 *A DEBT OF HONOUR* (CD,1a) C.P. Colnaghi. OPERA
COMIQUE 17/12/91 mat perf.* <u>Col. Desmond</u> Charles J.
Fulton; <u>Sir Hubert Hazeldean</u> A[lfred] Courtenay; <u>Aub-</u>
<u>rey</u> Ben Webster; <u>David</u> A. Heathcote. <u>Lady Hazeldean</u>
Mrs F. Copleston; <u>Sylvia</u> Marie Linden.<u>L & MGR</u> Edward
Compton; <u>Mus dir</u> W.A.Lutz; <u>Sm</u> C.W.A. Trollope; <u>Act mgr</u>
C. St. John Denton. *REV: E 19/12/91 p11; St 24/12/91*
p10.

91.363 *THE SPRING LEGEND* (Oa) C.P. Colnaghi (lib) &
Cotsford Dick (mus). OPERA COMIQUE 17/12/91 mat perf.*
<u>Dr Dosemoffen</u> Cairns James; <u>Sir Lancelot</u> George Pow-
er; <u>Fritz</u> W.R. Shirley; <u>Spitz</u> Sydney Barraclough.
<u>Bella Donna</u> Jessie Moore; <u>Bryonia</u> Edith Chester; <u>Pulsa-</u>
<u>tilla</u> Laura Linden; <u>Lischen</u> Blanche Leyton; <u>Seraphina</u>
<u>Lovering</u> Mrs F. Copleston. <u>L & MGR</u>, <u>Mus dir</u>, <u>Sm</u>, <u>Act</u>
<u>mgr</u> as for 91.362. *REV: E, St as for 91.362; SR 26/*
12/91 p724.

91.364 *THE LIGHT OF PENGARTH* (D,1a) Ina Leon Cassilis.
OPERA COMIQUE 17/12/91 mat perf.* <u>Will Devenish</u> W.R.
Shirley; <u>Jessie Crannock</u> Cairns James. <u>Minna</u> Laura
Linden. <u>L & MGR</u>, <u>Mus dir</u>, <u>Sm</u>, <u>Act mgr</u> as for 91.362.
REV: As for 91.362.

91.365 *OLIVER TWIST* (D,5a) George G. Collingham. OLYM-
PIC 21/12/91-27/1/92. 32 perf [w/mat 21/12/91; np 25/
12/91, 20/1/92].* <u>Bill Sykes</u> Bassett Roe; <u>Fagin</u> Henry
de Solla; <u>Monks</u> Harcourt Beatty; <u>Artful Dodger</u> James
A. Welch; <u>Noah Claypole</u> Frank M. Wood; <u>Charley Bates</u>
E. Trevor Warde; <u>Barney</u> Arthur Wright; <u>Sowerberry</u>
Henry Ludlow; <u>Bumble</u> T.C. Dwyer; <u>Giles</u> Ruston; <u>Brown-</u>
<u>low</u> Arthur Estcourt; <u>Toby Crackitt</u> [D.] J. Hennessy;
<u>Officer</u> Theodore Alker. <u>Nancy Sikes</u> Grace Hawthorne;
<u>Oliver Twist</u> Bertie Willis; <u>Rose</u> Henrietta Watson;
<u>Charlotte</u> Lesley Bell; <u>Mrs Sowerberry</u> Louisa Wyatt;
<u>Mrs Bumble</u> Emily Borthwick. <u>PP</u> Charles Wilmot; <u>L &</u>
<u>Mgr</u> W.W. Kelly; <u>Bm</u> H. Lawrence Harris; <u>Dir</u> Grace Haw-

thorne; <u>Bom</u> Arthur Frye; <u>Cond</u> William Robins; <u>Sec</u> C.J.
McCarthy; <u>Sm</u> Arthur Estcourt; <u>Asm</u> Arthur Wright; <u>Mach</u>
George Cawdery. *REV: E 26/12/91 p9; SR 26/12/91 p724;
St 24/12/91 p10-1, 11/2/91 p12; Ti 22/12/91 p4.*

91.366 *PALMISTRY* (Ca,1a) R.R. Lumley. PRINCE OF WALES'S
21/12/91-16/1/92. 23 perf [np 25/12/91].** <u>PP</u> Edgar
Bruce; <u>Mgr</u> Horace Sedger.

91.367 *ALONE IN LONDON* (D,4a) Robert Buchanan & Harriet Jay. PRINCESS'S 21/12/91-16/1/92. 23 perf [np 25/
12/91]. 1st perfd Olympic 2/11/85. <u>John Biddlecombe</u>
Henry Neville; <u>Richard Redcliffe</u> W.L. Abingdon; <u>Jen-
kinson</u> Wilfred E. Shine; <u>Walter Burnaby</u> Thomas Kings-
ton; <u>Mr Burnaby</u> Charles Steuart; <u>Spriggins</u> Fuller
Mellish; <u>Jack Woods</u> Thomas Verner; <u>Charlie Johnson</u>
Henry Bedford; <u>Robert</u> Louis Warner; <u>Inspector of
Police</u> G. Aubrey; <u>David</u> Percy Ames. <u>Ruth Clifton</u> Bea-
trice Selwyn; <u>Annie Meadows</u>/<u>Nan</u> Maud Elmore; <u>Liz
Jenkinson</u> Julia Warden/Esther Courtney; <u>Mrs Malony</u>
Mrs [H.?] Clifton; <u>Gipsy Tom</u>/<u>Tom Chickweed</u> Ellaline
Terriss; <u>Little Paul</u> Little May Blackburn; <u>Susan</u>
E. Roydall. <u>PP</u> Mrs Harriet Gooch; <u>L & Mgr</u> Sidney Her-
berte Basing; <u>Sc</u> H. Norman, C. Grimani & Sons; <u>Mach</u>
J.W. Cawdrey; <u>Sm</u> Isaac Cohen; <u>Mus dir</u> Michael Connelly;
<u>Asm</u> Thomas Verner; <u>Sec</u> Cecil Breton; <u>Act mgr</u> F. For-
bes; <u>Lime</u> [W.] Kerr; <u>Furn</u> Oetzmann; <u>Cost</u> Morris Angel;
<u>Pq</u> William Clarkson; <u>Dir</u> Isaac Cohen. *REV: E 26/12/91
p9; SR 26/12/91 p724; St 24/12/91 p10; Ti 22/12/91 p4.*

91.368 *HANS THE BOATMAN* (MC,3a) Clay M. Greene. STRAND
21/12/91-27/1/92. 28 mat perf [np 24-25/12/91, 2/1/
91, 15/1, 20/1/92]. 1st perfd Theatre Royal, Sheffield
7/3/87. <u>Hans</u> Charles Arnold; <u>Mr Farwell</u> George P. Hawtrey; <u>Yank Thursby</u> Austin Melford; <u>Darrell Vincent</u>
Edward O'Neill; <u>Lieut. Finch</u> Sydney Barraclough; <u>Reg-
inald Rowen</u> Lionel Rae; <u>Arthur Finch</u> A.R. Garland;
<u>Chauncey Grant</u> Alec C. MacKenzie; <u>Phil Scott</u> H. Buss.
<u>Jeffie</u> Alice Atherton; <u>Gladys Farwell</u> Agnes Knights;
<u>Little Hans</u> Little May Hannen; <u>Annie Rooney</u> Little
Daisy Stratton; <u>Baby Rooney</u> Alma Hannan. <u>PP</u> J.S.
Clarke; <u>Mgr</u> Willie Edouin; <u>Bm</u> J.T. Mackay Robertson;
<u>Sm</u> Charles Davies. *REV: E 26/12/91 p9; SR 26/12/91 p
724; St 24/12/91 p10; Ti 22/12/91 p4.*

91.369 *THE HONOURABLE HERBERT* (P,4a) C. Haddon Chambers. VAUDEVILLE 22/12/91-16/1/92. 26 perf [w/mat 26/12, 28/12/91, 2/1/92, 9/1/92; np 25/12/91].*
Pym Brady Thomas Thorne; Philip Tenby Arthur Elwood; Hon Harold Doring Sydney Brough; Lavender Charles Dodsworth; Waiter Oswald Yorke; Amner A. Vane-Tempest; Hon Herbert Doring H.B. Conway; Banks G. Robinson; Servant A. Austin. Mrs Doring Dorothy Dorr; Dorcas Collette Mary Collette; Lady Highfield Gertrude Warden; Simpson [Harriet] Trench; Florrie Summers Ella Banister. L & MGR Thomas Thorne; Act mgr Sydney Alport; Sm F[red] Grove; Sc Liberty, W.T. Hemsley; Sc dgn Wyburd; Cost Russell & Allen; Cost dgn Joyce; Mus dir Charles Dubois. REV: Ath 2/1/91 p31-2; E 26/12/91 p9; SR 2/1/92 p13; St 24/12/91 p10; Th 1/2/92 p95-6; Ti 23/12/91 p3.

91.370 *CINDER-ELLEN UP TOO LATE* (Bsq,3a) "A.C. Torr" [Fred Leslie] & W.T. Vincent. GAIETY 24/12/91-9/7/92. 181 perf [w/mat 2/1/92, 9/1, 16/1, 27/2, 12/3, 26/3, 2/4, 23/4, 7/5, 14/5, 21/5, 4/6, 2/7/92; np 25/12/91, 20/1/92, 15/4/92].* Prince Belgravia E.J. Lonnen; Sir Ludgate Hill Arthur Williams; Servant Fred Leslie; Peckham Harris; Gnorwood [C.] Walker; Footman Hill. Cinder-Ellen Nellie Farren/Kate James/ Letty Lind; Linconzina Sylvia Grey; Fettalana Florence Levey; Lord Taplow Maude Hobson; Lord Eastbourne Blanche Massey; Lord Soho Hetty Hamer; Sir Waterloo Bridge Janet Norton; Catherina Lillian Price; Grazina Maude Wilmot; Furnivalzina Violet Monckton; Griffina Eva Greville; Templina Adelaide Astor; Victorina Lily MacIntyre; Sir Peterborough Court Maud Boyd; Mrs Kensington Gore Emily Milly; Lord Whitefriars Dunville. MGR George Edwardes; Mus W. Meyer Lutz; Ch Katti Lanner, Willie Warde; Cost Miss Fisher, Alias; Cost dgn Wilhelm, Hugh Paterson; Dir Walter Raynham; Mus dir W. Meyer Lutz; Sm Frank Parker; Act mgr C.J. Abud; Bom A.P. Oxley; Pq C.H. Fox. REV: E 26/12/91 p11; SR 2/1/92 p16; Th 1/2/92 p96.

91.371 *HUMPTY DUMPTY; OR, THE YELLOW DWARF AND THE FAIR ONE WITH THE GOLDEN LOCKS* (Panto) Harry Nicholls & Augustus Harris. DRURY LANE 26/12/91-2/4/92. 147 perf [2 perf dy 28/12/91-17/2/92; M, W, S Mat there-

after].* Queen of Hearts Dan Leno; King of Hearts
Herbert Campbell; Humpty Dumpty Little Tich; Dumb
Waiter Charles Lauri; Japanese Doll John d'Auban;
Clown Harry Payne; Knave of Hearts Fred Walton; Twirl-
ey George Lupino; Buttons Tom Pleon; Fairy Oltatina
E.S. Vincent; Demon Cat Brothers Kitchen; Flunkey
Frank Damer; Porter Thomas Terriss; Harlequin Charles
Romaine; Pantaloon Tully Lewis; Policeman H. Forde.
Princess Allfair Marie Lloyd/Mabel Love; King Dulci-
mar Fanny Leslie; Maid of Hearts Retta Walton; Three
Fairy Queens Nora Williamson, Pattie Heywood, Florence
Paltzer; Japanese Doll Emma d'Auban; Court Jester
Madge Lucas; Columbine Annie Evans; Tit Bit Evelyn
Hughes. MGR Augustus Harris; Mus dir John Crook; Cost
Auguste, Harrisons, Angel, Landolf, Miss Collier,
Miss Palmer, Mrs Atkins; Armour Kennedy & Phillips,
Gutperle; Pq William Clarkson; Props [R.] Hicks, Lab-
hart; Chorus Master Stedman; Ch John d'Auban; Sm
Arthur P. Collins. *REV: E 2/1/92 p8; SR 2/1/92 p16;
Ti 28/12/91 p8.*

91.372 *CINDERELLA* (Panto) H. Buckstone Clair. NOVELTY
26/12/91-13/2/92. 58 perf [w/mat 26/12/91-2/1/92, 4/1,
6/1, 9/1, 11/1, 13/1, 16/1, 23/1, 30/1, 6/2, 13/2; np
20/1/92].* Baron Oofless H. Buckstone Clair; Jeames/
Clown W. Garratt; Gertrude Val Seymour; Pauline Frederick Ellis; Dr Syntax Owen Wynne; Grab'em A. St.
Laurence; Seize'em George Arnold; Lord Chamberlain
Reeves; Father Time Master [Buck] Williams; Harlequin
A. Whittaker; Pantaloon Holdun; A Masher G[eorge]
Arnold. Prince Peerless Bella Brian; Cinderella
Florrie Turner; Baroness Oofless Eleanor Lloyd; Dan-
dini Rose Crawford; Rosetta Alice Butler; Sir Algernon
Fitznooks Francis Rossiter; Sir Augustus Smyth Bea-
trice Hurst; Fairy Queen Patti Florence; Harebell Car-
lotta Parks; Rosebud Harriett Ware; Columbine Martini.
PD Mrs J.F. Brian; Sc [G.] Sewell, Edgerton, [A.]
Terraine. *REV: E 2/1/92 p9; SR 2/1/92 p16; St 31/12/
91 p17.*

91.373 *THE SWISS EXPRESS* (Farcical Panto,3a) Arthur
H. Gilbert & Charles Renad [or Read; adpt of *Le Voyage
en Suisse*]. PRINCESS'S 26/12/91-16/1/92 [19 mat perf];
18/1/92-3/2/92 [18 perf; w/mat 21/1, 23/1, 27/1, 30/1;

np 20/1/92]. Total 37 perf.* <u>Dr Gondimar Gull</u> Wilfred E. Shine/T.P. Haynes; <u>Dudely Green</u> Henry Dana; <u>Rhinoaven</u> Henry Bedford; <u>Mr Squeeze</u> L.J. Munro/T[homas] Verner; <u>M. Va Partout</u> J. Houker; <u>Gen. de Bayonette</u> Frederic; <u>Mandarin Ho-mi-hi</u> A. Guillaume; <u>Senor Bafflo-Bullos</u> R. Amedee; <u>Mlle Flirte</u> Julien; <u>Bob Rollingstone</u> Sidney Herberte Basing; <u>James</u> Charles Renad; <u>John</u> Rene Renad; <u>Gadabout</u> Frederic Renad; <u>Card Attendant</u> George Aubrey. <u>Lisette</u> Gladys Courtenay; <u>Jeanette</u> Alice Stuart; <u>Virginia Squeeze</u> Phyllis Broughton; <u>Mrs Squeeze</u> Mrs [H.] Clifton. <u>PP</u> Mrs Harriet Gooch; <u>L & Mgr</u> Sidney Herberte Basing; <u>Dir</u> Henry Neville; <u>Sm</u> Isaac Cohen; <u>Mus dir</u> Michael Connelly; <u>Mach</u> J.W. Cawdery; <u>Asm</u> Thomas Verner; <u>Sec</u> Cecil Breton; <u>Act mgr</u> F. Forbes. *REV: E 2/1/92 p8, 23/1/92 p9; St 21/1/92 p12.*

91.374 *THE DON* (C,3a) Mr & Mrs Herman C. Merivale. TOOLE'S 26/12/91. 1 perf.** <u>Mr Milliken</u> J.L. Toole; [Pappendick] John Billington; George Shelton; C.M. Lowne; Herbert Pearson; Frank J. Arlton; [Charles] Brunton. <u>Mrs Coventry Sparkle</u> Effie Liston; Eliza Johnstone; Irene Vanbrugh; Mary Brough. <u>MGR</u> J.L. Toole. <u>Comment</u>: Advertized in *Ti* for this date.

91.375 *A BROKEN SIXPENCE* (Ca,1a) Mrs G. Thompson & Kate Sinclair. TOOLE'S 26/12/91. 1 perf.** <u>MGR</u> J.L. Toole. <u>Comment</u>: Advertized in *Ti* for this date; for probable cast see 90.4.

91.376 *FORGIVENESS* (C.4a) J.W. Comyns Carr. ST. JAMES'S 30/12/91-10/2/92. 41 perf [w/S mat exc 2/1/92; np 20/1/92].* <u>Edward Hamilton</u> George Alexander; <u>Sir Edward Ferrars</u> Nutcombe Gould; <u>Tommy Muir</u> E.W. Gardiner; <u>Rev Maitland Muir</u> H.H. Vincent; <u>Hon Reginald Earle</u> Arthur Bourchier; <u>Abraham Plack</u> Herman de Lange; <u>Mr Tamworth</u> Fred A. Everill. <u>Mrs Badger</u> Dolores Drummond; <u>Mrs Meakin</u> Fanny Coleman; <u>Lucy Badger</u> Laura Green; <u>Nina Ferrars</u> Marion Terry. <u>L & MGR</u> George Alexander; <u>Sc</u> H.P. Hall, Walter Hann; <u>Mus & Mus dir</u> Walter Slaughter; <u>Cost</u> Russell & Allen, Savage & Perkins, Mme Yorke; <u>Furn</u> Frank Giles; <u>Pq</u> C.H. Fox; <u>Sm</u> Robert V. Shone; <u>Bm</u> Alwyn Lewis. *REV:*

Ath 2/1/92 p32; E 2/1/92 p11; SR 2/1/92 p12-3; St 7/1/ 92 p15-6; Th 1/2/92 p 97-8; Ti 31/12/91 p6.

*   *   *   *   *

92.1 *A FOOL'S PARADISE* (P,3a) Sydney Grundy. GARRICK
2/1/92-17/6/92. 147 perf [w/mat 23/1, 13/2, 20/2,
27/2, 5/3, 12/3, 26/3, 9/4, 14/5; mat only 30/4, 4/6,
11/6; np 20/1, 11-15/4]. 1st perfd Prince of Wales's,
Greenwich 7/10/87 [as *The Mousetrap*]. Earl of Norman-
tower Fred Kerr; Hon Tom Verinder Gilbert Hare/R[o-
land] Atwood; Philip Selwyn H.B. Irving; Price S.B.
Brereton; Sir Peter Lund, M.D. John Hare/Charles
Groves. Mrs Beatrice Selwyn Olga Nethersole; Mildred
Selwyn Beatrice Ferrar; Johnson Minna Blakiston; Kate
Derwent Kate Rorke. L & MGR John Hare; Bom E. Candler;
Act mgr C.G. Compton; Asm R[owley] Cathcart; Sc Will-
iam Harford; Cond A. Arnstein. *REV: Ath 9/1/92 p62;
E 9/1/92 p18; SR 9/1/92 p43; St 7/1/92 p15; Th 1/2/92
p98-9; Ti 4/1/92 p8.*

92.2 *MY DAUGHTER* (P,1a) Mrs S.B. Bancroft. GARRICK
2/1/92-16/1/92; 27/1/92-8/7/92. 154 perf [w/mat 13/2,
20/2, 27/2, 5/3, 12/3, 26/3, 9/4, 14/5; mat only
30/4; np 11-15/4, 4/6, 11/6, 18/6].* Cpt. Blake W.
Scott Buist; Rochie Charles Rock. Rosie Winifred Fraser; Mrs Blake Louise Moodie/Minna Blakiston; Lucy
Minna Blakiston/K[athleen] Hill. L & MGR, Bom, Act
mgr, Asm, Sc, Cond as for 92.1; Dir Mrs S.B. Bancroft.
REV: E, SR, St as for 92.1; Th 1/2/92 p99-100.

92.3 *THE MOUNTEBANKS* (CO,2a) W.S. Gilbert (lib) &
Alfred Cellier (mus). LYRIC 4/1/92-5/8/92. 221 perf
[w/S mat exc 19/3, 9/7; add mat 13/1, 21/1, 27/1, 3/2,

18/4, 6/7, 20/7, 27/7, 1/8, 3/8; np 20/1, 15/4].*
<u>Bartolo</u> Harry Monkhouse; <u>Arrostino Annegato</u> Frank
Wyatt; <u>Alfredo</u> J. Robertson; <u>Elvino di Pasta</u> J. Furn-
eaux Cook; <u>Giorgio Ravioli</u> Arthur Playfair; <u>Luigi
Spaghetti</u> Charles Gilbert; <u>Beppo</u> Gilbert Porteous;
<u>Risotto</u> Cecil Burt; <u>Pietro</u> Lionel Brough/Cairns James.
<u>Ultrice</u> Lucille Saunders/Jenny Dickerson; <u>Nita</u> Aida
Jenoure; <u>Minestra</u> Eva Moore; <u>Teresa</u> Geraldine Ulmar
[Mrs Ivan Caryll]/Jessie Moore. L & MGR Horace Sed-
ger; <u>Sc</u> T.E. Ryan; <u>Cost</u> Auguste, Cooling & Lawrence;
<u>Cost dgn</u> Percy Anderson; <u>Pq</u> William Clarkson; <u>Mach</u>
S. Trewen; <u>Props</u> Labhart; <u>Bm & Treas</u> William Greet;
Ch John d'Auban. *REV: Ath 9/1/92 p60; E 9/1/92 p11,
13/2/92 p10, 20/2/92 p8, 5/3/92 p9, 16/4/92 p13,
14/5/92 p18; SR 9/1/92 p42-3; St 7/1/92 p14-5; Th
1/2/92 p112-3; Ti 5/1/92 p7.*

92.4 *FIRST MATE* (DD,2a) "Richard Henry" [Richard Butler & H. Chance Newton]. SHAFTESBURY 4/1/92-16/1/92.
12 perf.** <u>Comment</u>: This is possibly a revival of
91.280 (q.v.).

92.5 *HENRY VIII* (5a) William Shakespeare. LYCEUM 5/1/
92-30/7/92; 1/10/92-5/11/92. 204 perf [mat only 30/4,
7/5, 14/5, 21/5, 28/5, 4/6, 11/6, 18/6, 25/6, 2/7,
9/7, 16/7, 23/7, 29/10, 5/11; np 20/1, 11-15/4]. 1st
perfd 1613. <u>Cardinal Wosley</u> Henry Irving/Arthur
Stirling; <u>Henry VIII</u> William Terriss; <u>Duke of Norfolk</u>
[Thomas E.] Wenman/[William] Haviland; <u>Griffith</u> [Hen-
ry] Howe; <u>Duke of Suffolk</u> [Frank] Tyars; <u>Cardinal
Campeius</u> [Allen] Beaumont; <u>Surveyor to Duke of Buck-
ingham</u> [William] Haviland/Acton Bond; <u>Sir Henry
Guildford</u> John Martin Harvey; <u>Gentleman</u> Johnson; <u>Duke
of Buckingham</u> Johnston Forbes-Robertson; <u>Cranmer</u>
Arthur Stirling/Vincent; <u>Lord Chamberlain</u> Alfred Bis-
hop; <u>Earl of Surrey</u> Clarence Hague; <u>Lord Sands</u> Gilbert
Farquhar/Johnson; <u>Cromwell</u> Gordon Craig; <u>Gardiner</u>
Lacy; <u>Gentlemen</u> Johnson/[W.J.] Yeldham, [John] Archer;
<u>Capucius</u> [R.P.] Tabb; <u>Sir Thomas Lovell</u> Stewart; <u>Sir
Anthony Denny</u> Davis; <u>Sir Nicholas Vaux</u> [W. Lionel]
Belmore; <u>Garter King at Arms</u> [W.] Belford; <u>Brandon</u>
Seldon; <u>Sgt. at Arms</u> Powell; <u>Messenger</u> [W.J.] Lorriss;
<u>Scribe</u> [T.] Reynolds; <u>Secretary</u> [H.W.] Cushing/[W.]
Marion. <u>Queen Katherine</u> Ellen Terry/Amy Roselle; <u>Anne</u>

Bullen Violet Vanbrugh; Old Lady [R.G.] Le Thiere/
Mrs Edward Saker; Patience Mrs Pauncefort. L & MGR
Henry Irving; Sc Joesph Harker, Hawes Craven, William
Telbin; Mus Edward German; Cost dgn Seymour Lucas,
Mrs J.W. Comyns Carr; Cost Auguste, Mrs Nettleship,
May & Co., Collinson & Lock, T[homas] Pratt & Sons,
Henry Heath, G. Pocock & Co., Kennedy & Co., Thurkle
& Co., Mrs Reid; Pq C.H. Fox; Furn Arnott; Mach Fill-
ery; Cond J. Meredith Ball; Chorus Master [R.P.]
Tabb; Act mgr Bram Stoker; Sm H.J. Loveday; Bom
Joseph Hurst. *REV: Ath 9/1/92 p61-2; E 9/1/92 p11, 8/*
10/92 p9; SR 9/1/92 p37-9, 30/1/92 p125-6, 6/2/92
p152, 5/3/92 p269-70; St 7/1/92 p14, 4/8/92 p11-2,
29/9/92 p12, 6/10/92 p12; Th 1/2/92 p101-2; Ti 6/1/92
p6.

92.6 *THE SHOWMAN'S DAUGHTER* (DD,3a) Mrs Frances Hodg-
son Burnett. ROYALTY 6/1/92-30/1/92. 22 perf [w/mat
27/3; np 20/1]. 1st perfd Theatre Royal, Worcester
12/10/91. Sir Arthur Bradwardine John Beauchamp;
Geoffrey Romney H. Reeves-Smith; Joe Hurst Will Dennis;
Adolphus Cadsby Harry Eversfield; Jakes Robert Nainby;
Partridge Lawrence Caird; James Cecil Rae. Lady Mont-
abin Ruth Rutland; Linda Hurst May Whitty; Mrs Bonney
Mrs Edmund Phelps; Amilla Bonney Catherine Clare.
PP Kate Santley; L Mrs Frances Hodgson Burnett; Mgr
J.T. Mackay Robertson. *REV: Ath 16/1/92 p96; E 9/1/92*
p16; SR 16/1/92 p71; St 14/1/92 p15; Th 1/2/92 p100-1;
Ti 7/1/92 p6.

92.7 *BEST MAN WINS* (F,1a) Mark Melford. ROYALTY 6/1/
92-30/1/92. 21 perf [np 20/1].** Farmer Kairns Robert
Nainby; Perks Richard Blunt; Jopper Valerie. Carlotta
[Catherine] Clare. PP, L, Mgr as for 92.6. *REV: St*
14/1/92 p15.

92.8 *THE COLLABORATORS* (Dramatic Joke,1a) C. Haddon
Chambers. 7/1/92-16/1/92. 9 perf.* Sydney Brough;
Charles Dodsworth. L & MGR Thomas Thorne. *REV: SR*
16/1/92 p71.

92.9 *HEARTSEASE* (D,5a) James Mortimer [adpt of Alexander Dumas, *La Dame aux Camélias*]. OLYMPIC 9/1/92,
11/1, 13/1, 16/1, 18/1, 21/1, 23/1, 25/1, 27/1/92.

9 mat perf. 1st perfd Princess's 5/6/75. <u>Armand Duval</u> Fuller Mellish; <u>M. Duval</u> Arthur Estcourt; <u>Comte de Varville</u> Bassett Roe; <u>Gaston Rieux</u> Harcourt Beatty; <u>Gustave</u> Henry de Solla; <u>Messenger</u> Theodore Alker; <u>Doctor</u> Henry Ludlow. <u>Nanine</u> Bertie Willis; <u>Mme Prudence</u> Louisa Wyatt; <u>Olympe</u> Lesley Bell; <u>Nichette</u> Henrietta Watson; <u>Maguerite Gautier (Camille)</u> Grace Hawthorne. <u>L & MGR</u> W.W. Kelly; <u>Pp</u> Charles Wilmot; <u>Bm & Treas</u> H. Lawrence Harris; <u>Dir</u> Grace Hawthorne; <u>Cond</u> William Robins; <u>Cost</u> Mme Bronte; <u>Sec</u> C.J. McCarthy; <u>Sm</u> T.C. Dwyer; <u>Asm</u> Arthur Wright; <u>Mach</u> George Cawdrey; <u>Bom</u> Arthur Frye. *REV: E 16/1/92 p9; SR 16/1/92 p71; St 14/1/92 p15; Ti 11/1/92 p10.*

92.10 *THE MAYFLOWER* (C,4a) F. Frankfort Moore [fnd on Longfellow's "The Courtship of Miles Standish"]. OPERA COMIQUE 9/1/92-14/1/92. 5 perf.* <u>Miles Standish</u> J.S. Blythe; <u>Elder Brewster</u> Sydney Paxton; <u>Israel Jones</u> Lewis Ball; <u>Roger Couant</u> Clarence Blakiston; <u>John Alden</u> Edward Compton; <u>Elizabeth Jones</u> Elinor Aickin; <u>Prudence Jones</u> Evelyn McNay; <u>Priscilla</u> Fortesque. <u>L & MGR</u> Edward Compton; <u>Sc</u> Joseph Harker; <u>Bm</u> J.H. Savile. *REV: E 16/1/92 p9; St 14/1/92 p14-5; Th 1/2/92 p106; Ti 11/1/92 p10.*

92.11 *THE NEW WING* (FC,3a) H. Arthur Kennedy. STRAND 9/1/92-9/4/92. 96 perf [w/S mat exc 9/1, 16/1, 23/1; add mat 17/2, 24/2, 2/3, 16/3, 23/3, 30/3, 6/4; np 20/1].** <u>Gen. Singleside</u> George P. Hawtrey; <u>Sir Edward Strangeways, Bart</u> Herbert Standing/Sydney Barraclough; <u>Bobbie Button</u> Herbert Ross; <u>Seth Jobbings</u> Austin Melford; <u>George Slab</u> Willie Edouin; <u>Roundel</u> Alec C. MacKenzie; <u>Nibbs</u> Master H. Buss. <u>Hester Singleside</u> Beatrice Lamb; <u>Flossie Trivett</u> Nina Boucicault; <u>Mrs Dexter</u> Fanny Robertson; <u>Louise Dexter</u> Olive. <u>PP</u> J.S. Clarke; <u>L</u> Willie Edouin; <u>Bm</u> J.T. Mackay Robertson; <u>Sm</u> Charles Davies; <u>Cond</u> Ernest Bucalossi. *REV: Ath 16/1/92 p95; E 16/1/92 p9; SR 16/1/92 p70; St 14/1/92 p14; Th 1/2/92 p106-7; Ti 11/1/92 p10.* <u>Comment</u>: Originally scheduled for performance on 21/12/91, but was apparently postponed until this date.

92.12 *THE COMPOSER* (MCa,1a) Arthur Chapman (lib) & J.M. Capel (mus). STRAND 9/1/92-9/4/92. 78 perf [np

20/1]. 1st perfd Theatre Royal, Richmond 29/10/91.
Jack Temple J.M. Capel. Nellie Venie Bennett; Mrs
Nimblepenny Lucia St. Ives [Mrs J.M. Capel]. PP, L,
Bm, Sm, Cond as for 92.11. *REV: Th 1/2/92 p108.*
Comment: As for 92.11.

92.13 *A CASE FOR EVICTION* (Ca,1a) S. Theyre Smith.
GARRICK 18/1/92-26/1/92. 7 perf [np 20/1]. 1st perfd
Court, Liverpool 22/9/82. Frank Stanley Pringle. Dora
Annie Webster; Mary E. Mitchell. L & MGR John Hare;
Bom E. Candler; Asm R[owley] Cathcart; Sc William
Harford; Act mgr C.G. Compton; Cond A. Arnstein.

92.14 *HIS LAST CHANCE* (Oa,1a) Herbert & Ethel Harraden.
PRINCESS'S 18/1/92-3/2/92. 14 perf [np 20/1].**
Charles Chester Sidney Herberte Basing. Alice Montrose
Ellaline Terriss. L & MGR Sidney Herberte Basing; Pp
Mrs Harriet Gooch; Mus dir Michael Connelly; Mach
J.W. Cawdrey; Asm T[homas] Verner; Bm L[ouis] F. Neth-
sole; Act mgr & Treas F. Forbes; Bom Cecil Breton.
REV: St 21/1/92 p12.

92.15 *JOHN LESTER, PARSON* (D,3a) Leighton Foster & Rider Knight. LYRIC 20/1/92. 1 perf.*Comment: Although
some sources indicate this play was performed, it
seems unlikely since the Lyric was closed on 20/1 because of a royal funeral. Perhaps a copyright perf
took place.

92.16 *HAMLET* (T,5a) William Shakespeare. HAYMARKET
21/1/92-28/5/92 [w/mat 5/3, 16/4; mat only 23/4, 30/4,
7/5, 14/5, 21/5, 28/5; np 11-15/4]; 4/6/92(m), 8/6(m),
11/6(m), 15/6(m), 22/6(m), 29/6(m), 6/7/92(2). 116
perf.** Claudius [F.H.?] Macklin; Hamlet H.B. Tree;
Polonius [Henry] Kemble; Horatio Arthur Dacre; Laertes Fred Terry/Robb Harwood; Rosencrantz C.M. Hallard;
Guildenstern [Charles F.] Caravoglia; Osric Ivan Watson; Marcellus Robb Harwood; Bernardo Crawley; Francesco Benn/F[rederick] Watson; Priest Charles Allan;
Ghost James Fernandez; 1st Gravedigger George Barrett;
2nd Gravedigger Edward Rose; 1st Actor [Charles] Hud-
son/Robinson; 2nd Actor Warden/Robinson/Garry; Court
Jester A[lfred] Wigley. Gertrude Rose Leclercq;
Ophelia Mrs H.B. Tree; Player Queen Claire Ivanova.

L & MGR H. Beerbohm Tree; <u>Sc</u> William Telbin, Walter
Hann, Walter Johnstone; <u>Mus</u> George Henschel; <u>Cost</u>
L. & H. Nathan; <u>Cost dgn</u> Karl; <u>Pq</u> William Clarkson;
<u>Bom</u> W.H. Leverton; <u>Elect</u> E. Wingfield Bowles; <u>Sm</u>
Edward Hastings; <u>Mus dir</u> Carl Armbruster; <u>Bm & Sec</u>
Frederick Harrison. *REV: Ath 30/1/92 p159; E 23/1/92
p10, 19/3/92 p10, 9/4/92 p12, 9/2/92 p7; SR 30/1/92
p126-7; St 28/1/92 p12; Th 1/3/92 p148-50; Ti 22/1/92
p9.*

92.17 *A NOBLE ATONEMENT* (D,4a) Ina Leon Cassilis.
OPERA COMIQUE 21/1/92 mat perf.* <u>Wilford Locksley</u>
Charles Lander; <u>Arthur Melville</u> H. Athol Forde; <u>Ed-</u>
<u>ward Smith</u> E.W. Thomas; <u>Roland West</u> Howard Sturge;
<u>Dolly Marchment</u> D.G. English; <u>Fendale</u> Bernard Copping;
<u>Joe Snedger</u> Frederic Jacques. <u>Marguerite Melville</u>
Annie Cathew; <u>Emily Smith</u> Florence Fordyce; <u>Dabbs</u>
Leila Rivers; <u>Morris</u> Adelaide Grace; <u>Rosamond Verner</u>
Lesley Bell. *REV: E 23/1/92 p10; St 28/1/92 p13.*

92.18 *THE SENTRY* (MF,1a) Felix Remo (lib) & T. Malcolm
Watson (lib) & Ivan Caryll (mus). LYRIC 22/1/92-27/6/
92. 134 perf [np 15/4].** <u>Tim O'Brien</u> Harry Parker/
Gilbert Porteous; <u>Col. Pettigrew</u> Cecil Burt/Charles
Gilbert; <u>Sgt.-Mjr.</u> Charles Crook. <u>Polly Burchett</u> Ellis
Jeffreys/Dora Thorne/Field-Fisher; <u>Mrs Pettigrew</u>
Florence Melville; <u>Peggy</u> Jessie Moore. L & MGR Horace
Sedger; <u>Bm & Treas</u> William Greet; <u>Mach</u> S. Trewen;
<u>Props</u> Labhart.

92.19 *THE GREY MARE* (FC,3a) George R. Sims & Cecil
Raleigh. COMEDY 23/1/92-19/3/92 [w/S mat exc 23/1,
30/1; add mat 9/3]; 30/5/92-2/7/92. 87 perf.* <u>John</u>
<u>Maxwell</u> Charles H. Hawtrey; <u>David Maxwell</u> Eric Lewis;
<u>Count de Chevrelle</u> James Nelson; <u>Collins</u> William Wyes;
<u>Stubbs</u> Ernest Cosham; <u>Algernon Maxwell</u> Gerald Gurney;
<u>Richard Beswick</u> W.F. Hawtrey; <u>Col. Gravacahn</u> Charles
H.E. Brookfield. <u>Julia Maxwell</u> Annie Irish/Cynthia
Brooke; <u>Marie</u> Adrienne Dairolles; <u>Hélène</u> Violet Arm-
bruster/Lizzie Ruggles; <u>Kate Stanhope</u> Lottie Venne/
Vane Featherston. MGR Charles H. Hawtrey; <u>Act mgr &</u>
<u>Sec</u> E.F. Bradley; <u>Asm</u> Charles Milton; <u>Mus dir</u> James
M. Glover. *REV: Ath 30/1/92 p159-60; E 30/1/92 p9;
SR 30/1/92 p122-3, 13/2/92 p183; St 28/1/92 p13; Th*

1/3/92 p150-1; Ti 25/1/92 p12.

92.20 *EAST LYNNE.* NOVELTY 23/1/92-6/2/92. 14 perf
[w/mat 23/1, 30/1, 6/2]. Comment: Advertized in the
Daily Telegraph.

92.21 *THAT LADY IN PINK* (Oa,1a) Ethel & Herbert Harra-
den. GAIETY 25/1/92-19/3/92. 48 perf.** Jack Morton
George T. Minshull. Florence Harcourt Linda Verner.
L & MGR George Edwardes; Sm Frank Parker; Act mgr
F.J. Harris; Mus dir W. Meyer Lutz; Bom A.P. Oxley.
Comment: Alternative title to *That Woman in Pink.*

92.22 *THERESE RAQUIN* (D,4a) A. Texeira de Mattos
[trans of Emile Zola]. CRITERION 26/1/92 mat perf.**
Laurent W.L. Abingdon; Camille Sydney Herberte Basing;
Grivet Herman de Lange; Michaud John Gibson. Mme
Raquin Elsie Chester; Suzanne Clarice Shirley; Thérèse
Raquin Laura Johnson. *REV: E 30/1/92 p10.*

92.23 *A HIGHLAND LEGACY* (P,1a) Brandon Thomas. COURT
27/1/92-2/4/92. 77 perf [w/W, S mat exc 2/3]. 1st
perfd Strand 17/11/88. Gordon Macdonnell Wilfred
Draycott; Tammy Tamson Macdonnell Brandon Thomas; Mr
Dobson W.L. Branscombe; Cavendish Howley Frank Lacy;
Job Fixem Compton Coutts. Mrs Butler Mrs Vaughan
Dawes; Clara Christine Noel. PP Mrs John Wood, Arthur
Chudleigh; Dir Brandon Thomas; Cond Edward Jones.
Comment: This play was originally scheduled for perf
on 2/12/91, but was apparently postponed until this
date.

92.24 *A LOST THREAD* (Sk) Mrs Hugh Bell. HAYMARKET
27/1/92 mat perf.** Sir George Seymour Arthur Dacre.
Lady Seymour Amy Roselle [Mrs Arthur Dacre]. L & MGR
H.B. Tree; Sm Edward Hastings; Mus dir Carl Armbruster; Bm & Sec F[rederick] Harrison; Bom W.H. Leverton.

92.25 *THE INTRUDER* (P,1a) [adpt of Maurice Maeterlinck,
L'Intruse]. HAYMARKET 27/1/92 mat perf.* Grandfather
H.B. Tree; Uncle James Fernandez; Father [F.H.?]
Macklin. 1st Daughter Mrs H.B. Tree; 2nd Daughter
Blanche Horlock; 3rd Daughter Thompson; Servant Ayl-

ward. L & MGR, Sm, Mus dir, Bm & Sec, Bom as for 92.
24. *REV: E 30/1/92 p10; SR 30/1/92 p121; St 28/1/92
p12-3; Ti 28/1/92 p6.*

92.26 *A QUIET RUBBER* (P,1a) Charles F. Coghlan. HAY-
MARKET 27/1/92 mat perf.** Lord Kilclare John Hare;
Charles Gilbert Hare; Mr Sullivan Charles Groves.
Mary Sullivan Lizzie Webster. L & MGR, Sm, Mus dir,
Bm & Sec, Bom as for 92.24. *REV: E, St, Ti as for
92.25.*

92.27 *THE CRITIC* (F,3a) R.B. Sheridan. HAYMARKET 27/
1/92 mat perf. 1st perfd Drury Lane 30/10/1779. Lord
Burleigh Arthur Cecil; Sentinel Willie Edouin; Sir
Walter Raleigh H[enry] Kemble; Governor of Tilbury
Fort Fred Leslie; Dangle [C.H.?] Hawtrey; Puff Henry
Neville; Sneer [Charles] Hudson; Earl of Leicester
Robb Harwood; Under Prompter [Alfred] Wigley; Sir
Christopher Hatton William Blakeley; Master of the
Horse Arthur Roberts; Beefeater [Charles] Allan;
Don Whiskerandos George Barrett; Sentinel Edward Rose.
Confidant Mrs E.H. Brooke; Tilburina Kate Phillips.
L & MGR, Sm, Mus dir, Bm & Sec, Bom as for 92.24.
REV: E. St, Ti as for 92.25.

92.28 *THE SILVER LINING* (WordlessSk) [C.D.] Marius.
HAYMARKET 27/1/92 mat perf.** [C.D.] Marius. Comment:
Apparently an alternative title for *The Silver Line.*

92.29 *MISS DECIMA* (OperaticC,3a) F.C. Burnand (lib)
[adpt fr Maxime Boucheron] & Edmond Audran (mus).
TOOLE'S 27/1/92-6/2/92. 13 perf [w/mat 29/1, 30/1,
6/2].** Peter Paul Rolleston Frank H. Celli; Marma-
duke Jessop Welton Dale; Bertie Brown A. St. John
Carr; Rev Dr Jeremie Jackson David James; The Cheval-
ier O'Flanagan Wilfred E. Shine; Donald McQuord R.
Sesnon; Jules H. Gordon; Waiter W. Botterill; Extras
Stanley Betjemann, George Williams, Sidney Burt,
Fred Emery, W. Joyce, H. Lanham. Rosa Napier MacRae;
Flora McDonald Lucy Buckstone; Decima Florence St.
John; La Senora Varganaz M.A. Victor; La Senorita
Inez Bertha Vere; Jeannie Macpherson Edith Fielding;
Coralie Beatrice Gordon; Extras Kate Bentley, Winifred
Newton, Nita St. Denys, Bertha Meyers, Vera Dudley,

Helen Fairlie, Hebe Cornell, Lorraine Drew, May Carleton, Mary Turner, Edith Falkland, Sylvia Phelps, Napier MacRae. L J.L. Toole; Dir Charles Wyndham; Bm & Sm S.H.S. Austin; A act mgr A.F. Henderson; Mus dir Archibald Evans; Cost Stagg & Mantle; Sc T.E. Ryan. *REV: E 30/1/92 p9; St 4/2/92 p13.* Comment: Included two new songs by Arthur Hervey & Audran.

92.30 *SAINTS AND SINNERS* (P,5a) H.A. Jones. VAUDEVILLE 27/1/92-20/2/92. 25 perf [w/S mat exc 20/2]. 1st perfd Prince of Wales's, Greenwich 17/9/84. Jacob Fletcher Thomas Thorne; George Kingsmill Arthur Elwood; Cpt. Eustace Fanshawe H.B. Conway; Samuel Haggard C.W. Somerset; Lot Burden Charles Dodsworth; Prabble E.M. Robson; Peter Greenacre Oswald Yorke; Jack Raddles/Uncle Bamberry Fred Grove; Leeson J[ohn] Wheatman; Porter A. Austin; Tom Marks G. Robinson. Letty Fletcher Dorothy Dorr; Lydia Kate Phillips; Mrs Partridge Rose Dudley; Fanny Parridge [Harriet] Trench. L & MGR Thomas Thorne; Act mgr Sydney Alport; Sm Fred Grove; Sc [W.T.] Hemsley, William Perkins, Liberty & Co.; Mus dir Charles Dubois. *REV: Ath 6/2/92 p192; E 30/1/92 p9; SR 13/2/92 p183; St 4/2/92 p12-3; Th 1/3/92 p151-2; Ti 28/1/92 p6.*

92.31 *EAST LYNNE* (4a) John C. Chute [adpt of Mrs Henry Wood's novel]. OLYMPIC 28/1/92-5/3/92. 48 perf [w/W, S mat; add mat 8/2, 15/2, 22/2, 29/2].** Archibald Carlyle Alfred B. Cross; Mr Dill Henry de Solla; Cpt. (later Sir Frances Levison) Bassett Roe; Bullock Frank M. Wood; Justice Hare Arthur Estcourt; Lord Mountsevern John C. Chute; Richard Hare Harcourt Beatty; Landlord Henry Ludlow. Little Willie Carlyle Ethel Patrick; Joyce Margaret Watson; Cornelia Carlyle Mrs Watty Brunton; Wilson Elsie Lanham; Barbara Hare Bertie Willis; Suzanne Winnie Wood; Little Lucy Emily d'Estelle; Lady Isabel/Mme Vine Lesley Bell. L & MGR W.W. Kelly; Pp Charles Wilmot; Bm & Treas H. Lawrence Harris; Dir John C. Chute; Cond William Robins; Props John Morris; AssistantBm Alfred Selwyn; Bom Arthur Frye; Sec C.J. McCarthy; Sm T.C. Dwyer; Asm Arthur Wright; Mach W. Gilbert.

92.32 *THE VICAR OF BRAY* (CO,2a) Sydney Grundy (lib) &
Edward Solomon. SAVOY 28/1/92-18/6/92. 143 perf [w/S
mat exc 11/6; add mat 8/6; np 15/4]. 1st perfd Globe
22/7/82. Rev William Barlow Rutland Barrington; Rev
Henry Sandford Courtice Pounds; Thomas Merton Richard
Green/Helier Lemaistre; Mr Bedford Rowe W.H. Denny;
John Dory W.S. Laidlaw; Peter Piper J. Bowden Haswell;
Samuel Spicer F. Barrett; 1st Huntsman J. Wilbraham;
2nd Huntsman Rudolph Lewis. Mrs Merton Rosina Brand-
ram; Nelly Bly Mary Duggan; Cynthia Louise Rowe/Amy
Farrell; Agatha Annie Cole; Blanche Cora Tinnie/Jose
Shalders; Winifred Lenore Snyder; Rose Janet Watts;
Gertrude Nellie Kavanagh. PP & MGR Richard d'Oyly
Carte; Bom C. Hawkins; Sc William Perkins, Joseph
Harker; Dir Charles Harris; Cond Edward Solomon/Fran-
cois Cellier; Sm W.H. Seymour; Ch John d'Auban; Act
mgr & Treas J.W. Beckwith; Cost dgn Percy Anderson;
Cost Miss Fisher, Auguste, Mme Leon, Angel & Son; Pq
William Clarkson; Props [H.] Skelly; Mach Sheldon;
Elect Lyons. *REV: Ath 6/2/92 p190; E 30/1/92 p11; SR
6/2/92 p149-50; St 4/2/92 p12; Th 1/3/92 p165-6; Ti
29/1/92 p3.* Comment: Thomas Merton was also played by
Robert Scott-Fishe.

92.33 *JUDAH* (P,3a) H.A. Jones. AVENUE 30/1/92-20/2/92.
22 perf [w/S mat exc 30/1].** Judah Llewellyn E.H.
Vanderfelt; Juxon Prall Cyril Maude; Earl of Asgarby
Charles J. Fulton; Mr Dethic Ernest Hendrie; Mr Pap-
worthy Ells Dagnall; Prall G.L. Leith; Roper W.H.
Barratt; Prof Jopp Sant Matthews. Vashti Dethic Olga
Brandon; Sophie Jopp Gertrude Warden; Mrs Prall Mrs
Ernest Clifton; Lady Eve Bessie Hatton. LI George
Paget; Bm George D. Day; Sm Charles [M.] Appleby; Sc
Walter Hann; Mus dir Wurm. *REV: Ath 6/2/92 p191-2; E
6/2/92 p9; SR 6/2/92 p152; St 4/2/92 p12; Th 1/3/92
p152-3; Ti 1/2/92 p14.*

92.34 *CAPTAIN BILLY* (Oa,1a) Harry Greenbank (lib) &
Francois Cellier (mus). 1/2/92-18/6/92. 119 perf [np
15/4].** Cpt. Billy Helier Lemaistre/W.S. Laidlaw;
Christopher Jolly C.R. Rose; Samuel Chunk Rudolph
Lewis. Widow Jackson [Agnes] Scott; Polly Janet Watts/
F[lorence] Easton. PP & MGR Richard d'Oyly Carte; Mus
dir Francois Cellier; Sm W.H. Seymour; Ch John d'Au-

ban; <u>Act mgr & Treas</u> J.W. Beckwith.

92.35 *BLUE-EYED SUSAN* (CO,2a) George R. Sims (lib) &
Henry Pettitt (lib) & F. Osmond Carr (mus). PRINCE OF
WALES'S 6/2/92-17/6/92. 122 perf [w/mat 13/2, 20/2,
27/2, 5/3, 12/3, 19/3, 26/3, 23/4, 21/5; np 15/4].*
<u>Doggrass</u> Arthur Williams/Fred Emney; <u>Gnatbrain</u> Chaun-
cey Olcott; <u>Raker</u> Fred Emney/A. Rolph; <u>Seaweed</u> Willie
Warde; <u>Hatchett</u> E.H. Haslem/[Harrison] Brockbank;
<u>Blue Admiral</u> E[rnest] Bantock; <u>Cpt. Crosstree</u> Arthur
Roberts; <u>Ben Bobstay</u> C. Royelle; <u>Quid</u> A. Rolph/Hunt;
<u>Jacob Twigg</u> A. Sneak; <u>German</u> Hunt/Percival; <u>French</u>
Trott; <u>Russian</u> [W.?] Palmer; <u>Italian</u> [A.?] Jackson;
<u>Spanish</u> [W.?] Clark; <u>Red Admiral</u> H[arry] Grattan;
<u>White Admiral</u> F. Weston. <u>William</u> Marian Burton/Wallace
Brownlow [sic]; <u>Dolly Mayflower</u> Grace Pedley; <u>Rosy
Morn</u> Katie Seymour; <u>Middy</u> Katie Barry/Phoebe Carlo;
<u>Blue Eyed Susan</u> Nellie Stewart; <u>Polly Primrose</u> Alice
Kingsley; <u>Violet Bank</u> Day Ford; <u>Daisy Meadows</u> Louie
Pounds; <u>Lily Lovelorn</u> [Kate] Cannon; <u>Pansy Blossom</u>
Violet Durkin; <u>May Rose</u> Collingwood. <u>PP</u> Edgar Bruce;
<u>Mgr</u> C.J. Abud; <u>Sc</u> Joseph Harker, Walter Hann; <u>Cost
dgn</u> Percy Anderson; <u>Cost</u> Miss Fisher, Alias, Cooling
& Lawrence, Harrisons; <u>Pq</u> C.H. Fox; <u>Mus dir</u> A[lfred]
Plumpton; <u>Dir</u> Hugh Moss; <u>Act mgr</u> Ernest Hallewell;
<u>Ch</u> Willie Warde; <u>Lime</u> [W.] Kerr; <u>Props</u> Brunton; <u>Treas</u>
W. Crellin. *REV: E 13/2/92 p11; SR 13/2/92 p181; St
11/2/92 p12; Th 1/3/92 p164-5; Ti 8/2/92 p10.*

92.36 *CALLED BACK.* NOVELTY 8/2/92-12/2/92. 5 perf.
<u>Comment</u>: Advertized in the *Daily Telegraph*.

92.37 *FOURTEEN DAYS* (C,3a) Henry J. Byron [adpt of
Edmond Gondinet & Alexandre Bisson, *Le Voyage d'Agré-
ment*]. CRITERION 10/2/92-19/3/92. 36 perf [w/mat
12/3, 19/3]. 1st perfd Criterion 4/3/82. <u>Peregrine
Porter</u> Charles Wyndham; <u>Claud Delafield</u> Walter Ever-
ard; <u>Brummles</u> William Blakeley; <u>Timothy Glibson</u>
George Giddens; <u>Arthur Spoonbill</u> S[tanley] Hewson;
<u>Col. Gunthorpe</u> Frank Atherley; <u>Jones</u> Sydney Valentine.
<u>Tippetts</u> F. Frances; <u>Fanny Simpson</u> K[athleen] Dene;
<u>Angelina Porter</u> Mary Moore. <u>L & MGR</u> Charles Wyndham;
<u>Sm</u> S.H.S. Austin; <u>Cond</u> Theo Ward; <u>Act mgr & Treas</u>
E. Harvey. *REV: Ath 20/2/92 p254; E 13/2/92 p11; SR*

13/2/92 p183; St 18/2/92 p12; Th 1/3/92 p153-4; Ti 12/2/92 p3.

92.38 *THE GREAT METROPOLIS* (Nautical Melo,5a) William Terriss & Henry Neville. PRINCESS'S 11/2/92-9/4/92. 60 perf [w/mat 13/2, 17/2, 25/2, 3/3, 9/3, 16/3, 23/3, 30/3, 6/4]. 1st perfd in New York 8/89. Jack Holt Henry Neville; Pony Simple Sydney Herberte Bas-Will Webster Fuller Mellish; Benjamin Bert Henry Bedford; Cpt. Carr T.P. Haynes; Matthew Quin Thomas Verner; Ned T[homas] Kingston; Dook Tom Terriss; Walter Mowbray W.L. Abingdon; Mr Holt C[harles] Steuart/John Carter; Dally C. Holmes; Servant Percy Ames; Coastguardsman George Aubrey. Nell Ellaline Terriss; Clara Maitland E. Brinsley Sheridan/Rosie Lewis; Fantine Skelton Waud; Mrs Carr Mrs [H.] Clifton; Gertrude Beatrice Selwyn; Servant Gladys Courtenay. L & MGR Sydney Herberte Basing; Pp Mrs Harriet Gooch; Mach J.W. Cawdrey; Sc H[arry] Potts, W. Finch Leicester; Mus dir Michael Connelly; Bm L[ouis] F. Nethersole; Sec & Bom Cecil Breton; Act mgr & Treas F. Forbes; Asm Thomas Verner; Cost Morris Angel; Furn Oetzmann. *REV: Ath 20/2/92 p254; E 13/2/92 p11; SR 20/2/92 p 214-5; St 18/2/92 p12; Th 1/3/92 p155-6; Ti 15/2/92 p14.*

92.39 *MAJOR HOPE* (Amusement,3a) Arthur Law. VAUDEVILLE 11/2/92 mat perf. 1st perfd Standard 2/10/82 [as *Hope*]. Mjr. Hope C.W. Somerset; George Clifford Nicol Pentland; Ernest Drayton Henry Pagden; Alphonso Smith H. Athol Forde; James Ernest Snail E.M. Robson. Mrs Arabella Washington Phipps Cicely Richards; Bertha Hope Agnes Verity; Maid M. Santry; Mrs Welsh Mrs Edmund Phelps. L & MGR Thomas Thorne; Dir C.W. Somerset; Bm Harrington Baily; Sm W. Cook. *REV: E 13/2/92 p13; St 18/2/92 p12; Th 1/3/92 p154-5.*

92.40 *LADY AUDLEY'S SECRET.* NOVELTY 13/2/92-19/2/92. c.6 perf. Comment: Advertized in the *Daily Telegraph.*

92.41 *THE SILVER SHIELD* (C,3a) Sydney Grundy. VAUDEVILLE 16/2/92 mat perf. 1st perfd Strand 19/5/85. Sir Humphrey Chetwynd Walter Russell; Dr Dozey John Beauchamp; Ned Chetwynd William Herbert; Mr Dodson Dick

Eric Lewis; <u>Tom Potter</u> Edward O'Neill. <u>Lucy Preston</u>
May Whitty; <u>Mrs Dozey</u> Mrs Edmund Phelps; <u>Alma Blake</u>
Annie Irish; <u>Susan</u> Mrs John Glendinning; <u>Wilson</u> Donald. *REV: E 20/2/92 p10; St 18/2/92 p12.*

92.42 *LADY FORTUNE* (CD,1a) Charles Thomas. COMEDY 18/
2/92-19/4/92. 52 perf [np 15/4]. 1st perfd Globe 17/
9/87. <u>Lord Ambleby</u> James Nelson; <u>Guy Mallory</u> Sam
Sothern; <u>Mr Jessup</u> William Wyes. <u>Mrs Cunliffe</u> Florence
Farr; <u>Kate Cunliffe</u> Violet Armbruster; <u>Sarah</u> Eva
Williams. <u>MGR</u> Charles H. Hawtrey; <u>Act mgr, Bm, Sec</u>,
E.F. Bradley; <u>Asm</u> Charles Milton; <u>Mus dir</u> James M.
Glover. *REV: E 20/2/92 p9.*

92.43 *A BOHEMIAN* (P,4a) Louis N. Parker. GLOBE 18/2/
92-12/3/92. 21 perf.* <u>Rev Hugo Bellairs</u> Fred A. Everill; <u>Cpt. Harold Bellairs</u> Murray Carson; <u>Rev Paul
Disney</u> E. Allan Aynesworth; <u>Norman Brooke</u> Lewis Waller; <u>Ambrose Clifford</u> T.W. Percyval; <u>Karl</u> Frederick
Victor. <u>Mrs Bellairs</u> Mrs [George] Canninge; <u>Olga
Clifford</u> Florence West; <u>Sybil Bellairs</u> Maude Millett.
<u>L & MGR</u> Murray Carson; <u>Sc</u> Walter Hann, [Richard C.]
Durant; <u>Dir & Sm</u> W[illiam] Lestocq; <u>Act mgr</u> W.H.
Griffiths; <u>Pq</u> William Clarkson; <u>Cost</u> Morris Angel;
<u>Furn</u> Oetzmann; <u>Asm</u> R.E. Warton; <u>Cond</u> John Storer;
<u>Treas</u> James A. Welch. *REV: E 20/2/92 p9; SR 27/2/92
p244; St 25/2/92 p13; Th 1/4/92 p199-200; Ti 22/2/92
p14.*

92.44 *HAND IN HAND* (CD,4a) Edward Darbey. NOVELTY 20/
2/92-27/2/92. 8 perf [w/mat 20/2, 27/2].** [<u>Edgar
Hartington</u>] Edwin Fergusson; [<u>Herbert Hartington</u>] H.
Buckstone Clair; W. Garrett; Owen Wynne; G.M. Slater.
<u>Jack the Waif</u> Marie Brian; Annie Travers; Alice Butler; Eleanor Lloyd. <u>Comment</u>: Source: *The Referee.*

92.45 *LADY WINDERMERE'S FAN* (P,4a) Oscar Wilde. ST.
JAMES'S 20/2/92-29/7/92; 31/10/92-30/11/92. 197 perf
[w/S mat exc 20/2, 16/7, 23/7; add mat 9/3, 23/3,
6/4, 27/4, 4/5, 11/5, 18/5, 8/6, 13/7, 16/11; mat
only 25/5; np 14-15/4].* <u>Lord Windermere</u> George
Alexander/Ben Webster; <u>Lord Augustus Lorton</u> H.H. Vincent; <u>Cecil Graham</u> Ben Webster; <u>Charles Dumby</u> A.
Vane-Tempest/Vernon Sansbury; <u>Mr Hopper</u> Alfred Holles;

Parker Vernon Sansbury/Russell Vaun; <u>Lord Darlington</u>
Nutcombe Gould. <u>Lady Strutfield</u> M[adge] Girdlestone;
<u>Duchess of Berwick</u> Fanny Coleman; <u>Lady Windermere</u>
Lily Hanbury/Winifred Emery; <u>Lady Agatha Carlisle</u>
Laura Graves/Edith Chester/Aileen O'Brian; <u>Lady Jed-
burgh</u> Bessie Page; <u>Mrs Cowper-Cowper</u> A[lice] de Win-
ton/Aileen O'Brian; <u>Lady Plimdale</u> Charlotte Gran-
ville; <u>Rosalie</u> Winifred Dolan; <u>Mrs Erlynne</u> Marion
Terry/Fanny Enson. <u>L & MGR</u> George Alexander; <u>Sc</u> H.P.
Hall, Walter Hann, William Harford; <u>Mus</u> Walter Slaughter; <u>Furn</u> Frank Giles & Co.; <u>Cost</u> Mme Savage, Mme
Purdue; <u>Pq</u> C.H. Fox; <u>Sm</u> Robert V. Shone; <u>Mus dir</u>
Walter Slaughter; <u>Bm</u> Alwyn Lewis. *REV: Ath 27/2/92
p285-6; E 27/2/92 p11; SR 27/2/92 p243-4; St 25/2/92
p12, 3/11/92 p12; Th 1/4/92 p200-1; Ti 22/2/92 p10.*

92.46 *DEBORAH* (P,5a) Langdon Elwyn Mitchell. AVENUE
22/2/92-26/2/92. 5 mat perf.* <u>Leviq St. Michael</u>
Charles J. Fulton; <u>Bastien St. Michael</u> Bernard Gould;
<u>Crawford</u> Austin Melford; <u>Alexander Marshall</u> Rudge
Harding; <u>John Dupre</u> Richard S. Boleyn. <u>Helen Marshall</u>
Beatrice Lamb; <u>Mrs St. Michael</u> Henrietta Cowen; <u>Cam-
ille St. Michael</u> Annie Webster; <u>Deborah</u> Marion Lea;
"Prologue" Elizabeth Robins. <u>LI</u> George Paget; <u>Sm</u>
George R. Foss; <u>Bm</u> George D. Day; <u>Cond</u> A. Vorzanger.
*REV: Ath 27/2/92 p286; E 27/2/92 p10; St 25/2/92 p12;
Th 1/4/92 p202; Ti 25/2/92 p11.*

92.47 *MY WIFE'S OUT* (F,1a) G.H. Rodwell. PRINCE OF
WALES'S 22/2/92-27/2/92. 6 perf. 1st perfd Covent
Garden 2/10/43. [Ernest] Bantock. Agnes Hewitt. <u>MGR</u>
C.J. Abud. <u>Comment</u>: Advertized in *Ti* simply as "farce"
for 26-27/2.

92.48 *A HAPPY PAIR* (Ca) S. Theyre Smith. CRITERION
23/2/92 mat perf.** <u>Mr Honeyton</u> Charles Wyndham. <u>Mrs
Honeyton</u> Mary Moore. <u>L & MGR</u> Charles Wyndham; <u>Sm</u> S.
H.S. Austin. *REV: St 25/2/92 p13.*

92.49 *THE HIGHWAYMAN* (C,1a) Justin Huntly McCarthy.
CRITERION 23/2/92 mat perf.** <u>Sir Harry Bellairs</u>
C.P. Colnaghi; <u>Lady Betty</u> Mrs Langtry. *REV: St 25/2/92
p13.*

92.50 *TIME IS MONEY* (Ca,1a) Mrs Hugh Bell & Arthur
Cecil. CRITERION 23/2/92 mat perf. 1st perfd Theatre
Royal, Newcastle 5/9/90. [Mr Graham] Charles H. Hawtrey. [Mrs Murray] Lottie Venne. Comment: It seems
probable this piece was cancelled at the last moment.

92.51 *THE LOQUACIOUS HUSBAND* Arthur Bourchier. CRITER-
ION 23/2/92 mat perf. 1st perf? Mr Gabbler Arthur
Bourchier. Mrs Gabbler Edith Chester. Comment: Although included in the V & A programme, I have been
unable to corroborate the existence of this play.

92.52 *BABY* (Ca) Lady Violet Greville. CRITERION 23/2/
92 mat perf.** Doddles George Belmore; Zachary Inkhorn Edwin Gilbert; Jack Turtledove Henry V. Esmond.
Selina Turtledove Eva Moore. *REV: St 25/2/92 p13.*

92.53 *TWO IN THE BUSH* (F) Murray Carson. GLOBE 23/2/
92-12/3/92. 17 perf.** Mjr. Frere James A. Welch;
Frederick Victor; John Willes. Nettie Carr Georgie
Esmond. L & MGR Murray Carson; Act mgr W.H. Griffiths.
Comment: This piece could have been perfd slightly
earlier: either this, or 91.361 was perfd 17/2-22/2.

92.54 *OUT OF THE WORLD* (DSk,1a) Herbert Burnett.
VAUDEVILLE 23/2/92 mat perf.* Col. Staunton W.F.
Stirling; Mr Stanley Alfred B. Cross; Simmoms Leonard
Calvert. Mabel Clarice Mylford. L & MGR Thomas Thorne;
Sm George R. Foss; Bm Tidd, J.J. Killingsworth; Pq
C.H. Fox; Cost Nathan. *REV: E 27/2/92 p9; St 25/2/92
p12.*

92.55 *ONLY A MODEL* (DSk,1a). VAUDEVILLE 23/2/92 mat
perf.* Laurence Arbuthnot Nicol Pentland; Col. Treherne Cecil Ramsey. Lilian Treherne Violet Russell;
Maggie Edith Gordon. L & MGR, Sm, Bm, Pq, Cost as for
92.54. *REV: As for 92.54.*

92.56 *MISTRESS PEG* (DSk,1a) Lita Smith. VAUDEVILLE
23/2/92 mat perf.* Stephen Taaffe A.E.W. Mason; Cpt.
J. Dash E. Yeronda Rae. Peg Woffington Clarice Mylford;
Lavinia Dallaway Mary Mordaunt; Pamela Oldbird Emily
Miller; Mary Smartly Agnes Ingreville. L & MGR, Sm,
Bm, Pq, Cost as for 92.54. *REV: As for 92.54.*

92.57 *COUSIN DICK* (Ca) Val C. Prinsep. PRINCE OF WALES'S 25/2/92 mat perf. 1st perfd Court 1/3/79. <u>Richard Dalston</u> Herbert Waring. <u>Constance Dalston</u> Estelle Burney; <u>Mary</u> Lillian Lee; <u>Florence Dalton</u> Dorothy Dene. <u>MGR</u> C.J. Abud; <u>Act mgr</u> W.H. Griffiths. *REV: St 3/3/92 p13.*

92.58 *SIXTEEN--NOT OUT* (C,2sc) James Blair. PRINCE OF WALES'S 25/2/92 mat perf.* <u>Winifred</u> Dorothy Dene; <u>Madge</u> Hetty Dene; <u>Kitty</u> Kathleen Dene; <u>Nora</u> Lena Dene. <u>MGR, Act mgr</u> as for 92.57. *REV: E 27/2/92 p11.*

92.59 *WALKER, LONDON* (C,3a) J.M. Barrie. TOOLE'S 25/ 2/92-14/7/93. 497 perf [w/S mat exc 27/2/92, 24/12/ 92, 1/4/93, 20/5, 27/5, 3/6, 10/6, 24/6, 1/7, 8/7/93; add mat 18/4/92, 18/5, 25/5, 6/6, 1/8, 26/12/92, 3/4/ 93; np 15/4/92, 27-31/3/93].* <u>Jasper Phipps</u> J.L. Toole/E.W. Garden; <u>Kit Upjohn</u> C.M. Lowne; <u>Andrew Mc-Phail</u> Seymour Hicks; <u>W.G.</u> Cecil Ramsey; <u>Ben</u> George Shelton. <u>Mrs Golightly</u> Effie Liston; <u>Bell Golightly</u> Irene Vanbrugh; <u>Nanny O'Brien</u> Mary Ansell/Alice Kingsley; <u>Sarah Rigg</u> Eliza Johnstone/Lydia Rachel; <u>Penny</u> Mary Brough. <u>L & MGR</u> J.L. Toole; <u>Sc</u> Joseph Harker; <u>Sm</u> John Billington; <u>Mus dir</u> William Robins; <u>Bm</u> George Lee; <u>Props</u> George Scarrott. *REV: Ath 5/3/92 p317; E 27/2/92 p11, 17/12/92 p9, 4/3/93 p9; SR 5/3/ 92 p272; St 3/3/92 p12, 15/12/92 p13; Th 1/4/92 p202-3; Ti 26/2/92 p10, 13/12/92 p6.*

92.60 *ONE TOUCH OF NATURE* (CD,1a) Benjamin Nottingham Webster. TOOLE'S 25/2/92-25/3/92. 26 perf. 1st perfd Adelphi 6/8/59. <u>William Penn-Holder</u> John Billington; <u>Belgrave</u> H[enry] Westland; <u>Beaumont Fletcher</u> Herbert Pearson; <u>Jones</u> Frank J. Arlton. <u>Constance Belmour</u> Cora Poole. <u>L & MGR, Sm, mus dir, Bm</u> as for 92.59. *REV: E 27/2/92 p11; St 3/3/92 p12.*

92.61 *A MODERN JUDAS* (D,4a) Nettie Cortelyon Guion. VAUDEVILLE 25/2/92 mat perf.* <u>Cpt. Leslie St. John</u> Frank Worthing; <u>Judas</u> Alfred Harding; <u>Medoc Slegman</u> Julian Cross; <u>Austin Dare</u> W.S. Parkes; <u>Gen. Grant</u> [Arthur?] Wellesley; <u>Karl Dare</u> Douglas Gordon; <u>Dr Scott</u> H[enry] Nelson; <u>Sgt.</u> Ballantyne; <u>Martin</u> S[idney] Burt; <u>Brown</u> W[illiam] Bonney; <u>Joe</u> G. Moore; Pic-

quot Grimes W. A[ubrey] Chandler; Doctor H[orn] Conyers. Madge Dare Amy McNeil; Esther V[iolet] Russell;
Grandma Dare Mrs W. Aubrey; Edna May Conrade; Meg
Megregor M. Porecky; Nanette R. Rellvitt; Chloe Henrietta Cross. *REV: E 27/2/92 p11; St 3/3/92 p13.*

92.62 *A SCRAP OF PAPER* (CD,3a) J. Palgrave Simpson
[adpt of Victorien Sardou, *Les Pattes de Mouche*].
PRINCE OF WALES'S 26/2/92 mat perf. 1st perfd St.
James's 22/4/61. Prosper Couramont Yorke Stephens;
Baron de la Glacière Herbert Waring; Anatole Sydney
Brough; Brismouche Lionel Brough; Baptiste Alfred
Matthews; François Bennett. Louise Gertrude Warden;
Mathilde Eva Moore; Zenobie Kate Hodson; Pauline
Margaret Brough; Mme Dupont Maria Saker; Suzanne de
Ruseville Helen Dauvray. PP Edgar Bruce; Mgr C.J.
Abud; Dir Lionel Brough; Act mgr Edward Minor. *REV:
E 27/2/92 p11; Th 1/4/92 p203-4.*

92.63 *BOX AND COX* (Romance,1a) John Maddison Morton.
CRITERION 27/2/92-2/3/92. 4 perf. 1st perfd Lyceum
1/11/47. James Cox William Blakeley; John Box David
Abbey. Mrs Bouncer Emily Vining. L & MGR Charles
Wyndham; Sm S.H.S. Austin; Cond Theodore Ward.

92.64 *FAST ASLEEP* (EccentricC,3a) C.H. Abbott [fnd on
W.S. Gilbert, "Wide Awake"]. CRITERION 1/3/92 mat
perf.* Mjr. Gen. Blister John Beauchamp; Hereward
T.G. Warren; Rev Hatley-Hylo Gilbert Trent; John
Blister William Wyes; James Blister E. Hardrie;
Jack Pointer George Giddens. Mrs Blister Mrs Edmund
Phelps; Sophia Mary Ansell; Mrs Harkaway Kate Phil-
lips; Jane Helen Lambert. DIR George Giddens. *REV:
E 5/3/92 p12; St 3/3/92 p12-3; Th 1/4/92 p204-5.*

92.65 *VIDA* (SocietyD,3a) Ina Leon Cassilis & Charles
Lander. PRINCE OF WALES'S 1/3/92 mat perf. 1st perfd
Londesborough, Scarborough 17/11/91. Sir Wilford
Falconer Frank [Kemble] Cooper; Lucien de St. Var
Léon Roche; Dr Murray John Clulow; Count Amadeo Mark
Paton; Arthur Leigh Harry Grattan; Herr Klein W.E.
Sauter; Dr Baretti Joseph Wilson. Muriel Vernon
Lilian Hingston; Evelyn Harley Clarice Shirley; Lady
Falconer Madge Johnstone; Louise Laroche Violet Ste-

vens; <u>Signora Rendano</u> Georgie Delapoer; <u>Vida Claver-</u>
<u>ing</u> Alice Lingard. <u>L & MGR</u> C.J. Abud; <u>Pp</u> Edgar Bruce;
<u>Act mgr</u> Douglas Tracy. *REV: E 5/3/92 p11; St 3/3/92*
p13.

92.66 *HAPPY RETURNS* (FC,3a) Fred Horner [fnd on Paul
Ferrier, *L'Article 231*]. VAUDEVILLE 1/3/92-27/4/92.
52 perf [w/mat 5/3, 12/3, 26/3, 2/4, 6/4, 18/4, 20/4,
23/4; np 11-16/4].* <u>Sir Robert Millward</u> Thomas
Thorne; <u>Horace Diprose</u> Cyril Maude; <u>Arthur Hemsley</u>
Charles S. Fawcett; <u>Ra-Ka-Too</u> Bill Edwards; <u>Henry</u>
<u>Farquhar</u> C.W. Somerset; <u>Bassett Doyle</u> C[harles] Dods-
worth; <u>Wilson</u> Oswald Yorke; <u>Gunter's man</u> J[ohn]
Wheatman. <u>Mrs Arthur Hemsley</u> Dorothy Dorr; <u>Mrs Alma</u>
<u>Beauchamp</u> Ella Banister; <u>Annette</u> [Harriet] Trench.
<u>L & MGR</u> Thomas Thorne; <u>Act mgr</u> Sydney Alport; <u>Sm</u> Fred
Grove; <u>Cond</u> Charles Dubois. *REV: Ath 5/3/92 p317-8;*
E 5/3/92 p10; SR 5/3/92 p272; Th 1/4/92 p205-6; Ti
4/3/92 p15.

92.67 *MEADOW SWEET* (C,1a) "Terra Cotta" [Miss Constance M. Prevost]. VAUDEVILLE 1/3/92-26/4/92. 44
perf [np 11-16/4].** <u>Benjamin Barnes</u> Fred Grove;
<u>John</u> Oswald Yorke; <u>Jacob</u> John Wheatman; <u>Fred Topliff</u>
Frank Gillmore. <u>Julia Topliff</u> K. Tyndall; <u>Margery</u>
<u>Meadows</u> Ella Banister. <u>L & MGR</u>, <u>Act mgr</u>, <u>Sm</u>, <u>Cond</u> as
for 92.66. *REV: SR 5/3/92 p272.*

92..68 *THE KISS* (Idyll,1a) Theodore de Banville [trans
John Gray]. ROYALTY 4/3/92. 1 perf.* <u>Pierrot</u> Bernard
Gould. <u>Urgele</u> Edith Chester. <u>L</u> Kate Santley; <u>Mgr &</u>
<u>Treas</u> J.T. Grein; <u>Act mgr</u> Charles Hoppe; <u>Sm</u> Herman de
Lange; <u>Mus dir</u> Jan Mulder; <u>Pq</u> William Clarkson; <u>Furn</u>
Oetzmann. *REV: Ath 12/3/92 p352; E 12/3/92 p8; SR*
12/3/92 p299-300; St 10/3/92 p12; Th 1/4/92 p206; Ti
5/3/92 p12. <u>Comment</u>: Independent Theatre Society.

92.69 *THE MINISTER'S CALL* (P,1a) Arthur Symons [fnd
on Frank Harris's story]. ROYALTY 4/3/92. 1 perf.*
<u>Rev John Letgood</u> Frank Worthing; <u>Deacon Knowell</u>
Rudge Harding; <u>Deacon Hooper</u> W[illiam] Bonney. <u>Mrs</u>
<u>Knowell</u> Gertrude Kingston. <u>L</u>, <u>Mgr & Treas</u>, <u>Act mgr</u>,
<u>Mus dir</u>, <u>Pq</u>, <u>Furn</u> as for 92.68. *REV: Ath, E, SR, St,*
Th as for 92.68. <u>Comment</u>: As for 92.68.

92.70 *A VISIT* (P,2a) Edward Brandes [trans William
Archer]. ROYALTY 4/3/92. 1 perf.* Kai Neergaard
Philip Cunningham; Emil Repholt Arthur Bourchier;
Servant W[illiam] Bonney. Florizel Olga Brandon. L,
Mgr & Treas, Act mgr, Mus dir, Pq, Furn as for 92.68.
REV: Ath, E, SR, St as for 92.68; Th 1/4/92 p207.
Comment: As for 92.68.

92.71 *THE BLACK FLAG; OR, ESCAPED FROM PORTLAND* (D,
4a) Henry Pettitt. OLYMPIC 7/3/92-19/3/92. 18 perf
[w/M, W, S mat]. 1st perfd Grecian 9/8/79. Jack
Glyndon Bassett Roe; Augustus Scarem Harcourt Beatty;
Harry Glyndon Alfred B. Cross; Cpt. Markby Alfred
Selwyn; Owen Glyndon Campbell Gollan; Cpt. Handysides
W.S.Parkes; Sim Lazarus Frank M. Wood; Jem Seaton
W[atty] Brunton, jr; John Locksley Wilton B. Payne.
Ned Bertie Willis; Mary Elsie Lanham; Ruth Mrs [Watty]
Brunton; Naomi Blandford Maud Milton; Topsy Carroll
Alice Yorke. L & MGR W.W. Kelly; Pp Charles Wilmot;
Bm & Treas H. Lawrence Harris; Sc W.H. Dixon; Cond
William Robins; Bom Arthur Frye; Cost E.J. Smith; Sec
C.J. McCarthy; Sm Arthur Estcourt; Asm Watty Brunton,
jr; Mach H. Hodges. *REV: E 12/3/92 p9; SR 12/3/92
p304; St 10/3/92 p12-3.*

92.71 *THE PLOWDENS* (C,4a) Otto Benzon & Edward Rose.
PRINCE OF WALES'S 8/3/92 mat perf.* C.W. Plowden
Charles Allan; Norman Ben Webster; Paul Herbert War-
ing; Watkins Roger Roberts; Mjr. Pauncefort Charles
Myers; Sir Hector Askell William Herbert. Mrs Plowden
Henrietta Lindley; Muriel Rose Nesbitt; Mary Hilda
Hervey; Cara Dale Isabel Ellissen. L & MGR C.J. Abud;
Pp Edgar Bruce; Dir Edward Rose; Furn Oetzmann; Sm
Roger Roberts; Act mgr G.F. Bashford. *REV: Ath 12/3/
92 p352; E 12/3/92 p11; SR 12/3/92 p304; St 10/3/92
p12; Th 1/4/92 p207-8; Ti 9/3/92 p10.*

92.73 *MR RICHARDS* (P,3a) Arthur Bourchier & James
Blair. SHAFTESBURY 10/3/92-12/3/92. 3 perf.* Harry
Chambers H. Reeves-Smith; Mr Richards Arthur Bourch-
ier; Viscount Wordsham E.W. Gardiner; Earl of Cromer
Ian Robertson; Mr Bentley Ells Dagnall; Harris G.L.
Leith; Nicholas Leggatt Edward Righton. Mrs Chambers
Lady Monckton; Lady Alice Carlton Rose Norreys; Mrs

Leggatt Mrs E.H. Brooke; Felicia P. Starbuck Helen
Leyton; Isabella Sophie Larkin. L & MGR John Lart;
Pp John Lancaster; Bom Watts; Lyr G.R. Askwith; Mus
Herbert Bunning, C.J. Hargitt; Sc Bruce Smith; Furn
Lyon; Cond C.J. Hargitt; Asm Thomas Sidney; Bm Gil-
bert Tate. *REV: Ath 19/3/92 p381; E 12/3/92 p9; SR
19/3/92 p332; St 17/3/92 p12; Th 1/4/92 p208-9; Ti
11/3/92 p5.*

92.74 *A GAY WIDOWER* (C,3a) Sylvain Mayer [adpt of
play by C. Laufs & Rudolf Kneisel]. VAUDEVILLE 11/3/
92 mat perf.* Abraham Penfold Cecil Ramsey; Harry
Liston Alfred B. Cross; Frank Harding Thomas Kingston;
Cpt. Languish Norman V. Norman; Ernest Fellowes Nicol
Pentland; John Baldwin C.W. Garthorne; Binns G. Rob-
inson; Penny Y. Ray. Kate Liston [Mary] Mordaunt;
Mabel Louise Peach; Ethel Alice Maitland; Sophie
Winter Ina Goldsmith; Eliza Birkett; Mrs Grist Mrs
Beaumont Nelson. *REV: E 12/3/92 p11; St 17/3/92 p12-3.*

92.75 *AN ENTHUSIAST* (DSk,1a) Olive Stettith. VAUDE-
VILLE 11/3/92 mat perf.* Paul Fabris Douglas Gordon.
Hon Mrs Stanfield Eleanor Bufton; Maud Stanfield
Olive Stettith; Sally Julia Warden. *REV: As for 92.74.*

92.76 *WINIFRED'S VOW* (C,3a) John Thomas Douglass (lib)
& Henry Parks (mus). NOVELTY 19/3/92-8/4/92. 18 perf.*
Prince Carl G.M. Slater; Von Steinitz W. Garrett;
Haarlem von Plonder H. Nelson Dickson; Fritz Varzin
A. Forde; Hans Hartwitz H. Buckstone Clair; Sgt.
Berglitz Owen Wynne; Frederic Lambourline E[dwin]
Fergusson. Frau Wanda Mrs J.F. Brian; Belinda Ida
Millais; Winifred Marie Brian. LYR Ida Millais. *REV:
E 26/3/92 p9; St 24/3/92 p12.*

92.77 *JANE* (F,3a) Harry Nicholls & W[illiam] Lestocq.
COMEDY 21/3/92-19/4/92. 29 perf [w/S mat; np 15/4].**
Charles Shackleton Charles H. Hawtrey; Mr Kershaw
William Wyes; Claude Master Richard Saker; Pixton
E.M. Robson; William Charles H.E. Brookfield. Mrs
Chadwick [Caroline] Ewell; Lucy Norton Ethel Matthews;
Jane Lottie Venne; Mrs Pixton M. Warlhouse. MGR
Charles H. Hawtrey; Act mgr, Bm, Sec E.F. Bradley;
Asm Charles Milton; Mus dir James M. Glover. *REV: SR*

26/3/92 p361; St 24/3/92 p12.

92.78 *QUEER STREET* (DD,2a) "Richard Henry" [Richard
Butler & H. Chance Newton]. GAIETY 21/3/92-9/7/92.
95 perf [np 15/4].* Wilson George T. Minshull; Chol-
ditch E[rnest] Bantock; Deudley Hill; Rasper C.
Walker/J. Graham. Mary Ethel Belnheim/Maud Hobson.
L & MGR George Edwardes; Sm Frank Parker; Act mgr F.J.
Harris; Mus dir W. Meyer Lutz; Bom A.P. Oxley. *REV:*
E 26/3/92 p9; SR 26/3/92 p361-2; Ti 22/3/92 p10.

92.79 *CALLED BACK* (D) John C. Chute. OLYMPIC 22/3/92-
2/4/92. 16 perf [w/mat M, W, S]. 1st perfd Devonshire
Park, Eastbourne 25/8/84. Gilbert Vaughan Alfred B.
Cross; Macari Campbell Gollan; Anthony March Harcourt
Beatty; Dr Ceneri Arthur Estcourt; Petroff W.S.
Parkes; Cpt. Varlamoff John C. Chute; Horatio Bangles
Watty Brunton, jr. Pauline March Lesley Bell; Teresa
Vanozzi Estelle Tyrrell; Priscilla Drew Mrs Watty
Brunton. BOM Arthur Frye. *REV: St 24/3/92 p12.*

92.80 *DONNA LUIZA* (Oa,1a) Basil Hood (lib) & Walter
Slaughter (mus). PRINCE OF WALES'S 23/3/92-13/5/92.
44 perf [np 15/4].* Don Alfonso del Fandango Taylor/
F. Weston; Lorenza [Harrison] Brockbank. Luiza Maggie
Roberts; Dolores Louie Pounds; Maria [Annie] Dwelly.
MGR C.J. Abud; Pp Edgar Bruce; Sm George Capel; Act
mgr Ernest Hallewell; Treas E[dward] Marshall. *REV:*
*E 26/3/92 p8; St 31/3/92 p13; Th 1/5/92 p269-70; Ti
24/3/92 p9.*

92.81 *THE CUSTOM HOUSE* (FC,3a) L.A.D. Montague. VAUDE-
VILLE 24/3/92 mat perf.* Anthony Crabb Cecil Crofton;
Edward Young John Clulow; Charles Cotfield Howard
Sturge; Chalker Ells Dagnall; Belgian Passenger Ivan
Watson. Mrs Young Lillie Belmore; Miss Tryphena Ogil-
vy Charlotte [E.?] Morland; Miss Montrevor Lilian
Daily; Mrs Brimblecombe Emily Dowton; Trimmins Marion
Lind. L & MGR Thomas Thorne; Bm Edwin Gilbert; Sc
W.T. Hemsley; Pd George Belmore; Pq William Clarkson;
Cost Morris Angel; Mus dir Charles Dubois. *REV: E 26/
3/92 p9; St 31/3/92 p13.*

92.82 *THE BREADWINNER* (P,3a) Alfred C. Calmour. AVENUE

26/3/92-1/4/92. 6 perf.* Hon Dudley Chancellor Lewis Waller; Dr Digby Fred A. Everill; Sir George Holroyd Charles [ie C.W.] Garthorne; Philip Trescott Arthur Elwood. Freda Alma Murray; Clari Harcourt Laura Linden; Mrs Digby Spenmore Mrs [George] Canninge; Bowden T. Roma; Mrs Armadale Olga Brandon. LI George Paget; Bm Charles Terry; Sec Field-Fisher; Cond Wurm. *REV: E 2/4/92 p7; SR 2/4/92 p388; St 31/3/92 p13; Th 1/5/ 92 p252-3; Ti 28/3/92 p4.* Comment: Possibly also perfd 2/4.

92.83 *LE NOZZI DI FIGARO* (O[4a]) W.A. Mozart. ROYALTY 26/3/92 mat perf.** Basilio Collwyn Thomas; Curzio M. Vander; Count Charles Edwards; Antonio [G.] Combe-Williams; Figaro Smallwood Metcalfe; Bartolo Archibald Bradford. Susanna Margaret Eden; Countess Winifred Ludlam; Cherubino Maria Garcia; Marcellina Edith Tancred; Barbarina Valerie Nelson. COND C.H. Allen Gill; Sm Edgar B. Skeet; Dir Gustave Garcia. *REV: E 2/4/92 p15; St 31/3/92 p13.*

92.84 *DAISY'S ESCAPE* (Ca,1a) A.W. Pinero. TOOLE'S 26/3/92-25/2/93. 340 perf [w/S mat exc 21/5, 24/12/ 92; add mat 18/4, 18/5, 25/5, 6/6, 26/12/92; np 15/4/ 92]. 1st perfd Lyceum 20/9/79. Augustus Caddell Laurence Irving/George Shelton; Tom Rossiter C.M. Lowne/ Herbert Pearson; Bullamore Frank J. Arlton; Tulk C[harles] Brunton/E.A. Coventry; Mjr. Mullett Henry Westland/John Billington. Daisy White Cora Poole/ Nerva Conynghame/Alice Kingsley; Mollie Beaumont Loveday/Mary Brough. L & MGR J.L. Toole; Sm John Billington; Mus dir William Robins; Asm & Prompter Frank J. Arlton; Bm George Lee. *REV: E 2/4/92 p11; Ti 28/3/92 p4.*

92.85 *CHRIS* (P,3a) Louis N. Parker. VAUDEVILLE 28/3/ 92-1/4/92. 5 mat perf.* Cpt. Phipps Herbert Waring; Hon Jack Branksome William Herbert; William Featherstone Sant Matthews; Rev Septimus Hervey-Hervey John Beauchamp; John Walters Frank Weathersby; James E.F. Siddons. Mrs Hervey-Hervey Henrietta Cowen; Mary Margaret Earl; Christine Featherstone Mrs Lancaster-Wallis. L & MGR Thomas Thorne; Act mgr E.B. Norman; Pd Mrs Lancaster-Wallis; Asm Frank Weathersby. *REV:*

Ath 2/4/92 p445-6; E 2/4/92 p11; SR 2/4/92 p388; St 31/3/92 p13; Th 1/5/92 p253-4; Ti 29/3/92 p12.

92.86 *MIDSUMMER DAY* (P,1a) Walter Frith. ST. JAMES'S 30/3/92-29/8/92; 28/1/92-30/11/92. 116 perf [np 14-15/4, 26/5].* Philip Merton H.H. Vincent; Lawrence Boyle Vernon Sansbury; Peterson Alfred Holles. Mrs Merton Fanny Enson; Muriel Merton Winifred Dolan; Parton Bessie Page. L & MGR George Alexander; Sm Robert V. Shone; Mus dir Walter Slaughter; Bm Alwyn Lewis. *REV: E 2/4/92 p7; St 7/4/92 p12; Ti 31/3/92 p7.*

92.87 *THEODORA* (P,6a,8tab) Robert Buchanan [adpt of Victorien Sardou's play]. OLYMPIC 4/4/92-9/4/92. 8 perf [w/mat 6/4, 9/4].** Justinian Bassett Roe; Andreas Julius Knight; Timocles W.E. Sauter; Agathon Henry Ludlow; Faber C.A. Gillig; Stryrax B[eresford] Whitcomb; Belisarius Arthur Estcourt; Marcellus Charles Lander; Euphratus Watty Brunton,jr; Caribert Harcourt Beatty; Mundus J. King; Pricus D.J. Hennessy; Grythes C[harles] Anson; Lycostrates Percy Wood; Amrou W.J. Monckton; Calchas John Franklin. Theodora Grace Hawthorne; Antonina Lesley Bell; Tamyris Ada Neilson. BOM Arthur Frye. *REV: St 7/4/92 p12.*

92.88 *THE UNKNOWN* (D,5a) [J.A. Stevens]. NOVELTY 9/4/92-c.29/4/92. c.18 perf. 1st perfd Surrey 31/7/82.

92.89 *THE MAELSTROM* (D,4a) Mark Melford. SHAFTESBURY 9/4/92-22/4/92. 10 perf [np 14-15/4]. 1st perfd Prince of Wales's, Southampton 16/3/91 [as *Hidden Terror*]. Lucius Tierce Mark Melford; Gibert Sarcliff John Beauchamp; Edward Hartleigh H. Reeves-Smith; Wolf Aylward C.W. Garthorne; Dr Summerton G.L. Leith; Ferguson R.J. Pakenham; Dr Fabert Giffard Stacey. Nora Appleford Decima Moore; Parker Helen Leyton; Mrs Grain Adeline Lester; Esther Claire Pauncefort; Rhoda Maggie Bowman; Gertrude Olga Brandon. L & MGR John Lart; Pp John Lancaster; Bom Watts; Sc Bruce Smith; Mus & Mus dir C.J. Hargitt; Sm Thomas Sidney; Bm & Treas Gilbert Tate. *REV: Ath 16/4/92 p512; E 16/4/92 p8; SR 16/4/92 p449-50; St 14/4/92 p10; Th 1/5/92 p 254-5; Ti 11/4/92 p8.*

92.90 *L'ENFANT PRODIGUE* (MP, without words,3a) Michel Carré, *fils* (lib) & André Wormser (mus). CRITERION 11/4/92-6/5/92. 27 perf [w/mat 13/4, 16/4, 18/4, 20/4, 23/4; mat only 25/4-6/5].** Pierrot, sr [V.] Courtes; Le Baron Enrico; Coloured Servant Jean Arceuil. Mme Pierrot E. Bade; Pierrot, jr Charoltte Raynard; Phrynette Francesca Zanfretta [Mrs Charles Lauri]. L & MGR Charles Wyndham; Pianist Landon Ronald; Mus dir Alfred Carpenter; Sm H. Agoust. *REV: E 16/4/92 p7; St 14/4/92 p10; Ti 12/4/92 p10.*

92.91 *SWEETHEARTS* (Dramatic Contrast,2a) W.S. Gilbert. ROYALTY 11/4/92-12/4/92. 2 perf. 1st perfd Prince of Wales's 7/11/74. Harry Spreadbrow Arthur Styan. Jenny Northcott Mrs Phillips. *REV: E 16/4/92 p9.*

92.92 *A SKIRT DANCE.* ROYALTY 11/4/92-12/4/92. 2 perf. Frank Lambert; Lambert. Countess Russell; Mrs Dick Russell.

92.93 *A PANTOMIME REHEARSAL* (Bsq,1a) Cecil Clay. ROYALTY 11/4/92-12/4/92. 2 perf.** Dick Deedes H. Leverson; Lord Arthur Pomeroy Frank Lambert; Cpt. Tom Robinson R.G. Leverson. Lady Muriel Mrs Phillips; Countess Russell. *REV: E 16/4/92 p9.*

92.94 *NIOBE (ALL SMILES)* (MythologicalC,3a) Harry & Edward Paulton. STRAND 11/4/92-21/7/93. 535 perf [w/W, S mat exc 13/4, 27/7, 24/12/92, 22/3/93; add mat 18/4, 6/6, 26/12,27/12/92, 23/3/93, 3/4, 22/5/93: np 15/4/92. 24/12/92. 31/2/93]. 1st perfd Prince of Wales's, Liverpool 1/9/90. Peter Amos Dunn Harry Paulton; Cornelius Griffin Forbes Dawson; Hamilton Tompkins George P. Hawtrey; Phillip Innings Herbert Ross; Parker G. Sillocks Alec C. MacKenzie. Niobe Beatrice Lamb; Caroline Dunn Ina Goldsmith; Helen Griffin Carlotta Zerbini; Hattie Griffin Georgie Esmond/Mabel Hardinge/Jessie Storey; Beatrice Sillocks Eleanor May; Madeline Mifton Isabel Ellissen/ Helen Ferrers; Mary Venie Bennett/Loraine Drew/Cynthia Brooke. PP J.S. Clarke; L Willie Edouin; Bm J.T. Mackay Robertson; Sm Charles Dubois; Cond Ernest Bucalossi. *REV: Ath 16/4/92 p512; E 16/4/92 p7; SR 16/4/92 p450; St 14/4/92 p10, 10/11/92 p13; Th 1/5/92 p255-6; Ti 12/4/92 p10.*

92.95 *NO CREDIT* (Ca,1a) Emily Coffin. STRAND 11/4/92-
21/7/93. 395 perf [np 15/4/92, 24/12/92, 31/3/93,
6/7/93].* Mr Grant George P. Hawtrey; Frank Gordon
Herbert Ross; Sir George Brinsley Alec C. MacKenzie.
Kitty Georgie Esmond; Barbara Venie Bennett/Ina Gold-
smith/Cynthia Brooke. PP, L, Bm, Sm, Cond as for 92.
94. *REV: E 16/4/92 p7; St 14/4/92 p10; Ti 12/4/92
p10.*

92.96 *THE MAGISTRATE* (F,3a) A.W. Pinero. TERRY'S 13/4/
92-4/6/92. 53 perf [w/S mat exc 4/6; add mat 18/4; np
15/4]. 1st perfd Court 21/3/85. Mr Posket Edward
Terry; Col. Lukyn [William] Mackintosh; Cis Farring-
don Henry V. Esmond; Achille Blond Herman de Lange;
Sgt. Lugg William Lugg; Mr Wormington Gilbert Trent;
Wyke W.E. Richardson; Mr/Bullamy Fred Cape; Cpt.
Horace Vale Klyde Maxwell; Inspector Messiter Albert
Sims; Constable Harris George Belmore; Isidore J.
Brabourne. Agatha Posket Fanny Brough; Beatie Tomlin-
son Annie Hill; Popham Alice Maitland; Charlotte
Ethel Matthews. PP & MGR Edward Terry; Bm H.T. Brick-
well; Sc T.W. Hall; Furn M.W. Edgley; Cost Viola
Clifford, S.E. Brown; Mus dir T[om] Smythe. *REV: E
16/4/92 p7; St 21/4/92 p12-3; Th 1/5/92 p257; Ti 14/
4/92 p4.*

92.97 *IN SEARCH OF AN ENGAGEMENT* (MSk) Nellie Ganthony. TERRY'S 13/4/92-30/5/92; 9/5/92-4/6/92. 44
perf [w/mat 18/4, 23/4, 30/4, 14/5; np 15/4].**
Nellie Ganthony. PP & MGR, Bm, Mus dir as for 92.96.

92.98 *THE TIN BOX* (FC,3a) George Manville Fenn. GLOBE
16/4/92-23/4/92. 8 perf [w/mat 18/4].* John Kedge
Walter Everard; Cpt. Robert Teale Austin Melford;
Lieut. Graham Teale E. Allan Aynesworth; Joseph Peach
Henry Vernon; Anthony Buzzard Arthur Helmore; Brace
George Hughes; Railway Porter T. Moore. Bella Kedge
Annie Hughes; Mrs Bolitho Eleanor Bufton; Minnie
Forde Sybil Baird; Clara Forde Beatrice Goodchild. L
& MGR Frederick Langley; Am Leonard Outram; Sm Robert
Soutar; Bm Frank Davis; Sc Richard C. Durant; Cond

John Storer. *REV: Ath 23/4/92 p543; E 23/4/92 p6; St 21/4/92 p12; Ti 18/4/92 p5.*

92.99 *A STRANGE GUEST* (Ca,1a) Frank Lange. GLOBE 16/4/92-23/4/92. 7 perf.* Joshua Bloghead Charles Grayson. Lady Pommeridge Kate Mills; Susan Cecily Banyard. L & MGR, Am, Sm, Bm, Cond, Sc as for 92.98. *REV: E, St as for 92.98.*

92.100 *JULIUS CAESAR* (T,5a) William Shakespeare. OLYMPIC 16/4/92-23/4/92. 7 perf [w/mat 23/4]. 1st perfd 21/9/1599. Brutus Edmund Tearle; Cassius Frederick Scarth; Marc Antony W.S. Hardy; Julius Caesar A. Gow Bentinck; Casca Jones Finch; Octavius Caesar Cyril Grier; Trebonius S.F Walker; Metellus John Saunders; Decius Alfred Paumier; Cinna E. Keilsel; Popilius Lenas Alfred Talboys; Titinius T.E. Simpson; Servius F.C. Alexander; Warro Charles Baker; Pindarus Cooke Beresford; Soothsayer Alfred Wilford; 1st Citizen E.B. Humphries; 2nd Citizen James Cooke; 3rd Citizen Murray. Lucius Georgina Harris; Flavius Minnie Goepel; Calphurnia [Marie] Glynne; Portia Theresa Osborne. L & MGR Edmund Tearle; Pp Charles Wilmot; Gen mgr Weldon Watts; Act mgr James Leslie. *REV: E 23/4/92 p7; St 21/4/92 p13.*

92.101 *THE LIFE WE LIVE* (D,4a) R. Fenton MacKay & Louis S. Denbigh. PRINCESS'S 16/4/92-28/4/92. 12 perf [w/mat 18/4].* Dick Redmond Charles Warner; Jonas Redmond Henry Bedford; George Esmond Ian Robertson; Harry Walter Gay; Terry O'Dowd Wilfred E. Shine; Charlie Noodle Harry Eversfield; Phil Burchill W.L. Abingdon; Sgt. Thorndyke Trant Fischer; Silas Redmond H. Nelson Dickson; Tom Welder C. Maitland; Giles Alfred Phillips; Red Mike F[rank] H. Westerton; Joey Sharp W[illie] Phillips; Sgt. of Police E. Ball; Policeman G[eorge] Aubrey; Cabman Percy Ames; Bailiff H. Francis; Warder H. George; Tom Thomas Verner; Jem Alfred Bernard. L & MGR Sidney Herberte Basing; Pp Mrs Harriet Gooch; Dir Charles Warner; Mus & Mus dir Michael Connelly; Asm Thomas Verner; Act mgr & Treas F. Forbes; Bm L[ouis] F. Nethersole; Mach J.W. Cawdrey; Sc [Richard] Halley, Grimani, [Julian] Hicks, Brown, [J.?] England; Cost Morris Angel. *REV: Ath*

23/4/92 p543; E 23/4/92 p6; St 21/4/92 p12; Th 1/5/ 92 p256-7; Ti 18/4/92 p5.

92.102 *A DOLL'S HOUSE* (P,3a) Henrik Ibsen [trans William Archer]. AVENUE 19/4/92-20/5/92. 30 perf [w/ mat 23/4, 30/4].** Torvald Helmer Charles Charrington; Nils Krogstad Herbert Flemming; Dr Rank Charles J. Fulton; Porter H[enry] Nelson; Einar Master Basil Deane; Bob Hilary Deane; Emmy Master Ambrose Deane. Nora Helmer Janet Achurch; Mrs Linden Marion Lea; Ellen Braekstad; Anna Florence Haydon. LI George Paget; Mgr Charles Charrington; Sc W.T. Hemsley; Furn Oetzmann; Sm George R. Foss; Bm Harrington Baily; Cond C.W. Lamartine. *REV: Ath 23/4/92 p543; E 23/4/92 p6; St 21/4/92 p12; Ti 20/4/92 p7.*

92.103 *BEATA* (DD,3a) "Austin Fryers" [W.E. Clery; adpt of Ibsen, *Rosmersholm*]. GLOBE 19/4/92-11/5/92. 22 perf [w/mat 30/4, 7/5; mat only 19-23/5].* Rosmer Leonard Outram; Rector Kroll Henry Vernon; Dr West Robert Soutar; Mortensgard George Hughes/ Austin Melford. Beata Frances Ivor; Helseth Susie Vaughan; Rebecca West Estelle Burney. L & MGR Frederick Langley; Dir Leonard Outram; Cost Stagg & Mantle; Am Leonard Outram; Sm Robert Soutar; Bm Frank Davis; Cond John Storer; Sc Richard C. Durant. *REV: Ath 23/ 4/92 p543; E 23/4/92 p8; St 21/4/92 p12; Th 1/5/92 p257-8; Ti 20/4/92 p7.*

92.104 *THE WIDOW* (FC,3a) Arthur Greville Bagot. COMEDY 21/4/92-7/5/92. 15 perf. 1st prof. Albert Godfrey Eric Lewis; Cpt. Jack Deakin Vincent Sternroyd; M. Gretot Arthur Grenville; James William Wyes; Charles Deakin Arthur Cecil. Mabel Deakin Violet Armbruster; Keriah MacNamara Lizzie Henderson; Mary Eva Williams; Lena Duprez Annie Irish. MGR Charles H. Hawtrey; Asm Charles Milton; Act mgr, Bm & Sec E.F. Bradley; Mus dir James M. Glover. *REV: 23/4/92 p9; St 28/4/92 p12-3; Th 1/5/92 p258; Ti 22/4/92 p4.*

92.105 *TIME IS MONEY* (Ca,1a) Mrs Hugh Bell & Arthur Cecil. COMEDY 21/4/92-7/5/92; 11/6/92(m). 16 perf.** Mr Graham Charles H. Hawtrey. Susan Vane Featherston; Mrs Murray Lottie Venne. MGR, Act mgr, Bm & Sec, Asm,

Mus dir as for 92.104. *REV: E, St, Ti as for 92.104.*

92.106 *A BREEZY MORNING* (Ca,1a) Eden Phillpotts.
COMEDY 21/4/92-7/5/92. 15 perf.** Mr Goldie Sam
Sothern. Mrs Goldie Florence Fordyce. MGR, Act mgr,
Bm & Sec, Asm, Mus dir as for 92.104.

92.107 *SWEET CUPID'S NET* (C,3a) Julian Cross. STRAND
21/4/92 mat perf.* Benjamin Blackheth Julian Cross;
Tom Margery Cecil Crofton; Clement Sutherland Frank
Gillmore; Langton Price, M.P. Henry Dana; Constable
Brill J.G. Campbell; James P. Morden; Waiter S[idney]
Burt. Abigail Blackheth Mrs E.H. Brooke; Rose Black-
heth Mary Mordaunt; Miss Bilkins Henrietta Cross;
Edith Beaumont Kate Ruskin. *REV: E 23/4/92 p9; St
28/4/92 p13.*

92.108 *A DESPERATE REMEDY* (P,1a) Harry P. Bruce.
STRAND 21/4/92 mat perf.* Arthur Ffolliot Nicol Pent-
land; Frank A.E.W. Mason. Blanche Ffolliot Essex Dane.
REV: As for 92.107.

92.109 *THE WHITE ROSE* (RD,4a) George R. Sims & Robert
Buchanan [fnd on Walter Scott, *Woodstock*]. ADELPHI
23/4/92-10/6/92. 42 perf.* Col. Markham Everard
Leonard Boyne; Oliver Cromwell Charles Cartwright;
Sir Harry Lee J.D. Beveridge; Jeremiah Holdfast Lio-
nel Rignold; Roger Wildrake Charles Dalton; Joseph
Tomkins Charles Collette; Charles Stuart Fuller
Mellish; Albert Lee Matthew Brodie; Gen. Harrison R.
Davis; Cpt. Pearson Howard Russell; Jolliffe Arthur
Leigh; Col. Yarborough George W. Cockburn; Mr Bletson/
Landlord H[arwood] Cooper, jr; Ezekiel Robins F.T.
Lingham; Ephraim Wood W. Northcote; Habakuk E. [F.]
Saxon; Corporal of the Guard F. [O.] Anderson. Alice
Lee Evelyn Millard; Elizabeth Cromwell Mrs Patrick
Campbell; Phoebe Mayflower Clara Jecks; Maid Alice
Bronse; Milkmaid [Helen] Vizetelly. PP & MGR A. & S.
Gatti; Sc Bruce Smith, William Perkins, Walter Hann;
Mus Henry Sprake; Mach H. Loftin; Pq William Clark-
son; Cost dgn Karl; Cost L. & H. Nathan; Furn J.S.
Lyon; Dir E.B. Norman; Mus dir Henry Sprake; Act mgr
& Treas Charles A. Jecks. *REV: Ath 30/4/92 p578; E
30/4/92 p11; SR 30/4/92 p510; St 28/4/92 p12; Th 1/6/*

92 p307-8; Ti 25/4/92 p10.

92.110 *PERIL* (C,3a) "Saville Rowe" [Clement Scott] &
B.C. Stephenson [adpt of Victorien Sardou, *Nos Intimes*]. HAYMARKET 23/4/92-5/7/92. 41 perf [w/mat 18/6,
25/6, 2/7; S only 23/4-28/5]. 1st perfd Prince of
Wales's 30/9/76. Sir Woodbine Grafton H. Beerbohm
Tree; Mr Crossley Beck [Henry] Kemble; Cpt. Bradford
Fred Terry; Sir George Ormond [F.H.] Macklin; Dr
Thornton Charles Allan; Percy Grafton A[lfred] Wigley; Meadows Robb Harwood; Kemp Edward Rose. Lady
Ormond Julia Neilson; Sophie Claire Ivanova; Lucy
Ormond Lizzie Webster; Miss Crossley Beck Rose Leclercq; L & MGR H.B. Tree; Sm Edward Hastings; Mus
dir Carl Armbruster; Bm & Sec F[rederick] Harrison;
Bom W.H. Leverton. *REV: Ath 30/4/92 p578; E 30/4/92
p9; SR 28/5/92 p624; St 28/4/92 p12; Th 1/6/92 p308;
Ti 25/4/92 p10.*

92.111 *ALONE IN THE WORLD* (D,4a) Prentiss Ingram.
PRINCESS'S 23/4/92-25/4/92. 2 mat perf;* trfd to
ROYALTY 2/5/92-5/5/92 [4 perf]. Total 6 perf. Jack
Marlowe Theo Balfour; Joseph Bolton Fred Wright, jr/
E.W. Colman; Reuben Bruce Maitland Marler; Andrew
Sharpus Hamilton Revelle; Sammy Snapper F[rank]
Weathersby; Ancient Sol P. MacNamara; Slippery Jim
Berlen; Bobb Linnett P. Trist; Antonio Pranzini E.
Daintree; Mike Logan R. Barry; Caleb Barwell A. Waller; James Carter G[eorge] Aubrey; Extras Rivington,
Dane, [Robert] Malone. Mrs Ferdinand Shaeffer
Naomi Hope; Mother Orsola Mrs Frank Huntley; Polly
Luwick Ida Sala; Mrs Barwell Hazeledean; Lena Shaeffer Louise Litta; Extras Howard, Birkbeck, [Isabel?] Rayner, Carlton, Canham. L & MGR Sidney Herberte
Basing; Pp Mrs Harriet Gooch; Asm F[rank] Weathersby;
Mus dir Michael Connelly; Act mgr E.D. Griffiths;
Dir Theo Balfour. *REV: E 30/4/92 p11; St 28/4/92 p13;
Ti 3/5/92 p10.*

92.112 *THE FIAT OF THE GODS* (Idyl of Parental Love,1a)
Leonard S. Outram. GLOBE 25/4/92-6/5/92. 11 perf.**
Galba Austin Melford; Flavian Leonard S. Outram.
Faustina Frances Ivor; Neodamia Sybil Baird. L & MGR
Frederick Langley; Am Leonard Outram; Sm Robert Sou-

tar; <u>Treas</u> Frank Davis; <u>Cond</u> John Storer; <u>Sc</u> Richard
C. Durant.

92.113 *RICHARD III* (T) William Shakespeare [adpt by
Colley Cibber]. OLYMPIC 25/4/92-6/5/92. 12 perf [w/
mat 30/5]. 1st perfd 1597. <u>Duke of Gloster</u> Edmund
Tearle; <u>Henry VI</u> Jones Finch; <u>Earl of Richmond</u> W.S.
Hardy; <u>Buckingham</u> Frederick Scarth; <u>Duke of Norfolk</u>
Charles Saunders; <u>Lord Stanley</u> A. Gow Bentinck; <u>Sir
Richard Ratcliffe</u> Cooke Beresford; <u>Earl of Oxford</u>
Arthur Lennard; <u>Lord Mayor of London</u> James Cooke; <u>Sir
James Blount</u> Ernest Chambers; <u>Sir William Catesby</u>
Cyril Grier; <u>Lieut. of the Tower</u> Charles Williams;
<u>Cpt. of the Guard</u> Frederick Kelsie; <u>Tressel</u> Alfred
Paumier; <u>Sir James Tyrrell</u> Alfred Talboys; <u>Bishop of
Ely</u> Arthur Wilson; <u>Bishop of Salisbury</u> Henry Orford;
<u>John Dighton</u> E. Rogers; <u>Miles Forest</u> T. Walker. <u>Ed-
ward, Prince of Wales</u> Georgina Harris; <u>Richard, Duke
of York</u> Minnie Goepel; <u>Duchess of York</u> Marie Glynne;
<u>Lady Anne</u> Theresa Osborne; <u>Elizabeth</u> Kate Clinton.
REV: E 30/4/92 p9; St 28/4/92 p13.

92.114 *THE NEW SUB* (P,1a) Seymour Hicks. COURT 27/4/
92-15/10/92. 161 perf [w/S mat exc 11/6, 25/6, 9/7,
16/7, 23/7, 30/7, 6/8, 13/8, 20/8, 27/8, 3/9, 1/10;
mat only 27/8, 3/9].* <u>Mjr. Ensor</u> Brandon Thomas;
<u>Cpt. Champion</u> W.G. Elliott/Wilfred Draycott; <u>Cpt.
Blount</u> C.P. Little; <u>Lieut. Crookenden</u> Compton Coutts;
<u>2nd Lieut. Dartlington</u> Ernest Bertram; <u>Private Mc-
Nally</u> [F.] Vaughan; <u>Surgeon-Mjr. Carruthers</u> Wilfred
Draycott/Sidney Warden. <u>Mrs Dartlington</u> Gertrude
Kingston. <u>L & MGR</u> Arthur Chudleigh; <u>Cost</u> Nathan; <u>Cond</u>
Edward Jones; <u>Dir</u> Brandon Thomas. *REV: E 30/4/92 p9;
St 5/5/92 p12; Ti 28/4/92 p10.*

92.115 *ROSENCRANTZ AND GUILDENSTERN* (Tragic Episode,
3tab) W.S. Gilbert. COURT 27/4/92-15/7/92. 77 perf
[w/S mat exc 11/6, 25/6, 9/7].** <u>King Claudius of
Denmark</u> Brandon Thomas; <u>Hamlet</u> Weedon Grossmith; <u>Ros-
encrantz</u> W.G. Elliott; <u>Guildenstern</u> C.P. Little; <u>1st
Player</u> W.L. Branscombe; <u>Polonius</u> R. Rochfort. <u>Queen
Gertrude</u> Gertrude Kingston; <u>Lady Player</u> May Palfrey;
<u>Ophelia</u> Decima Moore. <u>L & MGR</u> Arthur Chudleigh; <u>Dir</u>
W.S. Gilbert; <u>Cost</u> C.H. Fox; <u>Sc</u> W[illiam] Callcott.

REV: E, Ti as for 92.114; SR 30/4/92 p510.

92.116 *THE FRINGE OF SOCIETY* (C,4a) Charles Wyndham
& J. Moore [adpt of Alexandre Dumas, *fils, Demi-monde*].
CRITERION 30/4/92-25/7/92. 80 perf [w/S mat exc 30/4,
18/6, 25/6, 2/7, 9/7, 16/7, 23/7].* Sir Charles
Hartley Charles Wyndham; Arthur Cuthbert E.H. Vander-
felt; Joseph Poynder William Blakeley/David S. James
[ie David James, jr]; Duke of Mayfair Cyril Maude;
Phillips Frank Atherley; Russell C[harles] Terric.
Marion Carslow Mary Moore; Lady Carslow Carlotta
Addison; Mrs Joseph Poynder Ellis Jeffreys; Watson F.
Frances; Mrs Josephine Eve-Allen Mrs Langtry. L & MGR
Charles Wyndham; Sm S.H.S. Austin; Act mgr & Treas
E. Harvey; Cost Russell & Allen, Pitts & Richards,
Laferriere; Furn Oetzmann; Cond Theodore Ward. *REV:
Ath 7/5/92 p609; E 7/5/92 p7; SR 7/5/92 p537; St 5/5/
92 p12; Th 1/6/92 p309-10; Ti 2/5/92 p8.*

92.117 *HIGH LIFE BELOW STAIRS* (F,2a) Rev James Town-
ley. NOVELTY c.2/5/92-c/14/5/92. c/12 perf.** Philip
[George] Granville; Lord Duke H. Buckstone Clair; Sir
Harry G.M. Slater. Kitty Marie Brian; Lady Charlotte
Ida Douglas; Lady Bab Eleanor Lloyd; Cook Georgie
Harris. *REV: St 12/5/92 p13.*

92.118 *LADY AUDLEY'S SECRET.* NOVELTY c.2/5/92-c.14/5/
92. c.12 perf.

92.119 *A MUSICAL "SWARRY"* (MSk) Ben Nathan. TERRY'S
2/5/92-7/5/92. 7 perf [w/mat 7/5]. PP & MGR Edward
Terry; Bm H.T. Brickwell; Mus dir T[om] Smythe.

92.120 *NADIA* (P,4a) Lady Violet Greville [adpt of
Henri Greville's novel, *Les Epreuves de Raissa*]. LYRIC
3/5/92 mat perf.* Count Rezof Arthur Bourchier; Ivan
C[harles] Westmacott; Count Valerian Gretzky Frank
Gillmore; Michael Svensky E.J. Malyon; Sabatrine
Charles Thursby; Fadei Frank Motley Wood; Gen. Kleine
George Mudie; John James; Porof Julian Cross; Verger
Ernest Lyon. Princess Adine Helen Forsyth; Countess
Gretzky Henrietta Lindley; Mme Porof Adelaide Newton;
Nadia Olga Brandon. L & MGR Horace Sedger; Sm Julian
Cross; Asm E.J. Malyon; Cost L. & H. Nathan; Pq

C.H. Fox; <u>Furn</u> Oetzmann; <u>Mach</u> S. Trewen; <u>Props</u> Labhart; <u>Bm & Treas</u> William Greet. *REV: Ath 7/5/92 p609;
E 7/5/92 p10; St 5/5/92 p12-3; Ti 5/5/92 p14.*

92.121 *AN AMERICAN BRIDE* (D,4a) Sir William Young &
Maurice Noel. LYRIC 5/5/92 mat perf.* <u>Duke of St.</u>
<u>Heliers</u> Eric Lewis; <u>Jack Hilliard</u> Arthur Elwood; <u>Lord</u>
<u>Dorrington</u> Lewis Waller; <u>Jared Stagg</u> Charles Eaton;
<u>George Carston</u> Charles J. Fulton; <u>Maitland</u> G. East
E. Allan Aynesworth; <u>James McGuinis</u> Fred Kaye; <u>Billy</u>
B. Edwards; <u>Chandos</u> David Cowis. <u>Duchess of St. Hel-</u>
<u>iers</u> Henrietta Lindley; <u>Lady Hilda</u> Lilian Hingston;
<u>Violet Lanyon</u> Ethel Norton; <u>Stella Durand</u> Janette
Steer. <u>L & MGR</u>, <u>Furn</u>, <u>Pq</u>, <u>Mach</u>, <u>Bm & Treas</u> as for 92.
120; <u>Dir</u> Hugh Moss; <u>Mus</u> Lady Arthur Hill; <u>Props</u>
Mountain. *REV: E 7/5/92 p11; St 12/5/92 p12; Th 1/6/
92 p310-1.*

92.122 *A HOUSEHOLD FAIRY* (DomesticSk) Francis Talfourd. CRITERION 7/5/92-23/5/92. 14 perf.** <u>Julion</u>
<u>de Clifford</u> Frank Atherley. <u>Katherine</u> F. Frances.
<u>L & MGR</u> Charles Wyndham; <u>Sm</u> S.H.S. Austin; <u>Act mgr &</u>
<u>Treas</u> E. Harvey; <u>Cond</u> Theodore Ward.

92.123 *A STAGE COACH* (Ca,1a) Frederic de Lara. GLOBE
7/5/92-11/5/92. 4 perf. 1st perfd Ladbroke Hall 17/5/
87 [as *Another Matinee*]. <u>Richard de Vere Trevelyan</u>
Walter Everard; <u>Col. Bumpus</u> Austin Melford. <u>Mrs Tur-</u>
<u>tledove</u> Sophie Larkin; <u>Brown</u> Kate Mills; <u>May</u> Beatrice
Goodchild. <u>L & MGR</u> Frederick Langley; <u>Am</u> Leonard Out-
ram; <u>Sm</u> Robert Soutar; <u>Treas</u> Frank Davis; <u>Bm</u> George
Hughes; <u>Cond</u> John Storer; <u>Sc</u> Richard C. Durant. *REV:
E 14/5/92 p9; St 12/5/92 p13.*

92.124 *RICHELIEU* (P,5a) Edward Bulwer Lytton. LYCEUM
7/5/92, 14/5, 21/5, 8/6(m), 11/6, 18/6/92. 6 perf.
1st perfd Covent Garden 7/3/39. <u>Chevalier de Mauprat</u>
William Terriss; <u>Baradas</u> Frank K[emble] Cooper; <u>Hug-</u>
<u>uet</u> [Frank] Tyars; <u>Gaston</u> Acton Bond; <u>Cardinal Riche-</u>
<u>lieu</u> Henry Irving; <u>Joseph</u> Arthur Stirling; <u>Louis XIII</u>
[William] Haviland; <u>De Beringhen</u> Gilbert Farquhar;
<u>1st Secretary</u> Davis; <u>2nd Secretary</u> [John] Archer; <u>3rd</u>
<u>Secretary</u> [W.] L[ionel] Belmore. <u>Julie de Mortemar</u>
Jessie Millward; <u>Francois</u> Bessie Hatton; <u>Marian de</u>

de Lorme [Amy] Coleridge. L & MGR Henry Irving; Mus
dir J. Meredith Ball; Sm H.J. Loveday; Act mgr Bram
Stoker; Bom Joseph Hurst. *REV: Ath 14/5/92 p643; E
14/5/92 p9; St 12/5/92 p12; Ti 9/5/92 p8.*

92.125 *SI SLOCUM; OR, LIFE IN THE WILD WEST* (D) Clifton W. Tayleure. NOVELTY 7/5/92-c.14/5/92. c.7 perf.
1st perfd Amphitheatre, Liverpool 8/6/76 [as *Si Sol-
cum; or, Life on the Western Border*]. Si Slocum W.H.
Patterson; Ramirez Edwin Fergusson; Bledsoe H. Buckstone Clair; Jerry Harrison; Townsend George Granville; Wallace Foster G.M. Slater; Freddy Slocum
Master Buck Williams. Mickey Marie Brian; Grace
Townsend Ida Douglas; Mrs Slocum Phyllis Neville; Old
Woman Eleanor Lloyd; Patsey Georgie Harris. *REV: St
12/5/92 p13.*

92.126 *VIRGINIUS* (T,5a) James Sheridan Knowles. OLYM-
PIC 7/5/92-14/5/92. 8 perf [w/mat 14/5]. 1st perfd
Theatre Royal, Glasgow 1820; Covent Garden 17/5/20.
Virginius Edmund Tearle; Appius Claudius Frederick
Scarth; Caius Claudius Alfred Paumier; Dentatus Jones
Finch; Numitorius A. Gow Bentinck; Icilius W.S. Hardy;
Lucius Cyril Grier; Servius R. Parlby; Cornelius
Arthur Lennard; Marcus Cooke Beresford; Titus James
Cooke; Soldier James Newark. Servia Marie Glynne; Fe-
male Slave Calton; Virginia Theresa Osborne. L & MGR
Edmund Tearle; Pp Charles Wilmot; Act mgr James Les-
lie. *REV: E 14/5/92 p9.*

92.127 *ROBERT MACAIRE* (Melo,2a) Charles Selby. OLYMPIC
7/5/92-14/5/92. 8 perf [w/mat 14/5]. 1st perfd Adelphi
2/3/35. Germeuil Arthur Lennard; Dumont A. Gow Bentinck; Robert Macaire Edwin Lever; Jacques Strop Whimsical Walker; Charles Cooke Beresford; Pierre George
Collier; Sgt. Loupy Alfred Paumier; Louis James Newark; Francois R. Parlby. Marie Marie Glynne; Clementine Madge Wilson. L & MGR, Pp, Act mgr as for 92.126.

92.128 *FRA DIAVOLO* (O,3a) D.F.E. Auber. LYRIC 10/5/92
mat perf. 1st perfd Opéra-comique, Paris 28/1/30.
Fra Diavolo Wilfred Acfield; Lord Allcash Wyatt Keith;
Lorenzo Patrick O'Connor; Beppo Henry Land; Giacomo
Charles Hinchliff; Matteo Fred J. Vigay. Zerlina Jes-

sie Bradford; <u>Lady Allcash</u> Annie Fisher. *REV: E 14/5/
92 p12; St 12/5/92 p12-3.* <u>Comment</u>: Guildhall School
of Music.

92.129 *KARIN* (D,2a) Alfhild Agrell [trans Mrs Hugh
Bell]. VAUDEVILLE 10/5/92, 12/5/92. 2 mat perf.*
<u>Oscar Hjerne</u> Fuller Mellish; <u>Mr Milden</u> John Beauchamp;
<u>Niels</u> Herbert Ross; <u>Doctor</u> Ben Greet. <u>Karin</u> Elizabeth
Robins; <u>Mrs Hjerne</u> [Kate] Bateman [Mrs Crowe]; <u>Selma</u>
Florence Hunter. L & MGR Thomas Thorne; <u>Bm</u> G.F. Bash-
ford; <u>Sm</u> Ben Greet. *REV: Ath 14/5/92 p643; E 14/5/92
p11; St 12/5/92 p13; Th 1/6/92 p311-2; Ti 11/5/92 p5.*

92.130 *A CAPRICE* (DSk,1a) Justin Huntly McCarthy [ad-
pt of Alfred de Musset, *Un Caprice*]. VAUDEVILLE 10/5/
92, 12/5/92. 2 mat perf.* <u>M de Chavigny</u> Ian Robertson. <u>Mme de Léry</u> Marion Lea; <u>Mathilde</u> May Whitty.
<u>L & MGR</u>, <u>Bm</u>, <u>Sm</u> as for 92.129. *REV: Ath, E, St, Th as
for 92.129.*

92.131 *THE WAIF* (P,1a) Cotsford Dick [adpt of François
Coppée, *Le Passant*]. HAYMARKET 11/5/92(m); 30/5/92-
5/7/92. 33 perf. 1st perfd Princess's 10/87 [as *The
Stroller*]. <u>Zanetto</u> Mrs H.B. Tree; <u>Sylvia</u> Gertrude
Kingston. <u>L & MGR</u> H.B. Tree; <u>Cost</u> L. & H. Nathan; <u>Pq</u>
C.H. Fox, William Clarkson; <u>Sm</u> Edward Hastings; <u>Mus
dir</u> Carl Armbruster; <u>Bm & Sec</u> F[rederick] Harrison;
<u>Bom</u> W.H. Leverton. *REV: E 14/5/92 p11; St 12/5/92 p
13, 2/6/92 p12.*

92.132 *THE BROTHERS* (P,1a) Henry Byatt. HAYMARKET
11/5/92 mat perf. 1st perfd Vaudeville 10/3/87. <u>Rich-
ard Johnstone</u> Laurence Cautley; <u>William Johnstone</u>
W.L. Abingdon; <u>Servant</u> Stephen Caffrey. <u>Kitty</u> Annie
Hill. L & MGR, <u>Cost</u>, <u>Pq</u>, <u>Sm</u>, <u>Mus dir</u>, <u>Bm & Sec</u>, <u>Bom</u>
as for 92.131.

92.133 *THE PRIMROSE PATH* (D,4a) B.W. Findon. VAUDE-
VILLE 11/5/92 mat perf.* <u>Frank Trevor</u> Philip Cunning-
ham; <u>George Pollock</u> Herbert Flemming; <u>Mr Sangster</u>
C[harles] Dodsworth. <u>Blanche Colvin</u> Lucia Harwood;
<u>Miss Langley</u> Maude Brennan; <u>Jarvis</u> Mary Collette; <u>Maud
Trevor</u> Rose Norreys. *REV: E 14/5/92 p11; St 12/5/92
p13; Th 1/6/92 p312-3.*

92.134 *THE HEIR-AT-LAW* (C,5a) George Colman the Younger. ROYALTY 12/5/92. Rnd. 1st perfd Haymarket 15/7/1797. <u>Daniel Dowlas</u> G.T. Skilbeck; <u>Dick Dowlas</u> William [Gayer] MacKay; <u>Dr Pangloss</u> C.O. Skilbeck; <u>Henry Morland</u> Douglas Carnegie; <u>Stedfast</u> H. Seymour Hughes; <u>Zekiel Homespun</u> F.B. Weber; <u>Kenrick</u> Lionel Bethell; <u>John</u> Ernest F. Burchatt. <u>Lady Duberly</u> Cowper Coles; <u>Caroline Dormer</u> Beatrice Ward; <u>Cicely Homespun</u> Violet Goetze. <u>L</u> Kate Santley; <u>Sm</u> C.D. Hoblyn; <u>Sc</u> G. Ellerman; <u>Cond</u> Bradbury Turner; <u>Furn</u> Fox & Jacobs.

92.135 *PETTICOAT PERFIDY* (Ca,1a) Sir Charles L. Young. ROYALTY 12/5/92. Rnd. 1st perfd Court 21/5/85. <u>Mrs Norwood Jones</u> Jacques Hill; <u>Mrs Mountrevor</u> Italia Conti; <u>Juliette</u> Cowper Coles. <u>L</u>, <u>Sm</u>,<u>Cond</u>, <u>Furn</u> as for 92.134.

92.136 *VOTE FOR GIGGS* (FC,3a) [adpt of Albert Valabrègue's *L'Homme de Paille*]. VAUDEVILLE 12/5/92-20/5/92. 8 perf.* <u>Roderick Dimbley Giggs</u> Thomas Thorne; <u>Stumpy</u> C[harles] Dodsworth; <u>Sir John Plunkert</u> Charles S. Fawcett; <u>Andrew St. Clair</u> Oswald Yorke; <u>Mealy</u> J[ohn] Wheatman; <u>Jack Lightfoot</u> C.W. Somerset. <u>Mrs Agatha Muchmore</u> Emily Thorne; <u>Caroline</u> Gertrude Lovell; <u>Arabella Liggins</u> [Harriet] Trench; <u>Mrs McGregor</u> Eva Goodricke; <u>Mrs Carter</u> Rose Dudley; <u>Clementina</u> Mabel Love. <u>L & MGR</u> Thomas Thorne; <u>Act mgr</u> Sydney Alport; <u>Sm</u> Fred Thorne. *REV: E 14/5/92 p9; St 19/5/92 p12; Ti 14/5/92 p8.*

92.137 *REPARATION* (P,1a) J.T. Grein & C.W. Jarvis. VAUDEVILLE 12/5/92-20/5/92. 8 perf.* <u>Sir Thomas Foster</u> Fred Thorne; <u>Frank Holt</u> Frank Gillmore; <u>Mr Markham</u> C[harles] Dodsworth; <u>Mr Nesbitt</u> J[ohn] Wheatman. <u>Gertrude Foster</u> Ellen Thorne; <u>Miss Foster</u> Rose Dudley. <u>L & MGR</u>, <u>Act mgr</u>, <u>Sm</u> as for 92.136. *REV: E, St as for 92.136.*

92.138 *DAN THE OUTLAW* (D,3a) Jessie Robertson [revd ver]. NOVELTY 14/5/92 mat perf. 1st perfd Town Hall, Kilburn 29/12/88. <u>Norman de Vere</u> Charles Brooke; <u>Louis Delcroix</u> W. Garratt; <u>Eric Temple</u> Edwin Fergusson; <u>Jack Galbraith</u> G.M. Slater; <u>Jones</u> [G.] Sewell; <u>Parkes</u> Edgerton; <u>Harry Fenton</u> H. Hampton. <u>Kate Gal-</u>

braith Marie Brian; <u>Louisa Martin</u>/<u>Mme Varnhart</u> Eleanor Lloyd; <u>Bertha</u> Georgie Harris; <u>Servant</u> Reside;
<u>Marie de Vere</u> Jessie Robertson. *REV: E 21/5/92 p9;
St 19/5/92 p12.*

92.139 [deleted]

92.140 *CAVALLERIA RUSTICANA* (O[1a]) Pietro Mascagni.
COVENT GARDEN 16/5/92, 17/5, 19/5, 26/5, 1/6, 6/6,
18/6, 24/6; trfd to DRURY LANE 29/6, 6/7; trfd to
COVENT GARDEN 12/7, 18/7, 21/7; trfd to DRURY LANE
23/7, 27/7/92. 15 perf.** <u>Turiddu</u> Fernando de Lucia;
<u>Alfio</u> Eugene Dufriche. <u>Lola</u> Giulia Ravogli; <u>Lucia</u>
Mathilde Bauermeister; <u>Santuzza</u> Emma Calvé. L & MGR
Augustus Harris; <u>Cond</u> Luigi Mancinelli. *REV: Ath 21/
5/92 p675; E 21/5/92 p15; SR 28/5/92 p626; St 19/5/92
p12; Ti 17/5/92 p10.*

92.141 *PHILEMON ET BAUCIS* (O,2a) Charles Gounod.
COVENT GARDEN 16/5/92, 17/5, 19/5, 26/5, 1/6, 6/6,
18/6, 24/6; trfd to DRURY LANE 29/6, 6/7; trfd to
COVENT GARDEN 12/7, 20/7; trfd to DRURY LANE 27/7/92.
13 perf.** <u>Philemon</u> Sebastian Montariol; <u>Jupiter</u>
Pol Plançon; <u>Vulcan</u> Armand Castelmary. <u>Baucis</u> Sigrid
Arnoldson. L & MGR Augustus Harris; <u>Cond</u> Leon Jehin.
REV: As for 92.140.

92.142 *DIPLOMACY* (P,5a) Clement Scott & B.C. Stephenson [adpt of Victorien Sardou, *Dora*]. AVENUE 17/5/92
mat perf. 1st perfd Prince of Wales's 12/1/78. <u>Count
Orloff</u> de Lapasture; <u>Baron Stein</u> H. Leigh-Bennett;
<u>Henry Beauclerc</u> George Hockley; <u>Julian Beauclerc</u>
C. A[ubrey] Smith; <u>Algie Fairfax</u> J.C. Peyton; <u>Mark-
ham</u> H.W. Smithers; <u>Antoine</u> P.B. Chambers; <u>Shepherd</u>
Welsford. <u>Lady Henry Fairfax</u> Eveline Faulkner; <u>Mar-
quise de Rio-Zares</u> Mrs Horne; <u>Countess Zicka</u> Beryl
Faber; <u>Dora</u> Myrtie Faber; <u>Mion</u> Helen Luck. *REV: E
21/5/92 p9.* <u>Comment</u>: Brighton Green Room Club.

92.143 *A BURIED TALENT* (P,1a,3sc) Louis N. Parker.
COMEDY 19/5/92-28/5/92. 9 perf.** <u>Maris</u> Charles H.E.
Brookfield; <u>Pietro Casella</u> James Nelson; <u>Felix</u> Ernest
Cosham; <u>Graf von Friedberg</u> William Wyes. <u>Stella</u> Vane
Featherston. MGR Charles H. Hawtrey; <u>Act mgr, Bm, Sec</u>

E.F. Bradley; <u>Dir</u> F[rederick] Glover; <u>Asm</u> Charles Milton; <u>Mus dir</u> James M. Glover. *REV: E 21/5/92 p9; St 26/5/92 p15.*

92.144 *THE POET AND THE PUPPETS* (Travestie on *Lady Windermere's Fan*,4sc) Charles H.E. Brookfield. COMEDY 19/5/92-2/7/92. 40 perf [w.mat 11/6].* <u>A Poet</u> Charles H. Hawtrey; <u>Lord Pentonville/Hamlet/A Moralist/Spirit of Fair Arbitration</u> Charles H.E. Brookfield; <u>An Author/Lord Winterstock</u> Eric Lewis; <u>Parker</u> William Wyes; <u>A Realist/1st Young Man</u> Ernest Cosham; <u>Lord Gonbustus Often</u> James Nelson; <u>2nd Young Man/A Bard</u> W[illiam] Philp; <u>An Optimist</u> J[ohn] Phipps; <u>3rd Young Man</u> Harley Granville-Barker; <u>4th Young Man</u> Charles Milton. <u>Lady Winterstock</u> Cynthia Brook; <u>The "Duchess"</u> Lizzie Ruggles; <u>Fairy/Ophelia/Mrs Earlybird</u> Lottie Venne; <u>Mrs Nicey-Nicey</u> E. Goss; <u>Mrs Lummy-Lummy</u> E. Gordon; <u>Mrs McNaughtie-Naughtie</u> Lizzie Wilson; <u>Mrs Willoughby Myndear</u> Violet Austin; <u>Mrs Welly Nearly</u> Florence Wilson. <u>MGR</u>, <u>Act mgr</u>, <u>Bm</u>, <u>Sec</u>, <u>Asm</u>, <u>Mus dir</u>, <u>Dir</u> as for 92.143; <u>Ch</u> Mlle Marie; <u>Pq</u> Richards; <u>Cost</u> L. & H. Nathan. *REV: E, St as for 92.143; SR 28/5/92 p623-4; Ti 20/5/92 p10.*

92.145 *FAUST* (O,5a) Charles Gounod. COVENT GARDEN 20/5/92, 21/5, 24/5, 23/6, 4/7, 25/7/92. 6 perf.** <u>Faust</u> Anton van Dyck/Ben Davies; <u>Valentine</u> Ceste/Jean Lassalle/Eugene Dufriche/Victor Maurel; <u>Mephistopheles</u> Pol Plançon; <u>Wagner</u> Miranda. <u>Martha</u> Mathilde Bauermeister; <u>Marguerite</u> Emma Eames/Nellie Melba/Margaret MacIntyre/Sophie Traubmann; <u>Siebel</u> Passama/Agnes Janson. <u>MGR</u> Augustus Harris; <u>Cond</u> Enrico Bevignani. *REV: Ath 28/5/92 p704; SR 28/5/92 p626; St 26/5/92 p14; Ti 23/5/92 p8.*

92.146 *FORGET-ME-NOT* (P,3a) Herman C. Merivale & F.C. Grove. AVENUE 21/5/92-28/5/92. 7 perf. 1st perfd Lyceum 21/8/79. <u>Sir Horace Welby</u> Charles Charrington; <u>Prince Malleotti</u> Sant Matthews; <u>Barrato</u> Charles J. Fulton; <u>Robert</u> H. Edwards. <u>Stephanie de Mohrivart</u> Janet Achurch; <u>Alice Verney</u> Marion Lea; <u>Rose Verney</u> Alice de Wynton; <u>Mrs Foley</u> Kate Hodson. <u>LI</u> George Paget; <u>Mgr</u> Charles Charrington; <u>Sm</u> George R. Foss; <u>Bm</u> Harrington Baily; <u>Cond</u> C.W. Lamartine. *REV: E 28/5/92 p9; SR 28/5/92 p624; St 26/5/92 p15; Ti 23/5/92 p8.*

92.147 *ORFEO* (O,3a) C.W. Gluck. COVENT GARDEN 21/5/92,
31/5/92. 2 perf.** Orfeo Giulia Ravogli; L'Amor
Mathilde Bauermeister; Euridice Sofia Ravogli/Giulia
Valda. MGR Augustus Harris; Cond Enrico Bevignani.
*REV: E 28/5/92 p15; St 19/5/92 p12, 26/5/92 p14-5; Ti
23/5/92 p8.*

92.148 *OTHELLO* (T) William Shakespeare. OLYMPIC 21/5/
92-28/5/92. 7 perf.** Othello Edmund Tearle/Frederick
Scarth/J.S. Blythe; Iago Charles Pond; Brabantio A.R.
Hodgson; Duke of Venice James Cooke; Gratiano Arthur
Lennard; Montano Alfred Paumier; Cassio Frederick
Scarth; Julio James Newark; Lodovico A. Gow Bentinck;
Roderigo Cyril Grier; Antonio R. Parlby; Messenger
Cooke Beresford. Emilia Naomi Hope; Desdemona Kate
Clinton. *REV: E 28/5/92 p9; St 26/5/92 p16.*

92.149 *L'AMICO FRITZ* (O,3a) Pietro Mascagni. COVENT
GARDEN 23/5/92, 28/5, 9/6, 14/6, 1/7, 9/7; trfd to
DRURY LANE 16/7/92. 7 perf. 1st perfd Teatro Costanzi,
Rome 31/10/91. Fritz Fernando de Lucia; Rabbino Eu-
gene Dufriche; Hanezo Antonio de Vaschetti; Frederico
Iginio Corsi. Suzel Emma Calvé; Cattarina Mathilde
Bauermeister; Beppe Giulia Ravogli. MGR Augustus
Harris; Cond Enrico Bevignani. *REV: Ath 28/5/92 p704;
E 28/5/92 p11; SR 28/5/92 p625-6; St 26/5/92 p15; Th
1/6/92 p318; Ti 24/5/92 p5.*

92.150 *TOM AND JERRY* (SportingD). NOVELTY 23/5/92-c.
28/5/92. c.7 perf. Jem Hall; Joe Choyinski. Comment:
Source: *The Referee.*

92.151 *MY SWEETHEART* ([MC,3a]) [William Gill]. NOVELTY
23/5/92-c.28/5/92. c.7 perf.** Comment: As for 92.150.

92.152 *THERMIDOR* (D,4a) Victorien Sardou. OPERA COMI-
QUE 23/5/92-28/5/92. 7 perf [w/mat 28/5]. 1st perfd
Comédie-française, Paris 24/1/91. Labussiere C.-B.
Coquelin [ainé]; Martial Hugon [Edmond] Duquesne;
Ribout Bellucci; Lupin Laroche; Marteau J. Deroy;
Chateuil Lagrange, *fils*; Bérillon Darcey; Vasselin A.
Ramy; Bricard Bourgeotte; Samson Daumerie; Pecheur à

la ligne Barbeau; Jolibon Halbert; Tavernier Beru;
Wolf Verlet; Simonet Berney; Brault Level; Deburn
Andre; Gauthier Marie; Riviere Baron; Pierre Abel;
Jumelot Evrard; Un Crieur Gillet; Bouchard Cousin;
Gamin Faure. Fabienne Lecoultreuse Malvau; Françoise
Patry; Mlle Brault Kerwich; Gaspard Jeanne; Jacque-
line Jenny Rose; La Mariotte Bellucci; 1ere Lavandiere
Julie; 2eme Lavandiere Faure. L Edward Compton; Mgr
M.L. Mayer. *REV: Ath 28/5/92 p705; E 28/5/92 p9; SR
28/5/92 p626-7; St 26/5/92 p15; Ti 24/5/92 p5.*

92.153 *TWO YOUNG WIVES* (Ca) C. Vernon. CRITERION 24/
5/92-30/7/92. 56 perf [np 26-29/7].* Mr Leslie David
S. James; Mr Gordon Frank Atherley. Mrs Leslie F.
Frances. L & MGR Charles Wyndham; Sm S.H.S. Austin;
Act mgr & Treas E. Harvey; Cond Theodore Ward.

92.154 *AGATHA* (P,3a) Isaac Henderson. CRITERION 24/5/
92, 25/5, 27/5, 30/5, 31/5/92. 5 mat perf.* Col. da
Vigno Herbert Waring; Marchese Loreno Lewis Waller;
Signor Sebasti Laurence Cautley; Gen. Ricci Charles
J. Fulton; Servants J. Montagu, F[rederick?] Watson;
John Dow, U.S.A. Charles Wyndham. Gaeta Faviola Mary
Moore; Signora da Vigno Olga Nethersole; Contessa
Faviola Rose Leclercq; Leo Minnie Terry; Marchesa
Loreno Winifred Emery. L & MGR Charles Wyndham; Bm
G.F. Bashford; Mus & Cond Theodore Ward; Furn Oetzmann.
*REV: Ath 28/5/92 p705; E 28/5/92 p10; SR 28/5/92 p624;
St 26/5/92 p15-6; Th 1/7/92 p28-9; Ti 25/5/92 p8.*

92.155 *THE NOBLE ART* (F,3a) Eille Norwood. TERRY'S
25/5/92 mat perf. Theatre Royal, York 11/4/92. Andrew
Fullalove Arthur Williams; Charles Fullalove H.
Reeves-Smith; Bulwer Brady Sydney Brough; Prof Tranz
Julian Cross; Peter Sledge Sydney Valentine; Waters
Sidney Stuart; Call Boy Master Mansfield. Gertie
Fullalove May Whitty; Winifred Tiverton Katie Leech-
man; Tilly DuVal Lillie Belmore; Jenny Beatrice Good-
child. *REV: E 28/5/92 p11; St 26/5/92 p16; Th 1/7/92
p29.*

92.156 *DON PEDRO* (D,1a) Langdon Elwyn Mitchell. STRAND
26/5/92 mat perf.* Don Pedro Herbert Ross; Don Luis
Ernest Hendrie; Don Juan Ivan Watson. Donna Jacinta

Lizzie Webster. <u>L & MGR</u> Willie Edouin; <u>Pp</u> J.S. Clarke;
<u>Sm</u> Herman de Lange; <u>Bm</u> Charles Terry; <u>Cond</u> Ernest
Bucalossi. *REV: E 28/5/92 p11; St 2/6/92 p13; Th 1/7/
92 p29; Ti 27/5/92 p11.*

92.157 *IN THE SEASON* (CD,1a) Langdon Elwyn Mitchell.
STRAND 26/5/92 mat perf.* <u>Sir Harry Collingwood</u> Herbert Waring; <u>Edward Fairburne</u> Bernard Gould. <u>Sybil</u>
<u>March</u> May Whitty. <u>L & MGR</u>, <u>Pp</u>, <u>Sm</u>, <u>Bm</u>, <u>Cond</u> as for
92.156. *REV: E, St, Ti as for 92.156; Th 1/7/92 p30.*

92.158 *RUTH UNDERWOOD* (D,1a) Langdon Elwyn Mitchell.
STRAND 26/5/91 mat perf.* <u>Richard Underwood</u> Charles
Dodsworth; <u>Soldier</u> Bernard Gould; <u>Cpt.</u> Herbert Ross.
<u>Ruth Underwood</u> Marion Lea; <u>Elizabeth Underwood</u> Flo-
rence Haydon. <u>L & MGR</u>, <u>Pp</u>, <u>Sm</u>, <u>Bm</u>, <u>Cond</u> as for 92.
156. *REV: As for 92.157.*

92.159 *MANON* (O[5a]) Jules Massenet. COVENT GARDEN
27/5/92. 1 perf.** <u>Chevalier des Grieux</u> Ernest van
Dyck; <u>Comte des Grieux</u> Pol Plançon; <u>Lescaut</u> Eugene
Dufriche; <u>De Bretigny</u> Ceste; <u>Guillot</u> Miranda. <u>Rosette</u>
Agnes Janson; <u>Pousette</u> Mathilde Bauermeister; <u>Javotte</u>
Florenza; <u>Manon Lescaut</u> Eugenia Mravina. <u>MGR</u> Augustus
Harris; <u>Cond</u> Leon Jehin. *REV: Ath 4/6/92 p737; E 4/6/
92 p13; St 2/6/92 p12; Ti 31/5/92 p10.*

92.160 *LE PETIT CHAPERON ROUGE [LITTLE RED RIDING
HOOD]* (MP without words,3a) Charles de Sivry (mus) &
Albert de Sanson (lib) & Henry de Brisay (lib). ROY-
ALTY 27/5/92. 1 perf. <u>Jacques</u> Charles Hurbain; <u>Mend-
iant</u> L. Nitter; <u>M. Fernand</u> G[eorges] Treville; <u>Jules</u>
G. Marchaud; <u>Extras</u> Brown, [Robert] Malone, Hilary,
Clarke, Norton, Spencer. <u>Jenny</u> Aline Guyon; <u>Mme
Colichet</u> Irma Aubrys; <u>Rosa Tampon</u> Louise Dauville;
<u>Extras</u> Courtney, [Belle] Harcourt, Sherrington, Som-
erset, Nina Nicholson, Lily Nicholson, [Edith?] Dixey,
Carmen. <u>L</u> Kate Santley; <u>Dir</u> Vidal, de la Brousse; <u>Act
mgr & Treas</u> Henry L. Boss; <u>Cond</u> Coste; <u>Furn</u> Oetzmann;
<u>Bom</u> Arthur Dalby. *REV: E 4/6/92 p7; St 2/6/92 p13; Ti
30/5/92 p4.*

92.161 *MAKE-BELIEFS* (Duol) Dagmar Holberg & J.T. Grein
[adpt fr play by Otto Benzon]. ROYALTY 27/5/92.

1 perf.* <u>He</u> William Bonney. <u>She</u> Mary H. Keegan. <u>L</u>,
<u>Dir</u>, <u>Act mgr</u> & <u>Treas</u>, <u>Cond</u>, <u>Bom</u> as for 92.160. *REV:
As for 92.160.*

92.162 *HILDA* (P,3a). PRINCESS'S 28/5/92 mat perf.*
<u>Arthur Sydney</u> Julian Cross; <u>Gilbert</u> A. Wood; <u>Frank
Dundas</u> Foster Courtenay; <u>Dr Middlewitch</u> Cornwall. <u>Dai</u>-
<u>sy Gwynne</u> Kate Bealby; <u>Hilda Sydney</u> Marie Linden. <u>L</u>
& <u>MGR</u> Sidney Herberte Basing; <u>Dir</u> Julian Cross; <u>Mus</u>
Michael Connelly; <u>Cost</u> Mme Jules; <u>Furn</u> James Lyons.
REV: E 4/6/92 p7; SR 4/6/92 p657; St 2/6/92 p13.
<u>Comment</u>: V & A source indicates a perf on 2/5/92 mat;
all other sources indicate this date.

92.163 *WILL HE COME AGAIN* (F) Mrs Bernard Wishaw.
PRINCESS'S 28/5/92 mat perf. 1st perfd Avenue 3/3/91
[as *Two or One*]. <u>Douglas Macdougal</u> Foster Courtenay;
<u>James</u> H. Buss. <u>Emmy Campbell</u> Laura Linden. <u>L</u> & <u>MGR</u>,
<u>Mus</u>, <u>Cost</u>, <u>Furn</u> as for 92.162. *REV: E 4/6/92 p7.*
<u>Comment</u>: As for 92.162.

92.164 *CLEOPATRA* (D,5a) Victorien Sardou & Emile Moreau. ROYAL ENGLISH OPERA HOUSE 28/5/92-11/6/92. 15
perf [w/mat 4/6, 11/6]. 1st perfd Porte-Saint-Martin,
Paris 22/10/90. <u>Demetrius</u> Piron; <u>Dercetas</u> Duberry;
<u>Dellius</u> Fleury; <u>Kephren</u> Rebel; <u>Le Devin</u> Andre; <u>Mess-
ager</u> Munié; <u>Thyreus</u> [Henri] Deschamps; <u>Octave</u> Thefer;
<u>Olympus</u> Charton; <u>Amosis</u> Dupont; <u>Juba</u> Cartereau; <u>Gou-
verneur</u> Dubois; <u>Marchand</u> Latour; <u>Notable</u> Jean Tarebb;
<u>Strepsiade</u> Besson; <u>Un Esclave</u> Marchand; <u>Officier</u>
Charles; <u>Marc Antoine</u> Albert Darmont. <u>Cléopâtra</u>
Sarah Bernhardt; <u>Octavie</u> Jane Mea; <u>Charmiane</u> Simonson;
<u>Une Esclave</u> Merle; <u>Eros</u> Nadrey; <u>Iras</u> Gilberte Fleury;
<u>Dancers</u> Greet, Wright, Pasque, Mountcastle. <u>PP</u> Richard
d'Oyly Carte; <u>Dir</u> Henry E. Abbey, Maurice Grau; <u>Mus</u>
Xavier Leroux; <u>Cond</u> Andrew Levey; <u>Act mgr</u> G. Edwards
Minor. *REV: Ath 4/6/92 p739; E 4/6/92 p9; SR 4/6/92
p654-5; St 2/6/92 p12-3; Ti 30/5/92 p8.*

92.165 *ROMEO ET JULIETTE* (O[5a]) Charles Gounod. COV-
ENT GARDEN 30/5/92, 4/6, 21/6/92. 3 perf.** <u>Romeo</u>
Jean de Reske; <u>Frère Laurent</u> Edouard de Reske/Pol
Plançon; <u>Tybalt</u> Sebastian Montariol; <u>Mercutio</u> Eugene
Dufriche/Ceste; <u>Capulet</u> Pol Plançon/Eugene Dufriche;

Duc de Verone Alec Marsh. Stephano Agnes Janson/Faure; Gertrude Mathilde Bauermeister; Juliette Emma Eames/Nellie Melba. MGR Augustus Harris; Cond Luigi Mancinelli. *REV: Ath 4/6/92 p737; E 4/6/92 p13, 11/6/92 p13; St 2/6/92 p12, 9/6/92 p12; Ti 31/5/92 p10, 6/6/92 p12.*

92.166 *LA MEGERE APPRIVOISEE* (P,4a) Paul Delair [adpt of Shakespeare, *The Taming of the Shrew*]. OPERA COMIQUE 30/5/92-1/6/92. 3 perf [? mat on 4/6]. Petruccio C.-B. Coquelin [*ainé*]; Baptista Bellucci; Cambio Laroche; Grumio J. Deroy; Le Cuisinier Lagrange, *fils*; Hortensio [A.] Ramy; Le Tailleur Bourgeotte; Nathaniel Darcey; Philippo Daumerie; Nicolas Faure; Gregorio Moisson. Catherina Malvau; Cartis Patry; Bianca Kerwich. L Edward Compton; Mgr M.L. Mayer. *REV: Ath 4/6/92 p739; E 4/6/92 p7; SR 4/6/92 p655; St 2/6/92 p13; Ti 31/5/92 p5.*

92.167 *NICHOLSON'S NIECE* (FC,3a) Mrs Hugh Bell. TERRY'S 30/5/92 mat perf.* Mr Burton George Giddens; Rev Samuel Grigg Frank Atherley; Mr Lee Arthur Dacre; Jenks Ernest Hendrie. Mrs Tamworth Adria Hill; Mrs Burton Henrietta Cowen; Lucy Simpson Irene Rickards; Jane Mordaunt; Mrs Gradden Ethel Hope; Milly Vernon Maggie Grant. DIR George Giddens; Asm Frank Weathersby; Bm E.B. Norman; Furn Oetzmann; Ch John d'Auban. *REV: E 4/6/92 p8; St 2/6/92 p13.*

92.168 *LOHENGRIN* (O,4a) Richard Wagner. COVENT GARDEN 2/6/92, 7/6, 27/6, 2/7, 28/7/92. 5 perf.** Federico di Telramondo Eugene Dufriche/Jean Lassalle/Victor Maurel; Enrico l'Uccellatore Edouard de Reske/Pol Plançon; L'Araldo del Re Abramoff; Lohengrin Jean de Reske/Anton van Dyck/Sebastian Montariol. Elsa di Brabante Lillian Nordica/Nellie Melba; Ortruda Giulia Ravogli. MGR Augustus Harris; Cond Luigi Mancinelli. *REV: Ath 11/6/92 p769, 9/7/92 p74-5; E 4/6/92 p13, 9/7/92 p13; St 9/6/92 p12, 7/7/92 p12; Ti 4/6/92 p14.*

92.169 *LE GENDRE DE MONSIEUR POIRIER* (C,4a) Emile Augier & Jules Sandeau. OPERA COMIQUE 2/6/92. 1 perf [? mat on 4/6].** Poirier C.-B. Coquelin [*ainé*]; Edmond Duquesne; Bellucci; Laroche; Vatel [J.] Deroy;

Lagrange. Malvau; Bellucci. MGR M.L. Mayer,

92.170 *HERO AND LEANDER* (Musical & Dramatic Poem,3a)
Harold Kyrle Bellew. SHAFTESBURY 2/6/92-17/6/92. 14
perf. 1st perfd Prince's, Manchester 9/5/92. Leander
Kyrle Bellew; Naukleros Yorke Stephens; Aneros Lewis
Waller; Zesta E. Giradot; Diros G. Bellamy; Knater
Frederick Epitaux; Charaz Walford. Hero Mrs Brown
Potter; Ianthe Edith Chester; Zoe Nellie Murray; Meta
Daubeney; Zella Florence Friend [Mary Mannering]. PP
John Lancaster; L & Mgr John Lart; Bom Watts; Mus
William Robins; Sc I.K. McLennan; Ch Fannie Brown;
Dir Thomas W. Charles; Mus dir C.J. Hargitt; Sm Thomas
Sidney; Bm & Treas Gilbert Tate; Act mgr T.V. Twinn-
ing. *REV: Ath 11/6/92 p770; E 4/6/92 p9; St 9/6/92
p12-3; Th 1/7/92 p31-2; Ti 3/6/92 p7.*

92.171 *A PLAY IN LITTLE* (C,1a) Ian Robertson. SHAFTES-
BURY 2/6/92-17/6/92. 14 perf.* M Gerrard Ian Robert-
son; Marquis of Ripon Philip Cunningham; Philippe T,
Tindall. Marianne A[drienne] Dairolles. PP, L & Mgr,
Bom, Act mgr, Mus dir, Sm, Bm & Treas as for 92.170.
REV: Ath, E, St as for 92.170.

92.172 *THE COUNTY* (P,4a) Estelle Burney & Arthur Benham. TERRY'S 2/6/92 mat perf.* Duke of Allonby Herbert Waring; Dick Rawdon Henry V. Esmond; Hon Algernon Soames Herbert Ross; Col. Sumner Alfred Courtenay; Harrington Harrington Price W.L. Abingdon. Lady
Cynthia Graeme Annie Hughes; Lucy Price Henrietta
Cowen; Ann Lillian Lee; Mrs Harrington Price (Margot)
Estelle Burney; Mrs Algernon Soames Mrs Herbert Waring. PP Edward Terry; Mgr W.H. Griffiths; Dir George
R. Foss; Sc T.W. Hall. *REV: E 4/6/92 p9; SR 4/6/92
p657; St 9/6/92 p13; Th 1/7/92 p30-1; Ti 3/6/92 p7.*

92.173 *MISS IMPUDENCE* (Saynète) Edward A. Morton.
TERRY'S 2/6/92 mat perf.* Mr Baxter George R. Foss.
Miss Goslin Annie Hughes; Knight Lillian Lee. PP,
Mgr as for 92.172. *REV: E, St as for 92.172.*

92.174 *SOPHIA* (P,4a) Robert Buchanan [fnd on Henry
Fielding, *Tom Jones*]. VAUDEVILLE 2/6/92; 6/6/92-2/7/
92. 25 perf. 1st perfd Vaudeville 12/4/86. Tom Jones

Charles Warner; Squire Western Fred Thorne; Blifil
Oswald Yorke; Square Charles Dodsworth; Mr Allworthy
J.S. Blythe; Partridge Thomas Thorne; George Seagrim
J[ohn] Wheatman/Frank Gillmore; Copse A. Austin.
Sophia Maude Millett; Lady Bellaston Helen Vane; Miss
Western Sophie Larkin; Honour Kate Phillips; Molly
Seagrim Helen Forsyth; Susan Harriet Trench. L & MGR
Thomas Thorne; Sm Fred Thorne; Act mgr Sydney Alport.
REV: E 4/6/92 p9; Ti 7/6/92 p8.

92.175 *IL VASCELLO FANTASMA [DER FLIEGENDE HOLLANDER]*
(O,3a) Richard Wagner. COVENT GARDEN 3/6/92. 1 perf.**
Dalando Edouard de Reske; Erik Sebastian Montariol;
Il Pilota Gaudio Mansuede; L'Olandese Jean Lassalle.
Senta Margaret MacIntyre; Mary Mathilde Bauermeister-
MGR Augustus Harris; Cond Leon Jehin. *REV: Ath 11/6/
92 p769; E 11/6/92 p13; St 9/6/92 p12; Ti 4/6/92 p14.*

92.176 *CHAMILLAC* (C,5a) Octave Feuillet. OPERA COMI-
QUE 3/6/92. 1 perf.** Chamillac C.-B. Coquelin
[aîné]; Edmond Duquesne; Bellucci; Laroche; Lagrange;
[J.] Deroy. Malvau; Bellucci; Patry; Kerwich. MGR
M.L. Mayer.

92.177 *MARRIAGE* (P,3a) Brandon Thomas & Henry Keeling.
COURT 7/6/92, 21/6/92. 2 mat perf.* Sir Charles Jenks
W.G. Elliott; Hon Dudley Chumbleigh C.P.Little; Sir
John Belton Brandon Thomas; Quayle F. Vaughan. Hon
Mrs Dudley Chumbleigh Gertrude Kingston; Lady Belton
Ellaline Terriss. L & MGR Arthur Chudleigh; Sc W[ill-
iam] Callcott; Cond Edward Jones; Cost Mme Clemont,
Lewis & Allenby. *REV: Ath 11/6/92 p771; E 11/6/92 p8;
St 9/6/92 p13; Th 1/7/92 p32-3; Ti 8/6/92 p7.*

92.178 *SIEGFRIED* (O,3a) Richard Wagner. COVENT GARDEN
8/6/92, 13/6, 6/7; trfd to DRURY LANE 11/7/92. 4 perf.
1st perfd Bayreuth 16/8/76. Siegfried Max Alvary;
Mime Julius Lieban; Wotan, der Wanderer Grengg/Theo-
dore Reichmann; Alberich Lorent; Fafner Heinrich Wiegand. Stimma des Waldvogels Sophie Traubmann; Erda
Ernestine Schumann-Heink; Brunnhilde Rosa Sucher/Kath-
arina Klafsky. MGR Augustus Harris; Cond Gustav Mahler.
*REV: Ath 11/6/92 p769-70, 9/7/92 p75; E 11/6/92 p9,
9/7/92 p13; SR 25/6/92 p743; St 16/6/92 p12, 14/7/92*

p10; Ti 9/6/92 p6, 9/7/92 p7.

92.179 *PLOT AND PASSION* (D,3a) Tom Taylor. CRITERION
8/6/92 mat perf. 1st perfd Olympic 17/10/53. Henri
de Neuville Lewis Waller; Desmarets Cyril Maude;
Fouche Julian Cross; Marquise de Cevennes Howard
Sturge; Berthier G.H. Kersley; Jabot Charles Medwin;
Grisboulle Frank Rothsay. Cecile Adrienne Dairolles;
Mme de Fontanges Florence Fordyce. L & MGR Charles
Wyndham; Act mgr & Treas H[erbert] Blackmore: Mus dir
Theodore Ward; Sm Julian Cross. *REV: Ath 11/6/92 p771;
E 11/6/92 p7; St 9/6/92 p13.*

92.180 *NANCE OLDFIELD* (C,1a) Charles Reade. HAYMARKET
9/6/92 mat perf.** Nathan Oldworthy Brandon Thomas;
Alexander Oldworthy Gordon Craig. Susan Oldfield Kate
Phillips; Mrs Anne Oldfield Ellen Terry. L & MGR H.B.
Tree; Sm Edward Hastings; Mus dir Carl Armbruster;
Bm & Sec Frederick Harrison; Bom W.H. Leverton. *REV:
E 11/6/92 p9; St 16/6/92 p13.*

92.181 *STRATHLOGAN* (IrishD,5a) Charles Overton & Hugh
Moss. PRINCESS'S 9/6/92-13/6/92. 4 perf.* John, The
7th Earl of Strathlogan/Kenneth Kyrle Herbert Waring;
Inspector Robins Charles Steuart; Phil O'Hagan Henry
Bedford; Larry McQuirk Wilfred E. Shine; Hon Fred
Thistleton J.R. Crauford; Col. Desmond John Beauchamp;
Cornelius Roach T.P. Haynes; Dr Grieg Louis Warner;
Maurice O'Mara H. Reeves-Smith; Derrick O'Keefe Her-
bert Flemming; Sgt. Horrocks Tom Mowbray; Moolveen
Dan Fitzgerald; Constable George Aubrey; Dan Brady
Stephen Caffrey; Barney Oge Alfred Phillips; Simmons
William Clifford. Claire O'Mara Olga Brandon; Norah
McShane Dorothy Dorr; Vere Desmond Ada Ferrar; Kitty
Louise Litta; Sister Margaret Elizabeth Bessle; Nurse
Ethel Daymond; Servant Ida Sala. L & MGR Sidney Her-
berte Basing; Pp Mrs Harriet Gooch; Mus dir Michael
Connelly; Asm Thomas Verner; Mach J.W. Cawdrey; Am
Curzon Vincent; Act mgr & Treas F. Forbes; Sc W.T.
Hemsley; Dir Hugh Moss; Mus Warwick Williams. *REV: E
11/6/92 p7; SR 11/6/92 p685-6; St 16/6/92 p13; Th 1/7/
92 p33-4; Ti 10/6/92 p7.*

92.182 *REST* (P,1a) Henry V. Esmond. AVENUE 10/6/92 mat

perf.* <u>Phillippe</u> Philip Cunningham; <u>Pierre</u> Henry V.
Esmond; <u>Diego</u> C.M. Hallard. <u>Margot</u> Mrs E.H. Brooke;
<u>Nina</u> Annie Hughes. <u>LI</u> George Paget; <u>Mgr</u> Charles
Charrington; <u>Mus dir</u> C.W. Lamartine; <u>Sm</u> George Bel-
more; <u>Act mgr</u> Charles Roseley; <u>Pq, Cost</u> C.H. Fox.
REV: E 11/6/92 p9; St 16/6/92 p14.

92.183 *HER TRUE COLOURS* (Ca) W.A. Brabner. AVENUE
10/6/92 mat perf. 1st perfd Assembly Rooms, Ruthin
6/11/91. <u>Ralph Morrison</u> Henry Pagden. <u>Violet Verney</u>
Annie Irish. <u>LI</u>, <u>Mgr</u>, <u>Mus dir</u>, <u>Sm</u>, <u>Act mgr</u>, <u>Pq</u>, <u>Cost</u>
as for 92.182. *REV: As for 92.182.*

92.184 *THE HIGHWAYMAN* (Duol) Justin Huntly McCarthy.
AVENUE 10/6/92 mat perf.** <u>Sir Harry Bellairs</u> Henry
Dana. <u>Lady Betty Bassett</u> Phyllis Broughton. <u>LI</u>, <u>Mgr</u>,
<u>Mus dir</u>, <u>Sm</u>, <u>Act mgr</u>, <u>Pq</u>, <u>Cost</u> as for 92.182. *REV:*
As for 92.182.

92.185 *LES HUGUENOTS* (O,4a) Giacomo Meyerbeer. COVENT
GARDEN 10/6/92. 1 perf.** <u>Conte di San Bris</u> Edouard
de Reske; <u>Conte di Nevers</u> Tschernoff; <u>Marcello</u> Pol
Plançon; <u>Soldier</u> Iginio Corsi; <u>Tavannes</u> Gaudio Mansuede; <u>De Retz</u> Miranda; <u>Maurevert</u> Antonio de Vaschetti;
<u>De Cosse</u> Rinaldini; <u>Raoul</u> Sebastian Montariol. <u>Valen-
tina</u> Margaret MacIntyre; <u>Margherita di Valois</u> Eugenia
Mravina; <u>Urbano</u> Giulia Ravogli; <u>Dama d'Onore</u> Mathilde
Bauermeister. <u>MGR</u> Augustus Harris; <u>Cond</u> Enrico Bevignani. *REV: Ath 18/6/92 p800; E 18/6/92 p12; St 16/6/*
92 p12; Ti 13/6/92 p11.

92.186 *LA LUCE DELL'ASIA* (O) Isidore de Lara (mus) &
William Beatty-Kingston (lib). COVENT GARDEN 11/6/92,
20/6, 18/7/92. 3 perf.* <u>Il Principe Siddartha</u> Jean
Lassalle; <u>Atman</u> Pol Plançon; <u>Il Re Suddhodana</u> Alec
Marsh; <u>Mara</u> Miranda; <u>Primo Paesano</u> Iginio Corsi; <u>Se-
condo Paesano</u> Antonio de Vaschetti. <u>Devadatta</u> Nina
Burt; <u>Yosodhara</u> Emma Eames; <u>1ere Danseuse</u> Mabel Love.
<u>MGR</u> Augustus Harris; <u>Cond</u> Luigi Mancinelli. *REV: Ath*
18/6/92 p800; E 18/6/92 p9; SR 25/6/92 p743; St 16/6/
92 p12-3; Th 1/7/92 p42; Ti 13/6/92 p11.

92.186B *LA STATUE DU COMMANDEUR (DON JUAN UP TO DATE)*
(WordlessP) Paul Eudel (lib) & Evariste Mangin (lib)

& Adolphe David (mus). PRINCE OF WALES'S 11/6/92-26/
7/92. 50 perf [w/W, S mat exc 11/6; mat only 15-17/6;
some doubt whether perfd 11-14/6]. 1st perfd Cercle
funambulesque, Paris 14/1/92. La Statue du Commandeur A. Tarride; Don Juan H. Burguet; Count Prospero
Renoux; Don Luiz Albouy; Sganarelle V. Courtes.
Rosaura M. Chassin; Sylvia Litini. L & MGR C.J. Abud;
Pp Edgar Bruce; Mus dir Alfred Carpenter; Cost Baron,
Harrison; Pq William Clarkson; Dir Charles Lauri; Act
mgr Ernest Hallewell, Arthur Yates. *REV: Ath 18/6/92
p802; E 18/6/92 p7; SR 25/6/92 p744; St 16/6/92 p13;
Ti 13/6/92 p11.*

92.187 *MOSES & SON* (An Up-to-Date Mosaic,3a) J. Gordon.
ROYALTY 11/6/92. Rnd [perfd until at least 29/6].*
Solomon Moses Edward Righton; Aubrey Montagu Harry
Eversfield; Jacob Moses Master Sidney Westgate; Hon
Jack Bunting Gerald Maxwell; Col. Clapham Gore Fred
Shepherd; Griggs Robert Malone; Norfolk Howard Lennox
Pawle. Belle Doricourt Annie Irish; Mrs Moses Maria
Davis; Ruby Moses Emma Ritta; Rachel Eisenberger
Florence Birchell. L Kate Santley; Mgr Douglas Vernon;
Dir Edward Righton; Sc Richard C. Durant; Furn Oetz-
mann; Bm Edwin Herbert. *REV: E 18/6/92 p7; St 16/6/
92 p13-4; Ti 13/6/92 p11.*

92.188 *LA TOSCA* (D,5a,6tab) Victorien Sardou. ROYAL
ENGLISH OPERA HOUSE 13-15/6/92, 18/6(m), 24/6, 29/6(m),
4/7, 7/7, 16/7, 19/7, 23/7. 11 perf.** Baron Scarpia
Albert Darmont; Mario Cavaradossi Fleury; Cesare
Angelotti [Henri] Deschamps; Marquis Attavanti Munié;
Eusebe Charton; Spoletta Cartereau; Vicomte de Tre-
ville Thefer; Capreola Tarebb; Trivulce Duberry;
Schiarrone Piron; Paisiello Mallet; Ceccho Raymond;
Colometti Gaspard; Un Sergent Besson. Floria Tosca
Sarah Bernhardt; Reine Marie Caroline Jane Méa; Prin-
cess Orlonia Gilberte Fleury; Gennarino Seylor; Luc-
iana Nadrey; Un Monsignor Simonson. PP Richard d'Oyly
Carte; Dir Henry E. Abbey, Maurice Grau; Cond Andrew
Levey; Act mgr G. Edwards Minor. *REV: E 18/6/92 p9;
SR 18/6/92 p712-3; 30/7/92 p136-7; St 16/6/92 p13;
Ti 15/6/92 p13.*

92.189 *TRISTAN UND ISOLDE* (O[3a]) Richard Wagner. COV-

ENT GARDEN 15/6/92; trfd to DRURY LANE 18/6, 9/7/92.
3 perf. 1st perfd Munich 10/10/65. Tristan Max Alvary; Marke Heinrich Wiegand; Kurvenal Knapp; Melos
Simon; Steuermann Lorent; Hirt Landau. Isolde Rosa
Sucher/Ende-Andriessen/Katharina Klafsky; Brangane
Ernestine Schumann-Heink/Paula Ralph. MGR Augustus
Harris; Cond Gustav Mahler. *REV: Ath 18/6/92 p800,*
25/6/92 p833, 16/7/92 p106; E 18/6/92 p6; SR 25/6/92
p743-4; St 23/6/92 p10; Ti 18/6/92 p7.

92.190 *THE BOMBARDMENT OF ALEXANDRIA.* ROYALTY 15/6/92.
Rnd [perfd until at least 29/6].

92.191 *DON GIOVANNI* (O[2a]) W.A. Mozart. COVENT GAR-
DEN 16/6/92, 11/7; trfd to DRURY LANE 22/7/92. 3
perf.** Don Giovanni Victor Maurel/Eugene Dufriche;
Leporello Edouard de Reske; Masetto Caracciolo; Il
Commendatore Abramoff; Don Ottavio Dimitresco. Donna
Anna Minnie Terry/Giulia Valda/Louise Dotti; Donna
Elvira Lillian Nordica/Sofia Ravogli; Zerlina Zelie
de Lussan/Sigrid Arnoldson/Giulia Ravogli; 1ere Danseuse Giuri. MGR Augustus Harris; Cond Alberto Randegger. *REV: Ath 25/6/92 p832; E 18/6/92 p13, 30/7/*
92 p13; St 23/6/92 p10, 28/7/92 p10; Ti 18/6/92 p7,
25/7/92 p11.

92.192 *PAULINE BLANCHARD* (D,6a) Albert Darmont & Hum-
blot [fr novel by Jules Case]. ROYAL ENGLISH OPERA
HOUSE 16/6/92, 17/6/92. 2 perf. 1st Fr perf Odéon,
Paris 21/1/93. Blanchard Munié; Francois Marchal
Fleury; Marchal Piron; Cadet Rebel; Lamirel Gaspard;
Defuble [Henri] Deschamps; Pierre Thefer; Pothier
Charton; Chaponet Duberry; Gaugain Cartereau. Pauline
Blanchard Sarah Bernhardt; Angelina Gilberte Fleury;
Louise Marchal Marie Grandet; Thérèse Simonson; Tony
Seylor; Nicole Nadrey. PP Richard d'Oyly Carte; Dir
Henry E. Abbey, Maurice Grau; Cond Andrew Levey; Act
mgr G. Edwards Minor. *REV: Ath 25/6/92 p834; E 18/6/*
92 p9; St 23/6/92 p10.

92.193 *CARMEN* (O[4a]) Georges Bizet. COVENT GARDEN
17/6/92, 30/6/92. 2 perf.** Escamillo Jean Lassalle;
Dancairo Caracciolo; Remendado Rinaldini; Morales
Miranda; Zuniga Antonio de Vaschetti; Don José Jean

de Reske/Dimitresco. Carmen Blanche Deschamps-Jehin;
Frasquita Mathilde Bauermeister; Mercedes Agnes Janson; Michaela Emma Eames; 1ere Danseuse Giuri. MGR
Augustus Harris; Cond Leon Jehin. *REV: Ath 25/6/92
p832; E 25/6/92 p13; St 23/6/92 p10.*

92.194 *THEY WERE MARRIED* (C,4a) J.R. Crauford & Fred-
erick Hawley [fnd on story by Walter Besant]. STRAND
17/6/92 mat perf.* Percival Gerald Maxwell; Tom
Kemyss Philip Cunningham; Paul Perigal Stephen Caff-
rey; Lord Ferrier George Raiemond; Guy Ferrier J.R.
Crauford. Elsie Georgie Esmond; Maud Ferrier Alice
Ingram; Virginie Margaret Wallace; Violet Lovelace
Ada Ferrar; Mrs Hallows Ida Sala. *REV: E 18/6/92 p9;
St 23/6/92 p10-1.*

92.195 *WE ALL HAVE OUR LITTLE FAULTS* (F,1a) William
E. Suter. PRINCE OF WALES'S 18/6/92-25/6/92; 5/7/92.
8 perf. 1st perfd Grecian 6/10/64. Rollick Ells
Dagnall; Goosey Fred Walton; Gingernutt Reuben Inch.
Mrs Rollick Minnie Inch; Louisa Inch Madge Lucas.
PP Edgar Bruce; L & Mgr C.J. Abud; Act mgr Ernest
Hallewell, Arthur Yates.

92.196 *LA DAME AUX CAMELIAS* (D,5a) Alexander Dumas,
fils. ROYAL ENGLISH OPERA HOUSE 18/6/92-21/6; 22/6(m),
8/7, 9/7(m), 18/7, 23/7/92(m). 8 perf.** Arthur
Delorme; Armand Duval Fleury; Gaston Rieux Duberry;
Georges Duval Piron; M de Varville Rebel; St Gaudens
Munié; Gustave Thefer; Le Comte de Giray [Henri] Des-
champs; Docteur Charton; Commissionaire Cartereau;
Domestique Charles. Marguerite Gauthier Sarah Bern-
hardt; Olympe Gilberte Fleury; Prudence Marie Grandet;
Nichette Seylor; Nanine Simonson; Anais Merle; Adele
Nadrey. PP Richard d'Oyly Carte; Dir Henry E. Abbey,
Maurice Grau; Cond Andrew Levey; Act mgr G. Edwards
Minor. *REV: E 25/6/92 p9; Ti 20/6/92 p6.*

92.197 *A PAIR OF SPECTACLES* (C,3a) Sydney Grundy
[adpt of Eugene Labiche & Delacour, *Les Petites Oiseaux*]. GARRICK 20/6/92-5/8/92. 42 perf [w/mat 16/7].**
Benjamin Goldfinch John Hare/George Raiemond; Gregory
Charles Groves; Dick Sydney Brough; Percy Rudge Harding; Lorimer Henry Ashford/R[owley] Cathcart; Bar-

tholomew Charles Rock; <u>Joyce</u> R[owley] Cathcart/W.M.
Cathcart; <u>Shoemaker</u> W.M. Cathcart/Metcalfe. <u>Mrs Gold-
finch</u> Kate Rorke; <u>Lucy Lorimer</u> Winifred Fraser; <u>Char-
lotte</u> Minna Blakiston. <u>L & MGR</u> John Hare; <u>Bom</u> E. Candler; <u>Act mgr</u> C.G. Compton; <u>Asm</u> R[owley] Cathcart;
<u>Sc</u> William Harford; <u>Cond</u> A. Arnstein. *REV: E 25/6/92
p7.*

92.198 *BY THE MIDLAND SEA* (Episode) Justin Huntly Mc-
Carthy. CRITERION 21/6/92 mat perf.* <u>Harold, Lord
Mordred</u> Hamilton Revelle; <u>Cpt. Hamilton Banner</u> C.M.
Hallard; <u>Dr Penneth</u> Robb Harwood. <u>Lady Mordred</u> Rose
Norreys; <u>Mrs Wellington</u> Henrietta Lindley. <u>L & MGR</u>
Charles Wyndham. *REV: E 25/6/92 p7; Th 1/7/92 p77;
Ti 22/6/92 p12.*

92.199 *THE BALLAD-MONGER* (RP,1a) Walter Besant & Walter Pollock [adpt of Theodore de Banville, *Gringoire*].
CRITERION 21/6/92 mat perf.** <u>Gringoire</u> H. Beerbohm
Tree; <u>King</u> James Fernandez; <u>Olivier</u> Charles Allan;
<u>Simon</u> Robb Harwood. <u>Loyse</u> Mrs H.B. Tree; <u>Nicole</u> More-
land. <u>L & MGR</u> Charles Wyndham.

92.200 *MRS HILARY REGRETS* (Ca,1a) S. Theyre Smith.
CRITERION 21/6/92, 28/6/92. 2 mat perf.* <u>Dr Power</u>
Charles Wyndham; <u>Servant</u> [Charles] Terric. <u>Mrs Hil-
ary</u> Mary Moore. <u>L & MGR</u> Charles Wyndham. *REV: E 25/
6/92 p7, 2/7/92 p6; St 30/6/92 p11-2; Th 1/8/92 p77-
8; Ti 22/6/92 p12.*

92.201 *DAS RHEINGOLD* (O,[1a]) Richard Wagner. COVENT
GARDEN 22/6/92; trfd to DRURY LANE 27/6/92. 2 perf.
1st perfd Munich 22/9/69. <u>Loge</u> Max Alvary; <u>Wotan</u>
Grengg; <u>Donner</u> Zoltan Dome; <u>Froh</u> Simon; <u>Alberich</u>
Lissmann; <u>Mime</u> Julius Lieban; <u>Fasolt</u> Heinrich Wiegand;
<u>Fafner</u> Litter. <u>Fricka</u> Ende-Andriessen; <u>Freia</u> Katti
Bettaque; <u>Erda</u> Bianca Froehlich; <u>Woglinde</u> Sophie
Traubmann; <u>Wellgande</u> Paula Ralph; <u>Flosshilde</u> Ernestine
Schumann-Heink. <u>MGR</u> Augustus Harris; <u>Cond</u> Gustav Mah-
ler. *REV: Ath 25/6/92 p832-3; E 25/6/92 p6; SR 9/7/92
p44; St 30/6/92 p10; Ti 24/6/92 p14.*

92.202 *FEDORA* (D,4a) Victorien Sardou. ROYAL ENGLISH
OPERA HOUSE 22/6/92, 23/6, 25/6(m), 29/6, 2/7, 6/7,

9/7, 16/7(m), 22/7/92. 9 perf. 1st perfd Vaudeville,
Paris 12/12/82. Loris Ipanoff Albert Darmont; Siriex
Munié; Boroff [Henri] Deschamps; Gretch Rebel; Dr
Lorectk Gaspard; Desire Duberry; Tchileff Charton;
Rouvel Thefer; Cyrille Cartereau; Basile Piron. Prin-
cesse Fedora Sarah Bernhardt; Comtesse Olga Soukareff
Gilberte Fleury; Comtesse de Tournis Nadrey; Bune
Okar Merle; Demitri Seylor; Martta Simonson. PP
Richard d'Oyly Carte; Dir Henry E. Abbey, Maurice
Grau; Cond Andrew Levey; Act mgr G. Edwards Minor.
REV: E 25/6/92 p6. Comment: Cast from V & A programme
for 29/6/92.

92.203 *THE NOBLE ART* (F,3a) Eille Norwood. TERRY'S
22/6/92-19/7/92. 27 perf [w/S mat exc 25/6].** And-
rew Fullalove, J.P. Arthur Williams/William Cheesman;
Charles Fullalove H. Reeves-Smith; Prof Tranz Julian
Cross; Peter Sledge Sydney Valentine; Waters William
Cheesman; Call Boy Master Mansfield; Bulwer Brady
Eille Norwood. Gertie Fullalove Blanche Horlock;
Winifred Tiverton Kate Leechman; Tilly Du Val Beatrice
Goodchild; Jenny Ethel Norton. MGR & DIR Eille Nor-
wood; Pp & Mgr Edward Terry; Sm King Bolton; Mus dir
T[om] Smythe. *REV: St 30/6/92 p13; Ti 24/6/92 p14*.

92.204 *CHALK AND CHEESE* (Ca,1a) Eille Norwood. TERRY'S
22/6/92-19/7/92. 24 perf. 1st perfd Village Hall,
Esher 6/1/88. Walter Raymond Eille Norwood. Sybil
Raymond Ethel Norton; Perkins Irving. MGR & DIR, Pp &
Mgr, Sm, Mus dir as for 92.203.

92.205 *MRS HILARY REGRETS* (Ca,1a) S. Theyre Smith.
LYCEUM 23/6/92 mat perf.** Dr Power Charles Wyndham.
Mrs Hilary Mary Moore. L & MGR Henry Irving; Sm H.J.
Loveday; Mus dir J. Meredith Ball; Act mgr Bram Sto-
ker. *REV: E 25/6/92 p9; St 30/6/92 p10*.

92.206 *HUSH MONEY* (D,4a) Herbert Keith. TERRY'S 23/6/
92 mat perf.* Alan Sinclair Yorke Stephens; Frederick
Marshall W.L. Abingdon; Rev Mr Joy John Beauchamp;
Mr Chester J.R. Crauford; Jack Walton Orlando Barnett; Bates S[idney] Burt; Ericson Revell. Mrs West-
garth Cicely Richards; Amy Joy Mary Mordaunt; Evelyn
Dale Edith Gordon. *REV: Ath 9/7/92 p52; E 25/6/92*

p7; St 30/6/92 p12.

92.207 *THE ADVENTURERS* (C,3a) Edward Rose [adpt of
Emile Augier, *L'Aventurière*]. STRAND 24/6/92 mat perf.*
<u>Mjr. Shotley Carew</u> C.W. Somerset; <u>Basil Armathwaite</u>
Charles Myers; <u>Archie Venn</u> Harry Eversfield; <u>Harold</u>
Arthur Elwood. <u>Cissy</u> Alice Aldercron; <u>Rosa</u> Harriet
Trench; <u>Leila Carew</u> Claire Ivanova. <u>SM</u> Julian Cross;
<u>Bm</u> Arthur Hart. *REV: E 25/6/92 p10; St 30/6/92 p11;
Th 1/8/92 p78.*

92.208 *THE RING OF POLYCRATES* (DSk) Justin Huntly
McCarthy. STRAND 24/6/92 mat perf.* <u>Hamilton Cross</u>
Frank Gillmore; <u>Anthony Folijambe</u> Bassett Roe. <u>Mrs</u>
<u>Carew</u> Violet Thornycroft. *REV: E 2/7/92 p8; St 30/6/
92 p11; Th 1/8/92 p78-9.*

92.209 *LE PROPHETE* (O[5a]) Giacomo Meyerbeer. COVENT
GARDEN 25/6/92. 1 perf.** <u>Jean de Leyde</u> Jean de Res-
ke; <u>Zacherie</u> Edouard de Reske; <u>Oberthal</u> Pol Plancon;
<u>Jonas</u> Sebastian Montariol; <u>Mathisen</u> Miranda; <u>Sergent</u>
Armand Castelmary. <u>Berthe</u> Eugenia Mravina; <u>Fidès</u>
Blanche Deschamps-Jehin; <u>1ere Danseuse</u> Giuri. <u>MGR</u>
Augustus Harris; <u>Cond</u> Leon Jehin. *REV: Ath 2/7/92
p40; E 2/7/92 p13; SR 9/7/92 p44; St 30/6/92 p10; Ti
28/6/92 p8.*

92.210 *LEAH(THE FORSAKEN)*(5a) Albert Darmont. ROYAL
ENGLISH OPERA HOUSE 25/6/92-28/6/92. 3 perf. 1st
perfd Boston, 8/1/92. <u>Nathan</u> Albert Darmont; <u>Abraham</u>
Rebel; <u>Rudolph</u> Fleury; <u>Lorentz</u> Munié; <u>Hermann</u> Piron;
<u>Johann</u> Thefer; <u>Fritz</u> [Henri] Deschamps; <u>Lory</u> Duberry;
<u>Ludwig</u> Charton; <u>Grochen</u> Cartereau; <u>Muller</u> Tarebb.
<u>Leah</u> Sarah Bernhardt; <u>Madeleine</u> Jane Méa; <u>Gertrude</u>
Marie Grandet; <u>Rosel</u> Seylor; <u>Frank</u> Simonson; <u>La</u>
<u>Petite Leah</u> La Petite Andrée. <u>PP</u> Richard d'Oyly Carte;
<u>Dir</u> Henry E. Abbey, Maurice Grau; <u>Mus & Cond</u> Andrew
Levey; <u>Act mgr</u> G. Edwards Minor. *REV: Ath 9/7/92 p52;
E 2/7/92 p9; St 30/6/92 p10-1; Ti 27/6/92 p8.*

92.211 *SHAKESPEARE* (C,4a) Eden E. Greville. GLOBE
27/6/92-2/7/92. 6 perf. 1st perfd Grand Hall, Maiden-
head 27/5/91. <u>William Shakespeare</u> T.B. Thalberg;
<u>John Shakespeare</u> Henry Vernon; <u>Giles</u> Robert Soutar;

Tom Green Matthew Brodie; Earl of Sussex Frank Lindo;
Sir Thomas Lucy Arthur Helmore; Lord Southampton
Charles Medwin; Edmund Spenser J.J. Caversham; Ben
Jonson G. Lyon-Leith; Gabriel Spencer Douglas Gordon;
Hemynge Hugh Warren; Earl of Leicester Eugene Mayeur;
Sir Walter Raleigh F. Rawson Buckley; Harry Baillie
Arthur P. Bowyer; Constable H. Hudson; 1st Citizen
E.R. Beaumont. Mary Shakespeare Mrs Dion Boucicault;
Queen Elizabeth Beatrice Selwyn; Mistress Hobbins
Charlotte [E.] Morland; Maid of Honour Einna Cullum;
Dorothy Hilda Abinger; Elizabeth Throgmorton Mary H.
Keegan; Gipsy Lorraine Dreux; Mistress Page Kate Cal-
ton; Anne Hathaway Rose Norreys. L & MGR Frederick
Langley; Dir Paul M. Berton; Bm W.H. Griffiths, Geo-
rge Hughes; Mus & Mus dir John Storer; Asm Arthur P.
Bowyer; Sc E[dward] Banks, David Lee; Pq William
Clarkson; Furn Oetzmann; Cost L. & H. Nathan. *REV:
E 2/7/92 p7; St 30/6/92 p11; Th 1/8/92 p79; Ti 28/6/
92 p11.*

92.212 *THE COMPROMISING COAT* (Ca) J.T. Grein & C.W.
Jarvis. GLOBE 27/6/92-2/7/92. 6 perf.* Tom Thornton
Walter Everard; Frank Fairfield Douglas Gordon. Lucy
Hilda Abinger; Fanny Einna Cullum. L & MGR, Dir, Bm,
Mus dir, Asm as for 92.211. *REV: E, St as for 92.211.*

92.213 *DID YOU RING?* (FOa,1a) John W. Houghton (lib)
& J.W. Mabson (lib) & Landon Ronald (mus). PRINCE OF
WALES'S 27/6/92-26/7/92. 26 perf.* Tom Templer
Saxe. Kitty Amy Farrell; Suzan Kate James. L & MGR
C.J. Abud; Act mgr Georges Treville; Mus dir Landon
Ronald. *REV: E 2/7/92 p7; St 30/6/92 p12; Th 1/8/92
p90.* Comment: V & A source indicates 1st perf was
25/7/92.

92.214 *LE NOZZI DI FIGARO* (O[4a]). W.A. Mozart. COV-
ENT GARDEN 28/6/92, 15/7/92. 2 perf.** Il Conte
Edouard de Reske; Figaro Victor Maurel. Contessa
Emma Eames; Susanna Emma Teleky; Marcellina Mathilde
Bauermeister; Cherubino Sigrid Arnoldson. MGR Augus-
tus Harris; Cond Enrico Bevignani. *REV: Ath 2/7/92
p40-1; E 2/7/92 p13; SR 9/7/92 p44; St 30/6/92 p10;
Ti 2/7/92 p10.*

92.215 *A GHOST, NOT BY IBSEN* (DSk). CRITERION 28/6/92
mat perf.* <u>He</u> George Giddens; <u>It</u> Cyril Maude. <u>She</u>
Ellis Jeffreys. *REV: E 2/7/92 p6; St 30/6/92 p11-2;
Th 1/8/92 p84.*

92.216 *BY THE MIDLAND SEA* (Episode) Justin Huntly
McCarthy. CRITERION 28/6/92 mat perf.** <u>Lady Mordred</u>
Rose Norreys; <u>Mrs Wellington</u> Morland. *REV: E, St as
for 92.215.*

92.217 *OPPOSITION* (Oa,1a) "Richard Henry" [Richard
Butler & H. Chance Newton] (lib) & Ivan Caryll (mus).
LYRIC 28/6/92-5/8/92. 34 perf.* <u>Goswell Bloggs</u> Ar-
thur Playfair; <u>John Jones</u> Tom A. Shale; <u>William
Brown</u> Charles Gilbert; <u>Hodge</u> John Moore. <u>Cornelia
Culcher</u> Dora Thorne; <u>Rose</u> Emmeline Orford; <u>Clara</u> Jes-
sie Moore; <u>Susan Nipkins</u> Cissie Cranford. L & MGR
William Greet; <u>Mach</u> S. Trewen; <u>Props</u> Mountain; <u>Bm &
Treas</u> William Greet. *REV: E 2/7/92 p6; St 30/6/92
p11.*

92.218 *LADY BROWNE'S DIARY* (C,3a) Minnie Bell [adpt of
Octave Feuillet, *La Crise*]. STRAND 28/6/92 mat perf.*
<u>Sir Philip Browne</u> Herbert Waring; <u>Arthur Darrell</u> W.T.
Lovell; <u>Archibald</u> Ben Greet; <u>Jack</u> Basil Deane. <u>Lady
Browne</u> Lily Hanbury; <u>Gilby</u> Minnie Bell; <u>Margaret</u>
Hilary Deane. <u>L</u> Willie Edouin; <u>Bm & Act mgr</u> J.T.
Mackay Robertson; <u>Sm</u> Ben Greet; <u>Mus dir</u> Ernest Buca-
lossi. *REV: E 2/6/92 p6; St 30/6/92 p11; Th 1/8/92
p82-3.*

92.219 *THE GAVOTTE* (Ca) Minnie Bell. STRAND 28/6/92
mat perf.** <u>Sylvia</u> Sylvia Grey; <u>Dora</u> Maggie Garrett.
<u>L, Bm & Act mgr, Sm, Mus dir</u> as for 92.218. *REV: St
30/6/92 p11.*

92.220 *HIS SECOND WIFE* (P,3a) Vivian Hope. AVENUE
29/6/92 mat perf.* <u>Mr Eversleigh</u> Frank Gillmore; <u>Mr
Selby</u> E.M. Robson; <u>Harry</u> H. Tripp Edgar; <u>Everard Mor-
ton</u> H[enry] Dana; <u>John Craig</u> Charles S. Fawcett. <u>Mrs
Eversleigh</u> Alice de Winton; <u>Edith</u> Kate Ruskin; <u>Miss
Primley</u> Florence Hayden. <u>LI</u> George Paget; <u>Mgr</u> Charles
Charrington; <u>Sm</u> George R. Foss; <u>Mus dir</u> W.C. Lamartine;
<u>Bm</u> Harrington Baily. *REV: E 2/7/92 p6; St 30/6/92 p12;*

Th 1/8/92 p83.

92.221 *DIE WALKURE* (O[3a]) Richard Wagner. COVENT GAR-
DEN 29/6/92; trfd to DRURY LANE 4/7/92. 2 perf. 1st
perfd Munich 26/6/70. Sigmund Max Alvary; Wotan Theo-
dore Reichmann; Hunding Heinrich Wiegand. Brunnhilde
Ende-Andriessen/Katharina Klafsky; Sieglinde Katti
Bettaque; Fricka/Sigrune Ernestine Schumann-Heink;
Helmwige Sophie Traubmann; Waltraute Bianca Froehlich;
Grimgerte Simon; Gerhilde Kollar [Kohler?]; Ortlinde
Paula Ralph; Rossweisse Upleger; Schwertleitner Louise
Meisslinger. MGR Augustus Harris; Cond Gustav Mahler.
*REV: Ath 2/7/92 p41, 9/7/92 p75; E 2/7/92 p6; St 7/7/
92 p12; Ti 2/7/92 p10.*

92.222 *MAIDS AND MATRONS; OR, THE SEVEN AGES OF WOMAN*
(Monol) Robert Griffin Morris. CRITERION 29/6/92 mat
perf.* Miss O'Neill Potter. *REV: E 2/7/92 p6; Th 1/
8/92 p83.*

92.223 *LITTLE SUNBEAM* (CD,1a) Mrs Henry Wylde. LYRIC
30/6/92 mat perf.* Lord Conway Henry Doughty; Archie
Conway Sydney Barraclough; Mr Mont Orlando Barnett.
Miss De Vigne Mrs Carl Rosa; Susan Forster; Lady Con-
way Mrs Henry Wylde. *REV: E 2/7/92 p8; St 7/7/92 p13;
Th 1/8/92 p84.*

92.224 *FIDELIO* (O[3a]) Ludwig van Beethoven. DRURY
LANE 2/7/92; trfd to COVENT GARDEN 20/7/92. 2 perf.**
Pizzaro Lissmann; Rocco Heinrich Wiegand; Jacquine
Landau; Der Minister Zoltan Dome/Lorent; Florestan
Siedel. Leonore Katharina Klafsky; Marzelline Sophie
Traubmann. MGR Augustus Harris; Cond Gustav Mahler.
*REV: Ath 9/7/92 p74; E 9/7/92 p13; St 7/7/92 p13; Ti
4/7/92 p7.*

92.225 *THE PRIVATE SECRETARY* (FC,3a) Charles H. Hawtrey [adpt of Gustav von Moser, *Der Bibliothekar*].
COMEDY 4/7/92-4/11/92. 138 perf [w/W, S mat exc 6/7,
9/7, 13/7, 24/8]. 1st perfd Theatre Royal, Cambridge
14/11/83. Rev Robert Spalding W.S. Penley; Mr Cattermole W.F. Hawtrey; Douglas Cattermole Robb Harwood/
Charles H. Hawtrey; Harry Marsland Sam Sothern;
Sydney Gibson Harold Constable/Cecil H. Thornbury/

J[ames] Nelson; <u>Knox</u> A.W. Aysom; <u>Mr Marsland</u> H. Gordon Tomkins/Ernest Percy; <u>John</u> Newark/Wilton Heriot. <u>Eva Webster</u> Nina Boucicault/Violet Armbruster; <u>Edith Marsland</u> Violet Armbruster/Ethel Matthews; <u>Mrs Stead</u> C[aroline] Ewell; <u>Miss Ashford</u> Caroline Elton. MGR Charles H. Hawtrey; <u>Dir & Sm</u> F[rederick] Glover; <u>Act mgr</u> R.B. Dixon; <u>Mus dir</u> James M. Glover; <u>Bm</u> E.F. Bradley. *REV: E 9/7/92 p7; St 7/7/92 p13; Ti 5/7/92 p10.*

92.226 *THE HOMECOMING* (P,1a) Ernest Cosham. COMEDY 4/7/92-4/11/92. 107 perf.* <u>Alan Travers</u> Robb Harwood; <u>Mr Drydon</u> Harold Constable; <u>Charlie Harding</u> Sam Sothern. <u>Mrs Musgrave</u> Alice Yorke; <u>Stella</u> Nina Boucicault; <u>Martha</u> Florence Farr. MGR, <u>Act mgr</u>, <u>Mus dir</u>, <u>Sm</u>, <u>Bm</u> as for 92.225. *REV: E 9/7/92 p7; St 7/7/92 p 13-4; Th 1/8/92 p84.*

92.227 *NED'S CHUM* (P,4a) David Christie Murray. GLOBE 4/7/92 mat perf.** <u>John Furlong</u> David Christie Murray; <u>Mr Brocklehurst</u> Robert Soutar; <u>Ned Fellowes</u> H. Nye Chart; <u>Harold</u> Master Leo Byrne; <u>Dr Wentworth</u> J.R. Crauford; <u>Stuart Willougby</u> J.B. Gordon; <u>Bill Skiddaw</u> Charles Medwin; <u>Bob Clancy</u> F[rank] H. France; <u>Trooper</u> J. Brown Elliott. <u>Lucy Draycott</u> Violet Raye; <u>Araminta</u> Eily Mayo; <u>Servant</u> Einna Cullum; <u>Mrs Brocklehurst</u> Bella Fossette. <u>L & MGR</u> Frederick Langley; <u>Dir</u> Fred Stanmaur; <u>Mus</u> C.J. Hargitt; <u>Bm</u> George Hughes; <u>Mus dir</u> John Storer; <u>Sm</u> Robert Soutar; <u>Bom</u> T.W. Willis. *REV: E 9/7/92 p7; Ti 5/7/92 p10.*

92.228 *A LUCKY DOG* (FC,3a) Walter Sapte, jr. STRAND 4/7/92 mat perf.* <u>Harold Winyard</u> John Tresahar; <u>William Woodcock</u> Cyril Maude; <u>Benjamin Barrable</u> Fred A. Everill; <u>Milton Jones</u> Lawrence d'Orsay; <u>John Lucas</u> Charles S. Fawcett; <u>Joe Wiggs</u> J[ohn] Wheatman; <u>Cheevers</u> Charles Dodsworth; <u>Policeman</u> George Aubrey. <u>Servant</u> H[arriet] Trench; <u>Letitia Winyard</u> Fanny Robertson; <u>Marion Winyard</u> Annie Irish; <u>Atalanta Woodcock</u> Maud Milton. *REV: E 9/7/92 p8; St 7/7/92 p13; Th 1/8/92 p80; Ti 5/7/92 p10.*

92.229 *THE HIGHWAYMAN* (Duol) Justin Huntly McCarthy. STRAND 4/7/92 mat perf.** <u>Sir Harry Bellaire</u> Charles

Thursby. <u>Lady Betty Barrett</u> Mabel Love. *REV: E, St as for 92.228.*

92.230 *HAMLET UP TO DATE* (BsqSk) Mel B. Spurr. STRAND 4/7/92 mat perf. 1st perf? Mel B. Spurr. *REV: St 7/7/92 p13.*

92.231 *THE PICTURE DEALER* (FC,3a) Henry Reichardt & A. Goldsworthy. STRAND 4/7/92. 1st prof. <u>Comment</u>: Listed in Nicoll; ? perfd.

92.232 *ELAINE* (O[4a]) Hermann Bemberg. COVENT GARDEN 5/7/92, 8/7, 14/7, 18/7, 23/7/92. 5 perf.* <u>Lancelot</u> Jean de Reske/Sebastian Montariol; <u>Astolat</u> Pol Plançon; <u>Lavaine</u> Sebastian Montariol/Trieste; <u>Gauvain</u> Eugene Dufriche; <u>King Arthur</u> Ceste; <u>L'Ermite</u> Edouard de Reske. <u>Elaine</u> Nellie Melba; <u>Torre</u> Faure; <u>Reine Genievre</u> Blanche Deschamps-Jehin/Marie Brema; <u>Un Menestrel</u> Collard. <u>MGR</u> Augustus Harris; <u>Cond</u> Leon Jehin. *REV: Ath 9/7/92 p75; E 9/7/92 p13; SR 9/7/92 p44-5; St 7/7/92 p12-3; Th 1/8/92 p90; Ti 6/7/92 p9, 25/7/92 p11.*

92.233 *JO, THE WAIF* James Mortimer [adpt of Dickens's, *Bleak House*]. LYRIC 5/7/92 mat perf. 1st perf? <u>Sir Leicester Dedlock</u> Lawrence d'Orsay; <u>Inspector Bucket</u> Henry Bedford; <u>Mr Tulkinghorn</u> E. Girardot; <u>Rev Mr Chadband</u> Henry Crisp; <u>Mr Snagsby</u> Charles Dodsworth; <u>Mr Guppy</u> James A. Welch; <u>Crook</u> J. Francis; <u>Krooner</u> A.W. Gattie; <u>Beadle</u> A.G. Leigh. <u>Jo</u> Lydia Cowell; <u>Lady Dedlock</u> Maud Milton; <u>Mlle Hortense</u> Adrienne Dairolles; <u>Esther Summerson</u> Olive Stettith; <u>Mrs Snagsby</u> Kate Kearney; <u>Mrs Rouncewell</u> Fanny Robertson; <u>Mrs Piper</u> Kate Corcoran; <u>Rosa</u> Maggie Byron; <u>Guster</u> Louise Gourlay. <u>BM</u> William Greet; <u>Sm</u> A.G. Leigh. *REV: E 9/7/92 p9; St 7/7/92 p13; Th 1/8/92 p84-5.*

92.234 *AIDA* (O[4a]) Giuseppe Verdi. COVENT GARDEN 7/7/92. 1 perf.** <u>Il Re</u> Pol Plançon; <u>Amonasro</u> Victor Maurel; <u>Radamès</u> Dimitresco; <u>Un Messagiero</u> Rinaldini; <u>Ramfis</u> Edouard de Reske. <u>Aida</u> Margaret MacIntyre; <u>Una Sacerdotessa</u> Mathilde Bauermeister; <u>Amneris</u> Giulia Ravogli; <u>1ere Danseuse</u> Giuri. <u>MGR</u> Augustus Harris; <u>Cond</u> Enrico Bevignani. *REV: Ath 16/7/92 p106; E 9/7/*

92 p13; Ti 9/7/92 p7.

92.235 *LOVE, THE MAGICIAN* (P,3a) Josephine Rae &
Thomas Sidney. SHAFTESBURY 7/7/92 mat perf.* Geo-
ffrey Garth Frank Gillmore; Dick Crawford Philip
Cunningham; Pryden Potts Albert Bernard; Paul Ferroll
Lawrence d'Orsay; M Brisetout H. Tripp Edgar; Tom
Chetwoode Fred Knight; Wilfred Master Eric Field-Fish-
er. Hester Garth Irene Hayward; Lilith Markham Esme
Waldon; Mrs Davisson Fanny Robertson; Lena Davisson
Marjorie Christmas; Mary Dalry Florence Friend;
Morris Nina Brassey. L & MGR John Lart; Pp John Lan-
caster; Bom Watts; Dir Josephine Rae, Thomas Sidney;
Mus dir C.J. Hargitt; Sm Thomas Sidney. *REV: E 9/7/
92 p9; St 14/7/92 p11; Th 1/8/92 p82.*

92.236 *DER TROMPETER VON SAKKINGEN* (O[4a]) Victor
Nessler (mus) & Rudolf Bunge (lib). DRURY LANE 8/7/92,
14/7/92. 2 perf. 1st perfd Leipzig 4/5/84. Werner
Theodore Reichmann; Der Freiherr Heinrich Wiegand;
Conradin Lorent; Graf von Wildenstein Litter; Damian
Landau; Rector Manificus Maas; Haushofmeister Simon.
Baroness Maria Katti Bettaque; Gratin Ernestine
Schumann-Heink. MGR Augustus Harris; Cond Field.
*REV: Ath 16/7/92 p106; E 16/7/92 p13; St 14/7/92 p10;
Th 1/8/92 p91; Ti 9/7/92 p7.*

92.237 *THE GOLDFISH* (P,3a) W.G. van Nouhuys [trans
A. Teixeira de Mattos]. OPERA COMIQUE 8/7/92. 1
perf.* Herman Koorders W.L. Abingdon; Frans Koorders
Philip Cunningham; Van Rompel Edward Lennox; Arie
Joosten William Bonney; Fransen Rex Shirley; Gerrit
J. Fisher White. Marie Koorders Jessie Millward;
Greta Roskamp Maud Milton; Mrs van Borsden Mrs Edmund
Phelps; Stijntje Joosten Charlotte E. Morland; Door-
tje Ada Branson; Dina Mabel Hardy. L Edward Compton;
Dir & Treas J.T. Grein; Act mgr Charles Hoppe; Sm
Herman de Lange; Pq William Clarkson; Furn Oetzmann.
*REV: Ath 16/7/92 p107; E 16/7/92 p8; St 14/7/92 p10-1;
Th 1/8/92 p80-1; Ti 9/7/92 p7.* Comment: Independent
Theatre Society.

92.238 *FAUST UP TO DATE* (Bsq,2a) George R. Sims &
Henry Pettitt. GAIETY 11/7/92-20/8/92. 37 perf [w/mat

30/7]. 1st perf Gaiety 30/10/88. <u>Mephistopheles</u> Edmund Payne; <u>Lord Chancellor</u> George Honey; <u>Old Faust</u> H.C. Barry; <u>Valentine</u> Arthur Williams. <u>Marguerite</u> Florence St. John; <u>Young Faust</u> Amy Augarde; <u>Martha</u> Ada Dorée; <u>Siebel</u> Kitty Loftus; <u>Elsa</u> Cissy Fitzgerald; <u>Wagner</u> Jessie Harrison; <u>Donner</u> Winifred Hare; <u>Katrina</u> Rose Batchelor; <u>Gretchen</u> Alice Batchelor; <u>Totchen</u> Eva Greville; <u>Greta</u> Clara Vinanea; <u>Vivandiere</u> E. Percy. <u>L & MGR</u> George Edwardes; <u>Mus</u> W. Meyer Lutz, Auguste van Biene; <u>Pd</u> J.T. Tanner; <u>Sm</u> Frank Parker; <u>Act mgr</u> F.J. Harris, Joseph Zephan; <u>Sm</u> A.E. Dodson; <u>Gen mgr</u> J.T. Tanner; <u>Cond</u> W.F. Glover; <u>Bom</u> A.P. Oxley. *REV: E 16/9/92 p9; St 14/7/92 p11; Th 1/8/92 p82; Ti 12/7/92 p10.*

92.239 *FROU FROU* (C,5a) Henri Meilhac & Ludovic Halévy. ROYAL ENGLISH OPERA HOUSE 11/7/92-13/7/92. 4 perf [w/mat 13/7].** <u>M de Valreas</u> Fleury; <u>Domestique</u> Duberry; <u>M de Sartorys</u> Rebel; <u>Pitou</u> Thefer; <u>Baron de Cambri</u> [Henri] Deschamps; <u>Domestique</u> Cartereau; <u>Brigard</u> Angelo. <u>Gilberte</u> Sarah Bernhardt; <u>Louise</u> Jane Méa; <u>Baronne de Cambri</u> Gilberte Fleury; <u>Zanetto</u> Seylor; <u>Pauline</u> Merle; <u>Gouvernante</u> Nadrey. <u>PP</u> Richard d'Oyly Carte; <u>Dir</u> Henry E. Abbey, Maurice Grau; <u>Cond</u> Andrew Levey; <u>Act</u> mgr G. Edwards Minor. *REV: Ath 16/7/92 p107; E 16/7/92 p9; Ti 12/7/92 p10.*

92.240 *IDOLS OF THE HEART* (CD,1a) Janet Steer. CRITERION 12/7/92 mat perf. 1st perfd Shakespeare, Liverpool 21/2/90. <u>Lord Duncastle</u> Charles Eaton; <u>Derrick Sinclair</u> Frank Atherley. <u>Nurse Nancy</u> Alexes Leighton; <u>Editha</u> Mary Clayton; <u>Lady Irene Hamilton</u> Janet Steer. *REV: E 16/7/92 p9; St 14/7/92 p11; Th 1/8/92 p85.*

92.241 *A COWARDLY FOE* (D,1a) Wynn F. Miller. CRITERION 12/7/92 mat perf.* <u>Sir Arthur Greystock</u> Frank Atherley; <u>Ivan Metzikoff</u> Charles Eaton. <u>Lady Greystock</u> Janet Steer. *REV: As for 92.240.*

92.242 *DIE GOTTERDAMMERUNG* (O[Prol,3a]) Richard Wagner. COVENT GARDEN 13/7/92; trfd to DRURY LANE 18/7/92. 2 perf. 1st perfd Bayreuth 17/8/76. <u>Siegfried</u> Max Alvary; <u>Gunther</u> Knapp; <u>Alberich</u> Lissmann; <u>Manen</u> Lorent; <u>Hagan</u> Heinrich Wiegand. <u>Brunhilde</u> Katharina

Klafsky; <u>Gutrune</u> Katti Bettaque; <u>Waltrute</u> Ernestine
Schumann-Heink; <u>Woglinde</u> Sophie Traubmann; <u>Wellgunde</u>
Paula Ralph; <u>Flosshilde</u> Bianca Froehlich. MGR Augustus Harris; <u>Cond</u> Gustav Mahler. *REV: Ath 16/7/92 p*
106; E 16/7/92 p13; St 21/7/92 p10; Ti 14/7/92 p5.

92.243 *PHEDRE* (T,5a) Jean Baptiste Racine. ROYAL
ENGLISH OPERA HOUSE 14/7/92, 15/7, 21/7/92. 3 perf.
1st perfd Hotel de Bourgogne, Paris 1/1/1677. <u>Hip-</u>
<u>polyte</u> Albert Darmont; <u>Thesee</u> Rebel; <u>Thermamene</u>
Piron; <u>Panope</u> Thefer. <u>Phedre</u> Sarah Bernhardt; <u>Aricie</u>
Jane Méa; <u>Oenone</u> Marie Grandet; <u>Ismene</u> Simonson. <u>PP</u>
Richard d'Oyly Carte; <u>Dir</u> Henry E. Abbey, Maurice
Grau; <u>Cond</u> Andrew Levey; <u>Act mgr</u> G. Edwards Minor.
REV: E 16/7/92 p9; SR 16/7/92 p76; Ti 15/7/92 p3.

92.244 *FAITHFUL JAMES* (FC,1a) B.C. Stephenson. COURT
16/7/92-15/10/92. 84 perf [w/mat 10/9, 17/9, 24/9,
8/10, 15/10; mat only 27/8, 3/9]. 1st perfd Vestry
Hall, Turnham Green 24/10/89. <u>Admiral Vincent</u> Brandon
Thomas; <u>Henry Duncan</u> Wilfred Draycott; <u>Philip Mel-</u>
<u>ville</u> C.P. Little; <u>James</u> Weedon Grossmith; <u>Waiter</u>
Sidney Warden. <u>Mrs Melville</u> Sybil Grey; <u>Mrs Duncan</u>
Ellaline Terriss/May Palfrey. L & MGR Arthur Chud-
leigh; <u>Dir</u> Brandon Thomas; <u>Cond</u> Edward Jones. *REV:*
E 23/7/92 p7; St 21/7/92 p10; Th 1/8/92 p81-2; Ti
18/7/92 p10.

92.245 *TANNHAUSER* (O[3a]) Richard Wagner. COVENT GAR-
DEN 16/7/92, 22/7/92. 2 perf.** <u>Tannhauser</u> Max Alvary; <u>Landgraf</u> Heinrich Wiegand; <u>Walther von der Vo-</u>
<u>gelweide</u> Landau; <u>Biterolf</u> Litter; <u>Heinrich der</u>
<u>Schreiber</u> Simon; <u>Reimar von Zweter</u> Lorent; <u>Wolfram</u>
<u>von Eschinbach</u> Theodore Reichmann/Knapp. <u>Der Hirt</u>
Ernestine Schumann-Heink; <u>Venus</u> Katti Bettaque;
<u>Elisabeth</u> Katharine Klafsky. MGR Augustus Harris;
<u>Cond</u> Gustav Mahler. *REV: Ath 23/7/92 p139; E 23/7/92*
p13; St 21/7/92 p10; Ti 18/7/92 p8.

92.246 *PARTNERS FOR LIFE* (C,3a) Henry J. Byron. ROY-
ALTY 16/7/92 mat perf. 1st perfd Globe 7/10/71. <u>Tom</u>
<u>Gilroy</u> Edgar B. Skeet; <u>Horace Mervyn</u> Smallwood Met-
calfe;<u>Ernest</u> Percy Buckler; <u>Muggles</u> G. Combe-Williams;
<u>Goppinger</u> Gilbert Davies; <u>Sir Archibald Drelincourt</u>

Frederick Temple. <u>Fanny Smith</u> Lena Burnleigh; <u>Emily Mervyn</u> Mabel Archdall; <u>Priscilla</u> Edith Tancred. <u>DIR</u> Edgar B. Skeet, Gustave Garcia. *REV: E 23/7/92 p13; St 21/7/92 p10.*

92.247 *A HUNDRED YEARS AGO* (PastOa,1a) "Alec Nelson" [E.B. Aveling] (lib) & Henry J. Wood (mus). ROYALTY 16/7/92 mat perf.* <u>Soll Ball</u> William Philp; <u>Tom Ball</u> Frederick Bovill; <u>Joe Shortlands</u> Smallwood Metcalfe. <u>Liz Hendley</u> Margaret Warren; <u>Alice Hendley</u> Mary Brough. <u>COND</u> C.H. Allen Gill. *REV: E, St as for 92.246; Th 1/8/92 p83.*

92.248 *EUX* (Fantasy) Maurice Donnay. PRINCE OF WALES'S 18/7/92 mat perf. 1st perfd Bodinière, Paris 3/89. Georges Treville. Mlle M. Chassin. *REV: 21/7/92 p10.*

92.249 *DRESDEN CHINA* (Fantasy,1a) Alice Chapin & E.H. C. Oliphant. VAUDEVILLE 21/7/92 mat perf.* <u>Hermann</u> H. Tripp Edgar. <u>Gretchen</u> Kate Ruskin. <u>L & MGR</u> Thomas Thorne; <u>Mgr</u> Harrington Baily; <u>Pd</u> Fred Thorne; <u>Cond</u> Tom Smythe; <u>Ch</u> C. Romaine. *REV: E 23/7/92 p9; St 28/7/92 p10; Th 1/9/92 p129.*

92.250 *SHAME* (D,1a) Alice Chapin & E.H.C. Oliphant. VAUDEVILLE 21/7/92 mat perf.* <u>Dr Conway</u> Herbert Flemming; <u>Dr Hewett</u> Frank Gillmore. <u>Annie</u> Alice Chapin. <u>L & MGR</u>, <u>Mgr</u>, <u>Pd</u>, <u>Cond</u> as for 92.249. *REV: As for 92.249.*

92.251 *A ROLAND FOR AN OLIVER* (C,1a) Thomas Morton. VAUDEVILLE 21/7/92 mat perf. 1st perfd Covent Garden 29/4/19. <u>Sir Mark Chase</u> A. Wood; <u>Mr Selborne</u> Nicol Pentland; <u>Alfred Highflyer</u> Frank Gillmore; <u>Gamekeeper</u> Henry Nelson; <u>Fixture</u> Fred Thorne. <u>Mrs Selborne</u> Ellen Thorne; <u>Maria Darlington</u> Alice Chapin; <u>Mrs Fixture</u> Amy McNeil. <u>L & MGR</u>, <u>Mgr</u>, <u>Pd</u>, <u>Cond</u> as for 92. 249. *REV: E, St as for 92.249.*

92.252 *NYDIA, THE BLIND GIRL OF POMPEII* ([O,5a]) George Fox. DRURY LANE 23/7/92 mat perf. 1st perfd Crystal Palace 10/5/92. <u>Glaucus</u> Durward Lely; <u>Burbo</u> Gilbert King; <u>Olinthus</u> Walter Clifford; <u>Clodius</u> Joyce; <u>Arbaces</u> Henry Pyatt. <u>Ione</u> Giulia Valda; <u>Julia</u>

Welwyn; <u>Stratonice</u> Kate Vito; <u>Slave Girl</u> Dwyer; <u>Nydia</u>
Sigrid Arnoldson. <u>MGR</u> Augustus Harris; <u>Cond</u> Edward
Jones. *REV: E 30/7/92 p13; Ti 25/7/92 p11.*

92.253 *A ROYAL DIVORCE* (RD,5a) W.G. Wills & Grace
Hawthorne. PRINCESS'S 25/7/92-26/10/92. 152 perf
[w/mat 1/8, 3/8, 10/8, 17/8, 24/8, 29/8, 31/8, 5/9,
7/9, 12/9, 14/9, 19/9, 21/9, 24/9, 26/9, 28/9, 1/10,
3/10, 5/10, 8/10, 10/10, 12/10, 15/10, 17/10, 19/10,
22/10, 24/10, 26/10].** <u>Napoleon I</u> Murray Carson;
<u>Talleyrand</u> Henry de Solla/Beresford Whitcomb; <u>Marquis</u>
<u>de Beaumont</u> Harcourt Beatty; <u>Gen. Augereau</u> Henry Gray
Dolby; <u>Grimaud</u> Watty Brunton, jr; <u>Marshall Murat</u>
Beresford Whitcomb/Wordsworth Griffith; <u>Marshall Nay</u>
Henry Ludlow; <u>Brigadier Antoine</u> T.C. Martin; <u>Briga-</u>
<u>dier Pierre</u> D.J. Hennessey/Albert Rowton; <u>Brigadier</u>
<u>Jacques</u> A.W. Stead/D.J. Hennessey/H.J. Powell; <u>Lord</u>
<u>Keith</u> W.E. Sauter; <u>Dr Corvisart</u> H.J. Powell/D.J.
Hennessey; <u>Orderly</u> George Aubrey; <u>Bob Royal</u> H. Drum-
mond; <u>Officer</u> Theodore Alker. <u>Marie Louise</u> Lesley
Bell/Marie Dagmar; <u>Stephanie de Beauharnais</u> Margaret
Watson/Alice Livingston; <u>Blanche de Hervas</u> Frances
Wyatt/Madge Herrick; <u>Angelique de Varennes</u> Emelie
Ormesby; <u>Gouvernante</u> Louisa Wyatt; <u>Mme de Campan</u>
Madge Herrick/Michael; <u>Jeanne la Terreur</u> Chrissie
Eric; <u>Little King of Rome</u> Ethel Patrick; <u>Mother Lomas</u>
Helena Dixon; <u>Empress Josephine</u> Grace Hawthorne/Les-
ley Bell. <u>PP</u> Mrs Harriet Gooch; <u>Mgr</u> W.W. Kelly; <u>Bom</u>
Arthur Frye; <u>Act mgr</u> E.H. Robotham; <u>Sm</u> Watty Brunton,
jr; <u>Gen. agent</u> Warwick Major; <u>Bm</u> C.J. McCarthy; <u>Sec</u>
Miss G.A. Pearson; <u>Mus dir</u> E. Boggetti; <u>Mach</u> H. Hod-
ges; <u>Sc</u> Richard C. Durant, W.H. Dixon; <u>Cost</u> Morris
Angel; <u>Mus & Ch</u> William Robins; <u>Dir</u> Henry Herman.
REV: Ath 30/7/92 p172; E 30/7/92 p7; St 28/7/92 p10.

92.254 *THE JEALOUS WIFE* (C,5a) George Colman the
Elder. STRAND 26/7/92 mat perf.** <u>Mr Oakley</u> Herbert
Flemming; <u>Mjr. Oakley</u> John Beauchamp; <u>Charles Oakley</u>
Sydney Brough; <u>Mr Russet</u> Fred Thorne; <u>Lord Trinket</u>
Herbert Ross; <u>John</u> Alec C. MacKenzie; <u>Tom</u> Lionel Rae.
<u>Lady Freelove</u> Carlotta Leclercq; <u>Harriet Russet</u> Marie
Brooke; <u>Toilet</u> Nellie Thorne; <u>Mrs Oakley</u> Mrs G.B.W.
Lewis [Rosie Edouin]. *REV: E 30/7/92 p9; St 28/7/92
p10; Ti 27/7/92 p10; Th 1/9/92 p128.*

92.255 *THE POSTMAN* (Ca,1a) T. Edgar Pemberton. STRAND 26/7/92 mat perf.* John Archer Willie Edouin; Charlie Harvey Herbert Ross. Cherrie Tearle Isabel Ellissen; Mrs Searle Eleanor May; Dorcas Body Lily Belmore. *REV: E, St, Th as for 92.254.*

92.256 *HASTE TO THE WEDDING* (MC,3a,5tab) W.S. Gilbert (lib) & George Grossmith (mus) [mus ver of *Le Chapeau de Paille d'Italie*]. CRITERION 27/7/92-20/8/92. 22 perf.* Maguire Lionel Brough; Woodpecker Tapping Frank Wyatt; Uncle Bopaddy William Blakeley; Mjr.- Gen. Bunthunder Sydney Valentine; Cripps Welton Dale; Cpt. Bapp Frank Atherley; Duke of Turniptopshire David S. James; Cousin Foodle George Grossmith, jr; Jackson W.R. Shirley; Barns Fred Bond; Wilkinson Percy Brough. Marchioness of Market Harborough Ellis Jeffreys; Belea Crackinthorpe Sybil Carlisle; Anna Maria Maguire Marie Studholme; Mrs Leonora Bunthunder Day Ford; Patty Haidee Crofton. L & MGR Charles Wyndham; Sm S.H.S. Austin; Mus dir Theodore Ward; Act mgr & Treas E. Harvey; Cond George Grossmith; Cost C.H. Fox. *REV: E 30/7/92 p9; St 4/8/92 p12; Th 1/9/92 p132; Ti 28/7/92 p7.*

92.257 *THE BROKEN MELODY* (P,3a) Herbert Keen & "James Leader" [J.T. Tanner]. PRINCE OF WALES'S 28/7/92-27/ 8/92. 30 perf [w/S mat exc 30/7, 6/8].* Paul Borinski Auguste van Biene; Gen Ivanoff W.L. Abingdon; Dickson Fred Thorne; Dudley Mortimer Sant Matthews; Dr Magrath Stephen Caffrey; Hon Dick Spinnaker William Benson; Beaujour Frank Lacy; Benneton Leslie Murray. Duchesse de Vervier Olga Brandon; Mabel Blanche Horlock; Hon Mrs Spinnaker Adelaide Gunn; Mrs Dickson Mrs Campbell Bradley; Princess of Solento Aimee Mills. L & MGR C.J. Abud; Pp Edgar Bruce; Mus & Cond Carl Kiefert; Furn Oetzmann; Gen mgr J.T. Tanner; Act mgr E[rnest] Hallewell; Sm C.F. Bawtree. *REV: Ath 6/8/92 p212; E 30/7/92 p9; St 4/8/92 p12; Th 1/9/92 p123-4; Ti 29/7/92 p3.*

92.258 *THE WHITE LADY* (Ca). PRINCE OF WALES'S 28/7/92- 27/8/92; 15/10/92-4/11/92. 45 perf.* Harold Hernshaw Frank Lacy; Blake Charles McLagan; Guy Master Douglas Patrick. Mrs Waltham Adelaide Gunn. L & MGR, Pp, Gen

mgr, Act mgr, Sm as for 92.257. *REV: E, St as for 92.
257.*

92.259 *THE CROSS OF HONOUR* (Romantic Military D,5a)
Arthur Shirley & Maurice Gally [adpt of Léopold
Stapleaux, *Le Couçon*]. ROYALTY 29/7/92-c.13/8/92.
c.14 perf. 1st perfd Public Hall, New Cross 28/10/90
[as *False Witness*]. André Léonard Ronald Bayne;
Gen. de Bellegarde Albert E. Drinkwater; M de Savig-
nac H.A. Saintsbury; Calmette William Bonney; Dr
Leonard George Mallet; Dr Delaporte Douglas Gordon;
Antoine Chautard William Cheesman; Dominique H[enry?]
Nelson; Col. Rochemaure Lewis Wilson; Sgt. d'Aulnay
H. Wood; Col. Dardart Frederick Jones; Francois Ed-
ward Thane. Adrienne Delaporte Lilian Revell; Marie
Mary Jocelyn; Countess de Bellegarde Mrs Dalmaine.
L Kate Santley; Mgr Ronald Bayne; Sm A.E. Drinkwater;
Asm H. Nelson; Act mgr C. St. John Denton; A act mgr
Frederick Lloyd; Furn Oetzmann; Pq C.H. Fox; Dir
Ronald Bayne, Arthur Shirley; Sc Sydney Beltram,
George A. Toplis. *REV: Ath 6/8/92 p212; St 4/8/92
p12-3; Th 1/9/92 p124-5; Ti 30/7/92 p5.*

92.260 *ROUGH DIAMOND* (CD,1a) J.B. Buckstone. ROYALTY
29/7/92. Rnd. 1st perfd Lyceum 8/11/47. Sir William
Evergreen George Mallet; Lord Plato William Bonney;
Cousin Joe Albert E. Drinkwater; Cpt. Blenheim Douglas Gordon. Lady Plato Lilian Revell; Marjery Mary
Jocelyn. L, Mgr, Sm, Asm, Act mgr, A act mgr as for
92.259.

92.261 *THE LIGHTS OF HOME* (D,5a) George R. Sims &
Robert Buchanan. ADELPHI 30/7/92-17/12/92. 121 perf.*
Philip Carrington Harold Kyrle Bellew/Charles Dalton;
Edgar Garfield Charles Dalton/George W. Cockburn;
Jim Chowne Lionel Rignold/Eardley Turner; Dave Purvis
W.A. Elliott; Arthur Tredgold George W. Cockburn/
Thomas Kingston; Cpt. Petherick Howard Russell; Lieut.
Williamson Thomas Kingston/W. Northcote; Jack Steb-
bing Willie Drew; Joe Pendred J[ohn] Northcote; Jim
Atkins Harwood Cooper; Ned Parsons W. Northcote.
Sybil Garfield Evelyn Millard; Tress Purvis Mrs Pat-
rick Campbell/Dorothy Dorr; Martha Widgeon Clara
Jecks; Mrs Purvis Mrs Henry Leigh; Mrs Petherick

Ethel Hope. <u>PP & MGR</u> A. & S. Gatti; <u>Dir</u> E.B. Norman;
<u>Sc</u> Bruce Smith, William Perkins, Henry Emden; <u>Mus &</u>
<u>Mus dir</u> Henry Sprake; <u>Mach</u> H. Loftin; <u>Pq</u> William
Clarkson; <u>Cost dgn</u> Karl; <u>Cost</u> L. & H. Nathan; <u>Act mgr</u>
<u>& Treas</u> Charles A. Jecks. *REV: Ath 6/8/92 p212; E 6/*
8/92 p6; St 4/8/92 p12; Th 1/9/92 p125-6; Ti 1/8/92
p6.

92.262 *A LOST SHEEP* (FC,3a) Walter Parker & Arthur
Shirley. OPERA COMIQUE 30/7/92-5/8/92. 6 mat perf.
1st perfd Theatre Royal, Bradford 13/7/91. <u>Josiah</u>
<u>Duckweed</u> A. Wood; <u>Athanasius</u> Orlando Barnett; <u>Cpt.</u>
<u>Robert Rowser</u> Julian Cross; <u>Don Domingo</u> G.E. Bellamy;
<u>Mjr. Bangs</u> S[idney] Burt; <u>"Big Drink"</u> T[homas] Ver-
ner; <u>Donald Macgrab</u> Eardley Turner. <u>Ada Mayfield</u>
Florence Tyrrell; <u>Mrs Blacklock</u> Mrs Beaumont Nelson;
<u>Donna Lola</u> Aimee Lowther; <u>Donna Xarfia</u> Mary Mordaunt;
<u>Miss Dedshott</u> Henrietta Cross; <u>Mme Dazzle</u> Stella
Brooke; <u>Eliza</u> Julia Warden. *REV: Ath 6/8/92 p212; E*
6/8/92 p8; St 4/8/92 p13; Th 1/9/92 p127.

92.263 *MUSIC AT HOME* (Ca) Rose Seaton. OPERA COMIQUE
30/7/92-6/8/92. 7 perf. 1st perfd Opera House, Chatham 9/6/90. <u>Charles Vane</u> H.T. Bindloss. <u>Gabrielle</u>
<u>Rollo</u> Marquis; <u>Mme George</u> Brynalyn; <u>Mrs Charles Vane</u>
Rose Seaton. <u>L</u> Edward Compton; <u>Sm</u> J. Hermann Dickson;
<u>Act mgr</u> Francis Gosnay; <u>Bm</u> Tidd, J.J. Killingsworth;
<u>Bom</u> H. Hine. *REV: E 6/8/92 p6; St 4/8/92 p13.*

92.264 *THE UNDERSTUDY* (Duol) Elizabeth Bessle. OPERA
COMIQUE 30/7/92-6/8/92. 7 perf.* <u>Welldone Parrott</u>
Frank Lindo; <u>Call Boy</u> Master Field-Fisher. <u>Miss Earls-</u>
<u>court</u> Elizabeth Bessle. <u>L</u>, <u>Sm</u>, <u>Act mgr</u>, <u>Bm</u>, <u>Bom</u> as
for 92.263. *REV: As for 92.263.*

92.265 *MARRIAGE BELLS* (D,1a) Herbert Gough. OPERA
COMIQUE 30/7/92-6/8/92. 7 perf. 1st perfd Vaudeville
28/11/81. <u>Col. Hugh Beville</u> Henry Dana; <u>Percy Waldron</u>
C[harles] Cemally. <u>Jessie Faulkner</u> Cissie Wade; <u>Mrs</u>
<u>Faulkner</u> Florence Wade. <u>L</u>, <u>Sm</u>, <u>Act mgr</u>, <u>Bm</u>, <u>Bom</u> as
for 92.263. *REV: As for 92.263.*

92.266 *THE BAB-BALLAD MONGER; OR, THE MYSTERIOUS*
MUSICIAN AND THE DUKE OF DISGUISEBURY (Travestie) Frank

Lindo. OPERA COMIQUE 30/7/92-6/8/92. 7 perf.* Un-
limited Louis G.B. Prior; Organne Grindgroire Frank
Lindo; O'live'ere Richard Douglas. Drusilly Maggie
Garratt; Pages Amy Clifford, Eva Clifford. L, Sm,
Act mgr, Bm, Bom as for 92.263. *REV: As for 92.263.*

92.267 *OUR EMMIE* (CD,1a) Marwood Clark. OPERA COMIQUE
1/8/92-5/8/92. 5 mat perf.* Mr Sheldon Thomas Verner;
Dr Prescott Clinton Baddeley; Simon F[red] A. Gaytie.
Mrs Prescott Any Elstob; Emmie Italia Conti. *REV: As
for 92.263.*

92.268 *POOR MIGNONETTE* (Oa) Jacques Offenbach (mus)
& A. Schade (lib) & Percy Reeve (lyr) [adpt of Offen-
bach, *Pomme d'Api*]. CRITERION 2/8/92-3/12/92. 102
perf.* Rabasteus Sydney Valentine; Gustave Welton
Dale/W.R. Shirley. Catharine Haidee Crofton. L & MGR
Charles Wyndham; Sm S.H.S. Austin; Mus dir Theodore
Ward; Act mgr & Treas E. Harvey. *REV: E 6/8/92 p6;
St 4/8/92 p12; Th 1/9/92 p132.*

92.269 *BETSY* (C,3a) F.C. Burnand [adpt of Hennequin
& Najac, *Bébé*]. CRITERION 22/8/92-8/10/92. 46 perf
[w/S mat exc 27/8, 3/9, 8/10]. 1st perfd Criterion
6/8/79. Alexander Birkett William Blakeley/Mat Rob-
son; Richard Talbot George Giddens; Cpt. Redmond Mc-
Manus Sydney Valentine; Samuel Dawson David S. James/
Alfred Maltby; Adolphus Birkett Welton Dale; Barber
C. Edmonds/Aukett; Servant [Charles] Terric/H[enry]
Le Breton. Mrs Birkett Fanny Robertson; Betsy Jennie
Rogers; Mme Polenta Ellis Jeffreys; Mrs McManus
F. Frances; Nellie Bassett Marie Studholme; Grace
Peyton A. McRae. L & MGR, Sm, Mus dir, Act mgr & Treas
as for 92.268. *REV: E 27/8/92 p7; St 25/8/92 p11-2.*

92.270 *MARRIAGE BELLS* (C,1a) Herbert Gough. ROYALTY
3/9/92-16/9/92. 13 perf.** Col. Beville Henry Austin; Percy Charles Cemaly. Mrs Faulkner Florence
Wade; Jessie Faulkner Cissie Wade. *REV: E 10/9/92 p7;
St 8/9/92 p10.*

92.271 *MADGE* (CSk,1a) Florence Wade & Henry Austin.
ROYALTY 3/9/92-23/9/92. 20 perf [w/mat 17/9]. 1st
perfd St. George's Hall 10/3/91. Percy Parker Charles

Cemaly; <u>Henry Mervin</u> Henry Austin. <u>Miss Arbuthnot</u>
Florence Wade; <u>Abigail</u> Cissie Wade. *REV: As for 92.*
270.

92.272 *THE BAB-BALLAD MONGER; OR, THE MYSTERIOUS*
MUSICIAN AND THE DUKE OF DISGUISEBURY (Travestie,1a)
Frank Lindo. ROYALTY 3/9/92-23/9/92. 20 perf [w/mat
17/9].** <u>Organne Grindgoire</u> Frank Lindo; <u>Unlimited</u>
<u>Louis</u> Sheridan Lascelles; <u>O'live'ere</u> Richard [H.]
Douglass. <u>Drusilly</u> Lizzie Ruggles. *REV: As for 92.270.*

92.273 *CIGARETTE* (RO,3a) J. Haydn Parry (mus) & E.
Warham St. Leger (lib) & Barry Montour (lib). LYRIC
7/9/92-24/9/92; trfd to SHAFTESBURY 26/9/92-3/12/92.
88 perf [w/S mat exc 10/9, 24/9, 26/11; add mat
23/11, 30/11]. 1st perfd Theatre Royal, Cardiff 15/8/
92. <u>Nicotine</u> Charles Collette; <u>Claude</u> Joseph O'Mara;
<u>Marquis de Portale</u> Oswald Yorke; <u>Benzoline</u> A.J. Eve-
lyn; <u>Sgt. Mouston</u> Leslie Holland; <u>M. Bastian</u> Sheridan Lascelles; <u>Gaston</u> Alfred Warner; <u>Justin</u> Lyons.
<u>Mme de Vauricourt</u> Godfrey; <u>Violette</u> Albu/Jessie Brad-
ford; <u>Cigarette</u> Florence Bankhardt/Geraldine Ulmar
[Mrs Ivan Caryll]; <u>Comtesse de Montrouget</u> Hannah
Jones/Amadi/Helen Sugden; <u>Babette</u> May Lawrie; <u>Lady</u>
<u>Superior</u> Helen Vicary; <u>Mother Lou-Lou</u> Marion Erle;
<u>Clarisse</u> Jessie Bradford; <u>Julie</u> Celia Loseby. <u>L & MGR</u>
Horace Sedger; <u>Dir</u> Charles Collette; <u>Chorus Master</u>
Neill O'Donovan; <u>Sc</u> W.T. Hemsley; <u>Cost & Pq</u> Harrison;
<u>Cond</u> J. Haydn Parry; <u>Asm</u> Oswald Yorke; <u>Sec & Treas</u>
H.E. Marston; <u>Bm</u> W.H. Griffiths. *REV: E 10/9/92 p13;*
SR 10/9/92 p308-9; St 15/9/92 p12, 29/9/92 p12; Th
1/10/92 p182-3; Ti 8/9/92 p3.

92.274 *A PAIR OF LUNATICS* (DSk) W.R. Walkes. LYRIC
7/9/92-19/9/92. 11 perf.** <u>He</u> Oswald Yorke. <u>She</u>
Mary Collette. <u>L & MGR</u>, <u>Asm</u>, <u>Bm</u> as for 92.273.

92.275 *THE WEDDING EVE* (CO,3a) William Yardley (lib)
[adpt of Alexandre Bisson & Bureau-Jattiot, *La Veillée*
de Noces] & F. Toulmouche (mus) & Ernest Ford (mus)
& "Yvolde" (mus). TRAFALGAR SQUARE 10/9/92-11/11/92.
62 perf [w/S mat exc 10/9].* <u>Kernoe</u> Joseph Tapley/
William Philp; <u>Doulas</u> George Barrett; <u>Sacrovir</u> Arthur
Wilkinson/John Le Hay; <u>Katula</u> Leonard Russell; <u>The</u>

Seneschal William Elton; Vaton C. Royelle; Yeucensir
Arthur Norman. Yvonnette Decima Moore; Jeannette Ma-
bel Love; Elisabeth Kate Chard; Anne Marie Amie Douglas; Charlotte Yata Whynier. L & MGR Michael Levenston; Pp Mr & Mrs Frank Wyatt; Sm Thomas W. Charles;
Mus dir Ernest Ford; Act mgr George Manners; Bom
W[alter] Hamilton; Ch John d'Auban; Cost dgn Wilhelm;
Cost Miss Fisher, Auguste, Alias, Stagg & Mantle; Pq
William Clarkson; Pd Thomas W. Charles; Sc Walter
Hann, William Telbin, William Perkins. *REV: E 18/6/*
92 p8, 17/9/92 p15; St 15/9/92 p12, 3/11/92 p13; Th
1/10/92 p183-4; SR 17/9/92 p331-2. Comment: Opening
production of new theatre.

92.276 *OUR BOYS* (C,3a) Henry J. Byron. VAUDEVILLE
14/9/92-27/1/93; 11/2(m), 15/2(m), 18/2(m); 22/2/93-
4/3/93. 153 perf [w/S mat exc 17/9/92; add mat 26/12/
92, 4/1/93, 11/1, 18/1, 25/1, 22/2, 1/3/93; np 22-
25/12/92].** Perkyn Middlewick David James; Sir
Geoffrey Champneys William Farren; Talbot Champneys
E.W. Gardiner; Charles Middlewick H. Reeves-Smith;
Poddles Duncan Fleet; Kempster Howard. Mary Melrose
May Whitty; Violet Melrose Eva Moore; Belinda Cicely
Richards; Clarissa Champneys Sophie Larkin. L & MGR
A. & S. Gatti; Sc Bruce Smith; Furn Lyons; Pd David
James; Mus dir Henry Sprake; Asm Charles Ashford;
Act mgr & Treas L[ouis] F. Nethersole. *REV: Ath 24/*
9/92 p427; E 17/9/92 p11; St 22/9/92 p12; Ti 15/9/92
p7.

92.277 *THE QUEEN OF MANOA* (P,4a) C. Haddon Chambers
& W. Outram Tristram. HAYMARKET 15/9/92-17/10/92. 30
perf [w/mat 24/9, 1/10].* Armand Sevarro Lewis Wal-
ler; Baron Finot Cyril Maude; Lord Chudleigh Herbert
Flemming; Rt Hon Richard Malvern Edmund Maurice; Mjr.
Garrett Charles Collette/Graham Wentworth; Mr Hill
Rudge Harding; Mr Wildrake William Cheesman; Archi-
bald McNair J. Hastings Batson; Quaverly H.T. Bind-
loss; Lord Topsam Cave Chinn; Budleigh Know Orde;
Sir Charles Minster Kingscote; Allan Phillips; Ser-
vant Albert Sims. Dorothy Blair Marie Linden; Lady
Helmore Henrietta Lindley; Mrs Paddington Clover
Emily Cross; Lady Violet Malvern Mrs Langtry; Lady
Dashley Rose Nesbitt; Miss Undercliff [Agnes?] Ingre-

ville; <u>Mrs Manton</u> Kate Tyndale; <u>Mrs Macham</u> Anna Hardinge. <u>L</u> H. Beerbohm Tree; <u>Mgr</u> Mrs Langtry; <u>Sc</u> Walter Johnstone; <u>Cond</u> Carl Armbruster; <u>Bom</u> W.H. Leverton; <u>Pq</u> William Clarkson; <u>Elect</u> E. Wingfield Bowles; <u>Sm</u> Edward Hastings; <u>Bm & Sec</u> Frederick Harrison. *REV: Ath 24/9/92 p427; E 17/9/92 p9; SR 24/9/92 p360; St 22/9/92 p12; Th 1/10/92 p173-4; Ti 16/9/92 p7.*

92.278 *THE PRODIGAL DAUGHTER* (Sporting D,4a) Henry Pettitt & Augustus Harris. DRURY LANE 17/9/92-10/12/ 92;* trfd to COVENT GARDEN 12/12/92-14/1/93. 123 perf [w/S mat exc 17/9, 14/1; add mat 9/11, 27/12, 28/12/ 92, 2/1/93]. <u>Sir John Woodmere</u> Henry Neville; <u>Maurice Deepwater</u> James Fernandez; <u>Tom Blinker</u> Arthur Williams/George Barrett/Thomas Terriss; <u>Lord Banbury</u> Harry Nicholls/John L. Shine/Dalton Somers; <u>Hon Julian Bedford</u> Julius Knight; <u>Cpt. Harry Vernon</u> Leonard Boyne; <u>Miserable Jim</u> Charles Dodsworth/Frank Harrison; <u>Dudley Roper</u> John L. Shine/Charles Dodsworth; <u>Joseph Gunn</u> Frank Damer; <u>French Waiter</u> Campbell Gollan; <u>Mjr. Ormsby</u> Frank Harrison; <u>Mr Wood</u> James Francis; <u>Cpt. Woodstock</u> Standley Wade; <u>Sir Walter</u> Alfred Collins; <u>James</u> Thomas Terriss; <u>Garcon de Salle</u> Arthur Wilmot. <u>Dorcas Jentle</u> Fanny Brough; <u>Violet Woodmere</u> Blanche Horlock; <u>Rose Woodmere</u> Jessie Millward/Marie Illington; <u>Servant</u> G[eorgina] Cook. <u>L & MGR</u> Augustus Harris; <u>Mus & Mus dir</u> John Crook; <u>Sc</u> W. Caney, William Perkins, Joseph Harker; <u>Cost</u> Miss Collier, Gask & Co., Peter Robinson, Morris Angel; <u>Pq</u> William Clarkson; <u>Mach</u> J. Taylor; <u>Dir</u> Augustus Harris; <u>Sm</u> Arthur P. Collins; <u>Prompter</u> N[apier] Barry; <u>Sec & Treas</u> Fred G. Latham. *REV: Ath 24/9/92 p427; E 24/9/92 p9, 17/12/92 p9; SR 24/9/92 p360; St 22/9/92 p12, 15/12/92 p12; Th 1/10/92 p174-6; Ti 19/9/92 p8, 13/12/92 p6.*

92.279 *THE GREAT DEMONSTRATION* (F,1a) Israel Zangwill & Louis Cowen. ROYALTY 17/9/92-23/9/92. 7 perf [w/mat 17/9].* <u>Vernon Howard</u> Frank Lindo; <u>Bill Boggles</u> R[ichard] H. Douglass. <u>Mary</u> Lizzie Ruggles. *REV: E 24/9/92 p9; Th 1/10/92 p176.*

92.280 *COUSIN'S COURTSHIP* (DSk) Mary Collette. LYRIC 20/9/92-24/9/92;* trfd to SHAFTESBURY 26/9/92-13/10/

92; 24/11/92. 22 perf, <u>Jack</u> Oswald Yorke. <u>Effie</u>
Mary Collette. <u>PP</u> John Lancaster; <u>Gen mgr</u> W.H.
Griffiths; <u>Asm</u> Oswald Yorke; <u>Treas & Sec</u> H.E, Marston.
REV: E 1/10/92 p11; St 29/9/92 p12.

92.281 *THE BELLS* (3a) Leopold Lewis [adpt of Erckmann-
Chatrian, *Le Juif Polonais*]. LYCEUM 24/9/92-30/9/92;
29/10/92. 7 perf.** <u>Mathias</u> Henry Irving; <u>Christian</u>
William Terriss; <u>Walter</u> H[enry] Howe; <u>Hans</u> S[am]
Johnson; <u>President of the Court</u> F[rank] Tyars; <u>Dr
Zimmer</u> John Martin Harvey; <u>Notary</u> Gurney; <u>Clerk of
the Court</u> Lacy; <u>Mesmerist</u> [John] Archer. <u>Catherine</u>
Mrs Pauncefort; <u>Sozel</u> Kate Phillips; <u>Annette</u> [Amy]
Coleridge. <u>L & MGR</u> Henry Irving; <u>Bom</u> Joseph Hurst; <u>Sm</u>
H.J. Loveday; <u>Mus dir</u> J. Meredith Ball; <u>Act mgr</u> Bram
Stoker. *REV: Ath 1/10/92 p474; E 1/10/92 p9; SR 1/10/
92 p391; Th 1/11/92 p231-2; Ti 26/9/92 p11.*

92.282 *THE KING AND THE MILLER; OR, CRAMOND BRIG* (D,
1a) William H. Murray. LYCEUM 24/9/92-30/9/92; 29/10/
92. 7 perf.** <u>James V of Scotland</u> F[rank] Tyars;
<u>James Birkie</u> John Martin Harvey; <u>Jock Howieson</u> S[am]
Johnson; <u>Cpt. of King's Guard</u> [W. Lionel] Belmore;
<u>King's Page</u> Master Harwood. <u>Tibbie Howieson</u> Mrs
Pauncefort; <u>Marion</u> Foster. <u>L & MGR</u>, <u>Bom</u>, <u>Sm</u>, <u>Mus dir</u>,
<u>Act mgr</u> as for 92.281. *REV: E 1/10/92 p9.*

92.283 *HADDON HALL* (Light O,3a) Sydney Grundy (lib)
& Arthur Sullivan (mus). SAVOY 24/9/92-15/4/93. 204
perf [w/S mat exc 24/9; add mat 26/12/92; np 31/3/93].
1st perfd Theatre Royal, Wolverhampton 1892. <u>Rupert
Vernon</u> Rutland Barrington/J. Bowden Haswell; <u>The
MacCrankie</u> W.H. Denny; <u>Oswald</u> Charles Kenningham;
<u>Sir George Vernon</u> Richard Green; <u>John Manners</u> Courtice
Pounds/J[ohn] Macauley/[Bates] Maddison/Robert F.
Cunningham; <u>Sing-Song Simeon</u> Rudolph Lewis/J. Bowden
Haswell; <u>Kill Joy Candlemas</u> W.H. Leon; <u>Nicodemus
Knock-Knee</u> Arthur W. Fowles; <u>Barnabas Bellows-to-Mend</u>
George de Pledge; <u>Mjr. Domo</u> H. Gordon. <u>Dorothy Ver-
non</u> Lucile Hill/Florence Easton; <u>Dorcas</u> Dorothy Vane;
<u>Nance</u> Annie [Nita] Cole/May Bell; <u>Lady Vernon</u> Rosina
Brandram; <u>Gertrude</u> Claribel Hyde; <u>Deborah</u> Florence
Easton. <u>PP & MGR</u> Richard d'Oyly Carte; <u>Sc</u> William
Telbin, Hawes Craven, Joseph Harker, William Perkins;

Dir Charles Harris; Mus dir Francois Cellier; Cond
Arthur Sullivan; Sm W.H. Seymour; Ch John d'Auban;
Act mgr & Treas J.W. Beckwith; Cost dgn Percy Ander-
son; Cost Auguste, Mme Leon, B.J. Simmons, Angel &
Son, Alias; Pq William Clarkson; Props [H.] Skelly;
Mach Peter White; Elect Lyons; Lime [W.] Kerr. *REV:*
Ath 1/10/92 p456; E 1/10/92 p15, 8/4/93 p11; Sk 3/5/
93 p3; SR 1/10/92 p389-90; St 29/9/92 p12; Th 1/11/
92 p235-6; Ti 26/9/92 p11.

92.284 *THE WOODEN SPOON* (0a,1a) Gilbert Burgess (lib)
& Hope Temple (mus). TRAFALGAR SQUARE 26/9/92-11/11/
92. 41 perf.* Marquis d'Alverez William Philp; Pablo
Leonard Russell. Inez Violet Robinson; Mariana Millie
Vere. L & MGR Michael Levenston; Pp Mr & Mrs Frank
Wyatt; Sc E[dward] G. Banks; Sm Thomas W. Charles;
Mus dir Ernest Ford; Eng Arthur H. Vesey; Act mgr
Arthur Belmore. *REV: E 1/10/92 p9; St 29/9/92 p12;*
Th 1/11/92 p237.

92.285 *CINDER-ELLEN UP TOO LATE* [*SECOND EDITION*]
"A.C. Torr" [Fred Leslie] (lib) & W.T. Vincent (lib)
& W. Meyer Lutz (mus). GAIETY 1/10/92-17/12/92. 68
perf [w/mat 8/10].** Charles Hollywell Arthur Play-
fair; Sir Ludgate Hill Charles Danby; Servant Fred
Leslie; Peckham [H.C.] Barry; Gnorwood E.D. Wardes;
Footman Hill; Lord Leatherhead Fred Storey. Prince
Belgravia Maggie Duggan;Lincolnzina Sylvia Grey;
Fettalana Katie Seymour; Mrs Kensington Gore M. Hol-
mes; Mrs Bayswater Kate Welwyn; Sir Peterborough
Court Violet Durkin; Lord Taplow Florence Lloyd; Lord
Eastbourne Ethel Earle; Lord Soho Louie Pounds; Lord
Blackfriars N. Farringdon; Sir Waterloo Bridge Ivy
Hertzog/Lilly Harold; Templina Adelaide Astor/Maud;
Victorina Topsy Sinden; Grazina Alice Gilbert;
Griffina Eva Greville/Bob Robina; Cinder-Ellen Letty
Lind; Pages Phoebe Carlo, Lilian Sedgewick. L & MGR
George Edwardes; Add mus F. Osmond Carr, Scott Gatty,
Sidney Jones, Walter Slaughter; Cost Miss Fisher, J.
Harrison, Alias; Cost dgn Wilhelm, Hugh Paterson;
Pq C.H. Fox; Sc E.G. Banks; Mus dir W. Meyer Lutz;
Sm Frank Parker; Act mgr W.B. Fabian; Bom A.P. Oxley.
REV: E 8/10/92 p9; St 6/10/92 p12; Ti 3/10/92 p11.

92.286 *THE SNOWSTORM* (P,1a) Sidney Bowkett. GAIETY
1/10/92-17/12/92. 67 perf.* <u>Henry Fenton</u> George T.
Minshull. <u>Edith Kingsley</u> Maggie Roberts/Florence
Lloyd. L & MGR, Sm, Act mgr, Bom as for 92.285. *REV:
E, St as for 92.285.*

92.287 *THE AWAKENING* (C,3a) Arthur Benham. GARRICK
1/10/92-29/10/92. 25 perf.* <u>John Peyton</u> Herbert Waring; <u>Reginald Harley</u> Sant Matthews; <u>Montague Nichol-
son</u> E. Allan Aynesworth; <u>Dr Mason</u> Leonard Calvert;
<u>Carter</u> Douglas Bruce; <u>Hon Cecil Darbishire</u> Arthur
Elwood. <u>Lady Gertrude Harley</u> Vane Featherston; <u>Nurse</u>
Eva Williams; <u>Archie Ripon</u> Nina Boucicault; <u>Helen
Peyton</u> Estelle Burney. L John Hare; <u>Dir</u> John L. Moore;
Act mgr C.G. Compton; <u>Cond</u> de Tender; <u>Sc</u> William Harford; <u>Sm</u> Sant Matthews. *REV: Ath 8/10/92 p508; E
8/10/92 p9; St 6/10/92 p12; Th 1/11/92 p225; Ti 3/10/
92 p11.*

92.288 *A HUSBAND IN CLOVER* (F,1a) Herman C. Merivale.
GARRICK 1/10/92-29/10/92. 25 perf.** <u>Horace</u> Leonard
Calvert/Gerald Gurney. <u>Lydia</u> Eva Williams. L, <u>Dir</u>,
Act mgr, Sm, Sc, Cond as for 92.287. *REV: St 6/10/92
p12.*

92.289 *A LUCKY DOG* (FC,3a) Walter Sapte, jr. TERRY'S
3/10/92-26/11/92. 67 perf [w/W, S mat exc 5/10; add
mat 24/10, 31/10, 14/11, 21/11].** <u>William Woodcock</u>
G.W. Anson; <u>Harold Winyard</u> John Tresahar; <u>Milton
Jones</u> Lawrance d'Orsay; <u>John Lucas</u> Charles S. Faw-
cett; <u>Joe Wiggs</u> F. Hamilton Knight; <u>Benjamin Barrable</u>
Frederick Thorne; <u>Cheevers</u> Fred A. Gaytie; <u>Policeman</u>
George Aubrey; <u>Peter</u> Master Common. <u>Marion Winyard</u>
Helen Forsyth; <u>Letitia Winyard</u> Mrs [George] Canninge;
<u>Jane</u> Eveline Faulkner; <u>Atalanta Woodcock</u> Rose Norreys/
Marie Dagmar. PP Edward Terry; <u>Mgr</u> Sydney Alport; <u>Sm</u>
Fred Thorne; <u>Pq</u> C.H. Fox; <u>Cost</u> Harrison. *REV: Ath 8/
10/92 p508; E 8/10/92 p9; St 6/10/92 p12-3, 3/11/92
p12-3; Th 1/11/92 p226-7; Ti 4/10/92 p4.*

92.290 *QUEER STREET* (DD,2a) "Richard Henry" [Richard
Butler & H. Chance Newton]. TERRY'S 3/10/92-31/10/92.
25 perf.** <u>Cholditch</u> Fred Thorne; <u>Wilson</u> Frank Curzon; <u>Deedley</u> Fred A. Gaytie; <u>Rasper</u> F. Hamilton Knight

<u>Mary</u> Florence Kingsley; <u>Dorcas</u> Eveline Faulkner. <u>PP</u>,
<u>Mgr</u>, <u>Sm</u>, <u>Pq</u>, <u>Cost</u> as for 92.289. *REV: E 8/10/92 p9.*

92.291 *THE BARONESS* (CO,3a) Cotsford Dick.   ROYALTY
5/10/92-19/10/92. 14 perf [w/mat 15/10].* <u>Baron
Narcissus</u> Charles Conyers/William Foxon; <u>Grand Duke</u>
Charles E. Stevens; <u>Bruno</u> Fred Emney; <u>Hamilcar</u> George
Grossmith, jr; <u>Ambrose</u> Percy Brough; <u>Count Lorenzo</u>
[Charles J.?] Magrath; <u>Count Alfonso</u> William Foxon;
<u>Beppo</u> Lionel Brough. <u>Lauretta</u> Jessie Moore; <u>Isabella</u>
Olga Schuberth; <u>Marietta</u> Constance Wallace; <u>Angeolo</u>
Gladys Rees; <u>Rodolfo</u> Susie Nainby; <u>Ralooka</u> Marian
Asquith; <u>Tancredo</u> Gertrude Hope; <u>Gabrielle</u> Agnes Gig-
lio; <u>Dancer</u> Violet Dene. <u>L</u> Kate Santley; <u>Mgr</u> Douglas
Vernon; <u>Dir</u> J.T. Tanner; <u>Bom</u> J.E. Wace; <u>Cost & Pq</u>
C.H. Fox; <u>Sc</u> Richard C. Durant; <u>Ch</u> Miss H. Abrahams;
<u>Mus dir</u> S. Liddle; <u>Asm</u> Henry Lowther; <u>Bm</u> Edwin Her-
bert. *REV: E 8/10/92 p11; St 13/10/92 p12-3; Th 1/11/
92 p236-7; Ti 6/10/92 p10.*

92.292 *INCOGNITA* (CO,3a) F.C. Burnand (lib) & Charles
Lecocq (mus) & Harry Greenbank (lyr).   LYRIC 6/10/92-
13/1/93. 101 perf [w/S mat; add mat 26/12/92].*
<u>Dom Pedro</u> Harry Monkhouse/A.T. Hendon; <u>Morales</u> O'Don-
oghue John Child; <u>Baldomero</u> Charles Gilbert; <u>Don
Guzman</u> O'Grandi Fred Kaye; <u>Dom Gaetan</u> Wallace Brown-
low; <u>Ion Marquis d'Asparagossa</u> Cairns James; <u>Dom Fia-
sco d'Oporto</u> A.T. Hendon; <u>Marquis d'Azuera Braganza</u>
Tom A. Shale; <u>Usher</u> Henry J. Nordblom; <u>Lord Chamber-
lain</u> Francis Beaufort. <u>Josefa</u> Aida Jenoure/Emmeline
Orford; <u>Dona Scholastica</u> Susie Vaughan; <u>Lola</u> Mimi St.
Cyr; <u>Estella Tintemarra</u> M.A. Victor; <u>Princess Micaela</u>
Sedohr Rhodes/Aida Jenoure/Nellie Stewart/Dora Thorne;
<u>Anita</u> Dora Thorne; <u>Dolores</u> Emmeline Orford/Maud Mal-
colm Watson; <u>Pepa</u> Cissie Cranford; <u>Inez</u> Rose Hamil-
ton. <u>L, MGR & DIR</u> Horace Sedger; <u>Sc</u> Walter Hann, Jetley, R.C. McCleery; <u>Ch</u> John d'Auban; <u>Cost dgn</u> Edel;
<u>Cost</u> Stagg & Mantle, Auguste, Alias; <u>Pq</u> William
Clarkson; <u>Mus dir</u> Herbert Bunning; <u>Bm & Treas</u> William
Greet. *REV: E 8/10/92 p15; SR 15/10/92 p444; St 13/
10/92 p12; Th 1/11/92 p237-8; Ti 7/10/92 p7.*

92.293 *DOROTHY VERNON* (RD,4a) James Wimsett Boulding.
SAVOY 6/10/92 mat perf. 1st perfd Prince of Wales's,

Ashton 4/10/89. Sir George Vernon Ian Robertson; Sir Thomas Stanley Lawrance d'Orsay; Edward Stanley Orlando Barnett; Ben Shaw Henry Bedford; Will Dawson A. Wood; Praddle Roger Roberts; Podger Anning; Groom Laurence Hanray; John Manners Philip Cunningham. Luce Mrs Edmund Phelps; Cecily G[eraldine] St. Maur; Dame Maud Glamoye; Margaret Marion Lind; Dorothy Sydney K. Phelps; Extras Clara Guilford, Lorraine Dreux, Laura Statham, Maud McNaught, Beatrice Grenville. PP & MGR Richard d'Oyly Carte; Bm Terry & Co.; Ch Mrs Vincent Glass; Cond R[osabel] Watson; Sm E. Edmonds; Cost Nathan; Pq William Clarkson. *REV: E 8/10/92 p10; St 13/10/92 p12; Th 1/11/92 p227-8.*

92.294 *ORFEO* (O[3a]) C.W. Gluck. COVENT GARDEN 10/10/ 92, 13/10, 17/10, 19/10, 21/10, 26/10, 2/11, 11/11, 18/11, 23/11, 1/12, 6/12, 10/12, 14/12(m), 20/12/92 (m). 15 perf.** Euridice Sofia Ravogli; L'Amore Mathilde Bauermeister; Orfeo Giulia Ravogli; 1ere Danseuse Stichel. L & MGR Augustus Harris; Cond Enrico Bevignani. *REV: Ath 15/10/92 p524; E 15/10/92 p15; St 13/10/92 p12, 20/10/92 p12; Ti 11/10/92 p4, 2/12/92 p6.*

92.295 *CAVALLERIA RUSTICANA* (O,1a) Pietro Mascagni. COVENT GARDEN 10/10/92, 13/10, 17/10, 19/10, 21/10, 26/10, 2/11, 5/11, 9/11(m), 10/11, 12/11(m), 15/11, 17/11, 19/11(m), 21/11, 23/11, 30/11, 6/12, 8/12, 10/12, 14/12(m), 20/12(m), 22/12(m), 30/12/92(m), 3/1/93 (m), 10/1(m), 28/1, 2/2/93. 28 perf.** Alfio Pignalosa/Eugene Dufriche; Turiddu Giuseppi Cremonini/Ferruccio Giannini/Morello. Santuzza Del Torre/ Rosita Sala/Esther Palliser; Lucia Mathilde Bauermeister/Biancoli; Lola Olimpia Guercia. L & MGR Augustus Harris; Cond Enrico Bevignani/Wilhelm Field. *REV: Ath 15/10/92 p524; E 15/10/92 p15; St 13/10/92 p12, 20/10/92 p12, 2/2/93 p14; Ti 11/10/92 p4.*

92.296 *PINK DOMINOS* (C,3a) James Albery. CRITERION 10/10/92-18/11/92. 39 perf [w/S mat exc 12/11]. 1st perfd Criterion 31/3/77. Charles Greythorne Fred Kerr; Sir Percy Wagstaff Herbert Standing; Joskin Tubbs Alfred Maltby; Harry Greenlanes Welton Dale; Brisket Sydney Valentine; 1st Waiter H[enry] Le Bre-

ton; 2nd Waiter Aukett. Lady Maggie Wagstaff Ellis
Jeffreys; Sophie Sybil Carlisle; Mrs Tubbs Fanny
Robertson; Rebecca Agnes Hewitt; Miss Barron Stella
Maris. L & MGR Charles Wyndham; Sm S.H.S. Austin;
Mus dir Theodore Ward; Act mgr & Treas E. Harvey.
*REV: E 15/10/92 p9; St 13/10/92 p12; Th 1/11/92 p233;
Ti 11/10/92 p4.*

92.297 *IL TROVATORE* (O[4a]) Giuseppe Verdi. COVENT
GARDEN 11/10/92, 14/10/92. 2 perf.** Il Conte di
Luna Innocente de Anna; Ferrando Antonio de Vaschetti;
Ruiz Rinaldini; Manrico Ferruccio Giannini. Leonora
Rosita Sala; Azucena Olimpia Guercia/Tremelli; Inez
Mathilde Bauermeister. L & MGR Augustus Harris; Cond
Enrico Bevignani. *REV: Ath 15/10/92 p524; E 15/10/92
p15; St 13/10/92 p12; Ti 13/10/92 p5.*

92.298 *LOHENGRIN* (O[3a]) Richard Wagner. COVENT GAR-
DEN 12/10/92, 18/10, 27/10, 7/11/92. 4 perf.** Tel-
ramondo Eugene Dufriche; Enrico l'Uccellatore Armand
Castelmary; L'Araldo del Re Abramoff; Lohengrin
Giuseppe Cremonini. Elsa Nellie Melba; Ortruda Olimpia
Guercia/Giulia Ravogli. L & MGR, Cond as for 92.297.
REV: E, St, Ti as for 92.297; Ath 15/10/92 p524-5.

92.299 *CUT OFF WITH A SHILLING* (Ca,1a) S. Theyre
Smith. SHAFTESBURY 14/10/92-3/12/92. 42 perf [np 24/
11].** Col. Berners Charles Collette; Sam Gaythorne
Oswald Yorke. Kitty Mary Collette. PP John Lancaster;
Gen mgr W.H. Griffiths; Asm Oswald Yorke; Treas & Sec
H.E. Marston.

92.300 *FAUST* (O[5a]) Charles Gounod. COVENT GARDEN
15/10/92, 20/10, 31/10, 19/11(2), 7/12/92, 6/1/93(m),
4/2/93. 8 perf.** Valentino Pignalosa/Aramis; Wagner Antonio de Vaschetti/Eugene Dufriche; Mefistofele
Armand Castelmary; Faust Ferruccio Giannini/Giuseppe
Cremonini. Margherita Nellie Melba/Esther Palliser;
Siebel Olimpia Guercia; Marta Mathilde Bauermeister/
Biancoli. L & MGR Augustus Harris; Cond Enrico Bevig-
nani/Feld. *REV: Ath 22/10/92 p560, 26/11/92 p748; E
22/10/92 p15, 26/11/92 p15; St 20/10/92 p12, 24/11/92
p12, 9/2/93 p12-3; Ti 17/10/92 p8, 2/12/92 p6, 6/2/93
p12.*

92.301 *IN TOWN* (MF,2a) Adrian Ross (lib) & "James Leader" [J.T. Tanner] (lib) & F. Osmond Carr (mus). PRINCE OF WALES'S 15/10/92-24/12/92;* trfd to GAIETY 26/12/92-18/8/93. 297 perf [w/S mat exc 15/10/92, 20/5/93, 10/6, 17/6, 24/6, 1/7, 8/7, 22/7, 29/7, 5/8, 12/8/93; add mat 21/12/92, 19/7/93; np 31/3/93, 6/7/ 93]. Cpt. Arthur Coddington Arthur Roberts/Arthur Playfair/Forbes Dawson; Benoli Harry Grattan/E[rnest] Cosham; Rev Samuel Hopkins Ernest Bantock/George Mudie; Duke of Duffshire Eric Lewis/Eric Thorne; Lord Alexander Kincaddie Master Douglas Patrick; Hoffman Fritz Rimma; Fritz E. Frazer; Driver F. Lovell; Bloggins Vaughan. Lord Clanside Phyllis Broughton; Flo Fanshawe Sylvia Grey; Shrimp Jennie Rogers/Florence Thropp; Duchess of Duffshire Maria Davis; Lady Gwendoline Belle Harcourt/Jessie Moore; Bob Maud Hobson; Billie Blanche Massey; Lottie Hetty Hamer; Clara Kate Cannon; Lillie Nellie Simmons; Kitty Hetherton Florence St. John/Edna Grace; Lady Evangeline D[aisy] Gilpin. L & MGR George Edwardes; Pp Edgar Bruce; Bm F.J. Harris; Sc Banks, William Telbin; Cost dgn Wilhelm; Cost Miss Fisher, Auguste, J.A. Harrison, Howell & James; Pq William Clarkson; Furn Lyon; Mus dir Sidney Jones; Treas E[dward] Marshall. *REV: E 22/ 10/92 p8, 15/4/93 p9, 15/7/93 p6; SR 22/10/92 p474; St 20/10/92 p12-3, 13/4/93 p13; Ti 17/10/92 p13, 4/8/ 93 p10; Th 1/11/92 p230.*

92.302 *EUGENE ONEGIN* (O,3a,7tab) Petr Ilyich Tchaikovsky [lib trans by Mr & Mrs Sutherland Edwards]. OLYMPIC 17/10/92, 20/10, 21/10, 24/10, 26/10, 28/10, 31/ 10/92. 7 perf. 1st perfd Moscow 29/3/79; 1st prof Bolshoi, Moscow 23/4/81. Lensky Iver McKay; Prince Gremin Charles Manners; Eugene Onegin Eugene Oudin; Vladimir Lensky [Edwin] Wareham; Zaretsky H[arrison] Brockbank; Cpt. Boujanoff G[eorge] Tate; Triquet James Appleton. Tatiana Fanny Moody; Olga Lily Moody; Larina Selma; Philipievna A. Sviatlovsky. PP Charles Wilmot; Mgr Lago; Cond Henry J. Wood; Dir Paul M. Berton; Act mgr J.S. Fleming; Furn Oetzmann. *REV: Ath 22/10/92 p560-1; E 22/10/92 p15; St 20/10/92 p13; Th 1/11/92 p238-9; Ti 18/10/92 p4.* Comment: Cast from V & A programme for 28/10/92.

92.303 *AGATHA TYLDEN, MERCHANT AND SHIPOWNER* (P,4a)
Edward Rose. HAYMARKET 18/10/92-10/12/92. 52 perf
[w/S mat exc 22/10, 3/12, 10/12].* Hugh Ainsworth
Lewis Waller; Granam Macfarlane Cyril Maude; Lord
Cyprian St. Osyth W.T. Lovell/Herbert Flemming; Evans
Fred A. Everill; Max Sonderhausen Edmund Maurice;
Christopherson Rudge Harding; Jabez Thompson William
Cheesman. Agatha Tylden Mrs Langtry; Winifred Marsh
Marie Linden. L H. Beerbohm Tree; Bom W.H. Leverton;
Sc Walter Johnstone; Pq William Clarkson; Elect E.
Wingfield Bowles; Sm Edward Hastings; Cond & Mus dir
Carl Armbruster; Bm & Sec Frederick Harrison. *REV:*
Ath 22/10/92 p561-2; E 22/10/92 p8; SR 22/10/92 p474;
St 20/10/92 p12; Th 1/11/92 p228-9; Ti 19/10/92 p5.

92.304 *LA FAVORITA* (O,4a) Gaetano Donizetti. OLYMPIC
18/10/92, 19/10/92. 2 perf.** Alfonso Mario Ancona;
Baldassare Luigi Rossato; Don Gasparo [James] Appleton; Fernando Bernado Zerni. Leonora Domenici; Inez
Biancoli; 1ere Danseuse Louise Loveday. MGR Lago;
Cond Luigi Arditi. *REV: Ath 22/10/92 p561; E 22/10/92*
p15; St 20/10/92 p13; Ti 24/10/92 p8.

92.305 *THE GUARDSMAN* (FP,3a) George R. Sims & Cecil
Raleigh. COURT 20/10/92-14/1/93. 82 perf [w/S mat exc
22/10, 31/12/92, 7/1/93; np 23-25/12/92].* Sir James
Bramston Arthur Cecil; Cpt. Sir Eustace Bramston W.G.
Elliott; Archibald Clinton Wilfred Draycott; Gen.
Kenneth Blazer C.P. Little; Martin Compton Coutts;
Miles Robert Nainby; Downes E[rnest] Bertram; Hanbury
Hakes Weedon Grossmith. Daphne Lovat Ellaline Terriss;
Kitty Masters Agnes Thomas; Lucy Greville Isabel
Ellissen; Thompson Irene Rickards; Lady Jones Caroline
Hill. L & MGR Arthur Chudleigh; Sc W[illiam] Callcott;
Cond Edward Jones; Cost Russell & Allen, Lewis &
Allenby, C.H. Fox, L. Nathan; Furn Marler & Bennett.
REV: Ath 29/10/92 p600; E 22/10/92 p11; SR 29/10/92
p507; St 27/10/92 p12-3; Th 1/11/92 p229; Ti 21/10/
92 p3.

92.306 *CRAZED* (Musical Absurdity,1a) A.R. Phillips.
COURT 20/10/92-14/1/93. 73 perf [np 23-25/12/92]. 1st
perfd Assembly Rooms, Wood Green 1/10/92. Mr Brown
C.P. Little; Mr Smith Robert Nainby. Sally Sybil Grey.

L & MGR, <u>Cond</u> as for 92.305. *REV: E, St as for 92.305.*

92.307 *THE DUCHESS OF MALFI* (T,5a) John Webster [new
ver by William Poel]. OPERA COMIQUE 21/10/92, 25/10/
92. 2 mat perf. 1st perfd c.1619. <u>Daniel de Bosola</u>
Murray Carson; <u>Ferdinand</u> Sydney Barraclough; <u>Cardinal</u>
Bassett Roe; <u>Antonio</u> F. Rawson Buckley; <u>Delio</u> Frank
H. Westerton; <u>Castruccio</u> G.H. Kersley; <u>Roderigo</u> Rex
Shirley; <u>Silvio</u> C.W. Perkins; <u>Grisolan</u> Alex Bradley;
<u>Infant</u> Master Ambrose Deane. <u>Cariola</u> Miss Hall Caine;
<u>Julia</u> Alice de Winton; <u>Duchess of Malfi</u> Mary Rorke;
<u>Nurse</u> Gauntlett. <u>DIR & TREAS</u> J.T. Grein; <u>L</u> Edward
Compton; <u>Act mgr</u> Charles Hoppe; <u>Mus</u> William S. Vinn-
ing; <u>Ch</u> Miss Elliott, Arthur Dillon; <u>Cost</u> William
Clarkson, Samuel May; <u>Cost dgn</u> Jennie Moore; <u>Pq</u>
William Clarkson; <u>Lime</u> H. Parnell; <u>Mach</u> R. Warton; <u>Sc</u>
F. Taylor; <u>Dir</u> William Poel, Paul M. Berton; <u>Cond</u> C.W.
Lamartine. *REV: Ath 29/10/92 p599-600; E 29/10/92 p9;
SR 29/10/92 p507; St 27/10/92 p13; Th 1/11/92 p230-1;
Ti 22/10/92 p6.* <u>Comment</u>: Independent Theatre Society.

92.308 *CARMEN* (O[4a]) Georges Bizet. COVENT GARDEN
22/10/92, 3/11, 5/12, 9/12, 28/12(m), 12/1(m); trfd
to PALACE 1/2/93(m). 7 perf.** <u>Escamillo</u> Eugene
Dufriche; <u>Dancairo</u> Caracciolo/Iginio Corsi; <u>Remendado</u>
Rinaldini; <u>Morales</u> Iginio Corsi/Caracciolo; <u>Zuniga</u>
Antonio de Vaschetti/Caracciolo; <u>Don José</u> Durward
Lely/Barton McGuckin/Giuseppe Cremonini/Morello. <u>Car-</u>
<u>men</u> Zelie de Lussan/Giulia Ravogli; <u>Michaela</u> Sofia
Ravogli/Esther Palliser; <u>Frasquita</u> Mathilde Bauer-
meister/Biancoli; <u>Mercedes</u> Sara Palma/Agnes Janson/
Bertinetti; <u>1ere Danseuses</u> Riganti, Stichel. <u>L & MGR</u>
Augustus Harris; <u>Cond</u> Enrico Bevignani/Wilhelm Field;
<u>Maitre de Ballet</u> Balbiani. *REV: Ath 29/10/92 p598; E
29/10/92 p15; St 27/10/92 p12; Ti 12/12/92 p8.*

92.309 *BEEF TEA* (Oa,1a) Harry Greenbank (lib) & Wilfrid Bendall (mus). LYRIC 22/10/92-13/1/93; 20/1/93-
4/3/93; 16/3/93-15/4/93. 132 perf [np 27-31/3/93].*
<u>Richard Plum</u> Charles Gilbert/Charles Crook; <u>Cpt.</u>
<u>Cherry Blossom</u> Frank A. Walsh; <u>Reuben Caldicott</u> H.
Gregory. <u>Mrs Blossom</u> Elena Monmouth; <u>Lottie</u> Rose Hamilton. <u>L & MGR</u> Horace Sedger; <u>Mus dir</u> Herbert Bunning;
<u>Bm</u> William Greet. *REV: Ti 28/10/92 p5.*

92.310 *LOHENGRIN* (O[3a]) Richard Wagner. OLYMPIC 22/
10/92, 27/10/92. 2 perf.** Federico di Telramondo
Mario Ancona; Enrico l'Uccellatore Charles Manners;
L'Araldo del Re M. Worlock; Lohengrin Bernado Zerni.
Elsa di Brabante Emma Albani; Ortruda Rita Elandi. PP
Charles Wilmot; Mgr Lago; Cond Luigi Arditi; Act mgr
J.S. Fleming; Furn Oetzmann. *REV: Ath 29/10/92 p598;*
E 29/10/92 p15; Ti 24/10/92 p8.

92.311 *RIGOLETTO* (O[3a]) Giuseppe Verdi. COVENT GAR-
DEN 24/10/92. 1 perf.** Duke Giuseppe Cremonini;
Sparafucile Abramoff; Rigoletto Eugene Dufriche. Gilda
Nellie Melba; Maddalena Olimpia Guercia; Mathilde
Bauermeister. L & MGR Augustus Harris; Cond Enrico
Bevignani. *REV: Ath 29/10/92 p598; E 29/10/92 p15;*
St 27/10/92 p12; Ti 25/10/92 p11.

92.312 *IL BARBIERE DI SIVIGLIA* (O[2a]) Gioacchino
Rossini. COVENT GARDEN 25/10/92, 28/10, 11/11, 15/11,
18/11/92. 5 perf.** Figaro Mariano Padilla; Bartolo
Caracciolo; Basilio Armand Castelmary; Fiorello Iginio
Corsi; Almaviva Francesco Pandolfini. Rosina Emma
Nevada; Berta Mathilde Bauermeister. L & MGR, Cond as
for 92.311. *REV: Ath, E, St as for 92.311; Ti 27/10/*
92 p8.

92.313 *L'IMPRESARIO* [*DER SCHAUSPIELDIREKTOR*] (O,1a) W.A.
Mozart. OLYMPIC 25/10/92, 1/11/92. 2 perf. 1st perfd
Schonbrum Palace, Vienna 7/2/1786. Filippo Edwin
Wareham; Wolfgang G[eorge] Tate; L'Avvisatore del
Teatro Bartlett; Director Frank Richard Temple. Mlle
Herz Elena Leila; Mme Lange M. Marra. MGR Lago; Pp
Charles Wilmot; Cond Mascheroni; Act mgr J.S. Fleming.
REV: Ath 29/10/92 p598; E 29/10/92 p15; St 27/10/92
p12; Ti 26/10/92 p6.

92.314 *CAEDMAR* (RD,1a) Granville Bantock. OLYMPIC 25/
10/92, 1/11/92. 2 perf. 1st perfd Crystal Palace 18/
10/92 [Nicoll indicates title was *Caedmon*]. Caedmar
C[harles] Harding; Andred Isidore Marcil. Hulda Marie
Duma. MGR, Pp, Act mgr as for 92.313; Cond Granville
Bantock. *REV: As for 92.313.*

92.315 *DON GIOVANNI* (O[2a]) W.A. Mozart. COVENT GARDEN

29/10/92, 8/11, 24/11/92. 3 perf.** <u>Don Ottavio</u> Pedro Guetary; <u>Leporello</u> Caracciolo; <u>Il Commendatore</u> Abramoff; <u>Masetto</u> Rinaldini; <u>Don Giovanni</u> Mariano Padilla. <u>Donna Anna</u> Louise Dotti; <u>Donna Elvira</u> Mathilde Bauermeister; <u>Zerlina</u> Zelie de Lussan/Giulia Ravogli. L & MGR Augustus Harris; <u>Cond</u> Enrico Bevignani. *REV: Ath 5/11/92 p637; E 5/11/92 p15; St 3/11/92 p12; Ti 2/11/92 p10.*

92.316 *MOTHS* (RD,4a) Henry Hamilton [adpt of Ouida, *Moths*]. LYRIC 29/10/92 mat perf.** <u>Prince Zouroff</u> Richard S. Boleyn; <u>Ivan</u> Sydney Herberte Basing; <u>Duke of Mull & Cantyre</u> Sydney Brough; <u>Lord Jura</u> F.H. Macklin; <u>Raphael de Correze</u> Lewis Waller. <u>Princess Nadine Nelaguine</u> Henrietta Lindley; <u>Vere Herbert</u> Beatrice Lamb; <u>Duchess de Sonnaz</u> Adrienne Dairolles; <u>Fuschia Leach</u> Fanny Brough; <u>Lady Dolly Vanderdecken</u> Carlotta Addison. L & MGR Horace Sedger; <u>Pp</u> Henry J. Leslie; <u>Pq</u> William Clarkson; <u>Furn</u> Oetzmann; <u>Sm</u> R.S. Boleyn; <u>Bm</u> William Greet.

92.317 *MARITANA* (O[3a]) Vincent Wallace. OLYMPIC 29/10/92, 2/11/92. 2 perf.** <u>Don Caesar de Bazan</u> Charles Harding; <u>King</u> Charles Manners; <u>Don Jose de Santarem</u> Eugene Oudin; <u>Marquis de Montefiore</u> H[arrison] Brockbank; <u>Cpt. of Guard</u> L. Vallence; <u>Alcade</u> Isidore Marcil. <u>Maritana</u> Fanny Moody; <u>Lazarillo</u> Lily Moody; <u>Marchioness de Montefiore</u> Kate Vito. PP Charles Wilmot; <u>Mgr</u> Lago; <u>Cond</u> Henry J. Wood; <u>Act mgr</u> J.S. Fleming; <u>Furn</u> Oetzmann. *REV: E 5/11/92 p15; St 3/11/92 p12.*

92.318 *UNCLE TOM'S CABIN* (D,3a) Charles Hermann [adpt of Mrs H.B. Stowe's novel]. PRINCESS'S 29/10/92-19/11/92. 22 perf [w/W mat]. 1st perfd Theatre Royal, Manchester 1/2/53. <u>Phineas Fletcher</u> Charles Hermann; <u>Uncle Tom</u> M[aurice] Drew; <u>Simon Legree</u> Bassett Roe; <u>Dan Haley</u> J. Brooke; <u>George Harris</u> Leonard Outram; <u>St. Clair</u> Gilbert Yorke; <u>Nicodemus Marks</u> Stanislaus Calhaem; <u>Ephraim Skeggs</u> George B. Lee; <u>Sambo</u> Joe Holly; <u>Jumbo</u> F. Berry; <u>Quimbo</u> J. Kavala; <u>Moses</u> Augustus James; <u>Pete</u> Tom Miller; <u>Adolphus</u> J.D. Johnson; <u>Julius Caesar</u> A. Wilson. <u>Eliza Harris</u> Mrs Charles Hermann; <u>Cassy</u> Frances Ivor; <u>Aunt Ophelia</u> E. Brunton; <u>Topsy</u> Nellie Christie; <u>Aunt Chloe</u> Becky White; <u>Eva</u>

Edie King; Emmeline Casandra James; Dinah Kitty Port-
er; Mercy Mary St. Just. L & MGR Rollo Balmain; Cond
A. Vorzanger; Act mgr Alfred Bishop; Bm G.M. Polini.
REV: E 5/11/92 p9; St 3/11/92 p12.

92.319 *KIT MARLOWE* (P,1a) W.L. Courtney. ST. JAMES'S
31/10/92-26/11/92. 26 perf [w/mat 12/11, 26/11].**
Christopher Marlowe George Alexander; Thomas Nash
Vernon Sansbury; Edward Alleyn Alfred Holles; Henry
Chettle A. Vane-Tempest; Francis Archer H.H. Vincent.
Nan Edith Chester/Marion Terry. L & MGR George Alex-
ander; Sm Robert V. Shone; Bm Alwyn Lewis; Mus dir
Walter Slaughter. *REV: Ath 5/11/92 p637; E 5/11/92
p9; SR 19/11/92 p592; St 3/11/92 p12; Th 1/12/92 p
274-5.*

92.320 *TRISTAN UND ISOLDE* (O[3a]) Richard Wagner.
COVENT GARDEN 1/11/92, 5/11(m), 12/11, 16/11/92. 4
perf.** Tristan Alfred Oberlander; Kurvenal David
Bispham; King Marke Abramoff; Melot Karlyle; Shepherd
H. Phillips; Steersman Kaspar. Brungane Esther Pal-
liser; Isolde Pauline Cramer. L & MGR Augustus Harris;
Cond Carl Armbruster. *REV: Ath 5/11/92 p637; E 5/11/
92 p15; St 3/11/92 p12; Ti 2/11/92 p10, 7/11/92 p12.*

92.321 *WITHERED LEAVES* (Ca,1a) Frederick W. Broughton.
TERRY'S 1/11/92-26/11/92. 23 perf. 1st perfd Theatre
Royal, Sheffield 5/4/75. Tom Conyers Frank Curzon;
Sir Conyers Conyers Nicol Pentland; Cecil Vane W.
Lacy Barnett; Arthur Middleton Charles S. Fawcett.
May Rivers Evelyn Faulkner; Lady Conyers Carrie Cro-
nyn. MGR Sydney Alport; Sm Fred Thorne; Pq C.H. Fox;
Cost Harrison. *REV: E 5/11/92 p9; St 3/11/92 p13.*

92.322 *IL FLAUTO MAGICO [DIE ZAUBERFLOTE]* W.A. Mozart.
OLYMPIC 3/11/92. 1 perf. 1st perfd Theater auf der
Wieden, Vienna 30/9/1791. Sarastro Charles Manners;
Tamino F. Pearce; Monastatos G[eorge] Tate; Papageno
M. Worlock; L'Oratore Isidore Marcil; Due Uomini Ar-
mati Edwin Wareham, L. Vallence; Due Oratori James
Appleton, H[arrison] Brockbank. Astrifiammante Elena
Leila; Pamina Marie Duma; I Tre Geni Kate Vito,
C[ecile] Brani, R. Pounds; Papagena C[arla] Dagmar;
Tre Damigelle delle Regina M. Marra, Biancoli, A.

Sviatlovsky. PP Charles Wilmot; Mgr Lago; Cond Luigi Arditi; Act mgr J.S. Fleming; Furn Oetzmann. *REV: E 5/11/92 p15; St 10/11/92 p12; Ti 4/11/92 p7.*

92.323 *THE MARTYR* (F,1a) Templeton Lucas. VAUDEVILLE 3/11/92-4/3/93. 102 perf [np 22-25/12/92]. 1st perfd Court 22/1/72 [as *Browne the Martyr*]. Edward Browne Charles Ashford; Terebinth Topperton Duncan Fleet. Mrs Browne Marie Abington/Geraldine St. Maur. L & MGR A. & S. Gatti; Mus dir Henry Sprake; Asm Charles Ashford; Act mgr & Treas L[ouis] F. Nethersole. *REV: E 5/11/92 p9, 4/2/93 p9; St 10/11/92 p13; Ti 4/11/92 p7.*

92.324 *AIDA* (O[4a]) Giuseppe Verdi. COVENT GARDEN 4/ 11/92, 14/11/92. 2 perf.** Radames Ferruccio Giannini; Amonasro Eugene Dufriche; Il Re Antonio de Vaschetti; Il Messagiero Rinaldini; Ramfis Abramoff. Aida Nellie Melba; Sacerdotessa Mathilde Bauermeister; Amneris Giulia Ravogli/Olimpia Guercia. L & MGR Augustus Harris; Cond Enrico Bevignani. *REV: Ath 12/11/ 92 p672; E 12/11/92 p15; St 10/11/92 p12; Ti 7/11/92 p12.*

92.325 *THE ARABIAN NIGHTS* (FC,3a) Sydney Grundy [fnd on von Moser, *Haroun Alraschid*]. COMEDY 5/11/92-26/ 11/92. 21 perf [w/mat 19/11, 26/11]. 1st perfd Globe 5/11/87. Arthur Hummington Charles H. Hawtrey; Joshua Gillibrand W.S. Penley; Dobson William Wyes; Ralph Ormerod James Nelson. Mrs Hummington Vane Featherston; Mrs Gillibrand Lizzie Henderson; Daisy Maitland Nina Boucicault; Barbara Eva Williams; Rosa Colombier Lottie Venne. MGR Charles H. Hawtrey; Mus dir George Bonner; Asm Charles Milton; Bm E.F. Bradley. *REV: E 12/11/92 p8; SR 12/11/92 p565; St 10/11/ 92 p13; Th 1/1/93 p63; Ti 7/11/92 p12.*

92.326 *MY LORD IN LIVERY* (Ca,1a) S. Theyre Smith. COMEDY 5/11/92-26/11/92; 5/12/92-7/1/93. 48 perf [np 24-25/12/92]. 1st perfd Princess's 9/10/86. Lord Thirlmere James Nelson; Spiggott William Wyes; Hopkins Frederick Glover; Robert Master Turner. Sybil Amberley Vane Featherston; Laura Nancy Noel; Rose Eva Williams. MGR, Mus dir, Asm, Bm as for 92.325. *REV: E, St as for 92.325.*

92.327 *THE BOHEMIAN GIRL* (O[3a]) Michael Balfe. COVENT GARDEN 5/11/92, 10/11, 17/11/92. 3 perf.** <u>Thaddeus</u> Henry Piercy; <u>Count Arnheim</u> D. Ffrangcon Davies; <u>Florestan</u> Wilfred Esmond; <u>Devilshoof</u> Albert McGuckin. <u>Queen of the Gipsies</u> Agnes Janson; <u>Arline</u> Charlotte Walker. L & MGR Augustus Harris; <u>Cond</u> John Crook. *REV: E 12/11/92 p15; Ti 7/11/92 p12.*

92.328 *THE BURGLAR AND THE JUDGE* (P,1a) F.C. Phillips & Charles H.E. Brookfield. HAYMARKET 5/11/92-10/12/92. 31 perf.* <u>Mr Justice Gyves</u> Cyril Maude; <u>Parkhurst</u> William Cheesman; <u>Joe</u> Charles H.E. Brookfield/William H. Day. L H. Beerbohm Tree; <u>Mgr</u> Mrs Langtry; <u>Bom</u> W.H. Leverton; <u>Pq</u> William Clarkson; <u>Elect</u> E. Wingfield Bowles; <u>Sm</u> Edward Hastings; <u>Mus dir</u> Carl Armbruster; <u>Bm & Sec</u> Frederick Harrison. *REV: Ath 12/11/92 p673; E 12/11/92 p9; SR 12/11/92 p565; St 10/11/92 p12; Th 1/12/92 p277-8; Ti 7/11/92 p12.*

92.329 *YOU MUSTN'T LAUGH* (FC,3a) A. Lubimoff. OPERA COMIQUE 5/11/92-14/11/92. 9 perf [w/mat 12/11].* <u>Geoffrey Swift</u> T.B. Thalberg; <u>Pythagoras Teazle</u> Julian Cross; <u>Profundus Deep</u> Orlando Barnett; <u>Dr Pfefforkorn</u> Watty Brunton, sr; <u>Stephens McStopper</u> Frank McRae. <u>Seraphina</u> Annie Hughes; <u>Elizabeth Hopkins</u> Florence Haydon; <u>Ruby</u> Kate Bealby; <u>Florence Richmond</u> Florence Fordyce; <u>Annie</u> Thea Lesbrooke; <u>Laura</u> Honoria Ward; <u>Jane</u> Kathleen Bristowe; <u>Eliza</u> Maud Vivian; <u>Mrs Maria Grumble</u> Mrs Edmund Phelps; <u>Margharet</u> Little Daisy Stratton. MGR Robert Lody; L Edward Compton; <u>Cond</u> Charles Dubois; <u>Asm</u> Austin Leigh; <u>Act mgr</u> Francis Gosnay; <u>Treas</u> A.H. Morice; <u>Furn</u> Henry Deares; <u>Pq & Cost</u> William Clarkson; <u>Dir</u> Gospodin Lubimoff. *REV: Ath 12/11/92 p673; E 12/11/92 p8; St 10/11/92 p12; Ti 7/11/92 p12.* <u>Comment</u>: Title altered later to *A Close Shave.*

92.330 *MONSIEUR JACQUES* (Pathetic MP,1a) Morris Barnett. OPERA COMIQUE 5/11/92-14/11/92. 8 perf. 1st perfd St. James's 13/1/36. <u>Monsieur Jacques</u> Gospodin Lubimoff; <u>Sequence</u> Julian Cross; <u>Vivid</u> Austin Leigh; <u>Antonio</u> Watty Brunton, sr. <u>Nina</u> Helen Carroll. MGR, L, <u>Furn</u>, <u>Pq & Cost</u>, <u>Cond</u>, <u>Asm</u>, <u>Treas</u>, <u>Act mgr</u> as for 92. 329. *REV: E 12/11/92 p8; St 10/11/92 p12-3.*

92.331 *AULD LANG SYNE* (Ca) Basil Hood. PRINCE OF
WALES'S 5/11/92-30/3/93. 124 perf [np 3/3/93].* Hon
Jack Boothroyd Harry Grattan/F. Vaughan; George Fel-
lowes Graham Wentworth. Marion Blyth Maud Hobson;
Lucy Lilian Leath. L & MGR George Edwardes; Pp Edgar
Bruce; Bm F.J. Harris; Mus dir Sidney Jones; Sm [F.]
Vaughan; Treas E[dward] Marshall. *REV: E 12/11/92 p8.*

92.332 *DAVID* (P,4a) Louis N. Parker & "Thornton
Clark" [Murray Carson]. GARRICK 7/11/92-17/12/92. 38
perf [w/mat 19/11, 26/11].* Dr Wendover Murray Car-
son; David da Silva Herbert Waring; Col. Hood John
Beauchamp; Gilliar Grenfell [Alfred] Bucklaw. Paget
Lillian Lee; Dorothy Wendover Estelle Burney; Mrs
Grenfell Kate Bateman. L & MGR John Hare; Act mgr
C.G. Compton; Cond de Tender; Sc William Harford. *REV:*
Ath 12/11/92 p673-4, 26/11/92 p749-50; E 12/11/92 p8;
SR 26/11/92 p619; St 10/11/92 p12; Th 1/12/92 p275-7;
Ti 8/11/92 p10.

92.333 *A CAPRICE* (DSk,1a) Justin Huntly McCarthy.
GARRICK 7/11/92-17/12/92. 38 perf [w/mat 19/11, 26/
11].** Henri de Chavigny William Herbert. Mme de
L'Hery Estelle Burney; Mathilde Rose Nesbitt. L & MGR,
Act mgr, Cond, Sc as for 92.332. *REV: E 12/11/92 p8.*

92.334 *L'AMICO FRITZ* (O[3a]) Pietro Mascagni. COVENT
GARDEN 9/11/92, 21/11, 26/11, 30/11, 22/12/92(m),
3/1/93(m), 10/1(m), 28/1, 2/2/93. 9 perf.** Fritz
Giuseppe Cremonini/Ferruccio Giannini/Pedro Guetary;
Rabbino Eugene Dufriche/Pignalosa; Hanezo Antonio de
Vaschetti/Caracciolo; Federico Iginio Corsi. Beppe
Olimpia Guercia/Giulia Ravogli; Caterina Mathilde
Bauermeister/Biancoli; Suzel Del Torre. L & MGR Augus-
tus Harris; Cond Enrico Bevignani. *REV: Ath 12/11/92*
p672; E 12/11/92 p15; St 17/11/92 p12-3, 2/2/93 p14;
Ti 11/11/92 p12.

92.335 *KING LEAR* (T,5a) William Shakespeare. LYCEUM
10/11/92-1/2/93; 13/2, 20/2, 27/2, 6/3/93. 76 perf
[mat only 3/12/92, 24/12, 31/12/92, 14/1/93, 21/1].
1st perfd 1605. Lear Henry Irving/W.J. Holloway;
Edgar William Terriss; Edmund Frank [Kemble] Cooper;
Gloster Alfred Bishop; Kent W.J. Holloway; Cornwall

[Clarence] Hague; <u>Albany</u> [Frank] Tyars; <u>King of France</u>
Percival; <u>Burgundy</u> [Acton] Bond; <u>Curan</u> John Martin
Harvey; <u>Old Man</u> [Henry] Howe; <u>Fool</u> [William] Haviland;
<u>Oswald</u> Gordon Craig; <u>Physician</u> Lacy; <u>Knight</u> [R.P.]
Tabb; <u>Gentleman</u> Ian Robertson; <u>Officer</u> [W.J.] Lorriss;
<u>Herald</u> [W. Lionel] Belmore; <u>Messenger</u> Powell. <u>Goneril</u>
Ada Dyas; <u>Regan</u> Maud Milton; <u>Cordelia</u> Ellen Terry.
L & MGR Henry Irving; <u>Sc</u> Joseph Harker, Hawes Craven;
<u>Dgn</u> Ford Madox Brown; <u>Mus</u> J. Hamilton Clark, J. Mere-
dith Ball; <u>Cost dgn</u> Charles Cattermole, Mrs J.W. Comyns Carr; <u>Cost</u> Auguste, Mrs Nettleship, Mrs Reid; <u>Pq</u>
C.H. Fox; <u>Furn</u> Arnott; <u>Mach</u> Fillery; <u>Cond</u> J. Meredith
Ball; <u>Chorus Master</u> [R.P.] Tabb; <u>Sm</u> H.J. Loveday; <u>Act</u>
<u>mgr</u> Bram Stoker; <u>Bom</u> Joseph Hurst. *REV: Ath 19/11/92*
p712; E 12/11/92 p10; SR 19/11/92 p586-7, 10/12/92
676-7; St 17/11/92 p12; Th 1/12/92 p278-80; Ti 11/11/
92 p10.

92.336 *WHO IS SYLVIA?* (Ca,1a) "Austin Fryers" [W.E.
Clery]. OPERA COMIQUE 12/11/92 mat perf.* <u>Archie</u>
<u>Ford</u> Austin Fryers. <u>Nellie Foster</u> Florence Fordyce.
REV: E 19/11/92 p9.

92.337 *THE STATUE OF ALBEMARLE* (MF,1a) Mrs Bernard
Whishaw (lib) & Fred Whishaw (mus). TRAFALGAR SQUARE
16/11/92 mat perf.* <u>Waldegrave</u> Fred Whishaw; <u>Elphin-</u>
<u>stone</u> C. Royelle; <u>Horace</u> Brandreth; <u>Antony</u> H.C. Ma-
rillier; <u>Reginald</u> [Leon?] Baring; <u>Master of Albemarle</u>
<u>College</u> Arthur Somerville; <u>Senior Proctor</u> George T.
Minshull; <u>Junior Proctor</u> Richard H. Douglass; <u>Under-</u>
<u>graduates</u> Price, Summers, Johnson, James. <u>Priscilla</u>
Clare Solomon; <u>Gertrude</u> da Costa; <u>Jemima</u> Isabel Grey;
<u>Margaret</u> Isabel Rayner; <u>Gloriana</u> Hilda Burleigh; <u>Wini-</u>
<u>fred</u> M[ay] Carleton; <u>Katharine</u> Olive Owen; <u>Mistress</u>
<u>of Albemarle College</u> [Winifred] Newton; <u>Dorothy</u> Syl-
via Grey; <u>Undergraduates</u> [Helen] Fairlie, Ashmead,
Lane, Stewart, Kavanagh, Ida Wallace. PP Mr & Mrs
Frank Wyatt; <u>Bm</u> Arthur Blackmore; <u>Mgr</u> Michael Leven-
ston; <u>Cost</u> Harrison; <u>Pq</u> C.H. Fox; <u>Pd</u> George Capel;
<u>Mus dir</u> Orellana. *REV: E 19/11/92 p11; St 17/11/92 p13.*

92.338 *MA MIE ROSETTE* (Romantic CO,2a) George Dance
(lib) & Ivan Caryll (mus) [fr lib of Preval & Liorat,
& mus of Paul Lacome]. GLOBE 17/11/92-21/12/92 [w/

mat 17/12];* trfd to PRINCE OF WALES'S 26/12/92-25/
2/93 [w/S mat]. 94 perf. Henri IV of France Eugene
Oudin/Robert Scott-Fishe; Vincent Courtice Pounds;
Bouillon Frank Wyatt; Moustajon Cairns James; Col.
Cognac Lawrance d'Orsay; Segur Robert Scott-Fishe/Vera
Dudley; Winyar W. Rolph/A[lfred?] Warner. Rosette
Juliette Nesville; Martha Jessie Bond; Corisande
Jennie McNulty; Therese Florence Melville; Nichette
Day Ford/Lily Lewis; Clochette Marie Brooke/Blanche
Whyte; Petan Blanche Winter; Alphonse Rita Paton.
MGR John Lart, William Bonney; Cond Ivan Caryll; Dir
Thomas W. Charles; Bom Watts; Act mgr H.T. Brickwell;
Sc Bruce Smith; Cost dgn Howell Russell; Cost Alias,
Harrisons; Ch Mlle Rosa; Pq William Clarkson; Furn
Lyons; Treas A.S. Fehrman; Asm F. Highland. *REV: E
19/11/92 p10; SR 26/11/92 p620; St 24/11/92 p12-3;
Th 1/1/93 p56-7; Ti 18/11/92 p10.*

92.339 *THE COUNTY COUNCILLOR* (F,3a) H. Graham. STRAND
18/11/92 mat perf. 1st prof. Robert Faddicum E.W.
Garden; Detective-Inspector Catchpole Ernest Hendrie;
Dick Wellington Yorke Stephens; Tom Doubleton William
Bonney; Jack Wilding Roland Atwood; William Cripps
W[illiam] Lestocq; Cabman Charles Davies. Lottie Sin-
gleton Fanny Brough; Mrs Perks Nelly Williams; Mabel
Faddicum Maud Douglas; Kitty Nellie Dallas. L & MGR
Willie Edouin; Pp J.S. Clarke; Bm Lilford Arthur;
Cond Ernest Bucalossi. *REV: Ath 26/11/92 p749; E 19/
11/92 p11; SR 26/11/92 p619; St 24/11/92 p13; Th 1/1/
93 p56.*

92.340 *THE OLD LADY* (C,3a) C. Haddon Chambers. CRITER-
ION 19/11/92-3/12/92. 13 perf.* Col. Lund W.H. Vernon; Count de Chartres Herbert Standing; Charley Ara-
thoon Fred Kerr; Barker Sydney Valentine; McDoggerty
David S. James; Croupier Herman de Lange; Mr Smythe
Welton Dale. Mlle le Grande Rosina Filippi; Margery
Lund Ellis Jeffreys; Miss Lund Mrs John Wood. L & MGR
Charles Wyndham; Sm S.H.S. Austin; Cond A. Evans; Act
mgr & Treas E. Harvey; Sc Harry Potts; Furn W. White-
ley. *REV: Ath 26/11/92 p749; E 26/11/92 p9; SR 26/
11/92 p619; St 24/11/92 p12; Th 1/1/93 p57.*

92.340B *MASKS AND FACES* (C,3a) Tom Taylor & Charles

Reade. ROYALTY 21/11/92-25/11/92. 6 perf [w/mat 22/
11]. 1st perfd Haymarket 20/11/52. Sir Charles Poman-
der H. Seymour Hughes; Ernest Vane T. Comyn Platt;
Colley Cibber C.O. Skilbeck; Quin A. Cameron Skinner;
Triplet William [Gayer] MacKay; Lysimachus Triplet
Master Harry Rignold; Snarl Charles Wills; Soaper
J.B. Edwards; James Burdock Charles Steyne; Colander
Ernest F. Burchatt; Hunsdon W. Staunton; Call Boy/
Pompey Master Roland Bottomley. Mistress Vane Mrs
Herbert Morris; Kitty Clive Nellie Pollard; Mrs Trip-
let Beatrice Ward; Roxalana Triplet Rosina Begarnie;
Peg Woffington Mrs Arthur Ayers. L Kate Santley; Dir
H. Seymour Hughes; Ch Willie Warde; Cond Mortlake
Mann; Sm Alfred Phillips; Bm L.F. Chapuy; Pq William
Clarkson; Cost Nathan; Bom Arthur Frye. *REV: Referee
20/11/92 p2.*

92.341 *OTELLO* (O[4a]) Giuseppe Verdi. COVENT GARDEN
22/11/92, 25/11/92. 2 perf.** Otello Ferruccio
Giannini; Cassio Iginio Corsi; Rodrigo Rinaldini;
Ludovico Abramoff; Montano Antonio de Vaschetti; Un
Araldo Cernusco; Jago Eugene Dufriche. Emilia Olimpia
Guercia; Desdemona Nellie Melba. L & MGR Augustus
Harris; Cond Enrico Bevignani. *REV: Ath 26/11/92 p748;
E 26/11/92 p15; St 24/11/92 p12; Ti 21/11/92 p10, 14/
11/92 p7.*

92.342 *KIT MARLOWE* (P,1a) W.L. Courtney. DRURY LANE
24/11/92 mat perf.** Christopher Marlowe George
Alexander; Thomas Nash Vernon Sansbury; Edward Alleyn
Alfred Holles; Henry Chettle A. Vane-Tempest; Francis
Archer H.H. Vincent. Nan Marion Terry. L & MGR Augus-
tus Harris; Sm Arthur P. Collins; Asm N[apier] Barry;
Mus dir John Crook; Accompanists Walter Slaughter,
Walter Pallant, James M. Glover; Cost Mrs May, Harris-
son, Morris Angel; Pq William Clarkson, C.H. Fox;
Bom Walker. *REV: E 26/11/92 p9.*

92.343 *THE BURGLAR AND THE JUDGE* F.C. Phillips &
Charles H.E. Brookfield. DRURY LANE 24/11/92 mat
perf.** Mr Justice Gyves Cyril Maude; Parkhurst
William Cheesman; Joe Charles H.E. Brookfield. L &
MGR, Sm, Asm, Accompanists, Cost, Pq, Bom as for 92.
342. *REV: E 26/11/92 p9.*

92.344 *THE UP TRAIN* (Sk) C.P. Colnaghi. DRURY LANE
24/11/92 mat perf.** <u>Gentleman</u> Cairns James; <u>Porter</u>
W. Rolph. <u>Lady</u> Jessie Moore. <u>L & MGR</u>, <u>Sm</u>, <u>Asm</u>, <u>Accom-
panists</u>, <u>Cost</u>, <u>Pq</u>, <u>Bom</u> as for 92.342. *REV: E 26/22/
92 p9.*

92.345 *HOODMAN BLIND* (D,5a) H.A. Jones & Wilson Barrett. PRINCESS'S 26/11/92-10/12/92. c.13 perf. 1st
perfd Princess's 18/8/85. <u>Jack Yeulett</u> Rollo Balmain; <u>Ben Chibbles</u> George Barrett; <u>Mark Lezzard</u>
Bassett Roe; <u>Tom Lattiker</u> Leonard Outram; <u>Kridge</u>
Maurice Drew; <u>Mad Willy</u> Gilbert Yorke; <u>Mr Lendon</u> Edward Butler; <u>Jim Dadge</u> John Brooks; <u>Noah Quodling</u>
Stanislaus Calhaem; <u>Joe Swirrup</u> Bernard Mervyn;
<u>Ephraim Beever</u> Harding Thomas; <u>Jelks</u> Wensley Thomp-
son; <u>Abe Chawner</u> F. Laudry; <u>Inspector Jermin</u> H. Scott;
<u>Johnny Twite</u> Haliday; <u>Attendant</u> Felton; <u>Footman</u>
Crostley; <u>Policeman</u> G. Aubrey; <u>Bob Swirrup</u> Master Sus-
sums. <u>Nance Yeulett/Jess</u> Sara Mignon; <u>Tomtit</u> Maudie
King; <u>Polly Chibbles</u> Carlotta de Yonson; <u>Granny Quod-
ling</u> Mrs Edward Butler; <u>Mrs Beever</u> Marie Sutherland;
<u>Mrs Chawner</u> Eva Rayner; <u>Liz</u> Sinclair; <u>Kitty</u> Pauline
Edith Fuel; <u>Mrs Joe Swirrup</u> F. Waters; <u>Dancer</u> P. Lester; <u>Kit</u> Amy Rayner. <u>L & MGR</u> Rollo Balmain; <u>Pp</u> Mrs
Harriet Gooch; <u>Bm</u> G.M. Polini; <u>Bom</u> Arthur Frye; <u>Act
mgr</u> S. Pemberton; <u>Mus dir</u> Charles Dubois; <u>Asm</u> B[er-
nard] Mervyn; <u>Advertising mgr</u> C. Stuart. *REV: Ath
3/12/92 p788; E 3/12/92 p9; St 1/12/92 p12; Th 1/1/
93 p65; Ti 28/11/92 p12.*

92.346 *DOROTHY* (CO,3a) B.C. Stephenson (lib) & Alfred
Cellier (mus). TRAFALGAR SQUARE 26/11/92-17/12/92.
19 perf. 1st perfd Gaiety 25/9/86. <u>Geoffrey Wilder</u>
Joseph Tapley; <u>Harry Sherwood</u> Leonard Russell; <u>Squire
Bantam</u> J. Furneaux Cook; <u>Tom Strutt</u> John Le Hay; <u>John
Tuppitt</u> Frank Lacy; <u>Lurcher</u> William Elton. <u>Dorothy
Bantam</u> Decima Moore; <u>Mrs Privett</u> M.A. Victor; <u>Phyllis
Tuppitt</u> Lucy Carr Shaw; <u>Lady Betty</u> Yata Whynier;
<u>Lydia Hawthorne</u> Florence Dysart; <u>Dancer</u> Mabel Love.
<u>L & MGR</u> Michael Levenston; <u>Mus dir</u> Ernest Ford; <u>Pp</u>
Mr & Mrs Frank Wyatt; <u>Act mgr</u> Arthur Blackmore; <u>Eng</u>
Arthur H. Vesey; <u>Sc</u> E.G. Banks; <u>Ch</u> John d'Auban;
<u>Cost</u> Harrisons; <u>Pq</u> William Clarkson; <u>Bom</u> W[alter]
Hamilton. *REV: E 3/12/92 p9; St 1/12/92 p12; Th 1/1/*

93 p63-4; Ti 28/11/92 p12.

92.347 *THE SERIOUS FAMILY* (C,3a) Morris Barnett [adpt fr *Le Mari à la Campagne*]. NOVELTY 28/11/92-10/12/92; 17/12/92(m). 13 perf.** Cpt. Murphy Maquire Walter Howard; Charles Torrens Frank Beresford; Aminadab Sleek Matthews Monck; Frank Vincent Charles Hunting-don; Danvers Tyssil Young. Mrs Ormsby Delmaine Nora Meredith; Mrs Charles Torrens Anna Elstob; Emma Torrens Alice Buckland; Lady Sowerby Creamly Gordon Gray; Graham Maud Booth. L & MGR Matthews Monck. *REV: E 3/12/92 p9; St 1/12/92 p12-3.*

92.348 *FAMILY JARS* (F,1a) Joseph Lunn. NOVELTY 28/11/92. Rnd. 1st perfd Haymarket 26/8/22. Mr Porcelain Charles Lerigo; Benedict Frank Huntingdon; Delph J.W. Richards; Diggory Tyssil Young; Porter Marston. Emily Alice Buckland; Liddy Larragan Marie Martell. *REV: As for 92.347.*

92.349 *FROM GULF TO GULF* (P,4a) Henry John Smith. AVENUE 29/11/92 mat perf.* Earl of Montreal Graham Wentworth; Clarence Falkland T.B. Thalberg; Lawdon Campbell Gollan; Sir Francis Dale Wilfred Winton; Sir Henry Vane R. Lambert; Sir Percy Austin H. Wenman; Lord Esk Manners; Lord Fenwicke G.H. Kersley; Tracy Julian Cross; Stanly A. Wood; Job John Carter; Servant W. Chandler. Eveline Davies Webster; Lady St. Claire Kate Calton; Lady Marchmont F. Leclercq; Lady Vane D. Danvers; Nora Henrietta Cross. L George Paget; Mgr Harrington Baily; Dir Julian Cross; Cost Mrs May; Pq C.H. Fox; Furn Oetzmann; Cond T. Smyth. *REV: Ath 3/12/92 p788; E 3/12/92 p10; St 1/12/92 p13; Th 1/1/93 p58.*

92.350 *LIBERTY HALL* (C,4a) R.C. Carton. ST. JAMES'S 3/12/92-20/5/93. 182 perf [w/S mat exc 3/12; add mat 26/12, 28/12/92, 4/1/93, 11/1, 18/1, 25/1, 26/1, 1/2, 8/2, 22/2, 1/3, 8/3, 15/3, 3/4, 12/4, 19/4, 26/4/93; np 24/12/92, 30-31/3/93].* Mr Owen George Alexander; Mr Pedrick Nutcombe Gould/Murray Hathorn; J. Briginshaw H.H. Vincent; Hon Gerald Harringay Ben Webster; Mr Hickson Alfred Holles; Luscombe Vernon Sansbury/S. Norbury; Robert Binks Master Richard Sa-

ker; <u>William Todman</u> Edward Righton. <u>Crafer</u> Fanny Cole-
man; <u>Amy Chilworth</u> Maude Millett/Ailsa Craig; <u>Miss</u>
<u>Hickson</u> Aisla Craig/Winifred Dolan; <u>Blanche Chilworth</u>
Marion Terry/Charlotte Granville. L & MGR George
Alexander; <u>Sm</u> Robert V. Shone; <u>Bm</u> Alwyn Lewis; <u>Mus dir</u>
<u>& Mus</u> Walter Slaughter; <u>Furn</u> Frank Giles; <u>Cost</u> Mme
Savage, Mme Purdue, Mme Yorke; <u>Pq</u> C.H. Fox; <u>Sc</u> H.P.
Hall. *REV: Ath 10/12/92 p827; E 10/12/92 p9; Sk 10/5/*
93 p77; SR 10/12/92 p684-5; St 8/12/92 p12; Th 1/1/93
p58-60; Ti 5/12/92 p10.

92.351 *TO-DAY* (C,3a) Charles H.E. Brookfield [adpt
of Victorien Sardou & Emile de Najac, *Divorçons*].
COMEDY 5/12/92-7/1/93. 31 perf [w/mat 17/12, 31/12;
np 24-25/12].* <u>Bertie Twyford</u> Charles H.E. Brook-
field; <u>Arthur Dismore</u> James Nelson; <u>Chauncey Chatwin</u>
William Wyes; <u>Martin</u> Charles Milton; <u>Charles Prothero</u>
Charles H. Hawtrey; <u>Hughie</u> C[harles] Meyrick; <u>Claudie</u>
Harley Granville-Barker; <u>Johnnie</u> George Grossmith, jr;
<u>Cis</u> Arthur Royston; <u>Emile</u> Wilton Heriot; <u>Anglo-Indian</u>
H. Hudson; <u>American Tourist</u> E[rnest] Percy; <u>Epicure</u>
D. Richardson; <u>Admirer</u> E.H. Kelly; <u>Two Friends</u> G.E.
Shepheard, R[ussell] Vaun; <u>Portuguese</u> R. Malone, N.
Gilbert; <u>Very Young Man</u> L. Harbrod; <u>Page</u> Master Turn-
er; <u>Karl</u> Langham; <u>Hippolyte</u> Straahn; <u>Fritz</u> Schultze;
<u>Peter</u> Marsiduschk; <u>Saul</u> C. Manners; <u>Coloured Waiter</u>
Elliot. <u>Mrs Chauncey Chatwin</u> Vane Featherston; <u>Muriel</u>
<u>Airley</u> Ethel Matthews; <u>Miss Orme</u> Lizzie Henderson;
<u>Kitty Prothero</u> Lottie Venne; <u>Caroline</u> Henriette Polak;
<u>American Wife</u> Florence Farr; <u>American Daughter</u> M[ay]
Blayney; <u>Her Sister</u> A[lice?] Dukes; <u>Lady with open</u>
<u>mind</u> L. Ellis; <u>Syren</u> C. Carlyle; <u>English Lady</u> Ada
Mellor; <u>Lady of experience</u> M. Wilton. MGR Charles H.
Hawtrey; <u>Mus</u> Arthur Cecil; <u>Mus dir</u> George Bonner; <u>Asm</u>
Charles Milton; <u>Bm</u> E.F. Bradley. *REV: Ath 10/12/92*
p827; E 10/12/92 p9; SR 10/12/92 p685; St 8/12/92 p12;
Th 1/1/93 p60-1; Ti 6/12/92 p6.

92.352 *IRMENGARDA* (O,2a) Leonhard Emil Bach (mus) &
William Beatty-Kingston (lib). COVENT GARDEN 8/12/92,
30/12/92(m). 2 perf.* <u>Cuniberto</u> Pedro Guetary; <u>Il Re</u>
Antonio de Vaschetti/Caracciolo; <u>Burckhard</u> Abramoff/
Armand Castelmary; <u>Luca</u> Eugene Dufriche. <u>Irmengarda</u>
Giulia Valda; <u>Brigida</u> Olimpia Guercia. L & MGR Augus-

tus Harris; <u>Cond</u> Carl Armbruster. *REV: Ath 17/12/92 p863; E 10/12/92 p12; SR 17/12/92 p713; St 15/12/92 p12; Th 1/1/93 p63; Ti 9/12/92 p7.*

92.353 *THE SILENT BATTLE* [*AGATHA*] Isaac Henderson. CRITERION 8/12/92-25/1/93. 51 perf [w/S mat; add mat 21/12, 26/12, 28/12; mat only 24/12/92, 25/1/93].** <u>Col. da Vigno</u> Herbert Waring; <u>Filippo, Marchese Loreno</u> Frank Worthing; <u>Gen. Ricci</u> C.W. Somerset; <u>Signor Sebasti</u> E. Allan Aynesworth; <u>John Dow, U.S.A.</u> Charles Wyndham; <u>Servants</u> Hood/Kemp, [Charles] Terric. <u>Agatha, Marchesa Loreno</u> Winifred Emery; <u>Mercede, Da Vigno</u> Olga Nethersole/Janette Steer; <u>Costanza, Contessa Faviola</u> Rose Leclercq; <u>Leo, Da Vigno</u> Minnie Terry; <u>Gaeta Faviola</u> Mary Moore/Sybil Carlisle. <u>L & MGR</u> Charles Wyndham; <u>Sm</u> S.H.S. Austin; <u>Cond</u> A. Evans; <u>Act mgr & Treas</u> E. Harvey. *REV: E 10/12/92 p11; SR 17/12/92 p712; St 15/12/92 p12; Th 1/1/93 p64; Ti 12/ 12/92 p4.*

92.354 *HEADS OR TAILS* (Ca) J. Palgrave Simpson. CRITERION 8/12/92-24/1/93. 40 perf [np 24-25/12].** <u>Wrangleworth</u> Sydney Valentine; <u>Harold Dyecaster</u> Frank Atherley; <u>Christopher Quaile</u> David S. James. <u>Bridget</u> F. Frances; <u>Rosamond</u> Sybil Carlisle. <u>L & MGR</u>, <u>Sm</u>, <u>Cond</u>, <u>Act mgr & Treas</u> as for 92.353.

92.355 *UNCLE MIKE* (C,4a) Florence Warden. TERRY'S 8/12/92-7/1/93. 27 perf [w/mat 17/12, 26/12, 31/12; np 22-25/12].* <u>Michael Ventriss</u> Edward Terry; <u>Bunting</u> Fred Thorne; <u>Neville Stapleton Turner</u> Henry V. Esmond; <u>Claude Vereker</u> W.T. Lovell; <u>Stapleton Turner</u> Charles J. Fulton; <u>Sir Richard Ingleby</u> W[illiam] Calvert; <u>Egerton Curtis</u> C.M. Hallard; <u>Cabman</u> J. Brabourne; <u>Burton</u> H.R. Lambert; <u>Postman</u> E. Thorp; <u>Johnny Gibson</u> Master Mansfield. <u>Gwendolen Ingleby</u> Helen Forsyth; <u>Mrs Stapleton Turner</u> Alexes Leighton; <u>Madge Stapleton Turner</u> Annie Hill; <u>Midge Stapleton Turner</u> Lucy Webling; <u>Lady Ingleby</u> Carlotta Addison. <u>PP & MGR</u> Edward Terry; <u>Bm</u> H.T. Brickwell; <u>Cond</u> Thomas Smythe; <u>Sc</u> W.T. Hemsley; <u>Furn</u> Lyons; <u>Pq</u> William Clarkson; <u>Sm</u> George Belmore. *REV: Ath 17/12/92 p865; E 10/12/92 p11; SR 17/12/92 p712; St 15/12/92 p12; Th 1/1/93 p61; Ti 9/12/92 p10; TW93 p8.*

92.356 *ORPHEUS* (O,3a) C.W. Gluck. LYCEUM 9/12/92 mat
perf.** Orpheus Clara E. Butt; Euridice Maggie Purvis; Eros Ethel M. Cain. COND C. Villiers Stanford;
Dir Richard Temple. *REV: Ath 17/12/92 p863; SR 17/12/
92 p713-4.* Comment: Royal College of Music.

92.357 *WIDOWERS' HOUSES* (Didactic Realistic Play,3a)
G.B. Shaw. ROYALTY 9/12/92, 13/12/92. 2 mat perf.*
Harry Trench W.J. Robertson; Cokane Arthur Whittaker;
Sartorius T.W. Percyval; Lickcheese James A. Welch;
Waiter E.P. Donne; Porter W[illiam] Alison. Blanche
Florence Farr; Annie N. de Silva. DIR & TREAS J.T.
Grein; L Kate Santley; Act mgr Charles Hoppe; Sm
Herman de Lange; Cond C.W. Lamartine; Cost Morris
Angel; Pq William Clarkson; Furn Oetzmann. *REV: Ath
17/12/92 p865; E 17/12/92 p8; St 15/12/92 p12-3; Th
1/1/93 p61-2; Ti 10/12/92 p5.* Independent Theatre.

92.358 *JO.* NOVELTY 12/12/92-17/12/92. 6 perf.

92.359 *CHARLEY'S AUNT* (FC,3a) Brandon Thomas. ROYALTY
21/12/92-28/1/93; trfd to GLOBE 30/1/93-19/12/96.
1469 perf [w/W, S mat until 12/8/93, exc 21/12/92,
15/2/93, 22/3/93; w/S mat 30/9/93-23/6/94 exc 30/6/
94; w/S mat 5/1/95-22/6/95 exc 30/3/95, 13/4/95; w/
W mat 26/6/95-6/11/95 exc 3/7/95, 11/7/95; w/W, S mat
13/11/95-4/1/96 exc 21/12/95; w/S mat 11/1/96-20/6/96;
w/W mat 24/6/96-16/9/96 exc 8/7/96; w/W, S mat 23/9/
96-19/12/96; add mat 26/12/92, 11/7/93, 26/12/93,
16/5/94, 23/5/94, 30/5/94, 6/6/94, 13/6/94, 20/6/94,
26/6/94; mat only 19/8/93, 26/8/93, 2/9/93, 9/9/93,
16/9/93, 23/9/93, 23/12/93, 30/12/93, 4/4/96; np
31/3-1/4/93, 25/12/93, 23-24/3/94, 24-25/12/94,
12/4/95, 25/12/95, 5/2/96, 3/4/96]. 1st perfd Theatre
Royal, Bury St. Edmunds 29/2/92. Lord Fancourt Bab-
berley W.S. Penley/Edwin H. Wynne/F. Newton-Lindo/
Stanley Cooke; Col. Sir Francis Chesney Brandon Thom-
as/Walter Everard; Stephen Spettigue Ernest Hendrie/
Sydney Paxton; Charley Wykeham H[enry] Farmer/Alfred
C. Seymour; Brassett Cecil H. Thornbury; Jack Chesney
Percy Lyndal/H. Reeves-Smith; New Footman G. Graves/
Woodbridge. Donna Lucia d'Alvadorez Ada Branson; Amy
Spettigue Kate Gordon/Emmie Merrick/Audrey Ford; Ela
Delahay Emily Cudmore/Kate Graves/Annie L. Aumonier;

<u>Kitty Verdun</u> Nina Boucicault/Rhoda Kildare/Olga Schu-
berth/Mabel Lane. <u>L</u> Kate Santley; <u>Mgr</u> W.S. Penley;
<u>Dir</u> Brandon Thomas; <u>Bm</u> Henry Dana; <u>Am</u> Francis Gosnay;
<u>Mus dir</u> Franz Groenings; <u>Pq</u> C.H. Fox; <u>Furn</u> Oetzmann.
REV: Ath 31/12/92 p931; E 24/12/92 p9; Sk 22/2/93
p232-4, 17/5/93 p129-30; SR 24/12/92 p741, 28/7/94 p
100; St 22/12/92 p12, 26/12/95 p10-1; Th 1/2/93 p97-
8; Ti 22/12/92 p10.

92.360 *A LOVE GAME* (Ca) George Walter Browne. ROYALTY
21/12/92-14/1/93. 22 perf. 1st perfd Lyric, Ealing
17/2/85. <u>Jack May</u> Wilton Heriot. <u>Rosa Leigh</u> Edith
Lisle. <u>L</u>, <u>Mgr</u>, <u>Bm</u>, <u>Am</u>, <u>Mus dir</u>, <u>Pq</u>, <u>Furn</u> as for 92.
359. *REV: E 24/12/92 p9; St 22/12/92 p12.*

92.361 *THE LOST PARADISE* (P,3a) Henry C. De Mille
[fnd on Ludwig Fulda, *Das verlorene Paradies*]. ADEL-
PHI 22/12/92-11/3/93. 69 perf.* <u>Reuben Maitland</u>
Charles Warner; <u>Schwarz</u> Charles Dalton; <u>Benzel</u> George
W. Cockburn; <u>Ralph Standish</u> W.L. Abingdon; <u>Andrew
Knowlton</u> W.A. Elliott; <u>Bob Appleton</u> T.B. Thalberg;
<u>Fletcher</u> Sant Matthews; <u>Hyatt</u> Howard Russell; <u>Billy
Hopkins</u> Welton Dale; <u>Joe Barrett</u> J[ohn] Northcote.
<u>Polly Fletcher</u> Evelyn Millard/Mary H. Keegan; <u>Cinders</u>
Clara Jecks; <u>Nell</u> Grace Warner; <u>Mrs Knowlton</u> Ethel
Hope; <u>Julia</u> A[da] Rogers; <u>Kate</u> Marion Dolby; <u>Margaret
Knowlton</u> Dorothy Dorr. PP & MGR A. & S. Gatti; <u>Pd</u>
Thomas Oberle; <u>Mus</u> Frank Howson; <u>Sc</u> Bruce Smith; <u>Furn</u>
J.S. Lyon; <u>Pq</u> William Clarkson; <u>Cost dgn</u> Karl; <u>Cost</u>
L. & H. Nathan; <u>Sm</u> E.B. Norman; <u>Mus dir</u> Henry Sprake;
<u>Act mgr & Treas</u> Charles A. Jecks. *REV: Ath 31/12/92*
p931; E 24/12/92 p11; St 29/12/92 p11-2; Th 1/2/92
p99-100; Ti 23/12/92 p8.

92.362 *TROOPER CLAIRETTE* (MFC,3a) H. Raymond (lib)
& Antony Mars (lib) & Victor Roger (mus); adpt by
Charles S. Fawcett fr *Les Vingt-Nuit Jours de Clair-*
ette. OPERA COMIQUE 22/12/92-25/1/93. 38 perf [w/S
mat exc 24/12; add mat 26/12/92, 11/1/93, 18/1, 25/1/
93]. 1st perfd Prince of Wales's, Liverpool 31/10/92.
<u>The Captain</u> Willie Edouin; <u>Emile Duval</u> Percy F.
Marshall; <u>Gibard</u> Fred Mervin; <u>Michonnet</u> John Wilkinson; <u>Benoit</u> Richard Blunt; <u>Pepin</u> Charles Rock; <u>Vis-
count de Michodiere</u> Harry Eversfield; <u>Poiscau</u> James

A. Cook/A.R. Garland; <u>Jolliquet</u> Gilbert Porteous/James
A. Cook. <u>Berenice Pistachau</u> Madeline Shirley; <u>Octavie</u>
Hilda Abinger; <u>Rosalie</u> Lillie Belmore; <u>Charlotte</u> Eina
Cullum; <u>Virginie</u> Madge Ray; <u>Clairette</u> Alice Atherton;
<u>Estelle</u> Fay Darrell; <u>Annette</u> Stella Brandon/Kate
Jocelyn; <u>Aline</u> Dawn Griffiths; <u>Michotte</u> Jessie Cox.
<u>L</u> Edward Compton; <u>Mgr</u> Willie Edouin; <u>Bm</u> J.T. Mackay
Robertson; <u>Sc</u> Hedley Churchward; <u>Add mus</u> Ernest Buca-
lossi; <u>Mus dir</u> Ernest Bucalossi; <u>Act mgr</u> John B. Helm;
<u>Sm</u> James A. Cook. *REV: E 24/12/92 p9; St 29/12/92 p12;*
Th 1/2/93 p98-9; Ti 23/12/92 p8.

92.363 *LITTLE BO-PEEP, LITTLE RED RIDING HOOD AND*
HOP O' MY THUMB (Panto,14sc) Augustus Harris (lib) &
J. Wilton Jones (lib) & John Crook (mus). DRURY LANE
26/12/92-25/3/93. 138 perf [w/2 perf dy 27/12/92-14/
2/93; w/M, W, S mat 15/2/93-25/3/93].* <u>Daddy Thumb</u>
Dan Leno; <u>Dame Mary Quite Contrary</u> Arthur Williams/
John L. Shine/Thomas Terriss; <u>Granny Green</u> John
d'Auban; <u>Fee Faw Fum Esq</u> H.M. Clifford; The Craggs;
<u>Hop o'my Thumb</u> Little Tich; <u>The Wolves</u> Griffiths
Brothers; <u>Toddlekins</u> Fred Walton; <u>Mrs Fee Faw Fum</u>
E. Story Gofton; <u>Whipper</u> Bennett; <u>Snapper</u> Martell;
<u>Goody Thumb</u> Herbert Campbell; <u>Clown</u> Harry Payne;
<u>Squire Oofless</u> William Morgan; <u>Flopper</u> Thomas Terriss;
<u>Harlequin</u> Tom Cusden; <u>Pantaloon</u> Carl Waller; <u>Police-</u>
<u>man</u> Charles Ronaldson; <u>Swell</u> Frank Damer. <u>Little Bo</u>
<u>Peep</u> Marie Loftus; <u>Elfinella</u> Mabel Love; <u>Ariella</u> Ida
Heath; <u>Little Miss Muffit</u> Lizzie Wilson; <u>Little Red</u>
<u>Riding Hood</u> Marie Lloyd; <u>Nipper</u> Retta Walton; <u>Gnome</u>
<u>of the Glow Worm Glen</u> Emma d'Auban; <u>Marjery Daw</u>
Maude Wilmot; <u>Little Boy Blue</u> Ada Blanche; <u>Prince</u>
<u>Poppetty</u> Madge Lucas; <u>Johnny Green</u> C. Mabel Coates;
<u>Kissy Kissy</u> Eva Greville; <u>Flipper</u> Hettie Bennett;
<u>Polly Perkins</u> Emma Ward; <u>Little Polly Flinders</u> Blanche
Udell; <u>Sally Waters</u> Clara Douglas; <u>Gold Locks</u> Maclean;
<u>Tom the Piper's Son</u> Gertrude Kingston; <u>Dicory Dock</u>
Hertzogg; <u>Peter Piper</u> Cassell; <u>Betsy Wetsy</u> G[eorgie]
Cook; <u>Nicey Nicey</u> L. Scott; <u>Canoodolum</u> Menella;
<u>Popsy Wopsy</u> Hewitt; <u>Nyum Nyum</u> Rita Paton; <u>Tooty</u>
Gladys Rees; <u>Columbine</u> Annie Evans. <u>L & MGR & DIR</u>
Augustus Harris; <u>Sm</u> Arthur P. Collins; <u>Ch</u> John d'Au-
ban; <u>Sc</u> [Robert] Caney, Joseph Harker, Kautsky, Will-
iam Perkins; <u>Cost</u> Percy Anderson, Crage, Edel & Com-

elli, Auguste, Alias, Harrisons, B.J, Simmons, L, &
H. Nathan, Angel, Landolf, Miss Fisher, Miss Palmer,
Mrs Champion, Miss Collier; <u>Armour</u> Kennedy & Phillips,
Gutperle; <u>Pq</u> William Clarkson; <u>Mach</u> E.A. Taylor;
<u>Props</u> A. Jones, Labhart, [G.] Jackson; <u>Chorus Master</u>
Stedman; <u>Asm</u> N[apier] Barry; <u>Sec & Treas</u> Fred G. La-
tham. *REV: Ath 31/12/92 p931; E 31/12/92 p8; SR 31/12/*
92 p770; St 29/12/92 p12-3; Th 1/2/93 p102-3; TW93
p7-8.

92.364 *DICK WHITTINGTON* (Panto,12sc) Horace Lennard
(lib) & Oscar Barrett (mus). OLYMPIC 26/12/92-11/3/93.
120 perf [w/2 perf dy 27/12/92-14/2/93; w/M, W, S mat
15/2/93-11/3/93].* '<u>Liza</u> Victor Stevens; <u>Jack</u> Harry
Grattan; <u>Aldermann Fitzwarren</u> Fred Emney; <u>Cpt. Barn-
acle</u> Julian Cross; <u>Grand Chamberlain</u> Marius Girard;
<u>Nex, Spirit of Darkness</u> Deane Brand; <u>Cat</u> Charles
Lauri; <u>Boatswain</u> W.T. Riley; <u>Great Rat of Morocco</u> Mas-
ter Fred Farren; <u>Extras</u> W. White, Tom Lucerne, Frank
Sims, Ralph Foster, T. Montelli, John Bennett, H.E.
White, Walter Cranbourne, H. Brown, Besford, Robert
Lines, A. Bertram, Charles Wingrove, A. Marshall,
H.R. Franklyn, Tom Lovell, the Little Half. <u>Dick
Whittington</u> Edith Bruce; <u>Emperor of Morocco</u> Kate
Chard; <u>Spirit of the Bells</u> Amy Farrell; <u>1st Mate</u>
Florrie Harmon; <u>Azalea</u> Alice Bruce; <u>Mrs Fitzwarren</u>
Kate Sullivan; <u>Alice</u> Alice Brookes; <u>Spirit of Dreams</u>
Louise Loveday; <u>Roger</u> Amy Trevelyan; <u>Middy</u> Rosa Kelly;
<u>Cpt of Guard</u> Ethel Hawthorne; <u>Extras</u> Mary Campbell,
Lottie Brookes, Lily Stewart, Winifred Hastings,
Eugene Hamilton, Ada Taylor, Edith Shenstone, Ada May,
Vera Dudleigh, Edith Larimy, Helen Filliery, Maud
Guest, Violet Henderson, Alice James, Pattie Marshall,
Clara Clifton, Annie Wilson, Celia Loseby, Flossie
Holland, Lil Lynton, Ree Ansell, Dora Brandon, Dare
Darrell, Dorothy Selwyn, Henrietta Cross, Vera Neville,
Nellie Clifton, Lena Louis, Nellie Huntley, Emily
Archer, Nellie Lynn, Mary Anderson, Millie Herbert,
Ada Birket, Nora Cleland, Cissy Chamberlain, [Maud?]
de Vere, Ethel Francis, Alice Gresham, Florrie Mar-
shall, E. Hart, Rosa Poole, Celia Porch, M. Reeves,
Rose Perry, Amy Sergeant, Florence Seymour, Louie
Sylvester; Lydia Vivian, Clara Wells, Florence Coll-
ier, Sybil Arundale. <u>PP</u> Charles Wilmot; <u>Sc</u> Henry Em-

den, J. Pritchard Barrett; <u>Cost dgn</u> Wilhelm; <u>Cost</u>
Mme d'Orlean, Mrs May; <u>Ch</u> Katti Lanner; <u>Act mgr</u>
William Hogarth; <u>Props</u> F.C. Labhart, R. Eagle; <u>Bom</u>
Arthur Donald; <u>Mach</u> E. Littlejohns; <u>Lime</u> L.C. Par-
nell; <u>Gas</u> J. Jones; <u>Armour</u> Kennedy & Phillips, Kahn
& Hales; <u>Pq</u> William Clarkson; <u>Mus dir</u> James Weaver;
<u>Sm</u> Arthur Brunton; <u>Regisseur</u> J. Pritchard Barrett.
REV: SR 28/1/93 p98; St 29/12/92 p13, 26/1/93 p13;
Th 1/2/93 p104; TW93 p5-8.

92.365 *EAGLE JOE* (Melo,4a) Henry Herman. PRINCESS'S
26/12/92-5/1/93. 11 perf.* <u>Herr Rothenschlag</u> William
H. Day; <u>Tim O'Laney</u> Dan Fitzgerald; <u>Joseph McCloskey</u>
Rollo Balmain; <u>Charles Spencer</u> Leonard Outram; <u>Luke
Gregory</u> Alfred Bucklaw; <u>Boney Bob</u> Arthur Lyle; <u>Bill
Richardson</u> Charles A. Carlile; <u>Greaser John</u> Maurice
Drew; <u>Showman</u> F. Hemming; <u>Student</u> Willie Ash; <u>French
Waiter</u> Wensley Thompson; <u>Mexican</u> George Aubrey; <u>Count
de la Fere</u> Andrew Davidson; <u>Hoosier Dan</u> Cris Fenton;
<u>Longhorse Harry</u> J.F. Brent; <u>Black Peter</u> Lee Condy.
<u>Gamin</u> Dorothy Harwood; <u>Child</u> Little Florrie; <u>Nelly
Jackson</u> Mary Griffith; <u>Lisa</u> C[arlotta] de Yonson;
<u>Ysabel</u> Harwood; <u>Mme Rothenschlag</u> C. Claire; <u>Sarah</u>
[Sara] Mignon. <u>MGR</u> Rollo Balmain. *REV: Ath 31/12/92
p931; E 31/12/92 p8; St 29/12/92 p12; TW93 p8-9.*

92.366 *THE CHURCHWARDEN* (F,3a) C. Ogden & H. Cassell
[adpt of play by Rudolf Kneisel]; rev by Edward Terry.
TERRY'S 26/12/92-4/2/93. 42 perf [w/S mat exc 7/1/93;
add mat 26/12/92]. 1st perfd Theatre Royal, Newcastle
17/9/86. <u>Daniel Chuffy</u> Edward Terry; <u>Nathaniel Gad-
dam</u> Fred Thorne; <u>Mr Bearder</u> W[illiam] Calvert; <u>Frank
Bilton</u> Henry V. Esmond; <u>Alfred</u> George Belmore. <u>Mrs
Amelia Chuffy</u> Alexes Leighton; <u>Kate</u> Helen Forsyth;
<u>Amanda</u> Eily Desmond; <u>Jane</u> Laura Barradel. <u>PP & MGR</u>
Edward Terry; <u>Bm</u> H.T. Brickwell; <u>Cond</u> Tom Smythe; <u>Sm</u>
George Belmore. *REV: E 14/1/93 p11; St 12/1/93 p14.*

*   *   *   *   *

PLAYBILLS

1 8 9 3

93.1 *HYPATIA* (Classical P,4a) G. Stuart Ogilvie [adpt
of Kingsley's novel]. HAYMARKET 2/1/93-15/4/93. 104
perf [w/S mat; add mat 18/1, 25/1, 1/2, 8/2; np 27-
31/3].* Cyril [James] Fernandez; Arsenius Foss;
Peter the Reader [Charles] Hudson; James Garry; Paul
Charles Allan; Philammon Fred Terry; Orestes Lewis
Waller; Issachar H. Beerbohm Tree; Jopadab [Hamilton?]
Piffard; Marcus Hamilton Revelle; Theon [Henry] Kem-
ble; Hazael A[lfred] Wigley; Perimos Chandler; Kali-
phronos E. Holman Clark; Karos Crawley; Zenocles
Graham/Akerman May; 1st Citizen Mark Paton; Drusus
Horniman; Kalisthenes James A. Welch; 2nd Citizen
Rutland/Mayhew. Ruth Olga Brandon; Barea Charlotte E.
Morland; Helen Conyers d'Arcy; Suana Marion Grey;
Leda Constance Carew; Nerea Henrietta Leverett; Thy-
mele Ethel Johnson; Hypatia Julia Neilson. L & MGR
H.B. Tree; Dgn L. Alma-Tadema; Sc T.W. Hall, Walter
Hann, Walter Johnstone, Joseph Harker; Mus Hubert
Parry; Cost L. & H. Nathan; Cost dgn L. Alma-Tadema,
Karl; Bom W.H. Leverton; Pq William Clarkson; Sm Ed-
ward Hastings; Mus dir Carl Armbruster; Bm & Sec
Frederick Harrison. *REV: Ath 7/1/93 p31-2; E 7/1/93
p9; Sk 1/3/93 p301-2, 19/4/93 p685; SR 7/1/93 p14-5;
St 5/1/93 p14-5; Th 1/2/93 p105-6; Ti 3/1/93 p8, 10/
1/93 p10; TW93 p9-17.*

93.2 *THE COMING CLOWN* (Christmas Number,1a) Mark Melford. OPERA COMIQUE 2/1/93-25/1/93. 21 perf. 1st
perfd Royalty 21/12/86. Timothy Macovey Willie Ed-

ouin; <u>Tom Macovey</u> Harry Eversfield; <u>Mr Matlock</u> Richard
Blunt; <u>Burrors</u> Charles Rock; <u>Marsh</u> Master William/
Master C. Lawrence. <u>Mrs Macovey</u> Emily Dowton; <u>Nellie</u>
May St. Aubyn; <u>L</u> Edward Compton; <u>Mus dir</u> Ernest Buca-
lossi; <u>Act mgr</u> John B. Helm; <u>Sm</u> James A. Cook; <u>Mgr</u>
Wiilie Edouin; <u>Bm</u> J.T. Mackay Robertson.

93.3 *ROBIN GOODFELLOW* (C,3a) R.C. Carton. GARRICK 5/1/
93-11/2/93. 33 perf [mat only 4/2, 11/2].* <u>Valentine</u>
<u>Barbrook</u> John Hare/Gilbert Hare; <u>Stanley Trevenen</u>
Sydney Brough; <u>Rev Borthwick Soundy</u> Donald Robertson;
<u>Dr Milner</u> Gilbert Hare/Rowley Cathcart; <u>Hugh Rokeby</u>
Johnston Forbes-Robertson. <u>Constance</u> Rose Norreys;
<u>Mrs Bute Curzon</u> [Katherine] Compton; <u>Mrs Barbrook</u> Mrs
Edmund Phelps; <u>Emma</u> Helen Luck; <u>Grace</u> Kate Rorke. <u>L</u>
& <u>MGR</u> John Hare; <u>Sc</u> William Harford; <u>Mus dir</u> Andrew
Levey; <u>Act mgr</u> C.G. Compton; <u>Asm</u> Rowley Cathcart.
*REV: E 7/1/93 p9; SR 14/1/93 p42; St 12/1/93 p14; Th
1/2/93 p107-8; Ti 6/1/93 p8; TW93 p18-25.*

92.4 *WHO SPEAKS FIRST?* (Ca,1a) Charles Dance. ADELPHI
6/1/93-11/3/93. 56 perf. 1st perfd Lyceum 11/1/49.
<u>Cpt. Charles</u> George W. Cockburn; <u>Ernest Militant</u>
Howard Russell; <u>Potter</u> W. Northcote. <u>Mrs Ernest Mili-
tant</u> Mary H. Keegan; <u>Smart</u> Ada Rogers. <u>PP & MGR</u> A. &
S. Gatti; <u>Sm</u> E.B. Norman; <u>Act mgr & Treas</u> Charles A.
Jecks; <u>Mus dir</u> Henry Sprake.

93.5 *IN THREE VOLUMES* (Ca,1a) Arthur Law. PRINCE OF
WALES'S 6/1/93-25/2/93. 44 perf.* <u>Almeric Lobb</u>
Philip Cunningham. <u>Kate Tyrrell</u> Day Ford/Lily Lewis;
<u>Mrs Tyrrell</u> Jessie Moore. <u>PP</u> Edgar Bruce; <u>L</u> George
Edwardes; <u>Mgr</u> John Lart, William Boosey; <u>Act mgr</u>
E[rnest] Hallewell; <u>Sm</u> George Capel. *REV: E 14/1/93
p11; SR 14/1/93 p43; St 12/1/93 p14-5.*

93.6 *A WHITE LIE* (C,4a) Sydney Grundy [rev ver].
AVENUE 7/1/93-28/2/93. 51 perf [w/S mat exc 7/1, 14/
1]. 1st perfd Theatre Royal, Nottingham 8/2/89. <u>Sir</u>
<u>John Molyneux</u> W.H. Kendal; <u>George Desmond</u> F.H. Mack-
lin; <u>Cpt. Tempest</u> Cecil M. York; <u>Wheatcroft</u> G.P.
Huntley; <u>Dixon</u> H. Deane. <u>Lady Molyneux</u> Annie Irish;
<u>Hannah</u> Barbara Huntley; <u>Daisy</u> Empsie Bowman; <u>Kate</u>
<u>Desmond</u> Mrs W.H. Kendal; <u>Maid</u> Mary Clayton. <u>L</u> George

Paget; <u>Mgr</u> Kendal; <u>Sc</u> William Harford; <u>Cond</u> J. Hamilton Clarke; <u>Furn</u> Frank Giles. *REV: Ath 14/1/93 p61-2;*
E 14/1/93 p13; SR 14/1/93 p42-3; St 12/1/93 p14; Th
1/2/93 p106-7; Ti 9/1/93 p8; TW93 p25-6.

93.7 *KERRY* (D,1a) Dion Boucicault [adpt of Delphine de
Girardin, *La Joie Fait Peur*]. TERRY'S 9/1/93-4/2/93.
28 perf [w/S mat]. 1st perfd Prince's, Manchester
7/9/71 [as *Night and Morning*]. <u>Kerry</u> Edward Terry;
<u>Gerald Desmond</u> W.T. Lovell. <u>Cpt.</u> Coldham Alfred Ken-
drick; <u>Dr Mellish</u> William Calvert. <u>Blanche</u> Clara
Cowper; <u>Kate</u> Annie Hill. <u>PP & MGR</u> Edward Terry; <u>Bm</u>
H.T. Brickwell; <u>Mus dir</u> T[homas] Smythe; <u>Sm</u> George
Belmore. *REV: E 14/1/93 p11; St 12/1/93 p14; Ti 10/*
1/93 p10.

93.8 *FOR CHARITY'S SAKE* (MMonol) Frederick Bowyer (lib)
& Walter H. Hedgecock (mus). TERRY'S 9/1/93-4/2/93;
16/2/93-25/2/93. c.38 perf [w/S mat exc 18/2; ? perfd
24-25/1, 28/1].* Nellie Ganthony. <u>PP & MGR</u>, <u>Bm</u>, <u>Sm</u>,
<u>Mus dir</u> as for 93.7 *REV: E, St as for 93.7.*

93.9 *LA ROSIERE* (CO,3a) Harry Monkhouse (lib) & Edward
Jakobowski (mus). SHAFTESBURY 14/1/93-24/2/93. 41
perf [w/mat 21/1, 25/1, 1/2, 8/2, 15/2].* <u>Pierre</u>
<u>Pontois</u> William Elton; <u>Mjr. Victor Longueville</u> J.G.
Robertson; <u>Justin Bartenot</u> Frank Thornton; <u>Francis</u>
<u>Carnex</u> Albert James; <u>Cpt. Henri de l'Espard</u> Barring-
ton Foote; <u>Chief of Tzigani</u> C. Jamieson. <u>Adeline Du-</u>
<u>pret</u> Violet Cameron; <u>Hortense Ricouard</u> Lucille Saun-
ders; <u>Mme Marguerite Fontenay</u> Emily Miller; <u>Josephine</u>
Marie Halton; <u>Dancer</u> Minnie Thurgate, Rose Wyndham;
<u>Annette</u> Florence Leighton; <u>Julie</u> J[annette] Desborough;
<u>Barbolet</u> Elsa Gerard; <u>Victorine</u> Bertha James; <u>Marie</u>
Delamere; <u>Mimi</u> Louise Brown. <u>PP</u> John Lancaster; <u>Mgr</u>
Marie Halton, Harry Monkhouse; <u>Pd</u> Hugh Moss; <u>Sm</u> Al-
bert James; <u>Cond</u> Barter Johns; <u>Act mgr</u> W.H. Griffiths;
<u>Bom</u> W[alter] Hamilton; <u>Sc</u> W.T. Hemsley, Walter Hann;
<u>Ch</u> [Carlo?] Coppi; <u>Cost dgn</u> Edel; <u>Cost</u> Alias; <u>Pq</u>
William Clarkson. *REV: E 21/1/93 p9; SR 21/1/93 p72;*
St 19/1/93 p12, 16/2/93 p12; Th 1/3/93 p153-4; Ti
16/1/93 p6, 22/2/93 p2.

93.10 *CONFEDERATES* (D,1a) Henry Woodville. ROYALTY

16/1/93-28/1/93;* trfd to GLOBE 30/1/93-17/6/93.
130 perf [np 31/3-1/4]. Amos Hansen Cecil H. Thornbury; Dick Burton Wilton Heriot; Henry Leigh Henry
Farmer; Sgt. Doughty H. Gordon Tomkins. Nora Hansen
Mabel Lane. L Kate Santley; Mgr W.S. Penley; Bm
Henry Dana; Am Francis Gosnay; Sm Wilton Heriot; Mus
dir Franz Groenings. Comment: Nicoll indicates 1st
perf was Globe 25/2/97; see 97.42.

93.11 *THE MAGIC OPAL* (LO,2a) Arthur Law (lib) & Isaac
Albeniz (mus). LYRIC 19/1/93-4/3/93. 45 perf [w/S mat
exc 4/3].* Telemachus Ulysses Carambollas Harry
Monkhouse; Alzaga John Child; Pekito Tom A. Shale;
Arristippus Fred Kaye; Curro George Tate; Trabucos
Wallace Brownlow. Lolika Aida Jenoure; Olympia Susie
Vaughan; Zoe Emmeline Orford; Christina Dora Thorne;
Thekla Rose Hamilton/Maud Michael Watson; Martina
May Yohe; Irene Elena Monmouth; Alethia Cissy Cran-
ford; Leila Dolly Webb; Dancer Mlle Candida. L & MGR
& DIR Horace Sedger; Cond Herbert Bunning; Cost dgn
Karl; Cost L. & H. Nathan, G.B. Simmons, Alias; Bm
& Treas William Greet. *REV: Ath 28/1/93 p131; E 21/1/
93 p9; Sk 8/2/93 p95; SR 28/1/93 p97-8; St 26/1/93
p12; Th 1/3/93 p154-5; Ti 20/1/93 p6.*

93.12 *OVER THE WAY* (Ca,1a) T.W. Robertson [adpt of
Henri Murger, *Le Bonhomme Jadis*]. COURT 20/1/93-25/
2/93. 37 perf [w/S mat exc 21/1].* Mr Chirrup W.G.
Elliott; Alfred Hardy Wilfred Draycott. Jessie Ellaline Terriss/May Palfrey. L & MGR Arthur Chudleigh;
Sm T.W.S. Robertson; Bm Leonard Lillies; Mus dir Edward Jones. *REV: SR 28/1/93 p98; St 26/1/93 p12; Th
1/3/93 p155-6; Ti 23/1/93 p14; TW93 p27-8; E 28/1/93
p9.*

93.13 *THE BURGLAR AND THE JUDGE* (Comic Interlude).
F.C. Phillips & Charles H.E. Brookfield. COURT 20/1/
93-25/2/93. 37 perf [w/S mat exc 21/1].** Mr Justice
Gyves Weedon Grossmith; Parkhurst Sydney Warden; Joe
Charles H.E. Brookfield. L & MGR, Sm, Bm, Mus dir as
for 93.12. *REV: SR, Ti, TW93, E as for 93.12.*

93.14 *A PANTOMIME REHEARSAL* (MExt,1a) Cecil Clay.
COURT 20/1/93-25/2/93. 37 perf [w/S mat exc 21/1].**

Lord Arthur Percy Weedon Grossmith; Cpt, Tom Robinson
Charles H.E. Brookfield; Jack Deedes C.P. Little/W.G.
Elliott; Sir Charles Grandison Wilfred Draycott; Tom-
kins Quinton. Miss Violet Eva Moore; Lady Muriel
Beauclerc Irene Rickards; Miss May May Palfrey; Miss
Rose Ethel Wilson; Miss Lily Ellaline Terriss/Sybil
Grey. L & MGR, Sm, Bm, Mus dir as for 93.12. *REV: SR,
Ti, TW93, E as for 93.12.*

93.15 *THE SPORTSMAN* (FC,3a) W[illiam] Lestocq [adpt
of Georges Feydeau, *Monsieur Chasse*]. COMEDY 21/1/
93–15/4/93. 77 perf [w/S mat exc 21/1, 15/4; np 27/3–
1/4]. 1st prof. Dr Holroyd Charles Groves/William
Wyes; Mr Perkins W.F. Hawtrey; Bob Briscoe W.R. Shirley; Mr Robey Ernest Percy; Harry Briscoe Charles H.
Hawtrey. Mrs Fritchley Annie Goward; Mrs Robert Briscoe M. Wilton/Beatrice Ferrar; Mrs Briscoe Lottie
Venne; Emily Eva Williams. MGR Charles H. Hawtrey;
Bm E.F. Bradley; Mus dir George Bonner; Asm Charles
Milton. *REV: Ath 28/1/93 p131-2; E 28/1/93 p9; SR
28/1/93 p98; St 26/1/93 p12-3; Ti 23/1/93 p14; TW93
p26-7.*

93.16 *A WELSH HEIRESS* (Ca,1a) Tom Cullum. COMEDY 21/
1/93–15/4/93. 67 perf [np 27/3–4/1].* Tom Halliard
William Herbert; David Morgan William Wyes/Charles
Milton; Jim Evans Ernest Percy. Kate Tyrrel Vane
Featherston; Mrs Morgan Florence Haydon. MGR, Bm,
Mus dir, Asm as for 93.15. *REV: E, St as for 93.15.*

93.17 *A MUSICAL MONOLOGUE.* TERRY'S 24/1/93, 25/1, 28/
1/93(2). 4 perf. Dudley Causton. PP & MGR Edward
Terry.

93.18 *THE BAUBLE SHOP* (Play of Modern London Life,4a)
H.A. Jones. CRITERION 26/1/93–14/6/93. 133 perf [w/S
mat; np 30/3–5/4].* Viscount Clivebrook Charles
Wyndham; Earl of Sarum C.W. Somerset; Hon Charles
Cheviot E. Allan Aynesworth; Sir John Stradbroke Frank
Atherley/C[harles] Garry; Piers Bussey William Blake-
ley; Stoach Sydney Valentine; Ireson Frank Worthing/
C. Chinn; Matthew Keeber William H. Day; Body David
S. James; Mims S.H.S. Austin/Younge; Bence H[enry]
Lebreton. Lady Kate Ffennell Fanny Enson/F. Frances;

Lady Bellenden Louise Moodie; Gussy Bellenden Ellis
Jeffreys; Jessie Keeber Mary Moore. L & MGR Charles
Wyndham; Sm S.H.S. Austin; Act mgr & Treas E. Harvey;
Mus dir A. Evans; Sc W.T. Hemsley; Cost Russell &
Allen, Pitts & Richards. *REV: Ath 4/2/93 p163-4; E
28/1/93 p11, 25/2/93 p11; Sk 1/2/93 p4-5, 56; SR 4/2/
93 p125; St 2/2/93 p14-5; Th 1/3/93 p158-60; Ti 27/1/
93 p3; TW93 p28-37.*

93.19 *THE GUV'NOR* (C,3a) "E.G. Lankester" [Robert
Reece]. VAUDEVILLE 28/1/93-21/2/93. 23 perf [w/mat
1/2, 4/2]. 1st perfd Vaudeville 23/6/80. Macclesfield
David James; Butterscotch William Farren; Freddy E.W.
Gardiner; Theodore H. Reeves-Smith; Gregory Charles
Ashford; Jellicoe John Byron; The McToddy Edward Sid-
ney; Cabman Duncan Fleet; Mr Vellum Howard; Gunnell
Newton. Carrie Annie Hughes; Aurelia May Whitty;
Kate Marie Abington/Geraldine St. Maur; Mrs Maccles-
field Sophie Larkin; Polly Cicely Richards. L & MGR
A. & S. Gatti; Sc Bruce Smith; Furn Lyons; Pd David
James; Mus dir Henry Sprake; Asm Charles Ashford;
Act mgr & Treas L[ouis] F. Nethersole. *REV: Ath 4/2/
93 p164; E 4/2/93 p9; SR 4/2/93 p125; St 2/2/93 p15;
Th 1/3/93 p166-7; Ti 30/1/93 p14; TW93 p37-8.*

93.20 *BARTONMERE TOWERS* (C,3a) Rutland Barrington.
SAVOY 1/2/93 mat perf.* Sir Richard Beauly Cyril
Maude; Morton Cope Yorke Stephens; Richard Farquhar
William Herbert; Maurice Farquhar Philip Cunningham;
Hon Bertie Moline Frank Lacy; Sir James Hanbury Rut-
land Barrington; Dr Farquhar Charles J. Fulton;
Inspector Morrison [Arthur W.] Fowles; Johnson [Geo-
rge] de Pledge; Pawson [J. Bowden] Haswell; James
Lichfield. Mrs Johnson Rosina Brandram; Mary Hanbury
Lily Hanbury; Gertie Conyngham Helen Leyton; Lady
Hanbury Emily Cross. PP & MGR Richard d'Oyly Carte.
*REV: Ath 11/2/93 p194; E 4/2/93 p11; Sk 8/2/93 p95;
SR 4/2/93 p125; St 2/2/93 p15; Th 1/3/93 p161-2.*

93.21 *THE COUNTY COUNCILLOR* (FC,3a) H. Graham. TRA-
FALGAR SQUARE 4/2/93-28/4/93. 82 perf [w/mat 18/2,
25/2, 8/3, 15/3, 22/3, 3/4, 5/4, 12/4, 15/4, 19/4,
26/4; np 31/3].** Robert Faddicum E.W. Garden; Mr
Cripps Cyril Maude; Inspector Catchpole Mark King-

horne; Tom Doubleton E[dward] O'Neill; Jack Wilding
Harcourt Beatty; Cabman J[ohn] Willes; Dick Wellington Yorke Stephens. Lottie Singleton Fanny Brough;
Kitty Helen Leyton; Mrs Perks Nellie Williams; Mabel
Marie Lascelles; Melia Gertrude Price. L & PP Mr &
Mrs Frank Wyatt [Violet Melnotte]; Mgr Yorke Stephens, E.W. Garden; Bom F.J. Potter; Bm G.F. Bashford; Mus & Cond Arthur E. Godfrey; Ch Marriette
d'Auban. *REV: Ath 11/2/93 p194; E 11/2/93 p9; Sk
15/2/93 p186-7; SR 11/2/93 p153; St 9/2/93 p13; Th
1/3/93 p167; Ti 6/2/93 p4; TW93 p38.*

93.22 *WRITTEN IN SAND* (C,1a) Frederick W. Broughton.
TRAFALGAR SQUARE 4/2/93-3/3/93; 18/4/93-28/4/93. 36
perf [w/mat 19/4, 26/4]. 1st perfd Olympic 29/8/84.
Frank Seaton Harcourt Beatty; Fairfax Rendall E[d-
ward] O'Neill; Tom Potts J[ohn] Willes. Kate Shirley
Gertrude Price; Sister Winifred Marie Lascelles. L &
PP, Mgr, Bom, Bm, Cond as for 93.21. *REV: E 11/2/93
p9; St 9/2/93 p13.*

92.23 *BECKET* (T,Prol,4a) Alfred, Lord Tennyson [arr
Henry Irving]. LYCEUM 6/2/93-23/6/93; 5-6/7/93; 12-
13/7/93; 15/7(m), 21/22-7/93. 117 perf [mat only
8/4, 15/4, 22/4, 29/4, 6/5, 13/5, 20/5, 25/5, 27/5;
np 13/2, 20/2, 27/2, 6/3, 18/3, 27-31/3, 3/6, 7/6,
10/6, 14/6, 17/6, 24/6].* Thomas Becket Henry Irving;
Henry II William Terriss; King Louis of France Acton
Bond; Gilbert Foliot Lacy; Roger [Allen] Beaumont;
Bishop of Hereford [H.W.] Cushing; Hilary [John] Ar-
cher; John of Salisbury Alfred Bishop; Herbert of
Bosham [William] Haviland; Edward Grim W.J. Holloway;
Sir Reginald Fitzurse Frank [Kemble] Cooper; Sir
Richard de Brito [Frank] Tyars; Sir William de Tracy
[Clarence] Hague; Sir Hugh de Morville Percival;
De Broc [R.P.] Tabb; Richard de Hastings Seldon;
Youngest Knight Templar Gordon Craig; Lord Leicester
John Martin Harvey; Philip de Eleemosyna [Henry]
Howe; Herald [W. Lionel] Belmore; Geoffrey Master Leo
Byrne; Retainers [W.J.] Yeldham, W.J. Lorriss; Coun-
trymen [Sam] Johnson, [T.] Reynolds; John of Oxford
Ian Robertson; Servant Davis. Eleanor of Aquitaine
Genevieve Ward; Margery Kate Phillips; Rosamund de
Clifford Ellen Terry. L & MGR Henry Irving; Sc Will-

iam Telbin, Joesph Harker, Hawes Craven; <u>Mus</u> C. Villiers Stanford; <u>Mus dir</u> J. Meredith Ball; <u>Cost dgn</u>
Mrs J.W. Comyns Carr, Charles Cattermole; <u>Cost</u> Mrs
Nettleship, Thomas Pratt & Sons, Pocock Brothers,
Bieati, Auguste; <u>Chorus Master</u> [R.P.] Tabb; <u>Pq</u> C.H.
Fox; <u>Furn</u> Arnott; <u>Mach</u> Fillery; <u>Sm</u> H.J. Loveday; <u>Act</u>
<u>mgr</u> Bram Stoker. *REV: Ath 11/2/93 p193-4; E 11/2/93*
p10; Sk 8/2/93 p72-3, 15/2/93 p170, 189, 29/3/93 p
549; SR 11/2/93 p146-7, 4/3/93 p240; St 9/2/93 p12,
27/7/93 p10; Th 1/3/93 p162-3; Ti 7/2/93 p5, 24/7/93
p7; TW93 p39-54.

93.24 *MARIGOLD FARM; OR, THE SIMPLE SQUIRE AND THE*
EVIL EYE (LyrP,3a) Walter Sapte, jr. OPERA COMIQUE
7/2/93. Rnd.* <u>Squire Oakapple</u> R. de Fonblanque; <u>Com-</u>
<u>fit</u> Edward; <u>Stephen Cane</u> Oswald Yorke; <u>Baggetti</u> Briggs;
<u>Beadle</u> Balfour; <u>Mr Dawe</u> Graham; <u>Joe Splice</u> W. Archer;
<u>Villager</u> Horniman. <u>Mrs Dawe</u> [Sylvia?] Grey; <u>Sheba</u>
[Annie?] Schubert; <u>Marjory Dawe</u> [Alice?] Kingsley.
L Willie Edouin; <u>Bm</u> J.T. Mackay Robertson. <u>Comment</u>:
Nicoll indicates copyright perf.

93.25 *BETWEEN THE POSTS* (Ca,1a) Mrs Hugh Bell. COMEDY
9/2/93 mat perf. 1st perfd Theatre Royal, Newcastle
9/9/87 [as *L'Indécis*]. <u>Geoffrey Warburton</u> Arthur
Playfair. <u>Edith Neville</u> Esmé Beringer; <u>Maid</u> Skelton
Waud. <u>MGR</u> Charles H. Hawtrey; <u>Bm</u> E.F. Bradley. *REV:*
E 11/2/93 p11; St 16/2/93 p12.

93.26 *TIME IS MONEY* (Ca,1a) Mrs Hugh Bell & Arthur
Cecil. COMEDY 9/2/93 mat perf.** <u>Charles Graham</u>
Charles H. Hawtrey. <u>Susan</u> Vane Featherston; <u>Mrs</u>
<u>Murray</u> Lottie Venne. <u>MGR</u>, <u>Bm</u> as for 93.25. *REV: E,*
St as for 93.25; Ti 10/2/93 p9.

93.27 *AN UNDERGROUND JOURNEY* (Ca,1a) Mrs Hugh Bell
& Charles H.E. Brookfield. COMEDY 9/2/93 mat perf.*
<u>Duke of Peckham</u> Cyril Maude; <u>Railway Guard</u> William
Wyes. <u>Mrs Jennings</u> Fanny Brough. <u>MGR</u>, <u>Bm</u> as for 93.
25. *REV: E 11/2/93 p11; St 16/2/93 p12; Th 1/3/93 p*
160-1; Ti 10/2/93 p9; TW93 p54.

93.28 *SCHOOL* (C,4a) T.W. Robertson. OPERA COMIQUE
9/2/93 mat perf.** <u>Lord Beaufoy</u> Vernon Sansbury;

Jack Poyntz F.J. Nettlefold; Beau Farintosh C.W. Mc-
Cabe; Dr Sutcliffe D. Lewin Mannering; Mr Krux Roy-
ston Keith. Bella V. St. Lawrence; Naomi Tighe Nad-
age Doree; Mrs Sutcliffe Thea Symns; Tilly Jessie
Spiers; Milly Eva Hamblin; Laura Kate Robinson; Clara
Cassie Bruce; Kitty Evelyn Wells; Hetty Dorothy Ball.
REV: E 11/2/93 p10; St 16/2/93 p12.

93.29 *UNCLE SILAS* (D,4a) Seymour Hicks & Laurence S.
Irving [adpt of novel by Sheridan Le Fanu]. SHAFTES-
BURY 13/2/93 mat perf.* Dudley Ruthyn Seymour Hicks;
Austin Ruthyn Laurence S. Irving; Silas Ruthyn W[ill-
iam] Haviland; Charke E. Holman Clark; Wyatt [T.]
Reynolds; Hon Harry Chiffinch E.A. Coventry; Tom
Croft Gordon Craig; Wilton Ken Tom Hesslewood; John
Knatchbull Charles Westmacote; Digby Grist H. Nye
Chart; Pegtop Master Earle. Maud Ruthyn Violet Van-
brugh; Lady Knollys K[ate] Carlyon; Millicent Ruthyn
Irene Vanbrugh; Mme de la Rougiere Florence Cowell.
PP John Lancaster; Mgr Marie Halton, Harry Monkhouse;
Pq C.H. Fox; Cost L. & H. Nathan; Mus Dora Bright;
Sm Julian Cross; Cond J. Meredith Ball. *REV: E 18/2/
93 p10; SR 18/2/93 p179-80; St 16/2/93 p12; Th 1/3/93
p163-4.*

93.30 *LETTERS ADDRESSED HERE* (F,1a) H. Chance Newton.
SHAFTESBURY 14/2/93-24/2/93. 10 perf.* Domitian
Swire Albert James; Mars Gillikins Frank A. Walsh;
Mr Clewidge Sam Hill; Mr Tracshaw Harry Dorien; Mess-
enger Boy Master Alfred Pickett. Alfongs Minnie Thur-
gate; Mrs Clewidge J. Besborough; Mrs Tracshaw Flo-
rence Leighton; Daisy Armstrong Florence Barnes;
Esther Ann Swire Hettie Hertzfeld. DIR Hugh Moss;
Sm Albert James. *REV: E 18/2/93 p9; St 16/2/93 p12.*

93.31 *ALLENDALE* (C,3a) G.B. Burgin & Eden Phillpotts.
STRAND 14/2/93 mat perf.* Gilbert Crane Charles
Groves; Chizzleton Tubbs William Wyes; Lorrimer
Pount Cairns James; Harry Crane Julius Knight; Ram-
chunder Jhee W.E. Phillips. Amanda P. Warren Eva
Moore; Mrs Norton Folgate M.A. Victor; Letty Crane
Kate Ruskin; Martha Braddle Mrs H[enry] Leigh. PP
J.S. Clarke; L Willie Edouin; Bm J.T. Mackay Robert-
son; Sm Charles Davies; Cond Ernest Bucalossi. *REV:*

*E 18/2/93 p11; SR 18/2/93 p180; St 16/2/93 p12; Th
1/3/93 p164-5.*

93.32 *A LOST THREAD* (Sk,1a) Mrs Hugh Bell. STRAND
14/2/93 mat perf.** <u>Sir George Seymour</u> Arthur Dacre.
<u>Lady Seymour</u> Amy Roselle.<u>PP</u>, <u>L</u>, <u>Bm</u>, <u>Sm</u>, <u>Cond</u> as for
92.31. *REV: E, St as for 92.31.*

92.33 *FLIGHT* (P,4a) Walter Frith. TERRY'S 16/2/93-25/
2/93. 10 perf [w/mat 25/2].* <u>Ralph Sargent</u> Murray
Carson; <u>Philip Amherst</u> H.B. Conway; <u>Thomas Edward
Marley, alias Sargent</u> Edward Terry; <u>Weston Carr</u> Henry
V. Esmond; <u>Tanfield</u> W.T. Lovell; <u>Gascoigne</u> T.W. Per-
cyval; <u>Lord George Bond</u> Harry Eversfield; <u>Collins</u>
J. Brabourne; <u>Allen</u> H.R. Lambert. <u>Mrs Amherst</u> May
Whitty; <u>Blanche Templer</u> Annie Hill; <u>Sylvia Gascoigne</u>
Helen Forsyth. <u>PP & MGR</u> Edward Terry; <u>Bm</u> H.T. Brick-
well; <u>Sc</u> W.T. Hemsley; <u>Pq</u> William Clarkson; <u>Sm</u> George
Belmore; <u>Mus dir</u> T. Smythe. *REV: E 18/2/93 p9; Sk 22/
2/93 p244; St 23/2/93 p12; Th 1/3/93 p165; Ti 17/2/
93 p10; TW93 p63.*

93.34 *DIPLOMACY* (P,4a) Clement Scott & B.C. Stephenson
[adpt of Victorien Sardou, *Dora*]. 18/2/93-14/7/93
[w/S mat exc 1/4, 6/5, 13/5, 20/5, 3/6, 10/6, 17/6,
24/6; mat only 1/7, 8/7; np 31/3, 6/7]; 2/11/93-16/12/
93 [w/mat 16/12; mat only 6/12]. 174 perf.** <u>Count
Orloff</u> S.B. Bancroft; <u>Baron Stein</u> Arthur Cecil; <u>Henry
Beauclerc</u> John Hare/W. Scott Buist; <u>Julian Beauclerc</u>
Johnston Forbes-Robertson/W. Scott Buist; <u>Algie Fair-
fax</u> Gilbert Hare/Roland Atwood; <u>Markham</u> R[owley]
Cathcart; <u>Antoine</u> E[ugene] Mayeur; <u>Shepherd</u> R. Power.
<u>Lady Henry Fairfax</u> Mrs S.B. Bancroft/Mrs Edmund
Phelps; <u>Marquise de Rio-Zarès</u> Lady Monckton; <u>Comtesse
Zicka</u> Olga Nethersole/Margaret Ayrtoun/Elizabeth Ro-
bins; <u>Dora</u> Kate Rorke; <u>Mion</u> Helen Luck/Thérèse Des-
cours. <u>L & MGR</u> John Hare; <u>Act mgr</u> C.G. Compton; <u>Asm</u>
R[owley] Cathcart; <u>Cond</u> Andrew Levey; <u>Sc</u> William
Harford. *REV: Ath 25/2/93 p258; E 25/2/93 p11, 23/12/
93 p10; SR 25/2/93 p208, 11/11/93 p543; St 23/2/93
p12, 9/11/93 p13; Th 1/3/93 p165-6; Ti 20/2/93 p11;
TW93 p54-6, 259-261.*

93.35 *AN UNDERGROUND JOURNEY* (Ca,1a) Mrs Hugh Bell &

Charles H.E. Brookfield. TRAFALGAR SQUARE 18/2/93,
25/2/93. 2 mat perf.** <u>Duke of Peckham Rye</u> Cyril
Maude; <u>Railway Guard</u> E.W. Garden. <u>Mrs Jennings</u> Fanny
Brough. <u>PP & L</u> Mr & Mrs Frank Wyatt; <u>Mgr</u> Yorke Stephens, E.W. Garden; <u>Bm</u> G.F. Bashford; <u>Bom</u> F.J. Potter;
<u>Cond</u> Arthur E. Godfrey.

93.36 *THE MASTER BUILDER* (D,3a) Henrik Ibsen [trans
William Archer & Edmund Gosse]. TRAFALGAR SQUARE
20/2/93-3/3/93 [10 mat perf; np 25/2];* trfd to
VAUDEVILLE 6/3/93-25/3/93 [21 perf; w/S mat]. Total
31 perf. <u>Halvard Solness</u> Herbert Waring; <u>Dr Herdal</u>
John Beauchamp/Charles Allan/George R. Foss; <u>Ragnar
Brovik</u> Philip Cunningham; <u>Knut Brovik</u> H. Athol Forde/
Charles J. Fulton/Edward Rochelle. <u>Mrs Solness</u> Louise
Moodie/Elsie Chester; <u>Kala Fosli</u> Marie Linden; <u>Hilda
Wagnel</u> Elizabeth Robins. <u>PP & L</u> Mr & Mrs Frank Wyatt;
<u>Dir</u> Herbert Waring, Elizabeth Robins; <u>Mgr</u> Yorke
Stephens, E.W. Garden; <u>Cond</u> Dan Godfrey, jr; <u>Sm</u>
George R. Foss; <u>Bm</u> Charles Terry, G.F. Bashford; <u>Bom</u>
F.J. Potter. *REV: Ath 25/2/93 p258; E 25/2/93 p11,
11/3/92 p9; Sk 1/3/93 p291-2; SR 25/2/93 p208; St 23/
2/93 p12-3; Th 1/4/93 p212-4; Ti 21/2/93 p12; TW93
p56-63, 63-70.*

93.37 *THE STRIKE AT ARLINGFORD* (P,3a) George Moore.
OPERA COMIQUE 21/2/93. 1 perf.* <u>Baron Steinbach</u>
Charles J. Fulton; <u>Hamer</u> Charles Rock; <u>John Reid</u>
Bernard Gould; <u>Footman</u> Akerman May; <u>Fox</u> H.F. Spiers;
<u>Simon</u> M[ervyn] Herapath. <u>Lady Anne Travers</u> Florence
West; <u>Ellen Sands</u> Elsie Chester. <u>DIR & TREAS</u> J.T.
Grein; <u>L</u> Edward Compton; <u>Act mgr & Bm</u> Charles Hoppe;
<u>Sm</u> Herman de Lange; <u>Mus dir</u> W.C. Lamartine; <u>Furn</u>
Oetzmann; <u>Cost</u> Morris Angel; <u>Pq</u> William Clarkson.
*REV: Ath 25/2/93 p258; E 25/2/93 p9; Sk 1/3/93 p260;
SR 25/2/93 p208; St 23/2/93 p12; Th 1/4/93 p214-5;
TW93 p70-5.* <u>Comment</u>: Independent Theatre Society.

93.38 *OFF THE LINE* (D,1a) Clement Scott. TOOLE'S
27/2/93-10/5/93. 63 perf [w/S mat exc 6/5; add mat
3/4; np 27/3-1/4].** <u>Harry Coke</u> J.L. Toole; <u>Puffy</u>
Frank J. Arlton; <u>Jem Brass</u> Henry Westland. <u>Liz Coke</u>
Eliza Johnstone; <u>Mary Coke</u> Cora Poole. <u>L & MGR</u> J.L.
Toole; <u>Sm</u> John Billington; <u>Mus dir</u> William Robins;

<u>Bm</u> George Lee. *REV: St 2/3/93 p14.*

93.39 *THE IRONMASTER* (D,4a) A.W. Pinero [adpt of
Georges Ohnet, *Le Maître des Forges*]. AVENUE 2/3/93-
14/4/93. 35 perf [w/S mat exc 25/3, 8/4; np 27/3-4/4].
1st perfd St. James's 17/4/84. <u>Philippe Derblay</u>
W.H. Kendal; <u>Duc de Bligny</u> F.H. Macklin; <u>Moulinet</u>
J.E. Dodson; <u>Bechelin</u> Gilbert Farquhar; <u>Baron de Pré-
font</u> Oscar Adye; <u>Octave</u> H. Nye Chart; <u>Général de Pon-
tac</u> G.P. Huntley; <u>Young Gobert</u> Howard Sturge; <u>Old
Gobert</u> H. Deane; <u>Dr Servan</u> Owens; <u>Mouchot</u> Harris;
<u>Servant</u> Sharpe. <u>Baronne de Préfont</u> Annie Irish; <u>Mar-
quise de Beaupre</u> Florence Bennett; <u>Athenaiss</u> Adrienne
Dairolles; <u>Suzanne Derblay</u> Nellie Campbell; <u>Brigette</u>
Barbara Huntley; <u>Claire de Beaupre</u> Mrs W.H. Kendal.
<u>L</u> George Paget; <u>Mgr</u> W.H. Kendal; <u>Sc</u> William Harford;
<u>Mus dir</u> J. Hamilton Clarke; <u>Furn</u> Frank Giles. *REV:
Ath 11/3/93 p322; E 4/3/93 p9; Sk 8/3/93 p326-7; SR
18/3/93 p297; St 9/3/93 p12; Th 1/4/93 p216-7; Ti 4/
3/93 p15; TW93 p82-3.*

93.40 *BETWEEN THE POSTS* (Ca,1a) Mrs Hugh Bell [adpt
of *L'Indécis*]. GAIETY 3/3/93. 1 perf.** L & MGR
George Edwardes.

93.41 *ALEXANDRA* (P,4a). ROYALTY 4/3/93-11/3/93. 7
perf.* <u>Eric, Lord Knowlesford</u> Herbert Flemming; <u>Jack
Owthwaite</u> Edmund Maurice; <u>Dr Howarth</u> Charles Rock;
<u>Rev Charles Bevan</u> Gilbert Trent; <u>Van Noorden</u> Herman
de Lange; <u>Robert Ash</u> John Carter; <u>Anthony Want</u> Charles
Charrington; <u>Dicker</u> W.R. Staveley; <u>Waiter</u> C. Douglas
Cox. <u>Alexandra</u> Janet Achurch; <u>Lady Knowlesford</u> Mrs
Theodore Wright; <u>Mrs Bradley</u> Mabel Hardinge; <u>Chamber-
maid</u> Ida Sala; <u>Sara Chubb</u> Rose Nesbitt; <u>Mary Chubb</u>
L. Hudson; <u>Charlotte</u> Hetty Laurence. <u>L</u> Kate Santley;
<u>Mgr</u> Charles Charrington; <u>Bm</u> Harrington Baily; <u>Sm</u>
John Carter; <u>Sec</u> Gifford Stacey; <u>Bom</u> Glover; <u>Sc</u> Hed-
ley Churchward; <u>Mus dir</u> C.W. Lamartine. *REV: Ath
11/3/93 p322; E 11/3/93 p9; Sk 15/3/93 p414-5, 426;
St 9/3/93 p12-3; Th 1/4/93 p217-8; Ti 6/3/93 p8;
TW93 p75-82.*

93.42 *THE ARTFUL DODGE* (F,1a) E.L. Blanchard, TRAFAL-
GAR SQUARE 4/3/93-29/3/93; 17-18/4/93. 24 perf.**

Demosthenes Dodge E.W. Garden; Godfrey Grudge Mark
Kinghorne; Hon Frederick Fitz Fudge Harcourt Beatty;
Tim Trundle J[ohn] Willes; Nudge Tervin. Emily Wilton
Marie Lascelles; Susan Smudge Helen Leyton. L & PP
Mr & Mrs Frank Wyatt; Mgr Yorke Stephens, E.W. Garden;
Bm G.F. Bashford; Cond Arthur E. Godfrey; Bom F.J.
Potter.

93.43 *CORNEY COURTED* (0a,1a) Arthur Waugh (lib) &
Claude Nugent (mus) [adpt fr Charles Dickens, *Oliver
Twist*]. COMEDY 6/3/93 mat perf.* Mr Bumble R.G.
Legge. Mrs Corney Edith Chester. *REV: E 11/3/93 p10.*

93.44 *THE FAY O' THE FERN* (F) Robert George Legge.
COMEDY 6/3/93 mat perf. 1st perfd New, Oxford 4/2/93.
Chicele Benedoct Ben Greet; Byron Shalspeare Stratton
Rodney; Mjr. Auger F. Topham; Hammersmith Willis
Searle. Huon Constance Hellyer; Tib Mrs Tom Wilson;
Augusta Hilda Rivers; Daisy Florence Tanner; Elfia
Marie Wilson. *REV: 11/3/93 p10.*

93.45 *THE ISLE OF UTOPIA* (Ext) Claude Nugent (mus) &
George St. Cloud (lib). COMEDY 6/3/93 mat perf. 1st
perfd Park Theatre, Eastbourne 26/12/92. Mrs Bri-
tannia Ben Greet; Randley Standolf Columbus F. Top-
ham; Joseph Miller Stratton Rodney; Mjr.-Gen. Pri-
vate Thomas Atkins R.G. Legge; Jack Tar Willis Searle;
Jack O'Bullock G. Riddell; Hon Chevalier de Tivoli
Nutter; The Nipper Eyre; Mr 'Henry 'Awkins Wainwright.
Maiden of Bashful Fifteen Olga Schuberth; Match Makers
[Hilda] Rivers, [Constance] Hellyer, [Marie?] Wilson;
Sally Florence Tanner. *REV: E 11/3/93 p10.*

93.46 *THE AMAZONS* (FR,3a) A.W. Pinero. COURT 7/3/93-
8/7/93. 111 perf [w/mat 18/3, 25/3, 8/4, 15/4, 22/4,
13/5, 8/7; np 30-31/4, 6/7].* Barrington, Viscount
Litterly Fred Kerr; Andre, Count de Grival W.G.
Elliott; Rev Roger Minchin John Beauchamp; Fitton
W.H. Quinton; Youatt Compton Coutts; Orts R[obert]
Nainby; Galfred, Earl of Tweenwayes Weedon Grossmith.
Miriam, Marchioness of Castlejordan Rose Leclercq/
Emily Cross; Lady Wilhelmina Belturbet Ellaline
Terriss; Lady Thomasin Belturbet Pattie Browne; "Ser-
geant" Shutter Marianne Caldwell; Lady Noeline Bel-

turbet Lily Hanbury. L & MGR Arthur Chudleigh; Sc
T.W. Hall; Sm T.W.S. Robertson; Bm Leonard Lillies;
Mus & Mus dir Edward Jones. *REV: Ath 11/3/93 p322;*
E 11/3/93 p9; Sk 15/3/93 p395-6, 412-3, 5/4/93 p594-7;
SR 18/3/93 p297; St 9/3/93 p12; Th 1/4/93 p219-20;
Ti 8/3/93 p10; TW93 p83-7.

93.47 *THE FAIR EQUESTRIENNE; OR, THE CIRCUS RIDER*
(Sk,1a) E. Haslingden Russell. TRAFALGAR SQUARE 8/3/
93, 15/3/93. 2 mat perf. Prince's, Bristol 14/3/90.
Charles Kinghorn W.T. Lovell; Lord Loftus Percy
Brough. Lady Kitty Clare Cora Stuart. L & PP Mr & Mrs
Frank Wyatt; Mgr Yorke Stephens, E.W. Garden; Bm G.F.
Bashford; Bom F.J. Potter; Cond Dan Godfrey, jr. *REV:*
E 11/3/93 p9; St 9/3/93 p13.

93.48 *ORPHEUS* (O,3a) C.W. Gluck. LYCEUM 11/3/93 mat
perf.** Orpheus Clara E. Butt; Eurydice Maggie Purvis; Eros Ethel M. Cain; Wandering Spirit Blanche
Reynolds. L & MGR Henry Irving; Cond C. Villiers
Stanford; Bom Joseph Hurst. *REV: E 18/3/93 p8.* Comment: Royal College of Music.

93.49 *THE GOLDEN WEB* (CO,3a) Frederick Corder (lib)
& B.C. Stephenson (lib) & Goring Thomas (mus). LYRIC
11/3/93-15/4/93. 28 perf [w/mat 18/3, 8/4; np 27/3-
31/3]. 1st perfd Court, Liverpool 15/2/93. Dr Man-
acle Wallace Brownlow; Lord Silvertop Richard Temple;
Bullion J. Furneaux Cook; Spindle W.S. Laidlaw;
Geoffrey Norreys Tom A. Shale/Durward Lely; Smug
Arthur Wilkinson. Pamela Patch Amadi/Lina Hicks; Mrs
Scatterwell Dora Thorne/Cissy Cranford; Mrs Pounceby
Emmeline Orford; Amabel Alice Esty/Dora Thorne. L &
MGR & DIR Horace Sedger; Mus dir Herbert Bunning;
Bm & Treas William Greet. *REV: Ath 18/3/93 p355; E*
8/4/93 p9; Sk 22/3/93 p462-3, 19/4/93 p705-6; St 16/
3/93 p12, 13/4/93 p13; Th 1/4/93 p220-1; Ti 13/3/93
p11.

93.50 *A DOLL'S HOUSE* (P,3a) Henrik Ibsen. ROYALTY
11/3/93-25/3/93. 14 perf [w/mat 18/3; mat only 11/3,
25/3].** Torvald Helmer Charles Charrington; Nils
Krogstad Herbert Flemming; Dr Rank W.R. Staveley;
Porter [Henry] Nelson; Einar Master Basil Deane; Bob

Master Hilary Deane; Emmy Master Ambrose Deane. Nora
Helmer Janet Achurch; Mrs Linden Carlotta Addison;
Anna Ida Sala; Ellen Hetty Laurence. L Kate Santley;
Mgr Charles Charrington; Sc W.T. Hemsley; Mus dir
C.W. Lamartine; Bm Harrington Baily; Sm John Carter;
Sec Gifford Stacey; Bom Glover. *REV: E 18/3/93 p9;
SR 18/3/93 p297; St 16/3/93 p12; TW93 p87-88.*

93.51 *OUR PLAY* (Ca,1a) R.G. Graham. VAUDEVILLE 13/3/
93-18/3/93. 6 perf. 1st perfd Town Hall, Teddington
1/2/93. Sir John Blackham Charles J. Fulton; William
Shattock A. Wood; Charles Bourchier Philip Cunning-
ham. Sybil Kate Bealby. L & MGR A. & S. Gatti; Dir
Herbert Waring, Elizabeth Robins; Mus dir Henry
Sprake; Bm Charles Terry; Act mgr & Treas L[ouis] F.
Nethersole. *REV: E 18/3/93 p9; St 16/3/93 p12.*

93.52 *SOPHIA* (P,4a) Robert Buchanan [fnd on Henry
Fielding, *Tom Jones*]. TERRY'S 16/3/93 mat perf.**
Blifil D. Lewin Mannering; Tom Jones A. Dawson Mil-
ward; Mr Allworthy A.G. Brown; Squire Weston J.L.
Rowse; Partridge Martin J. Cahill; Square Cyril Ken-
yon. Sophia Kate Rorke; Mistress Honour Ellie Chester;
Lady Bellaston Mrs R. Evans; Molly Seagrim Adela Dray-
ton; Tabitha Western Marion Graham. PP & MGR Edward
Terry. *REV: St 23/3/93 p12.*

93.53 *DINNER FOR TWO* (Duo1) R.C. Carton. TRAFALGAR
SQUARE 22/3/93 mat perf. 1st perfd Theatre Royal,
Brighton 9/3/93. Stapleton Kidbrook Yorke Stephens;
Mjr. Powneby Cyril Maude; Achille J[ohn] Willes. L &
PP Mr & Mrs Frank Wyatt; Mgr Yorke Stephens, E.W.
Garden; Bm G.F. Bashford. *REV: E 25/3/93 p9; St 23/3/
93 p12.*

93.54 *THE FOOL'S REVENGE* (D,3a) Tom Taylor [fnd on
Victor Hugo, *Le Roi S'Amuse*]. TRAFALGAR SQUARE 23/3/
93 mat perf. 1st perfd Sadlers Wells, 18/10/59.
Guido Malatesta Bassett Roe; Serafino Dell'Aquila
Philip Cunningham; Baldassare Torelli Edmund Gurney;
Bertuccio Lionel Baxter; Gian Maria Ordelaffi Graham
Wentworth; Bernardo Ascolti Ivan Watson; Galeotto
Manfredi J.H. Barnes. Brigitta Dolores Drummond;
Fiordelisa Mabel Lane; Ascanio Nora Leslie; Frances-

ca Bentivoglio Maud Milton; Ginevra Ingram. DIR W.H.
Act mgr Francis Jerrard. *REV: E 25/3/93 p11; St 30/
3/93 p12; Th 1/5/93 p281-2.*

93.55 *MR JERICHO* (Oa) Harry Greenbank (lib) & Ernest
Ford (mus). SAVOY 24/3/93-15/4/93; 3/6/93-1/7/93. 45
perf [np 31/3].* Michael de Vere, Earl of Margate
George de Pledge/W.H. Leon; Horace Alexander de Vere,
Viscount Ramsgate Bates Maddison/Sidwell Jones; Mr
Jericho J. Bowden Haswell. Lady Bushey Agnes Scott;
Winifred Florence Easton. PP & MGR Richard d'Oyly
Carte. *REV: 1/4/93 p14; Ti 27/3/93 p8.*

93.56 *PETER THE SHIPWRIGHT* [*CZAR UND ZIMMERMANN*] (Co,
3a) Albert Lortzing. LYCEUM 25/3/93 mat perf. 1st
perfd Municipal Theatre, Leipzig 22/12/37. Peter I
Arthur Appleby; Peter Ivanhoff Philip Brozel; Herr
van Bett Arthur Barlow; Gen. Lefort John W. Foster;
Lord Syndham Fred B. Ranalow; Marquis of Chateauneuf
James Horncastle; Bridegroom Gerald Mirrielees. Widow
Brown Vena Galbraith; Maria Lilian Redfern; Bride
Gertrude Chandler. L & MGR Henry Irving; Cond G.H.
Betjeman; Bom Joseph Hurst. Royal Academy of Music.

93.57 *MAN AND WOMAN* (CD,4a) David Belasco & Henry C.
de Mille [rev T. Malcolm Watson]. OPERA COMIQUE 25/3/
93-22/4/93. 28 perf [w/S mat exc 25/3; add mat 3/4;
np 31/3].* Stephen Rodman Henry Neville/W.A. Elliott;
Col. Zachary T. Kipp Herbert Standing; Israel Cohen
Arthur Elwood; Calvin Stedman Charles J. Fulton;
Edward Seabury W.T. Lovell; Sam Delafield Sam Sothern;
Mr Pendleton Sant Matthews; William Prescott Arthur
Dacre; Cannon Edgar Monson; Lyman R. Webb Gerald God-
frey; Mr Reynolds W. Lawrence; Mr Bergman E.H. Kelly;
Mr Wayne Arthur Wilmot; Arnold Kirke Standley Wade;
Crawford Cecil Croft; Roberts Oscar Asche. Margery
Knox Eva Moore; Mrs Prescott M. Talbot; Dora Pres-
cott Lena Ashwell; Agnes Rodman Amy Roselle; Mrs
Delafield Nancy Noel; Lucy Annie Constance. L Edward
Compton; Mgr Amy Roselle; Bom Hamilton; Pq C.H. Fox;
Furn Maple & Co., J.S. Lyon; Cost Mme Josephine; Bm
J. Edward Hollingshead; Sc Walter Johnstone, W.T.
Hemsley; Mus dir Alfred J. Caldicott; Treas T.H.
O'Neil. *REV: Ath 1/4/93 p419-20; E 1/4/93 p14; Sk*

29/3/93 p508; St 30/3/93 p12; Th 1/5/93 p282-3; Ti
27/3/93 p8; TW93 p88-90.

93.58 *THE BABBLE SHOP; OR, LORD WYNDHAMERE'S FAN* (Bsq,
1a) Edward Rose. TRAFALGAR SQUARE 30/3/93-15/4/93.
21 perf [w/mat 3/4, 8/4, 15/4; np 31/3].* Hugo Hil-
derbrand Hengist de Sarum Cyril Maude; Lord Wyndhamere
Arthur Playfair; Stodge, M.P. E.W. Garden/J. Willes;
W. Sykes Mark Kinghorne; Caleb Plummer J[ohn] Willes;
Wireson E[dward] O'Neill; Beadle [Henry N.] Wenman.
Duchess of Higham Kickers Grace Huntley; Duchess of
Sou' Sou' Westmoreland Lizzie Ruggles; Duchess of
Marylebone Lizzie Wilson; "2 2 2 2 2" Helen Leyton;
Duchess of North Belgravia [Cissy?] St. George. L &
PP Mr & Mrs Frank Wyatt; Mgr Yorke Stephens, E.W.
Garden; Mus John Crook, Arthur E. Godfrey, Lionel
Monckton; Pq, Cost C.H. Fox; Bm G.F. Bashford. *REV:*
E 1/4/93 p14; Sk 12/4/93 p630; SR 2/4/93 p377; St 6/
4/93 p13; Th 1/5/93 p288; Ti 31/3/93 p8; TW93 p90-1.

93.59 *THE BLACK DOMINO* (D,5a) George R. Sims & Robert
Buchanan. ADELPHI 1/4/93-27/5/93. 49 perf.* Lord
Dashwood Charles Glenney; Joshua Honeybun Arthur
Williams/John Phipps; Cpt. Greville W.L. Abingdon;
Pierre Berton George W. Cockburn; Dr Maitland T.B.
Thalberg; Mjr. O'Flaherty John Le Hay; Chevenix Chase
Welton Dale; Jack Vavasour C.M. Hallard; Earl of
Arlington W. Dennis; Lord Drewcourt R.C. Stuart;
Charlie Watts Master H. Buss; James Honeybun W. North-
cote; Old Gentleman John Phipps; Sir George Johnson
Silverthorne; Inspector Howard Russell/Arthur Leigh;
Stokes Harwood Cooper; Bust of Homer [G.H.] Kersley;
Parker J[ohn] Northcote/John Phipps; Reynolds H.
Edgecumbe. Mildred Vavasour Evelyn Millard; Clarice
Berton Mrs Patrick Campbell/Olga Brandon; Rose Ber-
ton Bessie Hatton; Dolly Chester Clara Jecks; Mrs
Alabaster Ethel Hope; Maid Ada Rogers; Birdie Boston
Nita Carlyon; Gussie Conyers Stella Berridge; Granny
Norbury G. Conway. PP & MGR A. & S. Gatti; Sc Bruce
Smith, Walter Johnstone; Cost dgn Karl; Cost Nathan;
Ch John d'Auban; Mus & Mus dir Henry Sprake; Furn
J. Lyon; Pq William Clarkson; Sm E.B. Norman; Act mgr
& Treas Charles A. Jecks. *REV: Ath 8/4/93 p451-2; E*
8/4/93 p8, 20/5/93 p11; SR 8/4/93 p377-8; St 6/4/93

p12; Th 1/5/93 p285-6; Ti 3/4/93 p2; TW93 p91-6.

93.60 *OUR SMOKING CONCERT* (MSk) Mel B. Spurr. COURT
3/4/93-6/6/93. 56 perf. 1st perf? Mel B. Spurr.
L & MGR Arthur Chudleigh.

93.61 *THE BOHEMIAN GIRL* (O[3a]) Michael Balfe. DRURY
LANE 3/4/93, 6/4, 12/4, 15/4, 19/4, 25/4, 29/4/93.
7 perf.** Thaddeus [Robert] Eadie; Count Arnheim D.
Ffrangcon Davies; Florestan Wilfred Esmond; Devilshoof Albert McGuckin. Gipsy Queen Lucille Saunders;
Arline Albu/[Carla] Dagmar/Fanny Moody. L & MGR Augustus Harris; Cond Carl Armbruster; Bom [W.] Allcroft; Sec & Treas Fred G. Latham. *REV: Ath 8/4/93
p449-50; E 8/4/93 p15; St 6/4/93 p12; Ti 4/4/93 p5.*

93.62 *CAVALLERIA RUSTICANA* (O,1a) Pietro Mascagni.
DRURY LANE 3/4/93, 6/4, 12/4, 15/4, 19/4, 21/4,
25/4, 26/4, 29/4/93. 9 perf.** Turiddu Ferruccio
Giannini/Joseph O'Mara/Morello; Alfio Eugene Du-
friche/Pignalosa. Lola Olimpia Guercia; Lucia Bian-
coli; Santuzza Esther Palliser/Marie Duma. L & MGR,
Bom, Sec & Treas as for 93.61; Cond Wilhelm Feld.
*REV: Ath 8/4/93 p449-50; E 8/4/93 p15, 29/4/93 p15;
St 6/4/93 p12; Ti 4/4/93 p5.*

93.63 *UNCLE JOHN* (P,3a) George R. Sims & Cecil Ra-
leigh. VAUDEVILLE 3/4/93-22/4/93. 20 perf [w/mat
8/4, 15/4].* John Bryce Charles Groves; Charlie
Bryce H. Reeves-Smith; Bradford Julian Cross; Hon
Peter Penarth Lawrance d'Orsay; Gus Doyle Duncan
Fleet; Arthur Hastings E.W. Gardiner; Johnston John
Byron. Olive Penarth Rose Norreys; Polly Bryce Annie
Hughes; Jane Daisy England; Mary Lyddie Edmonds;
Lady Meynel Irene Rickards; Keziah Bryce Sophie Lar-
kin; Mrs Hilborough Geraldine St. Maur. L & MGR
A. & S. Gatti; Sc William Perkins; Sm & Pd William
Sidney; Furn J.S. Lyon; Mus dir Henry Sprake; Act mgr
& Treas L[ouis] F. Nethersole. *REV: Ath 8/4/93 p452;
E 8/4/93 p8; SR 8/4/93 p378; St 6/4/93 p12-3; Th 1/5/
93 p283-4; Ti 4/4/93 p5; TW93 p91-6.*

93.64 *CARMEN* (O[4a]) Georges Bizet. DRURY LANE 4/4/93,
8/4, 20/4, 24/4/93. 4 perf.** Escamillo Eugene Du-

friche/Pignalosa; <u>Zuniga</u> Antonio de Vaschetti; <u>Don
Jose</u> Morello; <u>Dancairo</u> Iginio Corsi; <u>Remendado</u> Rinal-
dini; <u>Morales</u> Caracciolo. <u>Carmen</u> Olimpia Guercia;
<u>Frasquita</u> Biancoli; <u>Mercedes</u> Florenza; <u>Michaela</u> [Carla]
Dagmar. <u>L & MGR</u> Augustus Harris; <u>Cond</u> Carl Armbruster;
<u>Bom</u> W. Allcroft; <u>Sec & Treas</u> Fred G. Latham. *REV: Ath
8/4/93 p450; E 8/4/93 p15, 29/4/93 p15; St 6/4/93 p12;
Ti 6/4/93 p9.*

93.65 *FAUST* (O[5a]) Charles Gounod. DRURY LANE 5/4/93,
27/4/93. 2 perf.** <u>Faust</u> Ferruccio Giannini/Joseph
O'Mara; <u>Valentine</u> Eugene Dufriche/Pignalosa; <u>Mephis-
topheles</u> Armand Castelmary; <u>Wagner</u> Antonio de Vaschetti. <u>Siebel</u> Olimpia Guercia; <u>Marta</u> Biancoli; <u>Mar-
guerite</u> Esther Palliser. <u>L & MGR</u>, <u>Bom</u>, <u>Sec & Treas</u> as
for 93.64; <u>Cond</u> Wilhelm Feld. *REV: Ath 8/4/93 p450;
E 8/4/93 p15; St 13/4/93 p12.*

93.66 *CLEVER ALICE* (C,3a) Brandon Thomas [adpt of
Adolf Willbrandt, *Die Maler*]. ROYALTY 6/4/93-21/4/93.
14 perf.* <u>Gerald Douglas</u> Charles Charrington; <u>James
Cook</u> Herbert Flemming; <u>Sir William Newgent</u> Edmund
Maurice; <u>Payne Williams</u> John Carter; <u>Corrington Selby</u>
Gilbert Trent; <u>Charles Verber</u> C.P. Little; <u>Claude
Couraine</u> Charles Rock; <u>Thomas Grace</u> W.R. Staveley.
<u>Alice</u> Janet Achurch; <u>Lady Altrood</u> Gertrude Kingston;
<u>Lady Lilton</u> Mrs Theodore Wright; <u>Grace</u> Ida Sala; <u>Lucy
Grace</u> Hettie Lawrence. <u>L</u> Kate Santley; <u>Mgr</u> Charles
Charrington; <u>Bom</u> Glover; <u>Sec</u> Gifford Stacey; <u>Sc</u> Hed-
ley Churchward; <u>Furn</u> Lyons; <u>Pq</u> C.H. Fox; <u>Mus dir</u> C.W.
Lamartine. *REV: E 8/4/93 p9; Sk 12/4/93 p631; St 13/
4/93 p13; Th 1/5/93 p286; Ti 8/4/93 p5; TW93 p97-8.*

93.67 *AN ENTERTAINMENT* John Le Hay. ADELPHI 8/4/93-
13/5/93. 31 perf. John Le Hay. <u>PP & MGR</u> A. & S. Gatti;
<u>Act mgr & Treas</u> Charles A. Jecks.

93.68 *THE CROSSING SWEEPER* (MSk) Basil Hood (lib) &
Walter Slaughter (mus). GAIETY 8/4/93-22/7/93. 90
perf [np 6/7].* <u>Bill</u> Edmund Payne. <u>Tom</u> Florence
Lloyd; <u>Nancy</u> Kate Cutler. <u>L & MGR</u> George Edwardes.
REV: E 15/4/93 p9; Sk 29/3/93 p521-2; St 13/4/93 p13.

93.69 *LOUIS XI* (5a) Dion Boucicault [adpt fr Casimir

Delavigne]. LYCEUM 8/4/93, 15/4, 6/5/93. 3 perf.**
Louis XI Henry Irving; The Dauphin John Martin Har-
vey; Duke de Nemours William Terriss; Philip de
Commines [Henry] Howe; Jacques Coitier Frank [Kemble]
Cooper; Tristan l'Ermite [Frank] Tyars; Oliver le
Dain [John] Archer; Francois de Paule [William] Havi-
land; Cardinal d'Alby [W.J.] Lorriss; Count de Dreux
[Acton] Bond; Montjoie Lacy; Monseigneur de Lude
[H.W.] Cushing; Count de Dunois [R.P.] Tabb; Marcel
[Sam] Johnson; Richard [T.] Reynolds; Didier [W.]
Marion; Officer of the Royal Guard Powell; Toison d'Or
[K.] Rivington; King's Attendant [W. Lionel] Belmore.
Marie Amy Coleridge; Martha Kate Phillips. L & MGR
Henry Irving; Cond J. Meredith Ball; Sm H.J. Loveday;
Act mgr Bram Stoker; Bom Joseph Hurst. *REV: E 15/4/93
p9; St 13/4/93 p12-3; TW93 p113-4.*

93.70 *THE LANDLADY* (Ca,1a) "Alec Nelson" [E.B. Ave-
ling]. VAUDEVILLE 8/4/93-22/4/93. 13 perf. 1st perfd
Shaftesbury 4/4/89. Bob Bateman Duncan Fleet; Leo-
nidas Gwynne Julian Cross. Nell Gwynne Daisy England.
L & MGR A. & S. Gatti; Sm William Sidney; Act mgr &
Treas L[ouis] F. Nethersole.

93.71 *MARITANA* (O[3a]) Vincent Wallace. DRURY LANE
10/4/93, 13/4/93. 2 perf.** Don Caesare de Bazan
Ben Davies; Don José D. Ffrangcon Davies; Charles II,
King of Spain Albert McGuckin; Marquis de Montefiore
Wilfred Esmond; Cpt. of the Guard Muller. Lazarillo
Lucille Saunders; Maritana Lucile Hill; Marchioness
de Montefiore Kate Vito. L & MGR Augustus Harris;
Cond Wilhelm Feld; Bom W. Allcroft; Sec & Treas Fred
G. Latham. *REV: E 15/4/93 p15; St 13/4/93 p12; Ti
13/4/93 p13.*

93.72 *LA JUIVE* (O[5a]) Fromental Halévy. DRURY LANE
11/4/93, 17/4, 22/4/93. 3 perf. 1st perfd Paris 23/2/
35. Eleazaro Ferruccio Giannini; Cardinal Brogni
Armand Castelmary; Il Principe Leopoldo Pedro Guetary;
Ruggero Antonio de Vaschetti; Alberto Caracciolo;
Araldo Cernusco. Rachele Gherlsen; La Principessa
Eudossia Carla Dagmar. L & MGR, Bom, Sec & Treas as
for 93.71; Cond Carl Armbruster. *REV: E, St, Ti as
for 93.71; Ath 15/4/93 p481; Th 1/5/93 p293-4.*

93.73 *THE MAGIC RING* [*THE MAGIC OPAL*] (CO,2a) Arthur
Law (lib) & Isaac Albeniz (mus). PRINCE OF WALES'S
11/4/93–19/5/93. 77 perf [w/S mat exc 15/4, 13/5].**
Telemachus Ulysses Caramtollas Harry Monkhouse; Curro
Arthur Watts; Arristippus Fred Kaye; Alzaga Edwin
Wareham; Pekito Frank A. Walsh; Trabucos Norman Sal-
mond. Zoe Lilian Stanley; Christina Anita Courtenay;
Irene Annie Laurie; Lolika Marie Halton; Martina
Susie Vaughan; Dancers Rosa, Wood, [Jennie] Rogers,
Young, Laubach, Selby, Reynolds, Shawe, Rooke. L & MGR
Edgar Bruce; Cond Albeniz; Act mgr C.P. Levilly; Cost
Miss Fisher, Auguste, L. & H. Nathan; Pq William
Clarkson. *REV: E 15/4/93 p11; St 13/4/93 p13; Th 1/5/
93 p294; Ti 13/4/93 p13.*

93.74 *MOROCCO BOUND* (MFC,2a) Arthur Branscombe (lib)
& Adrian Ross (lyr) & F. Osmond Carr (mus). SHAFTES-
BURY 13/4/93–5/1/94;* trfd to TRAFALGAR 8/1/94–10/
2/94. 295 perf [w/S mat 13/4/93–3/6/93; w/W mat 15/6/
93–20/7/93; w/S mat 9/9/93–10/2/94 exc 20/1/94; add
mat 12/8/93, 26/8, 26/12/93, 31/1/94; np 22–25/12/93,
20/1/94]. Spoofah Bey John L. Shine/Harry Grattan;
Vivian Sydney Barraclough/Templer Saxe/E.H. Haslam;
Dolly Alfred C. Seymour; Josiah Higgins Herbert
Sparling; Lord Percy Pimpleton George Grossmith, jr;
Sid Fakah Colin Coop/J. Jamieson/Richard Temple;
Musket Douglas Munro; Squire Higgins Charles Danby/
Harry Grattan. Hon Ethel Sportington Violet Cameron/
Florence Dysart/Hilda Glenn/Lilian Redfern/Maggie
Roberts; Comtesse de la Blague Jennie McNulty/Lizzie
Ruggles; Lady Walkover Agnes Hewitt; Rhea Porter
Marie Studholme/Maud Henri/Ruby Temple; Eva Sketchley
Eva Westlake/Maggie Ripley/ Maud Wellington; Nina
Featherstone Yata Whynier; Hilda Adlette Ruby Temple/
Lizzie Ruggles; Hon Maude Sportington Letty Lind/
Minnie Palmer. MGR F.J. Harris; Dir Frank Parker; Sc
E.G. Banks; Cost Harrison Ltd; Cost dgn Jean Paleo-
logue; Pq William Clarkson; Props Labhart; Ch Mariette
d'Auban; Mus dir Sidney Jones; Pp John Lancaster; L
H.J. Pearson. *REV: E 15/4/93 p11, 18/11/93 p9; Sk
19/4/93 p686, 22/11/93 p167, 17/1/94 p628; St 20/4/93
p13, 16/11/93 p13, 11/1/94 p15; Th 1/5/93 p294; Ti
17/4/93 p12, 5/8/93 p10; TW93 p104.*

93.75 *LOHENGRIN* (O[3a]) Richard Wagner. DRURY LANE
14/4/93, 18/4/93. 2 perf.** <u>Lohengrin</u> Morello; <u>Fred-</u>
<u>erico di Telramondo</u> Pignalosa; <u>Enrico l'Uccellatore</u>
Armand Castelmary; <u>L'Araldo del Re</u> Antonio de Vas-
chetti. <u>Ortruda</u> Olimpia Guercia; <u>Elsa di Brabante</u>
Esther Palliser/Gherlsen. <u>L & MGR</u> Augustus Harris;
<u>Cond</u> Carl Armbruster; <u>Bom</u> W. Allcroft; <u>Sec & Treas</u>
Fred G. Latham. *REV: Ath 22/4/93 p514; E 22/4/93 p15;*
St 20/4/93 p12; Ti 17/4/93 p8.

93.76 *THE SILVER SHELL* (P,4a) Henry J.W. Dam. AVENUE
15/4/93-3/6/93. 44 perf [w/mat 22/4; mat only 29/4].
1st perfd Prince of Wales's, Birmingham 2/12/92 [as
Prince Karatoff]. <u>Gen. Prince Karatoff</u> W.H. Kendal;
<u>Sir Richard Stanhope</u> F.H. Macklin; <u>Banham</u> J.E. Dod-
son; <u>Valdor</u> Cecil M. York; <u>Boris Ivanitch</u> Oscar Adye;
<u>Herr Schmidt</u> G.P. Huntley; <u>Paul Mouroff</u> Edmund Grace;
<u>Vasili</u> Howard Sturge; <u>Juge d'Instruction</u> George H.
Gray; <u>Agent de Police</u> V. Everard; <u>Constantin</u> A. Fau-
cet; <u>Andre</u> C. Norton; <u>Vladimir</u> H. Howard; <u>Ivan Petro-</u>
<u>vitch</u> Sydney Jerram; <u>Adolf</u> H. Deane; <u>Ladislas</u> Temple.
<u>Lady Armitage</u> Annie Irish; <u>Mrs Ladd</u> Florence Bennett;
<u>Lucille</u> Adrienne Dairolles; <u>Mrs Verney</u> Barbara Hunt-
ley; <u>Katharine Vail</u> Mrs W.H. Kendal; <u>Jack</u> Empsie
Bowman. <u>L</u> George Paget; <u>Mgr</u> Mr & Mrs W.H. Kendal; <u>Sc</u>
William Harford; <u>Furn</u> Frank Giles; <u>Mus dir</u> J. Hamilton Clarke. *REV: Ath 22/4/93 p515; E 22/4/93 p9; Sk*
26/4/93 p745; St 20/4/93 p12-3; Th 1/5/93 p287-8; Ti
17/4/93 p12; TW93 p98-104.

93.77 *THE MASTERPIECE* (Ca,1a) Mrs Hugh Bell. ROYALTY
15/4/93-21/4/93. 6 perf.* <u>Arthur Bromley</u> Herbert
Flemming. <u>Mrs Arthur Bromley</u> Gertrude Kingston; <u>Sarah</u>
Hetty Lawrence. <u>MGR</u> Charles Charrington; <u>Bom</u> Glover;
<u>Sec</u> Gifford Stacey; <u>Mus dir</u> C.W. Lamartine. *REV: E*
22/4/93 p9; St 20/4/93 p12.

93.78 *A DRAWN BATTLE* (Duol) T. Malcolm Watson. OPERA
COMIQUE 17/4/93-22/4/93. 6 perf.* <u>Ralph Kenyon</u>
Charles J. Fulton. <u>Patty Langton</u> Lena Ashwell. <u>L</u> Ed-
ward Compton; <u>Mgr</u> Amy Roselle; <u>Bom</u> Hamilton; <u>Bm</u> Ed-
ward Hollingshead; <u>Mus dir</u> Alfred J. Caldicott; <u>Treas</u>
T.H. O'Neil. *REV: E 22/4/93 p9; St 20/4/93 p12.*

93.79 *A WOMAN OF NO IMPORTANCE* (P,4a) Oscar Wilde.
HAYMARKET 19/4/93-16/8/93. 113 perf [w/S mat exc 15/7,
29/7; add mat 7/6; mat only 26/5, 12/8; np 6/7, 20-
22/7].* <u>Lord Illingworth</u> H.B. Tree/Frederick Harris-
on; <u>Sir John Pontefract</u> E. Holman Clark; <u>Lord Alfred
Rufford</u> Lawford; <u>Mr Kelvil</u> Charles Allan; <u>Ven Dr Dau-
beny</u> [Henry] Kemble; <u>Gerald Arbuthnot</u> Fred Terry;
<u>Farquhar</u> Hay; <u>Francis</u> [J.] Montagu. <u>Lady Hunstanton</u>
Rose Leclercq; <u>Lady Caroline Pontefract</u> R.G. Le
Thiere; <u>Lady Strutfield</u> Blanche Horlock; <u>Mrs Allenby</u>
Mrs H.B. Tree; <u>Hester Worsley</u> Julia Neilson/Lily
Hanbury; <u>Alice</u> Kelly; <u>Mrs Arbuthnot</u> Mrs Bernard Beere.
<u>L & MGR</u> H. Beerbohm Tree; <u>Sc</u> Walter Hann, Walter
Johnstone; <u>Pq</u> William Clarkson; <u>Elect</u> E. Wingfield
Bowles; <u>Bom</u> W.H. Leverton; <u>Sm</u> Edward Hastings; <u>Mus
dir</u> Carl Armbruster; <u>Bm & Sec</u> Frederick Harrison.
*REV: Ath 22/4/93 p515-6; E 22/4/93 p9, 13/5/93 p10;
Sk 26/4/93 p739-40, 744-5; SR 6/5/93 p482-3; St 20/4/
93 p12, 27/4/93 p12; Th 1/6/93 p332-3; Ti 20/4/93 p5;
TW93 p105-13.*

93.80 *DOT; OR, THE CRICKET ON THE HEARTH* Dion Boucicault. TOOLE'S 19/4/93, 26/4, 3/5/93. 3 mat perf.
1st perfd Winter Garden, New York 14/9/59. <u>Caleb
Plummer</u> J.L. Toole; <u>John Peerybingle</u> John Billington;
<u>Tackleton</u> George Shelton; <u>Edward Plummer</u> C.M. Lowne.
<u>Tilly Sloeboy</u> Eliza Johnstone; <u>Dot</u> Kate Phillips;
<u>Bertha</u> Irene Vanbrugh; <u>Mrs Fielding</u> Effie Liston;
<u>May Fielding</u> Cora Poole; <u>Spirit of Home</u> Beaumont
Loveday. <u>L & MGR</u> J.L. Toole; <u>Sm</u> John Billington; <u>Mus
dir</u> William Robins; <u>Bm</u> George Lee. *REV: Th 1/6/93
p339.*

93.81 *THE BIRTHPLACE OF PODGERS* (F,1a) John Holling-
shead. TOOLE'S 19/4/93, 26/4/93. 2 mat perf.** <u>Tom
Cranky</u> J.L. Toole; <u>Edmund Earlybird</u> Henry Westland;
<u>Alonzo Lexicon</u> Laurence Irving; <u>Old Maresnest</u> George
Shelton; <u>1st Photographer</u> H[erbert] Pearson; <u>2nd
Photographer</u> Frank J. Arlton; <u>Mortal Podgers</u> C[har-
les] Brunton. <u>Mrs Cranky</u> Eliza Johnstone; <u>Amelia</u>
Alice Kingsley; <u>Penelope Lexicon</u> Mary Brough. <u>L & MGR,
Sm, Mus dir, Bm</u> as for 93.80.

93.82 *THE LYONS MAIL* (Melo,3a) Charles Reade [adpt of

Emile Moreau, Giraudin, & Delacour, *Le Courrier de Lyon*]. LYCEUM 22/4/93, 29/4, 13/5, 20/5, 7/6, 14/6, 28/6/93. 7 perf.** Lesurques/Dubosc Henry Irving; Courriol William Terriss; Choppard S[am] Johnson; Fouinard [John] Archer; Durochat [W.J.] Lorriss; Jerome Lesurques Alfred Bishop; Dorval [Frank] Tyars; Didier [William] Haviland; Joliquet John Martin Harvey; Guerneau Gordon Craig; Lambert Lacy; Postmaster of Montgeron [Henry] Howe; Coco [T.] Reynolds; Postillion [J.H.] Allen; Commissary of Police [H.W.] Cushing; Guard [R.P.] Tabb; Waiter [W.] Marion; Julie Lesurques Amy Coleridge; Marie Foster; Niece to Postmaster Kate Phillips; Jeanette Jessie Millward. L & MGR Henry Irving; Sm H.J. Loveday; Act mgr Bram Stoker; Bom Joseph Hurst. *REV: E 29/4/93 p9; St 27/4/93 p12; TW93 p113-4.*

93.83 *THE BURGLAR AND THE JUDGE* (Farcical Interlude, 1a) F.C. Phillips & Charles H.E. Brookfield. PRINCE OF WALES'S 24/4/93-19/5/93. 23 perf.** Joe Charles H.E. Brookfield; Justice Gyves Fred Kaye; Parkhurst Francis Howard. L & MGR Edgar Bruce; Act mgr C.P. Levilly.

93.84 *ECHO* (C,3a) Arthur M. Heathcote. TRAFALGAR SQUARE 25/4/93 mat perf.* Alexis Jamblin G.K. Paley; Hugh A. Hamilton Revelle; Martin Drake Roy Horniman; Charley Coventry Howard Sturge; Mr Pargather Arthur M. Heathcote; Bruno Strangways A.F. Olphert; Mr Sallow S. Ellison; Mr Rudkin W.T. Durham; Mr Scalpin R[odney] Edgecumbe; Guests G.P. Matthew, G. Piddick; Footmen E.F. Abbott, B. Pares. Mrs Jamblin Mrs Edmund Phelps; Celia Lizzie Webster; Hester Kynaston Annie Webster; Miss Pegler Mrs [F.] Copleston; Guests Olive Molesworth, Cowper Coles, Eleanor Layton; Dona Ramona Agnes Hill. PP & L Mr & Mrs Frank Wyatt; Pq William Clarkson; Sm Julian Cross; Mus dir C.W. Lamartine; Bm Harrington Baily. *REV: E 29/4/93 p11; St 27/4/93 p12.* Comment: Some sources indicate an evening perf.

93.85 *IRMENGARDA* (O[2a]) Leonhard Emil Bach. DRURY LANE 21/4/93, 26/4/93. 2 perf.** Luca Eugene Dufriche; Cuniberto Pedro Guetary; Il Re Antonio de

Vaschetti; <u>Burckhard</u> Armand Castelmary. <u>Irmengarda</u>
Marie Duma; <u>Brigida</u> Olimpia Guercia. <u>L & MGR</u> Augustus
Harris; <u>Cond</u> Carl Armbruster; <u>Bom</u> W. Allcroft; <u>Sec &</u>
<u>Treas</u> Fred G. Latham. *REV: E 29/4/93 p15; St 4/5/93*
p12; Ti 27/4/93 p10. <u>Comment</u>: There is some doubt
whether the 21/4 perf was given.

93.86 *ADRIENNE LECOUVREUR* (P,5a) Henry Herman [adpt
of Eugene Scribe & Ernest Legouvé]. ROYALTY 26/4/93-
28/4/93. 3 perf. 1st perfd Court 11/12/80. <u>Michonnet</u>
Charles Charrington; <u>Maurice de Saxe</u> Herbert Flem-
ming; <u>Poisson</u> John Carter; <u>Abbé de Chazeuil</u> C.P.
Little; <u>Prince de Bouillon</u> Charles Rock; <u>Quinault</u>
W.R. Staveley; <u>Call Boy</u> Master Deane; <u>Servant</u> Gilbey
Trent. <u>Adrienne Lecouvreur</u> Janet Achurch; <u>Princess de</u>
<u>Bouillon</u> Florence Farr; <u>Duchesse d'Aumont</u> Ashton;
<u>Marquise de Sancerre</u> [Naomi?] Hope; <u>Mlle Jouvenot</u>
Paunceford; <u>Mlle Dangeville</u> Maria Graves; <u>Maid</u> Hetty
Laurence. <u>L</u> Kate Santley; <u>Mgr</u> Charles Charrington;
<u>Pq</u> C.H. Fox; <u>Furn</u> Lyons; <u>Bm</u> Harrington Baily; <u>Sm</u> John
Carter; <u>Sec</u> Gifford Stacey; <u>Bom</u> Glover; <u>Mus dir</u> C.W.
Lamartine. *REV: E 29/4/93 p9; SR 6/5/93 p483; Th 1/6/*
93 p339; Ti 28/4/93 p12; TW93 p122.

93.87 *JEALOUS IN HONOUR* (P,4a) "Basil Broke". GARRICK
27/4/93 mat perf.* <u>Prince Newski</u> Bernard Gould; <u>Col.</u>
<u>Strange</u> Sant Matthews; <u>Count von Bohrer</u> Edmund Mau-
rice; <u>Comte de Cerny</u> Gilbert Hare; <u>Hugh Ferrers</u> W.T.
Lovell; <u>Mr Nugent</u> Sydney Brough. <u>Mrs Strange</u> Mrs Edmund Phelps; <u>Alice Ferrers</u> Helen Luck; <u>Helen, Com-</u>
<u>tesse de Cerny</u> Kate Rorke. <u>L & MGR</u> John Hare; <u>Act mgr</u>
C.G. Compton; <u>Sm</u> R[owley] Cathcart; <u>Sc</u> William Harford; <u>Cond</u> Andrew Levey. *REV: E 29/4/93 p11; St 4/5/*
93 p12; Th 1/6/93 p334; Ti 28/4/93 p12; TW93 p123.

93.88 *A LAGGARD IN LOVE* (F,1a) Horace Lennard. TRA-
FALGAR 27/4/93 mat perf.* <u>Mr Battersby</u> Alfred Balfour; <u>Lord Marigold</u> Harry Grattan; <u>George Rose</u> Harcourt Beatty; <u>Alphonse</u> Wilton B. Payne. <u>Minnie</u>
<u>Battersby</u> Mabel Hardy; <u>Sarah</u> Millie Vere. *REV: E 29/*
4/93 p11; St 4/5/93 p12-3.

93.89 *A STAR TURN* (MSk) "Horthur Leuberts" (lib) &
A. Maurice (mus). TRAFALGAR 27/4/93 mat perf.* <u>Mr</u>

Starr-Turner Arthur Roberts. Miss Tapper Lola Radcliffe; Mrs Starr-Turner Phyllis Broughton. CH Mariette d'Auban. *REV: As for 93.88.*

93.90 *IN OLDEN DAYS* (Incident,1a) Mrs Agatha Hodgson.
TRAFALGAR 27/4/93 mat perf.** Jocelyn Durant Philip
Cunningham; Cpt. Desborough Edmund Gurney. Damaris
Nethercliffe Emilie Grattan. *REV: As for 93.88.*

93.91 *IL TROVATORE* (O[4a]) Giuseppe Verdi. DRURY LANE
28/4/93. 1 perf.** Ruiz Rinaldini; Ferrando Antonio
de Vaschetti; Il Conte di Luna Pignalosa; Manrico
Morello. Azucena Olimpia Guercia; Inez Biancoli;
Leonora Gherlsen. L & MGR Augustus Harris; Cond Wilhelm Feld; Bom W. Allcroft; Sec & Treas Fred G. Latham. *REV: E 6/5/93 p15; Ti 1/5/93 p11.*

93.92 *ALAN'S WIFE* (D,3a) Mrs Hugh Bell [fnd on story
by Glin Ameen]. TERRY'S 28/4/93, 2/5/93. 2 mat perf.*
Jamie Warren James A. Welch; Col. Stewart Mervyn
Herapath; Roberts Waller; 1st Warder Charles Gree-
ven; 2nd Warder/Hutton E.G. Waller. Jean Creyke
Elizabeth Robins; Mrs Holroyd Mrs E.H. Brooke; Mrs
Ridley Mrs Edmund Phelps; 1st Woman Mabel Hardy; 2nd
Woman Annie Saker. PD Herman de Lange; Furn Oetzmann;
Pq William Clarkson; Cost Morris Angel; Dir J.T.
Grein. *REV: Ath 6/5/93 p581-2; E 6/5/93 p8; St 4/5/93
p12; Th 1/6/93 p334-5; Ti 1/5/93 p4; TW93 p114-22.*
Comment: Independent Theatre Society.

93.93 *THEORY AND PRACTICE* (Duol) Arthur Benham.
TERRY'S 28/4/93, 2/5/93. 2 mat perf.* Philip Hunter
Bassett Roe. Mrs Hunter Estelle Burney. PD, Furn, Pq,
Cost, Dir as for 93.92. *REV: E, St, Th as for 93.92.*
Comment: Independent Theatre Society.

93.94 *REBECCA RUN MAD* (MSk,1a) H. Chance Newton.
SHAFTESBURY 29/4/93-10/7/93; 31/7/93-5/8/93. 68 perf.
1st perf? Wilfred of Ivanhoe/Sir O'Brian de Bore
Harry Grattan; Isaac of York Prof Hercat. Rebecca
Marie Studholme. MGR F.J. Harris; Pp John Lancaster;
L H.J. Pearson; Act mgr Arthur Blackmore; Sm Sidney
Jones.

93.95 *MR CYNIC* (Ca,1a) W.J. Locke & Graham Roper.
TRAFALGAR SQUARE 2/5/93 mat perf.* John Gargrave
Bassett Roe; Charlie Hamblyn Herbert Ross. Mrs For-
syth Winifred Fraser; Eva Merriton Eleanor Haddon.
REV: E 6/5/93 p8; St 4/5/93 p13.

93.96 *FAUST* (O[5a]) Charles Gounod. LYCEUM 3/5/93
mat perf.** Faust Bates Maddison; Mephistopheles
Edward Epstein; Valentine F. Stuart Hyatt; Wagner
Wyatt Keith. Marguerite Jessie Huddleston; Siebel
Jessie Browning; Martha Leonora Ellerton. COND Sir
Joseph Barnby; Chorus Master Neill O'Donovan; Dir
L.F. Chapuy; Ch Mrs Charles P. Smith. *REV: Ath 6/5/93
p580; E 6/5/93 p15.* Comment: Guildhall School of Music.

93.97 *HOMBURG* (Sk,1a) Joseph Hatton. TOOLE'S 3/5/93(m),
6/5(m), 10/5(m); 11/5-1/7/93. 52 perf [w/S mat exc
10/6, 17/6, 24/6, 1/7].* J.L. Toole/John Duncan
Campbell/Mark Loftus J.L. Toole; Col. Lord Saunders
Seymour Hicks; Eric Weldon Fletcher C.M. Lowne; Herr
Untersberg John Billington; Bandmaster von Schenken-
dorf Laurence Irving; Silas Short Herbert Pearson;
Donald Scott George Shelton; Lieut. Wilhelm von
Franken E.A. Coventry. Mrs Hopkins Eliza Johnstone;
Otis Hopkins Irene Vanbrugh; Freda von Franken Kate
Carlyon; Anna Hanz Alice Kingsley; Fraulein Liebestag
Beaumont Loveday. L & MGR J.L. Toole; Sc Joseph Har-
ker; Sm John Billington; Mus dir William Robins; Bm
George Lee. *REV: E 6/5/93 p9, 3/6/93 p7; Sk 10/5/93
p61; St 4/5/93 p13, 1/6/93 p14; Th 1/6/93 p339; Ti
4/5/93 p12.*

93.98 *MAM'ZELLE NITOUCHE* (MC,3a) Henri Meilhac (lib)
& Albert Millaud (lib) & Florimond Hervé (mus). TRA-
FALGAR SQUARE 6/5/93-18/8/93 [w/W mat exc 10/5, 21/6;
np 6/7]; 7/9/93-16/9/93 [w/S mat]. 113 perf. 1st perfd
Variétés, Paris 22/1/83. Celestin Frank Wyatt; Fernand
de Champlatreau Wallace Browlow/Leonard Russell;
Stage-manager of the Pontarcy Theatre Arthur Playfair/
Graham Wentworth; Loriot John Willes; Gustave George
Humphrey; Major Robert Pateman/Charles Glenney; 1st
Soldier Dudley Yates; Call-boy A.H. Brooke; Extras
Martin, Hider, Willis, Pinder. Mlle Corinne Violet
Melnotte; Lady Superior Elsie Chester; Sylvia Florence

Melville; Gimblette Dora Thorne; Janitress Delia Car-
lyle; Denise de Flavigny May Yohe/Sylvia Gerrish/
[Marie?] Elba; Extras Marion Martell, Maud Clifford,
Cissie Crawford, Francis Jocelyn, Denis Lunie, Chris-
tine Powis. PP & L Mr & Mrs Frank Wyatt; Mus dir Ivan
Caryll; Sc Bruce Smith; Cost Alias, Morris Angel, Mrs
May; Furn Lyon; Pq William Clarkson; Pd Frank Wyatt;
Bom F.J. Potter; Gen mgr Gilbert Tate; Act mgr & Treas
H[enry] Brandon; Asm Cairns James. *REV: E 13/5/93 p9,*
5/8/93 p7; St 11/5/93 p12, 14/9/93 p10; Th 1/6/93
p335-6; Ti 8/5/93 p8, 4/8/93 p10; TW93 p123-4.

93.99 *DIPLUNACY* (Travestie,1sc) F.C. Burnand. TRAFAL-
GAR SQUARE 6/5/93-10/6/93. 31 perf. 1st perfd Strand
14/2/78 [as *Dora and Diplunacy; or, A Woman of Un-*
common Scents]. Julian Beauclerc Arthur Playfair;
Baron Stein John Willes; Count Orloff Frank Wyatt;
Henry Beauclerc Cairns James. Dora Dora Thorne; Coun-
tess Henry Fairfax Violet Melnotte; Marquise de Rio-
Zarès Elsie Chester. PP & L, Mus dir, Sc, Cost, Furn,
Pq, Pd, Bom, Gen mgr, Act mgr & Treas, Asm as for 93.
98. *REV: E 13/5/93 p9; St 11/5/93 p12; Ti 8/5/93 p8;*
TW93 p124.

93.100 *FORBIDDEN FRUIT* (FC,3a) Dion Boucicault [fnd
on Hennequin & Delacour, *Les Dominos Roses*]. VAUDE-
VILLE 6/5/93-8/7/93. 56 perf [w/mat 14/6]. 1st perfd
Wallack's, New York 3/10/76. Cato Dove Charles Groves/
Arthur Williams; Mr Sgt. Buster Lionel Rignold; Cpt.
Derringer H. Reeves-Smith/W.L. Abingdon; Swalbach
Julian Cross; Podd J[ohn] Northcote; Victor Mark
Paton; Joseph H. Dixon; Tom S[idney] Burt; Ginger
Master Shaw; Conductor Lewis. Mrs Cato Dove Rose
Norreys; Zulu Lottie Venne; Mrs Arabella Buster
Maggie Duggan; Julia Perkins Daisy England. L & MGR
A. & S. Gatti; Pd & Sm William Sidney; Sc Bruce Smith;
Cost Nathan; Furn J.S. Lyon; Mus dir Henry Sprake;
Act mgr & Treas L[ouis] F. Nethersole. *REV: E 13/5/93*
p9; Sk 10/5/93 p64; St 11/5/93 p13; Th 1/6/93 p337-8;
Ti 8/5/93 p8; TW93 p123.

93.101 *SMOKE* (CD,1a) Benjamin Webster. VAUDEVILLE
6/5/93-8/7/93. 55 perf.** James Brown W. Northcote;
Reuben Armstrong Julian Cross; Richard Burton John

Northcote. <u>Abigail Armstrong</u> Geraldine St. Maur; <u>Ellen Armstrong</u> Daisy England. <u>L & MGR</u>, <u>Sm</u>, <u>Mus dir</u>, <u>Act mgr & Treas</u> as for 93.100 *REV: E, St as for 93.100.*

93.102 *TIME WILL TELL* (C,Prol,2a) Herbert Gardner. TRAFALGAR SQUARE 8/5/93 mat perf. 1st perfd Bridgewater House, 8/5/82. <u>Lord Adolphus Vautrien</u> William Herbert; <u>Thomas Clodworth</u> W[illiam] Lestocq; <u>Lord Fayniant</u> W.T. Lovell; <u>Specklebury</u> James A. Welch; <u>John Carr</u> Herbert Waring; <u>Duke of St. Lozels</u> Sant Matthews; <u>Count Achille Czernocski</u> A[rthur] Bromley-Davenport; <u>Smart</u> P. Rhodes. <u>Edith Ravenshaw</u> Vane Featherston; <u>Lettice</u> Eva Moore. <u>MGR</u> Arthur Bromley-Davenport. *REV: E 13/5/93 p12; SR 13/5/93 p516; St 11/5/93 p12-3; Ti 9/5/93 p11.*

93.103 *THE GREAT UNPAID* (FC,3a) Fred Horner [adpt of Alexandre Bisson, *La Famille Pont-Biquet*]. COMEDY 9/5/93-20/5/93. 12 perf [w/mat 13/5].* <u>Montague Clements</u> W.H. Vernon; <u>C. Knight-Williams</u> Cyril Maude; <u>Plantagenet Watts</u> Henry V. Esmond; <u>Herbert Somerset</u> E.W. Gardiner; <u>Bouillabaisse</u> Herman de Lange; <u>Wurzel</u> Frank M. Wood; <u>Albert Pettifer</u> Wilfred E. Shine. <u>Mrs Knight-Williams</u> M.A. Victor; <u>Eva Knight-Williams</u> Annie Hill; <u>Grace Walters</u> Beatrice Ferrar; <u>Mrs Montague Clements</u> Mary Rorke. <u>L</u> Comedy Theatre Co Ltd; <u>Sm</u> C. de Lange; <u>Mus dir</u> T[homas] Smythe; <u>Bm & Treas</u> H.T. Brickwell. *REV: Ath 13/5/93 p615; E 13/5/93 p9; Sk 17/5/93 p119; SR 13/5/93 p515-6; St 11/5/93 p12; Th 1/6/93 p338; Ti 10/5/93 p8; TW93 p124-5.*

93.104 *A MUSICAL ENTERTAINMENT* George Pritchard. COMEDY 9/5/93-20/5/93. 11 perf. George Pritchard. <u>L</u>, <u>Sm</u>, <u>Mus dir</u>, <u>Bm & Treas</u> as for 93.103. *REV: E 13/5/ 93 p9.*

93.105 *PAUL PRY* (C,3a) John Poole. TOOLE'S 10/5/93(m), 20/5/93(m); 3/7/93-14/7/93. 12 perf [np 6/7].** <u>Paul Pry</u> J.L. Toole; <u>Col. Hardy</u> John Billington; <u>Mr Witherton</u> George Shelton; <u>Old Stanley</u> Frank J. Arlon; <u>Simon</u> C[harles] Brunton; <u>Harry Stanley</u> C.M. Browne; <u>Frank Hardy</u> Henry Westland; <u>Grasp</u> Herbert Pearson. <u>Eliza</u> Irene Vanbrugh; <u>Phoebe</u> Eliza Johnstone; <u>Mrs Subtle</u> Effie Liston. <u>L & MGR</u> J.L. Toole; <u>Sm</u> John

Billington; Mus dir William Robins; Bm George Lee.

93.106 *JANE ANNIE; OR, THE GOOD CONDUCT PRIZE* (CO,2a)
J.M. Barrie (lib) & A. Conan Doyle (lib) & Ernest
Ford (mus). SAVOY 13/5/93-1/7/93. 50 perf [w/S mat
exc 13/5].* A Proctor Rutland Barrington; Sim Law-
rence Gridley; Greg Walter Passmore; Caddie Master
Harry Rignold; Tom Charles Kenningham; Jack Robert
Scott-Fishe; 1st Student J. Bowden Haswell; 2nd
Student Herbert Crimp; 3rd Student Sidwell Jones.
Bab Decima Moore; Jane Annie Dorothy Vane; Milly
Florence Perry; Rose Emmie Owen; Meg Jose Shalders;
Maud May Bell; Miss Sims Rosina Brandram. PP & MGR
Richard d'Oyly Carte; Cond Ernest Ford; Mus dir Fran-
cois Cellier; Dir Charles Harris; Sc William Perkins,
William Telbin; Sm W.H. Seymour; Ch John d'Auban;
Act mgr & Treas J.W. Beckwith; Cost dgn Wilhelm; Cost
Quitmann, Smardon, Mme Leon, Firmin & Sons, Angel &
Sons, Foster & Co.; Pq William Clarkson; Props [H.]
Skelly; Mach P[eter] White; Elect Lyons; Lime [W.]
Kerr. *REV: Ath 20/5/93 p648; E 20/5/93 p11; Sk 17/5/
93 p120; SR 20/5/93 p541-2; St 18/5/93 p10-1; Ti 15/
5/93 p8.*

93.107 *LOHENGRIN* (O[3a]) Richard Wagner. COVENT GAR-
DEN 15/5/93, 29/5, 3/6, 14/6, 23/6, 14/7, 22/7/93.
6 perf.** Lohengrin Francesco Vignas/Jean de Reske;
L'Araldo del Re Antonio de Vaschetti; Enrico l'Uccel-
latore Armand Castelmary/Pol Plançon/Edouard de Reske;
Telramondo Eugene Dufriche/Mario Ancona. Ortruda
Louise Meisslinger/Giulia Ravogli; Elsa di Brabante
Nellie Melba/Gherlsen/Lillian Nordica/Emma Albani.
L & MGR Augustus Harris; Cond Luigi Mancinelli. *REV:
Ath 20/5/93 p646-7, 3/6/93 p708, 1/7/93 p40; E 20/5/
93 p15, 1/7/93 p13; St 18/5/93 p10, 1/6/93 p12, 29/6/
93 p10; Ti 16/5/93 p10, 31/5/93 p10.*

93.108 *CAVALLERIA RUSTICANA* (O,1a) Pietro Mascagni.
COVENT GARDEN 16/5/93, 22/5, 26/5, 10/6, 26/6, 11/7,
18/7/93. 7 perf.** Turiddu Francesco Vignas; Alfio
Eugene Dufriche/Mario Ancona/Pignalosa. Lola Olimpia
Guercia/Giulia Ravogli/Pauline Joran; Santuzza Emma
Calvé; Lucia Mathilde Bauermeister/Biancoli. L & MGR,
Cond as for 93.107. *REV: Ath 20/5/93 p647; E 20/5/93*

p15; St 18/5/93 p10, 8/6/93 p12; Ti 20/5/93 p8.

93.109 *ORFEO* (O[3a]) C.W. Gluck. COVENT GARDEN 16/5/93, 22/5, 27/5, 5/6, 10/7/93; trfd to DRURY LANE 19/7/93. 6 perf.** <u>Orfeo</u> Giulia Ravogli; <u>L'Amore</u> Mathilde Bauermeister; <u>Euridice</u> Sofia Ravogli; <u>1ere Danseuse</u> Riganti. <u>L & MGR</u> Augustus Harris; <u>Cond</u> Enrico Bevignani. *REV: Ath 20/5/93 p647; E 20/5/93 p15; St 18/5/ 93 p10; Ti 20/5/93 p8.*

93.110 *CARMEN* (O[4a]) Georges Bizet. COVENT GARDEN 18/5/93, 30/5, 8/6, 12/6, 24/6, 30/6, 24/7/93. 7 perf.** <u>Don José</u> Albert Alvarez; <u>Zuniga</u> Caracciolo; <u>Remendado</u> Rinaldini; <u>Dancairo</u> Iginio Corsi/Coutellier; <u>Escamillo</u> Alexis Ghasne; <u>Morales</u> Iginio Corsi. <u>Carmen</u> Sigrid Arnoldson/Emma Calvé/Armand; <u>Michaela</u> Carla Dagmar/Sigrid Arnoldson/Lucille Hill; <u>Frasquita</u> Mathilde Bauermeister; <u>Mercedes</u> Florenza/Cecile Brani/Collard; <u>1ere Danseuses</u> Riganti, Stichel. <u>L & MGR</u>, <u>Cond</u> as for 93.109; <u>Maitre de Ballet</u> Balbiani. *REV: Ath 27/5/93 p679, 3/6/93 p708; E 20/5/93 p15, 3/6/93 p13; St 25/5/93 p12, 1/6/93 p12; Ti 20/5/93 p8, 31/5/ 93 p10.*

93.111 *WAITING* (Duol). CRITERION 18/5/93 mat perf.** [<u>Harry</u>] Harry Monkhouse. [<u>Phyllis</u>] Susie Vaughan. <u>L</u> Charles Wyndham; <u>Sm</u> S.H.S. Austin.

93.112 *MRS HILARY REGRETS* (Ca,1a) S. Theyre Smith. CRITERION 18/5/93 mat perf.** <u>Dr Power</u> Charles Wyndham. <u>Mrs Hilary</u> Mary Moore. <u>L</u>, <u>Sm</u> as for 93.112.

93.113 *I PAGLIACCI* (O[Prol,2a]) Ruggiero Leoncavallo [lib trans Frederick E. Weatherly]. COVENT GARDEN 19/5/93, 23/5, 27/5, 31/5, 5/6, 9/6, 13/6, 22/6, 10/7; trfd to DRURY LANE 19/7/93; trfd to COVENT GARDEN 28/7/93. 11 perf. 1st perfd Teatro dal Verme, Milan 21/5/92. <u>Canio</u> Fernando de Lucia/Morello; <u>Silvio</u> Richard Green; <u>Tonio</u> Mario Ancona; <u>Beppe</u> Charles Bonnard. <u>Nedda</u> Nellie Melba. <u>L & MGR</u> Augustus Harris; <u>Cond</u> Luigi Mancinelli. *REV: Ath 27/5/93 p678-9; E 27/ 5/93 p7; Sk 31/5/93 p227-8; SR 27/5/93 p566; St 25/5/ 93 p12, 8/6/93 p12, 15/6/93 p12-3, 22/6/93 p10; Th 1/7/93 p52-3; Ti 15/6/93 p11.*

93.114 *PHILEMON ET BAUCIS* (O[2a]) Charles Gounod. COV-
ENT GARDEN 19/5/93, 23/5, 26/5, 31/5, 9/6/93. 5 perf.**
Jupiter Pol Plançon; Vulcan Armand Castelmary; Phi-
lemon Charles Bonnard. Baucis Sigrid Arnoldson. L &
MGR Augustus Harris; Cond Enrico Bevignani. *REV: St
15/6/93 p12-3; Ti 20/5/93 p8.*

93.115 *FAUST* (O) Charles Gounod. COVENT GARDEN 20/5/93,
6/6, 15/6, 27/6, 15/7, 29/7/93. 6 perf.** Faust
Albert Alvarez/Salvaterra/Jean de Reske; Valentine
Alexis Ghasne/Jean Lassalle/Eugene Dufriche/Pignalosa;
Wagner Antonio de Vaschetti/Villani; Mephistopheles
Armand Castelmary/Edouard de Reske. Siebel Olimpia
Guercia/Marie Brema/Carla Dagmar; Marta Mathilde
Bauermeister; Marguerite Nellie Melba/Esther Palliser/
Lillian Nordica; lere Danseuses Riganti, Stichel. L &
MGR, Cond as for 93.114; Maitre de Ballet Balbiani.
*REV: Ath 27/5/93 p679, 10/6/93 p741; E 27/5/93 p15,
10/6/93 p15; St 25/5/93 p12, 8/6/93 p12, 22/6/93 p10,
29/6/93 p10; Ti 26/5/93 p8, 8/6/93 p6, 29/6/93 p10.*

93.116 *CAMILLE [LA DAME AUX CAMELIAS]* (D,5a) Alexan-
dre Dumas, *fils.* LYRIC 24/5/93, 27/5, 6/6, 21/6,
29/6, 7/7/93. 6 perf.** Armand Duval Flavio Ando;
Duval Ettore Mazzanti; Gaston de Rieux Antonio Galli-
ani; Saint-Gaudens Giachino Grassi; Gustave Riccardo
Caimmi; Comte de Giray Leo Orlandini; De Varville
Silvio Bonivento; Doctor Napoleone Bianco; Valet
Alfredo Geri; Messenger Pietro Batti. Marguerite
Gautier Eleanora Duse; Erminie Eleonora Ropolo; Mme
Duvernoy Giuseppina Solazzi; Nannetta Guglielmina
Magazzari; Olympia Gilda Bonivento. L & MGR Horace
Sedger; Dir Carl & Theodore Rosenfeld; Pd Flavio Ando;
Cond Herbert Bunning; Bm & Treas William Greet; Pq
William Clarkson; Furn Oetzmann. *REV: Ath 3/6/93 p
710; E 27/5/93 p9; Sk 31/5/93 p228-9; SR 27/5/93 p
571-2; St 1/6/93 p13; Ti 25/5/93 p5; TW93 p125-6.*

93.117 *ROMEO ET JULIETTE* (O[5a]) Charles Gounod. COV-
ENT GARDEN 25/5/93, 2/6, 20/6, 4/7, 17/7, 27/7/93.
6 perf.** Romeo Albert Alvarez/Jean de Reske; Capu-
let Eugene Dufriche/Pol Plançon; Duc de Verone
Caracciolo/Armand Castelmary; Gregorio Antonio de
Vaschetti/Villani; Bevoglio Rinaldini/Coutellier;

Mercutio Alexis Ghasne/Eugene Dufriche; Tybalt Charles
Bonnard; Friar Laurent Pol Plançon/Edouard de Reske.
Stephano Olimpia Guercia/Lucille Hill/Dagmar; Ger-
trude Mathilde Bauermeister; Juliette Nellie Melba.
L & MGR Augustus Harris; Cond Luigi Mancinelli. *REV:*
Ath 3/6/93 p708, 24/6/93 p806, 8/7/93 p74; E 27/5/93
p15; St 1/6/93 p12, 22/6/93 p10; Ti 26/5/93 p8, 22/6/
93 p10.

93.118 *MY AWFUL DAD* (C,2a) Charles J. Mathews. TERRY'S
25/5/93 mat perf. 1st perfd Gaiety 13/9/75. Sir
Adonis Evergreen Charles Collette; Dick Evergreen
E.W. Royce; Humphrey Lovekin Henry Crisp; Prince
Kortchokoff A.J. Evelyn; Cruetts Fred A. Gaytie; Nibs
Walter Arnauld; Fibs Arthur Estcourt; Dibs Trevor
Warde. Matilda Weddagain Florence Sinclair; Emma Meri-
gold Mary Collette; Mrs Briggs Mrs Henry Leigh;
Evangeline Clara de Vere Beatrice North; Charlotte
FitzPlantagenet Norah Neil. *REV: E 27/5/93 p8; St*
1/6/93 p14.

93.119 *A CASUAL ACQUAINTANCE* (CD,Prol,3a) J.F. Cooke.
TRAFALGAR SQUARE 25/5/93 mat perf.* Lord Garston
Hay; Thorton E[dmund] Maurice; Marsden W.L. Abingdon;
Talfourd Montague; Hotel Clerk H. Deane; 2nd Hotel
Clerk Arthur Coe; Postman [Rankin?] Duval; Interpre-
ter Ashby; American Ernest Percy; Ralph Thorton C.M.
Hallard; Mr Dunsford Stewart Dawson; Gerard Wilde
W.T. Lovell; Scrutton William Wyes; Detective Ernest.
Lady Garston Mrs Conyers d'Arcy; Mrs Thorton M. Tal-
bot; Mrs Harcourt Mrs B.M. de Solla; Miss Briggs
Constance Abbott; 3 Young Ladies Day Ford, Grace Con-
over, Hadden; Mrs Dunsford Mrs Edmund Phelps; Lucy
Dunsford Ettie Williams. DIR Edward Hastings. *REV:*
E 27/5/93 p8; St 1/6/93 p13; Ti 26/5/93 p8.

93.120 *FEDORA* (D,4a) Victorien Sardou. LYRIC 26/5/93,
31/5, 16/6/93. 3 perf.** Loris Ipanoff Flavio Ando;
De Sirieux Leo Orlandini; Gretch Giachino Grassi;
Rouvel Antonio Galliani; Loreck G. Tamberlani; Boroff
Riccardo Caimmi; Desiré Silvio Bonivento; Tschileff
Ettore Mazzanti; Dmitri E. Grammatica; Cyrill Napo-
leone Bianco; Ivan Alberto Buffi; Porter A. Alberici;
Basil Pietro Betti; Boleslay Lasinski M. Corstesi;

Dr Muller Alfredo Geri; Assistant of Physician B.
Tocco. Princess Fedora Romazoff Eleonore Duse; Count-
ess Olga Soukareff Guglielmina Magazzari; Mme de Tour-
nis Eleonora Ropolo; Baroness Ockar Gilda Bonivento;
Marka Cristina Buffi. L & MGR Horace Sedger; Dir Carl
& Theodore Rosenfeld; Pd Flavio Ando; Cond Herbert
Bunning; Bm & Treas William Greet. *REV: Ath 3/6/93
p710; E 3/6/93 p7; Ti 27/5/93 p8.*

93.121 *THE BELLS* (3a) Leopold Lewis [adpt of "Erck-
mann-Chatrian", *Le Juif Polonais*]. LYCEUM 27/5/93,
3/6, 10/6, 17/6, 24/6, 20/7/93. 6 perf.** Mathias
Henry Irving; Christian William Terriss; Hans [Sam]
Johnson; Walter [Henry] Howe; Mesmerist [John] Archer;
President of the Court F[rank] Tyars; Dr Zimmer John
Martin Harvey; Notary Gurney; Clerk of the Court Lacy.
Annette Amy Coleridge; Sozel Kate Phillips; Catherine
Maud Milton. L & MGR Henry Irving; Bom Joseph Hurst;
Sm H.J. Loveday; Act mgr Bram Stoker.

93.122 *A REGULAR FIX* (F,1a) John Maddison Morton.
LYCEUM 27/5/93, 3/6, 10/6, 17/6, 24/6/93. 5 perf.**
Hugh de Brass William Terriss; Surplus Alfred Bishop;
Charles Surplus John Martin Harvey; Abel Quick Acton
Bond; Smiler [John] Archer; Porter [T.] Reynolds. Mrs
Surplus N. de Silva; Emily Amy Coleridge; Mrs Deborah
Carter Foster; Matilda Jane Kate Phillips. L & MGR,
Bom, Sm, Act mgr as for 93.121.

93.123 *THE SECOND MRS TANQUERAY* (P,4a) A.W. Pinero.
ST. JAMES'S 27/5/93-28/7/93; 11/11/93-21/4/94. 223
perf [w/S mat exc 27/5/93, 15/7, 22/7, 11/11/93; add
mat 7/6/93, 21/6, 5/7, 6/12, 26/12/93, 3/1/94, 17/1,
24/1, 31/1, 14/2, 21/2, 28/2, 7/3, 14/3, 26/3/93; mat
only 20/12/93; np 6/7/93, 21-25/12/93, 7/2/94, 19-24/
3/94].* Aubrey Tanqueray George Alexander; Cayley
Drummle Cyril Maude/Henry V. Esmond; Frank Misquith
Nutcombe Gould/H.H. Vincent; Cpt. Hugh Ardale Ben
Webster; Sir George Orreyed Adolphus Vane-Tempest;
Gordon Jayne Murray Hathorn/Arthur Bromley-Davenport;
Morse Alfred Holles. Paula Tanqueray Mrs Patrick Camp-
bell/Charlotte Granville; Mrs Cortelyon Amy Roselle/
Charlotte Granville; Ellean Maude Millett; Lady Orre-
yed Edith Chester/Winifred Dolan/Lizzie Webster/Laura

Graves. L & MGR George Alexander; Sm H.H. Vincent; Mus
dir Walter Slaughter; Bm Robert V. Shone; Mus Walter
Slaughter; Furn Frank Giles; Cost Mme Savage, Mme Purdue, Mme Yorke; Pq William Clarkson; Sc H.P. Hall,
Walter Hann. *REV: Ath 3/6/93 p709-10; E 3/6/93 p9,*
28/4/94 p9; Sk 31/5/93 p230, 7/6/93 p284-5, 19/7/93
p625, 22/11/93 p167, 13/12/93 p343-5; SR 3/6/93
p601-2, 18/11/93 p568-9, 23/2/95 p249-51; St 1/6/93
p12-3, 16/11/93 p12; Th 1/7/93 p41-3; Ti 29/5/93 p8;
TW93 p126-37, 137-44, 202-13, 245-51, 292-7.

93.124 *UNCLE DICK'S DARLING* (CD,3a) Henry J. Byron.
TOOLE'S 27/5/93(m), 3/6/93(m). 2 mat perf.** Dick
Dolland J.L. Toole; Richard Chevenix John Billington;
Hon Claude Lorimer C.M. Lowne; Phipson Frank J. Arl-
ton; Roger C[harles] Brunton; Joe Lennard Henry West-
land. Mary Belton Irene Vanbrugh; Kate Renshaw Mary
Brough; Alice Landrail Beaumont Loveday; Mrs Torring-
ton Eliza Johnstone. L & MGR J.L. Toole; Sm John
Billington; Mus dir William Robins; Bm George Lee.
REV: E 3/6/93 p7; St 1/6/93 p14.

93.125 *FRASQUITA* (CO,2a) W. Meyer Lutz. GAIETY 29/5/
93 mat perf.* Don Bobadilla John Le Hay; Garduna
Eric Lewis; Pedro Charles Conyers; Leon Edmund Payne;
Sgt of Alguazils Fritz Rimma; Jose Fimiga G[odwin?]
Hunt. Col. of Carbineers Florence Lloyd; Cpt. of Carbineers Kate Cannon; Lieut. of Carbineers Violet
Durkin; Page Phoebe Carlo; Inez Costello Maggie Roberts; Manuella Louie Pounds; Teresa A[nnie] Dwelley;
Annetta Kate Cutler; Donna Isabella Maria Davis; Frasquita Juliette Nesville. DIR J.T. Tanner; Ch Mariette
d'Auban. *REV: E 3/6/93 p6; St 1/6/93 p13-4.*

93.126 *HEDDA GABLER* (P,4a) Henrik Ibsen [trans Edmund
Gosse]. OPERA COMIQUE 29/5/93(m), 30/5(m), 5/6, 6/6/
93. 4 perf.** George Tesman W. Scott Buist; Judge
Brack Charles Sugden; Ejlert Lovborg Lewis Waller.
Hedda Elizabeth Robins; Juliana Tesman Henrietta Co-
wen; Mrs Elvsted Marie Linden; Bertha Florence Hunter.
L Edward Compton; Act mgr & Bm Charles Hoppe; Mgr sec
J.T. Grein; Sm George R. Foss. *REV: E 3/6/93 p7; SR*
10/6/93 p630; St 1/6/93 p13; TW93 p148-52.

93.127 *CAPTAIN THERESE* (CO,3a) F.C. Burnand (lib) &
Gilbert A Beckett (lib) & Robert Planquette (mus).
CRITERION 30/5/93 mat perf.** Marquis de Vardeuil
George Temple; Philip de Bellegarde Scott Russell;
Vicomte Tancrede de la Touche James Leverett; Col.
Sombrero Walter Marnock; Sgt. Vadeboncoeur Carl Ris-
son; Sgt. La Tulipe Leon Baring; Mjr de la Gonfriere
John Lisbourne; Coupecourt A. Thomas; M. Duvat Fred
Emney. Cpt. Boulignac Florence Lynn; Lieut Compastro
Edith Stuart; Mme la Chanoinesse Nellie Christie;
Marceline Kate Drew; Claudine Eleanor Harwood; Therese
Emmott-Herbert. DIR Albert James; Cost Mrs S. May;
Gen mgr M Russell Rosse; Act mgr James A. Cook; Sm
H. Edlin. *REV: E 3/6/93 p7; St 1/6/93 p14.*

93.128 *LA LOCANDIERA* (C,3a) Carlo Goldoni. LYRIC
30/5/93, 2/6, 7/6, 27/6/93. 4 perf. 1st perfd 1753.
Cavaliere di Ripafatta Flavio Ando; Marchese di For-
linipopoli Ettore Mazzanti; Conte d'Albafiorita Sil-
vio Bonivento; Fabrizio Riccardo Caimmi; Servant
Nicolo Cortes. Miranvolina Eleonora Duse. L & MGR
Horace Sedger; Dir Carl & Theodore Rosenfeld; Pd
Flavio Ando; Cond Herbert Bunning; Bm & Treas William
Greet. *REV: Ath 3/6/93 p710; St 1/6/93 p13; Ti 31/5/
93 p10; TW93 p144.*

93.129 *CAVALLERIA RUSTICANA* (D,1a) Giovanni Verga.
LYRIC 30/5/93, 2/6, 7/6, 27/6/93. 4 perf. 1st perfd
Teatro Carignano, Turin 14/1/84. Turiddu Macca
Flavio Ando; Alfio Ettore Mazzanti; Uncle Brasi Gia-
chino Grassi. Santuzza Eleonora Duse; Lola Gugliel-
mina Magazzari; Nunzia Guiseppina Solazzi; Aunt Ca-
milla Cristina Buffi; Filomena Eleonora Ropolo;
Pippuzza Gilda Bonivento. L & MGR, Dir, Pd, Cond, Bm
& Treas as for 93.128. *REV: Ath, St, Ti as for 93.128.*

93.130 *ROSMERSHOLM* (P,4a) Henrik Ibsen. OPERA COMIQUE
31/5/93, 1/6(m), 7/6, 8/6/93. 4 perf.** Rosmer Lewis
Waller; Ulric Brendal Bernard Gould; Mortensgaard
W. Scott Buist; Kroll Athol Forde. Rebecca West Eliza-
beth Robins; Mme Helseth Frances Ivor. L Edward Comp-
ton; Act mgr & Bm Charles Hoppe; Mgr sec J.T. Grein;
Dir Elizabeth Robins; Furn Oetzmann; Cost Debenham &
Freebody; Sm George R. Foss. *REV: SR 10/6/93 p630;*

St 1/6/93 p13; TW93 p148-52.

93.131 *TICKLE AND SCRUBBS* (F) W.S. Penley & Frank
Wyatt. TRAFALGAR SQUARE 31/5/93 mat perf.* Mr Gars-
ton John Willes; Tickle Arthur Playfair; Scrubbs
Cairns James. Mrs Garston Irene Rickards. PP & L Mr
& Mrs Frank Wyatt. *REV: E 3/6/93 p7; St 1/6/93 p13.*

93.132 *LA JUIVE* (O[5a]) Fromental Halévy. COVENT GAR-
DEN 1/6/93. 1 perf.** Eleazar Ferruccio Giannini;
Cardinale Pol Plançon; Principe Leopoldo Charles Bonnard; Ruggero Antonio de Vaschetti; Alberto Caracciolo. Principessa Eudossia Sigrid Arnoldson; Rachele Italia Vasquez. L & MGR Augustus Harris; Cond
Enrico Bevignani; Sec & Treas Fred G. Latham. *REV:
Ath 10/6/93 p741; E 3/6/93 p13; St 8/6/93 p12; Ti
5/6/93 p8.*

93.133 *LEIDA* (D,3a) Josine Holland [trans A. Texeira
de Mattos]. COMEDY 2/6/93. 1 perf.* George Wielrave
Bassett Roe; Wertem Mervyn Herapath. Leida Martha
Conyngham; Geertje Charlotte E. Morland; Milkmaid
Grace Conover; Saar Henrietta Cowen. DIR Herman de
de Lange; Asm A. Nesbitt; Cost Morris Angel. *REV: Ath
10/6/93 p743-4; E 10/3/93 p7; Sk 7/6/93 p287; St 8/6/
93 p13; Th 1/7/93 p43-4; Ti 5/6/93 p12; TW93 p152-3.*
Comment: Independent Theatre Society.

93.134 *AT A HEALTH RESORT* (Ca,1a) H.M. Paull. COMEDY
2/6/93. 1 perf.* Duncan Macdona Gerald Maxwell;
Tellier Thomas Kingston; Waiter William Alison.
Sadie Tellier Gwynne Herbert; Lady Barrymore Helen
Lambert; Clara Barrymore Violet Thornycroft. *REV:
E, St, Ti, TW93 as for 93.133.* Comment: Independent
Theatre Society.

93.135 *THE MASTER BUILDER* (P,3a) Henrik Ibsen [trans
Edmund Gosse & William Archer]. OPERA COMIQUE 2/6/
93(m), 3/6(m), 9/6, 10/6/93. 4 perf.** Solness
Lewis Waller; Dr Herdal Charles Sugden; Knut Brovik
Leonard Outram; Ragnar Brovik W. Scott Buist. Hilda
Wangel Elizabeth Robins; Kaia Fosli Marie Linden;
Aline Solness Francis Ivor. L Edward Compton; Act mgr
& Bm Charles Hoppe; Mgr sec J.T. Grein; Dir Elizabeth

Robins; <u>Furn</u> Oetzmann; <u>Cost</u> Debenham & Freebody; <u>Sm</u>
George R. Foss. *REV: SR 10/6/93 p630; St 1/6/93 p13,
8/6/93 p13; TW93 p148-52.* <u>Comment</u>: Act IV of *Brand*
was also perfd.

93.136 *LES PECHEURS DE PERLES* (O[3a]) Georges Bizet.
COVENT GARDEN 3/6/93. 1 perf.**   <u>Nadir</u> Fernando de
Lucia; <u>Zurga</u> Mario Ancona; <u>Nuradah</u> Antonio de Vaschetti. <u>Leila</u> Emma Calvé. L & MGR Augustus Harris;
<u>Cond</u> Enrico Bevignani. *REV: Ath 10/6/93 p741; E 10/6/
93 p15; St 8/6/93 p12; Ti 5/6/93 p8.* <u>Comment</u>: Apparently Acts I & II only perfd.

93.137 *THE MERCHANT OF VENICE* (C,5a) William Shakes-
peare. LYCEUM 3/6/93, 10/6(m), 17/6(m), 24/6(m), 26-
27/6, 29-30/6, 17/7/93. 9 perf.**   <u>Shylock</u> Henry
Irving; <u>Bassanio</u> William Terriss; <u>Duke of Venice</u>
[Henry] Howe; <u>Antonio</u> [William] Haviland; <u>Prince of
Morocco</u> [Frank] Tyars; <u>Salanio</u> Lacy; <u>Salarino</u> John
Martin Harvey; <u>Gratiano</u> Frank [Kemble] Cooper; <u>Lorenzo</u>
Gordon Craig; <u>Tubal</u> [John] Archer; <u>Launcelot Gobbo</u>
S[am] Johnson; <u>Old Gobbo</u> [T.] Reynolds; <u>Gaoler</u> [H.]
Graham; <u>Leonardo</u> [W.] Marion; <u>Balthazar</u> [W.J.] Lorriss;
<u>Stephano</u> [W. Lionel] Belmore; <u>Clerk of the Court</u> Ian
Robertson. <u>Nerissa</u> Kate Phillips; <u>Jessica</u> [Amy] Cole-
ridge; <u>Portia</u> Ellen Terry. L & MGR Henry Irving; <u>Sc</u>
Hawes Craven, William Telbin, Walter Hann; <u>Sm</u> H.J.
Loveday; <u>Act mgr</u> Bram Stoker; <u>Bom</u> Joseph Hurst. *REV:
E 10/6/93 p8; Ti 5/6/93 p12.*

93.138 *AN INTERLUDE* (DSk,1a) Walter H. Pollock & Mrs
W.K. Clifford.   TERRY'S 3/6/93-9/6/93. 6 perf.* <u>Lord
Charles Vereker</u> Herbert Waring. <u>Miss Renton</u> Janet
Achurch. <u>MGR</u> Charles Charrington; <u>Mus dir</u> C.W. La-
martine; <u>Cost</u> Nathan; <u>Furn</u> Lyon; <u>Pq</u> C.H. Fox. *REV:
Ath 10/6/93 p744; E 10/6/93 p8; SR 10/6/93 p630-1; St
8/6/93 p12; Ti 5/6/93 p12; TW93 p153-5.*

93.139 *THE THREE WAYFARERS* (Legendary Trifle,1a)
Thomas Hardy. TERRY'S 3/6/93-9/6/93. 6 perf.* <u>Timothy
Sommers</u> Herbert Waring; <u>Hangman</u> Charles Charrington;
<u>Joseph Sommers</u> Gilbert Trent; <u>Shepherd</u> Stewart Dawson;
<u>Parish Constable</u> Fred Thorne; <u>Elijah</u> Charles Rock;
<u>Magistrate</u> John Carter; <u>Turnkey</u> Graham Blunt. <u>Damsel</u>

Janet Achurch/Mary Jocelyn; <u>Shepherd's wife</u> Annie
Hughes. <u>MGR</u>, <u>Mus dir</u>, <u>Cost</u>, <u>Furn</u>, <u>Pq</u> as for 93.138.
REV: As for 93.138.

93.140 *BECKY SHARP* (CD,1a) J.M. Barrie. TERRY'S 3/6/
93-9/6/93. 6 perf.* <u>Mjr. Dobbin</u> Charles Charrington;
<u>Joe Sedley</u> Edmund Maurice; <u>Fritz</u> Fred Thorne; <u>Max</u>
Charles Rock. <u>Amelia</u> Annie Hughes; <u>Becky Sharp</u> Janet
Achurch. <u>MGR</u>, <u>Mus dir</u>, <u>Cost</u>, <u>Furn</u>, <u>Pq</u> as for 93.138.
*REV: Ath, E, SR, Ti, TW93 as for 93.138; St 8/6/93
p12-3.*

93.141 *BUD AND BLOSSOM* (F,1a) Lady Colin Campbell.
TERRY'S 3/6/93-9/6/93. 6 perf.* <u>Johnny Elder</u> Herbert
Waring; <u>Mr Vanbrugh</u> Fred Thorne; <u>Charlie</u> Charles Rock;
<u>Bill</u> Stewart Dawson; <u>George</u> Gilbert Trent; <u>Harry</u>
Graham Blunt; <u>Monmorency</u> Master Harold Loveridge.
<u>Mrs Appleby</u> Lavis; <u>Mrs Gayworthy</u> Esmé Beringer; <u>Madge</u>
Mary Jocelyn; <u>Nelly Harold</u> Annie Hughes. <u>MGR</u>, <u>Mus dir</u>,
<u>Cost</u>, <u>Furn</u>, <u>Pq</u> as for 93.138. *REV: E, SR, St, Ti,
TW93 as for 93.138.*

93.142 *FOREIGN POLICY* (D,1a) A. Conan Doyle. TERRY'S
3/6/93-9/6/93. 6 perf.* <u>Foreign Secretary</u> Charles
Charrington; <u>Sir William</u> Edmund Maurice; <u>Prime Minis-
ter</u> Herbert Waring. <u>Lady Clara</u> Janet Achurch; <u>Miss Ida</u>
Esmé Beringer. <u>MGR</u>, <u>Mus dir</u>, <u>Cost</u>, <u>Furn</u>, <u>Pq</u> as for 93.
138. *REV: E, SR, St, Ti, TW93 as for 93.138.*

93.143 *A SCRAP OF PAPER* (C,3a) J. Palgrave Simpson
[adpt of Victorien Sardou, *Les Pattes de Mouche*].
AVENUE 5/6/93-23/6/93. 18 perf [w/mat 17/6].** <u>Col.
Blake</u> W.H. Kendal; <u>Sir John Ingram</u> F.H. Macklin; <u>Dr
Penguin</u> J.E. Dodson; <u>Archie Hamilton</u> W.R. Shirley;
<u>Thomas</u> H. Deane; <u>Jones</u> Moyse. <u>Lady Ingram</u> Annie Irish;
<u>Lucy Franklyn</u> Nellie Campbell; <u>Mrs Penguin</u> Sophie
Larkin; <u>Susan Hartley</u> Mrs W.H. Kendal; <u>Mrs Perkins</u>
Barbara Huntley; <u>Graham</u> Mary Clayton. <u>L</u> George Paget;
<u>Mgr</u> Mr & Mrs W.H. Kendal; <u>Sc</u> William Harford; <u>Furn</u>
Frank Giles; <u>Mus dir</u> J. Hamilton Clarke. *REV: E 10/6/
93 p8; SR 10/6/93 p630; St 8/6/93 p13; TW93 p162.*

93.144 *CALEB; OR, THE CURSE* (CD,3a) Miss S.A. Johnson.
TERRY'S 6/6/93 mat perf.* <u>Caleb Boyd</u> Henry Crisp;

Philip Cyril Harrison; <u>Andrew Grayham</u> Gerald Godfrey;
<u>Dr Mayflower</u> George Williams; <u>Thomas</u> E.W. Colman;
<u>Luke Marvel/Shifter</u> Arthur Estcourt; <u>Old Harry</u> Gregory;
<u>Artist's Model</u> Davidson; <u>Policeman XYZ 9,999,999</u> G.W.
Mortimer. <u>Jane</u> Jessie Danvers; <u>Mrs Hartrop</u> Lillian
Chester; <u>Lillian Wyndham</u> Jenny Owen; <u>Bryant</u> Kate
Sampey; <u>Mrs Bower</u> Evelyn Darrell; <u>Kate Grayham</u> Banew
Charles; <u>Thurza Grayham</u> Mary Righton. *REV: E 10/6/93
p9; St 8/6/93 p13.*

93.145 *THE FANCY FAIR* (MSk) Mel B. Spurr. COURT 7/6/
93-8/7/93. 28 perf [w/mat 24/6; np 6/7]. 1st perf?
Mel B. Spurr. <u>L & MGR</u> Arthur Chudleigh.

93.146 *TANNHAUSER* (O[3a]) Richard Wagner. COVENT GAR-
DEN 7/6/93, 17/6, 3/7/93. 3 perf.** <u>Tannhauser</u> Fran-
cesco Vignas; <u>Herman I</u> Heinrich Wiegand; <u>Biterolf</u>
Richard Green; <u>Wolfram</u> Mario Ancona; <u>Walther</u> Pedro
Guetary; <u>Heinrich</u> Iginio Corsi; <u>Reinmar</u> Antonio de
Vaschetti. <u>Venus</u> Gherlsen; <u>Pastore</u> Biancoli; <u>Elizabeth</u>
Emma Albani. <u>L & MGR</u> Augustus Harris; <u>Cond</u> Luigi
Mancinelli. *REV: Ath 10/6/93 p741; E 10/6/93 p15;
St 15/6/93 p12; Ti 8/6/93 p6.*

93.147 *DAVID GARRICK* (C,3a) T.W. Robertson. CRITERION
7/6/93(m); 15/6/93-19/7/93. 35 perf [w/S mat; np 6/7].
** <u>David Garrick</u> Charles Wyndham; <u>Simon Ingot</u> Will-
iam Farren; <u>Smith</u> William Blakeley; <u>Squire Chivey</u>
Sydney Valentine; <u>Jones</u> David S. James; <u>Brown</u> Ells
Dagnall; <u>Thomas</u> Johnson; <u>William</u> C[harles] Terric.
<u>Ada Ingot</u> Mary Moore; <u>Araminta Brown</u> Emily Miller;
<u>Mrs Smith</u> Emily Vining. <u>L & MGR</u> Charles Wyndham; <u>Sm</u>
S.H.S. Austin; <u>Act mgr & Treas</u> E. Harvey; <u>Mus dir</u> A.
Evans. *REV: E 22/7/93 p7.*

93.148 *OLIVIA* (P,4a) W.G. Wills. LYCEUM 7/6/93(m),
14/6(m), 1/7(m), 14/7. 4 perf.** <u>Dr Primrose</u> Henry
Irving; <u>Squire Thornhill</u> William Terriss; <u>Mr Burchell</u>
Frank [Kemble] Cooper; <u>Moses</u> Gordon Craig; <u>Farmer
Flamborough</u> [Henry] Howe; <u>Leigh</u> [Frank] Tyars; <u>Dick</u>
Master Leo Byrne. <u>Bill</u> Grace Webb; <u>Polly Flamborough</u>
Kate Phillips; <u>Phoebe</u> Foster; <u>Gipsy Woman</u> Ailsa Craig;
<u>Mrs Primrose</u> Maud Milton; <u>Sophia</u> Amy Coleridge; <u>Olivia</u>
Ellen Terry. <u>L & MGR</u> Henry Irving; <u>Mus</u> Sir Arthur

Sullivan; <u>Cond</u> J. Meredith Ball; <u>Sm</u> H.J. Loveday; <u>Act</u>
<u>mgr</u> Bram Stoker; <u>Bom</u> Joseph Hurst. *REV: SR 10/6/93*
p631.

93.149 *THE LUCKY BAG* (CO,1a) Louis N. Parker (mus) &
Mrs E.S. Willard ["Rachel Penn"] (lib). SAVOY 8/6/93
mat perf.* <u>Barney O'Toole</u> David S. James; <u>Postman</u>
Mervyn Herapath; <u>Cabman</u> Charles Garry. <u>Kate Adams</u> Eva
Moore. *REV: E 10/6/93 p9; Sk 14/6/93 p344; St 15/6/93*
p13. <u>Comment</u>: 93.149, 93.150 & 93.151 were licensed
by the Lord Chamberlain on 15/3/93, and originally
advertized for mat perf on 21/3/93.

93.150 *THE MERRY PIPER OF NUREMBURG* (Ent,1a) Mrs E.S.
Willard ["Rachel Penn"] (lib) & Louis N. Parker (mus).
SAVOY 8/6/93 mat perf.* <u>Piper</u> Frank H. Westerton.
<u>Sylvia</u> Anna Mather; <u>Martha</u> Mrs Theodore Wright. *REV:*
E, Sk, St as for 93.149; Ti 12/6/93 p4. <u>Comment</u>: As
for 93.149.

93.151 *PUNCH AND JUDY* (C,1a) Mrs E.S. Willard ["Rachel
Penn"] (lib) & Edward Jones (mus). SAVOY 8/6/93 mat
perf.* <u>Punch</u> John Le Hay; <u>Judy</u> James A. Welch; <u>Clown</u>
David S. James; <u>Doctor</u> Harry Grattan; <u>Parson</u> H[enry]
Besley; <u>Devil</u> Charles Garry; <u>Beadle</u> Claude Edmonds;
<u>Hangman</u> Mervyn Herapath; <u>Toby</u> Freddy Farren. <u>Baby</u>
Judy Kins.<u>Stage Business</u> Charles Lauri, R. Grattan.
REV: As for 93.149. <u>Comment</u>: As for 93.149.

93.152 *THE YOUNGER SON* (CD,4a) R.S. Sievier. GAIETY
9/6/93 mat perf.* <u>Frank Villiers</u> Herbert Waring; <u>Sir</u>
<u>Augustus Downey</u> Eric Lewis; <u>Squire Chester</u> John Beau-
champ; <u>Lord Lunar</u> H.H. Vincent; <u>Harold Chester</u> W.T.
Lovell; <u>Hawkes</u> H. Deane; <u>Michael O'Shaunessy</u> G. Fitz-
Gerald; <u>Reginald Roxwell</u> Ackerman May; <u>Herbert Askew</u>
<u>Chester</u> W.L. Abingdon; <u>Sams</u> G[raeme?] Goring. <u>Evelyn</u>
<u>Brookfield</u> May Whitty; <u>Lucie Amherst</u> Empsie Bowman;
<u>Winifred Chester</u> Eva Moore; <u>Mary Melford</u> Lena Ashwell.
<u>L & MGR</u> Georges Edwardes; <u>Dir</u> F.H. Macklin. *REV: E*
10/6/93 p11; Sk 14/6/93 p344; St 15/6/93 p13-4; Ti
12/6/93 p4.

93.153 *A DOLL'S HOUSE* (P,3a) Henrik Ibsen. LYRIC 9/6/
93, 14/6, 17/6. 3 perf.** <u>Helmer</u> Flavio Ando; <u>Dr Rank</u>

Leo Orlandini; <u>Krogstad</u> Ettore Mazzanti; <u>Porter</u> Al-
fredo Geri. <u>Nora</u> Eleonora Duse;<u> Mary Ann</u> Cristina
Buffi; <u>Mrs Linden</u> Guglielmina Magazzari; <u>Helen</u>
Eleonora Ropolo. <u>L & MGR</u> Horace Sedger; <u>Dir</u> Carl &
Theodore Rosenfeld. *REV: Ath 17/6/93 p776; E 17/6/93
p6; Sk 14/6/93 p344; St 15/6/93 p13; Ti 12/6/93 p4;
TW93 p155-61.*

93.154 *LA FAVORITA* (O[4a]) Gaetano Donizetti. COVENT
GARDEN 10/6/93, 13/7/93. 2 perf.** <u>Balthazar</u> Pol
Plançon/Armand Castelmary; <u>Don Gaspar</u> Coutellier;
<u>Fernand</u> Albert Alvarez; <u>Alfonse XI</u> Eugene Dufriche/
Alexis Ghasne. <u>Leonore</u> Armand; <u>Ines</u> Mathilde Bauermeister. <u>L & MGR</u> Augustus Harris; <u>Cond</u> Enrico Bevignani. *REV: Ath 17/6/93 p774; E 17/6/93 p13; St 15/6/93
p13; Ti 15/6/93 p11.*

93.155 *LES PLAIDEURS* (C,3a) Jean Baptiste Racine.
DRURY LANE 12/6/93. 1 perf. 1st perfd Hôtel de Bour-
gogne, Paris 11/1668. <u>L'Intime</u> E.-F.-J. Got; <u>Léandre</u>
Boucher; <u>Dandin</u> Leloir; <u>Petit Jean</u> Georges Berr; <u>Le
Souffleur</u> Roger; <u>Chicaneau</u> Pierre Laugier. <u>Isabelle</u>
Muller; <u>Comtesse</u> Amel. <u>L & MGR</u> Augustus Harris; <u>Dir</u>
Augustus Harris, Henry E. Abbey, Maurice Grau; <u>Rep</u>
C.J. Abud; <u>Sec & Treas</u> Fred G. Latham. *REV: Ath 17/6/
93 p775-6; E 17/6/93 p7; St 15/6/93 p12; Ti 13/6/93
p5; TW93 p168-71.* <u>Comment</u>: Comédie-Française.

93.156 *LE MALADE IMAGINARE* (C,3a) Molière. DRURY LANE
12/6/93. 1 perf. Palais-Royal, Paris 10/2/1673. <u>Argan</u>
E.-A.-H. Coquelin [*cadet*]; <u>Thomas</u> Jules Truffier;
<u>Purgon</u> Leloir; <u>Beralde</u> Martel; <u>Diafoirus</u> Joliet; <u>Ché-
ante</u> Samary; <u>Bonnefoy</u> Roger; <u>Fleurant</u> Falconnier.
<u>Angelique</u> Blanche Barretta; <u>Beline</u> Fayolle; <u>Toinette</u>
Kalb; <u>Louison</u> La Petite Gaudy. <u>L & MGR</u>, <u>Dir</u>, <u>Sec &
Treas</u>, <u>Rep</u> as for 93.155. *REV: As for 93.155.*

93.157 *BESS* (P,3a) Mrs Oscar Beringer. ST. JAMES'S
12/6/93 mat perf.** <u>Phil Summers</u> Henry V. Esmond; <u>Dr
Wenham</u> J.D. Beveridge; <u>Joe Summers</u> W.H. Vernon; <u>Am-
brose Comfort</u> Seymour Hicks; <u>Farmer Crabbage</u> Talbot
Fell; <u>Detective</u> Charles Milton; <u>Surgery Boy</u> Master Leo
Byrne. <u>Bess Summers</u> Genevieve Ward; <u>Keziah Crabbage</u>
Kate Phillips; <u>Nan Wenham</u> Esmé Beringer; <u>Mrs Wenham</u>

Helen Forsyth; <u>Pussie Summers</u> Caryl Field-Fisher. <u>L &
MGR</u> George Alexander; <u>Pd</u> Genevieve Ward; <u>Mus dir</u> Walter Slaughter; <u>Bm</u> Alwyn Lewis; <u>Pq</u> C.H. Fox; <u>Dir</u> W.H.
Vernon. *REV: E 17/6/93 p9; Sk 21/6/93 p438; SR 17/6/
93 p658; St 15/6/93 p13; Ti 13/6/93 p5.*

93.158 *TERRY; OR, TRUE TO HIS TRUST* (Racing D,1a)
Sutton Vane. TRAFALGAR SQUARE 12/6/93-15/7/93. 29 perf
[np 6/7]. 1st perfd Parkhurst 27/4/91. <u>Terry</u> Edward
Cranston; <u>Mjr. Kyte</u> Graham Wentworth. <u>Arrah Doyle</u>
Emmeline Orford. <u>PP & L</u> Mr & Mrs Frank Wyatt; <u>Pd</u>
Frank Wyatt; <u>Mus dir</u> Ivan Caryll; <u>Bom</u> H.T. Holliman;
<u>Gen mgr</u> Gilbert Tate; <u>Act mgr & Treas</u> H[enry] Bran-
don; <u>Asm</u> Cairns James.

93.159 *ST. RONAN'S WELL* (D,4a) Richard Davey & Walter
Herries Pollock [adpt of Scott's novel]. TRAFALGAR
SQUARE 12/6/93 mat perf.* <u>Francis Tyrrell</u> Frank
Worthing; <u>Lord Etherington</u> Gaston Mervale; <u>Mowbray of
St. Ronan</u> Edmund Gurney; <u>Mr Touchwood</u> Stewart Daw-
son; <u>Cpt. Jekyell</u> Charles Garry; <u>Mr Bindloose</u> Roth-
bury Evans; <u>Sir Bingo Binks</u> F. Cremlin; <u>Mr Merry-
weather</u> A. Yockney; <u>Cpt. McTurk</u> Akerman May; <u>Beenie</u>
Hawley Francks; <u>Toby</u> Master [Richard?] Saker. <u>Clara
Mowbray</u> Annie Rose; <u>Hannah Irwin</u> Sylvia Grey; <u>Megg
Dodds</u> Alexes Leighton; <u>Lady Penelope Pennyfeather</u>
Mrs Edward Saker; <u>Lady Binks</u> Claire Pauncefort; <u>Mrs
Blower</u> Mrs F. Copleston; <u>Eppie</u> [Nora] Leslie; <u>Nelly</u>
Margaret Eyre; <u>Dinah</u> Isabel Grey; <u>Maria</u> Emilie Grattan.
*REV: E 17/6/93 p6; SR 17/6/93 p658-9; St 15/6/93 p14;
Ti 13/6/93 p5.*

93.160 *DJAMILEH* (O,1a) Georges Bizet. COVENT GARDEN
13/6/93, 22/6, 26/6/93. 3 perf. 1st perfd Opéra Comique, Paris 22/5/72. <u>Haroun</u> Charles Bonnard; <u>Splen-
diano</u> Coutellier; <u>Marchand d'Escalves</u> Leonard. <u>Une
Almée</u> Riganti; <u>Djamileh</u> Gherlsen. <u>L & MGR</u> Augustus
Harris; <u>Cond</u> Alberto Randegger. *REV: Ath 17/6/93 p774;
E 17/6/93 p13; St 15/6/93 p13, 22/6/93 p10; Ti 15/6/
93 p11.*

93.161 *UN PERE PRODIGUE* (C,5a) Alexandre Dumas, *fils*.
DRURY LANE 13/6/93. 1 perf. 1st perfd Gymnase dramatique, Paris 30/11/59. <u>Le Comte de la Rivonnière</u> F.

Febvre; De Tournas E.-A.-H. Coquelin [*cadet*]; De Lig-
neray Prudhon; Andre de la Rivonnière Charles Gustave
Auguste Le Bargy; De Naton [Jules] Truffier; Joseph
Georges Berr; Garçon de Banque Roger; Cocher Hamel;
De Prailles Leitner; Domestique Falconnier; Domestique
[Emile] Dehelly. Hélène Reichenberg; Mme Godefroy
Blanche Adeline Pierson; Albertine de la Borde Marie
Louise Marsy; Mme de Chavry Persoons; Victorine Lynnes.
L & MGR Augustus Harris; Dir Augustus Harris, Henry
E. Abbey, Maurice Grau; Sec & Treas Fred G. Latham;
Rep C.J. Abud. *REV: Ath 17/6/93 p775-6; E 17/6/93 p7;
St 15/6/93 p12; Ti 15/6/93 p10; TW93 p168-71.* Comment:
Comédie-Française.

93.162 *HIS HIGHNESS; OR, EXCHANGE NO ROBBERY* (CO,3a)
Auscal Tate (mus) & Neil O'Donovan (mus) & John W.
Houghton (lib). OPERA COMIQUE 13/6/93 mat perf.*
Ferdinand Charles Conyers; Count Contarino Templar
Saxe; Baron Volpas Fred J. Vigay; Leopold Thomas Rey-
nolds; Giovanni L.F. Chapuy; Alessandro J. Ampfield.
Stephano Constance Adair; Florinda Beaumont Loveday;
Teresa Amadi; Gretchen Marie Faudelle; Minna Jessie
Bradford; Isabella Amy Loveday. L Edward Compton; Bm
Arthur Whittaker; Cond Neil O'Donovan; Ch Harry Barnes;
Chorus Master Ernest Thiel; Pq & Cost William Clark-
son. *REV: E 17/6/93 p9; St 15/6/93 p14.*

93.163 *PAR LE GLAIVE* (Verse D,5a,7tab) Jean Richepin.
DRURY LANE 14/6/93. 1 perf. 1st perfd Comédie-fran-
çaise, Paris 8/2/92. Pietro Strada Mounet-Sully;
Galeas Eugene Silvain; Ludwig Leloir; Guido Albert
Lambert, *fils*; Conrad le Loup Paul Mounet; Petruccio
Martell; Manetto Joliet; Metzler Dupont Vernon; Balbo
Roger; Hermann Villain; Ventura Samary; Gherardi
Clerh; Battista Falconnier; Karl Hamel; Rasponi
Pierre Laugier; Max Leitner; Pasquale [Emile] Dehelly.
Rinalda Julia Bartet; Bianca Adeline Dudlay; Orsola
Amel; Bettina Rachel Boyer; Chanteuse Bertiny; Laura
Drunzer; Rizzo La Petite Gaudy. L & MGR Augustus Har-
ris; Dir Augustus Harris, Henry E. Abbey, Maurice
Grau; Sec & Treas Fred G. Latham; Rep C.J. Abud. *REV:
Ath 17/6/93 p775-6; E 17/6/93 p7; St 15/6/93 p12; Ti
15/6/93 p10; TW93 p170-1.* Comment: Comédie-Francaise.

93.164 *THE ENEMY OF THE PEOPLE* (P,5a) Henrik Ibsen.
HAYMARKET 14/6/93(m), 21/6(m), 28/6(m), 20/7, 21/7,
22/7(2). 7 perf.* Dr Thomas Stockmann H.B. Tree;
Peter Stockmann [Henry] Kemble; Morten Kiil Charles
Allan; Aslaksen E.M. Robson; Hovstad James A. Welch;
Cpt. Horster Hamilton Revelle; Billing E. Holman
Clark; Eilif Master Skelly. Mrs Stockmann Mrs Theo-
dore Wright; Morten Dora Barton; Petra Lily Hanbury.
L & MGR H. Beerbohm Tree; Pq William Clarkson; Elect
E. Wingfield Bowles; Bom W.H. Leverton; Sm Edward
Hastings; Mus dir Carl Armbruster; Bm & Sec Frederick
Harrison. *REV: Ath 17/6/93 p776; E 17/6/93 p6; Sk
21/6/93 p433; SR 17/6/93 p659; St 15/6/93 p13, 27/7/
93 p10; Ti 15/6/93 p10; TW93 p162-8.*

93.165 *DEAREST MAMMA* (Ca,1a) Walter Gordon. CRITERION
15/6/93-19/7/93. 29 perf [np 6/7].** Harry Clinton
Frank Atherley; Nettle Croker C.W. Somerset; Browser
William Blakeley; Jones C[harles] Terric. Mrs Breeze-
ley Fussell M.A. Victor; Edith Clinton Ellis Jeffreys;
Mrs Honeywood F. Frances. L & MGR Charles Wyndham; Sm
S.H.S. Austin; Mus dir A. Evans; Act mgr & Treas E.
Harvey.

93.166 *DENISE* (P,4a) Alexandre Dumas, *fils*. DRURY
LANE 15/6/93, 20/6, 30/6/93. 3 perf. 1st perfd Théâtre-
français, Paris 19/1/85. Brissot E.-F.-J. Got; Andre
de Bardannes G.-H. Worms; Thouvenin Eugene Silvain;
Fernand de Thauzette Baillet; De Pontferrand Joliet;
Domestique Falconnier. Denise Julia Bartet; Mme
Brissot Pauline Granger; Mme de Thauzette Blanche
Adeline Pierson; Marthe de Bardannes Muller; Mme de
Pontferrand Amel; Clarisse Bertiny. L & MGR Augustus
Harris; Dir Augustus Harris, Henry E. Abbey, Maurice
Grau; Sec & Treas Fred G. Latham; Rep C.J. Abud.*REV:
Ath 24/6/93 p807; E 17/6/93 p7; St 22/6/93 p10, 29/6/
93 p10-1; Ti 19/6/93 p11; TW93 p168-71, 176-7.*

93.167 *A BLOT IN THE 'SCUTCHEON* (T,3a) Robert Browning.
OPERA COMIQUE 15/6/93 mat perf. 1st perfd Drury Lane
11/2/43. Thorold, Earl Tresham Louis Calvert; Austin
Tresham Lionel Dainer; Henry, Earl Mertoun Martin
Harvey; Gerard J. Fisher White. Mildred Tresham May
Harvey; Gwendolen Tresham N. de Silva. DIR Louis Cal-

vert; Sc Barratt. *REV: Ath 17/6/93 p6; St 22/6/93 p11; Ti 16/6/93 p8; TW93 p171.*

93.168 *POOR JONATHAN* (MC,2a) Charles H.E. Brookfield (lib) & Harry Greenbank (lyr) & Karl Millocker (mus) & Isaac Albeniz (mus). PRINCE OF WALES'S 15/6/93-30/6/93. 14 perf [mat only 24/6].* Jonathan Tripp Harry Monkhouse; Signor Piruetti Fred Kaye; Herr Steinbach W.H. Denny; Vandergold Sidney Tower; Ruggles/ Signor Screwlooski Arthur Wilkinson; Isidor Notador Frank Boor; Oyster Dick George de Pledge; Black Tom Montelli; Ginger Harry Joyce; Lord Garrick Bend Allerton; Hon Jack Hawser Watson. Marion Annie Schuberth; Dr Hatty Grant Violet Robinson; Linda Lettuce Mimi St. Cyr; Molly Jessie Bond; Guests Nellie Cozens, Blanche Wynter; Crystala Pallaza Clare Vanini; Giardina Covent Lillie McIntyre; Alberta Hall Anita Courtenay; Goldie Kipper Elsie Dare; Guests Annie Laurie, Florrie Sedohr, Lilian Stanley, Madge Lewis, Annie Selby; Dancer Mimi St. Cyr. L & MGR Edgar Bruce; Sc R.C. McCleery, Bruce Smith; Ch Mlle Rosa; Mus dir Isaac Albeniz; Cond J.H.H. Korte; Dir Thomas W. Charles; Cost Swan & Edgar, Miss Fisher, Alias; Furn Jetley; Pq William Clarkson; Act mgr C.P. Levilly. *REV: St 22/6/93 p10-1; Ti 16/6/93 p8.*

93.169 *LES EFFRONTES* (C,5a) Emile Augier. DRURY LANE 16/6/93, 21/6, 1/7, 8/7/93(m). 4 perf. 1st perfd Théâtre-français, Paris 10/1/61. Giboyer E.-F.-J. Got/ Jules Truffier; Vernouillet Baillet; Henri C.-G.-A. Le Bargy; Charrier de Feraudy; Marquis d'Auberive Leloir; De Sergine Albert Lambert, *fils*; General Martel; Baron Joliet; Vicomte d'Isigny Pierre Laugier; Domestiques Roger, Falconnier, Hamel. Clemence Muller; Vicomtesse Persoons; La Marquise Jane Hading; Femme de Chambre Drunzer. L & MGR Augustus Harris; Dir Augustus Harris, Henry E. Abbey, Maurice Grau; Sec & Treas Fred G. Latham; Rep C.J. Abud. *REV: Ath 24/6/93 p807; E 24/6/93 p7; St 22/6/93 p10, 29/6/93 p10-1; Ti 19/6/93 p11; TW93 p171.* Comment: Comédie-Française.

93.169A *LE FLIBUSTIER* (C,3a) Jean Richepin. DRURY LANE 17/6/93. 1 perf. 1st perfd Comédie-française, Paris 14/5/88. Mathurin Legoez E.-F.-J. Got; Jacquemin G.-H.

Worms; <u>Pierre</u> Paul Mounet; <u>Vieux Pecheur</u> Falconnier;
<u>Pecheur</u> Hamel. <u>Janik</u> Blanche Barretta; <u>Marie Anne</u>
Pauline Granger; <u>Une Vieille Femme</u> Jamaux; <u>Une Jeune</u>
<u>Fille</u> Drunzer. <u>L & MGR</u>, <u>Dir</u>, <u>Sec & Treas</u>, <u>Rep</u> as for
93.169. *REV: Ath 24/6/93 p807; E 24/6/93 p7; St 22/6/*
93 p10. <u>Comment</u>: As for 93.169.

93.169B *LES PRECIEUSES RIDICULES* (C,1a) Molière. DRURY
LANE 17/6/93. 1 perf. 1st perfd Petit-Bourbon, Paris
18/11/1659. <u>Mascarille</u> E.-A.-H. Coquelin [*cadet*];
<u>La Grange</u> Boucher; <u>Jodelet</u> Jules Truffier; <u>Un Violon</u>
Roger; <u>1er Porteur</u> Villain; <u>Du Croisy</u> Samary; <u>Gorgi-</u>
<u>bus</u> Clerh; <u>2me Porteur</u> Falconnier. <u>Cathos</u> Ludwig;
<u>Madelon</u> Kalb; <u>Marotte</u> Jamaux. <u>L & MGR</u>, <u>Dir</u>, <u>Sec &</u>
<u>Treas</u>, <u>Rep</u> as for 93.169. <u>Comment</u>: As for 93.169.

93.170 *GRINGOIRE* (C,1a) Theodore de Banville. DRURY
LANE 17/6/93. 1 perf. 1st perfd Théâtre-français,
Paris 23/6/66. <u>Louis XI</u> Eugene Silvain; <u>Gringoire</u>
Georges Berr; <u>Maitre Simon</u> Clerh; <u>Olivier le Dain</u>
Hamel. <u>Loyse</u> Richenberg; <u>Nicole</u> Lynnes. <u>L & MGR</u>, <u>Dir</u>,
<u>Sec & Treas</u>, <u>Rep</u> as for 93.169. *REV: Ath 24/6/93 p807;*
E 24/6/93 p7; Ti 19/6/93 p11. <u>Comment</u>: As for 93.169.

93.171 *ATLANTIS; OR, THE LOST LAND* (OExt,3a) Maurice
Dalton (lib) & Ernest Genet (lib) & Malby Haddow (mus).
OPERA COMIQUE 17/6/93. 1 perf. 1st perfd Gaiety 17/3/
86. <u>Tristram</u> Charles Conyers; <u>Uther</u> Fred Emney; <u>Earl</u>
<u>Dando</u> Leonard Russell; <u>Arthur</u> George Mudie; <u>Arnold</u>
Roland Carse; <u>Prof Septimus Solon Smith</u> Cairns James;
<u>John Tibbs</u> E.W. Royce; <u>Nonever</u> Carl Risson; <u>Wynot</u>
Montague Summers. <u>Juliana</u> Marie Faudelle; <u>Elaine</u>
Jessie Moore; <u>Perceval</u> Zamba. <u>L</u> Edward Compton; <u>Pd</u>
Cairns James; <u>Mus dir</u> Ernest Bucalossi; <u>Bm</u> Arthur
Whittaker; <u>Dir</u> Cairns James; <u>Cost & Pq</u> William Clark-
son. *REV: E 24/6/93 p6; St 22/6/93 p11.*

93.172 *ICI ON PARLE FRANCAIS* (F,1a) Thomas J. Williams.
TOOLE'S 17/6/93 mat perf.**

93.173 *L'AMICO FRITZ* (O[3a]) Pietro Mascagni. COVENT
GARDEN 19/6/93, 11/7, 18/7/93. 3 perf.** <u>Fritz</u> Fernando de Lucia/Francesco Vignas; <u>Rabbino</u> Eugene Du-
friche/Mario Ancona; <u>Hanezo</u> Antonio de Vaschetti; <u>Fed-</u>

erico Iginio Corsi. Beppe Pauline Joran; Caterina Mathilde Bauermeister; Suzel Emma Calvé. L & MGR Augustus Harris; Cond Pietro Mascagni. *REV: Ath 24/6/93 p806; E 24/6/93 p13; St 22/6/93 p10; Ti 22/6/93 p10.*

93.174 *LE DEMI MONDE* (C,5a) Alexandre Dumas, *fils.*
DRURY LANE 19/6/93. 1 perf. 1st perfd Gymnase dramatique, Paris 20/3/55. Oliver de Jaslin F. Febvre; De Naenjac G.-H. Worms; Richond de Feraudy; De Thonnerins Leloir; Domestiques Roger, Falconnier, Hamel. Marcelle Blanche Barretta; Suzanne d'Ange Marie Louise Marsy; Mme de Santis Ludwig; Vicomtesse de Verniere Fayolle; Femme de Chambre Jamaux. L & MGR Augustus Harris; Dir Augustus Harris,Henry E. Abbey, Maurice Grau; Sec & Treas Fred G. Latham; Rep C.J. Abud. *REV: Ath 24/6/93 p807; E 24/6/93 p7; Sk 28/6/93 p453; St 22/6/93 p10.* Comment: Comédie-Française.

93.175 *ANTONY AND CLEOPATRA* William Shakespeare.
LYRIC 19/6/93, 23/6, 26/6/93. 3 perf.** Marc Antony Flavio Ando; Octavius Caesar Silvio Bonivento; Lepidus Eduardo Mario; Enobarbus Ettore Mazzanti; Philo Giachino Grassi; Demetrius Pietro Alberici; Euphronius Napoleone Bianco; Mecaenas Nicolo Cortesi; Agrippa Leo Orlandini; Dolabella Pietro Maloni; Proculeius Nicolo Blanchi; Gallus Alfredo Geri; Thyreus Orlando Marconi; Alexas Antonio Galliani; Mardian Alberto Buffi; Seleucus Riccardo Caimmi; Soothsayer Paolo Zaroni; Clown Pietro Betti. Cleopatra Eleonora Duse; Octavia Gilda Bonivento; Charmian Guiseppina Solazzi; Iras Emma Grammatica. L & MGR Horace Sedger; Dir Carl & Theodore Rosenfeld. *REV: Ath 24/6/93 p807; E 20/6/93 p6; St 22/6/93 p10; Ti 21/6/93 p10; TW93 p172-6.* Comment: Italian version.

93.176 *THE ORDEAL* (D,1a) Tom S. Wotton. COMEDY 20/6/93 mat perf.* Arnold von Rabenstein Ernest Leicester; Moritz Wimelhaus F. Norreys Connell; Member of the Vehmgericht John P. Emery. Agatha Mary Stuart; Clara Emmie O'Reilly. COST Harrison. *REV: St 22/6/93 p11; Ti 21/6/93 p10.*

93.177 *TWO MEN AND A MAID* (D,4a) F.H. Purchase & James Webster. COMEDY 20/6/93 mat perf.* Gilbert Ellerton

Frank MacVicars; Dick Ellerton A. Austin Leigh; James
Fletcher Norman Clark. Ethel Rose Nesbitt; Annie Mar-
shall Florence Fordyce; Letitia Phipps Mary Stuart;
Kate Frayne; Phyllis Verner Nancy Noel. PQ William
Clarkson; Dir Henry Neville; Asm John P. Emery. *REV:*
St, Ti as for 93.176; Sk 28/6/93 p489.

93.178 *IL VASCELLO FANTASMA [DER FLIEGENDE HOLLANDER]*
Richard Wagner. COVENT GARDEN 21/6/93, 1/7/93. 2 perf.**
L'Olandese Jean Lassalle; Erik Morello; Il Pilota
Pedro Guetary; Dalando Edouard de Reszke. Senta Emma
Albani; Mary Mathilde Bauermeister. L & MGR Augustus
Harris; Cònd Luigi Mancinelli. *REV: Ath 24/6/93 p806;*
E 24/6/93 p13; St 29/6/93 p10; Ti 22/6/93 p10.

93.179 *HENRI III ET SA COUR* (D,5a) Alexandre Dumas,
père. DRURY LANE 22/6/93. 1 perf. 1st perfd Théâtre-
français, Paris 11/2/29. Duc de Guise F. Febvre;
Henri III G.-H. Worms; Ruggieri Eugene Silvain;
D'Epenon Boucher; Joyeuse Jules Truffier; Saint Megrim
Albert Lambert, *fils*; Cruce Martel; Brigard Roger;
Saint Paul Villain; Georges Clerh; La Chapelle Marteau
Falconnier; Bussy d'Amboise Hamel; Bussy Leclerc Pierre
Laugier; Antraguet Leitner; Saint Luc Emile Dehelly;
Du Halde Georges Berr. Catherine de Medicis Blanche
Adeline Pierson; Mme de Cosse Amel; Marie Nancy Mar-
tel; Arthur Bertiny; Duchess de Guise Brandès; Page
d'Antraguet Drunzer. L & MGR Augustus Harris; Dir
Augustus Harris, Henry E. Abbey, Maurice Grau; Sec &
Treas Fred G. Latham; Rep C.J. Abud. *REV: E 24/6/93*
p7; Sk 28/6/93 p453; St 29/6/93 p10-1; Ti 23/6/93 p10.
Comment: Comédie-Française.

93.180 *LE LUTHIER DE CREMONE* (C,1a) François Coppée.
DRURY LANE 23/6/93. 1 perf. 1st perfd Comédie-française, Paris 23/5/76. Philippo C.-G.-A. Le Bargy;
Sandro Samary; Maitre Ferrari Pierre Laugier. Giannina Du Minil. L & MGR, Dir, Sec & Treas, Rep as for
93.179. *REV: E 1/7/93 p7.* Comment: As for 93.179.

93.181 *FRANCILLON* (C,3a) Alexandre Dumas, *fils.* DRURY
LANE 23/6/93, 11/7/93. 2 perf. 1st perfd Théâtre-fran-
çais, Paris 17/1/87. Stanislas de Grandredon G.-H.
Worms/Le Bargy; Lucien de Riverolles Baillet; Celestin

de Feraudy; <u>Jean de Carillac</u> Jules Truffier; <u>Pinguet</u>
Samary; <u>Marquis de Riverolles</u> Pierre Laugier; <u>Henri</u>
<u>de Simeux</u> Leitner; <u>Domestique</u> Falconnier. <u>Francine de</u>
<u>Riverolles</u> Julia Bartet; <u>Thérèse Smith</u> Blanche Adeline
Pierson; <u>Annette de Riverolles</u> Muller; <u>Elisa</u> Kalb/
Ludwig. <u>L & MGR</u>, <u>Dir</u>, <u>Sec & Treas</u>, <u>Rep</u> as for 93.179.
REV: Ath 1/7/93 p42; E 1/7/93 p7; Sk 28/6/93 p453;
TW93 p176-9. <u>Comment</u>: As for 93.179.

93.182 *DEPIT AMOUREUX* (C,2a) Molière. DRURY LANE 24/6/
93 mat perf. 1st perfd Petit Bourbon, Paris 12/1658.
<u>Gros Rene</u> de Feraudy; <u>Mascarille</u> Georges Berr; <u>Eraste</u>
Samary; <u>Valere</u> Emile Dehelly. <u>Lucile</u> Muller; <u>Marinette</u>
Kalb. <u>L & MGR</u>, <u>Dir</u>, <u>Sec & Treas</u>, <u>Rep</u> as for 93.179.
REV: E 1/7/93 p7. <u>Comment</u>: As for 93.179.

93.183 *MADEMOISELLE DE LA SEIGLIERE* (C,4a) Jules San-
deau. DRURY LANE 24/6/93(m), 5/7/93. 2 perf.** <u>Le</u>
<u>Marquis de la Seiglière</u> F. Febvre/Leloir; <u>Bernard</u>
<u>Stamply</u> G.-H. Worms/Leitner; <u>Destournelles</u> E.-A.-H.
Coquelin [*cadet*]; <u>Raoul</u> Boucher; <u>Jasmin</u> Roger. Hélène
Blanche Barretta; <u>Baronne de Vaubert</u> Blanche Adeline
Pierson. <u>L & MGR</u>, <u>Dir</u>, <u>Sec & Treas</u>, <u>Rep</u> as for 93.179.
REV: E 1/7/93 p7. <u>Comment</u>: As for 93.179.

93.184 *ADRIENNE LECOUVREUR* (D,5a) Eugene Scribe &
Ernest Legouvé. DRURY LANE 24/6/93. 1 perf.** <u>Michon-</u>
<u>net</u> de Feraudy; <u>L'Abbé de Chazeuil</u> Jules Truffier;
<u>Prince de Bouillon</u> Leloir; <u>Maurice de Saxe</u> Albert
Lambert, *fils*; <u>Poisson</u> Joliet; <u>Quinault</u> Villain;
<u>L'Avertisseur</u> Roger; <u>Domestique</u> Falconnier. Adrienne
Lecouvreur Julia Bartet; <u>Princesse de Bouillon</u> Blanche
Adeline Pierson; <u>Athenais</u> Ludwig; <u>Mlle Dangerville</u>
Kalb; <u>Baronne</u> Persoons; <u>Marquise</u> du Minil; <u>Mlle Jou-</u>
<u>venot</u> Bertiny; <u>Femme de Chambre</u> Jamaux. <u>L & MGR</u>, <u>Dir</u>,
<u>Sec & Treas</u>, <u>Rep</u> as for 93.179. <u>Comment</u>: As for 93.179.

93.185 *FROU FROU* (C,5a) Henri Meilhac & Ludovic Halévy.
DRURY LANE 26/6/93. 1 perf.** <u>Brigard</u> de Feraudy;
<u>Valreas</u> C.-G.-A. Le Bargy; <u>Pitou</u> Georges Berr; <u>Baron</u>
Pierre Laugier; <u>Domestiques</u> Roger, Hamel; <u>Sartorys</u>
Leitner. <u>Louise</u> Blanche Barretta; <u>Gilberte</u> Marie
Louise Marsy; <u>Baronne</u> Ludwig; <u>Gouvernante</u> Amel; <u>Pau-</u>
<u>line</u> Bertiny; <u>George</u> La Petite Helanie. <u>L & MGR</u>, <u>Dir</u>,

Sec & Treas, <u>Rep</u> as for 93.179. *REV: Ath 1/7/93 p42;*
E 1/7/93 p7; Sk 5/7/93 p511. Comment: As for 93.179.

93.186 *JOHN THURGOOD FARMER* (P,1a) Henry Byatt.
GLOBE 26/6/93-28/3/94. 227 perf [np 19/8/93, 26/8,
2/9, 9/9, 16/9, 23/9, 23/-25/12, 30/12/93, 23-24/3/
94].* <u>Steve Armstrong</u> Wilton Heriot/Harry Farmer;
<u>John Thurgood</u> Cecil H. Thornbury; <u>Henry</u> Henry Besley/
E[dwin] H. Wynne/James Woodbridge. <u>Annie</u> Mabel Lane.
<u>L</u> W.S. Penley; <u>Bm</u> Henry Dana; <u>Am</u> Francis Gosnay; <u>Sm</u>
Wilton Heriot; <u>Mus dir</u> Franz Groenings; <u>Bom</u> H.W. Anderson. *REV: E 1/7/93 p6.*

93.187 *THE TAMING OF THE SHREW* (C,5a) William Shakespeare. DALY'S 27/6/93-10/7/93. 14 perf [w/S mat].**
<u>Petruchio</u> George Clarke; <u>Grumio</u> James Lewis; <u>Chris-
topher Sly</u> William Gilbert; <u>Lucentio</u> Creston Clarke;
<u>Gremio</u> Charles Leclercq; <u>1st Player/Tranio</u> Herbert
Gresham; <u>Hortensio</u> Sidney Herbert; <u>2nd Player/Pedant</u>
William Sampson; <u>Lord</u> John Craig; <u>Page</u> George Lesoir;
<u>Huntsmen</u> George Wharnock, Rankin Duval, Alfred Hick-
man; <u>Bapista</u> Henry Loraine; <u>Vincentio</u> Thomas Bridg-
land; <u>Biondello</u> Edward P. Wilks; <u>Tailor</u> Hobart Bosworth. <u>Katherine</u> Ada Rehan; <u>Curtis</u> Mrs G.H. Gilbert;
<u>Bianca</u> Frances Ross; <u>Widow</u> Lucie Celeste; <u>Hostess</u>
Adelaide Stirling. <u>MGR</u> Augustin Daly; <u>Bom</u> John Farrington; <u>Sc</u> T.E. Ryan, James Roberts, Walter Hann, H[enry]
Hoyt; <u>Mus dir</u> Henry Widmer; <u>Bm</u> George F. Bashford; <u>Pq</u>
William Clarkson. *REV: Ath 1/7/93 p42; TW93 p185-6;*
E 1/7/93 p9; Sk 28/6/93 p451-3, 5/7/93 p510-1; SR
1/7/93 p16-7; St 29/6/93 p11; Th 1/7/93 p101-2; Ti
28/6/93 p5. Comment: Opening production of new theatre.

93.188 *RUY BLAS* (D,5a) Victor Hugo. DRURY LANE 27/6/93.
1 perf. 1st perfd Renaissance, Paris 8/11/38. <u>Ruy</u>
<u>Blas</u> Mounet-Sully; <u>Don Cesar de Bazan</u> Baillet; <u>Don</u>
<u>Salluste</u> Paul Mounet; <u>Laquais</u> Jules Truffier; <u>Alcade</u>
Georges Berr; <u>Don Guritan</u> Martell; <u>Covadenga</u> Joliet;
<u>Camporeale</u> Dupont Vernon; <u>Alguazil</u> Roger; <u>Marquis del</u>
<u>Basto</u> Villain; <u>Ubilla</u> Samary; <u>Monztago</u> Clerh; <u>Manuel</u>
<u>Arias</u> Hamel; <u>Huissier</u> Falconnier; <u>Marquis de Santa</u>
<u>Crux</u> Pierre Laugier; <u>Marquis de Priego</u> Leitner; <u>Comte</u>
<u>d'Albe</u> Emile Dehelly. <u>La Reine</u> Julia Bartet; <u>Casilda</u>
Ludwig; <u>Camarera Mayor</u> Fayolle; <u>Duegne</u> Amel; <u>Page</u>

Drunzer. L & MGR Augustus Harris; Dir Augustus Harris,
Henry E. Abbey, Maurice Grau; Sec & Treas Fred G.
Latham; Rep C.J. Abud. *REV: Ath 8/7/93 p75; E 1/7/93
p7; Sk 5/7/93 p511.* Comment: Comédie-Française.

93.189 *TRISTAN UND ISOLDE* (O[3a]) Richard Wagner.
COVENT GARDEN 28/6/93; trfd to DRURY LANE 22/7/93. 2
perf.** Tristan Max Alvary; Kurvenal David Bispham;
King Marke Heinrich Wiegand; Melot Karlyle; Shepherd
H. Phillips. Brangane Esther Palliser; Isolde Fanny
Moran-Olden. L & MGR Augustus Harris; Cond Emil Stein-
bach. *REV: Ath 1/7/93 p40; E 1/7/93 p7; St 6/7/93 p
12; Ti 29/6/93 p10.*

93.190 *SOUVENT HOMME VARIE* (C,3a) Auguste Vacquerie.
DRURY LANE 28/6/93. 1 perf. 1st perfd Théâtre-fran-
çais, Paris 2/5/59. Troppa Georges Berr; Beppo Samary;
Valet Falconnier. Fideline Nancy Martel; Lydia Ber-
tiny. L & MGR Augustus Harris; Dir Augustus Harris,
Henry E. Abbey, Maurice Grau; Sec & Treas Fred G.
Latham; Rep C.J. Abud. *REV: E 1/7/93 p7.* Comment:
Comédie-Française.

93.191 *LE MONDE OU L'ON S'ENNUIE* (C,3a) Edouard Pail-
leron. DRURY LANE 28/6/93, 7/7/93. 2 perf.** Bellac
Prudhon; Roger de Céran Baillet; Paul Raymond Jules
Truffier; Géneral Martel; Saint Réault Joliet; Fran-
çois Roger; Toulonnier Villain; Virot Hamel; Des-
millets Pierre Laugier; Gaiat Leitner; Melchior de
Boynes Emile Dehelly. Jeanne Raymond Reichenberg;
Lucy Watson Emilie Broisat; Duchesse de Reville
Blanche Adeline Pierson; Suzanne de Villiers Ludwig;
Mme de Loudan Fayolle; Mme de Boynes Amel; Mme de Cé-
ran Persoons; Mme Ariego Nancy Martel; Mme de Saint
Réault Jamaux. L & MGR, Dir, Sec & Treas, Rep as for
93.190. *REV: E 1/7/93 p7; Sk 5/7/93 p511; St 6/7/93
p12.* Comment: As for 93.190.

93.192 *CHARLES I* (P,4a) W.G. Wills. LYCEUM 28/6/93(m),
7/7, 18/7/93. 3 perf.** Charles the First Henry Ir-
ving; Marquis of Huntley Alfred Bishop; Lord Moray
Frank [Kemble] Cooper; Oliver Cromwell William Terriss;
Ireton [Frank] Tyars; 1st Cavalier Lacy; 2nd Cavalier
[W. Lionel] Belmore; Attendant [R.P.] Tabb; Queen's

<u>Page</u> John Martin Harvey; <u>Prince James</u> Master Leo
Byrne. <u>Princess Elizabeth</u> Grace Webb; <u>Lady Eleanor</u>
Maud Milton; <u>Queen Henrietta Maria</u> Ellen Terry. <u>L &</u>
<u>MGR</u> Henry Irving; <u>Sc</u> Hawes Craven, Joseph Harker; <u>Cond</u>
J. Meredith Ball; <u>Sm</u> H.J. Loveday; <u>Act mgr</u> Bram Sto-
ker; <u>Bom</u> Joseph Hurst.

93.193 *RIGOLETTO* (O[3a]) Giuseppe Verdi. COVENT GAR-
DEN 29/6/93. 1 perf.** <u>Rigoletto</u> Pignalosa; <u>Spara-</u>
<u>fucile</u> Armand Castelmary; <u>Marullo</u> Cernusco; <u>Monterone</u>
Antonio de Vaschetti; <u>Borsa</u> Iginio Corsi; <u>Conte di</u>
<u>Ceprano</u> Rinaldini; <u>Il Duca</u> Fernando de Lucia. <u>Gilda</u>
Nellie Melba; <u>Maddalena</u> Giulia Ravogli; <u>Giovanna</u>
Mathilde Bauermeister. <u>L & MGR</u> Augustus Harris; <u>Cond</u>
Enrico Bevignani.

93.194 *L'ETE DE LA ST. MARTIN* (C,1a) Henri Meilhac &
Ludovic Halévy. DRURY LANE 29/6/93. 1 perf. 1st perfd
Français, Paris 1/7/73. <u>Noel</u> Prudhon; <u>Briqueville</u> De
Feraudy. <u>Adrienne</u> Blanche Barretta; <u>Mme Le Breton</u>
Fayolle. <u>L & MGR</u> Augustus Harris; <u>Dir</u> Augustus Harris,
Henry E. Abbey, Maurice Grau; <u>Sec & Treas</u> Fred G. La-
tham; <u>Rep</u> C.J. Abud. *REV: E 1/7/93 p7.* <u>Comment</u>: Comé-
die-Française.

93.195 *OEPIDE ROI* (T,5a) Sophocles [trans Jules Lacroix & E. Membrée(mus)]. DRURY LANE 29/6/93. 1 perf.
<u>Oedipe</u> Mounet-Sully; <u>Envoye du Palais</u> Eugene Silvain;
<u>Tiresias</u> Paul Mounet; <u>Coryphee</u> Martel; <u>Créon</u> Dupont
Vernon; <u>Messager de Corinthe</u> Villain; <u>Pretre de</u>
<u>Jupiter</u> Hamel; <u>Esclave de Laius</u> Albert Lambert, *fils.*
<u>1ere Jeune Fille Thebaine</u> Hadamard; <u>2eme Jeune Fille</u>
<u>Thebaine</u> Du Minil; <u>Jocaste</u> Lerou. <u>L & MGR</u>, <u>Dir</u>, <u>Sec &</u>
<u>Treas</u>, <u>Rep</u> as for 93.194. *REV: Ath 8/7/93 p75; E 1/7/*
93 p7; Sk 5/7/93 p511; SR 1/7/93 p16; St 6/7/93 p12;
TW93 p179-85. <u>Comment</u>: As for 93.194.

93.196 *FIREWORKS* (FC,3a) F.C. Phillips & Percy Fendall. VAUDEVILLE 29/6/93 mat perf.* <u>Rev Septimus Need-</u>
<u>ham</u> Alfred Maltby; <u>Hugo Fraser</u> W.T. Lovell; <u>Frederick</u>
<u>Grindley</u> Eric Lewis; <u>Tuffet</u> William Wyes; <u>James</u> Tre-
vor Warde. <u>Ada Pinkerton</u> Lottie Venne; <u>Mrs Fraser</u>
Gertrude Kingston; <u>Mrs Grindley</u> Ethel Matthews. *REV:*
E 1/7/93 p9; Sk 5/7/93 p510; St 6/7/93 p13.

93.197 *DIVORCONS* (C,3a) Victorien Sardou & Emile de
Najac. LYRIC 30/6/93, 5/7/93. 2 perf.** Des Pru-
nelles Flavio Ando. Cyprienne Eleonora Duse. L & MGR
Horace Sedger; Dir Carl & Theodore Rosenfeld. *REV:*
Ath 8/7/93 p75; St 6/7/93 p12; Ti 3/7/93 p4; TW93
p187.

93.198 *A WOMAN'S REVENGE* (D of Real Life,4a) Henry
Pettitt. ADELPHI 1/7/93-3/3/94. 206 perf [w/mat 7/9,
18/11, 26/12/93; np 18-25/12/93].* Frank Drummond
Charles Warner; Jephtha Grimwade Charles Cartwright;
Robert Overstone Herbert Flemming; John Overstone
John Carter; Sir John Blacklock Rudge Harding;
Justice Earle Howard Russell; Dick Chilton Arthur
Williams/E.W. Gardiner/William Younge; Martin Doyle
Arthur Leigh; Clerk of the Arraigns William Younge;
Usher Harwood Cooper. Mary Lonsdale Elizabeth Robins/
Mary Rorke; Mabel Wenworth Gertrude Kingston/Alma
Stanley; Maggie Westwood Florence L. Forster/Adah
Barton; Lottie Bromley Fanny Brough/Agnes Thomas/
Harrietta Polini; Little Mary Empsie Bowman/Amy Ray-
ner. PP & MGR A. & S. Gatti; Dir E.B. Norman; Furn
J. Lyon; Pq William Clarkson; Cost dgn Karl; Cost L.
& H. Nathan; Mus dir Henry Sprake; Act mgr & Treas
Charles A. Jecks. *REV: E 8/7/93 p6; Sk 19/7/93 p625;*
St 6/7/93 p12; Th 1/8/93 p102-3; Ti 3/7/93 p4; TW93
p187-8.

93.199 *L'AUTOGRAPHE* (C,1a) Henri Meilhac. DRURY LANE
1/7/93 mat perf.** Chastenay Baillet; Riscara Leloir;
Flavio Georges Berr. Julie Ludwig; Comtesse Nancy Mar-
tel. L & MGR Augustus Harris; Dir Augustus Harris,
Henry E. Abbey, Maurice Grau; Sec & Treas Fred G.
Latham; Rep C.J. Abud. Comment: Comédie-Française.

93.200 *LE GENDRE DE MONSIEUR POIRIER* (C,4a) Emile
Augier & Jules Sandeau. DRURY LANE 1/7/93 mat perf.**
Poirier E.-F.-J. Got; Montmeyran Baillet; Le Marquis
de Presles C.-G.-A. Le Bargy; Vatél De Feraudy;
François Roger; Chevassus Clerh; Verdelet Pierre Laugier; Domestique Falconnier. Antoinette Blanche Barretta. L & MGR, Dir, Sec & Treas, Rep as for 93.199.
Comment: Comédie-Française; V & A source indicates
an evening perf on 17/6.

93.201 *HAMLET: PRINCE DE DANEMARK* (D,5a,12tab) William Shakespeare [adpt Alexandre Dumas & Paul Meurice]. DRURY LANE 3/7/93. 1 perf.** Hamlet Mounet-Sully; 1er Fossoyeur E.-A.-H. Coquelin [*cadet*]; Le Roi Eugene Silvain; Horatio Baillet; Osric Jules Truffier; Rosencrantz Leloir; Laertes Samary; Le Spectre Martel; Francisco Joliet; Comedien Dupont Vernon; 2eme Fossoyeur Roger; Guildenstern Villain; Lucianus Falconnier; Bernardo Hamel; Polonius Pierre Laugier; Marcellus Leitner. Orphelie Reichenberg; Baptista Hadamard; La Reine Lerou; Prologue Drunzer. L & MGR, Dir, Sec & Treas,Rep as for 93.199. *REV: Ath 8/7/93 p75-6; E 8/7/93 p9; Sk 19/7/93 p625; SR 8/7/93 p44-5; St 6/7/93 p12; Ti 4/7/93 p5.* Comment: Comédie-Française.

93.202 *MUCH ADO ABOUT NOTHING* (C,5a) William Shakespeare. LYCEUM 3/7/93, 4/7, 8/7(m), 19/7/93. 4 perf.** Benedick Henry Irving; Claudio William Terriss; Don John [William] Haviland; Antonio H[enry] Howe; Dogberry S[am] Johnson; Leonato [Frank] Tyars; Borachio [Clarence] Hague; Seacoal [John] Archer; Don Pedro Frank [Kemble] Cooper; Friar Francis Alfred Bishop; Balthazar [Ian] Robertson; Conrade John Martin Harvey; Verges Seldon; Sexton [T.] Reynolds; Boy Master Leo Byrne; Oatcake [W.J.] Lorriss. Beatrice Ellen Terry; Margaret Kate Phillips; Ursula [Amy] Coleridge; Hero Jessie Millward. L & MGR Henry Irving; Cond J. Meredith Ball; Sm H.J. Loveday; Act mgr Bram Stoker; Bom Joseph Hurst. *REV: Sk 19/7/93 p625.*

93.203 *LES FEMMES SAVANTES* (C,5a) Molière. DRURY LANE. 4/7/93. 1 perf. 1st perfd Palais-royal, Paris 11/3/1672. Trissotin E.-A.-H. Coquelin [*cadet*]; Ariste Eugene Silvain; Clitandre Baillet; Vadius De Feraudy; Chrysale Leloir; Jullien Roger; Notaire Villain; Lepine Falconnier. Henriette Blanche Barretta; Armande Julia Bartet; Philaminte Blanche Adeline Pierson; Beline Fayolle; Martine Lynnes. L & MGR Augustus Harris; Dir Augustus Harris, Henry E. Abbey, Maurice Grau; Sec & Treas Fred G. Latham; Rep C.J. Abud. *REV: E 8/7/93 p9.* Comment: Comédie-Française.

93.204 *LA BATAILLE DE DAMES* (C,3a) Eugene Scribe & Ernest Legouvé. DRURY LANE 4/7/93. 1 perf. 1st perfd

Théâtre-français, Paris 17/3/51. Montrichard Prudhon;
De Grignon De Feraudy; Flavigneul Samary; Domestique
Roger; Brigadier Falconnier. Leonie Reichenberg;
Comtesse Emilie Broisat. L & MGR, Dir, Sec & Treas,
Rep as for 93.203. *REV: E 8/7/93 p9; Sk 19/7/93 p625.*
Comment: As for 92.203.

93.205 *THE MEDICAL STUDENT* (FC,3a) Beard Frances &
Herbert J. Laeland. STRAND 4/7/93 mat perf.* Mr
Burton Fred A. Everill; Tim James A. Welch; Sir Giles
de Feetum Lawrance d'Orsay; Dick J[ohn] Tresahar; Cab-
man Wyatt Keith; Looney J[ohn] Wheatman. Mrs Burton
Mrs H[enry] Leigh; Alice Mary Kingsley; Sophie Annie
Hill; Sarah Fanny Marriott; Anne H[enrietta] Cross.
PP J.S. Clarke; L Willie Edouin; Bm J.T. Mackay
Robertson; Sm Julian Cross; Act mgr Eugene O. Staf-
ford. *REV: E 8/7/93 p8; St 6/7/93 p13.*

93.206 *DIE WALKURE* (O[3a]) Richard Wagner. COVENT GAR-
DEN 5/7/93; trfd to DRURY LANE 15/7/93, 22/7/93.   3
perf.** Siegmund Max Alvary; Wotan Heinrich Wiegand;
Hunding David Bispham. Sieglinde Reuss Belce; Fricka/
Schwetleitner Louise Meisslinger; Helwige Gherlsen;
Gerhilde Carla Dagmar; Ortlinde Mathilde Bauermeister;
Brunnhilde Fanny Moran-Olden; Waltraute Cecile Brani;
Sigrune Marie Brema; Rossweisse Wilmore; Grimgerte
Aldridge. L & MGR Augustus Harris; Cond Emil Stein-
bach. *REV: Ath 8/7/93 p74; E 8/7/93 p13; St 13/7/93
p10; Ti 7/7/93 p14.*

93.207 *ARLEQUIN POLI PAR L'AMOUR* (Fair C,1a) Pierre
Carlet de Chamblain de Marivaux. DRURY LANE 5/7/93.
1 perf. 1st perfd 1720. Arlequin Jules Truffier;
Maitre de Danse Joliet; Berger Hamel; Triveliu Pierre
Laugier. Sylvia Muller; La Fee Nancy Martel; Une
Cousine Bertiny. L & MGR Augustus Harris; Dir Augus-
tus Harris, Henry E. Abbey, Maurice Grau; Sec & Treas
Fred G. Latham; Rep C.J. Abud. Comment: Comédie-Fran-
çaise.

93.208 *I RANTZAU* (O[4a]) Pietro Mascagni. COVENT GAR-
DEN 7/7/93. 1 perf. 1st perfd Teatro della Pergola,
Florence 10/11/92. Gianni Mario Ancona; Giacomo
Armand Castelmary; Fiorenzo David Bispham; Lebel

Iginio Corsi; <u>Georgio</u> Fernando de Lucia; <u>Luisa</u> Nellie
Melba; <u>Giulia</u> Mathilde Bauermeister. <u>L & MGR</u> Augustus
Harris; <u>Cond</u> Pietro Mascagni. *REV: Ath 15/7/93 p106-7;
E 8/7/93 p10, 15/7/93 p13; St 13/7/93 p10; Th 1/8/93
p112-3; Ti 10/7/93 p8.*

93.209 *L'ETINCELLE* (C,1a) Edouard Pailleron. DRURY
LANE 7/7/93. 1 perf. 1st perfd Français, Paris 13/5/
79. <u>Raoul</u> C.-G.-A. Le Bargy. <u>Mme de Renat</u> Julia Bar-
tet; <u>Antoinette</u> Bertiny. <u>L & MGR</u> Augustus Harris; <u>Dir</u>
Augustus Harris, Henry E. Abbey, Maurice Grau, <u>Sec &
Treas</u> Fred G. Latham; <u>Rep</u> C.J. Abud; <u>Comment</u> Comédie-
Française.

93.210 *A LA FRANCAISE* (F,1a) A. O'D. Bartholeyns.
AVENUE 8/7/93 mat perf.* <u>Raymond Digne</u> Louis Till;
<u>Raymond de la Guerre</u> G. de Maurier; <u>Banks</u> Sam Hemsley.
<u>Rosalie</u> Beverley Robinson. <u>PD</u> S.H.S. Austin; <u>Bm</u> F[ran-
cis] Jerrard. *REV: E 15/7/93 p7; St 13/7/93 p11.*

93.211 *A LORD IN WAITING* (C,1a) A. O'D. Bartholeyns.
AVENUE 8/7/93 mat perf.* <u>Mr Willoughby</u> Frank Worthing;
<u>Mr Sligo</u> J.B. Gordon; <u>Servant</u> Brash. <u>Fanny</u> Emilie
Grattan. <u>PD</u>, <u>Bm</u> as for 93.210. *REV: As for 93.210.*

93.212 *MILITARY MANOEUVRES* (Oa) A. O'D. Bartholeyns.
AVENUE 8/7/93 mat perf.* <u>John Barleymuckle</u> Sam Hems-
ley; <u>Barnaby Battlement</u> Fuller Allen; <u>Philip Fairnote</u>
Maurice Mancini; <u>Seth</u> Harry Grattan. <u>Sarah</u> Maria Sa-
ker; <u>Daisy</u> Haidee Crofton. <u>PD</u>, <u>Bm</u> as for 93.210. *REV:
As for 93.210.*

93.213 *LES HUGUENOTS* (O[5a]) Giacomo Meyerbeer. COV-
ENT GARDEN 8/7/93, 24/7/93. 2 perf.** <u>Raoul di Nangis</u>
Jean de Reszke; <u>Marcello</u> Edouard de Reszke; <u>Conte di
Nevers</u> Mario Ancona/Eugene Dufriche; <u>Huguenot Soldier</u>
Iginio Corsi; <u>De Retz</u> Caracciolo; <u>Maurevert</u> Antonio
de Vaschetti; <u>De Cosse</u> Rinaldini; <u>Conte di San Bris</u>
Jean Lassalle/Pol Plançon. <u>Margherita di Valois</u>
Sigrid Arnoldson/Lucille Hill; <u>Urbano</u> Guilia Ravogli;
<u>Dama d'Onore</u> Mathilde Bauermeister; <u>Valentina</u> Emma
Albani; <u>1ere Danseuse</u> Virginia Zucchi. <u>L & MGR</u> Augus-
tus Harris; <u>Cond</u> Enrico Bevignani. *REV: Ath 15/7/93
p107; E 15/7/93 p13; St 13/7/93 p10; Ti 10/7/93 p8.*

93.214 *HERNANI* (Verse D,5a) Victor Hugo. DRURY LANE
8/7/93. 1 perf. Lst perfd Français, Paris 25/2/30.
Hernani Mounet-Sully; Ruy Gomez Eugene Silvain; Don
Carlos C.-G.-A. Le Bargy; Don Garcie Georges Berr;
Lutzelbourg Martel; Hohenbourg Joliet; Duc de Gotha
Villain; Don Mathias Samary; Don Gil Falconnier; Duc
de Bavière Hamel; Don Ricardo Pierre Laugier; Don
Sanchez Leitner; Don Francisco Emile Dehelly. Dona
Sol Julia Bartet; Dona Josefa Amel; Marquise Jamaux;
Page Drunzer. L & MGR Augustus Harris; Dir Augustus
Harris, Henry E. Abbey, Maurice Grau. Sec & Treas
Fred G. Latham; Rep C.J. Abud. *REV: Ath 15/7/93 p108;*
E 15/7/93 p7; SR 15/7/93 p72; St 13/7/93 p10. Comment:
Comédie-Française.

93.215 *ENGAGED* (C,3a) W.S. Gilbert. ROYALTY 8/7/93
mat perf. 1st perfd Haymarket 3/10/77. Cheviot Hill
Edgar B. Skeet; Belvawney Wallace Douglas; Mr Symper-
son Percy Buckler; Mjr. McGillicuddy Smallwood Metcalfe. Belinda Treherne Edith Tancred; Minnie May
Bailey; Mrs. Macfarlane Muriel Hawley; Maggie Emily
Arnold; Parker Marie Garcia. *REV: E 15/7/93 p7; St*
13/7/93 p11.

93.216 *LA REINE JUANA* (Verse D,5a) Alexandre Parodi.
DRURY LANE 10/7/93. 1 perf. 1st perfd Théâtre-fran-
çais, Paris 6/5/93. Don Fernand d'Aragon Leloir; Don
Arias Albert Lambert, *fils*; Marquis de Denia Paul
Mounet; Fray Marcos Martel; Le Chef des Delegues des
Cortes Joliet; Mosen Ferrer Dupont Vernon; 1er Moine
Villain; Don Juan Samary; Don Tello Clerh; 2eme Moine
Falconnier; Envoyé de l'Empereur Hamel; Dr Soto Pierre
Laugier; Charles Quint Leitner; Don Enrique Emile
Dehelly. Donna Juana Adeline Dudlay; Donna Floresta
Brandès; Catalina La Petite Gaudy; Casilda Jamaux;
Estrella Drunzer. L & MGR Augustus Harris; Dir Augus-
tus Harris, Henry E. Abbey, Maurice Grau; Sec & Treas
Fred G. Latham; Rep C.J. Abud. *REV: Ath 15/7/93 p107;*
E 15/7/93 p7; Sk 19/7/93 p625; SR 15/7/93 p72; St 13/
7/93 p10; Ti 12/7/93 p5; TW93 p189-93. Comment: Comé-
die-Française.

93.217 *KING HENRY VIII* (HistP,5a) William Shakespeare.
LYCEUM 10/7/93, 11/7, 15/7/93.** Cardinal Wolsey

Henry Irving; Henry VIII William Terriss; Secretary
[W.] Marion; Griffith [Henry] Howe; Duke of Bucking-
ham Frank [Kemble] Cooper; Cranmer Vincent; Duke of
Suffolk [Frank] Tyars; Lord Chamberlain Alfred Bis-
hop; Capucius [R.P.] Tabb; Cardinal Campeius Lacy;
Earl of Surrey Clarence Hague; Garter, King-at-Arms
Bedford; Scribe [T.] Reynolds; Duke of Norfolk [Will-
iam] Haviland; Brandon Seldon; Lord Sands S[am] John-
son; Gardiner [John] Archer; Sir Henry Guildford
John Martin Harvey; Cromwell Gordon Craig; Sir Thomas
Lovell [W. Lionel] Belmore; Sir Anthony Denny Davis;
Sir Nicholas Vaux [H.W.] Cushing; Surveyor Doughty;
Sgt.-at-Arms [W.J.] Yeldham; Messenger [W.J.] Lorriss.
Queen Katherine Genevieve Ward; Anne Bullen [Amy]
Coleridge; Old Lady Maud Milton; Patience Mrs [Frank]
Tyars. L & MGR Henry Irving; Sc Joseph Harker, Hawes
Craven, William Telbin; Mus Edward German; Cond J.
Meredith Ball; Sm H.J. Loveday; Act mgr Bram Stoker;
Bom Joseph Hurst. *REV: E 15/7/93 p6.*

93.218 *ST. RONAN'S WELL* (RD,4a) Richard Davey & Walter
Herries Pollock [fr Scott's novel]. ROYALTY 10/7/93-
15/7/93; 28/7/93(m). 7 perf.** Francis Tyrell Frank
Worthing; Valentine Bulmer Gaston Mervale; Mowbray of
St. Ronan Edmund Gurney; Touchwood Henry Ashford; Cpt.
Jekyll Akerman May; Cpt. McTurk Hawley Francks. Miss
Mowbray Annie Rose; Lady Penelope Pennyfeather Mrs.
[F.] Copleston; Megg Dodds Alexes Leighton; Lady
Binks Katherine Stewart; Mrs Blower Mrs St. Hill;
Hannah Irwin Laura Hansen; Eppie [Nora] Leslie; Maria
Mary Jocelyn. MGR Annie Rose [Mrs Horace Neville]; Bm
W.J. Lancaster. *REV: E 15/7/93 p6; SR 15/7/93 p72;
St 13/7/93 p11.*

93.219 *THE HUNCHBACK* (P,5a) James Sheridan Knowles.
DALY'S 11/7/93-17/7/93. 7 perf [w/mat 15/7].* Sir
Thomas Clifford Arthur Bourchier; Master Walter George
Clarke; Modus Creston Clarke; Fathom William Gilbert;
Lord Tinsel Sidney Herbert; Thomas William Sampson;
Master Heartwell Thomas Bridgland; Master Wilford
John Craig; Gaylove Hobart Bosworth; Simpson Lloyd
Daubigny; Stephen Rankin Duval; Landlord George
Wharnock. Julia Ada Rehan; Helen Isabel Irving. MGR
Augustin Daly; Sc James Roberts, T.E. Ryan, John Reed,

Amalde, Walter Johnstone; <u>Bm</u> George F. Bashford; <u>Bom</u> John Farrington; <u>Pq</u> William Clarkson. *REV: E 15/7/93 p6; Sk 19/7/93 p624; SR 15/7/93 p72; St 13/7/93 p10; Th 1/8/93 p104-5; Ti 12/7/93 p5; TW93 p193-4.*

92.220 *THE MERCHANT OF VENICE* William Shakespeare. OPERA COMIQUE 11/7/93. 1 perf.** <u>Shylock</u> Herbert Waring; <u>Duke of Venice</u> P.C. Beverley; <u>Antonio</u> Bassett Roe; <u>Gratiano</u> Lionel Dainer; <u>Lorenzo</u> Oswald Yorke; <u>Tubal</u> S. Keaniss; <u>Salarino</u> F. Walford; <u>Salanio</u> Lorraine; <u>Launcelot Gobbo</u> A. Wood; <u>Old Gobbo</u> Edwin Shepherd; <u>Balthazar</u> C.F. Bawtree. <u>Portia</u> Ethel Verne; <u>Nerissa</u> Ethel Herbert; <u>Jessica</u> Ada Laurence. *REV: E 15/7/93 p6; St 13/7/93 p10-1.*

93.221 *PARALLEL ATTACKS* (Ca) Frederick James. STRAND 11/7/93(m); 31/7/93-18/8/93. 18 perf.* <u>Cpt. Alan Adair</u> Laurence Cautley; <u>Cpt. Philip Annersley</u> C. Aubrey Smith; <u>Lieut. Brunderson</u> J.R. Crauford. <u>Violet Fullerton</u> Beryl Faber; <u>Madge Fullerton</u> Mina Le Bert. *REV: E 15/7/93 p5; St 13/7/93 p11.*

93.222 *MIDGELET; OR, A DAY UP THE RIVER* (Ca) E. Benson. STRAND 11/7/93 mat perf.* <u>Harry Fielding</u> Alfred Harding. <u>Iris Vernon</u> Minnie Turner; <u>Midgelet</u> Lalor Shiel. *REV: As for 93.221.*

93.223 *THE LOAN OF A LOVER* J.R. Planché. STRAND 11/7/93 mat perf. 1st perfd Olympic 29/9/34. <u>Peter Spyk</u> Wilfred E. Shine; <u>Cpt. Armersfort</u> Gaston Mervale; <u>Swyzel</u> Gerald Godfrey; <u>Delve</u> Russell Crauford. <u>Gertrude</u> Grace Huntley; <u>Ernestine</u> Helen Lambert. *REV: As for 93.221.*

93.224 *BARBARA* (Ca,1a) Jerome K. Jerome. STRAND 11/7/93 mat perf.** <u>Cecil</u> H[enry] Doughty; <u>Finnicum</u> C.W.A. Trollope. <u>Barbara</u> Mina Le Bert; <u>Lillie</u> Edith Fielding. *REV: As for 93.221.*

93.225 *DIE MEISTERSINGER* (O[3a]) Richard Wagner. COVENT GARDEN 12/7/93, 21/7/93. 2 perf.** <u>Walter</u> Jean de Reszke; <u>Pogner</u> Heinrich Wiegand; <u>Beckmesser</u> David Bispham; <u>Fritz Kothner</u> Eugene Dufriche; <u>David</u> E. Charles Hedmont; <u>Hans Sachs</u> Jean Lassalle; <u>Kunz</u>

Vogelgesang Iginio Corsi; <u>Balthazar Zorn</u> Rinaldini;
<u>Augustin Moser</u> Coutellier; <u>Ulrich Eisslinger</u> Pedro
Guetary; <u>Konrad Nachtigal</u> Richard Green; <u>Herman Ortel</u>
Antonio de Vaschetti; <u>Hans Foltz</u> Cernusco; <u>Hans Sch-</u>
<u>wars</u> Caracciolo. <u>Maddalena</u> Mathilde Bauermeister; <u>Eva</u>
Emma Albani. <u>L & MGR</u> Augustus Harris; <u>Cond</u> Luigi
Mancinelli. *REV: Ath 15/7/93 p107; E 15/7/93 p13;*
St 20/7/93 p10; Ti 13/7/93 p10.

93.226 *LA JOIE FAIT PEUR* (C,1a) Delphine de Girardin.
DRURY LANE 12/7/93. 1 perf.** <u>Noel</u> E.-F.-J. Got;
<u>Adrien</u> Boucher; <u>Octave</u> Samary. <u>Blanche</u> Reichenberg;
<u>Mme Desaubiers</u> Blanche Adeline Pierson; <u>Mathilde</u> Du
Minil. <u>L & MGR</u> Augustus Harris; <u>Dir</u> Augustus Harris,
Henry E. Abbey, Maurice Grau; <u>Sec & Treas</u> Fred G.
Latham; <u>Rep</u> C.J. Abud. <u>Comment</u>: Comédie-Française.

93.227 *A HUSBAND IN CLOVER* (Ca,1a) Herman C. Merivale.
TRAFALGAR SQUARE 17/7/93–18/8/93; 7/9/93–16/9/93.
38 perf.** <u>Horace</u> Harcourt Beatty. <u>Lydia</u> Elsie Chester. <u>PP & L</u> Mr & Mrs Frank Wyatt; <u>Pd</u> Frank Wyatt;
<u>Bom</u> H.T. Holliman; <u>Gen mgr</u> Gilbert Tate; <u>Act mgr &</u>
<u>Treas</u> H. Brandon; <u>Mus dir</u> E. Vousden.

93.228 *LOVE IN TANDEM* (Eccentrice C,3a) Augustin Daly
[adpt of Bocage & de Courcy, *La Vie à deux*]. DALY'S
18/7/93–4/8/93. 19 perf [w/S mat; add mat 2/8]. 1st
perfd Daly's, New York 9/2/92. <u>Papa Skinastone</u> James
Lewis; <u>Donald Littlejohn</u> George Clarke; <u>Richard Tomp-</u>
<u>kinson Dymond</u> Arthur Bourchier; <u>Bob Packer</u> Herbert
Gresham; <u>Barry</u> William Greet; <u>Mr van Grooge</u> Thomas
Bridgland; <u>Young Bristow</u> John Craig; <u>Pitthammer, jr</u>
Hobart Bosworth; <u>Fiddley</u> Rankin Duval; <u>Barker-Prime</u>
Alfred Hickman. <u>Aprilla Dymond</u> Ada Rehan; <u>Countess</u>
<u>Alticheff</u> Mrs G.H. Gilbert; "<u>Cousin Tetty</u>" Isabel
Irving; <u>Mme Lauretta</u> Violet Vanbrugh; <u>Mme Mirales y</u>
<u>Penaflor y Casa-Floriday</u> Bustamente y Rosareina Lucie
Cleste; <u>Nadege</u> Florence Conron; <u>Mrs van Grooge</u> Olive
Barry; <u>Miss Brigham</u> Frances Ross; <u>Tilly Mixem</u> Eugenie
Upham; <u>Miss Gaggy</u> Catherine Carlisle; <u>Miss Greehn</u>
Adelaide Stirling. <u>MGR</u> Augustin Daly; <u>Cond</u> Henry Wid-
mer; <u>Bm</u> George F. Bashford; <u>Bom</u> John Farrington; <u>Pq</u>
William Clarkson. *REV: Ath 22/7/93 p139; E 22/7/93*
p7; Sk 26/7/93 p682; SR 22/7/93 p100; St 20/7/93 p10;

Th 1/8/93 p105-6; Ti 19/7/93 p5; TW93 p194-5.

93.229 *LOAN OF A LOVER* (F) J.R. Planché. DALY'S 18/7/
93-4/8/93. 16 perf.** <u>Peter Spyk</u> William Gilbert;
<u>Swysel</u> William Owen; <u>Delve</u> William Sampson; <u>Cpt. Amers-
fort</u> Sidney Herbert. <u>Ernestine</u> Percy Haswell; <u>Gertrude</u>
Catherine Lewis. <u>MGR</u>, <u>Bom</u>, <u>Bm</u>, <u>Pq</u>, <u>Cond</u> as for 93.228.
REV: E 22/7/93 p7.

93.230 *SIEGFRIED* (O,3a) Richard Wagner. COVENT GARDEN
19/7/93; trfd to DRURY LANE 24/7/93. 2 perf.** <u>Sieg-
fried</u> Max Alvary; <u>Der Wanderer</u> Heinrich Wiegand; <u>Mime</u>
Julius Lieban; <u>Alberich</u> David Bispham; <u>Fafner</u> Waldmann. <u>Brunnhilde</u> Fanny Moran-Olden; <u>Stimme des Wald-
vogels</u> Gherlsen; <u>Erda</u> Rose Olitzka. <u>L & MGR</u> Augustus
Harris; <u>Cond</u> Emil Steinbach. *REV: Ath 22/7/93 p139;
E 22/7/93 p13; Sk 26/7/93 p683; St 27/7/93 p10; Ti
24/7/93 p14.*

93.231 *AMY ROBSART* (O,3a) Isidore de Lara (mus) &
Augustus Harris (lib) & Frederick Edward Weatherley
(lib). COVENT GARDEN 20/7/93. 1 perf.* <u>Leicester</u>
Albert Alvarez; <u>Tressilian</u> Charles Bonnard; <u>Lambourne</u>
Armand Castelmary; <u>Varney</u> Jean Lassalle. <u>Amy Robsart</u>
Emma Calvé; <u>Queen Elizabeth</u> Armand. <u>L & MGR</u> Augustus
Harris; <u>Cond</u> Enrico Bevignani. *REV: Ath 29/7/93 p170-
1; E 22/7/93 p13; SR 29/7/93 p127; St 27/7/93 p10;
Th 1/9/93 p173-4; Ti 21/7/93 p8.*

93.232 *THE BURGLAR AND THE JUDGE* (Farcical Interlude,
1a) Charles H.E. Brookfield & F.C. Phillips. CRITERION
20/7/93 mat perf.** <u>Judge</u> Cyril Maude; <u>Burglar</u> Charles
H.E. Brookfield; <u>Servant</u> Robb Harwood. <u>L & MGR</u> Charles
Wyndham; <u>Bm</u> Harrington Baily; <u>Act mgr</u> E. Harvey; <u>Sm</u>
S.H.S. Austin, Julian Cross. *REV: E 22/7/93 p9; St
27/7/93 p10.*

93.233 *A VISIT TO A MUSIC HALL*. CRITERION 20/7/93 mat
perf. Bruce Smith. <u>L & MGR</u>, <u>Bm</u>, <u>Act mgr</u>, <u>Sm</u> as for
93.232. *REV: St 27/7/93 p10.*

93.234 *MRS HILARY REGRETS* (Ca,1a) S. Theyre Smith.
CRITERION 20/7/93 mat perf.** <u>Dr Power</u> Charles Wynd-
ham. <u>Mrs Hilary</u> Mary Moore. <u>L & MGR</u>, <u>Bm</u>, <u>Act mgr</u>, <u>Sm</u>

as for 93.232. *REV: As for 93.232.*

93.235 *A PAIR OF LUNATICS* (DSk) W.R. Walkes. CRITER-
ION 20/7/93 mat perf.** <u>He</u> George Alexander. <u>She</u>
Maud Millett. <u>L & MGR</u>, <u>Bm</u>, <u>Act mgr</u>, <u>Sm</u> as for 93.232.
REV: As for 93.232.

93.236 *PUPPETS* (Whimsicality) J.F. McArdle. CRITERION
20/7/93 mat perf.* <u>Bob Crump</u> G.W. Anson; <u>Cpt. Stour-
ton</u> Neville Doone; <u>Bubbage</u> Julian Cross; <u>Dionysius</u>
J.G. Taylor; <u>Binks</u> Aubrey. <u>Miss Phipps</u> Emily Miller;
<u>Georgina</u> Kate Calton; <u>Angelina</u> [Maude] Bowden; <u>Sera-
phina</u> Lucille Heaton; <u>Jemima Jane</u> H[enrietta] Cross.
<u>L & MGR</u>, <u>Bm</u>, <u>Act mgr</u>, <u>Sm</u> as for 93.232. *REV: As for
93.232.*

93.237 *THE THREE WAYFARERS* (Legendary Trifle) Thomas
Hardy. CRITERION 20/7/93 mat perf.** <u>Hangman</u> Charles
Charrington; <u>Shepherd</u> Stewart Dawson; <u>Elijah</u> Charles
Rock; <u>Parish Constable</u> Fred Thorne; <u>Timothy Summers</u>
Julian Cross; <u>Magistrate</u> John Carter; <u>Turnkey</u> Hart.
<u>Damsel</u> Mary Jocelyn; <u>Shepherd's Wife</u> Janet Achurch.
<u>L & MGR</u>, <u>Bm</u>, Act mgr, Sm as for 93.232. *REV: As for
93.232.*

93.238 *NANCE OLDFIELD* (C,1a) Charles Reade. LYCEUM
20/7/93. 1 perf.** <u>Nathan Oldworthy</u> Alfred Bishop;
<u>Alexander Oldworthy</u> John Martin Harvey. <u>Mrs Anne
Oldfield</u> Ellen Terry; <u>Susan Oldfield</u> Kate Phillips.
<u>L & MGR</u> Henry Irving; <u>Cond</u> J. Meredith Ball; <u>Sm</u> H.J.
Loveday; <u>Act mgr</u> Bram Stoker; <u>Bom</u> Joseph Hurst.

93.239 *THE ADVENTURES OF A NIGHT* (C,3a) Meyrick Milton [adpt of Pedro Calderon de la Barca, *Los Empenos
de Seis Horas*]. STRAND 21/7/93 mat perf. 1st perfd
Lyceum, Edinburgh 19/6/93. <u>Don Caesar</u> Meyrick Milton; <u>Don Pedro</u> W.H. Vernon; <u>Don Carlos</u> Luigi Lablache;
<u>Don Octavio</u> Fuller Mellish; <u>Justice</u> E.J. Malyon; <u>Ped-
rillo</u> Mark Kinghorne; <u>Arnesto</u> Hamilton Piffard; <u>Ge-
raldo</u> Fenton Boyd; <u>Silvio</u> Charles Herberte. <u>Donna
Bianca</u> May Whitty; <u>Donna Portia</u> Ada Ferrar; <u>Flora</u>
Cicely Richards. <u>SM</u> W.H. Vernon. *REV: Ath 29/7/93
p 171-2; E 22/7/93 p9; St 27/7/93 p10-1; Ti 24/7/93
p7.*

93.240 *LA FILLE DE MADAME ANGOT* (CO,3a) Charles Lecocq (mus) & Henry J. Byron (lib). CRITERION 22/7/93-
14/10/93. 85 perf [w/S mat exc 22/7]. 1st perfd Philharmonic 4/10/73. Larivaudière Sydney Valentine;
Louchard William Blakeley; Pomponnet Charles Davenport; Trenitz Welton Dale; The Beetle W. Melbourne/
Clifton Grove; The Grasshopper George Humphrey; Ange
Pitou Courtice Pounds; Guillaume Fred J. Vigay. Mlle
Lange Amy Augarde; Clairette Decima Moore/Nita Cla-
vering/Juliette Nesville; Aramante Haidee Crofton;
Javotte M.A. Victor; Hersilie Ellis Jeffreys/F. Fran-
ces; Babette F. Frances/Eva Westlake/Geraldine Wrang-
ham; Therese Bertha Vere; Delphine Day Ford/Edith
Fielding; La Papillon Maggie Gorst. L & MGR Charles
Wyndham; Sm S.H.S. Austin; Act mgr & Treas E. Harvey;
Mus dir John Crook; Sc William Perkins, Harry Potts,
R.C. McCleery. *REV: E 29/7/93 p7; Sk 2/8/93 p39, 30/
8/93 p249; St 27/7/93 p10; Ti 24/7/93 p7.*

93.241 *THE LADY OF LYONS* (D,5a) Edward Bulwer Lytton.
ROYALTY 24/7/93-5/8/93. 12 perf.** Claude Melnotte
Frank Worthing; Beausant Gaston Mervale; Col. Damas
Edmund Gurney; Landlord J.P. Millar; Glavis Hawley
Francks; Gaspar Douglas Gordon; Deschappelles Rothbury
Evans; Gervais Akerman May; Dupont J. Ricketts; Notary
G. French. Pauline Annie Rose; Widow Melnotte Alexes
Leighton; Mme Deschappelles Katherine Stewart. *REV:
29/7/93 p7; St 27/7/93 p11.*

93.242 *POOR MIGNONETTE* (Oa) Jacques Offenbach. CRI-
TERION 25/7/93-14/10/93. 71 perf.** Rabastens Gordon
Begg/S[am] Hemsley; Gustave Welton Dale. Catherine
Bertha Vere/Haidee Crofton. L & MGR Charles Wyndham;
Sm S.H.S. Austin; Act mgr & Treas E. Harvey; Mus dir
John Crook; Cost May; Pq C.H. Fox.

93.243 *THE SLEEPWALKER* (FC,3a) Charles Harry Abbott
[adpt of W.S. Gilbert, "Wide Awake"]. STRAND 25/7/93-
18/8/93. 26 perf [w/S mat; add mat 7/8]. 1st perfd
Prince of Wales's, Liverpool [rev ver of item 92.64].
Jack Pointer Charles S. Fawcett; Rev. Hatley Hylo
Harry Paulton; Hereward Herbert Ross; Mjr. Blister
Willie Edouin; John Blister Harry Eversfield; James
Blister Seymour Hicks. Sophia Blister Georgie Esmond;

Mrs Col. Harkaway Alma Stanley; Gwendoline Blister
Mrs G.B.W. Lewis; Sharp Clara Jecks. PP J.S. Clarke;
L Willie Edouin; Bm J.T. Mackay Robertson; Cond Ernest Bucalossi; Sm Charles Davies. *REV: Ath 29/7/93*
p172; E 29/7/93 p7; Sk 2/8/93 p10, 9/8/93 p72; St
27/7/93 p11; Ti 27/7/93 p14; TW93 p201-2.

93.244 *THE VEILED PROPHET [DER VERSCHLEIERTE PROFET]*
(O,3a) C. Villiers Stanford. COVENT GARDEN 26/7/93.
1 perf. 1st perfd Hanover 6/2/81. Azim Francesco
Vignas; Abdullah Villani; Watchman Pedro Guetary;
Caliph Antonio de Vaschetti; Mokana Mario Ancona.
Fatima Lucille Hill; Zelika Lillian Nordica. L & MGR
Augustus Harris; Cond Luigi Mancinelli. *REV: Ath*
29/7/93 p170-1, 5/8/93 p201; E 29/7/93 p13; SR 29/7/
93 p127-8; St 3/8/93 p10; Th 1/9/93 p174-6; Ti 27/7/
93 p11.

93.245 *A MODERN JULIET; OR, ROMEO REVISED* (DSk) "Tri-
plet". TERRY'S 26/7/93 mat perf.* Lady Isabel
Worthington Helena Dacre; Hon Florence Waterbury May
Palfrey. *REV: E 29/7/93 p9; St 27/7/93 p11.*

93.246 *DREGS* (D,1a) "Alec Nelson" [E.B. Aveling].
TERRY'S 26/7/93 mat perf. 1st perfd Vaudeville 16/5/
89. Frank Henry V. Esmond. Iris Eva Moore. *REV: E*
29/7/93 p9; St 27/7/93 p11.

93.247 *AN APRIL JEST* (Sk,1a) Arthur T. Weston. TERRY'S
26/7/93 mat perf.* Rose Rosalind Webling; Letty Lucy
Webling; Charles Warrington Peggy Webling. *REV: E 29/*
7/93 p9; St 27/7/93 p11.

93.248 *IRMENGARDA* (O[2a]) Leonhard Emil Bach. COVENT
GARDEN 28/7/93. 1 perf.** Luca Eugene Dufriche; Il
Re Antonio de Vaschetti; Burchhard Armand Castelmary;
Cuniberto Pedro Guetary. Irmengarda Marie Duma; Brig-
ida Olimpia Guercia. L & MGR Augustus Harris; Cond
Enrico Bevignani.

93.249 *A TRIP TO CHICAGO* (MFC,2a). VAUDEVILLE 5/8/93-
16/8/93; 6/9/93-21/10/93. 50 perf.* Mrs Johanna Mur-
phey John F. Sheridan; Mjr. Tiffin Charles Groves/
Mark Kinghorne; Benjamin Brewster Laurence Cautley;

Herbert Parke Sidney Brough/P.S. Champion; Charlie
Bleeter Lawrance d'Orsay; Alfonso Napoleon Bert
Williams; Peter Dunn Wilfred Carr. Mrs Herbert Parke
Helena Dacre/Rose Norreys/Alice de Winton; Mrs Car-
ter Parke Mrs Edward Saker/Marie Dagmar; Rose Amy
Thornton/Nellie Arline. L & MGR A. & S. Gatti; Bm &
Treas G.M. Polini; Sm William Sidney, Thomas Sidney;
Mus dir William Robins; Sc Bruce Smith; Pq William
Clarkson; Furn J.S. Lyons; Bom Sharpe. *REV: E 12/8/93
p7; St 10/8/93 p10; Ti 7/8/93 p11; TW93 p195-201.*

93.250 *SIXES* (Ca) Alfred Lindsay. VAUDEVILLE 5/8/93–
16/8/93; 6/9/93-23/9/93. 26 perf.* Hon Gilbert
Coldastone Lawrence d'Orsay; Cpt. Percy Shafto Laurence Cautley. Helen Forrester Helena Dacre; Bridget
Marie Dagmar. PP A. & S. Gatti. *REV: E, St as for
93.249.*

93.251 *PETERKIN; OR, THE LANDING OF THE FRENCH* (CO,3a)
L. Will Ladislaw (lib) & L. Camerana (mus). ROYALTY
4/9/93-8/9/93. 5 perf.* Matthias Habbijam Harry
Longden; Peter Jerrold Manville; Percy Lovel Thorpe
Sheffield; Hector Wellborn Antonio Metcalfe. Lucy
Precious Adeline Kyle; Priscilla Precious Maud Russell.
MGR Mario Moro; Pp G. Faller; Cond L. Camerana. *REV:
E 9/9/93 p7; St 7/9/93 p11; Ti 5/9/93 p6.*

93.252 *THE OTHER FELLOW* (F,3a) Fred Horner [adpt of
Georges Feydeau & Maurice Desvallières, *Champignol
Malgré Lui*]. COURT 9/9/93-15/11/93;* trfd to STRAND
18/11/93-27/11/93. 73 perf [w/mat 7/10, 21/10, 28/10,
4/11, 11/11, 22/11, 25/11]. Robert Champignol Charles
Groves; Cpt. Cameret Charles H.E. Brookfield/Harry
Paulton; Vicomte de St Fontaine Weedon Grossmith;
Lieut. Marbey Wilfred Draycott; Col. Fourrageot Her-
man de Lange; Camel William Wyes/C.P. Little; Sgt.
Compton Coutts; Corporal Robert Nainby/E.M. Robson;
Singleton Charles Burleigh; Arthur Seymour Hicks/Er-
nest Bertram; Joseph Sydney Warden/H[enry] Hudson;
Jerome Ernest Bertram; Sgt. of Gendarmes W.H. Quinton/
Howard; Barber Sidney; Prince of Valence Kelly/Cecil
Newton; Georges J[ames?] Anning; Moville Farley; Sam-
son Howard Finney; Martin W. Hack. Charlotte Pattie
Browne/Marianne Caldwell; Louise Ellaline Terriss;

Adrienne Madge McIntosh; Agnes Champignol Aida Jen-
oure/Pattie Browne. L & MGR Arthur Chudleigh; Sc T.W.
Hall; Cost Russell & Allen, Angel; Cond Edward Jones;
Sm T.W.S. Robertson; Bm Leonard Lillies. *REV: Ath 16/*
9/93 p396; E 16/9/93 p9, 25/11/93 p9; Sk 20/9/93 p384-
5, 29/11/93 p220; SR 16/9/93 p331; St 14/9/93 p9-10,
23/11/93 p12; Th 1/10/93 p224-5; Ti 11/9/93 p6; TW93
222-3.

93.253 *HIS LAST CHANCE* (0a,1a) Herbert & Ethel Harraden. COURT 9/9/93-15/11/93. 58 perf.** Charles Chester Seymour Hicks. Alice Montrose Ellaline Terriss.
L & MGR Arthur Chudleigh; Cond Edward Jones; Sm T.W.S.
Robertson. *REV: E 16/9/93 p9.*

93.254 *LA MASCOTTE* (CO,3a) Edmond Audran (mus) & H.B.
Farnie (lib) & Robert Reece (lib). GAIETY 9/9/93-14/
10/93; trfd to CRITERION 16/10/93-4/11/93. 56 perf
[w/S mat exc 9/9, 14/10].** Pippo Wallace Brownlow;
Prince Frittellini Charles Conyers; Rocco George
Mudie/Sam Hemsley; Laurent XVII Robert Pateman/Fred
Emney; Parafante E. Rosse; Matheo Fred Stanley/Sam
Hemsley/Henry Lebreton. Fiametta Phyllis Broughton;
Bianca Katie Seymour/Mabel Love; Bettina Florence St.
John; Tito Violet Monckton/Maude Hoppe; Angelo Lily
Harold/Warriner; Luigi Ethel Earle/Rutherford; Fin-
ella Maggie Gorst; Beppo Aimee Mills/Eva Westlake;
Carlo May Clarke/Rita Yorke; Guiseppe Madge Arrow-
smith; Georgio Wynne. L & MGR George Edwardes; Dir
J.T. Tanner; Cost J.A. Harrison; Pq C.H. Fox; Furn
Lyons; Mus dir W. Meyer Lutz; Act mgr E[dward] Mar-
shall; Bom A.P. Oxley. *REV: E 16/9/93 p11; St 14/9/*
93 p10; Th 1/10/93 p230-1; Ti 11/9/93 p14.

93.255 *DOLLARS AND SENSE* (C,3a) Augustin Daly. DALY'S
19/9/93-2/10/93. 14 perf [w/S mat]. 1st perfd Daly's,
New York 2/10/83. Eliphalet Lamb James Lewis; Jack
Hemmarsly George Clarke; Harry Latimer Arthur Bour-
chier; Pierce Tremont William Owen; Col. Jefferson
Quincy Briggs Charles Leclercq; Griggles Sidney Her-
bert; Roberts Edward P. Wilks. Phronic Ada Rehan;
Saphira Lamb Mrs G.H. Gilbert; Sybilia Briggs Lucie
Celeste; Hope Florence Conron; Mrs Tremont Frances
Ross; Jane Adelaide Stirling; Lyddy Sofia Hoffmann.

MGR Augustin Daly; Sc T.E. Ryan; Furn Maple; Sm George
Clarke; Prompter Henry Montague; Assistant Edward P.
Wilks; Mach H. Sheldon; Elect F. Hinton; Cond Henry
Widmer; Bom John Farrington, Edward Brown; Pq William
Clarkson; Bm George Bashford; Cost Harrisons. *REV:
Ath 23/9/93 p427; SR 23/9/93 p358; St 21/9/93 p10; Th
1/10/93 p225-6; Ti 20/9/93 p11; TW93 p223.*

93.256 *THE TEMPTER* (P,4a) H.A. Jones. HAYMARKET 20/9/
93-2/12/93. 73 perf [w/S mat; mat only 2/12].* The
Tempter H. Beerbohm Tree; Prince Leon of Auvergne
Fred Terry; Earl of Rougemont E. Holman Clarke; Sir
Gilbert Morbec Fuller Mellish; Sir Gaultier de Florac
A. Hamilton Revelle; Father Urban Fred A. Everill;
Drogo Pound G.W. Anson/Charles Allan; Host Charles
Allan/H. Russell; Master of the Vessel Baldie; Boats-
wain Wyatt; 1st Sailor Mark Paton; Cellarer Cowis;
Steersman Redmond; 2nd Sailor Robinson; Franklin
[J.] Montagu; 1st Beggar C. King/H. Russell. Lady
Isobel of Carmayne Julia Neilson/Lily Hanbury; Lady
Avis of Rougemont Mrs H.B. Tree; Sarah Pound Mrs E.H.
Brooke; Lettice Irene Vanbrugh/Lilian Stafford. L &
MGR H.B. Tree; Sc W.T. Hemsley, Joseph Harker, Walter
Hann; Mus Edward German; Bom W.H. Leverton; Dir Hugh
Moss; Sm Shelton; Elect E. Wingfield Bowles; Cost dgn
Karl; Cost L. & H. Nathan; Cond Carl Armbruster; Bm
& Sec Frederick Harrison. *REV: Ath 23/9/93 p427; E
23/9/93 p11; Sk 27/9/93 p438-9, 477, 18/10/93 p627,
19/9/94 p419; SR 23/9/93 p357-8; St 21/9/93 p10, 28/9/
93 p12; Th 1/11/93 p283-5; Ti 21/9/93 p3, 24/10/93
p4; TW93 p213-22, 224-30.*

93.257 *A LIFE OF PLEASURE* (D,5a) Henry Pettitt & Au-
gustus Harris. DRURY LANE 21/9/93-9/12/93;* trfd to
PRINCESS'S 11/12/93-17/2/94. 153 perf [w/S mat exc
23/9; add mat 9/11, 26/12/93, 1/1/94; np 25/12/93].
Desmond O'Brien Henry Neville; Cpt. Chandos Arthur
Dacre; Lord Avondale Frank H. Fenton; Isidore Scasi
William Elton; Michael Hanlan Stephen Caffrey; Sgt.
Perkins Clarence Holt; Sir John Berkley Robert Sou-
tar; Cpt. Danby Harry Nicholls; Dr Delamere Standley
Wade; Dennis O'Rourke Stanislaus Calhaem; Larry Doo-
lan Maurice Drew; Wilson James Francis; Inspector
C.L. Brocknor; Postman E.H. Brittan; Waiter T.W.

Bedells; Flag Officer W. Davis; Lieut. Crombie N[ich-
olas] Nomico; Lord Ealsford J.C. Beauvane; Check-
taker [Frank] MacVicars; Tompkins Alfred Balfour;
Private Smithers Joseph A. Cave; Harry Bolyn George
A. Seager; Orderly John Pollard; 1st Bailiff Henry
Cooper; 2nd Bailiff F. Maynard; Servant [H.] Lane
Bayliff. Norah Hanlen Mrs Bernard Beere/Emily S. Fitz-
roy; Lady Mary Clifford Lily Hanbury; Phyllis de
Belleville Laura Linden; Lady Nellborough R.G. Le
Thiere; Ethel Nita Carlyon; Grace Marie Hood; Lottie
St. Clair Dorothy Levick; Maud Murray Lizzie Wilson;
Josephine Kingston Clara Douglas; Laura Somerville
Emily S. Fitzroy; Daisy Pelham Gertrude Kingston;
Lady Brookfield Georgie Cook; Mabel Farquah Lillie
Teesdale; May Fielding Violet Malvern; Mlle Bocteau
Ethel Beaumont; Servant B. Talbot; Ethel Morton
Eweretta Lawrence. L & MGR Augustus Harris; Sm Arthur
P. Collins; Sc Robert Caney, William Perkins, Joseph
Harker, T.E. Ryan, J[ulian] Hicks; Mus James M.
Glover; Props G. Jackson, J. Jones; Cost Miss Collier,
Gask & Co., Mrs Besford, Miss Palmer, Angel, Deben-
ham & Freebody; Pq William Clarkson; Mach E.A. Taylor.
REV: Ath 30/9/93 p462; E 23/9/93 p9, 16/12/93 p7; Sk
20/9/93 p398-9, 4/10/93 p525; SR 30/9/93 p385; St 28/
9/93 p12, 14/12/93 p12; Th 1/11/93 p281-3; Ti 22/9/93
p8.

93.258 *SAMSON ET DALILA* (Biblical O,3a) Camille Saint-
Saëns. COVENT GARDEN 25/9/93. 1 perf. 1st perfd Wei-
mar 2/12/77. High Priest Eugene Oudin; Abimelech
Arthur Barlow; Samson Bernard Lane; An Old Hebrew/2nd
Philistine Charles Magrath; Philistine Messenger
James Gawthrop; 1st Philistine H. Lewis Thomas. Dalila
Edith Miller. COND Frederick H. Cowen; Pd Farley Sin-
kins. *REV: Ath 30/9/93 p460-1; E 30/9/93 p15; St 28/*
9/93 p12-3; Ti 27/9/93 p9.

93.259 *A MODERN DON QUIXOTE* (MF,2a) George Dance (lib)
& John Crook (mus). STRAND 25/9/93-14/10/93. 22 perf
[w/S mat; add mat 11/10]. 1st perfd Theatre Royal,
Nottingham 17/7/93. Don Quixote Arthur Roberts; San-
cho Panza E.W. Colman; Gen. Jenkinson Arthur Playfair;
Algernon Jenkinson Harry Phydora; Farmer Giles H.
Williamson; Jones Russell Wallett; Bishop of Gretna

Green Arthur Jackson. Maud Yata Whynier; Mabel Mabel
Love; Lilian Kitty Burns; Louie Louise Norman; Phoebe
Lizzie Aubrey; Hon Cecil Blake Doris Montford; Algernon Maud Santley; Margery Florence Hanley; Nellie
Evelyn Fitzgerald; Claude Gwendoline North; Mrs Crum-
pet Ada Doree. L Willie Edouin; Bm J.T. Mackay Robertson; Prop J.S. Clarke; Cost Alias; Pq William Clarkson; Sm Horace Lennard; Mus dir Sydney Ward. *REV: E*
30/9/93 p8; Sk 4/10/93 p486, 496; St 28/9/93 p13; Ti
26/9/93 p3; TW93 p233.

93.260 *THE MERRY BLACKSMITH* (Oa) E.C. Dunbar [adpt of
Longfellow's "The Village Blacksmith"]. VAUDEVILLE
25/9/93-21/10/93. 24 perf.* Jack Hardcastle E.C. Dun-
bar. Daisy Hardcastle Marie Thorne. L & MGR A. & S.
Gatti; Bm & Treas G.M. Polini; Sm William Sidney,
Thomas Sidney; Mus dir William Robins; Bom Sharpe.
REV: E 30/9/93 p8; St 28/9/93 p13.

93.261 *SOWING THE WIND* (C,4a) Sydney Grundy. COMEDY
30/9/93-31/1/93. 120 perf [w/S mat exc 30/9, 7/10;
mat only 23/12; np 25/12].* Mr Brabazan Brandon
Thomas; Mr Watkin Cyril Maude; Ned Annesley Sydney
Brough; Sir Richard Cursitor Edmund Maurice; Lord
Petworth Ian Robertson; Mr Deakin Will Dennis; Glos-
sop Chandler; Webb John Byron. Hon Mrs Fretwell
Rose Leclercq; Maud Fretwell Annie Hughes/Ettie Will-
iams; Bridget Mrs Campbell Bradley; Rosamund Winifred
Emery. L & MGR J.W. Comyns Carr; Sc William Telbin,
Walter Johnstone, Walter Hann; Bom Scarisbrick; Cost
dgn Karl; Cost L. & H. Nathan, Mrs Nettleship, Mrs
Alister; Pq William Clarkson; Furn Hampton; Sm Edward
Hastings; Mus dir Alfred J. Caldicott; Bm Silvanus
Dauncey. *REV: Ath 7/10/93 p498; E 7/10/93 p8, 21/10/*
93 p11; Sk 4/10/93 p486, 25/10/93 p661; SR 7/10/93
p412-3; St 5/10/93 p12; Th 1/11/93 p285-7; Ti 2/10/93
p11; TW93 p230-3.

93.262 *A MELODRAMA* (Skit). DRURY LANE 30/9/93, 12/10/
93. 2 mat perf. [Hero] George Grossmith, jr; [Vill-
ain] Robb Harwood; [Detective] Herbert Sparling;
[Faithful Servant] D[ouglas] Munro; A[lfred C.] Seymour. [Heroine] Letty Lind. *REV: St 19/10/93 p12.*

93.263 *THE FORESTERS* (Poetic C,4a) Alfred, Lord
Tennyson & Arthur Sullivan (mus) & Henry Widmer (mus).
DALY'S 3/10/93-12/10/93 [w/S mat]; 14/10(m), 16/10,
18/10, 20-21/10/93. 15 perf.* Robin Hood Arthur
Bourchier; Richard Coeur de Lion George Clarke; Little
John Herbert Gresham; Young Scarlet Lloyd Daubigny;
Prince John John Craig; Sir Richard Lea Henry Loraine;
Abbot Lloyd Lowndes; Sheriff of Nottingham Charles
Leclercq; Justiciary William Gilbert; Mercenary Camp-
bell Gollan; Walter Lea Robb Harwood; Friar Tuck
William Owen; Will Scarlet Hobart Bosworth; Old Much
Sidney Herbert; Pursuivant Rankin Duval; Three Lank
Retainers Thomas, George Lesoir, Alfred Hickman;
Three Merry Beggars Thomas Bridgland, Edward P. Wilks,
George Lesoir; Three False Friars William Sampson,
George Wharnock, Frederic Powell; Retainers & Fores-
ters Martin, [Rupert?] Lister, Leonard, Laming, Dear,
[Alfred?] Wigley, Moreton, Lidbury, Steward, Cheese-
man. Maid Marian Ada Rehan; Kate Catherine Lewis;
Titania Percy Haswell; Old Woman of the Hut Florence
Seymour; 1st Fairy Mrs Gaston Murray; Attendants on
Marian Olive Barry, Florence Conron, Helena Nelson,
Lulu Bosworth; Attendants on Titania Maud Sherman,
Kate Graves, May Young, Ray Maskell, Sofia Hoffman,
Lena Lorraine, Caroline Dagmar, Eugenia Upham, Made-
line Lack, Horiman, Olive Barry, [Lily?] Twyman,
Collis, Anderson. MGR Augustin Daly; Sm George
Clarke; Assistant Edward P. Wilks; Prompter Henry
Montague; Mach H. Sheldon; Elect F. Hinton; Cond Hen-
ry Widmer; Bom John Farrington, Edward Brown; Pq
William Clarkson; Bm George F. Bashford; Cost Harris-
ons. *REV: Ath 7/10/93 p498; E 7/10/93 p11; Sk 11/10/*
93 p543-4; SR 7/10/93 p413; St 5/10/93 p12; Th 1/11/
93 p287-8; Ti 4/10/93 p7; TW93 p233-7.

93.264 *TWO JOHNNIES* (FC,3a) Fred Horner [adpt of Albert Valabrègue & Maurice Ordonneau, *Durand et Durand*].
TRAFALGAR SQUARE 5/10/93-12/10/93. 8 perf [w/mat
11/10]. 1st perfd Theatre Royal, Northampton 27/4/
88. John Maggs Charles Glenney; Josiah Bulman Lionel
Rignold; Alexander Pepperton Percy F. Marshall; Thomas Brooding Graham Wentworth; J. Wilkes Fred Jacques;
Gorme Stanley Smith; John Maggs Frank Wyatt. Clara
Maggs Maud Elmore; Madge Clara Jecks; Hon Mrs Stan-

ley-Roxburgh Gladys Homfrey; Florence Marie Lascelles;
Stella Dashington Violet Melnotte. PP & L Mr & Mrs
Frank Wyatt; Pd Frank Wyatt; Cond Edward Crosse; Bom
H.T. Holliman; Gen mgr Gilbert Tate; Act mgr & Treas
H[enry] Brandon; Asm A.H. Brooke. *REV: E 7/10/93 p9;*
SR 21/10/93 p467; St 12/10/93 p13; Ti 6/10/93 p5;
TW93 p237-8.

93.265 *AULD LANG SYNE* (P,1a) Basil Hood. TRAFALGAR
SQUARE 5/10/93-12/10/93. 7 perf.** Hon Jack Boothroyd Fred Jacques; George Fellows Graham Wentworth.
Marion Blyth Maud Elmore. PP & L, Bom, Gen mgr, Act
mgr & Treas, Asm as for 93.264. *REV: E 7/10/93 p9.*

93.266 *UTOPIA (LIMITED); OR, THE FLOWERS OF PROGRESS*
(CO,2a) W.S. Gilbert (lib) & Arthur Sullivan (mus).
SAVOY 7/10/93-9/6/94. 245 perf [w/S mat exc 7/10/93;
add mat 27/12/93; mat only 30/5/94, 6/6/94; np 25/12/
93, 23/3/94].* King Paramount the First Rutland
Barrington; Scaphio W.H. Denny/W.H. Leon; Phantis
John Le Hay; Tarara Walter Passmore/Clarence Hunt; Mr
Goldbury Robert Scott-Fishe; Cpt. Sir Edward Corcoran
Lawrence Gridley; Lord Dramaleigh Scott Russell; Cpt.
Fitzbattleaxe Charles Kenningham; Calynx J. Bowden
Haswell; Sir Bailey Barrie Enes Blackmore; Mr Blush-
ington Herbert Ralland. Princess Zara Nancy McIntosh;
Princess Kalyba Florence Perry; Princess Nekaya Emmie
Owen; Lady Sophy Rosina Brandram/Agnes Scott; Salata
Edith Johnston; Melene May Bell/Madeline Galton;
Phylla Florence Easton/Howell-Hersee. PP & MGR Richard
d'Oyly Carte; Dir Charles Harris, W.S. Gilbert; Mus
dir Francois Cellier; Cond Arthur Sullivan; Sm W.H.
Seymour; Ch John d'Auban; Cost dgn Percy Anderson;
Cost Miss Fisher, Auguste, Mme Leon; Uniforms Firmin
& Sons, B.J. Simmons, Angel & Sons; Dresses Russell &
Allen; Judges Robes Ede & Son; Jewellery Parisian
Diamond Co.; Pq William Clarkson; Props [H.] Skelly;
Mach Peter White; Act mgr J.W. Beckwith; Sc Hawes
Craven; Lime [W.] Kerr; Elect Lyons. *REV: Ath 14/10/*
93 p528-9; E 30/9/93 p10, 14/10/93 p11; Sk 11/10/93
p541-2, 3/1/94 p526; SR 14/10/93 p438; St 12/10/93
p12; Th 1/11/93 p294-5; Ti 9/10/93 p6.

93.267 *IN STRICT CONFIDENCE* (Ca,1a) Paul Heriot. COM-

EDY 9/10/93-31/1/94. 97 perf [np 23-25/12/93].* Mr
Bittersweet W.T. Lovell; Andrew Edgways J. Byron.
Amelia Bittersweet Lena Ashwell. L & MGR J.W. Comyns
Carr; Bom Scarisbrick; Pq William Clarkson; Bm Sil-
vanus Dauncey. *REV: E 14/10/93 p8; St 12/10/93 p13.*

93.268 *LITTLE CHRISTOPHER COLUMBUS* (Bsq,2a) George R.
Sims (lib) & Cecil Raleigh (lib) & Ivan Caryll (mus).
LYRIC 10/10/93-20/10/94. 356 perf [w/S mat 10/10/93-
26/5/94 exc 24/3/94; w/S mat 22/9/94-20/10/94; add
mat 26/12/93, 26/3/94, 22/8, 29/8, 5/9/94; np 18-25/
12/93; 23/3/94].* O'Hoolegan E.J. Lonnen; Cpt. Jos-
eph H. Slammer Harry Parker/W.S. Laidlaw; Silas Block
J. Furneaux Cook; Mayor of Cadiz Henry Wright/H. Greg-
ory/Roland Carse; Don Juan George Tate/Jack Thompson;
Hotel Proprietor Roland Carse/Charles Crook; Head
Turk W.M. Birch. Pedro Kate Dudley/Marie Winter;
Sebastian Vinnie Cassell; Lopez Blanche Winter; Vigi-
lant Cutter Maud Vernon/Dorothy Webb; Mercedes Rose
Hamilton/M. Northcote; Lola Cissie Cranford/Dorothy
Wood; Salambo Smith Dora Thorne; Mysotes Calhoun
Millie Marsden/A. Maxwell; Guinevere Block Maud Hol-
land/Geraldine Ulmar/Effie Clements/Maud Michael Wat-
son; Pepita Eva Moore/Mabel Love; 2nd Mrs Block Ade-
laide Newton/John F. Sheridan [sic]; Chloe Jones Mimi
St. Cyr/Dorothy Wood/Alice Lethbridge; Hannah Maud
Leicester/Millie Marsden/Elena Monmouth; Little
Christopher May Yohe/Maud Holland/Florence St. John/
Addie Conyers; Penelope Vinnie Cassell/Gracie White-
ford; Dancing Girls Alice Gilbert, May Gore, Edith
Gardiner, Eva Greville. L & MGR & DIR Horace Sedger;
Cond Ivan Caryll; Ch John d'Auban; Sc R.C. McCleery,
Bruce Smith; Cost Alias, Harrisons; Cost dgn Edel;
Mach S. Trewen; Pq William Clarkson; Bm & Treas Will-
iam Greet. *REV: E 14/10/93 p8, 4/8/94 p7, 10/11/94
p9; Sk 18/10/93 p596, 600, 3/1/94 p513, 14/2/94 p114-
6, 14/3/94 p351-2; SR 11/8/94 p156; St 12/10/93 p12-3,
4/1/94 p15, 9/8/94 p12; Ti 11/10/93 p4, 1/1/94 p8,
4/8/94 p4; TW94 p302.* Comment: See item 94.250 for
details of a "transfer" of this piece.

93.269 *THE AMERICAN BRIDE* (D,4a) "Lawrence Olde" [Sir
William Young] & Maurice Noel. TERRY'S 11/10/93-7/11/
93. 24 perf.** Lord Dorrington Herbert Waring; Mait-

land G. East Frederick Kerr; Jack Hilliard Murray Car-
son; George Carston George R. Foss; James McGuinis
James A. Welch; Duke of St. Heliers Richard Blunt;
Chandos Robson Lambert; Jared Stagg Hamilton Piffard;
Billy Cooper. Lady Hilda Olga Brandon; Duchess of St.
Heliers Henrietta Lindley; Violet Lanyon Day Forde;
Stella Durand Janette Steer. L Edward Terry; Mgr Jan-
ette Steer; Bm Charles Terry; Cond Rosabel Watson;
Pq Charles Fox; Sc E.G. Banks; Cost Russell & Allen;
Furn Bartholinew & Fletcher; Sm George R. Foss. *REV:*
E 14/10/93 p8; Sk 18/10/93 p600; St 19/10/93 p13; Ti
12/10/93 p8; TW93 p240-2.

93.270 *THE LAST WORD* (C,4a) Augustin Daly [adpt of
Franz von Schoenthan, *Das Letzte Wort*]. DALY'S
13/10/93, 14/10, 17/10, 19/10, 21/10(m), 23-24/10/93.
7 perf.** The Secretary George Clarke; Alexander
Aircy James Lewis; Harry Rutherell Herbert Gresham;
Prof Rutherell William Owen; Boris Bouraneff Sidney
Herbert; Moses Mossop William Gilbert; Baron Stugve
Robb Harwood; Jordan William Sampson; Robert Edward
P. Wilks. Baroness Vera Ada Rehan; Faith Rutherell
Laura Graves/Percy Haswell; Winifred Isabel Irving;
Paul Sofia Hoffman; Mlle Lida Adelaide Sterling;
Molly Florence Conron. MGR Augustin Daly; Sm George
Clarke; Assistant Edward P. Wilks; Prompter Henry
Montague; Mach H. Sheldon; Elect F. Hinton; Cond
Henry Widmer; Bom John Farrington, Edward Brown; Cost
Harrisons; Pq William Clarkson; Bm George F. Bashford.
REV: E 21/10/93 p10; SR 21/10/93 p467; St 19/10/93
p12; Ti 14/10/93 p7; TW93 p238-40.

93.271 *A GAIETY GIRL* (MC,2a) Owen Hall (lib) & Harry
Greenbank (lyr) & Sidney Jones (mus). PRINCE OF
WALES'S 14/10/93-8/9/94;* trfd to DALY'S 10/9/94-
15/12/94. 397 perf [w/S mat exc 14/10/93, 9/6/94; np
25/12/93, 23/3/94]. Charles Goldfield C. Hayden
Coffin/W. Louis Bradfield; Sir Alfred Grey Eric Lewis/
George Mudie; Bobbie Rivers W. Louis Bradfield/Leed-
ham Bantock/Reginald Somerville/W. Louis Bradfield/
R.C. Stuart/J. Farren Soutar; Mjr. Barclay Fred Kaye/
George Grossmith, jr; Harry Fitzwarren Leedham Ban-
tock/Reginald Somerville; Romney Farquhar Lawrance
d'Orsay; Lance Gilbert Porteous/Smith; Auguste Fitz

Rimma/Charles Eaton; <u>Rev Montague Brierly</u> Harry Monk-
house/Rutland Barrington/Gilbert Porteous. <u>Rose</u>
<u>Brierly</u> Decima Moore/Kate Cutler; <u>Mina</u> Juliette Nes-
ville/Grace Palotta/Nina Martino; <u>Lady Edytha Aldwyn</u>
Kate Cutler/Louie Pounds; <u>Gladys Stourton</u> Marie Stud-
holme/Sadie Clinton; <u>Hon Daisy Ormsbury</u> Louie Pounds/
Ethel Sydney; <u>Alma Somerset</u> Maud Hobson/Blanche Mas-
sey/Marie Studholme; <u>Cissy Verner</u> Blanche Massey/Eva
Stanford/Alice Davis; <u>Haidee Walton</u> Ross Selwick/
Millie Malone/Batchelor/Florence Lloyd/Ada Maitland/
Violet Dene; <u>Ethel Hawthorne</u> Violet Robinson/Alison
Skipworth; <u>Lady Virginia Forest</u> Lottie Venne/Aide
Jenoure/Phyllis Broughton; <u>Lady Grey</u> Mrs Edmund Phelps/
Kate Hodson. <u>PP</u> Edgar Bruce; <u>Pd</u> George Edwardes; <u>Sc</u>
Walter Hann, William Telbin; <u>Cost</u> Miss Fisher, Au-
guste, Harrisons, Alias, Debenham & Freebody, Moy-
kopf, Morris Angel; <u>Cost dgn</u> Edel; <u>Mus dir</u> Sidney
Jones; <u>Sm</u> J.A.E. Malone; <u>Act mgr</u> C.P. Levilly. *REV:*
E 21/10/93 p8, 17/2/94 p11, 15/9/94 p8; Sk 11/10/93
p579, 18/10/93 p596-7, 1/11/93 p9, 8/11/93 p59, 14/2/
94 p111, 12/9/94 p363-5, 3/10/94 p512, 10/10/94 p569;
SR 21/10/93 p467; St 15/2/94 p13, 13/9/94 p13; Ti
16/10/93 p14, 11/9/94 p4; TW93 p242-5; TW94 p59-61,
244-5.

93.272 *MIAMI* (Melo O,3a) J. Haydn Parry (mus) & E.
Warham St. Ledger (lyr) [adpt by John Hollingshead
of J.B. Buckstone, *The Green Bushes*]. PRINCESS'S
16/10/93-28/10/93. 12 perf.* <u>Connor Kennedy</u> Courtice
Pounds; <u>George</u> Richard Temple; <u>Murtogh</u> Charles Ash-
ford; <u>Dennis</u> W.S. Osborn; <u>Jack Gong</u> A.J. Evelyn;
<u>Grinnidge</u> George Barrett. <u>Miami</u> Violet Cameron;
<u>Geraldine</u> Isabella Girardot; <u>Tigertail</u> Clara Jecks;
<u>Meg</u> Mrs B.M. de Solla; <u>Eveleen</u> May Wallace/Gabrielle
Ray; <u>Nelly</u> Jessie Bond. <u>DIR</u> John Hollingshead; <u>Sc</u>
W.T. Hemsley; <u>Cost dgn</u> E. Comelli; <u>Cost</u> Alias; <u>Pq</u>
William Clarkson; <u>Liveries</u> Angel; <u>Ch</u> Paul Valentine;
<u>Mus dir</u> Sydney Ward; <u>Sm</u> [E.] Edmonds; <u>Chorus dir</u> Neill
O'Donovan; <u>Mgr</u> T. Harris; <u>Act mgr</u> W.H. Griffiths;
<u>Treas & Sec</u> Walter Gooch; <u>Bom</u> Winkley. *REV: E 14/10/*
93 p10, 21/10/93 p8; Ath 21/10/93 p592; Sk 25/10/93
p652; St 19/10/93 p12-3; Ti 17/10/93 p5.

93.273 *THE LADY KILLER* (FC,3a) Charles S. Fawcett

[adpt of Alexandre Bisson, *115 Rue Pigalle*]. STRAND
17/10/93-17/11/93. 36 perf [w/W, S mat exc 18/10]. 1st
perfd Prince of Wales's, Liverpool 25/9/93. Sidney
Chuckle Cairns James; Bernard Brown Charles S. Faw-
cett; Dr Perfect Herbert Ross; Robert Robjohn Harry
Paulton; John Chuckle Willie Edouin. Sophie Lillian
Crauford; Carrie Conyers Jenny Dawson; Mrs Plumper
Annie Goward; Mrs Robjohn Mrs G.B.W. Lewis; Ina Rob-
john Georgie Esmond; Florence Chuckle Mina Le Bert;
Daisy Amy Gordon; Sarah Venie Bennett; May Stella
Berridge. PP J.S. Clarke; L & Mgr Willie Edouin; Bm
J.T. Mackay Robertson; Sm Charles Davies; Cond Ernest
Bucalossi. *REV: E 21/10/93 p8; Sk 25/10/93 p652; SR
21/10/93 p467; St 19/10/93 p13; Ti 18/10/93 p6; TW93
p262-3.*

93.274 *BINKS, THE DOWNY PHOTOGRAPHER* (Musical Absurd-
ity,1a) Nat Childs & Willie Edouin. STRAND 17/10/93-
17/11/93. 28 perf. 1st perfd Avenue 16/7/83 [as *A
Dream; or, Binks' Photographic Gallery*]. Horatio
Binks Willie Edouin; Charlie Dodsworth Cairns James;
Bertie Fortescue Herbert Ross; Chip Harry Eversfield;
Dickie Chumley Gordon Harvey; Muggins James A. Meade.
Ruby Chillington Alice Atherton; Flossie Jenny Daw-
son; Vesta Daisy Baldry; Polly Amy Gordon. PP, L &
Mgr, Bm, Sm, Cond as for 93.273. *REV: E, Sk, St as
for 93.273.* Comment: *Mary, The Child of Misfortune*
(DSk,1a) was perfd as part of this item.

93.275 *SIXES* (Ca) Alfred Lindsay. PRINCE OF WALES'S
18/10/93-22/12/93. 57 perf.** Hon Gilbert Coldastone
Lawrance d'Orsay; Cpt. Percy Shafto Lawrence Cautley.
Helen Forrester Marie Studholme; Bridget Marie Dag-
mar. PP Edgar Bruce; Sm R[eginald] Stockton; Act mgr
C.P. Levilly; Rep M. Edwards.

93.276 *THE ORIENT EXPRESS* (C,3a) F.C. Burnand [adpt of
Oscar Blumenthal & Gustav Kadelburg, *Die Orient Reise*].
DALY'S 25/10/93-11/11/93. 19 perf [w/S mat].* Augus-
tus Jellaby James Lewis; Odeseus Dioskobobulus George
Clarke; Robert Fetherston W.G. Elliott; Ernest Tre-
vor E. Allan Aynesworth; Sir Jasper Nickel William
Owen; Richard Glibb Herbert Gresham; Edwards Thomas
Bridgland. Hettie Fetherston Ada Rehan; Mrs Jellaby

Mrs G.H. Gilbert; <u>Nina</u> Isabel Irving; <u>Katrina Djoreska</u>
Catherine Lewis; <u>Frances</u> Adelaide Sterling. <u>MGR</u> Augustin Daly; <u>Sc</u> Walter Johnstone; <u>Furn</u> Maple; <u>Sm</u> George
Clarke; <u>Assist</u> Edward P. Wilks; <u>Prompter</u> Henry Montague; <u>Mach</u> H. Sheldon; <u>Elect</u> F. Hinton; <u>Cond</u> Henry Widmer; <u>Bom</u> John Farrington, Edward Brown; <u>Cost</u> Harrisons; <u>Pq</u> William Clarkson; <u>Bm</u> George F. Bashford. *REV:*
Ath 28/10/93 p298; E 28/10/93 p9; Sk 1/11/93 p8; SR
28/10/93 p493-4; St 26/10/93 p12, 2/11/93 p13; Ti 26/
10/93 p6; TW93 p256-7.

93.277 *THE RING OF POLYCRATES* (Ca) Justin Huntly Mc-
Carthy. DALY'S 25/10/93-11/11/93. 19 perf [w/S mat].**
<u>Hamilton Carew</u> Arthur Bourchier; <u>Antony Foljambe</u> Syd-
ney Herbert; <u>Jefferson</u> Hobart Bosworth. <u>Kitty Carew</u>
Percy Haswell. <u>MGR</u>, <u>Sm</u>, <u>Assist</u>, <u>Prompter</u>, <u>Mach</u>, <u>Elect</u>,
<u>Cond</u>, <u>Bom</u>, <u>Cost</u>, <u>Pq</u>, <u>Bm</u> as for 93.276. *REV: E 28/10/*
93 p9; St 26/10/93 p12.

93.278 *THE MELANCHOLY TRAGEDY OF DIDO AND AENEAS* (Bsq,
3a). STRAND 26/10/93 mat perf.* <u>Aeneas</u> Julian Cross;
<u>Achates</u> Robson Lambert; <u>Euryalus</u> Horn Conyers; <u>Api-</u>
<u>mines</u> Clifford Manners; <u>Stage-manager/Jupiter</u> J.S.
Blythe; <u>Prompter</u> Sidney Burt; <u>Lion</u> Fred Grove. <u>Iulus</u>
Matty Ney; <u>Dido</u> Mrs Gordon Gray; <u>Anna</u> Kate Calton;
<u>Attante</u> Alice Adair; <u>Venus</u> Violet Russell; <u>Juno</u> Lu-
cille Heaton; <u>Cupid</u> Maude Bowden; <u>Cromanthe/Euclytea</u>
Henrietta Cross; <u>Belthea/Gladelic</u> Hilda Burleigh;
<u>Cisiphrone/Ponecia</u> Agatha Leigh. *REV: E 28/10/93 p9;*
St 2/11/93 p13.

93.279 *A HARD CASE* (FC,3a) W. Carleton Dawe. TERRY'S
26/10/93 mat perf.* <u>Charles Meakham</u> Laurence Cautley; <u>Sir Frederick Freestone</u> H. Nye Chart; <u>Trencher</u>
Fred Thorne; <u>Lord Dasham</u> Willie Drew; <u>Hicks</u> Albert
Bernard. <u>Mrs Trencher</u> Sophie Larkin; <u>Belle</u> Jennie
Rogers; <u>Kate</u> Eva Moore. *REV: E 28/10/93 p11; St 2/11/*
93 p13.

93.280 *A QUESTION OF MEMORY* (P,4a) Michael Field.
OPERA COMIQUE 27/10/93. 1 perf.* <u>Ferencz Reny</u> Acton
Bond; <u>Stanislaus</u> A. Hamilton Revelle; <u>Haynam</u> John
Beauchamp; <u>Mausfeldt</u> Neville Doone; <u>Meyerhof</u> Charles
Rutland. <u>Ferencz's Mother</u> Mrs Theodore Wright; <u>Fina</u>

Mary H. Keegan; <u>Thelka</u> Hall Caine; <u>Elizabeth</u> Mrs
Charles Creswick; <u>L</u> F. Fowler; <u>Dir</u> J.T. Grein; <u>Asm</u>
Burton Cooke; <u>Act mgr</u> & <u>Bm</u> Charles Hoppe; <u>Pd</u> Herman
de Lange; <u>Cond</u> Edward Crosse; <u>Pq</u> & <u>Cost</u> William Clarkson, Morris Angel & Son; <u>Furn</u> Oetzmann. *REV: Ath 4/11/*
93 p635; E 4/11/93 p9; Sk 1/11/93 p8; St 2/11/93 p12;
Th 1/12/93 p341-2; Ti 28/10/93 p6; TW93 p251-5.
<u>Comment</u>: Independent Theatre Society.

93.281 *LE PATER* (PoetP,1a) François Coppée. OPERA
COMIQUE 27/10/93. 1 perf. 1st perfd Theatre des Gal-
eries, Brussels 14/1/90. <u>Le Curé</u> Ivan Watson; <u>Offic-</u>
<u>ier</u> Paul Duval; <u>Jacques Leroux</u> Paul M. Berton; <u>Zelie</u>
Charlotte E. Morland; <u>Voisine</u> Mabel Forrester; <u>Mlle</u>
<u>Rose</u> Anna Zetterberg. <u>L</u>, <u>Dir</u>, <u>Act mgr</u> & <u>Bm</u>, <u>Cond</u>, <u>Pq</u>
& <u>Cost</u>, <u>Furn</u> as for 93.280; <u>Pd</u> Paul M. Berton. *REV:*
Ath, E, St, Sk, Ti as for 93.280; Th 1/12/93 p342;
TW93 p255-6.

93.282 *DON JUAN* (Bsq,3a) James T. Tanner (lib) & Adrian Ross (lyr) & W. Meyer Lutz (mus). GAIETY 28/10/
93-16/6/94. 222 perf [w/S mat exc 28/10/93, 23/12/93,
3/2/94, 10/2, 17/2, 24/2, 3/3, 24/3, 7/4, 12/5, 26/5,
2/6, 9/6, 16/6/94; add mat 14/2/94, 21/2, 28/2, 23/4,
13/6/94; np 25/12/93, 23/3/94].* The Pasha Colin
Coop/Fred Vaughan; <u>Lambro</u> George Mudie/Robert Pateman;
<u>Pasha's Lieutenant</u> Edmund Payne/George Carroll; <u>Cecco</u>
Willie Warde; <u>Pedrillo</u> Arthur Roberts; <u>Sultan of Tur-</u>
<u>key</u> E.W. Royce; <u>Rodrigo</u> George Carroll. <u>Fernando</u> Con-
stance Collier/Maud Sutherland; <u>Gustavo</u> Kate Cannon;
<u>Frederico</u> Carrie Benton; <u>Don Juan</u> Millie Hylton/Louise
Montague; <u>Haidee</u> Cissy Loftus/Lettice Fairfax/Lilian
Stanley; <u>Isabella</u> Louise Montague/Ethel Earle; <u>Donna</u>
<u>Inez</u> Maria Davis/Lillie Belmore; <u>Cybele</u> Topsy Sinden;
<u>Zoe</u> Katie Seymour/Lettice Fairfax/ E[va?] Ellerslie/
Claire Solomon; <u>Donna Julia</u> Sylvia Grey/Katie Seymour;
<u>Manuel</u> Ethel Earle/Constance Collier/Violet Durkin;
<u>Mercedes</u> Patty Stanley; <u>Carlos</u> Lily Harold/Violet Dur-
kin/Lillian Price; <u>Leon</u> Violet Evelyn; <u>Enrique</u> Aimee
Mills/Violet Monckton; <u>Rodriguez</u> Florence Henderson;
Alphonso Hetty Hamer/Annie Vivian; <u>Angelo</u> Ethel Earle
<u>Mercedes</u> Pattie Stanley. <u>L</u> & <u>MGR</u> George Edwardes; <u>Sc</u>
E.G. Banks, William Telbin; <u>Cond</u> W. Meyer Lutz; <u>Cost</u>
Miss Fisher, Auguste, Harrisons; <u>Pq</u> C.H. Fox; <u>Ch</u>

Willie Warde, Mariette d'Auban; Dir J.T. Tanner; Act mgr E[dward] Marshall; Bom A.P. Oxley. *REV: E 4/11/93 p9, 27/1/93 p9, 14/4/94 p9 Sk 1/11/93 p8, 15/11/93 p123, 18/4/94 p618; St 2/11/93 p12, 19/4/94 p13; Ti 30/10/93 p10; TW93 p257-9; TW94 p108.* Comment: A "second edition" of this piece was introduced 12/4/94.

93.283 *FROG* (CD,3a) "Alec Nelson" [E.B. Aveling]. ROYALTY 30/10/93-1/11/93. 3 perf.* Fred Rogg Edmund Gurney; Paul Deville Alfred Bucklaw; Mr Graham Fred Grove; Arthur Rogg Douglas Gordon. Mrs Rogg Mrs Theodore Wright; Mary E. Brinsley Sheridan; Susan Nancy Noel; Alice Annie Rose [Mrs Horace Neville]. PD E.B. Aveling, Edmund Gurney. *REV: E 4/11/93 p9; Sk 8/11/93 p62; St 2/11/93 p12-3; Ti 31/10/93 p10; TW93 p261-2.*

93.284 *A HUNDRED YEARS AGO* (PastOa,1a) "Alec Nelson" [E.B. Aveling] (lib) & Henry J. Wood (mus). ROYALTY 1/11/93. 1 perf.** Sol Ball Collwyn Thomas; Tom Ball Gilbert Davies; Joe Shortlands Frank Fisher. Liz Hendley Winifred Ludlam; Alice Hendley Mabel Archdall. *REV: E 4/11/93 p9.*

93.285 *TOM, DICK AND HARRY* (FC,3a) Mrs R. Pacheco. TRAFALGAR SQUARE 2/11/93-6/1/94 [w/mat 16/12/93, 30/12/93; np 22-25/12/93]; trfd to STRAND 8/1/94-20/2/94 [w/W, S mat]. 105 perf. 1st perfd Theatre Royal, Manchester 24/8/93. Tom Stanhope Charles H. Hawtrey/Frank Curzon; Ned Moreland W.R. Shirley; Dick Winters Ernest Percy; Mathew Charles Milton; Oliver C[harles] Meyrick; Harry Winters Arthur Playfair; Gen. Rufus Stanhope John Beauchamp; Dr Wagner W.F. Hawtrey. Daisy Armitage Vane Featherston; Molly Somers Georgie Esmond/Kate Ruskin; Isabel Howard Eva Williams/Carrie Cronyn; Mrs Winters Sophie Larkin/Carlotta Zerbini. PP Mr & Mrs Frank Wyatt; Mgr Charles H. Hawtrey; Bm E.F. Bradley, H[enry] Brandon; Sc Leolyn Hart; Cost Mme Vanité; Cond Ernest Bucalossi; Asm Charles Milton. *REV: Ath 18/11/93 p705; E 4/11/93 p11; Sk 8/11/93 p63; SR 11/11/93 p543; St 9/11/93 p12; Ti 3/11/93 p10; TW93 p263.*

93.286 *BARBARA* (Ca,1a) Jerome K. Jerome. TRAFALGAR SQUARE 2/11/93-12/12/93. 35 perf.** Cecil Norton

W.R. Shirley; <u>Finnicane</u> Ernest Percy/Ernest Cosham.
<u>Lillie Lealand</u> Violet Lyster; <u>Barbara</u> Eva Williams.
<u>PP</u>, <u>Mgr</u>, <u>Bm</u>, <u>Sc</u>, <u>Cost</u>, <u>Cond</u>, <u>Asm</u> as for 93.285.
REV: E, St as for 93.285.

93.287 *THE SENTRY* (MF,1a) Ivan Caryll (mus) & Felix
Remo (lib) & T. Malcolm Watson (lib). LYRIC 4/11/93-
28/11/93. 21 perf.** <u>Col. Pettigrew</u> Henry Wright;
<u>Tim O'Brien</u> Harry Parker. <u>Peggy</u> Maud Holland; <u>Polly
Burchett</u> Dora Thorne; <u>Mrs Pettigrew</u> Adelaide Newton.
L & MGR Horace Sedger; <u>Cond</u> Ivan Caryll; <u>Bm & Treas</u>
William Greet.

93.288 *MIRZA* (D,4a) W. Bryant. OPERA COMIQUE 4/11/93-
9/11/93. 5 perf.* <u>Pierre Montal</u> Ivan Watson; <u>Cons</u>-
<u>tantine Ritz</u> Philip Cunningham; <u>Serge Voinoff</u> Charles
Rutland; <u>M Ritz</u> F. Llewelleyn; <u>Footman</u> Burton Cooke.
<u>Countess Dobronovoska</u> Maria Saker; <u>Mme de Montal</u> Hen-
rietta Cowen; <u>Mme Lesperon</u> Carlotta Zerbini; <u>Lezitre</u>
Rose Dupré; <u>Mirza</u> Nadage Doree. *REV: E 11/11/93 p9;
Sk 15/11/93 p119; St 9/11/93 p12; Ti 6/11/93 p12.*

93.289 *A SCREW LOOSE* (F,3a) Mark Melford. VAUDEVILLE
4/11/93-2/12/93. 26 perf [w/mat 25/11].* <u>Henry Strum</u>-
<u>mit</u> Frank Wyatt; <u>Sir Willifer Alladay</u> W.L. Abingdon;
<u>Mjr. Abbott</u> Arthur Elwood; <u>Dr Pounds</u> Fred Thorne;
<u>Constable Hodger</u> William Hargreaves; <u>Dr Pottle</u> Albert
Bernard; <u>Mr Peckham</u> Charles Hudson; <u>Gardener</u> Alfred
Phillips; <u>Butler</u> Harry Fenton. <u>Lady Alladay</u> Gertrude
Kingston; <u>Arabella Bestt</u> Alice de Winton; <u>Mrs Leary</u>
Kate Kearney; <u>Ellen</u> Delia Carlyle; <u>Mrs Henry Strummit</u>
Carrie Powell. L & MGR A. & S. Gatti; <u>Bm & Treas</u> G.M.
Polini; <u>Sm</u> William Sidney; <u>Mus dir</u> Arthur E. Godfrey;
<u>Sc</u> Bruce Smith; <u>Pq</u> William Clarkson; <u>Furn</u> J.S. Lyons;
<u>Bom</u> Sharpe. *REV: Ath 18/11/93 p705-6; E 11/11/93 p9;
Sk 15/11/93 p119; St 9/11/93 p12-3; Ti 6/11/93 p12;
TW93 p265.*

93.290 *THE BEST MAN WINS* (Fantastic Sk,1a) Mark Melford. VAUDEVILLE 4/11/93-2/12/93. 25 perf.** <u>Farmer
Kairns</u> William Hargreaves; <u>Perks</u> Alfred Phillips;
<u>Jopper</u> Fred Thorne; <u>Parson Yeulett</u> Rudge Harding.
<u>Charlotte Kairns</u> Ethel Waring. L & MGR, Bm & Treas,
<u>Sm</u>, <u>Mus dir</u>, <u>Bom</u> as for 93.289. *REV: E 11/11/93 p9;*

St 9/11/93 p13.

93.291 *MADAME FAVART* (CO,3a) Jacques Offenbach. CRI-
TERION 9/11/93-9/12/93. 32 perf [w/S mat]. 1st perfd
Folies-dramatiques, Paris 28/1/78. Marquis de Pont-
Sable David S. James; Sgt. Sam Hemsley; Hector de
Boispreau Charles Conyers; Biscotin Fred Emney; Mjr.
Cotignac H. Lewens; Charles Favart Wallace Brownlow.
Mme Favart Florence St. John; Suzanne Ellis Jeffreys;
La Cantiniere Maggie Gorst; Joli Coeur Eva Westlake;
Sans Quartier Madge Arrowsmith; De Meyrac Rita Yorke;
Larissolle Olga Durham; Babel Edith Fielding; Nicolas
M[aude] Hoppe. L & MGR Charles Wyndham; Sm S.H.S.Aus-
tin; Act mgr & Treas E. Harvey; Mus dir John Crook;
Cost Harrisons, Miss Fisher; Ch R.M. Crompton; Sc
W.T. Hemsley, Harry Potts, E.G. Banks. *REV: E 11/11/
93 p15; Sk 15/11/93 p119; SR 18/11/93 p569; St 16/11/
93 p12; Ti 11/11/93 p4.*

93.292 *MEASURE FOR MEASURE* (C) William Shakespeare.
ROYALTY 9/11/93, 10/11, 11/11(2), 18/11/93(2). 6 perf.
1st perfd 26/12/1604. DIR William Poel; Pq William
Clarkson; Props James Lyon; Cost dgn Jennie Moore;
Cost Victor Barthe, William Clarkson, Mays, Nathan;
L Kate Santley; Dgn R. Minton Taylor; Mus William S.
Vinning; Sc John Bull & Son; Building Construction
Macey & Sons; Lighting Sugg & Co.; Hon Treas C.E.J.
Jennings. *REV: SR 18/11/93 p568; St 16/11/93 p13;
TW93 p266-70.* Comment: A sixteenth century "recons-
truction" by the Shakespeare Reading Society.

93.293 *GUDGEONS* (C,3a) "Thornton Clark" [Murray Car-
son] & Louis N. Parker. TERRY'S 10/11/93-5/1/94. 62
perf [w/W, S mat exc 11/11, 15/11, 22/11; add mat
26/12; np 25/12].* Silas B. Hooper Murray Carson;
Howard K. Harrison Charles J. Fulton; Reginald Ffoll-
iott W.T. Lovell; Gover Richard Blunt; Arthur Smith
James A. Welch; James Ffolliott Treherne Herbert War-
ing. Bundy Charlotte E. Morland; Persis Harrison
Sybil Carlisle; Mrs Ffolliott Treherne Janette Steer/
Mrs Murray Carson. L & MGR Janette Steer; Pp Edward
Terry; Sc Richard C. Durant; Furn Lyons; Pq William
Clarkson; Mus dir Wurm; Asm R.E. Warton; Bm Gilbert
Tate; Pd Murray Carson. *REV: Ath 18/11/93 p705; E 18/*

11/93 p9, 23/12/93 p10; Sk 15/11/93 p119; SR 18/11/93
p569; St 16/11/93 p12-3; Th 1/12/93 p342-3; Ti 13/11/
93 p11; TW93 p270-3, 288.

93.294 *LEAP YEAR* (Ca) Frederick Kerr. TERRY'S 10/11/
93-5/1/94. 47 perf [np 25/12]. 1st perfd Ladbroke Hall
8/92. Tom Harcourt Beatty. Nellie Sybil Carlisle. L
& MGR, Pp, Bm, Mus dir, Asm as for 93.293. *REV: 18/11/*
93 p9; St 16/11/93 p13.

93.295 *MRS OTHELLO* (FC,3a) Fred Leslie & Arthur Shir-
ley [adpt of Maxime Boucheron & Ernest Morel, *Madame*
Othello]. TOOLE'S 11/11/93-23/12/93;*   trfd to
VAUDEVILLE 26/12/93-12/1/94. 66 perf [w/W, S mat exc
11/11/93, 15/11, 18/11/93; mat only 18-23/12/93; np
25/12/93]. Robert Blackmore Charles Glenney; Titan
Hercules Julian Cross/E.R. Rae; Ozmond Tiffler William
H. Day/J.G. Graham; Mr Hempe George Raiemond; Herbert
Gyle Percy F. Marshall; Adolphus Cecil Crofton; Tom-
asso Sidney Burt. Violet Blackmore Fanny Brough; Eliza
Cicely Richards; Alice Hempe Blanche Horlock/Henrietta
Cross; Carrie Gyle Mary Kingsley/Alice de Winton; Isa-
belle Hempe Gladys Ffolliott; Iris Hercules Maud
Abbott; Lucy Cottonham Alice Ravenscroft/Mabel Hardy;
Beaty Bauman Digby/Denis; Kathleen Henrietta Cross.
L & MGR J.L. Toole; Act mgr B. Holmes; Sm Julian Cross;
Mus dir Sydney Ward; Furn Oetzmann; Pq C.H. Fox; Cost
Morris Angel. *REV: Ath 18/11/93 p705; E 18/11/93 p9;*
Sk 22/11/93 p167, 170-1, 29/11/93 p221; St 16/11/93
p13; Ti 13/11/93 p11; TW93 p273-4.

93.296 *THE BROTHERS* (P,1a) Henry Byatt. TOOLE'S 11/11/
93-23/12/93; trfd to VAUDEVILLE 26/12/93-12/1/94. 53
perf [mat only 18-23/12; np 25/12].** Richard Johnston A. Kingsley; William Johnston Julian Cross;
Simpson William Lugg/E.R. Rae. Kitty Florence Mel-
ville/Henrietta Cross. L & MGR, Act mgr, Sm, Mus dir,
Furn, Pq, Cost as for 93.295; Mus Ernest Lake. *REV: E*
18/11/93 p9.

93.297 *THE SCHOOL FOR SCANDAL* (C) R.B. Sheridan [arr
Augustin Daly]. DALY'S 13/11/93-30/12/93. 49 perf
[w/S mat exc 23/12; add mat 20/12, 27/12; np 25/12].**
Sir Peter Teazle William Farren; Joseph Surface George

Clarke; <u>Charles Surface</u> Arthur Bourchier; <u>Sir Benjamin</u>
<u>Backbite</u> Sidney Herbert; <u>Sir Oliver Surface</u> William
Owen; <u>Sir Harry Bumper</u> Lloyd Daubigny/Alfred Hickman;
<u>Moses</u> James Lewis/William Sampson; <u>Crabtree</u> Charles
Leclercq; <u>Careless</u> Herbert Gresham; <u>Rowley</u> Thomas
Bridgland; <u>Snake</u> John Craig; <u>Trip</u> George Lesoir; <u>Ser-</u>
<u>vants</u> George Wharnock, Frederic Powell, William Samp-
son, Robb Harwood, Lloyd Lowndes. <u>Lady Teazle</u> Ada Re-
han; <u>Lady Sneerwell</u> Violet Vanbrugh; <u>Maria</u> Percy Has-
well; <u>Mrs Candour</u> Mrs G.H. Gilbert. <u>MGR</u> Augustin Daly;
<u>Sm</u> George Clarke; <u>Assist</u> Edward P. Wilks; <u>Prompter</u>
Henry Montague; <u>Mach</u> H. Sheldon; <u>Elect</u> F. Hinton; <u>Cond</u>
Henry Widmer; <u>Bom</u> John Farrington, Edward Brown; <u>Cost</u>
Harrisons; <u>Pq</u> William Clarkson; <u>Bm</u> George F. Bashford.
REV: Ath 18/11/93 p705; E 18/11/93 p9; Sk 15/11/93
p115, 22/11/93 p167; SR 18/11/93 p12; St 16/11/93 p12;
Th 1/12/93 p343-4; Ti 14/11/93 p10; TW93 p274-7.
Comment: The 1st perf of this particular arrangement.

93.298 *A VAIN SACRIFICE* (CD,3a) Walter F. Grogan.
STRAND 14/11/93 mat perf.* <u>Mark Conway</u> Norman V. Nor-
man; <u>Claude Wylmer</u> C. Leveson Lane; <u>Maurice Maclure</u>
H. Nye Chart; <u>Mr Temple</u> P. Darwin; <u>Mr Sanger</u> H. Tripp
Edgar; <u>Rivers</u> O. Greenwood; <u>Mr Campbell</u> George Norman;
<u>Mr Vane</u> W. Ashdown. <u>Gwendoline Temple</u> Hall Caine;
<u>Edith Wylmer</u> Violet Raye; <u>Servant</u> Alice Haydon; <u>Madge</u>
<u>Courtney</u> G[eraldine?] Olliffe; <u>Mrs Wylmer</u> Adelaide
Grace. <u>DIR</u> Norman V. Norman. *REV: E 18/11/93 p11; Sk*
22/11/93 p167; St 16/11/93 p12.

93.299 *CAPTAIN SWIFT* (P,4a) C. Haddon Chambers. HAY-
MARKET 15/11/93(m); 2/12/93-17/1/94. 44 perf [w/S mat
exc 2/12; mat only 23/12; np 11/12, 25/12].** <u>William</u>
<u>Wilding</u> H.B. Tree; <u>Harry Seabrook</u> Fuller Mellish/C.M.
Hallard; <u>Mr Gardiner</u> F.H. Macklin; <u>Mr Seabrook</u> Charles
Allan/Henry Kemble; <u>Marshall</u> Holman Hunt/E. Holman
Clark; <u>Michael Ryan</u> Mark Paton/Charles Allan; <u>Bates</u>
[J.] Montagu; <u>Servant</u> Ashby. <u>Mrs Seabrook</u> Lady Monck-
ton/Carlotta Addison; <u>Lady Staunton</u> Rose Leclercq/
Fanny Coleman; <u>Stella</u> Mrs H.B. Tree; <u>Mabel Seabrook</u>
Irene Vanbrugh. <u>L & MGR</u> H.B. Tree; <u>Bm & Sec</u> Frederick
Harrison; <u>Elect</u> E. Wingfield Bowles; <u>Bom</u> W.H. Leverton;
<u>Sm</u> Shelton; <u>Mus dir</u> Carl Armbruster. *REV: E 9/12/93*
p9; St 16/11/93 p12, 7/12/93 p13; Th 1/1/94 p49-51;

Ti 4/12/93 p7; TW93 p280-1.

93.300 'TWIXT CUP AND LIP (CD,1a) Walter Sapte, jr.
STRAND 18/11/93-25/11/93. 7 perf. 1st perfd Lyric,
Ealing 18/4/89. Sir Harry Roughton Charles Burleigh;
Mr Mallandale Howard Finney; Cuthbert Goode Ernest
Bertram; Mr Wilson Henry Hudson. Edith Mallandale
May Palfrey; Parker Eva Forrest. *REV: 25/11/93 p9; St
23/11/93 p12.*

93.301 THE VAGABOND; OR, A BAD PENNY (DD,1a) W[illiam]
Lestocq. CRITERION 21/11/93 mat perf. 1st perfd Vaudeville 13/7/82 [as A Bad Penny]. Richard Hyde W[ill-
iam] Lestocq; Harry Goodwin Fred Terry; Charles Hyde
William H. Day. May Hyde Ellaline Terry; Mary Marie
Dagmar. SM S.H.S. Austin, William H. Day. *REV: E 25/
11/93 p8; St 23/11/93 p12.*

93.302 MARY, THE CHILD OF MISFORTUNE (Bsq). CRITERION
21/11/93 mat perf.** Ralph Haverson Willie Edouin;
Prompter Harry Eversfield; Jack Shiver-my-Timbers
Herbert Ross. Mary Alice Atherton. *REV: As for 93.301.*
Comment: See 93.274.

93.303 GOODBYE (P,1a) Seymour Hicks. COURT 25/11/93-
16/1/94. 47 perf [w/S mat exc 25/11/93, 13/1/94; np
22-25/12/93].* Edward Winter William Herbert; 2nd
Lieut. Percy Winter Seymour Hicks; Alec Strangeways
Wilfred Draycott; Smith Robert Nainby; Roberts E.H.
Kelly. Mary Winter Ellaline Terriss/Marie Linden. L
& MGR Arthur Chudleigh; Bm Leonard Lillies; Mus dir
Edward Jones; Cost L. & H. Nathan; Furn Marler &
Bennet; Pq C.H. Fox; Sc T.W. Hall. *REV: Ath 2/12/93
p778-9; E 2/12/93 p9; Sk 6/12/93 p290; St 30/11/93
p13; Th 1/1/94 p46-8; Ti 27/11/93 p7; TW93 p278-80.*

93.304 A VENETIAN SINGER (CO,1a) B.C. Stephenson (lib)
& Edward Jakobowski (mus). COURT 25/11/93-8/12/93.
13 perf [w/mat 2/12].* Matteo Herbert Thorndike;
Gregorio Jack Robertson. Bianca Agnes Giglio; Paolina
Waldeck-Hall. L & MGR, Bm, Mus dir, Cost, Furn, Pq,
Sc as for 93.303; Ch Marriette d'Auban. *REV: As for
93.303 exc Ath.*

93.305 *UNDER THE CLOCK* (Ext,1a) Charles H.E. Brookfield & Seymour Hicks & Edward Jones (mus). COURT
25/11/93–16/1/93 [w/S mat exc 25/11/93, 13/1/94; np
22-25/12/93]; 27/1/94-3/3/94. 78 perf.* Sherlock
Holmes Charles H.E. Brookfield; Dr Watson Seymour
Hicks; Emile Nana Robert Nainby; Master of Ceremonies
William Wyes; Plaque of Goethe Harry Paulo; 1st Forester Hugh Gwynne; 2nd Forester Charles Simson. Statue
of Niobe Maude Wilmot; 3rd Mrs Tanqueray E. Lyall;
Hannah Lottie Venne. L & MGR, Bm, Mus dir, Cost, Furn,
Pq, Sc as for 93.303. *REV: Ath 2/12/93 p778-9; E 2/12/
93 p9; Sk 6/12/93 p290; SR 2/12/93 p626, 9/12/93 p651;
St 30/11/93 p13, 1/2/94 p13; Th 1/1/94 p46-8; Ti 30/
11/93 p7; TW93 p277-8.*

93.306 *THE BOHEMIAN GIRL* (O[3a]) Michael Balfe. DRURY
LANE 27/11/93 mat perf.** Thaddeus Ben Davies; Count
Arnheim D. Ffrangcon Davies; Florestan Wilfred Esmond;
Devilshoof Charles Manners. Queen of the Gipsies Rose
Olitzka; Buda Kate Vito; Arline Fanny Moody. L & MGR
Augustus Harris; Cond Wilhelm Feld. *REV: E 2/12/93
p8; Sk 29/11/93 p270; St 30/11/93 p13; Ti 28/11/93
p11.*

93.307 *ON TOUR.* Fred Horner. STRAND 27/11/93. 1 perf.
Comment: Advertized in *Ti* for this date. Possibly a
mis-print for *On Toast*, since the only other *On Tour*
was not perfd until 23/2/95 at Town Hall, Kilburn
(Nicoll).

93.308 *WEATHERWISE* (Unreality,1a) H. Chance Newton
(lib) & Ernest Ford (mus). LYRIC 29/11/93-4/7/94. 179
perf [np 18-25/12/93, 23/3/94].* Herodotus Dodderton
W.S. Laidlaw/Harry Parker/W. Bentley; Tom Yowick
George Tate; Harry Grayling Vernon Drew/Wilbur Gunn.
Pansy Maud Holland/Dora Thorne; Daisy Meadows Millie
Marsden. L & MGR Horace Sedger; Bm & Treas William
Greet. *REV: E 30/12/93 p7; St 4/1/94 p15.*

93.309 *A MELODRAMA* (Skit). SHAFTESBURY 30/11/93 mat
perf.** [Villain] Robb Harwood; Alfred C. Seymour;
[Faithful Servant] Douglas Munro; [Hero] George Grossmith, jr; [Detective] Herbert Sparling. [Heroine]
Letty Lind. *REV: St 7/12/93 p13.*

93.310 *ON THE BRAIN* Harry Pleon. SHAFTESBURY 30/11/
93 mat perf. 1st perfd Theatre Royal, Great Grimsby
23/7/88. Fred Wright, jr; Harry Pleon. *REV: St 7/12/*
93 p13.

93.311 *OLD CRONIES* (Ca,1a) S. Theyre Smith. DRURY
LANE 4/12/93 mat perf. 1st perfd St. James's 6/3/80.
Cpt. Pigeon Charles Groves; Dr Jacks George Raiemond.
L & MGR Augustus Harris; Sm Arthur P. Collins, Napier
Barry. *REV: E 9/12/93 p8; St 7/12/93 p13.*

93.312 *THE CONVICT'S ESCAPE* (DE,3sc) Arthur P. Collins
(lib) & James M. Glover (mus). DRURY LANE 4/12/93
mat perf. 1st perf? Frank H. Fenton. Alice Dukes.
L & MGR Augustus Harris. *REV: As for 93.311.*

93.313 *GENOVEVA* (O,4a) Robert Schumann (mus) & L.
Vance (lib[ver of lib of O.R. Reinick]). DRURY LANE
6/12/93 mat perf. 1st perfd Municipal Theatre, Leip-
zig 25/6/50. Hidulphus Robert E. Davies; Siegfried
Albert H. Archdeacon; Golo William Green; Drago
William Maynard; Balthasar Henry Bourchier; Caspar
George E. Rayment. Genoveva Una H. Bruckshaw; Mar-
garet Louise Kirkby Lunn. L & MGR Augustus Harris;
Cond C. Villiers Stanford; Dir Richard Temple. *REV:*
E 9/12/93 p8; SR 9/12/93 p648-9; Ti 7/12/93 p9.

93.314 *AN EASTER EGG* (Oa) "Willert Beale" [Walter
Maynard] (lib) & F. Sydney Ward (mus). TERRY'S 7/12/
93 mat perf.* Squire Hawthorn Robert F. Cunningham;
Jack Springfield David Oughton; Joe Douglas Munroe.
May Agnes Molteno; Dame Partlett Mrs B.M. de Solla;
Polly Nellie Murray. MGR & PD David Oughton; Mus dir
F. Sydney Ward, Augustus Bingham; Act mgr Gilbert
Tate; Sm R.E. Warton; Bm [Augustus] Bingham, Dawson,
A.H. Morice; Pq C.H. Fox, William Clarkson, Holtz;
Cost Angel. *REV: St 14/12/93 p13.*

93.315 *THE BLACK CAT* (P,3a) John Todhunter. OPERA
COMIQUE 8/12/93. 1 perf.* Arthur Denham Alfred Buck-
law; Cyril Vane Orlando Barnett; Fitzgerald Neville
Doone. Constance Denham Hall Caine; Blanche Tremaine
Mary H. Keegan; Miss Macfarlane Gladys Homfrey; Un-
dine Dora Barton; Jane Mabel Forrester. DIR J.T.

Grein; <u>L</u> F. Fowler; <u>Asm</u> Burton Cooke; <u>Act mgr</u> & <u>Bm</u>
Charles Hoppe; <u>Pd</u> Herman de Lange; <u>Furn</u> Oetzmann.
REV: Ath 16/12/93 p857-8; E 16/12/93 p11; St 14/12/93
p12-3; Th 1/1/94 p51-3; Ti 11/12/93 p12; TW93 p281-8.
<u>Comment</u>: Independent Theatre Society.

93.316 *THE DEBUTANTE* (Intermezzo) James D. Vyner.
OPERA COMIQUE 8/12/93. 1 perf.* W.L. Abingdon. Rose
Nesbitt. <u>DIR</u>, <u>L</u>, <u>Asm</u>, <u>Act mgr</u> & <u>Bm</u>, <u>Pd</u>, <u>Furn</u> as for
93.315. *REV: E 16/12/93 p11; St 14/12/93 p13.*
<u>Comment</u>: Independent Theatre Society.

93.317 *FAITHFUL JAMES* (F,1a) B.C. Stephenson. COURT
9/12/93-16/1/94. 35 perf [w/S mat exc 13/1/94; np 22-
25/12/93].** <u>Admiral Vincent</u> William Wyes; <u>James</u>
Robert Nainby; <u>Waiter</u> Sydney Warden; <u>Henry Duncan</u>
Wilfred Draycott; <u>Philip Melville</u> E.H. Kelly. <u>Mrs Dun-</u>
<u>can</u> Marie Linden; <u>Mrs Melville</u> Pattie Browne. <u>L</u> & <u>MGR</u>
Arthur Chudleigh; <u>Bm</u> Leonard Lillies; <u>Mus dir</u> Edward
Jones; <u>Cost</u> L. & H. Nathan; <u>Pq</u> C.H. Fox; <u>Furn</u> Marler
& Bennet; <u>Sc</u> T.W. Hall. *REV: E 16/12/93 p9; TW93 p278.*

93.318 *PICKWICK* (Oa,1a) F.C. Burnand (lib) & Edward
Solomon (mus). TRAFALGAR [SQUARE] 13/12/93-6/1/94.
14 perf [w/mat 16/1/94; np 22-25/12/93]. 1st perfd
Comedy 7/2/89. <u>Pickwick</u> C.P. Little; <u>Baker</u> Charles
H. Hawtrey; <u>Tommy</u> Master Stratton. <u>Mrs Bardell</u> Jessie
Bond. <u>PP</u> Mr & Mrs Frank Wyatt; <u>Mgr</u> Charles H. Hawtrey;
<u>Bm</u> H[enry] Brandon, E.F. Bradley; <u>Cond</u> Edward Solomon;
<u>Mus dir</u> Ernest Bucalossi. *REV: E 16/12/93 p9; SR 23/*
12/93 p709; St 21/12/93 p13.

93.319 *THE PIPER OF HAMELIN* (Fantastic O,2a) Robert
Buchanan (lib) & F.W. Allwood (mus). COMEDY 20/12/93-
9/2/94. 35 mat perf [perfd M-Fri only exc 1-2/2/94;
np 23-25/12/93].* <u>Pied Piper</u> Frank Wyatt/Arthur;
<u>Conrad the Cooper</u> Leonard Russell; <u>Mayor of Hamelin</u>
E.M. Robson; <u>Citizen Sauerkraut</u> Clarence Hunt; <u>Citi-</u>
<u>zen Bummelzug</u> W.J. Joyce; <u>Town Crier</u> H[arry] Longden;
<u>Town Clerk</u> F. Walsh. <u>Liza</u> Lena Ashwell; <u>Martha</u> Mrs
Campbell Bradley; <u>Hans</u> Gladys Doree; <u>Annchen</u> Ettie
Williams; <u>Deborah Meerschaum</u> Millicent Pyne; <u>Frau</u>
<u>Hasenfuss</u> A[ileen] O'Brian; <u>Frau Pumpernickel</u> Neva
Bond; <u>Frau Nussnacker</u> Gertrude Turner; <u>Fraulein Sch-</u>

metterling Blanche Whyte; <u>Fraulein Donnerwetter</u> Maud
Jackson. <u>L</u> J.W. Comyns Carr; <u>Sc</u> Walter Hann; <u>Cost dgn</u>
Karl, Mrs J.W. Comyns Carr; <u>Cost</u> L. & H. Nathan, Mrs
Alister, Mrs Nettleship; <u>Ch</u> Marriette d'Auban; <u>Pq</u>
William Clarkson; <u>Sm</u> Edward Hastings; <u>Mus dir</u> Alfred
J. Caldicott; <u>Bm</u> Silvanus Dauncey. *REV: Ath 30/12/93*
p923; E 23/12/93 p8; SR 23/12/93 p708; St 21/12/93
p13; Sk 27/12/93 p455, 466, 10/1/94 p573, 31/1/94 p
8-9; Th 1/2/94 p105-7; Ti 21/12/93 p8.

93.320 *MASTERS SANDFORD AND MERTON* F.C. Burnand (lib)
& Edward Solomon (mus). COMEDY 20/12/93-9/2/94. 35
mat perf [perfd M-Fri only exc 1-2/2/94; np 23-25/12/
93].* <u>William Barlow</u> Lionel Brough; <u>Sambo</u> Leonard
Russell; <u>Tommy Merton</u> E.M. Robson; <u>Harry Sandford</u>
Clarence Hunt. <u>Mlle Aurelie</u> Ada Doree; <u>Katie</u> Mrs Olga
Garland. <u>L & MGR</u>, <u>Ch</u>, <u>Sm</u>, <u>Mus dir</u>, <u>Bm</u> as for 93.319.
<u>Cost dgn</u> Karl; <u>Cost</u> L. & H. Nathan, Mrs Alister; <u>Sc</u>
Walter Johnstone. *REV: Ath, E, St, Th, Ti as for 93.*
319; Sk 27/12/93 p462; SR 23/12/93 p708-9.

93.321 *THE HEADLESS MAN* (C,3a) F.C. Burnand. CRITERION
21/12/93-10/3/94. 80 perf [w/S mat exc 23/12/93; add
mat 2/1/94, 11/1, 25/1/94; np 25/12/93]. 1st perfd
Criterion 27/7/89. <u>Sam Hedley</u> Charles Wyndham; <u>Gen.</u>
<u>Bletchingly</u> William Blakeley; <u>Wentworth Bracebridge</u>
J.G. Taylor; <u>Fred Otway</u> Frank Atherley; <u>Reginald Har-</u>
<u>court</u> Frank Worthing; <u>Mr Nupley</u> Sydney Valentine;
<u>Jenkins</u> C. Edmonds. <u>Mrs Torrington</u> Ellis Jeffreys;
<u>Mrs Gen. Bletchingly</u> F. Frances; <u>Mrs Hedley</u> Ethel
Matthews; <u>Miss Trimmer</u> E[mily] Miller; <u>Lydia March-</u>
<u>mont</u> May Blayney/Nancy Noel/Mabel Love; <u>Servant</u> A[nn-
ie] Saker. <u>L & MGR</u> Charles Wyndham; <u>Mus dir</u> A. Evans;
<u>Act mgr & Treas</u> E. Harvey. *REV: Ath 30/12/93 p923; E*
23/12/93 p11, 6/1/94 p1; SR 30/12/93 p740; St 4/1/94
p15; Ti 23/12/93 p7, 1/1/94 p8; TW93 p288-9.

93.322 *THE BENGAL TIGER* (F,1a) Charles Dance. CRITERION
21/12/93-9/2/94. 43 perf [np 25/12/93]. 1st perfd
Olympic 18/12/37. <u>Sir Paul Pagoda</u> C.W. Somerset; <u>Ed-</u>
<u>ward Henderson</u> Frank Atherley; <u>Arthur Onslow</u> C. Chinn/
Akermann May; <u>David</u> Sam Hemsley. <u>Miss Yellowleaf</u> M.A.
Victor; <u>Charlotte</u> Stella Maris. <u>L & MGR</u>, <u>Act mgr &</u>
<u>Treas</u>, <u>Mus dir</u> as for 93.321.

93.323 *BEAUTY'S TOILS* (FC,3a) Charles S. Fawcett [fnd
on W.B. Maxell, *Her Fatal Beauty*]. STRAND 21/12/93-
6/1/94. 17 perf [w/mat 23/12, 26/12, 27/12; np 25/12/
93].* <u>Duke of Middlewich</u> G[eorge] Humphrey; <u>Marquis</u>
<u>of Moydore</u> Gerald Moore; <u>Donald Quickshot</u> George
Giddens; <u>Sydney Cumming</u> Herbert Ross; <u>John Dryden</u>
Willie Edouin; <u>Saunders</u> Alec Mackenzie; <u>Mr Poser</u> Harry
Buss; <u>Policeman</u> Alfred P. Phillips; <u>Roberts</u> Robson
Lambert; <u>Organ Grinder</u> Alexander; <u>Piano Porter</u> Caleb
Porter. <u>Mrs Cumming</u> Mrs Dion Boucicault; <u>Ethel Cum-</u>
<u>ming</u> May Whitty; <u>Mrs Chandler</u> May Protheroe; <u>Jane</u>
Annie Goward; <u>Mrs Dryden</u> Emily Dowton; <u>Marion Lobb</u>
Miriam Clements. <u>L & MGR</u> Willie Edouin; <u>Pp</u> J.S. Clarke;
<u>Bm</u> J.T. Mackay Robertson; <u>Sm</u> C[harles] Davies; <u>Mus dir</u>
George W. Byng. *REV: St 28/12/93 p12; Ti 23/12/93 p7;*
TW93 p290.

93.324 *SIX PERSONS* (Duol) Israel Zangwill. HAYMARKET
22/12/93-21/4/94. 92 perf [np 23-25/12/93, 18-19/1/
94, 19-27/3/94].* <u>Charles</u> Frederick Kerr/E. Holman
Clark/A. Hamilton Revelle. <u>Eugenia</u> Irene Vanbrugh.
<u>L & MGR</u> H.B. Tree; <u>Bom</u> W.H. Leverton; <u>Sm</u> Shelton; <u>Mus</u>
<u>dir</u> Carl Armbruster; <u>Bm & Sec</u> Frederick Harrison;
<u>Elect</u> E. Wingfield Bowles. *REV: E 30/12/93 p10; Sk*
3/1/94 p516; SR 30/12/93 p740; St 28/12/93 p12; Th
1/2/94 p107; Ti 23/12/93 p7; TW93 p289-90.

93.325 *ADOPTION* (Ca,1a) "Richard Henry" [Richard But-
ler & H. Chance Newton]. PRINCE OF WALES'S 23/12/93-
3/3/94. 60 perf [np 25/12/93].** <u>Barnabus Blockle</u>
George Mudie/Frank A. Walsh; <u>Theodosius</u> Reginald
Stockton/Reginald Somerville; <u>Glumber</u> Gilbert Porteous.
<u>Barbara Blockle</u> Sybil Grey/Florence Rookie; <u>Constan-</u>
<u>tia</u> Florence Lloyd; <u>Whistler</u> Grace Palotta. <u>PP</u> Edgar
Bruce; <u>Sm</u> Reginald Stockton; <u>Act mgr</u> C.P. Levilly;
<u>Rep</u> M. Edwards. *REV: St 15/2/94 p13.*

93.326 *ROBINSON CRUSOE* (Panto) Harry Nicholls & Augustus Harris & James M. Glover (mus). DRURY LANE 26/12/
93-10/3/94. 116 perf [2 perf dy 27/12/93-10/2/94; W,
S mat thereafter; add mat 10/2, 15/2, 19/2].* <u>Will</u>
<u>Atkins</u> Herbert Campbell; <u>Man Friday</u> Little Tich;
<u>Snooks</u> Arthur Alexander; <u>Mrs Crusoe</u> Dan Leno; <u>Clown</u>
Harry Payne; <u>Dancer</u> John d'Auban; <u>Davy Jones</u> Charles

Dodsworth; <u>Queen</u> Ben Brown; <u>Invention</u> Henry Lorraine;
<u>King</u> [Charles?] Leclercq; <u>Cpt. Perkins</u> W. Poluski;
<u>Mate</u> S. Poluski; <u>Dancer/Harlequin</u> Albertieri; <u>Life</u>-
<u>guardsman/ Pirate Chief</u> Frank W. Damer; <u>Friday's Old</u>
<u>Father</u> [Stanislaus] Calhaem; <u>Prime Minister</u> Newland;
<u>Mirth</u> Joseph A. Cave; <u>Parrot</u> W. Jee; <u>Goat</u> T. Jee;
<u>Pantaloon</u> Carl Waller; <u>Policeman</u> Julian Girard. <u>Robin</u>-
<u>son Crusoe</u> Ada Blanche; <u>Dancer</u> Emma d'Auban; <u>Columbine</u>
Eva Clifton; <u>Dancer</u> Virginia Zucchi; <u>Polly Perkins</u>
Marie Lloyd; <u>Bessie Lightfoot</u> Maud Richardson; <u>Tommy</u>
<u>Boline</u> Lily Harold; <u>Perky Snooks</u> Julia Kent; <u>Spirit</u>
<u>of Pantomime</u> Nita Carlyon; <u>Recruiting Officiers</u> Mc-
Carthy, A. Reynolds. <u>L & MGR & DIR</u> Augustus Harris;
<u>Sm</u> Arthur P. Collins; <u>Ch</u> John d'Auban; <u>Sc</u> [Robert]
Caney, Joseph Harker, T.E. Ryan, Glendinning, William
Perkins; <u>Cost dgn</u> Percy Anderson, Crage, Comelli,
Edel; <u>Cost</u> Alias, Harrisons, B.J. Simmons, May, Will-
iam Clarkson, Angel, Landolf, Phillips & Son, Miss
Fisher, Miss Palmer, Miss Champion, Mrs Berford, Mrs
Manning, Miss Collier, Kennedy, Collater, White; <u>Pq</u>
William Clarkson; <u>Mach</u> E.A. Taylor; <u>Props</u> A. Jones,
Labhart; <u>Chorus Master</u> Stedman; <u>Asm</u> Napier Barry; <u>Bom</u>
[W.] Allcroft. *REV: Ath 30/12/93 p923; E 30/12/93 p7;
Sk 27/12/93 p462, 468, 3/1/94 p516, 10/1/94 p601, 14/
3/94 p378; SR 30/12/93 p740; St 28/12/93 p12, 15/3/94
p12; Ti 12/3/94 p6; TW94 p6-8.*

93.327 *CINDERELLA* (Fairy Panto,10sc) Horace Lennard
(lib) & Oscar Barrett (mus). LYCEUM 26/12/93-17/3/94.
126 perf [2 perf dy 27/12/93-10/2/94; M, W, S mat
thereafter].* <u>Thisbe</u> Victor Stevens; <u>Grand Chamber</u>-
<u>lain</u> Deane Brand; <u>Minister of War</u> William Lugg; <u>Baron</u>
<u>Pumpolino</u> Harry Parker; <u>Clorinda</u> Fred Emney; <u>Alidoro</u>
Richard Blunt; <u>Pedro</u> Charles Wallace; <u>Black Cat</u> Charle
Lauri; <u>Minister of Marine</u> Thomas Terriss; <u>Minister of</u>
<u>Finance</u> Willie Temple; <u>Minister of Agriculture</u> Guy
Waller; <u>Clown</u> Charles Lauri; <u>Pantaloon</u> Enrico Zanfretta; <u>Boots</u> H. Evans; <u>Harlequin</u> Harry Kitchen;
<u>Policeman</u> Fred Kitchen; <u>Ticket Inspector</u> George Aub-
rey. <u>Cinderella</u> Ellaline Terriss/Bessie Rignold;
<u>Prince Felix</u> Kate Chard; <u>Sylph Coquette</u> Minnie Terry;
<u>Fairy Godmother</u> Susie Vaughan; <u>Baroness</u> Clara Jecks;
<u>Fernando</u> Florrie Harmon; <u>Dandini</u> Alice Brookes; <u>Wood</u>
<u>Pigeon</u> Louise Loveday; <u>Fox</u> Francesca Zanfretta; <u>Fairy</u>

of the Slipper Violet Darrell; Fairy Potter Emily
Earle; Fairy Weaver Dora Barton; Fairy Electrician
Dorothy Harwood; Fairy Brassfounder Cassie Bruce;
Beauty Grace Leslie; Virtue Dora Rignold; Patience
Mary Barton; Industry Hilda Thorpe; Columbine Minnie
Tight. SC Henry Emden, J. Pritchard Barrett, Hawes
Craven; Ch Katti Lanner; Cost Wilhelm, Mrs S. May,
Miss Fisher, Auguste, Pocock Brothers; Props F.C.
Labhart, R. Eagle; Pq William Clarkson; Dir Oscar
Barrett; Sm Arthur Brunton; Regisseur J.R. Crauford;
Mus dir James Weaver; L Henry Irving; Bom Joseph
Hurst. *REV: Ath 30/12/93 p923; E 30/12/93 p7; Sk 27/
12/93 p462, 466, 3/1/94 p509, 516, 17/1/94 p622-3,
625, 21/3/94 p437; SR 30/12/93 p740; St 28/12/93 p12;
TW94 p1-6.*

93.328 *WALKER, LONDON* (C,3a) J.M. Barrie. TOOLE'S
26/12/93-27/1/94. 34 perf [w/S mat].** Jasper Phipps
J.L. Toole/Sydney Paxton; Kit Upjohn C.M. Lowne; An-
drew McPhail Laurence Irving; W.G. Cecil Ramsey; Ben
Frank J. Arlton. Mrs Golightly Kate Carlyon; Bell
Golightly Cora Poole; Nanny O'Brien Alice Kingsley;
Sarah Rigg Eliza Johnstone; Penny Mary Brough. L & MGR
J.L. Toole; Sm John Billington; Mus dir William Rob-
ins; Bm George Lee; Sc Joseph Harker; Props George
Scarrott.

93.329 *THE SPITALFIELDS WEAVER* (F) Thomas Haynes Bay-
ly. TOOLE'S 26/12/93-9/1/94. 13 perf.** Simmonds
J.L. Toole; John Billington. Florence Fordyce.

93.330 *BEST MAN WINS* (F,1a) Mark Melford. STRAND
26/12/93-9/1/94. 22 perf [2 perf dy 28/12/93-6/1/94;
mat only 8-9/1/94].** Kairns Alec C. Mackenzie;
Parson Jeulitt Robson Lambert; S[tephen?] Phillips;
Caleb Porter. Carlotta Kairns Ethel Waring. L & MGR
Willie Edouin. *REV: E 30/12/93 p10; St 4/1/94 p14-5.*
Comment: Some sources indicate 1st perf was 28/12/93.

93.331 *BINKS, THE DOWNY PHOTOGRAPHER* (Musical Absurdity,
1a) Nat Childs & Willie Edouin. STRAND 28/12/93-9/1/
94. 11 mat perf.** Muggins George Giddens; Bertie
Fortscue Herbert Ross; G[eorge] Humphrey; Alec Mc-

Kenzie; Willie Edouin; Chip Harry Buss; Robson Lam-
bert; Alfred P. Phillips. Ruby Chillington Alice
Atherton; Vesta Fanny Wentworth; Nancy Graeme; Jenny
Dawson; R. Penndennis; Stella Brandon; Cynthia Brooke.
L & MGR Willie Edouin. *REV: E 30/12/93 p10; St 4/1/
94 p14.* Comment: Possibly also perfd 26-27/12/93.

*   *   *   *   *

94.1 *THE COUNTRY GIRL* (C,3a) David Garrick [fnd on
William Wycherley, *The Country Wife*]. DALY'S 1/1/94-
6/1/94. 7 perf [w/mat 6/1]. 1st perfd Drury Lane 25/
10/1766. Squire Moody William Farren; Sparkish
George Clark; Harcourt Herbert Gresham; Belville E.
Allan Aynesworth; Old Will Thomas Bridgland; Servant
Frederic Powell. Peggy Thrift Ada Rehan; Alethea
Violet Vanbrugh; Lucy Catherine Lewis. L & MGR Augus-
tin Daly; Bom John Farrington, Edward Brown; Cost
Harrisons; Pq William Clarkson. *REV: Ath 6/1/94 p26;*
E 6/1/94 p9; Sk 10/1/94 p563; SR 6/1/94 p14-5; St 4/
1/94 p14; Th 1/2/94 p108-9; Ti 2/1/94 p8.

94.2 *A WOMAN'S WONT* (Ca). DALY'S 1/1/94-6/1/94. 6
perf.** Husband Sidney Herbert; Father-in-law James
Lewis; Servant William Sampson. Wife Isabel Irving;
Mother-in-law Mrs G.H. Gilbert; Servant Florence Conron. L & MGR, Bom, Cost, Pq as for 94.1. *REV: E 6/1/*
94 p9; St 4/1/94 p15.

94.3 *AN OLD JEW* (C,5a) Sydney Grundy. GARRICK 6/1/94-
3/2/94. 25 perf [mat only 24/1].* Julius Sterne John
Hare; Paul Venables Gilbert Hare; Bertie Burnside
W.L. Abingdon; Douglas Craik Eugene Mayeur; Wybrow
Walsingham Charles Rock; John Slater, M.A., LL.D.
G.W. Anson; James Brewster William H. Day; Willie
Wandle W. Scott Buist; Hon Rev Adolphus Finucane Gil-
bert Farquhar; Mr Polak Herman de Lange; Franconi
Gilbert Trent; Old Actor Robb Harwood; Fritz Gerald
du Maurier. Mrs Venables Mrs Theodore Wright; Eliza

Italia Conti; <u>Ruth Venables</u> Kate Rorke. <u>L</u> & <u>MGR</u> John
Hare; <u>Sc</u> William Harford; <u>Cond</u> Andrew Levey; <u>Asm</u>
R[owley] Cathcart; <u>Act mgr</u> C.G. Compton. *REV: Ath 13/*
1/94 p57-8; E 13/1/94 p9; Sk 17/1/94 p628; SR 20/1/94
p68-9; St 11/1/94 p15; Th 1/2/94 p109-12; Ti 8/1/94
p12; TW94 p9-21.

94.4 *A CASE FOR EVICTION* (Ca,1a) S. Theyre Smith.
GARRICK 6/1/94-4/4/94. 71 perf [mat only 24/1; np 19-
23/3].** <u>Frank</u> W. Scott Buist. <u>Dora</u> May Harvey/Helen
Luck; <u>Mary</u> Helen Luck/Italia Conti. <u>L</u> & <u>MGR</u>, <u>Sc</u>, <u>Asm</u>,
<u>Cond</u>, <u>Act mgr</u> as for 94.3. *REV: E, St as for 94.3.*

94.5 *TWELFTH NIGHT; OR, WHAT YOU WILL* (C,4a) William
Shakespeare. DALY'S 8/1/94-28/4/94. 111 perf [w/S
mat; add mat 28/2, 7/3, 14/3, 25/4; np 19-23/3]. 1st
perfd Middle Temple Hall 2/2/1601. <u>Orsino</u> John Craig;
<u>Sebastian</u> Sidney Herbert; <u>Antonio</u> Thomas Bridgland;
<u>Sea Cpt.</u> Hobart Bosworth; <u>Valentine</u> Alfred Hickman;
<u>Curio</u> Lloyd Lowndes; <u>Sir Toby Belch</u> James Lewis; <u>Sir</u>
<u>Andrew Aguecheek</u> Herbert Gresham; <u>Malvolio</u> George
Clarke; <u>Fabian</u> William Sampson/George Lesoir; <u>Feste</u>
Lloyd Daubigny; <u>Priest</u> Frederic Powell; <u>Officer</u> Camp-
bell Gollan. <u>Countess Olivia</u> Violet Vanbrugh; <u>Maria</u>
Catherine Lewis; <u>Viola</u> Ada Rehan; <u>Extras</u> Maud Sher-
man, Lena Loraine, Emma Gaston-Murray, Florence Con-
ron, Adelaide Sterling, Lulu Bosworth, Olive Barry,
Caroline Dagmar, Ida Molesworth, O'Doyne, Zippert,
Sophia Hoffman, Helena Nelson, May Young, Valda Glynn,
[E.] Oldcastle, Stevenson, Templar. <u>MGR</u> Augustin Daly;
<u>Bom</u> John Farrington, Edward Brown; <u>Cost</u> Harrisons;
<u>Pq</u> William Clarkson; <u>Sc</u> Walter Hann, Henry E. Hoyt;
<u>Ch</u> R.M. Compton; <u>Mus</u> Henry Widmer. *REV: E 6/1/94 p9;*
Sk 10/1/94 p564-5, 17/1/94 p628, 25/4/94 p672, 2/5/94
p21-3; SR 13/1/94 p42; St 11/1/94 p15; Th 1/3/94 p152-
3; Ti 9/1/94 p8; TW94 p22-31.

94.6 *DAISY'S ESCAPE* (Ca,1a) A.W. Pinero. TOOLE'S
10/1/94-27/1/94. 16 perf.** <u>Tom Rossiter</u> Herbert
Pearson; <u>Mjr. Mullet</u> Henry Westland; <u>Augustus Caddel</u>
Laurence Irving; <u>Bullamore</u> Frank J. Arlton; <u>Tulk</u>
C[harles] Brunton. <u>Daisy White</u> Cora Poole; <u>Mollie</u>
B[eaumont] Loveday. <u>L</u> & <u>MGR</u> J.L. Toole; <u>Sm</u> John Bill-
ington; <u>Mus dir</u> William Robins; <u>Bm</u> George Lee.

94.7 *UNCLE'S GHOST* (F,3a) Walter Sapte, jr. OPERA
COMIQUE 17/1/94-12/2/94. 30 perf [w/W, S mat exc 17/1].
1st perfd Prince of Wales's 15/6/87. John Smithson
John Tresahar; Cecil Crawley Charles Burleigh; Prof
Erasmus Pipjaw Alfred Maltby; Prof Sharp Lionel Wal-
lace; Prof Noodlechump Charles Lander; Dr Howe Ells
Dagnall; Dr Watt Brandon Hurst; Nobbs H. Norton;
Uncle Josiah Turbot Fred Thorne. Mrs Bartholomew Emily
Thorne; ? ? ? ? Carrie Coote; Ravinia Pipjaw E. Brins-
ley Sheridan; Jane May Nolon. L Farce Comedy Syndicate
Ltd; Bm Eugene O. Stafford; Mus & Mus dir W. Carlile
Vernon; Sm Ells Dagnall. *REV: E 20/1/94 p9; Sk 24/1/*
94 p681; St 25/1/94 p13; Th 1/3/94 p154-5; Ti 19/1/94
p4; TW94 p40.

94.8 *SUNSET* (1a) Jerome K. Jerome. OPERA COMIQUE 17/
1/94-12/2/94. 23 perf. 1st perfd Comedy 13/2/88.
Laurence Brandon Hurst; Azariah Stodd Lionel Wallace;
Rivers J.F. Graham. Lois Mary Kingsley; Joan May Nolon; Aunt Drusilla Henrietta Cowen. L, Bm, Mus & Mus
dir, Sm as for 94.7. *REV: E, St, Th as for 94.7.*

94.9 *THE CHARLATAN* (P,4a) Robert Buchanan. HAYMARKET
18/1/94-17/3/94. 60 perf [w/S mat].* Philip Woodville
H.B. Tree; Earl of Wanborough Nutcombe Gould; Lord
Dewsbury Fred Terry; Hon Mervyn Darrell Frederick
Kerr; Mr Darnley Charles Allan; Prof Marrables E. Hol-
man Clark; Butler Hay; Footman [J.] Montagu. Lady
Carlotta Deepdale Lily Hanbury; Mrs Darnley Mrs E.H.
Brooke; Olive Darnley Irene Vanbrugh; Madam Obnoskin
Gertrude Kingston; Isabel Arlington Mrs H.B. Tree.
L & MGR H.B. Tree; Sc Walter Hann; Bom W.H. Leverton;
Sm Shelton; Mus dir Carl Armbruster; Elect E. Wing-
field Bowles; Bm & Sec Frederick Harrison. *REV: Ath*
27/1/94 p122; E 20/1/94 p9; Sk 24/1/94 p680, 28/2/94
p242-3; SR 27/1/94 p94-5; St 25/1/94 p12-3; Th 1/3/94
p155-8; Ti 19/1/94 p3; TW94 p32-8.

94.10 *A GAUNTLET* (P,3a) Bjornsterne Bjornson [trans
Osman Edwards, adpt George P. Hawtrey]. ROYALTY 20/1/
94-24/1/94. 4 perf.* Riis W.A. Elliot; Mr Christen-
sen George P. Hawtrey; Alf Christensen Gaston Mervale;
Hoff Alfred Bucklaw; Peter Herbert George. Mrs Riis
Louise Moodie; Mrs Christensen Katherine Stewart;

<u>Marie</u> Eileen Munro; <u>Frederike</u> Cornelie Charles; <u>Kamma</u>
Florence Munro; <u>Hanna</u> Kate Graves; <u>Else</u> Frances Burleigh; <u>Olga</u> Maud Clifford; <u>Ortrude</u> Edith Maitland;
<u>Svava</u> Annie Rose. *REV: Ath* 27/1/94 p122; *E* 27/1/94
p9; *Sk* 24/1/94 p680; *St* 25/1/94 p13; *Th* 1/3/94 p158-
9; *Ti* 22/1/94 p4; *TW94* p38-40.

94.11 *PENELOPE* (MP,1a) George P. Hawtrey (lib) & Edward Solomon (mus) [adpt of William Brough & Andrew
Halliday, *The Area Belle*]. ROYALTY 20/1/94-24/1/94.
4 perf. 1st perfd Comedy 9/5/89. <u>Tosser</u> C.P. Little;
<u>Pitcher</u> George P. Hawtrey; <u>Walker Chalks</u> Aubrey Lum-
ley. <u>Mrs Croaker</u> Eileen Munro; <u>Penelope</u> Kate Santley.
REV: E, St, Th, Ti as for 94.10.

94.12 *A PAIR OF LUNATICS* (DSk) W.R. Walkes. LYRIC
25/1/94 mat perf.** <u>He</u> E.W. Gardiner. <u>She</u> Fanny
Brough. *REV: St* 1/2/94 p13.

94.13 *UNDER THE CLOCK* (Ext,1a) Charles H.E. Brookfield
& Seymour Hicks & Edward Jones (mus). LYRIC 25/1/94
mat perf.** [<u>Sherlock Holmes</u>] Charles H.E. Brookfield; [<u>Dr Watson</u>] Seymour Hicks; [<u>Master of Cere-
monies</u>] William Wyes. [<u>Hannah</u>] Lottie Venne. *REV: St*
1/2/94 p13.

94.14 *THE TRANSGRESSOR* (P,4a) A.W. Gattie. COURT 27/1/
94-7/4/94. 66 perf [w/S mat exc 27/1, 24/3; add mat
4/4; np 19-23/3].* <u>Eric Langley</u> Arthur Elwood; <u>Gerald
Hurst, M.D.</u> Seymour Hicks/Matthew Brodie; <u>Col. Foster</u>
James Fernandez; <u>Sir Thomas Horncliffe, Bart, J.P.</u>
Charles H.E. Brookfield; <u>Hon Rev Henry Meredith</u> Al-
fred Bucklaw; <u>Robert</u> David Cowis/Stuart. <u>Mrs Wood-
ville</u> Fanny Coleman; <u>Constance</u> Bessie Hatton; <u>Anne</u>
Minna Blakiston; <u>Sylvia</u> Olga Nethersole. <u>L & MGR</u>
Arthur Chudleigh; <u>Bm</u> Louis F. Nethersole; <u>Dir</u> Hugh
Moss; <u>Mus & Mus dir</u> Edward Jones; <u>Cost</u> Russell &
Allen, Mrs Nettleship, L. & H. Nathan; <u>Furn</u> Marler &
Bennett; <u>Pq</u> C.H. Fox; <u>Sc</u> T.W. Hall; <u>Act mgr</u> Leonard
Lillies. *REV: Ath* 3/2/94 p156; *E* 3/2/94 p11, 24/3/94
p11; *Sk* 31/1/94 p8, 21/2/94 p176-8, 4/4/94 p545; *SR*
10/2/94 p148-9; *St* 1/2/94 p13; *Th* 1/3/94 p159-61; *Ti*
29/1/94 p4; *TW94* p41-7.

94.15 *BEYOND* (Study of a Woman by a Woman) [fnd on story by Rene Maizeroy]. CRITERION 1/2/94 mat perf.* <u>Cpt. Fenton</u> Arthur Bourchier. <u>Mrs Fenton</u> Mrs Bernard Beere. *REV: E 3/2/94 p11; St 8/2/94 p13; Ti 2/2/94 p11.*

94.16 *THE DANCING MASTER* (Ca,1a) Max Pemberton & Milton Wellings. CRITERION 1/2/94 mat perf. 1st perfd Opera Comique 2/10/89. <u>Peter Winward</u> Charles Thursby; <u>Lord George Dale</u> Arthur Bromley-Davenport; <u>Dancer</u> Lambert. <u>Marjorie Lynton</u> Irene Vanbrugh; <u>Dancers</u> Roffrey, Conover, Stafford. <u>CH</u> Roffrey. *REV: E, St as for 94.15.*

94.16B *LISCHEN AND FRITZCHEN* (Oa) Jacques Offenbach. CRITERION 1/2/94 mat perf.** Mrs Godfrey Pearse. *REV: Ti 2/2/94 p11.*

94.17 *DICK SHERIDAN* (C,4a) Robert Buchanan. COMEDY 3/2/94-30/3/94. 49 perf [w/S mat exc 3/2, 17/3; add mat 14/3; np 19-23/3].* <u>Richard Brinsley Sheridan</u> H.B. Irving; <u>Dr Jonathan O'Leary</u> Brandon Thomas; <u>Lord Dazzleton</u> Cyril Maude; <u>Cpt. Matthews</u> Lewis Waller; <u>Sir Harry Chase</u> Sydney Brough; <u>Mr Linley</u> Edmund Maurice; <u>David Garrick</u> Will Dennis; <u>Mr Wade</u> F.M. Paget; <u>Cpt. Knight</u> Crawley; <u>Sir James Loder</u> H.J. Carvill; <u>Mr Abednego</u> John Byron; <u>Servant</u> Bertram; <u>Mr Linley's Servant</u> Anning. <u>Lady Miller</u> Vane; <u>Lady Pamela Stirrup</u> Lena Ashwell; <u>Lady Shuttleworth</u> Radclyffe; <u>Hon Mrs Elliott</u> Constance Brietzcke; <u>Miss Copeland</u> Ettie Williams; <u>Miss Beamish</u> Aileen O'Brian; <u>Mrs Lappett</u> Pattie Browne; <u>Miss Elizabeth Linley</u> Winifred Emery; <u>1st Lady</u> Carew. <u>L & MGR</u> J.W. Comyns Carr; <u>Sc</u> Walter Hann; <u>Cost dgn</u> Karl, Mrs J.W. Comyns Carr; <u>Cost</u> L. & H. Nathan, Mrs Nettleship; <u>Furn</u> Frank Giles, Emile Godfrey; <u>Pq</u> William Clarkson; <u>Ch</u> John d'Auban; <u>Sm</u> Edward Hastings; <u>Mus dir</u> Alfred J. Caldicott; <u>Bm</u> Silvanus Dauncey. *REV: Ath 10/2/94 p188; E 10/2/94 p9; Sk 7/2/94 p64, 28/2/94 p219, 7/3/94 p281, 298-9; SR 10/2/94 p149; St 8/2/94 p13; Th 1/3/94 p161-4; Ti 5/2/94 p7; TW94 p47-53.*

94.18 *CASTE* (C,3a) T.W. Robertson. GARRICK 5/2/94-4/4/94. 49 perf [w/mat 10/2, 17/2, 24/2; np 19-23/3].**

Hon George d'Alroy Johnston Forbes-Robertson; Cpt,
Hawtree W.L. Abingdon; Eccles G.W, Anson; Sam Gerridge
Gilbert Hare; Dixon George du Maurier. Marquise de St.
Maur Rose Leclercq; Polly Eccles May Harvey; Esther
Eccles Kate Rorke. L & MGR John Hare; Sc William Har-
ford; Cond Andrew Levey; Asm W.M. Cathcart; Act mgr
C.G. Compton. *REV: Ath 10/2/94 p188; E 10/2/94 p9;
Sk 14/2/94 p111, 21/3/94 p437; SR 10/2/94 p149; St
8/2/94 p12-3; Th 1/3/94 p164-5; Ti 6/2/94 p10; TW94
p53-8.*

94.19 *THE LEGACY* (C,1a) Frank Lindo. ROYALTY 6/2/94
mat perf.* Jack Martyn Douglas Gordon; Alfred Atte-
boy Robert Castleton; Jonas Sparley A.H. Brooke.
Agnes Hamilton Mary Clayton; Clara Sparley Marjorie
Christmas; Eliza Mary Bessle. L Kate Santley; Mgr
Annie Rose; Pd Frank Lindo; Act mgr A. Austin Leigh;
Asm A.H. Brooke; Mus dir Thomas P. Fish; Cost & Pq
Harrisons. *REV: E 10/2/94 p15; St 8/2/94 p13.*

94.20 *JUDITH SHAKESPEARE* (D,1a) "Alec Nelson" [E.B.
Aveling; fnd on novel by William Black]. ROYALTY 6/2/
94 mat perf.* Jack Orridge Rothbury Evans; Thomas
Quiny Frank Lacy; Frank Evans Ernest H. Patterson;
Willie Hart Lionel Calhaem. Judith Shakespeare Eva
Williams. L , Mgr, Asm, Act mgr, Mus dir, Cost & Pq
as for 94.19; Pd Henry Neville. *REV: E 10/2/94 p15;
St 8/2/94 p13.*

94.21 *TWO HEARTS* (D,1a) S.J. Adair Fitzgerald. ROYALTY
6/2/94 mat perf.* Dr Angus Williams Frank MacVicars;
Rev Josiah Darville W. Aubrey Chandler; Capel Arliss
Frederic de Lara. Heresta Aynsley Emilie Calhaem;
Jane Kate Bealby. L, Mgr, Asm, Act mgr, Mus dir, Cost
& Pq as for 94.19; Pd Stanislaus Calhaem; Mus John
Denham. *REV: E 10/2/94 p15; St 8/2/94 p13.*

94.22 [no entry]

94.23 *DEAREST MAMMA* (Ca,1a) Walter Gordon. CRITERION
10/2/94-10/3/94. 25 perf.** Harry Clinton Frank Atherley; Nettle Croker C.W. Somerset; Mr Browser William Blakeley; Jones C. Edmonds. Mrs Breezeley Fussell
M.A. Victor; Edith Clinton Stella Maris; Mrs Honey-

wood F. Frances. L & MGR Charles Wyndham; Act mgr &
Treas E. Harvey.

94.24 *THE LITTLE WIDOW* (F,3a) William Jarman. ROYALTY
15/2/94-10/3/94. 21 perf. 1st perfd Theatre Royal,
Liverpool 2/2/91. Mr Wilkins Potter Charles Sugden;
Dr Arthur Potter Welton Dale; Cpt. Rattlebrain Frank
Lacy; Auguste Bousieur A.E.W. Mason; Morton Ernest H.
Patterson. Mrs Wilkins Potter Sydney K. Phelps; Emily
Randall Emilie Grattan; Sophonisba Bousieur Jane
Gray; Mrs Constance Rattlebrain Minnie Palmer. BM
Francis Jerrard. *REV: E 17/2/94 p9; Sk 21/2/94 p214;
St 22/2/94 p14; Ti 17/2/94 p13; TW94 p58-9.* Comment:
Nicoll gives author's name as Fred Jarman.

94.25 *IN OLDEN DAYS* (Dramatic Incident,1a) Mrs Frances
Hodgson Burnett. ROYALTY 15/2/94-10/3/94. 21 perf.**
Jocelyn Durant A.E.W. Mason; Cpt. Desborough Harry
Grattan. Damaris Nethercliffe Emilie Grattan. BM
Francis Jerrard. *REV: E, St as for 94.24.*

94.26 *WAPPING OLD STAIRS* (CO,2a) Stuart Robertson (lib)
& Howard Talbot (mus). VAUDEVILLE 17/2/94-6/4/94. 43
perf [w/S mat exc 17/2, 24/3; add mat 26/3; np 19-23/
3]. 1st perfd Theatre Royal, King's Lynn 4/1/94.
Sir Wormwood Scrubbs Herbert Sparling; Mark Mainstay
Courtice Pounds; Cpt. Crook Henry Bourchier/Charles
Collette; Ben Brace Avon Saxon; Dick Fid Richard Tem-
ple/T.P. Haynes; Quartermaster William Vokes. Nancy
Joy Mary Turner; Molly Joy Hannah Jones; Daisy Pen-
nant Mary Hutton; Kate Capstan M[argaret?] Warren;
Betsy Binnacle L. Stewart; Susan Sinnett Jessie Bond/
Fanny Marriott; Nellie Caper Lennox; Annie Alport Amy
Bell; Bessie Bouncer Fane; Dolly Hawser Annie Laurie.
L A. & S. Gatti; Mgr Edward Curtice; Pd Richard Tem-
ple; Bm G.M. Polini/George Manners; Mus dir Sydney
Ward; Sc Richard C. Durant; Ch R.M. Compton; Pq & Cost
William Clarkson; Cost dgn W.D. Ironside; Bom Sharpe.
*REV: E 24/2/94 p9; Sk 21/2/94 p214; SR 24/2/94 p201;
St 22/2/94 p13-4; Ti 19/2/94 p11.*

94.27 *WET PAINT* (Ca,1a) Frederick Hay. VAUDEVILLE 19/
2/94-4/4/94. 34 perf [np 19-23/3].* Peter Penley
Herbert Sparling. Mrs Chiselhurst Annie Laurie; Polly

Geraldine Wrangham. L, Mgr, Bm, Mus dir, Bom as for
94.26. *REV: 24/2/94 p9.*

94.28 *DAN'L DRUCE, BLACKSMITH* (C,3a) W.S. Gilbert.
PRINCE OF WALES'S 20/2/94 mat perf. 1st perfd Haymar-
ket 11/9/76. Sir Jasper Coombe William Rignold; Dan'l
Druce William Mollison; Reuben Haines Sydney Valentine;
Geoffrey Winyard Fuller Mellish; Marple Julian Cross;
Joe Ripley Fred W. Permain; Sgt. Charles Medwin; Sold-
ier Lionel Wallace. Dorothy Nancy McIntosh. PP Edgar
Bruce. *REV: E 24/2/94 p9; Sk 21/2/94 p166; SR 24/2/*
94 p201; Th 1/4/94 p220-2.

94.29 *DINNER FOR TWO* (Duo1) R.C. Carton. LYRIC 21/2/
94 mat perf.** [Stapleton Kidbrook] Yorke Stephens;
[Mjr. Powneby] Cyril Maude. *REV: St 22/2/94 p13.*

94.30 *THE NEW BOY* (FC,3a) Arthur Law. TERRY'S 21/2/94-
14/4/94; trfd to VAUDEVILLE 16/4/94-2/3/95. 428 perf
[w/W, S mat exc 21/2/94, 28/2/94, 9/1/95; add mat
26/3/94, 7/5, 14/5, 10/12/94; np 23/3/94, 24-25/12/94].
1st perfd Devonshire Park, Eastbourne 1/2/94 [as *The*
Boy]. Archibald Rennick Weedon Grossmith/Arthur Hel-
more; Dr Candy John Beauchamp; Felix Roach J.D. Bev-
eridge/Frederick Volpé; Theodore de Brissac Sydney
Warden; Bullock Major Kenneth Douglas; Mr Stubber
T.A. Palmer. Mrs Rennick Gladys Homfrey; Nancy Roach
May Palfrey/Esmé Beringer; Susan Esmé Beringer/Alice
Beet. PP Edward Terry; Mgr Weedon Grossmith; Cond &
Mus dir C.J. Hargitt; Sc T.W. Hall; Furn Oetzmann;
Pq C.H. Fox; Bm A.F. Henderson; Sm C. Robinson. *REV:*
E 24/2/94 p9, 5/1/95 p10; Sk 28/2/94 p224, 28/3/94
p450-1, 7/11/94 p89; SR 24/2/94 p201, 28/7/94 p100;
St 1/3/94 p13; Th 1/4/94 p222-3; Ti 22/2/94 p10; TW94
p62-5.

94.31 *THE GENTLEMAN WHIP* (Ca,1a) H.M. Paull. TERRY'S
21/2/94-14/4/94; trfd to VAUDEVILLE 16/4/94-8/8/94.
144 perf [np 23/3]. 1st perfd Devonshire Park, East-
bourne 1/2/94. Mr Brown Frederick Volpé; Baxter Slade
Sydney Warden; Tom Ellicott J.R. Hatfield; Dixon
George Robinson. Lady Jane Verinder Helena Dacre;
Mabel Verender Esmé Beringer. PP, Mgr, Sc, Furn, Pq,
Bm, Sm, Mus dir as for 94.30. *REV: E 24/2/94 p9; St*

1/3/94 p13; TW94 p65.

94.32 *THE HEIRS OF RABOURDIN* (C,3a) Emile Zola [trans Alexander Teixeira de Mattos]. OPERA COMIQUE 23/2/94. 1 perf.* <u>Rabourdin</u> James A. Welch; <u>Chapuzot</u> Harding Cox; <u>Dominique</u> C.H. Hallard; <u>Le Doux</u> Douglas Gordon; <u>Dr Morgue</u> Charles Goodhart; <u>Isaac</u> F. Norreys Connell. <u>Vaussard</u> Mrs Arthur Ayers; <u>Fiquet</u> Mrs Lois Royd; <u>Eugenie</u> Lena Dene; <u>Charlotte</u> Mary Jocelyn. <u>L</u> F. Fowler; <u>Dir</u> J.T. Grein; <u>Asm</u> E.H. Kelly; <u>Act mgr & Bm</u> Charles Hoppe; <u>Mus dir</u> C.W. Lamartine; <u>Pd</u> Herman de Lange; <u>Furn</u> Oetzmann; <u>Pq</u> William Clarkson; <u>Cost</u> Mrs C. Alister. *REV: Ath 3/3/94 p287; E 3/3/94 p9; St 1/3/94 p13; Th 1/4/94 p223-4; TW94 p65-8.* <u>Comment</u>: Independent Theatre Society.

94.33 *THE WORLD* (D,5a) Henry Pettitt, Paul Meritt & Augustus Harris. PRINCESS'S 24/2/94-14/4/94. 50 perf [w/S mat exc 24/2; add mat 26/3; np 23/3]. 1st perfd Drury Lane 31/7/80. <u>Sir C. Huntingford</u> Charles Dalton; <u>Moss Jewell</u> William Elton; <u>Martin Bashford</u> Julian Cross; <u>Harry Huntingford</u> Charles Glenney; <u>Blackstone</u> Maurice Drew; <u>Pearson</u> Frank MacVicars; <u>Owen</u> Clarence Holt; <u>Langley</u> F. Mavard; <u>Hawkins</u> Joseph A. Cave; <u>Wyndham</u> Frank Damer; <u>Rushton</u> John Horsfall; <u>Detective</u> F.L. Robins; <u>Commissionaire</u> S. Williams; <u>Commisioner</u> John Durant; <u>Marshall</u> Nicholas Nomico. <u>Mabel Huntingford</u> Olga Brandon; <u>Ned Owen</u> Agnes Thomas; <u>Mary Blyth</u> Kate Tyndall; <u>Alice</u> Ethel Verne; <u>Miss McTab</u> Lydia Rachel. *REV: E 3/3/94 p9; St 1/3/94 p13; Th 1/4/94 p230-1; Ti 26/2/94 p12; TW94 p68-9.*

94.34 *THE BOHEMIAN GIRL* [(),3a)] Michael Balfe. DRURY LANE 26/2/94(m), 26/3, 7/4(m), 12/4, 19/4, 10/5/94(m). 6 perf.** <u>Thaddeus</u> Ben Davies/Henry Piercy; <u>Count Arnheim</u> D. Ffrangcon Davies; <u>Florestan</u> Wilfred Esmond; <u>Devilshoof</u> Charles Manners/Henry Pope. <u>Queen of the Gipsies</u> Rose Olitzka; <u>Buda</u> Kate Vito; <u>Arline</u> Fanny Moody/Carla Dagmar. <u>L & MGR</u> Augustus Harris; <u>Cond</u> James M. Glover. *REV: E 3/3/94 p15, 31/3/94 p15; St 1/3/94 p13, 29/3/94 p12, 19/4/94 p13; Ti 30/3/94 p8.*

94.35 *AS YOU LIKE IT* (PastC) William Shakespeare. PRINCE OF WALES'S 27/2/94, 14/3/94. 2 mat perf.**

Orlando Ada Ferrar; Adam Charlotte E. Morland; Jac-
ques Naomi Hope; Touchstone Sophie Larkin; Celia
Beatrice Selwyn; Audrey Lillie Belmore; Rosalind
Frances Ivor; Banished Duke Alexes Leighton; Duke
Frederick Annie Esmond; Oliver Amy McNeil; Charles
the Wrestler Gladys Ffolliott; Le Beau Laura Hansen;
William Sybil Baird; 1st Lord Ida Hazeldene; 2nd Lord
Helen Langton; Corin Ellen Rutland; Sylvius Mrs Gor-
don-Ascher; Amiens Agnes Best; Phoebe Mabel Goldsmith.
DIR Leonard Outram. *REV: E 3/3/94 p9; Sk 7/3/94 p321;
St 1/3/94 p13-4; Ti 28/2/94 p6; TW94 p69-72.*

94.36 *MRS DEXTER* (FC,3a) J.H. Darnley. STRAND 28/2/94-
10/3/94. 12 perf [w/mat 3/3, 7/3]. 1st perfd Court
Theatre, Liverpool 26/12/91. Mjr. Kildare, M.P.
Charles H. Hawtrey; Frank Fairfield, Q.C. Lionel Wal-
lace; Henry Thornton, Q.C. Wilfred Draycott; Hon
Timothy Townsend Gordon Harvey; Reginald Dexter, M.P.
W.F. Hawtrey; Mr Paxton Ernest Cosham; Fulton Sheri-
dan Lascelles; James Alec Mackenzie; Daniel Grimshaw
Willie Edouin. Mrs Dexter Fanny Brough; Mrs Kildare
Helen Conway; Mrs Thornton Eva Williams; Miss O'Hara
Alice Mansfield; Marie Ina Goldsmith. PP J.S. Clarke;
L Willie Edouin; Bm J.T. Mackay Robertson; Mus dir
F. Louis Schneider; Sm Charles Davies. *REV: E 3/3/94
p9; Sk 7/3/94 p321-2; St 8/3/94 p13; Th 1/4/94 p225-6;
Ti 1/3/94 p7; TW94 p72-3.*

94.37 *FOR CHARITY'S SAKE* (DC,1a) Charles S. Fawcett.
STRAND 28/2/94-10/3/94. 10 perf.** Nicholas Nubbles
W.F. Hawtrey; Mr Zebeedy Benjamin Catchpole Sheridan
Lascelles/Ernest Percy; Edward Fisher Gordon Harvey/
Charles Meyrick; Inspector Jones Alec Mackenzie/Char-
les Milton; Nick Ernest Cosham/W.R. Shirley. Charity
Eva Williams/Evelyn McNay. PP, L, Bm, Mus dir, Sm as
for 94.36. *REV: E 3/3/94 p9.* Comment: There is con-
siderable confusion over the production and cast for
this piece. It was initially advertized in *Ti* for
8/1/94, but all other evidence indicates this date.
The numerous cast changes are, however, puzzling.

94.38 *LIBERTY HALL* (C,4a) R.C. Carton. ST, JAMES'S
1/3/94 mat perf.** William Todman Edward Righton; Ho
Gerald Harringay Ben Webster; J. Briginshaw H.H. Vin-

cent; Mr Pedrick Nutcombe Gould; Mr Hickson Alfred
Holles; Robert Binks Master Frank Saker; Luscombe
Arthur Royston; Mr Owen George Alexander, Amy Chil-
worth Maude Millett; Crafer Fanny Coleman; Miss Hick-
son Lizzie Webster; Blanche Chilworth Marion Terry.
L & MGR George Alexander; Sm H.H. Vincent; Mus dir &
Mus Walter Slaughter; Bm Robert V. Shone; Furn Frank
Giles & Co.; Cost Mme Savage, Mme Purdue; Pq William
Clarkson; Sc H.P. Hall. *REV: St 8/3/94 p13.*

94.39 *FASHIONABLE INTELLIGENCE* (Duol) Percy Fendall.
COURT 5/3/94-7/4/94. 25 perf [np 19-23/3].* Mr Eger-
ton Charles H.E. Brookfield. Mrs Fitz Adam Lottie
Venne. L & MGR Arthur Chudleigh; Bm Louis F. Nether-
sole; Mus dir Edward Jones; Act mgr Leonard Lillies.
*REV: Ath 10/3/94 p322; E 10/3/94 p9; Sk 14/3/94 p378;
SR 10/3/94 p255; St 8/3/94 p13; Ti 6/3/94 p7; TW94
p79-80.*

94.40 *THE BEST MAN* (F,3a) Ralph R. Lumley. TOOLE'S
6/3/94-27/6/94; 30/6/94(m). 108 perf [w/S mat exc
10/3, 24/3, 16/6, 23/6; np 22-24/3].* Sir Lovel Gage
John Billington; Price Puttow J.L. Toole; Allen Skif-
ford C.M. Lowne; Walter Brewer E.A. Coventry; Minch
George Shelton; Williams Charles Brunton; Pemble
Frank J. Arlton. Mrs Mont Aubyn Beatrice Lamb; Brenda
Gage Florence Fordyce; Ada Jevons-Bailey Cora Poole;
Nina Skifford Alice Kingsley; Sarah Spooner Eliza
Johnstone. L & MGR J.L. Toole; Sm John Billington;
Mus dir William Robins; Bm George Lee; Sc Joseph Har-
ker; Furn Lyons. *REV: Ath 10/3/94 p322; E 10/3/94 p9;
Sk 14/3/94 p378, 381; SR 10/3/94 p255, 24/3/94 p310;
St 8/3/94 p13; Th 1/4/94 p226-8; Ti 7/3/94 p10; TW94
p75-6.*

94.41 *HESTER'S MYSTERY* (Ca,1a) A.W. Pinero. TOOLE'S
6/3/94-4/5/94. 49 perf [np 22-24/3].** Owen Silverdale Henry Westland; John Royle C.M. Lowne; Joel
Frank J. Arlton. Nance Butterworth Kate Carlyon; Hester Florence Fordyce. L & MGR, Bm, Sm, Mus dir as for
94.40. *REV: E 10/3/94 p9.*

94.42 *THE COTTON KING* (D,4a) Sutton Vane. ADELPHI 10/
3/94-5/5/94. 49 perf [w/mat 26/3; np 23/3].* Jack

Osborne Charles Warner; <u>Richard Stockley</u> Edward
O'Neill; <u>De Fonseca</u> Herbert Flemming; <u>James Shilling-
law</u> Charles Cartwright; <u>Benjamin Tupper</u> Arthur Williams; <u>Rev Mr Ponder</u> Lennox Pawle; <u>Dr Gilbert</u> Lyston
Lyle; <u>Silas Kent</u> John Carter; <u>George Piper</u> W. Northcote; <u>Peter Bell</u> Howard Russell; <u>Phillips</u> Tripp; <u>In-
spector Graham</u> Williamson. <u>Mrs Drayson</u> Mrs Dion Bou-
cicault; <u>Elsie Kent</u> Hall Caine; <u>Kitty Marshall</u> Alma
Stanley; <u>Susan</u> Harrison; <u>Hetty Drayson</u> Marion Terry/
Janet Achurch. <u>PP & MGR</u> A. & S. Gatti; <u>Dir & Sm</u> Char-
les Hudson; <u>Sc</u> Bruce Smith; <u>Mus & Mus dir</u> Edward Jones;
<u>Pq</u> William Clarkson; <u>Cost</u> L. & H. Nathan; <u>Bm & Treas</u>
G.M. Polini. *REV: Ath 17/3/94 p355-6; E 17/3/94 p11;
Sk 14/3/94 p336; SR 17/3/94 p282-3; St 15/3/94 p12-3;
Th 1/4/94 p228-30; Ti 12/3/94 p6; TW94 p76-9.*

94.43 *GO-BANG* (MFC,2a) Adrian Ross (lib) & Osmond
Carr (mus). TRAFALGAR [SQUARE]. 10/3/94-24/8/94. 166
perf [w/S mat exc 10/3; np 23/3].* <u>Jenkins</u> Harry
Grattan; <u>Sir Reddan Tapeleigh, K.C.S.I.</u> Arthur Play-
fair; <u>Lieut. Hon Augustus Fitzpoop</u> George Grossmith,
jr; <u>Wang</u> Sidney Howard/G. Jamieson/Fred Storey; <u>Narain</u>
Frederick Rosse/Edgar Stevens; <u>Dam Row</u> John L. Shine/
Arthur Playfair. <u>Helen Tapeleigh</u> Jessie Bond; <u>Lady
Fritterleigh</u> Agnes Hewitt; <u>Sarah Anne</u> Adelaide Astor;
<u>Belle Wedderburn</u> Maggie Roberts/Hilda Glenn; <u>Miss Flo
Wedderburn</u> Rubie Temple/Lydia Flopp; <u>Miss Di Dalrym-
ple</u> Letty Lind/Adelaide Astor; <u>Daisy Wedderburn</u> Maud
Lockett. <u>PP</u> Mr & Mrs Frank Wyatt; <u>Mgr</u> Arthur Black-
more; <u>Sc</u> E.G. Banks, T.E. Ryan; <u>Cost dgn</u> Edel; <u>Cost</u>
Stagg & Mantle, Swann & Edgar, Harrisons; <u>Ch</u> Mariette
d'Auban; <u>Pq</u> William Clarkson; <u>Props</u> Labhart; <u>Pd & Sm</u>
Frank Parker; <u>Treas</u> Horace Cole; <u>Mus dir</u> Carl Kiefert.
*REV: E 17/3/94 p9; Sk 14/3/94 p378, 28/3/94 p490, 11/
4/94 p563, 16/5/94 p137; SR 17/3/94 p283; St 15/3/94
p13; Ti 12/3/94 p4; TW94 p80-5.*

94.44 *FROU FROU* (P,5a) Henri Meilhac & Ludovic Halévy.
COMEDY 17/3/94(m); 31/3/94-15/6/94. 83 perf [w/mat
28/4, 19/5, 13/6; np 19-30/3].** <u>Henry de Sartorys</u>
Brandon Thomas; <u>Monsieur Brigard</u> Cyril Maude; <u>Le Vicomte Paul de Valreas</u> H.B. Irving; <u>Le Baron de Cambri</u>
Will Dennis; <u>Zanetto</u> Crawley; <u>Brigard's Servant</u> Barrett; <u>Servant in the Palazzo at Venice</u> Anning; <u>Foot-</u>

man Browne. Jack Gladys Doree; La Baronne de Cambri
Vane; Louise Brigard Marie Linden; Pauline Lena Ash-
well/Radclyffe; Governess Radclyffe/Aileen O'Brian;
Gilberte Brigard Winifred Emery. L & MGR J.W. Comyns
Carr; Sc Walter Johnstone; Furn Hampton & Sons,
E[mile] Godfrey; Pq William Clarkson; Sm Edward Hastings; Mus dir Alfred J. Caldicott; Bm Silvanus Dauncey. *REV: Ath 24/3/94 p387; E 24/3/94 p11; SR 24/3/94
p309-10; St 22/3/94 p12-3; Ti 19/3/94 p12; TW94 p106-
8.*

94.45 *CRAZED* (Musical Absurdity,1a) A.R. Phillips.
OPERA COMIQUE 22/3/94 mat perf.** Sophocles Smith
Charles Lander; Beethoven Brown F.W. Stanley. Sally
Kate Lovell. L S. & F. Fowler; Sec Arthur Hodges; Mus
dir Angelo A. Asher; Sm Arthur Shirley, Fred Stanley.
REV: St 29/3/94 p12.

94.46 [no entry]

94.47 [no entry]

94.48 *MARITANA* (O[3a]) Vincent Wallace. DRURY LANE
24/3/94, 5/4, 8/5/94(m). 3 perf.** Don José D. Ffrang-
con Davies; Don Caesar de Bazan Joseph O'Mara; King
W.H. Burgon; Cpt. Gilbert; Marquis Wilfred Esmond.
Maritana Lucille Hill; Lazarilleo Pauline Joran;
Marchioness Florenza. L & MGR Augustus Harris; Cond
James M. Glover. *REV: E 31/3/94 p15; St 29/3/94 p12;
Ti 26/3/94 p10.*

94.49 *ONCE UPON A TIME* (P,4a) Louis N. Parker & H.
Beerbohm Tree [adpt of Ludwig Fulda, *Der Talisman*].
HAYMARKET 28/3/94-21/4/94. 25 perf [w/S mat]. 1st
prof. The King H.B. Tree; Berenger Luigi Lablache;
Diomede Nutcombe Gould; Niccola Gilbert Farquhar; Ste-
fano Charles Allan; Panfilio E. Holman Clark; Ferrante
A. Hamilton Revelle; Basilio Hugh Dorrington; Omar
Fred Terry; Beppo F. Percival Stevens; Benedict John
Willes/Frederick Watson; Guido Frederick Watson/Fen-
ton Boydd; Baldino [William] Gayer Mackay; Pedro
D[avid] Cowis; Caspar Bert Thomas; Head Cook W[illiam]
Hargreaves; Officer of the Guard Edward Ritchie; Hab-
akuk Lionel Brough; Messenger Grafton. Magdalena

Julia Neilson; <u>Rita</u> Mrs H.B. Tree. <u>L & MGR</u> H.B. Tree;
<u>Bom</u> W.H. Leverton; <u>Mus & Mus dir</u> Carl Armbruster; <u>Sc</u>
Walter Hann; <u>Cost dgn</u> Karl; <u>Cost</u> L. & H. Nathan; <u>Pq</u>
William Clarkson; <u>Sm</u> Shelton; <u>Elect</u> E. Wingfield
Bowles; <u>Bm & Sec</u> Frederick Harrison. *REV: Ath 31/3/94*
p420; E 31/3/94 p9; Sk 18/4/94 p619; SR 31/3/94 p336-
7, 7/4/94 p365; St 5/4/94 p12-3; Th 1/5/94 p278-80;
Ti 29/3/94 p3; TW94 p85-91.

94.50 *IN THE EYES OF THE WORLD* (P,1a) A.C. Fraser
Wood. GLOBE 29/3/94-29/1/95. 261 perf [np 24-25/12].*
<u>Richard Carlton</u> H. Reeves-Smith; <u>Lord Wilfred Ponte-</u>
<u>fract</u> Harry Farmer/Wilton Heriot; <u>Horatio Parr</u> Cecil
H. Thornbury; <u>Wilks</u> Edwin H. Wynne/Henry Besley. <u>Lady</u>
<u>Mabel Wendover</u> Mabel Lane/Olga Schuberth. <u>L & MGR</u>
W.S. Penley; <u>Mus</u> John Farmer; <u>Bm</u> Henry Dana; <u>Am</u>
Francis Gosnay; <u>Treas</u> W.A. Tinney; <u>Sm</u> Wilton Heriot;
<u>Mus dir</u> Franz Groenings; <u>Bom</u> H.W. Anderson. *REV: E 7/*
4/94 p9.

94.51 *FAUST* (O[5a]) Charles Gounod. DRURY LANE 29/3/
94, 7/4, 14/4, 1/5(m), 12/5/94(m). 5 perf.** <u>Wagner</u>
Meskowitz; <u>Mephistopheles</u> Hugh Chilvers; <u>Faust</u> Joseph
O'Mara; <u>Valentine</u> Harrison Brockbank. <u>Marguerite</u>
Pauline Joran; <u>Matha</u> Florenza; <u>Siebel</u> Biancoli. <u>L &</u>
<u>MGR</u> Augustus Harris; <u>Cond</u> Armando Seppilli. *REV: Ath*
7/4/94 p452; St 5/4/94 p12; Ti 30/3/94 p8.

94.52 *A COMEDY OF SIGHS* (C,4a) John Todhunter. AVENUE
29/3/94-14/4/94. 16 perf [w/mat 7/4].* <u>Sir Geoffrey</u>
<u>Brandon</u> Bernard Gould; <u>Mjr. Chillingworth</u> Yorke Ste-
phens; <u>Rev Horace Greenwell</u> James A. Welch; <u>Williams</u>
Orlando Barnett. <u>Lady Brandon</u> Florence Farr; <u>Mrs</u>
<u>Chillingworth</u> Vane Featherston; <u>Lucy Vernon</u> Enid
Erle. <u>MGR</u> C.T.H. Helmsley; <u>Sc</u> W.T. Hemsley; <u>Furn</u>
Hampton & Sons; <u>Cost</u> M. & H. Nathan, Claude, Liberty
& Co., Benjamin; <u>Sm</u> George R. Foss. *REV: Ath 7/4/94*
p453; E 31/3/94 p9; Sk 28/3/94 p444-5; SR 7/4/94 p363;
St 5/4/94 p13; Th 1/5/94 p280-1; Ti 30/3/94 p10; TW94
p92-4.

94.53 *THE LAND OF HEART'S DESIRE* (P,1a) W.B. Yeats.
AVENUE 29/3/94-14/4/94; 24/4/94-12/5/94. 33 perf [w/
mat 7/4].* <u>Michael Bruin</u> James A. Welch/Orlando

Barnett; <u>James Bruin</u> A.E.W. Mason; <u>Father Hart</u> George
R. Foss. <u>Bridget Bruin</u> Charlotte E. Morland; <u>Mary
Bruin</u> Winifred Fraser; <u>Fairy Child</u> Dorothy Paget. <u>MGR</u>,
<u>Sc</u>, <u>Furn</u>, <u>Cost</u>, <u>Sm</u> as for 94.52. *REV: E 31/3/94 p9;*
Sk 25/4/94 p669, 714; St 5/4/94 p13; TW94 p91-2.

94.54 *AN ARISTOCRATIC ALLIANCE* (C,3a) Lady Violet Greville [adpt of Emile Augier & Jules Sandeau, *Le Gendre*
de Monsieur Poirier]. CRITERION 31/3/94-29/5/94. 59
perf [w/S mat exc 31/3].* <u>Gerald, Earl of Forres</u>
Charles Wyndham; <u>Firkin Potter</u> Charles Groves; <u>Anthony
Greenwood</u> J.G. Taylor; <u>Cpt. Marchmont</u> Frank Worthing;
<u>Monsieur Cordognac</u> Herman de Lange; <u>Jarvis</u> Markham.
<u>Lady Winnifred Skipton</u> Emily Fowler; <u>Rose Lea</u> Annie
Hughes; <u>Alice</u> Mary Moore. <u>L & MGR</u> Charles Wyndham;
<u>Act mgr & Treas</u> E. Harvey; <u>Sc</u> Hampton & Sons. *REV:*
Ath 7/4/94 p453-4; E 7/4/94 p9, 14/4/94 p8; Sk 4/4/94
p546, 549; St 5/4/94 p13-4; Th 1/5/94 p281-2; Ti 2/4/
94 p4, 3/4/94 p8, 4/4/94 p10; TW94 p94-6.

94.55 *MRS HILARY REGRETS* (Ca) S. Theyre Smith. CRI-
TERION 31/3/94-23/7/94. 98 perf.** <u>Dr Power</u> Frank
Atherley. <u>Mrs Hilary</u> F. Frances. <u>L & MGR</u>, <u>Act mgr &
Treas</u> as for 94.54. *REV: E 7/4/94 p9.*

94.56 *CARMEN* (O[4a]) Georges Bizet. DRURY LANE 31/3/94,
9/4, 17/4, 12/5/94. 4 perf.** <u>Escamillo</u> Richard
Green; <u>Zuniga</u> Hugh Chilvers; <u>Don José</u> Joseph O'Mara;
<u>Dancairo</u> Gilbert King; <u>Remendado</u> Wilfred Esmond;
<u>Morales</u> Stuart Wyatt. <u>Carmen</u> Rose Olitzka; <u>Michaela</u>
Carla Dagmar; <u>Frasquita</u> Biancoli; <u>Mercedes</u> Pauline
Joran. <u>L & MGR</u> Augustus Harris; <u>Cond</u> Armando Seppilli.
REV: Ath 7/4/94 p452; St 5/4/94 p12; Ti 2/4/94 p11.

94.57 *JAUNTY JANE SHORE* (Bsq,2a) "Richard Henry"
[Richard Butler & H. Chance Newton] (lib) & John
Crook (mus). STRAND 2/4/94-19/5/94. 58 perf [w/W, S
mat; add mat 14/5, 15/5].* <u>Richard, Duke of Glouces-
ter</u> Harry Paulton; <u>Edward IV</u> Edward Lewis; <u>Matthew
Shore</u> Fred Emney; <u>Waterbury</u> Arthur Nelstone; <u>Telefag</u>
Alfred P. Phillips; <u>Dato</u> Charles Lovell. <u>Grist</u> Grace
Huntley; <u>Catesby</u> Millie Marion; <u>Elisabeth Woodville</u>
Florence Daly; <u>Dame Ursula</u> Ada Doree; <u>Mary</u> Carrie
Coote; <u>Alicia</u> Hilda Hanbury; <u>Young Princes</u> Nellie &

Maggie Bowman; Jaunty Jane Shore Alice Atherton; Hast-
ings Emmeline Orford. PP J.S. Clarke; L Willie Ed-
ouin; Dir Willie Edouin; Cost dgn John W. Houghton;
Cost Alias, Auguste; Pq Fox; Mus dir J.J. Ross; Sm
Charles Davies. *REV: E 7/4/94 p9; Sk 11/4/94 p565;*
St 5/4/94 p13; Ti 3/4/94 p10; TW94 p103.

94.58 *MISS RUTLAND* (P of Modern Life,3a) Richard Pryce.
GAIETY 3/4/94 mat perf.* George Marston William Her-
bert; Hon John Massareen W.T. Lovell; Mr Layton Will-
iam Wyes; Mr Mordaunt Ernest Percy; Mr Le Marchant
Mules Brown; Mr Warburton Guy Lane Coulson; Morrisson
John Byron; Jackson James A. Welch; Call-boy R. Earle.
Helen Marston Frances Ivor; Lady Wroxeter Henrietta
Lindley; Mildred Luxmere Helen Forsyth; Miss Skelt
Jordan Mrs B.M. de Solla; Ethel Orient Evelyn Faulk-
ner; Florry Paget Olga Garland; Wilson Mabel Hardy;
Margaret Brown Mrs E.H. Brooke; Eleanor Rutland Ettie
Williams. L & MGR George Edwardes; Dir Edward Hast-
ings; Mus dir W. Meyer Lutz; Act mgr E[dward] Marshall;
Pq William Clarkson. *REV: E 7/4/94 p11; Sk 11/4/94*
p565; St 5/4/94 p13.

94.59 *THE FIEND AT FAULT* (Mediaeval Musical Mystery,
la) H. Sutherland Edwardes (lib) & William H. Taylor
(lib & mus) & F. Forster Buffen (mus). VAUDEVILLE 4/4/
94-6/4/94. 3 perf.* Enrico C. Emlyn Jones; Satanio
William Dever. Vera Madeleine Martinez. *REV: 7/4/94*
p9.

94.60 *THE LITTLE SQUIRE* (C,3a) Mrs William Greet &
Horace Sedger [adpt of novel by Mrs de la Pasture].
LYRIC 5/4/94-4/5/94. 22 mat perf [perfd M-Fri only].*
Claud Vernon Charles Sugden; Mr Wentworth Seymour;
Wilkinson W.S. Laidlaw; Granfer West Montelli; Cart-
ridge W. Bentley; Second Digger S. Williams;
1st Villager Charles Crook. Adrian de Coursay Dorothy
Hanbury; Mrs de Coursay Mary Rorke; Bessie Barton
Fanny Brough; Mrs Hardwick Rose Leclercq; Mrs Brown-
low Mrs Edmund Phelps; Cicely Hardwick Isa Bowman;
Lise de la Riviere Empsie Bowman; 1st Wife Dora Thorne;
2nd Wife Fenton. L & MGR Horace Sedger. *REV: E 7/4/94*
p11; Sk 11/4/94 p565, 2/5/94 p3, 17; St 12/4/94 p13;
Th 1/5/94 p282-4; Ti 6/4/94 p12; TW94 p102-3.

94.61 *MRS LESSINGHAM* (P,4a) "George Fleming" [Constance Fletcher]. GARRICK 7/4/94-15/5/94. 33 perf [mat only 5/5].* <u>Walter Forbes</u> Johnston Forbes-Robertson; <u>Mjr Edward Hardy, R.A., V.C.</u> John Hare/W. Scott Buist; <u>Hon Archie Hope-Glen</u> Sheridan Lascelles; <u>Charles B. Snead</u> Charles Rock; <u>James Vane</u> G.W. Hardy; <u>Master Bobby Snead</u> Master Frank Saker; <u>Farmer</u> Gerald du Maurier. <u>Lady Anne Beaton</u> Kate Rorke; <u>Lady Porteous</u> Dolores Drummond; <u>Mrs Lessingham</u> Elizabeth Robins; <u>Mrs Hope Glen</u> Helen Luck; <u>Harper</u> Emily Cross; <u>Mrs Snead</u> Ina Goldsmith. L & MGR John Hare; <u>Sc</u> William Harford; <u>Cond</u> Andrew Levey; <u>Asm</u> W.M. Cathcart; <u>Act mgr</u> C.G. Compton. *REV: Ath 14/4/94 p485; E 14/4/94 p9; Sk 18/4/94 p624, 658, 661, 23/5/94 p174; SR 14/4/94 p392-3; St 12/4/94 p13; Th 1/5/94 p284-6; Ti 9/4/94 p10; TW94 p96-102.*

94.62 *CAVALLERIA RUSTICANA* (O[1a]) Pietro Mascagni. DRURY LANE 12/4/94, 19/4, 26/4(m), 3/5(m), 10/5/94(m). 5 perf.** <u>Turridu</u> Joseph O'Mara; <u>Alfio</u> Harrison Brockbank/ D. Ffrangcon Davies. <u>Santuzza</u> Pauline Joran; <u>Lucia</u> Biancoli/Florenza; <u>Lola</u> Carla Dagmar. L & MGR Augustus Harris; <u>Cond</u> Armando Sepilli; <u>Sm</u> Arthur P. Collins; <u>A act mgr</u> Neil Forsyth. *REV: E 14/4/94 p15; St 19/4/94 p13, 3/5/94 p13.*

94.63 *FAUST* (P,5a) W.G. Wills [adpt of Goethe]. LYCEUM 14/4/94-7/7/94. 76 perf [w/mat 5/5, 12/5, 19/5; mat only 26/5, 31/5, 6/6, 16/6, 23/6, 7/7]. 1st perfd Lyceum 19/12/85. <u>Faust</u> William Terriss; <u>Valentine</u> Julius Knight; <u>Frosch</u> John Martin Harvey; <u>Altmayer</u> [T.] Reynolds; <u>Brander</u> [W. Lionel] Belmore; <u>Siebel</u> S[am] Johnson; <u>Student</u> [William] Haviland; <u>Citizens</u> [H.W.] Cushing, Seymour; <u>Mephistopheles</u> Henry Irving; <u>Witches</u> Seldon, Buckley, Forrest; <u>Soldier</u> [R.P.] Tabb; <u>Witch of the Kitchen</u> Clarence Hague; <u>He-Ape</u> Espinosa, jr; <u>She-Ape</u> [John] Archer. Bessy Kate Phillips; <u>Ida</u> Foster; <u>Alice</u> N. de Silva; <u>Catherine</u> Mrs Lacy; <u>Martha</u> M.A. Victor; <u>Margaret</u> Ellen Terry/ Jessie Millward. L & MGR Henry Irving; <u>Bom</u> Joseph Hurst; <u>Sc</u> William Telbin, Hawes Craven; <u>Mus</u> J. Hamilton Clarke, J. Meredith Ball; <u>Organist</u> Sayers; <u>Cost</u> Mrs Nettleship, Auguste, Mrs Reid; <u>Pq</u> Fox; <u>Furn</u> Arnott; <u>Mach</u> Fillery; <u>Sm</u> H.J. Loveday; <u>Act mgr</u> Bram

Stoker. *REV: E 21/4/94 p9; Sk 25/4/94 p672, 16/5/94
p115; SR 21/4/94 p416-7; St 19/4/94 p12-3; Ti 16/4/
94 p11; TW94 p103-6.*

94.64 *CHARMING MRS GAYTHORNE* (C,3a) Charles Smith
Cheltnam. CRITERION 19/4/94 mat perf.* Earl Pinch-
beck C.W. Somerset; Lord Groomsbury Yorke Stephens;
Sir Rupert Oakfield Frank MacRae; Hon Julian Fair-
main A.E.W. Mason; Reginald Brightwell Harley Gran-
ville-Barker; William Frank Vernon. Lord Oakfield
Essex Dane; Gabrielle Di Travers; Augustine Mary
Jocelyn; Mrs Gaythorne Mrs Ivy Dacre. L & MGR Charles
Wyndham. *REV: E 21/4/94 p11; Sk 25/4/94 p672; St
26/4/94 p13.*

94.65 *ARMS AND THE MAN* (RC,3a) G.B. Shaw. AVENUE
21/4/94-7/7/94. 75 perf [w/W mat exc 25/4, 2/5, 16/5].*
Mjr Paul Petkoff James A. Welch; Mjr Sergius Sara-
noff Bernard Gould; Cpt. Bluntschli Yorke Stephens;
Mjr Plechanoff A.E.W. Mason; Nicola Orlando Barnett.
Catherine Petkoff Mrs Charles Calvert; Raina Petkoff
Alma Murray; Louka Florence Farr. MGR C.T.H. Helmsley;
Sc W.T. Hemsley; Furn Hampton & Sons; Cost M. & H.
Nathan, Miss Fisher; Sm George R. Foss; Cond Wurm.
*REV: Ath 28/4/94 p550; E 28/4/94 p9; Sk 25/4/94 p673,
673; St 26/4/94 p12-3; Th 1/6/94 p322-3; Ti 23/4/94
p3; TW94 p109-18.*

94.66 *GENTLEMAN JACK* (D,5a) Charles T. Vincent & Will-
iam A Brady. DRURY LANE 21/4/94-11/5/94. 20 perf [w/mat
28/4,5/5]. 1st English perf.   Jack Royden James J.
Corbett; Joseph Royden William A. Brady; Mr Halliday
Ben Hendricks; George Halliday Cuyler Hastings; Bat
Houston John Donaldson; Schuyler Southgate Jay Wil-
son; Tom Carlton Frank Damer; Maxey Splash John McVey;
Manager Short J.H. Wren; Special Officer of the Roof
Garden Fred M. Harrison; Waiter at the Roof Garden
Bert Tuckman; President of the Olympic Club Dan Saw-
yer; Cpt. of Police Andrew Hayne; Mrs Morriarty Bud
Woodthorpe.   Polly Graham Sadie McDonald; Mrs Roy-
den Robertha Erskine; Alice Saunders Georgie Esmond;
Tootie Splash Florrie West. L Augustus Harris; Sm
Arthur P. Collins; A act mgr Neil Forsyth; Dir William
A. Brady; Cond James M. Glover; Mgr William A. Brady;

<u>Rep</u> Edward Thurnaer. *REV: E 28/4/94 p9; St 26/4/94
p12; Th 1/6/94 p337-8; Ti 23/4/94 p3.*

94.67 *BEST MAN WINS* (F,1a) Mark Melford. STRAND 21/4/
94-19/5/94. 25 perf.** <u>Farmer Kairns</u> Frank Meadows/
Mark Melford [?]; <u>Perks</u> Alfred P. Phillips; <u>Jopper</u>
Charles Davies; <u>Parson Yeulitt</u> E.W. Maule Cole. <u>Car-
lotta Kairns</u> Ethel Waring. <u>L</u> Willie Edouin; <u>Pp</u> J.S.
Clarke; <u>Dir</u> Willie Edouin; <u>Mus dir</u> J.J. Ross; <u>Sm</u>
Charles Davies.

94.67B *THE BIRTHPLACE OF PODGERS* (F,1a) John Holling-
shead. GAIETY 23/4/94 mat perf.** <u>Tom Cranky</u> J.L.
Toole; <u>Old Maresnest</u> George Shelton; <u>Edmund Earlybird</u>
Henry Westland; <u>Alonzo Lexicon</u> Frank J. Arlton; <u>Mor-
tal Podgers</u> Charles Brunton; <u>1st Photographer</u> Herbert
Pearson; <u>2nd Photographer</u> E.A. Coventry. <u>Mrs Cranky</u>
Eliza Johnstone; <u>Penelope Lexicon</u> Mary Brough; <u>Amelia
Maresnest</u> Alice Kingsley. <u>L & MGR</u> George Edwardes;
<u>Sm</u> J.A.E. Malone; <u>Act mgr</u> E[dward] Marshall. *REV:
E 28/4/94 p11; St 26/4/94 p13.*

94.67C *THE DANCING DERVISH* (Duol) F. Kinsey Peile.
GAIETY 23/4/94 mat perf.* <u>Viscount Hopemere</u> Lawrance
d'Orsay. <u>Ethel Macquay</u> Maud Hobson. *REV: St 26/4/94
p13.*

94.68 *A BUNCH OF VIOLETS* (P of Modern Life,4a) Sydney
Grundy [fnd on Octave Feuillet, *Montjoye*]. HAYMARKET
25/4/94-19/7/94; 8/10/94-3/11/94. 117 perf [w/S mat
exc 14/7, 13/10; add mat 16/5, 23/5, 30/5, 25/6, 4/7].*
<u>Sir Phillip Marchant</u> H.B. Tree; <u>Viscount Mount Sorrell</u>
Nutcombe Gould; <u>Hon Harold Inglis</u> C.M. Hallard; <u>Mark
Murgatroyd</u> Lionel Brough; <u>Jacob Schwartz</u> G.W. Anson/
Charles Allan; <u>Harker</u> E. Holman Clark; <u>Butler</u> Hay;
<u>Footmen</u> [J.] Montagu/Bert Thomas, Ferris; <u>Son of Toil</u>
John Willes. <u>Violet</u> Audrey Ford/Nancy Noel; <u>Mrs
Murgatroyd</u> Mrs H.B. Tree/Janette Steer; <u>Lady Marchant</u>
Lily Hanbury. <u>L & MGR</u> H.B. Tree; <u>Bom</u> W.H. Leverton;
<u>Sc</u> Walter Hann; <u>Sm</u> Shelton; <u>Mus dir</u> Carl Armbruster;
<u>Elect</u> E. Wingfield Bowles; <u>Bm & Sec</u> Frederick Harrison.
*REV: Ath 28/4/94 p550; E 28/4/94 p9, 13/10/94 p8; Sk
2/5/94 p8, 9/5/94 p65, 17/10/94 p623; SR 28/4/94 p444;
St 3/5/94 p13, 11/10/94 p12; Th 1/6/94 p324-6; Ti 26/*

4/94 p5; TW94 p118-26.

94.69 *PHILEMON AND BAUCIS* (O,2a) Charles Gounod.
DRURY LANE 26/4/94 mat perf.** Vulcan David Bispham;
Jupiter Charles Manners; Philemon Joseph O'Mara. Baucis Fanny Moody. L & MGR Augustus Harris; Cond Armando
Seppilli. *REV: St 3/5/94 p13; Ti 30/4/94 p12.*

94.70 *THE MASQUERADERS* (P,4a) H.A. Jones. ST. JAMES'S
28/4/94-30/7/94 [w/W, S mat 28/4-7/6 exc 28/4 2/5,
6/6, 4/7]; 10/11/94-22/12/94 [w/S mat 17/11-15/12;
add mat 21/11; mat only 22/12]. 139 perf.* David
Remon George Alexander/Arthur Royston/Leonard Boyne;
Sir Brice Skene Herbert Waring; Montagu Lushington
W.G. Elliott; Eddie Remon Henry V. Esmond; Lord Crandover Ian Robertson; Hon Percy Blanchflower A. Vane-
Tempest; Sir Winchmore Wills, M.D. Graeme Goring;
George Copeland Ben Webster/J.F. Cornish; Fancourt
Arthur Royston/F. Featherstone; Carter Guy Lane Coulson/F. Featherstone/Frank Dyall; Randall J.A. Bentham;
Rodney F. Kinsey Peile; Sharland Arthur Bromley-Davenport; Jimmy Stokes William H. Day/H.H. Vincent; Brinkler Alfred Holles; Thomson F.P. Loftus; Servant Theo
Stewart/Leslie Thompson/Frank Dyall/Edwards. Dulcie
Larondie Mrs Patrick Campbell/Evelyn Millard; Helen
Larondie Charlotte Granville; Charley Wisranger Irene
Vanbrugh; Lady Charles Reindean Beryl Faber; Lady
Crandover Mrs Edward Saker. L & MGR George Alexander;
Sc H.P. Hall; Furn Frank Giles & Co.; Pq William
Clarkson; Cost Mme Savage, Mme Purdue; Uniforms Sandon & Co.; Sm H.H. Vincent; Mus dir & Mus Walter
Slaughter; Bm Robert V. Shone. *REV: Ath 5/5/94 p590,
17/11/94 p685; E 5/5/94 p9, 4/8/94 p7, 17/11/94 p8;
Sk 2/5/94 p8, 9/5/94 p64, 106, 13/6/94 p361, 20/6/94
p420-1, 27/6/94 p480, 21/11/94 p202, 205; SR 5/5/94
p472, 17/11/94 p534-5; St 3/5/94 p13, 2/8/94 p10, 15/
11/94 p13; Th 1/6/94 p326-9; Ti 30/4/94 p12, 12/11/94
p14; TW94 p126-7, p127-36, p311-2.*

94.71 *AS YOU LIKE IT* (PastC,5a) William Shakespeare.
DALY'S 30/4/94-5/5/94. 8 perf [w/mat 2/5, 5/5].**
Duke Campbell Gollan; Frederick Thomas Bridgland;
Amiens Roland McQuarie; Jaques George Clarke; Lord/
Charles Hobart Bosworth; Le Beau Sydney Harcourt Her-

bert; <u>Oliver</u> John Dixon; <u>Orlando</u> John Craig; <u>Jacques</u>
Lloyd Lowndes; <u>Adam</u> William Farren; <u>Dennis</u> Rupert
Lister; <u>Touchstone</u> James Lewis; <u>Corin</u> Charles Leclercq; <u>Silvius</u> Alfred Hickman; <u>William</u> William Sampson. <u>Pages</u> Olive Barry, Florence Conron; <u>Hymen</u> Caroline Dagmar; <u>Celia</u> Sybil Carlisle; <u>Phoebe</u> Ida Molesworth; <u>Audrey</u> Catherine Lewis; <u>Rosalind</u> Ada Rehan.
<u>MGR</u> Augustin Daly; <u>Sc</u> Walter Hann, Bruce Smith; <u>Mus</u>
<u>& Cond</u> Henry Widmer; <u>Ch</u> R.M. Crompton; <u>Bom</u> John Farr-
ington, Edward Brown; <u>Cost</u> Harrisons; <u>Pq</u> William
Clarkson. *REV: E 5/5/94 p9; St 3/5/94 p14; Ti 2/5/94
p13, 7/5/94 p10.*

94.72 *KING KODAK* (MExt) Arthur Branscombe (lib) &
John Crook (mus) & Walter Slaughter (mus) & Edward
Solomon (mus) & Alfred Plumpton (mus) & Milton Wellings
(mus) & von der Fink (mus) & Lionel Monckton (mus).
TERRY'S 30/4/94-30/6/94. 62 perf [w/S mat exc 30/6].*
<u>James South</u> Edward Terry; <u>Dick Dashaway</u> Charles Dan-
by; <u>Admiral Sir William Broadsides, R.N.</u> George Gid-
dens/F.W. Trott/George Belmore; <u>M.T. Head</u> Compton
Coutts; <u>Hugh E. Foote</u> Huntley Wright; <u>Lord Deadbroke</u>
E.H. Kelly; <u>Lieut. Jack Broadsides, R.N.</u> George de
Pledge; <u>Harry Vernon</u> Jack Thompson; <u>Sgt. O'Flynn</u> F.W.
Trott/Greene Taylor; <u>Boleg Nula</u> W. Edwards. <u>Charlie</u>
<u>Broadsides</u> Ada Barry; <u>Hilda South</u> Violet Robinson/
Emelie Petrelli/Blanche Barnett; <u>Letitia Gushington</u>
Margaret Ayrtoun/Jessie Danvers; <u>Violet</u> Mabel Love;
<u>Lillie</u> Eva Levens; <u>Dora Nightingale</u> Lizzie Ruggles;
<u>Frankie Dashaway</u> Amy Saunders; <u>Millie Tarry</u> Blanche
Barnett/Marie Temple; <u>La Sifflaise</u> Errol Stanhope;
<u>Jennie Rossity</u> Violet Friend; <u>Eva Nescent</u> Marie Las-
celles; <u>Ella Gant</u> Irene du Foye; <u>Kitty Seabrooke</u> Kate
Vaughan/Maud Hill. <u>L & MGR</u> F.J. Harris, C.J. Abud;
<u>Ch</u> John d'Auban; <u>Sc</u> Walter Hann, E.G. Banks; <u>Cost</u> Miss
Fisher, Auguste, Alias, Harrison; <u>Props</u> Labhart; <u>Pq</u>
William Clarkson; <u>Pd</u> Thomas W. Charles; <u>Treas</u> H.T.
Brickwell; <u>Mus dir</u> John Crook; <u>Asm</u> R.H. Burnside. *REV:
E 5/5/94 p9; Sk 21/3/94 p437, 9/5/94 p65, 27/6/94 p459,
4/7/94 p511; St 3/5/94 p14; Ti 2/5/94 p13; TW94 p150-1.*

94.73 *PLOT AND PASSION* (D,3a) Tom Taylor. DALY'S 1/5/
94 mat perf.** <u>Fouché</u> Sydney Valentine; <u>Henri de Neu-</u>
<u>ville</u> Ernest Leicester; <u>Desmarets</u> J.G. Taylor; <u>Marquis</u>

de Cevennes Welton Dale; <u>Jabot</u> Wallace Douglas; <u>Gri-
bouille</u> F[rederic] Powell; <u>Berthier</u> Harold Mead.
<u>Cecile</u> Edith Lisle; <u>Marie de Fontanges</u> E. Oldcastle.
REV: E 5/5/94 p11.

94.74 *HER DEAREST FOE* (CD,4a) Henrietta Lindley [adpt
of Mrs Alexander's novel]. CRITERION 2/5/94 mat perf.*
<u>Col. Sir Hugh Galbraith</u> Frank Worthing; <u>Mjr.</u> Upton
Frank Atherley; <u>Robert Ford</u> Acton Bond; <u>Frank Reid</u>
A. Hamilton Revelle; <u>Adolphus Trapes</u> Sydney Valentine;
<u>Dr Slade</u> Charles Allan; <u>Edwards</u> C[harles] Terric.
<u>Lady Styles</u> Dolores Drummond; <u>Amy Leigh</u> Annie Webster;
<u>Mills</u> Mrs E.H. Brooke; <u>Mrs Travers</u> Henrietta Lindley.
<u>L & MGR</u> Charles Wyndham; <u>Dir</u> Henrietta Lindley; <u>Sm</u>
C. Edmonds; <u>Act mgr</u> E. Harvey. *REV: E 5/5/94 p9; St
3/5/94 p14.*

94.75 *ORFEO* (O[3a]) C.W. Gluck. DRURY LANE 3/5/94 mat
perf.** <u>Orfeo</u> Rose Olitzka; <u>Eros</u> Biancoli; <u>Eurydice</u>
Pauline Joran. <u>L & MGR</u> Augustus Harris; <u>Cond</u> Armando
Seppilli. *REV: St 10/5/94 p12; Ti 5/5/94 p8.*

94.76 *LA DAME AUX CAMELIAS* (P,5a) Alexandre Dumas.
PRINCE OF WALES'S 3/5/94 mat perf.** <u>Armand Duval</u>
Rothbury Evans; <u>Duval</u> J.S. Blythe; <u>Gaston Rieux</u>
Stuart Champion; <u>De Varville</u> Oswald Yorke; <u>Gustave</u>
Edgar Stevens. <u>Marguerite Gauthier</u> Anna Ruppert; <u>Nil-
chette</u> Ettie Williams; <u>Prudence</u> Catherine Stewart;
<u>Nanine</u> Earle; <u>Olympe</u> Olga Garland. *REV: E 12/5/94 p8;
Sk 16/5/94 p121; SR 12/5/94 p498.* <u>Comment</u>: Perfd in
English.

94.77 *A MELODRAMA*. TRAFALGAR [SQUARE]. 3/5/94 mat
perf.** <u>Hero</u> George Grossmith, jr; <u>Villian</u> Robb Har-
wood; <u>Faithful Servant</u> Douglas Munro; <u>Dog</u> Harem Jack;
<u>Detective</u> Herbert Sparling; <u>Child</u> A. Hurgon. <u>Heroine</u>
Letty Lind. <u>PP</u> Mr & Mrs Frank Wyatt; <u>Sm</u> F. Marchant,
Sydney Howard; <u>Mus dir</u> Carl Kiefert, Edward Jones,
[J.J.?] Ross, Alfred Carpenter; <u>Sec</u> E. Victor; <u>Treas</u>
H[orace] Cole; <u>Pq</u> William Clarkson; <u>Cost</u> Harrisons;
<u>Mgr</u> Arthur Blackmore; <u>Mus</u> Carl Kiefert.

94.78 *THE WILD DUCK* (P,5a) Henrik Ibsen. ROYALTY 4/5/
94-5/5/94. 3 perf [w/mat 5/5].* <u>Werle</u> George Warde;

Gregers Werle Charles J. Fulton; Old Ekdal Harding
Cox; Hialmar Ekdal W.L. Abingdon; Relling Laurence
Irving; Molvik Gilbert Trent; Graaberg Sydney Dark;
Petterson C.S. Skarratt; Jensen Charles Legassick;
Flor G. Armstrong; Balle Herbert Fletcher; Kaspersen
Herbert Maule. Gina Ekdal Mrs Herbert Waring; Hedvig
Winifred Fraser; Mrs Sorby Mrs Charles Creswick. DIR
J.T. Grein; L Kate Santley; Pd Herman de Lange; Mus
dir C.W. Lamartine; Furn Oetzmann; Pq William Clark-
son; Cost Morris Angel & Son; Act mgr Charles Hoppe.
*REV: Ath 12/5/94 p625; E 12/5/94 p11; Sk 9/5/94 p63;
St 10/5/94 p12-3; Th 1/6/94 p329-30; TW94 p136-43.*
Comment: Independent Theatre Society.

94.79 *DOMESTIC ECONOMY* (F,1a) Mark Lemon. TOOLE'S 5/5/
94-20/6/94. 44 perf [w/S mat exc 5/5, 12/5, 16/6].**
John Grumley J.L. Toole; Sgt. Tom Brown Herbert Pearson; Joey Master Alex Watson; Ginger Charles H. Brunton. Mrs Grumley Eliza Johnstone; Mrs Shackles Kate
Carlyon; Mrs Knagley Mary Brough; Peggy Brown Beaumont Loveday; Polly Lilly Earle. L & MGR J.L. Toole;
Sm John Billington; Mus dir William Robins; Bm George
Lee.

94.80 *LA SIGNORA DALLE CAMELIE [LA DAME AUX CAMELIAS]*
(D,5a) Alexandre Dumas, *fils*. DALY'S 7/5/94, 9/5,
11/5, 26/5(m), 30/5, 2/6(m), 4/6, 6/6, 11/6, 14/6/94.
10 perf.** Duval Cesare Rossi; Armando Duval Carlo
Rosaspina; Gaston de Rieux Napoleone Masi; Saint
Gaudens Antonio Colombari; Gustavo Luigi Galimberti;
Conte di Giray Paolo Cantinelli; Signor di Varville
Ferruccio Garavaglia; Dottore Ugo Piperno; Servo
Alfredo Geri; Portalettre Alfredo Sainati. Olimpia
Assunta Mezzanotte; Mme Duvernay Albertina Giordano
Pero; Ermina Ione Cristina; Nanetta Ines Cristina;
Margherita Eleonora Duse. PP & MGR Augustin Daly; Furn
Oetzmann; Bom Edward Brown; Bm John Farrington. *REV:
Ath 12/5/94 p624; E 12/5/94 p9; Th 1/6/94 p331-2; Ti
8/5/94 p10; TW94 p143-7.*

94.81 *A SILVER HONEYMOON* (DC) "Richard Henry" [Richard
Butler & H. Chance Newton]. TRAFALGAR 8/5/94-20/7/94.
64 perf.* Mathew Brumby Arthur Playfair; Rawstone
H.G. Dupres; Jim Edgar Stevens. Martha Hilda Glenn;

Lilian Maggie Roberts; Tadger Adelaide Astor. PP Mr
& Mrs Frank Wyatt; Mgr Arthur Blackmore; Treas Horace
Cole; Sm Frank Parker; Mus dir Carl Kiefert. REV: E
12/5/94 p9.

94.82 *A SOCIETY BUTTERFLY* (C of Modern Life,4a) Robert
Buchanan & Henry Murray. OPERA COMIQUE 10/5/94-22/2/94.
38 perf.* Charles Dudley William Herbert; Dr Coppee
Allan Beaumont; Cpt. Belton Fred Kerr; Lord Augustus
Leith Edward Rose; Mjr. Craigelder Henry J. Carvill;
Lord Ventnor Sydney Jerram; Herr Max H. Templeton;
Bangle Charles R. Stuart; Duchess of Newhaven Rose Le-
clercq; Lady Milwood Walsingham; Hon Mrs Stanley Lyd-
die Morand; Mrs Courtlandt Parke E. Brinsley Sheridan;
Miss Staten Ethel Norton; Rose Eva Williams; Marsh
Eva Vernon; Mrs Dudley Mrs Langtry. Characters in the
Intermezzo: Pans Fred Kerr. Hera Walsingham; Pallas
Lyddie Morand; Aenone Gladys Evisson; Aphrodite Mrs
Langtry. L S. & F. Fowler; Sc E.G. Banks; Cost dgn
Karl; Cost Nathan; Mus F.W. Allwood; Sm William Sidney;
Sec John Phipps; Bm Frederick Stanley. REV: Ath 19/5/
94 p655-6; E 12/5/94 p9; Sk 16/5/94 p116-7, 23/5/94
p209-10, 213, 20/6/94 p424; St 17/5/94 p13; Th 1/6/94
p332-4; Ti 11/5/94 p5; TW94 p147-50.

94.83 *GENTLE IVY* (P,4a) "Austin Fryers" [W.E. Clery].
STRAND 10/5/94 mat perf.* Lord Hartland Alfred B.
Cross; Hon Stuart Plowden Stanley Pringle; Lord Ruis-
lip H.A. Saintsbury; Hon Tom Bucklaw Rowland Atwood;
Job Polwyl Leonard Calvert; Rev Stephen Trefelyn Or-
lando Barnett. Ernie Bower Valli Valli; Mrs Polwyl
Susie Vaughan; Countess of Eglin Mrs Theodore Wright;
Lady Gwendoline Rose Nesbitt; Lady Adelaide Kate Beal-
by; Mrs Trefelyn Charlotte E. Morland; Miss Trefelyn
Mrs Gordon-Ascher; Ivy Bower Frances Ivor. DIR Fran-
cis Gosnay. REV: E 12/5/94 p11; St 17/5/94 p13-4.

94.84 *A LOVE LETTER* (DD,1a) Mrs E. Argent-Lonergau.
STRAND 10/5/94 mat perf.* Cpt Damborough Graham Went-
worth; John Vincent Flexmore. Lady Torchester Mary
Stuart; Hetty Clara Greet; Nurse Edith Ethel Selwyn.
REV: E 12/5/94 p11; St 17/5/94 p14.

94.85 *THE TWO ORPHANS* (D,5a) John Oxenford [adpt of

Adolphe d'Ennery & Cormon, *Les Deux Orphelines*]. ADEL-
PHI 12/5/94-18/6/94. 32 perf. 1st perfd Olympic 14/9/
74. <u>Count de Liniere</u> Herbert Flemming; <u>Marquis de
Presles</u> Lyston Lyle/Herbert Budd; <u>Armand</u> Ernest
Leicester; <u>Jacques</u> William Rignold; <u>Pierre</u> Charles
Cartwright; <u>Doctor</u> W[illiam] Cheesman; <u>Picard</u> David
S. James; <u>Martin</u> W. Northcote; <u>La Fleur</u> J[ohn] North-
cote; <u>Marais</u> Herbert Budd [or Hugh Dorington]; <u>Count
de Mailly</u> V. Everard; <u>Marquis d'Estrees</u> R. Norton [or
R. Strickland]; <u>Charlotte</u> R. Collins; <u>Jacquot</u> Nesbitt.
<u>Countess de Liniere</u> Alice Lingard; <u>Louise</u> Marion
Terry; <u>Henriette</u> Ellis Jeffreys; <u>La Frochard</u> Dolores
Drummond; <u>Marianne</u> Edith Cole; <u>Genevieve</u> Harrietta
Polini; <u>Florette</u> Alma Stanley; <u>Cora</u> Ailsa Craig. PP
A. & S. Gatti; <u>Dir</u> Charles Cartwright; <u>Ch</u> Henri De-
winne; <u>Mus & Mus dir</u> Edward Jones; <u>Bom</u> Arthur Frye;
<u>Bm & Treas</u> G.M. Polini; <u>Sm</u> Herbert Budd. *REV: Ath 19/
5/94 p655; E 19/5/94 p9; Sk 23/5/94 p209; St 17/5/94
p13; Th 1/6/94 p334-6; Ti 14/5/94 p10; TW94 p154-5.*

94.86 *JEAN MAYEUX* (Mimodrama,3a) Blanchard de la Bre-
têche & Charles Thony (mus). PRINCESS'S 12/5/94-19/5/
94. 7 perf.* <u>Jean Mayeux</u> Ed Vallot; <u>Alphonse</u> Jordan-
is; <u>Le Beau Leon</u> Depreter; <u>Robert Tissot</u> René Dubois;
<u>Marquis de la Lillière</u> Perrin; <u>Rouquin</u> Verdavainne;
<u>Auguste</u> Dechambre; <u>Baptiste</u> Moreau; <u>Superintendent of
Police</u> Deau; <u>Municipal Guard</u> Gaspard; <u>Rag Picker</u> Bord;
<u>M de St. Joyeuse</u> Gabriel; <u>Vicomte</u> Lalou; <u>M de Franes</u>
Denertis. <u>Chenille</u> Desiré; <u>Marquise de la Lillière</u>
Sandre; <u>Gadiche</u> Bignon; <u>Jeanne de la Lillière</u> Sergine;
<u>L'Ogress</u> Coltereau; <u>Caravane</u> Delorme; <u>Mlle Duchemin</u>
Valery; <u>Girodine</u> Fontaine; <u>La Grelee</u> Raspail; <u>La
Grande Lisa</u> Durand; <u>Mlle de Caravel</u> Breval; <u>Mlle de
Frasnes</u> Deschamps; <u>Mlle Lea de Guisnee</u> Guyonnet. PP
Mrs Harriett Gooch; <u>Cond</u> Charles Thony; <u>Sc</u> [Robert?]
Caney; <u>Pq</u> William Clarkson; <u>Mach</u> J.W. Cawdery; <u>Regiss-
eur</u> Depreter; <u>Bom</u> [E.J.] Ottley. *REV: Ath 19/5/94
p655; E 19/5/94 p9; Sk 23/5/94 p209; SR 19/5/94 p523;
St 17/5/94 p13; Th 1/6/94 p336-7; Ti 14/5/94 p10;
TW94 p153-4.*

94.87 *THE MAN IN THE STREET* (P,1a) Louis N. Parker.
STRAND 14/5/94-7/7/94. 48 perf.* <u>Jabez Gover</u> James
A. Welch; <u>Philip Adare</u> George R. Foss. <u>Minnie Adare</u>

Winifred Fraser. MGR C.T.H. Helmsley; Sm George R.
Foss. *REV: E 19/5/94 p11; St 17/5/94 p14; Ti 15/5/94
p3; TW94 p155.*

94.88 *MANON LESCAUT* (O[4a]) Giacomo Puccini. COVENT
GARDEN 14/5/94, 21/5/94. 2 perf. 1st perfd Teatro
Regio, Turin 1/2/93. Lescaut Antonio Pini-Corsi;
Des Grieux Umberto Beduschi; Geronte Vittorio Arimondi; Maestro di Ballo/Lampionajo M. Armandi; L'Oste/
Comandante di Marina Villani; Sgt degh Arcieri Antonio
de Vaschetti; Edmondo Pelagalli-Rosetti. Manon Lescaut
Olga Olghina; Il Musico Aurelia Kitzu. L & MGR Augustus Harris; Cond Armando Seppilli; Bom E. Hall; A act
mgr Neil Forsyth. *REV: Ath 19/5/94 p654-5; E 19/5/94
p8; SR 19/5/94 p525; St 17/5/94 p12-3; Ti 15/5/94 p3.*

94.89 *FAUST* (O[5a]) Charles Gounod. COVENT GARDEN 15/
5/94, 25/5, 2/6, 6/6, 18/6, 29/6, 10/7, 28/7/94. 8
perf.** Mephistopheles Pol Plançon/Edouard de Reske;
Valentine Henri Albers/Mario Ancona/Max Bouvet; Wagner Antonio de Vaschetti/Villani; Faust Emile Cossira/
Fernando de Lucia/Albert Alvarez/Jean de Reske. Márta
Mathilde Bauermeister; Marguerite Manette Simmonet/
Nuovina/Nellie Melba/Emma Eames; Siebel Pauline Joran/
Norcrosse/Giulia Ravogli. L & MGR, Bom, A act mgr as
for 94.88; Cond Enrico Bevignani. *REV: Ath 19/5/94
p655, 9/6/94 p750; E 19/5/94 p15, 2/6/94 p15, 9/6/94
p15; St 17/5/94 p13, 31/5/94 p10, 7/6/94 p12, 21/6/94
p13; Ti 17/5/94 p10, 28/5/94 p13, 4/6/94 p11.*

94.90 *ORFEO* ()[3a]) C.W. Gluck. COVENT GARDEN 16/5/94,
20/6, 26/7/94. 3 perf.** Orfeo Guilia Ravogli; Euridice Sofia Ravogli; L'Amore Mathilde Bauermeister.
L & MGR, Bom, A act mgr as for 94.88; Cond Enrico
Bevignani. *REV: E 19/5/94 p15; St 24/5/94 p12; Ti 17/
5/94 p10.*

94.91 *CAVALLERIA RUSTICANA* (O[1a]) Pietro Mascagni.
COVENT GARDEN 16/5/94, 22/5, 26/5, 30/5, 4/6, 12/6,
22/6, 11/7/94. 8 perf.** Turiddu Fernando de Lucia/
Morello/Joseph O'Mara; Alfio Mario Ancona/Eugene Du-
friche/David Bispham/P. Maggi. Santuzza Emma Calvé;
Lucia Mathilde Bauermeister; Lola Pauline Joran/Guilia
Ravogli. L & MGR, Bom, A act mgr as for 94.88; Cond

Luigi Mancinelli/Enrico Bevignani. *REV: E 19/5/94 p15;*
St 24/5/94 p12; Ti 17/5/94 p10.

94.92 *FACCIAMO DIVORZIO* [*DIVORCONS*] Victorien Sardou
& Emile de Najac. DALY'S 16/5/94, 17/5, 19/5, 21/5/94.
4 perf.** Clavignac Ferrucio Garavaglia; Des Prunelles
Carlo Rosaspina; Ademaro Napoleone Masi; Bafourdin
Paolo Cantinelli; Commissario di Polizia Antonio Co-
lombari; Bastiano Alfredo Sainati; Guiseppe Maggior-
domo Ugo Piperno; Primo Cameriere Luigi Galimberti;
Secondo Cameriere Alfredo Geri. Cyprienne Eleonora
Duse; Signora di Brionne Caterina Bella; Signora di
Valfontaine Assunta Mezzanotte; Signora di Lusignan
Albertina Giordano Pero; Guiseppina Ines Cristina.
L & MGR Augustin Daly; Furn Oeztmann; Mus dir Thomas
Smythe; Bom Edward Brown; Bm John Farrington. *REV: E*
19/5/94 p11; Sk 23/5/94 p209; SR 19/5/94 p523-4; St
24/5/94 p13; TW94 p151-3.

94.93 *MARRIAGE* (P,3a) Brandon Thomas & Henry Keeling.
COURT 17/5/94-14/7/94. 51 perf [mat only 14/7].**
Sir Charles Jenks Mackintosh; Sir John Belton, Bart
Sydney Brough; Hon Dudley Chumbleigh C.P. Little;
Quayle H[enry?] Hudson. Lady Belton Lena Ashwell; Hon
Mrs Dudley Chumbleigh Gertrude Kingston. L & MGR Ar-
thur Chudleigh; Act mgr Leonard Lillies; Bm S. Gray;
Cond Ernest Crooke; Furn Hampton & Sons, Lyons; Pq
C.H. Fox; Sc J. England, W[illiam] Callcott, T.W. Hall.
REV: Ath 26/5/94 p687; E 19/5/94 p11; Sk 23/5/94 p171,
30/5/94 p266, 269; SR 26/5/94 p554; St 24/5/94 p13;
Th 1/7/94 p30-1; Ti 18/5/94 p4; TW94 p155-8.

94.94 *THE CAPE MAIL* (D,1a) Clement Scott [adpt of
Jeanne qui pleure et Jeanne qui rit]. COURT 17/5/94-
14/7/94. 51 perf [mat only 14/7]. 1st perfd Prince
of Wales's, Liverpool 23/9/81. Cpt. Surgeon Hugh Travers Wilfred Draycott; Mr Quicke Sant Matthews; Bar-
tle W.H. Quinton. Mrs Preston Carlotta Addison; Mrs
Frank Preston Vane Featherston; Mary Preston Maude
Abbot; Mason Lilian Lee. L & MGR, Act mgr, Bm, Cond,
Furn, Pq as for 94.93; Sc T.W. Hall. *REV: Ath, E as*
for 94.93.

94.95 *PHILEMON ET BAUCIS* (O[2a]) Charles Gounod, COV-

ENT GARDEN 17/5/94, 22/5, 26/6, 5/7/94. 4 perf.**
Jupiter Pol Plançon/Max Bouvet; Philemon Charles Bon-
nard; Vulcan Armand Castelmary. Baucis Simmonet/Sig-
rid Arnoldson. L & MGR Augustus Harris; Cond Enrico
Bevignani; Bom E. Hall; A act mgr Neil Forsyth. *REV:
E 19/5/94 p15; St 24/5/94 p12; Ti 19/5/94 p9.*

94.96 *PAGLIACCI* (O[2a]) Ruggiero Leoncavallo. COVENT
GARDEN 17/5/94, 26/5, 30/5, 4/6, 12/6, 22/6, 6/7,
11/7/94. 8 perf.** Canio Fernando de Lucia/Charles
Bonnard/Philip Brozel; Tonio Mario Ancona/Eugene Du-
friche; Silvio Richard Green; Beppe Charles Bonnard/
Iginio Corsi. Nedda Sigrid Arnoldson/Lucille Hill/
Nellie Melba. L & MGR, Bom, A act mgr as for 94.95;
Cond Enrico Bevignani/Luigi Mancinelli. *REV: E 19/5/
94 p15, 28/7/94 p15; SR 28/7/94 p97-8; Ti 19/5/94 p9.*

94.97 *CARMEN* (O[4a]) Georges Bizet. COVENT GARDEN 18/
5/94, 24/5, 28/5, 8/6, 14/6, 2/7/94. 6 perf.** Don
José Emile Cossira/Albert Alvarez; Escamillo Henri
Albers; Dancairo Iginio Corsi/Charles Gilibert;
Remendado Rinaldini; Zuniga Villani. Carmen Emma
Calvé; Michaela Manette Simmonet/Florence Monteith;
Frasquita Mathilde Bauermeister; Mercedes Pauline
Joran/Cecile Brani; 1ere Danseuse Vanda Adler. L &
MGR, Bom, A act mgr, Cond as for 94.95. *REV: St 24/
5/94 p12; Ti 19/5/94 p9.*

94.98 *FALSTAFF* (O[3a]) Giuseppe Verdi. COVENT GARDEN
19/5/94, 23/5, 29/5, 1/6, 7/6, 16/6, 28/6, 9/7/94.
8 perf. 1st perfd Teatro alla Scala, Milan 9/2/93.
Fenton Umberto Beduschi; Ford Antonio Pini-Corsi;
Dr Caius M. Armandi; Bardolph Pelagalli-Rosetti; Pis-
tol Vittorio Arimondi; Falstaff Arturo Passina. Anne
Olga Olghina; Mistress Ford E. Zilli; Mistress Page
Aurelia Kitzu; Dame Quickly Giulia Ravogli. L & MGR,
Bom, A act mgr as for 94.95; Cond Luigi Mancinelli.
*REV: Ath 26/5/94 p686-7; E 26/5/94 p8; Sk 30/5/94
p232-3; SR 26/5/94 p552-3; St 24/5/94 p12-3; Ti 21/5/
94 p7, 2/6/94 p13.*

94.99 *MONEY* (C,5a) Edward Bulwer Lytton. GARRICK 19/
5/94-20/7/94; 27/10/94-22/12/94. 107 perf [w/mat 2/6,
9/6, 16/6, 23/6; mat only 5/12, 12/12, 22/12].**

Sir John Vesey John Hare/Charles Rock; Lord Glossmore
Arthur Bourchier; Sir Frederick Blount E. Allan
Aynesworth; Stout Henry Kemble/Charles Groves; Graves
Arthur Cecil; Evelyn Johnston Forbes-Robertson; Cpt.
Dudley Smooth Charles H.E. Brookfield; Old Member
Gilbert Hare/F. Percival Stevens/Gerald Paxton; Mr
Sharp Charles Rock; Toke Gerald du Maurier/Gilbert
Trent; Servant Albert Sims. Lady Franklin Mrs S.B.
Bancroft; Georgina Maude Millett; Clara Kate Rorke.
L & MGR John Hare; Sc William Harford, Walter John-
stone; Furn David L. Isaacs; Cond Andrew Levey; Asm
Henry Montague; Act mgr C.G. Compton. *REV: Ath 26/5/
94 p 687; E 26/5/94 p9, 3/11/94 p11; Sk 30/5/94 p259,
7/11/94 p63; SR 26/5/94 p554-5; St 24/5/94 p13, 1/11/
94 p13; Th 1/7/94 p32-3; Ti 21/5/94 p7, 29/10/94 p12;
TW94 p158-60.*

94.100 *THE NE'ER-DO-WELL* (D,1a) Sydney Bowkett. STRAND
22/5/94 mat perf.* Matthew Brenford Sydney Bowkett;
Alfred Dunscombe Robert Loraine; Rev Cyril Silver-
stone Ernest Percy. Clara Horton Maggie Roberts; Mary
May Fellowes; Madge Brenford Ray Pozner. *REV: E 26/
5/94 p11.*

94.101 *TIME, HUNGER AND THE LAW* (P,1a) Laurence B.
Irving. CRITERION 24/5/94 mat perf.* Ivan Ivanovitch
Saradoob Cyril Maude; Vasili Ivanovitch H.B. Irving;
Dimitri Konstantinovitch Laurence Irving; Grigori
Grigorivitch Cecil Ramsey; Misha T[om] Hesslewood;
Nikolai Innes; Peasants Anning, Hoole, [W?] Marion,
Davis; Policemen Taylor, Sullivan. Anna Ivanova
Dolores Drummond; Katyer Isa Bowman. L & MGR Charles
Wyndham; Mus Alfred J. Caldicott; Cost Nathan; Pq
William Clarkson; Act mgr E. Harvey. *REV: E 26/5/94
p11; St 31/5/94 p10; Ti 25/5/94 p12.*

94.102 *THE SUPER* (P,1a) Arthur M. Heathcote. CRITERION
24/5/94 mat perf.* Christopher Tweddle Arthur M.
Heathcote; Kenneth Adare Roy Horniman. Mrs Avery Mrs
Edmund Phelps. L & MGR, Act mgr as for 94.101. *REV:
E 26/5/94 p11.*

94.103 *CARMEN* (O[4a]) Georges Bizet. DRURY LANE 25/5/
94 mat perf.** Don José Bates Maddison; Escamillo

F. Stuart Hyatt; Zuniga C[harles] Hinchliff; Morales
W[illiam] Paull. Carmen Marie Alexander; Michaela
Jessie Bradford. L & MGR Augustus Harris. *REV: 2/6/
94 p7.*

94.104 *THE DANCING DERVISH* (Duol) F. Kinsey Peile.
LYRIC 29/5/94 mat perf.** Lord Hopemere Lawrance
d'Orsay. Ethel Macquay Maud Hobson; Maud Florence
Rooke. L & MGR Horace Sedger; Act mgr William Greet.
REV: E 2/6/94 p8; St 31/5/94 p10.

94.105 *THE CANDIDATE* (C,3a) Justin Huntly McCarthy
[adpt of Alexandre Bisson, *La Deputê de Bombignac*].
CRITERION 30/5/94-14/8/94. 73 perf [w/S mat exc 21/7,
28/7, 4/8, 11/8]. 1st perfd Royalty 2/3/88. Lord
Oldacre Charles Wyndham/Charles H. Hawtrey; Alaric
Baffin George Giddens; Barnabas Goodeve William
Blakeley; Amos Martlett C.W. Somerset; Cpt. Hazlefoot
Frank Worthing; Jacobs Markham. Dowager Countess
Osterley Fanny Coleman; Lady Oldacre Miriam Clements;
Mrs Amos Martlett Pattie Browne; Lady Dorothy Oster-
ley Mary Moore/Annie Hughes. L & MGR Charles Wyndham;
Act mgr & Treas E. Harvey; Cost Fenwick, Alice Riley,
Mme Eroom. *REV: E 2/6/94 p8; Sk 1/8/94 p42; St 7/6/
94 p12-3; Th 1/7/94 p33-4; Ti 31/5/94 p10; TW94 p166-
70.*

94.106 *LES HUGUENOTS* (O[5a]) Giacomo Meyerbeer. COVENT
GARDEN 31/5/94. 1 perf.** De Cosse/Huguenot Soldier
Iginio Corsi; Marcello Pol Plançon; Conte di San Bris
Eugene Dufriche; Conte di Nevers Henri Albers; Raoul
di Nangis Emile Cossira; Tavannes Rinaldini; De Retz
Antonio de Vaschetti; Maurevert Villani. Valentina
Ada Adini; Urbano Rose Olitzka; Dama d'Onore Mathilde
Bauermeister; Marguerite di Valois Manetta Simmonet;
lere Danseuses Palladino, Vanda Adler. L & MGR Augus-
tus Harris; Cond Enrico Bevignani; Bom E. Hall; A act
mgr Neil Forsyth. *REV: Ath 9/6/94 p750; E 2/6/94
p15; SR 9/6/94 p613; St 7/6/94 p12; Ti 2/6/94 p19.*

94.107 *LA LOCANDIERA* (C,3a) Carlo Goldoni. DALY'S
31/5/94, 7-8/6, 9/6(m), 12/6, 13/6/94(2). 7 perf.**
Marchese di Forlimpopli Cesare Rossi; Fabrizio Napoleone Masi; Cavaliere di Ripafratta Carlo Rosaspina;

Conte d'Albaflorita Paolo Cantinelli; Servo Alfredo
Sainati. Mirandolina Locandiera Eleonora Duse. L &
MGR Augustin Daly; Furn Oetzmann; Mus dir Thomas
Smythe; Bom Edward Brown; Bm John Farrington. *REV:*
E 26/5/94 p9; Sk 30/5/94 p259; SR 26/5/94 p555; St
31/5/94 p10.

94.108 *CAVALLERIA RUSTICANA* (D,1a) Giovanni Verga.
DALY'S 31/5/94, 7-8/6, 9/6(m), 12/6, 13/6/94(2). 7
perf.** Alfio Cesare Rossi; Turiddu Carlo Rosaspina;
Zio Antonio Colobari. Santuzza Eleonora Duse; Lola
Assunta Mezzanotte; Nunzia Albertina Giordano Pero;
Camilla Caterina Bella; La Zia Filomena Cesira Cris-
tina; Pipuzza Ines Cristina. L & MGR, Furn, Mus dir,
Bom, Bm as for 94.107. *REV: E 26/5/94 p9; Sk 30/5/94*
p259; SR 26/5/94 p555; St 31/5/94 p10; TW94 p160-6.

94.109 *LUCIA DI LAMMERMOOR* (O[3a]) Gaetano Donizetti.
COVENT GARDEN 5/6/94. 1 perf.** Enrico Eugene Du-
friche; Raimondo Antonio de Vaschetti; Arturo Iginio
Corsi; Normano Rinaldini; Edgardo Umberto Beduschi.
Lucia Nellie Melba; Alice Mathilde Bauermeister.
L & MGR Augustus Harris; Cond Luigi Mancinelli; Bom
E. Hall; A act mgr Neil Forsyth. *REV: St 7/6/94 p12;*
Ti 11/6/94 p8.

94.110 *MRS HILARY REGRETS* (Ca) S. Theyre Smith. CRI-
TERION 5/6/94, 14/6/94. 2 mat perf.** Dr Power
Charles Wyndham. Mrs Hilary Mary Moore. L & MGR
Charles Wyndham. *REV: E 9/6/94 p11, 16/6/94 p11; St*
21/6/94 p13.

94.111 *THE BALLAD-MONGER* (RP,1a) Walter H. Pollock
& Walter Besant [adpt of Theodore de Banville, *Grin-*
goire]. CRITERION 5/6/94 mat perf.** Gringoire
H.B. Tree; Louis XI Charles H.E. Brookfield; Olivier
le Dain Charles Allan; Simon Fourniez E. Holman Clark.
Loyse Mrs H.B. Tree; Nicole Mrs E.H. Brooke. L & MGR
Charles Wyndham. *REV: E 9/6/94 p11.*

94.112 *FASHIONABLE INTELLIGENCE* (Ca) Percy Fendall.
CRITERION 5/6/94 mat perf.** [Mr Egerton] Charles
H.E. Brookfield. [Mrs Fitz Adam] Lottie Venne. L &
MGR Charles Wyndham. *REV: 9/6/94 p11.*

94.113 *JOURNEYS END IN LOVERS MEETING* (Proverb,1a)
"John Oliver Hobbes" [Mrs P.M.T. Craigie] & George
Moore. DALY'S 5/6/94 mat perf.* Sir Philip Soupise
Johnston Forbes-Robertson; Cpt. Manamour William
Terriss. Lady Soupise Ellen Terry. PP & MGR Augustin
Daly; Bom Edward Brown; Bm John Farrington. *REV: E
9/6/94 p11; St 7/6/94 p13; Th 1/7/94 p34-6; TW94
p170-4.*

94.114 *THE BLACKMAILERS* (P,4a) John Gray & Andre
Raffalovitch. PRINCE OF WALES'S 7/6/94 mat perf.*
Admiral Sir Felbert Dangar Julian Cross; Mr Dangar
Felbert C[harles] Colnaghi; Edward Bond-Hinton A.
Bromley-Davenport; Guy Joscelyn Harry Eversfield;
Claud Price W.L. Abingdon; Servant to Hal Dangar
Frank Weathersby; Servant to the Bond-Hintons E. Bell-
enden; Hyacinth Halford Dangar Charles Thursby. Lady
Felbert Emily Miller; Hon Miss Alcyra Felbert Mary
Callan; Mrs Dangar Mrs Theodore Wright; Violet Bond-
Hinton M.T. Brunton; Susan Henrietta Cross; Camilla
Bond-Hinton Olga Brandon. PP Edgar Bruce; Bm Harring-
ton Baily; Dir Julian Cross; Furn W.F. Lyons; Pq Fox.
*REV: E 9/6/94 p11; Sk 13/6/94 p343; St 14/6/94 p13;
Th 1/7/94 p37-8; Ti 8/6/94 p8.*

94.115 *RIGOLETTO* (O[3a]) Giuseppe Verdi. COVENT GAR-
DEN 9/6/94, 21/6, 24/7/94. 3 perf.** Il Duca Fer-
nando de Lucia; Sparafucile Armand Castelmary;
Marullo Rinaldini; Monterone Antonio de Vaschetti;
Borsa Iginio Corsi; Conti di Ceprano Villani; Rigo-
letto Mario Ancona/Eugene Dufriche. Gilda Nellie
Melba; Giovanna Mathilde Bauermeister; Maddalena
Giulia Ravogli. L & MGR Augustus Harris; Cond Enrico
Bevignani; Bom E. Hall; A act mgr Neil Forsyth. *REV:
Ath 16/6/94 p782; E 16/6/94 p7; St 14/6/94 p12; Ti
11/6/94 p8.*

94.116 *WERTHER* (O[4a]) Jules Massenet. COVENT GARDEN
11/6/94, 23/6/94. 2 perf. 1st perfd Opernhaus,
Vienna 16/2/92. Werther Jean de Reszke; Albert Henri
Albers; Le Baili Armand Castelmary; Schmidt Iginio
Corsi; Johann Antonio de Vaschetti. Charlotte Emma
Eames; Sophie Sigrid Arnoldson. L & MGR, Bom, A act
mgr as for 94.115; Cond Luigi Mancinelli. *REV: Ath*

16/6/94 p782; E 16/6/94 p7; SR 16/6/94 p635-6; St
14/6/94 p12-3; Ti 12/6/94 p8.

94.117 *ROMEO ET JULIETTE* (O[5a]) Charles Gounod.
COVENT GARDEN 13/6/94, 19/6, 25/6, 3/7, 14/7, 20/7,
27/7/94. 7 perf.** Romeo Jean de Reszke; Capulet
Pol Plançon/Charles Gilibert; Mercutio Henri Albers;
Duc de Verone Armand Castelmary; Tybalt Charles Bonnard; Frère Laurent Edouard de Reske; Gregorio Antonio de Vaschetti; Benvoglio Rinaldini. Juliette Nellie
Melba; Gertrude Mathilde Bauermeister; Stephano
Lucille Hill/Carla Dagmar. L & MGR, Bom, A act mgr
as for 94.115; Cond Luigi Mancinelli. *REV: Ath 16/6/*
94 p782; E 16/6/94 p7; Sk 4/7/94 p529; SR 21/7/94
p72; Ti 16/6/94 p14.

94.118 *CHERRY HALL* (P,3a) Forbes Dawson. AVENUE 14/6/
94 mat perf.* Mr Trevor Charles Glenney; Lord Baynton, M.F.H. J.A. Rosier; Lord Elgar W.L. Abingdon;
Dr Taylor Gilbert Trent; Cpt. Porter J. Barker; Walter Stockson Lawrance d'Orsay; Jack Stockson Compton
Coutts; Michael James A. Warden; Reed E. Story Gofton; Footman W.H. Barratt. Lady Baynton Mrs Bennett;
Miss Metcalf Ettie Williams; Mrs Taylor Marjorie
Christmas; Mabel Vander Dora Baston; Maid Agnes Russell. *REV: Ath 30/6/94 p848; E 16/6/94 p11; St 21/6/*
94 p14.

94.119 *SIXES AND SEVENS* (Duol) E.H. Whitmore. CRITER-
ION 14/6/94 mat perf.* Cpt. George Hope Arthur Bourchier. Edith Cashdown Irene Vanbrugh. L & MGR Charles
Wyndham; Act mgr E. Harvey. *REV: E 16/6/94 p11; St*
21/6/94 p13.

94.120 *LOHENGRIN* (O[3a]) Richard Wagner. COVENT GARDEN
15/6/94, 27/6, 12/7, 23/7/94. 4 perf.** Lohengrin
Jean de Reszke; Enrico l'Uccellatore Edouard de Reszke;
Federico di Telramondo Mario Ancona/Arturo Pessina;
Araldo del Re Antonio de Vaschetti/Waldmann/Charles
Gilibert. Elsa di Brabante Nellie Melba/Emma Eames;
Ortruda Giulia Ravogli/Rose Olitzka. L & MGR Augustus
Harris; Cond Luigi Mancinelli; Bom E. Hall; A act mgr
Neil Forsyth. *REV: Ath 23/6/94 p814-5; E 23/6/94 p15,*
28/7/94 p15; SR 23/6/94 p661; St 21/6/94 p13; Ti 16/

6/94 p14.

94.121 *DULVERY DOTTY* (F,1a) Mrs Adams-Acton. TERRY'S
15/6/94-30/6/94. 14 perf. 1st prof. <u>Mr   Sandbird</u>
George Belmore; <u>Mr Joshua Sandbird</u> E.H. Kelly; <u>Mr</u>
<u>Quintin Westbrook</u> Huntley Wright. <u>Mrs Sandbird</u> Jessie
Danvers; <u>Polly Sandbird</u> Blanche Barnett; <u>Vera West-</u>
<u>brook</u> Lizzie Ruggles; <u>Susie</u> Eva Levens. L & MGR F.J.
Harris; <u>Pp</u> Edward Terry; <u>Treas</u> H.T. Brickwell; <u>Mus</u>
<u>dir</u> John Crook; <u>Asm</u> R.H. Burnside. *REV: E 23/6/94*
p11; St 21/6/94 p14.

94.122 *THE MIDDLEMAN* (P,4a) H.A. Jones. COMEDY 16/6/
94-23/6/94. 8 perf [w/mat 23/6].** <u>Sir Seaton Umfra-</u>
<u>ville</u> Bassett Roe; <u>Joseph Chandler</u> Royce Carleton;
<u>Cpt. Julian Chandler</u> W.T. Lovell; <u>Batty Todd</u> H[arry]
Cane; <u>Cyrus Blenkarn</u> E.S. Willard; <u>Jesse Pegg</u> F.H.
Tyler; <u>Dancer</u> F. Maxwell; <u>Epiphany Danks</u> Cecil Crof-
ton; <u>Mr Vachel</u> Thomas Sidney; <u>Dutton</u> C. Moore. <u>Lady</u>
<u>Umfraville</u> Mrs George Canninge; <u>Felicia Umfraville</u>
Violet Armbruster; <u>Mrs Chandler</u> Mrs H[arry] Cane;
<u>Maud Chandler</u> Keith Wakeman; <u>Mary Blenkarn</u> Agnes
Verity; <u>Nancy Blenkarn</u> Nannie Craddock. L & MGR J.W.
Comyns Carr; <u>Sm</u> T[homas] Sidney; <u>Bm</u> W.H. Griffiths;
<u>Bom</u> Scarisbrick; <u>Mus dir</u> J. Hamilton Clarke. *REV: Ath*
23/6/94 p816; E 23/6/94 p11; Sk 20/6/94 p400; SR 23/
6/94 p665-6; St 21/6/94 p13; Th 1/8/94 p67-9; Ti 18/
6/94 p8; TW94 p175-6.

94.123 *WALKER, LONDON* (C,3a) J.M. Barrie. TOOLE'S
16/6/94(m), 23/6(m), 29-30/6/94. 4 perf.**

94.124 *IZEYL* (Verse D,4a) Armand Sylvestre & Eugene
Morand & Gabriel Pierné (mus). DALY'S 18/6/94-26/6/94,
27/6(m), 5-6/7, 9-10/7, 12/7, 14/7(m), 16/7, 20/7,
21/7/94(m). 17 perf [add mat 26/6]. 1st perfd Renaissance, Paris 24/1/94. <u>Le Prince</u> Lucien-Germain Guitry; <u>Le Yoghi</u> de Max; <u>Scyndia</u> Deneubourg; <u>Le Tukkut-</u>
<u>tuti</u> Henri Deschamps; <u>Un Roi Vaincu</u> Montigny; <u>Un</u>
<u>Tisseur d'Etoffes</u> Angelo; <u>Un Mineur</u> Guiraud; <u>Le Le-</u>
<u>preux</u> Lacroix; <u>Un Pretre</u> Dupont; <u>L'Espion</u> Piron;
<u>L'Annonciateur</u> Bruniere; <u>Un Pecheur</u> Laroche; <u>Le Pau-</u>
<u>vre</u> Magnin; <u>1re Homme du Peuple</u> Kolb; <u>2me Homme du</u>
<u>Peuple</u> Bernard; <u>3me Homme du Peuple</u> Lami. <u>Izeyl</u> Sarah

Bernhardt; <u>La Princesse Harastri</u> Marthold; <u>Une Mère</u>
Marie Grandet; <u>1er Princesse</u> Mellot; <u>2me Princesse</u>
Seylor; <u>3me Princesse</u> Merle; <u>4me Princesse</u> Maille;
<u>5me Princesse</u> Dalcy; <u>6me Princesse</u> Scottez; <u>Yami Prin-</u>
<u>cesse</u> Boulanger; <u>Femmes du Peuple</u> Lacroix, Graci,
Brunet. <u>L & MGR</u> Augustin Daly; <u>Dir</u> Henry E. Abbey,
Maurice Grau; <u>Gen mgr</u> M.L. Mayer; <u>Mus dir</u> C.W. Lamartine; <u>Bom</u> Edward Brown; <u>Bm</u> John Farrington. *REV: Ath*
23/6/94 p815-6; E 23/6/94 p11; Sk 20/6/94 p416-9, 27/
6/94 p456-8; SR 23/6/94 p665; St 21/6/94 p13-4; Th 1/
8/94 p83-5; Ti 19/6/94 p10; TW94 p176-80.

94.125 *FOR GOOD OR EVIL* (P,3a) Mrs A.J. MacDonnell.
ROYALTY 18/6/94 mat perf.* <u>Col. Farquhar</u> Frank Adair;
<u>Sir Brian Ellerton</u> Rudge Harding; <u>Rev Mr Erroll</u>
S[heridan] Lascelles; <u>Tim Hagan</u> W.R. Shirley. <u>Lady</u>
<u>Sinclair</u> Mrs A.J. MacDonnell; <u>Kathleen</u> Violet Lyster;
<u>Fanny</u> Margot Werdermann. *REV: E 23/6/94 p11.*

94.126 *THE SPARE ROOM* (Curtain Raiser) Leopold A.D.
Montague. ROYALTY 18/6/94 mat perf.* <u>Guy</u> W.R. Shirley; <u>Uncle David</u> Orlando Barnett; <u>Cab-Runner</u> Henry
Gent. <u>Ethel</u> Winifred Whitworth; <u>Aunt Psyche</u> Mrs Jervis Waldy. *REV: E 23/6/94 p11.*

94.127 *THE JERRY BUILDER* (F,3a) Mark Melford. STRAND
18/6/94-30/6/94. 16 perf [w/W, S mat]. 1st perfd
Prince of Wales's, Southampton 13/6/92. <u>Jeremiah</u>
<u>Grubb</u> Willie Edouin; <u>Lord Cumberland</u> Cecil Paget;
<u>Joseph Baxter</u> Ernest Hendrie; <u>George</u> Robert Nainby;
<u>Arthur Baxter</u> Herbert Ross; <u>Percival Rodney</u> Douglas
Gordon; <u>Gussie Pollard</u> E.M. Sillward. <u>Mrs Amelia</u>
<u>Pollard</u> Susie Vaughan; <u>Lucy Rodney</u> Helen Conway; <u>Mrs</u>
<u>Newsome</u> Lucy Wilson; <u>Mattie Pollard</u> May Edouin; <u>Lady</u>
<u>Cumberland</u> Edith Hilton; <u>Mrs Billows</u> Emily Dowton;
<u>Dora</u> Grace Lane; <u>Minnie</u> Daisy Field; <u>Bridesmaid</u>
Rosita Tennyson. <u>L</u> Willie Edouin. *REV: Sk 27/6/94*
p459; St 21/6/94 p14; Th 1/8/94 p82-3; Ti 19/6/94
p10; TW94 p182-3.

94.128 *PARALLEL ATTACKS* (Ca,1a) Fred James. STRAND
18/6/94-11/10/94. 100 perf.** <u>Cpt. Alan Adair</u> Cecil
Paget; <u>Cpt. Philip Annersley</u> Herbert Ross; <u>Lieut.</u>
<u>Blunderson</u> E.M. Sillward. <u>Violet Fullerton</u> Grace

Lane; <u>Madge Fullerton</u> Florence A. Loveridge. <u>Pp</u> J.S.
Clarke; <u>L</u> Willie Edouin; <u>Mus dir</u> George Bonner; <u>Sm</u>
Charles Davies; <u>Act mgr</u> A[mand A.] Mascard.

94.129 *DIE WALKURE* (O[3a]) Richard Wagner. DRURY LANE
19/6/94, 14/7/94. 2 perf.** <u>Wotan</u> Heinrich Wiegand;
<u>Hunding</u> David Bispham; <u>Siegmund</u> Max Alvary. <u>Brunnhilde</u>
Katharina Klafsky; <u>Fricka</u> Rose Olitzka; <u>Helmwige</u>
Gelber; <u>Gerhilde</u> Carla Dagmar; <u>Ortlinde</u> Paula Ralph;
<u>Waltraute</u> Cecile Brani; <u>Sigrune</u> Esme Lee; <u>Rossweisse</u>
Pauline Joran; <u>Grimgerde</u> Aldridge; <u>Schwertleite</u> Savri-
Movicz; <u>Sieglinde</u> Gherlsen. <u>L & MGR</u> Augustus Harris;
<u>Cond</u> Otto Lohse; <u>Bom</u> [W.] Allcroft. *REV: Ath 23/6/94*
p815; E 23/6/94 p15; SR 23/6/94 p661; St 21/6/94 p13;
Ti 20/6/94 p10.

94.130 *SHALL WE FORGIVE HER?* (D,5a) Frank Harvey.
ADELPHI 20/6/94-18/8/94. 52 perf. 1st perfd Alexandra,
Sheffield 2/4/94. <u>Oliver West</u> Fred Terry; <u>Paul Els-</u>
<u>worth</u> F.H. Macklin; <u>Neil Garth</u> Charles Dalton; <u>Dr</u>
<u>McKerrow</u> Julian Cross; <u>James Stapleton</u> Herbert Flem-
ming; <u>Reggie</u> Harry Eversfield; <u>Jerry Blake</u> Herbert
Budd. <u>Grace</u> Julia Neilson/Harrietta Polini; <u>Aunt</u>
<u>Martha</u> Mrs Henry Leigh; <u>Joanna Lightfoot</u> Ada Neilson;
<u>Nellie</u> West Mabel Hardinge. <u>PP</u> A. & S. Gatti; <u>Sc</u> Bruce
Smith; <u>Dir</u> H.H. Vincent; <u>Sm</u> Herbert Budd; <u>Pq</u> William
Clarkson; <u>Cost</u> Stagg & Mantle, Morris Angel; <u>Furn</u> J.
Lyons; <u>Mus & Mus dir</u> Edward Jones; <u>Bom</u> Arthur Frye;
<u>Bm & Treas</u> Fred G. Latham. *REV: Ath 23/6/94 p816; E*
23/6/94 p8; Sk 27/6/94 p459; St 21/6/94 p13, 28/6/94
p13; Th 1/8/94 p69-71; Ti 21/6/94 p10; TW94 p180-2.

94.131 *LA NAVARRAISE* (O[2a]) Jules Massenet. COVENT
GARDEN 20/6/94, 26/6, 5/7, 16/7/94. 4 perf.* <u>Sgt.</u>
<u>Araguil</u> Albert Alvarez; <u>Remigio</u> Charles Gilibert;
<u>Gen. Garrido</u> Pol Plançon; <u>Ramon</u> Charles Bonnard; <u>Bus-</u>
<u>tamente</u> Eugene Dufriche. <u>Anita</u> Emma Calvé. <u>L & MGR</u>
Augustus Harris; <u>Cond</u> Philip Flon; <u>Bom</u> E. Hall; <u>A act</u>
<u>mgr</u> Neil Forsyth. *REV: Ath 23/6/94 p815; E 23/6/94*
p15; SR 23/6/94 p661-2; St 21/6/94 p13, 28/6/94 p12-3;
Ti 21/6/94 p10.

94.132 *NANCE OLDFIELD* (C,1a) Charles Reade. LYCEUM
20/6/94 mat perf.** <u>Nathan Oldworthy</u> Alfred Bishop;

<u>Alexander Oldworthy</u> John Martin Harvey. <u>Mrs Anne Old-</u><u>field</u> Ellen Terry; <u>Susan Oldfield</u> Kate Phillips. L &
MGR Henry Irving; <u>Bom</u> Joseph Hurst. *REV: E 23/6/94
p11; St 21/6/94 p13.*

94.133 *TRYING A MAGISTRATE* (Monol) J.L. Toole. LYCEUM
20/6/94 mat perf. 1st perfd Globe 17/12/77. J.L. Toole.
REV: As for 94.132.

94.134 *LA BASOCHE.* DRURY LANE 21/6/94. 1 perf.**
<u>Comment</u>: Advertized in *Ti* for this date.

94.135 *THE BOX LOBBY CHALLENGE* (C,5a) Richard Cumber-
land [adpt by W.R. Walkes]. ROYALTY 22/6/94 mat perf.
1st perfd Haymarket 22/2/1794. <u>Cpt. Waterland</u> H.A.
Saintsbury; <u>Jack Crotchet</u> E[rnest?] Lawford; <u>Sir</u>
<u>Toby Grampus</u> Douglas Gordon; <u>Fulsome</u> Edgar B. Skeet;
<u>Squire Robert</u> Fred Grove; <u>Old Crotchet</u> A. Ferrand;
<u>Joe</u> Walton; <u>William</u> F. Leque. <u>Lady Jane Danvers</u> Kath-
erine Stewart; <u>Diana Grampus</u> Lizzie Henderson; <u>Leti-</u>
<u>tia Rayner</u> Lilian Revell; <u>Theodosia</u> Mary Bessle;
<u>Lindamira</u> Davies-Webster; <u>Maria</u> Ellen Snow. <u>L</u> Kate
Santley; <u>Pd</u> George P. Hawtrey; <u>Act mgr</u> A. Austin
Leigh; <u>Asm</u> Edgar B. Skeet; <u>Pq</u> William Clarkson; <u>Cost</u>
Harrison; <u>Furn</u> Lyons; <u>Mus dir</u> Thomas P. Fish. *REV:
St 28/6/94 p14-5.*

94.136 *THE TEXAN* (Modern P,4a) Tyrone Power. PRINCESS'S
21/6/94-29/6/94. 8 perf.* <u>Sir Eardley Cumming</u> Rudge
Harding; <u>Cecil Cumming</u> Oswald Yorke; <u>Mjr. Gordon</u>
<u>Tyrrell</u> A[lbert] E. Drinkwater; <u>Dr Bryant</u> Ernest Co-
sham; <u>Jordan Wycke</u> Littledale Power; <u>Osborne</u> L. Lees;
<u>Crawley</u> Mark Paton; <u>Mr Busteed</u> Robert Munro; <u>William</u>
<u>Plainleigh</u> Tyrone Power. <u>Lady Cumming</u> May Howard; <u>Mrs</u>
<u>Gordon Tyrrell</u> Edith Crane; <u>Mrs Wycke</u> Katherine Stew-
art; <u>Maria Barker</u> Kate Hartley; <u>Bishop</u> Maggie Byron;
<u>Mlle Lucille</u> M. Shaw. <u>PP</u> Mrs Harriett Gooch; <u>Furn</u> A.
Ardley & Son; <u>Cost</u> Pitts & Richard, Mrs Selley, I.J.
Harries; <u>Bom</u> E.J. Ottley; <u>Sc</u> Richard C. Durant, Bruce
Smith; <u>Mus</u> W. [F.?] Glover; <u>Pq</u> William Clarkson; <u>Props</u>
Labhart; <u>Mach</u> J.W. Cawdrey; <u>Lime</u> L.C. Parnell; <u>Sm</u>
Frederick Loyd. *REV: E 23/6/94 p11; Sk 27/6/94 p459,
4/7/94 p554; SR 30/6/94 p692; St 28/6/94 p13; Th 1/8/
94 p71; TW94 p182.*

94.137 *DAISY'S ESCAPE* (Ca,1a) A.W. Pinero. TOOLE'S
21/6/94-27/6/94; 30/6/94(2). 8 perf.** Henry Westland; Herbert Pearson; George Shelton; Frank J. Arlton; Charles Brunton. Cora Poole; Beaumont Loveday.
Comment: See item 94.6 for probable roles.

94.138 *SIEGFRIED* (O[3a]) Richard Wagner. DRURY LANE
23/6/94, 5/7/94. 2 perf.** Der Wanderer Heinrich
Wiegand; Mime Rodemund; Alberich David Bispham; Fafner
Waldmann; Siegfried Max Alvary. Brunnhilde Katharina
Klafsky; Stimme des Waldvogels Gherlsen; Erda Rose
Olitzka; L & MGR Augustus Harris; Cond Otto Lohse;
Bom [W.] Allcroft. *REV: Ath 30/6/94 p846; E 30/6/94
p6; St 28/6/94 p13; Ti 25/6/94 p6.*

94.139 *MADAME SANS GENE* (P,4a) Victorien Sardou &
Emile Moreau. GAIETY 23/6/94-28/7/94. 38 perf [w/S
mat exc 23/6; add mat 27/6, 4/7]. 1st perfd Vaude-
ville, Paris 27/10/93. Napoléon Edmond Duquesne;
Fouché Lerand; Marechal Lefebvre Candé; De Neipperg
Grand; Savary, Duc de Rovigo Mangin; Despreaux Peu-
tat; Jasmin Gildes; De Saint-Marsan Rambert; Vabon-
train Aimé; Canouville Lauras; Constant Duvelleroy;
Duroc Schultz; De Lauriston Franck; Leroy Prevost;
Cop Moisson; Corso Gaillard; Arnault Abel. Reine
Caroline Verneuil/Avril; Mme de Bulow Suger; Princesse
Elisa Drunzer; Mme de Vintimille Avril; Mme de Rovigo
Melcy; Catherine Réjane; Mme de Canisy [Aimee] Sam-
uel; Mme de Talhouet Lerand; Toinon Mlle Jeanne/Netza;
Julie Aimee; La Rouossotte Suzanne; Mathurin Netza.
L & MGR George Edwardes; Sm J.A.E. Malone; Act mgr
E[dward] Marshall. *REV: Ath 30/6/94 p847; E 30/6/94
p7; Sk 27/6/94 p451, 456; 4/7/94 p520-1; SR 30/6/94 p692;
St 28/6/94 p14; Th 1/8/94 p72-3; Ti 25/6/94 p7; TW94
p183-5.*

94.140 *THE PROFESSOR'S LOVE STORY* (P,3a) J.M. Barrie.
COMEDY 25/6/94-10/8/94;* trfd to GARRICK 13/8/94-26/
10/94. 140 perf [w/W, S mat exc 27/6, 1/8; add mat
6/8; np 11/8]. Prof Goodwillie E.S. Willard; Dr Cosens H[arry] Cane; Dr Yellowlees Hugh Harting/Cecil
Crofton;Sir George Gilding Bassett Roe; Henders Royce
Carleton; Pete F.H. Tyler; Servants C. Moore, F. Maxwell. Agnes Goodwillie Mrs G[eorge] Canninge; Lucy

White Bessie Hatton; Effie Proctor Mrs H[arry] Cane;
Lady Gilding Keith Wakeman; Dowager Lady Gilding
Nannie Craddock. L & MGR J.W. Comyns Carr; Bom Scarisbrick; Mus dir J. Hamilton Clarke; Sm Thomas Sidney;
Bm W.H. Griffiths. *REV: Ath 30/6/94 p847; E 30/6/94*
p7, 18/8/94 p7; Sk 4/7/94 p510; SR 30/6/94 p692; St
28/6/94 p13-4; Th 1/8/94 p73-4; Ti 26/6/94 p6; TW94
p186-92.

94.141 *LA TOSCA* (D,5a) Victorien Sardou. DALY'S 25/6/
94, 26/6, 4/7(m), 11/7, 18/7/94. 5 perf.** Scarpia
Albert Darmont; Cavaradossi Laroche; Angelotti Angelo;
Trevilhac Deneubourg; Attavanti Henri Deschamps; Spo-
letta Deval; Trivulce Brunière; Eusebe Lacroix; Pais-
iello Lami; Schiaronne Piron; Capreola Dupont; Sgt.
Guiraud; Gen. Kolb; Ceccho Magnin; Procureur Bernard.
Tosca Sarah Bernhardt; Reine Marie Caroline Marthold;
Princesse Orlonia Saryta; Genarino Seylor; Luciana
Merle; Un Monsignor Dalcy. L & MGR Augustin Daly; Dir
Henry E. Abbey, Maurice Grau; Gen mgr M.L. Mayer; Bm
John Farrington; Bom Edward Brown. *REV: Ath 30/6/94*
p847; Sk 20/6/94 p393, 4/7/94 p510, 18/7/94 p637; St
28/6/94 p14.

94.142 *LA LOCANDIERA* (C,3a) Carlo Goldoni. AVENUE 26/
6/94 mat perf.** Carlo Col. Barrington Foote; Caval-
ière James Nelson; Fabrizio Col. H.L. Mitchell;
Count d'Albafiorita Lloyd Lowndes; Marquis of Forlipopoli C.W.A. Trollope. Mirandolina Mrs Dashwood. *REV:*
E 30/6/94 p15; St 28/6/94 p14.

94.143 *IN HONOUR BOUND* (C,1a) Sydney Grundy. AVENUE
26/6/94 mat perf.** Philip Graham Percy Downes; Sir
George Carlyon C.W.A. Trollope. Rose Dalrymple Edith
Young; Lady Carlyon Mrs Dashwood. *REV: As for 94.142.*

94.144 *TANNHAUSER* (O[3a]) Richard Wagner. DRURY LANE
26/6/94, 21/7/94. 2 perf.** Landgraf Heinrich Wiegand;
Wolfram David Bispham; Walther Simon; Biterolf [Jos-
eph?] Claus; Heinrich der Schreiber Rodemund; Reinmar Waldmann; Tannhauser Max Alvary. Elizabeth Katharina Klafsky; Venus Gherlsen; Hirt Paula Ralph. L &
MGR Augustus Harris; Cond Wilhelm Feld; Bom [W.] Allcroft. *REV: Ath 30/6/94 p846; E 30/6/94 p6, 28/7/94*

p15; Ti 27/6/94 p10.

94.145 *LA DAME AUX CAMELIAS* (D,5a) Alexandre Dumas, *fils*. DALY'S 27/6/94, 28/6, 30/6(m), 7/7, 11/7(m), 19/7/94. 6 perf.** Armand Duval Lucien-Germain Guitry; Commissionaire Piron; De Varville Angelo; Gaston Rieux Deneubourg; St. Gaudens Henri Deschamps; Comte de Giray Deval; Docteur Lacroix; Le Père Duval Montigny; Gustave Brunière; Arthur Guiraud; Domestique Kolb. Marguerite Gauthier Sarah Bernhardt; Prudence Marie Grandet; Olympe Saryta; Nichette Seylor; Nannine Merle; Anais Boulanger; Esther Dalcy; Adèle Maille; Groom Bellanger. L & MGR Augustin Daly; Dir Henry E. Abbey, Maurice Grau; Gen mgr M.L. Mayer; Mus dir C.W. Lamartine; Bom Edward Brown; Bm John Farrington. *REV: Sk 4/7/94 p510; TW94 p193-4.*

94.146 *A FAMILY MATTER* (C,3a) C.G. Compton & A. George Hockley. GARRICK 27/6/94 mat perf.* Rev John Conisbee Charles Groves; Gilbert C.M. Hallard; Rev William Richardson Alfred Bucklaw; Lord Eustace Leslie W. Granville; Col. Sir George Mitchell Howard Sturge; Bartram Albert Sims. Lady Conisbee Mary Rorke; Dulcie Winifred Fraser; Jean Ellis Jeffreys; Maid Pendennis. L & MGR John Hare. *REV: E 30/6/94 p15; Sk 4/7/94 p510; SR 30/6/94 p692; St 28/6/94 p14; Ti 29/6/94 p3.*

94.147 *IN TWO MINDS* (Ca,1a) Arthur M. Heathcote. GARRICK 27/6/94 mat perf.* Lady Margaret Minniver Annie Webster; Parkins Agnes Hill. L & MGR John Hare. *REV: E, St as for 94.146.*

94.148 *IN OLDEN DAYS* (Dramatic Incident,1a) Mrs Frances Hodgson Burnett. CRITERION 28/6/94 mat perf.** Jocelyn Durrant Frank Atherley; Cpt. Desborough Harry Grattan. Damaris Nethercliffe Emilie Grattan. *REV: E 30/6/94 p15; St 5/7/94 p13.*

94.149 *FOR CHARITY'S SAKE* (Sk) Frederick Bowyer & Walter H. Hedgecock. CRITERION 28/6/94 mat perf.** Nellie Ganthony. *REV: St 5/7/94 p13.*

94.150 *KING ROBERT OF SICILY* (Opera-tableaux,4a) Alfred J. Caldicott (mus). LYRIC 28/6/94 mat perf. 1st

perf? <u>King</u> Ben Webster; <u>Jester</u> Bert Thomas; <u>Pope</u> A.C.
Beverly; <u>Emperor</u> Ernest Percy; <u>Cardinal</u> Edward Ferris;
<u>Courtiers & Ambassadors</u> Harley Granville-Barker, Cal-
dicott, J. Bensbow, Brooke Stewart; <u>Monks</u> A.R. Gar-
land, T. Cabillas; <u>Sexton</u> F. [P.?] Loftus. <u>Singers</u>
Clara E. Butt, Mrs Albert Barker; <u>Empress</u> Ivy Dacre;
<u>Ladies of the Court</u> Christine Nethersole, Helen Petti-
can, Mitchell, Antoinette Elleston, Campbell; <u>Pages</u>
Grace Barker, Beverly; <u>Peasants</u> Garratt, Vere Cochran,
Merriel Watt Black, Lilian Stocker, Bessie Mercer,
Desmond, Phyllis Desmond. <u>COND</u> F. Welters; <u>Organist</u>
Allan; <u>Sm</u> W. Fielder. *REV: St 7/5/94 p13.*

94.151 *A NIGHT IN TOWN* (FC,3a) H.A. Sherburn. ROYALTY
28/6/94-11/7/94. 12 perf [mat only 11/7].** <u>Mr Babbicombe, Q.C.</u> Harry Paulton; <u>Fred</u> Cecil Ramsey; <u>Mr Dove-
dale</u> Hurdman Lucas; <u>Frank Darlington</u> Loring Fernie;
<u>Mr Culpepper</u> William Lockhart; <u>Jorkins</u> Compton Coutts;
<u>Simmons</u> Henry Nelson; <u>Policeman</u> Hubert Evelyn; <u>Pierotte</u>
Grahame Herrington. <u>Mrs Babbicombe</u> Emily Miller; <u>Mrs
Dovedale</u> Louisa Peach; <u>Mabel</u> Henrietta Cross; <u>Beatrice</u>
Florence Friend; <u>Polly Parker</u> Julia Warden; <u>Mrs Peg-
well</u> Blanche Eversleigh; <u>Maud Merrilon</u> Lucille Heaton;
<u>Lottie</u> K. McIver; <u>Nellie</u> Ada Palmer; <u>Bettie</u> Legh;
<u>Carrie Cuthbert</u> Kate Santley. <u>L & MGR</u> Kate Santley.
*REV: E 30/6/94 p7; Sk 4/7/94 p510; St 5/7/94 p14; Th
1/8/94 p75; TW94 p193.*

94.152 *VILLON, POET AND CUTTHROAT* (D,1a) S.X. Courte.
ROYALTY 28/6/94-11/7/94. 12 perf [mat only 11/7]. 1st
perfd Grand, Birmingham 12/4/94. <u>Francois Villon</u>
Loring Fernie; <u>Father Gervais</u> William Lockhart. <u>Helene</u>
Florence Friend. <u>L & MGR</u> Kate Santley. *REV: E, Sk,
St, TW94 as for 94.151.*

94.153 *FLOATING A COMPANY* (C,1a) Julian Cross. ROYALTY
28/6/94-11/7/94. 12 perf [mat only 11/7].* <u>Cpt. Car-
ruthers</u> Hurdman Lucas. <u>Rosalind Vernon</u> Henrietta
Cross. <u>L & MGR</u> Kate Santley. *REV: St 5/7/94 p14.*

94.154 *OFF THE LINE* (D,1a) Clement Scott. TOOLE'S
28/6/94-29/6/94. 2 perf.** [<u>Harry Coke</u>] J.L. Toole;
[<u>Jem Brass</u>] Henry Westland; [<u>Puffy</u>] Frank J. Arlton.
[<u>Mary Coke</u>] Cora Poole; [<u>Liz Coke</u>] Eliza Johnstone.

94.155 *PHEDRE* (T,5a) Jean Baptiste Racine. DALY'S
29/6/94, 30/6, 13/7/94. 3 perf.** <u>Hippolyte</u> Albert
Darmont; <u>Thesee</u> de Max; <u>Theramene</u> Piron; <u>Panore</u> Guiraud. <u>Phedre</u> Sarah Bernhardt; <u>Oenone</u> Marie Grandet;
<u>Ismene</u> Seylor; <u>Jeune Fille</u> Maille; <u>Aricie</u> Mellot. L &
MGR Augustin Daly; <u>Dir</u> Henry E. Abbey, Maurice Grau;
<u>Gen mgr</u> M.L. Mayer; <u>Mus dir</u> C.W. Lamartine; <u>Bom</u> Edward
Brown; <u>Bm</u> John Farrington. *REV: Sk 4/7/94 p510; Ti
2/7/94 p4; TW94 p194-5.*

94.156 *SIXES AND SEVENS* (Misunderstanding) E.H. Whitmore. LYRIC 29/6/94 mat perf.** <u>Cpt. George Hope</u>
Arthur Bourchier. <u>Edith Cashdown</u> Irene Vanbrugh. L &
MGR Horace Sedger; <u>Act mgr</u> William Greet; <u>Mach</u> S. Trewen; <u>Treas</u> Charles Warner; <u>Sec</u> W.A. Baskcomb. *REV: E
30/6/94 p10; St 5/7/94 p13-4.*

94.157 *SIGNA* (O[2a]) Gilbert Arthur à Beckett (lib)
& H.A. Rudall (lib) & Frederick H. Cowen (mus). COV-
ENT GARDEN 30/6/94, 6/7, 16/7, 24/7/94. 4 perf. 1st
perfd [in 3a] Teatro dal Verme, Milan 12/11/93. <u>Signa</u>
Ben Davies; <u>Bruno</u> Mario Ancona; <u>Sartorio</u> Armand Cas-
telmary/Vittorio Arimondi. <u>Gemma</u> de Nouvina/Sigrid
Arnoldson. L & MGR Augustus Harris; <u>Cond</u> Frederick H.
Cowen; <u>Bom</u> E. Hall; <u>A act mgr</u> Neil Forsyth. *REV: Ath
7/7/94 p40-1; E 7/7/94 p6; St 5/7/94 p12; Ti 2/7/94
p8.*

94.158 *TRISTAN UND ISOLDE* (O[3a]) Richard Wagner.
DRURY LANE 30/6/94, 12/7/94. 2 perf.** <u>Marke</u> Heinrich
Wiegand; <u>Kurnwenal</u> David Bispham; <u>Melot</u> Simon; <u>Hirt</u>
Karlyle; <u>Steuermann</u> Waldmann; <u>Tristan</u> Max Alvary.
<u>Isolde</u> Katharine Klafsky; <u>Brangane</u> Paula Ralph. L &
MGR Augustus Harris; <u>Cond</u> Otto Lohse; <u>Bom</u> [W.] All-
croft. *REV: E 7/7/94 p6; St 5/7/94 p12; Ti 2/7/94 p8.*

94.159 *LES ROIS* (D,4a) Jules Lemaitre. DALY'S 2/7/94,
3/7/94. 2 perf. 1st perfd Renaissance, Paris 7/11/
93. <u>Prince Hermann</u> Lucien-Germain Guitry; <u>Roi Christian XVI</u> de Max; <u>Prince Otto</u> Deval; <u>Comte Moellnitz</u>
Montigny; <u>Heilborn</u> Laroche; <u>Maubert</u> Angelo; <u>Prince
Renaud</u> Deneubourg; <u>Officier</u> Lami; <u>Huissier</u> Magnin; <u>Got-
lieb</u> Mevisto; <u>Alvarez</u> Brunière; <u>Officier d'Ordonnace</u>
Guiraud; <u>Little Christian</u> Le Petit Lacroix. <u>Princesse</u>

Wilhelmine Sarah Bernhardt; Frida de Talberg Marcelle
Valdey; Kate Saryta; Gouvernante Merle. L & MGR Augus-
tin Daly; Dir Henry E. Abbey, Maurice Grau; Gen mgr
M.L. Mayer; Mus dir C.W. Lamartine; Bom Edward Brown;
Bm John Farrington. *REV: Ath 7/7/94 p42; E 7/7/94 p7;
Sk 11/7/94 p572; St 5/7/94 p13; Th 1/8/94 p78-9; Ti
3/7/94 p10; TW94 p196-9.*

94.160 *A MODERN EVE* (P,3a) Malcolm C. Salaman. HAY-
MARKET 2/7/94 mat perf.* Sir Gerald Raeburn Charles
Allan; Eardley Hereford Fred Terry; Kenyon Wargrave
H.B. Tree; Melford Hay. Vivian Hereford Mrs H.B. Tree;
Mrs Mowbray Meryon Lottie Venne; Mrs Malleson Mrs
Dion Boucicault; Servant Conover. *REV: Ath 7/7/94
p41-2; E 7/7/94 p8; Sk 11/7/94 p572; SR 7/7/94 p17;
St 5/7/94 p12-3; Th 1/8/94 p76-7; Ti 4/7/94 p8; TW94
p199-202.*

94.161 *OUR FLAT* (FC,3a) Mrs H. Musgrave. STRAND 2/7/
94-11/10/94. 118 perf [w/W, S mat exc 4/7; add mat
6/8, 11/10]. 1st perfd Winter Gardens, Southport 10/
4/89. Reginald Sylvester Charles S. Fawcett; Clarence
Vane Forbes Dawson/Herbert Ross; Mr McCullum W.F.
Hawtrey/Ernest Hendrie; Bill George Gamble; Pinchard
Robert Nainby/Cecil Paget; Foreman Albert Sims/Charles
Davies; Stout Wilton Heriot/J.F. Graham/William Lugg/
E.M. Sillward; Joe Walter Hales. Margery Sylvester
May Whitty/Georgie Esmond; Lucy McCullum Georgie Es-
mond/Grace Lane; Bella Annie Goward; Clara Pryout
Alice Vicat/May Edouin; Mme Volant Laura Sedgwick/
Annie Esmond; Elsie Claremont Maud Graves/Florence A.
Loveridge. PP J.S. Clarke; L Willie Edouin; Bom Henry
L. Boss; Sm J.A.E. Malone; Cond Ernest Bucalossi; Bm
George Bryer. *REV: E 7/7/94 p7; St 5/7/94 p14; Th 1/
8/94 p81.*

94.162 *BOYS WILL BE BOYS* (Ca,1a) Joseph MacKay. STRAND
2/7/94. Rnd. 1st perfd Opera Comique 29/7/89. Sir
Giles Wapshot Richard Purdon/Wilton Heriot/J.F. Gra-
ham/William Lugg; Chatsworth Cholmondley Forbes Dawson; Alick Robert Nainby. Evelina Georgie Esmond. PP,
L, Bom, Sm, Cond, Bm as for 94.161. Comment: Although
V & A programmes exist for this play, newspapers
carried advertizements for item 94.128.

94.163 *LOHENGRIN* (O[3a]) Richard Wagner. DRURY LANE
3/7/94. 1 perf.** <u>Konig</u> Heinrich Wiegand; <u>Frederick</u>
<u>Telramund</u> Eugene Dufriche; <u>Herald</u> Waldmann; <u>Lohengrin</u>
Max Alvary. <u>Elsa</u> Katharina Klafsky; <u>Ortrud</u> Rose
Olitzka. <u>L & MGR</u> Augustus Harris; <u>Cond</u> Otto Lohse.
REV: Ath 7/7/94 p41; E 7/7/94 p6; SR 21/7/94 p71-2;
Ti 4/7/94 p5.

94.164 *MIRETTE* (O,3a) Michel Carré (lib) & Frederic
E. Weatherly (lyr) & Harry Greenbank (lib) & Andre
Messager; rev by Adrian Ross. SAVOY 3/7/94-11/8/94;
6/10/94-6/12/94. 101 perf [w/S mat exc 6/10; mat only
11/8].* <u>Gerard</u> Robert Scott-Fishe; <u>Baron Vanden Berg</u>/
<u>Burgomaster</u> John Coates/Richard Temple; <u>Notary</u>/<u>Max</u>
Herbert Ralland; <u>Picorin</u> Courtice Pounds; <u>Bobinet</u>
Walter Passmore; <u>Francal</u> Avon Saxon; <u>Bertuccio</u> Scott
Russell. <u>Mirette</u> Maud Ellicott/Kate Rolla/Florence St.
John; <u>Bianca</u> Florence Perry; <u>Dancing-girl</u> Emmie Owen;
<u>Marquise</u> Rosina Brandram. <u>PP & MGR</u> Richard d'Oyly
Carte; <u>Dir</u> Charles Harris, Frederic E. Weatherly, Harry
Greenbank; <u>Cond</u> Andre Messager; <u>Sc</u> Joseph Harker, Will-
iam Harford, T.E. Ryan; <u>Mus dir</u> Francois Cellier; <u>Ch</u>
John d'Auban; <u>Cost dgn</u> [E.] Comelli; <u>Cost</u> Alias, Au-
guste, Mme Leon, B.J. Simmons, Angel & Son; <u>Pq</u> William
Clarkson; <u>Props</u> [H.] Skelly; <u>Mach</u> Peter White; <u>Elect</u>
Lyons; <u>Sm</u> W.H. Seymour; <u>Act mgr & Treas</u> J.W. Beckwith.
REV: E 7/7/94 p7; Sk 11/7/94 p568-9, 10/10/94 p567,
568; St 5/7/94 p13; Th 1/11/94 p253; Ti 4/7/94 p5,
8/10/94 p3; TW94 p203-7; E 13/10/94 p15.

94.165 *L'ATTAQUE DU MOULIN* (O[4a]) Alfred Bruneau (mus)
& Louis Gallet (lib; trans Frederic E. Weatherly).
COVENT GARDEN 4/7/94, 13/7, 19/7/94. 3 perf. 1st perfd
Opéra Comique, Paris 23/11/93. <u>Dominique</u> Emile Cos-
sira; <u>Cpt. Ennemi</u> Henri Albers; <u>Merlier</u> Max Bouvet;
<u>Sentinelle</u> Charles Bonnard; <u>Tambour</u> Charles Gilibert;
<u>Jeune Homme</u> Villani; <u>Capitaine Française</u> Iginio Corsi;
<u>Sgt.</u> Van Acker. <u>Marcelline</u> Marie Delna; <u>François</u> de
Nouvina/Gherlsen; <u>Genevieve</u> Cecile Brani. <u>L & MGR</u> Au-
gustus Harris; <u>Cond</u> Philip Flon; <u>Bom</u> E. Hall; <u>A act</u>
<u>mgr</u> Neil Forsyth. *REV: Ath 7/7/94 p41, 14/7/94 p74-5;*
E 7/7/94 p6; Sk 11/7/94 p572; SR 7/7/94 p11-3; St 5/7/
94 p12, 12/7/94 p10; Ti 5/7/94 p10.

94.166 *FEDORA* (D,4a) Victorien Sardou. DALY'S 4/7/94, 7/7(m), 14/7, 21/7/94. 4 perf.** Lucien-Germain Guitry; Deval; Montigny; Laroche; Angelo; Deneubourg; Henri Deschamps; Lacroix. Sarah Bernhardt; Marcelle Valdey; Saryta; Seylor; Merle. L & MGR Augustin Daly; Dir Henry E. Abbey, Maurice Grau; Gen mgr M.L. Mayer. *REV: Th 1/8/94 p79-80.*

94.167 *MUCH ADO ABOUT NOTHING* (C,5a) William Shakespeare. LYCEUM 4/7/94, 5/7, 6/7/94(m). 3 perf.** Benedick Henry Irving; Borachio [Clarence] Hague; Don Pedro Frank [Kemble] Cooper; Conrade John Martin Harvey; Claudio Ben Webster; Friar Francis Sydney Valentine; Don John [William] Haviland; Balthazar Herbert Reeves; Leonato [Frank] Tyars; Antonio H[enry] Howe; Dogberry S[am] Johnson; Seacoal [John] Archer; Verges Lacy; Oatcake [W. Lionel] Belmore; Sexton [T.] Reynolds; Boy Master Leo Byrne. Hero Julia Arthur; Margaret Maud Milton; Ursula Ailsa Craig; Beatrice Ellen Terry. L & MGR Henry Irving; Sc Hawes Craven, W. Cuthbert, William Telbin; Cond J. Meredith Ball; Sm H.J. Loveday; Act mgr Bram Stoker; Bom Joseph Hurst.

94.168 *THE NEW LIFE* (P,1a) William Gayer MacKay. AVENUE 5/7/94 mat perf.* Dennis Wylde William Gayer MacKay; Robert Capper Herbert Flemming. Vera Wylde Mary Allestree. *REV: E 7/7/94 p10; St 12/7/94 p11.*

94.169 *IN THE DEPTHS OF THE SEA* (Musical Fantasy,1a, 2sc) William Gayer MacKay (lib & lyr) & Angela Goetze (mus). AVENUE 5/7/94 mat perf.* Sir James Barker Robert Legge; Algy Fitzroy Hamilton Revelle; John Doricus William Gayer MacKay. Lady Barker Carlingford; Maud Fitzroy Hilda Rivers; Sylvia Whiting Mrs Herbert Morris; Marina Jenny Featherstone; Ruby Mullett Juliet Groves. *REV: As for 94.168.*

94.170 *SUCH IS LOVE* (C,1a) Alfred M. Mond. AVENUE 5/7/ 94 mat perf.* Clarence Montagu Montgomery; Mr Greville Dawson Milward; Augustus Stanley Robert Legge; Servant Shiel. Mrs Rainer Cowper Coles; Daisy Rainer Braithwaite; Mrs Greville Mary Allestree. *REV: As for 94.168.*

94.171 *THE HOUSE OF LORDS* (0a,1a) Harry Greenbank (lib) & George W. Byng (mus) & Ernest Ford (mus). LYRIC 5/7/ 94-20/10/94; 29/10/94-3/11/94. 99 perf.* Duke of Hanover Square J. Furneaux Cook; Halifax Finsbury Wilbur Gunn; Mr Murgatroyd W.S. Laidlaw/F. Seymour. Duchess of Hanover Square Adelaide Newton; Lady Victoria Portobello Dora Thorne. L & MGR Horace Sedger; Bm Arthur Frye; Pq William Clarkson. *REV: E 14/7/94 p7; St 12/7/94 p11.*

94.172 *ELAINE* (O[4a]) Hermann Bemberg. COVENT GARDEN 7/7/94, 18/7/94. 2 perf.** Lancelot Jean de Reszke; L'Eremite Edouard de Reszke; Astolat Pol Plançon; Gauvain Eugene Dufriche; Travaine Charles Bonnard; Arthur Henri Albers. Elaine Nellie Melba; Reine Genievre Rose Olitzka; Torre Cecile Brani; Menestrel Biancoli. L & MGR Augustus Harris; Cond Luigi Mancinelli; Bom E. Hall; A act mgr Neil Forsyth. *REV: Ath 14/7/94 p75; E 14/7/94 p6; St 12/7/94 p10; Ti 9/7/94 p8.*

94.173 *FIDELIO* (O[3a]) Ludwig van Beethoven. DRURY LANE 7/7/94, 19/7/94. 2 perf.** Rocco Heinrich Wiegand; Jaquino Rodemund; Pizarro David Bispham; Fernando Waldmann; Florestan Max Alvary. Leonore Katharina Klafsky; Marzelline Gelber. L & MGR Augustus Harris; Cond Otto Lohse. *REV: Ath 14/7/94 p75; E 14/7/94 p6; St 12/7/94 p10-1; Ti 9/7/94 p8.*

94.174 *BECKET* (D,4a) Alfred, Lord Tennyson. LYCEUM 9/7/94-20/7/94. 11 perf [mat only 14/7].** Thomas Becket Henry Irving; Henry II William Terriss; King Louis of France Julius Knight; Gilbert Foliot Lacy; Roger Seldon; Hilary [John] Archer; John of Salisbury Alfred Bishop; Herbert of Bosham [William] Haviland; John of Oxford [H.W.] Cushing; Sir Reginald Fitzurse [Clarence] Hague; Sir Richard de Brito [Frank] Tyars; Sir William de Tracy [R.P.] Tabb; Sir Hugh de Morville [W. Lionel] Belmore; Richard de Hastings [Herbert] Innis; Youngest Knight Templar Buckley; Lord Leicester John Martin Harvey; Philip de Eleemosyna [Henry] Howe; Monk [K.] Rivington; Geoffrey Master Leo Byrne; Retainers Eardley Howard, Taylor; Countrymen [Sam] Johnson, [T.] Reynolds; Servant [W.] Marion.

Eleanor of Aquitaine Genevieve Ward; Margery Kate
Phillips; Rosamund de Clifford Ellen Terry. L & MGR
Henry Irving; Sc William Telbin, Joseph Harker, Hawes
Craven; Mus C. Villiers Stanford; Mus dir J. Meredith
Ball; Cost dgn Mrs J.W. Comyns Carr, Charles Catter-
mole; Cost Mrs Nettleship, Mrs Reid, Thomas Pratt &
Sons, Pocock Brothers, Bieati, Auguste; Pq Fox; Furn
Arnott; Mach Fillery; Sm H.J. Loveday; Act mgr Bram
Stoker; Bom Joseph Hurst. *REV: E 14/7/94 p7; Sk 18/7/*
94 p622; SR 14/7/94 p43-4; Th 1/8/94 p81-2; Ti 10/7/94
p10; TW94 p208-9.

94.175 *DER FREISCHUTZ* (O[3a]) C.M. von Weber. DRURY
LANE 10/7/94, 17/7/94. 2 perf. 1st perfd Schauspiel-
haus, Berlin 18/6/21. Kaspar Heinrich Wiegand; Otto-
kar David Bispham; Kilian Rodemund; Ehermit Waldmann;
Cuno [Joseph?] Claus; Samiel Simon; Max Max Alvary.
Agathe Katharina Klafsky; Aennchen Elise Kutscherra;
Brautjungfer Cecile Brani. L & MGR Augustus Harris;
Cond Otto Lohse. *REV: E 14/7/94 p6; St 12/7/94 p11;*
Ti 11/7/94 p11.

94.176 *TERSICHORE* (Ca,1a) Justin Huntly McCarthy.
LYRIC 12/7/94 mat perf.* Lord Mohun A. Hamilton Revelle; Master Oldacre Rudge Harding. Margaret Aida
Jenoure; Barbara Marianne Caldwell. *REV: E 14/7/94*
p10; St 19/7/94 p12-3.

94.177 *A DRAWN BATTLE* (Duol) T. Malcolm Watson. LYRIC
12/7/94 mat perf.** Mr Kenyon Lawrance d'Orsay. Miss
Langdon Marie Dagmar. *REV: As for 94.176.*

94.178 *WHO SPEAKS FIRST?* (F,1a) Charles Dance. PRIN-
CESS'S 12/7/94 mat perf.** Potter J.G. Taylor; Cpt.
Montgomery Walter Joyce; J.A. Rosier. Smart Clara
Jecks; Jerome. *REV: E 14/7/94 p16.*

94.179 *HE AND SHE* (Duol). PRINCESS'S 12/7/94 mat perf.
Frank M. Wood. Miss Roma.*REV: E 14/7/94 p16.* Comment:
Title is possibly an alternative for *A Pair of Luna-*
tics.

94.180 *VILLON: POET AND CUTTHROAT* (D,1a) S.X. Courte.
PRINCESS'S 12/7/94 mat perf.** Francois Villon Loring

Fernie. Helene Florence Friend. *REV: E 14/7/94 p16.*

94.181 *A SUCCESSFUL MISSION* (Duo1,1a). PRINCE OF
WALES'S 14/7/94 mat perf.* John Winton George Mudie.
Alice Gray Maude Hobson. *REV: E 21/7/94 p10; St 19/7/
94 p13.*

94.182 *AIDA* (O[4a]) Giuseppe Verdi. COVENT GARDEN
17/7/94, 25/7/94. 2 perf.** Ramfis Edouard de Reszke/
Morello; Il Re Pol Plançon; Amonasro P. Maggi/Mario
Ancona; Messaggiero Rinaldini; Radames Morello/Jean
de Reszke. Aida Ada Adini; Sacerdotessa Mathilde
Bauermeister; Amneris Giulia Ravogli. L & MGR Augustus
Harris; Cond Enrico Bevignani; Bom E. Hall; A act mgr
Neil Forsyth. *REV: Ath 21/7/94 p105; E 21/7/94 p13;
SR 21/7/94 p72, 28/7/94 p97-8; St 19/7/94 p12; Ti 19/
7/94 p10.*

94.183 *LA FEMME DU CLAUDE* (P,3a) Alexandre Dumas,
fils. DALY'S 17/7/94, 18/7/94(m). 2 perf. 1st perfd
Gymnase, Paris 16/1/73. Claude Ruper Lucien-Germain
Guitry; Cantagnac Deval; Daniel Montigny; Antonin
Laroche. Cesarine Sarah Bernhardt; Rebecca Mellot;
Edinie Marcelle Valdey. L & MGR Augustin Daly; Dir
Henry E. Abbey, Maurice Grau; Gen mgr M.L. Mayer;
Mus dir C.W. Lamartine; Bom Edward Brown; Bm John
Farrington. *REV: Ath 21/7/94 p107-8; E 21/7/94 p7; Sk
25/7/94 p678; SR 21/7/94 p72-3; St 19/7/94 p12; Ti
19/7/94 p14; TW94 p209-18.*

94.184 *AN ENEMY OF THE PEOPLE* (P,5a) Henrik Ibsen.
HAYMARKET 20/7/94. 1 perf.** Dr Thomas Stockmann
H.B. Tree; Peter Stockmann Charles Allan; Morton Kiil
Lionel Brough; Hovstad James A. Welch; Billing E. Hol-
man Clark; Aslaken E.M. Robson; Cpt. Horster A. Ha-
milton Revelle; Eiliff Master [G.?] Croxon. Mrs Stock-
mann Mrs Theodore Wright; Petra Lily Hanbury; Morten
Dora Barton. L & MGR H.B. Tree; Bom W.H. Leverton; Sm
Shelton; Mus dir Carl Armbruster; Elect E. Wingfield
Bowles; Bm & Sec Frederick Harrison. *REV: Sk 25/7/94
p678; SR 28/7/94 p99-100; St 26/7/94 p10; Ti 21/7/94
p7.*

94.185 *THE BALLAD MONGER* (RP,1a) Walter Besant & Wal-

ter Pollock. HAYMARKET 20/7/94. 1 perf.** <u>Louis XI</u>
James Fernandex; <u>Gringoire</u> H.B. Tree; <u>Olivier</u> Charles
Allan; <u>Simon</u> E. Holman Clark. <u>Loyse</u> Mrs H.B. Tree;
<u>Nicola</u> Mrs E.H. Brooke. <u>L & MGR</u>, <u>Bom</u>, <u>Sm</u>, <u>Mus dir</u>,
<u>Elect</u>, <u>Bm & Sec</u> as for 94.184. *REV: Sk, SR, St as for
94.184.*

94.186 *A LIFE POLICY* (P,4a) Helen Davis. TERRY'S 20/7/
94 mat perf.* <u>Col. Leigh</u> Charles Rock; <u>Lawrence Maber</u>
Herbert Flemming; <u>Dr Langley</u> Philip Cunningham; <u>Reg-</u>
<u>inald Lowthian</u> Rudge Harding; <u>Rev Mr Govette</u> F. Per-
cival Stevens; <u>Mr Kelp</u> Robb Harwood; <u>Dr Rogers</u> Albert
Sims; <u>Dr Drew</u> Harold Mead; <u>Detective</u> E.G. Woodhouse;
<u>John</u> R. Rivers. <u>Little Lawrence</u> Valli Valli; <u>Elsie</u>
Winifred Fraser; <u>Beatrice Morte</u> Mrs Herbert Waring;
<u>Mrs Lothian</u> Bertha Staunton; <u>Nurse Billings</u> Mrs Ed-
ward Saker; <u>Matilda</u> Rose Dudley. <u>PP</u> Edward Terry; <u>Dir</u>
Henry Montagu; <u>Furn</u> Frank Giles; <u>Bm</u> Harrington Baily.
*REV: Ath 28/7/94 p140; E 21/7/94 p9; Sk 25/7/94 p678;
St 26/7/94 p10-1.*

94.187 *THE LADY OF LONGFORD* (O[1a]) L.E. Bach (mus)
& Augustus Harris (lib) & Frederic E. Weatherly (lib).
COVENT GARDEN 21/7/94, 26/7/94. 2 perf.* <u>Earl of</u>
<u>Longford</u> Albert Alvarez; <u>Roundhead Col.</u> Edouard de
Reszke. <u>Countess of Longford</u> Emma Eames; <u>Little Muriel</u>
Evelyn Hughes. <u>L & MGR</u> Augustus Harris; <u>Cond</u> Luigi
Mancinelli; <u>Bom</u> E. Hall; <u>A act mgr</u> Neil Forsyth. *REV:
Ath 28/7/94 p138; E 28/7/94 p15; SR 28/7/94 p97-8; St
26/7/94 p10; Ti 23/7/94 p8.*

94.188 *THE MERCHANT OF VENICE* (C,5a) William Shakes-
peare. LYCEUM 21/7/94. 1 perf.** <u>Shylock</u> Henry Irving;
<u>Bassanio</u> William Terriss; <u>Duke of Venice</u> [Henry] Howe;
<u>Antonio</u> [William] Haviland; <u>Prince of Morocco</u> [Frank]
Tyars; <u>Salanio</u> Lacy; <u>Salarino</u> John Martin Harvey;
<u>Gratiano</u> Frank [Kemble] Cooper; <u>Lorenzo</u> [Clarence]
Hague; <u>Tubal</u> [John] Archer; <u>Launcelot Gobbo</u> S[am]
Johnson; <u>Old Gobbo</u> [T.] Reynolds; <u>Gaoler</u> Graham; <u>Leo-</u>
<u>nardo</u> [W.] Marion; <u>Balthazar</u> [K.] Rivington; <u>Stephano</u>
[W. Lionel] Belmore; <u>Clerk of the Court</u> [R.P.] Tabb.
<u>Nerissa</u> Kate Phillips; <u>Jessica</u> Amy Coleridge; <u>Portia</u>
Ellen Terry. <u>L & MGR</u> Henry Irving; <u>Sc</u> Hawes Craven,
William Telbin; <u>Cond</u> J. Meredith Ball; <u>Sm</u> H.J. Loveday;

Act mgr Bram Stoker. *REV: E 28/7/94 p9; Sk 1/8/94 p42;
SR 28/7/94 p100; St 26/7/94 p10; Ti 23/7/94 p8.*

94.189 *SIXES AND SEVENS* (Ca) E.H. Whitmore. LYCEUM
23/7/94 mat perf.** Cpt. George Hope Arthur Bourchier.
Edith Cashdown Irene Vanbrugh. L & MGR Henry Irving;
Bom Joseph Hurst; Bm Algernon Adye; Pq William Clarkson. *REV: E 28/7/94 p11.*

94.190 *NOT A BAD JUDGE* (CD,2a) J.R. Planché. ROYALTY
23/7/94. 1 perf. 1st perfd Lyceum 2/3/48. Marquis de
Treval Leslie Kenyon; Count de Steinberg William Lugg;
John Caspar Lavater W.L. Abingdon; Christian Thomas
Kingston; Betman Compton Coutts; Zug Ells Dagnall;
Rutley F[rank] Macrae; Notary Arthur Coe; Servant
Barrett. Louise Ettie Williams; Mme Betman Katherine
Stewart. MGR Edward Hastings. *REV: E 28/7/94 p9; St
26/7/94 p10.*

94.191 *THE LINEN DRAPER* (FC,3a) J.R. Brown & J.F.
Thornthwaite. ROYALTY 23/7/94. 1 perf.** Benjamin
Bazin E.M. Robson; Squire de Broke William Lugg; Cpt.
Harold de Broke Leslie Kenyon; Reginald Maitland
Compton Coutts; Lush Ells Dagnall; George Barrett.
Sarah Cicely Richards; Elinor Marsh Ettie Williams;
Mary Bazin Mary Raby; Mrs Maitland Katherine Stewart.
MGR Edward Hastings. *REV: As for 94.190.*

94.192 *HOME RULE* (CD,1a) J.G. Taylor. CRITERION 24/7/
94-15/9/94. 47 perf. 1st perfd Prince of Wales's,
Liverpool 19/3/77. Tom Bowles J.G. Taylor; John Veal
Frank Atherley; Ben Lanyard Fred J. Vigay. Nancy
Bowles Emily Vining; Mary Lanyard Annie Saker. L & MGR
Charles Wyndham; Act mgr & Treas E. Harvey.

94.193 *A FLYING VISIT* (Duol) Mrs William Greet. PRIN-
CESS'S 24/7/94 mat perf. 1st perfd Criterion 6/11/89.
Roland Atwood. Kate Bealby. PP Mrs Harriett Gooch;
Dir W.A. Baskcomb. *REV: St 26/7/94 p10.*

94.194 *IN HONOUR BOUND* (C,1a) Sydney Grundy. PRINCESS'S
24/7/94 mat perf.** Sir George Carlyon W.E. Bonney;
Philip Graham W.J. Montgomery. Rose Dalrymple Lillie
Hamilton; Lady Carlyon Louise Jordan. PP, Dir as for

94.193. *REV: St 26/7/94 p10.*

94.195 *THE PURITAN* (P,4a) David Christie Murray, Henry Murray & John L. Shine. TRAFALGAR 26/7/94 mat perf.* <u>Frank Milton</u> Charles Glenney; <u>Sir John Saunderson</u> W.L. Abingdon; <u>Baron de Marsac</u> Edward O'Neill; <u>James Burdock</u> John L. Shine; <u>Mr Duflos</u> Sant Matthews; <u>Col. Cheriere</u> George Warde; <u>Delbecchi</u> Harry Grattan; <u>Suisse</u> S. Hill; <u>Jean</u> H.G. Dupres; <u>Waiter</u> J. Mahoney. <u>Countess de Ricquiere</u> Florence Seymour; <u>Mary Milton</u> Winifred Fraser; <u>Leonide de Blanc</u> Mrs Theodore Wright; <u>Baroness de Marsac</u> Alice de Winton; <u>Mme Duflos</u> Agnes Hewitt; <u>Adele Duflos</u> Dora Barton. <u>PD</u> Herman de Lange; <u>Mus</u> Osmond Carr. *REV: Ath 4/8/94 p171; E 28/7/94 p11; St 2/8/94 p10.*

94.196 *LA BELLE ROSE.* LYRIC 28/7/94-8/8/94. 10 perf. <u>Comment</u>: Advertized in *Ti* for these dates.

94.197 *MISS RUTLAND* (P,3a) Richard Pryce. ROYALTY 28/7/94 mat perf.** <u>Comment</u>: Advertized in *Ti* for this date, but possibly not perfd.

94.198 *DIE MEISTERSINGER* (O[3a]) Richard Wagner. COVENT GARDEN 30/7/94. 1 perf.** <u>Pogner</u> Pol Plançon; <u>Hans Sachs</u> Mario Ancona; <u>Beckmesser</u> David Bispham; <u>Kunz Vogelgesang</u> Iginio Corsi; <u>Konrad Nachtigal</u> Richard Green; <u>David</u> Joseph O'Mara; <u>Fritz Kothner</u> Eugene Dufriche; <u>Balthazar Zorn</u> Rinaldini; <u>Herman Ortel</u> Antonio de Vaschetti; <u>Ulrich Eisslinger</u> Leonard; <u>Augustin Moser</u> Maestri; <u>Hans Foltz</u> Cernusco; <u>Walter von Stoltzing</u> Jean de Reszke; <u>Night Watchman/Hans Schwars</u> Villani. <u>Eva</u> Emma Eames; <u>Magdalena</u> Mathilde Bauermeister. <u>L & MGR</u> Augustus Harris; <u>Cond</u> Luigi Mancinelli; <u>Bom</u> E. Hall; <u>A act mgr</u> Neil Forsyth. *REV: Ath 4/8/94 p170; E 4/8/94 p13; SR 4/8/94 p126-7; St 2/8/94 p10; Ti 31/7/94 p5.*

94.199 *TO CALL HER MINE* (D,1a) Benjamin Landeck. LYRIC 30/7/94 mat perf. 1st perfd Surrey 18/12/93. <u>David</u> Ernest Leicester; <u>Fisherman</u> Ernest Norris. <u>Mary</u> Harriett Clifton; <u>Bess</u> Haidee Wright. *REV: E 4/8/94 p7.*

94.200 *WINNING A WIDOW* (Ca,1a). LYRIC 30/7/94 mat
perf. 1st perfd Soho 28/5/56. George Grossmith. Agnes
Hewitt. *REV: E 4/8/94 p7.*

94.201 *NEW YEAR'S EVE* (MMonol) Frank H. Lindo (lib)
& Algernon H. Lindo (mus). LYRIC 30/7/94 mat perf.
1st perfd Grosvenor Club, New Bond St 12/7/94. Sir
George Beauchamp George Tate. Mrs Kingsley Decima
Moore. *REV: E 4/8/94 p7.*

94.202 *THE TWO ORPHANS* (Bsq) John F. Sheridan. LYRIC
30/7/94 mat perf. 1st perf? Pierre E.J. Lonnen;
Louise John F. Sheridan; La Frochard Harry Grattan;
Doctor Montelli; La Fleur W.M. Birch; Julius Caesar
H.G. Dupres. Jacques Agnes Hewitt; Chevalier de Vaudrey Cissie Cranford; Marquis de Presles Millie Marsden; Henriette Gracie Whiteford. *REV: E 4/8/94 p7.*

94.203 *LOYAL* (P,1a) Henry T. Johnson. VAUDEVILLE 9/8/
94-14/12/94. 110 perf.* Col. Clulow Frederick Volpé;
King Charles II Thomas Kingston; Master Perkin Port-
soken Arthur Helmore; Robin Ruddock T.A. Palmer; Sgt.
Joel J.L. Mackay. Lilian Clulow Esmé Beringer/May
Palfrey; Cicely Alice Beet. L Weedon Grossmith; Mgr
A.F. Henderson; Dir Herman de Lange; Mus dir C.J. Hargitt. *REV: E 11/8/94 p7; Sk 15/8/94 p161; St 16/8/94
p10; TW94 p221.*

94.204 *LITTLE JACK SHEPPARD* (Bsq,3a) H.P. Stephens
(lib) & William Yardley (lib) & W. Meyer Lutz (mus)
& Alfred Cellier (mus) & Arthur Cecil (mus) & J.
Hamilton Clarke (mus) & Florian Pascal (mus). GAIETY
11/8/94-29/9/94. 49 perf [w/mat 25/8, 1/9, 12/9,
20/9, 26/9, 29/9]. 1st perfd Gaiety 26/12/85. Jonathan
Wild Seymour Hicks; Blueskin Charles Danby; Mr Wood
E.W. Royce; Abraham Mendez Frank M. Wood; Kneebone
W. Warde; Sir Roland Trenchard W[illiam] Cheesman.
Jack Sheppard Jessie Preston; Mrs Sheppard Lizzie
Collier; Thames Darrell Amy Augarde; Poll Stanmore
Florence Levey; Edgeworth Bess Violet Monckton; Kitty
Kettleby Georgina Preston; Mrs Wood Maria Jones;
Winifred Wood Ellaline Terriss; Cpt. Cuff Ethel Earle/
Nora Millington; Shotbolt Maud Sutherland; Ireton
Carrie Benton; Marvell Kate Cannon; Little Gog Raynor;

Little Magog Rossell; Arnold Lillie Henshawe. L & MGR
George Edwardes; Sc E.G. Banks, Walter Hann; Cost dgn
Ida & A. Chasemore; Cost Harrisons; Pq Fox; Ch Willie
Warde; Gas & Elect Effects George Poynton; Dir
Walter Raynham; Mus dir W. Meyer Lutz; Act mgr E[d-
ward] Marshall; Bom A.P. Oxley. *REV: E 18/8/94 p7;
Sk 15/8/94 p161, 5/9/94 p283, 285, 12/9/94 p361; St
16/8/94 p10; Th 1/9/94 p135-8; Ti 13/8/94 p7; TW94
p218-220.*

94.205 *HOT WATER* (FC,3a) H.B. Farnie [adpt of Henri
Meilhac & Ludovic Halévy *La Boule*]. CRITERION 15/8/
94-15/9/94. 32 perf [w/S mat exc 18/8]. 1st perfd
Criterion 13/11/76. Chauncery Pattleton Charles H.
Hawtrey; Sir Philander Rose Edward Righton; Martin
George Giddens; Corbyn J.G. Taylor; M'Lud William
Blakeley; Moddle Sydney Valentine; Usher William
Wyes/Ells Dagnall; Stage Manager Frank Atherley; Pi-
etro F[red J.] Vigay; Footman Nichols; Tiger Master
[Sidney?] Westgate. Mrs Pattleton Edith Chester; Mme
Marietta Miriam Clements/Katherine Drew; Lady Rose
Alice de Winton; Mrs Pitcher Emily Vining; Jane
Katherine Drew; Nina Annie Saker. L & MGR Charles
Wyndham; Cost Mme Eroom; Act mgr & Treas E. Harvey.
*REV: Ath 18/8/94 p236; E 18/8/94 p7; Sk 22/8/94 p178;
St 23/8/94 p10; TW94 p222-3.*

94.206 *THE FOUNDLING* (F,3a) W[illiam] Lestocq & E.M.
Robson. TERRY'S 30/8/94-26/10/94. 58 perf [w/mat 12/9,
19/9, 26/9, 3/10, 10/10, 17/10, 20/10, 24/10].* Mjr.
Cotton Charles Groves; Dick Pennell Sydney Brough;
Timothy Hucklebridge Huntley Wright; Jack Stanton
Oswald Yorke; Sir Nicholas Pennell George Warde.
Alice Meynall Ellis Jeffreys; Mrs Cotton Susie Vau-
ghan; Sophie Cotton Fanny Erris; Miss Ussher Minnie
Clifford; Tricky Little Maybud Emmeline Orford. PP
Edward Terry; Mgr W.J. Holloway; Sc Bruce Smith; Cost
dgn Marie Louise; Cost Marie Louise, Mme Wyndham;
Furn Longman & Co.; Mus dir James Weaver; Rep James
W. Mathews. *REV: E 1/9/94 p7; Sk 5/9/94 p291; St 6/9/
94 p12; Th 1/10/94 p191-2; Ti 31/8/94 p3; TW94 p232.*

94.207 *THEN FLOWERS GREW FAIRER* (P,1a) Sutton Vane.
TERRY'S 30/8/94-26/10/94. 50 perf. 1st perfd Lyric

Hall, Ealing 18/2/92. Jasper Hope George Warde; Lieut.
Fergus Boyne Oswald Yorke; Morgan Stanley Kenniss/
C.J. Easton. Felicia Hope Lizzie Webster; Beatrice
Gwynne Herbert. PP, Mgr, Mus dir, Rep as for 94.206.
REV: E, St as for 94.206.

94.208 *THE NEW WOMAN* (C,4a) Sydney Grundy. COMEDY 1/9/
94-5/2/95. 173 perf [w/W, S mat exc 1/9, 5/9, 8/9,
12/9, 26/12; np 24-25/12/94].* Gerald Cazenove Fred
Terry; Col. Cazenove Cyril Maude; Cpt. Sylvester J.G.
Graham; Mr Armstrong William Wyes; Percy Pettigrew
S[tuart] Champion; Wells J[ohn] Byron; Servant Mules
Brown. Lady Wargrave Rose Leclercq; Mrs Sylvester
Alma Murray; Enid Bethune Laura Graves; Victoria Vi-
vash Gertrude Warden; Dr Mary Bevan Irene Rickards;
Margery Armstrong Winifred Emery. L & MGR J.W. Comyns
Carr; Sc Walter Johnstone, Walter Hann; Bom Scarisbrick; Sm Edward Hastings; Bm Silvanus Dauncey; Mus
dir Alfred J. Caldicott. *REV: Ath 8/9/94 p331; E 8/9/
94 p9; Sk 5/9/94 p329, 12/9/94 p386, 17/10/94 p623,
5/12/94 p263, 12/12/94 supp p7-12, 6/2/95 p66-7; SR
8/9/94 p263-4; St 6/9/94 p12; Th 1/10/94 p186-7; Ti
3/9/94 p2, 30/11/94 p6; TW94 p223-32.*

94.209 *THE FATAL CARD* (P,5a) C. Haddon Chambers & B.C.
Stephenson. ADELPHI 6/9/94-16/3/95. 167 perf [w/mat
26/12/94, 12/1/95, 26/1, 9/2/95; np 24-25/12/94].*
Gerald Austen William Terriss; George Marrable Murray
Carson; Harry Burgess Harry Nicholls/Herbert Budd/
E.W. Gardiner; A.K. Austen Charles J. Fulton; James
Dixon W.L. Abingdon; Terence O'Flynn Richard Purdon;
Sulky Smith Cory Thomas; Harry Curtis Herbert Budd/
Blackburn; Hiram Webster Caleb Porter/Herbert Budd;
Cyrus Wackford Akerman May; Bully Jack W.A. Harrison/
W.B.D. Harrison; Dutch Winnigan W. Strickland; Cow
Boy W[illiam] Younge/Morley; Cattleman Walford; Mike
F. Boden. Margaret Marrable Jessie Millward; Mercedes
Vane; Cecile Austen Laura Linden; Penelope Austen
Sophie Larkin/Alice Carlton; Kate Three Stars [Irene?]
du Foye/Alice Carlton/Clara d'Alcourt; Servant in
Act III Retta Villis; Servant in Act IV Beatrice Hay-
den/L[eila?] Rivers. PP & MGR A. & S. Gatti; Bm Fred
G. Latham; Mus & Mus dir Edward Jones; Sc Joseph Har-
ker, T.W. Hall, Bruce Smith; Cost Jay, Mme Vanite,

Stagg & Mantle, Morris Angel & Son; Pq William Clarkson; Furn Frank Giles & Co.; Pd Fred G. Latham; Bom Arthur Frye. *REV: Ath 15/9/94 p363; E 8/9/94 p11; Sk 12/9/94 p341; SR 15/9/94 p290-1; St 13/9/94 p12-3; Th 1/10/94 p189-90; Ti 7/9/94 p3; TW94 p233-7.*

94.210 *THE QUEEN OF BRILLIANTS* (CO,3a) Brandon Thomas (lib) [adpt fr Gr of Theodor Taube & Isidor Fuchs] & Edward Jakobowski (mus). LYCEUM 8/9/94-18/10/94. 41 perf [w/S mat exc 8/9; add mat 17/10].* Florian Bauer Hubert Wilke; Della Fontana Arthur Williams; Lucca Rabbiato W.H. Denny; Grelotto John Le Hay; Mjr. Victor Pulvereitzer Avon Saxon/Max Eugene; Count Radaman Caprimonte Owen Westford;Moritz Fred Storey; Max Fred Wright, jr; Beppo Compton Coutts; Andrea Rupert Lister; Waiter Henry George; Fritz George Honey; Don Garcia James Pearson; Footman Hendon; Hackney Coachman Robert Stevens; Head Gardener John Evans; Dancers Fred Wright, jr, Fred Storey. Mme Englestein Amadi; Emma Lizzie Ruggles; Orsola Annie Meyers; Mirandola Florence Burle; Carola Sadie Wigley; Fioretta Lillie Comyns; Minna Susanne Leonard; Fraulein Kauf Zoe Gilfillan; Fraulein Schmidt Jessie Bradford; Head Matron Bertha Staunton; Bella Lillian Russell; Dancers Madge Greet, Helen Graeme, Biddy Rees, May Gore, Marion Gordon, Ethel Arundel; Ella Kitson; Gracie Leigh. L & MGR Henry Irving; Pd Charles Harris; Dir Henry E. Abbey, Maurice Grau; Bom Joseph Hurst; Sc Hawes Craven, Joseph Harker, William Perkins; Ch John d'Auban; Cond Paul Steindorff; Asm R.H. Burnside; Cost dgn A. Comelli; Cost Charles Alias, Auguste, Harrisons, B.J. Simmons, F. Westoby, Mme Gascoigne, Mrs Champion, Morris Angel & Son; Pq Mrs Charles Fox; Furn James Lyon & Son, Arnott; Mach W. Powell; Gen mgr C.J. Abud. *REV: E 15/9/94 p8; Sk 12/9/94 p344, 21/11/94 p184-5; SR 15/9/94 p290; St 13/9/94 p12, 25/10/94 p13; Th 1/ 10/94 p190-1; Ti 10/9/94 p10.*

94.211 *THE CHINAMAN* (FC,3a) John Tresahar. TRAFALGAR 13/9/94-4/10/94. 22 perf [w/W mat]. 1st perfd City, Sheffield 16/7/94. Hon Henry Reginald Hampton John Tresahar; Percy Fenton T.G. Warren; Ephraim Z. van Beekmann Graham Wentworth; Henri Gratin Frank Wyatt. Cotton Clara Jecks/Harry Bass; Julia Cicely Richards;

Constance Fenton Rhoda Halkett; Lucy Delia Carlyle;
Stella van Beekmann Edith Kenward. PP Mr & Mrs Frank
Wyatt; Mus dir Arthur E. Godfrey; Sm Graham Wentworth;
Cost Morris Angel & Son; Pq William Clarkson; Furn
James Lyons & Sons; Bm H[enry] Brandon. *REV: E 15/9/
94 p11; Sk 19/9/94 p400; St 20/9/94 p12-3; Th 1/10/94
p192-3; TW94 p240-44.* Comment: Nicoll indicates that
The Chinaman was the original title, as played at
Sheffield, and that the title at the Trafalgar was
Naughty Boys.

94.212 *THE ELECTRIC SPARK* Elizabeth Bessle [adpt of
Edouard Pailleron, *L'Etincelle*]. TRAFALGAR 13/9/94-
4/10/94. 19 perf. 1st perfd Olympic 8/5/89. Cpt.
Norreys Graham Wentworth. Lady Treherne Blanche Ripley; Geraldine Delia Carlyle. PP, Mus dir, Sm, Cost,
Pq, Furn, Bm as for 94.211. *REV: E 15/9/94 p11; St
20/9/94 p13.*

94.213 *LITTLE MISS CUTE* (Variety C,4a) Charles T. Vin-
cent; arr E.B. Norman. ROYALTY 14/9/94. 1 perf.*
Archie Forrester Gerald Spencer; Sir Arthur Radcliffe
Frank H. Fenton; Admiral Caroll Leslie Eardley Turner;
Edward Mountfort Edward Broughton; Count Giuseppe
Marani Ivan Watson; Jones Albert Sims; Filippo A.H.
Brooke. Lady Radcliffe Alexes Leighton; Helen Dean
Violet Armbruster; Mrs Leslie Ethel Hope; Miss Cute
Dexter Hope Booth; Edith Radcliff Italia Conti. L
Kate Santley; Bm C.G. Compton; Pd E.B. Norman. *REV:
E 22/9/94 p8; Sk 19/9/94 p400; St 20/9/94 p13; TW94
p244.*

94.214 *ON TOAST* (Ca,1a) Fred Horner. ROYALTY 14/9/94.
1 perf. 1st perfd Avenue 16/7/88. Peter Mapleson
Sheridan Lascelles; Mr Leigh Owen Harris; Joseph
Albert Sims. Mrs Leigh Violet Armbruster; Mrs Mapleson
Lillie Young. L, Bm as for 94.213. *REV: E, St as for
94.213.*

94.215 *THE DERBY WINNER* (D,4a) Augustus Harris, Cecil
Raleigh & Henry Hamilton. DRURY LANE 15/9/94-15/12/94;*
trfd to PRINCESS'S 26/12/94-16/2/95. 140 perf [w/S
mat 22/9-15/12; np 17-21/12, 25/12]. Earl of Desborough Arthur Bourchier/Rudge Harding; Col. Myles

Donelly James East; Mjr. Geoffrey Mostyn Charles Cart-
wright/Charles Dalton; Cpt. Lord Chisholm Rudge Hard-
ing; Rupert Leigh Charles Dalton/A. Hamilton Revelle;
Hon Guy Bagot Ernest Lawford/Standley Wade; Cyprian
Streatfield George Giddens/Maurice Drew; Joe Aylmer
Lionel Rignold/Charles Dodsworth; Dick Hammond Harry
Eversfield; Mr Langford Maurice Drew/Kenneth Black;
Mr Wilson Charles Hurst; Mr Wallace Henry Lorraine;
Waiter at the Railway Hotel James Francis/Spencer
Trevor; Boots at the Railway Hotel Jervis Vincent;
Auctioneer at Tattersal's Maurice Dudley; Guide at the
Law Courts Arthur Cowley; Usher at the Law Courts John
Lock/A. Leverett; Servant to Lord Desborough Digby
Roberts/Lyons; Waiter at the White Hart Hotel Charles
Danvers. Duchess of Milford Mrs John Wood; Countess
of Desborough Beatrice Lamb; Mrs Donelly Louise Moodie;
Annette Donelly Pattie Browne; Vivien Darville Alma
Stanley/Mrs Cecil Raleigh; Mary Aylmer Hetty Dene;
Nurse Lumley Amy Abbott; Harold, Viscount Fernside
Evelyn Hughes/Jessica Black; Lady Hilborough Lena
Delphine; Lady Mary Prestbury Lizzie Wilson; Countess
of Lingfield Georgie Cook; Duchess of Queenstown
Lydia Rachel; Lady Betty Tufnell L[ily] Brooking;
Lady Broadmoor L. Feverell; Lady Hilda Pentonville
E[thel] Beaumont; Hon Mrs Bentomond J. Talbot; Miss
Amelia P. Calhoun M. Thyler; Miss Grace O'Grady [May?]
St. Aubyn. L & MGR & DIR Augustus Harris; Bom W.
Allcroft; Sm Arthur P. Collins; Asm Frank Damer; A
act mgr Neil Forsyth; Mus James M. Glover; Sc Robert
Caney, William Perkins, Joseph Harker; Props Jackson
& Sons, J. Jones; Cost Miss Palmer, Mrs Besford, Mrs
Manning, Morris Angel & Son, Russell & Allen, Deben-
ham & Freebody; Pq William Clarkson; Mach E.A. Taylor.
REV: Ath 22/9/94 p395; E 22/9/94 p8, 23/2/95 p9; Sk
19/9/94 p400, 26/9/94 p455, 26/9/94 p498, 501, 14/11/
94 p114; SR 22/9/94 p322-3; St 20/9/94 p12, 27/12/94
p10; Th 1/10/94 p187-9; Ti 17/9/94 p10; TW94 p245-51.

94.216 *GRAF WALDEMAR* (P,5a) Gustav Freytag. OPERA
COMIQUE 15/9/94, 17/9/94. 2 perf. 1st perfd 1847.
Waldemar Graf Schenk Caesar Beck; Hiller William Karfiol; Fedor Iwanowitsch Furst Udaschkin Max Weilenbeck; Hugo Graf Schenk Heinrich Kamm; Box Ludwig Schubart; Rittmeister von Randor Siegfried Philippi; Hein-

rich von Sorben Albert Schmidt; Gordon Hugo Weitzel;
Der Bezirksvorsteher Hans Muller; Ein Nachwachter
Emil Moser; Gregor Fritz Weiler. Hans Elly Arndt;
Gertrude Eleonore von Driller; Georgine Furstin Udaschkin Milli Elsinger; Frau Box Frau Dr Heinold-Thomann; Kammerfrau Kathe Walden. DIR Charles F. Maurice.
REV: *Ath 20/10/94 p538; E 22/9/94 p9; Sk 19/9/94 p400,
26/9/94 p456-8, 10/10/94 p601; St 20/9/94 p13; Th 1/
10/94 p193-4; Ti 17/9/94 p10; TW94 p251-3, 253-6.*

94.217 *TILLI* (C,4a) Franz Stahl. OPERA COMIQUE 18/9/
94, 19/9, 22/9/94(m). 3 perf. Rebus Ernst Petersen;
Alfred Ludwig Schubart; Baron Strauss Max Weilenbeck;
Dr Phil Ernst Muller Ludwig Rusing; Karl Albert Sch-
midt. Thekla Frau Dr Heinold-Thomann; Tilli Anna Hocke;
Ella Toni Hoops; Corinna Elly Arndt; Friederike Kathe
Walden. *REV: E 22/9/94 p9; Sk 26/9/94 p455; St 27/9/
94 p12; Th 1/10/94 p194; Ti 19/9/94 p8.*

94.218 *DER PFARRER VON KIRCHFELD* (DD,5a) Ludwig Anzen-
gruber. OPERA COMIQUE 20/9/94, 21/9/94. 2 perf. 1st
perfd 5/11/70. Hell, Pfarrer von Kirchfeld Caesar
Beck; Graf von Hinterberg Heinrich Kamm; Wurzelsepp
Max Weilenbeck; Lux, Revierforster William Karfiol;
Der Pfarrer von St Jacob Ernst Petersen; Michl Bern-
dorfer Albert Schmidt; Thalmuller Loisl Ludwig Schu-
bart; Der Wirth Hugo Weitzel. Anna Eleanore von
Driller; Seine Braut Toni Hoops; Brigitte Frau Dr
Heinold-Thomann; Schullehrer Siegfried Philippi; Die
Wirthin Margarite Dittini; Hansl Elly Arndt. *REV: E,
Sk, St as for 94.217; TW94 p256.*

94.219 *ROBERT UND BERTRAM* (MP,4a) Gustav Rader. OPERA
COMIQUE 22/9/94, 24-25/9, 29/9/94(m). 4 perf. Robert
Charles F. Maurice; Bertram Ernst Peterson; Ipelmayer
Max Weilenbeck; Samuel Bandheim Ludwig Rusing; Erste
Albert Schmidt; Mehlmeyer William Karfiol; Polizei-
diener Carl Mantzel; Strambach Heinrich Kamm; Zweite
Hermann Schneider; Dritte Arthur Formes; Corporal
Paul Vielheim; Lips Willy Hammer; Erster Paul Horn;
Zweiter Ernst Heise; Brautvater Hermann Feller; Braeu-
tigam Fred Wahl; Jack Louis Zeiter; Louis Carl Fahr.
Michel Elly Arndt; Rosel Milli Elsinger; Isidora Toni
Hoops; Commerzeinrathm Forchheimer Frau Dr Heinold-

Thomann; <u>Frau Muller</u> Louise Zahn. *REV: E 29/9/94 p15; St 27/9/94 p12.*

94.220 *CLAUDE DU-VAL* (MP,2a) Frederick Bowyer (lib) & "Payne Nunn" (lib) & John Crook (mus) & Lionel Monckton (mus). PRINCE OF WALES'S 25/9/94-15/2/95. 142 perf [w/S mat exc 22/12/94, 9/1/95; add mat 17/10/94, 31/10/94; np 24-25/12/94]. 1st perfd Prince's, Bristol 23/7/94. <u>Sir Phillip Saxmundham</u> Eric Thorne/W.H. Denny; <u>Percy</u> Fitzroy Morgan/E.H. Kelly; <u>Sherlock Holmes-Spotter</u> H.O. Clarey/James Welsh; <u>Pincher, alias Lord Touchem</u> Charles E. Stevens/W.P. Dempsey; <u>Jasper</u> J. Winterbottom/J.W. Leonard/Leonard Russell; <u>Simon Wuzzle</u> Hayman/Laidman; <u>Jeames</u> Laidman/Danby/Sydney Watson; <u>Claude Duval</u> Arthur Roberts. <u>Johnny Albany</u> Georgie Edwards/Carrie Benton; <u>Harry Burlington</u> Maud Crichton/Poppy Haines; <u>Gussy Criterion</u> Ada Peppiatte/Edith Stuart; <u>Bertie Grafton</u> Marie Burdell/Flo Harrison; <u>Lady Joan Saxmundham</u> Amy Lyddon/Alice Aynsley Cook; <u>Gertie</u> Eva Ellerslie; <u>Dolly</u> Nellie Arline/Alice Holbrook/Simeta Marsden/Minnie Davenport; <u>Betty</u> Thornhill/Kitty Harcourt/Violet Leslie/Kitty Harcourt; <u>Letty</u> Louise Norman/Lily Dickinson/Lillian Farnie/Minnie Davenport; <u>Polly</u> Ida Young/Ellas Dee/A. Young; <u>Marjorie Saxmundham</u> Florrie Schuberth/Violet Robinson; <u>Lady Dorcas Chetwynd</u> Marie Halton/Alice Holbrook/Aida Jenoure. <u>PD</u> Arthur Roberts, E. Story Gofton; <u>Cost</u> Alias; <u>Pq</u> William Clarkson; <u>Ch</u> Willie Warde; <u>Furn</u> J.S. Lyon; <u>Cond</u> Ernest Allan; <u>Sm</u> E. Story Gofton; <u>Bm</u> J.W. Summers, C.P. Levilly; <u>Asm</u> Sidney Watson. *REV: E 29/9/94 p9; Sk 26/9/94 p456, 3/10/94 p512, 24/10/94 p679-80, 19/12/94 p352; SR 29/9/94 p352; St 27/9/94 p12-3; Th 1/11/94 p251-3; Ti 17/12/94 p10; TW94 p264-5.*

94.221 *DER MEINEIDBAUER* (P,3a) Ludwig Anzengruber. OPERA COMIQUE 26/9/94, 27/9, 1/10/94. 3 perf. 1st perfd 1871. <u>Mathias Ferner</u> Caesar Beck; <u>Grossknecht</u> Ludwig Rusing; <u>Franz</u> Albert Schmidt; <u>Adam Hollerer</u> Heinrich Kamm; <u>Toni</u> Ludwig Schubart; <u>Jacob</u> Siegfried Philippi; <u>Bader</u> William Karfiol; <u>Muckerl</u> Hugo Weitzel. <u>Vroni</u> Eleonore von Driller; <u>Crescenz</u> Anna Hocke; <u>Rosl</u> Elly Arndt; <u>Mirzl</u> Toni Hoops; <u>Burgerlies</u> Frau Dr Heinold-Thomann; <u>Waberl</u> Milli Elsinger; <u>Annerl</u> Kathe

Walden; <u>Bauenahn</u> Margarete Dittini; <u>Kathrin</u> Mizi Gruber. *REV: E 29/9/94 p15; Sk 3/10/94 p511; TW94 p265.*

94.222 *DURCH DIE INTENDANZ* (C,5a) E. Henke. OPERA
COMIQUE 28/9/94, 29/9, 2/10/94. 3 perf. Max Weilenbeck; Ludwig Rusing; Ernst Petersen; Siegfried Philippi; William Karfiol; Heinrich Kamm. Eleonore von
Driller; Anna Hocke; Frau Dr Heinold-Thomann.

94.223 *VERSPRECHEN HINTER'M HEERD* (MSk). OPERA COMI-
QUE 28/9/94, 29/9, 2/10/94. 3 perf. Charles F. Maurice. Elly Arndt.

94.224 *ODETTE* (P,4a) Clement Scott [adpt of Victorien
Sardou]. PRINCESS'S 29/9/94-12/10/94. 12 perf.*
<u>Lord Henry Trevene</u> Charles Warner; <u>Johnny Stratford</u>
Bernard Gould; <u>Philip Eden</u> Herbert Flemming; <u>Lord
Arthur Trevene</u> Eardley Howard; <u>Prince Nobitskoy</u> Roth-
bury Evans; <u>Dr Wilkes</u> Charles F. Lander; <u>Mr Hanway</u>
Gordon Tompkins; <u>Narcisse</u> Paul M. Berton; <u>Joseph</u>
Frederic Jacques; <u>Francois</u> W. Rosse. <u>Eva Trevene</u>
Ettie Williams; <u>Margaret Eden</u> Marie Cecil; <u>Lady Wal-
ker</u> E. Brinsley Sheridan; <u>Countess Varola</u> Mrs W.L.
Abingdon; <u>Mrs Hanway</u> Mrs B.M. de Solla; <u>Miss Bertram</u>
Rose Dupres; <u>Olga</u> Eva Valmard; <u>Odette</u> Mrs Anna Ruppert. <u>PP</u> Mrs Harriett Gooch; <u>Mgr</u> Mrs Anna Ruppert;
<u>Furn</u> Mawer & Stephenson; <u>Sc</u> Richard C. Durant; <u>Pq &
Cost</u> William Clarkson; <u>Props</u> Labhart; <u>Mach</u> J.W. Cawdery; <u>Lime</u> L.C. Parnell; <u>Mus dir</u> L. Térès. *REV: Ath
6/10/94 p465; E 6/10/94 p8; Sk 3/10/94 p511; St 4/10/
94 p14; Th 1/11/94 p255-6; Ti 1/10/94 p10; TW94 p259-
64.*

94.225 *A TRIP TO CHINATOWN* (MC,2a) Charles Hoyt.
TOOLE'S 29/9/94-15/12/94; trfd to STRAND 17/12/94-12/
1/95. 120 perf [w/W, S mat exc 29/9, 3/10, 10/10;
add mat 9/11, 27/12, 28/12; np 24-25/12]. 1st perfd
Hoyt's, New York 9/11/91. <u>Welland Strong</u> R.G. Knowles;
<u>Ben Gay</u> Herman de Lange; <u>Rashleigh Gay</u> Edgar Stevens;
<u>Norman Blood</u> Harry Hilliard; <u>Noah Heap</u> Albert Bernard/
Huntley Wright/H. Tripp Edgar; <u>Price</u> George Egbert;
<u>Slavin Payne</u> Fred Bousfield/Albert Bernard. <u>Willie
Grow</u> Clara Jecks/May Edouin; <u>Tiny Gay</u> Audrey Ford;
<u>Isabella Dame</u> Edith Vane; <u>Flirt</u> Georgie Wright; <u>Mrs</u>

Guyer Edith Bruce/Alice Atherton. L J.L. Toole; Mgr
H. Tripp Edgar; Sm Herman de Lange; Mus dir William
Robins; Gen mgr Gilbert Tate; Sc Joseph Harker, Bruce
Smith; Cost Mrs S. May, Morris Angel; Pq William
Clarkson; Mus Percy Gaunt, William Robins; Ch Georgie
Wright. *REV: E 6/10/94 p9, 22/12/94 p8; Sk 3/10/94
p511, 31/10/94 p12; St 4/10/94 p14-5, 1/11/94 p13,
20/12/94 p13; Th 1/11/94 p253-4; Ti 1/10/94 p10; TW94
p275-6.*

94.226 *RICHARD'S PLAY* (P,1a) Mary C. Rowsell & Joseph
J. Dilley. TOOLE'S 29/9/94-15/12/94; trfd to STRAND
17/12/94-1/1/95. 79 perf [np 24-25/12].** Richard
Maitland H. Tripp Edgar; Admiral Clipperton Albert
Bernard; Postboy Master [Alex] Watson. Sylvia Dela-
raine Madeline Rowsell; Prudence Kate Everleigh. L,
Mgr, Sm, Mus dir, Gen mgr as for 94.225. *REV: E 6/
10/94 p9.*

94.227 *TRUTHFUL JAMES* (FC,3a) James Mortimer & Charles
Klein. ROYALTY 2/10/94-13/10/94; trfd to STRAND 15/
10/94-27/10/94. 28 perf [w/mat 11/10, 17/10, 20/10,
24/10, 27/10]. 1st perfd Theatre Royal, Great Yarmouth
24/9/94. Nathaniel Tugstock G.W. Anson; Lemuel Bignold T.P. Haynes; James Verity Philip Cunningham; Guy
Pontefract Douglas Hamilton; James Selwyn Windham
Guise. Mrs Bignold Elsie Chester; Florence Bignold
Annie Ferrell; Ada Selwyn Carrie Coote; Sarah Tugstock Kate Kearney; Emma Roseby Mary Allestree; Eliza
Lydia Cowell. L Kate Santley. *REV: Ath 6/10/94 p465;
E 6/10/94 p8; Sk 3/10/94 p511, 10/10/94 p568; St 4/10/
94 p15; Th 1/11/94 p254-5; Ti 3/10/94 p3; TW94 p276.*

94.228 *A PIOUS FRAUD* (C,1a) James Mortimer [adpt of
Henri Meilhac & Ludovic Halévy, *L'Eté de St Martin*].
ROYALTY 2/10/94-13/10/94; trfd to STRAND 15/10/94-
27/10/94. 23 perf. 1st perfd Jodrell, 24/11/88 [as
A White Lie]. Sir George Allison Windham Guise; Her-
bert Allison Douglas Hamilton. May Carrie Coote; Miss
Martin Kate Kearney. L Kate Santley. *REV: E, St as
for 94.227.*

94.229 *THE CASE OF REBELLIOUS SUSAN* (C,3a) H.A. Jones.
CRITERION 3/10/94-23/3/95. 164 perf [w/S mat exc

22/12/94, 9/3/95; add mat 24/10/94, 31/10, 14/11,
21/11, 6/12, 13/12, 27/12/94; np 24-25/12/94, 25/2-
8/3/95].* Sir Richard Kato, Q.C. Charles Wyndham/
Frank Atherley; Admiral Sir Joseph Darby [Henry?]
Kemble; James Harabin C.P. Little; Fergusson Pybus
Fred Kerr; Lucien Edensor Ben Webster/A. Hamilton
Revelle; Mr Jacomb Ells Dagnall; Kirby Markham. Lady
Darby Fanny Coleman; Mrs Quesnel Gertrude Kingston;
Elaine Shrimpton Nina Boucicault; Lady Susan Harabin
Mary Moore/F. Frances. L & MGR Charles Wyndham; Cond
A. Evans; Act mgr & Treas E. Harvey; Cost Jays, Le-
ferriere, Mathilde Marie, Mme Eroom. *REV: Ath 13/10/
94 p501; E 6/10/94 p11; Sk 10/10/94 p568, 610, 613,
19/12/94 p368-9; SR 13/10/94 p407-8; St 11/10/94 p12;
Th 1/11/94 p249-51; Ti 4/10/94 p6, 11/3/95 p12; TW94
p266-75.*

94.230 *DER VEILCHENFRESSER* (C,4a) Gustav von Moser.
OPERA COMIQUE 3/10/94-5/10/94; 16/10, 19/10/94. 5
perf. Victor von Berndt Caesar Beck; Max Weilenbeck;
Heinrich Kamm; Siegfried Philippi; Ludwig Schubart;
Reinhardt von Feldt Albert Schmidt; Drill Sgt. Carl
Peters. Sophie von Wildenheim Eleonore von Driller;
Valeska Anna Hocke; Milli Elsinger; Elly Arndt; Frau
Dr Heinold-Thomann. *REV: E 6/10/94 p9; St 11/10/94
p13; Ti 8/10/94 p7.*

94.231 *DR KLAUS* (FC,5a) Adolph L'Arronge. OPERA COMI-
QUE 6/.10/94(2), 8/10/94; trfd to ROYALTY 11/12/94,
17/12/94. 5 perf. 1st perfd Wallner, Berlin 26/10/78.
Dr Ferdinand Klaus Caesar Beck; Leopold Griesinger
Max Weilenbeck; Max von Boden Heinrich Kamm; Paul
Gerstel Ludwig Schubart; Lubowski Ernst Petersen;
Behrmann William Karfiol; Colmar Siegfried Philippi.
Emma Klaus Anna Hocke; Julie Milli Elsinger; Anna
Elly Arndt; Marie Klaus Frau Dr Heinold-Thomann;
Marianne Kathe Walden; Auguste Minna Hunter; Frau von
Schlingen Marie Dittini. L J.D. Solomon; Cond Victor
Hollander; Gen mgr [R.] Mansell; Act mgr A.C. Miller.
REV: E 13/10/94 p12; St 11/10/94 p12-3; Ti 8/10/94 p7.

94.232 *KRIEG IM FRIEDEN* (FC,5a) Gustav von Moser &
Franz von Schonthan. OPERA COMIQUE 9/10/94-11/10/94;
trfd to ROYALTY 8/12/94. 4 perf. Caesar Beck; Ludwig

Rusing; Max Weilenbeck; Heinrich Kamm; Ludwig Schubart. Anna Hocke; Milli Elsinger; Martha Kruger; Toni
Hoops; Frau Dr Heinold-Thomann. *REV: E 13/10/94 p12.*

94.233 *MEIN LEOPOLD* (FC,3a) Adolph L'Arronge. OPERA
COMIQUE 15/10/94. 1 perf. 1st perfd Wallner, Berlin
23/12/73. Ernst Petersen; Ludwig Rusing; Max Weilen-
beck; Heinrick Kamm; Ludwig Schubart. Martha Kruger;
Milli Elsinger; Eleonore von Driller; Elly Arndt;
Frau Dr Heinold-Thomann. *REV: E 20/10/94 p9.*

94.234 *BEY OF MOROCCO* (Oa) [Victor Hollaender].OPERA
COMIQUE 17/10/94, 18/10/94. 2 perf. 1st perf? Ernst
Petersen; Siegfried Philippi; Charles F. Maurice.
Perl-Hollaender; Milli Elsinger; Elly Arndt; Toni
Hoops; Frau Dr Heinold-Thomann.

94.235 *STIFTUNGFEST* (FC,3a) Gustav von Moser. OPERA
COMIQUE 17/10/94, 18/10, 30/10/94. 3 perf. Ernst
Petersen; Ludwig Rusing; Ludwig Schubart; Siegfried
Philippi; Hugo Weitzel. Eleonore von Driller; Toni
Hoops; Frau Dr Heinold-Thomann.

94.236 *EDITHA'S BURGLAR* (1a) Edwin Cleary. HAYMARKET
18/10/94-3/11/94. 15 perf. 1st perfd Princess's 28/
10/87. Jack Lionel Brough; Edgar Lewis Charles Allan.
Editha Dora Barton. L & MGR H.B. Tree; Bom W.H. Leverton; Sm Shelton; Mus dir Carl Armbruster; Elect
E. Wingfield Bowles; Bm & Sec Frederick Harrison.

94.237 *MARRIED BY PROXY* (FC,3a) A.W. Yuill. TOOLE'S
18/10/94 mat perf. 1st perfd Theatre Royal, Greenock
19/1/94. Mjr. Chardin Clifford Bown; Albert Chardin
Edward Compton; Cpt. Lumley Robert Greville; Lieut.
Archer Harrison Hunter; Lieut. Pettigrew Auriol Fitz-
roy; Humphrey Reginald Dartrey; John John H. Brewer.
Mrs Hudson Bessie Thompson; Cecilia Hudson Sidney
Crowe; Olive Mitford Madeleine Meredith; Hemma Elsa
Wylde; Mrs Bummer Jessie Cross. L J.L. Toole; Sm
Herman de Lange, Lewis Ball; Cond William Robins; Gen
mgr Gilbert Tate; Bm J.H. Savile. *REV: Ath 27/10/94
p578; E 20/10/94 p8; St 25/10/94 p13.*

94.238 *THE LADY SLAVEY* (MC,2a) George Dance (lib) &

John Crook (mus). AVENUE 20/10/94-25/1/95. 94 perf
[w/S mat exc 20/10; add mat 26/12; np 22-25/12]. 1st
perfd Opera House, Northampton 4/9/93. Roberts Char-
les Danby/J.J. Dallas; Mjr. O'Neill Robert Pateman;
Vincent A. Evelyn Henry Beaumont/James Leverett; Lord
Lavender Herbert Sparling; Cpt. Fitz Norris George
Humphery. Flo Honeydew Jenny McNulty; Maud Adelaide
Astor/Lizzie Ruggles; Beatrice Blanche Barnett/Beatrice
Granville; Mme Pontet Elcho; Mme Louise [Irene] du
Foye; Liza Maryon/Rita Yorke/Julie Donna; Emma Phoebe
Turner/Desmond; Phyllis May Yohe. L & MGR William
Greet; Sm Reginald Stockton; Cond Henry J. Wood; Sc
E.G. Banks; Cost Mme Hayward, Jay, Morris Angel; Ch
Mariette d'Auban; Pq William Clarkson; Furn Lyons.
*REV: E 27/10/94 p8; Sk 31/10/94 p53, 28/11/94 p211,
28/11/94 supp p1-12, 19/12/94 p354-5; St 25/10/94
p12-3; Th 1/12/94 p316-7; Ti 22/10/94 p10; TW94 p286-
8.*

94.239 *A GAY WIDOW* (FC,3a) F.C. Burnand [adpt of Vic-
torien Sardou & Deslandes, *Belle Maman*]. COURT 20/
10/94-1/12/94. 41 perf [w/mat 10/11, 17/11, 24/11,
1/12].* Horace Dudley Charles H. Hawtrey; Peter
Rutherford Edward Righton; Algy Bruce Gilbert Hare;
Johnny Dunford H. Nye Chart; Hon Hugh Anstruther E.H.
Kelly; Vicomte de Barsac Wilfred Draycott; Col. Mumby
Fred Thorne; Dodd Compton Coutts; Mr Bentham Will
Dennis; Count Caramanti Robb Harwood; Uncle Popley
Fred Vaughan; Walworth Mumby Aubrey Fitzgerald; In-
spector Percy V. Everard; Robert W. Ritter Riley;
James C. Francis; Joseph Ernest Bertram. Nellie Dud-
ley Eva Moore; Mrs Pipwidge Mrs Charles Maltby; Ade-
lisa Mabel Hardinge; Countess Caramanti Violet Raye;
Miller Arlette Mowbray; Miss Witham Lydia Rachel; Mrs
Marbrook Lottie Venne. L Arthur Chudleigh; Act mgr
Leonard Lillies; Cond Henry Sprake; Furn Marler &
Bennett; Cost Russell & Allen; Pq C.H. Fox. *REV: Ath
27/10/94 p577-8; E 27/10/94 p8; Sk 24/10/94 p680; St
25/10/94 p12; Th 1/11/94 p256, 1/12/94 p315-6; Ti
22/10/94 p10; TW94 p276-81; Sk 21/11/94 p167.*

94.240 *OLD CRONIES* (Duol) S. Theyre Smith. COURT 20/
10/94-1/12/94. 37 perf.** Cpt. Pigeon Fred Thorne;
Dr Jacks Gilbert Hare. L, Act mgr, Cond as for 94.239.

94.241 *DER BIBLIOTHEKAR* (FC,4a) Gustave von Moser.
OPERA COMIQUE 20/10/94, 22/10, 25-26/10, 29/10, 1/11/
94. 6 perf. 1st perfd 1878. Macdonald Caesar Beck;
Marsland Max Weilenbeck; Gibson Ernst Petersen; Robert Ludwig Schubart; Harry Marsland Ludwig Rusing;
Lothair Macdonald Albert Schmidt; Leon Armadale Siegfried Philippi; Patrik Wadford William Karfiol; John
Hugo Weitzel; Commissionar Alexander Vincent; Execu-
tor August Kerger. Edith Eleonore von Driller; Sarah
Gildern Frau Dr Heinold-Thomann; Eva Webster Anna
Hocke; Frau Dickson Margarethe Dittini. L J.D. Solomon; Cond Victor Hollander; Gen mgr R. Mansell; Act
mgr A.C. Miller. *REV: E 27/10/94 p10; TW94 p288.*

94.242 *ROBBERY UNDER ARMS* (D,5a) Alfred Dampier &
Garnet Walch [adpt fr Rolf Boldrewood's romance].
PRINCESS'S 22/10/94-9/11/94. c.17 perf.* Cpt. Star-
light Alfred Dampier; Dick Marston Herbert Flemming;
Jim Marston Rothbury Evans; Sir Ferdinand Morringer
Paul M. Berton; Inspector Goring Henry Vibart;
Trooper McGinnis Bernard Gould; Trooper O'Hara George
Buller; Old Ben Marston Clarence Holt; George Store-
field Owen Harris; Moran Charles Charrington; Daly
Charles Lander; Black Jack E.G. Pout; Hulbert Swift;
Mr Baxter Fred Jacques; Champion Cook T. [C.] Dwyer;
Warrigal William Bonney; Bilbah Archer; King Billy F.
Forde; Lucky Jack Cohen; Clifford Edward Bonfield;
Dandy Green H. Powis; Harry the Reefer West; Dan
Robinson Garrett; Sam Dawson Scott; Arizona Bill Ed-
wards. Aileen Marston Mrs Anna Ruppert; Kate
Morrison Katherine Russell; Grace Storefield Rose
Dampier; Jennie Marie Cecil; Miss Euphrosyne Aspen
Carrie Daniels; Norah Mrs B.M. de Solla; Bella Barnes
Margaret Warren; Lady Passenger Erlynn. PP Mrs Harri-
ett Gooch; Mus dir L. Térès; Sm Frederic Jacques; Sc
Richard C. Durant; Pq & Cost William Clarkson; Mach
J.W. Cawdery; Lime L.C. Parnell; Mgr Arthur Yates.
*REV: E 27/10/94 p8; Sk 31/10/94 p11; St 25/10/94 p12;
Ti 23/10/94 p3; TW94 p281-6.*

94.243 *EINE PARTIE PIQUET* [Marc?] Fournier & Meyer.
OPERA COMIQUE 24/10/94. 1 perf. *REV: E 27/10/94 p10.*

94.244 *MAN SUCHT EINEN ERZIEHER* (C,2a) [Bohn?]. OPERA

COMIQUE 24/10/94. 1 perf. *REV: E 27/10/94 p10.*

94.245 *HERMANN UND DOROTHEA* (MF) A[lfred] Kalisch &
A. Weilrauch. OPERA COMIQUE 24/10/94. 1 perf. *REV:
E 27/10/94 p10.*

94.246 *THE BROKEN MELODY* (CD,3a) J.T. Tanner & Her-
bert Keen. OPERA COMIQUE 25/10/94 mat perf.** <u>Paul
Borinski</u> Auguste van Biene; <u>Gen. Ivanoff</u> H.A. Saints-
bury; <u>Dickson</u> William Benson; <u>Dudley Mortimer</u> George
Miller; <u>Beaujour</u> J.M. Capel; <u>Dr Magrath</u> Barton de
Solla; <u>Hon Dick Spinnaker</u> Charles McLagan; <u>Benneton</u>
W.J. Collinson. <u>Duchesse de Vervier</u> Emily Levertez;
<u>Mrs Dickson</u> Mrs Leslie Corcoran; <u>Hon Mrs Spinnaker</u>
Lillie Leigh; <u>Mabel</u> Lena Burnleigh. *REV: E 27/10/94
p11.*

94.247 *HIS EXCELLENCY* (CO,2a) W.S. Gilbert (lib) &
F. Osmond Carr (mus). LYRIC 27/10/94-6/4/95. 162 perf.
[w/S mat exc 27/10/94, 30/3/95, 6/4/95; add mat 14/
11/94, 21/11/94, 3/4/95; np 25/12/94].* <u>The Regent</u>
Rutland Barrington/Augustus Cramer; <u>Governor Griffen-
feld</u> George Grossmith; <u>Erling</u> Charles Kenningham;
<u>Tortennssen</u> Augustus Cramer; <u>Mats Munch</u> John Le Hay;
<u>Harold</u> Arthur Playfair; <u>Sentry</u> George Temple; <u>1st
Officer</u> Ernest Snow/Fred Garton; <u>2nd Officer</u> Frank
Morton. <u>Christina</u> Nancy McIntosh; <u>Nana</u> Jessie Bond/
Adeline Vaudrey; <u>Thora</u> Ellaline Terriss; <u>Dame Court-
landt</u> Alice Barnett; <u>Bianca</u> Gertrude Aylward/Augusta
Dewsnap; <u>Elsa</u> May Cross. <u>L</u> Horace Sedger; <u>Dir</u> W.S.
Gilbert; <u>Bm & Treas</u> C.P. Levilly; <u>Sc</u> T.E. Ryan; <u>Cost
dgn</u> Percy Anderson; <u>Cost</u> Miss Fisher, Mme Auguste,
B.J. Simmons, Firmin & Co., Cooling & Lawrence; <u>Pq</u>
William Clarkson; <u>Ch</u> John d'Auban; <u>Mus dir</u> C[arl]
Kiefert; <u>Sm</u> John Gunn; <u>Mgr</u> Arthur Fry. *REV: Ath 3/11/
94 p613; E 3/11/94 p15, 9/2/95 p11; Sk 31/10/94 p7,
7/11/94 supp p1-8; SR 3/11/94 p481; St 1/11/94 p12-3;
Th 1/12/94 p310-2; Ti 29/10/94 p12, 25/2/95 p10; TW94
p289-98.*

94.248 *HASEMANN'S TOECHTER* (C,4a) Adolph L'Arronge.
OPERA COMIQUE 27/10/94, 5/11/94. 2 perf. 1st perfd
Wallner, Berlin 23/12/73. <u>Hasemann</u> Ernst Petersen;
Albert Schmidt; Ludwig Rusing; Ludwig Schubart; Caesar

Beck. Albertine Frau Dr Heinold-Thomann; Eleonore
von Driller; Anna Hocke; Toni Hoops. *REV: E 3/11/94
p9.*

94.249 [no entry]

94.250 *LITTLE CHRISTOPHER COLUMBUS* George R. Sims (lib),
Cecil Raleigh (lib) & Ivan Caryll (mus). TERRY'S 29/
10/94-15/12/94. 59 perf [w/W, S mat exc 31/10; add
mat 19/11, 26/11, 6/12, 10/12].** O'Hoolegan E.J.
Lonnen; Silas Block J. Furneaux Cook; Don Juan Jack
Thompson; Cpt. Joseph H. Slammer W.S. Laidlaw; 2nd
Mrs Block John F. Sheridan; Mayor of Cadiz H. Gregory;
Head Turk W.M. Birch. Pedro Trevalyan; Lopez Reicke;
Guinevere Block Geraldine Ulmar; Dancer/Pepita Mabel
Love; Penelope Spry Gracie Whiteford; Vigilant Cutter
Dorothy Webb; Hannah Millie Marsden; Mercedes M.
Northcote; Officer of the Colombian Guard Cissie
Crauford; Salambo Smith Dora Thorne; Mysotes Calhoun
A. Maxwell; Chloe Dorothy Wood; Lola Maud Maude;
Little Christopher Addie Conyers; Dancing Girls &
American Tourists Blanche Astley, Alice Douglas,
Florrie Wilson, Eva Greville. PP Edward Terry; Ch
John d'Auban; Cost dgn Edel; Cost Alias, Harrison,
Mme Marle; Cond Ivan Caryll; Mus dir J. [H.H.] Korte;
Sm George Fielder; Bm H.T. Brickwell. *REV: St 1/11/94
p13.* Comment: See also item 93.268 of which this item
is a continuation, but with many cast-changes.

94.251 *TOECHING PAESEL.* OPERA COMIQUE 30/10/94. 1 perf.

94.252 *RAUB DER SABINERINNEN* (FC) Franz & P. von
Schonthan. OPERA COMIQUE 31/10/94, 3/11, 8/11/94; trfd
to ROYALTY 13/12/94. 4 perf. Ernst Petersen; Max
Weilenbeck; Ludwig Rusing; William Karfiol; Siegfried
Philippi. Eleonore von Driller; Toni Hoops; Frau Dr
Heinold-Thomann. *REV: E 10/11/94 p9.*

94.253 *ALL MY EYE-VANHOE* (Bsq,2a) Philip Hayman (lib)
& John Crook (mus) & Howard Talbot (mus) & Philip
Hayman (mus) & Edward Solomon (mus). TRAFALGAR 31/10/
94-7/11/94. 8 perf [w/mat 3/11].* Ivanhoe John L.
Shine; Will Scarlattina Harry Grattan; Robert Fitzoof
Fred Storey; Seedie Wreck Fred Wright, jr; Prior of

Jawfolke Abbey E.M. Robson; Sir Brandiboy Gilbert H.
M. Clifford; Mr Ithaacth James Stevenson; Prince
Johnnie Harold Eden. The Lady Soft Roeina Maggie Rob-
erts; Nell Guitar Alice Lethbridge; Tomba Clara Jecks;
Countess of Grundy Agnes Hewitt; Boilden Oiley, Esq
Bertha Meyers; Lady Alicia Fitzworse Nita Carlyon;
Rebecca Hothouse Peach Phyllis Broughton. PP Mr &
Mrs Frank Wyatt; Bm H[enry] Brandon, G[eorge] Manners;
Ch Anna Abrahams, Frank Parker; Sc [Fred?] Storey,
[W.P.] Warren; Cost dgn Lucien Besche, Comelli; Cost
Harrisons; Pq William Clarkson; Sm Frank Parker; Mus
dir Howard Talbot. *REV: E 3/11/94 p8; Sk 7/11/94 p63;
St 8/11/94 p12; Th 1/12/94 p318; Ti 1/11/94 p3; TW94
p298-300.*

94.254 *DIE RAUBER* (T,5a) Friedrich von Schiller.
OPERA COMIQUE 2/11/94, 6/11, 15/11/94. 3 perf. 1st
perfd Nationaltheater, Mannheim 13/1/1782. Franz
Max Weilenbeck; Caesar Beck. Amalia Eleonore von
Driller. *REV: E 10/11/94 p9; TW94 p300.*

94.255 *THE FUTURE MRS RANSOME* (Ca,1a) James Crowe.
AVENUE 7/11/94-25/1/95. 66 perf [np 22-25/12].* Gen.
Ransome Herbert Sparling; Admiral Ransome Arthur
Ring/Frank Sherlock/J. Newton; Jack Ransome Guy Wal-
ler. Marian Banks Elcho; Mrs Meeks Annie Montelli/
Kate Neverest. L & MGR William Greet; Sm Reginald
Stockton.

94.256 *NORA [A DOLL'S HOUSE]* Henrik Ibsen. OPERA COMI-
QUE 7/11/94, 9/11, 12/11/94. 3 perf.** Helmer Caesar
Beck; Rank Ludwig Rusing. Nora Eleonore von Driller.
REV: E 10/11/94 p9; Sk 14/11/94 p114; TW94 p310-1.

94.257 *JOHN-A-DREAMS* (P,4a) C. Haddon Chambers. HAY-
MARKET 8/11/94-27/12/94 [w/W, S mat exc 10/11, 14/11,
26/12; mat only 12/12; np 25/12]; 2/5/95-22/5/95
[w/mat 11/5]. 71 perf.* Harold Wynn H.B. Tree; Sir
Hubert Garlinge Charles Cartwright; Lord Barbridge
Charles Allan; Hon Rev Stephen Wynne Nutcombe Gould;
Percy de Coburn Herbert Ross; George Wanklyn Edmund
Maurice/Frank MacVicars; Cpt. Harding F. Percival
Stevens; 1st Mate John Willes/Edward Ferris; Boat-
swain Bert Thomas; 1st Steward [J.] Montagu; 2nd

Steward Lesly Thomson; **Butler** Hay. **Kate Cloud** Mrs Patrick Campbell/Lily Hanbury; **Lady Barbridge** R.G. Le Thiere; **Mrs Wanklyn** Janette Steer; **Servant** Conover. **L & MGR** H.B. Tree; **Sc** Walter Hann, Walter Johnstone; **Bm & Sec** Frederick Harrison; **Bom** W.H. Leverton; **Sm** Shelton; **Mus dir** Carl Armbruster; **Elect** E. Wingfield Bowles; **Pq** William Clarkson. *REV: Ath 17/11/94 p685; E 10/11/94 p11, 4/5/95 p10; Sk 14/11/94 p109, 111, 14/11/94 p154, 157, 21/11/94 p167, 21/11/94 supp p1-8; SR 10/11/94 p507; St 15/11/94 p12-3, 9/5/95 p13; Th 1/12/94 p313-5; Ti 9/11/94 p6, 3/5/95 p10; TW94 p302-10; TW95 p143.*

94.258 *ULTIMO* (F,5a) Gustave von Moser. OPERA COMIQUE 10/11/94, 13/11/94. 2 perf.

94.259 *THE JOKER* (FC,3a) M. Howard Tennyson. AVENUE 13/11/94 mat perf.* **Joseph Miller** Fred Thorne; **George Miller** H[enry?] Ashford; **Caryon Crowe** Alfred Maltby; **Felix** Lewis Fitzhamon; **Gerard Brewster** Cosmo Stuart; **James** W.H. Powell. **Mrs Caryon Crowe** Emily Thorne; **Penelope** Ethel Christine; **Mrs Lowe** E.M. Page; **Stella Lovel** E. Neilda; **Fannie** Annie Fox-Turner. **L & MGR** William Greet; **Bm** Harrington Baily. *REV: E 17/11/94 p7; Sk 21/11/94 p167; St 15/11/94 p13; Th 1/12/94 p317-8.*

94.260 *A KNIGHT ERRANT* (R,1a) Rutland Barrington (lib) & Alfred J. Caldicott (mus). LYRIC 14/11/94-12/1/95; 28/1/95. 52 perf [np 25/12/94].* **Baron de Boncoeur** Ernest Snow; **Sir Florian de Gracieux** W[illiam] Philp. **Lady Ermengarde** May Cross; **Armand** Alexander. **L** Horace Sedger; **Mgr** Arthur Fry; **Mus dir** C[arl] Kiefert; **Bm & Treas** C.P. Levilly; **Dir** Rutland Barrington; **Cost dgn** Percy Anderson; **Cost** B.J. Simmons. *REV: E 17/11/94 p8; Sk 21/11/94 p167-8; 19/12/94 p352-3.*

94.261 *DER STABSTROMPETER* (MF). OPERA COMIQUE 14/11/94, 16/11/94. 2 perf.

94.262 *WILHELM TELL* Friedrich von Schiller. OPERA COMIQUE 17/11/94; trfd to ROYALTY 1/12/94(m), 6/12/94. 3 perf. 1st perfd Weimar 17/3/04.

94.263 *THE WRONG GIRL* (FC,3a) H. Arthur Kennedy.
STRAND 21/11/94-15/12/94 [w/W, S mat exc 21/11];
18/12(m), 20/12(m), 21/12/94(m), 3/1/95(m). 33 perf.*
Cpt. Harry Montagu Forbes Dawson; George Glenfield
W[illiam] Blakeley; Oliver Chester Howard Russell;
Willoughby Chester Philip Cunningham; Willie Edouin
Willie Edouin; Isaac Lynx Dudley Cloran; Cobb Richard
Blunt. Gladys Gordon Violet Armbruster; Florence Cra-
ven Fanny Brough; Mrs Glenfield Helen Cresswell; Eva
Glenfield Daisy Bryer; Mrs Freemantle Wyville K.
Lucille Foote. PP J.S. Clarke; L Willie Edouin; Bom
A. [E.] Barnes; Mus dir George Bonner; Act mgr Amand
A. Mascard; Sm C[harles] Davies. *REV: E 24/11/94 p8;
Sk 29/8/94 p227, 236-7, 28/11/94 p217; St 29/11/94
p13; Th 1/1/95 p45-6; Ti 22/11/94 p5; TW94 p312-6.*

94.264 *THE QUEEN'S PRIZE* (Ca,1a) R. Fenton MacKay.
STRAND 21/11/94-15/12/94. 22 perf.* Cpt. Tom Dallis
Forbes Dawson; Col. Dallis Richard Blunt; Sgt. Jones
Charles Harvey; Lieut. Bob Graves Gordon Harvey. Cpt.
Kate Rivers K. Lucille Foote; Lieut Hettie Wren
Ettie Williams; Lucy Waveley Violet Armbruster. L,
Pp, Bom, Mus dir, Act mgr, Sm as for 94.263. *REV:
E, St, Ti as for 94.263.*

94.265 *THE SHOP GIRL* (MF) H.J.W. Dam (lib) & Ivan
Caryll (mus) & Adrian Ross (mus) & Lionel Monckton
(mus). GAIETY 24/11/94-29/5/96. 547 perf [w/S mat
exc 24/11/94, 22/12/94, 30/3/95, 6/4, 13/4, 9/11/95,
4/4/96, 23/5/96; add mat 19/12/94, 27/3/95, 3/4, 10/4,
23/5, 7/11/95; np 25/12/94, 12/4/95, 25/12/95, 3/4/
96].* Mr Hooley Arthur Williams/Harry Monkhouse/
Charles Danby/George Mudie; Charles Appleby Seymour
Hicks/Thomas Terriss/L[ouis?] MacKinder/George Rollit;
Bertie Boyd George Grossmith, jr/Fitzroy Morgan/Frank
Stayton; John Brown Colin Coop/Charles Lane; Sir
George Appleby Cairns James/Charles Lane/George Honey/
Harry Ashford/James Stevenson/George Mudie; Col.
Singleton Frank Wheeler/Coventry Davies/George Mudie/
W.J. Manning; Count St Vannen Robert Nainby; Mr Tweets
Willie Warde/Charles Lane; Mr Miggles Edmund Payne/
Robert Nainby/Frank Wheeler/Bertie Wright/L. MacKin-
der. Lady Dodo Singleton Helen Lee/Marie Halton/
Maud Sherman/Maggie Roberts/Grace Palotta; Miss Robin-

son Katie Seymour/Violet Lloyd/Lillie Rees; <u>Lady</u>
<u>Appleby</u> Maria Davis; <u>Ada Smith</u> Lillie Belmore/Alice
Barnett/Connie Ediss; <u>Faith</u> Lillie Dickinson/Florence
Neville/Pattie Stanley; <u>Hope</u> Agatha Roze/Patty Stan-
ley/Marie Yorke; <u>Charity</u> Lily Johnson/Agatha Roze/
Lily Johnson; <u>Maud Plantagenet</u> Maud Hill/Helen Lee/
Adelaide Astor/M. Glen/Carrie Coote; <u>Eva Tudor</u> Fannie
Warde/Mabel Bonton/Kate Adams/Krista Yudall; <u>Lillie</u>
<u>Stuart</u> Maud Sutherland/Marie Yorke/Maggie Roberts/
[Florence] Maitland; <u>Mabel Beresford</u> Violet Monckton/
[Florence] Maitland/Ethel Sydney/Louie Coote; <u>Agnes</u>
<u>Howard</u> Louie Coote; <u>Maggie Jocelyn</u> Maggie Ripley;
<u>Violet Deveney</u> Topsy Sinden; <u>Bessie Brent</u> Ada Reeve/
Ellaline Terrriss/Ethel Haydon/Claire Romaine/Kate
Cutler/Eva Moore; <u>Ada Wandesforde</u> Helen Lee; <u>Ada</u>
<u>Harrison</u> Lillie Henshaw/Florence Maitland; <u>Florence</u>
<u>White</u> Ada Belton; <u>Sylvia Perry</u> Maud Hoppe/Maud Suther-
land; <u>Birdie Waudesford</u> Maud Sutherland. L & MGR
George Edwardes; <u>Sc</u> Walter Johnstone, Walter Hann; <u>Ch</u>
Willie Warde; <u>Cost dgn</u> Wilhelm; <u>Cost</u> Miss Fisher,
Auguste, Harrisons, Morris Angel, Vanité, B. Benjamin
& Sons, Henry Heath; <u>Pq</u> C.H. Fox; <u>Furn</u> Oetzmann;
<u>Lighting</u> G[eorge] Poynton; <u>Dir</u> J.T. Tanner; <u>Cond</u> Ivan
Caryll; <u>Act mgr</u> Edward Marshall; <u>Bom</u> A.P. Oxley. *REV:*
E 1/12/94 p8; Sk 28/11/94 p215-7, 12/12/94 p299, supp
p1-6, 22/4/95 p571-2, 24/4/95 p667, 6/11/95 p79, 4/12/
95 p282, 288; SR 1/12/94 p598; St 29/11/94 p3, 28/11/
95 p12; Th 1/1/95 p41-3; Ti 26/11/94 p4, 19/4/95 p7;
TW94 p316-20; TW95 p131-2.

94.266 *THE WIFE OF DIVES* (CD,3a) S.X. Courte. OPERA
COMIQUE 26/11/94-8/12/94. 15 perf [w/mat 1/12, 5/12,
8/12]. 1st perfd Theatre Royal, Birmingham 27/8/94
[as *The Great Pearl Case*]. <u>Julius van Duccat</u> G.W.
Anson; <u>Lord Cyril Sieveking</u> Cosmo Stuart; <u>Rev Boaner-</u>
<u>ges Bodkin</u> Cecil Ramsey; <u>Humphries</u> Frank May; <u>Darryl</u>
<u>Dreighton</u> Charles Glenney. <u>Lady Haltwhistle</u> Carlotta
Addison; <u>Muriel Haltwhistle</u> Lucy Wilson; <u>Cecily Al-</u>
<u>lardyce</u> Florence Friend; <u>Mrs van Duccat</u> Olga Brandon.
L F. Fowler; <u>Mgr</u> Olga Brandon; <u>Mus dir</u> Wurm; <u>Pq</u>
William Clarkson; <u>Cost</u> Mrs Nettleship; <u>Furn</u> Lyon; <u>Bm</u>
Harrington Baily; <u>Sm</u> William [H.] Day. *REV: Ath 1/12/*
94 p760; E 1/12/94 p8; Sk 5/12/94 p263; SR 1/12/94
p598-9; St 29/11/94 p13; Th 1/1/95 p44-5; Ti 27/11/94

p10; TW94 p320-3.

94.267 *A FOLLY OF AGE* (C,1a) Arthur Ingram. OPERA COMI-
QUE 27/11/94-8/12/94. 11 perf.* Dick Ardingley Hurd-
man Lucas/W. Bonney; Richard Ardingley C[harles] Med-
win; Augustus Master Hal Baily; James Barlow L. Bean.
Violet Ardingley Zilla Nanson; Kate Beatrice Summers.
L, Mgr, Mus dir, Pq, Furn, Bm, Sm as for 94.266. *REV:*
E, St as for 94.266.

94.268 *ASHES* (P,3a) Edward Collins & Richard Saunders.
PRINCE OF WALES'S 30/11/94 mat perf.* Reginald Den-
ning Charles Glenney; Sir Everett Kerr Philip Cun-
ningham; Dr James Courtney Oswald Yorke; Mr Broadleigh
Stuart Champion; Frank Fairfax Richard Saunders; Mr
Frazer J.R. Hatfield; Cpt. Fawcett Lawrance d'Orsay.
Muriel Kerr Lucy Wilson; Comtesse de St. Maur Gwynne
Herbert; Mrs Ponsonby Robertha Erskine; Lady Constance
Kerr Alice de Winton. BM Herbert Blackmore. *REV: Ath*
8/12/94 p800; E 1/12/94 p10; Sk 5/12/94 p263; St 6/12/
94 p12; Th 1/1/95 p46.

94.269 *FAUST* (D). ROYALTY 30/11/94, 3/12/94. 2 perf.
Faust Caesar Beck; Mephistopheles Emil Katzorke. Gretchen Eleonore von Driller. *REV: Ti 1/12/94 p5.* Comment:
Nicoll lists this as the 1st perf of a play by an
unknown author.

94.270 *BEETHOVEN'S ROMANCE* (CD,4a) S.A. Raphael.
ROYALTY 1/12/94. 1 perf.* Ludwig van Beethoven John
Ennar; Stephan Breuning Victor Ellissen; Ferdinand
Ries Willie Hartog; Rudolf, Count Gallenburg William-
son; Prince Lichnowsky Cyril Bathurst; Moritz Bolz
C.M. Tulloch; Albert von Zierenheim Walter Tyrrell;
Lieut. von Falkenthal Robert Wilkins. Nannette Alber-
tine Smith; Lisa Susie Raphael; Elsa Schwarzfeld Alice
Christmas; Giulietta Guiccardi Margaret Halstan. *REV:*
E 8/12/94 p12; SR 8/12/94 p619-20; St 6/12/94 p12-3.
Comment: *St* indicates this was a copyright perf.

94.271 *SCHWABENSTREICH* Franz von Schonthan. ROYALTY
4/12/94, 10/12/94. 2 perf.

94.272 *DER PROBEPFEIL* (FC,4a) Oscar Blumenthal. ROY-

ALTY 5/12/94, 7/12, 8/12/94. 3 perf. 1st perfd 1883?
<u>Carl, Graf Dohnegg</u> Max Weilenbeck; <u>Baron Leopold v.d.</u>
<u>Egge</u> Emil Katzorke; <u>Hellmuth, sein Neffe</u> Ludwig Rus-
ing; <u>Bogumil Krasinski</u> Heinrich Kamm; <u>Rittmeister a.</u>
<u>D. von Dedenroth</u> Caesar Beck; <u>Spitzmuller</u> William
Karfiol; <u>Graf Longueville</u> Adolf Vogel; <u>Mjr. von Lank-</u>
<u>witz</u> Siegfried Philippi; <u>Ferdinand</u> Ludwig Schubart;
<u>Wilhelm</u> Hugo Weitzel; <u>Franz</u> Ferdinand Schmidt. <u>Grafin</u>
<u>Alexandra</u> Frau Dr Heinold-Thomann; <u>Beate</u> Anna Hocke;
<u>Hortense von Walnack</u> Martha Kruger; <u>Asta Walboth</u> Milli
Elsinger; <u>Melanie von Brauneck</u> Kathe Walden; <u>Charlotte</u>
Louise Simonis; <u>Lilly von Strehlen</u> Elly Arndt; <u>Alice</u>
<u>von Hohenfels</u> Paula Herz; <u>Pauline</u> Antonie Hoops. <u>L</u>
Kate Santley; <u>Dir</u> Charles F. Maurice, Arthur Frantz.
REV: E 8/12/94 p15; SR 29/12/94 p706-7.

94.273 *THE RED LAMP* (4a) W. Outram Tristram. HAYMARKET
6/12/94, 13/12/94. 2 mat perf.** <u>Paul Demetrius</u> H.B.
Tree; <u>Gen. Morakoff</u> Edmund Maurice; <u>Ivan Zazzulic</u>
Nutcombe Gould; <u>Prince Alexis Valerian</u> C.M. Hallard;
<u>Alan Villiers</u> Henry Neville; <u>Kertch</u> E. Holman Clark;
<u>Count Bohrenheim</u> Herbert Ross; <u>Turgan</u> F. Percival
Stevens; <u>Rheinveck</u> Parker Hanks; <u>Tolstoi</u> [William]
Gayer Mackay; <u>Officer of the Police</u> J. Montagu; <u>Ser-</u>
<u>vant</u> E[dward] Ferris. <u>Princess Claudia Morakoff</u> Janet
Achurch; <u>Mme Dannenberg</u> Mrs [Conyers?] d'Arcy; <u>Olga</u>
<u>Morakoff</u> Lily Hanbury; <u>Felise</u> Una Cockerell; <u>Countess</u>
<u>Voelcker</u> Mary Brough. <u>L & MGR</u> H.B. Tree; <u>Bom</u> W.H.
Leverton; <u>Sm</u> Shelton; <u>Mus dir</u> Carl Armbruster; <u>Elect</u>
E. Wingfield Bowles; <u>Pq</u> William Clarkson; <u>Bm & Sec</u>
Frederick Harrison. *REV: E 8/12/94 p15; TW94 p333-8.*

94.274 *THE BALLAD MONGER* (RP) Walter Besant & Walter
Pollock [adpt of Theodore de Banville, *Gringoire*].
HAYMARKET 6/12/94, 13/12/94. 2 mat perf.** <u>Gringoire</u>
H.B. Tree; <u>Louis XI</u> E. Holman Clark; <u>Olivier</u> Charles
Allan; <u>Simon</u> John Willes. <u>Loyse</u> Lily Hanbury; <u>Nicole</u>
Mrs E.H. Brooke. <u>L & MGR</u>, <u>Bom</u>, <u>Sm</u>, <u>Mus dir</u>, <u>Elect</u>,
<u>Pq</u>, <u>Bm & Sec</u> as for 94.273. *REV: E 8/12/94 p15.*

94.275 *DR BILL* (FC,3a) Hamilton Aidé [adpt of Albert
Carré, *Le Docteur Jojo*]. COURT 8/12/94-9/1/95. 26
perf [w/mat 15/12; np 22-25/12].** <u>Dr William Brown</u>
Charles H. Hawtrey; <u>Mr Firman</u> William H. Day; <u>Mr</u>

Horton Robb Harwood; George Webster E.H. Kelly; Baggs
F. Featherstone; Sgt. of Police C. Francis. Louisa
Brown Dora de Winton; Jennie Firman Violet Lyster;
Mrs Firman Dolores Drummond; Ellen Mabel Hardinge;
Miss Fauntleroy Edith Kenward; Mrs Horton Lottie
Venne. L & MGR Arthur Chudleigh. *REV: Ath 15/12/94
p838; E 15/12/94 p9; St 13/12/94 p12; Th 1/1/95 p43;
Ti 10/12/94 p6.*

94.276 *THE BIRTHDAY* (C,1a) George Pleydell Bancroft.
COURT 8/12/94-21/12/94. 12 perf.* Mr Leslie William
H. Day; Dr Wakefield Wilfred Draycott; Hubbard W.H.
Quinton. Ruth Leslie Dora de Winton; L & MGR Arthur
Chudleigh. *REV: Ath, E, St, Ti as for 94.275; Th 1/1/
95 p43-4; TW94 p332-3.*

94.277 *LOVE AND HONOUR* Campbell Clarke [adpt of Alexandre Dumas, *Monsieur Alphonse*]. GLOBE 11/12/94 mat
perf. 1st perfd Theatre Royal, Birmingham 30/6/75.
Cpt de Montaiglin John Beauchamp; M Octave H[enry] N.
Wenman; M Dieudonne Fred Vaughan; Remy W.H. Wills.
Mme Guichard Foley [Mrs T.E. Wenman]; Mme de Montaiglin Florence Charles; Adrienne Janet O'Mara. *REV: E
15/12/94 p11; St 13/12/94 p12-3.*

94.278 *VILLAIN AND VICTIM* (Duol) W.R. Walkes. HAYMAR-
KET 11/12/94 mat perf.* Adolphus Cyril Maude. Millicent Winifred Emery. L & MGR H.B. Tree.

94.279 *A SWARRY DANSONG* (MDuol) Rutland Barrington
(lib) & Edward Solomon (mus). HAYMARKET 11/12/94 mat
perf.** Robert Plushley Rutland Barrington. Harriet
Mantell Jessie Bond. L & MGR H.B. Tree.

94.280 *PENSION SCHOLLER* (3a) C. Laufs. ROYALTY 12/12/
94, 14/12, 15/12(m), 20/12, 27/12, 29/12/94(m). 6
perf. 1st perfd 1889? Philipp Klapproth Ernst Peter-
sen; Alfred Klapproth Ludwig Rusing; Ernst Kisling
Paul Eckhardt; Fritz Bernhardy Heinrich Kamm; Scholle
Max Weilenbeck; Eugen Rumpel Siegfried Philippi; Gro-
ber Emil Katzorke; Jean Hugo Weitzel. Ulrike Sprosser
Frau Dr Heinold-Thomann; Ida Anna Hocke; Franziska
Milli Elsinger; Josephine Kruger Martha Kruger; Amali
Pfeiffer Marie Dittini; Friederike Toni Hoops. L Kat

Santley; <u>Dir</u> Charles F. Maurice.

94.281 *THE CHIEFTAIN* (0,2a) F.C. Burnand (lib) & Arthur Sullivan (mus) [rev of their *The Contrabandista*,
perfd St George's Hall 18/12/67]. SAVOY 12/12/94-16/
3/95. 96 perf [w/S mat; add mat 27/12; np 25/12]. 1st
perf thus. <u>Count Vasquez de Gonzago</u> Courtice Pounds;
<u>Peter Adolphus Grigg</u> Walter Passmore; <u>Ferdinand de
Roxas</u> Robert Scott-Fishe/W.A. Peterkin; <u>Sancho</u> Richard
Temple; <u>José</u> M.R. Morand; <u>Pedro Gomez</u> Scott Russell;
<u>Blazzo</u> J. Bowden Haswell/F. Morrison; <u>Escatero</u> Powis
Pinder; <u>Pedrillo</u> Master Jeffrey Snelson. <u>Inez de Roxas</u>
Rosina Brandram/Spenser; <u>Dolly</u> Florence Perry; <u>Juanita</u>
Emmie Owen; <u>Maraquita</u> Edith Johnston; <u>Anna</u> Ada Newall;
<u>Zitella</u> Beatrice Perry; <u>Nina</u> Ethel Wilson; <u>Rita</u> Flo-
rence St. John. <u>PP & MGR</u> Richard d'Oyly Carte; <u>Mus
dir</u> Francois Cellier; <u>Dir</u> F.C. Burnand, Arthur Sulli-
van, Charles Harris; <u>Sm</u> W.H. Seymour; <u>Cond</u> Arthur
Sullivan; <u>Ch</u> John d'Auban; <u>Cost dgn</u> Comelli; <u>Cost</u>
Alias, Mme Auguste, Mme Leon, B.T. Simmons, Angel &
Son, Redfern & Co.; <u>Pq</u> William Clarkson; <u>Mach</u> Peter
White; <u>Elect</u> Lyons; <u>Act mgr & Treas</u> J.W. Beckwith.
*REV: E 15/12/94 p7; Sk 19/12/94 p354, 23/1/95 p601,
618-9, 621; SR 15/12/94 p658-9; St 20/12/94 p12-3; Th
1/1/95 p39-41; Ti 13/12/94 p10, 11/3/95 p12; TW94
p339-42.*

94.282 *LE ROI L'A DIT* (CO,3a) Leo Delibes. PRINCE OF
WALES'S 13/12/94 mat perf. 1st perfd Opéra Comique,
Paris 24/5/73. <u>Benoit</u> H. Winsloe Hall; <u>Marquis de
Moncontour</u> Albert H. Archdeacon; <u>Miton</u> Fritz Hart;
<u>Baron de Merlussac</u> Francis Harford; <u>Gautru</u> William
Maynard; <u>Pacome</u> Norman McLeod Jones. <u>Marquis de Fla-
rambel</u> Clementine Pierpoint; <u>Marquis de la Bluette</u>
Constance Sim; <u>Javotte</u> Marie Seigne; <u>Marquise de Mon-
contour</u> Louise Kirkby Lunn; <u>Philomele</u> Jessie Scott;
<u>Agathe</u> Grace Stanhope; <u>Chimene</u> Beatrice Lynton; <u>An-
gelique</u> Ena Bedford. <u>DIR</u> Richard Temple; <u>Cond</u> C.
Villiers Stanford. *REV: Ath 22/12/94 p869; E 15/12/94
p7; Ti 14/12/94 p10.* <u>Comment</u>: Royal College of Music.

94.283 *EINER VON UNSERE LEUT* O.F. Berg. ROYALTY 15/12/
94, 18/12, 21/12, 26/12/94(m). 4 perf.

94.284 *QUITE AN ADVENTURE* (Oa) Frank Desprez (lib)
& Edward Solomon (mus). SAVOY 15/12/94-29/12/94. 12
perf [np 25/12]. 1st perfd Olympic 7/9/81. <u>PP & MGR</u>
Richard d'Oyly Carte.

94.285 *HAL, THE HIGHWAYMAN* (P,1a) H.M. Paull. VAUDE-
VILLE 15/12/94-2/3/95. 65 perf [np 24-25/12].* <u>Hand-
some Hal</u> T[homas] Kingston; <u>Sir James Mortimer</u> Frederick Volpé; <u>Danby</u> Arthur Helmore; <u>Tim</u> J.L. MacKay.
<u>Celia Mortimer</u> Esmé Beringer; <u>Kitty Carter</u> Helena
Dacre. <u>L</u> Weedon Grossmith; <u>Mgr</u> A.F. Henderson; <u>Mus &
Mus dir</u> C.J. Hargitt; <u>Cost</u> L. & H. Nathan; <u>Pd</u> Herman
de Lange. *REV: E 22/12/94 p8; SR 22/12/94 p680; St
20/12/94 p13; Ti 17/12/94 p10; TW94 p338-9.*

94.286 *A STORY OF WATERLOO* (P,1a) A. Conan Doyle.
GARRICK 17/12/94 mat perf. 1st perfd Prince's, Bristol 21/9/94. <u>Corporal Gregory Brewster</u> Henry Irving;
<u>Sgt. Archie McDonald</u> Fuller Mellish; <u>Col. James Mid-
winter</u> [William] Haviland. <u>Norah Brewster</u> Annie Hughes
<u>L & MGR</u> John Hare; <u>Act mgr</u> C.G. Compton, E. Harvey;
<u>Sm</u> W.M. Cathcart; <u>Cond</u> Andrew Levey. *REV: SR 22/12/94
p679-80; Ti 18/12/94 p10; TW94 p343-4.*

94.287 *THE VICARAGE* (Fireside Story) Clement Scott
[adpt of Octave Feuillet, *Le Village*]. GARRICK 17/12/
94 mat perf. 1st perfd Prince of Wales's 31/3/77.
<u>George Clarke</u> S.B. Bancroft; <u>Rev Noel Haygarth</u> Arthur
Cecil; <u>Mason</u> Charles Rock. <u>Mrs Haygarth</u> Mrs S.B. Bancroft. <u>L & MGR</u>, <u>Act mgr</u>, <u>Sm</u>, <u>Cond</u> as for 94.286. *REV:
Ti 18/12/94 p10; TW94 p345.*

94.288 *EIN TOLLER EINFALL* C. Laufs. ROYALTY 19/12/94,
22/12(m), 29/12/94. 3 perf. 1st perfd 1886.

94.289 *THE MERRY WIVES OF WINDSOR* (C,5a) William
Shakespeare. HAYMARKET 20/12/94, 26/12/94.   2 mat
perf.** <u>Sir John Falstaff</u> H.B. Tree; <u>Fenton</u> C.M.
Hallard; <u>Justice Shallow</u> E. Holman Clark; <u>Master Slen-
der</u> Herbert Ross; <u>Mr Ford</u> Henry Neville; <u>Mr Page</u> Edmund Maurice; <u>Dr Caius</u> H[enry] Kemble; <u>Sir Hugh Evans</u>
E.M. Robson; <u>Host of "The Garter"</u> Charles Allan; <u>Pis-
tol</u> F. Percival Stevens; <u>Nym</u> [William] Gayer MacKay;
<u>Bardolph</u> [John] Willes; <u>Simple</u> Alfred Wigley; <u>John</u>

Rugby Williams. Robin Una Cockerell; Mistress Ford
Maud Milton; Mistress Page Lily Hanbury; Anne Page
Violet Armbruster; Mistress Quickly Mrs E.H. Brooke.
L & MGR H.B. Tree; Bom W.H. Leverton; Mus Sir Arthur
Sullivan; Ch Katti Lanner; Cost L. & H. Nathan; Sm
Shelton; Mus dir Carl Armbruster; Elect E. Wingfield
Bowles; Pq William Clarkson; Bm & Sec Frederick
Harrison.

94.290 *PAPAGENO*. ROYALTY 22/12/94, 24/12, 28/12/94.
3 perf.

94.291 *THE HOUSE THAT JACK BUILT* (Panto) H. Chance
Newton. OPERA COMIQUE 24/12/94-1/1/95. 7 mat perf [np
25/12].* Dame Alfred Balfour; Mr Tatters G.M. Slater;
Rat Master E. Martin; Cat Master Bertie Lloyd; Dog
Master Harry Gadsey; Maltster Master G. Ballennie;
Fiddle Master Alfred Pinnett; Dish Master Peter Ball-
ennie; Moon Master John Walters. Jack Tiny Grattan;
Jerribuildus Gwennie Hasto; Courage Nina Sevening;
Truth Lulu Valli; Falsehood Marie Dainton; Fear Fay
Rivington; Curate Dora Sevening; Dolly Dimple Pansy
Grattan; Spoon Daisy Maynard. MUS C.E. Howells. *REV:*
E 29/12/94 p7; St 27/12/94 p10; Ti 2/1/95 p10.

94.292 *EASTWARD HO!* (Operatic Bsq) C.M. Rodney (lib;
rev Willie Younge) & C.E. Howells (mus). OPERA COMI-
QUE 24/12/94-1/1/95. 7 mat perf [np 25/12]. 1st perfd
St George's, Walsall 31/7/93 [as *The Black Cat*].
Reginald Nanty Joseph McBride; Julian Ranter Fowler
Thatcher; Betterton Burge C.A. White; Muley Muzpha
George de Pledge; Beni Charles Baldwin; Mista Murphi
Gerald Hoole. Kitty Spangles Jenny Dawson; Gwendoline
Brougham Fanny Selby; Rhoda Royal Madge Annesley;
Tiny Maudie Brookman; Minnie Pateman Alice Beresford;
Bella Vavasour Maude Adams; Inez Brabazon Edith Hoppe;
Gladys Fontenbleu Lilian Stead; Vera Fancourt Florence
Lavender; Fasti Madge Rockingham; Zeffa Kate Ever-
leigh; Atcha Lilian Morgan; Balradour Rose Bernard;
Bebee Lilly Piercey. MGR H.P. Gatrell, John Donald.
REV: E 29/12/94 p7; Sk 2/1/95 p444; St 27/12/94 p10-1.

94.293 *GENTLEMAN JIM* (Ca,1a) W.R. Walkes. COURT 26/12/
94-9/1/95. 13 perf. 1st perfd Shakespeare, Liverpool

1/11/93. REV: Sk 2/1/95 p486.

94.294 *HANSEL AND GRETEL* (Fairy O,3a) Engelbert Humperdinck (mus) & Adelheid Welti (lib; fnd on Grimms' fairy tale). DALY'S 26/12/94-26/1/95;* trfd to GAIETY 28/1/95-1/3/95; trfd to PRINCESS'S 2/3/95-15/4/95; trfd to SAVOY 16/4/95-15/6/95. 168 perf [w/S mat exc 29/12, 2/3; add mat 1/1, 16/1, 23/1, 1/5, 8/5, 15/5; np 12/4; M-Fri mats only 28/1-1/3]. Peter Charles Copland. Gertrude Julia Lennox; Hansel Marie Elba; Gretel Jeanne Douste; Witch who eats children Edith Miller; Sandman Marie du Bedat; Dewman Jessie Huddleston. L & MGR Augustin Daly; Cond Luigi Arditi; Dir T.H. Friend; Furn Oetzmann; Bom [Edward] Brown; Bm John Farrington; Act mgr M. Edwards. *REV: Ath 29/12/94 p903; E 29/12/94 p7, 9/3/95 p9; Sk 2/1/95 p447, 30/1/95 p15, 3/4/95 p505, 1/5/95 p8; SR 29/12/94 p707-8; Th 1/2/95 p109-10; Ti 27/12/94 p4.*

94.295 *BASTIEN AND BASTIENNE* (O,1a) W.A. Mozart [trans Constance Bache]. DALY'S 26/12/94-26/1/95. 28 perf. 1st perfd Dr Anton Mesmer's Garden Theatre, Vienna 10/1768. Bastien Reginald Brophy; Colas Joseph Claus. Bastienne Jessie Huddleston. L & MGR, Cond, Dir, Furn, Bom, Bm, Act mgr as for 94.294. *REV: Ath 29/12/94 p903; E 29/12/94 p7; SR 29/12/94 p708; Ti 27/12/94 p4.*

94.296 *DICK WHITTINGTON* (Panto) Augustus Harris, Cecil Raleigh & Henry Hamilton. DRURY LANE 26/12/94-16/3/95. 123 perf [2 perf dy 27/12-9/2; w/M, W, S mat thereafter exc 4/3, 11/3; add mat 14/2].* Idle Jack Dan Leno; Fitzwarren Spry; Cat and Mate Brothers Griffiths; Steersman Percy Mordy; Mangold [Arthur] Hendon; Cabby Fawdon Vokes; Sexton J[oseph A.?] Cave; Baby Rat Master Griffiths; Clown & Policeman Griffiths Brothers; Harlequin Tom Cusden; Panteloon Carl Waller; Eliza the Cook Herbert Campbell. Alice Marie Montrose; Dick Whittington Ada Blanch; Mi-Yung-Man Lily Harold; Emperor of China Agnes Hewitt; Princess Ni-si-pi-si Queenie Lawrence; King Cat Eva Westlake; King Rat Madge Lucas; Fairy Christmas D[orothy] Wood; Fairy Blue Bell Lydia Flopp; Fairy Snowdrop Lily Morris; Cpt. of the Seagull Kate Dudley; Aides de Camp Arrowsmith, Gerard; Tee-To-Tum [Lena] Delphine; Pang-Si-Ku

Kemble; Ho-Che-Fow V. Murton/Nita Carlyon; Kin-Ya-Bow
E. Pritchard; Mjr. Domo A. Esmond; Zim-Dra-Fuz V[io-
let] Ellicott; Fond Mother Durkin; Columbine Buffy
Hoby. L & MGR & PD Augustus Harris; Sm Arthur P. Col-
lins; Ch John d'Auban, [Carlo?] Coppi; Mus James M.
Glover; Sc [Robert?] Caney, William Perkins, T.E.
Ryan, Bruce Smith, Joseph Harker; Cost dgn Comelli;
Cost Alias, Harrisons, B.J. Simmons, May, William
Clarkson, Angel, Landolff, Dowding, Auguste, Phillips
& Son, Miss Fisher, Miss Palmer, Mrs Champion, Mrs
Besford, Mrs Manning, Miss Collier, Kennedy & White;
Pq William Clarkson; Mach E.A. Taylor; Props A. Jones,
Jackson, Labhart; Electrical Effects Forrest & Sons,
Horgan & Crawshaw; Asm N[apier] Barry. *REV: E 29/12/
94 p6; Sk 2/1/95 p448-9, 451, 6/2/95 supp p1-8; St
3/1/95 p16-7; TW95 p1-3.*

94.297 *SANTA CLAUS* (Fairy Panto) Horace Lennard. LY-
CEUM 26/12/94-2/3/95. 58 perf [mats only exc 26/12].*
Santa Claus William Rignold; Sir Joseph Grimshaw Fred
Emney; Evadne Newfangle Victor Stevens; Richard Coeur
de Lion Charles Thorburn; Sheriff of Nottingham Harold
Coulter; Rufus Francis Hawley; Uriah Richard Blunt;
Friar Tuck Watty Brunton; Little John Picton Rox-
borough; Much the Miller's Son G. Durlach; Jack Reg-
inald Roberts; Notary E. Zanfretta; Steward Philippe;
Toy Soldiers Harry Kitchen, Fred Kitchen; Tatters
Charles Lauri; Nightmare Edouard Espinoza; Clown
Charles Lauri; Pantaloon E[nrico] Zanfretta; Harle-
quin Harry Kitchen; Nigger Servant Fred Kitchen; Tore-
ador [D.] Philippe; House Agent G[eorge] Aubrey; Ger-
man F. Maurice. Queen Mab Amy Farrell; Robin Good-
fellow Lily Twyman; Fantasy Ina Lucas; Truth Alice
Rene; Memory Bertha Staunton/Blanche Leigh; Hope H.
Nicholl; Jack Frost Cicely Turner; Holly Cassie Bruce;
Ivy H. Gallon; Mistletoe A[dela?] Drayton; Lady Gay
Grimshaw Susie Vaughan; Marian Lillie Comyns; Eric
Kitty Loftus; Rosamund Rosie Leyton/Cassie Bruce; Pert
Clara Jecks; Robin Hood Annie Schuberth; Alan-a-dale
Grace Lane; Will Scarlett Marie Lascelles; Polly Grace
Leslie; Dorothy Dislay; Moonbeam [Francesca] Zanfretta;
Lullaby Judith Espinoza; Fly Geraldine Somerset; Col-
umbine J. Price. L Henry Irving; Mus & Pd Oscar Bar-
rett; Sc Henry Emden, Hawes Craven; Ch Katti Lanner;

Cost dgn Wilhelm; Cost Mme d'Orlean, Mrs S. May, Miss
Fisher, Auguste, Pocock Brothers; Props F. [C.] Labhart, R. Eagle; Elect J.T. Niblett; Pq William Clarkson; Sm Henry Nelson; Regisseur Francis Hawley; Mus
dir James Weaver; Bom Joseph Hurst. *REV: E 29/12/94
p7, 23/2/95 p9; Sk 2/1/95 p442-3, 446, 450, 452, 454,
16/1/95 supp p1-12; TW95 p3-5.*

94.298 *LUMPACIVAGABUNDUS*. ROYALTY 26/12/94. 1 perf.
1st perfd 1833?

94.299 *MULLER UND MULLER*. ROYALTY 26/12/94, 27/12,
29/12/94. 3 perf.

94.300 *WALKER, LONDON* (C,3a) J.M. Barrie. TOOLE'S
26/12/94-2/2/95. 36 perf [w/mat 16/1, 30/1].** Jasper
Phipps J.L. Toole; Kit Upjohn C.M. Lowne; Andrew Mc-
Phail George Shelton; W.G. E.A. Coventry; Ben Frank
J. Arlton. Mrs Golightly Kate Carlyon; Bell Golightly
Cora Poole; Nanny O'Brien Alice Kingsley; Sarah Rigg
Eliza Johnstone; Penny Mary Brough. L & MGR J.L.
Toole; Sm John Billington; Cond William Robins; Bm &
Treas George Lee; Sc Joseph Harker; Props George
Scarrott.

94.301 *PAUL PRY* (C,3a) John Poole. TOOLE'S 26/12/94-
9/2/95. 41 perf [w/mat 23/1].** Paul Pry J.L. Toole;
Col. Hardy John Billington; Mr Witherton George Shel-
ton; Harry Stanley C.M. Lowne; Frank Hardy Henry
Westland; Old Stanley Frank J. Arlton; Grasp E.A.
Coventry; Simon C[harles] Brunton. Eliza Cora Poole;
Phoebe Eliza Johnstone; Mrs Subtle Kate Carlyon. L &
MGR, Sm, Cond, Bm & Treas as for 94.300.

94.302 *HAMLET* (T,5a) William Shakespeare. HAYMARKET
28/12/94, 29/12/94. 2 perf.** Hamlet H.B. Tree;
Ghost of Hamlet's Father James Fernandez; Claudius
Henry Neville; 1st Gravedigger Edward Righton; Polon-
ius E. Holman Clark; Horatio Bert Thomas; Laertes
C.M. Hallard; Rosencrantz [Charles F.] Caravoglia;
Guildenstern Lesly Thomson; Marcellus [William] Gayer
MacKay; Bernardo Edward Ferris; Priest Charles Allan;
2nd Gravedigger John Willes; 1st Actor F. Percival
Stevens; Francisco Williams; 2nd Actor [Frederick?]

Watson; Court Jester Alfred Wigley. Gertrude Frances
Ivor; Ophelia Gwendoline Floyd; Player Queen Hilda
Hanbury. L & MGR H.B. Tree; Sc William Telbin, Walter
Johnstone, Walter Hann; Mus George Henschel; Cost dgn
Karl; Cost L. & H. Nathan; Cond Carl Armbruster; Sm
Shelton; Bm & Sec Frederick Harrison. *REV: Ti 31/12/*
94 p8.

94.303 *SLAVES OF THE RING* (P,3a) Sydney Grundy. GAR-
RICK 29/12/94-16/1/95. 16 perf [mat only 16/1].*
Earl of Ravenscroft John Hare; Hon George Delamere
Arthur Bourchier; Mr Egerton, M.P. Will Dennis; Cpt.
Douglas Brandon Thomas; Harold Dundas Gilbert Hare;
Sir William Kennedy, Bart Charles Rock; Mr Tweedie,
M.R.C.S. Gerald du Maurier. Helen Egerton Kate Rorke;
Ruth Egerton Eleanor Calhoun; Mrs Egerton Mrs Dion
Boucicault; Mrs Winterbotham Kate Phillips. L & MGR
John Hare; Sc William Harford; Cond Andrew Levey; Asm
W.M. Cathcart; Act mgr C.G. Compton. *REV: E 5/1/95*
p11; Sk 9/1/95 p491, 505-6; SR 5/1/95 p10-1; Th 1/2/
95 p106-7; TW95 p5-12; St 31/12/94 p8.

94.304 *SIXES AND SEVENS* (Misunderstanding) E.H. Whitmore. GARRICK 29/12/94-16/1/95. 16 perf [mat only
16/1].** Cpt. George Hope Arthur Bourchier. Edith
Cashdown Violet Vanbrugh. L & MGR, Cond, Asm, Act mgr
as for 94.303. *REV: E 5/1/95 p11.*

94.305 *COX AND BOX* (Triumviretta) F.C. Burnand (lib)
& Arthur Sullivan (mus). SAVOY 31/12/94-16/3/95. 69
perf [w/mat 2/3, 9/3, 16/3]. 1st perfd Adelphi 11/5/67.
John James Box Scott Russell; James John Cox M.R.
Morand; Sgt. Bouncer Richard Temple. PP & MGR Richard
d'Oyly Carte; Sm W.H. Seymour; Act mgr & Treas J.W.
Beckwith.

*   *   *   *   *

95.1 *DIE FLEDERMAUS* (Oa,3a) Johann Strauss. ROYALTY
1/1/95-12/1/95; 19/1(m); 23-25/1/95. 15 perf. 1st
perfd Wieden, Vienna 5/4/74. [Eisentstein] Klein; [Alfred] Schulhof; Siegmund Katzorke; Ernst Petersen;
[Dr Falke] Heinrich Kamm; [Dr Blind] William Karfiol.
[Rosalinde] Caervary; [Adele] Borges Lenge; [Prince
Orloffsky] Hedwig von Loree; Frau Dr Heinold-Thomann;
[Ida] Brand. COND Victor Hollaender. *REV: Sk 9/1/95
p537; Ti 2/1/95 p10.*

95.2 *A HAPPY THOUGHT* (Ca,1a) H. Tripp Edgar. STRAND
2/1/95-12/1/95. 10 perf. 1st perfd Bijou 2/3/94.
John Wentworth H. Tripp Edgar; Jack Edgar Stevens;
Freddy Woodpeck Dudley Cloraine; Stranger Frank Stather. Kitty Wentworth Kate Ruskin. L Willie Edouin.
REV: E 5/1/95 p11.

95.3 *AN IDEAL HUSBAND* (P,3a) Oscar Wilde. HAYMARKET
3/1/95-6/4/95;* trfd to CRITERION 13/4/95-27/4/95.
124 perf [w/W, S mat exc 9/1, 13/4, 17/4, 24/4, 27/4;
add mat 19/2, 25/2, 21/3]. Earl of Caversham Alfred
Bishop/Charles Goodhart; Lord Goring Charles H. Hawtrey; Sir Robert Chiltern Lewis Waller; Vicomte de
Nanjac Cosmo Stuart; Mr Montford Henry Stanford;
Phipps Charles H.E. Brookfield; Mason H. Deane; Footmen Charles Meyrick, [Charles] Goodhart. Lady Chiltern
Julia Neilson; Lady Markby Fanny Brough/Vane Featherston; Lady Basildon Vane Featherston/Enid Spencer
Brunton; Mrs Marchmont Helen Forsyth; Mabel Chiltern

452

Maude Millett/Sydney Fairbrother; <u>Mrs Cheveley</u> Florence West. <u>L</u> H.B. Tree; <u>Mgr</u> Lewis Waller, H.H. Morell; <u>Sc</u> Walter Hann, William Harford; <u>Bom</u> W.H. Leverton; <u>Sm</u> Shelton; <u>Mus dir</u> Carl Armbruster; <u>Elect</u> E.
Wingfield Bowles; <u>Pq</u> William Clarkson. *REV: Ath 12/1/*
95 p57; E 5/1/95 p13; Sk 9/1/95 p495-8, 13/2/95 supp
p1-8; SR 12/1/95 p43-5; St 10/1/95 p15; Th 1/2/95
p104-5; Ti 4/1/95 p7; TW95 p14-9.

95.4 *THYRZA FLEMING* (P,4a) Dorothy Leighton [Mrs G.C.
Ashton Jonson]. TERRY'S 4/1/95-10/1/95. 7 perf [w/mat
8/1].* <u>Col</u>. Rivers Bernard Gould; <u>Bertie Earnshaw</u>
William Bonney; <u>John Heron</u> George Warde; <u>Bobby Falk-</u>
<u>land</u> Harry Buss; <u>Jenks</u> Osmond Shillingford; <u>Waiter</u>
George Shepheard. <u>Pamela Rivers</u> Winifred Fraser;
<u>Theophila Falkland</u> Agnes Hill; <u>Jones</u> A. Beaugarde;
<u>Martin</u> Papton/Gupton; <u>Chambermaid</u> Louise Cove; <u>Thyrza</u>
<u>Fleming</u> Esther Palliser. <u>PP</u> Edward Terry; <u>Dir</u> J.T.
Grein, Dorothy Leighton; <u>Pq</u> Fox; <u>Furn</u> Lyons; <u>Pd</u> Herman
de Lange; <u>Sm</u> W[illiam] Bonney; <u>Mus dir</u> T[homas] Smythe;
<u>Act mgr</u> Arthur Somerville; <u>Bom</u> J. Spratt. *REV: Ath*
12/1/95 p57; E 12/1/95 p11; Sk 9/1/95 p492; SR 26/1/95
p126; St 10/1/95 p15-6; Th 1/2/95 p107-8; TW95 p12-4.
<u>Comment</u>: Independent Theatre Society.

95.5 *GUY DOMVILLE* (P,3a) Henry James. ST. JAMES'S 5/1/
95-5/2/95. 32 perf [w/S mat exc 5/1; add mat 23/1].*
<u>Guy Domville</u> George Alexander; <u>Lord Devenish</u> W.G.
Elliott; <u>Frank Humber</u> Herbert Waring; <u>George Round</u>
Henry V. Esmond; <u>Servant</u> Frank Dyall. <u>Mrs Peverel</u>
Marion Terry; <u>Mrs Domville</u> Mrs Edward Saker; <u>Mary</u>
<u>Brasier</u> Evelyn Millard; <u>Fanny</u> Irene Vanbrugh; <u>Milliners</u>
Blanche Wilmot, Lucy Bertram/Violet Lyster. <u>L & MGR</u>
George Alexander; <u>Bom</u> Arnold; <u>Cost dgn</u> Percy Anderson;
<u>Cost</u> Mme Savage, Mme Purdue, Cooling & Lawrence; <u>Furn</u>
Frank Giles & Co.; <u>Pq</u> William Clarkson; <u>Mus & Mus dir</u>
Walter Slaughter; <u>Sc</u> H.P. Hall; <u>Sm</u> H.H. Vincent; <u>Bm</u>
Robert V. Shone. *REV: Ath 12/1/95 p57; E 12/1/95 p11;*
Sk 9/1/95p492, 501,538,541,16/1/95 p553-5; SR 12/1/95
p43-5; St 10/1/95 p16; Th 1/2/95 p105-6; TW95 p32-5;
Ti 7/1/95 p13.

95.6 *TOO HAPPY BY HALF* (C,1a) Julian Field. ST. JAMES'S
5/1/95-5/2/95; 25/5/95-19/6/95. 49 perf.* <u>Eric Verner</u>

Henry V. Esmond; Jack Fortescue Arthur Royston; James
E. Bentham. Maud Verner Evelyn Millard. L & MGR, Bom,
Sm, Mus dir, Bm as for 95.5. *REV: E, St as for 94.5;
Ath 12/1/95 p58.*

95.7 *KING ARTHUR* (P,Prol,4a) J.W. Comyns Carr, LYCEUM
12/1/95-3/5/95; 8/5(m), 11/5(m), 15/5(m), 18/5(m),
22/5(m), 25/5(m), 30/5(m), 1/6(m), 5/6(m), 8/6(m),
15/6(m), 8-10/7, 13/7/95(m). 105 perf [np 8-13/4].*
King Arthur Henry Irving/Frank Tyars; Sir Lancelot
Johnston Forbes-Robertson/Ben Webster; Sir Mordred
Frank Cooper/[William] Haviland; Sir Kay [Frank] Ty-
ars/Clarence Hague; Sir Gawaine Clarence Hague/[W.
Lionel] Belmore; Sir Bedevere Fuller Mellish; Sir
Agravaine Lacy; Sir Perivale Buckley; Sir Lavaine
Julius Knight; Sir Dagonet John Martin Harvey; Merlin
Sydney Valentine; Messenger [W. Lionel] Belmore;
Gaoler [R.P.] Tabb. Morgan Le Fay Genevieve Ward;
Elaine Lena Ashwell; Clarissant Annie Hughes; Spirit
of the Lake Maud Milton/Ailsa Craig; Guinevere Ellen
Terry/Maud Milton. L & MGR Henry Irving; Mus Arthur
Sullivan; Sc & Cost dgn Edward Burne-Jones; Bom Joseph
Hurst; Mus dir J. Meredith Ball; Cost Nathan, Mrs
Nettleship, Auguste; Pq Fox; Furn Arnott; Mach Fillery
Sm H.J. Loveday; Act mgr Bram Stoker. *REV: Ath 19/1/95
p93; E 19/1/95 p9; Sk 16/1/95 p547-50, 27/3/95 p461;
SR 19/1/95 p93-5; St 17/1/95 p12-3; Th 1/2/95 p96-101,
1/8/95 p104; Ti 14/1/95 p11; TW95 p20-32.*

95.8 *DER BETTELSTUDENT* (CO,3a) Karl Millocker. ROYALTY
12/1/95-22/1/95. 9 perf. 1st perfd Theater auf der
Wieden, Vienna 6/12/82. Schulhof; Siegmund Katzorke;
Ernst Petersen; Heinrich Kamm; William Karfiol. Hedwig
von Loree; Caervary; Borges Lenge; Frau Dr Heinold-
Thomann.

95.9 *KEEP YOUR OWN COUNSEL* (Duol) Henry Bellingham &
William Best. TERRY'S 14/1/95-26/1/95; 23/3/95-20/4/95
40 perf [w/mat 6/4, 13/4, 15/4, 20/4; np 12/4].* Mr
Pickering Sydney Brough/Harcourt Beatty. Dora Madge
McIntosh. PP & MGR Edward Terry. *REV: Ath 19/1/95
p108; E 19/1/95 p9; St 17/1/95 p13, 28/3/95 p13.*

95.10 *AN INNOCENT ABROAD* (F,3a) W. Stokes Craven.

TERRY'S 14/1/95-16/3/95. 64 perf [w/S mat; add mat
6/2]. 1st perfd Theatre Royal, Belfast 9/11/94. Tobias
Pilkington Edward Terry; Dick Leslie Kenyon; Jack
Summerville Harcourt Beatty; Dr Hanson Jack Thompson;
Bill Bouncer Ernest Hendrie; Dennis George Belmore;
Mr Knowles Robert Soutar; Wilber Gerald Mirrielees.
Mrs Pilkington Kate Mills; Lilly Eily Desmond; Cissy
Farnborough Madge McIntosh; Rose Jessie Danvers. PP &
MGR Edward Terry; Bm H.T. Brickwell; Sc H. Bruce Smith,
[Fred?] Storey, [W.P.] Warren; Furn Lyon; Mus dir
T[homas] Smythe; Sm George Belmore. *REV: Ath 19/1/95
p108; E 19/1/95 p9; St 17/1/95 p13; Th 1/2/95 p108-9;
Ti 15/1/95 p6; TW95 p35.*

95.11 *HIGH LIFE BELOW STAIRS* (MF,1a) Rev James Town-
ley. TERRY'S 14/1/95-16/3/95. 64 perf [w/S mat; add
mat 6/2].** Duke's Servant Edward Terry; Sir Harry's
Servant Ernest Hendrie; Lovell Sydney Brough/Leslie
Kenyon; Philip Jack Thompson; Tom Robert Soutar;
Kingston Gerald Merrielees; Coachman T. Eames. Lady
Bab's Maid Madge Ray; Lady Charlotte's Maid Madge Mc-
Intosh; Cook Eily Desmond; Chloe Blanche Astley;
Kitty Jessie Danvers. PP & MGR, Bm, Sm, Furn, Sc as
for 95.10; Ch John d'Auban; Cost & Pq William Clark-
son. *REV: E, St, Ti as for 95.10; TW95 p35-7.*

95.12 *DAISY'S ESCAPE* (Ca,1a) A.W. Pinero. TOOLE'S 16/
1/95 (m), 23/1(m), 30/1(m); 4/2/95-9/2/95. 9 perf.**

95.13 *A PAIR OF SPECTACLES* (C,3a) Sydney Grundy [adpt
of Eugene Labiche & Delacour, *Les Petites Oiseaux*].
GARRICK 17/1/95-2/3/95. 50 perf [w/mat 26/1, 2/2,
6/2, 9/2, 2/3; mat only 23/2, 9/3].** Benjamin Gold-
finch John Hare; Uncle Gregory Charles Groves/Charles
Rock; Percy E. Allan Aynesworth; Dick Gilbert Hare;
Lorimer Charles Rock; Bartholomew Gerald du Maurier;
Joyce George Raiemond/W.M. Cathcart; Another Shoe-
maker Roger Roberts. Mrs Goldfinch Kate Rorke; Lucy
Lorimer Mabel Terry Lewis/Winifred Fraser; Charlotte
Lilian Lee. L & MGR John Hare; Sc William Harford;
Cond Andrew Levey; Asm W.H. Cathcart; Act mgr C.G.
Compton. *REV: E 19/1/95 p11; Sk 20/2/95 p163; St 24/
1/95 p13; TW95 p37.*

95.14 *FADED FLOWERS* (P,1a) Arthur W. A'Beckett. GAR-
RICK 17/1/95-8/3/95. 43 perf [np 23/2]. 1st perfd Hay-
market 6/4/72. Harold Beresford Arthur Bourchier;
Robert Elton W. Scott Buist; Bobbie Master Horace
Terry. Ada Violet Vanbrugh/May Harvey. L & MGR, Sc,
Cond, Asm, Act mgr as for 95.13. *REV: E, St as for*
95.13.

95.15 *THE TABOO* (Fantastic O,2a) Mason Carnes (lib)
& Ethel Harraden (mus). TRAFALGAR 19/1/95-26/1/95.
7 perf. 1st perfd Theatre Royal, Leamington 22/5/94.
Papakaio Harry Paulton; Timaru Wilfred Howard; Ranoro
Kelson Truman; Bigmoko George Humphrey; Septimus
Octopus Sharp Frank Wyatt. Whangahia   Helena Dalton;
Wangathaia Maud Maude; Whangayonda Bertha Meyers;
Wattatauka Amadi; Orama Lettie Searle; Pateena Nellie
Murray; Kiwi Dorothy Wilmot; Vestida de Culteria y
Compania Lizzie St. Quinten. PP Mr & Mrs Frank Wyatt;
Cond Barter Johns. *REV: E 26/1/95 p10; St 24/1/95 p12-*
3; Th 1/2/95 p110-1; Ti 21/1/95 p11.

95.16 *THE HOUSE OF LORDS* (Oa,1a) Harry Greenbank
(lib) & Ernest Ford (mus) & George W. Byng (mus).
TRAFALGAR 21/1/95-26/1/95. 6 perf.** Henry, Duke of
Hanover Square Charles Crook; Halifax Finsbury V[er-
non?] Drew; Mr Murgatroyd Frederick Seymour. Emmeline
Carrie Fenton; Lady Victoria Portobello Maud Maude.
REV: E 26/1/95 p10.

95.17 *PAPA'S WIFE* (Duol) Seymour Hicks (lib) & F.C.
Phillips (lib) & Ellaline Terriss (mus). LYRIC 26/1/
95; 23/2/95-9/3/95. 14 perf.* Gerald Singleton Sey-
mour Hicks/Arthur Playfair; William Frank Morton.
Kate Wetherby Ellaline Terriss. L Horace Sedger; Mgr
Arthur Fry; Sm John Gunn; Mus dir Carl Kiefert; Bm &
Treas C.P. Levilly. *REV: E 2/2/95 p10; Sk 13/2/95*
p112; Ti 25/2/95 p10.

95.18 *SHALL WE FORGIVE HER?* (Melo,5a) Frank Harvey.
OLYMPIC 26/1/95-23/2/95. 24 perf.** Paul Elsworth
Frank Harvey; Neil Garth T.W. Benson; Oliver West
J. Carter Edwards; James Stapleton Charles Darrell;
Reggie Walton Arthur Raynor; Dr McHerrow E[dward]
Thane; Tony Blake Douglas Bruce. Grace West Mrs Frank

Harvey; Joanna Lightfoot Myra Rosalind; Nellie West
Alice Raynor; Aunt Martha Marie Anderson. MGR Charles
Wilmot; Sc W.T. Hemsley; Bm H.A. Freeman. *REV: Ath*
2/2/95 p174; E 2/2/95 p11; Sk 6/2/95 p64; St 31/1/95
p12.

95.19 *NANON* (CO,3a) [Richard Genee]. ROYALTY 26/1/95.
1 perf. 1st perfd 16/9/89. Comment: Advertized in *Ti*
for this date.

95.20 *THE JOURNEY'S END* (P,1a) Horace W.C. Newte.
GLOBE 30/1/95-12/9/96. 503 perf [np 12/4/95, 25/12/
95, 5/2/96, 3-4/4/96]. 1st perfd Ladbroke Hall 11/6/
91. Edwin Clements H. Reeves-Smith; Allan Blair
Sydney Paxton; Theophilus Briggs Cecil H. Thornbury.
Ethel Mabel Lane; Eleanor Emmie Merrick/Annie L.
Aumonier/Olga Schuberth. L W.S. Penley; Sc Bruce
Smith; Bm Francis Gosnay; Treas W.A. Tinney; Mus dir
Franz Groenings; Sm Wilton Heriot; Bom H.W. Anderson.

95.21 *AN ARTIST'S MODEL* (MC,2a) Owen Hall (lib) &
Harry Greenbank (lyr) & Sidney Jones (mus). DALY'S
2/2/95-25/5/95;* trfd to LYRIC 28/5/95-6/9/95.
214 perf [w/S mat exc 2/2; np 12/4, 27/5]. Rudolph
Blair C. Hayden Coffin; Sir George St. Alban Eric
Lewis; Archie Pendillon Yorke Stephens; Earl of
Thamesmead Lawrance d'Orsay; Algernon St. Alban J.
Farren Soutar; Carbonnet Maurice Farkoa; Apthorpe
Gilbert Porteous; Maddox Conway Dixon; James Cripps
E.M. Robson/John Le Hay; Smoggins William Blakeley.
Mme Amelie Lottie Venne; Adele Marie Tempest/Louise
Beaudet/Florence Perry; Lady Barbara Cripps Leonora
Braham/Kate Hodson; Lucien Nina Cadiz; Jessie Marie
Studholme; Rose Kate Cannon; Christine Alice Davis;
Ruby Kate Adams; Violet Lettice Fairfax; Geraldine
Hetty Hamer; Amy Cripps Louie Pounds/Lettice Fairfax;
Jane Sybil Grey; Miss Manvers Nellie Gregory; Daisy
Vane Letty Lind. L & MGR Augustin Daly; Pd James T.
Tanner; Cond Sidney Jones; Sc Glendenning; Ch John
d'Auban; Cost Miss Fisher, Redfern, Swan & Edgar,
Mme [Marthilde] Marie, Jay, Vanité, Scott Son &
Claxton, Morris Angel, Arthur Firmin & Co.; Pq Will-
iam Clarkson; Add mus Mr & Mrs Joseph Watson; Bom
[Edward] Brown; Bm John Farrington; Act mgr M. Ed-

wards. *REV: Ath 9/2/95 p193; E 9/2/95 p9, 5/10/95 p8;
Sk 6/2/95 p63-4, 98, 101, 20/3/95 p387, 8/5/95 p59,
78-9, 5/6/95 p303, 322, 26/6/95 p476, 9/10/95 p580;
St 7/2/95 p14-5, 30/5/95 p13, 3/10/95 p10; Th 1/3/95
p173-4; Ti 4/2/95 p8; TW95 p41-6.* Comment: These
roles were added at Lyric: <u>Hatfield</u> Sydney Ellison.
<u>Laura</u> Nellie Gregory; <u>Claire</u> Mary Collette; <u>Lucille</u>
Lydia Flopp. For cast of the "2nd Edition" see item
95.220B.

95.22 *THE BABES; OR, W(H)INES FROM THE WOOD* (Bsq,2a)
Harry Paulton, rev A.C. Shelley. STRAND 4/2/95-13/2/
95. 12 perf [w/W, S mat]. 1st perfd Theatre Royal,
Birmingham 9/6/84; 1st perf of rev ver. <u>Sir Rowland
Buttre</u> David S. James; <u>Bill Booty</u> J.J. Dallas; <u>Ralph
Reckless</u> Edgar Stevens; <u>Dr Bolus</u> J.D. Saunders;
<u>Police Inspector</u> Holland; <u>Dolly</u> Willie Edouin. <u>Tessie</u>
Alice Atherton; <u>Pattie Buttre</u> Elaine Gryce; <u>Bertie
Patchoulie</u> Mary Allestree; <u>Lady Buttre</u> Ada Palmer;
<u>Maude</u> Violet Neville; <u>Miss Specs</u> Annie Goward; <u>Victor</u>
Fanny Davenport; <u>Reginald</u> Agnes Pendennis; <u>Margery</u>
Pollie Bonheur; <u>Rosina</u> Ray Vivian; <u>Clementina</u> Ida
Young; <u>Queenie</u> Patty Thornhill. <u>L</u> Willie Edouin; <u>Mus</u>
W.C. Levey; <u>Ch</u> R.M. Crompton; <u>Sm</u> C[harles] Davies.
REV: E 9/2/95 p9; Sk 13/2/95 p112; St 7/2/95 p15.

95.23 *THE BIRTHPLACE OF PODGERS* (F,1a) John Hollingshead. TOOLE'S 4/2/95-9/2/95. 6 perf.**

95.24 *MARGATE* (FC,3a) Barton White. TERRY'S 5/2/95
mat perf.* <u>Gen. Piercy</u> Leslie Kenyon; <u>Tooting Beck</u>
Richard Purdon; <u>Arthur Vereker</u> Harcourt Beatty;
<u>Willie</u> E.H. Kelly; <u>Tobias Dodd</u> Robert Nainby; <u>Stephens</u>
Ells Dagnall; <u>Inspector of Police</u> Harry Norton; <u>Po-
liceman</u> Henry Benton. <u>Helen Vereker</u> Olga Kate Noyle;
<u>Mrs Beck</u> Dolores Drummond; <u>Kitty</u> Amelia Gruhn; <u>Paul-
ine</u> Ina Goldsmith; <u>Mrs Stephens</u> Katie Neville; <u>Mme
Tulipon</u> Mrs B.M. de Solla; <u>Eliza</u> Jessie Danvers. *REV:
Ath 9/2/95 p208; E 9/2/95 p8; Sk 13/2/95 p112; St
7/2/95 p15; Th 1/3/95 p174-5.*

95.25 *A LEADER OF MEN* (C,3a) Charles E.D. Ward. COM-
EDY 9/2/95-8/3/95. 26 perf [w/mat 16/2, 23/2].* <u>Lord
Killarney, M.P.</u> Will Dennis; <u>Robert Llewelyn, M.P.</u>

Fred Terry; <u>Archdeacon Baldwin</u> Joseph Carne; <u>Louis
Farquhar, M.P.</u> H.B. Irving; <u>Morton Stone, M.P.</u> William
Wyes; <u>Jack Carnforth</u> Sydney Brough; <u>Adolphus Poole</u>
Stuart Champion; <u>Llewelyn's Servant</u> J[ohn] Byron;
<u>Footman</u> M. Browne. <u>Lady Solway</u> R.G. Le Thiere; <u>Mrs
Alsager-Ellis</u> Alma Murray; <u>Barbara Deane</u> May Harvey;
<u>Mrs Dundas</u> Marion Terry. <u>L & MGR</u> J.W. Comyns Carr; <u>Bom</u>
Scarisbrick; <u>Sm</u> Edward Hastings; <u>Sc</u> Walter Hann, Wal-
ter Johnstone; <u>Mus dir</u> Alfred J. Caldicott; <u>Bm</u> Silvanus Dauncey; <u>Cost</u> Mrs Nettleship, Mrs Alister; <u>Furn</u>
Hampton, Emile Godfrey; <u>Pq</u> William Clarkson. *REV: Ath
16/2/95 p227; E 16/2/95 p9; Sk 13/2/95 p111, 154; SR
16/2/95 p216-8; St 14/2/95 p12; Th 1/3/95 p170-1; Ti
11/2/95 p10; TW95 p47-56.*

95.26 *THOROUGHBRED* (C,3a) Ralph R. Lumley. TOOLE'S
13/2/95-23/3/95; 15/4/95-8/6/95; 3/9/95-28/9/95. 111
perf [w/mat 1/5, 15/5, 22/5, 1/6, 5/6, 21/9].* <u>Lord
Sandacre</u> John Billington; <u>Hon Blenkinsopp Carlingham</u>
Fitzroy Morgan/Edward A. Coventry; <u>John Rimple</u> J.L.
Toole/Henry Westland/Rutland Barrington; <u>A.V. Decker</u>
C.M. Lowne; <u>Claude Nizril</u> Edward A. Coventry/Percy
Buckler; <u>Jeb Tosh</u> George Shelton; <u>Jennings</u> Frank J.
Arlton; <u>Wokeham</u> Master Alec Boles. <u>Hon Wilhelmina
Carlingham</u> Henrietta Watson/Florence Fordyce; <u>Miss
Pallingham</u> Cora Poole; <u>Mrs Rimple</u> Kate Carlyon/Eliza
Johnstone; <u>Delia Rimple</u> Florence Fordyce/Therese Nor-
blom. <u>L & MGR</u> J.L. Toole; <u>Sc</u> Joseph Harker; <u>Cost</u>
Harrison; <u>Sm</u> John Billington; <u>Cond</u> William Robins;
<u>Bm & Treas</u> George Lee. *REV: Ath 16/2/95 p227-8; E 16/
2/95 p9, 11/5/95 p9, 7/9/95 p9; Sk 20/2/95 p168; St
21/2/95 p13, 5/9/95 p12, 3/10/95 p10; Th 1/3/95 p171-
3; Ti 14/2/95 p3; TW95 p60-1.*

95.27 *THE SECRET* (F,1a) William Barrymore. TOOLE'S
13/2/95-23/3/95; 15/4/95-8/6/95. 82 perf. 1st perfd
Greenwich 11/4/68. <u>Dupuis</u> Henry Westland; <u>Valare</u> C.M.
Lowne; <u>Thomas</u> George Shelton; <u>Porter</u> C[harles] Brunton. <u>Cecile</u> Kate Carlyon; <u>Angelica</u> Alice Kingsley.
<u>L & MGR</u>, <u>Cond</u>, <u>Bm & Treas</u>,<u>Sm</u> as for 95.26. *REV: E 16/
2/95 p9.*

95.28 *THE IMPORTANCE OF BEING EARNEST* (Trivial Comedy
for Serious People,3a) Oscar Wilde. ST. JAMES'S 14/2/

95-8/5/95. 83 perf [w/S mat exc 16/2, 13/4; add mat 6/3, 13/3, 20/3, 27/3, 3/4, 15/4; np 27/2, 11-13/4].* John Worthing George Alexander; Algernon Moncrieffe E. Allan Aynesworth; Rev Canon Chasuble H.H. Vincent; Merriman Frank Dyall; Lane F. Kinsey Peile. Lady Bracknell Rose Leclercq/Mrs Edward Saker; Hon Gwendolen Fairfax Irene Vanbrugh; Hon Cecily Cardew Evelyn Millard/Violet Lyster; Miss Prism Mrs George Canninge. L & MGR George Alexander; Sc H.P. Hall, Walter Hann; Bom Arnold; Bm Robert V. Shone; Sm H.H. Vincent; Mus dir Walter Slaughter; Furn Frank Giles; Pq William Clarkson. *REV: Ath 23/2/95 p260; E 16/2/95 p11; Sk 20/2/95 p168, 210, 213; 20/3/95 p411-4; SR 23/2/95 p249-51; St 21/2/95 p12-3; Th 1/3/95 p169-70; Ti 15/2/95 p5; TW95 p56-60.*

95.29 *IN THE SEASON* (P,1a) Langdon Elwyn Mitchell. ST. JAMES'S 14/2/95-8/5/95. 68 perf [np 22/3, 11-13/4].** Sir Harry Collingwood Herbert Waring; Edward Fairburne Arthur Royston/F. Kinsey Peile. Sybil March Elliott Page. L & MGR, Bom, Bm, Sm, Mus dir as for 95.28. *REV: Ath, E as for 95.28.*

95.30 *A BREEZY MORNING* (Ca,1a) Eden Phillpotts. COMEDY 16/2/95-6/4/95. 43 perf.** Mr Goldie Sydney Brough/ Clarence Blakiston. Mrs Goldie May Harvey/Eva Williams. L & MGR J.W. Comyns Carr; Bom Scarisbrick; Sm Edward Hastings; Mus dir Alfred J. Caldicott; Bm Silvanus Dauncey.

95.31 *AN M.P.'S WIFE* (P,4a) Anon [adpt fr T. Terrell's novel, *A Woman of Heart*]. OPERA COMIQUE 16/2/95. 1 perf.* John Armytage, M.P. William Herbert; Sir Richard Macklin Frederic de Lara; Frank Everard Rothbury Evans; William Sparrow Percy Bell; Alexander Jephson J. Hastings Batson; Job Venables E[dward] Rochelle; Hired Waiter Adam Sprange; Robert Fenwick Charles Glenney. Ruth Elliott T. White/Alexes Leighton; Lady Calcott Alexes Leighton; Lucy Travers Alice Dukes; Rose Bellamy Ina Goldsmith; Elise Dorothy Lawson. *REV: Ath 23/2/95 p260; E 23/2/95 p9; SR 23/2/95 p249-51; St 21/2/95 p13; Th 1/3/95 p175-6; Ti 18/2/95 p12; TW95 p61-2.* Comment: There is some confusion over the length of run. Some sources indicate the play was perfd nightly until 23/2. However, it was advertized in *Ti* only for 16/2, and an advertizement in *The Referee* indicates the theatre was "to let" on 17/2.

95.32 *A STAGE COACH* (C,1a) Frederic de Lara. OPERA COMIQUE 16/2/95. 1 perf.** <u>Col. Bumpus</u> E[dward] Rochelle; <u>Robert de Vere Trevelyan</u> Frederic de Lara. <u>Mrs Turtledove</u> Alexes Leighton; <u>May</u> Alice Dukes; <u>Brown</u> Ina Goldsmith. *REV: E 23/2/95 p9.* <u>Comment</u>: As for 95. 31.

95.33 *MAN TO MAN* (D,5a) William Bourne. OLYMPIC 25/2/ 95-9/3/95. 12 perf. 1st perfd Queens, Manchester 24/ 3/84. <u>Matthew Ellerton</u> A. Holland; <u>Richard Ellerton</u> C.W. Spencer; <u>George Gordon</u> William Bourne; <u>Philip Ormond</u> Sydney Stirling; <u>Samuel Plumtree</u> Horace Stanley; <u>Bill Burkley</u> Arthur Rich; <u>Turner</u> W. Hassan; <u>Rogers</u> B. Hacking; <u>Martin</u> Russell; <u>Forde</u> P. Dawson. <u>Ned Doyle</u> D. Carlton; <u>Lavinia Dove</u> Clarrie Ash; <u>Ethel Maythorne</u> Amy McNeil; <u>Madge</u> A. Vennimore; <u>Mary</u> G. Norton. <u>MGR</u> Charles Wilmot; <u>Bm</u> H.A. Freeman. *REV: E 2/3/ 95 p9; St 28/2/95 p13.*

95.34 *DANDY DICK WHITTINGTON* (OB,2a) George R. Sims (lib) & Ivan Caryll (mus). AVENUE 2/3/95-13/7/95. 122 perf [w/S mat exc 2/3, 18/5, 1/6, 8/6, 15/6, 22/6, 29/6, 6/7, 13/7; np 11-13/4].* <u>Sir Achilles Fitzwarren</u> A.J. Evelyn; <u>Lady Fitzwarren</u> John F. Sheridan; <u>Cpt Fairfax, R.N.</u> James Barr/Roland Cunningham/ James Leverett; <u>Larry O'Brannagan</u> Henry Wright; <u>Koko Gaga</u> Robert Pateman; <u>Auguste</u> Frederick Vaughan; <u>Tom</u> Harold Patterson; <u>Phra Maha</u> H[enry] N. Wenman; <u>Song Kla</u> McBride; <u>Phung Tha</u> [T.A.] Shale; <u>Chanta Burce</u> Wilkes; <u>See Papat</u> Davies. <u>Alice</u> Ethel Haydon; <u>Lola</u> Bertha Meyers; <u>Sa Dee</u> Gracie Whiteford; <u>Willasee</u> Florence Levey; <u>Nuntahtari</u> Ellen Goss; <u>Chantawee</u> Maude Fisher/Lily McIntyre; <u>Jenny</u> I[rene] du Foye; <u>Zoe</u> L[ydia] Lisle; <u>Nina</u> Morgan; <u>Susan</u> Elcho; <u>Dick Whittington</u> May Yohe/Millie Hylton/Marie Alexander. <u>L & MGR</u> William Greet; <u>Bm & Treas</u> Tom Pitt; <u>Cond</u> Ivan Caryll; <u>Mus dir</u> Landon Ronald; <u>Ch</u> Willie Warde; <u>Cost dgn</u> Edel; <u>Cost</u> Alias; <u>Pq</u> William Clarkson; <u>Props</u> Labhart; <u>Sc</u> T.E. Ryan; <u>Pd</u> Frank Parker. *REV: E 9/3/95*

*p10; Sk 6/3/95 p276, 10/4/95 p579-82; St 7/3/95 p12-3;
Th 1/4/95 p236-7; Ti 4/3/95 p3.*

95.35 *GENTLEMAN JOE* (MF,2a) Basil Hood (lib) & Walter
Slaughter (mus). PRINCE OF WALES'S 2/3/95-28/3/96.
391 perf [w/S mat 9/3/95-11/5/95; w/W mat 22/5/95-29/
8/95; w/S mat 7/9/95-28/3/96; add mat 15/4/95, 18/7/
95; np 12/4/95, 25/12/95, 5/2/96].*   Gentleman Joe
Arthur Roberts; Lord Donnybrook William Philp/Wilfred
Wynnstay/Roland Cunningham; Hughie Jaqueson Evelyn
Vernon; Mr Ralli-Carr E.H. Kelly/St. John Hamund;
Dawson Eric Thorne; James Picton Roxborough; Mr Pil-
kington-Jones W.H. Denny;Photographer W.F. Brooks;
Postman G. Danby/S. Mantell/Ernest A. Thiel. William
Clara Jecks; Mrs Ralli-Carr Aida Jenoure/Phyllis
Broughton; Hon Mabel Cavanagh Kate Cutler/Lettie
Searle/Audrey Ford; Miss Lalage Potts Sadie Jerome;
Miss Pilkington-Jones Carrie Benton/May Adair/Florence
Linton; Miss Lucy Pilkington-Jones Audrey Ford/Winnie
Carl/Susie Reimers/Christine Salisbury; Ada Pilking-
ton-Jones Ellas Dee/Attie Chester/Kate Herman; Amy
Pilkington-Jones Eva Ellerslie/Attie Chester; Emma
Kitty Loftus/Ellas Dee; Cook A[nnie?] Wilson/Adelaide
Newton. PP Edgar Bruce; Pd Hugh Moss; Mus dir Herbert
Bunning; Sc Joseph Harker, T.E. Ryan; Cost Swan & Ed-
gar; Sm Clarence Hunt; Bm C.P. Levilly; Ch Willie
Warde; Pq William Clarkson. *REV: Ath 9/3/95 p322; E
9/3/95 p10; Sk 6/3/95 p276, 13/3/95 p378, 381, 11/12/
95 p333; SR 9/3/95 p313-5; St 7/3/95 p13, 14/11/95
p12-3; Th 1/4/95 p234-5; Ti 4/3/95 p11; TW95 p62-6,
346.* Comment: A sketch, entitled *A Trilby Triflet*,
was incorporated later. Cast: Svengali Arthur Roberts;
Taffy Philip Yorke; Laird W.H. Denny; Gecko Eric
Thorne. Trilby Kitty Loftus; Little Billie Clara Jecks.

95.36 *DINNER FOR TWO* (Duol) R.C. Carton. DALY'S 4/3/
95-24/4/95. 44 perf.** L & MGR Augustin Daly.

95.37 *SOWING THE WIND* (C,4a) Sydney Grundy. COMEDY
9/3/95-6/4/95. 30 perf [w/mat 16/3, 20/3, 23/3, 27/3,
3/4].** Mr Brabazon Brandon Thomas; Mr Watkin Cyril
Maude; Ned Annesley Sydney Brough; Lord Petworth H.B.
Irving; Sir Richard Cursitor C.W. Garthorne; Mr
Deakin Will Dennis; Glossop Chandler; Webb J[ohn] By-

ron. Rosamund Evelyn Millard; Hon Mrs Fretwell Kate
Phillips; Maud Fretwell Alice Kingsley; Bridget Mrs
E.H. Brooke. L & MGR J.W. Comyns Carr; Sm Edward
Hastings; Bm Silvanus Dauncey; Bom Scarisbrick; Mus
dir Alfred J. Caldicott; Cost dgn Karl; Cost L. & H.
Nathan, Mrs Nettleship, Mrs Alister; Furn Hampton,
E[mile] Godfrey; Pq William Clarkson. *REV: Ath 16/3/
95 p354; E 16/3/95 p9; Sk 20/3/95 p390; St 14/3/95
p13; Ti 11/3/95 p12; TW95 p74-5.*

95.38 *THAT TERRIBLE GIRL* (MFC,3a) J. Stephens. ROYALTY
9/3/95-22/3/95. 12 perf.* Phineas Chatterhawk Edward
Lauri; Horace Fairfax J.R. Hatfield; Dr Pilsbury
Barker F[rederick] Glover; Jack Babbitt Wyvel; U.R.
Slick Douglas Hamilton; Tim McSwat Stephen Bond;
Silas Saltzer George Giddens. Clover Atkins Hope
Booth; Prudence Primrose Kitty Leslie; Mrs van Schoo-
ler Ida Hazeldean; Pansy van Schooler Lillie McIntyre.
L Kate Santley; Sc E.G. Banks; Pd Frederick Glover;
Mus dir Henry Sprake; Bm H. Lawrence Harris; Bom A.
[E.] Barnes. *REV: E 16/3/95 p9; St 14/3/95 p13; Th
1/4/95 p237-8; Ti 11/3/95 p12; TW95 p94.*

95.39 *HER GUARDIAN* (Ca) J.R. Brown. ROYALTY 9/3/95-
23/3/95. 12 perf.* Mr Davenant J.R. Hatfield; Mr
Luttrell Wyvell; Mr Martineau Douglas Hamilton. Violet Fane Ida Heron; Miss Morant [Kitty] Leslie. L,
Mus dir, Bm, Bom as for 95.38. *REV: E 16/3/95 p9.*

95.40 *A LOVING LEGACY* (FC,3a) Fred W. Sidney. STRAND
12/3/95-10/4/95;   trfd to OPERA COMIQUE 15/4/95-20/
4/95. 39 perf [w/S mat exc 30/3; add mat 10/4, 17/4;
np 11-13/4]. 1st perfd Devonshire Park, Eastbourne
28/1/95. Harry Kingsley William H. Day; Edward Pom-
meroy Oswald Yorke; Savory Bird Alfred Maltby; Terence
Mark A. Kinghorne; Mohammed El Tebkir J.A. Rosier.
Mrs O'Rourke Lizzie Henderson; Kitty O'Rourke May
Whitty; May Nancy Noel; Susan Katie Lee. PP J.S.
Clarke; Mgr E.F. Bradley; Sc W.T. Hemsley; Cost Alias;
Furn Lyons; Pq William Clarkson; Act mgr R.B. Dixon;
Sm Charles Milton; Mus dir Howard Talbot; Bom H.T.
Holliman. *REV: Ath 16/3/95 p353-4; E 16/3/95 p9; St
14/3/95 p13, 18/4/95 p13; Th 1/4/95 p235-6; Ti 13/3/
95 p5; TW95 p95; Sk 20/3/95 p390, 3/4/95 p503.*

95.41 *SALT TEARS* (Serio-Comic D,1a) T.W. Speight.
STRAND 12/3/95-10/4/95. 26 perf. 1st perfd Royalty
24/7/73. Ben Briny H.R. Teesdale; Phil Shingle Robb
Harwood; Jim Riley's Father J. McKenzie. Ruth Mayfield Olga Garland; Lady Janet Trevor Ettie Williams.
PP, Mgr, Sc, Cost, Furn, Pq,Act mgr, Sm, Mus dir, Bom
as for 95.40. *REV: E 16/3/95 p9; St 14/3/95 p13.*

95.42 *THE NOTORIOUS MRS EBBSMITH* (P,4a) A.W. Pinero.
GARRICK 13/3/95-14/6/95. 86 perf [w/S mat exc 16/3,
13/4, 25/5, 1/6; add mat 15/4; mat only 8/6; np 11-
12/4, 13-14/5].* Duke of St. Olpherts John Hare;
Sir Sandford Cleeve Ian Robertson; Lucas Cleeve John-
son Forbes-Robertson/W. Scott Buist; Rev Amos Winter-
field Charles Aubrey Smith; Sir John Broderick Joseph
Carne; Dr Kirke Fred Thorne; Fortune Gerald du Maurier; Antonio Poppi Charles F. Caravoglia. Agnes Mrs
Patrick Campbell/Olga Nethersole; Gertrude Thorpe
Ellis Jeffreys; Sybil Cleeve Eleanor Calhoun/Helen
Ferrers; Nella Mary Halsey; Hephzibah Mrs Charles
Groves. L & MGR John Hare; Sc William Harford; Cond &
Mus Haydn Waud; Asm W.M. Cathcart; Act mgr C.G. Compton. *REV: Ath 16/3/95 p353; E 16/3/95 p11; Sk 20/3/95
p390, 433-4, 27/3/95 p493, 3/4/95 p499, 17/4/95 p617,
22/5/95 p184; SR 16/3/95 p346-7, 25/5/95 p693-4; St
21/3/95 p13; Th 1/4/95 p231-4; Ti 14/3/95 p10; TW95
p75-85, 85-94, 161-3.*

95.43 *A MAN'S LOVE* (P,3a) J.T. Grein & C.W. Jarvis
[adpt of J.C. de Vos]. OPERA COMIQUE 15/3/95, 16/3/
95(m). 2 perf. 1st perfd Prince of Wales's 25/6/89.
Frank Upworth Herbert Flemming. Georgie Mary Keegan;
Emily Winifred Fraser; Mary Jay Lupton. DIR J.T.
Grein, Dorothy Leighton; Pd Herman de Lange; Cond
F. L[ouis] Schneider; Sm Adam Sprange; Act mgr Arthur
Somerville; Am Frederick W. Spratt. *REV: E 23/3/95
p8; Sk 20/3/95 p390; SR 23/3/95 p379-80; Ti 16/3/95
p12; TW95 p95.* Comment: Independent Theatre Society.

95.44 *SALVE* (DSk,1a) Mrs Oscar Beringer. OPERA COMIQUE
15/3/95, 16/3/95(m). 2 perf.* Desmond Ogilvie William Haviland; Rex Ogilvie Matthew Brodie. Deborah
Ogilvie Mrs Theodore Wright. DIR, Pd, Cond, Sm, Act
mgr, Am as for 95.43. *REV: E, Sk, SR, Ti as for 95.43;*

St 21/3/95 p13; TW95 p95-6. Comment: As for 95.43.

95.45 *THE HOUSE OF LORDS* (Oa) Harry Greenbank (lib)
& Ernest Ford (mus) & George W. Byng (mus). PRINCE OF
WALES'S 16/3/95-11/4/95. 23 perf.** Henry, Duke of
Hanover Square J. Furneaux Cook; Halifax Finsbury
Vernon Drew; Murgatroyd Frederick Seymour. Emmeline
Adelaide Newton; Lady Victoria Portobello Dora Thorne.
PP Edgar Bruce; Sm Clarence Hunt; Bm C.P. Levilly;
Mus dir Herbert Bunning; Ch Willie Warde; Pq William
Clarkson.

95.46 *THE BLUE BOAR* (F,3a) Louis N. Parker & Murray
Parker. TERRY'S 23/3/95-20/4/95. 28 perf [w/mat 6/4,
13/4, 15/4, 20/4; np 12/4]. 1st perfd Court, Liver-
pool 31/8/94. Robert Honeydew Edward Terry; Cyril
Strawthwaite Harcourt Beatty; The Griffin George Bel-
more; Boots Leslie Kenyon. Dr Prendergast Fanny Brough;
Mrs Pounder Alexes Leighton; Millicent Madge McIntosh.
PP & MGR Edward Terry; Bm H.T. Brickwell; Mus dir
T[homas] Smythe; Sm George Belmore. *REV: Ath 30/3/95
p418; E 30/3/95 p8; Sk 27/3/95 p445; St 28/3/95 p13;
Th 1/5/95 p296-7; Ti 25/3/95 p10; TW95 p96.*

95.47 *ROSMERSHOLM* (P,4a) Henrik Ibsen [trans Le Comte
Prozor]. 25/3/95, 27/3(m), 28/3/95. 3 perf.** Rosmer
A.-F. Lugné-Poe; Kroll Ripert; Ulric Brendel Nargeot;
Mortensgaard Seruzier. Rebecca West Marthe Mellot;
Mme Helseth Suzanne Grey. DIR J.T. Grein, Dorothy
Leighton, A.-F. Lugné-Poe; Cond Louis F. Schneider;
Furn Lyon; Pq Fox; Act mgr Arthur Somerville, Gros;
Am Frederick W. Spratt. *REV: Ath 30/3/95 p417-8; Sk
17/4/95 p662; SR 30/3/95 p411-3; St 28/3/95 p12-3;
TW95 p104-9.* Comment: Independent Theatre Society &
Théâtre de l'Oeuvre.

95.48 *L'INTRUSE* (P,1a) Maurice Maeterlinck. OPERA
COMIQUE 25/3/95, 27/3(m), 28/3/95. 3 perf. 1st perfd
Theatre d'Art, Paris 21/5/91. L'Aieul A.-F. Lugné-
Poe; Le Père Ripert; L'Oncle Seruzier. 1ière Jeune
Fille Marthe Mellot; 2eme Jeune Fille Suzanne Despres;
3eme Jeune Fille Mme Durard; La Soeur de Charité
Louise Beraud. DIR, Cond, Furn, Pq, Act mgr, Am as
for 95.47. *REV: Ath, SR, St as for 95.47.* Comment: As

for 95.47.

95.49 *FOR FAMILY FAME; OR, THE SEA AND ITS DEAD*
(Nautico-Domestic D,4a) Bernard P. McDonald. ROYALTY
25/3/95 mat perf.* Earl of Riverdox Bernard P. Mc-
Donald; Hon Harold Dredgepool Ronald McDonald; George
Gaston George A. Powell; Crumpler Rex Shirley. Emme-
line Annie Hughes. L Kate Santley; Mus Allan Wyndham;
Cond R.P. Black; Furn Maple & Co. *REV: St 28/3/95 p13.*

95.50 *OLD CRONIES* (Duo1) S. Theyre Smith. ROYALTY 25/
3/95 mat perf.** Dr Jacks Ronald McDonald; Cpt.
Pigeon Bernard P. McDonald. *REV: St 28/3/95 p13.*

95.51 *IN AN ATTIC* (Ca,1a) J. Wilton Jones. ST. JAMES'S
25/3/95 mat perf.* Arthur Clarges Philip Cunningham;
Joe Dixon W.H. Denny. Rosalind Annie Hill. L & MGR
George Alexander; Bm Robert V. Shone; Treas Edward
Ledger; Dir William Nicholl. *REV: E 30/3/95 p11; St
28/3/95 p13.*

95.52 *PELLEAS ET MELISANDE* (D,5a) Maurice Maeterlinck.
OPERA COMIQUE 26/3/95, 29/3/95. 2 perf. 1st perfd
Bouffes-Parisien, Paris 16/5/93. Golaud A.-F. Lugné-
Poé; Arkel Ripert; Medecin Nargeant. Pelléas Marthe
Mellot; Melisande Suzanne Despres; Geneviève Suzanne
Gay; Petit Yniold Tessor; 1er Servante Bavier; 2e
Servante Sarvoix. DIR J.T. Grein, Dorothy Leighton,
A.-F. Lugne-Poe. *REV: Ath 30/3/95 p417-8; E 30/3/95
p11; SR 30/3/95 p411-3; St 28/3/95 p13; TW95 p109-11,
111-9.* Comment: Independent Theatre & Théâtre de
l'Oeuvre.

95.53 *SOLNESS LE CONSTRUCTEUR [THE MASTER BUILDER]*
Henrik Ibsen [trans Le Comte Proyor]. OPERA COMIQUE
27/3/95, 30/3/95(2). 3 perf.** Halvard Solness A.-F.
Lugné-Poé; Dr Herdal Ripert; Ragnar Brovik Nargeot.
Hilde Wangel Suzanne Despres; Mme Solness Suzanne
Gay; Kaia Fosli Marthe Mellot. DIR J.T. Grein, Dorothy
Leighton, A.-F. Lugné-Poé; Cond Louis F. Schneider;
Furn Lyon; Pq Fox; Act mgr Arthur Somerville, Gros;
Am Frederick W. Spratt; Mus Gabriel Fauré; Cost dgn
Lugné-Poé; Pd Maurice Maeterlinck. *REV: Ath, SR as
for 95.52; St 4/4/95 p12; TW95 p104-9.* Comment: As

for 95.52.

95.54 *FORTUNE'S FOOL* (DE) Henry Hamilton. HAYMARKET
28/3/95-6/4/95. 9 perf.* <u>Philip Challoner</u> Lewis
Waller. <u>L</u> H.B. Tree; <u>Bom</u> W.H. Leverton; <u>Mgr</u> Lewis
Waller; <u>Sm</u> Shelton; <u>Mus dir</u> Carl Armbruster; <u>Elect</u> E.
Wingfield Bowles. *REV: Ath 6/4/95 p452; St 4/4/95 p12;
Th 1/5/95 p300-1; Ti 29/3/95 p10.*

95.55 *THE NEWEST WOMAN* (MCa) Henry Chance Newton (lib)
& Georges Jacobi (mus). AVENUE 4/4/95 mat perf.*
<u>Melchizedeck Josser</u> Lytton Grey. <u>Girtonia Fitzgiggle</u>
Maud Holland. <u>L & MGR</u> William Greet; <u>Cond</u> Georges
Jacobi. *REV: E 6/4/95 p8.*

95.56 *A WOMAN'S CAPRICE* (Ca,1a) H.M. Lewis [adpt of
Gott sei dank; der Tisch ist gedeckt]. PRINCE OF
WALES'S 13/4/95-18/3/96; 16/4/96-20/6/96. 356 perf
[np 25/12/95, 5/2/96].* <u>Cpt. Flareuppe</u> Eric Thorne;
<u>Mr St. John Firmely</u> Evelyn Vernon/Roland Cunningham/
Wilfred Wynnstay; <u>William Jones</u> Picton Roxborough/
George Lake Grange/Philip Yorke. <u>Mrs Flareuppe</u> Ade-
laide Newton; <u>Mrs St. John Firmely</u> Ellas Dee/Kate
Herman; <u>May</u> Attie Chester/Simeta Marsden. <u>PP</u> Edgar
Bruce; <u>Sm</u> Clarence Hunt; <u>Bm</u> C.P. Levilly; <u>Mus dir</u>
Herbert Bunning; <u>Pq</u> William Clarkson. *REV: E 20/4/95
p8.*

95.57 *THE GIRL I LEFT BEHIND ME* (D,4a) Franklyn Fyles
& David Belasco. ADELPHI 13/4/95-10/8/95. 104 perf
[w/mat 15/4]. 1st English perf. <u>Gen Kennion</u> F.H.
Macklin; <u>Mjr. Burleigh</u> Charles J. Fulton; <u>Lieut.
Hawkesworth</u> William Terriss; <u>Lieut. Morton Parlow</u>
W.L. Abingdon; <u>Arthur Penwick, M.D.</u> E.W. Gardiner/
Harry Nicholls; <u>Private Jones</u> George W. Cockburn;
<u>John Ladru</u> Julian Cross: <u>Sgt. Dix</u> Ackerman May; <u>Mc-
Glynn</u> Richard Purdon; <u>Andy Jackson</u> Edwin Rorke. <u>Dick
Burleigh</u> Dora Barton; <u>Kate Kennion</u> Jessie Millward;
<u>Lucy Hawesworth</u> Hope Dudley/Cynthia Brooke/Blanche
Wolsley; <u>Fawn</u> Mary Allestree; <u>Wilber's Ann</u> Marie Mon-
trose/Nanette Comstock/Ethel Earle. <u>PP & MGR</u> A. & S.
Gatti; <u>Dir</u> Fred G. Latham; <u>Mus & Mus dir</u> John Crook;
<u>Sc</u> Joseph Harker, Bruce Smith; <u>Cost</u> Jay, Mme Perren,
Stagg & Mantle, Morris Angel & Son; <u>Pq</u> William Clark-

son; <u>Furn</u> Frank Giles; <u>Bom</u> Arthur Frye. *REV: Ath 20/
4/95 p514; E 20/4/95 p8, 22/6/95 p8; Sk 27/3/95 p461,
24/4/95 p668, 5/6/95 p304-5; SR 20/4/95 p507-8; St
18/4/95 p12, 20/6/95 p10-1; Th 1/5/95 p293-5; Ti 15/
4/95 p6; TW95 p119-23.*

95.58 *THE BOHEMIAN GIRL* (O,3a) Michael Balfe. DRURY
LANE 13/4/95, 20/4(m), 23/4, 3/5, 16/5/95. 5 perf.**
<u>Devilshoof</u> Charles Manners/Gilbert King; <u>Thaddeus</u>
John Child; <u>Count</u> Harrison Brockbank/D. Ffrangcon
Davies; <u>Florestein</u> Wilfred Esmond. <u>Arline</u> Fanny Moody/
Amy Sherwin; <u>Gipsy Queen</u> Rose Olitzka; <u>Nurse</u> Kate
Vito; <u>L & MGR</u> Augustus Harris; <u>Cond</u> James M. Glover;
<u>Sm</u> Arthur P. Collins; <u>A act mgr</u> Neil Forsyth. *REV:
Ath 20/4/95 p513; E 20/4/95 p15; St 18/4/95 p12; Ti
15/4/95 p6.*

95.59 *FAUST* (O[5a]) Charles Gounod. DRURY LANE 15/4/
95, 19/4, 24/4, 29/4, 4/5(m), 8/5, 14/5/95. 7 perf.**
<u>Mephistopheles</u> Charles Manners; <u>Valentine</u> Harrison
Brockbank; <u>Faust</u> Joseph O'Mara. <u>Marguerite</u> Fanny
Moody; <u>Siebel</u> Carla Dagmar. <u>L & MGR</u> Augustus Harris;
<u>Cond</u> Armando Seppilli. *REV: Ath 20/4/95 p513; E 20/4/
95 p15; St 18/4/95 p12; Ti 17/4/95 p3.*

95.60 *BEFORE THE DAWN* (P,1a) Henry Byatt. OPERA COMI-
QUE 15/4/95-20/4/95;*   trfd to STRAND 22/4/95-18/5/
95. 30 perf. <u>Sir John Radley, Bart</u> Matthew Brodie;
<u>Constable</u> H.R. Teesdale. <u>Sallie Gliberry</u> Katie Lee;
<u>Lena</u> Ettie Williams/Alice Rees. <u>MGR</u> E.F. Bradley.
REV: E 20/4/95 p8; St 18/4/95 p12-3.

95.61 *FANNY* (F,3a) George R. Sims & Cecil Raleigh.
STRAND 15/4/95-1/6/95. 55 perf [w/W, S mat exc 17/4].
1st perfd Prince of Wales's, Liverpool 8/4/95. <u>Cpt.
Gerald O'Brien</u> John L. Shine; <u>Prof Barnabas Bixley</u>
William H. Day; <u>Kellaway</u> Owen Harris; <u>Saunders</u> T.P.
Haynes; <u>Harold Gregory</u> Osmond Shillingford; <u>Bob Tap-
ping</u> George Blackmore; <u>George</u> J. Mahoney; <u>Joseph
Barnes</u> Robb Harwood. <u>Flo Barnes</u> Lydia Cowell; <u>Grace
Dormer</u> May Whitty; <u>Paquita O'Brien</u> Alma Stanley. <u>PP</u>
J.S. Clarke; <u>Mgr</u> John L. Shine; <u>Sc</u> W.P. Warren; <u>Mus
dir</u> Howard Talbot; <u>Sm</u> W.J. Robertson; <u>Bm</u> Arthur Fry.
REV: Ath 20/4/95 p514; E 20/4/95 p8; Sk 22/5/95 p195-8;

St 18/4/95 p12; Th 1/5/95 p297-9; Ti 16/4/95 p4; TW95 p123-8.

95.62 *THE BACKSLIDER* (Duol,1a) Osmond Shillingford. STRAND 15/4/95-20/4/95; 24/4(m), 27/4(m), 1/5(m), 4/5(m), 8/5(m), 11/5(m), 15/5(m), 18/5(m); 20/5/95-1/6/95 [w/W, S mat]. 30 perf.* <u>Antony Dolomite</u> Osmond Shillingford. <u>Mrs Agatha Dolomite</u> May Whitty. <u>PP</u>, <u>Mgr</u>, <u>Mus dir</u>, <u>Sm</u>, <u>Bm</u> as for 95.61. *REV: E, St, Th as for 95.61.*

95.63 *CARMEN* (O,4a) Georges Bizet. DRURY LANE 16/4/95, 20/4, 26/4, 1/5, 6/5/95. 5 perf.** <u>Don José</u> Philip Brozel; <u>Escamillo</u> Richard Green; <u>Remendado</u> Carlyle; <u>Morales</u> Percy Mordy; <u>Dancairo</u> Gilbert King; <u>Zuniga</u> Charles Hinchcliffe. <u>Carmen</u> Rose Olitzka; <u>Michaela</u> Florence Monteith; <u>Mercedes</u> Addison; <u>Frasquita</u> Ethel Gryce. <u>L & MGR</u> Augustus Harris; <u>Cond</u> Armando Seppilli; <u>Sm</u> Arthur P. Collins; <u>A act mgr</u> Neil Forsyth. *REV: Ath 20/4/95 p513; E 20/4/95 p15; St 18/4/95 p12; Ti 17/4/95 p3.*

95.64 *DELIA HARDING* (P,3a) J.W. Comyns Carr [adpt of Victorien Sardou]. COMEDY 17/4/95-17/5/95. 28 perf [w/mat 27/4].* <u>Sir Arthur Studley, C.B.</u> Cyril Maude; <u>Clive Studley</u> Fred Terry; <u>Stanley French</u> [William] Mackintosh; <u>Julian Ormsby</u> Gilbert Farquhar; <u>Percival Lumley</u> Lyston Lyle; <u>Sir Christopher Carstairs</u> Chandler; <u>Syndic of Bellagio</u> Will Dennis; <u>Clerk to the Syndic</u> Mules Brown; <u>Cpt. Simmonds</u> Clarence Blakiston; <u>Waiter</u> J[ohn] Byron. <u>Lady Carstairs</u> Rose Leclercq; <u>Mrs Venables</u> Dorothy Dorr; <u>Mrs Emmeline Jay</u> Eva Williams; <u>Janet Ross</u> Mrs E.H. Brooke; <u>Servant</u> Fleming Norton; <u>Delia Harding</u> Marion Terry. <u>L & MGR</u> J.W. Comyns Carr; <u>Bom</u> Scarisbrick; <u>Sc</u> Walter Johnstone; <u>Cost</u> Mrs Nettleship, Jay, Miss Ellis, Mme Vero; <u>Furn</u> Hampton & Sons, E[mile] Godfrey; <u>Pq</u> William Clarkson; <u>Sm</u> Edward Hastings; <u>Mus dir</u> Alfred J. Caldicott; <u>Bm</u> Silvanus Dauncey. *REV: Ath 27/4/95 p545; E 20/4/95 p8; Sk 24/4/95 p668; SR 20/4/95 p508-9; St 25/4/95 p12-3; Th 1/5/95 p295-6; Ti 18/4/95 p3; TW95 p128-30.*

95.65 *MARITANA* (O[3a]) Vincent Wallace. DRURY LANE

17/4/95, 10/5/95. 2 perf.** <u>King</u> Charles Manners;
<u>Don Caesar de Bazan</u> John Child; <u>Don José</u> D. Frangcon
Davies; <u>Cpt.</u> Carlyle; <u>Marquis</u> Wilfred Esmond. <u>Maritana</u>
Fanny Moody; <u>Marchioness</u> Kate Vito; E. Gorton; <u>Laza-</u>
<u>rillo</u> Jessie Gorton. <u>L & MGR</u> Augustus Harris; <u>Cond</u>
James M. Glover. *REV: Ath 20/4/95 p513-4; E 20/4/95*
p15; St 25/4/95 p12; Ti 19/4/95 p7.

95.66 *PAGLIACCI* (O[2a]) Ruggiero Leoncavallo. DRURY
LANE 18/4/95, 22/4, 25/4, 27/4(m), 30/4, 4/5, 7/5,
9/5, 11/5, 18/5(m), 22/5(m), 25/5/95(m). 12 perf.**
<u>Tonio</u> Harrison Brockbank; <u>Silvio</u> James Barr; <u>Beppe</u>
Percy Mordy; <u>Canio</u> Philip Brozel. <u>Nedda</u> Pauline Joran.
<u>L & MGR</u> Augustus Harris; <u>Cond</u> Armando Seppilli; <u>Sm</u>
Arthur P. Collins; <u>A act mgr</u> Neil Forsyth. *REV: E,*
St, Ti as for 95.65; Ath 27/4/95 p545.

95.67 *CAVALLERIA RUSTICANA* (O,1a) Pietro Mascagni.
DRURY LANE 18/4/95, 22/4, 25/4, 27/4(m), 30/4, 4/5,
7/5, 9/5, 11/5, 16/5, 18/5(m), 22/5(m), 25/5/95(m).
13 perf.** <u>Alfio</u> Harrison Brockbank/D. Frangcon
Davies; <u>Turiddu</u> Joseph O'Mara. <u>Santuzza</u> Esther Pal-
liser/Agnes Delaporte; <u>Lucia</u> Amadi; <u>Lola</u> Carla Dagmar.
<u>L & MGR</u>, <u>Cond</u>, <u>Sm</u>, <u>A act mgr</u> as for 95.66. *REV: As for*
95.66.

95.68 *THE LADIES' IDOL* (FC,3a) Arthur Law. VAUDEVILLE
18/4/95-15/6/95. 64 perf [w/S mat; add mat 15/5, 22/5,
5/6, 12/6]. <u>Lionel Delamere</u> Weedon Grossmith; <u>Duke of</u>
<u>Castleford</u> Sydney Warden; <u>Lord Finch Callowdale</u> C.P.
Little; <u>Sir Simon Roebuck</u> Arthur Helmore; <u>Mr Purley</u>
John Beauchamp; <u>Mr Wix</u> Frederick Volpé; <u>Mr Kurdle</u>
Thomas Kingston; <u>Mr Beamish</u> Kenneth Douglas/Hugh Gor-
ing; <u>Simmons</u> L. Power. <u>Duchess of Castleford</u> Gladys
Homfrey; <u>Countess of Groombridge</u> Helen Ferrers/K[ate]
Serjeantson; <u>Lady Helen Frant</u> Esmé Beringer; <u>Lady</u>
<u>Eugenia Rostrevor</u> K[ate] Serjeantson/Kathleen Francis;
<u>Lady Boyce</u> B. Crawford; <u>Mrs Somerville Smith</u> Beatrice
Hayden; <u>Miss Minniver</u> Alma Gordon; <u>Dora Vale</u> May Pal-
frey; <u>Mary</u> A[lice] Beet. <u>L</u> Weedon Grossmith; <u>Mgr</u> A.F.
Henderson; <u>Sc</u> T.W. Hall; <u>Cost</u> Mme Oliver Holmes; <u>Sm</u>
G. Robinson; <u>Mus dir</u> C.J. Hargitt; <u>Pq</u> Fox. *REV: Ath*
27/4/95 p545; E 20/4/95 p11; Sk 29/5/96 p251-4; SR
27/4/95 p549; St 25/4/95 p12; Th 1/5/95 p299-300;

Ti 19/4/95 p7; TW95 p130-1.

95.69 *HAL, THE HIGHWAYMAN* (P,1a) H.M. Paull. VAUDE-
VILLE 18/4/95-15/6/95. 51 perf.** Handsome Hal
Thomas Kingston; Sir James Mortimer T.A. Palmer; Tim
Kenneth Douglas. Kitty Carter A[lice] Beet; Celia
Kate Sejeantson. L, Mgr, Sm as for 95.68; Mus & Mus
dir C.J. Hargitt; Cost L. & H. Nathan; Pd Herman de
Lange. *REV: St 25/4/95 p12.*

95.70 *A DRAWN BATTLE* (Duol) T. Malcolm Watson. DALY'S
25/4/95-25/5/95. 27 perf.** L & MGR Augustin Daly.

95.71 *THE PASSPORT* (P,3a) B.C. Stephenson & William
Yardley [fnd on Col. Savage's novel, *My Official
Wife*]. TERRY'S 25/4/95-27/7/95; trfd to TRAFALGAR
29/7/95-24/8/95. 122 perf [w/S mat 4/5-8/6; w/W mat
12/6-21/8]. 1st prof. Ferdinand Sinclair Yorke Ste-
phens; Christopher Coleman Alfred Maltby; Bob Cole-
man Roland Atwood; Algy Grey Cecil Ramsey; Henry
Harris Compton Coutts; Pattison Richard Blunt; Schmir-
koff J.L. Mackay; George Greenwood George Giddens. Mrs
Coleman Fanny Coleman; Mildred Kate Tully; Violet
Tracey Grace Lane; Markham Cicely Richards; Mrs Darry
Gertrude Kingston. PP Edward Terry; L & MGR Henry
Dana; Mus dir H.A.J. Campbell; Furn Oetzmann; Pq Mrs
C.H. Fox; Cost Marshall & Snelgrove, Morris Angel; Sm
Standley Wade; Act mgr James W. Mathews. *REV: Ath 4/5/
95 p581; E 27/4/95 p9; Sk 1/5/95 p6, 49-50, 12/6/95
p364-5; SR 4/5/95 p580; St 2/5/95 p13; Th 1/6/95
p361-2; Ti 26/4/95 p10; TW95 p135-6.*

95.72 *BARON GOLOSH* (OB,2a) Adpt of Maurice Ordonneau
& Edmond Audran, *L'Oncle Celestin*; add mus by W. Meyer
Lutz. TRAFALGAR 25/4/95-8/6/95. 43 perf [w/S mat exc
27/4, 1/6, 8/6]. 1st perfd Star Theatre & Opera House,
Swansea 15/4/95. Baron Golosh E.J. Lonnen; Marreau
Harry Paulton/Charles Danby; Gustave Scott Russell;
Count Acacia Frank Wyatt; Viscount Acacia George Hum-
phrey; Ratinet W.S. Laidlaw; Hairdresser Stanley
Smith; Tailor V[ictor] M. Seymour; Bootmaker T.F.
Lovelace; Narcisse Ernest Down. Clementine Florence
Perry; Pamela M.A. Victor; Mme de Bellefontaine Violet
Melnotte; Madelon Alice Lethbridge; Therese Delia Car-

lyle; <u>Dressmaker</u> Alwyn; <u>Florist</u> [Marguerite?] Osland;
<u>Mme Margerine</u> Maud Maude; <u>Mme Gruyere</u> Violet Ella-
cott; <u>Mme Brie</u> Eva Murton; <u>Countess Acacia</u> Sylvia
Grey/Ada Reeve. <u>PP & L</u> Mr & Mrs Frank Wyatt; <u>Cond</u> W.
Meyer Lutz; <u>Add mus</u> Stuart Leslie; <u>Ch</u> John d'Auban;
<u>Sc</u> E.G. Banks; <u>Cost dgn</u> Comelli; <u>Cost</u> Harrisons; <u>Pq</u>
William Clarkson; <u>Furn</u> Lyons; <u>Sm</u> George Fielder; <u>Rep</u>
W.J. Glass; <u>Act mgr</u> Gilbert Tate, H[enry] Brandon.
REV: E 27/4/95 p9; Sk 1/5/95 p6, 22/5/95 p186, 12/6/
95 p353; St 2/5/95 p13; Th 1/6/95 p359-60.

95.73 *A HAPPY THOUGHT* (P,1a) H. Tripp Edgar. TRAFAL-
GAR 25/4/95-31/5/95. 32 perf.** <u>John Wentworth</u> H.
Tripp Edgar; <u>Jack Wentworth</u> Stanley Smith; <u>Freddy
Woodpeck</u> W.S. Laidlaw; <u>Stranger</u> Ernest Down. <u>Kitty
Wentworth</u> Kate Ruskin. <u>PP & L</u>, <u>Cond</u>, <u>Sm</u>, <u>Rep</u>, <u>Act
mgr</u> as for 95.72; <u>Mus</u> W. Carlyle Vernon. *REV: E 27/*
4/95 p9.

95.74 *A WOMAN'S NO* (P,1a) Somerville Gibney. TERRY'S
26/4/95-27/7/95. 80 perf.* <u>Hon Arthur Meyrick</u> Standley Wade; <u>Fawdon Lawless</u> Richard Blunt. <u>Minnie Law-
less</u> Kate Tully. <u>PP</u> Edward Terry; <u>L & MGR</u> Henry Dana
<u>Mus dir</u> H.A.J. Campbell; <u>Furn</u> Oetzmann; <u>Pq</u> Mrs C.H.
Fox; <u>Cost</u> Marshall & Snelgrove, Morris Angel; <u>Sm</u>
Standley Wade; <u>Act mgr</u> James W. Mathews.

95.75 *VANITY FAIR* (Caricature,3a) George W. Godfrey.
COURT 27/4/95-24/7/95; 23/9/95-2/11/95. 120 perf
[w/mat 4/5, 11/5, 25/5, 8/6, 3/7, 10/7, 24/7, 26/10;
mat only 2/11].* <u>Lord Arthur Nugent, G.C.B.</u> Arthur
Cecil; <u>Duke of Berkshire, K.G.</u> Charles Sugden; <u>Braba-
zon-Tegg</u> William Wyes/W.H. Quinton; <u>Harold Brabazon-
Tegg</u> H. Nye Chart; <u>Sir James Candy</u> Charles S. Faw-
cett; <u>Bertie Rosevere</u> A. Vane-Tenpest; <u>Sir Richard
Fanshawe</u> Wilfred Draycott/Howard Sturge; <u>Villars</u>
Howard Sturge; <u>Smiley</u> William Cheesman/H. Batson;
<u>Teale, Q.C.</u> F[rank?] MacDonnell; <u>Firmin</u> H.N. Ray;
<u>Clerk of Arraigns</u> [F.] Lane; <u>Footman</u> Lawrence/Widde-
combe; <u>Bill Feltoe</u> G.W. Anson/William Cheesman. <u>Lady
Jacqueline Villars</u> Helena Dacre; <u>Violet Brabazon-Tegg</u>
Nancy Noel; <u>Mrs Chetwynd</u> Frances Dillon; <u>Mrs Walrond</u>
Lucy Bertram/[Geraldine?] Wrangham; <u>Mrs Brabazon-Tegg</u>
Mrs John Wood/Susie Vaughan; <u>Viscountess of Castle-</u>

blaney Charlotte Granville. MGR Arthur Chudleigh; Sc
T.W. Hall; Mus dir Edward Jones; Act mgr Leonard Lillies; Furn Marler & Bennett; Pq C.H. Fox; Cost Russell
& Allen, Angel & Sons. *REV: Ath 4/5/95 p581-2; E 4/5/
95 p9, 28/9/95 p8; Sk 1/5/95 p6, 8/5/95 p105-6, 2/10/
95 p523; SR 4/5/95 p579-80; St 2/5/95 p12-3, 26/9/95
p12; Th 1/6/95 p358-9; Ti 29/4/95 p11; TW95 p132-5.*

95.76 *THE LILY OF KILLARNEY* (O[3a]) Julius Benedict.
DRURY LANE 27/4/95, 2/5, 11/5(m), 18/5/95. 4 perf.
1st perfd Covent Garden 8/2/62. Danny Mann W. Ludwig;
Myles-na-Coppaleen John Child; Corrigan Gilbert King;
Hardress Cregan Joseph O'Mara; Father Tom William
Devers. Eily O'Connor Fanny Moody; Anne Chute Mary
Glover; Mrs Cregan Amadi; Shelah Kate Vito. L & MGR
Augustus Harris; Cond James M. Glover. *REV: Ath 4/5/
95 p580; E 4/5/95 p15; St 2/5/95 p12; Ti 29/4/95 p11.*

95.77 *A HUMAN SPORT* (D,1a) "Austin Fryers" [W.E.
Cleary]. GLOBE 1/5/95 mat perf.* Herbert Groves
Philip Cunningham; Emile Foudriant Wilton Heriot; Old
Nip James A. Welch. Minnie Katherine Glover; Mrs
Chessle Mrs Theodore Wright. BM Francis Gosnay. *REV:
E 4/5/95 p11; Sk 8/5/95 p60; SR 4/5/95 p580; St 2/5/
95 p13; Th 1/6/95 p362.*

95.78 *ROMEO AND JULIET* (O,4a) Charles Gounod. DRURY
LANE 3/5/95 mat perf.** Friar Lawrence [B.] Griffiths-
Percy; Capulet Charles Hinchliff; Tybalt Frank J. As-
cough; Paris Richard Triggs; Mercutio F. Stuart Hyatt;
Duke of Verona Tom Powley; Gregorio Wyatt Keith; Romeo
Lloyd Chandos. Juliet Jessie Huddleston; Stephano
Minnie Hyem; Gertrude Annie Stoney. SM Wilfred Esmond;
Cond Sir Joseph Barnby. *REV: Ath 11/5/95 p617; E 4/5/
95 p15.* Comment: Guildhall School of Music.

95.79 *BYGONES* (P,1a) A.W. Pinero. LYCEUM 4/5/95-1/6/
95; 5/6, 8/6/95. 26 perf [np 11/5]. 1st perfd Lyceum
18/9/80. Hon Curzon Gramshawe Ben Webster; Rev Giles
Horncastle William Haviland; Prof Giacomo Mazzoni
Sydney Valentine. Bella Ailsa Craig; Ruby Annie Hughes.
L & MGR Henry Irving; Mach Fillery; Sm H.J. Loveday;
Mus dir J. Meredith Ball; Act mgr Bram Stoker; Bom
Joseph Hurst. *REV: E 11/4/95 p9; Sk 8/5/95 p60; SR*

11/5/95 p619-21; St 9/5/95 p12; Th 1/6/95 p350-3; Ti 6/5/95 p8.

95.80 *A STORY OF WATERLOO* (Sk,1a) A. Conan Doyle.
LYCEUM 4/5/95-1/6/95; 5/6, 8/6, 12/6(m), 27/7/95. 27
perf [np 11/5].** Corporal Gregory Brewster Henry
Irving; Sgt. Archie MacDonald, R.A. Fuller Mellish;
Col. James Midwinter Ben Webster. Nora Brewster Annie
Hughes. L & MGR, Mach, Sm, Mus dir, Act mgr,Bom as
for 95.79. *REV: E, Sk, SR, Th, Ti as for 95.79; St
9/5/95 p12, 1/8/95 p11; TW95 p137, 142-3.*

95.81 *DON QUIXOTE* (P,1a) W.G. Wills. LYCEUM 4/5/95-
1/6/95; 5/6, 8/6, 12/7/95(m). 27 perf [np 11/5].*
Master Quixada Henry Irving; Sancho Panza [Sam] John-
son; Father Perez [William] Haviland; Pedro [John]
Archer; Peasant [T.] Reynolds; Muleteers [W. Lionel]
Belmore, [K.] Rivington; Old Woman Herbert Innis.
Antonia N. de Silva; Maria Maud Milton; Dulcinea Mrs
Lacy; Girls Foster, K. Harwood, Ailsa Craig. L & MGR,
Mach, Sm, Mus dir, Act mgr, Bom as for 95.79; Cost
Auguste, Mrs Reid; Ch Espinosa; Furn Arnott; Sc Hawes
Craven. *REV: E, Sk, SR, Th, Ti as for 95.79; Ath 11/5/
95 p618; St 9/5/95 p12-3; TW95 p137-42.*

95.82 *A NEAR SHAVE* (MF) George D. Day (lib) & Edward
Jones (mus). COURT 6/5/95-27/7/95; 23/9/95-1/11/95.
107 perf.* Ebenezer Addleshaw G.W. Anson/William
Wyes/H.N. Ray; Josiah Giggins H.O. Cleary. Arabella
Pettifer Emmeline Orford/Blanche Wolsley. MGR Arthur
Chudleigh; Mus dir Edward Jones; Act mgr Leonard Lill-
ies; Furn Marler & Bennett; Pq C.H. Fox; Cost Russell
& Allen, Angel & Sons. *REV: E 25/5/95 p10, 28/9/95
p8; St 26/9/95 p12.*

95.83 *THREEPENNY BITS* (F) Israel Zangwill. GARRICK
6/5/95 mat perf. 1st perfd Opera House, Chatham 25/4/
95. Richard Westbourne Arthur Bourchier. Margaret
Linfield Violet Vanbrugh. L & MGR John Hare; Cond
Haydn Waud; Sm W.M. Cathcart; Bm G.F. Bashford. *REV:
Ath 11/5/95 p618; St 9/5/95 p13.*

95.84 *A QUIET RUBBER* (P,1a) Charles F. Coghlan. GAR-
RICK 6/5/95 mat perf.** Lord Kilclare John Hare;

Charles Gilbert Hare; Sullivan Charles Groves. Mary
Helen Luck. L & MGR, Cond, Sm, Bm as for 95.83. *REV:
St 9/5/95 p13.*

95.85 *THE VICARAGE* (Fireside Story) Clement Scott
[adpt of Octave Feuillet, *Le Village*]. GARRICK 6/5/95
mat perf.** George Clarke S.B. Bancroft; Rev Noel
Haygarth Arthur Cecil; Mason Charles Rock. Mrs Haygarth Mrs S.B. Bancroft. L & MGR, Cond, Sm, Bm as for
95.83. *REV: St 9/5/95 p13.*

95.86 *THE HOME SECRETARY* (P,4a) R.C. Carton. CRITERION
7/5/95-20/7/95. 72 perf [w/S mat 11/5-15/6; ·add mat
26/6].* Right Hon Duncan Trendel, M.P. Charles Wynd-
ham; Sir James Haylett, Q.C., M.P. Alfred Bishop;
Lord Blayver David S. James; Frank Trendel Sydney
Brough; Cpt. Chesnall Charles H.E. Brookfield; Mr
Thorpe-Didsbury, M.P. Herman de Lange; Rixon H. Deane;
Morris Lecaile Lewis Waller. Rhoda Trendel Julia Neilson; Lady Clotilda Bramerton Dolores Drummond; Esme
Bramerton Maud Millett; Mrs Thorpe-Didsbury Mary
Moore. L & MGR Charles Wyndham; Sc Walter Hann, John-
son; Cond A. Evans; Cost Lewis & Allenby, Jays, Pitts
& Richards, Mme Eroom; Furn Frank Giles; Act mgr &
Treas E. Harvey. *REV: Ath 11/5/95 p618; E 11/5/95
p9; Sk 15/5/95 p116, 162, 165; SR 18/5/95 p650-1; St
9/5/95 p13; Th 1/6/95 p356-8; Ti 8/5/95 p5; TW95 p144-
52.*

95.87 *LOVE AND DENTISTRY* (Duol) Herbert Swears. OPERA
COMIQUE 8/5/95 mat perf. 1st perfd Lecture Hall,
Greenwich 5/12/93. Herbert Swears. Lilian Maine. BM
A.F. Henderson; Dir David S. James. *REV: St 9/5/95
p13.*

95.88 *TOPSY-TURVY* (Monol). OPERA COMIQUE 8/5/95 mat
perf. 1st perf? Arthur Helmore. BM, Dir as for 95.87.
REV: St 9/5/95 p13.

95.89 *PAPA'S WIFE* (Duol) Seymour Hicks (lib) & F.C.
Phillips (lib) & Ellaline Terriss (mus). OPERA COMI-
QUE 8/5/95 mat perf.** Gerald Singleton Tom Terriss.
Kate Wetherby Ellaline Terriss. BM, Dir as for 95.87.
Comment: *St* indicates the Terrisses did not appear.

95.90 *THE SKYWARD GUIDE* (D,4a) Mrs Albert Bradshaw
[Anne M. Tree] & Mark Melford. ROYALTY 9/5/95 mat
perf.* <u>Albert Penrose</u> Loring Fernie; <u>Hamblen Temple-
ton</u> Harry Mountford; <u>Wilfred Barfoot</u> Frank Gordon;
<u>Tipper</u> A.D. Pierpoint; <u>Mr Craven</u> Roy Byford; <u>Christian
Strasse</u> Mark Melford; <u>Joseph</u> Robert Lintott; <u>Knubel</u>
James Ashburn; <u>Peter</u> Vincent Osborne; <u>Franz</u> Arthur
Edmunds; <u>Mr Beauley</u> Vansittart; <u>City Clerk</u> Cecil Rut-
land; <u>Paulio</u> George Albertazzi; <u>Gendarme</u> George W. Ab-
ron. <u>Vernon Strasse</u> Jackeydora Melford; <u>Aleppa</u> Ethel
Payne; <u>Adrea</u> Madge Lewis; <u>Hon Mrs Penrose</u> Ethel Arden;
<u>Leonora Garth</u> Dora de Winton; <u>Flavia Strasse</u> Annie
Stalman; <u>Ferda Colefield</u> Eva Willing; <u>Rosa</u> Ida Heron;
Jennie Gertrude Price; <u>Martha</u> Margaret Hayes. *REV:
St 16/5/95 p13; Th 1/6/95 p360-1.*

95.91 *WOOINGS AND WEDDINGS* (MSk) George Grossmith.
TOOLE'S 9/5/95-8/6/95. 31 perf [w/mat 15/5, 22/5,
1/6, 5/6]. 1st perf? or possibly an alternative title
for *Cups and Saucers*? George Grossmith. <u>L & MGR</u> J.L.
Toole; <u>Sm</u> John Billington; <u>Cond</u> William Robins; <u>Bm &
Treas</u> George Lee. *REV: St 16/5/95 p12-3.*

95.92 *THE TRIUMPH OF THE PHILISTINES; AND HOW MR JOR-
GAN PRESERVED THE MORALS OF MARKET PEWBURY UNDER VERY
TRYING CIRCUMSTANCES* (C,3a) H.A. Jones. ST. JAMES'S
11/5/95-19/6/95. 39 perf [w/S mat exc 11/5].* <u>Sir
Valentine Fellowes</u> George Alexander; <u>Willie Hessel-
tine</u> Henry V. Esmond; <u>Mr Jorgan</u> Herbert Waring; <u>Mr
Pote</u> E.M. Robson; <u>Mr Blagg</u> Ernest Hendrie; <u>Mr Modlin</u>
Arthur Royston; <u>Mr Skewett</u> James A. Welch; <u>Mr Wapes</u>
H.H. Vincent; <u>Mr Corby</u> Duncan Tovey; <u>Thomas Blagg</u>
Master Frank Saker; <u>Wheeler</u> Mark Paton. <u>Lady Beauboys</u>
Lady Monckton; <u>Alma Suleny</u> Elliott Page; <u>Angela Soar</u>
Blanche Wilmot; <u>Sally Lebrune</u> Juliette Nesville. <u>L &
MGR</u> George Alexander; <u>Bom</u> Arnold; <u>Furn</u> Frank Giles;
<u>Cost</u> Mme Savage, Mme Purdue; <u>Pq</u> William Clarkson; <u>Sc
dgn</u> William Morris & Co.; <u>Sc</u> H.P. Hall; <u>Bm</u> Robert V.
Shone; <u>Sm</u> H.H. Vincent; <u>Mus dir</u> Walter Slaughter.
*REV: Ath 18/5/95 p651; E 18/5/95 p9; Sk 15/5/95 p115-6,
162, 165; 19/6/95 p419-21; SR 18/5/95 p651-2; St 16/
5/95 p12; Th 1/6/95 p355-6; Ti 13/5/95 p7; TW95 p152-
61, 164-72.*

95.93 *OTELLO* (O[4a]) Giuseppe Verdi. COVENT GARDEN
13/5/95, 21/5, 29/5, 6/6, 18/6/95. 5 perf.** <u>Iago</u>
Arturo Pessina/Victor Maurel; <u>Cassio</u> Pelagalli-Rossetti; <u>Roderigo</u> Percy Mordy; <u>Montano</u> Richard Green;
<u>Lodovico</u> Vittorio Arimondi; <u>Otello</u> Francesco Tamagno.
<u>Desdemona</u> Emma Albani/Margaret MacIntyre; <u>Emelia</u> Rose
Olitzka. <u>L & MGR</u> Augustus Harris; <u>Cond</u> Luigi Mancinelli; <u>A act mgr</u> Neil Forsyth; <u>Bom</u> E. Hall. *REV: Ath*
18/5/95 p650, 22/6/95˙p814; E 18/5/95 p7, 22/6/95 p15;
Sk 22/5/95 p184; SR 18/5/95 p649-50; St 16/5/95 p12;
Ti 14/5/95 p10, 20/6/95 p6.

95.94 *MEFISTOFELE* (O[Prol,4a,Epi]) Arrigo Boito. COV-
ENT GARDEN 14/5/95. 1 perf.** <u>Mephistopheles</u> Pol
Plançon; <u>Wagner/Nereas</u> Iginio Corsi; <u>Faust</u> Fernando
de Lucia. <u>Margherita/Elena</u> Margaret MacIntyre; <u>Marta</u>
Aurelia Kitzu; <u>Pantalis</u> Agnes Janson. <u>L & MGR</u>, <u>Cond</u>,
<u>A act mgr</u>, <u>Bom</u> as for 95.93. *REV: Ath 18/5/95 p650;*
E 18/5/95 p7; Sk 22/5/95 p184; St 16/5/95 p12; Ti 17/
5/95 p10.

95.95 *LE PROPHETE* (O[5a]) Giacomo Meyerbeer. COVENT
GARDEN 15/5/95, 27/5/95. 2 perf.** <u>Oberthal</u> Vittorio
Arimondi; <u>Mathisen</u> Antonio Pini-Corsi; <u>Jonas</u> Iginio
Corsi; <u>Zaccaria</u> Armand Castelmary; <u>Jean de Leyden</u>
Francesco Tamagno. <u>Bertha</u> Gabrielle Lejeune; <u>Fidès</u>
Giulia Ravogli. <u>L & MGR</u>, <u>A act mgr</u>, <u>Bom</u> as for 95.93;
<u>Cond</u> Enrico Bevignani. *REV: Ath, E, Sk, Ti as for*
95.94.

95.96 *PAGLIACCI* (O,2a) Ruggiero Leoncavallo. COVENT
GARDEN 16/5/95, 20/6, 6/7, 12/7/95. 4 perf.** <u>Canio</u>
Fernando de Lucia/Philip Brozel; <u>Tonio</u> Mario Ancona/
Antonio Pini-Corsi; <u>Beppe</u> Charles Bonnard/Iginio Cor-
si; <u>Silvio</u> Jacques Bars. <u>Nedda</u> Fanny Moody/Pauline
Joran/Zelie de Lussan. <u>L & MGR</u>, <u>A act mgr</u>, <u>Bom</u> as for
95.93; <u>Cond</u> Armando Seppilli. *REV: Ath 25/5/95 p682,*
20/7/95 p107; E 18/5/95 p7, 22/6/95 p15, 6/7/95 p6,
20/7/95 p13; St 23/5/95 p10, 11/7/95 p10, 18/7/95 p10;
Ti 17/5/95 p10.

95.97 *PHILEMON ET BAUCIS* (O[2a]) Charles Gounod.
COVENT GARDEN 16/5/95, 20/7/95. 2 perf.** <u>Philemon</u>
Charles Bonnard/Philip Brozel; <u>Jupiter</u> Pol Plançon;

Vulcan Armand Castelmary. Baucis Marie Engle. L & MGR,
A act mgr, Bom as for 95.93; Cond Enrico Bevignani.
*REV: Ath 25/5/95 p682; E 18/5/95 p7, 27/7/95 p13; St
23/5/95 p10; Ti 17/5/95 p10.*

95.98 *LOHENGRIN* (O[3a]) Richard Wagner. COVENT GARDEN
17/5/95, 31/5, 23/7/95. 3 perf.** Lohengrin Theodore
Bertram/Francesco Vignas; Enrico l'Uccellatore Pol
Plançon; L'Araldo del Re Charles Gilibert; Telramondo
Mario Ancona/Victor Maurel. Elsa Emma Albani/Emma
Eames; Ortruda Rose Olitzka/Giulia Ravogli. L & MGR,
Cond, A act mgr, Bom as for 95.93. *REV: Ath 25/5/95
p682, 27/7/95 p139; E 25/5/95 p7, 27/7/95 p13; St 23/
5/95 p10, 25/7/95 p10; Ti 20/5/95 p8, 24/7/95 p10.*

95.99 *IL TROVATORE* (O[4a]) Giuseppe Verdi. COVENT GAR-
DEN 18/5/95, 23/5, 3/6, 13/6/95. 4 perf.** Ruiz
Iginio Corsi; Conti di Luna Arturo Pessina/Verdi;
Ferrando Vittorio Arimondi; Manrico Francesco Tamagno.
Leonora Margaret MacIntyre; Azuncena Giulia Ravogli;
Inez Mathilde Bauermeister. L & MGR, A act mgr, Bom
as for 95.93; Cond Armando Seppilli. *REV: Ath 25/5/
95 p682-3; E 25/5/95 p7.*

95.100 *FRA DIAVOLO* (O[3a]) D.F.E. Auber. COVENT GARDEN
20/5/95, 4/6, 14/6/95. 3 perf.** Fra Diavolo Fernando
de Lucia; Lord Rocburg David Bispham; Giacomo Vittorio
Arimondi; Beppo Antonio Pini-Corsi; Lorenzo Joseph
O'Mara; Matteo Antonio de Vaschetti. Zerlina Marie
Engle; Lady Pamela Amadi. L & MGR, A act mgr, Bom as
for 95.93; Cond Enrico Bevignani.*REV: Ath 25/5/95 p683;
E 25/5/95 p7; Sk 5/6/95 p296; St 23/5/95 p10; Ti 23/
5/95 p10.*

95.101 *THE PRUDE'S PROGRESS* (C,3a) Jerome K. Jerome &
Eden Phillpotts. COMEDY 22/5/95-27/7/95; trfd to
TERRY'S 29/7/95-14/9/95. 117 perf [w/W mat 5/6-24/7;
w/S mat 3/8-14/9; add mat 30/5, 1/6]. 1st perfd
Theatre Royal, Cambridge 10/5/95. Adam Cherry Edward
Righton; Jack Medbury W.T. Lovell/Oswald Yorke; Ted
Morris Ernest Leicester/G.H. Harker; Theodore Travers
Arthur Playfair; Ben Dixon Cyril Maude/Herbert Spar-
ling; Waiter James Anning. Nelly Morris Lena Ashwell/
Doris Templeton; Primrose Deane Ettie Williams; Mrs

Wheedles Alice Mansfield; Mrs Ben Dixon Fanny Brough/
Agnes Thomas; Mary K[athleen?] Hill. L & MGR J.W.
Comyns Carr; Bm E.F. Bradley; Sm & Pd Edward Hastings;
Mus dir Alfred J. Caldicott; Bom Scarisbrick. *REV: E
25/5/95 p8, 3/8/95 p7; Sk 29/5/95 p274, 277, 3/7/95
p531-4; SR 1/6/95 p727; St 23/5/95 p10, 30/5/95 p13;
Th 1/7/95 p46-7; Ti 23/5/95 p10; TW95 p181-3.*

95.102 *FALSTAFF* (O[3a]) Giuseppe Verdi. COVENT GARDEN
22/5/95, 10/6, 5/7/95. 3 perf.** Fenton Fernando de
Lucia/Georges Maugière; Ford Antonio Pini-Corsi; Dr
Caius Iginio Corsi; Pistol Vittorio Arimondi; Sir
John Falstaff Arturo Pessina/Victor Maurel; Bardolph
Pelagalli-Rossetti. Anne Zelie de Lussan; Mistress
Ford Pauline Joran; Mistress Page Aurelia Kitzu;
Dame Quickly Giulia Ravogli. L & MGR Augustus Harris;
Cond Luigi Mancinelli; A act mgr Neil Forsyth; Bom
E. Hall. *REV: Ath 25/5/95 p683, 15/6/95 p779; E 25/5/
95 p7; Sk 5/6/95 p296; St 30/5/95 p12, 13/6/95 p10;
Ti 23/5/95 p10, 12/6/95 p10.*

95.103 *PAPA'S WIFE* (MCa) Seymour Hicks (lib) & F.C.
Phillips (lib) & Ellaline Terriss (mus). GAIETY 23/5/
95 mat perf.** Gerald Singleton Seymour Hicks; Will-
iam C.D. Marius. Kate Weatherby Ellaline Terriss. L &
MGR George Edwardes; Sm A.E. Dodson; Treas & Act mgr
E[dward] Marshall. *REV: E 25/5/95 p15; St 30/5/95 p13.*

95.104 *CARMEN* (O[4a]) Georges Bizet. COVENT GARDEN
24/5/95, 2/7, 10/7, 18/7, 22/7, 27/7/95. 6 perf.**
Don Jose Fernando de Lucia/Albert Alvarez/Francesco
Vignas/Charles Bonnard; Remendado Pellagalli-Rossetti/
Iginio Corsi; Dancairo Iginio Corsi/Gilibert; Esca-
millo Mario Ancona/Henri Albers; Zuniga Antonio de
Vaschetti; Morales Antonio de Vaschetti/Jacques Bars.
Carmen Zelie de Lussan/Emma Calvé/Gemma Bellincioni;
Frasquita Mathilde Bauermeister; Mercedes Cecile
Brani; Michaela Marie Engle/Nellie Melba/Florence
Monteith. L & MGR Augustus Harris; Cond Enrico Bevig-
nani; A act mgr Neil Forsyth; Bom E. Hall. *REV: Ath
1/6/95 p714, 6/7/95 p39, 13/7/95 p75; E 1/6/95 p7,
6/7/95 p9, 13/7/95 p6; SR 1/6/95 p724-5; St 30/5/95
p12, 4/7/95 p10, 18/7/95 p10; Ti 27/5/95 p10, 4/7/95
p6, 11/7/95 p7.*

95.105 *FAUST* (O[5a]) Charles Gounod, COVENT GARDEN
25/5/95, 30/5, 7/6, 12/6, 17/6, 1/7, 17/7/95. 7 perf.**
Mephistopheles Pol Plançon; Valentine Henri Albers/
Victor Maurel/Mario Ancona; Wagner Charles Gilibert;
Faust Albert Alvarez. Marguerite Nellie Melba/Emma
Eames/Margaret MacIntyre; Siebel Fernanda Brazzi;
Marta Mathilde Bauermeister. L & MGR, A act mgr, Bom
as for 95.104; Cond Enrico Bevignani/Luigi Mancinelli.
*REV: Ath 1/6/95 p714, 6/7/95 p39; E 1/6/95 p7, 22/6/
95 p15, 6/7/95 p9; Sk 5/6/95 p294-6; St 30/5/95 p12,
20/6/95 p10, 4/7/95 p10; Ti 27/5/95 p10, 4/7/95 p6.*

95.106 *FEDORA* (P,4a) Herman Merivale [adpt of Victorien Sardou]. 25/5/95-19/7/95. 55 perf [w/S mat exc
25/5]. 1st perfd Haymarket 5/5/83. Count Loris Ipan-
off H.B. Tree; Jean de Siriex Nutcombe Gould; Pierre
Boroff Berte Thomas; Rouvel C.M. Hallard; Vernet
[William Gayer] Mackay; Laroche Edward Ferris; Dr
Loreck Edmund Maurice; Gretch E. Holman Clark; Bole-
las Lasinski Leslie; Tchileff Charles Allan; Desiré
Herbert Ross; Dmitri Lesly Thomson; Kirill F. Perci-
val Stevens. Princess Fedora Romazoff Mrs Patrick
Campbell/Mrs H.B. Tree; Countess Olga Soukareff Mrs
S.B. Bancroft; Baroness Ockar Hilda Hanbury; Mme de
Tournis Routh; Marka Aylward. L & MGR H.B. Tree; Bom
W.H. Leverton; Dir S.B. Bancroft; Sm Shelton; Mus dir
Carl Armbruster; Engineer E. Wingfield Bowles; Pq
William Clarkson; Furn Frank Giles & Co. *REV: Ath
1/6/95 p715; E 1/6/95 p9; Sk 5/6/95 p329-30; SR 1/6/
95 p725-6; St 30/5/95 p12-3; Th 1/7/95 p43-4; Ti 27/
5/95 p10, 26/6/95 p10; TW95 p172-9.*

95.107 *GISMONDA* (D,4a,5tab) Victorien Sardou. DALY'S
27/5/95-6/6/95. 12 perf [w/mat 1/6, 5/6].* Almerio
L.-G. Guitry; Zaccaria Franco Deval; L'Eveque Sophron
de Max; Stradella Angelo; Jacques de Lusignan Deneu-
bourg; Gregoras Montigny; Dom Bridas Chameroy; Giu-
stimani Laroche; Leonard de Tocco G. Montrose; Jac-
ques Crispo Duluard; Basiliades Gerard; Mataxas Piron;
Christofano Lacroix; Simonetti Castelli; Pasquale
Girod. Gismonda Sarah Bernhardt; Thisbe Patry; Donnata
Marie Grandet; Leonarda [Marcelle] Valdey; Agnello
Seylor; Cypriella Bellenger; Andrioli Berthilde;
Tiberio Desvergers; Epiphane Berthier; Pericles Gour-

nay; Nonnes Boulanger, La Croix, Resny; Francesco La
Petite Deschamps. L & MGR Augustin Daly; Dir Henry E.
Abbey, Maurice Grau; Gen mgr M.L. Mayer, C.J. Abud;
Mus dir T[homas] Smythe; Bom E[dward] Brown; Bm John
Farrington. *REV: Ath 1/6/95 p715; E 1/6/95 p9; Sk 5/6/
95 p322; SR 1/6/95 p726-7; St 30/5/95 p13; Th 1/7/95
p39-41; Ti 28/5/95 p8; TW95 p183-8.*

95.108 *ROMEO ET JULIETTE* (O[5a]) Charles Gounod.
COVENT GARDEN 28/5/95, 5/6, 22/6, 13/7, 19/7, 29/7/95.
6 perf.** Romeo Albert Alvarez; Tybalt Charles Bon-
nard; Mercutio Henri Albers; Capulet Charles Gilibert;
Duc de Verone Armand Castelmary; Gregorio Antonio de
Vaschetti; Benvoglio Iginio Corsi; Frere Laurent Pol
Plançon. Juliette Nellie Melba; Stephano Pauline
Joran; Gertrude Mathilde Bauermeister. L & MGR Augus-
tus Harris; Cond Luigi Mancinelli; A act mgr Neil
Forsyth; Bom E. Hall. *REV: Ath 1/6/95 p714; E 1/6/95
p7, 3/8/95 p13; St 30/5/95 p12; Ti 30/5/95 p8.*

95.109 *"MUSICAL SKETCH"*. M. Mercer Adams. COMEDY 1/6/
95. 1 perf. 1st perf? L & MGR J.W. Comyns Carr; Bm
E.F. Bradley. Comment: Advertized in *Ti* for this date.

95.110 *RIGOLETTO* (O[3a]) Giuseppe Verdi. COVENT GARDEN
1/6/95, 26/6, 26/7/95. 3 perf.** Rigoletto Mario An-
cona/Victor Maurel; Marullo Antonio de Vaschetti;
Borsa Iginio Corsi; Sparafucile Armand Castelmary;
Monterøne Charles Gilibert; Conte di Ceprano Pelagalli-Rossetti; Il Duca Fernando de Lucia/Charles
Bonnard. Gilda Nellie Melba; Giovanna Mathilde Bauermeister; Maddalena Giulia Ravogli. L & MGR Augustus
Harris; Cond Enrico Bevignani; A act mgr Neil Forsyth;
Bom E. Hall. *REV: Ath 8/6/95 p746-7; E 8/6/95 p8; St
6/6/95 p9; Ti 3/6/95 p11.*

95.111 *LA DAME AUX CAMELIAS* (D,5a) Alexandre Dumas,
fils. DRURY LANE 3/6/95, 8/6(m), 14/6/95; trfd to
SAVOY 3/7/95, 8/7/95. 5 perf.** Armando Duval Alfredo
de Sanctis; Duval Ettore Mazzanti; Gastone de Rieux
Antonio Galliani; Saint-Gaudens R. de Goudron; Conte
di Giray Silvio Bonivento; De Varville Dante Capelli;
Dottore Napoleone Bianco; Servo Alfredo Geri. Margherita Gauthier Eleonora Duse; Emina Antonietta Ber-

toldo; Mme Duvernoy Albertina Giordano Pero; Nanetta
Guglielmina Magazzari; Olimpia Gemma de Sanctis. L &
MGR Augustus Harris. *REV: Ath 8/6/95 p747-8; E 8/6/95
p11; Sk 29/5/95 p277, 12/6/95 p389; St 6/6/95 p9-10;
Th 1/7/95 p41-2; Ti 4/6/95 p7.*

95.112 *NANCE OLDFIELD* (C,1a) Charles Reade. LYCEUM
3/6/95, 4/6, 6-7/6; 10-14/6[w/mat 12/6]; 15-16/7,
20/7(m), 27/7/95. 14 perf.** Nathan Oldworthy Syd-
ney Valentine; Alexander Oldworthy John Martin Harvey.
Mrs Anne Oldfield Ellen Terry; Susan Oldfield Brenda
Gibson. L & MGR Henry Irving; Bom Joseph Hurst; Sm
H.J. Loveday; Mus dir J. Meredith Ball; Act mgr Bram
Stoker. *REV: St 13/6/95 p10, 1/8/95 p11.*

95.113 *THE BELLS* (3a) Leopold Lewis [adpt of "Erckmann-
Chatrian," *Le Juif Polonais*]. LYCEUM 3/6/95, 4/6,
6-7/6, 10-14/6/95. 9 perf.** Mathias Henry Irving;
Christian Frank [Kemble] Cooper; Walter [Henry] Howe;
Hans [Sam] Johnson; Dr Zimmer John Martin Harvey;
President of the Court F[rank] Tyars; Clerk of the
Court Lacy; Mesmerist [John] Archer; Notary Gurney.
Catherine Maud Milton; Sozel Ailsa Craig; Annette
Brenda Gibson. L & MGR, Bom, Sm, Mus dir, Act mgr as
for 95.112. *REV: Th 1/8/95 p103.*

95.114 *LA FEMME DU CLAUDE* (D,3a) Alexandre Dumas,
fils. DRURY LANE 5/6/95, 10/6/95. 2 perf.** Claudio
Alfredo de Sanctis; Cantagnac Ettore Mazzanti; Antonio
Ciro Galvani; Daniele Silvio Bonivento. Cesarina
Eleonora Duse; Rebecca Guglielmina Magazzari; Edmea
Guilda Bonivento. L & MGR Augustus Harris; A act mgr
Neil Forsyth; Act mgr [Gustave?] Amberg. *REV: Ath 8/6/
95 p747-8; E 8/6/95 p11; SR 8/6/95 p757-8; St 13/6/95
p10; Th 1/7/95 p41-2; Ti 6/6/95 p6; TW95 p188-92.*

95.115 *IZEYL* (Verse D,4a) Armand Sylvestre & Eugene
Morand ; mus by Gabriel Pierné. DALY'S 7/6/95, 8/6/
95(2). 3 perf.** Prince L.-G. Guitry; Le Yoghi de
Max; Scyndia Deneubourg; Tukkuttuti Chameroy; Roi
vaincu Castelli; Tisseur d'Etoffes Angelo; Mineur
Gerard; Lepreux Lacroix; Pretre Montigny; L'Espion
Andre; Annonciateur Duluard; Pecheur Laroche; Le Pau-
vre Piron; Hommes du Peuple [A.] Ramy, Kolb. Izeyl

Sarah Bernhardt; Princesse Harastri Patry; Mere·Marie
Grandet; 1er Princesse Seylor; 2me Princesse Bellenger; 3me Princesse Berthilde; 4me Princesse Desvergers; 5me Princesse Berthier; 6me Princesse Laurent;
Yami Boulanger; Femmes du Peuple Merle, Burckel, Lacroix. L & MGR Augustin Daly; Dir Henry E. Abbey,
Maurice Grau; Gen mgr M.L. Mayer, C.J. Abud; Mus dir
T[homas] Smythe; Bom E[dward] Brown; Bm John Farrington. *REV: Th 1/7/95 p39-41.*

95.116 *LA LOCANDIERA* (C,3a) Carlo Goldoni. DRURY LANE
7/6/95, 15/6(m); trfd to SAVOY 29/6(m), 5/7, 12/7/95.
5 perf.** Marchese di Forlipopoli Ettore Mazzanti;
Alfredo de Sanctis; Conte d'Albafiorita Silvio Bonivento; Cavaliere di Ripafretta Dante Capelli; Fab-
rizzio Ciro Galvani; Servatore Nicolo Cortesi. Mirandolina Eleonora Duse. L & MGR Augustus Harris. *REV:
St 13/6/95 p10; Th 1/7/95 p41-2; TW95 p193.*

95.117 *CAVALLERIA RUSTICANA* (D,1a) Giovanni Verga.
DRURY LANE 7/6/95, 15/6(m); trfd to SAVOY 29/6(m),
5/7, 12/7/95. 5 perf.** Compar Alfio Ettore Mazzanti;
Turiddu Macca Alfredo de Sanctis; Lo Zio Brasi R. de
Goudron. Santuzza Eleonora Duse; La Gna'Lola Gugliel-
mina Magazzari; Comare Camilla Gemma de Sanctis; La
Zia Filomena Antonietta Bertoldo; Pipuzza Gilda Boni-
vento. L & MGR Augustus Harris. *REV: Sk 3/7/95 p549;
St 13/6/95 p10, 11/7/95 p10, 18/7/95 p10; Th 1/7/95
p41-2.*

95.118 *A BREEZY MORNING* (Duol) Eden Phillpotts. LYRIC
7/6/95-12/7/95. 31 perf.** Bruce Goldie Frederick
Farnley. Mary Goldie Miriam Clement. PP Henry J. Leslie; L Horace Sedger; Bom [Walter] Hamilton; Act mgr
M. Edwards; Rep W.J. Glass.

95.119 *HAROLD; OR, THE NORMAN CONQUEST* (O,3a) Sir
Edward Malet(lib) & Frederic H. Cowen (mus). COVENT
GARDEN 8/6/95, 21/6, 9/7/95. 3 perf.* William David
Bispham; William Malet Richard Green; Alfnoth/Stigand
William Devers; Siward Jacques Bars; Harold Philip
Brozel. Edith Emma Albani; Princess Adela Louise
Meisslinger. L & MGR Augustus Harris; Cond Frederic
H. Cowen; A act mgr Neil Forsyth; Bom E. Hall. *REV:*

*Ath 15/6/95 p779; E 15/6/95 p7; Sk 12/6/95 p389; SR
15/6/95 p786-7; St 13/6/95 p9-10; Ti 10/6/95 p8, 22/6/
95 p14.*

95.120 *MAGDA [HEIMATH]* (P,4a) Herman Sudermann [trans
W. Remon]. DALY'S 10/6/95, 12/6(m), 15/6, 21/6/95. 4
perf. 1st perfd 7/1/93. Schwartz de Max; Hefferdingh
[Albert] Darmont; De Keller de Val; Max Deneubourg;
De Kelbs Chameroy; Beckmann Lacroix. Magda Sarah
Bernhardt; Augusta Marie Grandet; Francesca Patry;
Marie Bellenger; Therese Saryta; Mme de Klebs Merle;
Mme Elbrich Boulanger; Mme Schumann Burckel. L & MGR
Augustin Daly; Dir Henry E. Abbey, Maurice Grau; Gen
mgr M.L. Mayer, C.J. Abud; Mus dir T[homas] Smythe;
Bom E[dward] Brown; Bm John Farrington. *REV: Ath 15/6/
95 p780-1; E 15/6/95 p9; Sk 19/6/95 p398; SR 15/6/95
p787-9; St 13/6/95 p10; Th 1/7/95 p39-41; Ti 11/6/95
p10; TW95 p193-202.*

95.121 *LA TRAVIATA* (O[3a]) Giuseppe Verdi. COVENT GAR-
DEN 11/6/95, 15/6, 27/6/95. 3 perf.** Giorgio Germont
Mario Ancona/Arturo Pessina; Barone Duphol Jacques
Bars; Gastone Iginio Corsi; Dottore Grenvil Charles
Gilibert; Alfredo Fernando de Lucia/George Maugière.
Violetta Adelina Patti/Marcella Sembrich. Annina
Mathilde Bauermeister; Flora Bervoix Cecile Brani.
L & MGR Augustus Harris; Cond Luigi Mancinelli; A act
mgr Neil Forsyth; Bom E. Hall. *REV: Ath 15/6/95 p779-
80, 6/7/95 p38; E 15/6/95 p7, 29/6/95 p15; Sk 19/6/95
p408; St 13/6/95 p10, 4/7/95 p10; Ti 12/6/95 p10, 28/
6/95 p10.*

95.122 *LA TOSCA* (D,5a,6tab) Victorien Sardou. DALY'S
11/6/95, 13/6, 15/6(m), 20/6, 22/6/95. 5 perf.**
Trivulce Monrose; Spoletta Castelli; Schiarrone Piron;
Paisiello André; Capreola [A.] Ramy; Eusebe Lacroix;
Sgt. Gerard; Gen. Kolb; Ceccho Laurent; Procureur
Giraud; Scarpia [Albert] Darmont; Cavaradossi Laroche;
Angelotti Angelo; Attavanti Chameroy; Trevilhac Deneu-
bourg. Tosca Sarah Bernhardt; La Reine Marie Caroline
Burckel; Princesse Orlonia Saryta; Gennarino Seylor;
Luciana Merle; Monsignor Bellenger. L & MGR Augustin
Daly; Dir Henry E. Abbey, Maurice Grau; Gen mgr M.L.
Mayer, C.J. Abud; Mus dir T[homas] Smythe; Bom E[d-

ward] Brown; <u>Bm</u> John Farrington. *REV: Th 1/7/95 p39-41.*

95.123 *LA DAME AUX CAMELIAS* (D,5a) Alexandre Dumas, *fils.* DALY'S 12/6/95, 14/6, 22/6/95(m). 3 perf.**
<u>Armand Duval</u> L.-G. Guitry; <u>De Varville</u> Angelo; <u>Georges Duval</u> Montigny; <u>St. Gaudens</u> Chameroy; <u>Gaston Rieux</u> Monrose; <u>Gustave</u> Deneubourg; <u>Comte de Giray</u> Duluard; <u>Docteur</u> Lacroix; <u>Arthur</u> Gerard; <u>Commissionaire</u> Piron; <u>Domestique</u> Kolb. <u>Marguerite Gautier</u> Sarah Bernhardt; <u>Prudence</u> Patry; <u>Olympe</u> Saryta; <u>Nichette</u> Seylor; <u>Nanine</u> Merle; <u>Adele</u> Boulanger; <u>Andre</u> Lacroix; <u>Lucie</u> Desvergers; <u>Laure</u> Berthilde; <u>Groom</u> Berthier. <u>L & MGR</u>, <u>Dir</u>, Gen mgr, Mus dir, <u>Bom</u>, <u>Bm</u> as for 95.122. *REV: SR 15/6/95 p787-9; Th 1/7/95 p39-41.*

95.124 *MAGDA [HEIMATH]* Hermann Sudermann. DRURY LANE 12/6/95; trfd to SAVOY 27/6, 1/7, 6/7(m), 10/7, 13/7/95. 6 perf.**   <u>Selke</u> Ettore Mazzanti; <u>Max de Wendolovoski</u> Ciro Galvani; <u>Wefterding</u> Alfredo de Sanctis; <u>Barone Keller</u> Dante Capelli; <u>Prof Bermann</u> Napoleone Bianco; <u>Von Klehen</u> R. de Gourdran. <u>Magda</u> Eleonora Duse; <u>Maria</u> Guglielmina Magazzari; <u>Mana</u> Albertina Giordano Pero; <u>Francesco</u> Guilda Bonivento; <u>Sua Moglie</u> Gemina de Sanctis; <u>Terese</u> Antonietta Bertoldo. <u>L & MGR</u> Augustus Harris. *REV: Ath 15/6/95 p780-1; E 15/6/95 p9; Sk 19/6/95 p398; SR 15/6/95 p787-9; St 20/6/95 p9-10; Th 1/7/95 p41-2; Ti 13/6/95 p10; TW95 p193-202.*

95.125 *AN AVERAGE MAN; OR, HOW THE AVERAGE BECAME THE ABNORMAL* (D of Modern Life,4a) S.X. Courte. OPERA COMIQUE 13/6/95 mat perf. 1st perfd Pleasure Gardens, Folkstone 6/3/95. <u>Vivian Allardyce</u> Loring Fernie; <u>Robert Allardyce</u> Fred Grove; <u>John Allardyce</u> G[eorge] R. Foss; <u>Arthur Ingersoll</u> Alfred Kendrick; <u>Hon Bertie Thoytes</u> James Lindsay; <u>Montie Marlborough</u> Fred W. Permain; <u>Cecil Hampton</u> Hurdman Lucas; <u>Scout</u> Hugh Bodien. <u>Hon Dolly Thoytes</u> Kate Bealby; <u>Hilda Ffloyd Fanshawe</u> Marjorie Griffiths; <u>Winifred Dayne</u> Dora de Winton. <u>DIR</u> George R. Foss. *REV: E 15/6/95 p11; St 20/6/95 p10-1; Th 1/7/95 p45-6.*

95.126 *A NEAR SHAVE* (MF) George D. Day (lib) & Edward Jones (mus). TERRY'S 13/6/95 mat perf.** [Ebenezer

Addleshaw] G.W. Anson; [Josiah Giggins] H.O. Cleary.
[Arabella Pettifer] Emmeline Orford. *REV: St 20/6/95*
p10.

95.127 *SIXES AND SEVENS* (Misunderstanding) E.H. Whit-
more. TERRY'S 13/6/95 mat perf.** [Cpt. George Hope]
Arthur Bourchier. [Edith Cashdown] Violet Vanbrugh
[Mrs Arthur Bourchier]. *REV: St 13/6/95 p10.*

95.128 *A PRACTICAL JOKER* (Ca,1a) C.L. Hume. COMEDY
15/6/95-16/7/95. 27 perf.* Charles Dalrymple Arthur
Playfair; Dawson George P. Hawtrey. Adela Grey Doris
Templeton; Sybil Forsyth Lena Ashwell. L & MGR J.W.
Comyns Carr; Bm E.F. Bradley; Sm & Pd Edward Hastings;
Mus dir Alfred J. Caldicott; Bom Scarisbrick. *REV: E*
22/6/95 p8; Th 1/7/95 p47.

95.129 *A PAIR OF SPECTACLES* (C,3a) Sydney Grundy.
GARRICK 15/6/95. 1 perf.** Benjamin Goldfinch John
Hare; Uncle Gregory Charles Groves; Percy E. Allan
Aynesworth; Dick Gilbert Hare; Joyce Fred Thorne;
Lorimer Charles Rock; Bartholomew Gerald du Maurier;
Another Shoemaker T.W. Abbott. Mrs Goldfinch Kate
Rorke; Lucy Lorimer Nellie Thorne; Charlotte Lillian
Lee. L & MGR John Hare; Sc William Harford; Cond &
Mus Haydn Waud; Asm W.M. Cathcart; Act mgr C.G. Comp-
ton. *REV: E 22/6/95 p8; St 20/6/95 p10.*

95.130 *A QUIET RUBBER* (P,1a) Charles F. Coghlan. GAR-
RICK 15/6/95. 1 perf.** Lord Kilclare John Hare;
Sullivan Charles Groves; Charles Gilbert Hare. Mary
Sullivan Helen Luck. L & MGR, Sc, Cond & Mus, Asm,
Act mgr as for 95.129. *REV: As for 95.129.*

95.131 *LA PRINCESSE LOINTAINE* (P,4a) Edmond Rostand;
mus by Gabriel Pierné. DALY'S 17/6/95-19/6/95. 4 perf
[w/mat 19/6]. 1st perfd Renaissance, Paris 5/4/95.
Nicholose Laurent; Bertrand d'Allamanon L.-G. Guitry;
Frere Trophime Castell; Jeoffroy Rudel de Max; Squa-
ciafico Laroche; Erasme Chameroy; Chevalier aux Armes
Vertes Paris; Patron Montigny; Trobaldo le Calfat
Lacroix; Francois le Remolar Angelo; Pegofat [A.]
Ramy; Bruno Monrose; Bastagne Gerard; Juan le Portin-
galais Pelletier; Marais d'Aignes Mortes Magnin; Pilote

Piron; Mousse Camus. Princesse Melissande Sarah Bern-
hardt; Sorismonde Saryta. L & MGR Augustin Daly; Dir
Henry E. Abbey, Maurice Grau; Gen mgr M.L. Mayer, C.J.
Abud; Mus dir T[homas] Smythe; Bom E[dward] Brown; Bm
John Farrington. *REV: Ath 22/6/95 p815; E 22/6/95 p8;
Sk 26/6/95 p464; SR 22/6/95 p828-30; St 20/6/95 p10;
Th 1/7/95 p39-41; Ti 18/6/95 p8; TW95 p209-17.*

95.132 *DER VOGELHANDLER* (CO,3a) Karl Zeller (mus) &
M. West (lib). DRURY LANE 17/6/95, 19/6, 21/6, 27/6,
29/6/95. 5 perf. 1st perfd Wien, Vienna 10/1/91. Weps
Reer; Stanislaus Bernhardt; Suffle Richardi; Adam
Mahling; Schneck Weiss; Von Scharnagel Branck; Mau-
roner Gehring; Egydi Palm; Magerl Szwimberski; Zwill-
ing Dannenberg; Keller Umlauf; Wernleber Graff; Ein
Piguer Schvenner; Quendel Thalheim; Wurmchen Burger.
Christel Ilka von Palmay; Kurfurstin Farkas; Adelaide
Kornig; Comtesse Mimi Wienrich; Emmerenz Franke; Tette
Naumann; Nebel Worsh; Bauerin Sperling. L & MGR Augus-
tus Harris; Cond Doebber; A act mgr Neil Forsyth. *REV:
E 22/6/95 p9; St 20/6/95 p10; Th 1/7/95 p44-5; Ti 18/
6/95 p8; Ath 22/6/95 p814.* Comment: Ducal Court Company of Saxe-Coburg & Gotha.

95.133 *THE MERCHANT OF VENICE* (C,5a) William Shakes-
peare. LYCEUM 17/6/95-22/6/95; 29/6/95(m). 7 perf
[mat only 22/6].** Shylock Henry Irving; Bassanio
Frank [Kemble] Cooper; Duke of Venice [Henry] Howe;
Prince of Morocco [Frank] Tyars; Gratiano Ben Webster;
Antonio [William] Haviland; Launcelot Gobbo Sydney
Valentine; Salarino John Martin Harvey; Lorenzo Buck-
ley; Salanio Lacy; Clerk of the Court [R.P.] Tabb;
Tubal [John] Archer; Old Gobbo [T.] Reynolds; Goaler
G[eoffrey] Taylor; Leonardo [W.] Marion; Balthazar
[K.] Rivington; Stephano [W. Lionel] Belmore. Jessica
Ailsa Craig; Nerissa Maud Milton; Portia Ellen Terry.
L & MGR Henry Irving; Bom Joseph Hurst; Sm H.J. Love-
day; Mus dir J. Meredith Ball; Act mgr Bram Stoker.
REV: Th 1/8/95 p103.

95.134 *A MODERN HYPATIA: A DRAMA OF TODAY* (P,3a) Mabel
Collins. TERRY'S 17/6/95 mat perf.* Lord Arthur Dav-
enant Edmund Gurney; Lewin Alexis Acton Bond; Sir
George Martyn Frank Adair; Francis Rudge Harding; Dr

Vane Tylden Charles Sugden. Mrs Fitzpatrick Mrs Wilton; Rose Edith Crauford; Mrs Vane Tylden Agnes Hill; Servant Eileen Munro; Marcia Royal Mrs Theodore Wright. *REV: E 22/6/95 p11; Sk 26/6/95 p464; St 20/6/95 p10; Th 1/7/95 p47-8.*

95.135 *TWO WOMEN* (Dramatic Fragment) "One of Them." TERRY'S 17/6/95 mat perf.* Frank Villiers Leslie Delwaide; Collins Fenton. Lady Caroline Villiers Mrs Theodore Wright; Valerie de Lorme Mrs Wilton. *REV: E 22/6/95 p11; St 20/6/95 p10.*

95.136 *DIE EHRE* (D,4a) Hermann Sudermann. DRURY LANE 18/6/95, 22/6(m); trfd to SAVOY 29/6, 6/7/95. 4 perf. 1st perfd Lessing, Berlin 27/11/89. Muhlingk Lang; Carl Brauck; Lothar Brandt Vallentin; Hugo Hengel Herbert; Graf Trast Adolf Klein; Robert Heimoff; Der Alte Heinecke Weiss; Michalski Reer; Wilhelm Gehring; Johanne Thalheim; Indischer Deiner Palm. Amalie Kornig; Leonore Vogl; Seine Frau (Heinecke) Worsh; Auguste Naumann; Alma Linden; Hebenstreit Franke. L & MGR Augustus Harris. *REV: Ath 29/6/95 p847-8; E 22/6/95 p9; St 20/6/95 p10; Th 1/7/95 p44-5; Ti 19/6/95 p5; TW95 p217-8, 226-32.* Comment: Ducal Court Company of Saxe-Coburg & Gotha.

95.137 *IL BARBIERE DI SIVIGLIA* (O[2a]) Giocchino Rossini. COVENT GARDEN 19/6/95, 4/7/95. 2 perf.** Figaro Mario Ancona; Conte d'Almaviva Charles Bonnard; Basilio Vittorio Arimondi; Bartolo Antonio Pini-Corsi; Sargente Antonio de Vaschetti; Fiorello Iginio Corsi. Rosina Adelina Patti; Bertha Mathilde Bauermeister. L & MGR Augustus Harris; Cond Enrico Bevignani; A act mgr Neil Forsyth; Bom E. Hall. *REV: Ath 22/6/95 p814; E 22/6/95 p15, 6/7/95 p9; Ti 20/6/95 p6.*

95.138 *CAVALLERIA RUSTICANA* (O,1a) Pietro Mascagni. COVENT GARDEN 20/6/95, 25/6, 29/6(m), 6/7, 12/7, 24/7/95. 6 perf.** Turridu Francesco Vignas; Alfio Mario Ancona/David Bispham. Santuzza Gemma Bellincioni/Emma Calvé; Lola Giulia Ravogli/Aurelia Kitzu/Fernanda Brazzi; Lucia Mathilde Bauermeister. L & MGR, Cond, A act mgr, Bom as for 95.137. *REV: Ath 29/6/95 p846, 20/7/95 p107; E 22/6/95 p15, 29/6/95 p15, 13/7/95 p6,*

*20/7/95 p13; St 27/6/95 p12, 4/7/95 p10; Ti 22/6/95
p14.*

95.139 *HASEMANN'S TOCHER* (C,4a) Adolf L'Arronge.
DRURY LANE 20/6/95; trfd to SAVOY 4/7/95. 2 perf.**
Anton Hasemann Weiss; Wilhelm Knorr Reer; Hermann Kor-
ner Hanstein; Baron Zinnow Heimhoff; Klinkert Lang;
Eduard Klein Brauck; Dr Seller Richardi; Fritz Dannen-
berg; Lehmann Thalheim; Bartsch Gehring. Albertine
Worsh; Martha Naumann; Rosa Wienrich; Emilie Linden;
Frau Klinkert Kornig; Frau Gieseke Franke; Anna Sper-
ling; Dienstmadchen Cyriaci; Franziska Leitz. L & MGR
Augustus Harris. *REV: E 22/6/95 p9; St 27/6/95 p12;
Th 1/7/95 p44-5; Ti 21/6/95 p10.* Comment: Ducal Court
Company of Saxe-Coburg & Gotha.

95.140 *THE SECOND MRS TANQUERAY* (P,4a) A.W. Pinero.
ST. JAMES'S 20/6/95-3/7/95. 13 perf [w/mat 22/6].**
Aubrey Tanqueray George Alexander; Sir George Orreyed
E. Allan Aynesworth; Cpt. Hugh Ardale Herbert Waring;
Cayley Drummle Henry V. Esmond; Frank Misquith H.H.
Vincent; Gordon Jayne Mark Paton; Morse Fred Lomnitz.
Lady Orreyed Blanche Wilmot; Mrs Cortelyon Lady Monck-
ton; Paula Evelyn Millard; Ellean Irene Vanbrugh. L &
MGR George Alexander; Bm Robert V. Shone; Sm H.H. Vin-
cent; Mus dir & Mus Walter Slaughter; Furn Frank Giles
& Co.; Cost Mme Savage, Mme Purdue; Pq William Clark-
son; Sc H.P. Hall, Walter Hann; Bom Arnold. *REV: Ath
29/6/95 p848; Sk 26/6/95 p464; SR 29/6/95 p861; St 27/
6/95 p12; Ti 21/6/95 p10; TW95 p218-9.*

95.141 *DIE FLEDERMAUS* (CO,3a) Johann Strauss. DRURY
LANE 22/6/95, 28/6, 5/7, 10/7/95. 4 perf.** Eisen-
stein Mahling; Frank Reer; Alfred Burger; Dr Falke
Brauck; Dr Blind Richardi; Ali-Bey Palm; Ramusin Jena;
Murray Gehring; Lord Middleton Schonner; Cariconi
Thalheim; Frosch Weiss; Iwan Graff; Diener Dannenberg.
Rosalinde Dirkens-Drews; Orlofsky Naumann; Adele Far-
kas; Melanie Vogl; Felicita Cyriaci; Sidi Sperling;
Minni Rodmann; Faustine Worsh; Silvia Franke. L & MGR
Augustus Harris. *REV: St 27/6/95 p12; Th 1/7/95 p44-5;
Ti 24/6/95 p8.*

95.142 *DON GIOVANNI* (O[2a]) W.A. Mozart. COVENT GARDEN

24/6/95, 28/6/95. 2 perf.** <u>Don Ottavio</u> Philip Brozel;
<u>Masetto</u> Antonio Pini-Corsi; <u>Leporello</u> Armand Castel-
mary; <u>Il Commendatore</u> Charles Manners; <u>Don Giovanni</u>
Victor Maurel. <u>Zerlina</u> Adelina Patti; <u>Donna Anna</u> Ada
Adini; <u>Donna Elvira</u> Margaret MacIntyre. <u>L & MGR</u> Augustus Harris; <u>Cond</u> Enrico Bevignani; <u>A act mgr</u> Neil
Forsyth; <u>Bom</u> E. Hall. *REV: Ath 29/6/95 p846; E 29/6/
95 p13; SR 29/6/95 p858-60; Ti 25/6/95 p10.*

95.143 *HANSEL UND GRETEL* (O[3a]) Engelbert Humperdinck.
DRURY LANE 24/6/95, 2/7, 11/7/95. 3 perf.** <u>Der Vater</u>
Buttner. <u>Die Mutter</u> Wassiliewits; <u>Gretel</u> Farkas; <u>Han-
sel</u> Altona; <u>Knusperhexe</u> Scharnack; <u>Sanmachen/Thaumaun-
chen</u> Naumann. <u>L & MGR</u> Augustus Harris; <u>Cond</u> Doebber;
<u>Sm</u> Mahling; <u>A act mgr</u> Neil Forsyth. *REV: E 29/6/95
p6; St 27/6/95 p12; Th 1/7/95 p44-5; Ti 27/6/95 p6.*

95.144 *FAUST* (T,5a) W.G. Wills [adpt of Goethe]. LY-
CEUM 24/6/95-26/6/95. 3 perf.** <u>Mephistopheles</u> Henry
Irving; <u>Faust</u> Frank [Kemble] Cooper; <u>Valentine</u> Ben
Webster; <u>Student</u> [William] Haviland; <u>Witch</u> [Frank]
Tyars; Forrest; <u>Witch of Kitchen</u> Clarence Hague; <u>Frosch</u>
John Martin Harvey; <u>Altmayer</u> [T.] Reynolds; <u>Witch</u> G.
Black; <u>Brander</u> [W. Lionel] Belmore; <u>Soldier</u> [R.P.]
Tabb; <u>She-Ape</u> [John] Archer; <u>Siebel</u> S[am] Johnson; <u>He-
Ape</u> Espinosa, jr; <u>Witch</u> Buckley; <u>Citizens</u> [H.W.] Cush-
ing, Seymour. <u>Margaret</u> Ellen Terry; <u>Bessy</u> Maud Milton;
<u>Martha</u> [Alice?] Denvil; <u>Ida</u> Foster; <u>Catherine</u> Mrs
Lacy; <u>Alice</u> N. de Silva. <u>L & MGR</u> Henry Irving; <u>Mus</u>
J. Hamilton Clarke, J. Meredith Ball; <u>Sc</u> Hawes Craven,
William Telbin; <u>Cost</u> Mrs Nettleship, Auguste, Mrs
Reid; <u>Pq</u> Fox; <u>Furn</u> Arnott; <u>Mach</u> Fillery; <u>Sm</u> H.J. Love-
day; <u>Mus dir</u> J. Meredith Ball; <u>Act mgr</u> Bram Stoker;
<u>Bom</u> Joseph Hurst.

95.145 *ORFEO* (O[3a]) C.W. Gluck. COVENT GARDEN 25/6/95,
24/7/95. 2 perf.** <u>Orfeo</u> Giulia Ravogli; <u>Euridice</u>
Sophia Ravogli; <u>L'Amore</u> Mathilde Bauermeister. <u>L & MGR</u>
Augustus Harris; <u>Cond</u> Enrico Bevignani; <u>A act mgr</u> Neil
Forsyth; <u>Bom</u> E. Hall. *REV: E 29/6/95 p13; Ti 28/6/95
p10.*

95.146 *ALL OR NOTHING* (Episode) Hamilton Aidé. CRI-
TERION 25/6/95 mat perf. 1st perfd Queen Anne's-gate

17/7/80. Sir Henry Dashwood A. Hamilton Revelle; Servant A[rthur] Royston. Giulia, Lady Dashwood E[leanor] Calhoun. *REV: St 27/6/95 p12-3.*

95.147 *VILLAIN AND VICTIM* (Duol) W.R. Walkes. CRITERION 25/6/95 mat perf.** Adolphus Cyril Maude. Millicent Fanny Brough. L & MGR Charles Wyndham. *REV: St 27/6/95 p13.*

95.148 *SIXES AND SEVENS* (Misunderstanding) E.H. Whitmore. CRITERION 25/6/95 mat perf.** Cpt. George Hope Arthur Bourchier. Edith Cashdown Violet Vanbrugh. L & MGR Charles Wyndham.

95.149 *THE RAILROAD OF LOVE* (C,4a) Augustin Daly. DALY'S 25/6/95-1/7/95. 7 perf [w/mat 29/6]. 1st perfd Daly's, New York 1/11/87. Gen. Everett Edwin Varrey; Lieut. Howell Everett Frank Worthing; Phenix Scuttleby James Lewis; Adam Grinnidge George Clarke; Judge van Ryker Campbell Gollan; Benny Dumaresq Chester Devonne; Truffles Robert Shepherd; Crusty George Wharnock; Tom Hobart Bosworth. Mrs Eutycia Laburnam Mrs G.H. Gilbert; Viva van Ryker Sybil Carlisle; Cherry Jeanne Vorhees; Valentine Osprey Ada Rehan. L & MGR Augustin Daly. *REV: E 29/6/95 p7; Sk 3/7/95 p549; SR 29/6/95 p860-1; St 27/6/95 p13; Ti 26/6/95 p10; TW95 p233-4.*

95.150 *HEIMATH [MAGDA]* Hermann Sudermann. DRURY LANE 25/6/95; trfd to SAVOY 3/7/95(m). 2 perf.** Schwartze Adolf Klein; Max Brauck; Heffterdingk Lang; Muhler Heimoff; Beckman Richardi; Von Klebs Thalheim. Magda Wienrich; Marie Linden; Auguste Kornig; Franziska Worsh; Frau von Klebs Franke; Ellrich Leyk; Schumann Reichelt; Therese Sperling. L & MGR Augustus Harris. *REV: Ath 29/6/95 p848; E 29/6/95 p6; St 27/6/95 p12; Th 1/7/95 p44-5; Ti 26/6/95 p10.* Comment: Ducal Court Company of Saxe-Coburg & Gotha.

95.151 *DIE VERKAUFTE BRAUT [PRODANA NEVESTA; THE BARTERED BRIDE]*(CO3a) Bedrich Smetana. DRURY LANE 26/6/95 1/7, 6/7(m), 9/7/95. 4 perf. 1st perfd Czech, Prague 30/5/66. Kruschina Buttner; Micha Richardi; Wenzel Mahling; Hans Bernhardt; Kezal Gunther; Springer Reer;

Muff Jena. Kathinka Altona; Marie Wassiliewits; Agnes
Scarnack; Esmeralda Farkas. L & MGR Augustus Harris.
*REV: Ath 29/6/95 p846; E 29/6/95 p6; St 4/7/95 p10-1;
Th 1/7/95 p44-5; Ti 27/6/95 p6.* Comment: Ducal Court
Company of Saxe-Coburg & Gotha.

95.152 *THE STRANGE ADVENTURES OF MISS BROWN* (F,3a)
Robert Buchanan & "Charles Marlowe" [Harriet Jay].
VAUDEVILLE 26/6/95-5/9/95;* trfd to TERRY'S 7/10/95-
8/2/96. 256 perf [w/W, S mat 10/8/95-8/2/96; add mat
3/7/95, 17/7, 24/7, 31/7, 7/11, 11/11, 26-27/12, 30/12/
95, 6/1/96, 23/1/96; np 23-25/12/95]. Mjr. O'Gallag-
her John Beauchamp/Arthur Playfair; Private Docherty
L. Power; Herr von Moser Robb Harwood; Mr Hibbertson
Gilbert Farquhar; Sgt. Tanner Lionel Brough/Herbert
Standing; Cpt. Courtenay Frederick Kerr. Miss Romney
M.A. Victor; Angela Brightwell May Palfrey/Eva Moore;
Euphemia Schwartz Esmé Beringer/Adela Measor; Matilda
Jones Daisy Brough; Millicent Loveridge Jay Holford;
Clara Loveridge Grace Dudley/[Kate?] Cutler; Mrs
O'Gallagher Gladys Homfrey/Rosina Filippi; Emma Marion
Murray. L Weedon Grossmith; Mgr Frederick Kerr; Bm
A.F. Henderson; Sm W.J. Robertson; Mus dir C.J. Har-
gitt; Sc T.W. Hall. *REV: Ath 29/6/95 p848; E 29/6/95
p9; Sk 17/7/95 p643-5; SR 29/6/95 p861; St 4/7/95 p11,
10/10/95 p12; Th 1/8/95 p108-110; Ti 27/6/95 p6; TW95
p233.*

95.153 *BETWEEN THE POSTS* (Ca[1a]) Mrs Hugh Bell.
VAUDEVILLE 26/6/95-5/10/95; trfd to TERRY'S 7/10/95-
11/11/95. 119 perf.** Geoffrey Warburton John Buckstone. Edith Neville Adela Measor; Lucy Grace Dudley.
L, Mgr, Bm, Sm, Mus dir as for 95.152. *REV: E 29/6/95
p9.*

95.154 *LOUIS XI* (5a) Dion Boucicault [adpt of Casimir
Delavigne]. LYCEUM 27/6/95, 28/6, 3/7/95. 3 perf.**
Louis XI Henry Irving; Duke de Nemours Frank [Kemble]
Cooper; Philip de Commines Sydney Valentine; Tristan
L'Ermite [Frank] Tyars; Dauphin John Martin Harvey;
Francois de Paule [William] Haviland; Cardinal d'Alby
Gurney; Marcel [Sam] Johnson; Oliver le Dain [John]
Archer; Count de Dreux Fuller Mellish; Montjoie Lacy;
Jaques Coitier G. Black; Count de Dunois [R.P.] Tabb;

Richard Reynolds; <u>Didier</u> [W.] Marion; <u>Attendant</u> [W.
Lionel] Belmore; <u>Officer</u> Graham; <u>De Lude</u> [H.W.] Cushing; <u>Toison d'Or</u> [K.] Rivington. <u>Martha</u> Maud Milton;
<u>Marie</u> May Whitty. <u>L & MGR</u> Henry Irving; <u>Sm</u> H.J. Love-
day; <u>Mus dir</u> J. Meredith Ball; <u>Act mgr</u> Bram Stoker;
<u>Bom</u> Joseph Hurst. *REV: Th 1/8/95 p103.*

95.155 *MAN PROPOSES* (Ca,1a) Sydney Grundy. ST. JAMES'S
27/6/95 mat perf.** <u>Cpt. Huntingdon</u> E.W. Gardiner.
<u>Dina</u> Mary Rorke; <u>Bell Huntingdon</u> Kate Rorke. <u>MUS DIR</u>
Walter Slaughter; <u>Sm</u> H.H. Vincent.

95.156 *MARY JANE* (CSk) C.D. Adams. ST. JAMES'S 27/6/95
mat perf. James A. Welch. <u>MUS DIR</u>, <u>Sm</u> as for 95.155.

95.157 *SONIA* (Sk) E. Overbeck. ST. JAMES'S 27/6/95
mat perf. 1st perfd West, Albert Hall 9/5/95. <u>Count
Feodor Poltsky</u> H. Nye Chart. <u>Annette</u> Helen Vizitelly;
<u>Sonia Ivanovna</u> Violet Raye. <u>MUS DIR</u>, <u>Sm</u> as for 95.155.

95.158 *VILLAIN AND VICTIM* (Episode) W.R. Walkes. ST.
JAMES'S 27/6/95 mat perf.** <u>Adolphus</u> Cyril Maude.
<u>Millicent</u> Fanny Brough. <u>MUS DIR</u>, <u>Sm</u> as for 95.155.

95.159 *A MAGIC LANTERN ENTERTAINMENT* (Sk). ST. JAMES'S
27/6/95 mat perf. C.P. Little. <u>MUS DIR</u>, <u>Sm</u> as for 95.
155.

95.160 *QWONG HI* (FC,3a) R. Fenton MacKay. TERRY'S 27/
6/95 mat perf. 1st perfd Princess's, Bristol 1/4/95.
<u>Qwong Hi</u> Willie Edouin; <u>Frank Brett</u> Stewart Champion;
<u>Fred Earle</u> Douglass Hamilton; <u>Cpt. Lander</u> W.F. Haw-
trey; <u>Roy Lander</u> Harry Eversfield; <u>Verity</u> J. Graham;
<u>Bailiff</u> A[lfred?] Phillips. <u>Mrs Brett</u> Leslie Green-
wood; <u>Miss Diction</u> Helen Ferrers; <u>Lydia Winlock</u> Dora
de Winton; <u>Clarke</u> Annie Goward; <u>Queen Dimple</u> Daisy
Bryer; <u>Nettie Merrydue</u> May Edouin. *REV: E 29/6/95 p9;
Sk 3/7/95 p549; St 4/7/95 p11; Th 1/8/95 p111.*

95.161 *PETRUCCIO* (O,1a) Alick MacLean. COVENT GARDEN
29/6/95 mat perf.* <u>Rubino</u> John Child; <u>Petruccio</u>
Charles Manners; <u>Giovanni</u> William Devers. <u>Elvira</u> Fanny
Moody; <u>Her Mother</u> Edith Miller; <u>Mario</u> Tresder. <u>L &
MGR</u> Augustus Harris; <u>Cond</u> Philip Flon; <u>A act mgr</u> Neil

Forsyth; <u>Bom</u> E. Hall. *REV: Ath 6/7/95 p38-9; E 6/7/95 p9; SR 6/7/95 p9-10; St 4/7/95 p10; Ti 1/7/95 p8.*

95.162 *LES HUGUENOTS* (O[5a]) Giacomo Meyerbeer. COVENT GARDEN 29/6/95. 1 perf.** <u>Marcello</u> Pol Plançon; <u>Conte di Nevers</u> Mario Ancona; <u>Conte di St.</u> Bris Vittorio Arimondi; <u>Huguenot Soldier/De Cosse</u> Pellagalli-Rossetti; <u>Tavannes</u> Iginio Corsi; <u>Meru</u> Antonio de Vaschetti; <u>Raoul de Nangis</u> Francesco Tamagno. <u>Valentina</u> Emma Albani; <u>Urbano</u> Giulia Ravogli; <u>Dama d'Onore</u> Mathilde Bauermeister; <u>Margherita di Valois</u> Nellie Melba. <u>L & MGR</u>, <u>A act mgr</u>, <u>Bom</u> as for 95.161; <u>Cond</u> Luigi Mancinelli. *REV: Ath 6/7/95 p39; E 6/7/95 p9; St 4/7/95 p10; Ti 1/7/95 p8.*

95.163 *FIDELIO* (O[3a]) Ludwig van Beethoven. DRURY LANE 29/6/95(m), 4/7, 13/7/95. 3 perf.** <u>Fernando</u> Richardi; <u>Pizarro</u> Buttner; <u>Florestan</u> Bernhardt; <u>Rocco</u> Gunther; <u>Jacquino</u> Mahling; <u>1 Gefangener</u> Jena; <u>2 Gefangener</u> Burger. <u>Leonore</u> Scharnack; <u>Marzelline</u> Wassiliewits. <u>L & MGR</u> Augustus Harris; <u>Cond</u> Laugert; <u>Sm</u> Mahling. *REV: Ath 6/7/95 p39; E 6/7/95 p6; SR 20/7/95 p74-5; Th 1/7/95 p44-5; Ti 1/7/95 p12.* Comment: Ducal Court Company of Saxe-Coburg & Gotha.

95.164 *MA COUSINE* (C,3a) Henri Meilhac. GARRICK 1/7/95-6/7/95. 8 perf [w/mat 3/7, 6/7]. 1st perfd Variétés, Paris 27/10/90. <u>Champcourtier</u> [Armand] Numes; <u>Gaston</u> Maury; <u>Raoui Baron d'Arney-la-Hutte</u> Rambert; <u>Servant</u> Prevost. <u>Riquette</u> Réjane; <u>Clotilde, Baroness d'Arney-la-Hutte</u> Duluc; <u>Victorine Champcourtier</u> Avril; <u>Mme Berlandet</u> Claudia; <u>Rosalie</u> Simonson. <u>L</u> John Hare; <u>Dir</u> Henry E. Abbey, Maurice Grau; <u>Bm</u> C.J. Abud, G.F. Bashford; <u>Asm</u> W.M. Cathcart; <u>Cond</u> Haydn Waud. *REV: Ath 6/7/95 p40; E 6/7/95 p7; Sk 10/7/95 p564; SR 6/7/95 p12; St 4/7/95 p11; Th 1/8/95 p106-7; Ti 2/7/95 p10; TW95 p240-3.*

95.165 *BECKET* (D,4a) Alfred, Lord Tennyson. LYCEUM 1/7/95, 2/7/95. 2 perf.** <u>Thomas Becket</u> Henry Irving; <u>Henry II</u> Frank [Kemble] Cooper; <u>Herbert of Bosham</u> [William] Haviland; <u>Philip de Eleemosyna</u> [Henry] Howe; <u>John of Salisbury</u> Sydney Valentine; <u>Sir Reginald Fitzurse</u> [Frank] Tyars; <u>Sir Richard de Brito</u> [Clarence]

Hague; <u>Lord Leicester</u> John Martin Harvey; <u>Hilary</u>
[John] Archer; <u>Sir William de Tracy</u> [R.P.] Tabb;
<u>Richard de Hastings</u> Fuller Mellish; <u>Sir Hugh de Mor-</u>
<u>ville</u> [W. Lionel] Belmore; <u>Servant</u> [W.] Marion; <u>Roger</u>
G. Black; <u>John of Oxford</u> [H.W.] Cushing; <u>Gilbert Fol-</u>
<u>iot</u> Lacy; <u>King Louis</u> Buckley; <u>Monk</u> [K.] Rivington;
<u>Geoffrey</u> Master Leo Byrne; <u>Youngest Knight Templar</u>
E[ardley] Howard; <u>Extras</u> Gurney, Taylor, [Sam] John-
son, [T.] Reynolds. <u>Eleanor of Aquitaine</u> Mary Rorke;
<u>Margery</u> Brenda Gibson; <u>Rosamund de Clifford</u> Julia
Arthur. <u>L & MGR</u> Henry Irving; <u>Bom</u> Joseph Hurst; <u>Sc</u>
William Telbin, Joseph Harker, Hawes Craven; <u>Mus</u> C.
Villiers Stanford; <u>Mus dir</u> J. Meredith Ball; <u>Cost dgn</u>
Mrs J.W. Comyns Carr, Charles Cattermole; <u>Cost</u> Mrs
Nettleship, Mrs Reid, Thomas Pratt & Sons, Pocock
Brothers, Bieati, Auguste; <u>Pq</u> Fox; <u>Furn</u> Arnott; <u>Mach</u>
Fillery; <u>Sm</u> H.J. Loveday; <u>Act mgr</u> Bram Stoker.

95.166 *KIT MARLOWE* (P,1a) W.L. Courtney. CRITERION
2/7/95 mat perf.** <u>Christopher Marlowe</u> George Alexander; <u>Thomas Nash</u> Arthur Royston; <u>Edward Alleyn</u> Mark
Paton; <u>Henry Chettle</u> A. Vane-Tempest; <u>Francis Archer</u>
H.H. Vincent. <u>Nan</u> Irene Vanbrugh. <u>L & MGR</u> Charles Wyndham; <u>Mus</u> Walter Slaughter; <u>Treas</u> Edward Ledger; <u>Sm</u> C.
Edmonds. *REV: E 6/7/95 p8.*

95.167 *THE TWO GENTLEMEN OF VERONA* (C,4a) William
Shakespeare. DALY'S 2/7/95-8/7/95; 31/7/95(2). 9 perf
[w/mat 6/7]. 1st perfd 1595. <u>Duke of Milan</u> George
Clarke; <u>Proteus</u> Frank Worthing; <u>Valentine</u> John Craig;
<u>Sir Thurio</u> Sidney Herbert; <u>Sir Eglamour</u> Gerald Max-
well; <u>Antonio</u> Edwin Varrey; <u>Panthino</u> Charles Leclercq;
<u>Launce</u> James Lewis; <u>Speed</u> Herbert Gresham; <u>Host</u> Tyrone
Power; <u>1st Outlaw</u> Hobart Bosworth; <u>2nd Outlaw</u> Thomas
Bridgland; <u>3rd Outlaw</u> Campbell Gollan. <u>Sylvia</u> Maxine
Elliott; <u>Lucetta</u> Sybil Carlisle; <u>Ursula</u> Mallon; <u>Julia</u>
Ada Rehan. <u>L & MGR</u> Augustin Daly; <u>Cost dgn</u> Graham
Robertson; <u>Cost</u> Dazian & Co.; <u>Mus</u> Henry Widmer; <u>Sc</u>
Ernest Albert; <u>Sm</u> George Clarke; <u>Mus dir</u> Henry Widmer;
<u>Prompter</u> George Lesoir; <u>Bom</u> E[dward] Brown; <u>Bm</u> John
Farrington. *REV: Ath 6/7/95 p40; E 6/7/95 p7; Sk 3/7/
95 p508, 510, 10/7/95 p563-4; SR 6/7/95 p10-2; St 4/7/
95 p11; Ti 3/7/95 p10; TW95 p234-40.*

95.168 *DR KLAUS* (FC,5a) Adolph L'Arronge. SAVOY 2/7/95.
1 perf.** <u>PP & MGR</u> Richard d'Oyly Carte. <u>Comment</u>:
Ducal Court Company of Saxe-Coburg & Gotha.

95.169 *LE NOZZI DI FIGARO* (O[4a]) W.A. Mozart. COVENT
GARDEN 3/7/95, 11/7/95. 2 perf.** <u>Il Conte</u> Victor
Maurel; <u>Figaro</u> Mario Ancona; <u>Bartolo</u> Antonio Pini-
Corsi; <u>Basilio</u> Iginio Corsi; <u>Antonio</u> Antonio de Vas-
chetti; <u>Curzio</u> Maestri. <u>Contessa</u> Emma Eames; <u>Cherubino</u>
Marie Engle; <u>Marcellina</u> Mathilde Bauermeister; <u>Susanna</u>
Marcella Sembrich. <u>L & MGR</u> Augustus Harris; <u>Cond</u> Al-
berto Randegger; <u>A act mgr</u> Neil Forsyth; <u>Bom</u> E. Hall.
*REV: Ath 6/7/95 p39; E 6/7/95 p9; St 11/7/95 p10; Ti
4/7/95 p6.*

95.170 *DER WILDSCHUTZ* (CO,3a) Albert Lortzing. DRURY
LANE 3/7/95, 12/7/95. 2 perf. 1st perfd Leipzig 31/12/
42. <u>Graf</u> Buttner; <u>Baron</u> Burger; <u>Baculus</u> Richardi;
<u>Pancratino</u> Reer; <u>Ein Gast</u> Gehring; <u>Diener</u> Palm; <u>Ein
Koch</u> Thalheim. <u>Grafin</u> Scharnack; <u>Baronin</u> Farkas; <u>Nan-
ette</u> Pfeiffer; <u>Gretchen</u> Naumann. <u>L & MGR</u> Augustus
Harris; <u>Cond</u> Doebber. *REV: Ath 6/7/95 p39; E 6/7/95
p6; St 11/7/95 p10; Th 1/7/95 p44-5; Ti 4/7/95 p7.*
<u>Comment</u>: Ducal Court Company of Saxe-Coburg & Gotha.

95.171 *SAM'L OF POSEN* (CD,4a) George H. Jessop. GAIETY
4/7/95 mat perf.* <u>Samuel Plastrick</u> M.B. Curtis; <u>Mr
Winslow</u> Colin Coop; <u>Frank Bronson</u> Henry Vibart; <u>Jack
Cheviot</u> Sidney Brough; <u>Cuthbert Fitzurse</u> Lawrance
d'Orsay; <u>Uncle Goldstein</u> Julian Cross; <u>Conn Quinn</u>
Richard Purdon; <u>Henry Dentatus Brown</u> Robb Harwood;
<u>Snowball</u> W. Edwards. <u>Mlle Celeste</u> Albena de Mer; <u>Re-
becca</u> Mary Jocelyn; <u>Gladys</u> Constance Collier; <u>Mrs
Mulchay</u> Kate Kearney; <u>Ellen</u> Kate Cutler. <u>L & MGR</u>
George Edwardes. *REV: E 6/7/95 p6; Sk 10/7/95 p564-5;
St 11/7/95 p10-1; Th 1/8/95 p110-1.*

95.172 *MUCH ADO ABOUT NOTHING* (C,5a) William Shakes-
peare. LYCEUM 4/7/95-6/7/95. 3 perf [mat only 6/7].**
<u>Benedick</u> Henry Irving; <u>Don Pedro</u> Frank [Kemble] Cooper;
<u>Antonio</u> H[enry] Howe; <u>Claudio</u> Ben Webster; <u>Don John</u>
[William] Haviland; <u>Leonato</u> [Frank] Tyars; <u>Borachio</u>
[Clarence] Hague; <u>Conrade</u> John Martin Harvey; <u>Friar
Francis</u> Sydney Valentine; <u>Dogberry</u> [Sam] Johnson;

Verges Lacy; Seacoal [John] Archer; Oatcake [W. Lionel] Belmore; Sexton [T.] Reynolds; Balthazar Herbert Reeves; Boy Master Leo Byrne. Beatrice Ellen Terry; Hero Julia Arthur; Margaret Maud Milton; Ursula Ailsa Craig. L & MGR Henry Irving; Bom Joseph Hurst; Mus dir J. Meredith Ball; Sm H.J. Loveday; Act mgr Bram Stoker; Sc Hawes Craven, W. Cuthbert, William Telbin.

95.173 *THE IDLER* (P,4a) C. Haddon Chambers. ST. JAMES'S 4/7/95-10/7/95. 6 perf.** Mark Cross George Alexander; Sir John Harding Herbert Waring; Simeon Strong John Mason; Gen. Merryweather H.H. Vincent; Bennett Mark Paton. Lady Harding Evelyn Millard; Mrs Cross Lady Monckton; Mrs Glynn-Stanmore Elliott Page; Kate Merryweather Irene Vanbrugh. L & MGR George Alexander; Bm Robert V. Shone; Sm H.H. Vincent; Mus dir & Mus Walter Slaughter; Furn Frank Giles; Cost Mme Savage, Mme Purdue; Pq William Clarkson; Bom Arnold. *REV: Sk 10/7/95 p564; St 11/7/95 p10.*

95.174 *DER FREISCHUTZ* (O,3a) C.M. von Weber. DRURY LANE 6/7/95, 13/7/95(m). 2 perf.** Ottocar Buttner; Kuno Richardi; Caspar Jena; Max Bernhardt; Kilian Mahling; Samiel Wespi; 1 Jaeger Palm; 2 Jaeger Schvenner; 3 Jaeger Reer. Agathe Altona; Aennchen Wassiliewits; 1 Brautjungfer Pfeiffer. L & MGR Augustus Harris; Cond Langert. *REV: Ath 13/7/95 p75; E 13/7/95 p6; SR 20/7/95 p74-5; Th 1/7/95 p44-5; Ti 8/7/95 p10.* Comment: Ducal Court Company of Saxe-Coburg & Gotha.

95.175 *THE PALACE OF TRUTH* (Fairy O,3a) W.S. Gilbert. OPERA COMIQUE 6/7/95, 15/7/95. 2 perf. 1st perfd Haymarket 19/11/70. King Phanor Herbert Swears; Prince Philamir Gerald Lawrance; Chrysal Frank Towle; Zoram Harry Lawrence; Aristoeus Garrett Todd; Gelanor Kenyon Bright. Queen Altemire Lena Heinekey; Princess Zeolide Lilian Braithwaite; Mirza Marie Towle; Palmis Franklin Borrow; Azema Mrs R. Evans. L F. & S. Fowler; Pd H.A. Saintsbury; Mus dir C.A. Trew; Cost Harrisons, Nathan; Pq Fox; Furn Maple & Co.; Sm Erskine Loch; Bm Fred W. Spratt. *REV: St 11/7/95 p11.*

95.176 *DAY DREAMS* (P,1a) Herbert Swears. OPERA COMIQUE 6/7/95, 15/7/95. 2 perf. 1st perfd Eden, Brighton 5/

12/94. Sir Wilfred Ormond Dennis Eadie; Cpt. Danford
A.G. Brown; Morton Martin K. Cahill. Lady Ormond Lena
Heinekey; Hester Blake Marie Towle. L, Pd, Mus dir,
Cost, Pq, Furn, Sm, Bm as for 95.176. *REV: St 11/7/95*
p11.

95.177 *LUCIA DI LAMMERMOOR* (O[3a]) Gaetano Donizetti.
COVENT GARDEN 8/7/95, 16/7/95. 2 perf.** Enrico
Arturo Pessina/Antonio Pini-Corsi; Raimondo Vittorio
Arimondi; Arturo Pellagalli-Rossetti; Normano Iginio
Corsi/Maestri; Edgardo Francesco Vignas. Lucia Nellie
Melba; Alice Cecile Brani/Florenza. L & MGR Augustus
Harris; Cond Enrico Bevignani; A act mgr Neil Forsyth;
Bom E. Hall. *REV: Ath 13/7/95 p75; SR 20/7/95 p74-5;*
St 11/7/95 p10.

95.178 *BERUHMTE FRAU* (C,3a) Franz von Schoenthan &
Gustave Kadelburg. DRURY LANE 8/7/95. 1 perf. 1st
perfd Deutsches, Berlin 4/2/88. Roemer Herbert; Pal-
may H. Kadelburg; Traunstein Heimoff; Georg Brauck;
Diener Gehring. Agnes Kornig; Herma Linden; Wally Nau-
mann; Ottilie Wienrich; Hartwig Worsh; Seeman Franke;
Dienstmaldchen Sperling. L & MGR Augustus Harris. *REV:*
E 13/7/95 p6; St 11/7/95 p10; Th 1/7/95 p44-5.

95.179 *MADAME SANS-GENE* (Prol,3a) Victorien Sardou &
Emile Moreau. GARRICK 8/7/95-13/7/95. 8 perf [w/mat
10/7, 13/7].** Napoleon [Edmond] Duquesne; Marechal
Lefebvre Candé; De Neipperg Maury; Savary, Duc de
Rovigo [Armand] Numes; Fouché Gildes; Despreaux Du-
velleroy; De St. Marsan Rambert; Junot Montcharmont;
Roustan Andrelys; De Brigode Prevost; Vinaigre Gaill-
ard; Canouville Kemm; Jasmin Donnet; Cop Pelio; Con-
stant Courcelles; Vaboutran Darmand; De Lauristan
Chotard; Jolicoeur Charles; Rissout Lebeguinski; De
Mortemart Germain; Corso Leroy; De Fontanes Taillary;
Voisine André. Reine Caroline Avril; Princesse Elisa
Duluc-Maury; Mme de Bulow Aimée Samuel; Catherine
Réjane; Mme de Rovigo Mme Louise Dauville; Mme de
Vintimille Simonson; Mme de Canisy Darcy; Toinon
Netza; Roussotte Marcelle; Julie Ramie; Voisine
Claudia; Femme de Chambre Réné. L John Hare; Dir Henry
E. Abbey, Maurice Grau; Bm C.J. Abud, G.F. Bashford;
Asm W.M. Cathcart; Cond Haydn Waud. *REV: Ath 13/7/95*

p76; E 13/7/95 p7; Sk 17/7/95 p620; SR 13/7/95 p43; St 11/7/95 p11.

95.180 *A MIDSUMMER NIGHT'S DREAM* William Shakespeare. DALY'S 9/7/95-27/7/95. 21 perf [w/S mat; add mat 17/7]. 1st perfd 1592. Theseus George Clarke; Egeus Tyrone Power; Demetrius Frank Worthing; Lysander John Craig; Philostrate Hobart Bosworth; Quince Charles Leclercq; Snug Herbert Gresham; Bottom James Lewis; Flute Sidney Herbert; Snout William Sampson; Starveling Thomas Bridgland; Extras Stuart, [Robert] Shepherd, George Wharnock, Sherrard, [Rupert?] Lister. Hippolita Leontine/Lena Brophy/Adelaide Sterling; Hermia Maxine Elliott; Oberon Sybil Carlisle; Titania Percy Haswell; Fairy Sofia Hoffman; Puck, or Robin Goodfellow Lillian Swain; Helena Ada Rehan; Extras Helena Nelson, Lena Loraine, Jeanne Vorhees, Amy Stuart, Lulu Bosworth, Helen Bryant, Mariam Mansfield, Nina Felton, Lena Brophy, Kathleen Warren, Eveline Warren, Stevens, Lockie, Hill. L & MGR Augustin Daly; Sc Henry Hoyt, Walter Hann; Mechanical effects H. Sheldon, James Tait; Mus & Mus dir Henry Widmer; Cost dgn Bianchini; Cost Graham Robertson; Pq William Clarkson; Sm George Clarke; Prompter George Lesoir; Bom E[dward] Brown; Bm John Farrington. *REV: Ath 13/7/95 p76; E 13/7/95 p7; Sk 17/7/95 p620, 31/7/95 p20-1; SR 13/7/95 p43-5; St 11/7/95 p10; Ti 10/7/95 p7; TW95 p243-53.*

95.181 *CHARLES I* (P,4a) W.G. Wills. LYCEUM 11/7/95. 1 perf.** Charles I Henry Irving; Lord Moray Frank [Kemble] Cooper; Oliver Cromwell [Frank] Tyars; Marquis of Huntley Sydney Valentine; Queen's Page John Martin Harvey; Attendant [R.P.] Tabb; Ireton Lacy; 1st Cavalier [W. Lionel] Belmore; 2nd Cavalier [K.] Rivington; Prince James Master Leo Bryne; Princess Elizabeth Caryl Field-Fisher. Queen Henrietta Maria Ellen Terry; Lady Eleanor Maud Milton. L & MGR Henry Irving; Bom Joseph Hurst; Sc Hawes Craven, Joseph Harker; Cond J. Meredith Ball; Sm H.J. Loveday; Act mgr Bram Stoker.

95.182 *THE LYONS MAIL* (Melo,3a) Charles Reade [adpt of Emile Moreau, Giraudin & Delacour, *Le Courrier de Lyon*]. LYCEUM 12/7/95, 22-23/7/95. 3 perf.** Joseph

Lesurques/Dubosc Henry Irving; Postmaster of Montgeron
[Henry] Howe; Didier Ben Webster; Courriol [William]
Haviland; Jerome Lesurques Sydney Valentine; Choppard
S[am] Johnson; Dorval [Frank] Tyars; Joliquet John
Martin Harvey; Fouinard [John] Archer; Coco [T.]
Reynolds; Guard [R.P.] Tabb; Lambert Lacy; Postillion
[J.H.] Allen; Waiter [W.] Marion; Durochat [W. Lionel]
Belmore; Commissary of Police [H.W.] Cushing; Guerneau
Buckley. Jeanette Maud Milton; Julie Lesurques May
Whitty; Niece to Postmaster Ailsa Craig; Marie Foster.
L & MGR, Bom, Mus dir, Sm, Act mgr as for 95.181. *REV:*
Th 1/8/95 p103.

95.183 *TANNHAUSER* (O[3a]) Richard Wagner. COVENT GAR-
DEN 15/7/95, 25/7/95. 2 perf.** Wolfram Victor Mau-
rel; Hermann I Pol Plançon; Walther Charles Bonnard;
Heinrich Schrieber Iginio Corsi; Reinmar Antonio de
Vaschetti; Tannhauser Albert Alvarez; Biterolf Charles
Gilibert. Elizabeth Emma Eames; Venus Ada Adini;
Young Shepherd Mathilde Bauermeister. L & MGR Augustus
Harris; Cond Luigi Mancinelli; A act mgr Neil Forsyth;
Bom E. Hall. *REV: Ath 20/7/95 p107; E 20/7/95 p13;*
SR 20/7/95 p74-5; St 18/7/95 p10; Ti 16/7/95 p5.

95.184 *THE CORSICAN BROTHERS* (D,3a) Dion Boucicault
[adpt of Dumas, *Les Frères Corses*]. LYCEUM 15/7/95-
20/7/95. 6 perf [mat only 20/7].** Fabien dei Fran-
chi/Louis dei Franchi Henry Irving; Chateau Renaud
Frank [Kemble] Cooper; Montgiron Ben Webster; Alfred
Meynard [William] Haviland; Giordano Martelli [Frank]
Tyars; Colonna Sam Johnson; Griffo [John] Archer;
Boissec [T.] Reynolds; Beauchamp [W. Lionel] Belmore;
Orlando Sydney Valentine; Antonio Sanola John Martin
Harvey; Verner Lacy; Surgeon [K.] Rivington; Tomaso
[R.P.] Tabb. Emelie de l'Esparre Julia Arthur/May
Whitty; Mme de Franchi Mary Rorke; Coralie Maud Mil-
ton; Marie N. de Silva; Celestine Foster; Estelle
Brenda Gibson; Eugenie Davis. L & MGR Henry Irving;
Bom Joseph Hurst; Sc Hawes Craven, Joseph Harker; Cost
Auguste, Mrs Nettleship, Mrs Reid; Cost dgn Faustin;
Ch Espinosa; Pq Fox; Mach Fillery; Furn Arnott; Sm
H.J. Loveday; Mus dir J. Meredith Ball; Act mgr Bram
Stoker. *REV: E 20/7/95 p7; Sk 24/7/95 p682; Th 1/8/95*
p103.

95.185 *AFTER THE BALL* (Oa) F. Kinsey Peile. ST. JAMES'S
16/7/95 mat perf. * Mr Cyprian Smith F. Kinsey Peile.
Mrs Cyprian Smith Marie Halton. L & MGR George Alexander; Cond [Barter] Johns; Bm Robert V. Shone; Sm
H.H. Vincent; Mus dir Walter Slaughter. *REV: St 18/*
7/95 p10.

95.186 *OUR TOYS* (Fairy Vision in One Peep) William
Yardley. ST. JAMES'S 16/7/95 mat perf.* Lord Jennings
H.T. Rivers; Wooden Soldier W. Tabor; Our Mr Nash L.G.
Leverson. Fairy Chora Bigelow; China Shepherdess
Reeves; Little Red Riding Hood Kauffmann-Kendall; Our
Japanese Doll L. Kauffmann-Kendall; Lady Doll Mrs L.G.
Lever[son]. L & MGR, Bm, Sm, Mus dir as for 95.185;
Cond T.H. Frewin. *REV: St 18/7/95 p10.*

95.187 *JOURNEYS END IN LOVERS' MEETING* (Proverb,1a)
"J.O. Hobbes" [Mrs P.M.T. Craigie] & George Moore.
LYCEUM 17/7/95-19/7/95. 3 perf.** Sir Philip Soupire
Frank [Kemble] Cooper; Cpt. Maramour Ben Webster. Lady
Soupire Ellen Terry. L & MGR Henry Irving; Bom Joseph
Hurst; Sm H.J. Loveday; Mus dir J. Meredith Ball; Act
mgr Bram Stoker. *REV: E 20/7/95 p7; Sk 24/7/95 p682.*

95.188 *SHE STOOPS TO CONQUER* (C) Oliver Goldsmith.
COMEDY 18/7/95 mat perf.** Hardcastle H[enry] Kemble;
Jack Slang Eric Lewis; Tom Twist Charles H.E. Brook-
field; Tom Tickle Arthur Playfair; Stingo William Wyes;
Gregory Charles Dodsworth; Hastings W. Scott Buist;
Diggory Ells Dagnall; Roger Ernest Percy; Sir Charles
Marlowe Stanley Hope; Mat Muggins J[ohn] Byron: Tony
Lumpkin Edward Righton; Young Marlowe Cosmo Stuart;
Ralph Osman; Servant James Anning. Kate Hardcastle Mrs
Bernard Beere; Miss Neville Beatrice Selwyn; Maid Doris
Templeton; Mrs Hardcastle M.A. Victor. L & MGR J.W.
Comyns Carr. *REV: E 20/7/95 p9; St 25/7/95 p10.*

95.189 *SIXES AND SEVENS* (Misunderstanding) E.H. Whit-
more. COMEDY 18/7/95 mat perf.** Cpt. George Hope
Arthur Bourchier. Edith Cashdown Violet Vanbrugh. L &
MGR J.W. Comyns Carr. *REV: As for 95.188.*

95.190 *LA NAVARRAISE* (O[2a]) Jules Massenet. COVENT
GARDEN 20/7/95. 1 perf.** Araguil Charles Bonnard;

Remigio Armand Castelmary; Garrido Pol Plançon; Ramon
Jacques Bars; Bustamente Charles Gilibert. Anita Emma
Calvé. L & MGR Augustus Harris; Cond Philip Flon [or
Armando Seppilli];A act mgr Neil Forsyth; Bom E. Hall.
*REV: Ath 27/7/95 p139; E 27/7/95 p13; Sk 31/7/95 p57;
SR 3/8/95 p140-1; St 25/7/95 p10; Ti 22/7/95 p7.*

95.191 *TWICE FOOLED* (Ca,1a) "Lamda Mu." GAIETY 23/7/
95 mat perf.* Mr Parsons Green George Mudie; Penn
Colomb, Esq Eric Lewis. Mrs Parsons Green Phyllis
Broughton; Nina Marie Halton. *REV: E 27/7/95 p9; St
25/7/95 p10.*

95.192 *SIXES AND SEVENS* (Duol) E.H. Whitmore. GAIETY
23/7/95 mat perf.** Cpt. George Hope Arthur Bourchier.
Edith Cashdown Violet Vanbrugh. *REV: As for 95.191.*

95.193 *THE LUNATICS* (Sk) W. Walden. GAIETY 23/7/95 mat
perf. George Alexander. Irene Vanbrugh. *REV: As for
95.191.* Comment: This piece could possibly be W.R.
Walkes's *A Pair of Lunatics.*

95.194 *AFTER THE BALL* (Oa) F. Kinsey Peile. GAIETY
23/7/95 mat perf.** Mr Cyprian Smith F. Kinsey Peile.
Mrs Cyprian Smith Marie Halton. *REV: As for 95.191.*

95.195 *MACBETH* (T,5a) William Shakespeare. LYCEUM
24/7/95-26/7/95. 3 perf [mat only 24/7]. 1st perfd
Globe 20/4/1610. Macbeth Henry Irving; Macduff Frank
[Kemble] Cooper; Banquo [F.H.?] Macklin; Malcolm
Ben Webster; Duncan [William] Haviland; 1st Witch
Sydney Valentine; Caithness [Eardley] Howard; 2nd
Witch [Clarence] Hague; Lennox John Martin Harvey;
Fleance Master Leo Byrne; Porter [Sam] Johnson; 3rd
Witch [John] Archer; Sergeant [G.] Black; Siward [R.
P.] Tabb; Seyton Lacy; Doctor Fuller Mellish; Messen-
ger [W. Lionel] Belmore; Attendant [H.W.] Cushing;
Angus [T.] Reynolds; Ross Tyars; Menteith G[eoffrey]
Taylor; Officers [K.] Rivington, [W.] Marion; Murder-
ers Hemstock, Carter; Apparitions Baird, Master Leo
Byrne. Lady Macbeth Ellen Terry; Gentlewoman May
Whitty; Servant Foster; Donalbain Ailsa Craig; Hecate
Hallett; Apparition Holland. L & MGR Henry Irving;
Mus Arthur Sullivan; Mus dir J. Meredith Ball; Cost

<u>dgn</u> Charles Cattermole, Mrs J.W. Comyns Carr; <u>Cost</u>
Auguste, Helbronner, Mrs Reid, Kennedy & Co., Farwig
& Co., T. Hales; <u>Pq</u> Fox; <u>Furn</u> Arnott; <u>Mach</u> Fillery;
<u>Sm</u> H.J. Loveday; <u>Act mgr</u> Bram Stoker. *REV: Sk 31/7/
95 p57.*

95.196 *QWONG HI: THE "HEATHEN CHINEE"* (FC,3a) R. Fen-
ton MacKay. AVENUE 27/7/95-17/8/95. 25 perf [w/mat
31/7, 3/8, 7/8, 10/8, 14/8, 17/8].** <u>Qwong Hi</u> Willie
Edouin; <u>Frank Brett</u> Oswald Yorke; <u>Fred Earle</u> Forbes
Dawson; <u>Cpt. Lander</u> William F. Hawtrey; <u>Roy Lander</u>
Kenneth Douglass; <u>Verity</u> Ernest Cosham; <u>Bailiff</u> For-
rester. <u>Mrs Brett</u> Helen Ferrers; <u>Miss Diction</u> Beatrice
Day; <u>Lydia Winlock</u> Florence Fordyce; <u>Clarke</u> Lilian
Millward; <u>Queenie Dimple</u> Daisy Bryer; <u>Nettie Merrydue</u>
May Edouin. L & MGR William Greet; <u>Bm & Treas</u> Tom Pitt;
<u>Mus dir</u> Dr [John?] Storer. *REV: E 3/8/95 p7; St 1/8/
95 p11; TW95 p259-60.*

95.197 *NANCY AND CO* (FC,4a) Augustin Daly [adpt of
Julius Rosen]. DALY'S 29/7/95-30/7/95. 2 perf.**
<u>Ebenezer Griffing</u> James Lewis; <u>Kiefe O'Kiefe, Esq</u>
Frank Worthing; <u>Cpt. Paul Renseller</u> Sidney Herbert;
<u>Young Mr Sikes Stockslow</u> Herbert Gresham; <u>Julius</u> Will-
iam Sampson; <u>Taffy Brasher</u> Hobart Bosworth. <u>Huldah</u>
<u>Dangery</u> Mrs G.H. Gilbert; <u>Oriana</u> Maxine Elliott; <u>Daisy</u>
<u>Griffing</u> Percy Haswell; <u>Betsy</u> Helen Bryant; <u>Nancy</u> Ada
Rehan. *REV: E 3/8/95 p7; St 1/8/95 p11.*

95.198 *IN AN ATTIC* (Ca,1a) J. Wilton Jones. TRAFALGAR
29/7/95-24/8/95. 24 perf.** <u>Arthur Clarges</u> Guy Brandon; <u>Joe Dixon</u> Cecil Ramsey. <u>Rosalind</u> Marion Lind. <u>L</u>
<u>& MGR</u> Henry Dana; <u>Mus dir</u> H.A.J. Campbell; <u>Sm</u> Standley
Wade; <u>Act mgr</u> James W. Mathews. *REV: E 3/8/95 p7.*

95.199 *A DRAWN BATTLE* (Duol) T. Malcolm Watson. AVENUE
31/7/95.** <u>Comment</u>:This piece was advertized in both
the *Daily Telegraph* and the *Daily News*, but there is
some doubt whether it was actually perfd.

95.200 *WOMAN'S CAPRICE* (C,1a) H.M. Lewis [adpt of
Gott sei dank der Tisch ist gedeckt]. GAIETY 31/7/95
mat perf.** <u>Cpt. Flareuppe</u> Eric Thorne; <u>Mr St. John</u>
Evelyn Vernon; <u>William Jones</u> Picton Roxborough. <u>Mrs</u>

Flareuppe Adelaide Newton; Mrs St. John Firmely Ellas
Dee; May Attie Chester. L & MGR George Edwardes; Act
mgr E[dward] Marshall; Sm A.E. Dodson, REV: St 1/8/95
p11.

95.201 *LEAVE IT TO ME* (F,1a) Arthur Williams. GAIETY
31/7/95 mat perf.** Mr Easy George Mudie; Adolphus
Courtley Cairns James; Mr Quince Robert Nainby; Joe
Sprouts Arthur Williams. Amelia Easy Constance Collier;
Susan Muggins Katie Seymour. L & MGR, Act mgr, Sm as
for 95.200. REV: St 1/8/95 p11.

95.202 *DAGGERS DRAWN* (Ca,1a) Pryce Seaton. AVENUE 1/8/
95-17/8/95. 15 perf.** Sir George Grantley W.F. Hawtrey; Trip Ernest Cosham; Cpt. Jack Grantley Stanley
Kenniss. Ford Lilian Millward; Mrs Gerald Deering
Beatrice Day; Alice Deering Daisy Bryer. L & MGR William Greet; Bm & Treas Tom Pitt.

95.203 *SAVED FROM THE SEA* (D,4a) Arthur Shirley & Ben-
jamin Landeck. PRINCESS'S 3/8/95-13/9/95, 37 perf [w/
mat 5/8]. 1st perfd Pavilion 4/3/95. Dan Ellington
Charles Glenney; Jim Weaver Austin Melford; Peter
Scalcher Bassett Roe; Richard Fenton Frank Harding;
Billy Snooks Lionel Rignold; Jenkins Lennox Pawle;
Inspector Jenkins George Claremont; Chaplain George
Yates; Head Warder Freeman; 2nd Warder Jameson. Jack
Gladys White; Nancy Ellington Beaumont Collins; Mrs
Blake Harriet Clifton; Polly Blake Fannie Selby. PD
Isaac Cohén; Sc A. Terraine, [H.] Norman; Mus G.D.
Le Camera; Cost Morris Angel & Son; Sm John Douglass;
Mus dir W. Carlisle Vernon. REV: E 10/8/95 p7; St 8/8/
95 p12; Th 1/9/95 p165-7; Ti 5/8/95 p3.

95.204 *ALL ABROAD* (MF,2a) Owen Hall (lib) & James T.
Tanner (lib) & W.H. Risque (lyr) & Frederick Rosse
(mus). CRITERION 8/8/95-2/11/95. 86 perf [w/S mat exc
10/8, 2/11]. 1st perfd Theatre Royal, Portsmouth 1/4/
95. Mr Bowles Charles E. Stevens; Mr Beaver Horace
Mills; Baron Fontenay Herman de Lange; Ernest John
Coates; Maurice Meurice C.P. Little; Capshaw Lionel
Rae/L. Johnson; Skeggs G. Carroll; Gendarme Cecil
Frere; Adolphe L. Johnson/Lionel Rae; Tom Eltham
R[upert?] Lister; Reggie Andale C[harles] Mills; Jack

Smythe F[red?] Garton; Dancer William Vokes; Extras
H. Linwood, F[red?] Garton, C[harles?] Crook, L.
Wennesley, V. Calverwell, L. Winning, Connie Kate Cut-
ler; Blanche Leonide Amella; Chloe Feltop Nellie
Thorne; May Astor Lena Brophy; Mme Mostesquieu Ada
Reeve; Dancers Rosa Boote, Olive Dalmour, Rose Martin,
Pattie Thornhill; Extras Louise Lister, Daisy Gilpin,
May Romney, Lydia Lisle, Florence Cameron, Ada Max-
well, Maud Michel-Watson, Marguerite Osland, Bessie
Pelissier, Rose Heilbron. L & MGR Charles Wyndham;
Cost Redmayne, Pitts & Richards, Grace Watkin, Mme
Eroom, Thomas Giles & Co., Morris Angel; Sm Herman de
Lange; Asm C. Edmonds; Mus dir Carl Kiefert; Act mgr
& Treas E. Harvey. *REV: E 10/8/95 p7; Sk 14/8/95 p177,
11/9/95 p350, 378-9; St 15/8/95 p9; Th 1/9/95 p163-5;
TW95 p253-9.*

95.205 *A YOUNGSTER'S ADVENTURE* (Sk,1a) John S. Clarke.
STRAND 19/8/95-11/9/95. 28 perf[w/W, S mat].* Kit
Curtis Wilfred Clarke.   Lady Lyster Muriel Wylford;
Beckey Caroline Ewell; Ellen Nancy Noel. *REV: E 24/8/
95 p7; St 22/8/95 p11; TW95 p260.*

95.206 *NEW YORK DIVORCE* (F,3a) Wilfred Clarke [adpt of
Prête-moi ta Femme]. STRAND 19/8/95-11/9/95. 28 perf
[w/W, S mat].* Paul Roach Wilfred Clarke; Oliver Gold-
coyne Arthur Wood; Owen Cuttaway Arthur Helmore; Peter
Clincher Oswald Yorke; Caesar Smash Rankin Duval. Se-
lena Roach Muriel Wylford; Maud Eveltry Nancy Noel;
Honor Racket Marie Hudspeth. *REV: E, St as for 95.205;
Sk 28/8/95 p278; Th 1/9/95 p162-3; TW95 p260-1.*

95.207 [no entry]

95.208 *THE SWORDSMAN'S DAUGHTER* (D,4a) Brandon Thomas
& Clement Scott [adpt of Jules Mary & Georges Grisier,
Le Maître d'Armes]. ADELPHI 31/8/95-30/11/95. 80 perf
[w/mat 26/10].* Vibrac William Terriss; Jean Olgan
Charles J. Fulton; Baron de Chantoisel Harry Nicholls;
Dr Dubarry J.R. Crauford; Tommy Watkins Julian Cross;
Jacqout Breton Richard Purdon; Judge Melvil George R.
Foss; Count Henri de Rochfière W.L. Abingdon; Lieut.
Leverdier Vincent Sternroyd; Marescot Compton Coutts;
Leclair Edwin Rorke; Maurice Paul Berton; San Melito

A.W. Fitzgerald; Cartel Webb Darleigh; Prévot Caleb
Porter; Abbé Roland J.S. Blythe. Madeleine Jessie
Millward/Mary Allestree; Thérèse Vane Featherston;
Mrs Wilkins Marriott; Mme Breton Kate Kearney; Lizette
Mrs E.H. Brooke; Suzanne Mary Allestree/Marie Neilson;
Countess de Floriel Madge Leighton. PP & MGR A. & S.
Gatti; Sc Joseph Harker, Bruce Smith; Dir Fred G. La-
tham; Mus & Mus dir John Crook; Cost dgn Lucien
Besche; Cost Jay, Debenham & Freebody, Marshall &
Snelgrove, Miss Nathan, Morris Angel & Son; Pq William
Clarkson; Furn Frank Giles & Co.; Bom Arthur Frye; Asm
Caleb Porter; A act mgr Herbert Budd. *REV: Ath 7/9/95*
p331; E 7/9/95 p9; Sk 4/9/95 p298, 2/10/95 p549; St
5/9/95 p11-2; Th 1/10/95 p225-8; Ti 2/9/95 p4; TW95
p261-7.

95.209 *ALABAMA* (P,4a) Augustus Thomas. GARRICK 2/9/95-
12/10/95. 44 perf [w/W, S mat exc 4/9, 7/9, 11/9,
18/9]. 1st perfd Madison Square, New York 1/4/91.
Col. Preston James Fernandez; Harry Preston E.S. Willard; Lathrop Page Cecil Crofton; Raymond Page Bassett
Roe; Col. Moberley John Mason; Mr Armstrong W.T. Lovell; Squire Tucker F.H. Tyler; Decatur Harry Cane.
Carey Preston Agnes Miller; Mrs Page Marion Terry;
Atalanta Moberley Nannie Craddock; Mrs Stockton Keith
Wakeman. L John Hare; Mgr E.S. Willard; Bm W.H. Griffiths; Sc Walter Hann; Bom [E.] Candler; Cond Haydn
Waud. *REV: Ath 7/9/95 p331; E 7/9/95 p11; St 5/9/95*
p12; Ti 3/9/95 p3; TW95 p267-75.

95.210 *THE PRIVATE SECRETARY* (FC,3a) Charles H. Haw-
trey [adpt of Gustav von Moser, *Der Bibliothekar*].
AVENUE 3/9/95-26/10/95. 56 perf [w/S mat; add mat
23/10].** Mr Marsland Nicol Pentland; Harry Marsland
J.L. MacKay; Mr Cattermole William F. Hawtrey; Doug-
las Cattermole Charles H. Hawtrey; Rev Robert Spalding
Willis Searle; Sidney Gibson St. John Hamund; John
W.H. Taylor; Knox George Spencer; Gardener MacKenzie.
Edith Marsland Ada Mellon; Eva Webster Evelyn Harrison;
Mrs Stead Mrs Henry Leigh; Miss Ashford Caroline Elton.
L & MGR William Greet; Dir Charles H. Hawtrey; Sm
Frederick Glover; Mus dir Ernest Bucalossi; Bm C. Lid-
don Clark. *REV: E 7/9/95 p9; Sk 18/9/95 p412.*

95.211 *THE POSTSCRIPT* (C,1a) F. Hamilton Knight.
AVENUE 3/9/95-15/11/95. 58 perf [np 28/10-2/11]. 1st
perfd Prince of Wales's 14/2/88. <u>Col Sir Clive Butler</u>
Nicol Pentland; <u>Harold Treherne</u> Edward Ferris/J.R.
Hatfield. <u>Marjorie Fleming</u> Mary Clayton; <u>Mrs Treherne</u>
Dora Thorne. <u>L & MGR</u>, <u>Dir</u>, <u>Sm</u>, <u>Mus dir</u>, <u>Bm</u> as for 95.
210.

95.212 *DAISY'S ESCAPE* (Ca,1a) A.W. Pinero. TOOLE'S
3/9/95-27/9/95. 22 perf.** <u>Mjr. Mullet</u> H[enry] Westland; <u>Tom Rossiter</u> Frank J. Arlton; <u>Augustus Caddel</u>
George Shelton; <u>Bullamore</u> C[harles] Brunton; <u>Tulk</u>
T. Lowne. <u>Daisy White</u> Cora Poole; <u>Mollie</u> Mary Brough.
<u>L & MGR</u> J.L. Toole; <u>Sm</u> John Billington; <u>Cond</u> William
Robins; <u>Bm & Treas</u> George Lee. *REV: E 7/9/95 p9; St
5/9/95 p12.*

95.213 *THE CHILI WIDOW* (C,3a) Arthur Bourchier & Alfred Sutro [adpt of Alexandre Bisson & Fabrice Carré,
M. Le Directeur]. ROYALTY 7/9/95-21/3/96; 16/4/96-
27/4/96. 223 perf [w/S mat exc 7/9; add mat 4/12,
26/12/95, 27/1/96, 29/1/96; np 23-25/12/95; 5/2/96].*
<u>Sir Reginald Delamere</u> Arthur Bourchier; <u>Leslie Laven-
der</u> Cosmo Stuart/Charles Troode; <u>Duckworth Crabbe</u>
William Blakeley; <u>Frederick Martindale</u> Welton Dale/
W.G. Elliot; <u>Mathison Crawley</u> Frank Lindo; <u>Cecil
Fielding</u> Charles Troode/Gilbert Yorke/Herbert Shelley;
<u>Patrick O'Dwyer, M.P.</u> Ernest Hendrie; <u>Macpherson</u> Mark
Kinghorne; <u>Alfred Gentle</u> A. Bromley Davenport; <u>Will-
iam</u> Arthur Armstrong/Metcalf Wood; <u>Boy</u> S. Alexander/
A. Stuart. <u>Mrs Jeffreys</u> Sophie Larkin/Mrs Henry Leigh;
<u>Gladys de la Casa y Guales</u> Violet Vanbrugh; <u>Honor
Bliss</u> Kate Phillips; <u>Dulcie Martindale</u> Irene Vanbrugh.
<u>L & MGR</u> Arthur Bourchier; <u>Pp</u> Kate Santley; <u>Bom</u> W.E.
Blakeley; <u>Cond</u> Albert Fox; <u>Sc</u> W. Hemsley; <u>Cost</u> Mme
Vanité, Mrs Yorke, Mme Hayward; <u>Furn</u> Stagg & Mantle,
Frank Giles & Co.; <u>Pq</u> William Clarkson; <u>Bm</u> T. Stevens;
<u>Sm</u> Fred W. Permain; <u>Act mgr</u> Arthur Bertram. *REV: Ath
14/9/95 p364; E 14/9/95 p8; Sk 11/9/95 p355, 2/10/95
p532-3, 23/10/95 p692, 695, 18/12/95 p392; SR 12/10/
95 p470-2; St 12/9/95 p12, 19/12/95 p12; Th 1/10/95
p228-9; Ti 9/9/95 p10; TW95 p281-4.*

95.214 *BOGEY* (P,3a) Henry V. Esmond. ST. JAMES'S 10/9/

95-21/9/95. 12 perf [w/mat 18/9].* <u>Uncle Archie</u> But-
tanshaw Henry V. Esmond; <u>Jospeh Gradden</u> Fred Everill;
<u>Jamie Maclachlan</u> W.G. Elliot; <u>John Tiddy</u> Philp Cun-
ningham; <u>Noah Emens</u> Gaston Mervale; <u>Kennedy</u> W.R.
Staveley. <u>Marion Buttanshaw</u> Ethel Matthews; <u>Fairy</u>
<u>Buttanshaw</u> Eva Moore; <u>Maid</u> Lovell; <u>Miss Minden</u> Pattie
Bell. <u>L & MGR</u> George Alexander; <u>Bm</u> Oscar Barrett; <u>Sm</u>
W.R. Staveley; <u>Mus dir & Mus</u> Walter Slaughter; <u>Sc</u> H.
P. Hall; <u>Cost</u> Sara Perrin, Miss Hooper; <u>Furn</u> J.S.
Lyon; <u>Pq</u> William Clarkson, Fox; <u>Bom</u> Arnold. *REV: Ath
14/9/95 p364; E 14/9/95 p8; Sk 18/9/95 p446, 454-7;
St 12/9/95 p12; Th 1/10/95 p229-31; Ti 11/9/95 p4;
TW95 p275-81.*

95.215 *IN A LOCKET* (FC,3a) Harry & Edward A. Paulton.
STRAND 16/9/95-30/10/95. 50 perf [w/W, S mat exc 18/9;
mat only 30/10]. 1st perfd Grand, Birmingham 3/12/94
[as *A World of Trouble in a Locket*]. <u>Gen. Greville</u>
Clinton Baddeley; <u>Garnet Greville</u> Harold Child; <u>And-
rew Mallock</u> Laurence Cautley; <u>Alfred Bonner</u> W. Scott
Buist; <u>Marler</u> Frank M. Wood; <u>Comyns</u> James A. Welch;
<u>Middleton Simpkin</u> Harry Paulton. <u>Judith Simpkin</u> Annie
Hill; <u>Elaine Ferris</u> Gladys Evelyn; <u>Susan</u> Julia Warden; <u>Marian</u> Amy Elstob; <u>Cicely</u> Alice de Winton. <u>L</u>
Paulton Comedies Co. Ltd.; <u>Mgr</u> Harry Paulton; <u>Sc</u> E.G.
Banks; <u>Furn</u> W.E. Hardy & Co.; <u>Bm</u> J.B. Jackson; <u>Act
mgr</u> W.H. Clinton Baddeley; <u>Bom</u> A.E. Barnes. *REV: E
21/9/95 p8; Sk 25/9/95 p480-3; St 19/9/95 p10; Th 1/
10/95 p231-2; Ti 17/9/95 p10; TW95 p302-3.*

95.216 *A HANDSOME HUSBAND* (Ca,1a) Mrs J.R. Planché.
STRAND 16/9/95-5/11/95; 14/12/95-21/12/95. 49 perf
[np 30-31/10]. 1st perfd Olympic 15/2/36. <u>Henry
Wyndham</u> James A. Welch; <u>Henry Fitzherbert</u> Clinton
Baddeley. <u>Laura Wyndham</u> Agnes Paulton; <u>Amelia</u> Ida
Warrand; <u>Sophia Melford</u> Amy Elstob; <u>Jane</u> Winifred
Wood. <u>L</u>, <u>Mgr</u>, <u>Bm</u>, <u>Act mgr</u>, <u>Bom</u> as for 95.215. *REV: E
21/9/95 p8, 9/11/95 p10; St 19/9/95 p10.*

95.217 *CHEER, BOYS, CHEER* (D,5a) Augustus Harris &
Cecil Raleigh & Henry Hamilton. DRURY LANE 19/9/95-
14/12/95;* trfd to OLYMPIC 19/12/95-29/2/96. 177
perf [w/S mat 28/9-26/10; w/W, S mat 30/10/95-29/2/96
exc 18/12, 25/12/95; add mat 26/12/95; np 16-18/12,

25/12/95]. <u>Marquis of Chepstow</u> Henry Neville; <u>Lord
Archibald Kesteven</u> Sidney Howard; <u>George Hilyard</u>
A. Hamilton Revelle; <u>Reginald Fitzdavis</u> Charles Dal-
ton; <u>Wolff Meikstein</u> Lionel Rignold; <u>Oliver C. Brown</u>
George Giddens; <u>Cyrus Trueman</u> Austin Melford/Howard
Russell; <u>Rev Mr Nugent</u> William Rignold; <u>Forbes</u> [Frank?]
MacVicars; <u>John Knight</u> H. Tripp Edgar; <u>Corporal Thomp-
son</u> R.A. Lyons; <u>Sgt. Bucklaw</u> Frank Damer/Brooks; <u>Gib-
bens</u> Alfred Balfour/Digby Roberts; <u>Chandler</u> Arthur
Hendon/E. Rees; <u>Jackson</u> C[harles?] Danvers; <u>Policeman</u>
Alfred Robert/Arthur Hendon; <u>Porter</u> James Frances;
<u>Gordon Lee</u> Howard Russell/Biddles; <u>Philip Lee</u> A. Tre-
vor/Charles Ross; <u>Prof Schwinter</u> Herbert Charante/W.
Parker; <u>Signor Patrogilli</u> Court; <u>Sir Hilary Fanshaw</u>
Robert/Wilkins. <u>Lady Hilyard</u> Fanny Brough; <u>Lady Ugh-
tred</u> Mrs Cecil Raleigh/Marie Daltra [Mrs Lionel Rig-
nold]; <u>Kitty Parker</u> Pattie Browne; <u>Mrs Verity</u> Marie
Daltra; <u>Mrs Chomondeley</u> Fannie Ward; <u>Blanche Lindsey</u>
Eleanor Calhoun/[Gertrude] Gheen; <u>Miss Planquet</u> Mow-
brey/Harwood; <u>Miss Vernon</u> Kate Ruskin; <u>Miss Henshaw</u>
Edie Farquhar; <u>Miss Fitzwilliam</u> Gertrude Gheen; <u>Mrs
Bradshaw</u> Lydia Rachel; <u>Mrs Bentley</u> Amy Abbott; <u>Hotel
Clerk</u> De Groot; <u>Barmaid</u> Maud Francis/E. Cuthbert;
<u>Extras</u> V[iolet?] Crotty, E[ileen] Concanen, Margot
Werderman, G[eorgie] Cook, Lily Brooking, E. Budd,
L[izzie] Wilson, L. Donald, L. Feverell, E[thel]
Beaumont, J. Talbot, [F.] Glynn, E[thel] Salisbury,
A. Bliss. <u>L & MGR</u> Augustus Harris; <u>Sm</u> Arthur P.
Collins; <u>A act mgr</u> Neil Forsyth; <u>Mus & Cond</u> James M.
Glover; <u>Sc</u> Robert Caney, Schweitzer, Joseph Harker;
<u>Cost</u> Worth, Amelie Bosch & Co., Russell & Allen, Deb-
enham & Freebody, Miss Collier, Morris Angel & Son;
<u>Pq</u> William Clarkson; <u>Mach</u> E.A. Taylor; <u>Asm</u> Napier
Barry; <u>Pd</u> Augustus Harris. *REV: Ath 28/9/95 p427-8;
E 21/9/95 p11; Sk 25/9/95 p464, 466, 509-13, 25/12/
95 p440-1; SR 5/10/95 p438-9; St 26/9/95 p11-2, 26/
12/95 p11; Th 1/10/95 p221-4; Ti 20/9/95 p8; TW95
p301-2.*

95.218 *ROMEO AND JULIET* (T,5a) William Shakespeare.
LYCEUM 21/9/95-21/12/95. 79 perf [mat only 4/12,
11/12, 18/12, 21/12].** <u>Prince Escalus</u> Joseph Carne;
<u>Paris</u> Arthur Grenville; <u>Montague</u> Alfred Brydone/Syd-
ney Lawrence; <u>Capulet</u> George Warde; <u>Romeo</u> Johnston

Forbes-Robertson; <u>Mercutio</u> [Charles F.] Coghlan; <u>Ben-</u>
<u>volio</u> Frank Gillmore; <u>Tybalt</u> Will Dennis; <u>Friar Lau-</u>
<u>rence</u> Nutcombe Gould; <u>Friar John</u> Charles E. Senior;
<u>Balthazar</u> T.P. Williamson; <u>Sampson</u> Lennox Pawle/Guy
Coxon; <u>Gregory</u> George Canninge; <u>Peter</u> John Willes;
<u>Abraham</u> Charles Lloyd; <u>Apothecary</u> Ian Robertson. <u>Lady</u>
<u>Montague</u> M. Faber; <u>Lady Capulet</u> Mrs Edward Saker;
<u>Juliet</u> Mrs Patrick Campbell; <u>Nurse</u> Dolores Drummond.
<u>L</u> Henry Irving; <u>Mgr</u> Johnston Forbes-Robertson, Fred-
erick Harrison; <u>Sc</u> Hawes Craven, William Harford, T.
E. Ryan, Joseph Harker; <u>Cost</u> L. & H. Nathan, Mrs
Mason, <u>Mus</u> Edward Solomon; <u>Cond</u> Carl Armbruster; <u>Ch</u>
Espinosa; <u>Pq</u> Fox; <u>Props</u> [H.] Skelly; <u>Assistant Bm</u>
Horace Watson; <u>Sm</u> Ian Robertson; <u>Asm</u> George Riddell;
<u>Bom</u> Joseph Hurst. *REV: Ath 28/9/95 p427; E 28/9/95*
p11; Sk 25/9/95 p464-5, 498, 2/10/95 p566, 569, 16/10/
95 p631, 633, 639, 656-7; SR 28/9/95 p409-10; St 26/
9/95 p12; Th 1/10/95 p220-1; Ti 23/9/95 p5; TW95 p284-
95, 295-301.

95.219 *HARMONY* (DD,1a) H.A. Jones. ROYALTY 25/9/95-
5/12/95. 62 perf. 1st perfd Grand, Leeds 13/8/79 [as
Harmony Restored]. <u>Michael Kinsman</u> Mark Kinghorne;
<u>Frank Seaton</u> Arthur Armstrong; <u>Muggins</u> Charles Troode.
<u>Jenny</u> Ettie Williams. <u>L & MGR</u> Arthur Bourchier; <u>Pp</u>
Kate Santley; <u>Bom</u> W.E. Blakeley; <u>Cond</u> Albert Fox; <u>Bm</u>
T. Stevens; <u>Sm</u> Fred W. Permain; <u>Act mgr</u> Arthur Bertram. *REV: E 28/9/95 p8; Sk 2/10/95 p523; St 3/10/95*
p10.

95.220 *HER ADVOCATE* (P,3a) Walter Frith. DUKE OF
YORK'S [TRAFALGAR]. 26/9/95-30/11/95. 65 perf [w/S
mat exc 28/9, 5/10, 12/10; add mat 27/11].* <u>George</u>
<u>Abinger, Q.C.</u> Charles Cartwright; <u>Douglas Ferraby</u>
Oswald Yorke; <u>John Melcombe</u> [Arthur?] Holmes-Gore;
<u>Michael Dennis</u> J.H. Barnes/Forbes Dawson; <u>Dr Marshall</u>
C.W. Somerset; <u>Welsby</u> Cecil Ramsey; <u>Sgt. Black</u> Willie
Young; <u>Hon Mr Justice Vesey</u> Frederick Volpé/Charles
Karston; <u>Flack</u> Alfred Phillips; <u>Marker</u> D[ouglas] Nor-
man; <u>Mr Bodmin</u> S[pencer?] Trevor; <u>Mr Maclean</u> A.H.
Lyons; <u>Mr Blackstone, Q.C.</u> Lyston Lyle; <u>High Sheriff</u>
R. Vaughan; <u>Chaplain</u> P.J. Hillier; <u>Judge's Marshall</u>
F.W. Bedells; <u>Foreman of the Jury</u> A. Collins. <u>Mrs</u>
<u>Field</u> Gertrude Kingston; <u>Mrs Melcombe</u> Henrietta Wat-

son; <u>Blanche Ferraby</u> Lena Ashwell; <u>Female Warder</u>
[Minnie] Major.<u>L & MGR</u> Charles Cartwright, Henry Dana;
<u>Sc</u> Walter Johnstone, Bruce Smith; <u>Mus dir</u> Edward
Jones; <u>Cost</u> Mme [Mathilde] Marie, Nichols & Co.,
Morris Angel; <u>Furn</u> Oetzmann; <u>Lime</u> Digby; <u>Pq</u> William
Clarkson; <u>Sm</u> Standley Wade; <u>Act mgr</u> James M. Mathews.
REV: Ath 5/10/95 p462; E 28/10/95 p11; Sk 2/10/95
p524-5; SR 5/10/95 p439-40; St 3/10/95 p10, 21/11/95
p12; Th 1/11/95 p286-8; Ti 27/9/95 p3; TW95 p303-8.
<u>Comment</u>: A "Prologue" was added later, with the
following cast: <u>Hon Frank Calverley</u> H[enry?] Stanford; <u>Finch</u> T.P. Haynes. <u>Mrs Field</u> Gertrude Kingston;
<u>Eaton</u> Marion Lind.

95.220B *AN ARTIST'S MODEL* (MC,2a) Owen Hall (lib) &
Harry Greenbank (lyr) & Sidney Jones (mus). DALY'S
28/9/95-28/3/96. 178 perf [w/S mat exc 28/9, 25/1,
1/2, 8/2, 15/2; np 25/12].** <u>Rudolph Blair</u> C. Hayden Coffin; <u>Sir George St. Alban</u> Eric Lewis/E.W. Gar-
diner/Frank Walsh/Charles Ryley; <u>Earl of Thamesmead</u>
Lawrance d'Orsay/Rudge Harding; <u>Algernon St. Alban</u>
J. Farren Soutar/A[lfred] C. Seymour; <u>Carbonnet</u> Maurice Farkoa; <u>Apthorpe</u> Gilbert Porteous/Will Bishop;
<u>Maddox</u> Sydney Ellison/Conway Dixon; <u>Hatfield</u> S. Mor-
dy; <u>James Cripps</u> Fred Wright, jr/Leedham Bantock;
<u>Smoggins</u> William Blakeley/Walter Groves/T.P. Haynes/
Harry Monkhouse. <u>Adele</u> Marie Tempest; <u>Mme Amelie</u>
Lydia Thompson/Juliette Nesville/Sybil Grey; <u>Lady</u>
<u>Barbara Cripps</u> Ethel Hope/Mrs Edmund Phelps; <u>Lucien</u>
Nina Cadiz; <u>Jessie</u> Alice Davies; <u>Rose</u> Kate Cannon;
<u>Helen</u> K. Lucille Foote; <u>Laura</u> Nellie Gregory; <u>Lucille</u>
Lydia Flopp; <u>Claire</u> Mary Collette; <u>Mathilde</u> Ethel
Neild/Madge Rossell/Margaret Fraser; <u>Lena</u> Lettice
Fairfax; <u>Geraldine</u> Hetty Hamer; <u>Amy Cripps</u> Louie
Pounds/Laura Kearney; <u>Maud Cripps</u> Violet Lloyd; <u>Lily</u>
Mimi St. Cyr; <u>Daisy Vane</u> Letty Lind. <u>Comment</u>:"2nd
edition" of item 95.21.

95.221 *THE BIRTHPLACE OF PODGERS* (F,1a) John Hollingshead. TOOLE'S 28/9/95. 1 perf.** <u>Tom Cranky</u> J.L.
Toole.

95.222 *THE WRONG ADDRESS* (Duol). DUKE OF YORK'S [TRA-
FALGAR] 5/10/95-14/11/95. 35 perf.* <u>Hon John Bramp-</u>

ton Oswald Yorke. Mrs Alfred Franklin Henrietta Watson. L & MGR Charles Cartwright, Henry Dana; Mus dir Edward Jones; Sm Standley Wade; Act mgr James M. Mathews.*REV: E 12/10/95 p8; Sk 16/10/95 p681.*

95.223 *POOR MR POTTON* (F,3a) Clarence Hamlyn & H.M. Paull. VAUDEVILLE 10/10/95-2/12/95. 58 perf [w/W, S mat exc 16/10, 23/10].* Willoughby Potton Weedon Grossmith; Dick Harrowby Wilfred Draycott; Prof Schmidt John Beauchamp; Tom Dashwood Tom Terriss; Mr Dawson Frederick Volpé; Mr Batt Sydney Warden; Mr Kidby F. Saker. Mrs Dashwood Gladys Homfrey; Mrs Potton Florence Haydon; Catherine Dashwood May Palfrey/K[ate] Sejeantson; Pauline Dashwood Annie Chippendale; Barford A. Dale; Annie Alice Beet. L Weedon Grossmith; Bm A.F. Henderson; Mus dir & Mus C.J. Hargitt; Sc T.W. Hall. *REV: E 12/10/95 p10; Sk 16/10/95 p681, 6/11/95 p72-5; SR 19/10/95 p504-5; St 17/10/95 p12; Th 1/11/95 p290-1; Ti 11/10/95 p3; TW95 p308-12.*

95.224 *THE BURGLAR AND THE JUDGE* (F,1a) F.C. Phillips & Charles H.E. Brookfield. VAUDEVILLE 10/10/95-12/11/95. 29 perf.** Justice Gyves Tom Hesslewood; Parkhurst Sydney Warden; Joe Lawrence Irving. L, Bm, Mus dir & Mus as for 95.223. *REV: E 12/10/95 p10.*

95.225 *TANNHAUSER* (O[3a]) Richard Wagner. COVENT GARDEN 12/10/95, 19/10, 23/10, 26/10(m), 1/11, 5/11, 9/11/95. 7 perf.** Tannhauser E. Charles Hedmont; Wolfram von Echinbach David Bispham/Winfred Goff; Walther von der Vogelweide Reginald Brophy; Biterolf William Llewelyn; Heinrich Robert Eadie; Reinmar von Zwetter Whitney Tew; Hermann Alex Bevan. Elisabeth Alice Esty/Margaret MacIntyre/Marie Duma; Young Shepherd Clare Addison; Venus L. Recoschewitz/Rose Olitzka; Pages [Isa?] McCusker, Russell, Gray, Shortland. L & MGR Augustus Harris; Cond Wilhelm Feld; A act mgr Neil Forsyth. *REV: Ath 19/10/95 p541, 26/10/95 p576; E 19/10/95 p11, 26/10/95 p11; Sk 16/10/95 p636; SR 19/10/95 p502-3; St 17/10/95 p12, 24/10/95 p12; Ti 14/10/95 p10.*

95.226 *LOHENGRIN* (O[3a]) Richard Wagner. COVENT GARDEN 14/10/95, 18/10, 31/10, 7/11/95. 4 perf.** Lohen-

grin E. Charles Hedmont/Edwin Wareham; <u>Henry I</u> Franklin Clive/Alex Bevan; <u>Frederick Telramund</u> Winfred
Goff; <u>Herald</u> Wilson Sheffield. <u>Ortrud</u> Rose Olitzka/L.
Recoschwitz; <u>Elsa of Brabant</u> Alice Esty/Susan Strong;
<u>Gottfried</u> Clare Rothwell; <u>Pages</u> Russell, [Isa?] McCus-
ker, Gray, Clare Addison. L & MGR, <u>Cond</u>, A act mgr as
for 95.225. *REV: Ath 19/10/95 p541, 26/10/95 p576, 9/
11/95 p652; E 19/10/95 p11, 2/11/95 p15; SR 19/10/95
p502-3; St 17/10/95 p12, 24/10/95 p12; Ti 16/10/95
p4, 21/10/95 p12.*

95.227 *A BREEZY MORNING* (Duol) Eden Phillpotts. DALY'S
14/10/95-26/10/95. 12 perf.** <u>Bruce Goldie</u> Fred Upton.
<u>Mary Goldie</u> Miriam Clements. L & MGR Augustin Daly.

95.228 *A LION'S HEART* (Melo,Prol,5a) Arthur Shirley
& Benjamin Landeck. PRINCESS'S 14/10/95-19/10/95. 6
perf. 1st perfd Parkhurst 25/7/92. <u>Pierre Rizardo</u>
Charles Glenney; <u>Gaspard Dobre</u> William H. Day; <u>Timothy</u>
<u>Puggs</u> Leslie Thompson; <u>Ring Master</u> Charles Baldwin;
<u>Col. Robert de Villefort</u> E[dward] Rochelle; <u>Dick</u>
<u>Lorimore</u> George H. Harker; <u>Jack Bealby</u> Maitland Mar-
ler; <u>Dobson</u> Frank Harding; <u>Daddy Mason</u> George Yates;
<u>Cpt. Gavarnie</u> A[lfred] J. Byde; <u>Jean Loraine</u> George
Claremont; <u>Charlot</u> Charles Baldwin; <u>Pitou</u> Leslie
Thompson. <u>Louise/Marion Lorimore</u> Beaumont Collins;
<u>Gilbert</u> Josephine Woodin; <u>Bessie Lorimore</u> Fannie Sel-
by; <u>Sister Gertrude</u> Harriet Clifton; <u>Mme Le Coeminant</u>
Loveridge; <u>Louise</u> Alice Vitu. *REV: E 19/10/95 p8; Sk
23/10/95 p729; St 17/10/95 p12-3.*

95.229 *FAUST* (O[5a]) Charles Gounod. COVENT GARDEN
15/10/95, 19/10(m), 4/11/95. 3 perf.** <u>Faust</u> Philip
Brozel; <u>Mephistopheles</u> Charles Manners/Alex Bevan;
<u>Wagner</u> Arthur Welton; <u>Valentine</u> Winfred Goff. <u>Siebel</u>
Rose Olitzka; <u>Martha</u> Kate Lee; <u>Marguerite</u> Fanny Moody/
Alice Esty. L & MGR Augustus Harris; <u>Cond</u> Howard
Glover. *REV: Ath 19/10/95 p541; E 19/10/95 p11; St
17/10/95 p12.*

95.230 *THE BENEFIT OF THE DOUBT* (C,3a) A.W. Pinero.
COMEDY 16/10/95-27/12/95. 74 perf [w/S mat; add mat
6/11, 13/11, 20/11, 27/11; np 23-25/12].* <u>Claude</u>
<u>Emptage</u> Aubrey Fitzgerald; <u>Sir Fletcher Portwood, M.P.</u>

Cyril Maude; <u>Right Rev Antony Cloys, D.D., Bishop of</u>
<u>St. Olpherts</u> Ernest Cosham; <u>Alexander Fraser</u> J.G. Gra-
ham; <u>John Allingham</u> Leonard Boyne; <u>Denzil Shafto</u> J.W.
Pigott; <u>Peter Elphick</u> Stuart Champion; <u>Horton</u> Mules
Brown; <u>Quaife</u> John Byron. <u>Mrs Emptage</u> Henrietta Lind-
ley; <u>Justina Emptage</u> Esmé Beringer; <u>Theophila Fraser</u>
Winifred Emery; <u>Mrs Cloys</u> Rose Leclercq; <u>Olive Alling-</u>
<u>ham</u> Lily Hanbury; <u>Mrs Quinton Twelves</u> Eva Williams.
<u>L & MGR</u> J.W. Comyns Carr; <u>Bom</u> Scarisbrick; <u>Sc</u> Walter
Johnstone, Walter Hann; <u>Cost</u> Mrs Nettleship, Louie
Ellis, Mme Vero; <u>Furn</u> Hampton & Sons, E[mile] Godfrey;
<u>Pq</u> William Clarkson; <u>Sm</u> Edward Hastings; <u>Bm</u> Silvanus
Dauncey; <u>Mus dir</u> Alfred J. Caldicott. *REV: Ath 19/10/*
95 p542; E 19/10/95 p11; Sk 23/10/95 p737; St 24/10/
95 p12-3; SR 19/10/95 p503-4, 7/12/95 p761; Th 1/11/
95 p283-6; Ti 17/10/95 p6; TW95 p313-21; TW96 p73-7.

95.231 *THE VALKYRIE* [*DIE WALKURE*] (O[3a]) Richard
Wagner. COVENT GARDEN 16/10/95, 21/10, 24/10, 28/10,
2/11(m), 9/11/95(m). 6 perf.** <u>Siegmund</u> E. Charles
Hedmont/Edwin Wareham; <u>Wotan</u> David Bispham; <u>Hunding</u>
Alex Bevan. <u>Fricka</u> Rose Olitzka/L. Recoschewitz;
<u>Sieglinde</u> Susan Strong; <u>Brunnhilde</u> Lilian Tree; <u>The</u>
<u>Valkyries</u> Russell, [Clarice?] Sinico, Gray, Trefelyn,
[Kate] Lee, [Clare] Addison, [Isa?] McCusker, Rose
Olitzka. <u>L & MGR</u> Augustus Harris; <u>Cond</u> George Hen-
schel; <u>A act mgr</u> Neil Forsyth. *REV: E 19/10/95 p11;*
Sk 23/10/95 p729, 30/10/95 p4; SR 19/10/95 p502-3; St
24/10/95 p12; Ti 17/10/95 p6; Ath 19/10/95 p541.

95.232 *CARMEN* (O[4a]) George Bizet. COVENT GARDEN 17/
10/95, 22/10, 26/10/95. 3 perf.** <u>Don José</u> Philip
Brozel; <u>Escamillo</u> Winfred Goff; <u>Dancairo</u> Wilson Sheffield; <u>Remendado</u> Wilfred Esmond; <u>Zuniga</u> William Llewelyn; <u>Morales</u> Walter Harvey. <u>Michaela</u> Alice Esty;
<u>Carmen</u> Agnes Janson; <u>Frasquita</u> Clare Addison; <u>Merce-</u>
<u>des</u> Kate Lee. <u>L & MGR</u> Augustus Harris; <u>Cond</u> Wilhelm
Feld. *REV: Ath 26/10/95 p576; E 19/10/95 p11; Sk 30/*
10/95 p4; St 24/10/95 p12; Ti 21/10/95 p12.

95.233 *THE MERCHANT OF VENICE* (5a) William Shakespeare.
GAIETY 17/10/95 mat perf.** <u>Duke of Venice</u> Henry
Loraine; <u>Antonio</u> J.A. Rosier; <u>Bassanio</u> Frank Gillmore;
<u>Shylock</u> Charles Pond; <u>Salarino</u> Edward Ferris; <u>Gratiano</u>

Philip Cunningham; <u>Lorenzo</u> Arthur Grenville; <u>Launcelot</u> <u>Gobbo</u> J[ohn] Willes; <u>Old Gobbo</u> William Wyes; <u>Tubal</u> A[lfred?] Phillips; <u>Balthazar</u> J[ohn] Byron; <u>Stefano</u> James Anning; <u>Leonardo</u> Mules Brown; <u>Singer</u> Cassidy; <u>Portia</u> Ettie Williams; <u>Nerissa</u> Ella Tarrant; <u>Jessica</u> Mona K. Oram; <u>Singer</u> Emmie Law. <u>L & MGR</u> George Edwardes; <u>Dir</u> Edward Hastings; <u>Mus</u> Sir Henry Bishop; <u>Harpist</u> Stirling Jones; <u>Act mgr</u> E[dward] Marshall; <u>Cond</u> Alfred J. Caldicott. *REV: E 19/10/95 p11; Sk 23/ 10/95 p729; St 24/10/95 p13.*

95.234 *THE RISE OF DICK HALWARD* (P,3a) Jerome K. Jerome. GARRICK 19/10/95-9/11/95. 24 perf [w/S mat exc 19/10; add mat 30/10, 4/11].* <u>Dr Halward</u> F.H. Tyler; <u>Dick Halward</u> E.S. Willard; <u>Dan Graham</u> J.H. Barnes; <u>Reggie Philbrick</u> Henry V. Esmond; <u>Mr Carruthers</u> Harry Cane; <u>Valentine Carvalho</u> Bassett Roe; <u>Henry Duve</u> W.T. Lovell. <u>Mrs Carruthers</u> Fanny Coleman; <u>Madge</u> Marion Terry; <u>Enid Elphick</u> Annie Hughes; <u>Pamela</u> Winifred Fraser; <u>Servant</u> Violet Armbruster. <u>L</u> John Hare; <u>Mgr</u> E.S. Willard; <u>Bm</u> W.H. Griffiths; <u>Bom</u> E. Candler; <u>Cond</u> Haydn Waud. *REV: Ath 26/10/95 p577; E 26/10/95 p10; Sk 23/10/95 p737; St 24/10/95 p13; Th 1/11/95 p288-90; Ti 21/10/95 p12; TW95 p321-8.*

95.235 *THE HOME SECRETARY* (P,4a) R.C. Carton. SHAFTESBURY 21/10/95-13/11/95. 21 perf [mat only 13/11].** <u>Right Hon Duncan Trendel</u> Fred Terry; <u>Sir James Haylett</u> Henry Kemble; <u>Lord Blayver</u> F. Hamilton Knight; <u>Frank Trendel</u> Sydney Brough; <u>Mr Thorpe-Didsbury</u> E.J. Malyon; <u>Rixon</u> H. Deane; <u>Morris Lecaile</u> Lewis Waller; <u>Cpt. Chesnal</u> Charles H.E. Brookfield. <u>Rhoda</u> Julia Neilson; <u>Lady Clotilda Bramerton</u> Mrs Arthur Ayers; <u>Esme Bramerton</u> Maude Millett; <u>Mrs Thorpe-Didsbury</u> Lottie Venne/ Christine Mayne. <u>PP</u> John Lancaster; <u>L & Mgr</u> Lewis Waller, H.H. Morell; <u>Sm</u> E.J. Malyon; <u>Cond</u> de Tender; <u>Sec</u> Charles Meyrick. *REV: E 26/10/95 p10; Sk 30/10/ 95 p4; St 24/10/95 p13; Ti 22/10/95 p3.*

95.236 *THE FLYING DUTCHMAN* [*DER FLIEGENDE HOLLANDER*] Richard Wagner. COVENT GARDEN 25/10/95, 29/10/95. 2 perf.** <u>Van der Decken</u> [W.] Ludwig; <u>Erick</u> Dudley Buck; <u>Daland</u> William Llewelyn; <u>Helmsman</u> Reginald Brophy. <u>Senta</u> Marie Duma; <u>Mary</u> Kate Lee. <u>L & MGR</u>

Augustus Harris; Cond Wilhelm Feld. *REV: Ath 2/11/95*
p615; E 2/11/95 p15; Sk 23/10/95 p729, 30/10/95 p4;
St 31/10/95 p12; Ti 26/10/95 p10.

95.237 *THE BRIC-A-BRAC WILL* (CO,3a) S.J. Adair Fitz-
gerald (lib) & Hugh Moss (lib) & Emilio Pizzi (mus).
LYRIC 28/10/95-28/12/95. 62 perf [w/S mat exc 14/12;
add mat 26/12; np 25/12].* Duke Erico Lantazaro
Charles Conyers; Antonio Frank Wyatt; Paolo Harrison
Brockbank; Doge of Venice J.J. Dallas; Barnaba E.W.
Royce; Roberto Frank H. Celli; Beppo Stanley Patter-
son; Mudillo Watty Brunton, jr; Watchman Horn Conyers;
Extras H[enry] E. Garrod, E. Shale, R. Beresford, T.
France, G. Wells, J.W. Birtley, P.H. Kingsbury, T.T.
Moss, C. Flynn, T. Carling, T.J. Montelli, A. Romanes,
P[ercy?] Percival, G. Phillips, E. Rosoman, J. Rix,
H[arry] Dorien, R. Davies, G. Scholfield, H. Trevor.
Sylvia Kate Drew/Florence St. John; Chiara Susie
Vaughan; Lisette Fanny Marriott; Dancers Mabel Tilson,
Ada Wilkinson, Phyllis Desmond, Rose Doris, Kate
Doris, Jessie Collier, Kate Wyndham, Cassie King,
Alice Tyler, Lillie Wilkinson, Amy Ward, Connie Des-
mond; Extras Louise Forrester, Nancie Ellison, Nellie
Yorke, Winifred Davies, Ada Lennox, Beatrice Bailey,
Edith Merton, Marie Romanes, Ada Allen, Lillian Stead,
Honorine Scholfield, Agnes Matz, Gertrude Lonsdale,
Heloise Osland, Bessie Allayne, Ada Maxwell, Cordelia
Knight, Alice Ancliffe, Amy Douglas, Emily Greene,
Phoebe Cohen, Mabel Grey, Agnez Verney, Madeleine da
Costa. PP Henry J. Leslie; L Horace Sedger; Mgr Er-
nest Oswald; Bom Walter Hamilton; Dir Hugh Moss; Ch
Kate Paradise; Sc W.T. Hemsley, Bruce Smith; Mus dir
Arthur E. Godfrey; Cost dgn Karl; Cost L. & H. Nathan,
Alias, Harrisons; Pq William Clarkson; Props Shelley
& Sons, J.P. Killingback; Mach S. Trewen; Elect T.J.
Digby; Sm Tom Mowbray; Asm Horn Conyers; A act mgr
John B. Helm. *REV: E 2/11/95 p8; Sk 4/12/95 p288, 25/*
12/95 p440; St 31/10/95 p12, 12/12/95 p13; Ti 29/10/
95 p8.

95.238 *THE BOHEMIAN GIRL* (O[3a]) Michael Balfe. COVENT
GARDEN 30/10/95, 2/11/95. 2 perf.** Count Franklin
Clive; Florestein Wilfred Esmond; Thaddeus Reginald
Brophy; Devilshoof P. Hayes. Gipsy Queen Rose Olitzka;

<u>Arline</u> Margaret Ormerod. <u>L & MGR</u> Augustus Harris; <u>Cond</u>
Howard Glover. *REV: Ath 2/11/95 p615; E 2/11/95 p15;*
St 7/11/95 p12; Ti 2/11/95 p6, 4/11/95 p8. <u>Comment</u>:
Apparently only acts I & II were perfd.

95.239 *CAVALLERIA RUSTICANA* (O[1a]) Pietro Mascagni.
COVENT GARDEN 30/10/95, 8/11/95. 2 perf.** <u>Turiddu</u>
Edwin Wareham/Reginald Brophy; <u>Alfio</u> Wilson Sheffield.
<u>Santuzza</u> Lillian Tree; <u>Lola</u> [Isa?] McCusker/Margaret
Ormerod; <u>Lucia</u> Kate Lee. <u>L & MGR</u>, <u>Cond</u> as for 95.238.
REV: Ath 2/11/95 p615; E 2/11/95 p15, 9/11/95 p8; St
7/11/95 p12, 14/11/95 p12.

95.240 *TRILBY* (P,4a) Paul M. Potter [adpt of George
du Maurier's novel]. HAYMARKET 30/10/95-27/5/96 [w/
W, S mat exc 19/2/96, 13/5, 20/5, 27/5/96; add mat
10/2/96; np 25/12/95, 5/2/96, 19/2, 30/3-3/4/96];
1-3/6/96, 8-10/6, 15-17/6, 22-24/6, 29/6-1/7, 6-8/7
[w/W mat], 13-14/7/96. 254 perf. 1st perfd Theatre
Royal, Manchester 7/9/95. <u>Svengali</u> H. Beerbohm Tree;
<u>Talbot Wynne</u> Edmund Maurice/Percy Brough/Frank Mc-
Vicars; <u>Alexander McAlister</u> Lionel Brough; <u>William</u>
<u>Bagot</u> Patrick Evans/Henry V. Esmond; <u>Gecko</u> C.H. Hal-
lard; <u>Zouzou</u> Herbert Ross; <u>Dodor</u> Gerald du Maurier;
<u>Oliver</u> Berte Thomas; <u>Lorimer</u> William Gayer MacKay;
<u>Rev Thomas Bagot</u> Charles Allan; <u>Manager Kaw</u> E. Holman
Clark/F. Percival Stevens. <u>Trilby O'Ferrall</u> Dorothea
Baird; <u>Mrs Bagot</u> Frances Ivor; <u>Mme Vinard</u> Rosina
Filippi/Adrienne Dairolles; <u>Angele</u> Cicely Turner;
<u>Honorine</u> Agnes Russell; <u>Mimi</u> Olive Owen; <u>Desiree</u> Helen
Graeme; <u>Musette</u> Sadie Wigley; <u>Hortense</u> Madge Langton;
<u>Ernestine</u> Sybil Erlyn. <u>L & MGR & DIR</u> H.B. Tree; <u>Bom</u>
W.H. Leverton; <u>Ch</u> John d'Auban; <u>Sm</u> Shelton; <u>Mus dir</u>
Raymond Roze; <u>Eng</u> E. Wingfield Bowles; <u>Cost</u> L. & H.
Nathan; <u>Furn</u> Frank Giles; <u>Pq</u> William Clarkson; <u>Bm</u>
Fitzroy Gardner; <u>Asm</u> A[lfred] Wigley. *REV: E 2/11/95*
p11; Sk 11/9/95 p356, 25/9/95 p463, 9/10/95 p587, 30/
10/95 p11-2, 49-50, 6/11/95 p64, 105-6, 25/12/95 supp
p1-8; SR 9/11/95 p617-8; St 7/11/95 p12; Th 1/12/95
p344-5; Ti 31/10/95 p6; TW95 p328-35.

95.241 *THE LORD MAYOR* ("What You Will,"3a) W.E. Bradley, Harry Paulton & Edward A. Paulton. STRAND 1/11/
95-5/11/95. 5 perf [w/mat 2/11].* <u>Sir Martin Marlow</u>

Harry Paulton; <u>Martin Marlow, jr</u> W. Scott Buist; <u>Hon
Richard Gratwick</u> Harold Child; <u>Bristol</u> James A. Welch;
<u>Prof Grimweed</u> Laurence Irving; <u>Alderman Robbins</u> Clin-
ton Baddeley; <u>Alderman Harris</u> E[dward] A. Coventry;
<u>Henry H. Morgan</u> Newman Maurice; <u>Daniel B. Jackson</u>
Stanley Betjemann; <u>Inspector Handford</u> F.J. Waller;
<u>Gebel</u> C. Leighton; <u>Turner</u> E. Wilson; <u>Griffin</u> C. Mor-
dan. <u>Sabina Marlow</u> Gladys Evelyn; <u>Clarissa Marlow</u>
Agnes Paulton; <u>Lady Muriel Gratwick</u> Amy Elstob; <u>Cora</u>
Alice de Winton. L Paulton Comedies Co. Ltd.; <u>Mgr</u>
Harry Paulton; <u>Bm</u> J.B. Jackson; <u>Sc</u> E.G. Banks; <u>Furn</u>
W.E. Hardy & Co.; <u>Pq</u> William Clarkson; <u>Act mgr</u> W.H.
Clinton Baddeley. *REV: Ath 9/11/95 p653; E 9/11/95
p10; Sk 20/11/95 p172; St 7/11/95 p13; Th 1/12/95
p351-2; Ti 2/11/95 p6; TW95 p335-6.*

95.242 *MRS PONDERBURY'S PAST* (FC,3a) F.C. Burnand
[adpt of Ernest Blum & Raoul Toché, *Madame Mongodin*].
AVENUE 2/11/95-1/2/96. 90 perf [w/S mat exc 2/11,
9/11; add mat 26/12/95, 22/1/96; np 23-25/12/95].*
<u>Matthew Ponderbury</u> Charles H. Hawtrey; <u>Mervin Thorp</u>
Cosmo Stuart; <u>John Rumford</u> J.L. Mackay; <u>Hyacinth
Grayling</u> Willis Searle; <u>Peter</u> William F. Hawtrey.
<u>Mrs Ponderbury</u> Alma Stanley/Olliffe; <u>Ethel Peniston</u>
Ada Mallon; <u>Susan</u> Evelyn Harrison; <u>Countess de Moje-
ski</u> Lottie Venne. L & MGR William Greet; <u>Dir</u> Charles
H. Hawtrey; <u>Mus</u> Lionel Monckton; <u>Lyr</u> Harry Greenbank;
<u>Cond</u> Ernest Bucalossi; <u>Sm</u> Frederick Glover; <u>Bm</u> C.
Liddon Clark. *REV: Ath 9/11/95 p653; E 9/11/95 p10;
Sk 11/12/95 p351-4; SR 7/12/95 p760-1; St 7/11/95
p13; Th 1/12/95 p345-6; Ti 4/11/95 p10; TW95 p336-7;
TW96 p72-3.*

95.243 *THE SQUIRE OF DAMES* (C,4a) R.C. Carton [adpt
of Alexandre Dumas, *fils, L'Ami des Femmes*]. CRITER-
ION 5/11/95-21/3/96. 142 perf [w/W, S mat 20/11-21/
12; w/S mat 28/12/95-21/3/96; add mat 26/12/95, 29/1/
96; np 23-25/12/95, 5/2/96].*　<u>Mr Kilroy</u> Charles
Wyndham; <u>Col. Dennant</u> Frank Fenton; <u>Sir Douglas Thor-
burn</u> Bernard Gould; <u>Lord Eustace Chetland</u> Herman de
Lange; <u>Prof Dowle, F.R.S.</u> Alfred Bishop; <u>Baines</u>
R[upert] Lister; <u>Servant</u> C[harles] Terric. <u>Mrs Doyle</u>
Charlotte Granville; <u>Elsie</u> Beatrice Ferrar; <u>Zoe Nug-
getson</u> Fay Davis; <u>Adelaide Dennant</u> Mary Moore. L &

MGR Charles Wyndham; Cond Victor Hollander; Cost Paquin, Jay, Mme Eroom; Sm Herman de Lange; Act mgr & Treas E. Harvey. *REV: Ath 9/11/95 p653-4; E 9/11/95 p13; Sk 13/11/95 p119, 161-2; SR 9/11/95 p618; St 7/11/95 p12; Th 1/12/95 p346-8; Ti 6/11/95 p3; TW95 p337-45.*

95.244 *PAGLIACCI* (O[2a]) Ruggiero Leoncavallo. COVENT GARDEN 6/11/95, 8/11/95. 2 perf.** Canio Philip Brozel; Silvio Walter Harvey; Tonio David Bispham; Beppe Reginald Brophy. Nedda Margaret Ormerod. L & MGR Augustus Harris; Cond Wilhelm Feld. *REV: Ath 9/11/95 p652; E 9/11/95 p8; St 14/11/95 p12; Ti 7/11/95 p6.*

95.245 *THE PROFESSOR'S LOVE STORY* (P,3a) J.M. Barrie. GARRICK 6/11/95-7/3/96. 139 perf [w/W, S mat exc 13/11/95, 4/3/96; add mat 14/11/95, 21/11, 26-27/12/95, 16/1/96, 20/1/96; np 9/11/95, 23-25/12; mat only 6-8/11/95].** Prof Goodwillie E.S. Willard; Henders J.H. Barnes; Pete F.H. Tyler; Dr Cosens H[arry] Cane; Sir George Gilding Bassett Roe; Dr Yellowlees Cecil Crofton. Lucy White Annie Hughes; Agnes Goodwillie Mrs George Canninge; Lady Gilding Keith Wakeman; Effie Proctor Mrs H[arry] Cane; Dowager Lady Gilding Nannie Craddock. L John Hare; Mgr E.S. Willard; Bm W.H. Griffiths; Bom E. Candler; Cond Haydn Waud. *REV: E 9/11/95 p13; Sk 11/12/95 p341; St 7/11/95 p12-3.*

95.246 *THE MIKADO; OR, THE TOWN OF TITIPU* (Japanese O,2a) W.S. Gilbert (lib) & Arthur Sullivan (mus). SAVOY 6/11/95-4/3/96. 127 perf [w/S mat; add mat 4/12/95, 11/12, 18/12, 26/12/95, 1/1/96, 8/1, 15/1, 22/1/96; np 25/12/95]. 1st perfd Savoy 14/3/85. Nanki Poo Charles Kenningham; Mikado of Japan Robert Scott-Fishe/Richard Temple; Koko Walter Passmore; Pooh Bah Rutland Barrington; Pish-Tush Jones Hewson. Yum Yum Florence Perry; Pitti Sing Jessie Bond/Laurie Elliston; Peep Bo Emmie Owen; Katisha Rosina Brandram. PP & MGR Richard d'Oyly Carte; Cond Arthur Sullivan; Pd W.S. Gilbert, Arthur Sullivan; Bm J.W. Beckwith; Mus dir Francois Cellier; Dir Charles Harris; Sm W.H. Seymour; Ch John d'Auban; Cost dgn Wilhelm; Cost Mme Leon; Pq William Clarkson. *REV: E 9/11/95 p8; Sk 13/11/95 p119, 8/1/96 p563-6, 15/1/96 p613-20; Ti 7/11/*

95 p8.

95.247 *LIBERTY HALL* (C,4a) R.C. Carton. ST. JAMES'S
7/11/95-21/11/95. 16 perf [w/mat 13/11, 16/11, 20/
11].** <u>Mr Owen</u> George Alexander; <u>William Todman</u> E.M.
Robson; <u>Hon Gerald Harringay</u> E. Allan Aynesworth; <u>Mr
Pedrick</u> Arthur Royston; <u>J. Briginshaw</u> H.H. Vincent;
<u>Robert Binks</u> Master Jones; <u>Luscombe</u> Frank Dyall; <u>Mr
Hickson</u> F. Kinsey Peile. <u>Miss Hickson</u> Winifred Dolan;
<u>Crafer</u> Mouillot; <u>Amy Chilworth</u> Furtado-Clarke; <u>Blanche
Chilworth</u> Evelyn Millard. <u>L & MGR</u> George Alexander;
<u>Bom</u> Arnold; <u>Bm</u> Robert V. Shone; <u>Sm</u> H.H. Vincent; <u>Mus
& Mus dir</u> Walter Slaughter; <u>Furn</u> Frank Giles & Co.;
<u>Cost</u> Mme Savage, Mme Purdue; <u>Pq</u> William Clarkson; <u>Sc</u>
H.P. Hall. *REV: E 9/11/95 p14; SR 16/11/95 p652; St
14/11/95 p12.*

95.248 *THE RIVALS* (C,6a) R.B. Sheridan. COURT 11/11/
95-21/12/95. 42 perf [w/S mat exc 16/11; add mat 4/12].
1st perfd Covent Garden 17/1/1775. <u>Sir Anthony Ab-
solute</u> William Farren; <u>Cpt. Absolute</u> Sydney Brough;
<u>Faulkland</u> Charles Sugden; <u>Bob Acres</u> Arthur Williams;
<u>Sir Lucius O'Trigger</u> Brandon Thomas; <u>Fag</u> H. Nye Chart;
<u>David</u> W. Cheesman; <u>Coachman</u> W.H. Quinton; <u>Servant</u> F.
Lane; <u>Boy</u> Master Chapman. <u>Lydia Languish</u> Nancy Noel;
<u>Julia Melville</u> Violet Raye; <u>Lucy</u> Marie Hudspeth; <u>Mrs
Malaprop</u> Mrs John Wood. <u>MGR</u> Arthur Chudleigh; <u>Sc</u> T.W.
Hall; <u>Pd</u> Henry Neville; <u>Mus dir</u> F. Louis Schneider;
<u>Act mgr</u> Leonard Lillies; <u>Cost</u> Auguste, L. & H. Nathan;
<u>Pq</u> C.H. Fox; <u>Furn</u> Marler & Bennett. *REV: Ath 16/11/95
p689-90; E 16/11/95 p8; Sk 20/11/95 p172, 18/12/95
p401-3; SR 23/11/95 p685; St 14/11/95 p12; Th 1/12/
95 p349-50; Ti 12/11/95 p10; TW95 p346-51.*

95.249 *THE INTERVIEW* (Ca,1a) T.G. Warren. GARRICK
11/11/95-7/3/96. 99 perf [np 23-25/12/95].* <u>Martin
Grange</u> W.T. Lovell. <u>Natalie Morris</u> Keith Wakeman. <u>L</u>
John Hare; <u>Mgr</u> E.S. Willard; <u>Bm</u> W.H. Griffiths; <u>Bom</u>
E. Candler; <u>Cond</u> Haydn Waud. *REV: 16/11/95 p8.*

95.250 *AN OLD GARDEN* (P,1a) Hill Davies. TERRY'S
12/11/95-20/3/96. 116 perf [w/W, S mat 16/11-21/12;
np 23-25/12/95, 10-13/2/96]. 1st perfd Theatre Royal,
Brighton 14/10/95. <u>David Brice</u> W.J. Robertson; <u>Philip</u>

Melville John Buckstone/Osmond Shillingford. Mildred
Sandford Mona K. Oram; Rose Harmer Doris Templeton.
PP Edward Terry; L Frederick Kerr; Bm H.T. Brickwell;
Sm W.J. Robertson; Mus dir T[homas] Smythe. *REV: E*
16/11/95 p8, 22/2/96 p11; St 14/11/95 p13; TW95 p366.

95.251 *MERRIFIELD'S GHOST* (Ca,1a) H.M. Paull. VAUDE-
VILLE 13/11/95-11/1/96; 26/2/96-28/3/96. 77 perf [np
23-25/12/95].* Thomas Merrifield Frederick Volpé;
John Gordon Sydney Warden; Will Gordon Wilfred Dray-
cott/E[dward?] Ferris. Sylvia Merrifield Kate Serjeantson. L Weedon Grossmith; Bm A.F. Henderson; Mus
dir C.J. Hargitt. *REV: E 16/11/95 p8; Sk 20/11/95*
p172; SR 16/11/95 p652; St 21/11/95 p12; TW95 p352-3.

95.252 *A DARK SECRET: A TALE OF THE THAMES VALLEY* (D,
Prol,4a) John Douglass & James Willing, jr [fnd on
Sheridan Le Fanu, "Uncle Silas"]. PRINCESS'S 14/11/
95-24/1/96. c.61 perf. 1st perfd Standard 28/10/86.
Jonas Norton Robert Pateman; James Norton Arthur Wid-
decombe; Stephen E[dward] Rochelle; Cecil Raines G.
Leslie; Arthur Loates Frank Harding; Martin Brooke
George H. Harker; Dicken Hardacre George Yates; Jem
Slim Charles Baldwin/James Cooke; John Thomas Lesly
Thomson/William Aysom; Nat Jack Knifton; Yokel Beck-
ett; Bones Westacott; Wag Harding Wag Harding. May
Joyce Agnes Hewitt; Mme La Fontaine Amy Steinberg;
Nelly Norton Ida Millais; Lady Allcash Alice Vitu/
Ross; Madge Justin Harriett Clifton; Bessie Fanny Sel-
by; Mary Rae Rosenthal; Mrs Webster Ross/Alice Vitu;
Clasper Kate Vitu; A Gitana Kate [E.] Leslie; Extras
Marshall, Ross, Grainger, Powell, [Thea?] Lesbrooke,
Rivers. L & MGR James Crowdy; Sc Cecil E. Hicks, W.T.
Hemsley, J. Johnstone; Elect J.T. Niblett; Pd & Sm
John Douglass; Am Albert Gilmer; Treas Walter Good;
Mus dir Theodore Ward. *REV: E 16/11/95 p11; Sk 20/11/*
95 p172.

95.253 *NIOBE (ALL SMILES)* (C,3a) Harry & Edward A.
Paulton. STRAND 14/11/95-8/2/96. 103 perf [w/W, S mat;
add mat 26-27/12/95, 16/1/96, 23/1, 30/1/96; np 25/
12/95].** Peter Amos Dunn Harry Paulton; Cornelius
Griffin W. Scott Buist/Wilfred Clarke; Philip Innings
Harold Child; Jefferson Tompkins Clinton Baddeley;

Parker G. Sillocks Newman Maurice/T. Lawrence. Niobe
Beatrice Lamb; Helen Griffin Carlotta Zerbini; Made-
line Mifton Kate Connaught; Caroline Dunn Gladys
Evelyn/Angela Mayo; Beatrice Sillocks Ida Warrand/
Ida Heron; Hattie Griffin Agnes Paulton; Mary Winnie
Wood; Fanny B. Marsden. L Paultons Comedies Co. Ltd.;
Mgr Harry Paulton, Wilfred Clarke; Sc E.G. Banks;
Furn W.E. Hardy & Co.; Pq William Clarkson; Bm J.B.
Jackson; Mus dir Claude Fenigstein; Pp J.S. Clarke;
Bom A.E. Barnes. *REV: E 16/11/95 p11, 28/12/95 p7;
St 21/11/95 p12, 2/1/96 p16.*

95.254 *THE MAN IN THE STREET* (P,1a) Louis N. Parker.
STRAND 14/11/95-13/12/95. 26 perf.** Jabez Gover
James A. Welch; Philip Adare Harold Child. Minnie
Adare Agnes Paulton. L, Mgr as for 95.253. *REV: St
21/11/95 p12.*

95.255 *GIDDY GALATEA* (Operatic Trifle,1a) Henry Edlin
(lib) & Edward Jones (mus). DUKE OF YORK'S 15/11/95-
30/11/95. 14 perf.* Phidias Phixum Forbes Dawson;
Pygmalion Potts T.P. Haynes. Galatea Green Minnie
Thurgate; Daphne Potts Annie Dwelley. L & MGR Charles
Cartwright, Henry Dana; Mus dir Edward Jones; Sm
Standley Wade; Act mgr James M. Mathews. *REV: E 23/11/
95 p8; St 21/11/95 p12.*

95.256 *A MUSICAL ENTERTAINMENT.* AVENUE 16/11/95-29/
11/95. 12 perf. The Stavordales. L & MGR William
Greet; Dir Charles H. Hawtrey; Cond Ernest Bucalossi;
Sm Frederick Glover; Bm C. Liddon Clark.

95.257 *NANNIE* (C,2a) T.G. Warren. OPERA COMIQUE 16/11/
95-6/12/95. 20 perf [w/mat 23/11, 30/11].* Matthew
Burge Edward Sass; Sydney Wynne Oscar Adye; David
Geen J.G. Taylor. Nannie Geen Emily Cudmore; Jessie
Geen Emma Gwynne; Rose Dadden Stella Leigh; Eliza
Boon F. Montgomery. MGR Nellie Farren; Sc E.G. Banks;
Cost dgn E. Chasemore, Ida Chasemore; Cost Miss F.
Hadley, Miss A. Unite, Miss Moore, Alias; Pq William
Clarkson, Fox; Mus dir W. Meyer Lutz; Sec McCall
Chambers; Asm Harry Soutar; Bm W.H. Risque. *REV: E
23/11/95 p8; St 21/11/95 p11-2; Ti 18/11/95 p3; TW95
p351.*

95.258 *A MODEL TRILBY; OR, A DAY OR TWO AFTER DU MAURIER* (Bsq MSk,1a) Charles H.E. Brookfield (1ib) & William Yardley (1ib) & W. Meyer Lutz (mus). OPERA COMIQUE 16/11/95-1/2/96. 64 perf [np 24-25/12/95].* Durien Eric Lewis; Svengali Robb Hardwood; Taffy Farren Soutar; The Laird C.P. Little; Little Billee George Antley; Jacko Fred Storey; Thomas Bagot E.H. Kelly; The Stranger E.J. Scott. Zouzou Millie Le Capelaine; Dodor May Romney; Mme Vinard Helen Vicary/ F. Montgomery; Mrs Bagot Mary Stuart; Mimi Eva Hamblin; Musette Greville Moore; Trilby Kate Cutler; Dancers Lilian Hubbard, Nora Neville, Rose Vera, Marie Lovel, Beatrice Dunbar, Marie Beevor, Madge Greet. MGR, Sc, Cost dgn, Cost, Pq, Mus dir, Sec, Asm, Bm as for 95.257; Pd James T. Tanner; Ch Willie Warde. *REV: E 23/11/95 p8; Sk 13/11/95 p130-1, 20/11/95 p172-3, 25/12/95 p451; St 21/11/95 p11-2, 12/12/95 p13; Th 1/12/95 p350-1; Ti 18/11/95 p3; TW95 p351-2.*

95.259 *THE MANXMAN* (P,4a) Wilson Barrett [adpt of Hall Caine's novel]. SHAFTESBURY 18/11/95-30/11/95. 13 perf [w/mat 23/11]. 1st perfd Grand, Leeds 22/8/94. Philip Christian Lewis Waller; Pete Quilliam George W. Cockburn; Caesar Cregeen James Fernandez; Black Tom Henry Kemble; Ross Christian Charles H.E. Brookfield; Sir Edward Brookland F. Hamilton Knight; Mr Farrant F. Percival Stevens; Dr Mylechreest George Hippisley; Kelly Lesly Thomson; Jemmy y Lord H. Deane; Inspector Ballure C[harles] Goodhart. Lady Brookland Mrs Arthur Ayers; Cicely Cornwall Christine Mayne; Nancy Kate Phillips; Bella [Leonie] Norbury; Kate Cregeen Florence West. L & MGR Lewis Waller, H.H. Morell; Pp John Lancaster; Sc Walter Johnstone, [William] Harford, Walter Hann; Sm E.J. Malyon; Mus dir de Tender; Sec Charles Meyrick. *REV: E 23/11/95 p11; Sk 27/11/95 p244; SR 23/11/95 p684-5; St 21/11/95 p12; Th 1/12/95 p348-9; Ti 19/11/95 p5; TW95 p361-4; Ath 23/11/95 p725-6.*

95.260 *DIDO AND AENEAS* (O,3a) Henry Purcell. LYCEUM 20/11/95 mat perf. 1st perfd c.1689-90. Sailor Thomas Thomas. Dido Agnes Nicholls; Belinda Helen Jackson; 2nd Woman Alice M. Toothill; 1st Witch Morfydd Williams; 2nd Witch Jeannie Appleby; Spirit Anna Bergh;

Aeneas Ena Bedford; Sorceress Emlyn Davies. L Henry
Irving; Mgr Johnston Forbes-Robertson, Frederick
Harrison; Bom Joseph Hurst; Cond C. Villiers Stanford;
Pd Richard Temple; Ch B. Soutten; Pq William Clarkson.
REV: Ath 23/11/95 p725; E 23/11/95 p9; Ti 21/11/95 p8.
Comment: Royal College of Music.

95.261 *THE PASSPORT* (P,3a) B.C. Stephenson & William
Yardley [fnd on Col. Savage, *My Official Wife*]. DUKE
OF YORK'S 21/11/95, 26/11/95. 2 mat perf.** George
Greenwood George Giddens. Mrs Darcy Gertrude Kings-
ton. L & MGR Charles Cartwright, Henry Dana.

95.262 *THE MISOGYNIST* (P,1a) George William Godfrey.
ST. JAMES'S 23/11/95-14/12/95. 20 perf [w/mat 30/11].
1st perfd Theatre Royal, Manchester 25/10/95 [as *The
Woman Hater*]. Mr Corquodale George Alexander; Charlie
Denison E. Allan Aynesworth; Royd H.H. Vincent. Kitty
Denison Ellis Jeffreys/Mabel Hackney. L & MGR George
Alexander; Bom Arnold; Bm Robert V. Shone; Sm H.H.
Vincent; Mus dir Walter Slaughter. *REV: E 30/11/95
p11; Sk 27/11/95 p231; SR 30/11/95 p728-9; St 28/11/95
p12; Th 1/1/96 p43; Ti 25/11/95 p10; TW95 p364-6.*

95.263 *THE DIVIDED WAY* (P,3a) Henry V. Esmond. ST.
JAMES'S 23/11/95-14/12/95. 20 perf [w/mat 30/11].
1st perfd Theatre Royal, Manchester 31/10/95. Gen.
Humeden W.H. Vernon; Gaunt Humeden George Alexander;
Jack Humeden E. Allan Aynesworth; Jay Grist Herbert
Waring; Dr MacGrath H.H. Vincent; Mr Swendal E.M.
Robson; Kelly Frank Dyall. Phyllis Humeden Violet
Lyster; Mrs Kelly Mouillot; Lois Evelyn Millard. L &
MGR George Alexander; Bom Arnold; Bm Robert V. Shone;
Sm H.H. Vincent; Mus & Mus dir Walter Slaughter; Sc
H.P. Hall; Pq William Clarkson; Cost Mme Savage, Mme
Purdue; Furn Frank Giles & Co. *REV: Ath 30/11/95 p761;
E 30/11/95 p11; Sk 27/11/95 p248; SR 30/11/95 p728-9;
St 28/11/95 p12; Th 1/1/96 p41-3; Ti 25/11/95 p10;
TW95 p353-61.*

95.264 *AFTER ALL* (Vaud) Frank Desprez (lib) & Alfred
Cellier (mus). SAVOY 23/11/95-4/3/96; 4/4/96-8/8/96.
198 perf [w/mat 9/5/96, 30/5/96; np 25/12/95]. 1st
perfd Opera Comique 16/12/78. Pennyfather C. Herbert

Workman; <u>Selworthy</u> Jones Hewson. <u>Maria</u> Emmie Owen.
<u>PP & MGR</u> Richard d'Oyly Carte; <u>Sm</u> W.H. Seymour; <u>Act</u>
<u>mgr</u> J.W. Beckwith; <u>Mus dir</u> Francois Cellier.

95.265 *THE MISOGYNIST* (P,1a) G.W. Godfrey. DRURY LANE
28/11/95 mat perf.** <u>Mr Corquodale</u> George Alexander;
<u>Charlie Denison</u> E. Allen Aynesworth; <u>Royd</u> H.H. Vin-
cent. <u>Kitty Denison</u> Ellis Jeffreys. <u>L & MGR</u> Augustus
Harris; <u>A act mgr</u> Neil Forsyth; <u>Sm</u> Arthur P. Collins;
<u>Mus dir</u> James M. Glover; <u>Asm</u> Napier Barry.

95.266 *A DANGEROUS RUFFIAN* (F,1a) W.D. Howells. AV-
ENUE 30/11/95–2/1/96. 26 perf [np 23–25/12].* <u>Edward</u>
<u>Roberts</u> William F. Hawtrey; <u>Willis Campbell</u> J.L. Mac-
Kay; <u>Mr Bemis</u> William Wyes; <u>Dr Bemis, jr</u> E. Hatfield.
<u>Mrs Crashaw</u> Evelyn Harrison; <u>Bella</u> [Mary] Clayton;
<u>Mrs Roberts</u> Florence Harrington. <u>L & MGR</u> William
Greet; <u>Dir</u> Charles H. Hawtrey; <u>Cond</u> Ernest Bucalossi;
<u>Sm</u> Frederick Glover; <u>Bm</u> C. Liddon Clark. *REV: E 7/12/*
95 p8; Sk 11/12/95 p328; SR 7/12/95 p761-2; St 5/12/
95 p12; Th 1/1/96 p43-4.

95.267 *THE NEW BOY* (FC,3a) Arthur Law. VAUDEVILLE
3/12/95–11/1/96. 43 perf [w/W, S mat exc 4/12; add
mat 26/12; np 23–25/12].** <u>Archibald Rennick</u> Weedon
Grossmith; <u>Dr Candy</u> John Beauchamp; <u>Theodore de Bri-</u>
<u>zac</u> Sydney Warden; <u>Bullock Major</u> Kenneth Douglas;
<u>Felix Roach</u> J.D. Beveridge/Frederick Volpé; <u>Mr Stub-</u>
<u>ber</u> T.A. Palmer/T[om] Hesslewood. <u>Mrs Rennick</u> Gladys
Homfrey/Helen Kinnaird; <u>Nancy Roach</u> Lena Dene/May
Palfrey/Annie Hill; <u>Susan</u> Alice Beet. <u>L</u> Weedon Grossmith; <u>Bm</u> A.F. Henderson; <u>Sc</u> T.W. Hall; <u>Pq</u> Fox; <u>Sm</u>
G. Robinson; <u>Mus dir</u> C.J. Hargitt. *REV: Sk 11/12/95*
p328; St 5/12/95 p12.

95.268 *MR VERSUS MRS* (DSk) Arthur Bourchier & "Mountjoy" [F.B. Money Coutts?]. ROYALTY 4/12/95; 6–10/12/
95. 5 perf.* <u>Robert Challenger</u> Arthur Bourchier. <u>Hon</u>
<u>Mrs Featherleigh</u> Violet Vanbrugh. <u>L & MGR</u> Arthur
Bourchier; <u>Pp</u> Kate Santley. *REV: Sk 11/12/95 p328;*
St 5/12/95 p12; Th 1/1/96 p44.

95.269 *MADAME* (Absurdity,3a) James T. Tanner. OPERA
COMIQUE 7/12/95–1/2/96. 56 perf [w/S mat exc 7/12; add

mat 26/12; np 24-25/12].* <u>Mr Galleon</u> Eric Lewis;
<u>George Baxter</u> J. Farren Soutar; <u>Denton Jones</u> James G.
Taylor; <u>Cpt. Charles Cameron</u> Oscar Adye; <u>M Vivienne</u>
E.H. Kelly; <u>Charlemagne</u> E.J. Scott; <u>Jorkins</u> Horniman;
<u>Inspector</u> Culverwell. <u>Miss Baxter</u> Kate Tindall; <u>Edith
Galleon</u> F. Montgomery; <u>Mme Vivienne</u> Helen Vicary;
<u>Miss Godolphin</u> Emma Gwynne. <u>L & MGR</u> Nellie Farren;
<u>Sc</u> E.G. Banks; <u>Cost dgn</u> E. Chasemore, Ida Chasemore;
<u>Cost</u> Miss F. Hadley, Miss A. Unite, Miss Moore, Alias;
<u>Pq</u> William Clarkson, Fox; <u>Mus dir</u> W. Meyer Lutz; <u>Sec</u>
McCall Chambers; <u>Asm</u> Harry Soutar; <u>Bm</u> W.H. Risque.
*REV: E 14/12/95 p8; Sk 18/12/95 p253; St 12/12/95 p12-
3; Th 1/1/96 p44-5; Ti 9/12/95 p7; TW95 p377.*

95.270 *KITTY CLIVE (ACTRESS)* (C,1a) F. Frankfort
Moore. ROYALTY 11/12/95-21/3/96; 6/5/96-16/5/96; 8/6/
96-15/6/96; 4/7/96-31/7/96. 125 perf [np 23-25/12/95,
5/2/96].* <u>Jack Bates</u> Henry Vibart; <u>Landlord</u> Fred W.
Permain; <u>Kitty Clive</u> Irene Vanbrugh. <u>L & MGR</u> Arthur
Bourchier; <u>Pp</u> Kate Santley; <u>Cond</u> Albert Fox; <u>Bom</u> W.E.
Blakeley; <u>Bm</u> T. Stevens; <u>Sm</u> Fred W. Permain; <u>Act mgr</u>
Arthur Bertram. *REV: Ath 14/12/95 p844; E 14/12/95
p8; Sk 18/12/95 p392-3; St 19/12/95 p12; Th 1/1/96
p45-6; TW95 p377-8.*

95.271 *THE NEW HUSBAND* (Duol) Cotsford Dick. HAYMAR-
KET 16/12/95 mat perf.* <u>Mr Heliotrope</u> George Giddens;
<u>Servant</u> Master [G.] Croxon. <u>Mrs Heliotrope</u> Fanny
Brough. <u>L & MGR</u> H.B. Tree. *REV: E 21/12/95 p10; St
19/12/95 p12.*

95.272 *AFTER ALL* (MCa) Frank Desprez (lib) & Alfred
Cellier (mus). HAYMARKET 16/12/95 mat perf.** <u>H.
Selwyn</u> Jones Hewson; <u>Pennyfather</u> Rutland Barrington.
<u>Maria</u> Emmie Owen. *REV: As for 95.271.*

95.273 *ONE OF THE BEST* (D,4a) Seymour Hicks & George
Edwardes. ADELPHI 21/12/95-6/6/96. 163 perf [w/S mat
exc 21/12, 28/12/95, 4/4/96, 11/4, 16/5, 23/5, 30/5,
6/6/96; add mat 26/12/95, 6/4/96, 13/5/96; np 25/12/
95, 3/4/96].* <u>Dudley Keppel</u> William Terriss; <u>Philip
Ellsworth</u> W.L. Abingdon; <u>Lieut.-Gen. Coventry</u> Charles
J. Fulton; <u>Sir Archibald McGregor, K.C.B., A.D.C.</u>
Edward Sass/J.D. Beveridge; <u>Rev Dr Penrose</u> Julian

Cross; M Jules de Gruchy L. Delorme; Private Jupp
Harry Nicholls; Sgt. Henessy A.W. Fitzgerald/Albert
Skein/Strickland; Corporal Smythe [Guy?] Waller; Private (Hon) Montressor Richard Brennand; Private Ginger J. Cole; Private Snipe Webb Darleigh; Private
White Herrick; President of the Court H[ubert] Carter; Jason Jupp H. Athol Forde. Esther Coventry Jessie Millward/Henrietta Watson; Mary Penrose Edith
Ostlere; Kitty Spencer Vane Featherston; Mrs Spencer
Kate Kearney. PP & MGR A. & S. Gatti; Dir & Bm Fred
G. Latham; Mus & Mus dir John Crook; Sc Joseph Harker, Bruce Smith, William Harford; Cost Jay, Marshall
& Snelgrove, Mme Marte, Miss Goldfinch, Morris Angel
& Son; Furn Frank Giles & Co.; Pq William Clarkson;
Bom Arthur Frye; Asm Caleb Porter; A act mgr Herbert
Budd. *REV: Ath 28/12/95 p911; E 28/12/95 p7; Sk*
25/12/95 p477-8, 4/3/95 p243-6; SR 28/12/95 p867-9;
St 26/12/95 p10-1; Th 1/2/96 p98-100; Ti 23/12/95
p11; TW95 p378-82.

95.274 *TOMMY ATKINS* (Military D,4a) Benjamin Landeck
& Arthur Shirley. DUKE OF YORK'S 23/12/95-31/12/95.
9 perf [w/mat 26/12, 28/12; np 25/12]. 1st perfd
Pavilion 16/9/95. Harold Wilson Charles Cartwright;
Stephen Raymond Lyston Lyle; Ebenezer Skindle Lennox
Pawle; Cpt. Richard Maitland Edward O'Neill; Cpt.
Bob Sparrow Wilfred Forster; Colour-Sgt. Paddy Molloy
Richard Purdon; Private Mason G[eorge] W. Cockburn;
Col. Hardwick Pemberton Peach; Perkins Langley Handford; Arab Sheikh H. Gomer May; Tommy Trotman Harry
Buss; Private Harris Dalziel Heron; Orderly W. Richards; Surgeon Douglas Norman; Villager Alfred Collins.
Little Jack Jessica Black; Ruth Raymond Gertrude
Kingston; Elsie Wilson Constance Collier; Rose Selwyn Clare Harford; Margaret Maitland [Geraldine]
Olliffe; Kate Perkins Naomi Neilson; Martha Minnie
Major. L & MGR Charles Cartwright, Henry Dana; Cost
Morris Angel & Son, Miss West; Furn Oetzmann; Lime
Digby; Pq William Clarkson; Mus dir Edward Jones; Sm
Standley Wade; Act mgr James W. Mathews. *REV: Ath*
28/12/95 p911-2; E 28/12/95 p7; St 2/1/96 p16; Th
1/2/96 p102-3; Ti 24/12/95 p6; TW96 p8-9.

95.275 *THE SHAUGHRAUN* (Irish D,4a) Dion Boucicault.

NOVELTY 23/12/95-4/1/96. 12 perf [w/mat 26/12].**
<u>Robert Ffolliott</u> Leonard Yorke; <u>Cpt. Molyneaux</u> Ste-
phen Ewart; <u>Father Dolan</u> Harry Sainsbury; <u>Corry Kin-
chela</u> Robert Forsyth; <u>Harvey Duff</u> Tom Nerney; <u>Reilly</u>
Sidney Claire; <u>Sullivan</u> J.S. Marriott; <u>Mangan</u> J.
Williams; <u>Doyle</u> F. Franks; <u>Sgt. Jones</u> Edward Ranler;
<u>Conn</u> Chalmers MacKey. <u>Claire Ffolliott</u> Dorothy Coote;
<u>Arte O'Neill</u> Mary Hardacre; <u>Mrs O'Kelly</u> E.F. Brady;
<u>Bridget Mengan</u> Minnie Stokes; <u>Nancy Malone</u> Kate
Leicester; <u>Moya</u> Mariette Hyde. *REV: E 28/12/95 p7.*

95.276 *A HAPPY PAIR* (Ca,1a) S. Theyre Smith. STRAND
23/12/95-8/2/96. 41 perf [np 25/12].** <u>Mr Honeyton</u>
Wilfred Clarke. <u>Mrs Honeyton</u> Angela Mayo. <u>Pp</u> J.S.
Clarke; <u>Bom</u> A.E. Barnes; <u>Mgr</u> Harry Paulton, Wilfred
Clarke; <u>Bm</u> J.B. Jackson; <u>Mus dir</u> Claude Fenigstein.
REV: St 2/1/96 p16.

95.277 *CINDERELLA* (Panto) Augustus Harris & Cecil
Raleigh & Arthur Sturgess. DRURY LANE 26/12/95-21/3/
96. 179 perf [2 perf dy 27/12-22/2; w/M, W, S mat
24/2-21/3; add mat 27/2].* <u>The Baron</u> Herbert Camp-
bell; <u>The Baroness</u> Dan Leno; <u>Tutor</u> Lionel Rignold;
<u>Two Bailiff's Officers</u> Griffiths Brothers; <u>Clown</u> Tom
Lovell; <u>Policeman</u> M. Ring; <u>Pantaloon</u> Carl Waller.
<u>Prince</u> Ada Blanche; <u>Cinderella</u> Isa Bowman; <u>Dandini</u>
Alexandra Dagmar; <u>Angelina</u> Sophie Larkin; <u>Clorinda</u>
Emily Miller; <u>Fairy Godmother</u> Lily Harold; <u>French
Ambassador</u> Marguerite Cornille; <u>Lord Chamberlain</u>
Maggie Ripley; <u>Demon</u> L[illie] Comyns; <u>King Toy</u>
K[ate?] Jocelyn; <u>Spirit of Pantomime</u> Helen Lee; <u>Lord-
in-Waiting</u> Lena Delphine; <u>Cpt. of the Guard-at-Arms</u>
Harrison; <u>Master of the Ceremonies</u> E. Pritchard; <u>Mas-
ter of the Horse</u> M. Shields; <u>Prime Minister</u> V. Knight;
<u>Aide-de-Camp to the Prince</u> M. Bryer; <u>German Ambassador</u>
A. Fricker; <u>Italian Ambassador</u> H. Hastings; <u>Russian
Ambassador</u> Queenie Dudley; <u>Austrian Ambassador</u> L.
Feverell; <u>Harlequin</u> B[uffy] Hoby; <u>Columbine</u> E. Walker;
<u>Extras</u> H. Bliss, D. Franks, V[iolet?] Crotty, E. Bruce,
Lennard, E[thel] Salisbury, F. Glynn, E. Budd, Paget,
M[aud] Francis, J. Bayley, B. Park. L & MGR & PD
Augustus Harris; <u>Sm</u> Arthur P. Collins; <u>Am</u> Neil For-
syth; <u>Mus</u> James M. Glover; <u>Lyr</u> Mary Watson, Joseph
Watson, Constance Bache; <u>Ch</u> [Carlo] Coppi, John d'Au-

ban; <u>Sc</u> Joseph Harker, Bruce Smith, [Robert?] Caney,
J. Kautsky, Schweitzer, T.E. Ryan; <u>Cost dgn</u> Comelli;
<u>Cost</u> Alias, Harrisons, B.J. Simmons, Dore, Morris
Angel & Son, Landolff, Dowding, Auguste, Miss Fisher,
Miss Collier; <u>Asm</u> N[apier] Barry; <u>Pq</u> William Clarkson;
<u>Mach</u> E.A. Taylor; <u>Props</u> A. Jones, Jackson; <u>Elect</u> Hor-
gan, Crawshaw. *REV: E 28/12/95 p8; Sk 1/1/96 p491-2,
15/1/96 p591, 595, 22/1/95 p647, 661-8, 19/2/96 p173-
4; St 2/1/96 p14-5; Th 1/2/96 p103-4; Ti 27/12/95 p5;
TW96 p1-3.*

95.278 *ROBINSON CRUSOE* (Panto) Horace Lennard (lib)
& Oscar Barrett (mus). LYCEUM 26/12/95-22/2/96. 69
perf [mat only 26/12-25/1; 2 perf dy 27/1-8/2; w/M,
W, S mat 10/2-22/2].* <u>Mrs Crusoe</u> Victor Stevens;
<u>Dan'l Hopkins</u> Richard Blunt; <u>Will Atkins</u> Fred Emney;
<u>Larboard</u> Marius Girard; <u>Starboard</u> E[dward?] Morehen;
<u>Market Beadle</u> Roy Kennett; <u>Dog</u> Master L. Wilkes; <u>Goat</u>
Master Edwin Allen; <u>Parrot</u> Master A. Gough; <u>Cat</u> Master
H. Linwood; <u>Hullabaloo</u> Fred Storey; <u>Chut-Nee</u> W. Ritter
Riley; <u>Fiti-Fiti</u> Fred Kitchen; <u>Talkee-Talkee</u> [Enrico]
Zanfretta; <u>Em-Cee</u> Harry Kitchen; <u>Hanga-Mup</u> Philippe;
<u>Tripfoot</u> Master Herbert Lamartine; <u>Friday</u> Charles
Lauri; <u>Clown</u> James Le Fre; <u>Pantaloon</u> Albert de Voy;
<u>Harlequin</u> Frank Purcell; <u>Policeman</u> Fred Kitchen;
<u>Ticket Inspector</u> D. Philippe; <u>Sweep</u> Riley; <u>Car Atten-
dant</u> G[eorge] Aubrey. <u>Spirit of Adventure</u> Geraldine
Somerset; <u>Robinson Crusoe</u> Alice Brookes; <u>Polly Hopkins</u>
Grace Lane; <u>Cpt. Truman</u> Susie Vaughan; <u>Midshipmite</u>
Ida Muriel; <u>Sgt. of Marines</u> Lilian Holmes; <u>Oliver</u>
Mellor; <u>Randolf</u> E. Gibbons; <u>Geoffrey</u> May Haddon; <u>Mark</u>
L. Francis; <u>Nance</u> M. Mount; <u>Dora</u> Lena Lewis; <u>Maud</u> J.
Chamberlain; <u>Margery</u> L. Augarde; <u>Little Daisy</u> Ethel
Grace; <u>Nicee</u> Florence Herbert; <u>Picee</u> Mary Norton;
<u>Popsee</u> Catherine Williamson; <u>Wopsee</u> Blanche Doris;
<u>Ducksee</u> Pattie Marshall; <u>Kicksee</u> Constance Gordon;
<u>Princess Pretti-Pretti</u> [Francesca] Zanfretta; <u>Colum-
bine</u> Maud de Vere. <u>MGR & PD</u> Oscar Barrett; <u>L</u> Henry
Irving; <u>Sc</u> Henry Emden; <u>Ch</u> Katti Lanner; <u>Cost dgn</u>
Wilhelm; <u>Bom</u> Joseph Hurst; <u>Cost</u> Mme d'Orlean, Mrs S.
May, Pocock Brothers; <u>Props</u> F.C. Labhart, R. Eagle;
<u>Pq</u> William Clarkson; <u>Mus dir</u> James Weaver; <u>Regisseur</u>
J. Pritchard Barrett; <u>Sm</u> Henry Nelson; <u>Mach</u> R. Aff-
leck. *REV: E 28/12/95 p8; Sk 1/1/96 p491-2, 12/2/96*

p93, 108-12; St 2/1/96 p15; Th 1/2/96 p104-5; Ti 27/ 12/95 p5; TW96 p3-4.

95.279 *A WOMAN'S REASON* (D,3a) Charles H.E. Brookfield & F.C. Phillips. SHAFTESBURY 27/12/95-14/3/96. 80 perf [w/S mat exc 28/12/95, 7/3/96; add mat 15/1/ 96, 29/1, 6/2, 12/2/96; np 5/2/96, 19/2/96].* Lord Bletchley Charles H.E. Brookfield; Rev Cosmo Pretious Henry Kemble; Cpt. Crozier Charles F. Coghlan/George Hippisley/Nutcombe Gould; Stephen d'Acosta Lewis Waller; Algie Stewart Dawson; Mr McGeorge F. Hamilton Knight; Martin Tutt E.J. Malyon; James Lesly Thomson; Footman Charles Goodhart. Lady Bletchley Carlotta Addison/Mrs Arthur Ayers; Hon Nina Keith Mrs H.B. Tree; Agatha Pretious Maude Millett/Kate Cutler/Frances White; Curtice Violet Stevens; Leah d'Acosta Florence West. L & MGR Lewis Waller, H.H. Morell; Pp John Lancaster; Bom Potter; Sm E.J. Malyon; Mus dir O. de Tender; Sec Charles Meyrick. *REV: Ath 4/1/96 p27; E 4/1/96 p11; Sk 1/1/96 p489, 533-4, 29/1/96 p18-22; SR 4/1/96 p12-4; St 2/1/96 p15-6; Th 1/2/96 p100-2; Ti 28/12/95 p10; TW96 p4-7.*

95.280 *THE LATE MR CASTELLO* (F,3a) Sydney Grundy. COMEDY 28/12/95-20/2/96. 55 perf [w/S mat exc 28/12; add mat 15/1, 22/1, 29/1; np 5/2, 19/2].* Cpt. Trefusis Leonard Boyne/Stuart Champion; Sir Pinto Wanklyn Cyril Maude; Jack Uniacke J.G. Grahame; Spencer J[ohn] Byron. Mrs Bickerdyke Rose Leclercq; Mrs Castello Winifred Emery; Avice Esmé Beringer. L & MGR J.W. Comyns Carr; Bom Scarisbrick; Sc Walter Johnstone; Cost Mrs Nettleship, Jay; Furn Hampton & Sons, E[mile] Godfrey; Sm Edward Hastings; Mus dir Alfred J. Caldicott; Bm Silvanus Dauncey. *REV: Ath 4/1/96 p26-7; E 4/1/96 p11; Sk 1/1/96 p492; SR 4/1/96 p14; St 2/1/96 p15; Th 1/2/96 p97-8; Ti 30/12/95 p9; TW96 p7-8.*

95.281 *A BREEZY MORNING* (Duol) Eden Phillpotts. COMEDY 28/12/95-10/1/96. 12 perf.** Mr Goldie Clarence Blakiston. Mrs Goldie Eva Williams. L & MGR, Bom, Sm, Mus dir, Bm as for 95.280. *REV: E 4/1/96 p11.*

95.282 *JEREMY DIDDLER* (F,1a). SHAFTESBURY 30/12/95-

14/3/96. 64 perf [np 5/2, 19/2]. <u>Jeremy Diddler</u> C.W.
Somerset; [Charles] Goodhart; [Lesly] Thomson; [H.]
Deane; Trent. Frances White; Mrs Kitts/Mrs Arthur
Ayers. <u>L & MGR</u> Lewis Waller, H.H. Morell; <u>Pp</u> John
Lancaster; <u>Bom</u> Potter; <u>Sm</u> E.J. Malyon; <u>Mus dir</u> O. de
Tender; <u>Sec</u> Charles Meyrick.

*   *   *   *   *

96.1 *ALL ABROAD* (MF,2a) Owen Hall (lib) & James T. Tanner (lib) & Frederick Rosse (mus) & W.H. Risque (lyr). COURT 2/1/96-23/1/96. 21 perf [w/mat 11/1, 18/1].** Mr Bowles Willie Edouin; Mr Beaver Fred Kaye; Baron Fontenay David S. James; Ernest Templer Saxe; Maurice Meurice Charles Sugden; Caphshaw Lionel Rae; Adolphe [L.] Johnson; Skeggs George Elliston; Policeman Cecil Frere; Smythe Charles Mills; Extras Wilson, H.W. Mortimer, Eric Phillips, H. Brereton, C.R. Stewart, J. Brand. Connie May Edouin; Bessie Bell Blaney; Lottie Clive Daisy Bryer; Amy Beresford Maud Trautner; Gladys Colchester Edna Grace; Yvette Ethel Borlase; Mme Montesquieu Grace Palotta; Extras Jenny Holland, Murray, Olive Dalmour, Maud Wilmot, Marguerite Osland, Bessie Pelissier, Lydia Lisle, Waldorf, Walpole, Helena Waverley, Christian, Michel Watson, A. Dewsnap, Mary Leonard, Sybil Awdry, Darlington, Mori. L & MGR Arthur Chudleigh; Mus dir Carl Kiefert; Act mgr Leonard Lillies; Pd Willie Edouin. *REV: E 4/1/96 p11; St 9/1/96 p15; Ti 6/1/96 p11; TW96 p11-2.*

96.2 *A HIGHLAND LEGACY* (P,1a) Brandon Thomas. AVENUE 3/1/96-1/2/96. 26 perf.** Gordon McDonnell J.R. Hatfield; Tammy Tamson William F. Hawtrey; Mr Dobson Ernest Cosham; Cavendish Howley William Wyes; Job Fixem Willis Searle. Mrs Butler Honnor; Clara Dobson Evelyn Harrison. L & MGR William Greet; Dir Charles H. Hawtrey; Cond Ernest Bucalossi; Sm Frederick Glover;

<u>Bm</u> C. Liddon Clark.

96.3 *THE SIGN OF THE CROSS* (D,4a) Wilson Barrett.
LYRIC 4/1/96-30/1/97. 438 perf [w/W, S mat exc 4/1/96,
8/1, 19/2, 19/12/96; add mat 23/1/96, 30/1, 6/2, 18/2,
6-7/4, 25/5, 3/8, 30/11, 28/12/96, 11/1/97, 18/1/97;
np 5/2/96, 3/4, 16-17/11, 20/11, 23-24/11, 27/11,
1/12, 4/12, 7-8/12, 11/12, 21-25/12/96]. 1st perfd
Grand Opera House, St. Louis 27/3/95. <u>Marcus</u> Wilson
Barrett/H. Cooper Cliffe; <u>Nero</u> Franklyn McLeay; <u>Ti-
gellinus</u> Charles Hudson; <u>Licinius</u> Edward Irwin; <u>Gla-
brio</u> Ambrose Manning; <u>Philodemus</u> T.W. Percyval/Frank
Denton; <u>Metullus</u> G[eorge] Bernage; <u>Signinus</u> D[aniel]
McCarthy/Nelson Barry/ G. Dance; <u>Servillius</u> Horace
Hodges; <u>Strabo</u> Marcus St. John; <u>Viturius</u> C[harles]
Derwood; <u>Favius</u> Alfred Brydone/T. Wigney Percyval/
Alfred Brydone; <u>Titus</u> Stafford Smith; <u>Melos</u> Percy
Foster; <u>Extra</u> Clive Curry. <u>Berenis</u> Maud Hoffman/Lil-
lah McCarthy/Coronno Riccardo/Alida Cortelyou/Keith
Wakeman; <u>Dacia</u> Daisy Belmore/A. Linthicum; <u>Poppea</u>
Grace Warner; <u>Ancaria</u> Alida Cortelyou/Ada Ferrar/Olga
Brandon/Constance Collier/Ross Selwick; <u>Daones</u> Laura
Johnson/E. Lawrence/Rose Pendennis; <u>Julia</u> Cecilia
Wilman; <u>Cyrene</u> Gertie Boswell/E. Lawrence; <u>Edoni</u> Alice
Gambier; <u>Zona</u> Bessie Elma; <u>Catia</u> [Mignon] Shattinger/
Constance McGrath; <u>Mytelene</u> Rose Pendennis/M. Brierly;
<u>Stephanus</u> Haidee Wright; <u>Mercia</u> Maud Jeffries/Lillah
McCarthy/Constance Collier. <u>MGR</u> Wilson Barrett; <u>Sc</u>
Walter Hann, Stafford Hall; <u>Bm</u> A.E. Field, Arthur
Fry; <u>Mus</u> Edward Jones; <u>Pq</u> William Clarkson; <u>Ch</u> Mme
Cavallazzi; <u>Sm</u> Charles Cathcart; <u>Cost</u> Miss D. Bern-
stein; <u>Pp</u> Henry J. Leslie. *REV: Ath 11/1/96 p61; E
11/1/96 p9; Sk 8/1/96 p543, 547-9, 5/2/96 p63-7, 26/2/
96 p199, 27/5/96 p209; SR 11/1/96 p39-40; St 9/1/96
p14-5; Th 1/2/96 p91-3; Ti 6/1/96 p11; TW96 p9-11.*

96.4 *OUR GUARDIAN ANGEL* (RD,4a) Clarence Burnette.
NOVELTY 6/1/96-11/1/96. 6 perf. 1st perfd during pro-
vincial tour 8/95. <u>Cpt. Dunham Massey</u> C[larence] Bur-
nett; <u>Jack Darrell</u> Edward Bicker; <u>Joe Peggs</u> L.R.
Montgomery; <u>Sambo</u> Horace Barma; <u>Wan-Lee</u> C. Eldred-
Wood; <u>Gambier</u> Wallace Eastlake; <u>Simeon Crawl</u> Gilbert
Sandys; <u>Magistrate/Barney</u> Pat Alexander; <u>Mr Massey</u>
C. Blake; <u>Tom</u> Alfred Dixon. <u>Zadia</u> Ellen Cranston; <u>Lucy</u>

<u>Massey</u> Nita Snow; <u>Cora</u> Kittie Lofting; <u>Sarah</u> Clara
Reid; <u>Little Gambia</u>/<u>Little Lucy</u> Little Flossie Snow,
MGR & L T. Gilbert Perry, J. Tomsson. *REV: E 11/1/96
p9; St 9/1/96 p15.*

96.5 *THE PRISONER OF ZENDA* (RP,Prol,4a) Edward Rose
[adpt of Anthony Hope's story]. ST. JAMES'S 7/1/96–
18/7/96; 20/10/96–28/11/96. 255 perf [w/W, S mat exc
8/1/96, 1/4, 4/4, 3/6, 20/6, 27/6, 4/7, 11/7, 21/10,
28/10, 4/11/96; add mat 20/2/96, 2/3/96; np 5/2/96,
19/2, 2-3/4, 25/5/96].* <u>Prince Rudolf</u>/<u>Rudolf the
Fifth</u>/<u>Rudolf Rassendyll</u> George Alexander/Yorke Ste-
phens; <u>Duke Wolfgang</u>/<u>Michael, Duke of Streslau</u> Herbert
Waring/C. Aubrey Smith; <u>Gilbert, Earl of Rassendyll</u>
Charles Glenney/H.H. Vincent; <u>Horace Glynn</u> Vincent
Sternroyd; <u>Jeffreys</u> Henry Boyce/William H. Day; <u>Giffen</u>
F. Featherstone/W. Chandler; <u>Col. Sapt</u> W.H. Vernon/
H.H. Vincent; <u>Fitz von Tarlenheim</u> Arthur Royston;
<u>Cpt. Hentzau</u> Laurence Cautley/H.B. Irving; <u>Detchard</u>
William H. Day; <u>Bertram Bertrand</u> E. Allan Aynesworth;
<u>Marshall Strakencz</u> Henry Loraine; <u>Lorenz Teppich</u>
F[red] Lomnitz; <u>Franz Teppich</u> George P. Hawtrey; <u>Lord
Topham</u> George P. Bancroft/Louis Pleydell; <u>Ludwig</u> Ivo
Dawson/E. Standing/A.W. Munro; <u>Toni</u> Robert Loraine;
<u>Josef</u> Frank Dyall/Richard Dalton. <u>Amelia, Countess of
Rassendyll</u> Mabel Hackney; <u>Princess Flavia</u> Evelyn Mill-
ard/Julia Neilson; <u>Antoinette de Mauban</u> Lily Hanbury/
Ellis Jeffrey/Fay Davis; <u>Frau Teppich</u> Olga Brandon/
Kate Darvill. <u>L & MGR</u> George Alexander; <u>Bm</u> Robert V.
Shone; <u>Sm</u> H.H. Vincent; <u>Sec</u> R.G. Legge; <u>Mus & Mus dir</u>
Walter Slaughter; <u>Sc</u> H.P. Hall, Walter Hann, William
Telbin; <u>Furn</u> Frank Giles & Co.; <u>Cost</u> Mme Savage, Mme
Purdue, L. & H. Nathan; <u>Pq</u> William Clarkson; <u>Bom</u>
Arnold. *REV: Ath 11/1/96 p61; E 11/1/96 p9; Sk 8/1/96
p496, 15/1/96 p596, 29/1/96 p9, 11, 19/2/96 p153-9,
4/3/96 p254-5, 13/5/96 p130, 21/10/96 p568; SR 11/1/
96 p38-9, 31/10/96 p468; St 9/1/96 p15, 22/10/96 p13;
Th 1/2/96 p93-5; Ti 8/1/96 p10; TW96 p12-6, p295-6.*

96.6 *GAFFER JARGE* (Rustic Study,1a) Alicia Ramsay.
COMEDY 11/1/96–20/2/96. 41 perf [w/W, S mat exc 11/1,
12/2; np 5/2, 19/2].* <u>Gaffer Jarge</u> Cyril Maude; <u>Mas-
ter Tom</u> Clarence Blakiston; <u>Benson</u> J[ohn] Byron. <u>Mrs
Jones</u> Alice Mansfield/Mrs E.H. Brooke; <u>Susie</u> Jessica

Black. <u>L & MGR</u> J.W. Comyns Carr; <u>Bom</u> Scarisbrick; <u>Sm</u> Edward Hastings; <u>Bm</u> Silvanus Dauncey; <u>Mus dir</u> Alfred J. Caldicott. *REV: Ath 18/1/96 p96; E 18/1/96 p9; Sk 22/1/96 p648; St 16/1/96 p13; Th 1/2/96 p103.*

96.7 *OUR SAILOR LAD* (MC,3a) Frederick J. Kirke (lib) & George Dixon (mus). NOVELTY 13/1/96-18/1/96. 6 perf. 1st perfd Muncaster, Bootle 6/5/95. <u>Jonathan Lindsay</u> Herbert W. Kirke; <u>Sir Henry Vanborough</u> Harry Lowe; <u>William Birkett</u> Richard Harris; <u>Detective Serchley</u>/ <u>Alphonse de Bretton</u> Fred Byrne; <u>Jack Maitland</u> Fred J. Kirke. <u>Jim</u> Edith Claris; <u>Rita Valois</u> Madge Severn; <u>Mrs Loveman</u> Lily Seymour; <u>Nell Lindsay</u> E. Wynne Linton. <u>MUS DIR</u> William Nutter; <u>Cond</u> Henry T. Parkes. *REV: E 18/1/96 p9; St 16/1/96 p13.*

96.8 *MICHAEL AND HIS LOST ANGEL* (P,5a) H.A. Jones. LYCEUM 15/1/96-25/1/96. 10 perf.* <u>Rev Michael Feversham</u> Johnston Forbes-Robertson; <u>Sir Lyolf Feversham</u> M[urray?] Hathorn; <u>Edward Lashmar</u> Ian Robertson; <u>Andrew Gibbard</u> W[illiam] Mackintosh; <u>Rev Mark Doewray</u> Joseph Carne; <u>Withycombe</u> John Willes; <u>Organist</u> J.S. Crawley; <u>Organ Boy</u> Master Miller. <u>Audrie Lesden</u> Marion Terry; <u>Rose Gibbard</u> Sarah Brooke; <u>Mrs Cantelo</u> Henrietta Watson; <u>Fanny Clover</u> Mrs E.H. Brooke; <u>Anglican Sister</u> Jay Lupton. <u>MGR</u> Johnston Forbes-Robertson, Frederick Harrison; <u>L</u> Henry Irving; <u>Sc</u> Hawes Craven; <u>Mus</u> Edward German; <u>Cond</u> Carl Armbruster; <u>Cost</u> L. & H. Nathan, Thomas Pratt & Sons, Mrs Mason; <u>Assist</u> <u>Bm</u> Horace Watson; <u>Sm</u> Ian Robertson; <u>Asm</u> George Riddell; <u>Bom</u> Joseph Hurst. *REV: E 18/1/96 p9; Sk 22/1/ 96 p648, 693-4; SR 18/1/96 p70-1, 25/1/96 p98-100; St 23/1/96 p12; Th 1/2/96 p95-7; Ti 16/1/96 p6; TW96 p16-25.*

96.9 *TANNHAUSER* (O[3a]) Richard Wagner. DALY'S 20/1/ 96, 25/1, 28/1, 5/2, 11/2, 14/2/96. 6 mat perf.** <u>Wolfram</u> [W.] Ludwig/William Paull/Alec Marsh; <u>Hermann</u> Lemprière Pringle/A.S. Winckworth; <u>Walther</u> R[obert F.] Cunningham/Frank A. Wood; <u>Bitherolf</u> Dennis O'Sullivan/ George Fox; <u>Reinmar</u> Charles Tilbury; <u>Tannhauser</u> E.C. Hedmont/Barton McGuckin; <u>Heinrich</u> P. Somers. <u>Venus</u> Ina Gelber/Erna Gelber; <u>Shepherd Boy</u> Minnie Hunt; <u>Elizabeth</u> Ella Russell/Alice Esty. <u>L & MGR</u> Augustin

Daly; <u>Cond</u> Richard Eckhold; <u>Sm</u> H. Brooklyn; <u>Bm</u> John
Farrington; <u>Act mgr</u> M. Edwards; <u>Bom</u> E[dward] Brown.
*REV: Ath 25/1/96 p126, 1/2/96 p157; E 25/1/96 p10,
1/2/96 p10; St 23/1/96 p12-3, 30/1/96 p12; Ti 21/1/96
p9, 1/2/96 p4.* Comment: Royal Carl Rosa Opera Company.

96.10 *THE DAWN OF HOPE* (D,Prol,4a) Clarence Burnette
& Herbert B. Cooper. NOVELTY 20/1/96-25/1/96. 6 perf.*
<u>Tom Bravo/John Middleton, alias Tom Bravo</u> Herbert B.
Cooper; <u>Jacques Gauthier/Marquis de Rennes, alias Jac-
ques Gauthier</u> William E. Passmore; <u>John Marchmont</u>
G[ilbert] Arrandale; <u>Philip</u> F.L. Arthur; <u>O'Gorman</u>
James Mathewson; <u>Downey Bobbin</u> Victor Mason; <u>Jake</u> H.C.
Johnson; <u>Ernest Travers</u> H[erbert?] Maule; <u>Fichu</u> J.
Holland; <u>Police Constable</u> G. Laybourne. <u>Ann Cuthbert</u>
S. Fradelle; <u>Kitty Murphy</u> Rose Maitland; <u>Little Meg/
Jack</u> Frances Drew; <u>Granny Mitchell</u> Mrs E. Powers;
<u>Margaret</u> Gladys Gaunt. *REV: E 25/1/96 p13.*

96.11 *CARMEN* (O[4a]) Georges Bizet. DALY'S 21/1/96,
1/2, 12/2, 15/2/96. 4 mat perf.** <u>Escamillo</u> William
Paull/[W.] Ludwig; <u>Dancairo</u> A.S. Winckworth; <u>Remendado</u>
Frank A. Wood; <u>Morales</u> P. Somers; <u>Zuniga</u> Charles Tilbury; <u>Lilas Pastia</u> Felton; <u>Jose</u> Barton McGuckin. <u>Car-
men</u> Zelie de Lussan; <u>Michaela</u> Eva Relda/Minnie Hunt;
<u>Mercedes</u> Frances Graham; <u>Frasquita</u> Lettie Searle/
Lillie Williams/Elain Gryce. <u>L & MGR</u> Augustin Daly;
<u>Cond</u> Claude Jaquinot; <u>Sm</u> H. Brooklyn; <u>Bm</u> John Farring-
ton; <u>Act mgr</u> M. Edwards; <u>Bom</u> E[dward] Brown. *REV: Ath
25/1/96 p126; E 25/1/96 p10; St 23/1/96 p13; Ti 23/1/
96 p7.* Comment: Royal Carl Rosa Opera Company.

96.12 *JEANIE DEANS* (O,4a) Hamish MacCunn (mus) &
Joseph Bennett (lib) [fnd on Sir Walter Scott, *Heart
of Midlothian*]. DALY'S 22/1/96, 29/1/96. 2 mat perf.
1st perfd Lyceum, Edinburgh 15/11/94. <u>Davie Deans</u>
Alec Marsh; <u>John Dumble</u> Lemprière Pringle; <u>John, Duke
of Argyle</u> Frank Wood; <u>Constable</u> George Fox; <u>George
Staunton, alias Robertson</u> E.C. Hedmont. <u>Jeanie Deans</u>
Marie Duma; <u>Effie Deans</u> Alice Esty; <u>Madge Wildfire</u>
Edith Miller; <u>Queen Caroline</u> Minnie Hunt; <u>Janet Bal-
cristie</u> Lillie Williams; <u>Lady Suffolk</u> Eleanor Harwood.
<u>L & MGR</u>, <u>Sm</u>, <u>Bm</u>, <u>Act mgr</u>, <u>Bom</u> as for 96.11; <u>Cond</u> Ha-
mish MacCunn. *REV: E, St, Ti as for 96.11; Ath 25/1/*

96 p127, 1/2/96 p156-7. Comment: As for 96.11.

96.13 *LOHENGRIN* (O[3a]) Richard Wagner. DALY'S 23/1/
96, 30/1, 4/2/96. 3 mat perf.** Frederick [W.] Ludwig; Henry Lemprière Pringle; Herald Charles Tilbury;
Lohengrin Barton McGuckin. Elsa Ella Russell; Ortrud
Clara Poole; Pages Lillie Williams, Eleanor Harwood,
Brooklyn, Ellis. L & MGR, Sm, Bm, Act mgr, Bom as for
96.11; Cond Richard Eckhold. *REV: E 25/1/96 p10; St
30/1/96 p12; Ti 25/1/96 p7.* Comment: As for 96.11.

96.14 *MIGNON* (O[3a]) Ambroise Thomas. DALY'S 24/1/96
mat perf.** Lothario Alec Marsh; Laertes Frank A.
Wood; Giarno Charles Tilbury; Antonio Coleman; Wilhelm Robert F. Cunningham/E.C. Hedmont. Mignon Zelie
de Lussan; Frederick Frances Graham; Felina Eva Relda.
L & MGR, Cond, Sm, Bm, Act mgr, Bom as for 96.11. *REV:
Ath 1/2/96 p157; E 1/2/96 p10; St 30/1/96 p12; Ti 25/
1/96 p7.* Comment: As for 96.11.

96.15 *THE COLLEEN BAWN; OR, THE BRIDES OF GARRYOWEN*
(D,3a) Dion Boucicault [fnd on Gerald Griffen, *The
Collegians*]. PRINCESS'S 25/1/96-6/3/96. 36 perf.**
Myles-na-Coppaleen Richard Purdon; Hardress Cregan
Tom Terriss; Danny Mann Edward Rochelle/Robert Pate-
man; Kyrle Daly Frank Harding; Father Tom George W.
Cockburn/J. Powell; Mr Corrigan C[harles?] H. Kenney;
Bertie O'Moore G[eorge] Yates; Hyland Creagh W[illiam]
Aysom; Servant Beckett; Corporal Sullivan. Eily
O'Connor Beaumont Collins; Mrs Cregan Mrs Dion Bou-
cicault; Sheelah Harriett Clifton; Kathleen Creagh
Madge Herrick; Ducie Blennerhassett Alice Vitu; Anne
Chute Agnes Hewitt. MGR Albert Gilmer; Pd Mrs Dion
Boucicault, John Douglass; Sc Cecil E. Hicks, J.
Johnstone; Cost Morris Angel & Son; Pq William Clark-
son; Mus Thomas Baker; Sm John Douglass; Mus dir
Theodore Ward; Bom S.H. Macdonald. *REV: E 1/2/96 p9;
SR 1/2/96 p122-3; St 30/1/96 p12-3.*

96.16 *HERE SHE GOES* (Sk) Walter Sapte, jr. PRINCESS'S
25/1/96-6/3/96. 36 perf.* Boniface W[illiam] Aysom.
Emmeline Alice Vitu; Sarah Fannie Selby. MGR, Sm,
Mus dir, Bom as for 96.15. *REV: E 1/2/96 p9; St 30/
1/96 p13.*

96.17 *THE DAUGHTER OF THE REGIMENT* [*LA FILLE DU REGI-MENT*](O[2a]) Gaetano Donizetti. DALY'S 27/1/96 mat perf. 1st perfd Opéra Comique, Paris 11/2/40. Sgt. Suplice Lemprière Pringle; Bruno H. Brooklyn; Corporal Max George A. Fox; Tonio Frank A. Wood; Delve P. Somers. Marie Zelie de Lussan; Countess of Burkenfeldt Amadi; Babette Minnie Hunt. L & MGR Augustin Daly; Cond Claude Jaquinot; Sm H. Brooklyn; Bm John Farrington; Act mgr M. Edwards; Bom E[dward] Brown. *REV: Ath 1/2/96 p157; E 1/2/96 p10; St 30/1/96 p12; Ti 28/1/96 p6*. Comment: Royal Carl Rosa Opera Company.

96.18 *WHITTINGTON AND HIS CAT; OR, HARLEQUIN AND THE FAIRIES OF BOW BELLS* (Panto) C.J. Archer. NOVELTY 27/1/96-1/2/96. 6 perf. 1st perf? King Rat Whitmore Ledger; Gnaw-well Sam Ludham; Nibble-well Willie Garfield; Emperor of Morocco Sid Morton; Alderman Fitzwarren C.P. Amalia; Ben Badlot B.S. Monti; Thomas Master Bert Lloyd; Mysterious Mariner George Alderman; Bung Ben Stoddard; Dorothy Koridrop Arthur E. Aubert. Fairy Bowbell Pauline Alberga; Silvertone Isabel Johnson; Merry Peal Doll Chevalier; Joy Bell Ivy Graham; Wedding Chime Agnes Graham; Ding Dong Amy Power; Ting Ting Minnie Huen; Jingle Gracie Mervyn; Jangle Annie Edwards; Dick Whittington May Rosine; Masher Mate Jennie Bolton; Philip Lill Garfield; Tony Florence Jill; Roger Bettie Bond; Azis Dorothy Steer; Azwas Sarah Bootle; Alice Fitzwarren Marie Santley; Princess Poo-tee Pet A. Margot; Kitty Lottie Jones; Phoebe Sophie Worthing. *REV: E 1/2/96 p9*.

96.19 *THE FOOL OF THE FAMILY* (C,3a) Fergus Hume. DUKE OF YORK'S 30/1/96-1/2/96. 4 perf [w/mat 1/2].* Col. Cardington Robert Pateman; Peter Adolphus Grison Charles Cartwright; Basil Lambert H.B. Irving; Arthur Saville Wilfred Forster; Marlin Lyston Lisle. Rose Lambert Gertrude Kingston; Kitty Trevor Lena Ashwell; Cousin Tilly Marie Lyons. L & MGR Charles Cartwright, Henry Dana; Sc W.T. Hemsley, Bruce Smith; Furn Oetzmann; Cost [Mathilde] Marie, Miss Brown; Lime Digby; Pq William Clarkson; Act mgr James W. Mathews; Asm [A.H.?] Lyons. *REV: E 1/2/96 p13; SR 8/2/96 p148-9; St 6/2/96 p12-3; Th 1/3/96 p163-5; Ti 31/1/96 p10; TW96 p26-9*.

96.20 *FAUST* (O[5a]) Charles Gounod. DALY'S 31/1/96
mat perf.** <u>Mephistopheles</u> Alec Marsh; <u>Valentine</u>
William Paull; <u>Faust</u> E.C. Hedmont; <u>Wagner</u> Charles
Tilbury. <u>Marguerite</u> Alice Esty; <u>Siebel</u> Florence Graham; <u>Martha</u> Amadi. L & MGR Augustin Daly; <u>Cond</u> Claude
Jaquinot.*REV: E 8/2/96 p10; St 6/2/96 p12; Ti 1/2/96
p4.* <u>Comment</u>: Royal Carl Rosa Opera Company.

96.21 *THE FLYING DUTCHMAN* [*DER FLIEGENDE HOLLANDER*]
(O[3a]) Richard Wagner. DALY'S 3/2/96 mat perf.**
<u>Eric</u> Frank A. Wood; <u>Daland</u> Charles Tilbury; <u>Steersman</u>
R[obert F.] Cunningham; <u>Van der Decken</u> [W.] Ludwig.
<u>Senta</u> Ella Russell; <u>Mary</u> Amadi. L & MGR Augustin
Daly; <u>Cond</u> Richard Eckhold; <u>Sm</u> H. Brooklyn; <u>Bm</u> John
Farrington; <u>Act mgr</u> M. Edwards; <u>Bom</u> E[dward] Brown.
*REV: Ath 8/2/96 p189; E 8/2/96 p10; St 6/2/96 p12;
Ti 4/2/96 p11.* <u>Comment</u>: As for 96.20.

96.22 *ONE THOUSAND POUNDS REWARD; OR, THE SECRETS OF
LONDON* (Melo,Prol,3a) Charles Rogers. NOVELTY 3/2/96-
8/2/96. 6 perf. 1st perf? <u>Legrade/Frederick Ingle-
ford</u> David Collins; <u>Vincent Rainsworth</u> Charles Boult;
<u>Gilbert Lisle</u> Horatio Sinclair; <u>Ginger</u> L.C. Cody; <u>Dr
Hector</u> F. Holland; <u>Fred Ingleford</u> Henry Lonsdale;
<u>Inspector Gilbert</u> George Wilson; <u>Marquis of Charing
Cross</u> J.S. Taylor; <u>Fighting Jopp</u> Harding Thomas; <u>Pug</u>
Edwards; <u>Theophilus Furnside</u> Myall; <u>Sgt. Catchem</u> John
H. Harris; <u>President of the Coiners</u> J.K. Talbut;
<u>Williams</u> Harry Turner. <u>Dick Springthorne</u> Alice Met-
calfe; <u>Meg Ingleford</u> Cissy Podmore; <u>Kitty Springthorne</u>
Gertie Grenville; <u>Mrs McCarty</u> Milly de Vere; <u>Polly
Morris</u> Kathleen Graham; <u>Mme Sanson</u> Elaine Verner. *REV:
E 8/2/96 p11; St 6/2/96 p13.*

96.23 [no entry]

96.24 *HANSEL AND GRETEL* (O,3a) Engelbert Humperdinck.
DALY'S 6/2/96, 7/2, 13/2/96. 3 mat perf.** <u>Peter</u>
William Paull. <u>Gertrude</u> Amadi; <u>Hansel</u> Frances Graham;
<u>Gretel</u> Minnie Hunt; <u>Witch</u> Edith Miller; <u>Sandman</u>
Eleanor Harwood; <u>Dewman</u> Lettie Searle/Lily Williams.
L & MGR Augustin Daly; <u>Cond</u> Richard Eckhold. *REV:
Ath 15/2/96 p225; E 8/2/96 p10; St 13/2/96 p12; Ti 7/
2/96 p10.* <u>Comment</u>: Royal Carl Rosa Opera Company.

96.25 *PAGLIACCI* (O[2a]) Ruggiero Leoncavallo. DALY'S
8/2/96, 10/2/96. 2 mat perf.** <u>Tonio</u> Winfred Goff;
<u>Beppe</u> Frank A. Wood; <u>Silvio</u> George Fox; <u>Canio</u> E.C.
Hedmont/Barton McGuckin. <u>Nedda</u> Alice Esty. L & MGR
Augustin Daly; <u>Cond</u> Claude Jaquinot; <u>Sm</u> H. Brooklyn;
<u>Bm</u> John Farrington; <u>Act mgr</u> M. Edwards; <u>Bom</u> E[dward]
Brown. *REV: Ath 15/2/96 p225; E 15/2/96 p9; St 13/2/
96 p12; Ti 10/2/96 p4.* <u>Comment</u>: As for 96.24.

96.26 *CAVALLERIA RUSTICANA* (O,1a) Pietro Mascagni.
DALY'S 8/2/96, 10/2/96. 2 mat perf.** <u>Alfio</u> Dennis
O'Sullivan; <u>Turridu</u> Barton McGuckin/E.C. Hedmont.
<u>Santuzza</u> Ella Russell; <u>Lola</u> Minnie Hunt; <u>Lucia</u> Amadi.
<u>L & MGR</u>, <u>Cond</u>, <u>Sm</u>, <u>Bm</u>, <u>Act mgr</u>, <u>Bom</u> as for 96.25.
REV: As for 96.25. <u>Comment</u>: As for 96.24.

96.27 *CINDERELLA* (Fairy Panto) Frederick Charles.
NOVELTY 10/2/96-15/2/96. 6 perf. <u>Hilario</u> L. Platt;
<u>Malicio</u> R. Fairbanks; <u>1st Spirit</u> F[rank] Jennings;
<u>Baron Shiptalotte</u> Ridgewood Barrie; <u>Maudie</u> Charles
Lake; <u>Ethel</u> J.F. Odell; <u>Pimples</u> Herbert Garraway;
<u>Nobody's Baby Boy</u> Frank Dillon; <u>Bash/Mash</u> Otto, Hil-
ton. <u>Sunbeam</u> Daisy Clark; <u>Primrose</u> Nellie Vanderbilt;
<u>Roseleaf</u> Jessie Vanderbilt; <u>Daisie</u> Amy Milton; <u>Pansie</u>
Ella Dean; <u>Bluebell</u> Topsy Greet; <u>Violette</u> Maggie Da-
gon; <u>Sizeitte</u> Eileen O'Carrol; <u>Glewitte</u> Kitty Mayhew;
<u>Foillittie</u> Gipsy Frederick; <u>Kullorte</u> Isabel Gibson;
<u>Mettleite</u> Ada Ross; <u>Primite</u> Florrie Leslie; <u>Cinderella</u>
Lena Horwood; <u>Prince Perfect</u> Annie Craig; <u>Tofferini</u>
Madge Gilbert; <u>Lady Stiff as Starch</u> Emmeline Coss;
<u>Marquis de Cadie</u> Minnie Eldridge; <u>Viscount Nappe</u> Kitty
Mathew; <u>Little Dot</u> Lily Lake; <u>Little Tot</u> Marjorie
Talbot. *REV: E 15/2/96 p11.*

96.28 *THE NEW BARMAID* (MC,2a) Frederick Bowyer (lib)
& W. Edwardes-Sprange (lib) & John Crook (mus).
AVENUE 12/2/96-6/6/96; trfd to OPERA COMIQUE 8/6/96-
3/7/96. 138 perf [w/S mat exc 15/2, 30/5, 6/6, 13/6,
20/6, 27/6; add mat 6/4, 8/4; np 3/4]. 1st perfd
Opera House, Southport 1/7/95. <u>Cpt. Lovebury</u> Harrison
Brockbank; <u>Lieut. Bradley</u> Charles Rowan; <u>Col. Clay-
more</u> C.L. Wilford; <u>Bertie White</u> J.J. Dallas; <u>M Bousor</u>
Ells Dagnall; <u>Gussie</u> Jack Thompson; <u>Inspector Hart</u>
Brandreth; <u>Club Porter</u> Carling; <u>William White</u> John L.

Shine/E.J. Lonnen; Extras Gillett, Winning, B. Wensley, Seymour, L. Wensley, Stainlaus, Mignot, Rawdon, Pearce, Bentley, Charles, Williams, Cane, Bruce. Tommy [Agnes?] Ingreville; Ethel Joy Agnes Delaporte; Lady Moulton Maria Saker; Brenda Louth Maggie Hunt; Mabel Edith Denton; Kitty Edith Gain; Laura Marie Alexander; Dora Lottie Collins; Extras Singlehurst, Alexander, Trevor, Graves, [Edith] Gain, May Butler, Douglas, Wilson, Leslie, Rose, Franks, Carlisle, Reed, Phillimore, J. Butler, Hamilton, Clair, Beaufort, Leigh, Jessop, Meekle, Tremaine, Temple, L. Wilson, Percy. L Charles H. Hawtrey; Mgr Francis Howard, Alexander Loftus; Bm E.F. Bradley; Sm Ells Dagnall; Mus dir Ernest Bucalossi; Cost dgn Comelli; Cost Alias, Harrisons, Peter Robinson, Stagg & Mantle, Mme Follet, Morris Angel & Son; Pq William Clarkson; Ch Will Bishop, John d'Auban; Pd George Capel. *REV: E 15/2/96 p11, 13/6/96 p8; Sk 19/2/96 p144, 179-80, 17/6/96 p300; St 20/2/96 p12-3; Th 1/3/96 p165-6; Ti 13/2/96 p10; TW96 p35-8.*

96.29 *JEDBURY JUNIOR* (C,3a) Madeleine Lucette Ryley. TERRY'S 14/2/96-23/5/96. 105 perf [w/S mat exc 15/2, 9/5, 16/5, 23/5; add mat 18/3, 1/4, 8/4, 15/4, 22/4, 29/4, 6/5, 13/5, 20/5; np 3/4]. 1st perfd Empire, New York 23/9/95 [as *Christopher Junior*]. Christopher Jedbury, jr Frederick Kerr; Christopher Jedbury John Beauchamp; Mjr. Hedway J.L. MacKay; Tom Bellaby Arthur Playfair; Mr Glibb G.E. Bellamy; Mr Simpson Edward Beecher; Whimper Gilbert Farquhar; Job L. Power. Mrs Jedbury Emily Cross; Mrs Glibb Elsie Chester; Nellie Jedbury Eva Moore; Dora Hedway Maude Millett. PP Edward Terry; L Frederick Kerr; Sc Harry Potts; Pq William Clarkson; Furn James S. Lyon; Cond T[homas] Smythe; Bm H.T. Brickwell; Sm W.J. Robertson. *REV: Ath 22/2/96 p259; E 22/2/96 p11; Sk 19/2/96 p144, 179-80, 11/3/96 p289-91; SR 22/2/96 p198-9; St 20/2/96 p13; Th 1/3/96 p162-3; Ti 15/2/96 p12; TW96 p38-40.*

96.30 *ON 'CHANGE* (C) Eweretta Lawrence [adpt of Gustav von Moser, *Ultimo*]. STRAND 15/2/96-13/3/96. 27 perf [w/S mat exc 15/2]. 1st perfd Strand 1/7/85. James Burnett William Farren; Prof Peckering Peck Felix Morris; Tom W. Scott Buist; Joe Yorke Stephens;

Mouser James A. Welch; De Haas E.H. Kelly; Tiffin W.
Beckwith. Laomia E[nid] Spencer Brunton; Miss Peck
Alice Mansfield; Millie Gwendolen Floyd; Iris Eweretta
Lawrence. PP J.S. Clarke; Mgr W. Scott Buist; Act mgr
C.G. Compton. *REV: Ath 22/2/96 p259; E 22/2/96 p11;*
Sk 19/2/96 p144, 18/3/96 p342-3, 356; SR 22/2/96 p199;
St 20/2/96 p13; Th 1/3/96 p166-7; TW96 p40-1.

96.31 THE MAN IN THE STREET (Ca) Louis N. Parker.
STRAND 15/2/96-13/3/96. 24 perf [w/mat 9/3].** Philip
Adair W. Scott Buist; Jabez Gover James A. Welch.
Minnie Gwendolen Floyd. PP, Mgr, Act mgr as for 96.30.
REV: E, St as for 96.30.

96.32 SHADOWS OF A GREAT CITY (D,5a) Joseph Jefferson.
NOVELTY 17/2/96-22/2/96. 6 perf. 1st perfd Princess's,
Glasgow 28/2/87. Tom Cooper Edward Vivian; George Ben-
son Lionel d'Aragon; Abe Nathan W. Tullock; Jim Farren
A.E. Percival; Arkwright Percy Dale; Crouch W. Barker;
Hammond Edwin Clarke; Biggo C.W. Green; Messenger
Master Thorley. Annie Standish Augusta Tullock; Nellie
Standish Alice Rochefort; Biddy Roonan Agnes d'Ara-
gon; Mrs Higgins Lena Woodley; Little Nellie Standish
E. Tilley. L V. St. Lawrence; Mgr Walter Tyrrell. *REV:*
E 22/2/96 p11.

96.33 MRS PONDERBURY (FC,3a) F C. Burnand [adpt of
Ernest Blum & Raoul Toché, *Madame Mongodin*]. COURT
20/2/96-21/5/96. 85 perf [w/S mat exc 22/2, 28/3,
9/5; np 2-4/4]. 1st perfd Avenue 2/11/95 [as *Mrs*
Ponderbury's Past]. Matthew Ponderbury Charles H.
Hawtrey; Mervyn Thorpe Eric Lewis; John Rumford Bran-
don Thomas; Sir Rover Bearing William Wyes/William
Cheesman/W.H. Quinton; Col. Aversnack Aubrey Fitz-
gerald/Lawrence Grossmith; Dr Orlover E.W. Tarver;
Hyacinth Grayling Willis Searle; Peter William F. Haw-
trey/William Wyes. Countess de Mojeski Lottie Venne;
Ethel Peniston Violet Lyster; Lady Rover Bearing
Florence Haydon; Susan Evelyn Harrison; Mrs Ponderbury
Mrs John Wood. MGR Arthur Chudleigh; Bm Leonard Lil-
lies; Mus dir Carl Kiefert; Furn Marler & Bennett.
REV: E 22/2/96 p11; Sk 26/2/96 p226; St 27/2/96 p12.

96.34 A HIGHLAND LEGACY (P,1a) Brandon Thomas. COURT

20/2/96-21/5/96. 76 perf [np 2-4/4].** <u>Tammy Tamson</u>
Brandon Thomas; <u>Gordon McDonnell</u> E.W. Tarver; <u>Mr Dob-</u>
<u>son</u> William F. Hawtrey; <u>Cavendish Howley</u> William Wyes;
<u>Job Fixem</u> Willis Searle. <u>Mrs Butler</u> Florence Haydon;
<u>Clara Dobson</u> Violet Lyster. <u>L & MGR</u>, <u>Bm</u>, <u>Mus dir</u>,
<u>Furn</u> as for 96.33. *REV: E, St as for 96.33.*

96.35 *GOSSIP* (P,4a) Clyde Fitch & Leo Dietrichstein
[fnd on novel by Jules Clairette]. COMEDY 22/2/96-
21/3/96. 27 perf [w/mat 29/2, 7/3]. 1st perfd Palmer's,
New York 11/3/95. <u>Count Marcy</u> Leonard Boyne/Clarence
Blakiston; <u>Richard Stanford</u> Herbert Standing; <u>Thomas</u>
<u>Barry</u> J.W. Pigott; <u>Dr Robbins</u> E[rnest] Cosham; <u>Gaston</u>
<u>Berney</u> Stuart Champion; <u>Hallows</u> J[ohn] Byron; <u>Servant</u>
Mules Brown. <u>Mrs Stanford</u> Eleanor Calhoun; <u>Miriam</u>
<u>Stanford</u> Annette Skirving; <u>Mrs Cummings</u> Cara Daniels;
<u>Clara Cummings</u> Esmé Beringer; <u>Mrs Barry</u> Mrs Langtry.
<u>L & MGR</u> J.W. Comyns Carr; <u>Bom</u> Scarisbrick; <u>Sc</u> Walter
Johnstone; <u>Furn</u> Hampton, E[mile] Godfrey; <u>Cost</u> Mrs
Nettleship, Mme Nicolle, Louie Ellis, Mme Vero; <u>Pq</u>
William Clarkson; <u>Sm</u> Edward Hastings; <u>Mus dir</u> Alfred
J. Caldicott; <u>Bm</u> Silvanus Dauncey. *REV: Ath 29/2/96
p289-90; E 29/2/96 p11; Sk 26/2/96 p225-6; SR 29/2/96
p222-3; St 27/2/96 p12; Th 1/4/96 p228-30; Ti 24/2/96
p8.*

96.36 *THE LUCKY STAR* (D,4a) George Comer. NOVELTY 24/
2/96-29/2/96. 6 perf. 1st perfd Theatre Royal,Darling-
ton 1/8/87. <u>Squire Widdrington</u> W. Robertson Foulis;
<u>Sir Richard Malet</u> Arthur C. Percy; <u>Philip Esdaile</u>
Herbert Princep; <u>Col. Ashmore/Rev J. West</u> Reginald
Vernon; <u>Corporal Sharpe</u> Sid Proffit; <u>Denny Doyle</u>
Cecil Morand; <u>Bill Grudge</u> H. Anderson; <u>Bumble</u> Edward
Cheetham; <u>Hal Hawsley</u> William Anson; <u>Jack Marsden</u> J.
Harcourt; <u>Ali</u> Grant Taylor; <u>Ben Hassam</u> Ventor Gressor.
<u>Constance</u> Emma Rainbow; <u>Phoebe/Gippo</u> Wanda Zaleska;
<u>Sally Hawthorne</u> Mabel Percy Moore; <u>Minnie</u> Little
Denise. <u>L</u> V. St. Lawrence; <u>Mgr</u> Walter Tyrrell. *REV: E
29/2/96 p9; St 27/2/96 p13.*

96.37 *THE ROMANCE OF THE SHOPWALKER* (C,3a) Robert
Buchanan & "Charles Marlowe" [Harriet Jay]. VAUDEVILLE
26/2/96-28/3/96. 34 perf [w/S mat exc 29/2; add mat
18/3, 25/3]. 1st perfd Theatre Royal, Colchester 24/

2/96. Thomas Tompkins Weedon Grossmith; Earl of Dover-
dale Sydney Warden; Cpt. Dudley Sydney Brough; Samuel
Hubbard Frederick Volpé; Alexander McCollop David S.
James; Mr Catchem C[harles] H. Fenton; Conningsby
T[om] Hesslewood; Shopman Skinner/Herbert Sleath.
Lady Munro M. Talbot; Lady Evelyn May Palfrey; Lady
Mabel Nina Boucicault; Dorothy Hubbard Annie Hill;
Mrs Tompkins M.A. Victor. L Weedon Grossmith; Bm A.F.
Henderson; Sm William Holles; Mus dir C.J. Hargitt.
*REV: Ath 29/2/96 p290; E 29/2/96 p9; Sk 4/3/96 p234,
1/4/96 p429-32; SR 29/2/96 p223-4; St 27/2/96 p12,
5/3/96 p13; Th 1/4/96 p225-7; Ti 27/2/96 p10; TW96
p65-7.*

96.38 *FOR THE CROWN* (RP,4a) John Davidson [adpt of
François Coppée, *Pour La Couronne*]. LYCEUM 27/2/96-
30/5/96. 94 perf [w/S mat exc 29/2, 4/4; add mat
22/4, 6/5; np 3/4].* Stephen Ian Robertson; Prince
Michael Brancomir Charles Dalton; Constantine Bran-
comir Johnston Forbes-Robertson; Ibrahim William Mack-
intosh; Lazare Frank Gillmore; Ourosch J. Fisher
White; Turkish Prisoner J. Culver; Sentinel J[ohn]
Byron; Goatherd Murray Hathorn. Page Dora Barton;
Bazilide Winifred Emery; Anna Sarah Brooke/Jay Lup-
ton; Militza Mrs Patrick Campbell/Sarah Brooke. MGR
Johnston Forbes-Robertson, Frederick Harrison; L Henry
Irving; Bom Joseph Hurst; Mus & Cond Carl Armbruster;
Sc Walter Hann, Joseph Harker, Hawes Craven, T.E.
Ryan; Cost L. & H. Nathan; Assist Bm Horace Watson;
Sm Ian Robertson; Asm George Riddell. *REV: Ath 7/3/96
p321; E 29/2/96 p11; Sk 26/2/96 p201-2, 4/3/96 p234,
18/3/96 p318, 25/3/96 p383-90; SR 7/3/96 p248-50; St
5/3/96 p12-3; Th 1/4/96 p220-2; Ti 28/2/96 p5; TW96
p59-65.*

96.39 *THE SILVER HORSESHOE* (Romantic Naval D,5a) St.
Aubyn Miller. NOVELTY 2/3/96-7/3/96. 6 perf. 1st
perfd Aquarium, Brighton 4/2/95. Sir Geoffrey Feather-
stone Gilbert Verne; Cpt. Martin Stanton Stephen Vast;
Lieut. Arnold Featherstone W. Gustavus Bell; Lieut.
Archie Wentworth Ernest Mere; Rev Toby Muffins J.
Stimson Fitch; Hooky Pike R.B. Baldwyn; Joe Herman
Leslie Douglas; Walker Edward Sley; Cherrystone F.
Bartlett; Punch T. Rayne. Georgina Girton Emily Cus-

tance; <u>Lillian</u> Marion Herbert; <u>Zana</u> Flo Bartlett;
<u>Bess Lee</u> Marie Dorine. <u>L</u> V. St. Lawrence; <u>Mgr</u> Walter
Tyrrell. *REV: E 7/3/96 p11; St 5/3/96 p13.*

96.40 *SHAMUS O'BRIEN* (CO,2a) George H. Jessop (lib)
& C. Villiers Stanford (mus) [fnd on poem by Joseph
Sheridan Le Fanu]. OPERA COMIQUE 2/3/96-23/5/96. 82
perf [w/S mat exc 7/3; np 3/4].* <u>Shamus O'Brien</u> Denis
O'Sullivan; <u>Cpt. Trevor</u> W.H. Stephens; <u>Mike Murphy</u>
Joseph O'Mara; <u>Father O'Flynn</u> C[harles J.?] Magrath;
<u>Sgt. Cox</u> Frank Fisher; <u>Lynch</u> Garoghan; <u>Little Paudeen</u>
Master Ross. <u>Norah O'Brien</u> Louise Kirkby Lunn; <u>Peggy</u>
Winifred Ludlam; <u>Kitty O'Toole</u> Maggie Davies.   <u>L</u>
Nellie Farren; <u>Pd</u> Augustus Harris; <u>Cond</u> Henry J. Wood;
<u>Mgr</u> Shamus O'Brien Opera Company Limited; <u>Ch</u> R.M.
Crompton; <u>Sc</u> Robert Caney, Joseph Harker; <u>Cost dgn</u>
Comelli; <u>Cost</u> Alias; <u>Pq</u> William Clarkson; <u>Sm</u> Richard
Temple; <u>Act mgr</u> Wilfred Esmond. *REV: Ath 7/3/96 p320;
E 7/3/96 p11; Sk 11/3/96 p277, 8/4/96 p449, 463-6; St
5/3/96 p13; Th 1/4/96 p224-5; Ti 3/3/96 p12.*

96.41 *THE NEW HUSBAND* (Ca,1a) Cotsford Dick. GLOBE
3/3/96 mat perf.** <u>Mr Heliotrope</u> Cotsford Dick. <u>Mrs
Heliotrope</u> Kate Phillips. <u>L</u> W.S. Penley; <u>Treas</u> W[ill-
iam] Lestocq. *REV: E 7/3/96 p13.*

96.42 *VILLAIN AND VICTIM* (Sk) W.R. Walkes. GLOBE 3/3/
96 mat perf.** <u>Adolphus</u> Cyril Maude. <u>Millicent</u> Winifred Emery. <u>L</u>, <u>Treas</u> as for 96.41.

96.43 *THE BICYCLE* (Ca,1a) Mrs Hugh Bell. GLOBE 3/3/96
mat perf.* <u>Richard</u> Charles H. Hawtrey. <u>Amanda</u> Vane
Featherston; <u>Louise</u> Violet Lyster. <u>L</u>, <u>Treas</u> as for
96.41. <u>Comment</u>: This piece was included on the V & A
programme, but was possibly deleted before performance.
See item 96.51, which Nicoll indicates as being the
first perf of this piece.

96.44 *EAST LYNNE* (D,4a) Miss Heath & Wilson Barrett
[fnd on Mrs Henry Wood's novel]. PRINCESS'S 7/3/96-
28/3/96. 21 perf [w/mat 21/3, 28/3].* <u>Archibald
Carlyle</u> Payne/Magill Martyn; <u>Lord Mountsevern</u> Leonard
Yorke; <u>Justice Hare</u> Robert Medlicott; <u>Francis Levison</u>
Edward Rochelle; <u>Richard Hare</u> W. Taylor; <u>Lawyer Dill</u>

Percy Maynal; <u>Bullock</u> E.V. Campbell. <u>Little Willie</u> <u>Little Phillis</u>; <u>Little Isabel</u> Little Amy; <u>Barbara Hare</u> Adelaide Chippendale; <u>Cornelia Carlyle</u> Sophy Shenton; <u>Joyce</u> Madge Grey; <u>Susanne</u> Sydney Irving; <u>Wilson</u> Mowbray; <u>Lady Isabel/Mme Vine</u> Bessie Rignold. <u>GEN MGR</u> Albert Gilmer; <u>Am</u> Horace Gilmer; <u>Sm</u> John Douglass; <u>Treas</u> H. Bellamy Smith; <u>Mus dir</u> Theodore Ward; <u>Bom</u> S.H. MacDonald. *REV: E 14/3/96 p11; St 12/3/96 p13.*

96.45 *MY NEIGHBOUR'S WIFE* (F,1a) Alfred Bunn. PRINCESS'S 7/3/96-28/3/96. 21 perf [w/mat 21/3, 28/3]. 1st perfd Covent Garden 7/10/33. <u>Mr Somerton</u> Leonard Yorke; <u>Mr Smith</u> E.V. Campbell; <u>Mr Brown</u> Percy Meynal. <u>Mrs Somerton</u> Sophy Shenton; <u>Mrs Brown</u> Nellie Dare; <u>Mrs Smith</u> Hamilton. <u>GEN MGR</u>, <u>Am</u>, <u>Sm</u>, <u>Treas</u>, <u>Mus dir</u>, <u>Bom</u> as for 96.44. *REV: St 12/3/96 p13.*

96.46 *THE GRAND DUKE; OR, THE STATUTORY DUEL* (CO,2a) W.S. Gilbert (lib) & Arthur Sullivan (mus). SAVOY 7/3/96-10/7/96. 123 perf [w/S mat exc 7/3, 4/7; np 3/4].* <u>Rudolph</u> Walter Passmore; <u>Ernest Dummkopf</u> Charles Kenningham; <u>Ludwig</u> Rutland Barrington; <u>Dr Tannhauser</u> Scott Russell; <u>Prince of Monte Carlo</u> R[obert] Scott-Fishe; <u>Viscount Mentone</u> E. Carleton/ Basil Wood; <u>Ben Hashbaz</u> C[harles] Herbert Workman; <u>Herald</u> Jones Hewson. <u>Princess of Monte Carlo</u> Emmie Owen; <u>Baroness von Krakenfeldt</u> Rosina Brandram; <u>Julia Jellicoe</u> Ilka von Palmay/Florence Perry/Carla Dagmar; <u>Olga</u> Mildred Baker; <u>Gretchen</u> Ruth Vincent; <u>Bertha</u> Jessie Rose; <u>Elsa</u> Ethel Wilson; <u>Martha</u> Beatrice Perry/ Jessie Bond. <u>PP & MGR</u> Richard d'Oyly Carte; <u>Cond</u> Arthur Sullivan; <u>Bm</u> J.W. Beckwith; <u>Mus dir</u> Francois Cellier; <u>Dir</u> Charles Harris; <u>Sm</u> W.H. Seymour; <u>Sc</u> William Harford; <u>Ch</u> John d'Auban; <u>Cost dgn</u> Percy Anderson; <u>Cost</u> Miss Fisher, Auguste, Mme Leon, B.J. Simmons; <u>Pq</u> William Clarkson. *REV: Ath 14/3/96 p353; E 14/3/96 p9; Sk 11/3/96 p277, 18/3/96 p358, 15/4/96 p493, 515-21; St 12/3/96 p12-3; Th 1/4/96 p222-4; Ti 9/3/96 p7; TW96 p67-72.*

96.47 *THE STOWAWAY* (D,5a) Tom Craven. NOVELTY 9/3/96-14/3/96. 6 perf. 1st perfd Theatre Royal, Dewsbury 29/9/84. <u>Paul Inglis</u> R.B. Baldwyn; <u>Tom Inglis</u> W. Gustavus Bell; <u>Charles Etherington</u> Stephen Vast;

Percy Ewart J. Stimson Fitch; Job Hickey Leslie Doug-
las; Sandy Prowse George Reeves; Dicky Dials Alf
Russell; Freeman Richard Elfin; Servant H. St. Ruth.
Mrs Etherington Marie Dorine; Althea Dale Marion Her-
bert; Chucky Emily Custance. L V. St. Lawrence; Mgr
Walter Tyrrell. *REV: E 14/3/86 p11; St 12/3/96 p13.*

96.48 *IN AND OUT OF A PUNT* (Duol) Henry V. Esmond.
ST. JAMES'S 9/3/96 mat perf.* Hugh Henry V. Esmond.
Margaret Eva Moore. L & MGR George Alexander; Bm
Robert V. Shone; Sec R.G. Legge; Mus dir Walter
Slaughter. *REV: E 14/3/96 p13; St 12/3/96 p13.*

96.49 *THE MAN IN THE STREET* (Ca) Louis N. Parker. ST.
JAMES'S 9/3/96 mat perf.** Philip Adair W. Scott
Buist; Jabez Gover James A. Welch. Minnie Adair Gwen-
dolen Floyd. *REV: As for 96.48.*

96.50 *BLUE OR GREEN?* (Ca) Mrs Hugh Bell. COMEDY 12/3/
96 mat perf.* Sophia Larkings Carlotta Addison; Bet-
sinda Larkings Beatrice Herford; Telegraph Clerk
Robertson. *REV: E 14/3/96 p13; Sk 18/3/96 p356; St
19/3/96 p12; TW96 p77-8.*

96.51 *THE BICYCLE* (DSk) Mrs Hugh Bell. COMEDY 12/3/96
mat perf.** Dick Beauchamp Charles H. Hawtrey. Ara-
manda Vane Featherston; Louise Violet Lyster. *REV:
As for 96.50.* Comment: See comment for item 96.43.

96.52 *A HONEYMOON TRAGEDY* (Ca,1a) Mrs W.K. Clifford.
COMEDY 12/3/96 mat perf.* Count Dal Mezzio Acton
Bond; Waiter Charles Lloyd. Countess Dal Mezzio Mrs
Herbert Waring. *REV: As for 96.50.*

96.53 *SHADES OF NIGHT* (Fantasy,1a) Robert Marshall.
LYCEUM 14/3/96-30/5/96. 66 perf [np 3/4].* Cpt. Hon
Terence Trivett Frank Gillmore; Sir Ludovic Trivett
J[ohn] Willes. Winifred Yester Ethel Weyburn; Lady
Mildred Yester Henrietta Watson. MGR Johnston Forbes-
Robertson, Frederick Harrison; L Henry Irving; Bom
Joseph Hurst; Cond Carl Armbruster; Assist Bm Horace
Watson; Sm Ian Robertson; Asm George Riddell; Sc H.J.
Craven. *REV: Ath 21/3/96 p389; E 21/6/96 p11; Sk
25/3/96 p374; Th 1/4/96 p227-8; Ti 16/3/96 p11.*

96.54 *THE HUNCHBACK OF NOTRE DAME* [adpt of Victor Hugo]. NOVELTY 16/3/96-21/3/96. 6 perf. Claude Frollo Whitley Ward; Quasimodo Matthews Monck; Cpt. Phoebus Arthur Leslie; Clopin S. Edmond S. Linnit; Voopak H. Ely; Cpt. Ernest Ernest Leighsome; Tristran H.J. Noel. Gringoire Beatrice Lloyd; Jehan Fannie Sylvan; Esmeralda Norah Meredith; Mme Gondhurier Blanch Earle; Gudule Virginia Blackwood; Fleur-de-Lys Luddington; Gabrielle L. Gray; Marie Maudie Hastings; Ninette Desdemona Earle; Ninon McCarty; Edwina Davis; Meranee Patsy Trounsell. L V. St. Lawrence; Mgr Walter Tyrrell. *REV: E 21/3/96 p11.*

96.55 *THE DAY AFTER THE WEDDING* (Int,1a) [Marie Therese Kemble]. NOVELTY 16/3/96-[18/3/96. 3 perf]. 1st perfd Covent Garden 18/5/08. Comment: Mentioned in *St.*

96.55B *IN AND OUT OF A PUNT* (Duol) Henry V. Esmond. HAYMARKET 19/3/96 mat perf.** Hugh Henry V. Esmond. Margaret Eva Moore. L & MGR H.B. Tree; Sm Shelton; Bm Fitzroy Gardner. Comment: Source = V & A programme.

96.56 *TRICKY TRILBY.* NOVELTY [19/3/96-21/3/96. 3 perf]. Comment: Mentioned in *St*; however, I can find no other record of this play or performance.

96.57 *TRUE BLUE; OR, AFLOAT AND ASHORE* (Naval D,5a) Leonard Outram & Stuart Gordon. OLYMPIC 19/3/96-25/4/ 96. 34 perf [w/mat 21/3, 17/4; np 3/4].* Cpt. Drake J.F. Cornish; Lieut. Grey Maitland Alfred Bucklaw; Lieut. Mark Strachan William Rignold; Lieut. Jones Albert E. Raynor; Sub-Lieut. Algernon Skewes J.A. Bentham; Midshipman Easy Leon Lion; Assistant Engineer Duncan Tovey; John Lobbett Charles Wibrow; "Polly" Hopkins Jarvis Widdicomb; "Spud" Murphy Henry Bertram; Joe Cockles A. Gerard; Timothy Flatfoot Fred Solo; Corporal of the Watch Tom Taylor; Ward-Room Servant Charles Seymour; Governor of Gibraltar H.R. Teesdale; Governor of Algeciras F.A. Lane; Sir George Majoribanks--Monsieur Vandeloupe Leonard Outram/Frederic de Lara; Spero Xicluna Edward O'Neill; Spanish Hawker Percy Everard; Alfonso Bernard Stavordale; Carlos Roland Stewart; Rodriguez J. Beauvaine; Guardia Civil Stanislaus Calhaem. Midshipman Sprightly Marion Hunt-

ley; <u>Carlotta Malrayo</u> Mrs Raleigh; <u>Alice Majoribanks</u>
Laura Graves; <u>Daphne Bower</u> Mary Bates; <u>Rose Pringle</u>
Kate Phillips. <u>PP</u> Charles Wilmot; <u>Cost</u> Mrs May, J.
Hyman & Co., Russell & Allen, Stagg & Mantle; <u>L</u> Naval
Drama Syndicate; <u>Mgr dir & Pd</u> Leonard Outram; <u>Sc</u> W.T.
Hemsley, H. Mapleson, Fred Storey; <u>Pq</u> William Clark-
son; <u>Cond & Mus</u> B. Brigata Bucalossi; <u>Sec</u> W. Heron
Brown; <u>Sm</u> A.W. Fitzgerald; <u>Asm</u> T.N. Walter; <u>Bm</u> J.H.
Elliston; <u>Bom</u> S.J. Crookes. *REV: Ath 28/3/96 p422;*
E 21/3/96 p11; Sk 25/3/96 p374, 401; SR 28/3/96 p324-
6; St 26/3/96 p12; Th 1/5/96 p292-3; Ti 20/3/96 p10;
TW96 p79-82.

96.58 *OUTWARD BOUND* (MSk) Nellie Ganthony. TERRY'S
21/3/96-18/5/96. 49 perf [np 3/4].* Nellie Ganthony.
<u>PP</u> Edward Terry; <u>L</u> Frederick Kerr; <u>Cond</u> T[homas]
Smythe; <u>Bm</u> H.T. Brickwell; <u>Sm</u> W.J. Robertson.

96.59 *JANE SHORE; OR, A WOMAN'S PENANCE* (HistD,4a)
Violet Temple & T.N. Walter. NOVELTY 23/3/96-28/3/96.
6 perf. 1st perf? <u>Edward IV</u> Arthur Osborne; <u>Richard,</u>
<u>Duke of Gloucester</u> J.O. Stewart; <u>Lord William Hastings</u>
G.R. Cooper; <u>Sir William Catesby</u> L.G. Kean; <u>Sir Rich-</u>
<u>ard Radcliffe</u> Harry Crane; <u>William Shore</u> T.W. Law-
rence; <u>John Milverton</u> George Hammond; <u>Peter Buckram</u>
Henry J. Fowler; <u>Simon Muckleberry</u> Frank Stone; <u>Joel-</u>
<u>bert</u> T. Clements; <u>Malbouche</u> Bert Moore. <u>Queen Eliza-</u>
<u>beth Woodville</u> Maude Roberts; <u>Lady Wargrave</u> Eva Wil-
son; <u>Druisda</u> Lydia Fraser; <u>Jane Shore</u> Violet Temple.
<u>L</u> V. St. Lawrence; <u>Mgr</u> Walter Tyrrell. *REV: E 28/3/96*
p8; St 26/3/96 p12-3.

96.60 *JUDAS MACCABEUS* (O,5a) Abraham Goldfaden. NOVEL-
TY 30/3/96. 1 perf. <u>Judas Maccabeus</u> Goldsmith; <u>Anti-</u>
<u>ochus/High Priest</u> Fineberg; <u>Jason</u> Wallerstein; <u>Nic-</u>
<u>canor</u> Weisman; <u>Field Marshall</u> Magaddson; <u>Eleazar</u> Mas-
ter Sollie Keysor. <u>Hannah</u> J. Keysor; <u>Madia</u> Waxman.
<u>L</u> V. St. Lawrence; <u>Mgr</u> Walter Tyrrell, H. Fineberg;
<u>Sec</u> Godfrey Stargatt; <u>Cond</u> Prof Staub. *REV: E 4/4/96*
p9; St 2/4/96 p12-3.

96.61 *RABBI JOSELMAN* (O,5a) Abraham Goldfaden. NOVELTY
31/3/96. 1 perf. <u>Rabbi Joselman</u> Goldsmith; <u>Aaron</u> Herman; <u>Ulrich</u> Fineberg; <u>Kuntz</u> Wallerstein; <u>King Karl</u>

Weisman; <u>Pepercorn</u> Victor; <u>Brandth</u> Weisman; <u>Folger</u>
Magaddson. <u>Sara</u> J. Keysor; <u>Baruch</u> Waxman. <u>L</u>, <u>Mgr</u>,
<u>Sec</u>, <u>Cond</u> as for 96.60. *REV: As for 96.60.*

96.62 *THE PERSECUTION OF THE JEWS IN PORTUGAL* (MP).
NOVELTY 1/4/96. 1 perf. <u>Joseph</u> Fineberg; <u>Pardelouse</u>
Wallerstein; <u>Granville</u> Weisman; <u>King of Portugal/Rabbi</u>
<u>Aaron</u> Goldsmith; <u>Simon Aventove</u> Magaddson; <u>Pashow</u>
Victor. <u>Princess Elizabeth</u> Waxman; <u>Hannah</u> J. Keysor.
<u>L</u>, <u>Mgr</u>, <u>Sec</u>, <u>Cond</u> as for 96.60. *REV: E 4/4/96 p9.*

96.63 *KING SOLOMAN*. NOVELTY 2/4/96. Rnd. <u>Comment</u>:
Mentioned only in *Cyc*.

96.64 *FAUST* (O[5a]) Charles Gounod. DRURY LANE 4/4/96,
10/4, 17/4, 25/4(m), 30/4, 5/5/96. 6 perf.** <u>Faust</u>
E.C. Hedmont; <u>Mephistopheles</u> Charles Manners; <u>Wagner</u>
Hugh Gwynne; <u>Valentine</u> Wilson Sheffield. <u>Marguerite</u>
Fanny Moody; <u>Siebel</u> Louise Meisslinger; <u>Martha</u> Kate
Vito. <u>L & MGR</u> Augustus Harris; <u>Cond</u> Luigi Mancinelli.
REV: Ath 11/4/96 p486; E 11/4/96 p8; St 9/4/96 p13;
Ti 6/4/96 p8.

96.65 *THE GAY PARISIENNE* (MC,2a) George Dance (lib)
& Ivan Caryll (mus). DUKE OF YORK'S 4/4/96-27/3/97.
369 perf [w/S mat 11/4/96-30/5/96; w/W mat 10/6/96-
2/9/96; w/S mat 5/9/96-26/12/96; w/W, S mat 30/12/96-
24/2/97; w/S mat 27/2/97-27/3/97; add mat 15/4/96,
28/12/96, 22/2/97; np 25/12/96]. 1st perfd Opera
House, Northampton 1/10/94. <u>Ebenezer Honeycomb</u> Lionel Rignold; <u>Mjr. Fossdyke</u> W.H. Denny; <u>Tiger Tim</u>
William Butler; <u>Amos Dingle</u> Hubert Willis; <u>Tom Ever-</u>
<u>leigh</u> Edgar Stevens/Augustus Cramer; <u>Algernon P. Ducie</u>
James Francis/Neville Leese/C. Guildford; <u>Percy Toot-</u>
<u>ing</u> C. Guildford/F. Garton; <u>Cecil Smyth</u> P. Leslie/
Donald Hall/Henri Leoni/A. Turner; <u>Hans</u> Harry Kilburn;
<u>Fritz</u> Garth/Walter Butler; <u>Blatterwatter</u> Akerman May;
<u>Auguste Pompier</u> Frank Wheeler. <u>Mrs Honeycomb</u> Lillie
Belmore/Helen Kinnaird/Edith Stuart/M.A. Victor; <u>Nora</u>
Violet Robinson/Edith Courtney; <u>Mabel</u> Marion Dolby/
Nellie Gregory/S. Marsden; <u>Angela</u> Violet Ellicott;
<u>May</u> Edith Stuart/Helen Kinnaird; <u>Ethel</u> E. Carlton/
Florence Ellis/May Harrison; <u>Gladys</u> Edith Bartlett;
<u>Maud</u> Edith Mada; <u>Edith</u> Rose Montgomery/Clare Leighton/

Florrie Glynn; Violet Ivy Hertzog; Rose Maud Hoppe;
Gretchen Harriet Wood/Edith Milton; Anna Edith Mil-
ton; Ruth Louie Freear/Peggy Pryde; Julie Bonbon Ada
Reeve/Violet Dene/Clara Thropp; Dancers Beatrice
Grenville, Nora Neville, Violet Dene, Lillie McIntyre.
GEN MGR Michael Levenston; Mgr Horace Sedger; L York
Dramatic Syndicate Limited; Sc E.G. Banks, William
Telbin; Cond Sidney Jones; Ch Will Bishop; Cost dgn
A. Comelli; Cost Alias; Bm James A. Cook; Pq William
Clarkson. *REV: E 11/4/96 p10; Sk 15/4/96 p498, 29/4/
96 p15-7; St 9/4/96 p13; Th 1/5/96 p291-2; Ti 6/4/96
p8; TW96 p298-305.*

96.66 *THE STAR OF INDIA* (D,5a) George R. Sims & Arthur
Shirley. PRINCESS'S 4/4/96-16/5/96. 38 perf [w/mat
6/4].* Sir Roland Stanmore Lyston Lyle; Cpt. Stan-
more Clifton Alderson; Mark Stanmore George Young;
Dick Hatfield Walter Beaumont; Lieut. Dollamore Sid-
ney Howard; Mr Wentworth A.E. Matthews; Corporal
O'Sullivan Charles H. Kenny; Aleem Khan Robert Pate-
man; Arthur Hopkins J.T. MacMillan; Vernon Hopkins
Frank Wyatt; Tom Tully F[red] Colson; Jim Green H.
Wade; Dan Williams George Yates; Subadar Hira Singh
Gerald Morley; Superintendent Willoughby Charles Fran-
more; Cpt. Fordyce Grey; Mjr. Wallace Lyster. Kate
Armiger Hettie Chattell; Mrs Wentworth Kate Tyndall;
Dora Wilton Nellie Gregory; Oriana Sydney Fairbrother;
Clarry Beamish Helen Farrington; Mrs Beamish Harriett
Clifton; Mrs Musters Helen Vicary; Maraquita Agnes
Hewitt; Extras Violet Forester, Beatrice Parke, Marie
Aubrey, Lily Floyd, Holmes, Lily Gordon, Lilian Mow-
bray. MGR Albert Gilmer; Sc Cecil E. Hicks, H[enry]
Brooke, J. Johnstone; Mus & Mus dir Theodore Ward;
Cost Viola, Stagg & Mantle, Morris Angel & Son, Gains-
borough; Pd & Sm John Douglass; Am Horace Gilmer;
Treas H. Bellamy Smith; Bom S.H. MacDonald. *REV: Ath
11/4/96 p486; E 11/4/96 p10; St 9/4/96 p13; Th 1/5/96
p285-7; Ti 6/4/96 p8; TW96 p82-6.*

96.67 *CAVALLERIA RUSTICANA* (O,1a) Pietro Mascagni.
DRURY LANE 6/4/96, 11/4(m), 16/4, 18/4, 22/4, 28/4/96.
6 perf.** Alfio Wilson Sheffield; Turiddu E.C. Hedmont. Santuzza Lilian Tree; Lucia Amadi; Lola Jessie
Huddleston. L & MGR Augustus Harris; Mus dir Luigi

Mancinelli. *REV: Ath 11/4/96 p486; E 11/4/96 p8; St 9/4/96 p13; Ti 8/4/96 p4.*

96.68 *PAGLIACCI* (O,2a) Ruggiero Leoncavallo. DRURY LANE 6/4/96, 11/4(m), 16/4, 18/4, 22/4, 28/4, 4/5/96. 7 perf.** <u>Tonio</u> Richard Green; <u>Silvio</u> Theodore Byard; <u>Beppe</u> Reginald Brophy; <u>Canio</u> Philip Brozel. <u>Nedda</u> Pauline Joran. L & MGR, <u>Cond</u> as for 96.67. *REV: As for 96.67.*

96.69 *BELOW LONDON BRIDGE* (D,4a) Richard Dowling. NOVELTY 6/4/96-11/4/96. 6 perf.* <u>Frank Jeaters</u> W[ill-iam] Felton; <u>John Crane</u> Augustin Symonds; <u>Ben Sherwin</u> Frank Stanvill; <u>Jim Natchbrook</u> W[illiam] Adams; <u>George Sayers</u> C. Lewis; <u>Hilliers</u> W.M. Franks; <u>Bill Smith</u> H. Roberts; <u>Artificer</u> W. Johnson. <u>Edith Orr</u> Ethel Fennar; <u>Mrs Orr</u> Mrs Gordon-Gray; <u>Widow Natchbrook</u> Ina Leon Cassilis; <u>Mrs Natchbrook</u> Katie Parry; <u>Mary Jeaters</u> V. St. Lawrence; <u>Mgr</u> Walter Tyrrell. *REV: E 11/4/96 p11; St 9/4/96 p13-4.*

96.70 *THE NEW AGENT* (MCa) R.H. Lindo (lib) & A[lger-non H.] Lindo (mus). NOVELTY 6/4/96-11/4/96. 6 perf.* <u>Montague Antonio</u> R. Henry; <u>Sir John Blasi</u> W.M. Franks; <u>William</u> W[illiam] Adams. <u>Lady John Blasi</u> Katie Parry; <u>Tottie Oliver</u> Violet Neville. L, Mgr as for 96.69. *REV: E 11/4/96 p11.*

96.71 *THE BOHEMIAN GIRL* (O[3a]) Michael Balfe. DRURY LANE 7/4/96, 15/4, 18/4/96(m). 3 perf.** <u>Thaddeus</u> Herbert Grover/Reginald Brophy; <u>Devilshoof</u> Charles Manners/G.H. Snazelle; <u>Count Arnheim</u> Wilson Sheffield; <u>Florestein</u> Wilfred Esmond. <u>Arline</u> Fanny Moody/Agnes Molteno; <u>Gipsy Queen</u> Louise Meisslinger; <u>Nurse</u> Kate Vito. L & MGR Augustus Harris; <u>Mus dir</u> Luigi Mancinelli; <u>Cond</u> J.M. Glover. *REV: E 11/4/96 p8, 18/4/96 p9; St 9/4/96 p13; Ti 8/4/96 p4.*

96.72 *A MOTHER OF THREE* (F,3a) Clotilde Graves. COMEDY 8/4/96-4/6/96. 61 perf [w/S mat; add mat 22/4, 29/4, 13/5].* <u>Prof Murgatroyd</u> Felix Morris/Charles H.E. Brookfield; <u>Sir Wellington Port, K.C.B.</u> Cyril Maude; <u>Napier Outram Port</u> Stuart Champion; <u>Cpt. Tuckle</u> Clarence Blakiston; <u>Cheveley Thrupp</u> Cosmo Stuart.

Lady Port Rose Leclercq; Amelia MacKenzie; Sooza Annie
Goward; Cassiopeia Esmé Beringer; Vesta Lily Johnson;
Aquila Audrey Ford; Mrs Murgatroyd Fanny Brough. L &
MGR J.W. Comyns Carr; Bom Scarisbrick; Pd Charles H,
Hawtrey; Sm Frederick Glover; Mus dir Alfred J. Cald-
icott; Bm Silvanus Dauncey. *REV: Ath 11/4/96 p486-7;
E 11/4/96 p10; Sk 15/4/96 p534, 27/5/96 p192-3; SR
11/4/96 p374; St 16/4/96 p13; Th 1/5/96 p289-90; Ti
9/4/96 p6; TW96 p114-5.*

96.73 *THE GUINEA STAMP* (P,1a) Cyril Hallward. COMEDY
8/4/96-4/6/96. 50 perf.* Sir Charles Trefusis Ernest
Cosham; Jack Manners Cosmo Stuart; Cecil Arbuthnot
Stuart Champion. Mabel Trefusis May Edouin; Nellie
Robinson Jessie Bateman. L & MGR, Bom, Sm, Mus dir,
Bm as for 96.72. *REV: E, St as for 96.72.*

96.74 *CARMEN* (O[4a]) Georges Bizet. DRURY LANE 8/4/96,
13/4, 29/4, 2/5(m), 6/5/96. 5 perf.** Escamillo
Richard Green; Don José Philip Brozel; Remendado Wil-
fred Esmond; Morales Williams Devers; Dancairo Wilson
Sheffield; Zuniga William Llewelyn. Carmen Pauline
Joran; Michaela Amy Sherwin; Mercedes Jessie Huddle-
ston; Frasquita Clara Addison. L & MGR Augustus Harris;
Mus dir & Cond Luigi Mancinelli. *REV: Ath 11/4/96 p486;
E 11/4/96 p8; St 16/4/96 p12; Ti 10/4/96 p8.*

96.75 *HANSEL AND GRETEL* (O[3a]) Engelbert Humperdinck.
DRURY LANE 9/4/96, 20/4, 24/4, 4/5, 9/5/96(m). 5
perf.** Peter Charles Copland. Hansel Marie Elba;
Gertrude Julia Lennox; Gretel Jessie Huddleston;
Witch Louise Meisslinger; Dewman Edith Johnston; Sand-
man Sylvia Delrita. L & MGR, Mus dir as for 96.74.
*REV: Ath 18/4/96 p520-1; E 11/4/96 p8, 25/4/96 p15;
St 16/4/96 p12; Ti 10/4/96 p8.*

96.76 *THE SIN OF ST. HULDA* (RD,4a) G. Stuart Ogilvie.
SHAFTESBURY 9/4/96-25/4/96. 17 perf [w/mat 11/4,
18/4].* Otho Charles Cartwright; Heinric Lewis Wal-
ler; John Knipperdolling Henry Kemble; Manteuffel
Kenneth Black; Count Ulric George Hippisley; Joachim
Edmund Covington; Herman Charles Goodhart; Ernest
Frank McDonnell; Wilhelm A. Anderson; Konrad Lesly
Thomson; Nikolaus H. Deane; Franz Henry Nelson;

Stortebecker Gilbert Trent; <u>Tipstaff</u> Henry; <u>Hugo</u> A.
Chenery; <u>Herald</u> Frank Morley; <u>Officer</u> James Spiller;
<u>Maximilian</u> Frank Thornton. <u>Dame Friederike</u> Annie Web-
ster; <u>Liese</u> Helena Dacre; <u>Marte</u> E. Brinsley Sheridan;
<u>Elizabeth</u> Mrs Arthur Ayres; <u>Hedwig</u> Marie Lyons; <u>Ann</u>
Lillian Brennard; <u>Elsa</u> Annie Burton; <u>Maria</u> Leonie
Norbury; <u>Gretchen</u> Rachel; <u>Doris</u> Dorothy Harwood; <u>St.</u>
<u>Hulda</u> Kate Rorke. L & MGR Lewis Waller, H.H. Morell;
<u>Pp</u> John Lancaster; <u>Bom</u> David; <u>Sc</u> William Harford,
Walter Johnstone, Walter Hann; <u>Cost dgn</u> Mrs J.W. Comyns Carr, Karl; <u>Cost</u> Mrs Nettleship, J. & L. Nathan;
<u>Pq</u> Fox; <u>Sm</u> E.J. Malyon; <u>Asm</u> A.J. Bowyer; <u>Mus dir</u> O.
de Tender; <u>Sec</u> Charles Meyrick. *REV: Ath 18/4/96 p521-*
2; E 11/4/96 p10; Sk 15/4/96 p498; SR 18/4/96 p396-7;
St 16/4/96 p13; Th 1/5/96 p287-9; Ti 10/4/96 p8; TW96
p106-14.

96.77 *SEALED TO SILENCE* (D) F. Moir Bussy & H.M.
Holles. STRAND 10/4/96. <u>Comment</u>: Probably a copyright
perf.

96.78 *TANNHAUSER* (O,3a) Richard Wagner. DRURY LANE
11/4/96, 14/4, 27/4, 7/5, 9/5/96. 5 perf.** <u>Tann-</u>
<u>hauser</u> E.C. Hedmondt/Philip Brozel; <u>Hermann</u> Alex
Bevan; <u>Wolfram</u> David Bispham; <u>Walther</u> Reginald Bro-
phy; <u>Biterolf</u> William Llewelyn; <u>Heinrich</u> Robert Eadie;
<u>Reinmar</u> Ormonde. <u>Elizabeth</u> Marie Duma; <u>Venus</u> Lilian
Tree; <u>Young Shepherd</u> Clara Addison; <u>Pages</u> [Margherita]
Kowska, Bliss, Shortland, Guerrier. L & MGR Augustus
Harris; <u>Mus dir & Cond</u> Luigi Mancinelli; <u>Sm</u> Arthur
P. Collins; <u>Am</u> Neil Forsyth. *REV: Ath 18/4/96 p521;*
E 18/4/96 p9; St 16/4/96 p12; Ti 13/4/96 p8.

96.79 *BIARRITZ* (MF,2sc) Jerome K. Jerome (lib) & Adrian Ross (lib) & F. Osmond Carr (mus). PRINCE OF
WALES'S 11/4/96-20/6/96. 71 perf [w/S mat exc 11/4].*
<u>John J. Jenkins</u> Arthur Roberts; <u>Johannes</u> Fred Kaye;
<u>Gen Tomassino</u> Eric Thorne; <u>Rodney Kemp</u> Roland Cunning-
ham/Augustus Cramer; <u>Duke of Melton Mowbray</u> Algernon
Newark; <u>Dr Arlistreete</u> L.F. Chapuy; <u>Honcurable John-</u>
<u>nie</u> Harold Eden; <u>Gendarme</u> Walker Marnock. <u>Tessie</u>
<u>Carew</u> Phyllis Broughton; <u>Charley Bargus</u> Millie Hylton;
<u>Enriqua</u> Ellas Dee/Attie Chester; <u>Babette</u> Pierette
Amella; <u>Duchess of Melton Mowbray</u> Harrie Doreen; <u>Mrs</u>

Carew Adelaide Newton; Florence Eva Ellerslie; Jane
Julia Kent; Elizabeth Carrie Benton; Janet Kittie
Loftus; Extras Attie Chester, Christine Salisbury,
Nelly Alwyn, Fanny Harris, Florence Linton, Lucille,
Grahame, Mary Turner, Florrie Schubert. PP Edgar Bruce;
Sc [T.E.] Ryan, R.C. McCleery; Cost Sarah Mayer, A.
Morhange; Mus dir Herbert Bunning; Sm Clarence Hunt;
Act mgr C.P. Levilly. *REV: E 18/4/96 p8; Sk 15/4/96
p498; SR 18/4/96 p397-8; St 16/4/96 p12-3; Th 1/5/96
p290-1; Ti 13/4/96 p8; TW96 p116-22.*

96.80 *EAST LYNNE* (D). NOVELTY 13/4/96-18/4/96. 6 perf.
Francis Levison Augustin Symonds; Archibald Carlyle
William Felton; Lord Mount Severn Pemberton Peach;
Justice Hare Frank Stanville; Richard Hare W[illiam]
Adams; Dill W.M. Francks; Officer George Abel. Little
Willie Glennie Wood; Barbara Hare Ethel Fennar; Miss
Carlyle Eva Dudley; Joyce Katie Parry; Wilson Violet
Neville; Lady Isabel V. St. Lawrence. L V. St. Law-
rence; Mgr Walter Tyrrell. *REV: E 18/4/96 p8; St 16/
4/96 p13.*

96.81 *MONSIEUR DE PARIS* (P,1a) Alicia Ramsay & Rudolph
de Cordova. ROYALTY 16/4/96-5/5/96. 16 perf [np 28/4].
1st perfd Gaiety, Hastings 6/4/96 [as *The Executioner's Daughter*]. Georges Delpit Mark Kinghorne; Henry
Le Febvre Henry Vibart. Mere Lisette Mrs Henry Leigh;
Jacinta Violet Vanbrugh. L & MGR Arthur Bourchier;
Pp Kate Santley; Mus & Cond Albert Fox; Bm T. Stevens;
Sm Fred W. Permain; Act mgr Arthur Bertram; Bom W.E.
Blakeley. *REV: Ath 25/4/96 p554; E 18/4/96 p8; Sk
22/4/96 p551; SR 25/4/96 p473-5; St 23/4/96 p13; Th
1/5/96 p293-4; TW96 p139-40.*

96.82 *THE LADY OF LONGFORD* (O[1a]) Leonhard Emil Bach
(mus) & Augustus Harris (lib) & Frederick E. Wertherly
(lib). DRURY LANE 20/4/96, 24/4, 9/5/96(m). 3 perf.**
Earl of Longford Reginald Brophy; Roundhead Col. Alex
Bevan. Countess of Longford Pauline Joran; Muriel
Valli Valli. L & MGR Augustus Harris; Cond Wilhelm
Feld. *REV: Ath 25/4/96 p553; E 25/4/96 p15; St 23/4/
96 p12; Ti 22/4/96 p12.* Comment: "Given in English
for the first time" (*Ti*).

96.83 *AT BAY* (D,Prol,4a) Charles Lander & Ina Leon Cassilis. NOVELTY 20/4/96-25/4/96. 6 perf, 1st perfd Ladbroke Hall 9/4/88. Laurence Dudley William Felton; Vernon Gray Augustin Symonds; Sam Watson W.M. Franks; Jerry Hackett George Abel; Edward Darrell Watty Brunton, sr; Philip Darrell Pemberton Peach. Lucy Darrell Daisy England; Alice Katie Parry; Mrs Hackett Ina Leon Cassilis; Ethel Dudley V. St. Lawrence. L V. St. Lawrence; Mgr Walter Tyrrell. *REV: E 25/4/96 p8; St 23/4/96 p13.*

96.84 *LOHENGRIN* (O,3a) Richard Wagner. DRURY LANE 21/4/96, 25/4, 1/5/96. 3 perf.** Lohengrin E.C. Hedmondt; Henry I Alex Bevan; Herald Wilson Sheffield; Frederick Telramund David Bispham. Elsa of Brabant Fanny Moody; Ortud Louise Meisslinger. L & MGR Augustus Harris; Mus dir & Cond Luigi Mancinelli; Sm Arthur P. Collins; Am Neil Forsyth. *REV: Ath 25/4/96 p553; E 25/4/96 p15; St 23/4/96 p12, 30/4/96 p12; Ti 22/4/ 96 p12.*

96.85 *THE ROGUE'S COMEDY* (P,3a) H.A. Jones. GARRICK 21/4/96-30/5/96. 41 perf [w/S mat exc 23/5, 30/5; add mat 20/5, 27/5].* Bailey Prothero E.S. Willard; Mr Lambert W.T. Lovell; Sir William Clarabut Cecil Crofton; Sir Thomas Dovergreen Sydney Brough; Lord John Bucklow David S. James; Marquis of Bicester George Canninge; Mr Sydenham J.R. Crauford; Mr Reffell A.B. Tapping; Mr Hubbock George Willoughby; Mr Chester Webber; Mr Pinniger W. Levy; Robert Cushing Herbert Standing; Palmer F. Hamilton Knight; 1st Footman Albert Sims; 2nd Footman L. Wenman; Servant at Lady Dovergreen's G. Smith/G.James. Miss Jennison Geraldine Olliffe; Lady Clarabut Lady Monckton; Nina Clarabut Cora Poole; Lady Dovergreen Robertha Erskine; Mrs Sydenham Mrs H[arry] Cane; Mrs Reffell Keith Wakeman; Miss Proye Ellen Meyrick. L John Hare; Mgr E.S. Willard; Act mgr W.H. Griffiths; Bom [E.] Candler; Cond Haydn Waud. *REV: Ath 25/4/96 p554; E 25/4/96 p8; Sk 29/4/96 p4; SR 25/4/96 p426-8; St 23/4/96 p12-3; Th 1/5/96 p284-5; Ti 22/4/96 p12; TW96 p122-6.*

96.86 *MY ASTRAL BODY* (F,3a) Charles Hudson & Nicholas Colthurst. COURT 22/4/96 mat perf.* Clarke Cariston

Yorke Stephens; Clarke Cariston's Astral Body [W.?]
Beckwith; Albert Thayer C. [M.] Lowne; David Meredith,
J.P. Ernest Hendrie; Naingre Phu J.F. Cornish; Bullam
Pore W. Lee. Mildred Cariston Fanny Coleman; Anne
Meredith [Sydney?] Fairbrother; Kate Harland Helen
Petrie. MGR Arthur Chudleigh; Pd John Douglass; Mus
dir Carl Kiefert. *REV: E 25/4/96 p11; St 23/4/96 p13;
Th 1/6/96 p353-4.*

96.87 *MARITANA* (O[3a]) Vincent Wallace. DRURY LANE
23/4/96. 1 perf.** King Charles Manners; Don José
William Devers; Don Caesar John Child; Cpt. Wino-
gradoff; Marquis W. Esmond. Maritana Fanny Moody;
Lazarillo [Jessie?] Browning; Marchioness Kate Vito.
L & MGR Augustus Harris; Mus dir Luigi Mancinelli.
REV: E 25/4/96 p15; St 30/4/96 p12.

96.88 *MARY PENNINGTON, SPINSTER* (C,4a) W.R. Walkes.
ST. JAMES'S 24/4/96 mat perf.* Timothy Hale Cyril
Maude; George Armstrong Frank H. Fenton; Algy Blom-
field Sydney Brough; Dr Hale's Servant W. A[ubrey]
Chandler. Mary Pennington Kate Rorke; Lady Maitland
Olga Brandon; Prudence Dering Mary Jerrold; Mrs Pen-
nington's Servant Furtado-Clarke. L & MGR George
Alexander; Dir E.W. Gardiner; Bom Arnold. *REV: Ath
2/5/96 p593; E 25/4/96 p11; Sk 29/4/96 p4; St 30/4/96
p12-3; Th 1/6/96 p354-5; TW96 p126-8.*

96.89 *THE GEISHA: A STORY OF A TEAHOUSE* (Japanese
MP,2a) Owen Hall (lib) & Harry Greenbank (lyr) & Sid-
ney Jones (mus). DALY'S 25/4/96-28/5/98. 760 perf
[w/S mat exc 25/4/96; add mat 24/2/97, 24/6/97; mat
only 24/12/97; np 25/12/96, 16/4/97, 22/6, 25/12/97,
8/4/98].* Reginald Fairfax C. Hayden Coffin/Conway
Dixon/John Coates; Dick Cunningham W. Louis Bradfield/
Ernest Snow/J. Farren Soutar; Arthur Cuddy Leedham
Bantock/E.L. Fraser/Donald Hall/Edmund Sherras; George
Grimston Sydney Ellison; Cpt. Katana William Philp/
Frank Boor/Maurice Farkoa; Takemine Fred Rosse/Colin
Coop/Williams; Wun Hi Huntley Wright/Fred Wright, jr;
Marquis Imari Harry Monkhouse/Rutland Barrington/W.H.
Rawlins. O Mimosa San Marie Tempest/Elise Cooke/
Jessica Lait/Maggie May/Hilda Moody; Juliette Diamant
Juliette Nesville/Mary Fawcett/Elsie Cross/Mabel Dun-

can; <u>Nami</u> Khristine Yudall/Rhoda Windrum/F[lorence?]
Rooke; <u>O Kiku San</u> Emilie Herve/Maggie May/Florence
Lauri/Jessica Lait/F[lorence?] Collingbourne/Eva
Clarke/Gertie Carlow/Marie Fawcett; <u>O Hana San</u> Mary
Fawcett/Mary Collette/C. McGill/Gertie Carlow; <u>O Kin-
koto San</u> Elise Cook/Grace Arundale/Gertrude Palmer/
M[arguerite] Roche; <u>O Komuraski San</u> Mary Collette/
Toby Claude/Marguerite Roche; <u>Lady Constance Wynne</u>
Maud Hobson/Gladys Homfrey; <u>Marie Worthington</u> Blanche
Massey/Lucille Grahame; <u>Ethel Hurst</u> Hetty Hamer/Lucy
Golding/Maie Saqui; <u>Mabel Grant</u> Alice Davis; <u>Louie
Plumpton</u> Margaret Fraser/Kate Cannon; <u>Molly Seamore</u>
Letty Lind; <u>Tommy Stanley</u> Lydia Flopp/Fanny Dango.
<u>L & MGR</u> Augustin Daly; <u>Cond</u> Sidney Jones/Victor
Champion/Ernest Ford; <u>Sc</u> William Telbin; <u>Ch</u> Willie
Warde; <u>Sm</u> Brian England; <u>Cost dgn</u> Percy Anderson;
<u>Cost</u> Miss Fisher, Jays, Alias, Harrison, Mrs Bigelow,
Cooling & Lawrence, Cole, Morris Angel; <u>Furn</u> Franck,
Marian, Anton Benda; <u>Lime</u> [W.] Kerr; <u>Pq</u> William Clark-
son; <u>Add mus</u> Lionel Monckton; <u>Bm</u> John Farrington; <u>Act
mgr</u> M. Edwards; <u>Bom</u> E[dward] Brown. *REV: E 2/5/96 p8;
Sk 29/4/96 p4, 42, 13/5/96 p89, 99, 2/12/96 p232-4;
St 30/4/96 p12; Th 1/6/96 p350-2; Ti 27/4/96 p12; TW
96 p130-1.* <u>Comment</u>: The following roles were added
during the course of the production: <u>Hon Gerald St.
Pancras</u> Lawrance d'Orsay/Arthur Appleby/Scott Russell.
<u>Miss Foster</u> M[arie] Yorke/Mabel Tempest; <u>Miss Waters</u>
J. Morell/O[live] Morell.

96.90 *TWO OF A TRADE.* AVENUE 27/4/96-6/6/96. 36 perf.*
<u>LI</u> Charles H. Hawtrey; <u>Mgr</u> Francis Howard, Alexander
Loftus. <u>Comment</u>: Nicoll indicates that the Lord Chamberlain issued the licence for this piece for 21/5/96.

96.91 *OUR BOYS* (C,3a) Henry J. Byron. NOVELTY 27/4/96-
2/5/96. 6 perf.** <u>Sir Geoffrey Champneys</u> Edward Beasley; <u>Talbot Champneys</u> Arthur S. Wood; <u>Perkyn Middle-
wick</u> John S. Wood; <u>Charles Middlewick</u> William Felton;
<u>Kempster</u> W.M. Francks. <u>Poddles</u> Adah Lacroft; <u>Belinda</u>
Nellie Glyn; <u>Clarissa Champneys</u> Kate Robberds; <u>Violet
Melrose</u> Octavia Kenmore; <u>Mary Melrose</u> V. St. Lawrence.
<u>L</u> V. St. Lawrence; <u>Mgr</u> Walter Tyrrell; <u>Sm</u> Pemberton
Peach. *REV: E 2/5/96 p8-9; St 30/4/96 p13.*

96.92 *DREAM FACES* (Dramatic Fancy,1a) Wynn Miller.
NOVELTY 27/4/96-2/5/96. 6 perf.** Robert William
Felton; Philip William Adams. Lucy Alice Darrell; Mar-
garet V. St. Lawrence. L, Mgr, Sm as for 96.91. *REV:
As for 96.91.*

96.93 *THE NEW BABY* (F,3a) Arthur Bourchier [adpt of
H.F. Fisher & J. Jarno, *Der Rabenvater*]. ROYALTY 28/
4/96-16/5/96. 19 perf [w/S mat exc 16/5]. 1st prof
Gaiety, Hastings 6/4/96. Col. Wilberforce Walker
Arthur Bourchier; Commodore van Gutt William Blakeley;
Petruchio Gomez W.G. Elliott; Harry Charles Troode.
Drusilla Walker Alice Mansfield; Patience van Gutt
Mrs B.M. de Solla; Faith Irene Vanbrugh; Kate Gomez
Katherine Stewart; Pascoe Lilian Millward. L & MGR
Arthur Bourchier; Pp Kate Santley. *REV: Ath 2/5/96
p593; E 2/5/96 p8; Sk 6/5/96 p50-1, 86; SR 25/4/96
p473-5; St 30/4/96 p12; Th 1/6/96 p353; Ti 29/4/96
p13; TW96 p133-6.*

96.94 *A NIGHT OUT* (FC,3a) Seymour Hicks [adpt of
Georges Feydeau & Maurice Desvallières, *Hôtel du Libre
Echange*]. VAUDEVILLE 29/4/96-9/10/97. 525 perf [w/W,
S mat 9/5/96-30/5/96; w/W mat 3/6/96-6/10/97 exc 26/8/
96; add mat 26/12/96, 19/4/97, 15/5, 22/5/97; np 25/
12/96, 16/4/97, 22/6/97]. 1st perfd Theatre Royal,
Newcastle 13/4/96 [as *A Night in Paris*]. Joseph Ping-
let George Giddens; Paillard Charles Sugden; Mathieu
William Wyes; Maxime Aubrey Fitzgerald/George Gros-
smith, jr/Aubrey Fitzgerald; Brochard Joseph Carne;
Boulot Gus Danby; Bastien E.W. Thomas/Cairns James;
Ernest Herbert Peters; Botticelli Neville Doone. Mar-
celle Fannie Ward/Sybyl Grey; Angelique Mrs Edmund
Phelps; Victorine Pattie Browne/Sybyl Grey; Lady Eva
Murton; Hyacynthe Lottie Sargent/Clara Earle; Violette
E. Barrington/Gladys Deroy; Marguerite Eileen Concan-
en/D. Danby; Rose Edith Henderson/Betty MacDonald/
Mary Walker/Maud Deane. L & MGR A. & S. Gatti; Sm
George Fielder; Bm W.H. Risque; Pd Seymour Hicks; Sc
William Harford, Joseph Harker; Cond George Arnold;
Cost Jay & Co., Mrs Bigelow, Mme Elaine, Morris Angel
& Son; Pq William Clarkson; Furn Oetzmann. *REV: Ath
2/5/96 p593; E 2/5/96 p8; Sk 12/8/96 p107-9; SR 25/4/
96 p473-5; St 7/5/96 p12, 19/11/96 p13; Th 1/6/96*

p352-3; Ti 30/4/96 p6; TW96 p137-9. Comment: Nicoll
gives Charles H. Klein as the author of this piece.
However, the evidence appears to support Hicks as the
correct author.

96.95 *PAPA'S WIFE* (Ca,1a) Seymour Hicks (lib) & F.C.
Phillips (lib) & Ellaline Terriss (mus). VAUDEVILLE
29/4/96-10/11/96. 168 perf.** Gerald Singleton Tom
Terriss/J. Farren Soutar/Neville Doone; William E.W.
Thomas/Gus Danby. Kate Weatherby Grace Lane. L & MGR,
Sm, Bm, Cond as for 96.94. *REV: E 2/5/96 p8; St 7/5/*
96 p12.

96.96 *A CLERICAL ERROR* (P,1a) H.A. Jones. LYCEUM 1/5/
96 mat perf.** Rev Richard Capel Wilson Barrett; Dick
Capel Edward Irwin; Perry Ambrose Manning. Minnie
Heritage Maud C. Jeffries. L Henry Irving; Mgr Johnston Forbes-Robertson, Frederick Harrison. *REV: E 2/5/*
96 p11; St 7/5/96 p9; Th 1/6/96 p355-6.

96.97 *WHO'S TO WIN HIM?* (Ca,1a) Thomas J. Williams.
CRITERION 1/5/96. 1 perf. 1st perfd Lyceum 20/1/68.
Cyril Dashwood Seymour Hicks; Prattleton Primrose
Harry Nicholls; Squire Brushleigh John L. Shine. Rose
Kate Rorke; Sylvia Dorothea Baird; Minuetta Annie
Hughes; Arabella Fay Davis; Musidora Maude Millett.
L & MGR Charles Wyndham; Mus dir Victor Hollander;
Bom G. Mills. *REV: E 9/5/96 p11; St 7/5/96 p9.*

96.98 *DAVID GARRICK* (C,3a) T.W. Robertson. CRITERION
1/5/96. 1 perf.** David Garrick Charles Wyndham;
Simon Ingot C.W. Somerset; Squire Chivey Ells Dagnall;
Smith William Blakeley; Brown Alfred Maltby; Jones
E.W. Gardiner; Garrick's Servant J.H. Barnes; Ingot's
Servant Kenneth Douglas. Mrs Smith Emily Vining; Ara-
minta Brown Emily Miller; Ada Ingot Mary Moore. L &
MGR, Mus dir, Bom as for 96.97. *REV: St 7/5/96 p9.*

96.99 *DIE WALKURE* (O[3a]) Richard Wagner. DRURY LANE
2/5/96, 8/5/96. 2 perf.** Siegmund E.C. Hedmondt;
Hunding Alex Bevan; Wotan David Bispham. Sieglinde
Marie Duma; Fricka Louise Meisslinger; Brunnhilde
Lilian Tree; Valkyries Russell, Marini, Brani, Tre-
felyn, Lee, [Clare] Addison, [Isa?] McCusker, Louise

Meisslinger; L & MGR Augustus Harris; Mus dir Luigi
Mancinelli. *REV: Ath 9/5/96 p627; St 7/5/96 p12; Ti
4/5/96 p10.*

96.100 *THE TICKET-OF-LEAVE MAN* (D,4a) Tom Taylor.
NOVELTY 4/5/96-9/5/96. 6 perf. 1st perfd Olympic 27/
5/63. Robert Brierly Frank Lindo; James Dalton William
Felton; Hawkshaw Augustin Symonds; Melton Moss George
Abel; Green Jones T. West Carnie; Gibson W[atty] Brun-
ton; Maltby Leonard Shepherd; Brunton [William] Adams.
Sam Willoughby Katie Parry; Emily St. Evremond Kate
Brunton; Mrs Willoughby Kate Robberds; May Edwards V.
St. Lawrence. L V. St. Lawrence; Mgr Walter Tyrrell;
Bom Edward Hastings, jr. *REV: E 9/5/96 p10; St 7/5/96
p12.*

96.101 *SWEET LAVENDER* (DD,3a) A.W. Pinero. OPERA COMI-
QUE 7/5/96 mat perf.** Dick Phenyl Dennis Eadie;
Geoffrey Wedderburn W. Sewell Singer; Clement Hale
E.J. Heseltine; Dr Delaney F. Moore; Horace Bream
L.C. Graves; Bulger H. Goring. Mrs Gilfillian Mary
Stuart; Minnie Mabel Archdall; Ruth Rolt Mrs Herbert
E. Ford; Lavender Edith Stewart. *REV: 14/5/96 p13.*

96.102 *MOTHS* (RD,4a) Henry Hamilton [adpt of Ouida's
novel]. ST. JAMES'S 7/5/96 mat perf.** Prince Zouroff
Charles Cartwright; Duke of Mull & Cantyre Vincent
Sternroyd; Lord Jura Arthur Elwood; Raphael de Cor-
reze Frank H. Fenton; Ivan G. N[ix] Webber. Vere
Herbert Kate Rorke; Princess Nadine Nelaguine Enid
Spencer Brunton; Duchesse de Sonnaz Beverley Sit-
greaves; Lady Dolly Vanderdecken Kate Phillips; Fus-
chia Mrs Clement Scott. L & MGR George Alexander; Bm
Robert V. Shone; Sm H.H. Vincent, A.B. Tapping; Sec
R.G. Legge; Mus dir Walter Slaughter; Sc H.P. Hall;
Cost Jay, Mme Jeannette; Pq William Clarkson; Bom
Arnold. *REV: E 9/5/96 p13; St 14/5/96 p13.*

96.103 *HENRY IV, PART I* (HistP,4a) William Shakespeare.
HAYMARKET 8/5/96(m), 13/5(m), 20/5(m); 28/5-11/7/96.
29 perf [perfd ea Th-S only, w/S mat; mat only 4/7,
11/7].** Sir John Falstaff H.B. Tree; King Henry IV
William Mollison; Henry, Prince of Wales Frank Gillmore; Prince John of Lancaster Berte Thomas; Earl of

Westmoreland F. Percival Stevens/Romaine; Thomas
Percy Fred A. Everill; Henry Percy Charles Allan;
Henry Percy, surnamed Hotspur Lewis Waller; Edmund
Mortimer C.M. Hallard; Sir Walter Blunt Frank McVicars/
F. Percival Stevens; Sir Richard Vernon A.E. Hippis-
ley; Poins Herbert Ross/Gerald du Maurier; Owen Glen-
dower E. Holman Clark; Douglas Henry Vibart; Francis
D.J. Williams; Bardolph Lionel Brough; Gadshill Gerald
du Maurier/Lesly Thomson; Peto [William] Gayer Mac-
Kay; Sheriff Arthur Coe; 1st Messenger J. [A.] Rosier;
2nd Messenger [J.] Montagu; 1st Traveller T. Shannon/
B. Thorn; 2nd Traveller Grafton; Hotspur's Servant
Yardley. Lady Hotspur Mrs H.B. Tree; Lady Mortimer
Marion Evans; Mistress Quickly Kate Phillips/Alice
Kingsley. L & MGR H.B. Tree; Bom W.H. Leverton; Sc
Walter Johnstone, [Hugh?] Freemantle, Walter Hann;
Mus & Mus dir Raymond Roze; Pd H.B. Tree, Louis Cal-
vert; Sm Shelton; Eng E. Wingfield Bowles; Cost L. &
H. Nathan; Pq William Clarkson; Bm Fitzroy Gardner.
*REV: Ath 16/5/96 p659; E 9/5/96 p13; Sk 13/5/96 p94-5,
24/6/96 p341, 358-9; SR 16/5/96 p500-2; St 14/5/96
p12-3; Th 1/6/96 p344-6; Ti 9/5/96 p14, 29/5/96 p6;
TW96 p86-106, 141-50, 159-69.*

96.104 *A MATCHMAKER* (C,4a) Clotilde Graves & Gertrude
Kingston.SHAFTESBURY 9/5/96-22/5/96. 12 perf.* Archi-
bald Rolles Lewis Waller; Marquess of Westbourne C.P.
Little; Hon Charles Soper E.W. Gardiner; Bishop of
Dorminster Kenneth Black; Earl of Cranboisie Lesly
Thomson; Bingley Bligh, M.P. Alfred Maltby; Waite
Gilbert Trent; Roberts Charles Ross. Wilhelmina
Florence West; Georgiana Ridout Beatrice Ferrar; Flora
[Enid] Spencer Brunton; Ethel Daisy Brough; Betty
Bullen Nina Boucicault; Lady Louisa Holdawle Fanny
Coleman; Mrs Waite Mrs Arthur Ayers; Margaretta Lena
Ashwell; Mrs Lane Gertrude Kingston. L & MGR Lewis
Waller, H.H. Morell; Bom David; Furn Lyons; Cost Na-
than, Ethel Walters, Jay, [Marie?] Louise; Pq Fox; Bm
Charles Meyrick; Sm E.J. Malyon; Asm A.J. Bowyer; Mus
dir O. de Tender. *REV: Ath 16/5/96 p659; E 16/5/96 p9;
Sk 13/5/96 p93, 20/5/96 p173; SR 23/5/96 p524-5; St
14/5/96 p13; Th 1/6/96 p349-50; Ti 11/5/96 p10; TW96
p150-5.*

96.105 *ROMEO ET JULIETTE* (O[5a]) Charles Gounod. COV-
ENT GARDEN 11/5/96, 19/5, 3/6, 12/6, 18/6, 11/7, 20/7,
28/7/96. 8 perf.** Romeo Jean de Reszke/Albert Alva-
rez; Frère Laurent Pol Plançon/Edouard de Reszke;
Capulet Charles Gilibert/Pol Plançon/Armand Castel-
mary; Mercutio Henri Albers/Jacques Bars; Tybalt Jac-
ques Bars/Charles Bonnard/B. Piroia; Duc de Verone
Armand Castelmary/Alex Bevan; Gregorio Antonio de
Vaschetti; Benvoglio Rinaldini. Gertrude Mathilde
Bauermeister/Jessie Huddleston; Juliette Emma Eames/
Nellie Melba. L & MGR Augustus Harris; Cond Luigi
Mancinelli; Am Neil Forsyth; Bom E. Hall; Sm Arthur P.
Collins. *REV: Ath 16/5/96 p657, 27/6/96 p851; E 16/5/*
96 p7, 20/6/96 p18; Sk 20/5/96 p135, 24/6/96 p379; SR
16/5/96 p499-500; St 14/5/96 p12; Ti 12/5/96 p12, 19/
6/96 p10.

96.106 *FETTERED LIVES* (D,5a) Harold Whyte. NOVELTY
11/5/96-16/5/96. 6 perf. 1st perfd Britannia 31/7/93.
Mark Meredith William Felton; Joe Hazleton Leonard
Shepherd; Ned Goodman George Abel; Dick Denam [Ed-
ward] Beasley; Hawkey Smart Jones; Black Ben W.M.
Franks; Inspector Blake [F.] Stephens; Peter Podge
Bernard; Constable Hoolan Wynn; Joe Wurzel F. Ashby.
Madge Markley Helena Head; Nelly Goodman Kate Brunton;
Little Alice Alice Williams; May Ingles V. St. Law-
rence. L V. St. Lawrence; Mgr Walter Tyrrell. *REV: E*
16/5/96 p9; St 14/5/96 p13.

96.107 *VENUS* (Farcical Sk) Jessie Robertson. NOVELTY
11/5/96-16/5/96. 6 perf.* Simon Gubbins Edmund Gwenn.
Laura Gubbins Lilian Clayton; Sarah Gubbins Jessie
Robertson. L, Mgr as for 96.106. *REV: As for 96.106.*

96.108 *CAVALLERIA RUSTICANA* (O[1a]) Pietro Mascagni.
COVENT GARDEN 12/5/96, 21/5, 29/5, 17/6, 17/7/96. 5
perf.** Turiddu Fernando de Lucia/Giuseppe Cremonini;
Alfio Mario Ancona/Antonio Pini-Corsi. Santuzza Mar-
garet MacIntyre/d'Alma; Lola Fernanda Brazzi; Lucia
Mathilde Bauermeister. L & MGR Augustus Harris; Cond
Enrico Bevignani; Am Neil Forsyth; Bom E. Hall; Sm
Arthur P. Collins. *REV: Ath 16/5/96 p658; E 16/5/96*
p7; Sk 20/5/96 p135, 10/6/96 p256; St 14/5/96 p12; Ti
14/5/96 p12.

96.109 *HANSEL AND GRETEL* (O[3a]) Engelbert Humperdinck. COVENT GARDEN 12/5/96, 21/5, 1/6/96. 3 perf.**
Peter David Bispham. Hansel Marie Elba; Gertrude Lilian Tree; Witch Louise Meisslinger; Gretel Jessie
Huddleston; Dewman Mathilde Bauermeister; Sandman
Fernanda Brazzi. L & MGR, Am, Sm, Bom as for 96.108;
Cond Luigi Mancinelli. *REV: Ath 16/5/96 p658; E 16/5/
96 p7; Sk 20/5/96 p135; St 14/5/96 p12; Ti 14/5/96
p12.*

96.110 *MR VERSUS MRS* (Incident) Arthur Bourchier &
F.B. Money Coutts [?="Mountjoy"]. HAYMARKET 12/5/96
mat perf.** Robert Challenger Arthur Bourchier. Mrs
Featherleigh Violet Vanbrugh. L & MGR H.B. Tree; Mus
dir Raymond Roze; Cost L. & H. Nathan; Pq William
Clarkson; Bom W.H. Leverton; Bm Fitzroy Gardner. *REV:
E 16/5/96 p8; Ti 13/5/96 p14.*

96.111 *MRS HILARY REGRETS* (Ca,1a) S. Theyre Smith.
HAYMARKET 12/5/96 mat perf.** Dr Power Charles Wynd-
ham; Preston C[harles] Terric. Mrs Hilary Mary Moore.
L & MGR, Mus dir, Bom, Bm, Cost, Pq as for 96.110.
REV: E 16/5/96 p8; Ti 13/5/96 p14.

96.112 *LA FAVORITA* (O[4a]) Gaetano Donizetti. COVENT
GARDEN 13/5/96, 23/5/96. 2 perf.** Fernando Giuseppe
Cremonini; Baldassare Pol Plançon; Alfonso Mario An-
cona; Gaspar B. Piroia. Inez Mathilde Bauermeister;
Leonora Eugenia Mantelli. L & MGR Augustus Harris;
Cond Enrico Bevignani; Am Neil Forsyth; Bom E. Hall;
Sm Arthur P. Collins. *REV: Ath 16/5/96 p658; E 16/5/
96 p7; Sk 20/5/96 p135; SR 16/5/96 p449-500; St 21/5/
96 p12; Ti 14/5/96 p12.*

96.113 *JO* (D,3a) J.P. Burnett [adpt of Charles Dickens,
Bleak House]. DRURY LANE 13/5/96-30/5/96. 16 perf. 1st
perfd Prince of Wales's, Liverpool 8/11/75 [as *Bleak
House*]. Sir Lester Dedlock Rudge Harding; Mr Tulkinghorn Howard Russell; Mr Snagsby Alfred Balfour; Mr
Chadband Robb Harwood; Mr Guppy Charles Stuart; Mr
Bucket [Frank?] McVicars; Coroner F[red] Grove; Servant H. Clark; Beadle Young. Lady Dedlock Alma Stanley; Hortense Ada Lee; Esther Joan Burnett; Mrs Roun-
cell Fanny Robertson; Rosa Kathleen Gordon; Guster

Katie Lee; Jenny Mary Bates; Mrs Snagsby Mrs Vernon
Paget; Jo Jennie Lee. L & MGR Augustus Harris; Pd
J.P. Burnett; Sm Arthur P. Collins; Am Neil Forsyth.
*REV: E 16/5/96 p9; Sk 20/5/96 p133-4, 27/5/96 p218;
SR 23/5/96 p523-4; TW96 p155-6.*

96.114 *PHILEMON ET BAUCIS* (O[2a]) Charles Gounod.
COVENT GARDEN 14/5/96. 1 perf.** Philemon Charles
Bonnard; Vulcan Armand Castelmary; Jupiter Charles
Gilibert. Baucis Marie Engle. L & MGR Augustus Harris;
Cond Enrico Bevignani; Am Neil Forsyth; Bom E. Hall;
Sm Arthur P. Collins. *REV: Ath 23/5/96 p691; E 16/5/
96 p7; Sk 20/5/96 p135; St 21/5/96 p12; Ti 18/5/96 p9.*

96.115 *PAGLIACCI* (O[2a]) Ruggiero Leoncavallo. COVENT
GARDEN 14/5/96, 29/5, 1/6, 17/6, 17/7/96. 5 perf.**
Canio Fernando de Lucia/Charles Bonnard; Tonio Mario
Ancona; Silvio Jacques Bars/Richard Green; Beppe B.
Piroia. Nedda Margaret Reid/Pauline Joran. L & MGR,
Am, Bom, Sm as for 96.114; Cond Armando Seppilli/En-
rico Bevignani. *REV: Ath, E, St, Ti as for 96.114.*

96.116 *FAUST* (O[5a]) Charles Gounod. COVENT GARDEN
15/5/96, 25/5, 6/6, 25/6, 3/7, 9/7/96. 6 perf.**
Mephistopheles Pol Plançon/Edouard de Reszke; Wagner
Charles Gilibert; Valentine Henri Albers/Mario Ancona;
Faust Charles Bonnard/Jean de Reszke/Albert Alvarez.
Siebel Fernanda Brazzi; Martha Mathilde Bauermeister;
Marguerite Emma Eames/Nellie Melba/Margaret MacIntyre.
L & MGR, Am, Bom, Sm as for 96.114; Cond Luigi Man-
cinelli/Landon Ronald/Enrico Bevignani. *REV: Ath 23/
5/96 p691, 30/5/96 p722; E 23/5/96 p7, 30/5/96 p7, 27/
6/96 p18; Sk 27/5/96 p184; St 21/5/96 p12, 28/5/96
p13, 2/7/96 p10; Ti 18/5/96 p9.*

96.117 *ROMEO AND JULIET* William Shakespeare. PRINCE
OF WALES'S 15/5/96 mat perf.** Escalus Edward Ferris;
Paris Acton Bond; Montague F. Dyall; Capulet Austin
Melford; Mercutio W.H. Vernon; Benvolio Oswald Yorke;
Tybalt Frederick Volpé; Friar Laurence Arthur Stir-
ling; Friar John Sydney Laurence; Balthazar Roy
Horniman; Sampson Mark Kinghorne; Gregory John Byron;
Peter Ernest Hendrie; Abraham F.G. Thurstans; Apothe-
cary R[udolph?] de Cordova; Dancers H.F. Overbury,

Michael Dure, Reginald Galloway. Romeo Esmé Beringer; Lady Montague Agnes Hill; Lady Capulet Frances Ivor; Juliet Vera Beringer; Nurse Mrs E.H. Brooke; Dancers Lily Linfield, May Daly, Lluellyn. DIR Mrs Oscar Beringer, W.H. Vernon; Mus William Wallace, Charles Gounod; Fights Cpt. Hutton; Ch Lily Linfield [Mrs Lys Baldry]; Cost dgn Karl, Mrs Louise Jopling; Cost L. & H. Nathan, Liberty; Pq William Clarkson. *REV: E 16/5/ 96 p11; Sk 13/5/96 p104-5, 20/5/96 p135; St 21/5/96 p13, 25/6/96 p10; TW96 p155.*

96.118 *LOHENGRIN* (O[3a]) Richard Wagner. COVENT GARDEN 16/5/96, 22/5, 28/5, 22/6, 21/7/96. 5 perf.** Lohengrin Giuseppe Cremonini/Jean de Reszke; Enrico l'Uccellatore Pol Plançon/Vittorio Arimondi/Edouard de Reszke; Telramondo Mario Ancona/David Bispham; L'Araldo del Re Charles Gilibert/Holmes. Elsa Emma Albani/Emma Eames [?]/Lola Beeth; Ortruda Eugenia Mantelli/Louise Meisslinger/Rose Olitzka. L & MGR Augustus Harris; Cond Luigi Mancinelli; Am Neil Forsyth; Bom E. Hall; Sm Arthur P. Collins. *REV: Ath 23/ 5/96 p691, 30/5/96 p722; E 23/5/96 p7, 30/5/96 p7; Sk 27/5/96 p184, 3/6/96 p248, 1/7/96 p388; St 21/5/96 p12; Ti 18/5/96 p9, 25/5/96 p8.*

96.119 *ROSEMARY* (P,4a) Louis N. Parker & Murray Carson. CRITERION 16/5/96-25/7/96; 6/10/96-26/12/96; 13/ 2/97-20/3/97. 195 perf [w/S mat exc 16/5/96, 11/7, 18/7, 25/7, 26/12/96, 13/2/97; add mat 15/7/96, 21/10, 28/10, 11/11, 18/11, 9/12, 16/12/96; mat only 2/12/96; np 24-25/12/96].* Sir Jasper Thorndyke Charles Wyndham; Prof Jogram J.H. Barnes; Cpt. Cruickshank, R.N. Alfred Bishop; William Westwood Kenneth Douglas; George Minifee James A. Welch/A.E. George; Abram F.H. Tyler; Stilt Walker John Byron/A.E. George/C. Edmonds. Mrs Cruickshank Carlotta Addison; Mrs Minifee Emily Vining; Priscilla Annie Hughes/M[ary?] Jocelyn; Dorothy Cruickshank Mary Moore. L & MGR Charles Wyndham; Sc Walter Hann; Cost Harrison, Mrs Mason; Cost dgn H.G. Glendoni; Bom [G.] Mills; Sm Percy Hutchison; Mus dir Victor Hollaender; Act mgr & Treas E. Harvey. *REV: Ath 23/5/96 p692; E 23/5/96 p10, 10/10/96 p10, 27/3/97 p10; SR 23/5/96 p525; St 21/5/96 p12-3, 8/10/ 96 p13, 18/2/97 p15; Th 1/6/96 p347-9; Ti 18/5/96 p9;*

TW96 p156-9.

96.120 *RIGOLETTO* (O[3a]) Giuseppe Verdi. COVENT GAR-
DEN 18/5/96, 23/6/96. 2 perf.** Il Duca Fernando de
Lucia/Giuseppe Gremonini; Sparafucile Vittorio Ari-
mondi; Borsa Iginio Corsi; Marullo Rinaldini; Monte-
rone Antonio de Vaschetti; Rigoletto Mario Ancona;
Conte di Ceprano Cernusco. Gilda Emma Albani/Nellie
Melba; Giovanna Mathilde Bauermeister; Contessa di
Ceprano Cecile Brani; Maddalena Eugenia Mantelli/
Fernanda Brazzi; Paggio Edith Johnston. L & MGR Augus-
tus Harris; Cond Enrico Bevignani; Am Neil Forsyth;
Bom E. Hall; Sm Arthur P. Collins. *REV: Ath 23/5/96
p691, 27/6/96 p851; E 23/5/96 p7, 27/6/96 p18; Sk 27/
5/96 p184; St 21/5/96 p12, 25/6/96 p10; Ti 21/5/96
p14.*

96.121 *A RING OF IRON* (D,4a) Frank Harvey. NOVELTY
18/5/96-23/5/96. 6 perf. 1st perfd Theatre Royal,
Portsmouth 15/9/84. Sir John Grahame Charles Hartley;
Wilfred Meredith Bernard Copping; Sam Thorpe George
Abel; Timothy Clinker T. West Carnie; Burly Mike [F.]
Stephens; Dr Grant W[atty] Brunton; Stanley W. Ste-
vens; Stevens H. Moore. Geraldine Bellew [Marion?]
Herbert; Nancy Drake Kate Brunton; Selina Thorpe
[Adah] Lacroft; Florence Meredith [E.L.] Maddock[s];
Nurse Bland Elsie Trevor; Mary Gordon V. St. Lawrence.
L V. St. Lawrence; Mgr Walter Tyrrell. *REV: E 23/5/96
p8; St 21/5/96 p13.*

96.122 *THE NEW MODEL* (Dancing Sk). NOVELTY 18/5/96-
23/5/96. 6 perf.* Wilfred Lydon. Norah Grey. L, Mgr
as for 96.121; Ch John d'Auban. *REV: St 21/5/96 p13.*

96.123 *THE SPAN OF LIFE* (Melo,4a) Sutton Vane. PRIN-
CESS'S 18/5/96-27/6/96. 37 perf [w/mat 25/5]. 1st
perfd Grand, Islington 6/6/92. Richard Blunt Ernest
E. Norris; Dunstan Leech Austin Melford; Nutty Brown
Herbert Vyvyan; Dismal Brown/Dapper Brown/Tipton Perch
Leonhardt Troupe; Inspector Fergusson George Yates;
Joshua Gurnett Charles Franmore; Abel Perry Fred Col-
son; Azrek Gerald Kennedy. Cecil Blunt Dolly Love;
Cecil Jelf Gladys White; Mrs Jelf Harriett Clifton;
Shrove Tuesday Sydney Fairbrother; Kate Heathcote Kate

Tyndall. MGR Albert Augustus Gilmer; Am Horace Gilmer; Treas H. Bellamy Smith; Sm George T. Minshull; Mus dir Theodore Ward. *REV: E 23/5/96 p8; St 21/5/96 p13.*

96.124 *THE FORTUNE OF WAR* (Sk) F.C. Phillips. CRITERION 19/5/96 mat perf.* Dick Harcourt W.L. Abingdon. Finette Lottie Venne; Lucille Dorothy Wood. DIR William Herbert; Sm Herman de Lange; Act mgr E. Harvey. *REV: E 23/5/96 p10; St 21/5/96 p13.*

96.125 *MAN PROPOSES* (P,1a) Sydney Grundy. CRITERION 19/5/96 mat perf.** Cpt. Huntington E.W. Gardiner. Dinah Nina Boucicault; Bell Huntington Kate Rorke. DIR, Sm, Act mgr as for 96.124. *REV: As for 96.124.*

96.126 *THE BURGLAR AND THE JUDGE* (P,1a) F.C. Phillips & Charles H.E. Brookfield. CRITERION 19/5/96 mat perf.** Justice Gyves Cyril Maude; Burglar Charles H.E. Brookfield; Parkhurst Sidney Warden. DIR, Sm, Act mgr as for 96.124. *REV: E 23/5/96 p10; St 21/5/ 96 p12.*

96.127 *MR VERSUS MRS* (Incident) Arthur Bourchier & "Mountjoy." CRITERION 19/5/96 mat perf.** Robert Challenger Arthur Bourchier. Hon Mrs Featherleigh Violet Vanbrugh. DIR, Sm, Act mgr as for 96.124.

96.128 *THE OTHER WOMAN* (Duol) Ellis Kingsley. CRITERION 19/5/96 mat perf. Silvie Grahame Kate Rorke; Enid Vivian Winifred Emery. Comment: The V & A programme has an "X" against this item, which could indicate it was deleted at the last moment. Nicoll gives the 1st perf of this piece as Her Majesty's 11/11/97 (see item 97.252).

96.129 *FORTUNE'S FOOL* (Monol) Henry Hamilton. CRITERION 19/5/96 mat perf.** Philip Challoner Lewis Waller. DIR, Sm, Act mgr as for 96.124. *REV: St 21/5/96 p13.*

96.130 *FRA DIAVOLO* (O[3a]) D.F.E. Auber. COVENT GARDEN 20/5/96, 26/5/96. 2 perf.** Fra Diavolo Fernando de Lucia; Beppo Antonio Pini-Corsi; Giacomo Vittorio Arimondi; Lorenzo B. Piroia/Joseph O'Mara; Matteo Antonio de Vaschetti; Lord Rocburg David Bispham.

Lady Pamela Pauline Joran; Zerlina Marie Engle. L &
MGR Augustus Harris; Cond Enrico Bevignani; Am Neil
Forsyth; Bom E. Hall; Sm Arthur P. Collins. *REV:*
Ath 23/5/96 p696; E 23/5/96 p7; Sk 3/6/96 p248; St
28/5/96 p12-3; Ti 21/5/96 p14.

96.131 *JOSIAH'S DREAM; OR, THE WOMAN OF THE FUTURE*
(FC,3a) Charles Rogers. STRAND 21/5/96-10/6/96. 19
perf [w/mat 23/5].* Josiah Jenkins Sidney Harcourt;
Algy Gushington Graham Wentworth; John Hardy George
Raiemond; William Richard Blunt; Charlie Templeton
J.A. Bentham. Caroline Ada Branson; Georgina Lettice
Fairfax; Johanna Bucklaw Mary Allestree; Frederica
Florence L. Forster. PP J.S. Clarke; Mgr W. Spencer.
REV: Ath 30/5/96 p724; E 23/5/96 p11; Sk 3/6/96 p248,
250; St 28/5/96 p13; Th 1/7/96 p40-1; Ti 22/5/96 p10;
TW96 p179.

96.132 *GOOD-BYE* (P,1a) Henry T. Johnson. STRAND 21/5/
96-10/6/96. 18 perf.* Lieut. Stanley Tibbets C.M.
Lowne; Lieut. Jack Melrose J.A. Bentham; Angus Crosby
Richard Blunt; Trooper Kitson Francis Hawley. Florence
Forester Mary Allestree; Hetty Florence L. Forster.
PP, Mgr as for 96.131. *REV: E 23/5/96 p10; St 28/5/96*
p13. Comment: Title changed to *The Muff of the Regi-*
ment on 27/5/96.

96.133 *SIGNAL LIGHTS* (Dramatic Novelty,5a) W.J.
Thompson. NOVELTY 25/5/96-30/5/96. 6 perf. 1st perfd
Metropole, Birkenhead 30/7/94. Ralph Dennison Gra-
ham Davis; Squire Ellis Arthur Gibbons; Jaques Farris
Wilfred Grahame; Pierre Marks Richard Cowell; Bob
Henderson Lewis J. Ward; Sheriff P. Wilton; Warden
O.J. Hindley; Pinkie M. Eddie Powers. Romp Henderson
Minnie Oscar Gray; Maillie Ellis Maud Fergusson. L
V. St. Lawrence. *REV: E 30/5/96 p8; St 28/5/96 p13.*

96.134 *TANNHAUSER* (O[3a]) Richard Wagner. COVENT GAR-
DEN 27/5/96, 4/6, 16/6, 24/6, 13/7/96. 5 perf.**
Hermann I Pol Plançon; Wolfram Mario Ancona/Henri
Albers; Walther B. Piroia; Heinrich Iginio Corsi;
Biterolf Charles Gilibert; Reinmar Antonio de Vas-
chetti; Tannhauser Albert Alvarez. Elizabeth Emma
Eames/Lola Beeth; Venus Ada Adini; Pastore Mathilde

Bauermeister. L & MGR Augustus Harris; Cond Luigi Mancinelli; Am Neil Forsyth; Bom E. Hall; Sm Arthur P.
Collins. *REV: Ath 30/5/96 p722-3; E 30/5/96 p7; Sk
3/6/96 p248, 24/6/96 p379; St 4/6/96 p10.*

96.135 *THE MIKADO; OR, THE TOWN OF TITIPU* (Japanese
O,2a) W.S. Gilbert (lib) & Arthur Sullivan (mus).
SAVOY 27/5/96, 4/6, 10/6, 17/6, 24/6, 4/7/96. 6 mat
perf.** Pooh-Bah Rutland Barrington; Nanki Poo Char-
les Kenningham; Mikado Robert Scott-Fishe; Pish-Tush
Jones Hewson; Koko Walter Passmore. Pitti Sing Jessie
Bond; Yum Yum Florence Perry; Peep Bo Emmie Owen;
Katisha Rosina Brandram. PP & MGR Richard d'Oyly
Carte. *REV: E 30/5/96 p7.*

96.136 *'TWIXT NIGHT AND MORN* (Dramatic Study,2Epi-
sodes) Edward Martin Seymour. AVENUE 28/5/96 mat perf.*
Man Edward O'Neill. Woman Florence Fordyce. L Charles
H. Hawtrey; Mgr Ernest Oswald, Alexander Loftus; Cond
Norfolk Megone; Pq & Cost William Clarkson; Sm Hugh
Bulkeley; Bm A. Donald; Act mgr C. St. John Denton.
REV: E 30/5/96 p11; St 4/6/96 p11.

96.137 *HIS RELATIONS* (FC,3a) H.A. Saintsbury. AVENUE
28/5/96 mat perf.* Mjr.-Gen. Faraday Walter McEwan;
Edward Fitz-Coolington H.A. Saintsbury; Frederick Lake
J. Farren Soutar; Thomas Pinker W[illiam] Cheesman;
Matthew Barlings Frank M. Wood; Morgan Graham Price.
Gertie Fitz-Coolington Florence Fordyce; Rose Maydue
Audrey Ford; Jennings Marianne Caldwell; Jenny Mont-
gomery Dorothy Chesney. L, Mgr, Cond, Pq & Cost, Sm,
Bm, Act mgr as for 96.136. *REV: E 30/5/96 p11; Sk
3/6/96 p248; St 4/6/96 p11; Th 1/7/96 p42; Ti 20/5/96
p6.*

96.138 *FUNNIBONE'S FIX* (F,1a) Arthur Williams. GAIETY
28/5/96 mat perf. 1st perfd Surrey 27/3/80. Septimus
Snubwell George Mudie; Ferdinand Funnibone Arthur
Williams; Cecil Cooke Robert Nainby; Mr Winkletoes
Colin Coop; Mr Russetblue Lane; Printer's Boy Master
Johnny Hutchings. Widow Smith Annie Dwelly; Milly
Snubwell Emily Spiller. *REV: E 30/5/96 p8.*

96.139 *DIE MEISTERSINGER* (O[3a]) Richard Wagner. COV-

ENT GARDEN 30/5/96, 5/6, 9/6, 15/6, 8/7/96. 5 perf.** Walther Jean de Reszke; Hans Sachs Edouard de Reszke; Pogner Pol Plançon; Beckmesser David Bispham; Fritz Kothner Charles Gilibert; Kunz Vogelgesang Iginio Corsi; Balthazar Zorn Rinaldini; Augustin Moser B. Piroia; Ulrich Eissilinger Jacques Bars/Maestri; Konrad Nachtigal Trabucco; Herman Ortel Antonio de Vaschetti; Hans Foltz Cernusco; Hans Schwars Alex Bevan/ Armand Castelmary; David Charles Bonnard. Eva Emma Eames; Maddalena Mathilde Bauermeister. L & MGR Augustus Harris; Cond Luigi Mancinelli; Am Neil Forsyth; Bom E. Hall; Sm Arthur P. Collins. *REV: Ath 6/6/96 p754; E 6/6/96 p7; Sk 10/6/96 p256; St 4/6/96 p10; Th 1/7/96 p42-3; Ti 1/6/96 p12.*

96.140 *MAMZELLE NITOUCHE* (MC,3a) Henri Meilhac & Albert Millaud & Florimond Hervé. COURT 1/6/96-31/7/96. 55 perf [w/mat 6/6, 1/7].** Mjr. Count of Castle Gibus Robert Pateman; Celestin Louis MacKinder; Fernand de Champlatreux Joseph Tapley; Loriot J[ohn] Willes; Robert Lawrence Grossmith; Gustave E.W. Tarver; Stage Manager Arthur Playfair; Call-boy Master Trebell. Corinne Florence Levey; Lady Superior F[lorence] Haydon; Janitress Delia Carlisle; Sylvia Louisa Velda; Lydia Florrie Wilson; Zimblette Carl; Denise May Yohe. MGR Arthur Chudleigh; Add mus Carl Kiefert, J.H. Yorke; Lyr Clifton Bingham, E.W. Bowles; Cost dgn Comelli; Cost Alias; Pq William Clarkson; Sc T.W. Hall; Ch Mme Rosa; Pd Robert Pateman; Bm Leonard Lillies. *REV: E 6/6/96 p9; Sk 10/6/96 p255; SR 20/6/ 96 p623; St 4/6/96 p10; TW96 p179.*

96.141 *UNCLE THATCHER* (P,1a) Clive Brooke. COURT 1/6/ 96-14/7/96. 38 perf.* Matthew Arbutson J[ohn] Willes; John Lawder Roy Horniman; Frank Ainsley E.W. Tarver; Dick Thatcher William F. Hawtrey. Mrs Ainsley Florence Haydon; Agnes Violet Lyster. MGR, Bm as for 96.140. *REV: E 6/6/96 p8; St 4/6/96 p11.*

96.142 *THE COLLEEN BAWN; OR, THE BRIDES OF GARRYOWEN* (DD,3a) Dion Boucicault. NOVELTY 1/6/96-6/6/96. 6 perf.** Hardress Cregan H.J. Pennefather; Kyrle Daly Temple E. Crozier; Hyland Creagh H.P. Brodie; Mr O'Moore T.W. Franks; Servant Beresford Carl; Father

Tom George Belmore; Mr Corrigan George Abel; Danny
Mann John Duggan; Myles-na-Coppaleen Edward Beasley.
Mrs Cregan Elsie Trevor; Anne Chute Eleanor Head;
Sheelah Jessie Danvers; Kathleen Creagh Limecole;
Ducie Biennerhasset E. Cook; Eily O'Connor V. St.
Lawrence. L V. St. Lawrence; Mgr Walter Tyrrell. *REV:
E 6/6/96 p8-9; St 4/6/96 p11.*

96.143 *THE VICTORIA STAKES* (DSk) E. Skuse. NOVELTY
1/6/96-6/6/96. 6 perf.* Bessie Eva Brooke; Alice Frances Brooke. L, Mgr as for 96.142. *REV: As for 96.142.*

96.144 *MARTHA* (O[4a]) Friedrich von Flotow. COVENT
GARDEN 2/6/96, 11/6/96. 2 perf.** Plunketto Edouard
de Reszke; Tristano Antonio Pini-Corsi; Sceriffo
Antonio de Vaschetti; Lionello Guiseppe Cremonini.
Martha Marie Engle; Nancy Eugenia Mantelli. L & MGR
Augustus Harris; Cond Enrico Bevignani; Am Neil Forsyth; Bom E. Hall; Sm Arthur P. Collins. *REV: Ath
6/6/96 p754; E 6/6/96 p7; St 4/6/96 p10; Ti 3/6/96
p12.*

96.145 *THE QUEEN'S PROCTOR; OR, DECREE NISI* (C,3a)
Herman C. Merivale [adpt of Victorien Sardou & Emile
de Najac, *Divorçons*]. ROYALTY 2/6/96-31/7/96. 59 perf
[w/S mat exc 6/6, 20/6; add mat 16/6]. 1st prof. Sir
Victor Crofton, Bart., M.F.H. Arthur Bourchier; The
O'Paque, M.P. Henry Bayntun/Henry Vibart; Caesar
Borgia W.G. Elliott/Charles Troode; Joseph Papplecombe
Ernest Hendrie; Reddie Mark Kinghorne; Thompson Char-
les Troode/Fred W. Permain; Stokes Henry Kitts/Met-
calfe; Gardener Metcalfe Wood; Boy Master Bottomley.
Lady Crofton Violet Vanbrugh; Lady Roller E. Scott
Daymar; Hon Miss Pilkington Helen Rous; Mrs Maydew
Mabel Beardsley; Williams Katharine Stewart. L & MGR
Arthur Bourchier; Pp Kate Santley; Cost Wolmershaus-
en, Mme Guy, Mme Hayward, Russ & Co.; Pq William
Clarkson; Furn Frank Giles & Co.; Bom W.E. Blakeley;
Bm T. Stevens; Sm Fred W. Permain; Act mgr Arthur
Bertram; Mus dir Albert Fox. *REV: Ath 6/6/96 p755;
E 6/6/96 p8; Sk 10/6/96 p259, 17/6/96 p338, 8/7/96
p437-9; SR 6/6/96 p576; St 4/6/96 p10, 6/8/96 p12; Th
1/7/96 p38-9; Ti 3/6/96 p12; TW96 p178-9.*

96.146 *MAGDA* (P,4a) Hermann Sudermann [trans Louis N.
Parker]. LYCEUM 3/6/96-19/6/96. 15 perf [mat only
13/6]. 1st perf this trans. Leopold Schwartze James
Fernandez; Lieut. Max von Wendlowski Frank Gillmore;
Heffterdingk Johnston Forbes-Robertson; Dr von Keller
W. Scott Buist; Prof Beckman Murray Hathorn; Von
Klebs J. Fisher White. Magda Mrs Patrick Campbell;
Marie Sarah Brooke; Augusta Mrs E.H. Brooke; Franziska
von Wendlowski Alice Mansfield; Frau von Klebs Bessie
Page; Frau von Ellrich Abbott Fuller; Frau Schumann
De Burgh; Theresa Marianne Caldwell. MGR Johnston
Forbes-Robertson, Frederick Harrison; L Henry Irving;
Bom Joseph Hurst; Sc Hawes Craven; Cond Carl Armbrus-
ter; Cost Mrs Mason; Assist Bm Horace Watson; Sm Ian
Robertson; Asm George Riddell. *REV: Ath 13/6/96 p788;
E 6/6/96 p8; Sk 10/6/96 p266, 294; St 11/6/96 p12; SR
6/6/96 p575-6; Th 1/7/96 p35-6; Ti 4/6/96 p5; TW96
p170-7.*

96.147 *A RESCUED HONOUR* (C,3a) Arthur Fry. AVENUE 4/6/
96 mat perf.* Bertie Clifford Charles Weir; Noah
Drayton Cecil Morton York; Dr Deprez Webb Darleigh;
Fred Hanbury Gordon Harvey; Uncle Harvey George Mudie;
Holmes L.W. Ryder; Richard Barton Albert E. Raynor;
Reuben Drake Owen Harris; Tommy Tabor George Marlowe.
Clara Clifford Agnes Knights; Agnes May Cross; Aunt
Harvey Isabel Grey; Peggy Barton Charlotte E. Morland;
Simpson Violet Ackhurst; Alice Barton Decima Moore.
REV: E 6/6/96 p11; St 11/6/96 p13; Th 1/7/96 p41-2.

96.148 *CARMEN* (P,4a) Henry Hamilton [adpt of Prosper
Merimee's novel]. GAIETY 6/6/96-20/6/96. 15 perf [w/
mat 13/6, 18/6].* Don José Libengoa Charles Dalton;
Don Manoel Sarceda Thomas Kingston; Lucas Mendez
Luigi Lablache; Bernal d'Aila J.R. Crauford; Priest
Acton Bond; Pedro Diaz George Humphrey; Dancaire
George R. Foss; Remendado Graeme Goring; Lilas Pas-
tia Albert Sims; Beppo T[homas?] Courtice. Dolores
Lena Ashwell; Lisa Eva Williams; Anita Helena Dacre;
Teresa Alexes Leighton; Inez May Marshall; Juana
Madge Meadows; Carmen Olga Nethersole. L & MGR George
Edwardes; Pd Thomas A. Hall, Olga Nethersole; Sc W.T.
Hemsley; Mus Frank A. Howson; Ch Espinoza; Cost Mrs
Nettleship, L. & H. Nathan; Pq William Clarkson; Bm

Louis F. Nethersole; <u>Asm</u> W. Postance; <u>Mus dir</u> J.H.H. Korte; <u>Bom</u> A.P. Oxley. *REV: Ath 13/6/96 p788; E 13/6/96 p8; Sk 10/6/96 p255; SR 13/6/96 p597-8; St 11/6/96 p13; Th 1/7/96 p37-8; Ti 8/6/96 p13; TW96 p187-9.*

96.149 *ADRIENNE LECOUVREUR* (P,5a) Eugene Scribe & Ernest Legouvé. COMEDY 8/6/96-10/6/96; 17/6/96, 19/6/96. 5 perf [mat only 10/6].** <u>Maurice, Prince de Saxe</u> Duval; <u>Michonnet</u> Lacroix; <u>Abbé de Chazeuil</u> Jean Dara; <u>Prince de Bouillon</u> Chameroy; <u>Quinault</u> Brunière; <u>Poisson</u> [A.] Ramy; <u>Valet</u> Kolb; <u>L'Avertisseur</u> Gerard. <u>Adrienne Lecouvreur</u> Sarah Bernhardt; <u>Princess de Bouillon</u> Patry; <u>Duchesse d'Aumont</u> A[ndree] Canti; <u>Mlle Jouvenot</u> Seylor; <u>La Baronne</u> Boulanger; <u>Mlle Dangeville</u> Berthilde; <u>La Marquise</u> Desvergers; <u>La Comtesse</u> Gerber; <u>Femme de Chambre</u> Fournier. <u>L</u> J.W. Comyns Carr; <u>Mgr</u> Charles H. Hawtrey; <u>Dir</u> M.L. Mayer. *REV: E 13/6/96 p8; Sk 17/6/96 p300; St 11/6/96 p12-3; Ti 9/6/96 p12; TW96 p189-90.*

96.150 *LA TRAVIATA* (O[3a]) Giuseppe Verdi. COVENT GARDEN 8/6/96. 1 perf.** <u>Alfredo</u> Fernando de Lucia; <u>Giorgio Germont</u> Mario Ancona; <u>Barone Duphol</u> Antonio de Vaschetti; <u>Gastone</u> Iginio Corsi; <u>Dottore Grenvil</u> Charles Gilibert; <u>Il Marchese</u> Rinaldini. <u>Violetta</u> Emma Albani; <u>Flora Bervoix</u> Cecile Brani; <u>Annina</u> Mathilde Bauermeister. <u>L & MGR</u> Augustus Harris; <u>Cond</u> Enrico Bevignani; <u>Am</u> Neil Forsyth; <u>Bom</u> E. Hall; <u>Sm</u> Arthur P. Collins. *REV: Ath 13/6/96 p787; E 13/6/96 p18; Sk 17/6/96 p299; St 11/6/96 p12; Ti 12/6/96 p4.*

96.151 *THE MYSTERY OF THE HANSOM CAB* (D,4a) Fergus Hume & Arthur Law. NOVELTY 8/6/96-13/6/96. 6 perf. 1st perfd Princess's 23/2/88. <u>Mark Frettleby</u> George Belmore; <u>Brian Fitzgerald</u> H.J. Pennefather; <u>Roger Moreland</u> Temple E. Crozier; <u>Oliver Whyte</u> W.M. Franks; <u>Kilsip</u> George Abel; <u>Gorby</u> Edward Beasley; <u>Jailor</u> R[obert] Smith; <u>Carlton</u> L[eonard] Shepherd; <u>Felix Rolleston</u> G[eorge] Graham; <u>Cabman</u> J.Johnson; <u>Newsboy</u> A. Falcon. <u>Made Frettleby</u> Eleanor Head; <u>Dora Featherweight</u> D[aisie] Cook; <u>Mother Guttnersnipe</u> Elsie Trevor; <u>Rosanna Moore</u> E.L. Maddocks; <u>Mrs Sampson</u> Jessie Danvers; <u>Sal Rawlins</u> V. St. Lawrence. <u>L</u> V. St. Lawrence; <u>Mgr</u> Walter Tyrrell. *REV: E 13/6/96 p8; St 11/6/96 p13.*

96.152 *THE STEPSISTER* (DC,1a) Walter Sapte, jr. NOVEL-
TY 8/6/96-13/6/96. 6 perf. 1st perfd Comedy 4/6/87.
Temple E. Crozier; [Edward] Beasley. Mary V. St. Lawrence; Sarah Adah Lacroft; Limecole. L, Mgr as for
96.151. *REV: St 11/6/96 p13.*

96.153 *TRIAL BY JURY* (CO,1a) W.S. Gilbert (lib) &
Arthur Sullivan (mus). GAIETY 9/6/96 mat perf.**
Judge Rutland Barrington; Counsel Eric Lewis; Defen-
dant Charles Kenningham; Usher Robert Scott-Fishe;
Foreman of the Jury W.S. Penley; Associate W.S. Gil-
bert; Extras W. Louis Bradfield, J.J. Dallas, Jones
Hewson, Mark Kinghorne, Walter Passmore, William
Philp, Scott Russell, W.H. Seymour, John L. Shine,
J. Farren Soutar, Herbert Standing, A.B. Tapping,
Herbert Waring, James A. Welch, Charles H. Hawtrey,
Henry V. Esmond, Charles Glenney, J.H. Barnes, Lewis
Waller, W[illiam] Lestocq, Sydney Harcourt, Laurence
Cautley, E. Allan Aynesworth, Charles Dalton, Bassett
Roe, E.W. Gardiner, Paul Arthur, William Herbert,
W.L. Abingdon, Arthur Elwood, Ernest Leicester, Yorke
Stephens, Cory James. Plaintiff Florence St. John;
Extras Phyllis Broughton, Kate Cutler, Mary Desmond,
Florence Dysart, Ethel Haydon, Edith Johnson, Eva
Moore, Emmie Owen, Grace Palotta, Florence Perry,
Violet Robinson, Kristine Yudall, Lily Twyman, Werde-
mann, [Ina] Repton, [Daisy?] Gilpin, Rose Wilson,
Adams, [Ada] Newall, Reiness, Bemister, [Ruth] Vin-
cent, Castelle, de Lacy, M[ildred] Baker, [Laurie]
Elliston. MUS DIR Ivan Caryll; Act mgr E[dward] Mar-
shall; Sm J.A.E. Malone, B. Shelton, W.H. Seymour,
Guy Waller; Cost Morris Angel & Son, Harrison; Pq
William Clarkson, C.H. Fox; Bom A.P. Oxley; Cond
Francois Cellier; Pd W.S. Gilbert. *REV: E 13/6/96 p9.*

96.154 *IN AND OUT OF A PUNT* (Ca) Henry V. Esmond.
GAIETY 9/6/96 mat perf.** Hugh Henry V. Esmond. Margaret Eva Moore. ACT MGR, Sm, Cost, Pq, Bom as for
96.153. *REV: E 13/6/96 p9.*

96.155 *MORE THAN EVER* ([Bsq]1a) Arthur Matthison (lib)
& W. Meyer Lutz (mus). GAIETY 9/6/96 mat perf. 1st
perfd Gaiety 1/11/82. Sir Crimson Fluid Harry Monkhouse; Shambles Arthur Williams; Kangy Frank Wheeler;

Arsenico della Morte W.L. Abingdon; Policeman Harry
Nicholls. Lady Aqua Tofana Clara Jecks. ACT MGR, Sm,
Cost, Pq, Bom as for 96.153; Cond W. Meyer Lutz. *REV:*
E 13/6/96 p9.

96.156 *MAGDA.* Hermann Sudermann. COMEDY 10/6/96, 18/
6/96. 2 perf.** Pasta Angelo; Deval; Deneubourg;
Castelli; Chameroy. Magda Sarah Bernhardt; Patry; Sey-
lor; [Marcelle] Valdey; [Andree] Canti. L J.W. Comyns
Carr; Mgr Charles H. Hawtrey; Dir M.L. Mayer. *REV:*
Ath 13/6/96 p788; St 18/6/96 p10-1.

96.157 *AIDA* (O[4a]) Giuseppe Verdi. COVENT GARDEN 10/
6/96, 10/7, 15/7/96. 3 perf.** Radames Albert Alva-
rez/Lucignani; Amonasro Mario Ancona; Il Re Vittorio
Arimondi/Armand Castelmary; Messaggiero Rinaldini;
Ramfis Pol Plançon/Edouard de Reszke/Vittorio Ari-
mondi. Aida Ada Adini/Margaret MacIntyre; Amneris
Eugenia Mantelli; Sacerdotessa Mathilde Bauermeister.
L & MGR Augustus Harris; Cond Enrico Bevignani; Am
Neil Forsyth; Bom E. Hall; Sm Arthur P. Collins. *REV:*
Ath 13/6/96 p787, 18/7/96 p106; E 13/6/96 p18, 18/7/
96 p19; Sk 17/6/96 p299; St 18/6/96 p10, 16/7/96 p10;
Ti 12/6/96 p4, 13/7/96 p4.

96.158 *THE GREATEST OF THESE* (P,4a) Sydney Grundy.
GARRICK 10/6/96-18/7/96. 39 perf [w/mat 17/6, 24/6,
1/7, 8/7, 18/7]. 1st perfd Grand, Hull 13/9/95. Mr
Armitage, J.P. W.H. Kendal; Rev Luke Dormer H[enry]
Kemble; Philip Curzon Nutcombe Gould; Lawrence Armi-
tage Rodney Edgecumbe. Grace Armitage Nellie Camp-
bell; Mrs Cragg Mrs Charles Sennett; Servant Frances
Owen; Mrs Armitage Mrs W.H. Kendal. L John Hare; Bom
E. Candler; Sc William Harford; Cond Haydn Waud. *REV:*
Ath 13/6/96 p788; E 13/6/96 p10; Sk 17/6/96 p300; SR
13/6/96 p599; St 18/6/96 p10; Th 1/7/96 p34-5; Ti
11/6/96 p9; TW96 p180-7.

96.159 *LA TOSCA* (D,5a) Victorien Sardou. COMEDY 11/6/
96-13/6 [w/mat 13/6]; 20/6/96(m). 5 perf.** Baron
Scarpia Deval; Mario Cavaradossi Deneubourg; Atta-
vanti Chameroy; Angelotti Angelo; Eusebe Lacroix;
Spoletta Castelli; Trevilhac Jean Dara; Schiarrone
Piron; Trivulce Brunière; Capreola [A.] Ramy; Sgt.

Gerard; <u>Procureur</u> Colon; <u>Gen.</u> Kolb; <u>Ceccho</u> Pitou;
<u>Paisiello</u> Bary. <u>Floria Tosca</u> Sarah Bernhardt; <u>La Reine</u>
Andree Canti; <u>Gennarino</u> Seylor; <u>La Princesse</u> Boulanger;
<u>Luciana</u> Berthilde; <u>Suivante</u> Desvergers; <u>Monsignor</u>
Gerber; <u>Suivante</u> Fournier. <u>L</u> J.W. Comyns Carr; <u>Mgr</u>
Charles H. Hawtrey; <u>Dir</u> M.L. Mayer. *REV: St 18/6/96*
p11.

96.160 *THE SUNBURY SCANDAL* (FC,3a) Fred Horner.
TERRY'S 11/6/96-16/6/96. 5 perf.* <u>Sir John Quaill,</u>
<u>Q.C., M.P.</u> Frederick Kerr; <u>William Joyce</u> E.W. Garden;
<u>Carl Rottenstein</u> Robb Harwood; <u>Cpt. Wilfred Quaill</u>
Wilfred Draycott; <u>Horace Binks</u> G.E. Bellamy; <u>James</u>
<u>Ostler, Esq., J.P.</u> Gilbert Farquhar; <u>Magistrate's</u>
<u>Clerk</u> L. Power; <u>Tompkins</u> Herbert E. Terry; <u>Inspector</u>
<u>Joyce</u> W.J. Robertson; <u>Police Sgt.</u> John Gomah. <u>Lady</u>
<u>Quaill</u> Fanny Brough; <u>Hon Constance Cowley</u> Maude
Millett. <u>L & MGR</u> Frederick Kerr; <u>Pp</u> Edward Terry; <u>Bm</u>
H.T. Brickwell; <u>Sm</u> W.J. Robertson; <u>Mus dir</u> T[homas]
Smythe; <u>Sc</u> Fred Storey, Harry Potts; <u>Furn</u> S.T. Waring
& Sons, Lyons & Co.; <u>Cost</u> Redfern; <u>Pq</u> William Clarkson. *REV: E 13/6/96 p11; Sk 17/6/96 p300, 338; St*
18/6/96 p11; Th 1/7/96 p39-40; Ti 12/6/96 p10; TW96
p190. <u>Comment</u>: Although Nicoll indicates this was the
1st perf, a note in *TW96* indicates the play was perfd
"three nights previously at Eastbourne."

96.161 *AN OLD GARDEN* (P,1a) Hill Davies. TERRY'S 11/
6/96-16/6/96. 5 perf.** <u>David Brice</u> W.J. Robertson;
<u>Peter Melville</u> Wilfred Draycott. <u>Mildred Sanford</u> Mona
K. Oram; <u>Rose Harmer</u> Doris Templeton. <u>L & MGR</u>, <u>Pp</u>,
<u>Bm</u>, <u>Sm</u>, <u>Mus dir</u> as for 96.160. *REV: E, St as for 96.*
160.

96.162 *PLAYING THE GAME* (MFC,3a) William Younge (lib)
& Arthur J. Flaxman (lib) & Fred Eplett (mus). STRAND
12/6/96-15/6/96. 3 perf.* <u>Earl Penruddock</u> J.S. Blythe;
<u>Lord Peter Penruddock</u> J.W. Bradbury; <u>Col. Michael</u>
<u>O'Clancey</u> Rupert Rusden; <u>Emmerson O'Clancey</u> Deane
Brand. <u>Countess Penruddock</u> Marion Sterling; <u>Lady Amy</u>
<u>Penruddock</u> Violet Darrell; <u>Mrs O'Clancey</u> Nellie New-
ton; <u>Lady Nesta Danby</u> Kate Chard. <u>PP</u> J.S. Clarke; <u>L</u>
W. Spencer. *REV: E 20/6/96 p8; St 18/6/96 p11; Th 1/*
7/96 p41; TW96 p190.

96.163 *DIE WALKURE* (O[3a]) Richard Wagner. COVENT GAR-
DEN 13/6/96, 19/6/96. 2 perf.** Siegmund Albert Al-
varez; Wotan Henri Albers; Hunding Armand Castelmary.
Fricka Fernanda Brazzi; Sieglinde Lola Beeth; Schwertleitner Rose Olitzka; Brunnhilde Eugenia Mantelli;
Rossweise Cecile Brani; Waltraute Louise Meisslinger;
Ortlinde Mathilde Bauermeister; Gerhilde [Clare] Addison; Siegrune Louise Kirkby Lunn; Helmwiege Ella
Russell. L & MGR Augustus Harris; Cond Luigi Mancinelli; Am Neil Forsyth; Bom E. Hall; Sm Arthur P.
Collins. *REV: Ath 20/6/96 p818; E 20/6/96 p18; Sk 17/
6/96 p299; SR 27/6/96 p647-8; St 18/6/96 p10; Ti 15/6/
96 p10.*

96.164 *FEDORA* (D,4a) Victorien Sardou. COMEDY 15/6/96,
17/6/96(m). 2 perf.** Loris Ipanoff Deval; Loreck
Chameroy; De Sirieux Angelo; Tchileff Lacroix; Gretch
Castelli; Cyrille Piron; Boroff [A.] Ramy; Rouvel
Jean Dara; Desire Bruniere; Basile Gerard; Portier
Kolb; Lazinski Giraud. Princesse Fedora Romazoff
Sarah Bernhardt; Mme de Tournis [Andree] Canti; Marka
Berthilde; Dimitri Seylor; Baronne Ockar Boulanger;
Olga Soukareff [Marcelle] Valdey. L J.W. Comyns Carr;
Mgr Charles H. Hawtrey; Dir M.L. Mayer. *REV: Ti 17/6/
96 p12.*

96.165 *MR BARNES OF NEW YORK* [Hal Collier-Edwards?].
NOVELTY 15/6/96-20/6/96. 6 perf.** Mr Burton Barnes
Bernard Copping; Baron von Guisebach Edward Beasley;
Jacopo A. George; Cpt. de Belloc G[eorge] Graham;
Tomasso George Belmore; Mateo R[obert] Smith; Edwin
Gerard Anstruther C[harles] Lillford-Delph; George
Fellows Arthur George Abel; Charles Marion Phillips
E.H. Brooke; Count Danella Temple E. Crozier; Antonio
Paoli Beresford Carl; Andrea W.M. Franks. Enid Ans-
truther C. Bracher; Maud Chartris Jessie Danvers;
Lady Chartris Elsie Trevor; Marina Paoli V. St. Law-
rence. L V. St. Lawrence; Mgr Walter Tyrrell. *REV:
E 20/6/96 p8; St 18/6/96 p12.*

96.166 *THE NEW MODEL*. NOVELTY 15/6/96-20/6/96. 6
perf.** E.H. Brooke; Leonard Annesley. Norah Grey.
L, Mgr as for 96.165. *REV: As for 96.165.*

96.167 *LA DAME AUX CAMELIAS* (D,5a) Alexandre Dumas,
fils. COMEDY 16/6/96, 19/6(m), 20/6/96. 3 perf.**
Armand Duval Deval; Gaston Rieux Angelo; Saint Gaudens
Chameroy; Docteur Lacroix; De Varville Castelli; G.
Duval Piron; Comte de Giray [A.] Ramy; Gustave Brun-
ière; Arthur Gerard; Commissionaire Bary; Domestique
Kolb. Marguerite Gauthier Sarah Bernhardt; Olymphe
Andree Canti; Nichette Seylor; Nannine Boulanger;
Adele Berthilde; Clara Desvergers; Prudence Patry;
Groom Gerber; Marie Fournier. L J.W. Comyns Carr; Mgr
Charles H. Hawtrey; Dir M.L. Mayer.

96.168 *DEAREST MAMMA* (Ca,1a) Walter Gordon. ROYALTY
16/6/96-3/7/96. 16 perf.** Uncle Browser William
Blakeley; Harry Clinton Charles Troode; Nettle Croker
Metcalfe Wood; Jones Fred W. Permain. Mrs Breezely
Fussell Helen Rous; Edith Clinton Mabel Beardsley;
Mrs Honeywood Katherine Stewart. L & MGR Arthur Bour-
chier; Pp Kate Santley; Bm T. Stevens; Sm Fred W.
Permain; Act mgr Arthur Bertram; Mus dir Albert Fox.

96.169 *ESMERALDA* (O,4a) A. Goring Thomas. DRURY LANE
18/6/96 mat perf.** Phoebus de Chateaupers Ernest
Burry; Claude Frollo [B.] Griffiths-Percy; Quasimodo
[F.] Stuart Hyatt; Marquis de Chevereuse Wyatt Keith;
Gringoire Richard Triggs; Clopin Alec Lee. Lady Lois
Margaret Mos; Esmeralda Jessie Bradford; Fleur-de-Lys
Mabel Engelhardt. L & MGR Augustus Harris; Cond Neill
O'Donovan. *REV: Sk 24/6/96 p379.* Comment: Guildhall
School of Music.

96.170 *LUCIA DI LAMMERMOOR* (O[3a]) Gaetano Donizetti.
COVENT GARDEN 20/6/96, 29/6/96. 2 perf.** Edgardo
Giuseppe Cremonini; Enrico Mario Ancona; Raimondo
Vittorio Arimondi; Arturo Iginio Corsi; Normano Rinaldini. Lucia Nellie Melba; Alice Mathilde Bauermeister. L & MGR Augustus Harris; Cond Enrico Bevignani; Am Neil Forsyth; Bom E. Hall; Sm Arthur P.
Collins. *REV: Ath 27/6/96 p851; E 27/6/96 p18; SR
27/6/96 p647-8; St 25/6/96 p10; Ti 22/6/96 p13.*

96.171 *THE SCHOOL FOR SCANDAL* (C,5a) R.B. Sheridan.
LYCEUM 20/6/96-24/7/96. 32 perf [w/mat 1/7, 15/7].**
Sir Peter Teazle William Farren; Sir Oliver Surface

Edward Righton; <u>Sir Benjamin Backbite</u> Cyril Maude;
<u>Joseph Surface</u> Johnston Forbes-Robertson; <u>Charles
Surface</u> Fred Terry; <u>Crabtree</u> Arthur Wood; <u>Careless</u>
Frank Gillmore/Sydney Brough; <u>Rowley</u> Charles Dods-
worth/Charles Rock; <u>Moses</u> Fred Thorne; <u>Snake</u> Sydney
Warden; <u>Trip</u> Norman Forbes; <u>Sir Harry Bumper</u> Jack
Robertson; <u>Sir Toby</u> J.S. Crawley; <u>Servant to Joseph</u>
Clifford Soames; <u>Lady Sneerwell's Servant</u> Sydney Law-
rence/Burchill. <u>Lady Teazle</u> Mrs Patrick Campbell; <u>Mrs
Candour</u> Rose Leclercq; <u>Lady Sneerwell</u> Henrietta Wat-
son; <u>Maria</u> Sarah Brooke; <u>Lady Teazle's Servant</u> Italia
Conti. <u>MGR</u> Johnston Forbes-Robertson, Frederick
Harrison; <u>L</u> Henry Irving; <u>Cond</u> Carl Armbruster; <u>Cost</u>
L. & H. Nathan, Mrs Mason; <u>Assist Bm</u> Horace Watson;
<u>Sm</u> Ian Robertson; <u>Asm</u> George Riddell; <u>Bom</u> Joseph
Hurst. *REV: Ath 27/6/96 p852; E 27/6/96 p8; Sk 24/6/
96 p343, 8/7/96 p462; SR 27/6/96 p648-50; St 25/6/96
p10, 30/7/96 p9; Th 1/7/96 p36-7; Ti 22/6/96 p13; TW
96 p191-9.*

96.172 *CALLED BACK* (4a). NOVELTY 22/6/96-27/6/96. 6
perf. <u>Gilbert Vaughan</u> Temple E. Crozier; <u>Anthony
March</u> George Abel; <u>Dr Ceneri</u> George Belmore; <u>Paolo
Macari</u> Bernard Copping; <u>Louis Petroff</u> Edward Beasley;
<u>Arthur Kenyon</u> C[harles] Lillford-Delph; <u>Cpt. Varla-
moff</u> George Graham; <u>Officer</u> Robert Smith; <u>Ivan</u> W.M.
Franks. <u>Paul</u> Daisie Cook; <u>Mary Vaughan</u> Helena Head;
<u>Priscilla Drew</u> Elsie Trevor; <u>Pauline</u> V. St. Lawrence.
<u>L</u> V. St. Lawrence; <u>Mgr</u> Walter Tyrrell. *REV: E 27/6/96
p8.*

96.173 *THE LOTTERY TICKET* (F,1a) [Samuel Beazley].
NOVELTY 22/6/96-27/6/96. 6 perf. 1st perfd Drury Lane
13/12/26. <u>Charles</u> George Graham. <u>Mrs Corset</u> Jessie
Danvers. <u>L</u>, <u>Mgr</u> as for 96.172. *REV: E 27/6/96 p8.*

96.174 *KISS IN THE DARK* (F,1a) J.B. Buckstone. NOVELTY
22/6/96-27/6/96. 6 perf.** <u>L</u>, <u>Mgr</u> as for 96.172. *REV:
E 27/6/96 p8.*

96.175 *ON THE MARCH* (MC,2a) William Yardley (lib) &
Cecil Clay (lib) & B.C. Stephenson (lib) & John Crook
(mus) & Edward Solomon (mus) & Frederic Clay (mus).
PRINCE OF WALES'S 22/6/96-5/9/96. 77 perf [w/S mat].

1st perfd Theatre Royal, Sheffield 18/5/96. Fitzaller-
ton Scroggs Thomas E. Murray; Col. McAlister Cecil
Ramsey; Cpt. Felix McAlister Templer Saxe; Lieut.
Jack Ferris Charles H.E. Brookfield; Sgt. Struggles
Horace Mills; Corporal Rush Cecil Freare; Cpt. King
G.L. Wilson; Dancer G. Elliston; Extras Atkins, Drew,
Jameson, Seymour, [Wilfred?] Wynnstay, Luke, Brooke,
Pennington, Gregory, Tyler, Rose. Edith de Bang
Maud Boyd/Winifred Hare; Florence Pringle Frances
Earle; Elfrida Molyneux Augusta Walters; Maggie Wel-
land Alice Atherton; Dancers Martin, Rundell; Extras
Chesters, Carswell, Herman, Grahame, Humphreys, D.
Russel, C[hristine] Salisbury, E[thel] Borlase, B.
Benson, Clifden, Barker, J. Salisbury, M. Turner,
Linton, Melton, Rosa, Douglas, Stirling, Boyce, Wood,
Dexter, Pryce, Haines, Hargreaves, Seymour, Seymour
[sic], Faulkner, Maurice, Spencer, Margot. MGR Cissy
Grahame; Pd Frank Parker; Ch George F. Marion, Will
Bishop; Cost Jays, Marie Watkin, Alias, Morris Angel,
Cooling & Lawrence; Sc Bruce Smith; Mus dir George W.
Byng; Bm C.P. Levilly. *REV: E 27/6/96 p8; Sk 1/7/96
p389; SR 27/6/96 p650; St 25/6/96 p10; Th 1/8/96 p95-
6; Ti 23/6/96 p13; TW96 p199-201.*

96.176 *A HUSBAND'S HUMILIATION* (Ca,1a) Annie Hughes.
CRITERION 25/6/96 mat perf.* George Wildfire Edmund
Maurice; Mr Bicillus Herbert Ross; Servant Lesly
Thomson. Mrs Wildfire Annie Hughes. L & MGR Charles
Wyndham. *REV: E 27/6/96 p12.*

96.177 *MRS HILARY REGRETS* (Ca) S. Theyre Smith. CRI-
TERION 25/6/96 mat perf.** Dr Power Charles Wyndham.
Mrs Hilary Mary Moore. L & MGR Charles Wyndham. *REV:
E 27/6/96 p12.*

96.178 *KITTY CLIVE--ACTRESS* (C,1a) F. Frankfort
Moore. CRITERION 25/6/96 mat perf.** Jack Bates Henry
Vibart; Landlord Fred W. Permain. Kitty Clive Irene
Vanbrugh. L & MGR Charles Wyndham. *REV: E 27/6/96 p12.*

96.179 *THE MERCHANT OF VENICE* (5a) William Shakespeare. DUKE OF YORK'S 25/6/96 mat perf.** Duke of
Venice Charles Franmore; Antonio Edward Ferris; Shylock Charles Pond; Bassanio Frank Gillmore; Salarino

H. Tripp Edgar; Salanio C.B. Reston; Gratiano Philip
Cunningham; Lorenzo Graham Browne; Launcelot Gobbo
J[ohn] Willes; Old Gobbo William Wyes; Tubal L.F.
Chapuy; Balthazar Mules Brown. Portia Ettie Williams;
Nerissa Mrs Bennett; Jessica Kate Ruskin. MGR Michael
Levenston; Dir Edward Hastings. *REV: Sk 8/7/96 p459;
St 2/7/96 p10-1.*

96.180 *MAJOR RAYMOND* (P,4a) Philip Havard. TERRY'S
25/6/96 mat perf.* Mjr. Raymond W.L. Abingdon; Mr
Dyson Frederick Volpé; Sir John Beale Julian Cross;
Michael Kennedy G[eorge] Hippisley; Oliver Fleming
Oswald Yorke; Bernard, Viscount Ashbrooke C.M. Lowne;
Frewin Guy Waller; Isaac Rubinstein Sydney Burt; Binks
S.F. Harrison. Molly Dyson Eva Moore; Lady Dorothea
Gunthorpe Madge Raye; Mrs Graham Nora Carewe; Tomkins
Alice Chippendale; Mrs Rubinstein Davis Webster;
Rachel Rubinstein Lena Cross; Maud Graham Beatrice
Baily; Mrs Fleming Mary Raby. *REV: Ath 4/7/97 p42;
E 27/6/96 p11; Sk 1/7/96 p389; St 2/7/96 p10; Th 1/8/
96 p97-8.*

96.181 *TRISTAN UND ISOLDE* (O[3a]) Richard Wagner.
COVENT GARDEN 26/6/96, 30/6, 4/7, 14/7/96. 4 perf.**
Tristan Jean de Reszke; Marke Edouard de Reszke;
Kurvenal David Bispham; Melot B. Piroia; Der Hirt
Edwin Wareham; Steurmann Antonio de Vaschetti. Bran-
gane Louise Meisslinger; Isolde Emma Albani. L Augus-
tus Harris; Cond Luigi Mancinelli; Am Neil Forsyth;
Bom E. Hall; Sm Arthur P. Collins. *REV: Ath 4/7/96
p41; E 4/7/96 p7; Sk 1/7/96 p388; SR 4/7/96 p10-2;
St 2/7/96 p10; Ti 29/6/96 p12, 17/7/96 p7.*

96.182 *TERROR OF PARIS* (D,4a) E. Hill-Mitchelson &
Charles H. Longden. NOVELTY 29/6/96-4/7/96. 6 perf.
1st perfd Victoria Opera House, Burnley 2/7/94. Du-
mont Charles Bush; Henri Martin John Davidson; Cpt.
Brigand Albert Ward; Larouche Charles H. Longden;
Pierre Valjean A. Clifton-Alderson; Daddy J.W. Lyne;
Bruno J.N. Hitchin; Gaston Mortimer S. Hastings; Pi-
card Frederick Ross; Sgt. Toupe C.H. Henderson; Coupe
E. Stocks; Alphonse T. Dyson. Marguerite Florence
Charles; Claire Ethel Griffies; Estelle Dolly Dott-
ridge. L V. St. Lawrence; Mgr Walter Tyrrell; Bm &

<u>Treas</u> Mortimer S. Hastings; <u>Cond</u> Henry Parks; <u>Sm</u>
George Abel; <u>Bom</u> Edward Hastings, jr. *REV: St 9/7/96
p13.*

96.183 *THE GRIP OF IRON* (D,4a) Arthur Shirley [adpt
of Adolphe Belot, *Les Etrangleurs*]. PRINCESS'S 29/6/96-
11/7/96. 12 perf. 1st perfd Surrey 17/10/87 [as *The
Stranglers of Paris*]. <u>Jagon</u> Fred Powell; <u>Lorentz de
Ribas</u> James E. Thompson; <u>Paul Blanchard</u> Charles East;
<u>Alphonse de Coucon</u> Arthur E. Godfrey; <u>Dodot</u> Gus
Wheatman; <u>Robert de Belfort</u> Wilfred Carr; <u>De Baudin</u>
Charles Girdlestone; <u>Loustalot</u> Andrew Liston; <u>Gover-
nor of Prison</u> Sidney White; <u>Cpt. of the Raven</u> Gilbert
Jones; <u>Warden of the Raven</u> Harry Richmond; <u>Warden of
La Grande Roquette</u> William Pollard; <u>Footman</u> Thomas
Griffin; <u>Prison Barber</u> William Griffen; <u>Cpt. Guerin</u>
Amos Townsend. <u>Sophie Blanchard</u> Florence Nelson; <u>Cora</u>
East Robertson; <u>Marie Guerin</u> Frances Ruttledge; <u>Bab-
ette</u> Cissie Liston; <u>Zelie de Ribas</u> Florence Townsend;
<u>La Goulet</u> Nellie Arline; <u>Mlle de Charal</u> Annie Garrett;
<u>Mlle Delaney</u> Phyllis Kent; <u>Mlle Mevree</u> Beatrice
Holmes; <u>Mlle Legros</u> Annie Newman. <u>MGR</u> Albert Gilmer.
REV: E 4/7/96 p8; Sk 8/7/96 p459; St 2/7/96 p11.

96.184 *WOMAN'S PROPER PLACE* (Duol) J. Wilton Jones
& Gertrude Warden. ST. JAMES'S 29/6/96. 1 perf.*
<u>Comment</u>: There is some doubt whether this item was
perfd, since, for example, the performance times for
96.5 remained unchanged in newspaper advertisements.

96.185 *HER FATHER'S FRIEND* (RP,3a) H.A. Rudall. SAVOY
29/6/96 mat perf.* <u>Marquis de Tournac</u> George W. Cock-
burn; <u>Dermont</u> Sydney Paxton; <u>Maurice</u> Harrison Hunter;
<u>Père Jerome</u> H.A. Saintsbury; <u>"Tiger"</u> Jacques Charles
Dodsworth; <u>Gen. Hansberger</u> George Riddell; <u>Camille</u>
Clarence Fitzclarence; <u>1st Soldier</u> Albert E. Raynor;
<u>2nd Soldier</u> William Burchill; <u>3rd Soldier</u> Ferdinand
Conti; <u>Extras</u> Lance Holt, William Luff, E.H. Brooke,
Phillips. <u>Rosette</u> Kate Turner; <u>Aline</u> Italia Conti.
<u>PP & MGR</u> Richard d'Oyly Carte; <u>Pd</u> Hugh Moss; <u>Asm</u> H.
Walter; <u>Cost</u> Mme Hubert, L. & H. Nathan; <u>Pq</u> William
Clarkson; <u>Furn</u> J.S. Lyon; <u>Act mgr</u> C. St. John Denton;
<u>Sec & Gen Am</u> Ferdinand Conti; <u>Mus dir</u> Benjamin Barrow.
REV: Ath 4/7/96 p42; E 4/7/96 p11; Sk 8/7/96 p459; St

2/7/96 p10; Th 1/8/96 p99-100.

96.186 *THE PITY OF IT* (Incident,1a) Ian Robertson.
SAVOY 29/6/96 mat perf.* <u>Alec Bond</u> Ian Robertson;
<u>Jack Hilliard</u> Sydney Brough. <u>Anne</u> Violet Royal; <u>Rhoda
Irwin</u> Italia Conti. PP & MGR, <u>Cost</u>, <u>Pq</u>, <u>Furn</u>, <u>Act
mgr</u>, <u>Sec & Gen Am</u>, <u>Mus dir</u> as for 96.185. *REV: E, St
as for 96.185.*

96.187 *MEFISTOFELE* (O[Prol,4a,Epi]) Arrigo Boito.
COVENT GARDEN 1/7/96, 6/7/96. 2 perf.** <u>Faust</u> Giu-
seppe Cremonini/Fernando de Lucia [?]; <u>Wagner/Nereas</u>
Rinaldini; <u>Mefistofele</u> Edouard de Reszke. <u>Margherita/
Elena</u> Margaret MacIntyre; <u>Marta/Pantala</u> Eugenia Man-
telli. <u>L</u> Augustus Harris; <u>Cond</u> Luigi Mancinelli; <u>Am</u>
Neil Forsyth; <u>Bom</u> E. Hall; <u>Sm</u> Arthur P. Collins. *REV:
Ath 4/7/96 p41; E 4/7/96 p7; Sk 8/7/96 p424; St 9/7/
96 p12; Ti 3/7/96 p7.*

96.188 *THE MUMMY* (F,3a) George D. Day & Allan Reed.
COMEDY 2/7/96 mat perf. 1st prof. <u>Rameses</u> Lionel
Brough; <u>Prof Jeremy Garsop</u> William Cheesman; <u>Ezra van
Tarsel Smythe</u> Robb Harwood; <u>Jack Tibbs</u> Stuart Cham-
pion; <u>North Marston</u> Clarence Blakiston. <u>Alvena Garsop</u>
Alice Mansfield; <u>Eva Garsop</u> Lily Johnson; <u>Mabel Wood-
ruff</u> Jessie Bateman; <u>Cleopatra</u> Annie Goward; <u>Hattie
van Tassel Smythe</u> Charlotte G. Walker. *REV: Ath 11/7/
96 p76; E 4/7/96 p11; SR 11/7/96 p37; St 9/7/96 p12;
Th 1/8/96 p98.*

96.189 *CARMEN* (O[4a]) Georges Bizet. COVENT GARDEN
2/7/96, 7/7/96. 2 perf.** <u>Escamillo</u> Mario Ancona;
<u>Remendado</u> B. Piroia; <u>Dancairo</u> Charles Gilibert; <u>Don
José</u> Albert Alvarez; <u>Morales</u> Jacques Bars; <u>Zuniga</u>
Trabucco. <u>Michaela</u> Emma Eames/Margaret Reid; <u>Fras-
quita</u> Mathilde Bauermeister; <u>Mercedes</u> Cecile Brani;
<u>Carmen</u> Zelie de Lussan. <u>L</u> Augustus Harris; <u>Cond</u> En-
rico Bevignani; <u>Am</u> Neil Forsyth; <u>Bom</u> E. Hall; <u>Sm</u>
Arthur P. Collins. *REV: Ath 11/7/96 p75; E 4/7/96 p7;
St 9/7/96 p12; Ti 3/7/96 p7.*

96.190 *BEHIND THE SCENES* (C,3a) George P. Hawtrey &
Felix Morris [adpt of *The First Night*; trans fr *Le
Père de la Debutante*]. COMEDY 4/7/96 mat perf.* <u>Jack</u>

Cardew Cosmo Stuart; <u>Achille Talma Dufard</u> Felix Morris; <u>Ferdinand Schreiber</u> William F. Hawtrey; <u>Alexan-</u>
<u>der Huggett</u> Ernest Cosham; <u>John Duncan</u> Frederick Vol-
pé; <u>Mr Wilson</u> Harry Ford; <u>Mr Vaughan</u> William Aysom;
<u>Mr Bennett</u> Frank Lacy; <u>Mr Bucalossi</u> Ernest Bucalossi;
<u>Jeffreys</u> C. King; <u>Tommy</u> R. Earle. <u>Miss Pettigrew</u>
Alice Beet; <u>Miss Hamilton</u> Gertrude Henriquez; <u>Miss</u>
<u>Dufard</u> Sarah Brooke; <u>Maud Beresford</u> Alma Stanley.
REV: Ath 11/7/96 p76; E 11/7/96 p9; Sk 15/7/96 p503;
SR 11/7/96 p37; St 9/7/96 p12; Th 1/8/96 p100; Ti 6/
7/96 p10.

96.191 *SIBERIA* (P,5a) Bartley Campbell. NOVELTY 6/7/
96-11/7/96. 6 perf. 1st perfd California, San Francisco 26/11/82. <u>Michael Jaracoff</u> Bernard Copping;
<u>Loris Ipanoff</u> C[harles] Lillford-Delph; <u>Nicolai Nei-</u>
<u>goff</u> Temple E. Crozier; <u>Michael Sparta</u> Leonard Shep-
herd; <u>Count Stanislaus</u> B. George; <u>Ivan Nordoff</u> George
Abel; <u>Lieut. Smailoff</u> George Grahame; <u>Lieut. Portoff</u>
E[dward] Beasley; <u>David Janoski</u> W.M. Franks; <u>Priest</u>
[F.] Ashby; <u>Michael Trolsky</u> George Belmore; <u>Peter</u>
<u>Moreoff</u> R[obert] Smith; <u>Nordovitch</u> H. Kelly; <u>Peter</u>
<u>Christovich</u> [H.P.] Brodie. <u>Marie Janoski</u> [E.L.] Mad-
docks; <u>Countess Stanislaus</u> [Eleanor] Head; <u>Princess</u>
[Elsie] Trevor; <u>Vera</u> Jessie Danvers; <u>Drovina</u> [Daisie]
Cook; <u>Sarah Janoski</u> V. St. Lawrence; <u>L</u> V. St. Law-
rence; <u>Mgr</u> Walter Tyrrell. *REV: E 11/7/96 p9; St*
9/7/96 p13.

96.192 *LADY FORTUNE* (CD,1a) Charles Thomas. NOVELTY
6/7/96-11/7/96. 6 perf.** <u>Kate Cunliffe</u> V. St. Lawrence. <u>L</u>, <u>Mgr</u> as for 96.191. *REV: As for 96.191.*

96.193 *THE LIAR* (C,2a) Samuel Foote. ROYALTY 9/7/96,
15/7, 23/7/96. 3 mat perf.** <u>Sir James Elliot</u> Charles
Troode; <u>Old Wilding</u> Ernest Hendrie; <u>Young Wilding</u>
Arthur Bourchier; <u>Papillon</u> Henry Vibart; <u>John</u> Metcalfe Wood; <u>William</u> Alexander Stuart. <u>Miss Grantham</u>
Irene Vanbrugh; <u>Miss Godfrey</u> Helen Rous. <u>L & MGR</u>
Arthur Bourchier; <u>Pp</u> Kate Santley. *REV: Ath 18/7/96*
p108; E 11/7/96 p10; Sk 15/7/96 p135; SR 18/7/96 p61-
2; St 16/7/96 p10; Ti 10/7/96 p10; TW96 p219.

96.194 *MONSIEUR DE PARIS* (P,1a) Alicia Ramsay & Ru-

dolph de Cordova. ROYALTY 9/7/96, 15/7, 23/7/96. 3
mat perf.** <u>Jacinta</u> Violet Vanbrugh. <u>L</u> & <u>MGR</u>, <u>Pp</u> as
for 96.193. <u>Comment</u>: Remainder of cast probably as
for 96.81.

96.195 *THE LITTLE GENIUS* (CO,2a) Augustus Harris (lib)
& Arthur Sturgess (lib) & Eugen von Taund (mus) &
James M. Glover (mus) & Landon Ronald (mus). SHAFTES-
BURY 9/7/96-21/11/96. 128 perf [w/mat 5/8, 16/9, 26/9,
30/9, 7/10, 17/10, 21/10, 31/10, 4/11, 11/11, 18/11].*
<u>Lord Lomond</u> C.P. Little; <u>Chevalier Tween</u> E.J. Lonnen;
<u>Signor Gordoni</u> Arthur Williams/Ells Dagnall; <u>Mr Knox</u>
William Cheesman/Eardley Turner; <u>Edward Lord Calmore</u>
Harrison Brockbank; <u>Lord Jermyn</u> Cecil Lawrence; <u>Bath-
ing Machineman</u> A.T. Hendon; <u>Footmen</u> S. White, G.
Shuter/S. Hill, F. Lewis; <u>Extras</u> F.A. Noyce, S. White,
F. Griffiths, F. Court, H. Foster, J. Truscott, G.
Shuter, G. Hill, F. Lewis, J. Svermeski. <u>Georgie Knox</u>
Maggie Roberts/Lillian Menelly; <u>Arabella</u> Kate Phillips;
<u>Lady Plantagenet</u> Birdie Sutherland; <u>Hon Miss Edith
Byng</u> Edith Johnston/[E.] Wrangham; <u>Miss Mount Gore</u>
Lillian Menelly/[E.] Wrangham; <u>Lady Mabel Clare</u> Nell
Gwynne/C[arrie] Benton; <u>Miss Sackville</u> Edith Meurice;
<u>Paolo</u> Annie Dirkens/Florence St. John; <u>Extras</u> E.
Lange, E. Lynes, H. Hamilton, V. Herbert, A. McFar-
lane, D. Maitland, N. Thorley, H. Keene, E. Wrangham,
D. Temple, M. Temple, F. Harrison, G. Gordon, L. Wil-
son, A. Thomas, F. Blake, L. Marsden, L. Dudley, C.
Berton, V. Fowler. <u>PP</u> John Lancaster; <u>L</u> Theatrical
Enterprises Limited; <u>Mgr</u> A.H. Chamberlyn; <u>Dir</u> Herbert
Love; <u>Gen mgr</u> H.T. Brickwell; <u>Rep of H. Love</u> T.B.
Davis; <u>Ch</u> Will Bishop; <u>Cost</u> Alias, Miss Fisher, Peter
Robinson, Miss Collier, Miss Doughty, Westoby & Co.,
Morris Angel; <u>Sc</u> Joseph Harker; <u>Pq</u> William Clarkson;
<u>Mus dir</u> James M. Glover; <u>Sm</u> Ells Dagnall; <u>Asm</u> Beres-
ford Whitcomb. *REV: E 11/7/96 p10; Sk 24/6/96 p382,
15/7/96 p466-7, 11/11/96 p94; St 16/7/96 p10, 10/9/
96 p12; Th 1/8/96 p96-7; Ti 10/7/96 p10, 7/9/96 p4;
TW96 p257-8; E 12/9/96 p10.* <u>Comment</u>: A "second edition" was introduced on 5/9/96. The following role
was added during the production: <u>Lady Mount Gore</u> L.
Dudley.

96.196 *THE COUNTESS GUCKI* (C,3a) Augustin Daly [adpt

of Franz von Schonthan]. COMEDY 11/7/96-27/7/96. 18
perf [w/mat 15/7, 18/7, 23/7, 25/7]. 1st perfd Daly's,
New York 28/1/96. Court Counsellor von Mittersteig
James Lewis; Gen. Suvatscheff Edwin Stevens; Bruno
von Neuhoff Charles Richman; Cousin Leopold Sidney
Herbert; Baumann William Haseltine; Wensel Robert
Shephard. Clementina Mrs G.H. Gilbert; Lilli Helma
Nelson; Rosa Mabel Gillman; Countess Hermana Trachan
Ada Rehan. MGR Charles H. Hawtrey; L J.W. Comyns Carr;
Mus dir William Withers; Sm Herbert Gresham; Bm Arthur
Rehan; Bom Scarisbrick. REV: Ath 18/7/96 p107-8; E
18/7/96 p8; Sk 15/7/96 p139; SR 18/7/96 p61; St 16/7/
96 p10; Th 1/8/96 p92-3; Ti 13/7/96 p12; TW96 p212-9.

96.197 *THE MIKADO; OR, THE TOWN OF TITIPU* (Japanese
O,2a) W.S. Gilbert (lib) & Arthur Sullivan (mus).
SAVOY 11/7/96-17/2/97. 226 perf [w/S mat; add mat
30/12/96, 6/1/97, 13/1, 20/1, 27/1/97; np 25/12/96].**
Mikado Richard Temple/Robert Scott-Fishe/Jones Hewson;
Pooh-bah Rutland Barrington/Fred Billington/Jones Hew-
son; Ko-Ko Walter Passmore; Nanki-Poo Charles Kenning-
ham/Scott Russell; Pish-Tush H.G. Gordon/Jones Hewson.
Katisha Rosina Brandram/Kate Talby; Pitti-Sing Jessie
Bond/Bessie Bonsall; Yum Yum Florence Perry/Emmie
Owen; Peep-Bo Emmie Owen/Beatrice Perry. PP & GEN MGR
Richard d'Oyly Carte; Bm J.W. Beckwith; Mus dir Fran-
cois Cellier; Dir Charles Harris; Sm W.H. Seymour.

96.198 *MY GIRL* (Domestic MP,2a) James T. Tanner (lib)
& Adrian Ross (lyr) & F.Osmand Carr (mus). GAIETY
13/7/96-28/11/96; trfd to GARRICK 1/12/96-16/1/97.
185 perf [w/S mat exc 18/7, 1/8; np 30/11, 25/12]. 1st
perfd Theatre Royal, Birmingham 13/4/96 [as *The Cler-
gyman's Daughter*]. Rev Arthur Mildreth Charles Ryley;
Theo Paul Arthur/W. Louis Bradfield; Alexander McGregor John Le Hay; Dr Tertius Huxtable Fred Kaye; Lord
Barum Lawrance d'Orsay/Paul Arthur; Leopold van Fon-
tein W.H. Rawlins; Saunders Leslie Holland/W.H. Pow-
ell/Tom Terriss; Weekes Willie Warde/Alfred Asher;
Mayor of Porthampton Colin Coop/Tim Ryley/Robert
Nainby; John Fahee W. Downes. Lady Bargrave Maria
Davies/Christine Mayne/N. Langton; Beatrix Ethel Hay-
don/Sybil Carlisle/Mabel Warren/Florence Dysart; Rebecca Marie Montrose/Nellie Murray; Phoebe Toodge

Katie Seymour/Lillian Menelly/Blanche Astley; Melissa
Banks Ethel Sydney/Florence Dysart/Florence Lloyd/
Christine Mayne; Mayoress Connie Ediss/Lillie Belmore;
Dorothy Kate Adams/Sophie Elliott/Maud Santley; Mary
Ada Maitland/Edith Singlehurst/Retta Villis; Miss
Veriner Florence Lloyd/Lucille Grahame/Margaret Fra-
zer/Annie Vivian; Mrs Porkinson Grace Palotta/Retta
Villis/Mabel Warren/Lucille Grahame; May Ellaline
Terriss/Ethel Sydney/Isa Bowman; Dancers Maggie Cross-
land, Lottie Williams, Margaret Fraser. L & MGR
George Edwardes; Sc Walter Hann, William Telbin; Cost
dgn Wilhelm; Cost Redferns Limited, Miss Fisher,
Harrisons, Henry Heath & Co.; Ch Willie Warde; Pq
William Clarkson; Mus dir J.H.H. Korte; Sm J.A.E.
Malone; Act mgr E[dward] Marshall; Bom A.P. Oxley.
REV: E 18/7/96 p8, 5/12/96 p10; Sk 22/7/96 p542, 546,
9/9/96 p265, 21/10/96 p547-9; St 16/7/96 p10, 3/12/96
p15; Th 1/8/96 p94-5; Ti 14/7/96 p11; TW96 p219-24.

96.199 *THE ARABIAN NIGHTS* (FC,3a) Sydney Grundy.
NOVELTY 13/7/96-18/7/96. 6 perf.** Arthur Hummingtop
Graham Wentworth; Ralph Ormerod Temple E. Crozier;
Joshua Gillibrand Besley Beltram; Dobson W.M. Franks.
Mrs Hummingtop [E.L.] Maddocks; Mrs Gillibrand Elsie
Trevor; Daisy Maitland Jessie Danvers; Barbara Daisy
Cook; Rosa Colombier V. St. Lawrence. L V. St. Law-
rence; Mgr Walter Tyrrell. *REV: E 18/7/96 p9; St 16/*
7/96 p11.

96.200 *A BED OF ROSES* (C,1a) H.A. Jones. NOVELTY 13/
7/96-18/7/96. 6 perf. 1st perfd Globe 26/1/82. Peter
Vellacott George Belmore; Charles Vellacott C[harles]
Lillford-Delph; George Dalyson Temple E. Crozier;
Basker W.M. Franks. Dora Vellacott Daisy Cook; Amy
Brendon [E.L.] Maddocks. L, Mgr as for 96.199. *REV:*
E 18/7/96 p9.

96.201 *DRINK* (D,7a) Charles Reade. PRINCESS'S 13/7/96-
30/7/96. 16 perf.** Coupeau Charles Warner; Lantier
S.B. Brereton; Gouget Alec Frank; Poisson Frederic
Jacques; Mes Bottes Lloyd Townrow; Bibi Alfred Phillips; Bec Sali E. Smith; Jacques W. Jones; Pierre
Colombe E. Lilly; Pierre H. Carlin; Adolphe John Cook-
son. Virginie Madge Denzil; Little Nana Holly Lyons;

Mme Rouge Agnes Byron; Gervaise Stella Leigh; Phoebe
Sage Minnie Rayner; Juliette E. Lyons; Delphine E.
Papera; Louise Minnie Ruby. MGR Albert Gilmer; Sc
Richard C. Durant, R. Messider; Am Horace Gilmer; Sm
George T. Minshull; Treas H. Bellamy Smith; Mus dir
Theodore Ward. *REV: E 18/7/96 p8; St 16/7/96 p11; Ti
14/7/96 p11.*

96.202 *THE HONOURABLE MEMBER* (CD,3a) A.W. Gattie.
COURT 14/7/96 mat perf.* Samuel Ditherby, M.P. G.W.
Anson; Luke Heron W. Scott Buist; James Hubbock George
Bernage; Beamer James A. Welch; Williams Graham
Browne; Davies Thomas Courtice. Mrs Ditherby Mrs Ed-
mund Phelps; Mrs Hubbock Mrs A.R. McIntosh; Margery
Douglass Madge McIntosh. MGR Arthur Chudleigh. *REV:
Ath 18/7/96 p108; E 18/7/96 p11; Sk 22/7/96 p542; SR
18/7/96 p62; St 16/7/96 p10-1; Th 1/8/96 p98-9; Ti
15/7/96 p4.*

96.203 *THE LITTLEST GIRL* (P,1a) Robert Hilliard [adpt
of Richard Harding Davis's story, "Her First Appearance"]. COURT 15/7/96-31/7/96. 15 perf.* Van Bibber
Robert Hilliard; Davenport Roy Horniman; Mr Carruthers
Sidney Howard. Littlest Girl Alice Cecile. L & MGR
Arthur Chudleigh. *REV: Ath 25/7/96 p140; E 18/7/96
p8; St 23/7/96 p10.*

96.204 *THE BALLADMONGER* (RP,1a) Walter Besant & Walter
Pollock. HAYMARKET 15/7/96. 1 perf.** Gringoire H.B.
Tree; Louis XI James Fernandez; Olivier Charles Allan.
Loyse Mrs H.B. Tree; Nicole Frances Ivor. L & MGR
H.B. Tree; Sm Shelton; Asm Alfred Wigley; Prompter
D.J. Williams; Bm Fitzroy Gardner; Furn Frank Giles;
Pq William Clarkson; Mus dir Raymond Roze; Bom W.H.
Leverton; Eng E. Wingfield Bowles; Cost L. & H. Na-
than. *REV: E 18/7/96 p8; Ti 16/7/96 p5.*

96.205 *MANON* (O[5a]) Jules Massenet. COVENT GARDEN
16/7/96, 22/7/96. 2 perf.** Chevalier des Grieux
Albert Alvarez; Lescault Henri Albers; Guillot Mor-
fontain Charles Gilibert; De Bretigny Jacques Bars;
Garde Rinaldini; Garde Antonio de Vaschetti; Comte
des Grieux Pol Plançon. Manon Nellie Melba; Poussette
Mathilde Bauermeister; Javotte Cecile Brani; Rosette

Sanda. L̲ Augustus Harris; C̲o̲n̲d̲ Luigi Mancinelli; A̲m̲
Neil Forsyth; B̲o̲m̲ E. Hall; S̲m̲ Arthur P. Collins. *REV:*
Ath 25/7/96 p137; E 18/7/96 p19; St 23/7/96 p10; Ti
17/7/96 p7.

96.206 *LES HUGUENOTS* (O[5a]) Giacomo Meyerbeer. COVENT
GARDEN 18/7/96, 24/7/96. 2 perf.** M̲a̲r̲c̲e̲l̲l̲o̲ Pol Plan-
çon; C̲o̲n̲t̲e̲ ̲d̲i̲ ̲N̲e̲v̲e̲r̲s̲ Mario Ancona; C̲o̲n̲t̲e̲ ̲d̲i̲ ̲S̲a̲n̲ ̲B̲r̲i̲s̲
David Bispham; H̲u̲g̲u̲e̲n̲o̲t̲ ̲S̲o̲l̲d̲i̲e̲r̲ Jacques Bars; T̲a̲v̲a̲n̲n̲e̲s̲
Rinaldini; D̲e̲ ̲C̲o̲s̲s̲e̲ Iginio Corsi; D̲e̲ ̲R̲e̲t̲z̲ Antonio de
Vaschetti; M̲a̲u̲r̲e̲v̲e̲r̲t̲ Trabucco; R̲a̲o̲u̲l̲ ̲d̲i̲ ̲N̲a̲n̲g̲i̲s̲ Lucig-
nani. M̲a̲r̲g̲h̲e̲r̲i̲t̲a̲ ̲d̲i̲ ̲V̲a̲l̲o̲i̲s̲ Nellie Melba/Marie Engle;
U̲r̲b̲a̲n̲o̲ Fernanda Brazzi; D̲a̲m̲a̲ ̲d̲'̲O̲n̲o̲r̲e̲ Mathilde Bauermeister; V̲a̲l̲e̲n̲t̲i̲n̲a̲ Emma Albani. L̲, A̲m̲, B̲o̲m̲, S̲m̲ as for
96.205; C̲o̲n̲d̲ Enrico Bevignani. *REV: Ath 25/7/96 p137;*
E 25/7/96 p10; Sk 29/7/96 p5; St 23/7/96 p10; Ti 20/
7/96 p15.

96.207 *TRILBY* (4a) [American ver of G. du Maurier's
novel]. NOVELTY 20/7/96-25/7/96. 6 perf. T̲a̲l̲b̲o̲t̲
W̲y̲n̲n̲e̲ C[harles] Lillford-Delph; S̲a̲n̲d̲y̲ ̲M̲c̲A̲l̲l̲i̲s̲t̲e̲r̲
George Belmore; W̲i̲l̲l̲i̲a̲m̲ ̲B̲a̲g̲o̲t̲ Donald Stuart; S̲v̲e̲n̲g̲a̲l̲i̲
Trant Fischer; G̲e̲c̲k̲o̲ J. Willoughby; Z̲o̲u̲z̲o̲u̲ Temple E.
Crozier; D̲o̲d̲o̲r̲ W.M. Franks; R̲e̲v̲ ̲T̲h̲o̲m̲a̲s̲ ̲B̲a̲g̲o̲t̲ Bernard
Copping; M̲a̲n̲a̲g̲e̲r̲ Robert Smith; A̲t̲t̲e̲n̲d̲a̲n̲t̲ ̲o̲f̲ ̲t̲h̲e̲ ̲T̲h̲e̲-
a̲t̲r̲e̲ [H.] P. Brodie; D̲o̲c̲t̲o̲r̲ B[eresford] Carl. M̲m̲e̲
V̲i̲n̲a̲r̲d̲ Mrs Stanislaus Calhaem; M̲r̲s̲ ̲B̲r̲a̲n̲d̲ Elsie Tre-
vor; T̲r̲i̲l̲b̲y̲ V. St. Lawrence. L̲ V. St. Lawrence; M̲g̲r̲
Walter Tyrrell. *REV: E 25/7/96 p9; St 30/7/96 p10.*

96.208 *MY COUSIN* (Ca,1a) J.J. Hewson. NOVELTY 20/7/96-
25/7/96. 6 perf. 1st perfd Theatre Royal, Belfast
16/10/85. J̲o̲h̲n̲ ̲P̲e̲r̲r̲y̲b̲l̲e̲ G[eorge] Belmore. L̲, M̲g̲r̲ as
for 96.207. *REV: St 30/7/96 p10.*

96.209 *DON GIOVANNI* (O[2a]) W.A. Mozart. COVENT GAR-
DEN 23/7/96, 27/7/96. 2 perf.** D̲o̲n̲ ̲O̲t̲t̲a̲v̲i̲o̲ Giuseppe
Cremonini; L̲e̲p̲o̲r̲e̲l̲l̲o̲ Antonio Pini-Corsi; I̲l̲ ̲C̲o̲m̲m̲e̲n̲-
d̲a̲t̲o̲r̲e̲ Vittorio Arimondi; M̲a̲s̲e̲t̲t̲o̲ Rinaldini; D̲o̲n̲
G̲i̲o̲v̲a̲n̲n̲i̲ Mario Ancona. D̲o̲n̲n̲a̲ ̲A̲n̲n̲a̲ Emma Albani; Z̲e̲r̲-
l̲i̲n̲a̲ Margaret Reid; D̲o̲n̲n̲a̲ ̲E̲l̲v̲i̲r̲a̲ Margaret MacIntyre.
L̲ Augustus Harris; C̲o̲n̲d̲ Enrico Bevignani; A̲m̲ Neil
Forsyth; B̲o̲m̲ E. Hall; S̲m̲ Arthur P. Collins. *REV: Ath*
1/8/96 p170-1; E 25/7/96 p10; Sk 29/7/96 p5; St 30/7/

96 p9; Ti 24/7/96 p5.

96.210 *THE WORLD AGAINST HER* (D,5a) Frank Harvey. NOVELTY 27/7/96–1/8/96. 6 perf. 1st perfd Theatre Royal, Preston 11/1/87. <u>Gilbert Blair</u> Bernard Copping; <u>James Carlton</u> Gilbert Arrandale; <u>Robert Danvers</u> Henry Bertram; <u>Simon Clegg</u> C[harles] Lillford-Delph; <u>Harold Vernon</u> Temple E. Crozier; <u>Bob Millett</u> Newman Maurice; <u>Dick Markland</u> Percy Murray; <u>Heslop</u> Robert Smith; <u>Thwaites</u> W.M. Franks. <u>Servant</u> Daisy Cook; <u>Liz</u> Winifred Wood; <u>Jenny Clegg</u> Thea Lesbrook; <u>Lucy Danvers</u> Katie Brunton; <u>Sally Millett</u> Elsie Trevor; <u>Ned</u> Gladys Whyte; <u>Annie</u> Maudie Hastings; <u>Madge Carlton</u> V. St. Lawrence. <u>L</u> V. St. Lawrence; <u>Mgr</u> Walter Tyrrell. *REV: E 1/8/96 p8.*

96.211 *LOVE ON CRUTCHES* (C,3a) Augustin Daly [fnd on play by Heinrich Stobitzer]. COMEDY 28/7/96–8/8/96. 15 perf [w/W, S mat]. 1st perfd Daly's, New York 25/11/84. <u>Sydney Austen</u> Charles Richman; <u>Guy Roverley</u> Sidney Herbert; <u>Dr Epenetus Quattles</u> James Lewis; <u>Mr Bitteredge</u> Herbert Gresham; <u>Podd</u> William Haseltine; <u>Bells</u> Robert Shephard. <u>Annie Austen</u> Ada Rehan; <u>Eudoxia Quattles</u> Mrs G.H. Gilbert; <u>Mrs Margert Gwynn</u> Sybil Carlisle; <u>Besta</u> Helma Nelson; <u>Netty</u> Gerda Wisner. <u>MGR</u> Charles H. Hawtrey; <u>L</u> J.W. Comyns Carr; <u>Bom</u> Scarisbrick. *REV: Ath 1/8/96 p172; E 1/8/96 p8; Sk 5/8/96 p48; St 30/7/96 p9-10; Th 1/9/96 p155-6; Ti 29/7/96 p9; TW96 p225-7.*

96.212 *OTHELLO* (T,5a) William Shakespeare. COVENT GARDEN 30/7/96. 1 perf.** <u>Duke of Venice</u> Charles Bernard; <u>Brabantio</u> L.F. Chapuy; <u>Gratiano</u> C[harles] Steyne; <u>Lodovico</u> H. Tripp Edgar; <u>Montano</u> Walter Howe; <u>Othello</u> Charles Pond; <u>Cassio</u> Graham Browne; <u>Iago</u> Hermann Vezin; <u>Roderigo</u> Harry Cane; <u>Antonio</u> Mules Brown; <u>Messenger</u> W. Brandon. <u>Desdemona</u> Ettie Williams; <u>Emilia</u> Mrs Bennett. <u>L</u> Augustus Harris; <u>Pq</u> William Clarkson; <u>Pd</u> Edward Hastings; <u>Bom</u> Edward Hall. *REV: E 1/8/96 p9; St 6/8/96 p12.*

96.213 *IN SIGHT OF ST PAUL'S* (D,4a) Sutton Vane. PRINCESS'S 1/8/96–19/9/96. 44 perf [w/mat 3/8].* <u>Mr Chichester</u> E. Story Gofton; <u>Tom Chichester</u> Ernest Lei-

cester; <u>Harry Chichester</u> George Hippisley; <u>John Grid-</u>
<u>stone</u> Austin Melford; <u>Fretly Burnsides</u> Walter Howard;
<u>Gillie Fletcher</u> Lyston Lyle; <u>David Treacher</u> Harry
Cane; <u>Dennis Sheridan</u> A. Rymon; <u>Jim Palfrey</u> Herbert
Vyvyan; <u>Inspector Clarkson</u> Gerald Kennedy; <u>Prescott</u>
Chris Walker; <u>Amos</u> C. Astley; <u>Chelsea Pensioner</u> Thomas
Kean; <u>Greenwich Pensioner</u> S. Foley; <u>Drummer Boy</u> George
Yates. <u>Cynthia Dell</u> Keith Wakeman; <u>Beatrice Moreland</u>
Alice Yorke; <u>Countess Fellstar</u> Flora Wills; <u>Mrs Bur-</u>
<u>lington Marsh</u> Mary Bates; <u>Lady Snow</u> Lily Gordon; <u>Rose</u>
Winifred Lang; <u>Becky Vetch</u> Florrie Millington; <u>Gracie</u>
<u>Chichester</u> Sydney Fairbrother; <u>Aileen Millar</u> Kate
Tyndal; <u>Extras</u> Maud Mellor, Violet Roper, Sybil Camp-
bell, Dorothy Campbell, Kate Smith, Eva Wharncliffe,
Reeca Val Cees, Daisy Colson. <u>MGR</u> Albert Augustus Gil-
mer; <u>Sc</u> Cecil E. Hicks, J. Johnstone, Conrad Trisch-
ler; <u>Cost</u> Alias, Morris Angel & Son; <u>Pq</u> William
Clarkson; <u>Pd</u> W. Calder, George T. Minshull; <u>Am</u> Horace
Gilmer; <u>Sm</u> George T. Minshull; <u>Treas</u> H. Bellamy Smith;
<u>Mus dir</u> Theodore Ward. *REV: Ath 8/8/96 p204; E 8/8/96*
p8; Sk 12/8/96 p87; St 6/8/96 p12; Th 1/9/96 p156-7;
Ti 3/8/96 p11.

96.214 *AFTER DARK: A TALE OF LONDON LIFE* (D,4a) Dion
Boucicault. NOVELTY 3/8/96-8/8/96. 6 perf.** <u>Old Tom</u>
Henry Bertram; <u>Dicey Morris</u> Newman Maurice; <u>Gordon</u>
<u>Chumley</u> Bernard Copping; <u>Bellingham</u> Percy Murray;
<u>George Medhurst</u> Temple   E. Crozier; <u>Crumpet</u> C[har-
les] Lillford-Delph. <u>Eliza</u> V. St. Lawrence; <u>Rose</u>
<u>Egerton</u> Thea Lesbrooke. <u>L</u> V. St. Lawrence; <u>Mgr</u> Walter
Tyrrell. *REV: St 6/8/96 p13.*

96.215 *LOST IN NEW YORK* (CD,5a) Leonard Grover. OLYM-
PIC 3/8/96-12/9/96. 36 perf.* <u>Arthur Wilson</u> George
H. Harker; <u>Horatio Chester</u> William Lee; <u>"Hackensack"</u>
<u>George</u> A[lfred] B. Cross; <u>Martin Purcell Tramp</u> Char-
les E. Edwards; <u>Anon Ally</u> C. Stuart Johnson; <u>Dr Ar-</u>
<u>nold</u> Robert Escott; <u>Mate of the Steamer "Bellevue"</u>
James E. Fish; <u>Guard of the Insane Asylum</u> E.A. June.
<u>Mrs Henrietta Wilson</u> Maggie Hunt; <u>Jennie Wilson</u> Lily
B. Sinclair; <u>Caroline Peabody</u> Lesley Bell; <u>Matron of</u>
<u>the Insane Asylum</u> Mrs S[tanislaus] Calhaem; <u>Marie</u>
Esther Phillips; <u>Little Susie</u> Petite Lucy. *REV: Ath*
8/8/96 p204; E 8/8/96 p8; Sk 12/8/96 p87; St 6/8/96

p12; Th 1/9/96 p158-9; Ti 4/8/96 p4.

96.216 *THE SINS OF THE NIGHT* (D,5a) Frank Harvey.
NOVELTY 10/8/96-15/8/96. 6 perf. 1st perfd Theatre
Royal, Barnsley 30/3/93. Squire Thorne Henry Bert-
ram; Tim Dexter Charles Lillford-Delph; Leslie Thorne
Bernard Copping; Giles Ridger Newman Maurice; Harold
Thorne Oswald True; John Marchant Percy Murray; Man-
uel Ramez Temple E. Crozier/Harold Child; Draco Robert
Smith; Pablo W[ilfred] M. Franks/Robert Smith. Jenny
Daisy Cook; Cynthia Mayne Thea Lesbrooke; Abemma
Winifred Wood; Dolly Peachblossom Cicely Wynne/Katie
Brunton; Rosa V. St. Lawrence. L V. St. Lawrence; Mgr
Walter Tyrrell; Pq William Clarkson; Furn J.S. Lyons;
Sc E.V. & A. Williams; Cost Morris Angel & Son; Pd
Newman Maurice; Bom Edward Hastings, jr. *REV: E 15/8/
96 p8, 11; St 13/8/96 p10.* Comment: Temple E. Crozier
was accidentally killed during the first perf.

96.217 *ICI ON PARLE FRANCAIS* (F,1a) Thomas J. Williams. NOVELTY 10/8/96. 1 perf.** Victor Dubois Temple
E. Crozier; Mjr. Rattan Bernard Copping. Anna Maria
V. St. Lawrence. L, Mgr as for 96.216. *REV: St 13/8/
96 p10.*

96.218 *WEATHER OR NO* (Musical Duol) Adrian Ross (lib)
& William Beach (lib) & Bertram Luard Selby (mus).
SAVOY 10/8/96-17/2/97; 2/3/97-24/4/97. 209 perf [np
25/12/96; 16-17/4/97].* He Scott Russell. She Emmie
Owen/Beatrice Perry. PP & MGR Richard d'Oyly Carte;
Mus dir Francois Cellier; Sm W.H. Seymour; Act mgr
J.W. Beckwith. *REV: E 22/8/96 p9; St 20/8/96 p12; Ti
18/8/96 p6.* Comment: Nicoll indicates 1st perf = 15/8.

96.219 *THE MUMMY* (F,3a) George D. Day & Allan Reed.
COMEDY 11/8/96-5/9/96. 23 perf.** Rameses Lionel
Brough; Prof Jeremy Garsop Frederick Volpé; Ezra van
Tassel Smythe Ernest Percy; Jack Tibbs Stuart Cham-
pion; North Marston Clarence Blakiston. Alvena Gar-
sop Noney Seabrooke; Mabel Woodruff Doris Templeton;
Cleopatra Annie Goward; Hattie van Tassel Smythe
Elliot Page. MGR & PD Charles H. Hawtrey; L J.W. Co-
myns Carr; Sm Frederick Glover; Mus dir Ernest Buca-
lossi; Bom Scarisbrick; Bm C. Liddon Clark; Act mgr

Arthur Donald. *REV: E 15/8/96 p8; Sk 19/8/96 p168; St 13/8/96 p10; Ti 12/8/96 p5; TW96 p227-30.*

96.220 *THE GUINEA STAMP* (P,1a) Cyril Hallward. COMEDY 11/8/96-5/9/96. 23 perf.** Sir Charles Trefusis Ernest Cosham; Jack Menzies Clarence Blakiston; Cecil Arbuthnot Stuart Champion. Mabel Trefusis Noney Seabrooke; Nellie Robinson Maud Abbott. MGR, L, Sm, Mus dir, Bom, Bm, Act mgr as for 96.219. *REV: E, St as for 96.219.*

96.221 *AN ENGLISHWOMAN* (D,5a) St. Aubyn Miller. NOVELTY 17/8/96-22/8/96. 6 perf. 1st perfd Opera House, Chatham 1/1/94. Cpt. Frank Earlsworthy Oswald True; Mjr. Jasper Gordon Bernard Copping; Fred Chatsworth Jack Haddon; Arthur Grahame C[harles] Lillford-Delph; Rev Robert Evergreen Harold Child; Silas Mayne Percy Murray; Lord Henry Mallinghurst Arthur Elton; Pipkins Newman Maurice; Dr Woodgate Robert Smith; Sgt. Davidson Henry Bertram; Police Officer Beresford Carl; Landlord Harry Danby; Matthew Rudge Charles Sutton. May Wildmere Daisy Cook; Grace Warner Thea Lesbrooke; Rose Winifred Wood; Sylvia V. St. Lawrence. L V. St. Lawrence; Mgr Walter Tyrrell. *REV: E 22/8/96 p9; St 20/8/96 p12.*

96.222 *A BLIND MARRIAGE* (P,4a) Francis Francis. CRITERION 20/8/96-3/10/96. 45 perf [w/S mat exc 22/8].* Jefferson D. Hurd Herbert Standing; Lord Langdale Herbert Waring; Jim Spencer Charles J. Fulton; Dolly Talbot Henry V. Esmond; Gussy Talbot Arnold Lucy; Servant C[harles] Terric. Mrs Saville Carlotta Addison; Miss Saville Eva Moore; Linda Logan Kate Rorke. L & MGR Charles Wyndham; Pd Herbert Standing; Sc H[arry] Potts; Mus Percy Standing; Bom [G.] Mills; Sm W.J. Robertson; Cond Victor Hollaender; Act mgr & Treas E. Harvey. *REV: Ath 29/8/96 p299; E 22/8/96 p10; Sk 26/8/96 p179; St 27/8/96 p12; Th 1/9/96 p157-8; Ti 21/8/96 p8; TW96 p230-6.*

96.223 *NEWMARKET* (Racing C with music,3a) Mrs Frank Taylor & Ernest Boyde Jones. OPERA COMIQUE 22/8/96-17/10/96. 58 perf [w/W mat exc 26/8; add mat 29/8, 5/9]. 1st perfd Prince's, Manchester 22/6/96. Lord

Kempton Wilfred Forster; Col. Stockbridge Forbes Daw-
son/Aubrey Fitzgerald; Tom Snaffle Willie Edouin;
Ronald Mayver Fred Featherstone/Charles Stuart/Sydney
Cosby; M Brisson Laurence Caird/J. Brabourne; Ferdie
Craddock Kenneth Altamont; Sir William Ascotte Aubrey
Fitzgerald/George Humphrey; Charlie Fenn George A.
Seager; Jemmy Smart Littledale Power; Billie Price
Bryant Rashlie; Sam Bale Fred Topham/Paul Boswell;
Nap Jones Paul Boswell; Bob Cordyce George Gregory;
Dick Groundsell George Curtiss; Tim Crop Henry Wynne;
Clerk of the Scales Victor M. Seymour/L.C. Dudley.
Poppy Snaffle May Edouin; Lady Ascotte Sadie Jerome/
Alice Skipworth; Lady Windsor Kate Serjeantson/Flo-
rence Harwood; Lady Sandown J. Butler; Alexandra
Parkes Stafford; Mrs Nap Jones Greene Taylor; Kitty
Virginia Boswell; Maggie Rose Hamilton; Mrs Charles
Fenn Winnie Carl. MGR DIR Alexander Loftus; L Nellie
Farren; Bm Augustus R. Garland; Cost Morris Angel &
Son, Westoby & Son, Stagg & Mantle; Pq William Clark-
son; Sc E.G. Banks; Mus dir Ernest Woodville; Asm
John Harwood. *REV: Ath 29/8/96 p299; E 29/8/96 p10;
Sk 26/8/96 p179, 16/9/96 p313; St 27/8/96 p12; Th 1/
10/96 p218-9; Ti 24/8/96 p6.*

96.224 *MY ARTFUL VALET* (FC,3a) James Mortimer [adpt
of Henri Chivot & Alfred Duru, *Le Truc d'Arthur*].
TERRY'S 22/8/96-3/10/96. 48 perf [w/W, S mat exc 22/8,
29/8]. 1st perfd Globe 10/11/91 [as *Gloriana*]. Leopold
Fitz-Jocelyn J.G. Graham; Timothy Chadwick Alfred
Maltby; Count Evitoff Ivan Watson; Baron Kronikoff
Rupert Lister; Mjr. Stonideff John Byron; Spinks James
A. Welch; Richards Frank Saker. Mrs Gloriana Lover-
ing Edith Blande; Jessie Chadwick Maggie Byron; Kitty
Lydia Cowell. PP Edward Terry; Mgr James A. Welch;
Bom W.R. Field; Sm Henry Loutter; Act mgr Charles
Hoppe; Mus dir T[homas] Smythe; Furn Lyon; Pq William
Clarkson. *REV: Ath 29/8/96 p299; E 29/8/96 p10; Sk
26/8/96 p177; St 27/8/96 p12; Th 1/10/96 p221-2; Ti
24/8/96 p6; TW96 p236-7.*

96.225 *THE MAN IN THE STREET* (P,1a) Louis N. Parker.
TERRY'S 22/8/96-3/10/96. 37 perf.** Jabez Gover
James A. Welch/John Byron; Philip Adare Rupert Lister.
Minnie Adare Madge McIntosh. PP, Mgr, Bom, Sm, Act

mgr, <u>Mus dir</u>, <u>Furn</u>, <u>Pq</u> as for 96.224. *REV: E, St as for 96.224.*

96.226 *THE STRIKE* (D) Dion Boucicault. NOVELTY 24/8/96-29/8/96. 6 perf. 1st perfd Lyceum 15/9/66 [as *The Long Strike*]. <u>Richard Radley</u> Bernard Copping; <u>Mr Moneypenny</u> C[harles] Lillford-Delph; <u>Noah Learoyd</u> Percy Murray; <u>John O'Reilly</u> Harold Child; <u>Jack Roberts</u> Newman Maurice; <u>James Allen</u> Oswald True; <u>Cpt. Wolf</u> T. Jackson; <u>Davis</u> T. Jones; <u>Court Crier</u> Thomas; <u>Crankshaw</u> Henry Bertram; <u>Granger</u> Harry Danby; <u>Tom Beresford</u> Carl; <u>Brooke</u> Jack Haddon; <u>Spurrier</u> W. Simpson; <u>Armitage</u> F. Sharpe; <u>Sir John Fairfield</u> Robert Smith. <u>Lizzie Ashby</u> Winifred Wood; <u>Sally Naylor</u> Daisy Cook; <u>Susan</u> Olive Wynne; <u>Maggie</u> Templeton; <u>Mrs Allen</u> Elsie Trevor; <u>Betsy</u> [Margaret] Marshall; <u>Nellie Learoyd</u> Thea Lesbrooke. L V. St. Lawrence; <u>Mgr</u> Walter Tyrrell. *REV: E 29/8/96 p11; St 27/8/96 p13.*

96.227 *BOYS TOGETHER* (D,4a) C. Haddon Chambers & J.W. Comyns Carr. ADELPHI 26/8/96-5/12/96. 91 perf [w/mat 7/10, 21/10, 4/11].* <u>Frank Villars</u> William Terriss; <u>Hugo Forsyth</u> W.L. Abingdon; <u>Earl of Harpendon</u> C.W. Somerset; <u>Tom Wrake</u> J.D. Beveridge; <u>Viscount Ayot</u> Harry Nicholls; <u>Rudolph Klein</u> [William] Mackintosh; <u>Hassan</u> Luigi Lablache; <u>Col. Lannock</u> Oscar Adye; <u>Hon Fred Cholmondley</u> James Lindsay; <u>Cpt. Lyster</u> E[dmund] Covington; <u>Herbert Askew</u> Alban Attwood; <u>Reginald Lane</u> J.W. MacDonald; <u>Orderly</u> Pollard; <u>Peters</u> Webb Darleigh; <u>Gurney</u> J. Cole; <u>Ginger Smith</u> Alfred Phillips; <u>Agha Fula</u> Cyril Melton; <u>Arab Messenger</u> Caleb Porter. <u>Ethel Wood</u> Jessie Millward; <u>Lady Ayot</u> Alice Kingsley; <u>Mrs Babbage</u> Kate Kearney; <u>Miriam</u> Nesbitt. PP & MGR A. & S. Gatti; <u>Dir & Bm</u> Fred G. Latham; <u>Mus & Mus dir</u> John Crook; <u>Sc</u> William Harford, William Perkins, Bruce Smith, Walter Hann; <u>Pq</u> William Clarkson; <u>Furn</u> Hampton & Co.; <u>Cost dgn</u> Lucien Besche; <u>Cost</u> Morris Angel & Son, Jay, Mrs Nettleship, Marshall & Snelgrove; <u>Bom</u> Arthur Frye. *REV: Ath 5/9/96 p332; E 29/8/96 p10; Sk 26/8/96 p218, 2/9/96 p222, 7/10/96 p453-6; St 3/9/96 p12; Th 1/10/96 p216-8; Ti 27/8/96 p4; TW96 p245-50.*

96.228 *MONTE CARLO* (MC,2a) Sydney Carlton (lib) & Harry Greenbank (lyr) & Howard Talbot (mus). AVENUE

27/8/96-6/11/96. 76 perf [w/S mat exc 29/8; add mat
7/10, 14/10, 21/10, 28/10, 4/11]. 1st prof. Sir Ben-
jamin Currie Charles Rock; Gen. Frederick Boomerang
Eric Lewis; Fred Dorian Richard Green; James E.W.
Garden; Harry Verinder A. Vane-Tempest; Prof Lorrimer
Robb Harwood; Belmont Guy Fane; Standring C.L. Wil-
ford; Cpt. Rossiter W.H. Kemble; Croupier Roland
Carse; Francois Edward Espinosa; Extras Vaughan,
Roberts, Fitzgerald, Brook, Arnold, Wigley, Heads-
worth, Pearson, Melville. Mrs Carthew Lottie Venne/
Aida Jenoure; Dorothy Kate Cutler; Ethel Hettis Lund;
Gertie Gelatine May Belfrey; Bertie Gelatine Venie
Belfrey; Little Jemima Lalor Shiel; Midshipman Kitty
Abrahams; Suzanne Emmie Owen; Extras Gaumore, Carlton,
Kavanagh, Cross, Gain, Dannett, Sefton, Baun, Boyce,
Winter, Hensey, Cooper, Stirling, Millbank, Stuart,
d'Albertson, [Ada?] Peppiatte, Wood, Stafford, Bond,
Dennett. MGR Henry Dana, H.J. Wilde; L Charles H. Haw-
trey; Bom [Arthur] Fry; Sc W.T. Hemsley, Bruce Smith;
Pd Fred Mervin; Ch Edward Espinosa; Cond Howard Tal-
bot; Cost Marshall & Snelgrove, Pitts & Richards,
Stagg & Mantle, Redfern, Gainsborough, Mlle Ellaline,
Westoby, Clarkson; Pq William Clarkson; Lime Digby;
Sm Standley Wade. *REV: Ath 5/9/96 p331; E 29/8/96 p13;*
Sk 2/9/96 p222, 23/9/96 p366-70; St 3/9/96 p12; Th
1/10/96 p219-20; Ti 28/8/96 p4; TW96 p250-2.

96.229 *OUTWARD BOUND* (MSk) Nellie Ganthony. CRITERION
27/8/96-3/10/96. 36 perf [w/mat 29/8, 5/9, 12/9].**
Nellie Ganthony. L Charles Wyndham; Bom [G.] Mills;
Sm W.J. Robertson; Cond Victor Hollaender; Act mgr &
Treas E. Harvey.

96.230 *THE WANDERER'S RETURN* (DD,2a). NOVELTY 31/8/96-
5/9/96. 6 perf. Joshua Vere Bernard Copping; Arthur
Temple Harold Child; Philip Fanshawe Jack Haddon;
Christopher Chirrup Newman Maurice; Jack Nightingale
Percy Murray; Jacob Thorne Oswald True; Roger Wheat-
ley Beresford Carl; Stubble Robert Smith; Ralph T.
Jackson; Giles W. Thompson; Clump Harry Danby; Butter-
cup [H.?] Anderson; Hedgerow [Horatio?] Sinclair.
Mary Perkins Daisy Cook; Phoebe Pride [Margaret] Mar-
shall; Susan Whitecross Olive Wynne; Rose Maythorne
Sinclair; Emily Thea Lesbrooke; Alice Vere V. St.

Lawrence. L V. St. Lawrence; Mgr Walter Tyrrell. *REV:*
E 5/9/96 p10; St 3/9/96 p13.

96.231 *OLIVER TWIST*. NOVELTY 31/8/96-5/9/96. 6 perf.
Bill Sykes Percy Murray; Fagin Bernard Copping; Dod-
ger Newman Maurice; Charlie Bates Harold Child; Monks
Jack Haddon; Bumble Robert Smith. Oliver Maudie Hastings; Nancy Sikes V. St. Lawrence. L, Mgr as for 96.
230. *REV: As for 96.230.*

96.232 *THE WAGES OF SIN* (DD,4a) Frank Harvey. NOVELTY 7/
9/96-12/9/96. 6 perf. 1st perfd Theatre Royal, Coventry
3/8/82. George Brand Bernard Copping; Stephen Marler
Percy Murray; Josiah Deane Henry Bertram; Harry Went-
worth Harold Child; Ned Drummond Newman Maurice; Jud-
son Jack Haddon; Darley Blunt [Cecil] Hill. Servant
Polly Jackson; Rose Deane Daisy Cook; Mrs Jemima
Bloggs Elsie Trevor; Juliana Bloggs [E.L.] Maddocks;
Barbara Dale Thea Lesbrooke; Jenny [Margaret] Marshall;
Ruth Hope V. St. Lawrence. L, Mgr as for 96.230. *REV:*
E 12/9/96 p10; St 10/9/96 p12.

96.233 *AN ARTIST'S MUDDLE*. NOVELTY 7/9/96-12/9/96. 6
perf. Newman Maurice; Bernard Copping. Olive Wynne.
L, Mgr as for 96.230. *REV: St 10/9/96 p12.*

96.234 *A BACHELOR'S ROMANCE* (P,4a) Martha Morton.
GAIETY 11/9/96 mat perf.* L & MGR George Edwardes.

96.235 *THE MUFF OF THE REGIMENT* (P,1a) Henry T. John-
son. GLOBE 14/9/96-5/2/97. 124 perf [np 25/12/96].
1st perfd Strand 21/5/96 [as *Goodbye*]. Lieut. the Hon
S. Tibbitts Wilton Heriot; Lieut. Jack Melrose Harry
Farmer; Trooper Kitson Duncan Tovey; Angus Crosby
Sydney Paxton. Florence Forester Blanche Wolsley;
Hetty Lettice Fairfax. L W.S. Penley. *REV: E 26/12/96*
p8.

96.236 *THE KING OF CRIME* (D,4a) Arthur Shirley & Benjamin Landeck. NOVELTY 14/9/96-19/9/96. 6 perf. 1st
perfd Surrey 19/12/92 [as *Midnight; or The Bells of*
Notre Dame]. Ronjarne Samuel Livesay; Gandelu Gustavus Livesey; Simon Albert Ward; Louis Marcarot Clarence Temple; Mick Maloney Sam Roberts; M Folgat Os-

wald Douglas; <u>Perpignan</u> Edwin Maydew; <u>Taberet</u> S.S.
Wilford; <u>Bordogne</u> S. Bale; <u>Baptiste</u> J. Morris; <u>Toto</u>
Fred Lawrence. <u>Henriette</u> Madge Devereux; <u>Mathilde</u>
Frances Alleyne; <u>Mere Crochard</u> Violet Vivian; <u>Cla-</u>
<u>risse</u> Rose Maitland; <u>Mme Maurivert</u> Susie Gordon;
<u>Mimi Patenfair</u> Rosie Leigh. L V. St. Lawrence; <u>Mgr</u>
Walter Tyrrell. *REV: E 19/9/96 p10; St 17/9/96 p12.*

96.237 *LORD TOM NODDY* (MP,2a) George Dance (lib) &
F. Osmond Carr (mus). GARRICK 15/9/96-14/11/96. 62
perf [w/S mat]. 1st perfd Theatre Royal, Bradford
6/4/96. <u>Lord Tom Noddy</u> Little Tich; <u>Magnum</u> Cecil
Frere; <u>Col. Ben Nevis</u> Picton Roxborough; <u>Solomon van</u>
<u>Delle</u> H.C. Barry; <u>Lieut. Crowshaw, R.N.</u> George Paul-
ton; <u>Augustus A. Jackson</u> Sidney Harcourt. <u>Miss Ben</u>
<u>Nevis</u> Gladys Ffolliott; <u>Polly Primrose</u> Kate James;
<u>Marion Forsyth</u> Sybil Arundale; <u>Constance Forsyth</u>
Katie Leechman; <u>Angela</u> Violet Friend; <u>Maud</u> Dora Nel-
son; <u>Ethel</u> Maud Traunter; <u>Florrie</u> Maidie Hope; <u>Bea-</u>
<u>trice</u> Olive Dalmour; <u>Marguerite</u> Germaine de Marco;
<u>May</u> Edna Grace; <u>Gladys</u> Edith Singlehurst; <u>Nurse Phoebe</u>
Mabel Love. L William Greet; Sc Henry Emden, William
Harford; Pd George Dance; <u>Mus dir</u> Barter Johns; Ch
Will Bishop; <u>Cost dgn</u> A. Comelli; <u>Cost</u> Alias; Pq Will-
iam Clarkson; <u>Bom</u> [E.] Candler; <u>Act mgr</u> W.H. Griffiths;
Sm W.H. Davies. *REV: E 19/9/96 p10; Sk 16/9/96 p350,*
23/9/96 p381, 388, 28/10/96 p1, 26-30; St 17/9/96 p12;
Th 1/10/96 p220-1; Ti 16/9/96 p8; TW96 p252-7.

96.238 *THE BACKSLIDER* (Duol) Osmond Shillingford.
CRITERION 17/9/96-3/10/96. 15 perf.** <u>Antony Dolomite</u>
Percy Standing. <u>Mrs Agatha Dolomite</u> M. Lockie. L Char-
les Wyndham.

96.239 *THE DUCHESS OF COOLGARDIE* (D,5a) Euston Leigh
& Cyril Clare. DRURY LANE 19/9/96-26/11/96. 67 perf
[w/S mat exc 19/9, 26/9].* <u>Big Ben</u> Charles Glenney;
<u>Myles Hooligan</u> John L. Shine; <u>Sailor Jack</u> Laurence
Cautley/Edward O'Neill; <u>Bendigo Bill</u> Edward O'Neill/
Clarence Holt/William Rider; <u>Yorkshire Dick</u> C.M. Lowne;
<u>Cpt.</u> E.H. Vanderfelt; <u>Tom Airy</u> Oswald Yorke/M. Warren;
<u>Hiram Vannicker</u> Claud Llewellyn; <u>Melbourne Jerry</u>
Watty Brunton, jr; <u>Herr von Schwop</u> E. Story Gofton;
<u>Lord Glendargle</u> Ernest Bertram; <u>MacDonald</u> Isaacson;

Warden of Coolgardie Hermann Vezin. Sybil Gray Hilda
Spong/Rose Meller; Wallaroo Laura Johnson; Kathleen
O'Mara Laura Linden; Harry Valli Valli/Faulkner; Nel-
lie Grey Edith Jordan. L Executors of Augustus Harris;
Sm Arthur P. Collins; Act mgr Neil Forsyth; Mgr John
Coleman; Mus James Weaver; Ch Paul Valentine; Sc J.
Johnstone, [Robert] Caney; Cost Mrs Thornhill, Miss
Collier; Mach E.A. Taylor; Props [A.?] Jones; Pq
William Clarkson; Bm John Chute. *REV: Ath 26/9/96
p428; E 26/9/96 p10; Sk 16/9/96 p312, 23/9/96 p353,
356, 4/11/96 p45, 72-3; SR 5/10/96 p367-8; St 24/9/96
p12; Th 1/10/96 p215-6; Ti 21/9/96 p8; TW96 p258-9.*

96.240 *IVANHOE; OR, REBECCA, THE JEWESS* (HistD,5a)
[Thomas Dibdin?; fnd on Walter Scott's novel]. NOVELTY
21/9/96-26/9/96. 6 perf. 1st perfd Surrey 20/1/20.
Cedric of Rotherwood Henry Bertram; Ivanhoe Bernard
Copping; Isaac of York Newman Maurice; Sir Brian de
Bois Guilbert Percy Murray; Richard I Robert Smith;
Wamba Harold Child; Friar Tuck Frank Ashton; De Bracy
Harry Danby; Sir Reginald Front de Boeuf Cecil Hill;
Lucas de Beaumanor Charles Hilding; Gurth Jack Haddon.
Lady Rowena Cybel Wynne; Elgitha [Margaret] Marshall;
Ulrica Thea Lesbrooke; Rebecca V. St. Lawrence. L V.
St. Lawrence; Mgr Walter Tyrrell. *REV: E 26/9/96 p11;
St 24/9/96 p13.*

96.241 *ICI ON PARLE FRANCAIS* (F,1a) Thomas J. Williams.
NOVELTY 21/9/96-26/9/96. 6 perf.** Spriggins Newman
Maurice; Mjr. Regulus Rattan Bernard Copping; Victor
Dubois Harold Child. Anna Marie [Margaret] Marshall;
Mrs Spriggins Elsie Trevor; Angelina Daisy Cook; Julia
Cybel Wynne. L, Mgr as for 96.240. *REV: E 26/9/96 p11.*

96.242 *CYMBELINE* (C,5a) William Shakespeare. LYCEUM
22/9/96-12/12/96; 16/12/96(m); 26/12/96-2/1/97; 23/1/
97-29/1/97. 88 perf [w/mat 26/12/96, 30/12/96, 2/1/97;
mat only 11/11/96, 25/11, 2/12, 5/12, 9/12, 12/12/96,
27/1/97]. 1st perfd Globe 1610. Cymbeline F.H. Macklin; Cloten Norman Forbes; Posthumus Leonatus Frank
[Kemble] Cooper; Belarius Frederic Robinson; Guiderius
Ben Webster; Arviragus Gordon Craig/John Martin Harvey; Pisanio [Frank] Tyars; Cornelius Lacy; Two British Cpt. [John] Archer, Needham; Two British Lords

Clarence Hague, [W. Lionel] Belmore; <u>Iachimo</u> Henry
Irving/H. Cooper Cliffe; <u>Philario</u> Fuller Mellish;
<u>Caius Lucius</u> H. Cooper Cliffe/[W. Lionel] Belmore;
<u>Roman Cpt.</u> [R.P.] Tabb. <u>Queen</u> Genevieve Ward; <u>Helen</u>
Mrs Tyars; <u>Imogen</u> Ellen Terry/Julia Arthur. <u>L & MGR</u>
Henry Irving; <u>Sc</u> Hawes Craven, Joseph Harker; <u>Dgn</u>
Lawrence Alma Tadema; <u>Cost dgn</u> Karl, Mrs Nettleship;
<u>Cost</u> Karl, Mrs Nettleship, Auguste; <u>Mus</u> J. Hamilton
Clarke; <u>Props</u> Arnott; <u>Mach</u> Fillery; <u>Pq</u> Fox; <u>Mus dir</u>
J. Meredith Ball; <u>Sm</u> H.J. Loveday; <u>Bom</u> Joseph Hurst;
<u>Act mgr</u> Bram Stoker. *REV: Ath 26/9/96 p427-8; E 26/9/*
96 p10; Sk 30/9/96 p418-9, 30/9/96 p434; SR 26/9/96
p339-41; St 24/9/96 p12; Th 1/10/96 p212-5; Ti 23/9/
96 p4; TW96 p260-76.

96.243 *TWO LITTLE VAGABONDS* (Melo,5a) George R. Sims
& Arthur Shirley [adpt of Pierre Decourcelle, *Les*
Deux Gosses]. PRINCESS'S 23/9/96-29/5/97. 276 perf
[w/W, S mat 3/10/96-13/3/97 exc 7/10/96, 23/12/96,
3/2/97; w/W mat 17/3/97-26/5/97 exc 14/4/97; add mat
28-29/12/96, 31/12/96, 1/1/97, 11/1, 18/1, 25/1, 29/1,
4/2, 19/4/97; np 25/12/96, 16/4/97]. 1st prof. <u>George</u>
<u>Thornton</u> Ernest Leicester; <u>Cpt. Darville</u> Lyston Lyle/
Clifton Alderson; <u>John Scarth</u> Walter Howard/M. Sabine
Pasley; <u>Bill Mullins</u> Edmund Gurney/S. Major Jones;
<u>Dido Bunce</u> Chris Walker/W. Getston Carey; <u>Leeson</u> Her-
bert Vyvyan; <u>Hargitt</u> Gerald Kennedy/Edward Warden; <u>Dr</u>
<u>Lynn</u> C. Astley; <u>Job Gargoyle</u> F. Lloyd; <u>Whiffin</u> Thomas
Kean; <u>Footman</u> A. Rymon; <u>Cough Drop</u> Edward W. Coleman/
Harry Barford. <u>Barbara Scarth</u> Mena Le Bert/Eva
Williams; <u>Sister Randall</u> Eva Williams/May Thorne; <u>Maid</u>
<u>Servant</u> Dorothy Campbell; <u>Biddy Mullins</u> Marie Hassell/
Marie Foley/Blanche Stanley; <u>Marion Thornton</u> Gerald-
ine Olliffe/Hilda Spong; <u>Wally</u> Sydney Fairbrother/
Beryl Mercer; <u>Dick</u> Kate Tyndall/Ida Laurence/Bracewell.
<u>MGR</u> Albert Gilmer; <u>Sc</u> Cecil E. Hicks, Henry Brooke,
W.T. Muir, Ernest Howard, R. Flannagan, C. Rider No-
bie; <u>Sm & Pd</u> George T. Minshull; <u>Cost</u> Morris Angel &
Son, <u>Pq</u> William Clarkson; <u>Am</u> Horace Gilmer <u>Treas</u> H.
Bellamy Smith; <u>Mus dir</u> Theodore Ward. *REV: Ath 3/10/*
96 p459-60; E 26/9/96 p10; Sk 30/9/96 p430, 14/10/96
p498-501, 17/2/97 p150; SR 5/10/96 p368; St 1/10/96
p12; Th 1/11/96 p273-4; Ti 24/9/96 p4.

96.244 *TEDDY'S WIVES* (FC,3a) Fergus Hume [adpt of
W.D. Calthorpe, *The Mormon*]. STRAND 24/9/96-30/12/96.
109 perf [w/W, S mat exc 23/12, 26/12; np 25/12]. 1st
perfd Theatre Royal, Eastbourne 4/4/96. Hon Teddy
Miles Mallaby; Oliver Walford Gerald Moore; The McNab
Fred Thorne; Solomon Isaccs Cecil H. Thornbury; Choldy
J[ohn] Wheatman. Mrs Cottingham Emily Thorne; Nora
Audrey Ford; Mrs Crupples Alice Mansfield; Hon Mrs
Miles Maude Millett. PP J.S. Clarke; L & Mgr Mallaby;
Sm J[ohn] Wheatman; Mus dir W.T. Gliddon; Bm C. Lid-
don Clark; Act mgr Sam Hemsley; Bom S.J. Crookes.
*REV: E 26/9/96 p13; Sk 30/9/96 p168; St 1/10/96 p12;
Th 1/11/96 p278-9; Ti 25/9/96 p3; TW96 p277.*

96.245 *DREAM FACES* (P,1a) Wynn Miller. STRAND 24/9/96-
30/12/96. 84 perf [w/mat 19/12; np 25/12].** Philip
Percy Brough; Robert Royston Keith. Margaret Mrs J.W.
Boughton; Lucy Muriel Ashwynne. PP, L & Mgr, Sm, Mus
dir, Bm, Act mgr, Bom as for 96.244. *REV: E, St as
for 96.244.*

96.246 *SEALED TO SILENCE* (D,5a) Smedley Norton & H.
Vickers Rees. NOVELTY 28/9/96-10/10/96. 12 perf.*
Horace Desmond Bernard Copping; Frank Danbrook J.Wid-
decombe; Zachariah Wolfenstein Percy Murray; George
Grainger Jack Haddon; Ikey Moses Newman Maurice; Hon
Bertie Broker Harold Child; Detective Sgt. Hustler
Harry Danby; Christopher Tiddlebit John Warner;
Michael Angelo Baxter Beresford Carl; Dr Johnstone F.
Walker; Sir James Crouch Henry Bertram; Magistrate's
Clerk Shirley Wentworth; Counsel for Prosecution Rob-
ert Smith; Counsel for Defence Rossiter; Policeman
Cotter; Stage-door Keeper Fairleigh Ashton. Newsboy
Laura Weston; Madge Fairley Cybel Wynne; Dolly Dash-
away Edith Leyland; Mrs Prudhoe Thea Lesbrooke; Mrs
Blimber Elsie Trevor; Nelly Maudie Hastings; Mary
[E.L.] Maddocks; Sadie Cranberry Daisy Cook; Pollie
[Margaret] Marshall; Mildred Antrobus V. St. Lawrence.
L V. St. Lawrence; Mgr Walter Tyrrell; Dir Newman
Maurice. *REV: E 3/10/96 p10; St 1/10/96 p12-3.*

96.247 *MR MARTIN* (P,3a) Charles H. Hawtrey. COMEDY
3/10/96-13/11/96. 41 perf [w/S mat exc 3/10].* Sir
Charles Sinclair Henry Kemble; Harry Sinclair W.T.

Lovell; <u>Martin Heathcote</u> Charles H. Hawtrey; <u>George</u>
<u>S. Martin</u> Charles H.E. Brookfield; <u>Hon George Bam-</u>
<u>fylde</u> Frederick Volpé; <u>Algy Pakenham</u> Alfred Matthews;
<u>Mr Kilfoyle</u> William F. Hawtrey; <u>Watkins</u> H. Deane;
<u>Footman</u> Henry Stephenson. <u>Mona Carew</u> Jessie Bateman;
<u>Hon Mrs George Bamfylde</u> Marjorie Griffiths; <u>Tiny</u>
<u>Merridew</u> Nina Boucicault; <u>Sophia O'Flanagan</u> Rose Le-
clercq; <u>Maudie Vavasour</u> Lottie Venne. <u>MGR</u> Charles H.
Hawtrey; <u>Sc</u> E.G. Banks; <u>Mus dir</u> Ernest Bucalossi; <u>Sm</u>
Frederick Glover; <u>Bm</u> C. Liddon Clark; <u>Act mgr</u> Arthur
Donald. *REV: E 10/10/96 p10; Sk 7/10/96 p440; SR 17/*
10/96 p416-7; St 8/10/96 p12; Th 1/11/96 p274-5; Ti
5/10/96 p11; TW96 p282-3.

96.248 *A WHITE STOCKING* (C,1a) Edward Ferris & Arthur
Stewart. COMEDY 3/10/96-13/11/96; 19/11/96-26/2/97.
120 perf [np 24-25/12/96].* <u>Mr Stapleton</u> William F.
Hawtrey/H[enry] Stephenson/Frederick Volpé; <u>Cpt. Fav-</u>
<u>ersham</u> George Hippisley; <u>Peter</u> H. Deane. <u>Lydia Staple-</u>
<u>ton</u> Elliot Page/Maud Abbott. <u>MGR</u>, <u>Mus dir</u>, <u>Sm</u>, <u>Bm</u>,
<u>Act mgr</u> as for 96.247. *REV: E, Sk, St as for 96.247;*
Ath 10/10/96 p493-4.

96.249 *THE WHITE SILK DRESS* (MF,2a) Henry J.W. Dam
(lib) & A[lick?] MacLean (mus) & R[eginald] Somerville
(mus). PRINCE OF WALES'S 3/10/96-19/2/97. 132 perf
[w/S mat 10/10/96-2/1/97; np 25/12/96].* <u>Jack Hammers-</u>
<u>ley</u> Arthur Roberts; <u>Sir James Turner</u> Eric Thorne/Char-
les Rock; <u>Lord Macready</u> E.H. Kelly/Harold Eden; <u>Mjr.</u>
<u>Penyon</u> J. Furneaux Cook/Isidore Marcil; <u>Prof Beasley</u>
Walter Uridge; <u>Cousin Charles Hammersley</u> Harold Eden;
<u>Angus McWhirter</u> George Traill; <u>Skinderson</u> William
Cheesman; <u>Bolingbroke</u> L.F. Chapuy/Eric Thorne; <u>Bellamy</u>
Lawrence Caird/Arthur T. Hendon; <u>Office Boy</u> Master
Harry Rignold. <u>Mary Turner</u> Decima Moore/Lucille Gra-
hame/Stella Gastelle; <u>Mrs Pennington</u> Ellas Dee; <u>Lady</u>
<u>Turner</u> Singleton; <u>Lady from Algiers</u> Mrs E.H. Brooke;
<u>Miss Talbot</u> Eva Ellerslie; <u>Miss Essex</u> Pierrette Amel-
la; <u>Edith Hammersley</u> Carrie Benton; <u>Mrs Bailey</u> Kitty
Loftus. <u>PP</u> Edgar Bruce; <u>Sc</u> W.T. Hemsley; <u>Mus dir</u>
George W. Byng; <u>Sm</u> Clarence Hunt; <u>Act mgr</u> C.P. Levilly.
REV: Ath 10/10/96 p493-4; E 10/10/96 p10; Sk 7/10/96
p440, 478; SR 17/10/96 p417-8; St 8/10/96 p12-3; Th
1/11/96 p276-7; Ti 5/10/96 p11; TW96 p278-80.

96.250 *THE BELLE OF CAIRO* (MP,2a) Cecil Raleigh (lib) & F. Kinsey Peile (lib, lyr, mus). COURT 10/10/96-19/12/96. 71 perf [w/S mat exc 10/10].* Earl of Bulcester Charles Wibrow; James Parker Arthur Nelstone; Cook's Guide F.D. Pengelly; Mr Stallabrass Victor M. Seymour; Mr Patching H.V. Surrey; Luigi [Roy] Horniman; Duval Bey Eugene Mayeur; Cpt. Sir Gilbert Fane, Bart John Peachey; Mjr. Trevor Philip Leslie; Lieut. Marchmont E.W. Tarver; Surgeon Cpt. Cree Roy; Ali Ibrahim Michael Dwyer. Lady Molly Rosemere Ethel Earle; Lady Ermyntrude Rosemere Milly Thorne; Susan Smith Maud Wilmot; Maud Stallabrass Rieke; Martha Stallabrass Loraine; Mary Stallabrass Bliss; Mrs Patching Grace Dudley; Barbara Giulia Warwick; Nepthys May Yohe. L & MGR Arthur Chudleigh; Sc Henry Emden; Ch Arthur Nelstone; Cost dgn Percy Anderson; Cost Liberty & Co., Auguste, Simmons, Morris Angel & Sons, Mrs Bigelow, Cooling & Lawrence; Pq William Clarkson; Mus dir Carl Kiefert; Bm Leonard Lillies. REV: E 17/10/96 p10; Sk 14/10/96 p482-3, 524, 11/11/96 p89, 110-1; St 15/10/96 p12; Th 1/11/96 p277-8; Ti 12/10/96 p11; TW96 p280-2.

96.251 *A CROWN OF THORNS* (D,4a) Gilbert Elliott. OLYMPIC 10/10/96-17/10/96. 7 perf. 1st perfd County, Reading 9/3/93 [as *The Love King*]. Count Maurice Vauthier Gilbert Elliott; Henry Lefrane Dudley Clinton; Baron Holstein William Felton; Froude John Ottaway; Picot Harry Paulton, jr; Hans John J. MacMahon; Abbé Lavalle Louis Ford; Officer of the Directoire Charles M. Holmes; Dr Ricardo A. Robertson. Countess Vauthier Mrs Walter Edwin; Salonara Alice de Winton; Ninette Georgie Wright; Marie Millicent Marsden; Mother Bagnolet Emily Edwin; Mathilde, Princess of Zodiac Agnes Hewitt. REV: E 17/10/96 p10; St 15/10/96 p12-3; Th 1/11/96 p279.

96.252 *A WOMAN'S GUILT* (D,3a) Bernard Copping. NOVELTY 12/10/96-17/10/96. 6 perf.* Mr Beresford Henry Bertram; Noel Beresford Jack Haddon; Salter Newman Maurice; Musgrave Harold Child; Storman Robert Smith; Sidney Mivart Bernard Copping. Olga Zettmar Amy F. Millar; Polly Cybel Wynne; Mary Anne Marie McDowell; Forewoman Margaret Marshall; Dora Grahame V. St. Lawrence. L V. St. Lawrence; Mgr Walter Tyrrell. *REV: E 17/10/96 p10; St 15/10/96 p13.*

96.253 *SNATCHED FROM DEATH* (Melo,1a) Stephanie Baring & Walter Beaumont. NOVELTY 12/10/96-17/10/96. 6 perf.* Daniel Ray Bernard Copping; George Romaine Jack Haddon; Bill Higgins Newman Maurice; Long Jim Robert Smith; Judge Lynch Cecil Hill. Flash Jess Stephanie Baring; Nelly Dane Cybel Wynne. L, Mgr as for 96.252. *REV: As for 96.252.*

96.254 *UNDER THE RED ROBE* (P,4a) Edward Rose [adpt of Stanley Weyman's novel]. HAYMARKET 17/10/96-2/6/97. 253 perf [w/W, S mat exc 17/10, 21/10/96, 2/6/97; np 24-25/12/96, 3/3/97, 16/4/97; mat only 12-15/4/97].* Gil de Berault Herbert Waring; Richelieu Sydney Valentine; Henri de Cochefort Hamilton Revelle; Marquis de Pombal J.L. MacKay; De Fargis Albert Mayer; Cpt. Larolle Cyril Maude; Lieut. Bernard Gould; Sir Thomas Brunt Dawson Milward; Clon E. Holman Clarke; Louis Clarence Blakiston; Sgt. Rupert Lister; Malpas Cecil Hope/H.H. Welch; Landlord Leslie Victor; Monk Mules Brown; Secretary D.J. Smith; Major Domo Harley Granville-Barker; Doorkeeper Cosmo Hamilton/W.H. Thorne. Renee de Cochefort Winifred Emery/Beryl Faber; Mme de Cochefort Eva Moore; Mme Zaton Fanny Coleman; Suzette Rhoda Halkett; Waitress Annie Saker/Crawford. L Frederick Harrison; Mgr Frederick Harrison, Cyril Maude; Sc Walter Johnstone, Joseph Harker, Walter Hann; Cost L. & J. Nathan, Mrs Nettleship; Cost dgn Karl; Bom W.H. Leverton; Mus & Cond Alfred J. Caldicott; Fights B. Bertrand; Sm G[eorge] Gamble; Bm Horace Watson. *REV: Ath 24/10/96 p572; E 24/10/96 p10; Sk 21/10/96 p532-5, 28/10/96 p42, 11/11/96 p116-7, 25/11/96 p185; SR 24/10/96 p441-2; St 22/10/96 p12-3; Th 1/11/96 p271-3; Ti 19/10/96 p8; TW96 p283-9.*

96.255 *NOT GUILTY* (Melo,5a). NOVELTY 19/10/96-24/10/96. 6 perf. Nick Chaddox Percy Murray; Harry Grafton Bernard Copping; Oswald Brandon Jack Haddon; Jacob Grafton Watty Brunton, sr; Timothy Sprouts Newman Maurice; Ernest Saville Harold Child; Lord Elmore Harry Simpson; Mr Burton Stewart Adair; Lord Chief Justice Frank Jennings; Mr Stanton Robert Smith; Jim

Cecil Hill; Clerk of the Court [Horatio] Sinclair;
Lieut. Willoughby Wallace Widdecombe; Wattles Harry
Danby; Ferris Henry Bertram; Hurst Beresford Carl.
Sarah Lawler Katie Brunton; Nelly Chaddox V. St. Law-
rence; Margaret Thea Lesbrooke. L V. St. Lawrence;
Mgr Walter Tyrrell. *REV: E 24/10/96 p11; St 22/10/96
p13.*

96.256 *LOVE IN IDLENESS* (C,3a) Louis N. Parker & Ed-
ward J. Goodman. TERRY'S 21/10/96-19/12/96. 65 perf
[w/S mat; add mat 25/11, 2/12, 9/12, 16/12]. 1st perfd
Theatre Royal, Brighton 13/3/96. Mortimer Pendlebury
Edward Terry; Frank W.E. Ashcroft; Rushey Platt, Esq,
M.P. Gilbert Farquhar; Jack Fenton Sydney Brough;
Eugene Gondinot Herman de Lange. Maggie Hilda Rivers;
Louise Gondinot Beatrice Ferrar; Abigail Bright Bella
Pateman; Mrs Trott Kate Mills; Martha Jessie Danvers.
PP Edward Terry; Bm H.T. Brickwell; Sec Clifford King;
Sm George Belmore; Bom W.R. Field; Sc Leolyn Hart;
Furn Lyon & Co.; Pq William Clarkson. *REV: Ath 31/10/
96 p612; E 24/10/96 p10; Sk 28/10/96 p14-5; SR 31/10/
96 p467-8; St 29/10/96 p12; Th 1/11/96 p279-80; Ti
22/10/96 p5; TW96 p289-93.*

96.257 *A WOMAN'S PROPER PLACE* (Duol) J. Wilton Jones
& Gertrude Warden. TERRY'S 21/10/96-19/12/96. 53 perf
[w/mat 24/10].** Richard Montague Robertson W.E.
Ashcroft. Mrs Richard Montague Robertson Beatrice
Ferrar. PP, Bm, Sec, Sm, Bom as for 96.256. *REV: E,
St as for 96.256.*

96.258 *WHEN GEORGE THE FOURTH WAS KING* (P,1a) LYCEUM
24/10/96 mat perf. 1st perfd Theatre Royal, Birmingham 17/9/96. William Garden Charles Groves; Joshua
Dade Gilbert Hare; Harry Joliffe Frank Gillmore.
Mary Mona K. Oram. L & MGR Henry Irving; Sm H.J. Loveday; Mus dir J. Meredith Ball; Act mgr Bram Stoker;
Bom Joseph Hurst; Sc William Harford.

96.259 *CASTE* (C,3a) T.W. Robertson. LYCEUM 24/10/96
mat perf.** Eccles John Hare; George d'Alroy Frank
Gillmore; Sam Gerridge Gilbert Hare; Cpt. Hawtree
Frederick Kerr; Dixon E. Vivian Reynolds. Polly May
Harvey; Marquise de St. Maur Susie Vaughan; Esther

Eccles Mona K. Oram. L & MGR, Sm, Mus dir, Act mgr,
Bom, Sc as for 96.258. *REV: Ti 26/10/96 p8; TW96 p293-
4.*

96.260 *HIS LITTLE DODGE* (C,3a) Justin Huntly McCarthy
[adpt of Georges Feydeau & Maurice Hennequin, *Le Sys-
tème Rebardier*]. ROYALTY 24/10/96-16/1/97. 81 perf
[w/S mat exc 24/10/96, 2/1/97, 9/1, 16/1/97; add mat
25/11/96; np 24-25/12/96].* Sir Hercules Little Fred
Terry; Hon Mandeville Hobb Weedon Grossmith; Pollaby
Petlow Alfred Maltby; Grice Frank Dyall. Lady Miranda
Little Ellis Jeffreys; Candy Leila Repton. L Kate
Santley; Mgr George Alexander; Act mgr R.G. Legge;
Bom Horne; Sc Frank Giles; Sm Frank Dyall; Mus dir
William Robins; Sec Winifred Dolan. *REV: Ath 31/10/96
p612; E 31/10/96 p10; Sk 28/10/96 p5, 4/11/96 p86,
18/11/96 p138-9; SR 31/10/96 p468; St 29/10/96 p12;
Th 1/12/96 p337-8; Ti 26/10/96 p8; TW96 p296-7.*

96.261 *THE STORM* (P,1a,2tab) Ian Robertson. ROYALTY
24/10/96-14/11/96. 19 perf.* Le Barrier Henry V. Esmond; Pascal H.B. Irving. Louisette Dorothy Hammond.
L, Mgr, Act mgr, Bom, Sm, Mus dir, Sec as for 96.260;
Sc H[arry] Potts. *REV: E 31/10/96 p10; SR 31/10/96
p468; St 29/10/96 p12-3; TW96 p297.*

96.262 *THE YORKSHIRE LASS; OR, THE ROLL OF THE DRUM*
(D,4a) J. Wilton Jones. NOVELTY 26/10/96-31/10/96.
6 perf.** Jack Selwyn Jack Haddon; Dick Blosser New-
man Maurice; Steve Milson Percy Murray; Maurice
Thorne Harold Child; Cpt. Digby Bernard Copping; Gen.
Selwyn Stewart Adair; Joe Bargess Cecil Hill; Gabriel
Helmsley Robert Smith; Inspector Exley Harry Danby.
Little Jack Maudie Hastings; Patty Katie Brunton;
Kate Grantley Cybel Wynne; Elsie Thea Lesbrooke;
Faith Helmsley V. St. Lawrence. L V. St. Lawrence;
Mgr Walter Tyrrell. *REV: E 31/10/96 p10; St 29/10/96
p13.*

96.263 *MY NEIGHBOUR'S WIFE* (F,1a) Alfred Bunn. NOVELTY
26/10/96-31/10/96. 6 perf.** Bernard Copping; Harold
Child; Newman Maurice. Elsie Trevor; [E.L.] Maddocks;
[Marie] McDowell. L, Mgr as for 96.263. *REV: As for
96.262.*

96.264 *NUMBER ONE ROUND THE CORNER* (F,1a) William
Brough. COURT 28/10/96-19/12/96. 46 perf. 1st perfd
Lyceum 12/3/54. <u>Flipper</u> Arthur Nelstone; <u>Nobbler</u> Char-
les Wibrow; <u>2nd Floor Lodger</u> [Roy] Horniman. L & MGR
Arthur Chudleigh; <u>Bm</u> Leonard Lillies.

96.265 *THE LADY OF LYONS; OR, LOVE AND PRIDE* (D,5a)
Edward Bulwer Lytton. NOVELTY 2/11/96-7/11/96.   6
perf.** <u>Claude Melnotte</u> Bernard Copping; <u>Col. Dumas</u>
John Brooks; <u>Beauseant</u> Jack Haddon; <u>Glavis</u> Harold
Child; <u>Deschappelles</u> Stewart Adair; <u>Landlord</u> Cecil
Hill; <u>Gaspar</u> Robert Smith; <u>Cpt. Gervais</u> Frank Jenn-
ings; <u>Cpt. Dupont</u> Harry Danby; <u>Mjr. Desmoulins</u> Charles
Franklyn; <u>Notary</u> Beresford Carl. <u>Mme Deschappelles</u>
Elsie Trevor; <u>Widow Melnotte</u> Cybel Wynne; <u>Janet</u> [Ma-
rie] McDowell; <u>Pauline</u> V. St. Lawrence. L V. St. Law-
rence; <u>Mgr</u> Walter Tyrrell. *REV: E 7/11/96 p10; St*
5/11/96 p13.

96.266 *THE MARRIED BACHELOR.* NOVELTY 2/11/96-7/11/96.
6 perf.** Newman Maurice; John Brooks. Cybel Wynne;
Elsie Trevor. <u>L</u>, <u>Mgr</u> as for 96.265. *REV: St 5/11/96*
p13.

96.267 *POOR OLD PERKINS* (FC,3a) Percival H.T. Sykes.
STRAND 3/11/96 mat perf.* <u>John Thomas Perkins</u> Harry
Paulton, jr; <u>Cpt. Frank Stone</u> Percy Murray; <u>Lieut.</u>
<u>James Rill</u> George Holwood; <u>Signor Bertini</u> Harold
Child. <u>Mrs Perkins</u> Ada Murray; <u>Ada Perkins</u> Ada St.
Ruth; <u>Blanche Merton</u> Mrs Ivy Dacre; <u>Mary Trotter</u> Thea
Lesbrooke; <u>Signora Bertini</u> Laurel King. *REV: E 7/11/*
96 p13; St 5/11/96 p12; Th 1/12/96 p339.

96.268 *FOR THE CZAR* (T,1a) Percival H.T. Sykes. STRAND
3/11/96 mat perf.* <u>Karl Monomachos</u> Percy Murray; <u>Ivan</u>
<u>Vasilivitch</u> Charles Bernhardt; <u>Vladimir Roumanoff</u> Ha-
rold Child; <u>Sgt. Schkovsky</u> Cecil Hill; <u>Petra Fedoto-</u>
<u>vitch</u> Thea Lesbrooke; <u>Alexina Roumanoff</u> Cybel Wynne.
REV: E, St as for 96.267; Sk 25/11/96 p184.

96.269 *DONNA DIANA* (Poetical C,4a) Westland Marston
[adpt of Moreto, *El Desden con el Desden*]. PRINCE OF
WALES'S 4/11/96, 5/11/96. 2 mat perf. 1st perfd
Princess's 2/1/64. <u>Don Caesar</u> Arthur Bourchier; <u>Don</u>

Luis Henry Vibart; Don Gaston Charles Troode; Don
Diego Mark Kinghorne; Perin W.G. Elliott. Donna Fenisa
Mabel Beardsley; Donna Laura E. Scott Daymar; Flor-
etta Irene Vanbrugh; Donna Diana Violet Vanbrugh;
Dancers Beatrice Rosslyn, D. Clarke, M[ollie?] Clarke,
Mabel Grey. PP Edgar Bruce; Mus & Cond Albert Fox;
Cost John Simmons & Sons; Ch Ernest d'Auban; Pd Ar-
thur Bourchier. *REV: Ath 7/11/96 p645; E 7/11/96 p13;
Sk 11/11/96 p94-5, 130; SR 7/11/96 p492-4; St 5/11/96
p12; Th 1/12/96 p338-9; Ti 5/11/96 p10; TW96 p305.*

96.270 *THE TWO ORPHANS* (D,5a) [John Oxenford]. NOVEL-
TY 9/11/96-13/11/96. 6 perf.** Count de Linière John
Brooks; Marquis de Presles Harold Child; Armand, Chev.
de Vaudrey Charles Alleyne; Jacques Jack Haddon;
Pierre Bernard Copping; Dr Stuart Adair; Picard New-
man Maurice; Martin Harry Danby; Lafleur Robert James;
Marais Cecil Hill; Count de Mailly Beresford Carl;
Marquis d'Estrees J. West Carnie. Countess de Linière
Elsie Trevor; La Frochard Lizzie Nelson; Marianne Cy-
bel Wynne; Genevieve [Marie] McDowell; Florette Mar-
garet Marshall; Julie Lillie Gordon; Cora Nellie Han-
lon; Adelle Ailda Thorpe; Henriette/Louise V. St.
Lawrence. L V. St. Lawrence; Mgr Walter Tyrrell; Dir
Newman Maurice. *REV: E 14/11/96 p10; St 12/11/96 p15.*

96.271 *ROUND A TREE* (P,1a) W.H. Risque. VAUDEVILLE
11/11/96-9/10/96. 282 perf [np 25/12/96, 18/1/97,
16/4, 22/6/97].* Grundy Neville Doone; Lobbett Cairns
James; Sam George Grossmith. Mrs Grundy Sibyl Grey;
Josephine Florence Lloyd/Lottie Sargeant/Phyllis
Broughton. L & MGR A. & S. Gatti; Sm George Fielder;
Bm W.H. Risque; Cond F. Sydney Ward; Sc William Perkins. *REV: E 14/11/96 p10; St 19/11/96 p13; Th 1/12/
96 p339-40; Ti 12/11/96 p6.*

96.272 *JOURNEYS END IN LOVERS' MEETING* (Proverb,1a)
"J.O. Hobbes" [Mrs P.M.T. Craigie] & George Moore.
DRURY LANE 12/11/96 mat perf.** Sir Philip Soupire
Frank [Kemble] Cooper; Cpt. Maramour Ben Webster.
Lady Soupire Ellen Terry. L Executors of Augustus
Harris; Mgr John Coleman; Act mgr Neil Forsyth; Bm
John Chute.

96.273 *THE MANXMAN* (P,5a) Wilson Barrett [adpt of
Hall Caine's novel]. LYRIC 16/11/96, 17/11, 20/11,
23-24/11, 27/11, 1/12, 4/12, 7-8/12, 11/12, 19/12/96
(m). 12 perf.** Pete Quilliam Wilson Barrett; Philip
Christian Austin Melford/T. Wigney Percyval; Ross
Christian Horace Hodges; Caesar Cregeen Ambrose Man-
ning; Monty Missitt George Howard; Prof Mawley George
Bernage; Black Tom Stafford Smith; Johnnie C[harles]
Derwood; Dr Mylechreest Percy Foster; Jonique Jelly
Marcus St. John. Kate Cregeen Maud Jeffries; Miss
Christian Alice Gambier; Nancy Daisy Belmore; Bella
Kelly Rose Pendennis. L & MGR William Greet; Pp Henry
J. Leslie; Mus Sydney Jones; Sc Stafford Hall; Bm A.E.
Field; Sm Charles Cathcart; Mus dir Edward Jones.
*REV: Ath 21/11/96 p723-4; E 21/11/96 p10; Sk 25/11/96
p184; SR 5/12/96 p584; St 19/11/96 p12; Th 1/12/96
p334-5; Ti 17/11/96 p6; TW96 p321-2.*

96.274 *A WOMAN OF THE PEOPLE* (Romantic Melo,[4a])
Benjamin Webster. NOVELTY 16/11/96-21/11/96. 6 perf.
1st perfd Amphitheatre, Liverpool 17/2/77. Bertrand
Charles Alleyne; Remy Newman Maurice; Appiant Bernard
Copping; Theobald de Buissière Jack Haddon; Dr Leblome
Harold Child; Guillaume Cecil Hill; Guesmenu Harry
Danby; Official of Asylum Beresford Carl. Sophie Cy-
bel Wynne; Catherine Margaret Marshall; Marguerite
Marie McDowell; Charlotte May Blanchard; Berlinguette
Cora Ennis; Marie V. St. Lawrence. L V. St. Lawrence;
Mgr Walter Tyrrell. *REV: E 21/11/96 p10; St 19/11/96
p13.*

96.275 *SURE TO WIN* (Sporting P,1a) W.H. Goldsmith.
NOVELTY 16/11/96-21/11/96. 6 perf.* Job Mainprize
Robert Smith; Fred Denton Bernard Copping; Dennis
Blackland Jack Haddon; Richard Ainslie T. West Carnie.
Mary Mainprize Margaret Marshall. L, Mgr as for 96.
274. *REV: As for 96.274.*

96.276 *IN AND OUT OF A PUNT* (Ca,1a) Henry V. Esmond.
ROYALTY 16/11/96-16/1/97. 52 perf [np 24-25/12/96].**
Hugh Henry V. Esmond/Frank Dyall. Margaret Leila Rep-
ton. L Kate Santley; Mgr George Alexander; Bom Horne;
Mus & Lyr Algernon H. Lindo; Sm Frank Dyall; Mus dir
William Robins; Sec Winifred Dolan; Act mgr R.G.

Legge.

96.277 *THE HAVEN OF CONTENT* (P,4a) T. Malcolm Watson.
GARRICK 17/11/96 mat perf. 1st perfd Prince's, Bris-
tol 22/10/96. Clive Northcote Ernest Leicester; Lord
Henry Silcroft Julius Knight; James Fenton, M.P. John
Beauchamp; Mr Vulliamy A.E. George; Mr Cheadley R.E.
Warton; Evans R.J. Beauchamp; Saunders Lesly Thomson.
Lady Jane Sudeley [Charlotte?] Granville; Mrs Fenton
M. Talbot; Chris Haidee Wright. *REV: Ath 21/11/96*
p724; E 21/11/96 p7; Sk 25/11/96 p184; St 19/11/96
p12-3; Th 1/12/96 p335-7; TW96 p314-9.

96.278 *A WHITE ELEPHANT* (F,3a) R.C. Carton. COMEDY
19/11/96-26/2/97. 99 perf [w/S mat exc 21/11/96; add
mat 20/1/97, 3/2/97; np 24-25/12/96].* Joseph Ogden
Charles H.E. Brookfield/H.S. Stephenson; Earl of Baw-
combe Eric Lewis; Hon Stacey Gillam Charles H. Hawtrey; Mr Tweed Henry Kemble; Robert Peploe Cecil Ramsey; Charles Glenthorne W.T. Lovell; Bigsby William
F. Hawtrey/Frederick Volpé/H[enry] Stephenson/H.Deane.
Lady Gwendolen Ogden [Katherine] Compton; Letitia Ogden Alice Mansfield; Emily Rawston Nina Boucicault;
Celestine Nina Cadiz; Mrs Jauncey Mrs Charles Calvert;
Mrs Cyrus N. Dowker Lottie Venne. MGR Charles H. Hawtrey; Mus dir Ernest Bucalossi; Sm Frederick Glover;
Bm C. Liddon Clark; Act mgr Arthur Donald. *REV: Ath*
28/11/96 p765; E 21/11/96 p13; Sk 25/11/96 p184, 10/
2/97 p105-7; SR 5/12/96 p584-5; St 26/11/96 p15; Th
1/12/96 p333-4; Ti 20/11/96 p6; TW96 p319-21.

96.279 *WHEN THE CAT'S AWAY* (Oa) A. Kenward Matthews
(lib) & Bond Andrews (mus). GARRICK 19/11/96 mat
perf.* Miss Ogle Huntley Wright; Charley Scott Russell; Bertie Templar Saxe. Miss Cynthia Minnie Thurgate; Miss Beatrice Lettice Fairfax; Agnes Fannie
Marriott. *REV: E 21/11/96 p9; St 26/11/96 p15.*

96.280 *THE TRANSFERRED GHOST* (Ca) Neville Lynn (lib)
& John Crook (mus). GARRICK 19/11/96 mat perf.*
Benjamin Nicholas Hayes/Ghost F. Vincent Walker; Al-
gernon Pottinger Jones Frank A. Walsh. Madeline An-
gela Hayes Cassie Bruce; Mrs Simkin Mary Desmond.
REV: As for 96.279.

96.281 *A STATE TRIAL* (Duol) Laurence S. Irving. GAR-
RICK 19/11/96 mat perf.* James II Ben Greet. Mary
Plowden Maggie Bowman. *REV: E 21/11/96 p9; St 26/11/
96 p15.*

96.282 *RIZPAH MISERY* (Monol) Mrs Vere Campbell. GAR-
RICK 19/11/96 mat perf. 1st perfd Grand, Glasgow 6/2/
94. Hermann Vezin. Laura Johnson. *REV: St 26/11/96
p15.*

96.283 *THE MAID OF YESTERDAY* (Duol) Mrs Vere Campbell.
GARRICK 19/11/96 mat perf. 1st perfd Queens Gate,
South Kensington 11/5/96. Sir Aubert Sedgwick Acton
Bond. Maude Allandale Laura Johnson. *REV: St 26/11/
96 p15.*

96.284 *LITTLE EYOLF* (D,3a) Henrik Ibsen [trans Will-
iam Archer]. AVENUE 23/11/96-27/11/96 [5 mat perf];
30/11/96-19/12/96 [w/S mat; mat only 16/12; np 7/12].
25 perf.* Alfred Allmers Courtenay Thorpe/W. Scott
Buist; Eyolf Master Stewart Dawson; Engineer Borgheim
C.M. Lowne. Rita Allmers Janet Achurch/Mrs Patrick
Campbell; Asta Allmers Elizabeth Robins; The Rat Wife
Mrs Patrick Campbell/Florence Farr. L Charles H. Hawtrey; Mgr F.J. Harris; Act mgr C.G. Compton; Dir
Elizabeth Robins; Pd George R. Foss; Bom H. Callan.
*REV: Ath 28/11/96 p765-6; E 28/11/96 p13; Sk 2/12/96
p212-3, 16/12/96 p317; SR 28/11/96 p563-5, 12/12/96
p623-5; St 26/11/96 p15, 10/12/96 p13; Th 1/1/97 p40-
1; Ti 24/11/96 p10; TW96 p306-14, 322-4, 329-30, 342.*

96.285 *A BAFFLED CRIME* (CD,4a) Charles W. McCabe.
NOVELTY 23/11/96-28/11/96. 6 perf.* Stephen Travers
Bernard Copping; Cyril Travers Harold Child; Martin
van Gelda Charles Alleyne; Jack Ainslie Jack Haddon;
Bertie Lane T. West Carnie; Dr Richard Taylor Robert
Smith; Jem Slade Ernest Nelson; Gus Gordon Newman
Maurice; Tommy Fribsley Master Victor St. Aubin; Lieut.
of the Tartar Frank Jennings; Porter Harry Danby;
Arthur Colson Stuart Adair; Saunders Beresford Carl;
Detective Cecil Hill. Dolly Vavasour Katie Brunton;
Maud Montmorency Marie McDowell; Mrs Marthy Fribsley
Elsie Trevor; Nelly Travers/Jessie Travers V. St.
Lawrence. L V. St. Lawrence; Mgr Walter Tyrrell. *REV:*

E 28/11/96 p10; St 26/11/96 p17.

96.286 *ROBERT MACAIRE.* NOVELTY 23/11/96-28/11/96. 6
perf. Robert Macaire Bernard Copping. Jacques Strop
Newman Maurice. L, Mgr as for 96.285. *REV: E 28/11/96
p10.*

96.287 *THE BELLS* (D,3a) Leopold Lewis [adpt of Erck-
mann-Chatrian, *Le Juif Polonais*]. LYCEUM 25/11/96,
5/12, 12/12, 14-15/12/96. 5 perf.** Mathias Henry
Irving; Christian Frank [Kemble] Cooper; Walter [John]
Archer; Hans [Sam] Johnson; Dr Zimmer John Martin
Harvey; Notary Gurney; President of the Court F[rank]
Tyars; Clerk of the Court [Sidney] Lacy; Mesmerist
Rendall. Catherine Maud Milton; Sozel Edith Craig;
Annette Brenda Gibson. L & MGR Henry Irving; Bom
Joseph Hurst; Sm H.J. Loveday; Mus dir J. Meredith
Ball; Act mgr Bram Stoker. *REV: E 28/11/96 p13; St 3/
12/96 p14; Ti 26/11/96 p5.*

96.288 *JOURNEYS END IN LOVERS' MEETING* (Proverb,1a)
"J.O. Hobbes" [Mrs P.M.T. Craigie] & George Moore.
LYCEUM 25/11/96. 1 perf.** Sir Philip Soupire Frank
[Kemble] Cooper; Cpt. Maramour Ben Webster. Lady Sou-
pire Ellen Terry. L & MGR, Bom, Sm, Mus dir, Act mgr
as for 96.287. *REV: E 28/11/96 p13; St 3/12/96 p14-5;*

96.289 *THE KISS OF DELILAH* (P,3a) George Grant & James
Lisle. DRURY LANE 27/11/96, 28/11/96. 2 perf.* Maxi-
milian Robespierre Hermann Vezin; Collot d'Herbois
Brooke Warren; Hannibal Legendre Sam Johnson; Coupe
Tete Edward O'Neill; Guyzot Palmer; Chapuy Philip
Darwin; Jacques Morgan; Pierre Arthur Vezin; Sgt. of
the National Guard Woburn; Francois Joseph Talma T.B.
Thalberg. Herminie Vanhove Hilda Spong; Estelle Beau-
pas Edith Jordan. L Executors of Augustus Harris; Mgr
John Coleman; Act mgr Neil Forsyth; Cost Mrs S. May,
Charles May; Mus dir James Weaver. *REV: Ath 5/12/96
p804; Sk 2/12/96 p212; SR 5/12/96 p584-5; St 3/12/96
p15; Th 1/1/97 p39-40; TW96 p327-8.*

96.290 *LOST IN LONDON* (D,4a) Watts Phillips. NOVELTY
30/11/96-5/12/96. 6 perf. 1st perfd Adelphi 16/3/67.
Gilbert Featherstone Jack Haddon; Sir Richard Loader

Ernest Nelson; Job Armroyd Bernard Copping; Benjamin
Blinker Newman Maurice; Thomas Harry Danby; Topps
Frank Jennings; Jim Master Willie Hill; Jack Longbones
Cecil Hill; Dick Rayne Beresford Carl. Nelly Daisy
England; Tiddy Dragglethorpe Elsie Trevor; Mme d'Alton
Marie McDowell; Florence Margaret Marshall. L V. St.
Lawrence; Mgr Walter Tyrrell. *REV: E 5/12/96 p10; St
3/12/96 p15.*

96.291 *AS YOU LIKE IT* (C,5a) William Shakespeare. ST.
JAMES'S 2/12/96-20/3/97. 115 perf [w/W, S mat; mat
only 2/12/96, 17/3/97, 20/3/97; np 21-25/12/96, 3/3/
97].** Duke James Fernandez; Frederick C. Aubrey
Smith; Amiens Bertram Wallis; Jaques W.H. Vernon/H.H.
Vincent; 1st Lord H.H. Vincent/L. Roberts; 2nd Lord
George P. Bancroft; Le Beau Vincent Sternroyd; Charles
J[ames] Wheeler; Oliver H.B. Irving; Jaques de Bois
R[obert] Loraine; Orlando George Alexander; Adam
Henry Loraine; Dennis A.W. Munro; Touchstone Henry V.
Esmond; Corin William H. Day; Silvius Arthur Royston;
William George P. Hawtrey. Hymen Julia F. Opp; Rosa-
lind Julia Neilson; Celia Fay Davis; Phoebe Dorothea
Baird/Ellis Jeffreys; Audrey Kate Phillips. L & MGR
George Alexander; Sc T.E. Ryan, H.P. Hall, Walter
Hann; Mus Edward German, Walter Slaughter; Cost dgn
Graham Robertson; Cost L. & H. Nathan; Ch Espinosa;
Bm Robert V. Shone; Sm H.H. Vincent; Mus dir Walter
Slaughter; Pq William Clarkson; Props Robinson; Bom
Arnold. *REV: Ath 12/12/96 p846; E 5/12/96 p13, 13/3/
97 p10; Sk 9/12/96 p256-7, 280, 6/1/97 p415, 439-42;
SR 5/12/96 p585-6; St 3/12/96 p15, 11/3/97 p12; Th
1/1/97 p37-8; Ti 3/12/96 p6; TW96 p331-7.*

96.292 *A PRINCESS OF ORANGE* (D,1a) Fred James. LYCEUM
3/12/96 mat perf.* Cpt. Wilford Blount Ernest Leicester; Don Fernand de Medillo Luigi Lablache. Louise,
Princess of Orange May Whitty. MUS DIR J. Meredith
Ball, J.M. Capel, Edward Jones, F. Sydney Ward; Bm
W.B. Fabian; Sm Charles Cruikshanks; Asm J.F. Cornish,
Sidney Harcourt, Ernest E. Norris; Cost L. & H. Nathan, Harrisons, Morris Angel & Son; Pq William Clarkson, C.H. Fox; Mach Fillery; Furn Arnott; Bom Joseph
Hurst; L & Mgr Henry Irving. *REV: E 5/12/96 p13; St
10/12/96 p12; Th 1/1/97 p41-2.*

96.293 *CHATTERTON* (1a) H.A. Jones & Henry Herman. LY-
CEUM 3/12/96 mat perf. 1st perfd Princess's 22/5/84.
Chatterton Wilson Barrett; Nat Boaden Ambrose Manning.
Mrs Angel Mrs George Owen; Cecilia Daisy Belmore; Lady
Mary Maud C. Jeffries. MUS DIR, Bm, Sm, Asm, Cost,
Pq, Mach, Furn, Bom, L & Mgr as for 96.292; Cond Ed-
ward Jones. *REV: E, St as for 96.292.*

96.294 *AN IDYLL OF THE CLOSING CENTURY* (Duol) Estelle
Burney. LYCEUM 3/12/96 mat perf.* Hayes Dormer Cyril
Maude. Hon Millicent Warreyne Winifred Emery. MUS DIR,
Bm, Sm, Asm, Cost, Pq, Mach, Furn, Bom, L & Mgr as
for 96.292. *REV: As for 96.292.*

96.295 *TRIAL BY JURY* (CO,1a) W.S. Gilbert (lib) &
Arthur Sullivan (mus). LYCEUM 3/12/96 mat perf.**
Judge Rutland Barrington; Counsel Harrison Brockbank;
Defendant Charles Kenningham; Usher Frank Wheeler;
Foreman of Jury Walter Passmore; Associate Charles
Cruikshanks; Extras [Charles] Childerstone, G.H. Daw-
son, B[arton?] de Solla, Jones Hewson, Cory James,
Henry Sanders, Scott Russell, W.H. Seymour, Hilton
St. Just, A.B. Tapping, Chris Walker, Akerman May,
Oscar Adye, Charles Fulton, Frederic Jacques, W.T.
Lovell, M.R. Morand, Sydney Paxton, T. Gideon Warren,
[Avon?] Hastings, [Dudley?] Jepps, [C. Herbert] Work-
man, Castle, [Joseph?] Ruff, Ard, Marsland, Edwin
Walton, William Luff. Plaintiff Florence Dysart;
Extras Bella Bashall, Annie Beaufort, Phyllis Brough-
ton, Edith Cartwright, Mary Desmond, Agnes Hill,
Edith Johnston, Eva Moore, Werdermann, Ina Repton,
Violet Robinson, Kristine Yudall, Mrs Gordon-Ascher,
Gladys O. Ffolliott, Mary Bates, Christine Beauclerc,
Clara Nicholls, Rose Wilson, [Daisy] Gilpin, Adams,
[Ada] Newall, [Pattie?] Reimers, Bemister, [Ruth]
Vincent, Castelle, de Lacy, M[ildred] Baker, [Mar-
guerite?] Moyse, Murray, [Laurie] Elliston, [Bessie?]
Bonsall, Kate Osborne, Agnes Imlay. MUS DIR, Bm, Sm,
Asm, Cost, Pq, Mach, Furn, Bom, L & Mgr as for 96.292;
Cond J. Meredith Ball. *REV: E, St as for 96.292.*

96.296 *THE CIRCUS GIRL* (MP) James T. Tanner (lib) &
W. Palings (lib) & Ivan Caryll (mus) & Lionel Monckton (mus). GAIETY 5/12/96-7/5/98. 494 perf [w/S mat

exc 5/12/96, 12/6/97, 24/7, 31/7, 7/8, 14/8, 21/8,
28/8, 18/9/97, 30/4/98, 7/5/98; add mat 10/2/97, 17/2,
24/6/97; np 24-25/12/96, 16/4/97, 22/6, 20-25/12/97,
4-9/4/98]. 1st prof thus. Copyright perf Gaiety 27/5/
96 [as *In the Ring*]. Dick Capel Seymour Hicks/W.H.
Powell; Sir Titus Wemyss Harry Monkhouse/Ells Dagnall;
Drivelli Arthur Williams/C. Roper Lane; Hon Reginald
Gower Lionel MacKinder/W. Louis Bradfield; Auguste
Willie Warde; Adolphe Bertie Wright/E[dward] W. Cole-
man/Alfred Asher/Harry Phydora; Albertoni Colin Coop;
Commissaire of Police Robert Nainby; Vicomte Gaston
Maurice Farkoa/Robert Selby; Toothpick Pasha Arthur
Hope/Herbert Clayton/Milroy Cooper/Fernley Swift;
Rudolph E.D.Wardes/Percy Lockner; Proprietor of Cafe
Leslie Holland/W.H. Powell/Ed Sellward/Charles Lane;
Flobert Robert Selby/George Farrow; Cocher W.F.
Brooke; Sgt. de Ville Fred Ring/W.J. Manning; Valli-
and W.H. Powell/F.W. Ring/Charles Lane/H. Bernhardt;
Biggs Edmund Payne/Horace Mills. Lucille Katie Sey-
mour/Coralie Blythe/Madge Greet/Florence Lauri; "La
Favorita" Ethel Haydon/Maidee Hope/Frances Earle;
Mrs Drivelli Connie Ediss; Lady Diana Wemyss Maria
Davis/Annie Dwelly; Marie Grace Palotta/Mabel Duncan/
Nina Cadiz; Louise Lily Johnson/Alice Betelle/Lily
Johnson/Marjorie Glenn; Liane Louie Coote; Emilie
Alice Betelle/Maud Wilmot/Marie Saqui; Juliette Maidie
Hope/Madge Greet/Florence Percival/Edith Denton/So-
phie Elliott/Florence Schuberth/Rose Brady; Comtesse
d'Epernay Ada Maitland/Birdie Sutherland/Margherita
Kowska/Norma Whalley/Mabel Duncan; Marquise de Mille-
fleurs Kathleen Francis/Kate Adams/Rose Brady/Mar-
jorie Pryor/Rosie Boote; Rose Gompson Alice Neilson/
Mabel Warren/Frances Earle/Margaret Fraser; Dora Wem-
yss Ellaline Terriss/Ethel Haydon/Lily Johnson/Grace
Dudley; Dancers Maggie Frazer, Ethel Nield, Lottie
Williams, Madge Greet. L & MGR George Edwardes; Lyr
Harry Breenbank, Adrian Ross: Cost dgn Comelli; Cost
C. Alias, Auguste, Harrisons, Miss Fisher; Ch Willie
Warde; Pq Gustave, William Clarkson; Sc T.E. Ryan,
William Telbin; Cond Ivan Caryll; Sm J.A.E. Malone;
Act mgr Edward Marshall. *REV: E 12/12/96 p10; Sk 9/
12/96 p256, 30/12/96 p412, 17/2/97 p157-60, 3/3/97
p245-8, 17/11/97 p134; St 10/12/96 p12-3, 13/1/98 p14;
Th 1/1/97 p38-9; Ti 7/12/96 p12; TW96 p340-1.* Comment:

The following role was added during the course of the
production: <u>Marie Beaville</u> Mabel Duncan/Marie Saqui/
Dora Dudley.

96.297 *THE KING AND THE MILLER* (D,1a) William H. Murray. LYCEUM 5/12/96, 12/12, 14-15/12/96. 4 perf.**
<u>James V</u> F[rank] Tyars; <u>James Birkie</u> John Martin Har-
vey; <u>Jock Howieson</u> [Sam] Johnson; <u>Cpt. of King's
Guard</u> Lacy. <u>King's Page</u> [Maud?] Holland; <u>Tibbie Howie-
son</u> Eleanor Aicken; <u>Marion</u> Foster. L & MGR Henry Irving; <u>Bom</u> Joseph Hurst; <u>Sm</u> H.J. Loveday; <u>Mus dir</u> J.
Meredith Ball; <u>Act mgr</u> Bram Stoker.

96.298 *HENRY DUNBAR; OR, A TALE OF TWO LIVES* (D,4a)
[Tom Taylor?]. NOVELTY 7/12/96-12/12/96. 6 perf. 1st
perfd Olympic 9/12/65 [as *Henry Dunbar; or, A Daugh-
ter's Trial*]. <u>Joseph Wilmot</u> Henry Allison; <u>Clement
Austin</u> H.J. Spencer; <u>Alfred Lovel</u> Leonard Ross; <u>Henry
Carter</u> R. Somers; <u>Major Vincent</u> George; <u>Leary Pal</u>
E.F. Graves; <u>Hartoff</u> Henry Rivers; <u>Tibbs</u> Allendale;
<u>Messenger</u> T. Fenton; <u>Henry Dunbar</u> Frank Teams. <u>Laura
Dunbar</u> Ethel Strange; <u>Mary Madden</u> Annie Fisher; <u>Mar-
garet</u> Annesley. L V. St. Lawrence; <u>Mgr</u> Walter Tyrrell.
REV: E 12/12/96 p10.

96.299 *GOOD FOR NOTHING* (CD,1a) J.B. Buckstone. NOVEL-
TY 7/12/96-12/12/96. 6 perf.** <u>L</u>, <u>Mgr</u> as for 96.298.

96.300 *WOMAN'S WORLD* (C,3a) James P. Hurst. COURT 8/
12/96 mat perf.* <u>Keith Dunlop</u> Joseph Carne; <u>Ulric
Falshawe</u> George Hippisley; <u>Sebastian Meggeson</u> Compton
Coutts; <u>Kelland Smith</u> Frederick Volpé; <u>Hilary Glynn</u>
Ivan Watson. <u>Constance Glynn</u> Esmé Beringer; <u>Lucy Mait-
land</u> Jessie Bateman; <u>Anna Gurbs, M.D.</u> M. Talbot; <u>Jane
McKillop</u> Alice Beet; <u>Charlotte Bap</u> Marie Lyons; <u>Mrs
Lascelles</u> [Enid] Spencer Brunton; <u>Barbara Earp</u> Adela
Weekes. L & MGR Arthur Chudleigh; <u>Pd</u> A.B. Tapping;
<u>Mus dir</u> Carl Kiefert; <u>Bm</u> Leonard Lillies. *REV: Ath 12/
12/96 p846; E 12/12/96 p13; Sk 16/12/96 p317; St 10/
12/96 p13; Th 1/1/97 p42-3; TW96 p337-40.*

96.301 *A NIGHT OFF* (C,4a) Augustin Daly. ROYALTY 8/12/
96 mat perf.** <u>Prof Babbit</u> Frank Hole; <u>Jack Mulberry</u>
Reginald Dance; <u>Dr Damask</u> Herbert Swears; <u>Lord Mul-</u>

berry Graham Wentworth; Snap Guildford Dudley. Mrs
Babbitt Mrs St. Hill; Angelica Damask Lilian Braithwaite; Susan Marian Moore; Nisbe Sybil Carlisle. MGR
George Alexander; Bm Luther Munday; Sm Guildford Dudley; Act mgr Harold Veasey. *REV: St 10/12/96 p13.*

96.302 *THE ANTI-MATRIMONIAL SOCIETY* (Ca,1a) Emily
Beauchamp. STRAND 8/12/96 mat perf. 1st perfd Gaiety,
Dublin 9/3/76. Col. Lovelace Trevor Lowe; Cpt. Frank
Grahame Jack Warrington; Pat O'Connor Charles Kenny.
Ethel Lovelace Valde Wynne; Clara Biggs Cynthia Gran-
ville; Elsie Manley Ruby Wyndham; Ina Fortescue V.
Le Dain; Jessie Arundel Marie Thornhill; Laura Mait-
land Marie Bates; Annie Singleton Beatrice Parke;
Maud Mayflower Josephine Bennett; Cissy Scissors Aud-
rey Littleton; Selina Pringle Mrs Stanislaus Calhaem.
PP J.S. Clarke; Bm Balsir Chatterton. *REV: E 12/12/96
p13; St 10/12/96 p13.*

96.303 *YES OR NO?* (P,3a) Emily Beauchamp. STRAND 8/12/
96 mat perf. 1st perfd Theatre Royal, Dublin 2/5/77.
Mr Dunlop Charles Seymour; Sir Ralph Cleverley, Bart.
Aubrey Fitzgerald; Jack Westaway Trevor Lowe; John
Winter Calvert. Katrine Dunlop Eileen Munro; Milly
Mayfield Mrs Bennett; Matilda MacIntyre Emily Beau-
champ. PP, Bm as for 96.302. *REV: As for 96.302.*

96.304 *SWEET NANCY* (P,[3a]) Robert Buchanan [adpt of
Rhoda Broughton, "Nancy"]. CRITERION 10/12/96 mat
perf.** Gen. Sir Roger Tempest Edmund Maurice; Frank
Musgrave C.M. Hallard; Mr Gray Charles Rock; Alger-
non Gray [John] Martin Harvey; Bobby Kenneth Douglas;
The Brat Master Grose; Pemberton Claude Edmonds. Mrs
Gray Henrietta Cowen; Barbara Gray Lena Ashwell;
Nancy Gray Annie Hughes; Theresa Gray Marion Bishop;
Mrs Huntley Helen Ferrers. L & MGR Charles Wyndham.
*REV: E 12/12/96 p11; Sk 16/12/96 p317; St 17/12/96
p15; TW96 p341-2.*

96.305 *AN OLD SONG* (P,1a) Rev Freeman Wills & A. Fitz-
maurice King. CRITERION 10/12/96 mat perf. 1st perfd
Great Hall, Tunbridge Wells 2/8/94. Rouget de Lisle
[John] Martin Harvey; Ravachol [W.] Lionel Belmore.
Signora Sara Rosetti May Whitty; Angele N. de Silva.

L & MGR Charles Wyndham. *REV: E, Sk, St as for 96.304.*

96.306 *FALSTAFF* (O,3a) Giuseppe Verdi. LYCEUM 11/12/96
mat perf.** Sir John Falstaff J. Mansel Lewis; Fenton Leon Zaguty; Forel R. Emlyn Davies; Dr Caius Joseph Boddy; Randolph Fritz B. Hart; Pistol Harry
Dearth. Mistress Ford Eleanor Jones; Anne Agnes H.
Nicholls; Mistress Page Morfydd J. Williams; Dame
Quickly Muriel Foster. L & MGR Henry Irving; Bom Joseph Hurst; Cond C. Villiers Stanford; Pq William
Clarkson; Pd Richard Temple; Ch B. Soutten. *REV: Ath
19/12/96 p881; E 12/12/96 p17; Ti 12/12/96 p10.*

96.307 *ENGLAND'S GLORY; OR, A STORY OF WATERLOO* (P,4a)
Henry Allison. NOVELTY 14/12/96–19/12/96. 6 perf. 1st
perfd Parkhurst 20/8/94. Ned Thornhill Herbert Cecil;
Cpt. Le Fanu John H. Manley; Admiral Fairweather T.H.
Gregory; Dr Wiseheart Henry Allison; Lieut. Harrin-
gay Rex Lloyd; Pompey Leonard Sheen; Old Daddy Gibbon
Tayleur; French Officer Allendale. Viscount Cho'mond-
eley Alice Sanger; Dora Fairweather Vera Douglas; Bess
Thornhill Annesley. L V. St. Lawrence; Mgr Walter
Tyrrell. *REV: E 19/12/96 p10; St 17/12/96 p15.*

96.308 *COMPLICATIONS* (F). NOVELTY 14/12/96–19/12/96.
6 perf. Rex Lloyd; Frank Gibbon; F.C. Brooke. Flo
Chamberlain; Alice Sanger. L, Mgr as for 96.307. *REV:
St 17/12/96 p15.*

96.309 *THE EXTRAORDINARY BEHAVIOUR OF MRS JALLOWBY*
(FC,3a) Clive Brooke. NOVELTY 18/12/96 mat perf.*
Mjr.-Gen. Orcas Jallowby J. Norton-Wilson; Harry A.
Yockney; Wibbler Cecil Compton; Lincoln Beale Graham
Wentworth; Arthur Jallowby Clive Brooke. Mrs Orcas
Jallowby Isabel Grey; Charlotte May Rosine; Annabel
Chevenix Belvore; Estelle Jallowby Eleanor Lane. L,
Mgr as for 96.308. *REV: Ath 26/12/96 p916; E 19/12/96
p13; St 24/12/96 p11; Th 1/1/97 p43-4.*

96.310 *UNCLE THATCHER* (P,1a) Clive Brooke. NOVELTY
18/12/96 mat perf.** Cecil Compton; J. Norton-Wilson;
A. Yockney; Clive Brooke. Isabel Grey; Belvore. L,
Mgr as for 96.307. *REV: E, St as for 96.309.*

96.311 *RICHARD III* (T,5a) William Shakespeare. LYCEUM 19/12/96; 27/2/97-7/4/97. 35 perf [mat only 31/3/97, 7/4/97].** Richard, Duke of Gloster Henry Irving; King Edward IV Gordon Craig; George, Duke of Clarence H. Cooper Cliffe; Henry, Earl of Richmond Frank [Kemble] Cooper; Cardinal Bouchier [H.W.] Cushing; Duke of Buckingham F.H. Macklin; Duke of Norfolk Lacy; Lord Rivers Fuller Mellish; Lord Hastings Ben Webster; Lord Stanley Frederick Robinson; Lord Lovel [John] Archer; Marquis of Dorset [Eardley] Howard; Bishop of Ely [T.] Reynolds; Sir Richard Ratcliff [W. Lionel] Belmore; Sir William Catesby [Frank] Tyars; Sir James Tyrrell Clarence Hague; Sir Robert Brackenbury John Martin Harvey; Lord Mayor of London [R.P.] Tabb; Officer [K.] Rivington; 1st Murderer Norman Forbes; 2nd Murderer William Farren, jr. King's Page Edith Craig; Edward, Prince of Wales Lena Ashwell; Richard, Duke of York Gertrude Norman; Elizabeth Maud Milton; Duchess of York Mary Rorke; Lady Anne Julia Arthur; Margaret Genevieve Ward. L & MGR Henry Irving; Sc Hawes Craven, Joseph Harker; Cost dgn E. Hamilton Bell; Cost Auguste, Mrs Nettleship, Mrs Reid; Mus dir & Mus J. Meredith Ball; Props Arnott; Mach Fillery; Pq Fox; Sm H.J. Loveday; Bom Joseph Hurst; Act mgr Bram Stoker. *REV: Ath 26/12/96 p915, 6/3/97 p322; E 26/12/96 p8, 6/3/97 p10; Sk 23/12/96 p325, 342-3, 30/12/96 p375; SR 26/12/96 p671-3; St 24/12/96 p10-1, 4/3/97 p12; Th 1/1/97 p35-7; Ti 21/12/96 p11, 1/3/97 p11; TW96 p342-51.* Comment: "Owing to a sprain received by Sir Henry Irving he will be unable to play for a few days, and the Lyceum Theatre will therefore be closed this evening [21 December], and to-morrow and Wednesday evenings" *(Ti)*. As noted above, the production was not resumed until 27 February.

96.312 *JEDBURY JUNIOR* (C,4a) Madeleine Lucette Ryley. GLOBE 21/12/96-5/2/97. 51 perf [w/W, S mat exc 13/1/97, 30/1, 3/2/97; add mat 24/12/96; np 25/12/96].** Christopher Jedbury, jr H. Reeves-Smith; Christopher Jedbury, sr Sydney Paxton; Mjr. Hedway Gordon Tompkins; Tom Bellaby Wilfred Draycott; Mr Glibb F. Newton Lindo; Mr Simpson Wilfred Heriot; Whimper Harry Farmer; Job Duncan Tovey. Mrs Jedbury, sr Claire

Pauncefort; Mrs Glibb Mabel Lane; Nellie Jedbury Emmie
Merrick; Dora Hedway Annie L. Aumonier. L W.S. Penley.
REV: E 26/12/96 p8; St 24/12/96 p11; Ti 22/12/96 p4.

96.313 *THE EIDER-DOWN QUILT* (FC,3a) Tom S. Wotton.
TERRY'S 21/12/96-27/3/97. 99 perf [w/S mat; add mat
22/1/97, 24/2, 10/3/97; np 25/12/96, 3/3/97].* Alberto
de Bologna Herman de Lange; Sir John de Caudebec, J.P.
Nicol Pentland; Cpt. Bernard Arthur Playfair; Dick
A.E. Matthews; Peter Mumforth Frederick Volpé/Frank
J. Arlton; Colenutt Charles Terric. Sybil Audrey Ford;
Lucy Pemberton Ethel Matthews; Rosamund Dennison
[Enid] Spencer Brunton; Patricia Fanny Brough/Alice
Beet. PP Edward Terry; Mgr Arthur Playfair; Bm E.F.
Bradley; Sm Dennis Bryan; Mus dir W. Meyer Lutz; Pd
Charles Cartwright; Cost Redfern, Mme [Sara?] Perrin,
Miss Brown; Sc Leolyn Hart; Furn Lyon; Pq William
Clarkson. *REV: E 26/12/96 p8; Sk 30/12/96 p383, 3/2/
97 p70-1; SR 2/1/97 p12; St 24/12/96 p11; Th 1/2/97
p102-3; Ti 22/12/96 p4; TW96 p358.*

96.314 *IN MARY'S COTTAGE* (P,1a) Charles Beckwith.
TERRY'S 21/12/96-9/1/97. 17 perf [np 25/12/96].*
Dick Grantley Sydney Brough; Mark Bassett Charles
Terric. Mrs Purritt Mrs Campbell Bradley; Jane Spark
Dora Barton; Mary Winifred Fraser. PP, Mgr, Bm, Sm,
Mus dir as for 96.313. *REV: E, St as for 96.313.*

96.315 *BLACK EY'D SUSAN; OR, ALL IN THE DOWNS* (Nautical D,2a) Douglas Jerrold. ADELPHI 23/12/96-8/5/97.
118 perf [w/mat 26/12/96, 2/1/97, 9/1, 16/1, 23/1,
30/1, 27/2, 19/4/97; np 25/12/96, 18/1/97, 12-17/4/97].
1st perfd Surrey 8/6/29. William William Terriss;
Cpt. Crosstree Charles J. Fulton; Hatchett Oscar
Adye; Raker H. Trant Fischer; Doggrass J.D. Beveridge;
Admiral Luigi Lablache; Jacob Twig Cyril Melton; Gnat-
brain Harry Nicholls; Blue Peter Charles Fisher; Sea-
weed Jarvis Widdicombe; Quid Webb Darleigh; Lieut.
Pike William Dempsey; Midshipman Denton; Ploughshare
Vincent. Susan Jessie Millward; Dolly Mayflower Vane
Featherstone. PP & MGR Agostino & S. Gatti; Dir & Bm
Fred G. Latham; Mus T.W. Blewitt; Sc William Har-
ford, William Perkins; Cost L. & H. Nathan, Morris
Angel & Sons; Furn Hampton & Sons; Ch John d'Auban;

Mus dir John Crook; Bom Arthur Frye; A act mgr Herbert Budd. *REV: Ath 2/1/97 p26; E 26/12/96 p8; Sk 23/12/96 p340; SR 2/1/97 p12; St 31/12/96 p14-5; Th 1/2/97 p97-8; Ti 24/12/96 p3; TW96 p357-8.*

96.316 ALL THAT GLITTERS IS NOT GOLD (DC,2a) Thomas Morton & John Maddison Morton. ADELPHI 23/12/96-8/5/ 97. 110 perf [np 25/12/96, 18/1/97, 12-17/4/97]. 1st perfd Olympic 13/1/51.   Sir Arthur Lassells Luigi Lablache; Jasper Plum J.D. Beveridge; Stephen Plum Charles J. Fulton; Frederick Plum Oscar Adye; Toby Twinkle Harry Nicholls; Harris Jarvis Widdicomb. Lady Valeria Margaret Halstan; Lady Leatherbridge Kate Kearney; Martha Gibbs Vane Featherston. PP & MGR, Dir & Bm, Furn, Mus dir, Bom, A act mgr as for 96.315; Cost Peter Robinson, Miss Goldfinch, Morris Angel & Sons. *REV: Ath, E, SR, St as for 96.315; Sk 30/12/96 p373.*

96.317 RED RIDING HOOD (Panto) Victor Stephens. NOVELTY 24/12/96-6/2/97. 63 perf [2 perf dy 24/12/96-16/1/ 97; w/M, W, S mat 18/1/97-6/2/97].* Baron Graball Andy Rowan; Wicked Wolf Charles Brighten; Fox Harold Child; Granny Newman Maurice; Simple Simon T. West Carnie; Locks Beresford Carl; Bumble Cecil Hill. Cupid Little Rosie Weston; Jack Ray Cantor; Jill K. Beresford; Fairy Gossamer Lucy Murray; Fernando Ivy Thurloe; Robin Goodheart May Lovegrove; Margery Daw E.L. Maddocks; Coquette Amy [F.] Millar; Armando Carlton; Violet Edith Lyddon; Dolly Mayflower Fanny McKay; Elsie Florrie Vokes; Marguerita Lola Ritchie; Dora Buttercup M[argaret] Marshall; Polly Dimple J. Hill; Daffodil Louisa Janson; Snowdrop Nelly Mead; Moss Rose Cassie Seagrist; Heartsease Gipsy Woolf; Hyacinth Violet Pagis; Narcissus Lena Pagis; Little Red Riding Hood Rose Moncrieff. L V. St. Lawrence; Mgr Walter Tyrrell. *REV: E 26/12/96 p11; St 31/12/96 p17; Ti 28/12/96 p8.*

96.318 THE PILGRIM'S PROGRESS (Mystery P,with mus,4a) George C. Collingham [fnd on John Bunyan]. OLYMPIC 24/12/96-4/1/97. 12 perf [w/W, S mat; np 25/12/96].* Apollyon W.L. Abingdon; Gloriosus Frank H. Celli; Fairspeech Arnold Lucy; Holdworld Quinton Pearson;

Thankless Gilbert Buckton; Vainhope W.E. Sauter; Dives
Jack Cole; Pamper Gilbert Porteous; Graspall Edwin
Shepherd; Slave George Wallis; Slave Guy Fane; Ra-
phael Courtenay Thorpe; Faithful George W. Cockburn;
Death Lesly Thomson; Giant Despair John Webb; Bertram
W. Melville; Simple H.J. Cole; Mammon Dudley Clinton;
Timeserver Reginald Waller; Presumption Hubert Evelyn;
Sloth J.R. Melton; Slave L.T. Thomas. Speranza Esmé
Beringer; Isolde Roma St. John Brenon; Iris Frances
Stuart Innes; Malignily Laura Johnson; Fidelia Juli-
ette d'Ervieux; Melusina Emily [S.] Fitzroy; Sabra
Irene San Carolo; Crafty Maud St. John; Dame Gossip
Nettie Hooper; Mistress Timorous Maud Locker; Christ-
ian Grace Hawthorne; Mme Bubble Mary Milton; Flori-
monde Vera Beringer. MGR DIR & PD Henry J. Leslie;
L Anglo American Theatrical Syndicate Ltd; Sc Bruce
Smith, W. Harker, E.G. Banks, Richard C. Durant,
William Perkins; Cost dgn Comelli; Cost Alias, Sim-
mons, Harrison, Nathan, Besford; Ch [Carlo] Coppi;
Pq William Clarkson; Elect T.J. Digby; Mus W. Meyer
Lutz, Henry J. Leslie; Pp Mrs Charles Wilmot; Mus dir
W. Meyer Lutz; Sm Guy Waller; Bm Alfred Cuthbert. *REV:
Ath 2/1/97 p26; E 26/12/96 p11; SR 2/1/97 p11-2; St
31/12/96 p15; Th 1/2/97 p101-2; Ti 25/12/96 p3; TW96
p352-7.*

96.319 *THE KEY TO KING SOLOMON'S RICHES, LIMITED*
(Rhodesian D,4a) Abbey St. Ruth. OPERA COMIQUE 24/12/
96-2/1/97. 8 perf [np 25/12/96].* Hugh Baring E.H.
Vanderfelt; Coppall F[rank?] MacDonnell; Lazarus J.A.
Arnold; Crawler Gilbert Yorke; Harry Grice Ernest
Bertram; Hans van Zyl Frederick Lane; Col. Yates Per-
cy Murray; Pat Murphy Harry Paulton, jr; McLimo John
H. Manley; Downey Bernard Liell; Rhodes Lawrence Ster-
ner; Jarge Rawgreen W.P. Warren-Smith; Adolphus Zas-
harias Sillytoe Norman Graham; Arnott Stuart Adair;
Slumper F. Mason; Gutter Broker Thomas Verner; Sig-
mund G. Sarjeant; Klass Stroud. Sam Agnes Paulton;
Farni Thea Lesbrooke; Ruth Baring Abbey St. Ruth;
Cissy Grant Mabel Hardinge; Mme Raphael Thornton;
Matilda Perkins Mrs Mat Robson; Jane Marianne Caldwell; "The Matabele Quartette" Lal Price, Nancy Stew-
art, Emma Parry, Phyllis Desmond. L Abbey St. Ruth;
Sc Leolyn Hart; Cost Morris Angel & Son; Pq William

Clarkson; Props Hall, Meade; Furn Lyon; Mus & Mus dir
[W.] Carlile Vernon; Sm T[homas] Verner; Bm Horace
St. Ruth. *REV: E 26/12/96 p11; Sk 30/12/96 p373; St
31/12/96 p15; Th 1/2/97 p103-4; Ti 25/12/96 p3.*

96.320 *ALADDIN* (Panto) Arthur Sturgess (lib) & Horace
Lennard (lib) & Oscar Barrett (mus). DRURY LANE 26/
12/96-27/3/97. 138 perf [2 perf dy 28/12/96-13/2/97;
w/M, W, S mat 15/2/97-6/3/97; w/W, S mat 10/3/97-27/
3/97; add mat 18/2/97, 25/2/97].* Mrs Twankay Dan
Leno; Abanazar Herbert Campbell; Chief Constable Fred
Griffiths; Washee-Washee Joe Griffiths; Slave of the
Lamp Paul Cinquevalli; Emperor Walker Marnock; Grand
Vizier Fritz Rimma; Dancing Master Ernest d'Auban;
Lord Chamberlain G. Angelo; Tax Collector Cleveland;
Constable E.G. Chasemore; Dog Master Goff; Coiffeur
Leo Mars; Canvasser Sawyers; Glover [George?] Aubrey.
Milliner Ebb Darcia; Aladdin Ada Blanche; Princess
Badroulbadour Decima Moore; Sau-See Clara Jecks; Pe-
koe Helene Pillans; Spirit of Life Florence Darley;
Genius of the Ring G[eraldine] Somerset; Slave of the
Ring Grigolati; Extras C. Gaisford, L[ily] Milbank,
Levy, L[ena?] Delphine, A. Gordon, [Gertrude] Cla-
ridge, Miro, K. Beardshaw, D[ora?] Rignold, M[aud?]
Rignold, G. Briscoe, [L.] Marsden, Taylor, E[thel]
Beaumont, Archer, B. Talbot, O. Vaughan, D[aisy]
Sedger, E. Pritchard, M[aude] Vinton, E. Ward, J.
Jones, H. West, J. Goodman, J. Ibberson. L Executors
of Augustus Harris; Mgr & Pd Oscar Barrett; Sm Arthur
P. Collins; Act mgr Neil Forsyth; Mus dir James Wea-
ver; Sc Henry Emden, Joseph Harker, Robert Caney, J.
Pritchard Barrett, William Telbin; Ch Katti Lanner,
John d'Auban; Cost dgn Wilhelm; Cost Auguste, Miss
Fisher, Harrisons, B.J. Simmons, J. Phillips & Son,
Miss Collier, Mme d'Orlean, Alias; Props Labhart, A.
Jones, Jackson, R. Eagle; Pq William Clarkson. *REV:
E 2/1/97 p11; Sk 13/1/97 p461-3; SR 23/1/97 p87-9; St
31/12/96 p14, 1/4/97 p13; Th 1/2/97 p104-5; Ti 28/12/
96 p8; TW96 p358-60.*

96.321 *THE HOLLY TREE INN* (P,1a) Mrs Oscar Beringer
[adpt of Charles Dickens]. TERRY'S 28/12/96-18/2/97;
25/2/97. 30 mat perf [perfd M-Th only exc 1/2, 8/2,
15/2].** Harry Master Stewart Dawson; Jabez Cobbs

George Belmore; <u>Cpt. Walmer</u> Sydney Brough; <u>Tom</u> Charles
Seymour. <u>Norah Valli</u> Valli; <u>Betty</u> Beatrice Ferrar;
<u>Mrs Cobbs</u> Kate Mills. <u>PP</u> Edward Terry; <u>Cond</u> W. Meyer
Lutz; <u>Bm</u> N. Reed; <u>Sm</u> George Belmore; <u>Cost</u> Peter Robinson. *REV: E 2/1/97 p13; Sk 27/1/97 p35; SR 2/1/97
p12; St 31/12/96 p15; TW97 p6-7.*

96.322 *LOVE IN IDLENESS* (C,3a) Louis N. Parker & Edward J. Goodman. TERRY'S 28/12/96-18/2/97; 25/2/97.
30 mat perf [perfd M-Th only exc 1/2, 8/2, 15/2].**
<u>Mortimer Pendlebury</u> Edward Terry; <u>Frank</u> W.E. Ashcroft;
<u>Rushey Platt</u> Gilbert Farquhar/George Belmore; <u>Jack
Fenton</u> Sydney Brough; <u>Eugene Gondinot</u> Herman de Lange/
Gilbert Farquhar. <u>Maggie</u> Hilda Rivers; <u>Louise Gondi-
not</u> Beatrice Ferrar; <u>Abigail Bright</u> Bella Pateman;
<u>Mrs Trott</u> Kate Mills; <u>Martha</u> Florence Leclercq. <u>PP</u>,
<u>Cond</u>, <u>Bm</u>, <u>Sm</u> as for 96.321; <u>Sc</u> Leolyn Hart; <u>Furn</u>
Lyon; <u>Pq</u> William Clarkson. *REV: E, St as for 96.321.*

96.323 *BETSY*(C,3a) F.C. Burnand [adpt of Hennequin &
Najac, *Bébé*. CRITERION 29/12/96-13/2/97. 47 perf [w/
S mat; mat only 13/2].** <u>Alexander Birkett</u> Alfred
Bishop; <u>Adolphus Birkett</u> Aubrey Boucicault; <u>Cpt. Mc-
Manus</u> J.H. Barnes; <u>Richard Talbot</u> Kenneth Douglas;
<u>Samuel Dawson</u> James A. Welch; <u>Barber</u> C[laude] Edmonds.
<u>Mrs Birkett</u> Carlotta Addison; <u>Mrs McManus</u> M. Clayton;
<u>Mme Polenta</u> Sybil Carlisle; <u>Nellie Bassett</u> Marion
Bishop; <u>Grace Peyton</u> Deroy; <u>Servant</u> Dora Fellowes;
<u>Betsy</u> Annie Hughes. <u>L & MGR</u> Charles Wyndham; <u>Sm</u> Percy
Hutchison; <u>Bom</u> [G.] Mills; <u>Mus dir</u> Victor Hollaender;
<u>Act mgr & Treas</u> E. Harvey. *REV: E 2/1/97 p13; SR 2/
1/97 p12; TW97 p5-6.*

96.324 *WHY WOMEN WEEP* (Ca,1a) Frederick W. Broughton.
CRITERION 29/12/96-12/2/96. 40 perf.** <u>Arthur Chan-
dos</u> F.H. Tyler; <u>Frank Dudley</u> Kenneth Douglas; <u>Fritz</u>
A.E. George. <u>Dora</u> Sybil Carlisle; <u>Madge</u> E. Randolph.
<u>L & MGR</u>, <u>Sm</u>, <u>Bom</u>, <u>Mus dir</u>, <u>Act mgr & Treas</u> as for 96.
323. *REV: E 2/1/97 p13.*

*   *   *   *   *